DICTIONARY

OF

NATIONAL BIOGRAPHY

1912—1921

THE DICTIONARY of NATIONAL BIOGRAPHY

Founded in 1882
by
GEORGE SMITH

1912–1921

Edited by H. W. C. Davis
and
J. R. H. Weaver

With an Index covering the years 1901–1921
in one alphabetical series

OXFORD UNIVERSITY PRESS

Oxford University Press, Walton Street, Oxford OX2 6DP

Oxford New York Toronto
Delhi Bombay Calcutta Madras Karachi
Kuala Lumpur Singapore Hong Kong Tokyo
Nairobi Dar es Salaam Cape Town
Melbourne Auckland

and associated companies in
Beirut Berlin Ibadan Nicosia

Oxford is a trade mark of Oxford University Press.

First published 1927
Tenth impression 1985

ISBN 0 19 865202 x

Printed in Great Britain
at the University Press, Oxford
by David Stanford
Printer to the University

PREFATORY NOTE

THIS volume contains the lives of notable persons who died in the years 1912–1921. It has been planned on less ample lines than the Supplement which was published by Messrs. Smith, Elder in 1912, under the editorship of the late Sir Sidney Lee. That work, dealing with the obits of eleven years, included 1,660 lives and extended to 2,035 pages. It was a bold and attractive experiment. If, however, the same policy of selection were to be pursued throughout the present century, the result would be to add about 15,000 lives (and nearly 20,000 pages of print) to the main work, which (with the three supplementary volumes published in 1901) contains a little more than 30,000 substantive articles. *Est modus in rebus.* A continuation on such a scale would be beyond the means of most of those for whose use such a work is primarily intended. The editors have endeavoured to reduce in some degree the average length of articles, so far as this could be done without sacrificing essential facts. But, whenever it was possible and seemed desirable to obtain personal appreciations of the kind that only contemporaries can supply, room has been found for such material, in the belief that it may be useful to the future historian of this age.

The period of time which these biographies cover is more than a hundred years. The late Lord Wemyss was born in 1818; Francis Bashforth, the mathematician, and Alexander Campbell Fraser, the metaphysical philosopher, in 1819. The decade 1820–1829 is represented by a substantial list of names, among which appear those of Joseph Arch, the pioneer of agricultural trade-unionism, Sir Nathaniel Barnaby, the naval designer, Sir Sandford Fleming, Sir Edward Fry, Lord Halsbury, Augustus Jessopp, Lord Lindley, Lord Lister, Lord Llandaff, Lord Peel, Lord Mount Stephen, Sir Charles Tupper, Alfred Russel Wallace and John Westlake, the international lawyer. With the next decade, 1830–1839, we enter the full stream of the era which this volume chiefly represents: this is the decade which produced Elizabeth Garrett Anderson, Sir Francis Burnand, Joseph Chamberlain, Lord Courtney of Penwith, Sir William Crookes, Emily Davies, William De Morgan, Sir Michael Hicks Beach (Lord St. Aldwyn), Thomas Hodgkin, Shadworth Hodgson, Sir John Lubbock (Lord Avebury), Sir John Mahaffy, Sir Clements Markham, Sir James Murray, the lexicographer, Sir Andrew Noble, Sir Edward Poynter, Lord Roberts, Henry John Roby, Frederic Seebohm, Walter Skeat, Philip Webb, Lord Welby, William Hale White ('Mark Rutherford'), Lord Wolseley, and Sir Evelyn Wood.

From these instances it will be evident that the spirit of the early

Victorian age was still a living force in the second decade of the present century. Many articles in this volume relate to men and women whose characters matured and whose convictions were fully formed before 1870. Some of these illustrious survivals may owe a part of their current reputation to the fact that they survived so long. But a career must be judged as a whole; the effect of a life's work is cumulative; and a man's personal influence must be gauged, in some degree, by its duration as well as by its intensity. The Nestors of any period are to be remembered as links between the vivid present and the dissolving past, as the repositories of unwritten tradition, and faithful critics of their innovating juniors.

A biographical dictionary which covers four years and a half of European war might be expected to abound in names taken from that glorious, heart-rending roll of honour which records the names of 946,000 citizens of the British Empire. But the loss which that list represents to the Empire at large, and to Great Britain and Ireland in particular—since these sister islands contributed to the roll of honour more than 743,000 names—is not to be measured by those careers which a Dictionary of National Biography can chronicle. In the war years the hopes of the future were sacrificed to meet the imperious necessities of the present, and every battle took heavy toll of the young, more especially of those who had proved their powers of leadership in thought and action; so that we may say, with Pericles: *ἡ νεότης ἐκ τῆς πόλεως ἀνῄρηται ὥσπερ τὸ ἔαρ ἐκ τοῦ ἐνιαυτοῦ εἰ ἐξαιρεθείη*.[1] Such biographies as those of Rupert Brooke, Julian Grenfell, Francis Ledwidge, Henry Moseley, and Frederick Septimus Kelly illustrate the richness and variety of the promise which sympathetic observers could perceive in that devoted generation.

Other aspects of the war, and national losses of other kinds which it occasioned, are revealed in the lives of Admirals Sir Robert Arbuthnot, Sir Christopher Cradock, Sir Horace Hood, and Captain Fryatt; of Lord Kitchener, drowned at sea, and Lord Lucas, killed by a fall from the air; of Generals Sir Thompson Capper, Sir Beauchamp Duff, Charles Fitzclarence, V.C., John Gough, V.C., Sir James Grierson, Sir Stanley Maude; of Nurse Edith Cavell, Sir Victor Horsley, Dr. Elsie Inglis, Arthur Wavell. The lives of Albert Ball, V.C., William Leefe Robinson, V.C., and Reginald Warneford, V.C., are included to illustrate the brilliant audacity which characterized the Royal Air Force in the war.

The acknowledgements of the Editors are due in particular to the following, for valuable criticisms and suggestions: Sir Hugh P. Allen, Sir Hugh K. Anderson, Sir Vincent Baddeley, Mr. C. F. Bell, Mr. E. I.

[1] The youth have been taken away out of the city, as if the spring were taken out of the year.

Carlyle, Mr. H. C. Colles, Admiral Sir Reginald Custance, Mr. Geoffrey Dawson, Brigadier-General J. E. Edmonds, Sir Charles Firth, Mr. S. Vesey FitzGerald, Sir Archibald Garrod, Mr. Stephen Gaselee, Sir Edmund Gosse, Sir Edward Grigg, the Bishop of Durham, the Dean of St. Paul's, Earl Jellicoe, Professor A. B. Keith, Lord Kilbracken, the Archbishop of York, the late Dr. Walter Leaf, Sir Richard Lodge, Professor J. W. Mackail, Mr. Justice Mackinnon, Major-General Sir Frederick Maurice, Mr. W. G. Newton, the Earl of Onslow, Professor A. F. Pollard, Professor R. S. Rait, Sir Harry Reichel, Mr. Bruce Richmond, Mr. C. P. Scott, Sir Charles S. Sherrington, Sir Squire Sprigge, the Bishop of Oxford, Dr. J. R. Tanner, and Professor G. M. Wrong.

In preparing the volume the Editors have had the advantage of the assistance of Miss Margaret Toynbee, B.A., formerly exhibitioner of St. Hugh's College, Oxford. Their thanks are due in special measure to the Rev. H. E. D. Blakiston, D.D., President of Trinity College, Oxford, Mr. C. R. L. Fletcher, and Dr. D. G. Hogarth for valuable help on the proof-sheets, and to the Officials of the Oxford University Press, who have assisted the work at every stage with criticism and advice.

LIST OF CONTRIBUTORS

1912–1921

F. W. A. .... Frederick William Andrewes.
A. W. A. .... Arthur Wilfred Ashby.
A. J. A. ...... Arthur Jacob Ashton.
J. H. A. ...... James Hartley Ashworth.
C. T. A. ...... Christopher Thomas Atkinson.
C. A. .... Claude Aveling.

V. W. B. .... Vincent Wilberforce Baddeley.
C. B. .... Cyril Bailey.
J. C. B. ...... John Cann Bailey.
G. B. .... Graham Balfour.
K. C. B. ..... Kenneth Champain Bayley.
R. P. B. .... Richard Perry Bedford.
R. J. B. ...... Ralph Jermy Beevor.
H. B–e. ...... Harold Begbie.
A. C. B. ...... Archibald Colquhoun Bell.
C. F. B. ...... Charles Francis Bell.
M. H. B. ..... Malcolm Henry Bell.
J. H. B. ...... John Henry Bernard.
B. W. B. .... Benjamin Wolfe Best.
L. B. .... Laurence Binyon.
H. E. D. B. ... Herbert Edward Douglas Blakiston.
A. T. B. ...... Arthur Thomas Bolton.
T. B. .... Tancred Borenius.
H. B–t. ..... Helen Bosanquet.
G. F. B. ...... Godfrey Fox Bradby.
J. R. B. ...... John Rose Bradford.
A. C. B–y. .... Andrew Cecil Bradley.
W. H. B. ..... William Henry Brayden.
H. F. B. B–S. Herbert Francis Brett Brett-Smith.
R. B. .... Robert Bridges.
J. L. B. ...... James Leslie Brierly.
M. S. B. ...... Martin Shaw Briggs.
H. B. .... Henry Broadbent.
R. H. B. ..... Robert Henry Brodie.
F. H. B. ..... Frank Herbert Brown.
G. E. B. ..... George Earle Buckle.
E. C. B. ...... Edward Cuthbert Butler.

G. A. R. C. ... Geoffrey Arthur Romaine Callender.
J. B. C. ...... John Brainerd Capper.
E. I. C. ...... Edward Irving Carlyle.
C. M. C. ...... Cecil Maurice Chapman.
H. B. C. ..... Hugh Boswell Chapman.
R. W. C. ..... Robert William Chapman.
H. B. C–n. ... Henry Buckley Charlton.
H. H. C. ..... Harold Hannyngton Child.
W. M. C. ..... William Macbride Childs.
V. C. .... Valentine Chirol.
H. Ch. .... Hugh Chisholm.
L. W. C. ..... Lawrence Wensley Chubb.
A. C. .... Alfred Cochrane.
G. D. H. C. ... George Douglas Howard Cole.
H. C. C. ...... Henry Cope Colles.
I. D. C. ...... Ian Duncan Colvin.
A. C–R. ...... Arthur Compton-Rickett.
R. S. C. ...... Robert Seymour Conway.
G. A. C. ...... George Albert Cooke.
S. A. M. C. ... Sydney Arthur Monckton Copeman.
A. E. C. ...... Arthur Ernest Cowley.
W. L. P. C. ... William Lang Paige Cox.
A. S. C. ...... Andrew Storrar Cunningham.
B. C. .... Brysson Cunningham.
M. C. .... Myra Curtis.

D. D. .... David Davies.
H. W. C. D. .. Henry William Carless Davis.
G. D. .... Geoffrey Dawson.
W. E. L. D.... Wilfred Ernest Lytton Day.
J. E. G. de M. James Edward Geoffrey de Montmorency.
H. F. D. ..... Henry Fitz-Gibbon Deshon.
H. B. D. ..... Harold Bailey Dixon.
C. D. .... Campbell Dodgson.
F. G. D. ..... Frederick George Donnan.
F. W. D. ..... Frank Watson Dyson.

H. E. E. ..... Hugh Edward Egerton.
P. G. E. ...... Percival George Elgood.
G. E. .... Godfrey Elton.
J. A. E. ...... James Alfred Ewing.

W. B. F. ..... William Bates Ferguson.
A. W. F. ..... Adam Wightman Fergusson.

List of Contributors

J. B. F. ...... John Benjamin Firth.
S. V. FG. ..... Seymour Vesey Fitz-Gerald.
A. P. M. F. ... Arthur Percy Morris Fleming.
W. F. .... William Foster.
J. H. F. ...... John Henry Fowler.
F. F. .... Frank Fox.
J. F. .... John Fraser.
W. H. F. ..... Walter Howard Frere.

E. G. .... Edward Garnett.
A. E. G. ..... Archibald Edward Garrod.
K. F. G. ..... Kenneth Francis Gibbs.
B. W. G. ..... Benedict William Ginsburg.
R. J. G. ...... †Rickman John Godlee.
H. S. G.–R. .. Harry Stuart Goodhart-Rendel.
G. S. G. ...... George Stuart Gordon.
E. G–e. ...... Edmund Gosse.
W. L. G. ..... William Lawson Grant.
W. F. G. ..... William Forbes Gray.
G. G. .... †George Greenhill.
E. F. B. G. ... Ellinor Flora Bosworth Grogan.
J. A. G. ...... James Andrew Gunn.
E. J. G. ...... Edward John Gwynn.
S. G. .... Stephen Lucius Gwynn.

H. M. H. ..... Henry Mendelssohn Hake.
F. de H. H. ... Francis de Havilland Hall.
P. H. .... Philip Hanson.
H. B. H. ..... Harold Brewer Hartley.
H. H. .... Henry Head.
R. D. H. ..... Robert Drew Hicks.
G. F. H. ..... George Francis Hill.
N. L. H. ..... Nina Louisa Hills.
C. N. H. ..... Cyril Norman Hinshelwood.
F. W. H. ..... Francis Wrigley Hirst.
D. G. H. ..... †David George Hogarth.
B. H. H. ..... †Bernard Henry Holland.
A. F. H. ..... Arthur Fenton Hort.
A. H. .... Archibald Hurd.
J. S. H. ...... Julian Sorell Huxley.
L. H. .... Leonard Huxley.
A. M. H. ..... Albert Montefiore Hyamson.

G. V. J. ...... Graham Vernon Jacks.
J. H. J. ...... James Hopwood Jeans.
F. T. J. ...... Fryn Tennyson Jesse.
K. J-B. ...... Katharine Jex-Blake.
A. H. J. ...... †Arthur Henry Johnson.
F. C. J. ...... Fanny Cecilia Johnson.
H. J. .... Hilda Johnstone.
H. A. J. ...... Henry Albert Jones.
C. J. .... Henry Chapman Jones.
J. N. J. ...... †John Newell Jordan.

A. B. K. ..... Arthur Berriedale Keith.
E. A. K. ..... Edmund Arbuthnott Knox.

H. L. .... Horace Lamb.
P. A. L. ...... Philip Aislabie Landon.
A. F. L. ...... Alan Frederick Lascelles.
J. B. L. ...... John Bowring Lawford.
R. W. L. .... Robert Warden Lee.
S. L. .... Shane Leslie.
E. G. T. L. ... Edward George Tandy Liddell.
W. A. L. ..... †William Alexander Lindsay.
R. L. .... Reginald Littleboy.
W. L. .... Walter Lock.
R. L–e. ...... Richard Lodge.
H. V. L. ..... Harrington Verney Lovett.
P. L. .... Percy Lubbock.
H. W. L. ..... †Henry William Lucy.
H. E. L. ..... †Henry Elford Luxmoore.

A. B. M. ..... Alexander Beith Macaulay.
G. M. .... George Macdonald.
C. K. M. ..... Charles Kincaid Mackenzie, Lord Mackenzie.
F. D. M. ..... Frank Douglas Mackinnon.
H. P. M. ..... Hugh Pattison Macmillan.
J. R. M. ..... John Richard Magrath.
H. D. A. M. .. Henry Dewsbury Alves Major.
D. O. M. ..... Dougal Orme Malcolm.
J. J. M. ..... James Joseph Mallon.
R. R. M. ..... Robert Ranulph Marett.
E. M. .... Edward Howard Marsh.
C. C. M. ...... Cyril Charles Martindale.
H. W. M. .... †Henry William Massingham.
P. E. M. ..... Percy Ewing Matheson.
T. M. .... Theobald Mathew.
F. M. .... Frederick Barton Maurice.
H. R. M. ..... Hugh Robert Mill.
A. A. M. ..... Alan Alexander Milne.

List of Contributors

M. M. .... May Morris.
H. W. M–e. .. Henry William Moule.
G. H. M. ..... George Herbert Murray.

E. B. N. ..... Evan Baillie Noel.

F. W. O. ..... Frederick Wolff Ogilvie.
S. L. O. ...... Sidney Leslie Ollard.
C. T. O. ...... Charles Talbut Onions.
O. .... Richard William Alan Onslow, Earl of Onslow.
C. V. O. ...... Charles Venn Owen.

F. P. .... Frederick Page.
S. P. .... †Stephen Paget.
E. P. .... Edith Palliser.
J. L. P. ...... John Leslie Palmer.
J. P. .... John Parker.
A. S. P. ...... Arthur Samuel Peake.
E. H. P. ..... Ernest Harold Pearce.
J. R. P. ...... John Roland Peddie.
G. P. .... George Peel.
N. P. .... Norman Penney.
A. B. P. ...... Arthur Beresford Pite.
A. P. .... †John Arthur Platt.
B. J. P. ...... Benjamin John Plunket.
R. I. P. ...... Reginald Innes Pocock.
A. W. P. ..... Alfred William Pollard.
R. E. P. ...... Rachael Emily Poole.
D'A. P. ...... D'Arcy Power.
C. H. C. P. ... Charles Harris Curtis Prentice.
L. L. P. ..... Langford Rice Price.
H. A. P. ..... Harold Arthur Prichard.
A. O. P. ...... Arthur Octavius Prickard.
A. S. P-P. .... Andrew Seth Pringle-Pattison.
E. S. P. ...... Edward Schroder Prior.
L. C. P. ...... Louis Claude Purser.

R. S. R. ...... Robert Sangster Rait.
G. D. R. ..... George Daniel Rawle.
A. W. R. ..... Arthur William Reed.
W. R. .... William Rees.
V. H. R. ..... Vernon Horace Rendall.
H. W. R. ..... Herbert William Richmond.
C. H. R. ..... Charles Henry Roberts.
P. E. R. ..... Paul Ernest Roberts.
S. C. R. ...... Sydney Castle Roberts.
W. D. R. ..... William David Ross.
R. N. R. B.... Robert Neal Rudmose Brown.
E. F. R. ..... †Edward Francis Russell.
E. R. .... Ernest Rutherford.
A. D. R. ..... Albert Daniel Rutherston.

M. S. .... Michael Sadleir.
M. E. S. ...... Michael Ernest Sadler.
A. W. S. ..... †Arthur Warren Samuels.
E. M. S. ...... Ernest Mason Satow.
W. R. S. ..... William Robert Scott.
J. H. S. ...... James Herbert Seabrooke.
W. B. S. ..... William Boothby Selbie.
L. A. S. B. ... Lewis Amherst Selby Bigge.
C. S. S. ...... Charles Scott Sherrington.
W. S. S. ..... Walter Sydney Sichel.
H. S. .... Herbert Sidebotham.
P. S. .... Percy Simpson.
K. S. .... Kenneth Sisam.
C. A. S. ...... Charles Aitchison Smith.
D. N. S. ...... David Nichol Smith.
A. S. .... Arthur Smithells.
J. A. S. ...... John Alfred Spender.
M. H. S. ..... Marion Harry Spielmann.
F. P. S. ...... Frederick Puller Sprent.
J. H. S–y. .... James Herbert Srawley.
H. W. S. .... Henry Wickham Steed.
H. S–n. ...... Herbert Stephen.
M. T. B. S. ... Margaret Thyra Barbara Stephen.
E. S. .... Eugene Stock.
T. B. S. ...... Thomas Banks Strong.
H. S–t. ...... Henry Sturt.
S. .... John Andrew Hamilton, Baron Sumner.

H. T. .... Henry Tanner.
A. H. T. ..... Alexander Hamilton Thompson.
R. C. T. ...... Reginald Campbell Thompson.
J. A. T. ...... John Arthur Thomson.
J. J. T. ...... Joseph John Thomson.
A. J. T. ...... Arnold Joseph Toynbee.
P. J. T. ...... Paget Jackson Toynbee.
C. H. T. ...... Cuthbert Hamilton Turner.
H. H. T. ..... Herbert Hall Turner.

W. C. U. ..... William Cawthorne Unwin.

P. V. .... †Paul Vinogradoff.

H. C. W. ..... Henry Charles Wace.
E. M. W. ..... Edward Mewburn Walker.
E. A. W. ..... Eric Anderson Walker.
E. W. .... Ernest Walker.
W. S. W. ..... William Stewart Wallace.

List of Contributors

T. H. W. .... Thomas Herbert Warren.
F. W. .... Foster Watson.
P. W. .... †Philip Watts.
W. T. W. .... William Templeton Waugh.
J. R. H. W. .. John Reginald Homer Weaver.
J. W. .... Joseph Wells.
E. A. W–r. ... Emil Alphonse Werner.
C. W. .... Charles Whibley.
F. E. W....... Frederick Ernest Whitton.
F. W. W. .... Frederic William Whyte.
C. H. W. ..... Cyril Hackett Wilkinson.
B. W. .... Arthur Frederic Basil Williams.
G. P. W. ..... Griffith Price Williams.
H. W. W. .... Herbert Wrigley Wilson.
B. C. A. W. .. Bertram Coghill Alan Windle.
T. J. W. ..... Thomas James Wise.
A. F. R. W. .. Alexander Frederick Richmond Wollaston.
D. W. .... Dudley Wright.
E. M. W–g. ... †Edward Murray Wrong.
G. M. W. ..... George Mackinnon Wrong.

MEMOIR OF SIR SIDNEY LEE

THE present volume of the DICTIONARY includes the biographies of persons of note who died in the period 1912–1921. It therefore contains no life of Sir Sidney Lee, who died 3 March 1926. An article upon him will be included in the next decennial volume, which is intended to appear about 1935.

It seemed to the present editors that as a memoir of George Smith, the founder of the Dictionary, was prefixed to the First Supplement, although he died some months later than the date fixed as the limit of that work, so it was desirable to preface this volume with some account of the second Editor of the Dictionary. It also seemed desirable that this preface should take the form of an explanation of the nature of the task which occupied so large a part of Lee's life, and of its connexion with his writings in general.

Sidney Lee was born 5 December 1859. His father, Lazarus Lee, was a London merchant. He was educated at the City of London School under Dr. Edwin Abbott, obtained an exhibition at Balliol College, Oxford, and matriculated in October 1878. He was awarded a third class in classical moderations in 1880, and a second class in modern history in Trinity Term 1882. He matriculated and took his degree as Solomon Lazarus Lee, but subsequently changed the first name and dropped the second altogether. Whilst still an undergraduate he wrote two articles on Shakespearian subjects which attracted the attention of scholars. One, entitled 'The Original of Shylock', which appeared in the *Gentleman's Magazine* for February 1880, was an attempt to show that the trial of Dr. Lopez in 1594 for a plot against Queen Elizabeth suggested the study of Jewish character which Shakespeare embodied in *The Merchant of Venice*. The other was a new study of *Love's Labour 's Lost*, printed in the same periodical for October 1880.[1] Through these articles he became known to Dr. Furnivall, who commissioned him to edit the romance of Huon of Bordeaux (translated from the French by Lord Berners about 1530) for the Early English Text Society; the first volume of this appeared in 1883. Lee was thinking of applying for a lectureship in English which was about to be established at the university of Groningen, when the foundation of this Dictionary afforded him an opportunity for employment in England.

There was great need of such a Dictionary. The present generation scarcely realizes the difficulties which the lack of such a tool imposed upon scholars. Standard foreign collections of universal biography gave very unsatisfactory lives of Englishmen. English collections of the same kind—those of Chalmers and Rose for example—were obsolete or very imperfect. As for a collection of national biography, the seven folio volumes of *Biographia Britannica*, published in 1747–1766, were long out of date, and the

[1] These developed into two papers printed in the *Transactions* of the New Shakspere Society: 'The Topical Side of the Elizabethan Drama', 22 October 1886, and 'Elizabethan England and the Jews', 10 February 1888.

attempt of Dr. Kippis to produce a revised and enlarged edition of that work came to an untimely end with the letter F in 1793. Mr. John Murray, about 1856, had announced a new 'Biographia Britannica', compiled by various writers and edited by Dr. William Smith, but the project ended with the list of names to be included under the letter A. It was, therefore, very fortunate that in 1882 a publisher of great enterprise, genuine interest in literature, and ample means conceived the scheme which developed into the DICTIONARY OF NATIONAL BIOGRAPHY. Mr. George Smith's first idea was a Dictionary of Universal Biography, with many editors and contributors, English and foreign. 'From that wild attempt', said he, 'I was saved by the knowledge and sound judgement of Mr. Leslie Stephen.' In November 1882 Stephen was appointed editor, and on 23 December he published in the *Athenæum* the announcement of 'A New Biographia Britannica'. It was a very clear and concise statement of the editor's programme.

'Apart from precedent', Stephen wrote, 'one or two principles are clear. We should aim at giving the greatest possible amount of information in a thoroughly business-like form. Dates and facts should be given abundantly and precisely; it is of primary importance to give in all cases, and upon a uniform plan, a clear reference to the primary authorities; and in the case of literary biographies it is important to give a full bibliographical notice. It would, however, be easy to ensure failure by attempting too much. We must exclude much if the Dictionary is not to break down under its own weight. We must in the first place exclude (with certain exceptions) names which are only names. A biographical dictionary must be a collection of biographies, and cannot be a full catalogue of names. This, I may add, implies a limit to the bibliographical part of the work....'

'We shall have to deal with a great mass of information. Biographies of this kind may err by being too diffuse or too meagre. . . . We must of course aim at being condensed. Philosophical and critical disquisition, picturesque description, and so forth, are obviously out of place and must be rigorously excised. . . . On the other hand, it is a mistake to economise space by omitting any useful information. And when we ask what information comes under that head, it is not easy to draw the line. Elaborate analysis of character or exposition of critical theories is irrelevant; but a reader may fairly ask to have characteristic anecdotes in their most authentic form, and a clear statement of the view taken by a statesman of political controversies or of the position in the history of literature of a remarkable poem. . . .'

'I have been asked whether anything in the way of "literary style" is to be admitted. If style means superfluous ornament, I say emphatically, no. But style, and even high literary ability, is required for lucid and condensed narrative, and of such style I shall be anxious to get as much as I can. A biography written with a single eye to giving all the information presumably desirable by an intelligent reader may be not only useful, but intensely interesting, and even a model of literary art. . . .'

'Finally I have one remark to add. The editor of such a work must, by the necessity of the case, be autocratic. He will do his best to be a considerate autocrat.'

The next thing to be done was to find a good sub-editor. Stephen said that he wanted 'a man of knowledge, good at abstracting, looking up authorities, and so forth, and an efficient whip in regard both to printers and contributors'. Various candidates for the post were considered, but Furnivall, who, as a Trinity Hall man had influence with Stephen, strongly recommended Lee, and after an interview Lee was chosen. In him Stephen found more than he had demanded: an assistant whose zeal never flagged, and whose ability was greater than he expected; a subordinate whose loyalty to his editor laid the foundation of a lasting friendship.

Lee began his duties in March 1883. 'The Dictionary', wrote Stephen about that time, 'is more or less launched and, like other work, so far as my experience has gone, it is rather a humbug; that is, one talks a great deal and lets other people talk more about the immensity of the task, and after all one finds it to be really simple when it is once got a little into order.' A system was devised and gradually elaborated by the light of experience. The first task was the compilation of a list of the names to be included. Up to the beginning of the letter M this was done by Mr. Thompson Cooper, one of the authors of *Athenae Cantabrigienses*, whose collection of biographical data proved of great service. 'An ideal Dictionary', said Stephen, 'would be a complete codification or summary of all the previously existing collections. . . . It is bound first of all to include all the names which have appeared in any respectable collection of lives, and in the next place to supplement this by including a great many names which for one reason or another have dropped out, but which appear to be approximately of the same rank.' Lists compiled in this way appeared at intervals in the *Athenæum* from June 1883 onwards. Eventually they came out twice a year, each consisting of the 900 or 1,000 names which it was meant to include in the next two volumes of the Dictionary. Readers were invited to suggest additions, and in order that the editor might judge the value of their suggestions, to refer him at the same time to the sources of information available. By this means the co-operation of scholars was ensured, and the number of omissions greatly reduced. The revised lists, printed in pamphlet form, were sent to intending contributors, who were asked to say what articles they would undertake. As soon as their offers were received, the editor assigned the articles, and when there were several applicants for the same article decided between them. In the first list it was stated that the editor, in assigning articles to contributors, would 'inform them what space can be allowed for each name'. But that plan was soon abandoned: it became the exception, not the rule. In the case of the 'great lives', Stephen told a contributor, 'I have found it best to suggest a limit, not of course quite absolute, but as the amount to be aimed at.' The scale was fixed by comparison; if so-and-so could be adequately dealt with in twenty pages, twenty or at most twenty-five would suffice for a man of equal rank. But this method could not be applied to the minor lives. Often the editor could not know till the article came in what there was to say about the man; and so instead of fixing a limit beforehand he cut down the article to the size which the facts justified him in allowing.

Stephen was thoroughly convinced of the importance of these minor articles. Looking back on his editorial work he said: 'The judicious critic is well aware that it is not upon the lives of the great men that the value of the book really depends. It is the second-rate people—the people whose lives have to be reconstructed from obituary notices or from references in memoirs or collections of letters; or sought in prefaces to posthumous works; or sometimes painfully dug out of collections of manuscripts; and who really become generally accessible through the Dictionary alone—that provide the really useful reading. Nobody need look at Addison or Byron or Milton in a dictionary. He can find fuller and better notices in any library; and the biographer must be satisfied if he has put together a useful compendium of all the relevant literature.' [1]

Stephen's articles on the men he named show what excellence such a compendium might attain. Many of the 378 articles which he contributed were of this kind. Lee's 870 articles included a far larger proportion of lives of second-rate people in which research was required. The wide range of the articles which Lee contributed to the early volumes of the Dictionary is remarkable. They begin with Prince Arthur and some fourteenth-century bishops, and end with nineteenth-century politicians; but the best of them are those dealing with men of the Tudor times such as Ascham and Caxton. Their merit was at once recognized. R. C. Christie in an elaborate review of the first ten volumes of the Dictionary, after praising Stephen's Byron as unsurpassable, added: 'There is no contributor whose initials we are more glad to see than Mr. S. L. Lee. We may always depend upon his accuracy and research. . . . Mr. Lee's bibliographical information and his references to authorities leave nothing to be desired.' [2]

As contributors they made an admirable team. Stephen's great lives and Lee's minor lives, Lee's knowledge of the sixteenth and seventeenth centuries and Stephen's knowledge of the eighteenth and nineteenth, supplemented each other. They divided the editorial work between them. Stephen, who disliked proof-correcting and did it badly, dealt with the original manuscripts, and Lee with the proofs. 'My greatest worry', wrote Stephen in April 1884, 'is struggling against the insane verbosity of the average contributor. I never knew before how many words might be used to express a given fact. I read piles of MS., cutting right and left, and reducing some copy to a third of its original mass.' [3] In a circular to the contributors in April 1888, he complained that the average length of lives was increasing, and urged writers to condense their own articles. 'If they find—as may probably be the case—that he has been more ruthless than formerly in the excision of superfluous words (or of words which to him appear to be superfluous) they may be comforted by remembering that such work is even more annoying to the Editor than to his victims; and is in fact by many degrees the most irksome part of his duty. He only discharges it under a sense of necessity, and can say conscientiously that he does not spare his own manuscripts more than those of his contributors.'

[1] *Studies of a Biographer*, 1898, p. i. [2] *Quarterly Review*, vol. clxiv, pp. 357, 364.
[3] F. W. Maitland, *Life and Letters of Leslie Stephen*, 1906, p. 383.

Meanwhile Lee's small clear handwriting—clearer then than it became afterwards—became familiar to contributors on the margin of the proofs returned to them. He made corrections, verified or queried doubtful statements, inserted fresh information, and as far as possible enforced uniformity in minor matters of method. The printed list of about a hundred and twenty of the commonest books of reference in the form in which it was desirable to cite them was probably devised by him. For, as Professor A. F. Pollard observes: 'Detail was more congenial to him than to his chief', and 'he had a passion for precision.' [1]

A more difficult part of Lee's business was to keep the contributors up to time. To the general public the most remarkable feature of the Dictionary of National Biography was the regularity with which the quarterly volumes appeared. Its publication was to have commenced in October 1884, but the first issue had to be postponed till January 1885. After that there was no failure, and to secure this continuous flow of printed matter was Lee's special function. The dilatoriness of contributors was the earliest obstacle. By a printed circular in April 1886 they were reminded that the default of a few contributors might compel the postponement of a volume. Henceforth an article must be sent in within six months from the date of its assignment, and if it had not been delivered within a year from the assignment, the editor considered that he was free to make a new arrangement. It was Lee's business to see to the observance of this rule, to remind delinquents of their crime, and to keep the editor informed of the result. The price of punctuality was eternal vigilance.

The struggle to produce the Dictionary told upon Stephen, who was unused to office life, and found the continuous drudgery a greater strain than did the younger man. He grew nervous and depressed under his burden, and it became too heavy for him. 'That damned thing goes on', he wrote in January 1888, 'like a diabolical piece of machinery, always gaping for more copy, and I fancy at times that I shall be dragged into it and crushed out into slips.' Shortly afterwards he fell ill, and in the autumn of 1889 he had a more serious breakdown. On each occasion he was absent from the office for three months or longer. Lee had to do the editor's work as well as his own, and to take great responsibility without possessing adequate authority. 'I feel always', wrote Stephen, 'that the credit of getting on with such punctuality is due to you.' For a moment Stephen thought of proposing to drop one quarterly issue on account of his illness, but decided to make an arrangement which would diminish his labour. He told a friend that he had put the Dictionary 'into commission', and done it 'upon such terms that if I have to retire, it will, I think, be able to go on under the present management' (December 1889).[2] Lee's name as joint editor appeared with that of Stephen on the title page of the volume issued in March 1890, and of the four following volumes. Then, on 14 May 1891, he told Lee: 'For the future you must say *editor* and not editors, and my name must be removed from the title page of the next volume.' [3] From volume xxvii onwards Lee's name appeared alone.

[1] 'Sir Sidney Lee and the Dictionary of National Biography', in the *Bulletin* of the Institute of Historical Research, June 1926, p. 5.

[2] Maitland, pp. 394, 401, 403.

[3] Maitland, *ibid.*

To both men their eight years' collaboration had been a great advantage. 'My greatest piece of good fortune', said Stephen, 'was that from the first I had the co-operation of Mr. Sidney Lee as my sub-editor. Always calm and confident when I was tearing my hair over the delay of some article urgently required for the timely production of our next volume, always ready to undertake any amount of thankless drudgery, and most thoroughly conscientious in his work, he was an invaluable helpmate. When he succeeded to my post after a third of the task was done I felt assured that the Dictionary would at least not lose by the exchange. He had moreover more aptitude for many parts of the work than I can boast of, for there were moments at which my gorge rose against the unappetizing, but I sorrowfully admit the desirable, masses of minute information which I had to insert. I improved a little under the antiquarian critics who cried for more concessions to Dryasdust, but Mr. Lee had no such defect of sympathy to overcome.'[1] Lee always expressed his obligations to Stephen with equal emphasis. 'Leslie Stephen', he said at Cambridge in 1911, 'was the master under whom I served my literary apprenticeship, and it was as his pupil that I grew to be his colleague and his friend. He gave me my earliest lessons in the writing of biography, and in speaking of its principles I am guided by his teaching.' This was not a mere figure of speech: Stephen's doctrine and Stephen's practice were continually referred to in Lee's writings and conversation. Their friendship continued till Stephen's death in 1904.

At the time when Lee became editor the initial difficulties of the enterprise had been overcome. The arrangements for the production of the Dictionary had been systematized, the machinery worked with less friction, and the output was better and more uniform in quality. A review of the first twenty-two volumes of the Dictionary, published in October 1890, showed that in the opinion of good judges there had been a marked improvement since the start. 'There is a steady advance in brevity and conciseness. . . . There is a high average of methodical and scholarly work', said the reviewer.[2] Some other biographical dictionaries which began well fell off as they approached their conclusion. Editors and proprietors revealed their desire to bring the work to an end as soon as possible, and to omit all the names that could decently be omitted. The Dictionary was saved from this fate by the unwearied industry of Lee, and the resolve of Mr. Smith to spare no expenditure necessary to produce a book of lasting value. The result was that the Dictionary continued to improve, and it is an axiom with those who habitually use it that in accuracy and fullness the lives in the later volumes are superior to those in the early part.

But this improvement was purchased at an increasing cost. Originally it was intended that the Dictionary should be completed in fifty volumes. At first this seemed feasible. In April 1886 Stephen announced that the letters A and B would not exceed their proper proportion by more than 100 pages. In April 1888 he sounded an alarm. The average length of

[1] Leslie Stephen, *Some Early Impressions* [ed. 1924], p. 160.

[2] *English Historical Review*, vol. v, p. 787. Compare the article on the first ten volumes in the *Quarterly Review*, vol. clxiv.

the lives had increased. 'The explanation seems to be the satisfactory one, that more information has been given, not that a greater number of words has been employed to give the same amount of information. The fact, however, makes some difference in calculations as to the probable length of the whole work.' Accordingly he begged contributors to condense their articles. In 1890 the two editors repeated the appeal, and suggested various expedients for saving space. In 1895, when the letter P had been reached, Lee perceived clearly that not less than sixty volumes would be necessary.

'While I gratefully acknowledge the zeal and ability which contributors have brought to the service of the Dictionary, I cannot ignore a tendency on the part of some writers to expand their manuscripts beyond reasonable limits. Every effort is made in the Editor's office to remove superfluous detail before the articles are published, but greater condensation might possibly be secured if some writers co-operated rather more actively in the work of abridgement. I would invite contributors, after completing an article, to peruse it carefully with a view to determining whether each of the facts recorded is fairly certain to be useful to those who may be expected to consult the Dictionary. . . . The practice of introducing the last scrap of information that patient research can reveal is not to be condemned lightly, but if the Dictionary is to be confined within manageable bounds information of trivial interest must be sacrificed. To present the essential facts in the career of the subject of the memoir so as to suggest readily to the reader the character and value of his achievements, is the only practicable aim.'[1]

Lee was himself too much inclined to the fault he mentioned to be a very effective preacher. Stephen was pleased to receive a new scrap of information and to take it into account in an article. Lee liked to hunt for one and to put it in. He had also a tendency to give a somewhat excessive number of bibliographical details. Nor did his own style ever attain the conciseness which marked Stephen's. But the expansion of the Dictionary was mainly due to other causes: to the exertions of the staff and the contributors.

The home of the Dictionary was the top floor of No. 14, Waterloo Place, next door to the premises of Smith, Elder, & Co., which were No. 15, and connected with the publisher's office by a speaking tube. The small back room of the flat was the editor's sanctum. The large front room looking into Waterloo Place was the workshop; several large tables, many ink-pots, piles of proofs and manuscript on chairs and tables, a little pyramid of Stephen's pipes at one end of the chimney piece, a little pyramid of Lee's pipes at the other end. The narrow side room opening out of it held on its shelves a fine assortment of reference books, sets of the *Gentleman's Magazine* and of *Notes and Queries*, Wood, Le Neve, and other biographical collections.

The number and composition of the editor's staff varied at different dates. When Stephen fell ill more help was needed, so Mr. C. L. Kingsford and Mr. W. A. J. Archbold became in succession assistant sub-editors. Later Mr. Thomas Seccombe replaced Mr. Archbold, and in January 1893

[1] Circular 9, November 1895.

Mr. A. F. Pollard began work in the office. Mr. E. I. Carlyle became an additional sub-editor in 1896, and Mr. H. E. Murray was clerk in charge of the Dictionary throughout its publication. When Lee became editor he introduced stricter rules about attendance. 'The rule for assistant editors was three hours each morning at the Museum and four each afternoon in Waterloo Place,' with proof-reading at home in the evenings when it was required. They wrote a considerable number of articles themselves. Their work upon the articles of other people was not confined to the elimination of verbiage and the correction of erroneous statements; they inserted fresh biographical facts, information about portraits, and bibliographical details. Some articles were partially rewritten; a paragraph or a column was often added; once the assistant editors increased a three-page life to nine pages. To another life Lee added about ten pages, and his initials appeared at the end beside those of the original author. An article which was completely rewritten in the office became anonymous, and anonymity was also the custom when an author found the alterations more than he was willing to accept.[1] These improvements, while they brought the Dictionary nearer to Lee's ideal standard, swelled its bulk considerably.

The zeal of the contributors worked towards the same result. The Dictionary had given a great stimulus to research, which was reflected in their articles. Nearly three-quarters of the work was written by about a hundred regular contributors. They were most of them specialists studying some particular branch of knowledge or some particular period of history. They learnt more and more about their subjects as the Dictionary went on, and put more and more learning into their articles. They felt personally interested in the success of the undertaking. 'It was a curious fact', said Mr. Smith in 1894, 'that everybody who had taken part in the production of the Dictionary had manifested a strong liking for it. Editors, assistant editors, contributors, all seemed to have formed a kind of comradeship with the common object of making the work as perfect as possible; and this affection for the work was not a transitory one, it was the same under Mr. Sidney Lee as it was under Mr. Leslie Stephen. In truth they all liked the Dictionary and were proud of it.'

The contributors fostered their esprit de corps by dining together. Some of these entertainments were festivities like college gaudies. There was a dinner at Richmond at the Star and Garter in July 1888. Mr. Smith entertained the contributors by fifties at his home in Park Lane in 1892, and to the number of 200 at the Whitehall Rooms in 1897. The contributors entertained Mr. Smith at the Westminster Palace Hotel in 1894. Finally, the Lord Mayor gave a dinner at the Mansion House on 30 June 1900, to celebrate the conclusion of the Dictionary. At these gatherings the usual toasts were the proprietor, the editor, and the contributors. The speakers jested about their trade like the grave-diggers in *Hamlet.* Canon Ainger told them that the editor's motto was 'No flowers, by request.' Sir E. Maunde Thompson compared his brother contributors to the Murderers' Club in De Quincey: each man looked at his neighbour

[1] See 'A Statistical Account' of the Dictionary in vol. lxiii, pp. ix–x, and *Bulletin* of the Institute of Historical Research, June 1926, p. 6.

and said, 'Shall I have your life or will you have mine?' The proprietor reassured them all by declaring that provision had been made for carrying on the Dictionary 'in the event of my—may I say, lamented—demise'.

Mr. Smith was not sorry when the Dictionary ended, but the contributors felt as if the whole Round Table were dissolved. They were vexed, too, that no public honour was bestowed upon Smith by the government, and were much gratified subsequently when his picture was placed in the National Portrait Gallery. Both editors had been 'considerate autocrats': a testimonial from the contributors had been presented to Stephen in 1891; Lee received a presentation of silver in 1900. These mutual congratulations were justified. The verdict of a foreign scholar is that the Dictionary is 'la meilleure, sans contredit, des Biographies nationales'.[1] Neither Stephen nor Lee could keep the work to the intended scale, but it preserved nevertheless a certain harmony and consistency of character; it was not a fortuitous concourse of articles, but bore evidence of design throughout. It reflected the aims of the three men responsible for its making: Smith's bold plan for a comprehensive national record, Stephen's desire to summarize lucidly and concisely whatever of importance was already known, Lee's zeal for adding to knowledge.

The sixty-third and last volume of the Dictionary appeared in October 1900; but Lee had several more labours to perform. As soon as the main work was published, what is known as the First Supplement was taken in hand, and the last of the three volumes composing it was issued in October 1901. It contained the lives of some 200 persons whose names had been accidentally omitted from the original lists, and of a much larger number who had died while the Dictionary was coming out. The practice of the editors during those fifteen years had been to include lives of the latter class whenever their place in the alphabet permitted. Sometimes the printing of the volume in hand was suspended in order to insert the memoir of an eminent man suddenly deceased. For instance, Roundell Palmer, Earl of Selborne, died on 4 May 1895. A four-page article upon him by Mr. J. M. Rigg was included in volume xliii, which appeared at the end of June. But John Bright, who died in March 1889, and Gladstone, who died in May 1898, had to wait for the Supplement because the letter B had been concluded in 1886 and G in 1890. About eight hundred articles of this class were now added. In the list of authorities given at the end of them the words 'personal knowledge' and 'private information' frequently appear. Part of Lee's skill as an editor lay in the judicious selection of writers who possessed this knowledge or could procure this information. His acquaintance not only with men of letters but with men of mark in all walks was unusually wide, and as editor he had acquired a reputation for trustworthiness and discretion which secured him access to private papers and confidences from public men. These qualifications stood him in good stead when he came to the most difficult part of his task.

It had been intended that the limit of the Dictionary should be the last day of the year 1900, but the death of Queen Victoria on 22 January 1901 furnished a better historical landmark. At the earnest request of Mr. Smith, Lee undertook to write the Queen's life for the Supplement. Fate

[1] C. V. Langlois, *Manuel de Bibliographie historique*.

also imposed upon him the duty of writing the life of Mr. Smith himself, who died on 6 April 1901. So while the life of the founder served as a preface to the three volumes, that of the Queen formed the epilogue.

Lee had known Mr. Smith for nearly eighteen years, there were fragments of an autobiography available, and the family supplied all the additional facts required. He grouped round the figure of the publisher the great writers whose books he had printed, and made the story of his career a chapter in the history of Victorian literature.

The article on the Queen presented problems far less easy to handle, and Lee undertook it with many misgivings. The life of a constitutional sovereign is a long series of external events minutely chronicled, behind which the will and character of the individual lie concealed. The reticence of living witnesses and the absence of documentary materials increased the obscurity. Neither the Queen's letters nor the portions of her diary, since published, were then available. 'The only part of the Queen's career which has been fully dealt with is her married life', wrote Lee. Information about her part in political events, her private opinions, and her feelings during the last forty years of her reign was scanty or lacking altogether. Lee sought help from private sources, and employed the reminiscences he obtained to eke out and interpret his imperfect materials. He claimed to have stated facts accurately, to have judged them with sympathy as well as candour, and to have respected alike public interests and private feelings. The article was published as a book in 1902, and reached a third edition in 1904. Its production in 1901 was a remarkable feat.

The completion of the Supplement made it possible to plan and produce what was originally entitled the Index and Epitome, and is now styled the Concise D.N.B. It appeared about March 1903. During the summer of 1904 it was followed by the volume of Errata, presented gratis to all subscribers to the Dictionary. The three hundred pages of small print which it contains show what scrupulous care Lee devoted to maintaining the accuracy of the Dictionary. There were inevitably many real errors besides accidental misprints. Stephen accepted the fact philosophically. 'A book of which it is the essence that every page should bristle with facts and dates is certain to have errors by the thousand.' [1] Lee's attitude was more apologetic. He industriously accumulated the corrections made in reviews and periodicals, and those sent to him by critical readers, penitent contributors, or aggrieved relatives. This often involved correspondence with the author of the article as well as with the critic. The validity of each objection had to be examined, and proof required, before any alteration was made. Lee repeatedly pledged himself that all proved errors of fact should be corrected as soon as opportunity offered. Some were corrected in reissues from the stereotyped plates; more, when the sixty-six volumes of Dictionary and Supplement were compressed into twenty-two in the edition of 1908–1909. These small but continuous repairs in the fabric of the Dictionary—the process of reparation Lee called it—were all that it was possible to do without resetting the type. Lee was conscious that time, the progress of historical research, and the publication of new historical materials would eventually render a new edition necessary. When that

[1] *Some Early Impressions*, p. 161.

would be undertaken he could not pretend to know, and he returned with fresh ardour to his study of Shakespeare and the Elizabethan age as soon as the Dictionary and the Supplement were issued.

For the next eight years Lee's time was almost exclusively devoted to those two subjects. The article on Shakespeare which he had contributed to volume li of the Dictionary had expanded into the *Life of Shakespeare*, published in 1898. The book reached its sixth edition in 1908, and was rewritten and enlarged to twice its original size in 1915. The history of Shakespeare's native town, which Lee had originally published in 1885, was similarly revised and enlarged in 1906. A visit to America in 1903 resulted in the volume of lectures, entitled *Great Englishmen of the Sixteenth Century*, in which he attempted to show the working of the spirit of the Renaissance in English life. He wrote also, for an American periodical, a series of articles entitled, 'The Call of the West',[1] which traced the influence of the discovery of America on thought and action in England. Lee also turned his attention to the text of Shakespeare. He published a facsimile reproduction of the first folio of Shakespeare's Plays in 1902, and similar reproductions of the Poems and the Sonnets in 1905, followed in 1910 by an edition of Shakespeare in twenty volumes,[2] to which he contributed annotations throughout, prefaces to some of the plays, and a general introduction. At the same time he took up with vigour the study of comparative literature, writing a history of the Sonnet in Italy and France and an account of the development of that form of composition in Elizabethan literature. Last of all, in a series of lectures delivered at Oxford in 1909, entitled *The French Renaissance in England*, he showed in detail the debt of Tudor writers to French authors with regard both to form and ideas.

In 1910 the time came for the preparation of a second Supplement. Mr. Smith regarded the Dictionary not as an enterprise completed once for all, but as a work which was to be permanently maintained and continued. In Lee's phrase it was to be 'a living organism'. At stated intervals new biographies were to be added to commemorate those worthy of inclusion in the national record who had died since its last issue. To carry out her husband's wishes Mrs. George Smith undertook to defray the cost of three more volumes to include persons deceased between January 1901 and December 1911.

Lee was engaged on the production of the SECOND SUPPLEMENT from October 1910 to December 1912. It was a more laborious business than the first Supplement, for the three volumes dealt with 1,635 names instead of about 1,000, and contained over 2,200 pages as against 1,400. The editor's labour was increased by the fact that he no longer had his old staff to help him. He had to find new assistants and to train them while the work was actually in progress. Of the regular contributors who had written about three-quarters of the original Dictionary, few were still available. About a score of them are commemorated in the Dictionary or the Supplements, and the list of the dead included men like Joseph

[1] Published in *Scribner's Magazine* for 1907.

[2] Published originally by the University Press of Cambridge, Massachusetts, in 1907–1910, and reissued in England as *The Caxton Shakespeare* in 1910.

Knight who had written over 500 articles on dramatists or actors, and Sir Alexander Arbuthnot who wrote most of the articles on Anglo-Indian officials. Specialists on earlier periods were frequently reluctant to undertake lives of nineteenth-century personages, and two who had each written about a volume for the original Dictionary contributed only one article apiece to the Supplement. Fortunately Sir John Laughton was able to continue his series of naval articles, and Colonels Vetch and Lloyd their military series, and other old contributors were available. But there were many new hands, and therefore Lee reissued the rules for contributors in an enlarged form, and made his ten commandments into twelve. Lee himself wrote the lives of several Shakespearian scholars, and of some of his old contributors, besides an article upon Leslie Stephen which would have earned Stephen's approval. But his chief contribution was a life of King Edward VII, sixty pages in length, marked by the same qualities as his account of Queen Victoria. It was sufficiently critical in its views to rouse some controversy, but it was so obviously honest that the King's own papers were subsequently placed at Lee's disposal for the purpose of writing a fuller biography. Without adequate evidence that he was in error he would alter nothing ; objections raised to statements in the article would be duly considered when the book was written.

Lee was also called upon to answer people who objected to the Supplements on principle. They said that lives of persons so recently deceased were premature ; that they were impressions, not considered verdicts, lacked historical perspective, and must be based on insufficient documentary evidence. However, the only rule laid down by Stephen in the original prospectus was that the eminent man should be dead ; he was not required to have been dead for a generation, or some convenient number of years. Stephen's practice conformed to his principle. Henry Fawcett died 6 November 1884, and Stephen published the life of his friend in 1885. Stephen's brother Fitzjames died 11 March 1894, and the preface to Leslie's life of him is dated 1 May 1895. Neither friendship, nor blood, nor nearness of time, affected the justice of his account of the two men. Time would have made the lives no better ; it might have dimmed the clearness of his memories ; it might have prevented the lives from being written, since he died in 1904. In Stephen's view the danger was in delay, not in haste. 'Any one', wrote Stephen, 'who like me has had much to do with biography must have been painfully impressed by the singular rapidity with which its materials vanish. Again and again I have had to lament the fact.'[1] Stephen's view was Lee's too. In defending what he termed 'recent biography' he asserted that the first-hand evidence of living contemporaries was 'the most essential ingredient' in any biography.[2] He instanced Boswell's Johnson and Lockhart's Scott to prove that the earliest biographies were the best, and quoted Johnson's warning against postponement. 'If a life be delayed till interest and envy are at an end, we may hope for impartiality, but obtain little intelligence.'[3]

[1] *Some Early Impressions*, p. 8.

[2] See 'At a Journey's End' in the *Nineteenth Century* for December 1912, and 'The Perspective of Biography', published by the English Association in September 1918.

[3] *The Rambler*, No. 60.

In a lecture Lee examined the different kinds of bias which a biographer had to guard against, the family bias, the official bias, the ethical bias, hero-worship, and most insidious of all, the historical bias. This last was a tendency to forget the distinction between history and biography, and to drown the man's life in the story of his times, under pretence of showing the influence of his environment on him. It was the business of the historian, not of the biographer, to determine the man's importance to his time. The biographer recorded the man's deeds; he was the witness not the judge, and he was not called upon to anticipate the historian's verdict.

At first sight the frequent lack of documentary evidence seems a more serious objection. For political reasons the papers of statesmen and diplomatists are often kept private for a long period of years. Disraeli's correspondence was held back for more than thirty years after his death, Peel's for more than forty years. Of late, however, there has been a tendency to shorten the interval between the death of a public man and the appearance of the official biography with its copious extracts from his diaries and letters. Morley's *Life of Gladstone* appeared five years after Gladstone's death. Three Victorian statesmen died between 1906 and 1908: Gathorne-Hardy, Goschen, and the eighth Duke of Devonshire; their biographies were published in time to be used in the articles in the second Supplement. The objection therefore affected only a limited number of the particular class of lives it touched. Lee rightly held that an event so uncertain as the date when documents become accessible should not be made an argument either for postponement or omission.

The difficulty caused by the lack of documents does not affect 'recent biography' only. It is a perennial difficulty, and affects the biographies of men who died centuries ago. The Dictionary contains lives of William Cecil, Lord Burghley, and his son Robert, of Robert Harley, Earl of Oxford, and of William, Lord Grenville. When those articles were written neither the Cecil papers at Hatfield, nor the Harley papers at Welbeck, nor the Grenville papers at Dropmore had been calendared by the Historical Manuscripts Commission, and all need revision by the light of this new evidence. The historian does not abstain from writing the history of a reign because some of the documents which he wants are not accessible. The biographer is often in a similar position. Each does the best he can with the materials he is able to obtain, knowing that part of what he writes is merely provisional.

For the editor of a biographical dictionary the solution of the problem was simple. The Dictionary was an indispensable aid for workers of every kind; it was an instrument for the advancement of knowledge, to be perfected as more became known, not to be held back till all was known. By disregarding superstitions in order to facilitate the study of our own time Lee did a great service to historical scholarship.

Lee continued to act as editor of the Dictionary for four years after the completion of the Second Supplement, that is, to conduct the necessary correspondence and to supervise the reissue of volumes when required. Owing to the death of Mr. Reginald Smith in December 1916, the firm of Smith, Elder, & Co. was dissolved early in the following year, and in June 1917 the heirs of the founder presented the copyright and stock of the Dictionary to the University of Oxford. With the change in its proprietorship Lee's connexion with the undertaking came to an end.

The rest of Lee's life was largely occupied by teaching and university administration. From 1913 to 1924 he was professor of English literature in the East London College, which formed part of the University of London. He resigned his professorship, owing to ill-health, in the summer of 1924, published the first volume of his *Life of King Edward VII* in March 1925, and was endeavouring to complete the second volume at the time of his death. He died on 3 March 1926, and was buried at Stratford-on-Avon.

C. H. FIRTH

DICTIONARY

OF

NATIONAL BIOGRAPHY

(TWENTIETH CENTURY)

PERSONS WHO DIED 1912–21

ABERCORN, second DUKE OF (1838–1913). [See HAMILTON, JAMES.]

ABNEY, SIR WILLIAM DE WIVELESLIE (1843–1920), photographic chemist and education official, the eldest son of the Rev. Edward Henry Abney, vicar of St. Alkmund's, Derby, afterwards prebendary of Lichfield, by his wife, Catharine, daughter of Jedediah Strutt, of Greenhall, Belper, was born at Derby 24 July 1843. He was educated at Rossall School, and in 1861 obtained a commission in the Royal Engineers through the Royal Military Academy. The first few years of his service were spent in India, where he was attached to the Sappers and Miners, Bombay, until transferred (1865) to the public works department. In 1867 he returned to England on sick leave and was stationed at Chatham, where in 1871 he was appointed assistant to the instructor in telegraphy at the school of military engineering. A few months afterwards he was appointed instructor in chemistry and photography, a department which in 1874 became a separate school under his sole charge. In 1877 Abney, who had been gazetted captain in 1873, left Chatham and entered the science and art department at South Kensington (afterwards incorporated in the Board of Education) as inspector of science schools. From this time his work followed two distinct, but concurrent, courses, in both of which he was enthusiastic, persevering, and eminently successful.

When Abney joined the science and art department there were not half a dozen practical laboratories, suitable for teaching purposes, connected with it; but at the end of seven years more than a hundred were in existence. Having retired from the army in 1881, he was appointed assistant director for science in 1884 and director in 1893. By 1903, owing to Abney's initiative, practical work in connexion with the teaching of science had made such progress that there were more than a thousand chemical or physical laboratories, besides laboratories for mechanics, metallurgy, and biology, connected with the department. In 1899 Abney was made principal assistant secretary to the Board of Education, and held the position, which is that of chief official in the science division, until he retired in 1903 under the changes brought about by the Education Act of that year. He then became scientific adviser to the Board and a member of the advisory council for education to the War Office.

As a youth Abney had been interested in photography, and, as soon as the opportunity offered, he began scientific investigation of its numerous problems. He soon made a reputation as a leading exponent of practical photography, and as early as 1874 he was given sole charge of the arrangements for photographic observations of the transit of Venus, and went himself to Egypt to observe it. In experimental photography he aimed at devising methods of measurement, and he applied them in researches relating to the intensities of various sources of illumination, to the opacity of photographic deposits, to the exposure efficiency of shutters of various types, and to allied subjects. He was also a pioneer in the advancement of photographic emulsion-making; it was due mainly to discoveries made by Charles Bennett and Abney in this country and by D. B. van Monckhoven, of Ghent, that a rapid gelatine emulsion was first produced (1878–9), making 'instantaneous' photography possible. Abney also introduced, in 1881, the gelatino-citro-chloride emulsion printing process, the forerunner of the modern printing-out paper. His treatise, *Photography with Emulsions*, was long the standard work on the subject. Hardly less important were Abney's investigations (1877) of the alkaline development of the photographic image, and his introduction in 1880 of a new developing agent, hydroquinone.

But Abney's most notable experimental work related to spectro-photography, colour analysis, and colour vision. He re-drew the three-colour sensation curves associated with the Young-Helmholtz theory of colour vision, and as early as 1880 succeeded in making photographic plates sensitive to the red and infra-red; with these he mapped this region of the solar spectrum with an accuracy comparable to that of the standard maps of the normal solar spectrum prepared by A. J. Ångstrom and H. A. Rowland. He made thousands of these specially sensitive plates for use in his chemical and astronomical investigations.

Abney was awarded in 1882 the Rumford medal of the Royal Society, of which he had been elected a fellow in 1876. He was made a C.B. in 1888, and K.C.B. in 1900. He was president of the Royal Photographic Society from 1892 to 1894, in 1896, 1903, and 1905; of the Royal Astronomical Society, 1893–1895; and of the Physical Society, 1895–1897. In the autumn of 1920 he went to Folkestone because of his failing health, and died there on 3 December.

Abney married twice: first, in 1864 Agnes Mathilda (who died in 1888), daughter of Edward W. Smith, of Tickton Hall, Yorkshire, by whom he had one son and two daughters; secondly, in 1890 Mary Louisa, daughter of the Rev. E. N. Meade, D.D., of St. Mary's Knoll, Scarborough-on-Hudson, U.S.A., by whom he had one daughter.

The diversity of Abney's scientific labours makes it difficult to give an adequate review of them. Over one hundred of his papers are recorded in the Royal Society's *Catalogue* and as many more are to be found in the *Photographic Journal* and kindred publications. His experimental work lacked nothing for completeness and precision, yet he had little liking for meticulous refinement in research, and his methods were remarkable for their ingenious simplicity. He underrated the advances made (1891) in sensitometry by F. Hurter and V. C. Driffield, yet his *Instruction in Photography* (1870) and his *Treatise on Photography* (1875), in their latest editions, still rank among the most valuable photographic textbooks in the English language. His investigations of the problems of colour vision he summarized in his *Trichromatic Theory of Colour* (1914). He was a keen traveller, and wrote an account of *Thebes, and its Five Great Temples* (1876) and was joint author, with C. D. Cunningham, of *The Pioneers of the Alps* (1888).

[*Proceedings* of the Royal Society, vol. xcix, A, 1921; *Photographic Journal*, January 1921; *British Journal Photographic Almanac*, 1922; *The Times*, 4 December 1920; personal knowledge.] C. J.

ALCOCK, Sir JOHN WILLIAM (1892–1919), airman, was born at Manchester 6 November 1892, the eldest child and eldest son of John Alcock, horsedealer, by his wife, Mary Whitelegg, both of that city. He was educated at the parish school, St. Anne's-on-Sea, and entered the Empress motor works in Manchester as an apprentice in 1909. Flying soon attracted him, and in 1910 he went to Brooklands, where, as mechanic to the French pilot Maurice Ducrocq, he learned the art of 'tuning' an aeroplane. Alcock took his aviator's certificate in November 1912, and was then employed by the Sunbeam motor-car company as a racing pilot.

In November 1914 Alcock joined the Royal Naval Air Service as a warrant-officer instructor, serving mostly at the Royal Naval Flying School at Eastchurch, Kent. He received his commission as flight sub-lieutenant in December 1915, but was retained at Eastchurch until December 1916, when he was posted to No. 2 wing in the Eastern Mediterranean. From his base at Mudros he took part in many long-distance bombing raids. On 30 September 1917, flying a single-seater Sopwith 'camel', he earned the distinguished service cross for a gallant and skilful attack on three enemy seaplanes, two of which crashed into the sea. At 8.15 p.m. on the same day, Alcock left on a Handley Page aeroplane to bomb Constantinople. He was over the Gallipoli peninsula when the failure of one of his two engines compelled him to turn back. He covered sixty miles with one engine, but was then forced to alight in the sea, near Suvla Bay. Alcock and his crew of two were afloat on their craft for two hours, but their Verey lights failed to attract the attention of the British destroyers, and as the aeroplane now began to sink, they left it and struck out for the land. They got ashore after an hour in the water, and lay concealed throughout the night, but at noon were made prisoners by the Turks.

Alcock was released and returned to England after the armistice, and he left the Royal Air Force in March 1919 with warden, 8 January 1836. Alma was the name of his godfather. His father died when the boy was four years old, and his mother, who was left with a large family, sent him to be educated in the gymnasium at Leeuwarden. Even in childhood he was devoted to drawing, and at fourteen painted his opus i, ' Portrait of my Sister ', the first of a prodigious series, each numbered in orderly fashion in Roman numerals, ending only two months before his death with opus ccccviii, ' Preparations '. His early attempts displayed such promise that in 1852 he went to Antwerp, and entered the academy. He soon attracted the attention of Louis Delaye, professor of archaeology, who confirmed in him a passion for that science, which profoundly influenced his work for the rest of his life; and in Delaye's studio, in 1858, he painted his first notable effort in this direction, ' Clotilde at the Tomb of her Grandchildren ' (opus viii). Later he became the pupil of Hendrik Leys, working on that master's pictures as well as on his own, and studying, to use his own words, ' the combinations that form a picture, and how pictures are made '. The first that he painted under these auspices was ' The Education of the Children of Clovis ' (opus xiv, 1861), of which Leys remarked ' That marble is cheese ', a stricture which can never again have been passed on Alma-Tadema. In 1864 he sent to the Paris salon his first contribution, ' Egyptians, Three Thousand Years Ago ' (opus xviii); this obtained a gold medal, and also brought him into touch with J. L. Gérôme, who revealed to him the medium which he himself employed, which Alma-Tadema always used thereafter. In 1863, on his marriage, he settled in Brussels, but the death of his wife in 1869 and the favourable reception of his pictures at the Royal Academy decided him to remove to London, where he finally settled in October 1870.

By this time Alma-Tadema had attained full command of his powers. The first picture which he painted in London, ' From an Absent One ', was opus lxxxvi —the hand obeying the dictates of the mind with an easy assurance without which his astonishing productiveness would have been impossible. In 1871 he completed eleven pictures; in 1872 thirteen; in 1873 thirteen; in 1874 twenty-one, including the two large and elaborate works, ' A Sculpture Gallery ' (opus cxxv) and ' A Picture Gallery ' (opus cxxvi); in 1875 seventeen; in 1876 only nine, but among these was the great ' Audience at Agrippa's ' (opus clxi). In few of the following years was his output less prolific. Impeccable drawing, and a sound and sane handling of his materials, whether water-colour or oil, characterized all Alma-Tadema's productions; and he seemed rather to play with, than to work at the artistic problems he set himself to solve. He excelled in the representation of textures, and lavished beautiful accessories of every kind upon his canvases. His wide and profound knowledge of archaeology ensured an accuracy which never became pedantic, whether he was dealing with ancient Egypt, Greece, or Rome, or with the Merovingian period which first attracted him. His greatest triumphs, however, were obtained in his reconstructions of imperial Rome, an achievement which was fitly recognized when, in 1906, on the recommendation of the Institute of British Architects, he was awarded the royal gold medal for the promotion of architecture. His skill was happily utilized by Sir Henry Irving, who persuaded him to design the scenery for *Cymbeline* in 1896 and for *Coriolanus* (as produced in 1901), and later by Sir Herbert Beerbohm Tree [q. v.] in productions of *Julius Caesar* and *Hypatia*.

Long before this his fellow artists had been prompt to acknowledge Alma-Tadema's high desert. In 1876, three years after he had received from Queen Victoria letters of denization, he was elected an associate of the Royal Academy, and in 1879 a full academician. Officialdom endorsed the verdict of his brother artists when, in 1899, he was knighted, and in 1907 appointed one of the members of the order of merit. Nor were more tangible proofs of appreciation lacking. No public gallery of any importance in Europe, America, or Australia is without at least one example of his handiwork, nor can any private collection of modern art be deemed representative which has nothing of his to show, while excellent reproductions exist of many of his pictures.

Alma-Tadema's social success was rapid and complete. Gifted with a genial and attractive personality, he was a well-known figure in many and various circles, and few people of importance living in, or visiting, London, failed to find their way to the fine house which he built for himself in St. John's Wood, and, if musicians, to leave their autographs on his famous piano-lid. He died 25 June 1912 at Wiesbaden, where he was undergoing treatment for an internal complaint.

Alma-Tadema married twice: first, in 1863 Marie Pauline (died 1869), daughter of

Eugène Gressin de Bois Girard, of Sancerre, France, by whom he had two daughters; secondly, in 1871 Laura Teresa (died 1909), daughter of George Napoleon Epps [q. v.].

[*Art Annual*, 1886 and 1910; Georg Ebers, *Lorenz Alma-Tadema*, 1885; Cosmo Monkhouse, *British Contemporary Artists*, 1899; private information. Portrait, *Royal Academy Pictures*, 1896.] M. H. B.

ALVERSTONE, Viscount (1842–1915), judge. [See Webster, Richard Everard].

ANDERSON, ELIZABETH (1836–1917), better known as Mrs. Elizabeth Garrett Anderson, physician, was born in London 9 June 1836, the second daughter of Newson Garrett, merchant, of Aldeburgh, Suffolk, by his wife, Louisa, daughter of John Dunnell. She was educated at a school at Blackheath, kept by the Misses Browning, aunts of the poet, Robert Browning, and women of considerable powers. She was early impressed by the desirability, for women no less than for men, of an engrossing interest in life, as well as of economic independence. Her attention was already attracted by the idea of the fitness of women for medical studies and the need for their services as doctors when, in March 1859, she attended three lectures on the question of the admission of women to the medical profession, given by Dr. Elizabeth Blackwell [q. v.], an Englishwoman who, after much difficulty, had graduated M.D. in the United States and had just been admitted to the recently formed British medical register. Stimulated in her desire for medical training by contact with Dr. Blackwell, Elizabeth Garrett found two problems confronting her: the difficulty of obtaining the necessary training; and that of inducing a qualifying body to examine her when trained. She obtained some casual teaching and experience at the Middlesex Hospital and began to study in earnest in 1860. But in spite of the kindness of individual doctors, her efforts to enter upon a regular course were frustrated, both by the London hospitals to which she applied, and by the universities of Edinburgh and St. Andrews, where most of the professors and students were violently opposed to the opening of medical courses to women.

After much alternating hope and disappointment, during which she was constantly supported by the practical help and championship of her father, Miss Garrett was at length advised that the Society of Apothecaries could not, by its charter, refuse to admit her to its examinations. She thereupon obtained from the Society the authorization to get her medical education privately from teachers of recognized medical schools, took the examinations of the Society, and in 1865 obtained its licence to practise, thus qualifying as a medical practitioner. The Society of Apothecaries, however, altered forthwith its constitution, so as to debar from qualification in the future those who had not been trained in a medical school. It looked as if the long fight had been fruitless in general results, and as if women would have to go to foreign universities for their medical qualifications. But Miss Garrett now had the right to practise, and in 1866 she opened a dispensary for women and children in Marylebone, which was quickly appreciated, and which before long was converted into a small hospital where women could obtain the medical services of those of their own sex. Known for many years as the New Hospital for Women, Euston Road, its name was changed in 1918 to the Elizabeth Garrett Anderson Hospital. It was the first hospital staffed by medical women.

In 1870, just before the outbreak of the Franco-Prussian War, Miss Garrett obtained the M.D. degree of the university of Paris, both the Emperor Napoleon III and the British ambassador, Lord Lyons, giving her sympathy and support in her enterprise. In November 1870 she was a candidate for the London School Board; the husbands of her patients in Marylebone formed themselves into committees to support her candidature, with the result that her name appeared at the head of the poll with 47,000 votes, the highest vote, it is said, ever recorded in these elections; the poet Browning was among her enthusiastic supporters. In 1871 she married James George Skelton Anderson (died 1907), of the Orient steamship line, whose sympathy and co-operation constituted a great factor in her further success.

Thanks in great measure to the excellence of the work done by Mrs. Garrett Anderson, the British examining bodies gradually opened their examinations to women. After the foundation in 1874 of the London School of Medicine for Women by Dr. Sophia Louisa Jex-Blake [q. v.], the requirement of training in a large general hospital was met by the London (afterwards the Royal) Free Hospital admitting women as students to its wards. If the battle was not yet completely won, at least the outposts had been carried; but for many years Mrs. Garrett Anderson remained the only woman admitted to membership of the British Medical Association, to which she was elected in 1873. Her activities in her chosen sphere were unceasing; for twenty-three years (1875–1897) she was lecturer on medicine at the London School of Medicine for Women, and for twenty years (1883–1903) its dean, while she acted as senior physician to the New Hospital for Women for over a quarter of a century (1866–1892); in 1896–1897 she was president of the East Anglian branch of the British Medical Association.

Possessed of sound judgement as well as natural wit, Mrs. Garrett Anderson aimed at the maintenance of health rather than the cure of disease. Like her friend Miss Sarah Emily Davies [q. v.], the first mistress of Girton College, Cambridge, she desired to improve the whole social and political status of women, believing that the real opposition lay, not, as was sometimes said, between serious study and domestic habits, but between serious study and frivolity. Her own interests were many and varied: gardening, outdoor life generally, music, foreign travel, art needlework. She spoke and wrote frequently on the subjects which she had at heart. Her interest in housing and sanitation found scope during her term of office as mayor of Aldeburgh (1908–1909), where she always had her country home. She was ever an ardent champion of women's suffrage, and a warm supporter of the work of her sister, Mrs. Millicent Garrett Fawcett.

Mrs. Garrett Anderson possessed in a high degree the qualities necessary for pioneers. During the early struggles an opponent wrote of her: 'She has great calmness of demeanour, a large amount of firmness, usually a good deal of fairness and coolness in argument, a pleasant countenance, a decided but perfectly feminine manner, and attire at once apart from prevalent extravagance and affected eccentricity.' By her wise statesmanship, steady pressure, and high ideals she was instrumental in securing the admission of women to various qualifying bodies and to important medical societies, and in ensuring the equality of their status with that enjoyed by men. She died at Aldeburgh 17 December 1917, and is buried in the churchyard there, beside her father and mother. She left one son, Sir Alan Garrett Anderson, K.B.E., and one daughter, Dr. Louisa Garrett Anderson, C.B.E., who organized the first hospital managed by women at the front in the European War, and was subsequently head of the military hospital in Endell Street, London.

[*The Times*, 18 December 1917; Elizabeth Blackwell, *Pioneer Work in Opening the Medical Profession to Women*, 1895 and 1914; Millicent Garrett Fawcett, *What I Remember*, 1924; Barbara Stephen, *Emily Davies and Girton College*, 1927; private information and letters; personal knowledge.] F. C. J.

ANDERSON, MARY REID (1880–1921), women's labour organizer, was born at Glasgow 13 August 1880, the eldest daughter of John Duncan Macarthur, proprietor of a drapery establishment, by his wife, Anne Elizabeth Martin. She was educated at a school in Glasgow, and afterwards studied for a time in Germany at Diez a. d. Lahn. On her return she entered her father's business and became interested in the conditions of shop employees. Moved by their grievances she joined in 1901 the shop assistants' union, and through her interest in this organization was led to work for the improvement of women's labour conditions in general. Becoming known to Sir Charles Dilke [q. v.] and to Miss Gertrude Tuckwell, the honorary secretary to the Women's Trade Union League, Miss Macarthur was appointed, through their influence, general secretary to the League (1903), a position in which she at once came into prominence. She now began to organize women workers everywhere and, managing always to lend dramatic quality to her struggles, obtained wide publicity and sympathy for her cause. Much of her work was connected with the extension of the trade union movement. She created a very large number of local unions, and later stabilized these small organizations by amalgamating them to form the National Federation of Women Workers (1906), of which she became secretary. Another side of her activities was concerned with the question of sweated labour and the establishment of a minimum wage for sweated women workers. In 1906 she assisted in forming the National Anti-Sweating League, of which she became a prominent member, impressing the select parliamentary committee on work in the home (1907) by her evidence in favour of a legal minimum wage. Her work for the women chain-makers of Cradley Heath was especially notable. She was elected by them as a workers' representative on the chain-making trade board (1909), and after this board had fixed legal minimum rates of wages she led in 1910 a memorable strike of the women in order to compel the employers to pay the new rates of wages without the delay permitted by the Trade Boards Act of 1909.

In 1911 Miss Macarthur married Mr. William Crawford Anderson, chairman of the executive committee of the Independent Labour Party, and from 1914 to 1918 member for the Attercliffe division of Sheffield. In 1914, at the request of Queen Mary, Mrs. Anderson became honorary secretary of the central committee on women's employment, and in this office, and as a member of the committee of the Prince of Wales's fund, and of numerous reconstruction and other committees, such as the national insurance advisory committee, she rendered important service to the country during the European War. She exerted a powerful influence on behalf of munition workers, and was one of the authors of the Wages (Temporary Regulation) Act (1918), under which wages were stabilized after the armistice. At the general election of 1918 she spoke in many constituencies on behalf of the labour party, and standing herself as labour candidate for the Stourbridge division of Worcestershire, was nearly successful in winning the seat.

The deaths of both her parents not long after the general election was followed by the death from pneumonia of her husband in February 1919. In search of distraction Mrs. Anderson visited America. In 1920 she paid a second visit to attend as a representative of Great Britain the first labour conference convened under the League of Nations. This conference, and the possibility which it revealed of alleviating the lot of the workers throughout the world, rekindled her faith and ardour, and she returned to England to arouse enthusiasm for the 'labour charter' which she had helped to fashion at Washington. In her oratory, which was always moving, there was detected at this period a new and deeper note which her friends attributed to the maturity that comes of suffering. But at the zenith of her powers she became ill and underwent an operation which revealed the presence of a malignant ailment from which there was no hope of recovery. A second operation was attempted, without success, and she died at Golders Green 1 January 1921, leaving one daughter.

[Mary A. Hamilton, *Mary Macarthur: A Biographical Sketch*, 1925; personal knowledge.] J. J. M.

ANSON, Sir WILLIAM REYNELL, third baronet (1843-1914), warden of All Souls College, Oxford, was born at Walberton, Sussex, 14 November 1843, the eldest son of Sir John William Hamilton Anson, second baronet, by his wife, Elizabeth, daughter of Major-General Sir Denis Pack [q. v.]. After three years at a private school at Brighton he went to Eton in 1857, becoming there after a time the pupil of Edmond Warre [q. v.], afterwards head master. From Eton he passed in 1862 to Balliol College, Oxford, and after taking first classes in classical moderations and the final classical school he was elected to a fellowship at All Souls College in 1867, an event which was to determine his subsequent career. For a few years after this he read for the bar and practised on the home circuit; but in 1874, within a year of succeeding to the baronetcy, he returned to Oxford as Vinerian reader in English law. In 1881 he was elected warden of his college, the first layman to hold that office.

Anson's election occurred at a difficult moment in the history of All Souls. The Statutory Commission of 1877 had recently introduced far-reaching reforms in the tenure of fellowships and the disposal of college revenues, and it seemed doubtful how far the historic continuity of All Souls could be retained. For Anson the duty of his college was clear; it lay in the loyal acceptance of the new order, combined with the preservation of what was permanently valuable in the spirit of the old. He believed, and he set himself as warden to prove, in words which he had used himself in speaking of his friend and colleague, John Andrew Doyle [q. v.], 'that there was room for a college of an exceptional type, devoting itself through its professoriate and its library to university purposes, encouraging advanced study by the endowment of research, securing through a system of prize fellowships the continued interest in academic life of men engaged in public work, and yet retaining its old character as a collegiate society'. His own temperament, which was cautious without being obstructive, made him admirably qualified to be the leader of such a policy. How well he succeeded in it can be fully appreciated only by the members of the college that he guided so wisely during the thirty-three years of his wardenship.

It was characteristic of Anson that he at once recognized that the exceptional opportunities attaching to the headship of All Souls laid peculiar obligations upon him. He possessed just the qualities necessary to give him a commanding position in university affairs. A man of real learning, he was also a man of affairs, with a wide knowledge of the world outside Oxford; holding strong opinions himself, he was invariably courteous and tactful in expressing them, and patient of those who honestly differed from him; precise and orderly in his habits of mind, he was completely free from pedantry. For the first eighteen years of his wardenship he was a resident in Oxford, a frequent speaker in congregation and convocation, an active member of numerous boards and delegacies, a sincere, if cautious, friend of university reform. In addition to the multifarious duties of his office he voluntarily undertook from 1886 to 1898 the tuition, in law, of undergraduates of Trinity College. It was also during these busy years that he produced the works of legal literature which are his chief claim to public remembrance; he published *The Principles of the English Law of Contract* in 1879; part I of *The Law and Custom of the Constitution* in 1886; and part II of the same work in 1892.

In 1898 Anson became vice-chancellor of the university, but he held the office for six months only; for in April 1899 a vacancy occurred in the parliamentary representation of the university, and his friends urged him to come forward in the unionist interest. He had already made one unsuccessful attempt to enter parliament, as liberal candidate for West Staffordshire in 1880; but even at that time his liberalism had been rather that of Lord Hartington and Mr. Goschen than that of Mr. Gladstone, and in 1886 he had been one of the minority who seceded from their party on the question of Home Rule. Anson had abandoned his political ambitions, though not his keen interest in contemporary politics; and he saw that at the age of fifty-four a political career of the first rank was hardly open to him. He was elected without opposition, and continued to represent the university in parliament until his death. He proved himself an ideal university member, and was moreover admirably equipped, by his researches into the history of parties and by his unrivalled knowledge of the working of the constitution, to play a useful part in the counsels of his party; but he lacked some of the qualities necessary to the successful party leader. His voice was somewhat weak for public speaking; his physique had never been robust; his political opinions, though strong, were never extreme. Certainly his best parliamentary work was done on subjects that fall more especially within the province of a university burgess rather than on general political questions; and on the former, as the House soon recognized, he spoke with authority.

In the summer of 1902 Anson was appointed parliamentary secretary to the Board of Education, a position which at once brought him into the forefront of the controversy aroused by Mr. Balfour's Education Bill of that year. In retrospect it is now generally admitted that this Bill laid well and truly a foundation for the subsequent development of public elementary education; but at the time certain proposals in it, particularly those for giving rate-aid to the voluntary schools, were bitterly resented by a large number of nonconformists in the country, and were opposed with all the arts of parliamentary obstruction by a section of the opposition in the House. The controversy was discreditable to the extreme partisans on both sides, who displayed a narrow sectarian rancour in which the real interests both of religion and of education seemed to be forgotten. Anson, though he enjoyed the administrative work of his office and entered with zest into the parliamentary struggle, could not be altogether happy in such an atmosphere. Moreover his office was a subordinate one without a seat in the Cabinet; and the policy for which he was responsible in the House of Commons was not in all respects what he would have framed himself; indeed the Bill was already in committee when he took office. In the following year his principal business was the London Education Bill, with which also he was far from satisfied. He remained at the Board of Education until the resignation of the Balfour ministry in 1905, engaged mainly in the work of administrative reorganization entailed by the new Acts, and in the ungrateful task of dealing with the 'passive resistance' movement which followed the attempts to enforce the Act of 1902 in some parts of the country. By the time he left office he had rendered services of great value to the country and to his party, for which, by an oversight of the party leaders, resented more by his friends than by himself, he received no public recognition; and it was not till 1911 that he received the belated honour of a privy councillorship at the coronation of King George V.

During the remainder of Anson's life his party was in opposition. He took a prominent part in the debates on the abortive liberal Education Bills of 1906–1908; but after that his interventions became rarer. He was, however, in full sympathy with his party in the bitter constitutional struggle that arose out of Mr. Lloyd George's Finance Bill of 1909; he lent the support of his authority as a constitutional lawyer to the action of the House of Lords in rejecting the Bill; and he deeply resented what he regarded as the mutilation of the constitution by the passing of the Parliament Act of 1911, and the policy of Mr. Asquith's government in forcing their Home Rule Bill through parliament under the powers obtained under that Act. He died at Oxford after a short illness 4 June 1914. He never married.

Anson found time for many forms of public service outside the academic and the political fields. He was chancellor of the diocese of Oxford (1899–1912), chairman of the Oxfordshire Quarter Sessions (1894–1914), a trustee of the British Museum, and of the National Portrait Gallery, a bencher of the Inner Temple, fellow of Eton College, and chairman of the council of Oxford House in Bethnal Green. But a mere recital of his activities gives a very imperfect idea of his personality; a churchman, a scholar, a lawyer, a politician, he was above all a friend; his courtesy and sympathy made young and old feel at home in his company; his humour left no sting except when it was pointed at what seemed to him low or mean; his generosity, often exercised anonymously, seemed to have no limits.

In his *Principles of the English Law of Contract* Anson set himself to 'delineate the general principles which govern the contractual relation from its beginning to its end'. He asked and answered with admirable lucidity just those questions that an intelligent student would ask about the subject. The book possesses two eminent merits: it directs the student's attention to general principles, avoiding doubtful or exceptional rules and the peculiarities of the special contracts; and it teaches him method. It has remained the indispensable introductory text-book on the subject. Sixteen editions have been published in this country, it has been translated into German, and an American edition has been widely used. But the book is also memorable because it heralded a new conception of legal education. The scientific study of English law dates practically from the latter half of the nineteenth century; when Anson began to lecture on it, he was the only teacher of English law in Oxford; and, in spite of Blackstone's example, almost all books on English law were then written with a professional, and not an educational, purpose. Anson himself was one of a band of pioneers who by their own personal teaching and by their admirable text-books dealt a mortal blow to the superstition that English law cannot be taught; and to help in ending the centuries-old divorce between English law and the English universities was no slight service to both. His *Law and Custom of the Constitution* has the same merits of orderly arrangement and perfectly lucid expression, but its aim is different. It is not primarily a book for the beginner, but a full and accurate description of the constitution from a special point of view carefully chosen and continuously adhered to by the author. The two parts of the work deal respectively with *Parliament* and *The Crown*; in each his attitude is that of a scientific inquirer investigating and demonstrating the anatomy of a highly complex organism; yet he never allows the reader to forget that what he is examining is not a piece of dead mechanism, but a living body with a history of past development and a future of which the trend can sometimes be dimly forecast. It was the actual working of the constitution in the present that he had set himself to describe, and he strictly subordinated to this its other aspects; yet he well knew that it is only for purposes of analysis and exposition that the law and the history of the constitution can be dissociated. No other writer on the constitution has chosen to observe it from exactly the angle chosen by Anson; and his work has therefore a distinctive object and method, which, together with its admirably thorough execution, ensure it a place in the permanent literature of the English constitution. Five editions of it have appeared. Besides his legal works, Anson published in 1898 the *Autobiography and Political Correspondence of Augustus Henry, 3rd Duke of Grafton.*

Anson's portrait, painted by Sir H. von Herkomer in 1895, hangs in the hall of All Souls, and a recumbent effigy by John Tweed has been placed in the college chapel.

[*A Memoir of Sir William Anson*, edited by H. H. Henson, 1920; *The Times*, 5 and 6 June 1914; personal knowledge.] J. L. B.

ARBER, EDWARD (1836–1912), man of letters, the youngest son of Thomas Arber, architect, of London, by his wife, Eleanor Newell, was born at 29 George

Street, Hanover Square, 4 December 1836. He was educated at private schools in and around London, and after a year at a school in Paris entered the civil service as a clerk in the Admiralty office in 1854. He had already shown an interest in English literature, and in 1858 he began to attend at King's College the lectures of Henry Morley [q. v.], under whose influence this interest grew into a lifelong devotion to the subject. From this time forward he gave such leisure as a civil servant had to the study of English literature, especially of the Tudor and Stuart periods, until in 1878, feeling that his life was being wasted, he retired from the Admiralty, and was appointed English lecturer at University College, London, under Professor Morley. In 1881 he was made professor of English at the Mason College, Birmingham, where he did much to popularize the study of English by his personal influence in lecturing and teaching as well as by his writing; both there and at London University he was mainly responsible for the introduction into the curriculum of the study of old and middle English texts. In 1894 he retired from teaching and lived in London, with the position of emeritus professor of English language and literature in the university of Birmingham. From 1880 he was a fellow of King's College, London.

From the first Arber had perceived that the study of English was gravely handicapped by the lack of reliable texts at a reasonable price, and with characteristic energy he determined to supply the deficiency himself. The Early English Text Society, founded by Frederick James Furnivall [q. v.] in 1864, was doing much to make middle English literature accessible, and Arber set himself, in his own words, ' to *represent* the later literature by giving, at as cheap a price as can be, exact texts, sometimes of books already famous, sometimes of those quite forgotten '. On 1 January 1868 Milton's *Areopagitica* was published at the price of 6*d*., the first of a series of thirty volumes known as Arber's ' English Reprints ' (1868–1871). They were immediately successful, and were afterwards followed by *An English Garner* (8 vols., 1877–1896) and ' The English Scholar's Library ' (16 vols., 1878–1884) as well as by several volumes dealing with the early history of America. All these contain reprints of works written between the time of Caxton and that of Addison, some of which still remain the only easily available texts. But Arber's most important contributions to English studies were the *Transcript of the Registers of the Company of Stationers of London, 1554–1640* (5 vols., 1875–1894), and the *Term Catalogues, 1668–1709* (3 vols., 1903–1906), edited from the quarterly lists of the booksellers. These contain much material formerly quite inaccessible, and are essential for any detailed study of the Elizabethan and Restoration periods.

All these volumes, like most of Arber's work, were printed privately and distributed by himself. The critical and historical introductions prefixed to his Reprints, if at times ill-arranged, and occasionally coloured by his violently protestant sympathies, display very considerable knowledge, as well as the energy and enthusiasm without which he could never have succeeded in his lifelong task. If his work does not always reach the standard of accuracy demanded by modern scholarship, it must be remembered that he was a pioneer in this field; and it is largely owing to the labours of such men as Arber that the exact study of English has been made possible. Much of his work was done in the Bodleian Library, and in 1905 he received the honorary degree of doctor of letters from the university of Oxford. On 23 November 1912 he was knocked down by a taxicab whilst crossing Kensington High Street, and killed instantaneously.

Arber married in 1869 Marion, only daughter of Alexander Murray, who had published the first few volumes of the Reprints. He left two sons, of whom the elder, E. A. N. Arber, became demonstrator in palaeobotany in the university of Cambridge, and died in 1918.

[Private information.] R. L.

ARBUTHNOT, Sir ROBERT KEITH, fourth baronet (1864–1916), rear admiral, the eldest son of Sir William Wedderburn Arbuthnot, third baronet, by his wife, Alice Margaret, daughter of the Rev. Matthew C. Tompson, vicar of Alderminster, Worcestershire, was born at Alderminster 23 March 1864. Entering the navy in 1877 Arbuthnot won the Goodenough medal for the sub-lieutenant who passes the best examination of the year, served in the royal yacht, and was in 1885 promoted from it to the rank of lieutenant. In 1897 he became commander, and in 1897–1898 served under the director of naval intelligence. Afloat and ashore he gained a high reputation as an energetic and scientific officer. He was injured by an accident to a 6-inch gun in 1901, and in 1903–1904 was flag-captain at Portsmouth to Sir John (afterwards Lord) Fisher. Thenceforward he was continuously employed. In 1910 in a speech at a private dinner, he expressed his fear of the imminence of war with Germany; this speech, which was reported, gave great offence to the Kaiser, and was made the subject of formal complaint by the German government. The Admiralty in consequence was obliged to punish Arbuthnot by removing him from his ship, *Lord Nelson* ; but it immediately appointed him to serve on the submarine committee, and a few months later in the same year made him commodore of the third destroyer flotilla, where he did work in which he excelled, the training of young officers.

In October 1913, a year after his promotion to rear-admiral, Arbuthnot was appointed second in command of the second battle squadron, flying his flag in the *Orion*, and this position he held in the grand fleet at the outbreak of the European War. He was at sea with the six battleships of the squadron, under Vice-Admiral Sir George Warrender [q. v.], when German battle-cruisers bombarded Hartlepool and Scarborough on 16 December 1914, and his squadron, with Admiral Beatty's force of four battle-cruisers, had a narrow escape from the German high seas fleet, eighteen dreadnoughts strong. On that occasion Arbuthnot made a determined effort to bring to action the German light craft which passed near the British battleships. Shortly afterwards (January 1915) he was appointed to an independent command, that of the first cruiser squadron, comprising four old-type armoured cruisers of large displacement but low fighting quality. In this squadron, with his flag in the *Defence*, he was serving at the battle of Jutland on 31 May 1916. By the battle-orders his position was in advance of the screen of destroyers covering Admiral Jellicoe's twenty-four battleships, and was therefore well ahead of the latter. The orders laid down that the first duty of the British cruisers, in the event of a fleet action, was to engage the enemy cruisers. As the afternoon drew on the air was full of wireless signals indicating the proximity of Beatty's battle-cruiser force in action with the Germans, and at 4.51 p.m. Jellicoe signalled to the Admiralty, ' Fleet action is imminent '. A haze overhung the water and it was difficult to see clearly. Presently from the south-east came bright crimson flashes and detonations as the battle drew nearer to Jellicoe's main force. At 5.46 p.m. Arbuthnot signalled to Jellicoe, then about four miles distant, the general position of the enemy ; he was fast closing in on the Germans ; but still from his ships only the flashes of guns could be seen in the mist and smoke. At 5.53 p.m. he signalled to his squadron to ' open fire and engage the enemy '. Near him were four German light cruisers of Rear-Admiral Boedicker's second scouting group and the twelfth half-flotilla of destroyers screening the German battle-cruisers. It was the obvious duty of the British cruiser force and destroyers to deal with this German advance guard, and they attacked with such vigour that Boedicker's force did not detect or signal to the German command the approach of Jellicoe's twenty-four battleships. By the grand fleet battle-orders, in the event of bad visibility, the battle-fleet was to deploy by the wing nearest to the enemy, and not away from the enemy as it subsequently did, for reasons explained in the British official history [Corbett, iii, 359–363]. Arbuthnot with *Defence* and *Warrior* pushed in on the German light craft in execution of his task. Fiercely engaged with the German light cruiser *Wiesbaden*, he passed across the bow of Beatty's flagship *Lion*, only 200 yards or so away, and put his adversary out of action. He must have seen that Beatty was heavily engaged, but all the evidence shows the smoke and mist to have been so troublesome that the German heavy ships were difficult to make out. At this critical moment Arbuthnot was suddenly sighted by the German battle-cruiser *Lützow* and battleships *Grosser Kurfürst*, *Markgraf*, *Kronprinz*, and *Kaiser*, which opened a crushing fire on him at a range of 7,000 yards and upwards. At least two salvoes caught his ill-protected ship ; ' a huge furnace ' was seen to glow for some seconds under her fore-turret, and then there rose from her to a great height a pillar of flame and smoke in which Arbuthnot and every soul in the *Defence* perished (6.20 p.m.).

Arbuthnot was an officer of the highest moral and physical courage—' as gallant and determined as ever lived ' (Admiral Jellicoe)—who knew how to maintain strict discipline without losing the affection of his subordinates. A vigorous thinker, he had attracted the notice of Lord Fisher, though he was not in complete sympathy with all Lord Fisher's policy. He died, as Jellicoe's dispatch stated, doing his duty nobly, and performing a task of great difficulty as leader of the cruisers which were covering the battle-fleet. From this task with all its dangers he was the last man to shrink.

Arbuthnot, who was posthumously awarded the K.C.B., married in 1897 Lina, daughter of Colonel A. C. Macleay, and left one daughter.

A portrait of Arbuthnot is included in Sir A. S. Cope's picture 'Some Sea Officers of the Great War', painted in 1921, in the National Portrait Gallery.

[Battle of Jutland official dispatches; H. W. Fawcett and G. W. W. Hooper, *The Fighting at Jutland*, 1921; Sir Julian S. Corbett, (Official) *History of the Great War. Naval Operations*, vols. ii, iii, 1921, 1923; (Official) *Narrative of the Battle of Jutland*, 1924; O. Groos, *Der Krieg in der Nordsee*, vol. v, 1925 (the German official history); private information.] H. W. W.

ARCH, JOSEPH (1826–1919), politician, the younger son of John Arch, a farm worker of Barford, near Warwick, by his wife, Hannah Sharard, was born at Barford 10 November 1826. He was the descendant of people who for several generations had been farm or estate labourers and domestic servants. After three years' attendance at the village school he began work on a farm at nine years of age. But with the help of his mother he continued his education in simple subjects at home during his later boyhood and youth. From the age of nine to forty-six, when he took up the task of organizing the farm workers, Arch was working in woods and on farms, partly in the neighbourhood of his birthplace but mainly in distant parts of England and Wales. After the age of eighteen he was rarely a stationary and regular worker, for he was engaged intermittently in skilled tasks. He gained a high reputation for skill in his work, especially as a hedge-cutter; and he obtained an intimate personal knowledge of the conditions of labour and of life of his fellow workers throughout the country.

In 1847 Arch married Mary Ann Mills, the daughter of a mechanic in the neighbouring village of Wellesbourne, and they had a family of seven children. Soon after his marriage he became a lay preacher of the Primitive Methodist Connexion. He thus gained an experience of public speaking. Having obtained some acquaintance with the methods of the industrial labour movement, on his visits to his home he took opportunities of suggesting to his neighbours that the only effective method of improving their conditions was to be found in combination. But Arch was not alone in the idea of promoting a trade union for agricultural labourers. A union was started in Herefordshire in 1871, and in other areas there had been sporadic efforts to combine. The great movement began, however, when a group of labourers invited Arch to address a meeting at Wellesbourne on 7 February 1872. From that day the movement spread rapidly. The Warwickshire Agricultural Labourers' Union was formed on 29 March and, unions having sprung up in other counties, the National Agricultural Labourers' Union was founded just two months later; in December of that year the Warwickshire Union was affiliated to the National. On its formation Arch was appointed organizing secretary of the National Union, and later he was elected president.

For some time 'the revolt of Hodge' created a large amount of public and political interest, and not a little consternation. The Union leaders began using the strike weapon. Their opponents replied with lock-outs. But from an early stage the Union assisted and encouraged the migration of workers to industrial areas. Arch was everywhere its most prominent representative and spokesman. In 1875 he went to Canada as the guest of the Canadian government to examine conditions of labour and to arrange a scheme for assisting the emigration of farm workers. In 1880 he stood as liberal candidate for Wilton, Wiltshire, and was defeated. But in 1885 he contested the North-West division of Norfolk and was returned to parliament. In the following year he was defeated by his former opponent. From 1873 to 1886 Arch had devoted himself mainly to the activities of the National Union, but he was always a keen liberal and an active party supporter. On the occasion of the Home Rule split he remained with the Gladstonian party. From 1886 onwards he was much engaged in miscellaneous political activities. The Union at this time was weakening, for the membership, which had reached over 86,000 in the early part of 1874, fell to 20,000 in 1880, and was only about 5,000 in 1889. Arch's interest in it was waning also. He vacillated between belief in industrial combination and in political action—always on the liberal side—as methods of improving the lot of the farm workers. In 1892 he was again elected member for North-West Norfolk. Although the Union was again active and its membership increasing for a time, Arch was 'moving in the political sphere' and his parliamentary duties 'gave him no choice but to look on'. He continued to represent North-West Norfolk as a liberal until 1902, but as the Union declined and finally disappeared Arch's political influence declined also.

Arch's wife died in 1894, and in 1899 he married Miss Miriam Blomfield. On retiring from public life he settled in the family cottage at Barford, where he died 12 February 1919. Always a poor man and always limited in outlook, Arch was never able, except in 1872, to give an effective lead to opinion; yet by his perseverance and energy he did more than any other man of his time to improve the conditions of the agricultural workers; and for some years, especially from 1872 to 1886, he exercised considerable influence in matters relating to agriculture and rural life.

[Joseph Arch, *Autobiography*, edited by the Countess of Warwick, 1898.] A. W. A.

ARDILAUN, first Baron (1840–1915), philanthropist. [See Guinness, Sir Arthur Edward.]

ARGYLL, ninth Duke of (1845–1914), governor-general of Canada. [See Campbell, John Douglas Sutherland.]

ARROL, Sir **WILLIAM** (1839–1913), engineering contractor, was born at Houston, Renfrewshire, 13 February 1839, the son of Thomas Arrol, who began life as a spinner and afterwards became manager at the works of Messrs. Coats, thread manufacturers, at Paisley. At the age of nine Arrol began work in the bobbin department of Messrs. Coats, but disliking factory work was apprenticed in 1853 to Thomas Reid, a blacksmith at Paisley; in 1863 he became foreman at the works of Laidlaw and Son, boiler and bridge manufacturers, at Glasgow. Five years later (1868) he was able to set up as a boiler-maker on his own account, and in 1872 began the construction of the Dalmarnock ironworks, near Glasgow, which in time covered 20 acres, employed 5,000 men, and became the largest structural steelworks in the United Kingdom. Among early contracts were two for the Caledonian Railway; one, a five-arched bridge at Bothwell, the other, a heavy viaduct carrying the main line over the Clyde into Glasgow.

Before 1870 direct railway communication between the north of Scotland and England was barred by the estuaries of the Tay and Forth. At that time plans were approved for a long girder bridge over the Tay and a suspension bridge over the Forth. The Tay bridge was built in 1870–1877, and a beginning made with that over the Forth, the contract for the latter being placed with the Dalmarnock firm. But on 28 December 1879, during an exceptionally heavy storm, the centre spans of the Tay bridge were blown down, together with a railway train which was crossing at the time. A new Tay bridge of eighty-five spans, designed by William Henry Barlow [q. v.], was constructed by Arrol's firm in 1882–1887; and a cantilever bridge of a new type was designed by (Sir) John Fowler [q. v.] and (Sir) Benjamin Baker [q. v.] for the Forth. In 1883 the firm of Tancred, Arrol, & Co. was formed to undertake the construction of the Forth bridge, and it was completed in 1890. On the site of the bridge the estuary narrows to about a mile across and is divided into channels, 200 feet in depth, by the island of Inchgarvie. The bridge consists of two main spans, each one-third of a mile (1,710 feet) in length, and side spans. Larger at that time than any rigid or stable bridge, and little exceeded by any similar structure since, the design of the Forth bridge was governed by the condition that the erection had to be effected without scaffolding, by building out from the piers. For its construction there were required 51,000 tons of steel, 65,000 cubic yards of concrete, 49,000 cubic yards of rubble, and 750,000 cubic feet of granite. The piers were sunk by excavation in compressed air. The total length of the bridge is 8,295 feet, the height above high-water level 150 feet, and the height of the towers 361 feet. Great as is the credit due to the engineer designers, much is due also to the constructors, without whose courage, resource, and mechanical skill, the bridge could not have been built in the time, and at the moderate cost of £3,000,000.

Arrol added a designing department to the Dalmarnock works, and constructed many other bridges, including the steel work for the Tower bridge, London (1886–1894), the Nile bridge at Cairo (1904–1908), and the Wear bridge at Sunderland (1905–1909). The first is interesting owing to the size of the bascules, which open for the passage of ships; they each weigh 1,200 tons, and are moved by hydraulic power.

Arrol, who was knighted in 1890, did not take a large part in public affairs. He was deputy lieutenant for the county of Glasgow, J.P. for the county of Ayr, and for fourteen years (1892–1906) he represented South Ayrshire in parliament as a liberal-unionist. In 1885 he bought the estate of Seafield, at Ayr, built a house there, took pleasure in gardens, and collected pictures. He died there 20 February 1913.

Arrol was married three times: first, in 1864 to Elizabeth Pattison (died 1904); secondly, in 1905 to Miss Hodgart (died 1910), of Lockerbank, Ayr; thirdly, in 1910 to Elsie, daughter of James Robertson, of London. He had no children.

[Philip Phillips, *The Forth Bridge*, 1889; *Proceedings* of the Institution of Mechanical Engineers, February, 1913; *Transactions* of the Institution of Engineers and Ship-builders in Scotland, vol. lvi, 472, 1912–1913; *Engineering*, 21 February 1913.] W. C. U.

ASHBOURNE, first Baron (1837–1913), lord chancellor of Ireland. [See Gibson, Edward.]

AUSTIN, ALFRED (1835–1913), poet laureate, the second son of Joseph Austin, wool-stapler, of Leeds, by his wife, Mary, sister of Joseph Locke, M.P. [q. v.], was born at Headingley, Leeds, 30 May 1835. Of a Roman Catholic family, he was educated at Stonyhurst College (1849–1852) and then at Oscott College, whence in 1853 he graduated B.A. of London University. Called to the bar by the Inner Temple in 1857, he joined the Northern circuit; but in 1858, having already published a verse-tale and a novel, he abandoned law for literature. The meagre notice given in the *Athenæum* to his satire, *The Season* (1861), drew from him a sequel abusing that journal and its editor, William Hepworth Dixon. Austin's faith in his poetic genius wavered somewhat in 1862, when a narrative poem entitled *The Human Tragedy*, which he gave out as the first draft of a *magnum opus*, was coldly received. He published no more verse till 1871, but turned again to novel-writing, though with little success. After his marriage in 1865 to Hester, daughter of Thomas Homan-Mulock, of Bellair, King's county, he sought an opening in political journalism. He contested Taunton unsuccessfully in 1865 and Dewsbury in 1880, standing in the conservative interest. From 1866 to 1896 he was leader-writer to the *Standard*, and occasionally acted as its special correspondent abroad, for example at the Vatican Council of 1869–1870, with the Prussian army in 1870, and at the Congress of Berlin in 1884. His chief concern was with foreign affairs. An early enthusiast for Polish and Italian patriots, his hatred of Russia made him a devoted follower of Disraeli. In 1870 he rejoiced when the Prussian sword, 'the World's salvation, smote its insulter to the knee' (*Interludes*), and by 1876 he thought Garibaldi an 'unmitigated nuisance'. In 1883 he and William John Courthope [q. v.] became joint editors of the newly founded *National Review*, and Austin carried on the work for eight years after Courthope's resignation in 1887.

From 1863 Austin was a fairly regular contributor to the critical reviews. In this way, by 1870, he had given public expression to his view that Hugo, Tennyson, Browning, Morris, Arnold, Clough, and Swinburne were indifferent poets, because they were either 'feminine' or lyrical, and lyric he called 'essentially childish'. He urged that no poem was great unless it was an epic or dramatic romance on a theme combining love, patriotism, and religion. In 1867 he had settled at Swinford Old Manor, near Ashford, Kent, in a domestic circle conscious of the privilege of cherishing a great poet. Feeling himself again 'the adopted heir of Art and Nature', he returned to poetry, and besides extending his *Human Tragedy* to the range of the ideal great poem, between 1871 and 1908 he published twenty volumes of verse. In 1894, a prose work, *The Garden that I Love*, achieved wide popular success; and because of this, or because of his journalistic services to Lord Salisbury's party, he was made poet laureate on 1 January 1896. Although the appointment was humorously criticized, the laureate's reverence for authority and for official ceremony gave him partial qualifications; but in commemorating certain national events he only revealed his own lack of all sense of the ludicrous. On the whole, his laureate pieces are better than most of their kind, although the first of them—an *Ode* in *The Times* (12 January 1896) hailing the news of the Jameson Raid—is as bad as the worst. To the end he believed that only the malice of critics and the *odium theologicum* prevented the world from taking him at his own high valuation. He never formally left the Church of Rome, but 'vicarage gardens' and 'hamlets hallowed by their spires' attached him sentimentally to the Church of England. He died without issue at Swinford Old Manor 2 June 1913.

By mingling earlier work with every new volume, Austin added to the apparent bulk of his writings. Probably he is best in his prose 'garden-diaries', casual but often pompous jottings, half reverie, half autobiography, mainly devoted to the charm of his Kentish home or of his Italian holidays: they are not as solemnly sentimental as his poems. His novels are thin in story, abundant in moralizing, and luscious in sentiment. His criticism is profuse in the false attribution to others of precisely those faults which he failed to recognize in himself. His verse never frees itself from his admiration of Scott and Byron: but Scott never taught him the way to tell a tale, and Byron could not save him from invariably being 'an uncompromising moralist' (*The Season*). Not content with a talent for singing simply of country and countryside, he attempted to treat philosophic themes in epic and dramatic form. *The Conversion of Winckelmann* and *Fortunatus the Pessimist* are minor successes: but he had no gift for characterization and his narrative dwells inordinately on tales of sighing lovers 'with teardrops trembling on the cheek'. Perpetually revolving truisms, he could never give them the semblance of new or valuable truths.

There is a portrait of Austin by Leslie Ward ('Spy') in the National Portrait Gallery.

The following is a list of Austin's works:

I. Verse. (*a*) Satires: 1. *The Season* (1861). 2. *My Satire and its Censors* (1861). 3. *The Golden Age* (1871).

(*b*) Narrative: 4. *Randolph* (1854). 5. *The Human Tragedy* (1862); this was withdrawn from circulation, and an expanded version appeared in 1876, and revised versions of this in 1889 and 1891. 6. *Madonna's Child* (1873); this became Act 2 of *The Human Tragedy* in 1876. 7. *Rome or Death* (1873); this became Act 3 of *The Human Tragedy* in 1876, giving to the original story a setting in the Garibaldian wars, and leading to an Act 4 which extends the setting to include phases of the Franco-German War. 8. *Leszko the Bastard: a Tale of Polish Grief* (1877), a reshaping of no. 4 above.

(*c*) Collections of Lyric and Narrative: 9. *Interludes* (1872). 10. *Soliloquies in Song* (1882). 11. *At the Gate of the Convent* (1885). 12. *Love's Widowhood* (1889). 13. *English Lyrics* (edited by William Watson, 1890). 14. *Lyrical Poems* (1891). 15. *Narrative Poems* (1891). 16. *The Conversion of Winckelmann* (1897). 17. *Songs of England* (1898). 18. *A Tale of True Love* (1902). 19. *The Door of Humility* (1906); this is a reflective poem in lyric verse with a shadowy narrative framework. 20. *Sacred and Profane Love* (1908).

(*d*) Dramatic Poems: 21. *The Tower of Babel* (1874 and 1890). 22. *Savonarola: a Tragedy* (1881). 23. *Prince Lucifer* (1887). 24. *Fortunatus the Pessimist* (1892). 25. *England's Darling* (1896); this is the laureate's diploma piece on Alfred the Great. 26. *Flodden Field: a Tragedy* (1903); this is the only one of the dramas capable of being staged, and was performed without success at His Majesty's Theatre in June 1903.

II. Prose. (*a*) Novels: 1. *Five Years of It* (2 vols., 1858). 2. *An Artist's Proof* (3 vols., 1864). 3. *Won by a Head* (3 vols., 1866).

(*b*) Political: 4. *Russia before Europe* (1876); second edition entitled *Tory Horrors: a letter to Gladstone* (1876). 5. *England's Policy and Peril: a letter to Beaconsfield* (1877). 6. *Hibernian Horrors: a letter to Gladstone* (1880).

(*c*) Critical: 7. *A Vindication of Lord Byron* (1869); this first appeared in *The Standard*. 8. *The Poetry of the Period* (1870), eight papers reprinted from *Temple Bar* (1869). 9. *New and Old Canons in Criticism* (*Contemporary Review*, 1881). 10. *A Vindication of Tennyson* (*Macmillan's Magazine*, 1885), a reply to Swinburne's *Tennyson and Victor Hugo*, later reprinted in *The Bridling of Pegasus* (no. 13 below). 11. *The End and Limits of Objective Poetry*, a preface to the second edition of *Prince Lucifer* (1887). 12. *The Position and Prospects of Poetry*, a preface to the third edition of *The Human Tragedy* (1889). 13. *The Bridling of Pegasus* (1910), a collection of essays written in the preceding thirty years, the most noteworthy being an attack on Wordsworth.

(*d*) Personal and Miscellaneous: 14. *A Note of Admiration to the editor of the Saturday Review* (1861), part of the quarrel about *The Season*. 15. *The Garden that I Love* (1894). 16. *In Veronica's Garden* (1895). 17. *Lamia's Winter Quarters* (1898). 18. *Spring and Autumn in Ireland* (1900), reprinted from *Blackwood's Magazine* (1894–1895). 19. *The Poet's Diary* (1904). 20. *Haunts of Ancient Peace* (1902). 21. *The Garden that I Love*, Second Series (1907). 22. *Autobiography* (2 vols., 1911).

[Austin's *Autobiography*; J. O. in the *Athenæum*, 7 June 1913; S. P. Sherman, *On Contemporary Literature*, 1917.]

H. B. C-n.

AVEBURY, first Baron (1834–1913), banker, man of science, and author. [See Lubbock, Sir John.]

BAINBRIDGE, FRANCIS ARTHUR (1874–1921), physiologist, was born 29 July 1874 at Stockton-on-Tees, the elder son of Robert Robinson Bainbridge, chemist, of that town, by his wife, Mary Sanderson. Educated at the Leys School, Cambridge, he proceeded to Trinity College, Cambridge, where he studied physiology and took a first class in both parts of the natural science tripos (1895–1897). He then entered St. Bartholomew's Hospital, London, obtaining his M.B. degree at Cambridge in 1901 and the M.D. in 1904.

Bainbridge's work at this period, excellent though it was, gave no suggestion of the abilities which he was later to display. Medicine did not appeal to him, and for a time, seeing no opening in pure physiology, he devoted himself to pathology and bacteriology. In 1905 he became Gordon lecturer on pathology at Guy's Hospital, and in 1907 he went as assistant bacteriologist to the Lister Institute of Preventive Medicine, where his work on food-poisoning bacilli gained wide recognition, and was later embodied in his Milroy lectures at the Royal College of Physicians (1912). In 1911 he became professor of physiology at Durham University and was now able to give undivided attention to the subject which he loved best. His success here was immediate, and when, in 1915, a chair of physiology was instituted at St. Bartholomew's Hospital, he was recalled to fill the post, which he occupied till his premature death, which took place in London on 21 October 1921. He was elected F.R.S. in 1919. He married in 1905 Hilda Winifred, daughter of the Rev. Edward Thornton Smith, of Bickley, Kent, by whom he had one daughter.

Bainbridge was of slight physique and had indifferent health. He was not an impressive teacher, though his lucidity of mind rendered him a very successful one. But he was a brilliant experimenter, bestowing careful thought beforehand on a proposed research, and possessing both ingenuity in devising experiments and high technical skill in carrying them out. Thus his contributions to physiological science were of lasting value. Chief among them were his early work on the mechanism of lymph formation, that on urinary secretion and on the effect on the body of partial removal of the kidneys, and, above all, his later studies on the circulation, in which he established the law that increase of pressure on the venous side of the heart accelerated the rate of the beat. Apart from numerous scientific papers, his most important publication was a monograph on *The Physiology of Muscular Exercise*, a masterly review of the subject (1919).

[*The Times*, 29 October 1921; *Proceedings* of the Royal Society, vol. xciii, B, 1922; private information; personal knowledge.] F. W. A.

BALFOUR OF BURLEIGH, sixth BARON (1849–1921), statesman. [See BRUCE, ALEXANDER HUGH.]

BALL, ALBERT (1896–1917), airman, was born at Nottingham 21 August 1896, the elder son of Sir Albert Ball, estate agent, sometime mayor of the city, by his wife, Harriet Mary Page, of Derby. He was educated at Trent College, Long Eaton, Derbyshire, where he showed himself a sensitive, conscientious boy, with a disturbing passion for collecting pistols. He left school in December 1913, and bought an interest in two engineering companies at Nottingham. On the outbreak of the European War in August 1914 he volunteered for the Nottinghamshire and Derby regiment, Territorial Force, and within two weeks of joining was promoted sergeant. He was granted his commission in October, and spent the winter in training. Chafing at the delay in getting to France, he transferred to a cyclists' corps near Ealing, but aviation caught his fancy, and he entered at Hendon for a course of training. He had to do his flying at dawn in order to be back in camp at Ealing for the 6.0 a.m. parade. He passed out in October 1915, and went to Norwich for training as a flying officer. He was a careful rather than a brilliant pilot. He survived some serious crashes, and having completed his training at the Central Flying School, Upavon, Wiltshire, was seconded to the Royal Flying Corps in January 1916, when he was sent to Gosport as instructor.

Ball flew overseas on 18 February 1916 in order to join No. 13 squadron, and spent his early days chiefly in artillery reconnaissance, which he described as 'great sport'; but he felt the responsibility for his observer's life. Although he was by temperament a single-seater pilot, his two-seater machine drove down, during April, two enemy aeroplanes and destroyed one. In May he was given a single-seater, from which on the 15th he destroyed his first German aeroplane. By the end of the month he was attracting notice. After a short leave in England he returned to France and joined his squadron, No. 11, ten days before the opening of the Somme battle (1 July). Before the battle ended the British air service had established an ascendancy over the enemy which was never afterwards lost, and Ball was the spearhead of this achievement. But the strain told on him, and on 17 July he was wisely transferred to a two-seater squadron, No. 8. On 1 August he was promoted lieutenant, and on the 15th of the same month he was back with No. 11; the next day, on his Nieuport machine, he attacked five enemy aeroplanes, destroying one and forcing two down. On 22 August, his last day with No. 11 squadron, he flew into an enemy formation of twelve machines, crashed two of them, set fire to another, returned for ammunition, attacked fourteen more, ran out of petrol, landed just clear of the trenches, slept by his machine, and flew next morning to No. 60, his new squadron. His audacity and skill were remarkable. By the end of the month he was the leading Allied pilot, and on 1 September he destroyed four more enemy machines. He was promoted captain on 13 September.

Ball's extraordinary success had a heartening effect on the British infantry. When the Somme campaign ended, he was sent home to infuse his spirit and methods into flying officers in training. He was in England from 4 October 1916 until 7 April 1917, when he flew out with No. 56 squadron, arriving for the Arras offensive which opened on 9 April. His method now was to lead his patrol on S.E. 5 (scout experimental) machines and, in addition, to go out alone on his Nieuport. On 3 May he had destroyed thirty-eight enemy machines, one more than the record of the leading French airman, Georges Guynemer. On 5 May, after shooting down two Albatross scouts, he wrote home, describing his spare time, 'I dig in the garden and sing.' Two days later, 7 May 1917, Ball made his last flight. The reports are conflicting. He flew into a formation led by the German airman, Manfred Freiherr von Richthofen, fought three of the enemy, and, it would seem, sent two down before he himself was hit. He was buried at Annoeullin, east of La Bassée. His posthumous Victoria cross award (June 1917) credited him with a record of forty-three aeroplanes and one balloon destroyed and a large number sent down out of control. Ball was awarded the military cross (1916), the distinguished service order with two bars (1916), the croix de guerre and legion of honour (1917), and the Russian order of St. George, fourth class (1917).

Ball was a cheerful young soldier, of gentle manners and vigilant conscience. 'I hate this killing business,' he wrote; but he fought with an almost religious fervour. When he was flying his aeroplane was as much a part of him as were his sensitive hands. He was the greatest fighting pilot of the air service, and his personality has contributed much to its traditions of efficiency and self-sacrifice.

[W. A. Briscoe and H. R. Stannard, *Captain Ball, V.C.*, 1918; official records; personal knowledge.] H. A. J.

BALL, Sir ROBERT STAWELL (1840–1913), astronomer and mathematician, was born at Dublin 1 July 1840, the eldest son of Robert Ball, LL.D. [q.v.], a clerk in Dublin Castle and a well-known naturalist, by his wife, Amelia Gresley Hellicar, of Bristol. He was educated at Tarvin Hall, near Chester, under Dr. J. Brindley, and in 1857 entered Trinity College, Dublin, shortly after the death of his father. In the course of a distinguished university career he gained a scholarship, the Lloyd exhibition, a university studentship and prizes in the fellowship examinations of three successive years (1863–1865). Between 1865 and 1867 he was tutor to the sons of the third Earl of Rosse [q.v.] at Birr Castle, Parsonstown, King's county, and there he first came in contact with practical astronomy through making regular observations of nebulae with Lord Rosse's celebrated six-foot reflector, then, and till long after, the largest in the world. After two years of this congenial work, Ball was appointed professor of applied mathematics and mechanism in the Royal College of Science, Dublin, which had recently been founded by government. He had a natural gift for teaching, and a notable feature of his instruction was the extensive use of experimental apparatus in mechanics, on a system derived from Robert Willis [q.v.]. His growing reputation at this time is attested by his election as a fellow of the Royal Society (1873).

Ball's association with the Royal College of Science came to an end in 1874, and thereafter his life was filled by two astronomical appointments: first (1874–1892), as Andrews professor of astronomy in the university of Dublin and royal astronomer of Ireland, and secondly (1892–1913), as Lowndean professor of astronomy at Cambridge, in succession to John Couch Adams [q.v.]. During his earlier years at the Dunsink Observatory he was an energetic observer with the refractor, but it can now be realized that the plan of his work was unfortunate in conception. In choosing the subject of stellar parallaxes for investigation he was following in the footsteps of his predecessor at Dunsink, F. F. E. Brünnow, but instead of confining his programme to a small number of stars, he spread a wide net in the hope of discovering, by relatively few observations, such stars as might give evidence of exceptional proximity. As the working list included a high proportion of red giants, for reasons natural at the time but now understood to be particularly illusory, it is not surprising that the results were purely negative. From 1880 onwards Ball's activity as a visual observer declined. His right eye, which first gave serious trouble in 1883, became quite useless within the next ten years and was removed in 1897; in the second place, other occupations began to take a larger share of his time.

At Cambridge, where he held a fellowship at King's College, Ball's academic lectures were highly appreciated, and he undertook there his last important work, a *Treatise on Spherical Astronomy* (1908). While at Dunsink he had installed a reflecting telescope for photographic work, the mirror being presented by Dr. Isaac Roberts [q. v.], and the Cambridge observatory under his direction received an important addition to its equipment in the shape of a photographic refractor in the coudé form.

The other occupations to which allusion has been made took two forms, and were mainly responsible for Ball's reputation in the world at large. Between 1877 and 1906 he published no less than thirteen popular works on astronomy. Of these the most considerable and the most successful was *The Story of the Heavens* (first edition, 1886). But it was as a popular lecturer that he came in contact with the widest circle. In this capacity Ball showed all the qualities which make for success. He delivered courses of Christmas lectures at the Royal Institution, and for many years he lectured under the auspices of the Gilchrist Trust. Lecturing tours also took him to America in 1884, 1887, and 1901.

But Ball's real reputation will not rest on his achievements as a popularizer of science, great as they were, nor even as an astronomer, in which capacity he lacked the advantages of professional training, though his energy and enthusiasm went far to supply the deficiency. It must be based on his work as a mathematician, in which he found his most absorbing interest and to which he devoted much of his leisure. Here he was fortunate in finding early a topic which gave a unity to all his researches. This was the theory of screw motions and their relations. Two books, *The Theory of Screws: A Study in the Dynamics of a Rigid Body* (1876) and *A Treatise on the Theory of Screws* (1900), incorporated at different stages the results obtained in a series of twelve great memoirs, published mainly by the Royal Irish Academy, of which he was secretary from 1877 to 1880 and a vice-president from 1885 to 1892. Even after the formal treatise, in the period extending up to his seventieth year, four additional memoirs were published on the same subject. Ball was a geometrician rather than an analyst, as would be expected of one who had received his early training in the Dublin school of his time. He has been ranked by Professor E. T. Whittaker as 'one of the two or three greatest British mathematicians of his generation'. His presidential address to Section A of the British Association in 1887 was notable and characteristic.

Ball's activities and interests were most varied. He was president of the Royal Astronomical Society from 1897 to 1899 and of the Mathematical Association in 1899 and 1900. He was scientific adviser to the Irish Lights Board from 1882 till his death, and rarely missed the annual tour of inspection by the commissioners. He took the most active interest in the affairs of the Royal Zoological Society of Ireland, of which his father had been honorary secretary; he was elected president in 1890 and held the office until he left Dublin for Cambridge. From his father also he had inherited a love of botany, and took a delight in the gardens attached to the observatories at which he resided. At Dunsink in particular, where the grounds are extensive, he indulged a hobby for practical farming, and experimented on pasture land with artificial manures, at that time a comparatively new method in Ireland. Though mainly English by descent, in appearance he was the typical Irishman of convention, and his geniality and sense of humour, which were always combined with shrewdness, made him universally popular. He was knighted in 1886. He died at Cambridge 25 November 1913.

Ball married in 1868 Frances Elizabeth, daughter of W. E. Steele, afterwards director of the National Museum of

Ireland. He had four sons and two daughters.

[W. Valentine Ball, *Reminiscences and Letters of Sir Robert Ball,* 1915 ; *Proceedings* of the Royal Society, vol. xci, A, 1915.]

BARBELLION, W. N. P. (pseudonym), diarist and biologist. [See CUMMINGS, BRUCE FREDERICK.]

BARING, EVELYN, first EARL OF CROMER (1841–1917), statesman, diplomatist, and administrator, was the sixth son of the second marriage of Henry Baring, M.P., with Cecilia, eldest daughter of Admiral William Windham, of Felbrigge, Norfolk. He was born 26 February 1841 at Cromer Hall, Norfolk. His father died in 1848, and Evelyn was brought up by his mother, a remarkable lady who is said to have sung Anacreon to her children. Destined for the Artillery, he passed through the Rev. F. A. Bickmore's hands into the Ordnance School, Carshalton. After objection had been taken to his defective eyesight, he entered at Woolwich in August 1855, and three years later was commissioned, and accompanied his battery to the Ionian Islands, a station which was to affect his future life. The local vernacular, which he learned passably, led him on to read Homer and Anacreon with M. Romanos, a Corfiote scholar; at Corfu he met his future wife, Ethel Stanley, then seventeen years old, the daughter of Sir Rowland Stanley Errington, of the elder Roman Catholic line of the Stanleys and holder of an ancient baronetcy; and there, too, becoming aide-de-camp to the high-commissioner, Sir Henry Knight Storks [q.v.], he was introduced to diplomacy. The times were stirring: he assisted at the reception of Otho, the fugitive king of Greece, at the welcome offered by a British squadron to the new king, George, and at the transference of the Islands to the Greek crown. He followed his chief to Malta and thence in 1864 on a special mission to Jamaica, taking occasion to spend some weeks in General Grant's camp before Petersburg. By the time young Baring had returned by way of Malta to England, in 1867, he had seen men and cities and acquired a working knowledge of at least three foreign languages.

He entered the Staff College, where, to judge by his three *Staff College Essays* published in 1870, he must have been a student of unusual industry, intelligence, and knowledge. Passing next into that department of the War Office which later became the Intelligence Division, he translated for publication two German manuals, one on 'Kriegspiel', the other on military training. Memories of his *libido sciendi* and almost inconvenient zeal long survived in the office. Nevertheless Captain Baring, when offered, in 1872, a choice between military or civil employ, chose the latter, and went out to India with his cousin, Lord Northbrook, the viceroy, as private secretary. He found his reward in varied experience of every headquarter department, and of much provincial administration, especially during the Bengal famine of 1874, which he investigated in Behar. His hand is said to be discernible in many of his chief's dispatches, and he wrote the official memoir on the Northbrook viceroyalty. In May 1876 he returned, with the decoration of C.I.E., to London. His mother had died in 1874 and the home at 11 Berkeley Square was broken up. He resumed work at the War Office and, in June, married Miss Errington, their union having been facilitated by inheritances on both sides. Sir Louis Mallet of the India Office and others in the Whitehall world had marked him for civil promotion; but he was little known outside. Some astonishment was expressed, therefore, early in 1877 that Mr. Goschen, commissioned by the holders of Egyptian bonds to advise Khedive Ismail how to meet his liabilities, should nominate Captain Baring, R.A., to be first British commissioner of the *Caisse de la Dette.* The inquiring public, knowing no more than that he had a way with him which had fluttered Indian dovecotes and earned him the nickname of Overbaring, wondered what other qualifications, besides his family connexion, he might have for diplomatic finance.

In April 1876 Egypt, owing to the criminal extravagance of Khedive Ismail since 1863, failed to pay her foreign coupon, and had to submit her finance to international control. France, whose nationals held at home the bulk of the bonds and in Egypt the most important material interests, was the power chiefly interested; and her government, regarding the situation with complacency as a guarantee of French dominance, gratified financiers and electors by claiming her full pound of flesh. The British government, with fewer bondholders, but more humanitarians to consider, preferred to leave on Ismail the onus of skinning Egypt by methods for which it hoped to avoid responsibility. A year earlier it had refused to nominate any commissioner. Now, apprehensive of the imminent Berlin Congress, it accepted Baring.

The British commissioner joined the Caisse in March 1877, but kept in the background awhile to study the sources of revenue, ignorance of which had brought Goschen's 'settlement' to nothing. Little seen in Cairo society, he soon knew more than his colleagues, and his masterful will began to impose itself. He it was who, early in 1878, inspired the damning exposure of provincial maladministration which led to the four members of the Caisse being constituted by the powers a special commission of inquiry under Sir Charles Rivers Wilson [q. v.] and Riaz Pasha. Their inquisition proved at once too much for the prime minister, and by the spring of 1879 for Ismail. The first report was followed by a show of compliance, to be nullified presently by a military mutiny fomented *ad hoc*. It was succeeded by a second report, drafted by Baring in March 1879, which declared Egypt bankrupt, and proposed liquidation. Ismail repudiated the imputation, beat the patriotic drum, and closured the inquiry. Baring waited a month to see if any power would intervene, and finding none, resigned his membership of the Caisse and went home. Hardly was he in London before Bismarck roused the powers to action. Ismail was unseated in June and Tewfik was preferred in his room. France and Great Britain revised and revived their dual control, and Baring was summoned, from thoughts of standing in the liberal interest for East Norfolk, to see Lord Salisbury, and to consider the post of British controller. He hesitated, but, being advised by Mr. Gladstone to eschew home politics, accepted, and went out to join M. de Blignières in September.

Ignoring the formalists at the Quai d'Orsay, Major Baring agreed quickly with his colleague to pool functions rather than delimit them, and proceeded to set the direction and pace of the control. The country, he held, must be 'morally healed' by administrative reform before being politically regenerated. By March 1880 he had put the work in hand, but not without offering to France the unpleasant spectacle of a British controller openly preferring fellahin to bondholders and dominating the dual control. Under the circumstances it is hardly surprising that, after little more than six months' tenure, he should have been offered another post, which, perhaps, his government, committed to France in the matter of the dual control, did not intend him to decline. He was asked by Lord Ripon to be financial member of the viceroy's council in India, and on acceptance he went home in April. Repassing Cairo in early December he warned Riaz to keep his eye on the army, but was assured all was well. He reached Bombay before Christmas.

Baring's earlier sojourn in India had left a memory, and his Egyptian fame had preceded him. A suggestion of autocracy in his brusque speech and manner excited the ready jealousy of the Civil Service. 'They seem to regard me', he wrote, 'as an Incarnation of the Devil and the India Office.' But his conservative attitude in financial matters quickly conciliated the opposition. There was nothing sensational in any of his three budget statements, but much to show his appreciation of the Indian peasant's singular dependence on the state, and of the balance of profit and loss under progress of the European type—the sort of calculation which would always interest Baring. It was a period of monetary stringency, of heavy calls for the recent Afghan War, of depreciated currency and an unsatisfactory fiscal system. But the financial member, deprecating revolutionary changes, had not only established his authority, but had won sympathy from natives as well as British when, in August 1883, he received a fresh call. The pot that he had left simmering in 1880 had boiled up and over.

After a series of events which need not be recounted here, Great Britain found herself saddled with sole responsibility for constructing in Egypt an administration to replace one that she had destroyed. A few months' experience of chaos under the khedivial restoration, and reports from Lord Dufferin, who had been commissioned to outline a policy, convinced Whitehall that it must find some one to patch up the civil administration before troops could be withdrawn. Since there was no longer any question of dual control, Baring, who had been in correspondence with Sir Garnet Wolseley, the commander of the British troops in Egypt, might be entrusted with the mission. He landed at Alexandria on 11 September 1883.

Thus Sir Evelyn—for he had been gazetted K.C.S.I.—came to the chief task of his life at forty-two. Not a man of genius, he possessed unusually powerful and versatile talents, whose full exercise was ensured both by a strong character matured in a varied school of experience, and also by the vigorous physical constitution of a tall upstanding man. Level judgement was the qualification he most valued, and quick to discern it in other men, he was, as a rule, magnificently served. Though an optimist, he suspected enthusiasm; fantasy, rhapsody, and all kinds of unstable exuberance he cordially disliked. Whiggery, inborn and confirmed by his career, convinced him of his right to lead. Lord Rosebery once told him he was 'a good man to go tiger-shooting with'; but perhaps in other adventures he was a better leader than colleague, his strength of purpose presenting, as was said of him, 'a rather granitic surface to persuasion'. But he was no Cato to champion causes well lost, and, at his own moment, he could be the soul of reasonable compromise; and he was always confident that past experience of his loyalty, which never defrauded a subordinate of credit due, would reassure those whom he might be compelled to sacrifice for the time being. His air of conscious superiority and his habitual disinclination for small talk made him appear somewhat difficult of approach; but 'le Grand Ours', as Cairene society nicknamed its master, could be genial enough and keenly appreciate cultivated converse and both humour and wit.

He was British agent and consul-general, with plenipotentiary diplomatic rank, the junior of the other similarly accredited representatives of the powers; but as representative of the one power occupying the country in force, he was *de facto* to impose the British will. To be a tyrant were easy; to be aught else than a failure would tax all the talents. He began in an evil hour. A summer of epidemic cholera had bared the nakedness of the land and its leaders. He found Charles Clifford Lloyd [q.v.] established as 'inspector-general of reforms', compromising the whole situation by futile attacks on the jealous ministry of the interior, and dissipating what local cordiality had been bred by the Dufferin report. Two days before Baring landed, the hapless William Hicks [q.v.] had set forth to perish (5 November) at Shekan, near el-Obeid, and the news of his catastrophe arrived soon afterwards.

The year-old revolt in the Sudan had suddenly passed beyond Egyptian capacity of control. Baring did not grasp yet the full significance of the Hicks disaster, for he could still indite to Lord Granville a forecast of a speedy reduction of the British garrison and its withdrawal to Alexandria, and promise a *politique de replâtrage* on Dufferin lines; but he did see at once that it raised a most serious question of finance. Was Egypt to cripple herself still further by undertaking other adventures of this sort? Avoidance of bankruptcy was his first commandment; and his reason and experience forbade increase of taxation as a means. The Egyptian ministers, blind to inevitable consequences, were eager to throw the little good money they had after the bad already sunk in the Sudan. Such waste Baring decided must at all hazards be prevented. A characteristic request for instructions, which he himself dictated in the second part of the telegram, went to London to be answered promptly by orders to 'advise' the government of Egypt to withdraw for a time from the Sudanese provinces. The pride of the pashas was outraged; the prime minister resigned; the khedive protested. But, as Lord Milner said, Baring, when his mind was made up, intervened 'with an emphasis which broke down all resistance'. It was his first grave intervention, and he clinched it by procuring from Lord Granville the famous dispatch which defined what the occupying power intended should be understood by its representative's 'advice' on all occasions. One concession he made, however, and this he had cause to regret. He allowed Valentine Baker [q.v.] to undertake with a raw *gendarmerie* the ignominious Suakin expedition which faltered and failed at el-Teb.

To prescribe withdrawal was one thing; to withdraw another. Some garrisons and civilians in the equatorial region were known to be already shut in. The rest could not leave safely without efficient organization and leading. The political question about the Sudan had made much noise; the practical problem was widely canvassed. British responsibility, which had been disclaimed for Hicks, by what Baring held then and later to be a criminal error, could not be ignored for a result of British 'advice'. Little was known at Cairo, and less in London, about actual conditions in the Sudan. The popular name of General Charles George Gordon [q.v.], who had served in various parts of the world since the termination of his governorship of the Sudan in 1879, was suggested to ministers. Baring knew little of him except by report; but he suspected an embodiment of much that he admired—courage, magnetism, military genius—and of more that he disliked—fantasy, fanaticism, action on impulse. He had an alternative in his mind—an Egyptian ex-governor, whose fortunes would entail less British responsibility—and twice he refused to agree to Gordon.

Then finding withdrawal from the Sudan too unpopular in Egypt for any decent Egyptian to wish to undertake it, and himself left alone in his objection to Gordon, he gave way and asked for the man he mistrusted. How Gordon left London on 18 January 1884, commissioned by an informal meeting of ministers to proceed up the Nile (Baring vetoed his going to Suakin, and lived to repent) and to report from Khartoum on ways and means of withdrawal; how, bethinking himself on the voyage that evacuation must not mean abandonment, he asked for the supreme command, was supported in his request by Baring, and in the latter's presence interviewed his blood-foe, Zobeir, with a view to calling him up later to take over evacuated Khartoum; how he pledged himself to arrange withdrawal as soon as possible, and to submit in all things to Baring's instructions—these facts are well known. Less certain is it what happened to bring Gordon's mission to naught after he had departed up the river with Colonel Stewart. Meanwhile, over and above the arduous task of listening to Gordon at the end of a wire and of endeavouring, by analysis of ten messages a day, to recommend to London what an erratic Bayard really desired. Baring had the finance, and consequently the irrigation, of Egypt ever on his mind. To increase the taxable area, not the taxes, was his policy, but to that end capital must first be found for new canals and drains. Further, the clamour for Alexandrian indemnities, overdue since 1882, threatened a financial crisis, which could hardly fail to end in fresh international control. Baring took a bold line. In the face of an annual deficit he projected a loan, and referred the proposal to London for discussion in the summer. All other matters of reform he deferred *sine die*, whether at the ministry of the interior, whence he suffered Nubar Pasha to oust Clifford Lloyd, or in justice, or education, or sanitation, or the army.

What could not stand over was withdrawal from the Sudan. By the end of March 1884 it was clear that the mission of Gordon had only added to the imprisoned Egyptians a man, in whom all Europe was interested, for some one else to rescue. The question now, wrote Baring to the Foreign Office, 'is how to get Gordon and Stewart out of Khartoum'. He saw no way but a British relief expedition, to which, since February, Gordon had been trying to force the hand of Whitehall. By whose fault, if any one's, things had come to this pass, it is not easy to determine. Gordon, faithful to a self-imposed duty not to abandon the Sudan to the Mahdi's mercies, made no serious effort to withdraw, waiting assent to one proposition after another, which he made through Baring to London, to be, one after the other, rejected. He might not have Zobeir, because Mr. Gladstone and the British public would not hear of a slave-raider being preferred to power under their joint ægis. He was not to retire southwards, because so he would be committing Egypt to hold equatorial provinces. Turkish troops must not be used except under conditions that the Sultan would not accept. A British-Indian force operating about Suakin was able to relieve Tokar at the end of February; but only if the road were opened by co-operation from Gordon's end could it send a flying column to Berber. Baring tardily supported this last scheme, but failed to persuade the War Office. Gordon, proclaiming to the Sudan that a British advance-guard was even now at Wadi Halfa, dug himself in. His fighting instinct, his pride of race, his sense of high command, made him refuse all thought of abandoning Khartoum to howling savages, in whose permanent cohesion he did not believe. He railed at Baring and every one else, sent off Stewart, and held on. Mr. Gladstone's government reluctantly admitted Baring's logic, and referred to the War Office the question by what route the relief should go.

Baring himself, over-worked and exasperated by international intrigue, came home in April to push his loan, and hurry the relief expedition, which, however, was delayed till the autumn. The loan, also, hung fire, France refusing to strengthen British hands in Egypt; and Baring had to return in the autumn only to take in financial sail. Nor dared he hope anything from the mission of his cousin, Lord Northbrook, who arrived presently to report to Mr. Gladstone on 'the exigencies of Egyptian finance'. Cordially sympathizing with the ex-viceroy's desire to free Egypt from internationalism and foreign privileges, Baring watched without surprise another report go the way of many predecessors to the pigeon-hole. That winter saw the zenith of French obstruction and the nadir of Egyptian powers. The Caisse ignored Lord Northbrook's recommendation that Egypt should have the spending of her own savings, and pocketed all the surplus of provincial receipts; Nubar and Baring suffered a fall when together they tried to suppress the scurrilities of a Franco-

Egyptian journal, the *Bosphore Egyptien.* Over the turn of the year 1884 hung the lengthening shadow of impending tragedy at Khartoum, which Baring could only watch as a spectator, chafing at the heavy cost of the straining relief force. He cared little that the world imputed to him and to (Sir) Edwin Egerton, his *chargé d'affaires* during the past summer, futilities which they had had to transmit from London, such as the 'hope of Her Majesty's Government' that the trapped hero would 'remain some time longer at Khartoum', or Mr. Gladstone's faith in an appeal to 'the Mahdi's reason'. But, when the worst was known, in the early days of February 1885, he did care profoundly that, against his own judgement, he had sent Gordon to his death.

It was never Baring's way to cry over spilt milk; and insisting, when none remained to be rescued, on effectual evacuation of all the Sudan except Suakin, he turned once more to finance and irrigation. In this (Sir) Colin Scott-Moncrieff, in that (Sir) Edgar Vincent, had forged ahead, in spite, rather than by grace, of Nubar, whose hostility increased towards both and towards Baring who championed them. Nubar continued, however, to work with the latter, in fair accord, in order to lighten the peasant's burden by remission of the *corvée* for canal clearance. But if he detected any hand put out to touch the sanctuary of the interior his jealousy blazed forth.

Yet it was in this sad summer of 1885 that the dawn broke. The powers, outworn by the importunities of their nationals, consented after all on reasonable terms to a loan of nine millions, wherewith Egypt might pay the indemnities and spend a million on works of irrigation. Unwittingly France further lightened Baring's burden by procuring the dispatch of Sir Henry Drummond Wolff [q.v.] to negotiate with the Sultan a British withdrawal in three years' time. When he came on from Constantinople to Egypt at the end of the year, he absolved Baring from so much responsibility for external affairs that for nearly two years the latter could see to the laying out of his hard-won million which was to bring in cent. per cent. from the land; and he could even think of calling other plans for reform out of abeyance—plans for justice, police, and so forth. Nubar scented danger to the interior and stiffened. He had watched Granville's star pale in London and Salisbury's rise. How would it fare with Baring now? Nubar challenged him in 1887 over the succession to Valentine Baker in the command of the police and affronted him to his face in London, only to discover that, in the everlasting flux of parties, the imperial policy of Great Britain remains ever the same. Once his man was down, Baring compromised the quarrel. There was not money yet for any serious reform at the interior; and also—it was his way.

The dawn brightened. Thanks to new canals and a patched-up barrage, the yield from arable lands steadily swelled a revenue on which no extraordinary call had been made for three years. The Treasury accounts of 1888 all but balanced; in 1889 a surplus appeared; while the victory of (Lord) Grenfell at Toski guaranteed relief from further expenditure on Nubian defence. With luck in avoiding other entanglements Egypt had won her race against bankruptcy and international control. Two years earlier, the British occupation had been stabilized by the Sultan's refusal, at the instigation of France, to ratify the clause of the Wolff Agreement giving right of re-entry after withdrawal; and since then foreign capital had entered Egypt more boldly. With Nubar gone and Riaz in his room, Baring could attend to railways, justice, education, and other matters crying for reform, with money in hand and promise of more. He procured the almost complete abolition of the *corvée*, and on the advice of (Sir) John Scott [q.v.], constrained Riaz to abolish the 'brigandage commissions' which had dealt as courts-martial with agrarian crime, by use of torture and the forbidden *kurbash.* Now that more and better judges could be paid, he directed official attention to reform of the native courts, and, in 1890, at the price of the resignation of Riaz, had Scott created adviser to the department of Justice. Signs of approval and support had been lavished by Whitehall. He was gazetted C.B. in 1885, K.C.B. in 1887, and G.C.M.G. a twelvemonth later. Force of character, unflinching reasonableness, strength to compromise, and intellectual superiority had already given him dominance over every one in Egypt, his diplomatic colleagues not excepted. The French consul-general, the Marquis de Reverseaux, confessed it more candidly than the Quai d'Orsay could approve.

Baring's work was growing under his hand, and his *politique de replâtrage* was beginning to be forgotten in a policy of perfection. Greater projects were in his mind than were consistent with any immediate realization of the end for which he had pressed at first. 'The Egyptians', he now held, 'should only be permitted to govern themselves after the fashion in which Europeans think they ought to be governed'; and no longer expecting this consummation from the existing generation of Egyptian officials, his mind postponed evacuation *sine die*, and grew somewhat less averse from the introduction of more British officials. But to the end he would always require very good reason for every British official the more, well knowing the danger of tutelage retarding, rather than promoting, the political education of a backward people. His own personal authority, which, backed by the small army of occupation, was the one effective power in the country, taking the place of an organized system, had to be exerted through the action of his forceful personality upon another, sagacious but not forceful—that of the Khedive Tewfik. 'I had not to govern Egypt,' he was to write, 'but to assist in the government without the appearance of doing so, and without any legitimate authority over the agents with whom I had to deal.' Only the khedive could without friction make his labours of practical effect. Therefore, he attached supreme (as the event showed, too great) importance to continued co-operation with a prince of Tewfik's character and disposition; and he received with lively consternation, as he himself confessed, the sudden intelligence, in 1892, that the khedive was dying. To forestall the Sultan or any other would-be wrecker, he lost not a moment in summoning Tewfik's eldest son from Europe. By European reckoning Abbas would still be a minor for some months to come; but Baring grasped at a suggestion that a Moslem prince's age should be counted by lunar years, and Abbas was duly installed. The Sultan laid by his rival candidate against a better day, and ordered a firman of investiture to be sent to Cairo. The delays and mysteries of its dispatch, arrival, and communication made sport for the world, whose amusement reached its height when the precious document proved to deprive Egypt of Sinai. Baring supported Abbas, and the chanceries tackled the Porte, with the usual result. When the dust had subsided, Abbas ruled all that his father had ruled, with Baring overruling as before, but under the new style of Baron Cromer.

For awhile all seemed well. Cromer buttressed the young khedive against the Sultan's commissioner, Mukhtar Pasha—sole and sore legacy of the Wolff negotiations—as effectively as against the Sultan himself. But as Abbas began to feel his feet, he turned from the authoritative tutor to counsellors of the closet. Tigrane Pasha expounded nationalism in admirable French, and Abbas wondered that an Armenian could be 'so good an Egyptian'. The country, said Tigrane, had now acquired all the knowledge and all the resources requisite for its admission to the comity of nations. Let the occupying power be dismissed with thanks. But its *congé* could be given effectually by the sovereign alone. Therefore a deputation of notables should go quietly to Constantinople, and the khedive must follow to confirm their prayers. The Sultan would grant anything to get the British out of Egypt.

Cromer suffered Abbas to listen and obey; for he foresaw how Abdul Hamid would deal at Constantinople with such inconvenient precedents as a nationalist deputation, and a visit from an autonomous viceroy. He knew something of Turks, and to learn their tongue had been at pains which he declined to expend on Arabic, thinking the Turkish of the local pashas would help him, where the vernacular of the million might embarrass. As he expected, Abbas returned in autumn, sore and sulky, ready to vent his spleen in peevish complaints of British officials. These carried to Cromer incessant protests against the consequent insolence of subordinates; but he refused to move, and even compromised the dismissal of his ally, Mustapha Fehmi. It was not reasonable to expect as yet the confidence and friendship, which Tewfik, his equal in age and greatly beholden to him in the past, had shown. Moreover, the British public, which Cromer understood and kept always in view, would not, in the case of a boy still in his 'teens, distinguish necessary firmness from unnecessary bullying on any issue yet raised. Lord Rosebery, a reputed radical, had come to the Foreign Office in London, and Cromer saw that Nubar's mistake was being repeated by Tigrane. He had but to wait, and a better occasion would be offered by the court cabal.

It came in January 1894. On parade at Wadi Halfa, before the sirdar, and the listening ranks, Abbas rebuked British officers whom, to a man, their countrymen held to have performed a miracle in creating an army out of fellahin. The sirdar, Kitchener, tendered his resignation, and Cromer cleared decks for action. With no more demur than any previous foreign secretary.

Lord Rosebery remitted as orders from Her Majesty's government the instructions suggested to him by its representative in Egypt; and a British battalion, homeward bound, was diverted from the Canal and marched to Cairo for an outward and visible sign. Abbas ate his bitter words, and nationalism went to ground again. Reviewing his stewardship in after years Cromer judged this to be the last round he had to fight against official obstruction; and in fact all serious opposition above ground ceased henceforward. Abbas, saying he understood that he might sit on the box of the state coach, but not touch the reins, consoled himself with private finance. Ministers, lapsing into ciphers, took their tone from Mustapha Fehmi, who replaced Nubar in the autumn of 1895. Cromer, once more confident of the future, reverted to the great projects of Tewfik's last years. Surveys for a Nile dam were put in hand with the cordial approval of every husbandman in Egypt, and a curtain of masonry began to rise above the cataract. Cromer had intended to await its completion and the expansion of revenue which was certain to follow, before allowing the eager sirdar to begin the realization of an even greater project, the reconquest of the Sudan. But the disaster of Adowa in 1895, leading Italy to press for some Egyptian action in the rear of Abyssinia, caused London to force Cromer's hand. Money was tight and only by a majority vote was half a million obtained from the commissioners of the Caisse, the French and the Russian commissioners forming the minority. With this the sirdar got to work, and when, on a subsequent appeal, the courts declared that the grant must be refunded to the Caisse, Cromer hardly persuaded the British Treasury to cover a debt incurred by following British instructions. Preparations were made with much secrecy. After noting the progress of the Upper Egypt railway to Sohag, to Girgeh, to the crossing of the river at Nag Hamadi, Cromer added, in his published report for 1896, that, while the restoration of Karnak engaged his attention, he had 'nothing of military interest' to write about. Then, suddenly, Egypt heard that there was an up-Nile campaign afoot, and that Kitchener was bound for Dongola, which, though few but soldiers knew the fact, was no place to stay in long. Cromer had urged Suakin as first objective, but had been overruled.

Throughout the further advances, which that first step inevitably entailed—to Abu Hamed, to the Atbara, and to Omdurman—the British agent, recalling his half-forgotten military terminology and tactics, and sinking a habitual distrust of soldier strategists, which he shared with Lord Salisbury, had to play minister of war, as well as to support the sirdar against both the Egyptian Cabinet and Whitehall. On all policy and plans of the campaign he was asked for and gave advice. Kitchener, if not congenial to Cromer's heart, satisfied his head (though there was to be some friction later, when the sirdar had become governor-general of the Sudan), and from Dongola in 1896 to Fashoda in 1898 Cromer accorded him his absolute trust. The conduct of the last and most perilous act of the campaign, the Fashoda meeting with the Frenchman, Marchand (Cromer had long ago warned Kitchener and London that it might happen), he was content to leave to his subordinate with only the briefest general instruction. In the final hour of their joint triumph, he was far away in northern Scotland beside the sick-bed of his wife.

He returned in the autumn of 1898, to enforce the singular Anglo-Egyptian arrangement which he had devised for excluding internationalism from the reconquered Sudan; and troubled consuls-general were advised that their nationals south of the twentieth parallel must look to British protection alone. Cromer intentionally discouraged the company promoter and all others who might exploit native populations. Lady Cromer survived her return to Cairo by a few weeks only. Bereaved and alone, her husband went to Khartoum in December to find comfort where capitulations and mixed courts were not. In Egypt, however, the clouds of internationalism were breaking. The Franco-British Agreement of 1899, defining zones of influence in Africa, cleared the way for the definitive pact of 1904, by which the burden of dualism was lifted from most of the foreign-controlled administrations just in time to save the railways. It looked as if the capitulations themselves might go, as Cromer had desired long and devoutly, because he held autonomy impossible in Egypt until there were not only more good citizens but more citizens—until, in fact, the resident Europeans both obeyed and made Egyptian laws. But this consummation he would not live to see.

He bestrode the local world with none to let or hinder. The Boer War disturbed Egypt no more than the Armenian massacres had done. While some Moslems undoubtedly welcomed our early ill success, the resident Greeks supported us from first to last. Cromer had seen land assessment revised, land survey completed, land tax lowered, a land bank created, and the interior and education subjected to advisers since 1896. His long postponement of educational reform has often been criticized ; and even so intelligent an Egyptian patriot as Sheikh Mohammed Abdu accused him of keeping the people ignorant in the interest of British imperialism. His own explanation was that he waited till money was plentiful before embarking on experiments in pedagogy, none of the systems proposed at an earlier stage being suitable to Egyptian conditions or promising finality. He used to cite results of our education system in India as instances of the eddies which too rapid a current can produce in the stream of progress ; and he was particularly averse from the creation of an urban intelligentsia. In the sphere of primary education progress was retarded by the lack of qualified teachers, and by religious tradition and prejudice ; and it was not before Cromer's last years in Egypt that much advance could be attempted. Even then but little reduction resulted in the obstinate illiteracy of the fellahin.

Cromer's formal relations with Abbas, whose attitude was improved by a visit to London, remained friendly, and a step in the peerage in 1899 assured him that his word was still law in Downing Street. In 1901 he was created an earl, and he gratified his friends by marrying Lady Katherine Thynne, second daughter of the fourth Marquess of Bath. By his first wife he had had two sons ; now a third was born. A little volume of his *Paraphrases from the Greek Anthology* had been issued privately before his second marriage ; an enlarged edition, published later, was received with favour as the diversion of a man of affairs. In Cairo he had attained to a sort of Pharaonic apotheosis, becoming ' The Lord ' simply ; and sly profanity rang changes on this style. But one thing was already troubling his peace—the ever-growing clamour of nationalists in a hurry. The old whig was not surprised ; but he grew more and more apprehensive, lest those at home whom he called sentimental radicals should listen and try to hustle his administrative jog-trot. His health, hitherto robust, began to deteriorate in 1905, indisposing him to listen to a suggestion that he should take the Foreign Office in the Campbell-Bannerman ministry formed late in that year. In 1906 an unexpected ebullition of Egyptian sympathy with a second attempt by Abdul Hamid to revise the Sinaitic boundary added to his uneasiness, though he minimized its import ; and atop of it came a wave of native anger at certain death-sentences passed upon natives of the Delta village of Denshawai, who had been convicted of attacking a shooting party of British officers. These sentences he himself (he was in England at the time) judged too severe. He landed from leave in the autumn to find Egyptian society turned topsy-turvy by bubble-speculation and buzzing with malevolent criticism. Ill with chronic indigestion and feeling his age, he held on a little longer. King Edward wrote with his own hand to dissuade the old proconsul from resignation ; but Cromer felt too much enfeebled to face the political experiment of speeding up autonomy, which he suspected to be imminent. He delivered an apologia and a counsel of perfection in the Cairo opera house in May 1907, and then went down the side of the ship which he had rescued, refitted, and piloted for nearly a quarter of a century.

Parliament acknowledged handsomely his great use of great talents. Universities offered degrees and societies their presidential chairs. But it was from a private study, out of touch with Whitehall, that he watched his first successor, Sir (John) Eldon Gorst [q. v.], sail the new course he had foreseen would be set, and his second, Lord Kitchener, abruptly put up the helm and steer for such direct control, as he himself had often threatened but never practised. As health returned he began to attend the House of Lords, where he made a maiden speech in February 1908, and took the lead of the free traders. Subsequently he spoke fairly often, and was listened to with respect ; but he had no natural gift of oratory, and nervousness in public speaking never left him. In that same year appeared the account of his stewardship (*Modern Egypt*, 2 vols.) which his first wife had encouraged him to write. The style of the book has the unhurried lucidity of diplomatic dispatches. The British public read it avidly, but Egyptians looked askance at a mirror held up to their nature.

Lord Cromer's old love of the Greek and Roman classics deepened and the range of his reading broadened with his increased leisure. He searched the past assiduously for modern instances, and from the chair of the Classical Association delivered, in 1910, an address on

Ancient and Modern Imperialism which makes the best of his smaller books. Chance in 1912 led the editor of the *Spectator* to encourage him to review new books. Three consequent volumes of *Political and Literary Essays* attest omnivorous reading, a memory singularly retentive of all stages in a long experience, and an apostolic desire to impart all that he knew, or thought. Impatient of inactivity, he was eager at seventy years to preach free trade or denounce anti-vivisection and votes for women. The public, which had long labelled him man of action, was a little disconcerted by this fresh foliage budding on the eve of winter; and malice sneered that the new laurels were torn from his old crown. But unheeding he went on his masterful way, fulfilling a green old age.

In 1913 he broke long silence about Egypt by calling attention, in the *Nineteenth Century and After*, to the continued curse of the capitulations. Next year the outbreak of the European War found him ready to do any service that still in him lay. From various experience he expounded German policy and methods, and in 1915 issued a supplement to his *Modern Egypt*, embodying notes, long discreetly suppressed, on his relations with Abbas Hilmi, ex-khedive. A more arduous service was to be his last. He was invited, in 1916, to preside over the Dardanelles Commission; and overcoming a Thucydidean distaste for such inquisitions in time of war, he put on government harness again. Assiduous in attendance at the sittings, he would summon the commission to meet at his own house if he were forbidden to go out of doors. After one such meeting in December he collapsed. During rallies he demanded always the draft report, and in January 1917 seemed about to renew his lease of life. But the flicker was brief, and on the 29th, a month short of his seventy-sixth birthday, he died.

Lord Cromer's portrait was painted by J. S. Sargent, R.A., in 1903; a memorial tablet, with a medallion portrait in relief on the base, was designed by Sir W. Goscombe John, R.A., for Westminster Abbey; there are also drawings made by William Strang in 1908 and J. S. Sargent in 1912.

[Lord Sanderson, Memoir in *Proceedings* of the British Academy, 1917; Lord Cromer, *Annual Reports*, 1884–1906; *Modern Egypt*, 2 vols., 1908; *Abbas II*, 1915; minor writings, especially 'Capitulations in Egypt', *Nineteenth Century and After*, July 1913, and *Ancient and Modern Imperialism*, 1910. Appreciations published by colleagues and contemporaries from A. Milner, *England in Egypt*, 1892, to Sir J. Rennell Rodd, *Social and Diplomatic Memories*, ii, 1923; personal knowledge; private information.]

D. G. H.

BARNABY, Sir NATHANIEL (1829–1915), naval architect, the eldest son of Nathaniel Barnaby, by his wife, Anna Fowler, was born at Chatham 25 February 1829. His father was an inspector of shipwrights at Sheerness dockyard. Here, at the age of fourteen, young Barnaby became a shipwright apprentice; and after five years of apprenticeship won a scholarship at the Portsmouth central school of mathematics and naval construction (1848). On leaving the school in 1852 he was appointed draughtsman in the royal dockyard at Woolwich; two years later he became overseer of the *Viper* and the *Wrangler*, ships building in the Thames for service in the Crimean War. In 1854 he was appointed to the naval construction department of the Admiralty; there he assisted in the preparation of the designs for the last of the wooden sailing 'line of battle' ships and also in the design of the *Warrior*, the first British iron-armoured seagoing battleship.

When Sir Edward James Reed [q. v.], who had married Barnaby's sister, became chief constructor of the navy in 1863, he made Barnaby head of his staff, and in this capacity Barnaby worked on most of Reed's designs, including that of the *Monarch*, Reed's conception of a fully-rigged seagoing turret ship as compared with the *Captain* (which subsequently capsized) designed by Captain Cowper Phipps Coles [q. v.].

On Sir Edward Reed's retirement from the Admiralty in 1870, his work was carried on for a short time by a council of construction with Barnaby as president. In 1872 Barnaby was appointed chief naval architect, a title changed in 1875 to director of naval construction. As successor to Reed he had to deal with the designs of the *Devastation* and *Thunderer* and of the *Fury*, afterwards named *Dreadnought*: the first two vessels, of 9,330 tons displacement, with no sail power, had an 'all big gun' armament of four 12-inch 35-ton muzzle-loading guns, two in each of two turrets at the ends of the vessel; the *Fury* was of similar general design but somewhat larger with increased armour protection. In one bold stride Reed had evolved a design embodying the most important features of many battleships down to the time of the modern *Dreadnought* (launched 1906), if not indeed to the present day. His designs were much criticized at the time of the loss of the *Captain* (7 September 1870) which they were thought to resemble. A committee of investigation was appointed, and Barnaby proposed certain modifications in the *Devastation* and *Thunderer*, to which Reed objected; the Admiralty, however, adopted them. In the *Dreadnought*, the third vessel of the class, of 10,820 tons, carrying four 12·5-inch 38-ton muzzle-loading guns, further changes were made which met Reed's objections.

Barnaby's first important design for a battleship was that for the *Inflexible* of 11,400 tons displacement. She had moderate sail power, and a one calibre armament of four 16-inch 80-ton muzzle-loading guns, two in each of two turrets placed *en échelon* in a central citadel 110 feet long, protected with armour 24 inches thick. The ends of the vessel were without side armour but were fitted internally with belts of cork upon strong under-water decks. This design met with severe criticism from Reed, who objected that the cork protection could be shot away and the ship rendered unstable. A committee, however, reported favourably on the design. The *Inflexible* was laid down in 1874; four similar but smaller vessels, *Ajax*, *Agamemnon*, *Colossus*, and *Edinburgh*, were laid down somewhat later—the last in 1879.

Barnaby's next design was that for the *Collingwood*, laid down in 1880. She and five similar vessels, varying somewhat in gun power, and all without sail, were known as the *Admiral* class. The first five of the vessels had four powerful breech-loading guns, then introduced for the first time, mounted in pairs in barbettes at either end of the ship on the middle line, as in the *Devastation* design; between the barbettes six 6-inch breech-loaders were carried along the sides of the ship, which were protected by a belt of armour 18 inches thick over nearly half the length of the ship. The *Benbow*, the sixth vessel of this class, had a single 16·25-inch breech-loading gun in a barbette at each end of the ship, and ten 6-inch breech-loading guns along the sides of the vessel between the barbettes.

Barnaby designed various armoured vessels, ranging from battleships to cruisers, including the *Impérieuse*, *Warspite*, *Shannon*, *Nelson*, and *Northampton*. His cruiser designs were specially noteworthy. The cruisers *Iris* and *Mercury*, laid down in 1875 and 1876, were the first vessels for the royal navy built entirely of steel, which he advocated and introduced. His 'protected' cruisers of the *Mersey* class, laid down in 1883 and 1884, were the first of a powerfully armed type of swift vessels protected from end to end by a strong deck, below water at the sides of the ship, but above water at the middle line. His 'belted' cruisers of the *Orlando* class, laid down 1885–1886, were somewhat larger and more heavily armed and armoured; for many years they were in good repute for general all round qualities. He also designed the cruisers *Rover*, *Bacchante*, the *Leander* class, and *Comus* class. As regards special vessels, Barnaby designed the *Vesuvius*, the first British vessel fitted with a tube for discharging torpedoes under water; the torpedo-ram *Polyphemus*, armed with under-water torpedo tubes; and the *Rattlesnake*, the forerunner of the torpedo boat destroyer class.

Barnaby was one of the founders of the Institution of Naval Architects; he presented many papers, and took an active part in discussing those relating to warship design. He wrote the articles *Navy* and *Shipbuilding* in the *Encyclopædia Britannica* (ninth edition), and published *Naval Development in the Nineteenth Century* (1902) and other works on naval construction. He read papers before the Iron and Steel Institute in order to promote improvement in the manufacture of steel for shipbuilding purposes. As a debater he was skilful and convincing. The foundation of the royal corps of naval constructors was largely due to him, and he became its first head. He was strongly in favour of designs for the leading classes of merchant vessels being such as to make those vessels of use in war.

Barnaby was made C.B. in 1876 and K.C.B. in 1885; he also received several foreign decorations. On account of ill-health he retired from office in 1885. In private life he devoted much time to the Sunday school work of the Baptist chapel at Lee, Kent, and wrote several hymns for it. He died at Lewisham 15 June 1915, and was buried in St. Margaret's churchyard at Lee. He married in 1855 Sarah (died 1910), daughter of John Webber, of Birmingham, by whom he had one son and two daughters.

[Admiralty records; *Transactions* of the Institution of Naval Architects; personal knowledge.] P. W.

BARNES, JOHN GORELL, first BARON GORELL, of Brampton (1848–1913), judge, was born at Walton-on-the-Hill, near Liverpool, 16 May 1848, of a Derbyshire stock. His great-grandmother was a daughter of Edward Gorell, of Hazle Hall, Yorkshire, not far from Leeds, a dissenter belonging to the sect founded by John Glas [q. v.] and Robert Sandeman [q. v.]. His grandfather, John Gorell Barnes, was a landowner near Chesterfield and a colliery proprietor who combined shrewd business abilities with a passion for social reform. Henry, the third son of this John Gorell Barnes, founded a forwarding agency and shipping business at Liverpool, and married in 1847 Georgiana, daughter of the Rev. Richard Smith, rector of Staveley, Derbyshire, whose father, also Richard Smith, had been fellow and dean of Trinity College, Cambridge. The future judge was the eldest child and elder son of this marriage. He was educated privately, and after his father's sudden death in 1865 the boy, not yet seventeen, was sent to Peterhouse, Cambridge, the college of Dr. Edward John Routh [q. v.], who had married Hilda Airy, a daughter of Sir George Airy, astronomer royal, and a niece of Henry Barnes. Barnes, despite his youth, was classed as a senior optime in January 1868. Cambridge, its steady practical thinking, its athletics and social pleasures, left a definite mark upon his life. He was made an honorary LL.D. in 1898 and an honorary fellow of Peterhouse the next year.

After a short period in his father's old firm, Barnes was articled to a firm of solicitors in Liverpool, but a few years later was advised in the office to go to the bar. He entered at the Inner Temple in 1873, and after reading in equity chambers became a pupil in October 1874 of (Sir) James Charles Mathew [q.v.], the leading commercial junior in the Temple at that time. He worked in Mathew's chambers till shortly before Mathew became a judge in 1881. Barnes, who had been called to the bar in 1876, at once succeeded to Mathew's great junior practice; and to this he gradually added a substantial admiralty practice and a great deal of mercantile work on the Northern circuit. He soon became a familiar figure in the Court of Appeal, the House of Lords, and the Privy Council. He always found time, however, to pay close attention to the work of the men in his crowded pupil room. After seven years of ceaseless work, he took silk in self-protection (1888) and made an immediate mark as a weighty, industrious, and popular leader, whose temper nothing could ruffle. In June 1892 he was, rather unexpectedly, made a judge of the probate, divorce, and admiralty division in succession to Sir Francis Henry Jeune [q. v.], afterwards Lord St. Helier, who had just succeeded Sir Charles Parker Butt as president. In February 1905 Barnes succeeded Jeune as president of the division, a position which he held till February 1909, when he was raised to the peerage as Baron Gorell, of Brampton, near Chesterfield. As president, he had already sat from time to time in the Court of Appeal and on the Judicial Committee of the Privy Council; and from July 1909 to July 1912 he sat regularly in the House of Lords and delivered many judgments of moment.

Barnes found time and energy for much extra-judicial work. He was a member of a committee appointed by the lord chancellor to consider improvements in the High Court. He was chairman of the county courts committee which reported in 1909 and laid the basis for some of the proposals of the royal commission on divorce. In 1909 he also acted as an arbitrator in the dispute between the Great Eastern Railway Company and its employees; and in the same year he was chairman of the copyright committee, the report of which led to the passing of the Copyright Act of 1911. The nomination in 1909 of the royal commission on divorce and matrimonial causes was due to the strong opinion which he expressed, in the House of Lords, that the law which he had administered as a judge for sixteen years needed a large measure of amendment. Lord Gorell was the chairman of the commission, and every class of thought and social outlook was represented by the commissioners or by the numerous witnesses whose services they utilized to secure an absolutely exhaustive inquiry into the social, legal, theological, and medical aspects of the marriage tie. The majority report recommended an extension of the grounds for divorce so as to include desertion, cruelty, incurable insanity, habitual drunkenness, and penal servitude for life in commutation of a death sentence. The minority report rejected any extension of the grounds of divorce; but there was a large volume of reforms in law and procedure common to the two reports, including far-reaching proposals relating to nullity of marriage, presumption of death for purposes of remarriage, equality of the sexes for divorce purposes, and restraints on the publication of reports of divorce cases. The majority report was signed 30 January 1912 and the commission came to an end in the following November. Lord Gorell's health was then rapidly breaking. He died at Mentone 22 April 1913 and was buried at Brampton beside his grandfather, John Gorell Barnes.

The broad characteristics of Lord Gorell's character and work are exemplified by his brief, rapid, and smoothly successful career at the bar; by his many reported arguments and reported judgments in the court of first instance, the Court of Appeal, the Privy Council, and the House of Lords; by his extra-judicial work and his speeches in the House of Lords. As a judge of first instance his judgments were very rarely reversed, and all of them are models of industry, insight, and common sense. The foundation of a commercial court was the joint idea of Sir James Charles Mathew and himself. Barnes, soon after his appointment to the probate, divorce, and admiralty division, announced that he was prepared to deal with cases raising points of insurance law, and his court was therefore largely resorted to by commercial solicitors. The establishment of the commercial court from 1 March 1895 under Mathew was a successful development of Barnes's experiment [see *Weekly Notes*, 2 March 1895].

Barnes combined a great enthusiasm for any work that he undertook with an unusual capacity for mastering complicated facts. His keen and profound intelligence was never satisfied until the broad principle governing any particular set of circumstances had been fully exposed. In field after field of law he showed these qualities, with the result that many of his judgments are distinct contributions to the growth of English law. His work on the divorce commission revealed his passionate desire to see justice made available for all classes of the community. He was no politician, but he represented the best thinking of the old school of liberal thought. Like his paternal grandfather, he was a reformer. From the Gorells he inherited an almost gloomy mysticism that seemed at times to dominate his outlook on life. Yet normally he was a very cheerful man who loved the pleasant things of life. As a friend and a judge he was kindly, genial, enthusiastic, full of praise for all good work, considerate to the bar, penetrating, intensely human.

Barnes married in 1881 Mary Humpston, eldest daughter of Thomas Mitchell, of West Arthurlee, Renfrewshire, who also was of Derbyshire descent; they had two sons and one daughter. He was succeeded by his elder son, Henry Gorell Barnes, second Baron Gorell, a barrister of considerable promise, who in May 1914 introduced in the House of Lords a Bill incorporating the common elements of the two reports of the divorce commission. He was killed in action at Ypres in January 1917, and was succeeded as third baron by his younger brother, Ronald Gorell Barnes.

[J. E. G. de Montmorency, *John Gorell Barnes, first Lord Gorell: a Memoir*, 1920; personal knowledge. Portrait, *Royal Academy Pictures*, 1896.] J. E. G. de M.

BARNETT, SAMUEL AUGUSTUS (1844–1913), divine and social reformer, the elder son of Francis Augustus Barnett, of Bristol, was born at 5 Portland Square, Bristol, 8 February 1844. His father was a man of wealth, the first manufacturer of iron bedsteads; his mother, Mary Gilmore, came of an old merchant family in Bristol. Educated at home, he went in June 1862 to Wadham College, Oxford, which was chosen because of the tory and protestant prejudices of the warden, Benjamin Parsons Symons. These did not appeal to young Barnett, and he never felt that he had got the best out of Oxford; 'I made the mistake of using my time to grind at books rather than to know men.' But he remained devotedly attached to Oxford and to Wadham, and not the least of his claims to be remembered is that he, as much as any man of his generation, brought his university into living relation with the social and moral life of England.

He took a second class in law and modern history in 1865, and then, after two years of teaching, travelled in America, a visit which 'knocked all the toryism out of me'. In December 1867 he became curate at St. Mary's, Bryanston Square, London, to William Henry Fremantle (afterwards dean of Ripon). He was at once introduced to his life's work, the problems of a great city. Here in 1869 was founded the Charity Organization Society, through which he made the acquaintance of Miss Octavia Hill [q. v.] and through her met his future wife, Henrietta Octavia, daughter of Alexander Rowland, of Champion Hall, Kent, who shared and inspired his work for forty years. They were married in January 1873, and went to St. Jude's, Whitechapel, a parish, in the words of its bishop, 'the worst in the diocese, inhabited mainly by a criminal population'. Barnett's connexion with Whitechapel lasted throughout his life, though he resigned St. Jude's in 1894, when made a canon of Bristol. In 1895 he was a select preacher at Oxford, and at Cambridge in 1889 and 1905, and from 1906 to 1913 canon, and finally sub-dean, of Westminster. He died at Hove 17 June 1913; the funeral service was at St. Jude's but there is a memorial to him in the Abbey. He had no children.

Barnett's life is best recorded by his activities. He was before all things a religious man; his aim was 'to decrease not suffering but sin'. Conscious of the failure of the church services, he tried to give them a higher reality, and in his 'worship hour' every Sunday evening from 8.30 to 9.30, he sought to reach by music and by non-biblical readings those who would not come to church. His attempt was condemned as unorthodox, but he had the warm support of the suffragan, Dr. Walsham How [q. v.]. Barnett was a pioneer in other forms of teaching. His art exhibitions, begun in 1881, introduced East London to good pictures, and resulted in the building of the Whitechapel art gallery; he was never more himself than when expounding pictures to crowds of listeners. His parish library, from the first a centre of good reading, developed, through the students' library at Toynbee Hall, into the Whitechapel public library. He was also a pioneer in bringing primary school teachers to Oxford; out of the vacation courses held there from 1885 onwards developed the Oxford day training college. In his own parish schools he was one of the first to introduce handwork (in 1886) and pictures, and so to anticipate the work of the 'art for schools' association and of the association for promoting technical education (1887). The first pupil-teacher centres were held in his schools (1885). All these activities and others now generally adopted were promoted by his education reform league, founded in 1884.

Barnett knew that education could not succeed unless the material conditions of the people were improved. He pressed for the destruction of insanitary dwellings, and had a large share in promoting the Artisans' Dwellings Act of 1875. He was a guardian in Whitechapel for twenty-nine years from 1875, and chairman for twelve years, and the administration of poor relief there was everywhere taken as a model. He was one of the first to advocate universal pensions (1883), and to urge the danger of unemployment and the need of special study as to its causes and its remedies. Largely thanks to him the Mansion House relief fund in 1893 was much less mischievous than that of 1885–1886. The 'children's country holiday' fund, started by him and Mrs. Barnett in 1877, has been one of the greatest blessings to East London.

But probably the work by which Barnett will be remembered is university settlements. The *Bitter Cry of Outcast London* in 1883 had stirred public sympathy, and in an article in the *Nineteenth Century* of February 1884 he put forth proposals for bringing university men into the life of cities, which have been adopted and developed all over the civilized world. On the basis of these proposals Toynbee Hall was founded in 1884, and he was its first warden (1884–1896).

There was indeed no movement for social or moral improvement in which Barnett did not take a prominent part; in many he was the prime mover. He was an effective speaker, but his strength lay in his personality. He had a unique power of discovering what was best in a man and of helping to make it effective. His friends looked on him as a 'prophet'; many whose names are unknown would agree with M. Clemenceau's remark in 1884, that Barnett was one of the 'three really great men' he had met in England. He was a good writer; his letters to his mother from Egypt, when Herbert Spencer was one of the party, will live for their literary merits, and few men have had a greater gift for summing up a principle or a line of action; his works are a storehouse of quotations; the most important are *Practicable Socialism* (1888), *Religion and Progress* (1907), *Religion and Politics* (1911), *Worship and Work* (1913), and *Vision and Service* (1917), the two last-named edited by Mrs. Barnett. His portrait, painted by G. F. Watts in 1887, is in the possession of Mrs. Barnett; a copy hangs in Wadham College hall. He was also painted with Mrs. Barnett by Sir H. von Herkomer in 1909; this portrait is now at Barnett House, the institution founded at Oxford to encourage, what he had always urged, the study of social problems.

[*Life* by Mrs. Barnett, 2 vols., 1918; Annual Reports of Toynbee Hall and St. Jude's, Whitechapel; personal knowledge.]

J. W.

BARRY, Sir JOHN WOLFE WOLFE- (1836–1918), civil engineer. [See Wolfe-Barry.]

BARTHOLOMEW, JOHN GEORGE (1860–1920), cartographer, born at 10 Comely Green Place, Edinburgh, 22 March 1860, was the elder son of John Bartholomew, whose father founded a firm of map-engravers and publishers, by his wife, Anne, daughter of John McGregor, of Greenock. He was educated at Edinburgh High School and University, but did not take his degree; he entered at an early age the draughtsman's office in his father's firm, receiving instruction in cartography from his father and from E. G. Ravenstein. In 1889, on the removal of the firm to new premises in Park Road, where the name 'Edinburgh Geographical Institute' was adopted, he took over the entire management, and the rest of his life was devoted mainly to his work as a cartographer.

Bartholomew gave much thought to the perfecting of the technical processes of map-production as well as to the planning of new geographical works; and by keeping in touch with the latest progress of discovery and research he avoided the tendency of some map-makers to content themselves with following in the footsteps of their predecessors. The two great atlases of Scotland and of England and Wales, published in 1895 (second edition 1912) and 1903 respectively, are among the most important of his works, embodying an immense amount of geographical and statistical research; but his most ambitious undertaking was probably the *Physical Atlas of the World*, planned to appear in several volumes, of which, however, only two, dealing respectively with *Meteorology* (1899) and *Zoogeography* (1911), were actually published. The summit of his achievement is perhaps reached in '*The Times*' *Survey Atlas of the World*, which was produced under his direction and was the result of some fifteen years' work, though not actually completed until 1921, after his death. The large output of the firm also included, in addition to the ordinary tourist and political maps and school atlases, a number of physical and statistical maps of great scientific value, among which may be mentioned those illustrating the results of the *Challenger* expedition, and the series of bathymetrical surveys of the Scottish lakes; for both of these Bartholomew worked in association with his friend, Sir John Murray [q. v.] the oceanographer. Bartholomew's work as a map-maker is distinguished both by accuracy in detail and by skill in craftsmanship; but his most important contribution to the science of cartography was his extension and improvement of the system of layer colouring for marking contours, a system by which his maps attain a high degree of delicacy and effectiveness. His skilful use of colour for other purposes, as for instance in population maps, is also noteworthy.

Although never strong in health Bartholomew was a hard worker. Apart from maps, he produced, among other works, a valuable *Survey Gazetteer of the British Isles* in 1904. He took an active interest in the social and intellectual life of Edinburgh, and had a genius for friendship. He was one of the founders in 1884 of the Royal Scottish Geographical Society, of which he was joint honorary secretary from the beginning until his death; and it was largely owing to his efforts that a lectureship in geography was established in Edinburgh University in 1908. He received the Victoria medal of the Royal Geographical Society in 1905 and the honorary degree of LL.D. of the university of Edinburgh in 1909.

Bartholomew married in 1889 Janet, daughter of A. Sinclair Macdonald, J.P., of Cyder Hall, near Dornoch, Sutherlandshire, by whom he had three sons and two daughters. Having gone to Portugal in the winter of 1919–1920 owing to increasing ill-health, he died at Cintra 13 April 1920; and was buried in the cemetery of São Pedro.

Bartholomew is worthy of a high place among British cartographers, his work forming perhaps the most notable individual contribution to British map-making since that of John Cary, just a century earlier.

[*Geographical Journal*, June 1920; *Scottish Geographical Magazine*, 15 July 1920; private information.] F. P. S.

BARTON, Sir EDMUND (1849–1920), Australian statesman, the youngest son of William Barton, stock and share broker, of Sydney, by his wife, Mary Louisa Wydah, was born at Glebe, Sydney, 18 January 1849. He was educated at Sydney grammar school, and after a brilliant career at Sydney University was called to the bar in 1871. In 1879 he entered the New South Wales legislative assembly as member for Sydney University; he subsequently represented in the assembly Wellington (1880–1882), East Sydney (1882–1887, 1891–1894), and Hastings and Maclay (1898–1900). He served as speaker of the legislative assembly from 1883 to 1887. From 1887 to 1891, and again in 1897–1898, he was a member of the legislative council. Although opposed to him politically, Barton agreed with Sir Henry Parkes [q. v.] in his advocacy of Australian federation; and when the latter retired from the premiership and to a great extent from public life in 1891, it was to Barton's hands that he entrusted the leadership of the movement. Barton had been a member of the federal convention which met at Sydney in March 1891, and when, in October of that year, he accepted the post, which he had already held in 1889, of attorney-general of New South Wales under (Sir) George Richard Dibbs [q.v.], it was only on the assurance that he should have a free hand in the conduct of the federal movement. Although, however, he was successful in securing the assent of the assembly (to which he had returned in June 1891) to resolutions approving of the main principles of the Constitution Bill drafted at the Sydney convention, there was little enthusiasm about the subject; and when Barton resigned office in December 1893 on personal grounds, little progress had been made towards carrying through the proposed measure.

It was now clear that if success was to be achieved, it must be by appealing directly to the people and not to their parliaments. In accordance with this policy, Barton in July 1893 had established the Sydney Federation League; and it was owing to the public opinion aroused by this and similar bodies throughout Australia that the conference of premiers met at Hobart in February 1895 and finally gave the desired impetus to the movement. When, in pursuance of the decision of the Hobart conference, an election was held for the proposed federal convention, Barton was returned at the head of the poll for New South Wales; and at the meeting of the convention at Adelaide on 18 March 1897 he was chosen to draw up the preliminary resolutions and to act as leader of the convention. As chairman both of the constitutional and drafting committees he was largely responsible for the new Constitution Bill as it emerged from the convention; whilst his invariable tact and good sense greatly facilitated its labours. But in his own colony he was less successful, and the numerous amendments made to the Bill by the legislative council (to which he had returned as a member in 1897) caused him to disclaim all responsibility for that body's proceedings. None the less he worked strenuously at the subsequent meetings of the federal convention at Sydney (September 1897) and Melbourne (January 1898), and took a leading part in the campaign at the referendum in New South Wales on 3 June 1898. That a sufficient majority was not then obtained was no fault of his; and when federation finally triumphed in New South Wales under the leadership of Sir George Houstoun Reid [q.v.], it was to Barton that the credit of that triumph belonged.

In 1900 Barton went to London as leading member of the deputation which watched the passage of the Commonwealth of Australia Constitution Bill through the imperial parliament; and after its enactment he became the first prime minister of the Australian Commonwealth (January 1901), Sir William John Lyne [q.v.], the New South Wales premier, having been unable to find colleagues when invited by Lord Hopetoun, the governor-general, to form a ministry. With the premiership Barton held the portfolio of foreign affairs. In 1903, when the Australian high court of justice came into being, Barton, who had been created G.C.M.G. in 1902, took a judgeship, assigning with characteristic self-abnegation the post of chief justice to Sir Samuel Walker Griffith.

Barton's position as Commonwealth premier had been a most difficult one, since he was in command of a crew of captains who were accustomed to leadership in their respective states. Moreover, the government was a coalition, containing one member from Western Australia (Sir John, afterwards Baron, Forrest, q.v.) who was a strong conservative, and another from South Australia (Charles Cameron Kingston, q.v.) whose radicalism tended towards sympathy with working-class aspirations. Again, in New South Wales and Victoria the tariff question had been the main issue in party politics; but the policy of the new ministry, which found its embodiment in the Customs Tariff Act of 1902, was of necessity a compromise between the views of the free-traders of New South Wales and the extreme protectionists of Victoria.

Both as a statesman and as a judge Barton won the respect and affection of all who knew him. He tempered natural dignity with charm of manner; and in spite of the years spent in politics, his mastery of both constitutional and common law was universally recognized.

He married in 1877 Jean Mason, daughter of David Ross, of Newcastle, New South Wales, and had four sons and two daughters. He died at Medlow, in the Blue Mountains, New South Wales, 6 January 1920.

[*The Times*, 8 January 1920; *Year Book of Australia*, 1901; B. R. Wise, *The Making of the Australian Commonwealth*, 1913; John Quick and Robert R. Garran, *Annotated Constitution of the Australian Commonwealth*, 1901; H. G. Turner, *The First Decade of the Australian Commonwealth*, 1911; Chief Justice Knox in *Commonwealth Law Reports*, 1919–1920.] H. E. E.

BASHFORTH, FRANCIS (1819–1912), ballistician, was born at Thurnscoe, near Doncaster, 8 January 1819, the eldest son of John Bashforth, who farmed the glebe at Thurnscoe. He was educated at Brampton Bierlow and afterwards at Doncaster grammar school, whence he entered St. John's College, Cambridge, as a sizar, in 1840. He was second wrangler in 1843, when John Couch Adams [q.v.] was senior wrangler. Although not at all intimate as undergraduates, the two mathematicians became firm friends in after-life. Bashforth was elected a fellow of his college in 1843, and was ordained deacon in 1850 and priest in 1851. In 1857 he accepted the college living of Minting, near Horncastle, of which he remained rector until 1908. In 1905 he was made an honorary fellow of his college.

After taking his degree Bashforth spent three years in practical civil engineering, working partly in London and partly with one of the new railway companies which were then being formed throughout the country. He was engaged on the survey of projected lines, and in this way gained that practical experience in careful measurement which afterwards proved so valuable to him in his experiments in gunnery. Bashforth was anxious to obtain a post as professor of mathematics in the provinces, but such appointments were rare in those days. In 1864, however, he was appointed professor of applied mathematics to the advanced class of artillery officers at Woolwich, which afterwards developed into the Royal Artillery College.

Bashforth's main interest lay in the science of ballistics, and it is upon a series of experiments made by him between the years 1864 and 1880 that our present knowledge of air-resistance is founded. Great Britain entered the Crimean War with military equipment of a type which dated from the Peninsular campaigns. The muzzle-loading musket, 'Brown Bess', and the cast iron smooth-bore cannon, firing a spherical solid shot, were still employed. The ineffectiveness of such artillery in the Crimea in general, and the exigencies of the siege of Sebastopol in particular, called for more powerful weapons, and a beginning was made there with the Lancaster rifled guns which had a bore of oval section twisted longitudinally. These guns fired an oval shell, but they were not a success because many burst on service, probably owing to the shell jamming in the bore. In the preface to his *Mathematical Treatise on the Motion of Projectiles* (1873) Bashforth says, 'Feeling that the satisfactory solution of any question in gunnery depends upon the construction of a trustworthy chronograph, it therefore became my duty to recommend that a proper instrument should be procured, and that a systematic course of experiments should be undertaken to determine, in the first instance, the resistance of the air to the motion of projectiles'. He accordingly set to work to construct the chronograph, first tried in November 1865, which bears his name; and the military authorities carried out at Shoeburyness, Essex, under his direction, experiments which enabled him to determine the air-resistance. His results are set out in the treatise above mentioned, and he described his experiments in his *Report on the Experiments made with the Bashforth Chronograph*, (*1865–1870*), published by the government in 1870.

Bashforth's ballistic experiments and the theory based upon them required continual amplification, and he received much assistance from his pupils. But in 1872, finding that under a new scheme of army reorganization the scope and importance of his post were to be reduced, he resigned his position at Woolwich. Thereafter he resumed his clerical duties at Minting, the living of which he had been allowed by the indulgence of his bishop to retain. Nevertheless, in 1873 he was appointed adviser to the War Office on questions relating to the science of artillery; and in 1878 he was requested by the government to lend his chronograph and give his assistance in a new series of experiments to be carried out with both very high and very low velocities. The invitation gave Bashforth much satisfaction, and he superintended the working out of the results of a large number of experiments made in the years 1878 to 1880. His *Final Report* was published in 1880, and he received from the government a grant of £2,000 for his work. He utilized his leisure by preparing, in conjunction with Professor Adams, a treatise on *Capillary Action* (1883), and he also published *The Bashforth Chronograph* (1890). Bashforth married in 1869

Elizabeth Jane, daughter of the Rev. Samuel Rotton Pigott, vicar of Bredgar, Kent, by whom he had one son. In 1908 he retired to Woodhall Spa, Lincolnshire, where he died 13 February 1912. Bashforth's name will always be bracketed with that of Benjamin Robins [q.v.]; they are the two principal English authorities on the science of ballistics.

[*Yorkshire Weekly Post*, 16 February 1912; Memoir by J. H. Hardcastle in *Arms and Explosives*, August 1912; *The Eagle* (magazine of St. John's College, Cambridge), vol. xxxiii, 215–16, 1912, xxxiv, 109–11, 257–60, 1913; private information.] G. G.

BATTENBERG, Prince LOUIS ALEXANDER of (1854–1921), admiral of the fleet. [See Mountbatten, Louis Alexander.]

BEACH, Sir MICHAEL EDWARD HICKS, first Earl St. Aldwyn (1837–1916), statesman. [See Hicks Beach.]

BEECHING, HENRY CHARLES (1859–1919), dean of Norwich, man of letters, was born 15 May 1859 at 16 Dorset Street, London. He was the second son of James Plumer George Beeching, and came of a Sussex family of shipowners and bankers who had long held land at Bexhill. His mother was Harriet, daughter of William Skaife, of Knaresborough, whose family had lived for many generations near Pately Bridge, Yorkshire. In 1875 he went to the City of London School, where he came under the influence of Dr. Edwin A. Abbott, for whom he always retained an affectionate regard. In October 1878 he went up to Balliol College, Oxford, as an open exhibitioner, and soon became one of a circle which included J. W. Mackail, J. St. Loe Strachey, (Sir) Clinton Dawkins, (Sir) Rennell Rodd, and (Sir) Sidney Lee. His enthusiasm for English literature, and more especially for English poetry, was stimulated by his Balliol friendships, and his own gift for writing verse was early apparent. He contributed to an undergraduate periodical called *Waifs and Strays*, and in 1879 published, in conjunction with Mackail and J. B. B. Nichols, a small volume of poems entitled *Mensae Secundae*; this was followed later by *Love in Idleness* (1883) and *Love's Looking-glass* (1891), both of which were written with the same collaborators. He graduated B.A. in 1883.

In 1882 Beeching was ordained deacon, and became curate of St. Matthew's, Mossley Hill, Liverpool, where he remained until 1885. In that year he accepted the living of Yattendon, a small village in Berkshire, which he held for fifteen years. He was able to devote much of his time to literary work, particularly to the study of the English poets. In 1895 he published his best-known volume of verse, *Love in a Garden and Other Poems*. In 1896 he began to contribute anonymously to the *Cornhill Magazine*, of which his friend St. Loe Strachey was then editor, *Pages from a Private Diary*; these were published in book-form, also anonymously, in 1898; the second edition (1903) bore the pseudonym 'Urbanus Sylvan'. In 1900 his edition of Milton was published by the Clarendon Press.

In 1900 Beeching gave up his work as a country clergyman, and became chaplain of Lincoln's Inn and professor of pastoral theology at King's College, London. Two years later he was appointed canon of Westminster, a most congenial post for a man of his tastes. He was select preacher at Oxford in 1896–1897 and again in 1912–1913; at Cambridge in 1903, 1909, and 1912; and at Dublin in 1905. In 1906 he published *Provincial Letters and other papers*, and in 1909 a life of Francis Atterbury. During this London period he also produced several volumes of sermons and lectures, including *Religio Laici* (1902), *The Bible Doctrine of Atonement* (1907), and *William Shakespeare . . . a reply to Mr. George Greenwood, M.P.* (1908). He also edited two volumes of sermons and lectures by his friend Alfred Ainger [q.v.].

In 1911 Beeching was appointed dean of Norwich. He became keenly interested in the history and services of his cathedral, and took an active part in the life of the city. His health began to fail in 1918, and on 25 February 1919 he died at Norwich from heart failure. His ashes were buried in Norwich Cathedral on 3 March. He married in 1890 Mary, daughter of the Rev. A. J. Plow, and niece of Robert Bridges, afterwards poet laureate, and had three daughters.

Beeching was eminent both as churchman and man of letters. A man of wide sympathies and varied interests, he was beloved and successful alike as country rector, canon of Westminster, and dean of Norwich. As a preacher he showed learning and eloquence. He was a liberal churchman, but no controversialist, and he had a deep love for the ritual and liturgy of the Church of England. He will be best remembered as an essayist and critic of charm and distinction, with a prose style that reveals great delicacy of judgement, sure literary taste, and a rare vein of humour. His own poetry, though slender in volume, is marked by technical skill, by polished wit, and by the verbal dexterity which made his epigrams famous. With his lovable personality, his charm of manner, and his gift of humour, Beeching was a man of many friends, one of whom called him 'the wisest and wittiest of my Balliol contemporaries'.

A coloured drawing, made by William Strang in 1908, is in the possession of Miss Phyllis Anne Beeching. A small pastel drawing by Arthur Batchelor belongs to Mrs. Beeching, and a drawing by Bowyer Nichols to Mrs. Guest-Williams, of Trowell Rectory, near Nottingham.

[*Cornhill Magazine*, April 1919; *Oxford Magazine*, 7 March 1919; *The Times*, 26 February 1919; *Church Times*, 28 February 1919; *Eastern Daily Press*, 26 February and 3 March 1919; Memoir by Sir Sidney Lee and bibliography by G. A. Stephen in *Norwich Public Library Readers' Guide*, vol. vii, no. 6, April 1919; private information.]

F. P. S.

BELCHER, JOHN (1841–1913), architect, the eldest of the ten children of John Belcher, a London architect, by his first wife, Anne Woollett, a descendant of Philip Woollett, father of the eighteenth-century engraver, William Woollett [q.v.], was born at 3 Montague Terrace, Trinity Square, London, 10 July 1841. The family were members of the 'Catholic Apostolic', or 'Irvingite', Church, in which Belcher was a minister throughout his life. He was educated at private schools and at Luxemburg, and after spending a few months in Paris as an architectural student (1862–1863) he became partner to his father in a good city practice in 1865.

After his father's retirement in 1875 Belcher soon gave evidence of individuality in his building in the City. At the corner of the new Queen Victoria Street he boldly adopted French Gothic for business premises (1871), and later on (1876) he introduced a 'Queen Anne' building at the Bucklersbury corner of the same block. He built two versions of the hall of the Curriers Company in London Wall; the first building was bought and pulled down by Messrs. Rylands, whose adjoining warehouses in Wood Street Belcher also designed; the second (1874), which also has been dismantled, had a French Gothic elevation to London Wall, reminiscent of Jacques Cœur's house at Bourges. As a designer, Belcher was at home in domestic work, and of much that he did his own house on Champion Hill, Camberwell, is a good example (1885). For the Earl of Eldon he reconstituted the old mansion of Stowell Park, Gloucestershire, and prepared a scheme for gardens—one of the first endeavours to revive an architectural garden without serpentine paths and formal beds (1886).

Belcher's artistic sympathy quickly responded to the spirit of the day, when Italian renaissance was succeeding to the Gothic revival. The palaces of Genoa aroused his enthusiasm, and their influence lasted, giving opportunity for the use of sculpture and mural decoration, and liberty in employing the classic tradition. The offices of the Institute of Chartered Accountants, which he built in 1890 on an obscure site behind Moorgate Street, at once made his fame, and became a landmark in City architecture; the sculptured frieze, placed at the foot of the columns, was executed by his lifelong friend, (Sir) William Hamo Thornycroft, R.A., and Harry Bates adorned the basement with terms and corbels. The architect was here seen to be not only courageous but in sympathy with the sculptor. The design for the Victoria and Albert Museum in 1891 added to Belcher's reputation. Colchester town hall (1898), with a picturesque campanile, was also a success. Electra House, Finsbury (1902), is a fine classical mass with good sculpture at the entrance, and the Winchester House elevation to London Wall is original and profuse in its combination of the two arts. Messrs. Mappin and Webb's shop in Oxford Street (1907) and a building at the west corner of St. James's Street and Piccadilly (1908) were novel attempts to employ vertical lines without a classical order, and have little of the usual sculpture. Whiteley's stores in Bayswater (1912) were the first example of a new architectural interpretation of the requirements of business, and the house of the Royal Society of Medicine in Wimpole Street (1913) showed the restraint and dignity which the occasion demanded. The offices of the Zoological Society of London in Regent's Park (1913) mark a later development in the direction of modern French treatment. Lord Ashton gave Belcher the opportunity for a purely monumental building: the Ashton Memorial (1906) in the Williamson park at Lancaster is reminiscent of Wren's method at Greenwich. Holy Trinity church, Kingsway, London, is original in the recessing of the front on a semicircular plan (1910).

Belcher's work is the striking outcome of a traditional education in classical architecture stimulated to revolt by the Gothic revival, and producing an eclecticism which opened the way for new alliances with sculptors and painters, untrammelled by convention. He was quick to respond to new movements, and had the courage of his convictions. His work, therefore, represents the approach of architecture to the arts and crafts movement in renaissance building, as does that of his friend John Dando Sedding [q.v.] in Gothic. He was an original member of the Art Workers' Guild, and his presidency of the Royal Institute of British Architects in 1904 proved a valuable link between the two societies. He published a small book of essays, *Essentials in Architecture* (1893), and collaborated with Mervyn E. Macartney in publishing an important collection of photographs of houses, entitled *The Later Renaissance in England* (1897–1899) ; this has had considerable influence on contemporary building.

Belcher was elected A.R.A. in 1900 and R.A. in 1909. The Royal Institute of British Architects nominated him in 1907 for the royal gold medal of architecture. He married in 1865 Florence, daughter of Matthew Parker, a minister, of Dublin. They had no children. He died at Redholm, Champion Hill, Camberwell, 8 November 1913, and is buried in Norwood cemetery. An excellent portrait by F. Dicksee, R.A., hangs in the gallery of the Institute.

[*Journal* of the Royal Institute of British Architects, 22 November and 6 December 1913 ; personal knowledge.] A. B. P.

BENSON, RICHARD MEUX (1824–1915), divine, and founder of a religious order, the second son of Thomas Starling Benson, of Champion Lodge, Surrey, by his second wife, Eliza, only child of Richard Meux, was born at his father's London residence, Bolton House, Russell Square, 6 July 1824. His father, who was high sheriff of Surrey (1814), had no profession and gave much time to hunting, shooting, and fishing. His mother, to whom he was devoted and to whom he owed his religious training, was descended from Anne, sister of Edward IV, as well as from the seventeenth-century divine, Robert Sanderson, bishop of Lincoln [q.v.]. Through his mother Benson was also a cousin of the first Lord Brougham. After Benson's birth his father lived at North Cray Place, Kent, until 1833 when he removed to Sketty Park, near Swansea. In 1837 the family occupied a château near Boulogne, and from 1839 to 1861 their home was the Manor House, Teddington, Middlesex, where Mr. Benson died in 1858 and his widow in 1859.

Richard Benson was educated at home with his elder brother, Henry Roxby, afterwards General Benson, who fought in the Crimea, commanded the 17th Lancers, and died in 1890. His education was sufficiently thorough to enable him, while still a youth, to escort his half-sister, Sarah Benson, to Germany in 1841, and to make a long foreign tour with her in 1843. Proceeding from Germany to Italy the brother and sister wintered in Rome, where they had the entrée to distinguished society. Benson saw much of the leading Italian theologians of the day, and used to walk with De Rossi, the archaeologist, then a youth of his own age. Cardinal Acton [q.v.] and other cardinals paid them some attention, and they had a private audience with the pope, Gregory XVI, who conversed not of theology but of Italian cities. Benson set himself to study thoroughly the Roman Church, but his studies did nothing to shake the beliefs in which he had been educated and he attended regularly the Anglican services then held in a hayloft outside the Porta del Popolo. Later they visited Naples, Venice, and Karlsbad, where Benson left his sister while he went to Dresden and Prague.

In October 1844 Benson went up to Christ Church, Oxford ; in 1846 he was nominated by Dr. Pusey to a studentship and admitted on 24 December with Henry Parry Liddon, George William Kitchin, and George Ward Hunt. He retained his studentship till his death. He took his B.A. degree (second classes in *literae humaniores* and mathematics) in 1847, and gained the Kennicott scholarship for Hebrew in 1848, in which year he was ordained deacon by Bishop Wilberforce at Cuddesdon and became assistant curate of St. Mark's, Surbiton, close to his home. He was ordained priest, by the same bishop, and graduated M.A. in 1849. In 1850 he became vicar of Cowley, two miles from Oxford, then a small village, although the parish extended as far as Magdalen bridge. He lived a life of study and devotion, eagerly promoted the practice of retreats, was a close friend of Henry Parry Liddon [q.v.], then vice-principal of Cuddesdon, and was much consulted by Anglicans inclined to become Roman Catholics.

(Sir) Francis Cowley Burnand [q.v.] went to live with Benson for a time, but ultimately seceded to the Church of Rome.

In 1859, his parents being dead, Benson proposed to give himself to missionary work in India, but the marking out of Cowley Common as a site for an Oxford suburb caused Bishop Wilberforce to press Benson to give up the plan, and he devoted himself to providing for the new district. A sermon preached by John Keble at Wantage on 22 July 1863 [No. 5 in *Sermons Preached on Various Occasions*, 1880] moved Benson to think of founding a community for men, and in 1865 he laid his plan before Bishop Wilberforce, who agreed to be responsible for the episcopal oversight of the work and to give a preacher's licence to any priest who joined the community. On 27 December 1866 the society of mission priests of St. John the Evangelist was formally constituted by Benson, S. W. O'Neill (a former Eton master), and C. C. Grafton (later bishop of Fond du Lac), each of whom took a life vow of celibacy, poverty, and obedience. Benson was at once elected superior and still held that office in 1884, when the bishop of Oxford (Dr. Mackarness) became visitor and formally approved the statutes and the rule. About the beginning of 1866 Benson had removed from Cowley village to a house not far from the iron church which he had erected in the new district in 1859. In 1868 the Society moved into the mission house in Marston Street. In 1870 old Cowley was separated ecclesiastically from the new district, which was created a parish as Cowley St. John with Benson as its vicar. In November of that year Benson went to America to establish a branch house in Boston, to preach missions and conduct retreats. He returned in September 1871. In 1886 he resigned his vicarage, and in 1890 his office as superior, in which he was succeeded by Robert Lay Page. He went to India, and after working there proceeded again to Boston in 1892. He returned to Cowley in 1899 and remained there till his death.

Benson had a frame described as compact of 'catgut and iron' and he was rigorously ascetic, spending whole nights in prayer and writing, and even in his ninety-first year fasting a whole day. As a preacher he had no popular gifts; he was at his best in conducting retreats or addressing his community, being eloquent, original, and fertile in illustration. In theology he was whole-heartedly loyal to the Anglican position as representing his conception of true catholicism. He disliked one-sided teaching and over-definition and had no sympathy with later doctrinal developments, e. g. of Reservation 'after the Roman manner'. He had a wide and cultivated mind; literature, art, poetry, music, and history, all appealed to him. But his one real interest was that of an apostle and a missionary. His organization of the community life for men was a great achievement; many years before his death the 'Cowley Fathers' had become an honoured name in the Church of England, and the Society was established in India and in South Africa as well as in the United States. The success of his work made Benson unquestionably 'one of the greatest spiritual forces in the English Church during the latter half of the nineteenth century' [Bishop Hall in *Letters*, p. 1].

In appearance Benson was short, thin, and wiry; in later years he was much bent with rheumatism and his very white face was deeply lined. Eventually he became deaf and blind, but he was still mentally vigorous and his spiritual influence in no way lessened. Naturally reserved and shy and by training austere, he was exceedingly tender-hearted and had a swift sense of humour. He died at the Mission House, Cowley, 14 January 1915, and is buried in the cemetery adjoining the parish church of St. Mary and St. John.

Of Benson's many books, *Redemption* (a course of sermons, 1861), two expository works, *The Wisdom of the Son of David* (1860) and *The Divine Rule of Prayer* (1866), as well as his well-known *Manual of Intercessory Prayer*, pt. i (1863), belong to the period before the founding of the community at Cowley. His *Bible Teachings* (1875) illustrates the balance of his eucharistic teaching; his devotional works, *Benedictus Dominus* (1876), *The Final Passover* (1884, 1893–1895), and *Spiritual Readings* (1879, 1882), exhibit his deep spiritual insight. His later years were devoted to a commentary on the Psalms, *The War Songs of the Prince of Peace* (1901).

[G. Congreve and W. H. Longridge, *Letters of Richard Meux Benson*, 1916, and *Further Letters*, 1920; *Church Times*, 8 August 1924; private information; personal knowledge.]

S. L. O.

BENSON, ROBERT HUGH (1871–1914), Catholic writer and apologist, the fourth son and youngest child of Edward White Benson [q.v.], afterwards archbishop of Canterbury, by his wife, Mary Sidgwick (a second-cousin), was born

18 November 1871 at Wellington College, of which his father was the first head master. In 1872 Edward Benson was appointed chancellor of Lincoln cathedral and removed to Lincoln; in 1877 he became bishop of the new diocese of Truro, and in 1882 archbishop of Canterbury, from which date the Bensons had Lambeth Palace and Addington Court, near Croydon, for their homes. These romantic surroundings ever coloured the imagination of Robert Hugh Benson, and he inherited, and early displayed, a high-strung and dramatically responsive temperament. In 1882 he went to a preparatory school at Clevedon, Somerset, and in 1885 gained a scholarship at Eton, where he stayed till 1889. Not idle, he yet showed no interest in study, nor any remarkable religious sense, but ended by winning the Hervey prize for a poem on Father Damien. At Wren's collegiate establishment, where he prepared unsuccessfully for a year for the Indian civil service, *John Inglesant* made a lasting impression on him. In October 1890 he went up to Trinity College, Cambridge, where he remained for three years. Here he was only moderately successful in classics, but he began theology, as he had decided to take orders. Wagner, Swedenborg, mesmerism, and climbing in the Alps were among his interests.

Prepared for the diaconate by Charles John Vaughan, dean of Llandaff, Benson was ordained deacon in 1894, not without a sharp mental struggle due, seemingly, to a fear of the irrevocable. After a retreat in which Fr. Basil Maturin [q.v.], still an Anglican, gave him much spiritual and intellectual help, he was ordained priest in the Church of England (1895), and till the autumn of 1896 he worked in the Eton mission at Hackney Wick among poor people who loved him more than he liked them. After his father's death in October 1896 he went to Egypt, whence Anglicanism 'seemed provincial'. From May 1897 till June 1898 he was curate at Kemsing, near Sevenoaks, but fled, for discipline, to the Community of the Resurrection at Mirfield, Yorkshire. Benson's views about the sacraments developed fast, but some lectures by Canon (afterwards Bishop) Gore unsettled him: he began to see no alternative but authority or scepticism.

In 1903 Benson returned to his home and in September of that year was received into the Roman communion at Woodchester, Gloucestershire. He had already written *The Light Invisible*, semi-mystical fiction (1903); in 1904 appeared *By What Authority?*, a vivid story of the Elizabethan religious revolution. The months from November 1903 to June 1904 were spent at San Silvestro, Rome, and, after ordination, he returned to England, and at Llandaff House, Cambridge, read theology and wrote *The King's Achievement* (1905) on Henry VIII, *The Queen's Tragedy* (1906) on Mary Tudor, and *The History of Richard Raynal, Solitary* (1906), fiction disguised as history, being an account of a hermit in Henry VI's reign. He migrated in 1905 to the Rectory, Cambridge, and there wrote novels of modern life: *The Sentimentalists* (1906), *The Conventionalists* (1908)—studies of rather abnormal, and also of very average, temperaments; *A Mirror of Shalott* (1907), *The Papers of a Pariah* (1907)—studies of catholic ritual as from without; and *The Lord of the World* (1907), a sensational description of the coming of Anti-Christ. Lesser works of this period are *A City set on an Hill* (1904) and *An Alphabet of Saints* (1905).

Benson bought and quaintly adorned an old house at Hare Street, Buntingford, Hertfordshire, where he lived from 1908 till his death, carving, embroidering, gardening, entertaining friends, and writing. The books belonging to this period are: *The Necromancers* (1909) on spiritualism, *A Winnowing* (1910), *None other Gods* (1910), *The Coward* (1912), *Come Rack, Come Rope* (1912), *An Average Man* (1913), *Oddsfish* (1914) on Charles II, *Initiation* (1914) a study of pain, and *Loneliness* (1915). He also printed some sermons, *The Religion of the Plain Man* (1906), *Christ in the Church* (1911), *The Friendship of Christ* (1912), and *Paradoxes of Catholicism* (1913), four short religious plays, some war prayers and poems, and a life of Archbishop Becket (1910), the last partly in collaboration with Mr. Frederick Rolfe, with whom he struck up a tempestuous friendship.

Benson was immensely popular as a preacher, although his manner was violent owing to his stammer, and his voice shrill. He visited Rome and America more than once, preaching and lecturing, had a vast correspondence, and poured forth press articles on innumerable subjects; but he lacked leisure, patience, and health to deal adequately with his materials. *By What Authority?*, at once well-documented, vigorous, and tender, and *None other Gods*, with strong characterization, varied incident, and many mystical touches, not superadded to but expressed through the normal, are perhaps the best specimens of his two styles of writing. But his astounding vitality was infused into all his books; the charm of his boyish enthusiasm won him a welcome everywhere; his friendships were fervent; but they were none too lasting when he lost interest, save within his family where the influence of his mother remained paramount with him. Athirst for experience, he used fully every lesson he had learned, yet his piety remained childlike and his faith fierce. In 1911 he was made private chamberlain to Pope Pius X. His death was due to pneumonia supervening on false angina, and to the ruin of his nervous system by feverish yet systematic overwork. He died at Salford 19 October 1914, in the presence of his brother, Arthur Christopher Benson, to whom he was devoted,

[C. C. Martindale, *The Life of Monsignor Robert Hugh Benson*, 1916; A. C. Benson, *Hugh*, 1914; letters; private information.]

C. C. M.

BERESFORD, Lord CHARLES WILLIAM DE LA POER, Baron Beresford (1846–1919), admiral, was born at Philipstown, King's county, 10 February 1846, the second son of the Rev. John de la Poer Beresford, fourth Marquess of Waterford, by his wife, Christiana, fourth daughter of Charles Powell Leslie, M.P., of Glaslough, county Monaghan. He was educated at Bayford School, Hertfordshire, and at Stubbington House, near Fareham. He entered the *Britannia* as a naval cadet in December 1859, and in March 1861 was appointed to the *Marlborough*, flagship in the Mediterranean and one of the finest of the old wooden line of battleships. He was rated midshipman in June 1862. He was transferred in July 1863 to the *Defence*, a new ironclad, and after less than a year was appointed as senior midshipman to the *Clio*, corvette, in which he made a voyage to the Falkland Islands and round Cape Horn to Honolulu and Vancouver. In December 1865 he was transferred to the *Tribune* at Vancouver, promoted sub-lieutenant 1866, and in the following February transferred to the *Sutlej*, flagship on the Pacific station. In the following June he returned home in her and joined the *Excellent*, gunnery school ship. After eight months in the royal yacht *Victoria and Albert*, which gave him his promotion to lieutenant in October 1868, he was appointed to the *Galatea*, frigate (captain, Prince Alfred, Duke of Edinburgh), in which he made a voyage of two and a half years, visiting the Cape, Australia, New Zealand, Japan, China, India, and the Falkland Islands. In November 1872 he was appointed flag lieutenant to Sir Henry Keppel, commander-in-chief at Plymouth, and remained there till August 1874, when he was sent for a few months to the *Bellerophon*, flagship of the North American station. At the general election of 1874 Lord Charles was returned to parliament for Waterford in the conservative interest, and retained the seat until 1880. In September 1875 he went as aide-de-camp to the Prince of Wales on his tour in India and was promoted commander in November of that year. In May 1877, after a short period in the *Vernon* for torpedo instruction, he was appointed commander to the *Thunderer*, Channel squadron, till June 1878. A year later he was appointed to the command of the royal yacht *Osborne*, a post which he retained till November 1881. During these years, 1874–1881, he was chiefly known as a dashing sportsman, a personal friend of the Prince of Wales, and a prominent popular figure in smart society.

At the beginning of 1882 Lord Charles took command of the *Condor*, gunboat, under Sir Beauchamp Seymour (afterwards Lord Alcester), commander-in-chief of the fleet that bombarded Alexandria (11 July) during the Egyptian crisis; he took the leading part in engaging and silencing Fort Marabout in that operation. After the bombardment he was sent ashore under Captain John (afterwards Lord) Fisher and appointed provost-marshal and chief of police, and restored order with admirable efficiency, nerve, and tact. He was promoted captain and mentioned in dispatches for gallantry for these services. He was offered an appointment on the staff of the khedive and also that of war correspondent of the *New York Herald*, but Sir Garnet (afterwards Viscount) Wolseley refused to release him. He then returned home and remained on half-pay till August 1884, when he was appointed to the *Alexandra*, to act on the staff of Lord Wolseley during the Nile expedition for the relief of Khartoum. He was afterwards placed in command of the naval brigade on the Nile, with which he took part in the battle of Abu Klea on 17 January 1885. He also commanded the expedition which went to the rescue of (Sir) Charles William Wilson [q.v.] in the *Safieh*, when he kept his ship steadily engaged under heavy fire while his engineer, Mr. Benbow, repaired her disabled boiler (4 February). He was commended in the House of Commons, and described by Lord Wolseley in his dispatch as ' an officer whose readiness and resource and ability as a leader are only equalled by his daring'. For these services he was made C.B.

Lord Charles came home in July 1885, and was returned to parliament for East Marylebone, and re-elected in 1886. The Prince of Wales, with whom he had become very intimate, urged Lord Salisbury, on the formation of the conservative government, to give him political office, but the prime minister preferred to appoint him fourth naval lord of the Admiralty under Lord George Hamilton. He proved a difficult colleague and early showed himself hostile to the policy of the Board. He found fault with the shipbuilding programme and with the organization and pay of the intelligence department, and objected to the supreme authority of the first lord in naval administration. At length he resigned in January 1888. For the next two years he was a constant and outspoken critic of naval affairs in the House of Commons, until, in December 1889, he was appointed to the command of the *Undaunted*, armoured cruiser, on the Mediterranean station, resigning his seat in parliament. He returned to England in June 1893, to take command of the Medway dockyard reserve till March 1896. In 1897 he was appointed aide-de-camp to Queen Victoria, and in September of that year was promoted to flag rank and won for his party, at a by-election at York, a seat which he retained till January 1900, when he was sent to the Mediterranean as second in command under Sir John Fisher. In the meantime, in 1898–1899, he had gone to China on a special mission on behalf of the Associated Chambers of Commerce, and had published his report in a spirited volume entitled *The Break-up of China* (1899). In the Mediterranean he worked in general harmony with his chief, whose reforming zeal he shared and at that time approved; but he earned a rebuke from the Admiralty for allowing the publication in the press of a letter highly critical of Admiralty policy. In February 1902, on returning to England, he was returned to parliament for Woolwich. He was promoted vice-admiral in October 1902, and early in 1903 he again left the House of Commons in order to take up the chief command of the Channel squadron, being promoted K.C.B. in the following June. In March 1905 he hauled down his flag, and two months later went to the Mediterranean as commander-in-chief, with the acting rank of admiral, to which he was promoted in November 1906.

After two years in the Mediterranean Lord Charles was made commander-in-chief of the Channel fleet, then the principal fleet of the navy, including as it did fourteen battleships. It was a time when, in order to meet the growing German danger, the naval forces in home waters were being gradually but radically reorganized by Sir John Fisher, then first sea lord. Beresford was out of sympathy with many of the changes, and relations between him and Whitehall became exceedingly strained: the gradual development of the home fleet, comprising some fully-manned vessels and some reserve ships with nucleus crews, as an independent command in peace time caused him great irritation; and at last, in March 1909, he was ordered to haul down his flag and come on shore, the Channel fleet being abolished as a separate command and absorbed into the greatly enlarged home fleet. Beresford at once challenged the whole policy of the Board of Admiralty and its organization of the fleets in a long polemical document addressed to the prime minister, Mr. Asquith. This was referred to a sub-committee of the Committee of Imperial Defence, composed of the prime minister and four secretaries of state. The report of this committee was published in August 1909, and on the whole vindicated the action and policy of the Admiralty, though in certain respects its wording seemed to justify some of Beresford's criticisms. Beresford published an account of his views in 1912 in a book called *The Betrayal*. He was again returned to parliament, as a member for Portsmouth, in 1910, and held the seat till January 1916, when he was raised to the peerage as Baron Beresford, of Metemmeh and of Curraghmore. He was placed on the retired list in February 1911, and received the G.C.B. He died of apoplexy while staying at Langwell, Caithness, 6 September 1919, and was honoured with a state funeral in St. Paul's Cathedral.

Beresford was one of the most remarkable personalities of his generation: brave, high-spirited, an enthusiastic sportsman, of noble birth, and possessed of ample private means, he touched life at many points, and to the general public was the best-known sailor of his day. He had some of the faults as well as many of the virtues of his Irish ancestry, and although he was passionately devoted to the navy and to his country, his love of publicity and impatience of control sometimes led him into conduct that was alien from the strict traditions of the service.

In parliament and on the platform, while not strong in argument, he was an attractive and forceful speaker and was popular with all parties, confining himself as a rule to naval topics in which he was especially interested. Owing partly to his variety of interests and partly to his quarrels with authority, he had until late in life comparatively little actual sea experience; but from the day in January 1900 on which he hoisted his flag in the Mediterranean, when nearly fifty-four, he was for the greater part of nine years continuously afloat. He soon showed himself an able and active flag officer; and he commanded the most important of the fleets of the country during a period of great naval development, when the position of foreign affairs was often critical, with an energy and ability that won general recognition from the service. He maintained and enhanced the fighting efficiency of the squadrons and flotillas placed in his charge, and devoted immense personal care to the welfare of the great body of men under his orders. He fully understood and practised the art of delegating authority, and he won the devoted loyalty of all ranks by his frank recognition of merit and his readiness to overlook minor faults when the intention of the action was good and sound. He was ambitious to reach the highest position in his profession, and it was unfortunate that the last years of his command were clouded by what came to be a personal antagonism between himself and that other great sailor, Lord Fisher, with whom, until 1903, he had been on terms of amity and in full agreement on naval policy. But a man of his geniality and good humour could not long nurse resentment; and in his entertaining autobiography, *Memories*, published in 1914, all traces of this regrettable dispute have practically disappeared. An admirable host, in London and general society he enjoyed a well-deserved and universal popularity.

Beresford married in 1878 Mina, daughter of Richard Gardner, M.P. for Leicester, and left two daughters.

There is a portrait of Beresford by C. W. Furse in the National Portrait Gallery.

[Admiralty records; Lord Charles Beresford, *Memories*, 1914.] V. W. B.

BERTIE, FRANCIS LEVESON, first VISCOUNT BERTIE OF THAME (1844–1919), diplomatist, was born 17 August 1844 at Wytham Abbey, Berkshire, the second son of Montagu Bertie, sixth Earl of Abingdon, by his wife, Elizabeth Lavinia, only daughter of George Granville Vernon Harcourt, M.P., of Nuneham Courtney, Oxfordshire. He was educated at Eton, and entered the Foreign Office by competitive examination in 1863. There he remained for forty years. From 1874 to 1880 Bertie was parliamentary private secretary to the Hon. Robert Bourke, afterwards Baron Connemara [q.v.], under-secretary of state for foreign affairs. In 1878 he was attached, as acting second secretary, to the special embassy of the Earl of Beaconsfield and the Marquess of Salisbury to the Congress of Berlin. From 1882 to 1885 he was acting senior clerk at the Foreign Office, and senior clerk from 1889 to 1894. In the latter year Bertie was appointed assistant under-secretary of state for foreign affairs, a position which he held until 1903 when, after his long term of service at the Foreign Office, he was sent as ambassador to Rome. He only remained there a year, being transferred at the beginning of 1905 to Paris, where he remained for thirteen years, his term of service being twice prolonged.

When Bertie came to Paris, the Anglo-French *entente*, concluded 8 April 1904, was barely nine months old. The Russo-Japanese War was still raging, though Russia was practically defeated. France was the ally of Russia, and Great Britain of Japan. Germany, believing France to have been weakened by the Russian disasters, and wishing to break the French *entente* with England, suddenly raised the question of Morocco, in which France had been promised British diplomatic support. The German Emperor's visit to Tangier, 31 March 1905, was intended to prove to France the worthlessness of British assurances. In this crisis Bertie's firm straightforwardness was conspicuously revealed; and, despite the ejection of M. Delcassé from the French Foreign Office at the instance of Germany, Bertie's composure helped the French government to recover from panic and to follow the policy which triumphed at the Algeciras Conference of 1906.

During the European crisis brought on by the Austro-Hungarian annexation of Bosnia-Herzegovina in October 1908, Bertie's aim was to preserve the Anglo-French *entente*. Though he distrusted the Russian foreign minister, Isvolsky, by dint of plain speaking and upright conduct he kept the confidence of the French government as fully as that of his own. Later on, when a policy of economic and financial co-operation, as a prelude to political co-operation, between France and

Germany was favoured by M. Caillaux, Bertie understood at once that the effect would be to subordinate France to Germany and to make of France, under German influence, an instrument of anti-British designs. He stood by France throughout the Agadir crisis of July 1911, and subsequently combated the French and German tendencies which sought to estrange France from England during the years 1912 and 1913. In so doing he made not a few enemies ; but in all sections of French society—from the aristocratic Faubourg Saint-Germain to the Republican Left—his personal influence was such that succeeding French governments constantly sought his advice.

In the crisis of July 1914 Bertie's apparent imperturbability was severely tested. As late as 27 July he felt confident that France would not go to war on account of Serbia, even if Russia did so. When war came, he hoped (3 August) that Great Britain would give naval aid to France without taking part in the land war. His dispatches show little trace of the ordeal through which he was passing. Down to his retirement in April 1918 he remained a fixed and constant element in the ebb and flow of the military and political intercourse that was carried on through other than diplomatic channels. For a long period he suffered from the subtle opposition of the semi-official British personages in Paris who supplied sundry British ministers with special information. He resigned, owing to ill-health, in April 1918, and left Paris in June. He died suddenly in London, after a short illness, 26 September 1919.

Few diplomatists of the first rank ever sought public recognition less than Bertie, or disliked it more. He respected neither persons nor reputations until personal experience had enabled him to judge of them. His mind was shrewd and his language blunt, his demeanour hearty without effusiveness, and his uprightness unfailing. Lord Grey of Fallodon, his chief from 1906 to 1916, wrote in the preface to Bertie's *Diary* : 'He had the gift of making himself trusted, and he had it in a rare degree. . . . The Foreign Office in London felt sure that a friendly policy with France would be carried out, with him as its intermediary, in the most efficient and wholesome manner.' M. Clemenceau, who placed implicit trust in him, gave him, on his retirement, such proofs of esteem on behalf of France as a British ambassador can rarely have received.

Bertie was created K.C.B. in 1902, G.C.M.G. in 1904, G.C.B. in 1908, and a privy councillor in 1903. He also received the grand cordon of the French legion of honour. He was raised to the peerage under the title of Baron Bertie of Thame, in 1915, and advanced to a viscounty on his retirement in 1918. He married in 1874 Lady Feodorowna Cecilia (died 1920), daughter of Henry Richard Charles Wellesley, first Earl Cowley [q.v.], by whom he had one son, Vere Frederick (born 1878), who succeeded his father as second viscount.

The diary which Lord Bertie kept in Paris during the years of the European War was edited by Lady Algernon Gordon Lennox under the title of *The Diary of Lord Bertie of Thame, 1914–1918*, 2 volumes (1924).

[Lord Bertie's *Diary* ; *British Documents on the Origins of the War*, vol. xi, ed. J. W. Headlam-Morley, 1926 ; personal knowledge.] H. W. S.

BETHAM-EDWARDS, MATILDA BARBARA (1836–1919), novelist and writer on French life. [See EDWARDS.]

BIDDULPH, SIR ROBERT (1835–1918), general, was born in London 26 August 1835, the second son of Robert Biddulph, M.P., J.P., of Ledbury, Herefordshire, by his wife, Elizabeth, daughter of the philanthropist, George Palmer, M.P. [q.v.], of Nazing Park, Essex. He entered the Royal Military Academy, Woolwich, in 1850, and passed into the Royal Artillery in 1853. In the following year he went to the Crimea and was engaged in the battles of Alma and Balaclava and the siege of Sebastopol. In the Indian Mutiny Biddulph was on the staff of Sir Colin Campbell as brigade major during the siege and capture of Lucknow. At this period he first met Garnet (afterwards Viscount) Wolseley, with whom he formed a life-long friendship. After Lucknow he joined the staff of Sir James Hope Grant [q.v.] as deputy assistant adjutant-general, Oudh field force, and, with the rank of captain, accompanied his chief to China in 1860. He was engaged in all the actions of the campaign which terminated in the fall of Peking. He subsequently returned to India, and was promoted major in 1861 and three years later lieutenant-colonel.

Biddulph returned to England in 1865 and served as assistant boundary commissioner for the Reform Act (1867). In 1871 he was summoned from the staff at Woolwich to be private secretary to Mr. (afterwards Viscount) Cardwell, secretary of state for war, in which post he had much to do with the introduction of the 'modern system' of army organization. He had previously thought deeply upon the question of army reform, and his chief, who recognized his exceptional qualities, appointed him assistant adjutant-general at the War Office, where he remained until 1878, having been promoted colonel in 1872. In 1878 he was selected for special service in Cyprus under Sir Garnet Wolseley, and in the following year he went to Constantinople as commissioner to arrange the financial details under the Anglo-Turkish Convention of 1878. On Wolseley's departure for South Africa a few months later, Biddulph succeeded him as high commissioner and commander-in-chief in Cyprus, where his main activities included the reformation of the currency, reorganization of the administration of justice, revision of taxation, the destruction of the locust scourge, and the construction of public works. In 1883 he was promoted major-general. He was very much respected and liked by the inhabitants of Cyprus, and the home government offered him a higher appointment in Natal; but, for family reasons, he was obliged to decline the post, and came home in 1886 in order to take up the post of inspector-general of recruiting. He was made lieutenant-general in the following year and general in 1892.

In 1893, having in the meanwhile filled the posts of director-general of military education (1888–1893) and quartermaster-general (January 1893), Biddulph was appointed governor and commander-in-chief at Gibraltar, where he remained nearly seven years. Here he again turned his mind to currency reform, and was also responsible for the re-arming of the fortress and the construction of new harbour and dockyard works. He returned to England in 1900, and later was president of the court set up to inquire into the supply of remounts during the Boer War. In 1904, the year in which he published *Lord Cardwell at the War Office*, he was appointed army purchase commissioner. He was the last person to hold that office, and it fell to him to complete one of Cardwell's great reforms, the abolition of the purchase of commissions. In 1914 he succeeded Lord Roberts as master gunner of St. James's Park. He died in London 18 November 1918. His career was connected principally with administration, but his military qualities were also very considerable. Throughout his life he was guided by strong religious principles. He was created K.C.M.G. (1880), G.C.M.G. (1886), and G.C.B. (1899). He married in 1864 Sophia (died 1905), daughter of the Rev. Anthony Lewis Lambert, rector of Chilbolton, Hampshire, and widow of Richard Stuart Palmer, of Calcutta. They had four sons and six daughters.

[*The Times*, 20 November 1918; private information.] C. V. O.

BINNIE, Sir ALEXANDER RICHARDSON (1839–1917), civil engineer, born in London 26 March 1839, was the eldest son of Alexander Binnie, wholesale clothier, of 77 Ladbroke Grove, London, by his wife, Hannah, daughter of Isaac Carr, of Johnby, Cumberland. He was educated privately, and articled in 1858 to Terence Woulfe Flanagan, civil engineer, and on the latter's death to John Frederic La Trobe-Bateman [q.v.] with whom he continued as assistant until 1862. From 1862 to 1866 Binnie was employed in railway construction in mid-Wales, and in 1867, after examination, he was appointed an executive engineer in the Public Works Department of India. He was stationed at Nagpur, and while there in 1873 carried out the works for the supply of that city with water from Ambajheri. In conjunction with Major Lucey Smith, he discovered coal at Warora in the Chanda district. This led to the construction of the Wardha–Warora branch of the Great Indian Peninsula Railway and to the opening up of the coal-field, for which Binnie received the commendation of the government of India. The Warora colliery was worked from 1871 till 1906.

In March 1875 Binnie was appointed chief engineer for waterworks to the city of Bradford. He repaired and reconstructed the Stubden, Leeshaw, and Leeming reservoirs, and designed and constructed the reservoirs at Barden and Thornton Moor. He also prepared the plans and sections for the Nidd Valley water scheme, which, however, was not actually carried out till after he had left Bradford.

In March 1890 Binnie was appointed chief engineer to the London County Council, a position which he held till 1901. During this time he superintended the construction of the Blackwall and Greenwich tunnels under the Thames and the Barking Road bridge over the Lea. In 1891, with Sir Benjamin Baker [q.v.], he prepared a report to the London County Council on the main drainage of London, and began the work of addition and reconstruction, therein recommended, which was completed after his retirement. He also designed the necessary works for widening the Strand and for the construction of the thoroughfares of Aldwych and Kingsway connecting it with Holborn. In 1897, on the completion of the Blackwall tunnel, he was knighted.

On the termination of his engagement with the County Council, Binnie commenced private practice at Westminster. In 1906 he reported to the government of Ireland on the Bann and Lough Neagh drainage, and from 1905 to 1907 he acted as chairman of the viceregal commission on the arterial drainage of Ireland. He visited Malta in 1909 in order to report on the water supply. In 1910 and 1911 he reported on the water supply and drainage of Petrograd, and in 1913 on the water supply of the city of Ottawa.

Binnie became a member of the Institution of Civil Engineers in 1865, and was elected president in 1905. In 1913 he published an important work on *Rainfall Reservoirs and Water Supply*, based on lectures which he had delivered at the request of the Chadwick trustees. A few years before his death, which took place at Beer, Devon, on 18 May 1917, an illness necessitated the amputation of one of his legs. He was buried at Brookwood cemetery. He married in 1865 Mary (died 1901), daughter of Dr. William Eames, physician, of Londonderry, by whom he left two sons and three daughters.

[*The Times*, 19 May 1917; *Proceedings* of the Institution of Civil Engineers, vol. cciii, 1916–1917; private information.] E. I. C.

BIRDWOOD, Sir GEORGE CHRISTOPHER MOLESWORTH (1832-1917), Anglo-Indian official and author, the eldest son of General Christopher Birdwood, Indian army, by his wife, Lydia Juliana, daughter of the Rev. Joseph Taylor, of the London Missionary Society, was born at Belgaum in the Bombay Presidency 8 December 1832. His family had long been connected with the Indian army and public services. He was sent at the age of seven to England to be educated, and went first to the Plymouth new grammar school, then to the Dollar Academy, and finally to the university of Edinburgh where he took his M.D. degree. In 1854 he was appointed to the Bombay establishment of the Indian medical staff, and he took part as a naval surgeon in the Persian expedition of 1856–1857. During the following ten years, whilst practising in Bombay and holding professorships of anatomy and physiology and of botany and materia medica at the Grant medical college, he laid the foundations of his future work by devoting himself to the study of many unexplored aspects of Indian life, social, economic, and scientific. He was registrar to the newly founded university of Bombay, curator of the government museum, secretary to the Bombay branch of the Royal Asiatic Society, and one of the founders of the Victoria botanical gardens and the Victoria and Albert museum at Bombay. His manifold activities in Bombay, which found recognition in his appointment as sheriff of the city in 1864, were cut short by ill-health, and he returned to England in 1868, as he told his friends, to die, but in fact, only to begin a long career of valuable service as an interpreter to his own countrymen of Indian life, art, and culture, and as a friend to Indians, for whom he aimed at promoting opportunities of social and intellectual intercourse with England. He was special commissioner of the Bombay government for the Paris exhibition of 1867; and, after he had recovered his health at home, he was appointed to assist Dr. John Forbes Watson [q.v.] in the annual exhibitions at South Kensington, of which the first was held in 1871. In 1878 he was posted as special assistant in the statistics and commerce department of the India Office, and he was in charge of the Indian sections of the chief international exhibitions down to that of Chicago in 1893. He retired from official work in 1902.

Birdwood's literary output both before and after his retirement was enormous, but the bulk of it was in the somewhat scattered form of reports, papers in the transactions of learned societies, contributions to magazines and newspapers, and introductions or appendixes in the books of others. The range of his writings was as wide as his interests. He was an authority on Indian art—more so perhaps than on Indian philology and etymology, in which he sometimes gave free rein to his whimsical imagination and love of paradox, though he was an accomplished Sanskrit scholar. To the study of Indian life and Indian folk-lore he brought a store of recondite information and solid learning. Besides special treatises on Indian botanical subjects, his two most important works were his *Report on the Miscellaneous Old Records of the India Office* (1879), and *The Industrial Arts of India* (1880); perhaps his most characteristic work is the volume of essays, entitled *Sva* (1915), giving to the mystic

'Svastika' an interpretation which some authorities dispute. Birdwood had an important share in the foundation of 'primrose' day (19 April). The oriental strain in Lord Beaconsfield's character appealed strongly to him, and it was a letter of his to *The Times* shortly before the first anniversary of the statesman's death which led popular sentiment to associate the primrose with his memory [see W. F. Monypenny and G. E. Buckle, *Life of Benjamin Disraeli*, vi. 630–1].

Birdwood, who was knighted in 1881, and made K.C.I.E. in 1887, died at Ealing 28 June 1917. He married in 1856 Frances Anne, daughter of Edward Tolcher, R.N., of Plympton St. Mary, and had three sons and two daughters.

[India Office *List*; *Journal of Indian Art and Industry*, vol. viii, January 1899; *Journal* of the Royal Society of Arts; files of *The Times*; private letters.] V. C.

BISHOP, EDMUND (1846–1917), liturgiologist and historian, was born at Totnes, 17 May 1846, the youngest child of Michael Bishop, by his wife, Susan Quick. He had his schooling at Exeter and in Belgium. On leaving school at seventeen he became, for a year, literary secretary to Thomas Carlyle, and in 1864 entered the Education Office. In 1867 he was received into the Church of Rome. During these years, before and after office hours, he frequented the British Museum, examining manuscripts systematically on a large scale. He discovered, transcribed, analysed, and annotated the 'Collectio Britannica' of some 300 papal letters of the fifth to the eleventh centuries, most of them previously unknown. Finding no means of publishing the work in England, he presented it to the editors of the *Monumenta Germaniae Historica*. Paul Ewald in *Neues Archiv* for 1880, in a lengthy appreciation of this remarkable find, signalized the 'infinite pains . . . thorough palæographical knowledge . . . brilliant conjectures . . . and surety of the restitutions of passages unintelligibly corrupt', which marked Bishop's work. This at once established his reputation on the Continent; it drew from Mommsen and the editors of the *Monumenta* a handsome written tribute, and put Bishop henceforth in constant communication with the group of *Monumenta* scholars. Bishop was a self-made scholar; but his contact as a young man with these eminent historical critics and with others, such as the Comte Riant, was to him a sufficient inspiration.

In 1885 Bishop retired from the Education Office, and shortly afterwards went to the Benedictine monastery of Downside, near Bath, with the intention of becoming a monk; his health, however, proved too frail for the life. He stayed on at Downside till 1889, and till the end of his life spent several months there almost every year. From 1893 until 1901 he resided and worked with Dom (afterwards Cardinal) Gasquet in a house near the British Museum. Growing much enfeebled in health, he passed his last fifteen years with his sister at Barnstaple, where he died 19 February 1917. He was unmarried.

Though his interests and his accumulations of knowledge ranged widely over many fields, it is principally as a liturgical scholar that Edmund Bishop will be known. It may safely be said that he knew the western liturgies in their entire sweep as no one else in his day. He had an unrivalled knowledge of the minutest details, but liturgy interested him primarily, not as texts, nor as ceremonial, but as the expression of the religious sense of the various peoples and ages; thus he regarded liturgy as a branch of the history of religion. His outstanding single contribution was the identifying of the Roman mass book of Gregory the Great, the central point, backwards and forwards, for the history of the liturgy in the west. His principal studies on the Roman liturgy, along with many other of his essays of varied character, were published at Oxford in 1918 in *Liturgica Historica*. He produced two other substantial pieces of work: an investigation of the early English calendars in the *Bosworth Psalter* (1908); and the *Appendix* to the *Liturgical Homilies of Narsai* (*Texts and Studies*, 1909), containing an epoch-making study on the 'Epiclesis'. But the products that bear Bishop's name are far from being the measure of his contributions to learning. Other scholars' books grew out of his encouragement, advice, and gifts of material. An inquiry would call forth a letter that was a treatise involving days of labour. The amount of his work thus buried in the books of others cannot be estimated.

As a scholar Bishop has been justly compared with F. J. A. Hort, and, like Hort, he was a man of singular charm, striking appearance, and old-world courtesy. His piety was simple and sincere. His library, bequeathed to Downside, where he is buried, is a speaking record of the man; a unique collection, illustrating liturgy, made with exquisite knowledge and endless care, it was a life-long work of joy.

[Notices collected in the *Downside Review*, October 1917 and October 1918 ; *Journal of Theological Studies*, April 1917 ; *Church Quarterly Review*, 1918 ; *The Christian Altar* (reprinted, 1906, from the *Downside Review*) with bibliography to 1906 attached ; personal knowledge.] E. C. B.

BLAKE, EDWARD (1833–1912), Canadian lawyer and politician, the eldest son of William Hume Blake, of Cashel Grove, co. Galway, by his wife, Catharine Hume, was born at Adelaide, Upper Canada, 13 October 1833. His father had settled in Canada in 1832, and became chancellor of Upper Canada. Blake was educated at Upper Canada College and the university of Toronto, and was called to the bar in 1856. He occupied through life an unrivalled position among Canadian barristers ; but his chief title to fame rests on his political career. He entered political life in 1867 at the birth of the new Dominion of Canada as liberal member for West Durham in the Dominion House of Commons, and for South Bruce in the Ontario House. At the early age of thirty-eight he became prime minister of Ontario (1871). Within less than a year, however, he resigned office (1872) and retired from the Ontario House in order that he might devote himself to federal politics. In the Dominion House of Commons he contributed greatly to the defeat of Sir John Macdonald [q.v.] over the so-called 'Pacific scandal' in 1873 ; and he ultimately became minister of justice in the administration of Alexander Mackenzie [q.v.]. His occupancy of this office, from 1875 to 1877, was of no little significance for the constitutional history of Canada and the British Empire. He brought about a considerable diminution in the powers and prerogatives of the governor-general, in regard especially to the pardoning power and the reservation of bills for the signification of the royal pleasure. In this respect he may be said to have put the coping-stone on the edifice of self-government in the Dominions.

In 1880, two years after the defeat and resignation of the Mackenzie administration, Blake succeeded Mackenzie as leader of the liberal opposition. He led the liberal party through the wilderness of two general elections, that of 1882 and that of 1887, but in neither of these was he successful in shaking the hold of Sir John Macdonald on the country. In 1888, discouraged by failure, he therefore retired in favour of (Sir) Wilfrid Laurier [q.v.]; and in 1892 he abandoned Canadian politics for British. He became the nationalist member for South Longford in the British House of Commons, and he continued to sit in the imperial parliament until 1907. In the councils of the Irish nationalist party he exerted a decided influence, especially in keeping agitation within constitutional bounds ; but he never succeeded in obtaining in the British parliament the position due to his abilities and his record. In his later years it was rather as a lawyer than as a politician that he was eminent. He argued many important constitutional cases before the Judicial Committee of the Privy Council, and by his vigour of character and his legal knowledge did much to shape its decisions. He died at Toronto 2 March 1912.

It is remarkable that hardly any British statesman of equal standing has spent a shorter time in public office than Edward Blake. For this there were various reasons. Blake was lacking in certain qualities essential to the politician. He had little humour, and a rather mordant wit. His really warm humanity lacked the geniality which distinguished his great foeman, Sir John Macdonald. For these reasons he never attracted to himself any large personal following. But he was a man of great abilities, and in point of political idealism he was almost too far in advance of the Canada of his day.

Blake married in 1858 Margaret, daughter of the Rt. Rev. Benjamin Cronyn, bishop of Huron ; there were three sons and one daughter of the marriage.

[J. C. Dent, *The Canadian Portrait Gallery*, 1880 ; J. S. Willison, *Sir Wilfrid Laurier and the Liberal Party*, 1903 ; private information.] W. S. W.

BOOTH, CHARLES (1840–1916), shipowner and writer on social questions, was the third son of Charles Booth, corn merchant, of Liverpool, by his first wife, Emily Fletcher, of Liverpool. Both his parents were Unitarians. Henry Booth [q.v.] and James Booth [q.v.] were his uncles. He was born at Liverpool 30 March 1840, and educated there at the Royal Institution School. After some training in the Liverpool office of Lamport and Holt's steamship company, he began his long and successful career as shipowner at the age of twenty-two, when he joined his eldest brother Alfred as partner in Alfred Booth & Co. Later, the Booth steamship company was formed, of which Booth himself was chairman until 1912. With but few intervals, Booth was actively engaged in his business to the end of his life.

Booth's opinions on industrial matters owed much, he believed, to the influence of Comte. The positivist, Henry Crompton [q.v.], was his cousin, and Edward Spencer Beesly was married to a cousin. He insisted upon the importance in industry of enterprise and of leadership, and he was afraid of socialism mainly because, under it, business transactions would no longer be 'tried in the court of profit and loss' [*Life and Labour: Industry*, v, 72–8]. He grew up with the Trade Union movement, and in general sympathy with its earlier policy, but its later developments he regarded with misgiving [*Industrial Unrest and Trade Union Policy*, 1913]. In politics Booth was never a keen partisan: as a young man he was a radical; afterwards he became a unionist, and was a member of the unofficial Tariff Commission of 1903–1904.

Booth had always taken an interest in the welfare of working men, but it was not until he was past middle age that there began to appear the works which established his reputation as a writer on social questions. In his first paper, *Occupations of the People* (1886), he sought to portray the industrial complexion of Great Britain and Ireland by rearranging the census figures of 1841–1881. This canvas he found too large, and he turned to London, publishing in *The Tower Hamlets* (1887) the beginnings of his 'inquiry into the condition and occupations of the people of London', which continued without intermission for sixteen years. The earlier part appeared as *Labour and Life of the People* (1889), and the whole as *Life and Labour of the People in London* (1891–1903), comprising *Poverty*, four volumes, *Industry*, five volumes, *Religious Influences*, seven volumes, and a *Final Volume*. Booth's volumes appeared at a critical time in the history of English social reform. A lively interest was being taken in the problems of pauperism, and it was coming to be recognized that benevolence, to be effective, must be scientific. Fitful investigations, such as those of Henry Mayhew [q.v.], had been made into the condition of the London poor, but there were as yet few data upon which reforms could be built with confidence. Booth's object was to fill this gap; his *Life and Labour* was designed to show 'the numerical relation which poverty, misery, and depravity bear to regular earnings and comparative comfort, and to describe the general conditions under which each class lives'. His work was based partly—at the suggestion of Joseph Chamberlain—on the records of School Board visitors, partly on his own inquiries, and partly on information collected, under his direction, from the Charity Organization Society and from other bodies in touch with London pauperism. Among the many who helped him to compile his material, and edit it, were his wife's cousin, Miss Beatrice Potter (Mrs. Sidney Webb) and (Sir) Graham Balfour for the earlier volumes, and Ernest Aves for the later. [The manuscript note-books containing the detailed evidence on which *Life and Labour* was founded are in the possession of his widow.] It was no proper part of Booth's plan to analyse economic changes or to trace the course of social development. His object was to give an accurate picture of the condition of London as it was in the last decade of the nineteenth century. In this light, his *Life and Labour* was recognized as perhaps the most comprehensive and illuminating work of descriptive statistics which had yet appeared.

With one exception—old age pensions—Booth was hesitant in urging particular social reforms; although he put together a few conclusions in the *Final Volume* of his *Life and Labour*, and made recommendations, published in his *Poor Law Reform* (1910), to the Poor Law Commission of 1905–1909, from which he himself had had to retire owing to ill-health. His public advocacy of old age pensions began in 1891 with a paper to the Royal Statistical Society; and subsequently he devoted much time to writing and speaking in favour of old age pensions, especially by endowment, rather than by insurance as advocated by William Lewery Blackley [q.v.] [*The Aged Poor: Condition*, 1894, and other books]. The passing of the Old Age Pensions Act in 1908 was largely due to the part which he had played in converting public opinion. His main criticism of the Act was that pensions were granted not to all, but only to those whose incomes fell below a certain level.

Booth married in 1871 Mary, only daughter of Charles Zachary Macaulay, and granddaughter of Zachary Macaulay [q.v.]. There were three sons and four daughters of the marriage. Booth was president of the Royal Statistical Society (1892–1894), fellow of the Royal Society (1899), and a privy councillor (1904). In 1906 he received the first honorary degree given by the new university of Liverpool.

He died 23 November 1916 at his home, Gracedieu Manor, Whitwick, and was buried at Thringstone, Leicestershire. A tablet to his memory, the work of Sir Charles Nicholson, Bart., was unveiled in 1920 in the crypt of St. Paul's Cathedral by (Sir) Austen Chamberlain.

[Booth's published works; *Charles Booth, A Memoir*, anon., 1918 (by his widow); private information.] F. W. O.

BOOTH, WILLIAM (1829–1912), popularly known as 'General' Booth, founder of the Salvation Army, was born at Sneinton, a suburb of Nottingham, 10 April 1829. His father, a speculative builder, was of a dark and taciturn nature; his handsome and dignified mother (Mary Moss) was obviously of Jewish descent. The boy, who was the only son, never stayed long at any one school, and at thirteen years of age, on account of family poverty, was apprenticed to a pawnbroker in a squalid part of Nottingham. In after years he spoke of this experience with great bitterness; but it is clear that he proved himself an admirable assistant to his employer, who soon singled him out for special confidence. Before he had been a year in this shop, his father, whose business undertakings had gone from bad to worse, died rather suddenly, and Mrs. Booth and her daughters moved into a small fancy-shop in Goosegate, Nottingham, where their struggle with penury made a dark impression on William's mind. He always spoke of his 'blighted childhood'.

The boy drifted out of the Church of England and into Wesleyan circles, but was not at the outset affected by this change of religious atmosphere. His heart seems to have been stirred for the first time by the fervid oratory of Feargus O'Connor [q.v.], who visited Nottingham during the election of 1842. That election witnessed a collision between chartists and soldiers, and William ranged himself on the side of the chartists. He was deeply affected, he tells us, by the daily spectacle of ragged children crying for bread at that time in the streets of Nottingham. But methodism was creeping into his blood, and two years later, with his conscience tortured by a small piece of sharp-practice in which he had overreached some of his fellow assistants at the pawnbroker's shop, he made public confession of his sin and underwent the experience of conversion (1844). Had it not been for this burden of conscience, and the lightening effect of confession, it is possible that he might have become an orator of radicalism; as it was, religion made him, from a political point of view, one of the hardest conservatives of his generation.

Two years after his conversion, on recovering from a fever which brought him to death's door, Booth joined a group of youthful revivalists who conducted religious services in the streets of Nottingham. He was then seventeen years of age, distinguished by his height, his pale face, his black hair, and his passionate voice. In 1849 he went to London in search of better-paid work. He tried to escape from the business he hated, but no one wanted him, and he was at last obliged to go as assistant to a pawnbroker in Walworth. He took at this time several vows which witness to great earnestness of mind and a certain grimness of spiritual intention. His letters of this period are likewise full of fiery zeal. He almost starved himself in order to send money back to his mother and sisters. His scanty leisure was devoted to religion, and he began to attract the attention of some local methodists, one of whom, a rich boot-manufacturer, persuaded him to become a lay-preacher. It was this boot-manufacturer who introduced him into the family of a carriage-builder living in Clapham, where he discovered the woman who was so powerfully to influence his subsequent career.

Catherine Mumford [see Booth, Catherine], daughter of the carriage-builder, was an invalid who spent most of her life on a sofa. She had cultivated her mind to a degree unusual among people in suburban circles. She saw the greatness of Booth's nature, but deplored his lack of culture. She criticized his sermons, recommended him books, and tried to steady the wild flame of his religious aspiration. But her religion at that time was stamped with the respectability of suburbanism. She was a true child of the dissenting chapel. Booth gave her a wider outlook and gradually weaned her mind from its subservience to public opinion. He admitted his lack of learning, but nothing, not even her persuasions, could tame his 'love for souls'. That was the master passion of his life. The suburban bluestocking took fire from the provincial ignoramus whose mind was as inferior to hers, as her spirit was inferior to his spirit. They became engaged, and Booth, who in 1852 had become an itinerant preacher of the Methodist New Connexion, consulted her by letter about his sermons, sent her his linen for mending, and constantly exhorted her to widen her sympathies and to approve of revivalist methods. Their love-letters must be of interest to any student of the nineteenth century who looks below the political and economic surface.

The lovers were married in 1855. Booth had then established something of a reputation as a travelling preacher of methodism, but his violent methods in the pulpit had made him powerful enemies. At the end of nine years in the ministry, rather than submit to the authority of his church, he broke with methodism, and launched out as an independent revivalist (1861). Mrs. Booth joined in this work, and it was at her suggestion that Booth came to London in 1865 and started the Christian Mission in Whitechapel. Thirteen years later, when he was nearly fifty years of age, William Booth accidentally converted his 'Christian Mission' into the 'Salvation Army' merely by the use of a metaphor (1878). One day in describing the Christian Mission in the presence of his son Bramwell, he used the phrase 'a volunteer army'. The son objected, since the new volunteer movement was just then the subject of some ridicule, declaring that he was a 'regular' or he was nothing. Booth altered the offending phrase to 'a salvation army', and from that alteration came the military titles (against which he fought for some time) and the military uniform (which he himself only gradually and grudgingly adopted), destined to transform the Whitechapel mission into a worldwide engine of revivalism.

Almost at once public attention was drawn to a new force in the religious life of the nation. Booth became the champion of 'the bottom dog'. He was sick of respectable people. His sympathies were genuinely on the side of the depressed, and as genuinely he believed that eternal punishment was the fate of all those who perished without the experience of conversion. But this grim theology was mitigated by a love for the degraded poor of great cities which was something new in modern England's religious life. Booth 'saved' these people in battalions, and proved to all the churches that the religious instincts of the urbanized people were much the same as in Wesley's day at the dawn of the industrial revolution. He beat his showman's drum in what he believed to be the service of the Light of the World, and speedily became the target of ridicule and calumny, the stormy centre of much rioting. But he pushed steadily forward, helped by his wife and children, and drew multitudes to 'the penitent's form'. Deeper acquaintance with the problem he was so impulsively attacking led him to become a social reformer. In 1890 he published a book called *In Darkest England and the Way Out*. It was largely written by the journalist W. T. Stead [q.v.], and altogether lacking in Booth's impressive Doric; but it created a sensation, and in spite of a very bitter and rather ridiculous attack by T. H. Huxley, Booth was liberally financed by the British public to look after the souls and bodies of 'the dim millions'.

He always held that you cannot make a man clean by washing his shirt, and his social work was chiefly an excuse for getting at the souls of men; but he had real and deep pity for the distressed poor, and he admitted the influence of environment. He was indirectly responsible for a much more intelligent attention on the part both of the churches and the politicians to the physical conditions of human life. It is characteristic of him that he hung back from a crusade for sexual purity which his son Bramwell persuaded W. T. Stead to undertake in the *Pall Mall Gazette*, and that he desired the rescue work of the 'Army' to be solely in the hands of women. In spite of all his platform outspokenness, he was a timorous administrator of the 'Army', and used his autocracy chiefly to safeguard its spiritual activities. His son Bramwell was the real organizer. Booth used to call him his Melanchthon.

His days were clouded by family secessions, and almost brought to wreck by the sufferings of his wife as she lay dying from cancer. In the end he was overtaken by blindness, but continued to visit many and far countries of the world where the Salvation Army flag was flying, evoking extraordinary enthusiasm from the multitudes, receiving the hospitality of kings and ambassadors. In those days, with his strong Jewish features, his flowing white beard, his wild looks, and his tall attenuated frame, the venerable man was something of a patriarchal figure in British public life. He died in London 20 August 1912. His wife, by whom he had three sons and four daughters, had died in 1890.

Booth is much more interesting as a man than as a founder of anything new in religion or politics. He was entirely ignorant of theology, unacquainted with any language except his own, and entertained an almost savage prejudice against science and philosophy. In everything intellectual he was an obscurantist of the most pronounced type, and in everything religious a 'hebraist' of uncompromising narrowness. He condemned cricket and football as sharply as card-playing and horse-racing. Further there was something of the casuist in his nature which enabled him, with no shock to his conscience, to conciliate the mammon of unrighteousness in the interest of his philanthropy. He had warm friends among bookmakers, commercial millionaires and various aristocrats, who showed scant evidence in their lives of the repentance which he so sternly demanded of his converts. He never appeared before these people except as a prophet of God, but the urgent need of their money for his emigration schemes, his farm colonies, his shelters, and his halls, induced him to tone down the thunders of Sinai to the *piano* note of a somewhat chaffing and good-natured admonition. Once, however, he made Cecil Rhodes kneel down and pray with him in a railway carriage. Among those who applauded him were churchmen of such eminence as Lightfoot, Westcott, and Liddon, while Archbishop Benson laboured hard to bring the 'Army' into the orthodox fold of the Church of England. He had an interview with King Edward VII, whom he liked greatly, and he took tea with Mr. Gladstone at Hawarden. The King asked what the churches now thought of him ; he replied with a grim humour, 'Sir, they imitate me'.

His diaries reveal the secret of his attraction, if they do not account for the remarkable success of his propaganda. With a narrow and almost cunning mind, a turbulent and autocratic heart, something great yet childlike in the man's nature was for ever at war with the universe, demanding mercy for mankind and peace for himself. The emotional side of his character was always at strife with the acute or commercial instincts of his nature, and perhaps the heart which so truly loved children and so earnestly sympathized with 'the lowest of the low', was never quite completely convinced of the justice of the divine ordering of this world. Every now and then there are records in his diaries, particularly at the time of his wife's sufferings, which have something of the stark honesty and the searching realism of the Book of Job. Some aspects of his turbulent character—in particular, its wild fervour and its genius for advertisement—may probably be explained by the blend in his veins of Jewish and midland blood.

It is worth recording that this vehement person who, as it were, unroofed the slum to Victorian respectability, and spoke of himself as a moral scavenger netting the very sewers, was of a singularly delicate constitution. He had a physical horror of dirt, even of shabbiness, and from his youth up was noticeable for a meticulous attention to personal cleanliness, both of body and linen. Noxious smells made him ill. The sight of depravity tore at his heart. The sufferings of children, even the memory of them, brought tears to his eyes. It was this extreme sensitiveness to squalor and suffering which made him so effective in unveiling the dark places of civilization. He saw sharply what others scarcely saw at all, and he felt as an outrage what others considered to be natural.

That there was something in his nature which made him restless, harsh, autocratic, and sometimes even angrily explosive, he readily admitted. He called it 'Booth blood'. In the main his higher self triumphed over these dangerous tendencies, and he probably changed more lives for the better than any other religious emotionalist for many hundreds of years. William James, the psychologist, quotes Booth as an authority for the doctrine 'that the first vital step in saving outcasts consists in making them feel that some decent human being cares enough for them to take an interest in the question whether they are to rise or sink'.

A portrait of Booth by D. N. Ingles was placed, on loan, in the National Portrait Gallery in 1925.

[Harold Begbie, *Life of William Booth*, 2 vols., 1920 ; personal knowledge.]

H. B-E.

BOTHA, LOUIS (1862–1919), South African soldier and statesman, was born 27 September 1862 at Honigfontein, near Greytown, Natal. He was the ninth child of a family of six sons and seven daughters born to Louis Botha and his wife Salomina, the youngest daughter of Gerrit Reinier van Rooyen. Both the parents were children of 'voortrekkers' from Cape Colony into Natal, and till 1869, when Louis was seven years old, they lived as British subjects on the farm, Onrust, nine miles from Greytown. The family then migrated to the Orange Free State and finally settled down on a farm near Vrede. Here Louis and the other young children had a limited amount of schooling from neighbouring teachers, but his education chiefly consisted in learning the South African farmer's craft on a large mixed farm of some 5,000 acres, where ostriches, sheep, cattle, and horses were kept and some rough crops raised. On such a farm every member of a large household had to take his share in looking after the cattle and sheep, breaking in the horses, shooting game for the family pot, and supervising the Kaffirs. Here Louis Botha learned to understand and sympathize with the Kaffirs of South Africa and to speak familiarly the two chief native languages, Sesuto and Zulu. Here he acquired that unerring eye for country which served him in such good stead in later years; and here was developed his deep and affectionate appreciation of his own people in the rough and tumble of a large family ruled patriarchally by a notable father and mother who were leaders in their own neighbourhood.

Botha was eighteen years old when he started on his first independent adventure. With a bundle of food and clothes put up by his mother to strap on to his horse, he set forth at the beginning of winter in charge of the family's sheep and cattle to find better pasture in the warm low-lying lands on the borders of Zululand. It was a long month's trek across the Drakensberg, a trek not without its perils, and he undertook it every winter for four years. Zululand in those days, owing to the exile of the paramount chief, Cetywayo, and to Sir Garnet Wolseley's division of the country among several petty chieftains, was in a state of unrest and turmoil, and on one occasion at least all Botha's presence of mind was needed to avert a serious peril. One of these chieftains, hot from the murder of a missionary, suddenly appeared in Botha's camp with his impi and truculently demanded some of his flock. Young Botha, who had only one cartridge left, quietly lighted his pipe and then, after reproving them for their unceremonious approach, offered them one sheep on condition that they cleared off at once, which they did in a much chastened mood. During these sojourns on the Zululand border he made the acquaintance of Lukas Meyer, then landrost of Utrecht, and in 1884 was one of the first to respond to Meyer's call for volunteers to restore Cetywayo's son, Dinizulu, to his father's possessions, on promise of a large tract of land in Zululand as a reward for the volunteers. After a short campaign conducted by Meyer with 800 Boers and some 16,000 of Dinizulu's Zulu adherents, Dinizulu's chief adversary, Usibepu, was routed and Dinizulu restored to his father's position. In accordance with the agreement, a large and rich tract of Zululand on the borders of Natal and the Transvaal was assigned to the volunteers, who formed the 'New Republic' with Meyer as president. Botha, who had already acquired the confidence of his companions by his presence of mind and resourcefulness, was chosen as one of the commissioners to delimit the farms. He himself obtained Waterval, a farm in the neighbourhood of the new capital, Vryheid, and thither in 1886 he brought his bride, Annie Emmet, eldest daughter of John Cheere Emmet, a descendant of the Irish patriot, Robert Emmet; she was a sister of one of his comrades in the Zulu expedition. Three sons and two daughters were born of the marriage. Botha's father died in 1885 and his mother in 1887, and he never afterwards lived in the Free State, but settled down to a very happy married life at Waterval, busying himself with his own farm-work and with local affairs. He was made field-cornet of his district and also kept the local post-office in his house. But the New Republic was short-lived. It had difficulties with both its neighbours, the Transvaal and Natal; had been cut off by the British from an approach to the sea at St. Lucia Bay, where Botha had originally laid out the township; and finally in 1888 cast in its lot with the Transvaal.

P. J. Joubert, the commandant-general, came down to Vryheid to take over the new province, and made Botha's acquaintance. Five years later, during the great contest for the presidency, Botha and his friend Meyer enthusiastically supported Joubert against Kruger. Otherwise the even tenor of Botha's happy farm life was undisturbed till in 1895, when the government of Swaziland had been handed over to the Transvaal, he was appointed a native commissioner. Here he distinguished himself by his energetic fight against the scandalous liquor traffic with the natives; but he resigned the appointment after six months and returned to his more congenial duties as field-cornet and native commissioner at Vryheid. At the end of that year, when (Sir) Leander Starr Jameson [q.v.] invaded the Transvaal, he was called upon to mobilize the burgher force of his frontier district; and, though strongly opposed to Kruger's illiberal Uitlander policy, the main cause of the projected rising in Johannesburg, he is stated to have strongly urged the shooting of Jameson; it is also on record that in later years, when this advice was reported to him, Jameson remarked, 'Yes, Botha was always right'.

In 1897 Botha entered political life as member for his district in the first volksraad, appearing at the head of the poll in opposition to a Kruger candidate. In the volksraad he distinguished himself as a supporter of Joubert's liberal views on the Uitlander franchise, and vigorously opposed the corrupt concessions of the Kruger régime, especially the Pretoria water concession and the dynamite monopoly, which he was called upon to investigate as a member of the volksraad committee. But though against the president's policy, and one of the minority of seven who voted against the ultimatum of 9 October 1899, he cast all doubts aside when war was declared (11 October 1899), and went off to muster his commando at Vryheid.

The war soon proved the mettle of this quiet, wise man. As a simple field-cornet he accompanied Lukas Meyer's commandos for the invasion of Natal, but from the outset showed a dash and an understanding of aggressive action which brought him to the front. He led the first reconnoitring party across the Buffalo river, distinguished himself at the battle of Dundee, and on 30 October, when Lukas Meyer fell sick, was promoted to be assistant-general. Shortly afterwards he was put in command of the southern force investing Ladysmith. But Botha was not content to sit quietly before Ladysmith; with some of the other younger Boers he was always pressing Joubert, the commander-in-chief, to push on and possibly even reach the sea before the British reinforcements arrived. Thus urged, Joubert crossed the Tugela in November, sweeping round Estcourt with two columns, and during this advance Botha ambushed an armoured train near Chievely and took prisoner Mr. Winston Churchill. However, as British reinforcements began to arrive, Joubert re-crossed the river, and, being invalided himself, left Botha in command of the Tugela defences. Sir Redvers Buller [q.v.], on taking over command of the British forces in Natal at the end of November, decided to reach Ladysmith by a frontal attack on the Boer centre opposite Colenso. Botha, with that rare instinct for reading his opponent's mind, one of his most remarkable characteristics as a general, divined that Buller would choose this course and, weakening his widely extended flanks, concentrated nearly all his strength on his centre. In this position, on a semicircle of hills north of the Tugela, he had dug himself in so securely and so imperceptibly that the advancing British troops were at his mercy. To make assurance doubly sure he gave orders that not a shot should be fired by his men until the enemy were actually crossing the Tugela. The Boers, however, when the British guns under Colonel Charles James Long came forward into action in an exposed position just south of the Tugela, could no longer restrain themselves and, besides putting the battery out of action, so clearly revealed the enormous strength of their position that Buller gave up his intended frontal attack.

Botha seems at once to have realized the crushing effect of this reverse on Buller, and once more urged an immediate advance, but he was overruled by the elder Boers. Unfortunately for the Boer people Botha was not yet master of their military decisions, and the Boer force facing Buller was divided into independent commands with no single general supreme. However, when it came to actual fighting, Botha's clear vision and practical resource enabled him to impose his will on his colleagues. At Tabanyama, his prompt call for volunteers saved the Boer right flank. Again, when the British force had climbed Spion Kop on 24 January 1900 and many of the burghers had begun a panic-stricken retreat, Botha brought up guns to shell the British detachment, rallied his men, and directed the succession of counter-attacks which finally dislodged the British. He showed once more the same spirit during the last desperate fighting before Ladysmith in February, when Buller was working round on the eastern flank. At Vaalkrantz his energy forced Buller to retire, though it could not induce his burghers to follow up the success; and though for a moment he despaired as the British advanced, he soon returned to his normal attitude and telegraphed to Kruger after a Boer success, 'With the help of the Lord, I expect that if only the spirit of the burghers keeps up as it did to-day, the enemy will suffer a great reverse.' But in the last stage Botha was constantly hampered by Meyer, who had returned to the field and was in nominal command; and after Pieter's Hill (27 February) his attempts to rally the burghers for one more stand were frustrated by Joubert himself, who gave the signal for a general retreat.

On the day of Pieter's Hill General Piet Cronje surrendered at Paardeberg, and a month later Joubert died, whereupon Botha, the most prominent of the young, eager, and capable Boers, was promoted to be commandant-general of the Transvaal. He at once began to infuse new energy into the fighting forces of his countrymen. He sent a peremptory telegram to the landrosts of the eastern districts, bidding them send up all the shirkers to join their commandos: 'Act on this immediately,' he concluded, 'because every minute lost is in itself a wrong which you are doing to your country and kindred;' and he went himself to see that his orders were obeyed. He also made better use of the many foreign volunteers from Europe, hitherto looked at askance by the burghers, by enrolling them into special corps. Then he took over his reorganized commandos from Natal to the Free State to resist Lord Roberts's triumphant march north in May; but, with hardly 10,000 men to oppose to Roberts's 100,000, he had successively to abandon the positions taken up at Zand river and elsewhere, making his last stand for Johannesburg and Pretoria at Doornkop. Just before this battle (29 May 1900) it had been proposed in the volksraad to destroy the mines, but Botha, who was always a clean fighter, threatened to lay down his command if this were done. After the surrender of Pretoria, Botha retired to Diamond Hill, whence Roberts attempted to dislodge him on 12 June. In this, his last engagement with Roberts, he profited from his experience of the field-marshal's favourite enveloping tactics and, by putting most of his strength on the wings, held up the British attacks long enough to secure for his forces a safe retreat along the line of railway.

After Diamond Hill Botha saw that the only hope left to the Boers was to abandon regular tactics and begin a guerilla war, so as to render the British positions insecure in every district of the country. He sent off the commandos to their own districts, where they could operate to the best advantage, himself remaining in the south-eastern Transvaal, chiefly because it was his own country, but also to keep in touch with the peripatetic government. At Bergendal on 27 August with a few well-entrenched troops he kept Buller long enough on the railway to enable himself to get the government away into the fastnesses of Lydenburg. Though separated during the next eighteen months from his chief subordinates by vast tracts of country, and often also by lines of blockhouses and ever tightening cordons of British troops, Botha was rarely out of communication with his scattered commandos, chiefly owing to his excellent system of intelligence by means of natives and hardy Boer messengers. Periodically, too, he held conferences of his chief lieutenants to decide on the main operations for the succeeding few months. One of his chief exploits in the field was his sudden raid to the borders of Natal in September and October 1901. Thither he attracted a great many British troops from other quarters where they were sorely needed, and, after leading them a most exhausting dance, escaped through the only exit they had left open. Immediately after this he suddenly swooped down from a distance of seventy miles, thirty of which he marched in one day, to Bakenlaagte, where he defeated and put out of action Colonel George Elliot Benson's force, long the terror of the south-eastern Transvaal (30 October). Naturally during these months of constant movement he had several hair-breadth escapes from capture, but he was well served by devoted adherents and not less by his own quickness, due to early training, in noting the slightest sign of danger on the veld.

After the first seven months of the war, Botha, though always the heart and soul of the Boer defence, never lost sight of any opportunity for making peace. Before Diamond Hill, at Middelburg in February 1901, when he had his first interview with Lord Kitchener, and on one or two other occasions he showed himself willing to discuss terms. His chief aim was of course to preserve his people's threatened independence, but he also had a secondary object, that if independence proved impossible, the struggle should not be allowed to drift on till there were no people left to maintain a national identity even in a state of dependence. Accordingly in March 1902, when the Transvaal was almost at its last gasp, he willingly seized the olive branch offered by Kitchener. He was convinced by that time that the Boers could not win, and he realized better than any that, short of winning, they could not hope to retain their independence. At the Vereeniging conference of May 1902, when delegates from all the commandos still fighting in the Transvaal and the Free State met to discuss terms, he clinched the matter by his sane utterance: 'Terms may still be secured which will save the language, customs, and ideals of the people. The fatal thing is to secure no terms at all and yet be forced to surrender. We are slipping back; we must save the nation.' 'We must save the nation!'—that was his main idea in all the negotiations with Kitchener and Lord Milner, when he fought with success, after the great points of the language and eventual self-government had been granted, for the £3,000,000 to be devoted to restoring the burghers to their farms; and with the same idea, when it looked as if the chief Free Staters might stand aloof from the majority in favour of peace, he and General J. H. De La Rey persuaded the irreconcilable Free State leader, Christian De Wet, to bring in his people too for the sake of national unity.

'We are good friends now,' said Kitchener on 31 May 1902, as he shook hands with the general whom he had learned to respect as a formidable and straight antagonist. Kitchener's countrymen very soon came to the same opinion. Botha's great purpose for the remainder of his life was doubtless to 'save his nation'; but by that he meant not merely to restore its material prosperity and to preserve its national consciousness, but also to observe faithfully the troth plighted at Vereeniging, when it agreed to become a member of the British Empire. Nothing confirmed this resolution of Botha so much as his kindly and informal reception by King Edward (17 August 1902), when he went over to England to plead for the Boer orphans and widows. Botha then acquired a respect and devotion to the king who showed such courtesy to a recent foe, and also to the nation whom this king represented. But this mission, undertaken with De Wet and De La Rey, failed in its principal object of obtaining through charity large funds for his country's needs. On his return to South Africa he abandoned his Vryheid farm, Waterval, which had been destroyed during the war, and bought another at Rusthof, near Standerton; but he spent most of his time in his house at Pretoria, where he was accessible at all hours to his people, listening to their complaints and giving them advice and more material help for the restoration of their farm life. His attitude towards Crown Colony government was one of reserve: he consistently refused to give any formal advice or accept a seat on the legislative council, on the ground that the imperial government should take full responsibility for its actions; on the other hand he did not stay apart in sullen resentment. When Mr. Joseph Chamberlain [q.v.] came out, he met him socially and was never backward in making representations to him or to Lord Milner on what he considered grievances of his countrymen (principally the question of Dutch teaching in the schools), and on the question of assistance to the returned burghers. In January 1905, on the eve of the promulgation of the Lyttelton constitution, with other leading Boers he founded 'Het Volk', an organization intended to keep up the national feeling of the Boers and to secure their effective co-operation. In this organization he brought together for the first time the 'hands up' and 'bitter end' sections of his countrymen. At the inaugural meeting Botha once more emphasized the fact that the flag question had been irrevocably settled, but he demanded in return enough trust from the imperial government to give them responsible government at once.

Within two years this had been granted by Sir Henry Campbell-Bannerman's government (31 July 1906), and Botha found himself not only with a majority in the new parliament but called upon to form a ministry under the British Crown. One of his first actions was a striking illustration of the attitude he intended to adopt towards the mother-country. In 1907 on behalf of the Transvaal he presented to Queen Alexandra the Cullinan diamond, the largest hitherto found, to be incorporated in the crown jewels. In domestic politics also he showed his determination to govern not merely as the leader of the Boers but as the responsible minister for both the white races in the Transvaal. Though he sent home the Chinese labourers on the Rand, whose importation he had opposed from the outset, he repatriated them gradually, so as to cause as little disorganization as possible in the industry, and helped to secure a more plentiful supply of native labour. But his main achievement during his ministry was to persuade the Transvaal to go whole-heartedly into the movement for closer union. At the Union Convention of 1908–1909 he naturally headed the Transvaal delegation, which was far better equipped with information and more decided on its policy than any of the other three. In this Convention the strength of the combination of Botha with his chief lieutenant, General Johannes Smuts, first showed its force in South African politics. To this remarkable combination Smuts contributed intellectual range, ingenuity of resource, suppleness of demeanour, and considerable sympathy with the English no less than the Boer mind; Botha for his part was no scholar and relied much on the knowledge of 'Jan', as he called the younger man; many of the problems of civil administration with which he had to deal were strange to him at the outset; and, though he could speak English in private talk, he nearly always made his public speeches in Dutch; on the other hand, he had a great gift of piercing to the core of a problem when the facts had been presented to him, and it would have been almost as true to say of him as of Chatham: 'The first time I come to him about any matter I find him extremely ignorant; the second time I come to him I find him completely informed upon it.' He had also the gift of inspiring confidence, largely because he himself had so generous a belief and love for his fellow men, and thereby drew out the best from all with whom he was thrown into contact; but with this gentle quality he had the power of hitting hard when necessary, and no one took liberties with him twice.

At the Union Convention the determination of Botha and the Transvaal delegation to make a real union and not merely a loose confederation carried the day. As Sir George Herbert Farrar, one of the English delegates, said, 'British and Boer had been brought together by the wise and tolerant action of General Botha and General Smuts, and to-day they stood together asking to join in a union of South Africa.' This tendency was marvellously strengthened by the alliance struck up at the Convention between Botha and Dr. Jameson, whom Botha had once wanted to shoot. Both instinctively felt that they were struggling towards the same end—the reconciliation of the races on the common ground of their interest in South Africa. Botha had not always an easy task with some of his own countrymen during the discussions, and even when the language and the native questions had been settled satisfactorily to Boer aspirations, the question of the capital might have wrecked everything had not Botha finally taken aside the Transvaal supporters of Pretoria, and appealing to the trust reposed in their statesmanship by King Edward and the British people, persuaded them to accept the compromise of two capitals.

Botha was chosen as first prime minister of the Union of South Africa (10 May 1910) and held that office till his death. He and Jameson had discussed the feasibility of a coalition ministry of their two parties; but it was found impossible, and Botha formed a purely party ministry. Yet when the care of all South Africa was committed to him he had no more idea of governing solely in the interests of the Dutch section than before in the Transvaal. When his colleague, General J. B. M. Hertzog, went about the country stirring up strife by his speeches against the British element of the population and Botha's proposals for naval defence, Botha re-formed his ministry in December 1912, excluding Hertzog, and in the following year won a striking victory over him and his ally, De Wet, at the congress of the South African party. The two most serious difficulties with which Botha's ministry had to deal before the European War were the question of Indian immigrants and the unrest on the Rand. Indians originally brought to Natal as indentured labourers claimed the right, through their spokesman, M. K. Gandhi, to settle in the country as citizens when their periods of indenture were completed. Smuts, who took over the chief management of this question, had some difficult passages with the able Indian leader, and also had to deal with the opposition of the Indian government; but a satisfactory compromise was reached in 1914, and Gandhi returned to his own country, declaring himself satisfied. The unrest on the Rand was an even more serious matter. In July 1913 there was a general strike of the white miners and considerable fear of a native rising also; while, owing to the pending reorganization of the Union forces, imperial troops alone were available. After a collision between them and the Johannesburg mob, Botha and Smuts, much against their will, felt bound to sign an inconclusive agreement with the strikers; and in the following January another still more serious strike paralysed the railways. This time Botha and Smuts were well prepared. Martial law was proclaimed, the burgher force to the number of 60,000 was called out, nine of the labour leaders were seized and deported from the country without trial, and the strike collapsed. These drastic and arbitrary measures, and especially the deportations, aroused much criticism both in England and in South Africa. But the South African parliament was satisfied that the right course had been taken, if not in the best way, and passed the Indemnity Act brought in by the government.

On the declaration of war against Germany in August 1914, many of the Dutch who followed the banner of Hertzog were disposed to take up the attitude that it was none of their business, and that South Africa should remain neutral. But Botha never had any hesitation as to the right course to pursue. He at once suggested to the imperial government that, as they needed all their troops in Europe, the imperial garrison should be withdrawn from South Africa and the Union left to look after its own defence.

This offer was gladly accepted, and it was conveyed to Botha that the best help the Union could give would be to invade German South-West Africa. This also Botha agreed to do; but it is characteristic of his cautious and deliberate methods that for some weeks the English in South Africa were left in suspense, as no public announcement of his intentions was issued. From the outset he had seen that he would have to tread warily with his own people; and before he could deal with the Germans he was suddenly faced by a serious revolt. Christian Frederick Beyers, the commandant-general of the burgher forces, De Wet in the Free State, and Solomon G. Maritz, commanding on the German frontier, took up arms against the policy of active intervention in the war, some of them in concert with the Germans. Botha's own distress at this revolt of his own people, many of whom had recently been his trusted companions in arms, and his unflinching determination to do his duty are plain from his answer to a deputation from Pretoria: 'For myself I am willing to submit to any personal humiliation if this is necessary rather than take arms against my own people, many of whom fought with me through the war. But I will not betray my trust, and if, after I have tried every method of negotiation, they still refuse to come in, I will move out against them with the commandos that I know will stand by me.' It was characteristic too of Botha that, when he did take the field against the rebels, he called out the commandos almost exclusively from the Dutch districts, to avoid the danger of renewing a racial conflict. On 28 October he smote Beyers's main force near Rustenberg so effectually that it never recovered. The leader, after wandering about with small detachments, was drowned in the Vaal on 8 December. A week earlier De Wet was captured after a long flight through the desert, his forces in the Free State having been scattered by Botha on 11 November. By the end of February 1915 the last rebels had surrendered. In dealing with the delinquents Botha showed clemency; a few of those who had broken their military oath were shot, the other leaders, including De Wet, were given comparatively short terms of imprisonment, while the rank and file were dismissed to their homes.

Botha's campaign against German South-West Africa, in which he himself took the chief command, was one of the prettiest pieces of strategy in the war. He himself advanced from Swakopmund against the main German forces at Windhoek, while three columns under Smuts entered the country from south, east, and west and drove all opposing force towards Botha at Windhoek. The actual fighting was not serious, but the country with its sand-storms, its villainous tracks, and its vast desert spaces in which many of the wells had been poisoned by the Germans, was a more serious obstacle than the enemy. Botha's careful arrangements and the fine marching and fighting qualities called out among the South African troops, this time drawn from both races, by the confidence felt in their commander, surmounted all difficulties. The campaign, which had begun in March 1915, was concluded in the following July by the unconditional surrender of the German forces and of their colony. Botha gave generous terms to the Germans, both military and civilians, and signalized the moment of victory by issuing a proclamation in which he deprecated some anti-German rioting at Johannesburg, and stated that the war was being waged against the German government, but not against individual Germans, and that it was unworthy of the nation to forget its dignity.

To the Versailles Peace Conference of 1919 Botha went with Smuts as delegates for South Africa. Though under continuous medical treatment, Botha attended assiduously both the full meetings and the committees, and took a firm line in supporting the rights of the Dominions. He impressed all the delegates as one of the most commanding figures of the Conference, and whenever he spoke his opinion carried great weight. His hearers were, indeed, deeply moved by a speech from Botha pleading for compromise and lenient terms, in which he reminded them that 'he also came from a conquered nation'. After signing the treaty he returned as quickly as he could to South Africa. But he was already a dying man. Shortly after reaching Pretoria he died, on 27 August, within a month of completing his fifty-seventh year.

Botha visited England several times after the Boer War, in 1902 in a private capacity, in 1907 when he had just assumed office in the Transvaal, in 1909 with the scheme for South African union, in 1911 for imperial conferences, and lastly at the time of the Peace of Versailles. Whenever he was in London his chief preoccupation was to guard the interests of South Africa. In 1907 he secured an advantageous loan from the imperial government; and in 1911 he worked out with Viscount Haldane the scheme for a South African defence force, which proved so valuable both to South Africa and to the Empire a few years later. The more he came to London the more surely he won the regard of Englishmen. His few brief speeches, always given in Dutch, sounded a note of sincerity and gallant courtesy and of convincing loyalty to the Crown. In his own country the verdict of the immense majority of both English and Dutch was the same. Some of those who, like Hertzog, parted company with him, thought him too deferential to the English element in the population: but all felt him to be essentially a simple God-fearing man, with an attractive nature, not clever, but of great wisdom, patience, and loving-kindness. He was at his best and certainly happiest in his own beautiful farm, where he lived a patriarchal life with his family, entertaining simply and always the best of hosts. Smuts, the colleague most unlike him in most ways but the one who knew and loved him best, said at his graveside: 'His was the largest, most beautiful, sweetest soul of all my land and days.'

A portrait of Botha is included in J. S. Sargent's picture 'Some General Officers of the Great War', painted in 1922, in the National Portrait Gallery. Another portrait, painted by J. Blair Leighton from photographs and information supplied by relations and friends, was presented to the House of Commons by Sir W. Mitchell Cotts in 1925.

[Sir J. F. Maurice and M. H. Grant, (Official) *History of the War in South Africa*, 1906–1910; '*The Times*' *History of the War in South Africa*, 1900–1909; G. S. Preller (editor), *General Botha*, Pretoria, 1920; H. Spender, *General Botha*, 1916; P. J. Sampson, *Capture of De Wet*, 1915; W. Whittall, *With Botha and Smuts in South Africa*, 1917; Ian Colvin, *Life of Jameson*, 1922; Earl Buxton, *General Botha*, 1924; *Cape Times*; private information; personal knowledge.] B. W.

BOURCHIER, JAMES DAVID (1850–1920), correspondent of *The Times* in the Balkan Peninsula, was born at Baggotstown, Bruff, co. Limerick, 18 December 1850, the fourth son of John Bourchier, of Baggotstown, a property which had descended from father to son since 1651; his mother was Sarah Aher, of La Rive, Castlecomer, co. Kilkenny. Bourchier was an exhibitioner at Trinity College, Dublin, and took his degree there (1873), with a gold medal for classics. He subsequently won a scholarship at King's College, Cambridge, and was placed seventh in the first class of the classical tripos (1876). In 1888, after ten years as a master at Eton, where his deafness proved a handicap, Bourchier went to Roumania and Bulgaria on a mission for *The Times*, definitely joining its staff in 1892. For fifteen years he made his headquarters at Athens, afterwards at Sofia. Active in mind and body, a linguist and a musician, and, in spite of his deafness, excellent company, Bourchier knew every one of note in the Balkans and was behind the scenes of Balkan politics for a generation. He wrote excellently on archaeology and travel, as well as on politics. His sympathy with patriots and with the oppressed, together with his honesty of purpose, fearlessness, and power of identifying himself with a cause, won for him a unique place in the Balkan Peninsula. He often served as intermediary between the Cretan insurgents and the Greek authorities, and he acted unofficially as confidential adviser to Prince George of Greece when, in 1898, the latter became high commissioner of Crete. When the Bulgarian peasants in Macedonia rose against the Turks in 1903, Bourchier brought their sufferings and the justice of their cause before the public with great insistence and ability. In 1911–1912 he was entrusted by King George of Greece and M. Venizelos on one side, and by King Ferdinand of Bulgaria and M. Gueshov on the other, with many of the secret negotiations preceding the Balkan alliance. Bourchier regarded this alliance as the only remedy for Balkan troubles. Much as he deplored the part played by Bulgaria in the second Balkan War and in the European War, he did not withdraw his sympathy from the Bulgars, whose national character he warmly admired.

In 1915 Bourchier went to Roumania and later to Odessa and Petrograd, reaching England early in 1918. He then retired from *The Times*, and devoted himself to the forlorn attempt to secure what seemed to him a just and final settlement in the Balkans. He died at Sofia 30 December 1920, and was buried with high honours at Rilo monastery. He was unmarried.

[Bourchier's diaries and papers; his contributions to *The Times*, 1888–1920, and to the *Quarterly*, *Fortnightly*, and other Reviews; his articles on Balkan subjects in the *Encyclopaedia Britannica* (11th edition); Lady Grogan, *Life of J. D. Bourchier*, 1924; private information; personal knowledge.]

E. F. B. G.

BOWES, ROBERT (1835–1919), bookseller, publisher, and bibliographer, was born at Stewarton, Ayrshire, 22 August 1835, the third son of Robert Bowes, of that town, by his wife, Margaret, daughter of Duncan Macmillan. As a youth he joined his uncles, Daniel Macmillan [q.v.] and Alexander Macmillan in their bookselling and publishing business at Cambridge, and one of his earliest activities was a share in the formation of the Cambridge Working Men's College, of which Alexander Macmillan and Francis Gerald Vesey, archdeacon of Huntingdon, were secretaries. Shortly after this the connexion of the Macmillans with Frederick Denison Maurice, Charles Kingsley, and Thomas Hughes began. Between 1858 and 1863 Bowes was in charge of the newly opened London depôt; in the latter year the publishing business was wholly transferred to London and Bowes returned to Cambridge, where he remained at the head of the bookselling business (known until 1907 as Macmillan & Bowes and afterwards as Bowes & Bowes) until his death, 9 February 1919. In 1868 he married Fanny, youngest daughter of Augustine Gutteridge Brimley, alderman and once mayor of Cambridge; he had one son, George Brimley Bowes, who succeeded him as head of the business, and two daughters.

In the civic and educational life of Cambridge Robert Bowes took a prominent part. He was a town councillor for nine years, an officer in the Volunteers, retiring with the rank of honorary major in 1889, a governor of the Old Schools and of the Perse School, a member and twice chairman of the Free Library committee, and an officer of the Local Lectures Association. He was also treasurer of the Cambridge Antiquarian Society from 1894 to 1909, and in 1870 joined in helping F. D. Maurice and others to form an association in Cambridge for promoting the higher education of women. This step ultimately led to the establishment of Newnham College.

Bowes was not merely a bookseller, but a bookman, and several well-known books appeared with his publishing imprint, such as *Lapsus Calami* (1891), by James Kenneth Stephen, and John Willis Clark's *Concise Guide to Cambridge* (1898) as well as his edition of David Loggan's *Cantabrigia Illustrata* (1905). But his greatest work was done in the field of Cambridge bibliography. In company with Henry Bradshaw [q.v.] he became an enthusiastic researcher into the work of John Siberch [q.v.], the first Cambridge printer; and his *Biographical Notes on the University Printers in Cambridge* (1886, originally a paper read before the Cambridge Antiquarian Society in 1884) was pioneer work based on original sources. This was followed in 1894 by *A Catalogue of Books printed at or relating to the University, Town, and County of Cambridge from 1521 to 1893*, a monumental work which remains the standard authority on the subject, and in 1906 he collaborated with Mr. George John Gray in a monograph on John Siberch. In 1918 the public orator of the university, Sir John Sandys, fittingly presented for the degree of M.A., *honoris causa*, 'bibliopolam honestissimum, virum de Cantabrigia praeclare meritum, Robertum Bowes'.

[Memoir by G. J. Gray reprinted from *The Cambridge Chronicle*, 20 March 1918; private information.] S. C. R.

BOYD CARPENTER, WILLIAM (1841–1918), bishop of Ripon. [See CARPENTER.]

BRACKENBURY, SIR HENRY (1837–1914), general and writer on military subjects, was born at Bolingbroke, Lincolnshire, 1 September 1837. He was the youngest son of William Brackenbury, of Aswardby, Lincolnshire, formerly lieutenant in the 61st Regiment, by his wife, Maria, daughter of James Atkinson, of Newry, county Down, and widow of James Wallace. Their third son was Major-General Charles Booth Brackenbury [q.v.]. Henry Brackenbury's schooling was interrupted by youthful vagaries. He was at Tonbridge School from 1846 to 1849, and afterwards went to Eton, where he was from 1850 to 1852 in the house of the Rev. Charles Wolley (afterwards Wolley-Dod). He was then sent to Canada, but a brief probation in a notary's office in Quebec led to no satisfactory result, and it was not until he entered the Royal Military Academy at Woolwich in 1854 that he settled down to work. The Crimean War caused a demand for officers, and Brackenbury had not served the full number of courses before he received a commission in the Royal Artillery in April 1856.

When the news of the Indian Mutiny arrived in England, Brackenbury was accepted for active service, and he sailed for India at the end of August 1857. After some campaigning with General Whitlock's column he was invalided home in 1858. He soon obtained some minor positions at Woolwich, and was gazetted adjutant of the depôt brigade in 1860. Among his interests at this time was cricket, and his name is to be found in one or two regimental matches of the period. Early in his career as a soldier he began to devote himself to writing. He had a facile pen and a retentive memory, and narrow means gave him the necessary incentive to literary and journalistic work. Beginning with two papers on early ordnance for the *Proceedings* of the Royal Artillery Institution, he continued to contribute articles, chiefly upon technical subjects, to various periodicals. He made a special study of military history and administration; and when Mr. (afterwards Viscount) Cardwell went to the War Office in 1868, Brackenbury wrote in support of the minister's proposals for army reform. In 1868 he was appointed professor of military history at Woolwich Academy, and visited some of the European battlefields in order to add to his knowledge of the subject.

The Franco-German War afforded Brackenbury opportunities of a different kind. In the autumn of 1870 a British National Society for Aid to the Sick and Wounded was established under the presidency of Colonel Robert James Loyd Lindsay (afterwards Baron Wantage), and Brackenbury was invited to superintend the distribution of relief at the seat of war. He carried out this work capably and impartially, and was decorated for his services by both belligerents. He returned to England at the end of January 1871 and resumed his duties at Woolwich.

When the Ashanti expedition was planned in the autumn of 1873, and the command given to Sir Garnet (afterwards Viscount) Wolseley, Brackenbury wrote offering to serve under him in any capacity. Wolseley took him to Ashanti as his assistant military secretary, and in his autobiography [*The Story of a Soldier's Life*, vol. ii, 80] records his appreciation of Brackenbury's services. Wolseley became Brackenbury's consistent patron and supporter. In 1875 he was promoted brevet lieutenant-colonel, and in July 1878 accompanied Wolseley to Cyprus. His chief returned almost at once, but Brackenbury remained to organize a force of military police, as well as to remodel the prisons of the island. In the following year (1879) he acted as Wolseley's military secretary in Zululand, with Sir George Pomeroy Colley as chief of the staff. The victory of Lord Chelmsford [q.v.] at Ulundi (4 July) ended the war before Wolseley could join the troops in the field; but Brackenbury was present at the capture of the Zulu king, Cetywayo, and on Colley's recall to India succeeded that officer as head of Wolseley's staff, and took part in the successful expedition against the chief, Sekukuni, in the north of the Transvaal.

From Africa Brackenbury sailed direct to India, having accepted the position of private secretary to the viceroy, the first Earl of Lytton. He held this appointment only a short time, for the viceroy resigned on the fall of the conservative government in the spring of 1880. Although their official association was so brief, Lytton and Brackenbury remained close friends. In 1881 Brackenbury was offered and accepted the post of military attaché to the British embassy in Paris. While on leave in England in May 1882, he was dispatched by the government to Ireland, where agrarian and political troubles had culminated in the Phoenix Park murders. His position was indefinite at first, but subsequently he was appointed under-secretary for police and crime. The arrangement was not a success, and his early resignation gave offence to the military authorities, who placed him on half-pay and refused him permission to serve with Wolseley in the expedition against Arabi Pasha (August 1882). His career suffered only a temporary interruption, for in 1884 Wolseley selected him for the Egyptian campaign for the relief of General Gordon, and in September he was appointed deputy assistant adjutant and quartermaster-general at Cairo. He joined Wolseley at Korti on 24 December and started up the Nile, with the rank of brigadier-general and second in command of the river column. On the death of General William Earle [q.v.] at Kirbekan on 10 February 1885, Brackenbury succeeded to the command of the column, which was recalled to Korti a few days later. After further service in Egypt he came home in August, and was promoted major-general.

Important appointments for Brackenbury followed. He was deputy assistant quartermaster-general and head of the intelligence branch at head-quarters for five years from 1 January 1886; from 1891 to 1896 he was military member of the council of the viceroy of India; and from 1896 to 1899 president of the ordnance committee. But his greatest opportunity came at the close of his military career. Soon after the outbreak of the South African War (October 1899) the provision of munitions on a large scale was found to require an effective organizer at the War Office. The post of director-general of ordnance was offered to Brackenbury, and was held by him during the continuance of the war. His efficiency in the position met with general acknowledgment.

Brackenbury was made C.B. in 1880, promoted K.C.B. in 1894, and received the K.C.S.I. in 1896. In 1900 he was promoted G.C.B., and he was made a privy councillor on his retirement in 1904. He died at Nice 20 April 1914. He was twice married: first, in 1861 to Emilia (died 1905), daughter of Edmund Storr Halswell, F.R.S., and widow of Reginald Morley; secondly, in 1905 to Edith, daughter of Louis Desanges, who survived him. There was no issue of either marriage.

Brackenbury was an able man, with considerable capacity for organization. He wrote well upon military subjects, and was a competent student of the art of war as it was known in the nineteenth century. His published books were *The Last Campaign of Hanover* (1870), *The Tactics of the Three Arms* (1873), *Narrative of the Ashantee War* (2 vols., 1874), *The River Column* (1885), and *Some Memories of my Spare Time* (1909).

[Private information.] A. C.

BRADDON, MARY ELIZABETH (1837–1915), novelist. [See MAXWELL, MARY ELIZABETH.]

BRASSEY, THOMAS, first EARL BRASSEY, of Bulkeley, Cheshire (1836–1918), was born at Stafford 11 February 1836, the eldest son of Thomas Brassey [q.v.], railway contractor, of Buerton, Cheshire. He was educated at Rugby and University College, Oxford, where he took honours in the school of law and modern history (1859). His father's railway enterprises led to school holidays being spent partly at Portsmouth, where he acquired his love of the sea and interest in maritime affairs, partly in France, where he obtained a sound knowledge of the French language. Other holidays and Oxford vacations were spent in yachting cruises, a pastime in which he took great interest throughout his life. He was elected to the Royal Yacht Squadron a year after leaving Oxford. Brassey decided not to follow his father's profession but to join the parliamentary bar, and he became a pupil of John Buller, the leading parliamentary draftsman of the day. He was called to the bar in 1866, but soon abandoned a legal career for politics. Having already stood unsuccessfully as a liberal for Birkenhead in 1861, he was elected for Devonport in June 1865, but, before taking his seat, was defeated at the general election a few weeks later. He failed at a by-election at Sandwich in 1866, but was successful at Hastings in 1868 and retained that seat until 1886.

From his entry into parliament until 1880 Brassey worked hard and laboriously at the subjects in which he was interested: wages, the condition of the working classes, and employers' liability; naval matters of every department, administration of the dockyards, naval pay, shipbuilding and designs, organization of the naval reserves, and the creation of the Royal Naval Volunteer Artillery (1873). He compiled useful volumes entitled *Work and Wages* (1872), *Foreign Work and English Wages* (1879), *British Seamen* (1877), *The British Navy* (1882–1883), an encyclopaedic work in five volumes, and *Sixty Years of Progress* (1904). The character of his work and his conception of his duty in public life are aptly described in his own preface to *The British Navy*: 'Few men have entered the House of Commons with more slender share of what are usually described as parliamentary talents than the humble individual who writes the present introduction; and if, by devotion to special subjects, he has gained the confidence of the public, his experience may perhaps encourage others.'

There is no doubt that Brassey's untiring industry contributed greatly to the reforms in naval administration and maritime policy that were being evolved as the conditions of the old sailing navy and marine rapidly passed away. Besides his parliamentary work he published articles in the leading reviews, wrote letters to *The Times*, issued pamphlets and read papers and lectures at public institutions, nearly always on labour questions or naval and marine affairs. He spent part of every parliamentary recess at sea in his yacht; and in 1876–1877 he accomplished a tour round the world, an account of which is given in his first wife's popular book, *Voyage in the 'Sunbeam'* (1878). The later voyages of the *Sunbeam* Brassey described in his book *'Sunbeam' R.Y.S.*, published a few months before his death. He was the first private yachtsman to be given the certificate of master mariner after examination. Although he was never happier than when afloat in his yacht, he never undertook a long voyage unless it was to fulfil some public purpose; and in 1916 he handed over the *Sunbeam* to the government of India for hospital work during the war.

In 1880 Brassey joined Mr. Gladstone's second administration as civil lord of the

Admiralty, and held this office for four years. In 1881 he was created K.C.B. in recognition of his services to the naval reserves, and in 1884 he was made parliamentary secretary to the Admiralty, a position which he held until the end of that parliament (1885). As civil lord his administrative responsibility was limited to the control of the works department and of Greenwich Hospital. He was more interested in other branches of naval affairs, and employed himself in writing detailed memoranda on all kinds of subjects for the benefit of his colleagues, who appreciated his keen interest in naval matters; but his productions, while full of facts, seldom led up to any concrete conclusion, and the effect of them was rather to ventilate the subject than to produce any tangible results. His short term as parliamentary secretary and spokesman of the Admiralty did not add to his reputation, for he was no parliamentary debater nor quick at taking up points made against his department in the House of Commons. Brassey was not included in Mr. Gladstone's 1885 government. He supported the Home Rule policy, and was defeated at Liverpool in the general election of 1886. In that year first appeared *Brassey's Naval Annual*, which has been for many years the most authoritative survey of naval affairs throughout the world. He was raised to the peerage as Baron Brassey, of Bulkeley, Cheshire, on Mr. Gladstone's resignation (1886).

Brassey served as lord-in-waiting to Queen Victoria from 1893 to 1895, when he was appointed governor of Victoria. His administration of Victoria coincided with the movement for the federation of the Australian colonies, and he played a considerable part in bringing this measure into effect. The Queen's assent to the Commonwealth Act was given a few months after his departure (1900). He won a large measure of popularity among the people of Victoria and displayed his usual industry in lecturing and speaking on naval defence, imperial federation, and industrial subjects.

After his return to England Brassey was an incessant advocate, both at the Institute of Naval Architects, of which he was president (1893–1896), and in the House of Lords, of the employment of armed merchant ships as cruisers for the protection of British trade routes. His instinct was always to make the best use of material ready to hand rather than embark on the expense of new weapons. He preferred re-arming old battleships and subsidizing merchant cruisers to new construction, and using fishermen as reservists to increasing the personnel of the navy. He did not altogether appreciate the inadequacy of these measures in the days when scientific development had so far advanced and formidable rivals were creating powerful modern fleets.

In 1906 Brassey was promoted G.C.B., and in 1908 he was appointed lord warden of the Cinque Ports, a distinguished and congenial office which he retained for five years. At the coronation of King George V (1911) he was created Earl Brassey and Viscount Hythe. He died in London 23 February 1918.

Brassey was married twice: first, in 1860 to Anna (died 1887), only child of John Allnutt, of Charles Street, Berkeley Square; she was a devoted helper in his parliamentary career and in his yachting voyages; by her he had one son, Thomas Allnutt, second Earl Brassey, and four daughters; secondly, in 1890 to the Hon. Sybil de Vere Capell, youngest daughter of Viscount Malden, and granddaughter of the sixth Earl of Essex, by whom he had one daughter. The second Earl Brassey, a generous benefactor to the Bodleian Library and to Balliol College, Oxford, died without issue in 1919, and the title became extinct.

Lord Brassey was a rich man, of no outstanding ability but with great powers of industry, and of kindly, genial, and equable temperament. Throughout a long public life he spared neither time nor money in the public interest and in promoting the patriotic causes which he had most at heart. To his conscientious and persistent advocacy the royal navy, the naval reserves, the mercantile marine, and imperial federation are greatly indebted.

[Lord Brassey's own numerous publications and compilations; private information.] V. W. B.

BRIDGES, Sir WILLIAM THROSBY (1861–1915), general, was born 18 February 1861, at Greenock, where his father, Captain William Wilson Somerset Bridges, R.N., was then stationed. Of an Essex family, Captain Bridges married a daughter of Charles Throsby, of New South Wales. Their son William was educated at a school in Ryde, Isle of Wight, at the Royal Naval School, Greenwich, at Trinity College School, Port Hope, Canada (his father having retired to that Dominion), and at the Canadian Military College, Kingston. While he was at the Military College his parents removed to New South Wales, where he ultimately joined them, obtaining a civil appointment in the roads and bridges department of that state. In 1885 he obtained a lieutenancy in the New South Wales Permanent Artillery and was posted in charge of the Middle Head forts at Sydney. After a rather purposeless period, a school of gunnery was established at Middle Head, and from this point onwards Bridges's remarkable energy found adequate outlet. He was made a captain in 1890, and served as a major in the Boer War: he was present at the relief of Kimberley (15 February 1900), and was engaged at Paardeberg (27 February), and in several other actions. On his return to Australia he joined the head-quarters staff and served successively as assistant quartermaster-general (1902), chief of intelligence (1905), chief of the general staff and Australian representative on the Imperial General Staff in London (1909), commandant, Royal Military College, Duntroon (1910), and inspector-general of the Commonwealth military forces (1914). He was promoted lieutenant-colonel in 1902, colonel in 1906, and brigadier-general in 1910, and awarded the C.M.G. in 1907. With characteristic thoroughness he visited military schools in America, Belgium, Great Britain, Canada, France, and Germany before commencing his duties at the college at Duntroon. At the outbreak of the European War (1914) he was selected to command the first Australian contingent, with the rank of major-general, and he was in command of the first Australian division on the Gallipoli Peninsula, where he was mortally wounded by a sniper 15 May 1915. He died at sea, five days later, on board a hospital ship. His body was taken back to Australia and interred in the grounds of the Military College at Duntroon.

In the foundation of the Royal Military College, Duntroon, Bridges played a very prominent part, and it is in this connexion that his name will chiefly be remembered, for, under his able leadership, Duntroon ranked as one of the finest military colleges in the world. He was gazetted K.C.B. 17 May 1915, the notice appearing four days after his death. He was tall, thin, and loose-limbed, with a stoop at the shoulders which proclaimed him a student; a slow but deep thinker; so shy that he appeared to be dour and brusque in manner, a trait productive of a like nervousness in his subordinates; somewhat intolerant of opposition; a man of singularly few words; never one to seek for favours; always quietly efficient. He married in 1885 Edith Lilian, daughter of Alfred Dawson Francis, of Moruya, New South Wales. There were four children of the marriage.

[*The Times*, 24 May 1915; Commonwealth of Australia Official Records; *Official History of Australia in the War of 1914–1918*, vol. i, 1923.] C. V. O.

BRIGHT, JAMES FRANCK (1832–1920), master of University College, Oxford, was born in London 29 May 1832, the second son of Richard Bright, M.D. [q.v.], the discoverer of the true causes and nature of 'Bright's disease'. His mother, his father's second wife, was Eliza, daughter of Captain Benjamin Follett, of Topsham, Devon, and sister of Sir William Webb Follett [q.v.], solicitor-general in both of Sir Robert Peel's administrations, and attorney-general in 1844. Bright went in that year to Rugby, which was then under the headmastership of Archibald Tait, the future archbishop of Canterbury, and still inspired with the traditions of Dr. Arnold. There he made some lifelong friendships with men of future mark, more especially with George Joachim Goschen (afterwards Viscount Goschen), Thomas Jex-Blake (subsequently head master of Rugby), and Horace Davey (afterwards Baron Davey of Fernhurst). In 1850 he went up to University College, Oxford, then under the mastership of Dr. Frederick Plumptre, and in December 1854 obtained a first class in the school of law and modern history. He had originally intended to follow his father's profession of medicine, but finally decided to take holy orders. He was ordained deacon in 1856 and priest in 1876, and became B.D. and D.D. in 1884.

Meanwhile Bright had been offered a temporary post as a junior master at Marlborough College. The head master, Dr. George Cotton [q.v.], was so well pleased with his work that in 1855 he promoted him to the mastership of the modern school, which had just been started. Bright has left an account of the school when Cotton was appointed head master in 1852. 'It was', he wrote, 'in a very bad state: there was a great deal of bullying of a severe character; one boy, for instance, was periodically half-hanged; another tall ruffian used to take a small boy into Savernake forest, and, giving him twelve yards' start, proceeded to pot him with a pistol.' There was also a fixed hostility to the masters. The organization of games was scarcely perceptible. The arrangement of the school buildings lent itself to disorder—immense dormitories and schoolrooms in which certain privileged boys were allowed to sit out of school hours, where they cooked illicit meals, but where it was nearly impossible to read or study; and an enormous big-school room, the scene of all sorts of pranks and bullying, into which all the unprivileged were crowded. Something had been done by Cotton with the help of E. S. Beesly and other masters before the arrival of Bright, who at once joined the reformers. He was specially successful in improving the relations between the masters and the boys, in reorganizing the schoolrooms, and in introducing changes after the model of his old school, Rugby. Finding that there was a deficiency of suitable books on English history for boys, Bright also began his well-known *History of England.* In 1860 he opened Preshute House, the first private house to be established at Marlborough, and in 1864 married Emmeline Theresa, daughter of the Rev. Edmund Dawe Wickham, vicar of Holmwood, Surrey. At Marlborough he remained to see the great prosperity of the school under the new head master, George Granville Bradley [q.v.], appointed in 1858.

Bradley's departure from Marlborough to University College, Oxford, in 1870 was a great loss to Bright, but it was the death of his wife in 1871 which finally induced him to abandon his school work. She was a very clever, lively woman, who had been of the greatest assistance to him and to whom he was deeply attached. In 1872, therefore, he retired, intending to devote himself to literary work, and especially to the completion of the second volume of his *History of England*; but in 1873 Bradley offered him the post of lecturer in modern history at University College, with the promise of a fellowship, while Balliol and New College also agreed to add him to their staffs.

When Bright took up his new post (he was elected a fellow in 1874) the condition of University College was not very satisfactory. In the later days of Dr. Plumptre the college had been distinguished rather for athletics, especially on the river, than for success in the schools. Dr. Bradley had therefore raised the standard of the entrance examination. In consequence many of the sons of the old *clientèle* had failed to obtain admission, yet the college had not succeeded in attracting many men of high intellectual calibre. The college was therefore declining in numbers and in reputation, while the relations between the tutors and the undergraduates were by no means friendly. Among other insubordinate practices in fashion was that of screwing up the dons in their rooms. In time, however, Bradley's reforms had due effect, and in the revival of the prosperity of the college the new members whom he added to his staff, especially Bright and Samuel Henry Butcher [q.v.], gave him valuable assistance.

Bright's character well fitted him for the work of conciliating the undergraduates. With great elevation of mind and high principle he combined a genuine sympathy for every form of wholesome energy, physical and intellectual, and was ever ready with encouragement and advice. In the university Bright took a prominent part in the division of the old school of law and modern history, and in the establishment of intercollegiate lectures open to all members of the university. Adopted first by the modern history tutors, the latter reform was eventually extended to the other faculties, and proved advantageous. If it resulted in some overcrowding of lecture rooms, it undoubtedly improved the character of the lectures by allowing each tutor to devote himself to fewer subjects. Bright's own lectures, more particularly those on foreign history during the eighteenth century, were well attended, and were appreciated for their breadth of treatment.

So invaluable had been Bright's work as a tutor, and for some time as dean of the college, that, when Bradley was called to the deanery of Westminster in 1881, Bright was elected to succeed him as master. Henceforth he devoted most of his time to the general administration of the college and to university work, while he spent his leisure moments in completing his *History of England.* In the improvement of the college he was materially assisted by his great friend Arthur Dendy, bursar of the college, R. W. Macan, who succeeded him as master, and H. M. Burge, eventually bishop of Oxford, his son-in-law. He took a leading part in the conversion of 'the hall' and no. 90 High Street into the Durham buildings, in the extension of the dining-hall, and in the restoration of its fine hammer-beam roof. On his retirement from the mastership he appropriated his pension to the assistance of poor students of his college, and in his will left £2,500 for the same purpose.

Bright was an active member of the

hebdomadal council of the university. He strenuously supported the proposal, not adopted until 1920, to throw open the theological degrees to others than members of the Church of England, and he was a firm and generous advocate of university education for women. He also took an active part in municipal affairs, and was a member of the city council from 1897 to 1901. He initiated the experiment of a technical school and presented a site in St. Clement's for the purpose. He was also treasurer of the Radcliffe infirmary (1883–1893).

Bright felt deeply the death (1905) of his sister-in-law, Miss Wickham, who had controlled his house and helped him in his literary work since his wife's death, and in the following year he resigned his mastership. He retired to Hollow Hill, a house belonging to his son-in-law, William Carr, of Ditchingham Hall, Norfolk. Here he took a leading part in county work as J.P. and poor law guardian. He died 22 October 1920, in his eighty-ninth year. He had four daughters.

Bright was in theology of the progressive school, and in politics a liberal with certain radical tendencies. Although somewhat visionary, changeable in his opinions, and apt at times to be discouraged, it was his moral elevation and his sincerity which earned him general respect, while his affectionate nature endeared him to his friends, who included persons of every shade of religious and political thought.

In addition to his *History of England* (5 vols., 1875–1904), Bright published *Lives* of Maria Theresa and Joseph II in the 'Foreign Statesmen' series (1897).

[*The Times*, 25 October 1920; private information; personal knowledge.]

A. H. J.

BROOKE, Sir CHARLES ANTHONY JOHNSON (1829–1917), second raja of Sarawak, was born at Berrow, Somerset, 3 June 1829, being the second son of the Rev. Francis Charles Johnson, vicar of White Lackington, by his wife, Emma Frances Brooke, sister of the first raja, Sir James Brooke [q.v.]. From the grammar school at Crewkerne he entered the royal navy in 1842, and after ten years, spent mostly afloat, resigned his commission and joined Sir James Brooke, who in 1841 had assumed the government of Sarawak and the title of raja.

For more than twelve years Charles Johnson lived amongst the head-hunting tribes, the erstwhile pirates of Sekrang and Sarebas. By instinct a leader of men, his high courage and physical activity quickly won him the respect and attachment of this warlike people. The Chinese insurrection of 1857 was a test of the stability of the raja's rule. It afforded a striking proof of loyalty on the part of his native subjects, and the timely arrival at Kuching of Charles Johnson with the Dayaks, who had readily rallied to his call, brought about a speedy suppression of the rebellion. During the latter part of his uncle's reign, Charles Johnson acted as heir-apparent, and much administrative responsibility passed into his hands. On the death of the raja in 1868 he succeeded to the title, and added to his own the surname of Brooke.

Progress and development marked the reign of the second raja. He built surely and well on the foundation laid by his uncle, abolishing slavery, and devoting his energies to the advancement of agriculture and education. In 1888 he was created G.C.M.G., and by treaty with Great Britain secured protection against foreign aggression and full recognition of the internal independence of Sarawak. The rebuilding of Kuching, the construction of roads, waterworks, wireless installations, and a railway were further achievements which helped to lift the country from poverty and primitive savagery to the prosperous level of a modern state. Although he occupied the position of an untrammelled despot, his sole ambition was the well-being of his subjects. For nearly seventy years he laboured on their behalf, and the little nation thus built up stands as a remarkable monument to his memory.

Leaving Sarawak in 1916, he died at his English home, Chesterton House, Cirencester, 17 May 1917, and was buried beside the first raja at Sheepstor, Devonshire. He married in 1869 Margaret Lili, daughter of Clayton de Windt, of Blunsdon Hall, Highworth, Wiltshire, by whom he had five sons and one daughter; he was succeeded as raja by his eldest surviving son, Charles Vyner Brooke.

[Charles Brooke, *Ten Years in Sarawak*, 1866; Alleyne Ireland, *The Far Eastern Tropics*, 1905; S. Baring Gould and C. A. Bampfylde, *A History of Sarawak*, 1909; correspondence and personal knowledge, 1875–1917.]

H. F. D.

BROOKE, RUPERT CHAWNER (1887–1915), poet, was born at Rugby 3 August 1887, the second of three brothers. His father was William Parker Brooke, a master at Rugby School, and his mother was Mary Ruth Cotterill. His school life, in his father's house at Rugby, was normal and happy. He played cricket and football for the school, read widely in English, wrote quantities of verse in the obsolescent manner of the 'nineties, and won prizes with poems on *The Pyramids* and *The Bastille*. In 1906 he went to King's College, Cambridge, where he soon entered into the full swim of university life and became a popular and conspicuous figure. Young Cambridge, in his mind, was to be the centre of the most vital movements in literature, art, drama, and social progress ; and to this end he worked. He was a member of the 'Apostles', and became president of the University Fabian society, which he hoped to convert from what seemed to him a hard and selfish outlook to an ideal based on sympathy rather than on class warfare, and on faith in what he called 'the real though sometimes overgrown goodness of all men'. He took a leading part in founding the Marlowe society, and acted in its performances of *Dr. Faustus* and *Comus*. He read for the classical tripos, but worked harder at English. 'There are only three things in the world,' he said,—'one is to read poetry, another is to write poetry, and the best of all is to live poetry.' His most distinctively favourite poet was Donne, and he made a careful study of the Elizabethans, winning the Harness prize with an essay, *Puritanism in the Early Drama*, and a fellowship at King's (1912) with a dissertation on John Webster.

After taking his degree in 1909, Brooke made himself a second home at the Old Vicarage, Grantchester, where he settled down for the next three years to a life of reading and bathing, varied by visits to London, Munich, and Berlin, and by a term at Rugby during which he acted as house-master after the sudden death of his father early in 1910. In December 1911 he published a volume of *Poems*, which aroused a good deal of interest, and next year he wrote a one-act play, *Lithuania*, which showed considerable dramatic power. Meanwhile he was spending more and more time in London. His remarkable and prepossessing good looks and his evident goodwill made him an attractive figure, and he was beginning to be known among a large and varied circle of interesting friends as a man of exceptional promise and charm—'a creature', as was written of him by Henry James, 'on whom the gods had smiled their brightest'.

In May 1913 Brooke set out for a year of travel, beginning with New York and Boston, and then going across Canada and down to San Francisco. He next sailed to Hawaii, and after short visits to Samoa, Fiji, and New Zealand he stayed for some months in Tahiti, whence he sent home several poems for publication in *New Numbers*, a quarterly in which he joined forces with Lascelles Abercrombie, John Drinkwater, and Wilfrid Gibson. These poems, together with his essay, *Some Niggers*, show how willingly and completely he had yielded himself to the spirit of the island life.

In June 1914 he came home across America, intending to settle down at Cambridge. The War came in August, and he has left a record of his feelings on hearing the news, when 'as he thought "England and Germany", the word "England" seemed to flash like a line of foam'. In September he was given a commission in the Royal Naval Division, and he took part in the Antwerp expedition in October. 'Apart from the tragedy', he wrote, 'I've never felt happier or better in my life than in those days in Belgium. And now I've the feeling of anger at a seen wrong to make me happier and more resolved in my work.' After Antwerp the division went to Blandford for training, and about Christmas he wrote the five war-sonnets which appeared in the last issue of *New Numbers*, and quickly became known. On 28 February 1915 the division sailed for the Dardanelles and spent some time 'drifting about', as he said, 'like a bottle in some corner of the bay at a seaside resort'. Sir Ian Hamilton at Port Said offered Brooke a post on his staff, but he preferred to stay with his platoon. Soon after this he was attacked by blood-poisoning, which his constitution, weakened by a sunstroke, was unable to resist ; and after two days' illness he died and was buried at Scyros on 23 April. He had left directions that the profits of his writings were to be divided among three of his brother poets. 'If I can set them free to any extent', he said, 'to write the poetry and plays and books they want to, my death will be more gain than loss.' He was unmarried.

Besides the *Poems* of 1911 and the posthumous volume *1914 and other Poems*, there have been published Brooke's fellowship dissertation, *John Webster*, a work of scholarship and insight, and the *Letters from America* which he wrote for the *Westminster Gazette*, and of which in especial the sections on *Niagara* and *The Rockies* show him as an accomplished writer of prose. Mention must also be made of the fine quality of his familiar letters, many of which appear in the memoir prefixed to his *Collected Poems* (1916). But his main reputation will rest on the two small books of verse. Of the pieces in the earlier volume, many were written under the ' ninetyish ' influence already mentioned, and were condemned by the author himself for ' unimportant prettiness ' ; a few, which at the time attracted disproportionate attention, were studies in ugliness and the bravado of precocious disillusionment ; but the best, such as *Dining-room Tea* and *The Fish*, had the qualities of ' adventurousness, curiosity, and life-giving youthfulness ', of ' sharpness and distinctness ' of vision, which led Walter de la Mare to class him as a poet of the intellectual imagination. These qualities, together with a peculiar power of combining humour with poetic beauty and tenderness of feeling, as in *The Old Vicarage* and *Tiare Tahiti*, are still more marked in the second volume, which also showed ever-increasing technical ability, for instance in an easy mastery over the octosyllabic couplet, and in certain slight and subtle novelties in the construction of the sonnet. It remained for the few fragments written on the way to the Dardanelles to show that his instrument had fallen from his hands at the moment when he had brought it to perfection.

[Memoir by Edward Marsh prefixed to *Collected Poems*, 1916 ; Walter de la Mare, *Rupert Brooke and the Intellectual Imagination*, 1919 ; John Drinkwater, *Rupert Brooke, an Essay* (privately printed 1916); private information.] E. M.

BROOKE, STOPFORD AUGUSTUS (1832–1916), divine and man of letters, the eldest son of the Rev. Richard Sinclair Brooke, incumbent of the Mariners' church, Kingstown, Ireland, by his wife, Anna, daughter of the Rev. T. Stopford, D.D., was born at Glendoen, near Letterkenny, co. Donegal, 14 November 1832. He was educated at Trinity College, Dublin, where he took prizes in English verse, and graduated in 1856. In 1857 he was ordained, and appointed to a curacy at St. Matthew's, Marylebone. In the following year he married Emma Diana, daughter of Thomas Wentworth Beaumont, M.P., of Bretton Park, Yorkshire ; by her he had two sons and six daughters. His wife died in 1874. Shortly after his marriage he resolved to give up his curacy and search for a field of larger opportunity. But though his reputation as a preacher was already considerable, his religious views, judged by the standard of the day, were dangerously broad, and for a short time he was without employment. In the autumn of 1859, however, he was appointed to the curacy of St. Mary Abbots, Kensington, of which Archdeacon John Sinclair [q.v.] was then vicar. Here he remained four years, and it was during this period that he began work on his *Life* of Frederick William Robertson. His power and influence as a preacher grew rapidly ; but he chafed under ecclesiastical authority—though at the time he had no idea of secession from the Church of England—and this drove him to look for a position of greater independence.

After the marriage of the Princess Royal to Prince Frederick (afterwards Crown Prince) of Prussia in 1858, it was decided to appoint an Anglican chaplain who should be attached both to their court and to the British embassy in Berlin. Brooke applied for the post, his application was accepted, and he went out to Berlin in 1863. His position there, however, was not what he had been led to expect ; there was friction with the English church already established in Berlin ; and he did not care for his surroundings. At the end of 1864 he resigned and returned to London to seek further clerical work and arrange for the publication of the *Life* of Robertson which he had completed while in Berlin. His *Life and Letters of the late Frederick W. Robertson*, published in 1865, two years after *Essays and Reviews*, was at once recognized as a work of exceptional power, and of great importance as a broad church document. It was bitterly attacked by the evangelical party.

In 1866 Brooke became minister of the proprietary chapel of St. James, York Street, a position which gave him a greater independence and freedom than he had enjoyed hitherto. The congregation, small at first, within a year filled the place to overflowing. After preaching several times before Queen Victoria, he was appointed a chaplain-in-ordinary in 1867. He remained at St. James's chapel for nine years, during the last of which he wrote his *Primer of English Literature* (1876), of which Matthew Arnold said to him, ' You have made a delightful book, and one which may have a wide action—the thing which one ought to desire for a good product almost as much as its production.' Half a million copies of this book had been sold by 1917. On the expiration of the lease of St. James's chapel, Brooke's friends presented him

(1876) with the lease of Bedford chapel, Bloomsbury, where he remained, drawing large congregations, till 1895. Meanwhile he had found that none of the accepted systems of theology could give him the complete freedom of self-expression which he desired ; and in 1880 he seceded from the Church of England. Though sympathizing to a certain extent with the tenets of Unitarians, he never attached himself definitely to any religious denomination.

During this period Brooke produced his *Life and Writings of Milton* (1879) and a lyrical drama, *Riquet of the Tuft* (1880), and during the 'eighties he was preparing his *History of Early English Literature* (1892). He also published at this time selections of sermons and a volume of *Poems* (1888). For a short time (1881–1884) he was principal of the Men and Women's College in Queen Square. But as he approached the age of sixty, his health failed, and preaching became more and more arduous to him, till in 1895 he was compelled to give up his work at Bedford chapel. In a few years, however, the vitality of youth returned to him, and he continued his literary work with renewed vigour. Between 1893 and 1913 he published seventeen volumes, and from 1900 to 1905 he gave a memorable series of lectures on English poetry at University College, London. For many years he continued occasionally to preach in Unitarian churches both in London and in the provinces. In the later years of his life he took up painting, in which he attained a high degree of excellence. He continued to live in London till 1913, when he retired to Ewhurst, where he died 18 March 1916 in his eighty-fourth year.

Of Brooke's other literary works the most important are : *Theology in the English Poets—Cowper, Coleridge, Wordsworth, Burns* (1874), *Notes on Turner's 'Liber Studiorum'* (1885), *Tennyson, his Art and Relation to Modern Life* (1894), *The Poetry of Robert Browning* (1902), *On Ten Plays of Shakespeare* (1905), *Studies in Poetry* (1907), *Ten more Plays of Shakespeare* (1913). He also published several volumes of sermons.

[L. P. Jacks, *Life and Letters of Stopford Brooke*, 2 vols., 1917. Portrait, *Royal Academy Pictures*, 1905.] G. V. J.

BROUGHTON, RHODA (1840–1920), novelist, was born near Denbigh 29 November 1840. She was the daughter of the Rev. Delves Broughton, a younger son of an old Staffordshire family, by his wife, Jane, daughter of George Bennett, Q.C., of Dublin. When Rhoda was still a child her father was presented to the living of Broughton, Staffordshire, where the Elizabethan manor-house, which was one of the family seats, was placed at his disposal. Here Rhoda, who was the youngest of a family of three daughters and one son, passed her girlhood. The old house which forms the background of her first story was drawn from Broughton Hall, and her life in the Staffordshire village furnished her with material for some of the best scenes in her novels. Under the guidance of her father, a man of wide reading, she acquired the intimate knowledge of English poetry which makes itself apparent throughout her work.

Mr. Broughton died in 1863, his wife having predeceased him, and Rhoda made her home, first with her two sisters at Surbiton, and afterwards with her sister Eleanor, who married Mr. William Charles Newcome, of Upper Eyarth, near Ruthin, Denbighshire, in 1864.

In 1867 she began her literary career with the publication of two novels, *Cometh Up as a Flower* and *Not Wisely but too Well*. The first of these books captivated the reading public with the freshness of its dialogue and the frank abandonment of its characters to emotions which the novels of the period usually treated with greater discretion. Its successor struck the same note more emphatically, and these early works gave Miss Broughton a reputation for audacity which she lost in later years when literary fashions had overtaken her and passed her by.

From this time she published on an average a novel every two years. Among the best known are : *Good-bye, Sweetheart* (1872), *Nancy* (1873), *Joan* (1876), *Belinda* (1883), *Doctor Cupid* (1886), *Foes-in-law* (1900), and *A Waif's Progress* (1905). Her private life was uneventful. In 1878 she took a house at Oxford with Mrs. Newcome, then a widow. The two sisters made for themselves a distinguished position in Oxford society, and Rhoda's vitality, sincerity, and pungent wit gained her the friendship of some of the most notable people of her day. Her freedom of speech was combined with a marked conventionality of outlook ; and her deep regard for the manners and breeding of the class into which she was born made her a keen and amusing critic of modern fashions.

In 1890 the sisters moved to Richmond. Mrs. Newcome died there in 1894, and after a few years Miss Broughton joined a cousin at Headington Hill, near

Oxford, where, but for occasional visits to London, she lived till her death on 5 June 1920.

As a novelist Rhoda Broughton appealed more to the general reader than to the critic. She did not take the art of fiction seriously, and her style was somewhat slipshod. Her gifts were, however, genuine and they developed with exercise. Her later novels, less sentimental in theme than those of her youth, contain some excellent light comedy, and her books are an entertaining record of country house life during the latter half of the nineteenth century.

[*The Times*, 7 June 1920; *Fortnightly Review*, vol. cviii, pp. 262–78; private information.] M. C.

BROWN, PETER HUME (1849–1918), historian, was born at Tranent, Haddingtonshire, 17 December 1849, and educated in the Free Church school at Prestonpans, which he entered at the age of eight and left only in 1869. His father died in 1852, his mother in 1866, and for the last three years of his school-life he was in the guardianship of unsympathetic relations, acting as a pupil-teacher and presumably sentenced to the career of a schoolmaster. From 1869 to 1872 he was teaching in Wales and at Newcastle-upon-Tyne; but in 1872 he matriculated at Edinburgh University with the idea of becoming a minister. This plan, however, he abandoned in 1874; he left Edinburgh in the hope of obtaining private tutorships which would give him opportunities of continental travel. But his first and only post of this kind took him no farther afield than the south-west of England. Weak health forced him to modify his plans: he returned to Edinburgh and graduated there in 1875. There were two Edinburgh professors to whom, in after years, he acknowledged his obligations, David Masson [q. v.], the biographer of Milton, and Alexander Campbell Fraser [q. v.], the editor of Berkeley; but the most fruitful friendship which he formed in his student days was that with his contemporary, Richard (afterwards Viscount) Haldane, and his true masters were Goethe, Renan, and Sainte-Beuve. On graduating Hume Brown opened a private school in Edinburgh, and in 1879 he married; but, after the untimely death of his wife (1882), he closed his school, went into lodgings in Edinburgh, and devoted himself to historical and literary studies, making a livelihood by private tuition. For the next sixteen years life went hardly with him; but he gradually established his reputation as an historian. In 1890 he published a biography of George Buchanan, the humanist, and in 1892 an edition of Buchanan's vernacular writings. Three years later appeared his biography of John Knox (1895), which is chiefly remarkable for a resolute avoidance of theological controversy and for the emphasis which it lays upon the political aspects of the reformer's life-work. Neither work was written for the general public; but, in the opinion of the best judges, they designated Hume Brown as the natural successor to David Masson, when the latter resigned the editorship of the *Register of the Privy Council of Scotland* in 1898. In 1899 Hume Brown published the first volume of his *History of Scotland*; in 1901 he was appointed to Sir William Fraser's chair of ancient history in the university of Edinburgh. These appointments relieved him of financial anxieties at an age when large undertakings are rarely planned with any confidence that they will be completed. Hume Brown, however, organized his life with method and with forethought. In the course of the next seventeen years he completed his *History*, continued the publication of the *Register*, and wrote two admirable courses of lectures on *Scotland in the Time of Queen Mary* (1904) and *The Legislative Union of England and Scotland* (1914). He also undertook and finished the *Life of Goethe* which he himself regarded as his *magnum opus*. Preliminary studies, on the *Youth of Goethe*, appeared in 1913; the *Life*, completed just before his death, was posthumously published in 1920. He died, of cerebral haemorrhage, on 30 November 1918, in his Edinburgh home at the foot of the Braid Hills.

By profession an historical expert, by inclination a student of the human microcosm, and at heart profoundly sceptical of ideas which express themselves in the political framework of society, Hume Brown possessed something of the ironic quality which amused him in Erasmus, much of the aphoristic wisdom which he reverenced in Goethe; but his salient characteristics were the insatiable curiosity and almost unbounded tolerance which made Sainte-Beuve, in his opinion, the king of literary critics. As a writer he was too cautious, or unduly respectful to his public; he contented himself, in print, with expressing his mature conviction in precise and polished sentences. In conversation it was otherwise; he talked of subjects on which his mind was not yet made up, hazarded conjectures, lapsed into paradox or quiet and genial malice, argued the moot points, would even generalize with a half-humorous reluctance. His influence on younger men was remarkable; in matters intellectual he was a sort of father-confessor to whom they turned instinctively for guidance.

[Notices by G. Macdonald in *Proceedings* of the British Academy, vol. viii, and by C. H. Firth in *Scottish Historical Review*, January 1919; personal knowledge.] H. W. C. D.

BRUCE, ALEXANDER HUGH, sixth BARON BALFOUR OF BURLEIGH in the Scottish peerage (1849–1921), statesman, born at Kennet, Alloa, 13 January 1849, was the only son of Robert Bruce, of Kennet (1795–1864), M.P. for Clackmannanshire, by his second wife, Jane Hamilton, daughter of Sir James Fergusson, of Kilkerran, fourth baronet. His ancestor, Robert Balfour, fifth Baron Balfour of Burleigh [q.v.], was attainted in 1716, and the title was restored in 1869. He was educated at Loretto and Eton, and graduated in 1871 at Oriel College, Oxford. On attaining his majority he began a strenuous public career. In 1876 he became a representative peer for Scotland, and sat in the Lords in that capacity until his death. His shrewdness, business ability, and sound knowledge of local government were early recognized; and his biography is largely a record of his work on commissions, the reports of which became authoritative documents. He was chairman of the educational endowments commission (1882–1889), the metropolitan water-supply commission (1893–1894), the rating commission (1896), the royal commission on food supply in time of war (1903), the royal commission on closer trade relations between Canada and the West Indies (1909), and the committee on commercial and industrial policy after the War (1916–1917). In 1888–1889 he was lord-in-waiting to Queen Victoria, and from 1889 to 1892 parliamentary secretary to the Board of Trade. Entering the third Salisbury Cabinet in 1895 as secretary for Scotland, an office which he held for eight years, he showed himself one of the ablest administrators that country has ever produced; his unwearied efforts to further the welfare of Scotland by wise and beneficent legislation were universally recognized. During his term of office the Scottish Parish Councils Act became operative, while his legislative achievements included the codification and amendment of the Public Health Acts (Scotland) 1897; the establishment of the congested districts board (1898); and an Act (1899) simplifying and cheapening the promotion of private Scottish bills by municipalities and other corporate bodies. In 1903 the tariff reform controversy caused him to leave the government and to join the unionist free trade group. In 1904 he was appointed lord warden of the stannaries, in virtue of which he presided over the council of the duchy of Cornwall during the minority of the Prince of Wales.

In his later years Balfour of Burleigh was perhaps the most outstanding figure in the public life of Scotland. In 1896 he became lord rector of Edinburgh University; in 1900 chancellor of St. Andrews University; and in 1917 chairman of the Carnegie trust for the universities of Scotland. In the affairs of the Church of Scotland he took a leading part. He organized the fund for aged and infirm ministers, and was at all times a stout defender of the connexion between church and state. But his most enduring work was done in connexion with the movement for union between the Church of Scotland and the United Free Church, a project which, largely owing to his advocacy and statesmanship, was brought within measurable distance of accomplishment before his death. He was the author of *An Historical Account of the Rise and Development of Presbyterianism in Scotland* (1911).

Balfour of Burleigh became a privy councillor in 1892, a knight of the Thistle in 1901; G.C.M.G. in 1911; and G.C.V.O. in 1917. He was D.C.L. of the university of Oxford (1904) and an honorary LL.D. of the four Scottish universities. In 1876 he married Lady Katherine Eliza Hamilton-Gordon, youngest daughter of the fifth Earl of Aberdeen, by whom he had two sons and three daughters. He died 6 July 1921 at his residence, 47 Cadogan Square, London. Balfour of Burleigh had a commanding presence and much charm of manner. Without brilliance, he yet represented the best type of public servant—conscientious, purposeful, and with a gift for mastering complicated details and presenting them lucidly and cogently.

[The *Scotsman*, 7 July 1921; *British Monthly*, December 1904; Lady Frances Balfour, *A Memoir of Lord Balfour of Burleigh*, 1925; personal knowledge.] W. F. G.

BRUCE, VICTOR ALEXANDER, ninth EARL OF ELGIN and thirteenth EARL OF KINCARDINE (1849–1917), statesman and sometime viceroy of India, was the eldest son of James Bruce, eighth Earl of Elgin [q.v.], by his second wife, Lady Mary Louisa Lambton, daughter of the first Earl of Durham, author of the famous report on Canadian government. He was born 16 May 1849 at Monklands, near Montreal, his father being then governor-general of Canada. He was educated first at Glenalmond—very strenuous and Spartan in its earliest days—and afterwards, like his father, at Eton, in Dr. Warre's house. While there he succeeded his father, who died at Dharmsala, in the Punjab Hills, on 20 November 1863, after little more than eighteen months' tenure of the viceroyalty. From Eton he went to Balliol College, Oxford, where he graduated with a second class in *literae humaniores* in 1873, and was captain of the college cricket eleven. He proceeded M.A. in 1877. For some twenty years after leaving Oxford he lived chiefly at his Fifeshire seat, taking a very active part in county and Scottish affairs, and specially in the promotion of education. He accepted the chairmanship of the Scottish liberal association; and adhering to Mr. Gladstone at the time of the Home Rule split, he was in the short-lived government of 1886, first as treasurer of the household and then as first commissioner of works.

His party returned to power in 1892, and in the following year Elgin was offered the Indian viceroyalty in succession to Lord Lansdowne, when it had been refused by Sir Henry Norman [q.v.]. Lord Rosebery testified publicly (May 1899) to the difficulty he found in overcoming Elgin's objections, based chiefly on a modest estimate of his own powers. His recognition of his own limitations was so far justified that he cannot be reckoned among the outstanding governors-general of India. His personal influence on affairs was weakened by a retiring disposition and a self-distrust, from which there sprang a subservience to Whitehall that has, perhaps, no parallel in viceregal records. Though his influence on affairs was thus less positive than was fitting, his period of office will live in history as marking a momentous change in the conditions of British rule in India.

An acute observer has well said that when Elgin landed at Bombay in January 1894, there seemed to be no reason why the comfortable system of control then in vogue should not continue upon the same lines for a period measured by decades. But beneath the unruffled surface, new currents of thought were forming and were steadily gaining momentum. Intellectual Indians were ceasing to accept the solid fact of British control without question and without criticism, and Elgin's quinquennium by no means fulfilled its early promise of placidity [Lovat Fraser, *India under Curzon and After*, 1911, chap. 1]. The initial trouble was financial. The continued fall of the rupee exchange had caused large deficits; and, as measures already taken to secure stabilization could only mature by degrees, import duties were levied for revenue purposes. In order to meet Lancashire views, cotton goods were excluded, in the first instance, from the schedule. A heated controversy was evoked; in which for the first time the non-official European residents joined the Indian politicians in vehement agitation against government action. The viceroy, with marked failure of imagination, wrote to the secretary of state, Sir Henry Fowler, that the outcry was 'unreasonable and unreasoning' [*Life of Lord Wolverhampton*, 1912]. For a blunt ruling in the legislature (27 December 1894) that all official members must obey the 'mandate' of the India Office he was bitterly attacked in both the English-owned and the Indian press. A subsequent compromise on the cotton duties allayed the storm, but failed to satisfy Indian opinion.

Elgin's tenure was marked also by persistent and costly trouble on the Frontier. The delimitation of the Afghan boundary had made it necessary to establish a political agency in Chitral, and in 1895 a local rising was followed by the destruction of a Sikh detachment, and the British agent, (Sir) George Scott Robertson [q. v.], was besieged in the Chitral fort. After his relief there was a prolonged controversy as to the expediency of retaining control. In 1897 the Waziris rose in revolt, and the Tochi Valley had to be occupied by a British force. Then followed the attack of the Swat tribes upon the Malakand, the raids of the Mohmands upon villages near Peshawar, and the seizure of the Khyber Pass by the Afridis. In a few days the North-West Frontier was aflame from Tochi to Buner, and it took 60,000 troops and a six months' campaign to extinguish the conflagration. Elgin was charged, on the one hand, with indecision while the fate of the Khyber Pass was in the balance, and, on the other, with exercising little independent judgement in regard to the alleged 'forward' policy of the military authorities. The commander-in-chief, Sir George White, described him at this time as 'straight, clever and considerate'

[Sir M. Durand, *Life of Sir George White*, 1915].

Soon after Elgin's arrival, India had entered upon a cycle of lean years. The monsoon rains of 1895 were deficient and those of 1896 failed almost completely. Then followed the most intense and severe famine that had been known under British rule. By the spring of 1897 over four million people were receiving relief, and the mortality was extremely heavy. Moreover, in the autumn of 1896, bubonic plague was detected in the Bombay slums. Carried into the interior of the Western Presidency by a *trek* of the mill hands, it spread thence to almost all parts of India, and has since been endemic. The preventive measures instituted were deeply resented in Western India, where sanguinary riots occurred and two officers were deliberately murdered. A school of revolutionary extremists now grew up [*Report of Sedition Committee*, 1918]; sedition trials had to be instituted, and the law on the subject was strengthened.

Elgin was hardly fitted to be at the helm in such stormy seas. A man with the driving power of John Lawrence might be careless of dress and deficient in the instinct for ceremonial without detriment to his prestige; Elgin, apart from his public spirit, his chivalry, and his high sense of duty, had little to counteract the handicaps of reserve of manner, habitual silence, a retiring disposition, a certain homeliness in his aspect and bearing, a curious dislike of riding and on public occasions even of driving, and a general inaptitude for social leadership. He neither looked the great part which he had accepted so reluctantly, nor trusted himself in it. Yet he gave proof of no small administrative capacity in such matters as railway extension and famine relief.

Returning home at the beginning of 1899, Elgin received the Garter. He promptly resumed his local work in Scotland and was re-elected convener of the Fife county council. In September 1902 he accepted the chairmanship of a royal commission to inquire into the military preparations for the South African War, and into allegations of extravagance and contractual fraud. He carried through the inquiry with such judgement and dispatch that a unanimous report, which suggested methods of home defence later embodied in the territorial system, was presented in the following July. In 1905 he was chairman of the important commission necessitated by the decision of the House of Lords in the appeal of the Free Church against the union of the two large non-established Presbyterian bodies in Scotland. The recommendations of the commission were embodied in an Act passed a few months later; and Lord Elgin became chairman of a second commission charged with giving detailed effect to the recommendations of the first. Subsequently, at the request of the founder, he became chairman of the Carnegie trust for the Scottish universities, and he held this office till his death. He was chancellor of the university of Aberdeen from 1914.

Elgin was selected for the colonial secretaryship when Sir H. Campbell-Bannerman formed his ministry on the eve of the great liberal victory of January 1906. He shared in the steps, such as the grant of full autonomy to the Transvaal, which led a few years later to the union of South Africa. His cautious temperament never responded with enthusiasm to certain aspects of radical thought on overseas problems. We have Lord Morley's testimony [*Recollections*, 1917, ii, 207, 211] that Elgin was unsympathetic towards his proposals for Indian constitutional reforms. Moreover, Elgin publicly dissociated himself from the charges which had been brought against the unionist government at the general election with reference to the importation of Chinese labour for the Transvaal mines. Elgin was somewhat overshadowed by his brilliant under-secretary, Mr. Winston Churchill, whose speeches on departmental matters were as aggressive and stimulating as his own were cautious and pedestrian. So there was no great surprise when Mr. Asquith, on becoming prime minister in April 1908, did not include Elgin in the reconstituted Cabinet. Refusing the marquisate offered him, but avoiding any public indication of wounded pride, Elgin returned with zest to his first and deepest attachment to parochial, county, and Scottish affairs. In these at least he was not wavering or self-distrustful, and his devoted, useful service was recognized and appreciated on all hands.

In 1876 Elgin married Lady Constance Carnegie, daughter of the ninth Earl of Southesk, by whom he had six sons and five daughters; she died in 1909. His second wife, whom he married in 1913, was Gertrude Lilian, daughter of Commander William Sherbrooke, of Oxton Hall, Nottinghamshire, and widow of Captain Frederick Ogilvy, R.N. He died at his seat Broomhall, Dunfermline, Fifeshire, 18 January 1917. He was survived by five sons and four daughters, and another son was born posthumously. He was succeeded by his eldest son, Edward James Bruce, who served as a territorial officer in the European War.

[Works cited above; Parliamentary debates; Indian official reports; V. Smith, *Oxford History of India*, 1919; P. E. Roberts, *Historical Geography of India*, part II, 1920; *The Times, Scotsman, Aberdeen Free Press, Dundee Advertiser*, 19 January 1917; *Manchester Guardian, Times of India*, 20 January 1917; confidential papers; personal knowledge.] F. H. B.

BRUCE, WILLIAM SPEIRS (1867–1921), polar explorer and oceanographer, was born in London 1 August 1867, the fourth child of Samuel Noble Bruce, M.R.C.S., of Edinburgh, by his wife, Mary, daughter of L. Wild Lloyd, and grandson of the Rev. William Bruce, minister of the Swedenborgian church, Hatton Garden. On his father's side he was of Scottish and Norse descent. On leaving Norfolk county school, North Elmham, Bruce went to Edinburgh University to read medicine, but he never qualified. The close association of Edinburgh with the *Challenger* expedition (1872–1876) turned his interests to the sea and exploration. In 1892–1893 he sailed as surgeon in the Dundee whaler *Balaena* for the South Shetlands and Graham Land, where he made researches in zoology and discovered the first evidence in favour of the Antarctic anticyclone. After fruitless attempts to raise funds for the exploration of South Georgia, he took charge in 1895 of the high-level meteorological observatory on Ben Nevis, but left it in 1896 to join the Jackson-Harmsworth expedition in Franz Josef Land, where he stayed a year, engaged in biological work. He made short voyages in 1898 with Major Andrew Coats in the *Blencathra* to Kolguev, Novaya Zemlya, and the Barents Sea, and with the Prince of Monaco in the *Princesse Alice* to Bear Island, Hope Island, and Spitzbergen. In 1899, with the Prince of Monaco, he explored and charted Red Bay, Spitzbergen.

Feeling that now he had gained the necessary experience in polar work, Bruce announced in 1900 his plans for a Scottish national Antarctic expedition to explore the Weddell Sea. Funds were raised in Scotland, and the expedition sailed in November 1902. The *Scotia* spent two summers in oceanographical and biological work in the Weddell Sea and South Atlantic. Coats Land was discovered in March 1904 and proved to be part of the Antarctic continent. The intervening winter was spent at the South Orkneys, where an observatory was built which has since been maintained by the Argentine Republic. Gough Island was biologically explored. The expedition returned home in July 1904 with large biological collections from waters down to 2,900 fathoms and voluminous hydrographical and meteorological observations. Seven volumes of Bruce's *Report on the Scientific Results of the Voyage of S.Y. 'Scotia', 1902–1904* contained most of the results, but lack of means prevented the completion of the series. Other results were published by the Royal Society of Edinburgh. Bruce then turned his attention to Spitzbergen, and with the help of the Prince of Monaco had small expeditions engaged in the survey of Prince Charles Foreland in 1906, 1907, and 1909. He made a vain effort in 1910–1911 to raise funds for a new Antarctic expedition which was to include a traverse of Antarctica. In 1912, 1914, 1919, and 1920 he was again in Spitzbergen, engaged in the exploration of the coal-bearing regions to which he had drawn attention in 1898. A whaling enterprise in the Seychelles occupied him in 1915–1916.

Bruce founded in Edinburgh in 1907 the Scottish oceanographical laboratory, and hoped to expand it into a great institute of oceanography comparable with that in Monaco. He undertook the whole burden of upkeep and maintained the laboratory for many years at great personal sacrifice. But failing health combined with want of means compelled him in 1920 to abandon the scheme. The library and collections were presented to various institutions in Edinburgh. He died at Edinburgh 28 October 1921. In accordance with his wishes his body was cremated and the ashes were scattered in the Southern Ocean off South Georgia on 2 April 1923. Bruce married in 1901 Jessie, daughter of Alexander Mackenzie, merchant, of Nigg, Ross-shire; they had a son and a daughter. Bruce's contributions to scientific societies were numerous; but, with small regard for the spectacular side of exploration, he avoided publicity and wrote little of popular interest. He received the honorary degree of LL.D. from Aberdeen University (1906) and the gold medal of the Royal Scottish Geographical Society (1904), the Patron's medal of the Royal Geographical Society (1910), the Neill prize and medal of the Royal Society of Edinburgh (1913), and the Livingstone medal of the Hispanic Society of America (1920).

[R. N. Rudmose Brown, *A Naturalist at the Poles: Life and Voyages of W. S. Bruce*, 1923; *Proceedings* of the Royal Society of Edinburgh, 1922; *Scottish Geographical Magazine*, 1897–1921 *passim*; personal knowledge.] R. N. R. B.

BRUNTON, Sir THOMAS LAUDER, first baronet (1844–1916), physician, the third son of James Brunton, by his wife, Agnes, daughter of John Stenhouse, of White Lee, was born at Hiltonshill, Roxburghshire, 14 March 1844. Educated privately, he entered the university of Edinburgh, where he had a distinguished academic career, graduating M.B., C.M. with honours in 1866. For a year after graduation he acted as house-physician in Edinburgh Infirmary. In 1867, as Baxter scholar, he began a period of travel and study, working successively in Vienna, Berlin, Amsterdam, and Leipzig, and laying the foundations of European friendships which were shaken only in the last years of his life.

Returning to England in 1870, he was appointed lecturer in *materia medica* and pharmacology at the Middlesex Hospital, and in the following year to the same position at St. Bartholomew's. Regarding this as a responsibility that involved more than the mere delivery of lectures, and in emulation of the pharmacological laboratories that were just beginning to be established in Germany, he secured as his first laboratory the only place available, a hospital scullery, measuring twelve feet by six. He remained on the active staff of St. Bartholomew's as casualty physician for four years, as assistant physician for twenty years, and as physician for nine. During this time he gradually became an acknowledged leader of the medical profession, with a more than European reputation. His fruitful researches and his wide knowledge of scientific and medical literature, his friendships with British and foreign workers, his personal charm and integrity, added to his fame—at least with the general public—as the most widely known consulting physician in London, gave him a peculiar and powerful influence as a connecting link between the practice of medicine and the sciences upon which it is based.

Brunton's own investigations covered a wide field, but his main interest was in the treatment of disease. His M.D. thesis (1867) on *Digitalis, with some Observations on the Urine*, embodying the results of six months' experiment on himself, started a life-long interest in problems of the circulation. His greatest single contribution to practical medicine was made in 1867 while he was still a house-physician in Edinburgh. He had been observing closely a patient who was suffering from nightly attacks of *angina pectoris*, and noticed that, during the attacks, the blood pressure rose. 'It seemed probable that the great rise in tension was the cause of the pain, and it occurred to me that if it was possible to diminish the tension by drugs, instead of by bleeding, the pain would be relieved. I knew, from unpublished experiments by Dr. A. Gamgee [q.v.], that nitrite of amyl had this power, and therefore tried it on the patient. My expectations were perfectly answered.' Amyl nitrite immediately secured, and has since retained, a position of first importance in the treatment of this disease. From 1870 to 1890 Brunton and his collaborators published many important papers on digitalis, nitrites, inorganic salts, enzymes, on the relation between chemical constitution and physiological action, and on many other problems. His publications and addresses were full not only of new observations but also of explanations and suggestions, many of far-reaching importance and in advance of his time.

Brunton was also—and for his time this was equally important—a great teacher and organizer of knowledge. His lectures at St. Bartholomew's were described by one who attended them as 'the most interesting and instructive of all the lectures given there at that time'. His *Textbook of Pharmacology and Therapeutics* (1885) was the first complete treatise on the subject from the standpoint of physiology, and few pioneer text-books in any science can have attained such a high level of excellence. It was translated into several languages. Brunton delivered the Lettsomian lectures in 1886, the Goulstonian lecture in 1877, the Croonian lectures in 1889, and the Harveian oration in 1894.

He had imperial as well as academic interests. He was one of the founders of the national league for physical education, and a steadfast and active advocate of national health, school hygiene, and military training. In a letter to Brunton in 1915 Sir Douglas (afterwards Earl) Haig wrote, 'You and I have often talked about the certainty of this war, and have done, each of us, our best to prepare in our own spheres for it'.

Brunton had married in 1879 Louisa Jane, daughter of the Ven. Edward A.

Stopford, archdeacon of Meath. They had three sons and three daughters. The death of his devoted wife in 1909, and of his second son (killed in action in France in 1915) clouded the last years of his life. Of somewhat frail build, he was impressive only when he spoke. His learning, originality, and practical skill entitle him to rank as one of the founders of modern pharmacology. This, combined with his enthusiasm, his capacity for friendship, and unfailing kindness of heart made him an outstanding and cosmopolitan figure for over a quarter of a century. He died in London 16 September 1916.

[Notices in the *British Medical Journal*, 1916, vol. ii, p. 440; *Lancet*, 1916, vol. ii, p. 572; *Proceedings* of the Royal Society, vol. lxxxix, B, 1915–1916 (portrait); personal knowledge.] J. A. G.

BULLEN, ARTHUR HENRY (1857–1920), English scholar, the second son of George Bullen, LL.D. [q.v.], by his first wife, Eliza Martin, born in London 9 February 1857, was educated at the City of London School under Dr. Edwin Abbott, and at Worcester College, Oxford, where he matriculated as an open classical scholar in 1875. He was noted even at school for his knowledge of the Elizabethan and nineteenth-century writers, and especially of Lamb and Swinburne, for an extraordinary memory and ear for poetry, and faculty of reciting it. The magnificent collection of seventeenth-century English books in Worcester College library confirmed his early tastes. He was a good Greek and Latin scholar and took a first class in classical moderations, but only a third in *literae humaniores*, for which he read little except English literature. On leaving Oxford he taught in a school at Margate, but soon abandoned teaching for literary work. He wrote many articles for the early volumes of this DICTIONARY, chiefly on English authors of the sixteenth and seventeenth centuries, a period of which Sir Leslie Stephen pronounced his knowledge to be 'very remarkable, and, in some respects, probably unsurpassed'. During the years 1881–1890 he produced, in four dozen volumes, the bulk of his life-work as an editor, including the dramatic works of Day, Marlowe, Middleton, Marston, Nabbes, Peele, and Davenport, the sixteen plays (five of them from manuscripts) in the four earlier volumes of *Old English Plays*, the poems of Thomas Campion (whom he rescued from obscurity), and his well-known collections of Elizabethan and Caroline lyrics. In February and March 1889 Bullen delivered in Oxford lectures (never published) on Drayton, Dekker, Campion, and Breton; but after the failure of his application in that year for the chair of English at University College, London, he set up as publisher, a career for which he had excellent literary intuition but small business capacity. In partnership with H. W. Lawrence (1891–1900) and subsequently with F. Sidgwick (1902–1907), he issued a large number of works, including the poets of the 'Muses' Library' series. In 1904 he founded at Stratford-on-Avon the Shakespeare Head Press, which he carried on until his death. Here from 1904 to 1907 he edited and printed, with brief but not unimportant notes, the ten volumes of his Stratford Town Shakespeare. During 1906 he edited for Lord Northcliffe the revived *Gentleman's Magazine*, to which he contributed much original matter; but his main work was now the publishing of other men's books. His influence on younger scholars was stimulating and fruitful, and to him English scholarship is indebted for such works as R. B. McKerrow's edition of Nashe and W. W. Greg's *Henslowe's Diary*. He died at Stratford 29 February 1920. He had married in 1879 Edith, daughter of William John Goodwin, head of the map department of the Ecclesiastical Commissioners, by whom he had two sons and three daughters. *Weeping-Cross*, a posthumous volume of short poems by him, with a portrait, appeared in 1921.

As an editor Bullen modernized his texts, but did great work in publishing early plays and lyrics, many of which he himself discovered in manuscript. As a textual critic his greatest achievement was the interpretation of the mysterious 'Oncaymaeon' of *Doctor Faustus*, I. i. 12, which had baffled all previous editors, as the Aristotelian ὂν καὶ μὴ ὄν. Recognized early by Swinburne and J. A. Symonds, and by such European scholars as Beljame, Jusserand, and Delius, his work gradually won him fame at home, and he enjoyed a civil list pension for some years before his death. His unflagging energy in popularizing the dramatists and song writers of the sixteenth and seventeenth centuries has had an influence on English scholarship, and on English poetry, which it is easier to appreciate than to define.

[Letters; printed testimonials at the British Museum; memoir (by the writer) prefixed to Bullen's third (posthumous) edition of *Shakespeare's Sonnets*, 1921; private information.] H. F. B. B-S.

BURGH CANNING, HUBERT GEORGE DE, second MARQUESS and fifteenth EARL OF CLANRICARDE (1832–1916), Irish landed proprietor, was born 30 November 1832, the younger son of Ulick John De Burgh, first Marquess and fourteenth Earl of Clanricarde, by his wife, Harriet, only daughter of George Canning, the statesman. Educated at Harrow, he entered the diplomatic service in 1852, and was for ten years attaché at Turin, retiring as second secretary in 1863. In 1867, as Viscount Burke, he was returned to parliament in the liberal interest as member for county Galway. But Gladstone's Irish Land Act displeased him, and he resigned in 1871. The seat was won by Colonel Nolan, a Home Ruler, after a fierce contest in which the Clanricarde interest was thrown against the popular candidate. In 1862 De Burgh had assumed by royal licence the additional surname of Canning, as heir of his maternal uncle, Earl Canning. His elder brother's death in 1867 made him heir to the marquisate, to which he succeeded in 1874.

The rest of Lord Clanricarde's life was spent in resisting the movement to limit the Irish landlord's power. His campaign was conducted at a distance, as he never visited his large property—some 56,000 acres—in East Galway, but lived continuously in the Albany, Piccadilly. Having great wealth and living penuriously (although he amassed art treasures and jewels, of which he was a connoisseur), he could not be seriously inconvenienced by the tenants' combined refusal to pay rent: and he fought them by the weapon of eviction, and by using all the devices of the law to restrict the operation of the Land Act of 1881. In 1886 the 'plan of campaign', according to which rents were paid to representatives of the Land League and not to the landlord, was started on his estate, and fresh disturbances followed. Of his 1,159 tenants 186 were evicted; many 'emergency men' were installed in the vacant holdings, and there was a crop of murders. The saying attributed to him, 'Do they think they will intimidate me by shooting my bailiffs?', dramatically expressed the facts. After the Wyndham Land Purchase Act of 1903 he was urged to sell, but refused absolutely. Ministers of both parties recognized that Lord Clanricarde was deliberately thwarting the policy of parliament, which had first established dual ownership and then aimed at complete land purchase. The case for the Town Tenants' Act in 1907 was based largely on the fact that a solvent tenant of Lord Clanricarde's in Loughrea had been evicted expressly because his political activities were disapproved; and the compulsory powers of purchase given to the Congested Districts Board by the Act of 1909 were chiefly aimed at expropriating this landlord. But Lord Clanricarde fought the matter from court to court until a decision of the Land Court in July 1915 transferred the estate (except the demesne) to the Board at a price of £238,211.

Lord Clanricarde died in the Albany 12 April 1916. His estates were never highly rented, but he held desperately to the old order in which the landlord could wield arbitrary power over his tenants, and he was careless alike of public opinion, which universally condemned his conduct, and of the consequences, which left his estates, in the words of Mr. Birrell, 'haunted with the ghosts of murdered men'.

Lord Clanricarde never married, and in the absence of a direct heir the marquisate became extinct. The earldom, however, passed by special remainder to his cousin, George Ulick Browne, sixth Marquess of Sligo.

[*The Times*, 14 April 1916; Hansard, *Parliamentary Debates*; personal knowledge.]

S. G.

BURNAND, SIR FRANCIS COWLEY (1836–1917), playwright, author, and editor of *Punch*, was born 29 November 1836, the only son of Francis Burnand, a London stockbroker, by his wife, Emma Cowley. Through his mother he claimed descent from the poetess and dramatist, Hannah Cowley [q.v.]. After three years at Eton, he matriculated in 1854 at Trinity College, Cambridge, where he devoted himself mainly to theatricals, founding the Cambridge Amateur Dramatic Club, usually known as the A.D.C. It was at first intended that he should read for the bar; but the fact that a living, purchased by one of the family, had become vacant, made it seem advisable that he should take orders. He accordingly went to Cuddesdon Theological College to prepare for ordination, but a further acquaintance with theological matters led him to accept the Roman Catholic faith (December 1858), and, contrary to the hopes of Cardinal Manning, to seek in a secular direction a means of livelihood. He was called to the bar in 1862; but the attraction of the footlights set him on the road which was to lead to the editorship of *Punch*. When he shocked Manning by saying that he had no vocation for the priesthood, but that he fancied he had a vocation for the stage, he was only speaking the truth. The stage had always called to him. But he had at this time no vocation for writing, no inner call to express himself by means either of play or book. Such vocation, as it happened, was not required. He was to be playwright, not dramatist. Gay good-humour, agility of mind, a facility which, however, spared no industry, were equipment enough for the theatrical world he set out to conquer. It was an easy-going world in those days, with no heights for the young to scale more inspiring than the well-timed burlesque of a popular drama or the skilful naturalization of a popular French farce. Before he had finished with it, Burnand had more than a hundred such burlesques and adaptations to his name. Of these *Black-eyed Susan* (1866) and *The Colonel* (1881) were the most successful; and if they are not destined for immortality, it can at least be claimed for them that they survived triumphantly the origins from which they sprang.

Contemporaneously with these plays went on his work for the lighter periodicals of his day, especially *Fun*, which he helped Henry James Byron [q.v.] to found; and his first contribution to *Punch* in 1863 was followed shortly afterwards by an invitation to join the staff. His work for *Punch* was more original, though in this again, for the most part, he was happier when somebody else had provided him with a point of support. With the exception of his best-known book, *Happy Thoughts* (1866), one of the most popular series which has ever appeared in *Punch*, his burlesques of other writers (especially the *New History of Sandford and Merton*, 1872, and *Strapmore* by 'Weeder', 1878) were his chief contribution to the humour of his time. This was a time when 'humorists' were not only labelled as such, but were qualified inevitably as 'genial'. To be genial, in fact, was almost enough. For the rest, italics and exclamation-marks were recognized badges of wit, periphrasis was in itself jocular, and an appropriate quotation from Dickens was proof to the most sceptical that the writer was a jolly good fellow. In this school the pun naturally held high esteem. There was no mistaking a pun; it was, from the fact of its being there, a genial contribution to the entertainment. Burnand contributed much in this line; and if a great deal of it was no more than a formal acknowledgement of his reputation as a humorist, there were to be found here and there real flashes of brilliance. One much-quoted saying of his was in answer to the charge that *Punch*, in his time, was not so good as it used to be—'It never was'.

There is no doubt that under Burnand's editorship, which began in 1880 and lasted twenty-six years, the reputation of *Punch* increased considerably. It grew less intolerant of opinions with which it disagreed; it became more catholic in its appeal; it began to discard its air of a Family Joke and aspired to be the National Institution which it has since been proclaimed. Yet he always kept for it a note of irresponsibility; and although this irresponsibility has lost most of its humour for a later generation, it has left behind it a pleasant feeling that the editor (as the editor of such a paper should) enjoyed his work, and that even as the controller of 'the most famous humorous paper in the world' he refused to take himself too seriously.

Burnand was twice married: first, in 1860 to Cecilia Victoria (who died in 1870), daughter of James Ranoe; by her he had five sons and two daughters; secondly, in 1874, to Rosina, widow of Paysan Jones, of Liverpool, by whom he had two sons and four daughters. In 1902 he was knighted, the first writer on *Punch* to receive that distinction, and in 1906 he retired from the editorship. He died at Ramsgate 21 April 1917, at the age of eighty.

[F. C. Burnand, *Records and Reminiscences*, 1903; M. H. Spielmann, *The History of Punch*, 1895; private information.]

A. A. M.

BURNHAM, first Baron (1833–1916), newspaper proprietor. [See Levy-Lawson, Edward].

BUTLER, HENRY MONTAGU (1833–1918), head master of Harrow school, dean of Gloucester, master of Trinity College, Cambridge, was born at Gayton, Northamptonshire, 2 July 1833. He was the ninth child and youngest (fourth) son of Dr. George Butler [q.v.], the Harrow head master of Byron's boyhood. His grandfather was the Rev. Weeden Butler, the elder [q.v.], head of a noted school at Chelsea, and a friend of Burke, whom Montagu Butler was to idolize. Both his father and his uncle, Weeden Butler, the younger [q.v.], were Cambridge graduates. Trained under the Rev. Edward Wickham at Hammersmith, he was placed by his father in 1846 in the house of Dr.

Charles John Vaughan [q.v.], then head master of Harrow, where his uncle, William Oxenham, was under-master. He speedily won distinction as a scholar and the regard both of Dr. Vaughan and of many of his contemporaries, among them John (afterwards fifth Earl) Spencer and (Sir) George Otto Trevelyan who introduced him to Macaulay. Despite delicate health he played in the school cricket eleven, while as head of the school he earned both popularity and respect. From Harrow he went in 1851 to Trinity College, Cambridge, of which in his first term he was elected a minor scholar. Here again he won many prizes and many friends. His tutor was William Hepworth Thompson [q.v.], and he read, among others, with Richard Shilleto [q.v.]. He became president of the Union Society, and senior classic (1855), and in that year was elected fellow of his college. His gifts and aims fitted him for a parliamentary career, and in 1856 he was appointed private secretary to William Francis Cowper (afterwards Lord Mount-Temple), vice-president of the committee of Council on education. He was also chosen secretary to the royal commission for rebuilding the National Gallery. He travelled much with his friends, was a member of the Alpine club, an enthusiast for Italy, and a student of Dante.

Shortly after a tour taken in the East (1857–1858), he was ordained to the curacy of Great St. Mary's, Cambridge. But immediately afterwards the Harrow head-mastership fell vacant, and Butler was elected at the age of twenty-six (1859). He had great obstacles to overcome—an old-fashioned set of masters (with exceptions, notably Brooke Foss Westcott, afterwards bishop of Durham), some rooted prejudices, and the fact that he followed Vaughan, who had concealed an iron hand in a velvet glove. But gradually he prevailed, through his tact and firmness, through his public spirit and devotion to Harrow both in work and games, through his understanding of boys and men, his winning manners, generosity, and sense of humour. Vaughan had brought stimulus to Harrow: Butler added atmosphere. His reign of twenty-six years proved him a sympathetic head master. He recognized modern needs, but in their sanest perspective; and he reconciled the inspirations of the past to the aspirations of the hour. As brother-in-law of Sir Francis Galton [q.v.] he kept in touch with science and gave it a formal place in the curriculum, while he insisted that a 'modern school' should be really efficient. In music he welcomed and recognized (1863) John Farmer [q.v.], and thus arose a cycle of Harrow school songs, of which Edward E. Bowen [q.v.] was chief librettist. Among other masters whom he gathered round him were Reginald Bosworth Smith [q.v.] and Frederick William Farrar [q.v.], and throughout he kept touch with the greater world and with friends such as Tennyson, Matthew Arnold, Charles Kingsley, and Ruskin. His anniversaries of heroes and heroism created a spell of tradition, and he seldom lost sight of an old pupil. Anglo-Indian associations attracted him also through his first marriage (1861) with Georgina Isabella Elliot, granddaughter of Hugh Elliot [q.v.], the diplomatist.

Butler was anything but a pedagogue, yet neither was he the cruel humanitarian who spares the rod: honest stupidity never incurred his contempt; his main defect, perhaps, was an over-sensitive refinement. His verses, grave or gay, his broadminded sermons, exerted a real influence, and he was one of the best after-dinner speakers of his day. As a writer of Latin verse his facility was extraordinary. Of Harrow he made a miniature Parnassus. All his talents were dedicated to the school, and he presided brilliantly over its tercentenary celebrations (1871). In 1885, two years after his first wife's death, he was appointed dean of Gloucester, and ceased to direct, though never to influence, the destinies of the school; in 1901 he was elected a governor by the masters.

In 1886 Butler accepted the mastership of Trinity College, Cambridge. There his successes were repeated. His affection for the college was deep, and his personal qualities quickly won recognition. His hospitalities became a tradition. The annual reunions of old Trinity men were largely due to his initiative. Already, as a young graduate, and in the spirit of Frederick Denison Maurice [q.v.], he had co-operated in a short-lived experiment of classes for working-men. This interest he had never lost; it was now pursued in manifold activities. In other enterprises he was recognized both by the university and by the town as a natural leader, and he became a real link between religious bodies of various views and different denominations. He was vice-chancellor of the university for the years 1889–1890. On his eightieth birthday the fellows of his college presented him with an address of warm appreciation.

Butler married as his second wife in

1888 Agnata Frances, the daughter of Sir James Ramsay, of Bamff, baronet. She was placed by the examiners above the senior classic at Cambridge in 1887. By his two marriages Butler had five sons and three daughters.

Among Butler's chief publications are his volumes of school and university sermons (1861, 1866, 1898, 1899), *Ten Great and Good Men* (1909), *Chatham as an Orator* (Romanes lecture, 1912), *Some Leisure Hours of a Long Life* (1914). He died at Cambridge 14 January 1918.

There is a portrait of Butler by Sir Hubert von Herkomer at Harrow, and another by Sir William Orpen at Trinity College, Cambridge.

[E. Graham, *The Harrow Life of Henry Montagu Butler, D.D.*, 1920 ; J. R. M. Butler, *Henry Montagu Butler : Master of Trinity College, Cambridge, 1886–1918,* 1925 ; *The Tercentenary of Harrow School,* 1871 ; P. M. Thornton, *Harrow School,* 1885 ; Hallam, Lord Tennyson, *Tennyson and his Friends,* 1911 ; notices in the *Lives* of Archbishop Benson, 1899, Bishop Westcott, 1903, Dean Farrar, 1904, and Sir R. C. Jebb, 1907 ; in the *Memoir* of H. Sidgwick, 1906 ; and in the *Collections and Recollections* of G. W. E. Russell, 1898 ; private information ; personal knowledge.] W. S. S.

BUTLIN, Sir HENRY TRENTHAM, first baronet (1845–1912), surgeon, the fourth son of the Rev. William Wright Butlin, vicar of Penponds, Cornwall, by his wife, Julia Crowther Trentham, was born at Camborne 24 October 1845. He was educated at home until, at the age of nineteen, he went to London and entered as a student at St. Bartholomew's Hospital, having decided, like his paternal grandfather, to enter the medical profession. After qualification (1867) he had the good fortune to obtain the post of house surgeon to (Sir) James Paget [q. v.], and like many other pupils of that great surgeon Butlin was profoundly influenced by his example and teaching. After he had held the usual junior offices, he was elected an assistant surgeon to the Hospital in 1881, in due course was appointed full surgeon in 1892, and in 1897 a lecturer in surgery at the Hospital school. Many of his pupils retain a grateful recollection of Butlin's clinical teaching, which was based upon a wide knowledge of morbid anatomy. He was never too busy to help a perplexed student. For twelve years he had charge of the throat department, and played a great part in its development, and in the advancement of British laryngology in general.

Besides St. Bartholomew's and its school, other professional bodies and movements claimed Butlin's services. He took much interest in the reconstructed university of London, and was the first dean of its faculty of medicine. He held in succession the offices of councillor, treasurer, and president of the British Medical Association, and in the last capacity he presided over the annual meeting held in London in 1910. After serving as councillor, he was elected in 1909 to the presidency of the Royal College of Surgeons, the blue ribbon of British surgery, but was compelled by failing health to resign that office shortly before his death. The university of Durham conferred on him the honorary degree of D.C.L., and that of Birmingham an honorary LL.D. He was created a baronet in 1911.

Whatever task Butlin undertook he carried out with all his energies and with conspicuous success. He had a very strong sense of duty, and his own interest or advancement were of no account as compared with the cause which he had at heart. His high standards and personal qualities won for him the respect and affection of those with whom he had to do ; so, in virtue of duty well done, there came to him, unsought, the highest places and honours in his profession. To those who knew him best it was a constant source of surprise that with a frame so slight and so little robust, he was able to carry on so many activities and with such efficiency.

Yet, in addition to his hospital and other public work, and the demands of a large practice as operating surgeon and laryngologist, Butlin always found time for scientific investigation, and all through his busy life he produced papers, addresses, and monographs, dealing, for the most part, with the favourite subjects of his study, namely the pathology of carcinoma and sarcoma. His last contribution thereto, which embodied highly original views, was read for him before the Royal College of Surgeons in the last months of his life. He was also the author of a well-known book upon *Diseases of the Tongue* (1885). An excellent lecturer, and an orator of the school of Paget, Butlin had taken trouble to train himself in public speaking, and could deliver an address, or a Hunterian oration, without notes, in admirable form, and with good emphasis.

Outside his profession, Butlin had many interests. He was a man of cultured taste, had a keen appreciation of art, was a good linguist, and liked to spend his holidays in travel in France, Spain, or Italy. He was fond of horses, and riding and driving were among his favourite recreations. He died in London 24 January 1912.

Butlin married in 1873 Annie Tipping, daughter of Henry Balderson, merchant, of Hemel Hempstead, and to his wife's helpful co-operation he liked to attribute much of his success in life. They had two daughters and a son who, succeeding his father as second baronet, joined the army whilst an undergraduate at Trinity College, Cambridge, and was killed in action in the European War in 1916.

[Obituary notice by C. B. Lockwood in St. Bartholomew's Hospital *Report*, vol. xlviii, 1912; *Lancet*, 1912, vol. i, p. 331; *British Medical Journal*, 1912, vol. i, p. 276; private information; personal knowledge.]

A. E. G.

BUTTERWORTH, GEORGE SAINTON KAYE (1885–1916), composer, was born 12 July 1885 at 16 Westbourne Square, London. He was the only child of (Sir) Alexander Kaye Butterworth, solicitor and subsequently general manager of the North Eastern Railway Company, by his wife, Julia Marguerite, daughter of George Wigan, M.D., of Portishead, Somerset. John Kaye, bishop of Lincoln [q. v.], was his great-grandfather, and John and Joseph Butterworth [q. v.] were ancestors in the direct male line. His first school was at Aysgarth, Yorkshire, whence he entered Eton as a king's scholar in 1899. He took part with credit in the intellectual, social, and athletic life of the school: music he studied with T. F. Dunhill, as well as with Christian G. Padel in York. From 1904 to 1908 he was in residence at Trinity College, Oxford; he took a third class in the honour school of *literae humaniores*, and was a prominent figure in musical circles, holding the presidency of the University Musical Club during the period October 1906 to March 1907.

After leaving Oxford, having abandoned his original intention of adopting the bar as a profession, Butterworth acted for a short time as one of the musical critics of *The Times*; and in 1909 accepted a teaching post at Radley College. In 1910 he returned to London, and worked for a few months at the Royal College of Music, studying the organ with Sir Walter Parratt, the piano with Herbert Sharpe, and theory with Charles Wood. The greatest influence on his musical ideals was derived from an intimate friendship with Ralph Vaughan Williams, whom he had first met in his Oxford days. He enlisted on the outbreak of war in August 1914, and was subsequently given a commission in the Durham Light Infantry. He was killed in action at Pozières, in the first battle of the Somme, 5 August 1916. He had won the military cross in the previous month and was again recommended for it shortly before his death.

Butterworth was greatly attracted by English folk-music, and gave much time to research in this field; he was also a prominent worker for the English Folk-Dance Society, of which he was one of the founders. He collected and arranged an album of Sussex folk-songs; and, in conjunction with Cecil J. Sharp, published several books of country and morris dances. His original compositions, few in number but of very distinctive quality, include about twenty songs (more than half to words from A. E. Housman's *A Shropshire Lad*), a suite for strings, and four orchestral pieces, three of which are idylls partially based on folk-song material, and the fourth a rhapsody thematically connected with some of the *Shropshire Lad* songs. This rhapsody (first produced under Arthur Nikisch at the Leeds festival of 1913) is his masterpiece, combining singularly individual imaginativeness with great command of orchestral technique; moods at once simple and intense made special appeal to him, and he expressed them with a sensitive intimacy that gives his work a notable place in contemporary English music.

[*Memoir*, privately printed, 1918; private information; personal knowledge.] E. W.

BUXTON, Sir THOMAS FOWELL, third baronet (1837–1915), governor of South Australia, born 26 January 1837, was the eldest son of Sir Edward North Buxton, second baronet, by his wife, Catherine, second daughter of Samuel Gurney, of Upton, Essex. His grandfather, Sir Thomas Fowell Buxton [q.v.], was the friend of Sir James Mackintosh, William Wilberforce, and Zachary Macaulay, and succeeded Wilberforce as the leader of the anti-slavery movement. Buxton was educated at Harrow and at Trinity College, Cambridge, and in 1858 succeeded his father as third baronet. In 1865 he was returned to parliament in the liberal interest as one of the members for King's Lynn, and he represented that constituency until 1868. His subsequent attempts to enter parliament, in 1874 (Westminster), 1876, 1879 (North Norfolk), 1880 (West Essex), were unsuccessful. He had a multitude of social interests: the British and Foreign Anti-Slavery Society, of which he was elected president in 1899, the Volunteer movement, the welfare of African natives, the betterment of elementary schools, the Church Missionary Society, Missions to Seamen, and the Commons Preservation Society. He was closely associated with the movement begun in 1866 for saving Epping Forest, and was a generous contributor to the fund raised to enable a labourer named Willingale to contest the legality of enclosures at Loughton.

In 1895 Buxton was appointed governor of South Australia. The choice was a happy one. The colony owed its foundation very largely to the efforts of men like the Buxtons—the members of the South Australian Association in London. This association included many people who had some of the spirit of the later Fabian socialists and who planned to set up in a new land a model state which would not reproduce the social inequalities of older countries. Many of the early South Australian settlers were people who had given up good positions in the home country in pursuit of this ideal. Their influence persisted in after generations, and Buxton, as governor of the colony, found himself in a sympathetic atmosphere. He retired from the governorship on completing his term of office in 1898, and in 1899 was created G.C.M.G. in recognition of his services. He died at Cromer 28 October 1915.

Buxton married in 1862 Lady Victoria Noel (died 1916), youngest daughter of the first Earl of Gainsborough, and had five sons and five daughters. He was succeeded in the baronetcy by his eldest son, Thomas Fowell Victor (1865–1919).

[G. W. E. Russell, *Lady Victoria Buxton: a Memoir, with some account of her Husband*, 1919.] F. F.

BYWATER, INGRAM (1840–1914), Greek scholar, the only son of John Ingram Bywater, a clerk in the Customs, was born in London 27 June 1840. He was educated at University College School and King's College School, London, and at Queen's College, Oxford, where he matriculated as a scholar in 1858. In 1863 he was elected to an open fellowship at Exeter College.

As an undergraduate Bywater was the pupil of Jowett and Robinson Ellis, and the friend of Pater and Swinburne. As a young Fellow he became intimate with Mark Pattison and his accomplished wife; and this intimacy was influential in forming his tastes. The Pattisons were fond of foreign travel, and Bywater visited in their company many of the libraries and museums of Europe. Pattison was a collector of early printed books; and Bywater's regular Sunday visits to his lodgings were doubtless devoted to bibliography as well as to tobacco and desultory conversation. Pattison was also an uncompromising advocate of the claims of learning, who expressed with more truth than moderation the view that the atmosphere of Oxford was inimical to study: 'a Fellowship is the grave of learning'. Bywater's opinions were more moderate, and the expression of them more conciliatory; but he did not conceal his view that recognition and support were too grudgingly accorded to research at Oxford, and that the college tutorial system in particular left too little leisure, and too little initiative, either to the student or to his teachers.

During the twenty years of Bywater's life as a tutor most of his time was given to teaching and to the studies for which he became famous. The publication in 1877 of his edition of the Fragments of Heraclitus won for him an assured position in the world of European scholarship, and he was invited by the Prussian Academy of Sciences to edit the works of Priscianus Lydus (published 1886). His relations with continental scholars, notably with Professor Jacob Bernays, of Bonn, were cordial and fruitful.

Charles Cannan [q.v.] used to say that though Bywater was doubtless an eminent Aristotelian, it was to be deplored that he had not become a bookseller, in which profession he must have been preeminent. Actually, he might well have become librarian of the Bodleian. The curators, of whom Pattison was one, and Coxe, the veteran librarian, were anxious to secure him; and he accepted, experimentally, the post of sub-librarian. He found, however, that the duties were too irksome. He was expected to read manuscripts as a matter of routine, and shrank from the prospect: 'those who care for MSS. *per se* are usually dull dogs'. He therefore resigned. Pattison deplored the decision; but Pattison had himself declared that 'the librarian who reads is lost'; Bywater was not prepared to be merely the cause of learning in others. He declined also the headship of Exeter College, offered to him in 1887.

In 1884 Bywater was appointed to a newly created readership in Greek. In 1885 he married. His wife was a member of the well-known Devonshire family of

Cornish, and the widow of Hans William Sotheby, formerly fellow of Exeter College. She was a lady of ample means and varied accomplishments, both literary and artistic. The Bywaters lived in term-time at a house on the edge of the University Parks, and in vacation at Mrs. Bywater's London house, 93 Onslow Square. This was Bywater's real home until his death; and here, with his wife's help, he gradually increased his remarkable collection of early classical books.

In 1893 Benjamin Jowett died, and Mr. Gladstone nominated Bywater, whose claims were supported by the powerful testimony of German scholars, to be regius professor of Greek in his place. The great popularizer and translator was thus succeeded by a scholar more purely scientific. Bywater occupied the chair until 1908. He continued to lecture, especially upon the *Republic* of Plato and the *Poetics* of Aristotle. Those who believe that the particularism of colleges, or the exigencies of examinations, prevent the University from making the most of its professors, have noted that a mere handful of undergraduates attended in the Schools the lectures which formerly had crowded the hall of Exeter College.

Mrs. Bywater died in 1908, and Bywater in the same year resigned his professorship and retired to his house in London. In 1909 he published the crowning labour of his Aristotelian studies, the monumental edition of the *Poetics*. Thereafter he undertook no large work of his own; but he continued to contribute occasional articles to the *Journal of Philology* (of which he had been an editor since 1879), and to help scholars in many fields by reading the proofs of their work. He died in London 17 December 1914. He had no children. His portrait by J. S. Sargent is in the National Portrait Gallery.

As an editor of Greek texts Bywater was certainly the first of the English scholars of his generation. He had a wide familiarity with manuscripts, an unrivalled knowledge of the history of classical learning and the editorial art, and a fine sense of what he liked to call the *Sprachgebrauch*. To these he added untiring industry, and a keen insight into the logical sequence of his author's thought. It has been objected to his interpretations of Aristotle, that he was too much a grammarian and too little a philosopher; but this apparent limitation was due not to narrowness but to a considered scepticism. In the preface to the *Poetics* he reminds us 'that the very idea of a Theory of Art is modern, and that our present use of this term "Art" does not go further back than the age of Winckelmann and Goethe'. This was with oblique reference to the work on the *Poetics* of Samuel Henry Butcher [q.v.], much of which Bywater regarded as irrelevant. In private he was more outspoken: 'You must not expect from me anything about Fine Art, for I don't think Aristotle said anything about it.'

The best judges, in estimating the value of Bywater's published work, have rightly laid stress on the perfection of its form. They have pointed to the laborious accuracy of his indexes, and to the fine judgement which by a silent change in the punctuation made an obscure passage plain. But his editions of Heraclitus and Aristotle, and even the ampler commentary on the *Poetics*, reflect one side only of his vast learning and his catholic humanism. His profound veneration for the genius of Aristotle was untinged by superstition. His statement to a newspaper interviewer was characteristic: 'My chief work has been on Aristotle, a philosopher who influences people to this day without their knowing it. . . . It is astonishing how profound in many ways was Aristotle's knowledge of science. . . . In everything that relates to animal life he is extremely good.' And he was heard to quote with approval a saying of H. W. Chandler, that 'the first half-dozen chapters of any book of Aristotle are really very well done'.

Much of his best work was anonymous, and hardly known except to those who benefited by it. He was a delegate of the University Press from 1879 until his death, and few publishers can have been so assiduous in reading the manuscript, or the proofs, of solid books. His immense bibliographical knowledge and his great practical wisdom were enough in themselves to assure him power and usefulness as a learned publisher; but on very many enterprises of scholarship he was not content merely to advise or to decide. He read with care the proofs of the long series of Oxford Classical Texts, of which he and Charles Cannan were the promoters, and his influence and example guided the critical methods of the editors. To the *Oxford English Dictionary* he contributed much that would otherwise hardly have been found. 'Murray,' he said, 'asked me for an early instance of *poetria* ('poetry'), and when I tell you that I found it at last in a seventh-century scholium to the Epistles of Horace, you may imagine that it took me some time; but I am sometimes lucky on Sundays.'

Bywater was president of the Oxford Aristotelian Society from its inception in the early 'eighties until his leaving Oxford in 1908. The society met in his rooms weekly during term, and it is stated that in twenty-five years he did not miss half a dozen meetings. The procedure was to construe and discuss, chapter by chapter, one of the more important writings of the Philosopher. The knowledge and the methods which the society inculcated in its members had a far-reaching influence upon philosophical studies in Oxford.

In University politics Bywater was a 'liberal' and a reformer. To national and international affairs his attitude was sceptical; his prejudices were conservative—'the vulgar radicalism of my youth' was his own phrase—but he had no illusions. He had learned much from the Germans, and had done much to introduce German scientific methods into English scholarship; but in later years he recognized and deplored the growing chauvinism which prevented even the best of the Germans from admitting that they could learn anything from an English book.

Bywater was a prince of bibliophiles; for there was nothing about a book that he did not know, and no kind of value that he did not appraise. For this reason the collection which he bequeathed to the Bodleian Library, and which there bears his name, is much more than a collection of rare and beautiful books. It is, as he himself wrote, 'a conspectus in its limited way of the literature of learning from the age of Bessarion to that of the Ἐπίγονοι of Scaliger and Casaubon'; and it is also a real part of the work of a great humanist. In his London home, surrounded by these books, Bywater was most himself. 'It was there,' writes one of the most devoted of his younger friends, 'that he was a great teacher. It was not merely that he was a master of his subject—and of one's own; but one felt powerfully the stimulus of a temperament from which what may be called the casual impurities of intellectual life—pedantry, hurry, irrelevance, pretentiousness, cleverness—had been purged away.'

[Memoir by W. W. Jackson, 1917, reissued with addenda, 1919 (to the bibliography add the inaugural lecture of 1894, published 1919); personal knowledge.] R. W. C.

CADOGAN, GEORGE HENRY, fifth Earl Cadogan (1840–1915), statesman, was born at Durham 9 May 1840. He was the eldest son of Henry Charles, the fourth Earl, by his wife, Mary, daughter of Gerald Valerian Wellesley, prebendary of Durham and brother of the first Duke of Wellington. He was educated at Eton and at Christ Church, Oxford, and as a young man accompanied the Prince of Wales on various tours at home and abroad. At the general election of 1868, as Viscount Chelsea, he stood unsuccessfully for the borough of Bury, in the conservative interest. He was elected for Bath in 1873, but in the same year went to the House of Lords in consequence of his father's death. Disraeli made him under-secretary of state for war in 1875, and under-secretary for the Colonies in 1878. During the second Salisbury administration (1886–1892) he was lord privy seal, and responsible for Irish business in the House of Lords. In the session of 1887 he introduced the Irish Land Act of that year, and in April he joined the Cabinet. He was at this time the trusted adviser of Queen Victoria in regard to her domestic affairs. For his political and other services he received the Garter in July 1891.

When the third Salisbury administration was formed (June 1895) Lord Cadogan became lord-lieutenant of Ireland with a seat in the Cabinet. He was warmly interested in Mr. Gerald Balfour's Land Act of 1896, and pressed the Treasury until he obtained more liberal terms of purchase for Irish tenants than that department was at first inclined to allow. Afterwards he turned to the subject of Irish education. He appointed commissions to investigate intermediate education (1899) and university education (1901); and he sponsored the Act of 1899 which created a new department of agriculture, industries, and technical instruction for Ireland. He dealt quietly but firmly with the agitations which were stimulated in Ireland by the South African War. He was accused of weakness by *The Times* newspaper (1902), which drew an unfavourable and unfair contrast between his tendencies and those of the chief secretary, Mr. George Wyndham [q.v.], who had succeeded Mr. Gerald Balfour in 1900. But Lord Cadogan enjoyed the full confidence of Lord Salisbury, by whom he was twice dissuaded from resigning. Though he was in favour of pacifying agrarian discontent by the concessions embodied in the Wyndham Land Bill of 1902, he consistently urged the Cabinet to proclaim disaffected areas and to proceed against seditious newspapers. He resigned in July 1902, at the same time as Lord Salisbury, and retired into private life.

Lord Cadogan was honourably distinguished for his interest in the welfare of the population of Chelsea, where, as lord of the manor, he held a large estate. In conjunction with Lord Iveagh he spent enormous sums on model dwellings for workmen and on other schemes of social betterment. In 1900 he was elected as the first mayor of Chelsea.

He married twice: first, in 1865 Lady Beatrix Jane Craven (died 1907), daughter of the second Earl of Craven; and secondly in 1911 his cousin, Countess Adèle Palagi, granddaughter of Sir George Cadogan, brother of the fourth Earl. By his first wife he had six sons and two daughters. He died in London 6 March 1915.

[Private information.] H. W. C. D.

CALDERON, GEORGE (1868–1915), dramatist, was born in London 2 December 1868, the fifth son of the painter Philip H. Calderon, R.A. [q.v.]. He was educated at Rugby and Trinity College, Oxford. He was called to the bar in 1894, but turned to literature and journalism for support. He spent the years 1895–1897 at St. Petersburg, whence he returned with a profound knowledge of Russian and a lasting bent towards Slavonic studies. In 1900 he married Katharine, widow of his college friend, Archibald Ripley, and daughter of John Hamilton, of Brown-hall, county Donegal. He lived thenceforward at Hampstead. They had no children. From 1900 to 1903 he held a post on the library staff of the British Museum. His literary work, at first mainly critical, included two stories in a vein of ironic extravaganza, *Downy V. Green* (1902) and *Dwala* (1904). His first play, *The Fountain*, was produced by the Stage Society in 1909; it was followed by *The Little Stone House* (1911), *Revolt* (1912), and a few shorter pieces. In 1906 he spent some months in the South Seas, the result of which was a long-pondered volume of impressions, *Tahiti*. This, with two volumes of his collected plays, was published (1921–1922) after his death. Among these plays, in strong contrast with the rest, is a tragedy in blank verse, *Cromwell: Mall o' Monks*.

Calderon's gift as a dramatist, though he did not live to develop it fully, was made up of much fertility in ideas, a quick eye for modern character, and a remarkable command of vivid and expressive dialogue—to which should be added a sense of romantic beauty which was occasionally allowed to appear with penetrating effect. His plays were carefully designed for the conditions of the stage, and it was perhaps an accident that none of them had a popular success. But his work was always to some extent hampered by his great versatility. He was primarily a man of letters; but he might equally have been, he largely was, a scholar, a publicist, an adventurer. He gave much time and labour to a study of Slavonic dialects and folk-lore, and to the light so thrown upon primitive religion; but the work which he planned on this subject was still fragmentary when he died. He was an exceptional linguist, often occupied by researches in many languages, and in the science of language itself. He also took an active and enterprising part in various public affairs, notably during the coal strike of 1912. Moreover, he possessed unusual talents as a musician, a draughtsman, and an actor, had he cared to cultivate them seriously. His keen delight in travel and his impressionability are admirably shown in his *Tahiti*. But his published work imperfectly represents a many-sided man, and one whose character was as rare and deep as his gifts were conspicuous.

On the outbreak of war in 1914 Calderon was determined, in spite of his age, to reach the fighting-line. He went to France as an interpreter, was wounded in the first battle of Ypres, and in May 1915 was sent, with a commission in the Oxfordshire and Buckinghamshire Light Infantry, to the Dardanelles, where he was attached to the King's Own Scottish Borderers. He was reported wounded and missing in the action of 4 June 1915, and in the absence of any further news was afterwards presumed killed on that date.

[Percy Lubbock, *George Calderon: a Sketch from Memory*, 1921; personal knowledge.] P. L.

CALLAGHAN, Sir GEORGE ASTLEY (1852–1920), admiral, was born in London 21 December 1852, the third son of Captain Frederic Marcus Callaghan, J.P., of Lotabeg, co. Cork, by his wife, Georgina Frances, daughter of Captain James Hodgson, of the East India Company's service. He entered the royal navy in January 1866 in H.M.S. *Britannia*, and was promoted sub-lieutenant in April 1872 and lieutenant in 1875. His first appointment as lieutenant was to the *Ruby*, East Indies station. During this commission one of the ship's boats capsized in the Irrawady, and Callaghan earned the commendation of the Admiralty by his gallant behaviour, which saved the lives of several of the crew. In 1880 he returned home in order to qualify in gunnery, and was afterwards on the staff of the port gunnery schools. In 1885 he was again appointed to the *Ruby*, this time as first and gunnery lieutenant on the South-East coast of America station. He was promoted to commander in 1887, and in 1888 was appointed to the *Bellerophon*, the flag-ship on the North American station, in which ship he returned home in 1892. In the same year he was given the command of the *Alacrity*, yacht of the commander-in-chief, China station, and he received his promotion to captain in 1894.

From now onward Callaghan's rise in the service was steady and rapid. He served for three years (1894–1897) as naval adviser to the inspector-general of fortifications at the War Office. In July 1897 he took command of the *Hermione*, at first in the Channel squadron and later on the China station, where he remained until 1901, having been given command of the *Endymion*, a first-class cruiser, in 1899. While he commanded the *Endymion* the Boxer rebellion broke out in 1900. Admiral Sir Edward Hobart Seymour was then commander-in-chief on the China station; and, on the decision of the powers to intervene, brigades were landed from various ships to endeavour to push through to the relief of the legations in Peking. This being found impracticable with the small force at his command, Admiral Seymour returned to Tientsin. In the following month a combined naval and military relief force was formed under Lieutenant-General Sir Alfred Gaselee [q.v.]. Callaghan was given the command of the British naval brigade which, after severe fighting and much hardship from the heat, succeeded in entering Peking in time to relieve the legations. For this service he was specially mentioned in dispatches and received the C.B. (1900).

After commanding the *Edgar* in manœuvres as senior officer of the cruisers, Callaghan was appointed to the *Caesar*, first-class battleship, on the Mediterranean station, at the time when Sir John (afterwards Baron) Fisher [q.v.] was commander-in-chief. He returned in 1903 to be captain of Portsmouth dockyard. This shore service lasted only one year, as, by his own request, he was sent again to sea so that his last year as captain should be spent in familiarizing himself with the most recent developments in the fleet. He commanded the *Prince of Wales* in the Mediterranean during 1904-1905 and was at this time also made aide-de-camp to King Edward VII.

In July 1905 Callaghan was promoted to rear-admiral, and he hoisted his flag in H.M.S. *Illustrious* as rear-admiral in the Channel fleet in 1906. From this time he was in uninterrupted command afloat for eight years. The years immediately preceding the European War were a time of strenuous activity in the navy. Lord Fisher was urging and carrying out his reforms and redistributions, shifting the centre of power from the Mediterranean, and forming fresh divisions for defence and attack in home waters. In these schemes Callaghan was to bear an important part from the outset. In 1907 he was given the command of the new fifth cruiser squadron, the 'tip of the spear' as it was designated, hoisting his flag in the *Leviathan*, and afterwards transferring it to the newly built *Shannon*. Having spent eighteen very strenuous months in bringing his squadron up to a high pitch of efficiency, Callaghan hoisted his flag in the *Duncan* as second in command of the Mediterranean station (1908). During this command he received the K.C.V.O. (1909) and was also made grand officer of the Crown of Italy for his services in connexion with the Messina earthquake. He became vice-admiral in 1910 and, returning to home waters, immediately hoisted his flag in the *King Edward VII*, commanding the second division of the home fleet. The next year he was made commander-in-chief, home fleets, with the acting rank of admiral. This great command, of the largest naval fighting force which, up to that time, had ever acted under one flag, he held during the three years of incessant preparation prior to war, his appointment being extended in December 1913 for the further period of one year. His fleet flagships were successively *Neptune*, *Hercules*, and *Iron Duke*. He was awarded the G.C.V.O. after the inspection of the fleet by King George V at Weymouth in 1912, and the grand cordon of the legion of honour on President Poincaré's official visit to the fleet in 1913.

In July 1914 Callaghan was in command of the mobilized naval forces at Portsmouth on the occasion of another royal inspection, when 460 ships assembled under his flag. This great fleet was about to disperse when the European situation became critical. Callaghan was summoned to the Admiralty, the fleet meanwhile leaving for Scapa Flow. At the Admiralty the disposition of the fleet and the plan of operations in the event of war were discussed with him. Sir John Rushworth (afterwards Earl) Jellicoe had already been appointed to succeed Callaghan in December when the latter's extension of command would be fulfilled, and Callaghan welcomed the intimation that Sir John should immediately act as his second in command. But, after Callaghan had gone north, Mr. Winston Churchill and Prince Louis of Battenberg [q.v.], the first sea lord, came to the conclusion that, if war broke out, Jellicoe should at once take over the supreme command; they were doubtful if Callaghan's physical strength would be equal to the immense strain. Sir John Jellicoe on leaving London for the fleet at Scapa Flow was given sealed instructions directing him to take over the command. Soon after midnight on 3–4 August, when war was certain, telegrams were sent to both admirals informing them of the decision and instructing Callaghan to haul down his flag and hand over the command. Much sympathy was felt throughout the fleet for Callaghan, and protests were made by all the principal admirals who had served under him, and by Sir John Jellicoe himself. It was a bitter disappointment to Callaghan not to command in war the fleet to which he had devoted his energies and abilities for so long, and he left amid the regret of all those under his command. Although it was not his fortune to wield the weapon which he had brought to so fine an edge, he could at least lay it down knowing it was ready and in place to meet, with a heavy reckoning, anything which the enemy could attempt. Callaghan was immediately appointed for special service at the Admiralty and also first and principal naval aide-de-camp to the King. This was followed on 1 January 1915 by his appointment as commander-in-chief at the Nore, a post which he held until March 1918. He received the G.C.B. in 1916, and in April 1917 he was promoted to the rank of admiral of the fleet and flew his flag as such for one year, a unique record in the annals of naval history.

When Callaghan hauled down his flag in March 1918 he had completed fifty-two years' service, of which only eleven in all had been spent in shore billets; while for the last twelve years he had kept his flag flying continuously, except for the few months at the beginning of the War. He was thus essentially and primarily a seaman, with a remarkable knowledge, learnt by continual and exceptional experience, of tactics, of gunnery, and of cruiser and destroyer operations. His fairness, judgement, common sense, equable temperament, modesty, and charm of manner, apart from his great fleet knowledge, rendered him a fine commander-in-chief. His successor in command of the grand fleet, Sir John Jellicoe, on many public occasions testified handsomely to the high state of efficiency in which he found the fleet when Callaghan was so abruptly relieved by him. Callaghan's naval service ended, he was in 1919 appointed by the King Bath King of Arms, and he officiated at the historic chapter of the Order of the Bath held in Westminster Abbey in the spring of 1920.

He died in London 23 November 1920 at the age of sixty-eight, and was accorded a public funeral in Westminster Abbey. He married in 1876 Edith Saumarez, daughter of the Rev. Frederick Grosvenor, rector of Dunkerton, Bath, and had one son and three daughters.

[Admiralty records; Sir Julian S. Corbett, (Official) *History of the Great War. Naval Operations*, vol. i, 1920.] V. W. B.

CAMPBELL, JOHN DOUGLAS SUTHERLAND, ninth Duke of Argyll (1845–1914), governor-general of Canada, was the eldest son of George Douglas, the eighth Duke, by his wife, Lady Elizabeth Georgiana Sutherland Leveson-Gower, eldest daughter of the second Duke of Sutherland. He was born at Stafford House, London, 6 August 1845, and educated at the Edinburgh Academy, Eton, St. Andrews, and Trinity College, Cambridge. As Marquess of Lorne he entered parliament in 1868, the liberal member for Argyllshire, and for three years was private secretary to his father, then secretary of state for India. In 1871 he married Princess Louise, fourth daughter of Queen Victoria. In 1878 he was appointed governor-general of Canada. His period of office was uneventful, his chief constitutional problem arising soon after his arrival in Canada. Mr. Luc Letellier, lieutenant-governor of Quebec, had dismissed a provincial conservative government on grounds thought inadequate by the Dominion conservative ministry, and Sir John Macdonald, the prime minister, recommended Letellier's removal. Lord Lorne showed reluctance, and on Macdonald's advice consulted the Colonial Office; he was instructed to act on the opinion of his constitutional advisers. Relations between the governor and prime minister were cordial, Macdonald writing, 'Lord Lorne is a right good fellow, and a good Canadian'. He was conscientious, interested in the country and a fair speaker, but did not show a strong personality.

In 1883 Lord Lorne returned to England, contested Hampstead unsuccessfully at the next general election, and followed his father out of the liberal party on the question of Home Rule. His intimacy with the court and his friendship with Macdonald in Canada had prepared the way for such a change. In 1892 he contested an election at Bradford; in 1895 he became unionist member for South Manchester. He succeeded to the dukedom of Argyll in April 1900. In April 1914 he developed double pneumonia while in the Isle of Wight, and died on 2 May, leaving no issue. He was succeeded in the title by his nephew, Niall Diarmid Campbell, grandson of the eighth Duke.

The Duke of Argyll's interests were less of a political than of a dilettante literary character. He seldom spoke in parliament, and never held ministerial office. Possibly his relation with the Crown made a party career difficult. After 1883 he continued to take an interest in Canadian affairs, especially in immigration, and wrote several books about Canada and a pamphlet advocating imperial federation. He also published fiction, volumes of verse, a life of Palmerston, and two volumes of reminiscences.

[Writings, especially *Passages from the Past*, 1907; S. Lee, *Queen Victoria*, 1902: J. S. Willison, *Sir Wilfrid Laurier and the Liberal Party*, 1903; O. D. Skelton, *Life and Times of Sir A. T. Galt*, 1920; J. Pope, *Memoirs of Sir John Macdonald*, 1894, and *Correspondence of Sir John Macdonald*, 1921. Portrait, *Royal Academy Pictures*, 1906.]

E. M. W-G.

CANNAN, CHARLES (1858–1919), scholar and university publisher, was born 2 August 1858, the elder son of David Alexander Cannan, a native of Kirkcudbrightshire, by his wife, Jane Dorothea Claude, of Huguenot descent. He was educated at Clifton College, while John Percival [q.v.] was head master, and at Corpus Christi College, Oxford, of which he was a scholar. In 1884 he was elected fellow of Trinity College, where Percival had become president in 1878. Cannan became classical tutor and dean in 1884, and junior bursar in 1887. At Trinity he quickly made his mark as an original and unconventional tutor and lecturer—his lectures on 'Mods.' logic were especially remembered—and his influence was felt in the social and athletic no less than in the intellectual life of the college. He was an unusual dean. His doctrine was that discipline should be enforced without the imposition of penalties; and once, when driven to 'gate' an undergraduate, he declared that this was failure, and that he ought to resign. To not a few of his pupils Cannan communicated something of his interest in the Aristotelian writings, the study of which remained for some forty years the chief occupation of his leisure. In his youth he read a good deal in poetry and polite literature; his share in the *Oxford Book of English Verse* has been recorded by its compiler. But later his reading, when dictated by choice, was commonly either a newspaper or Aristotle. He read the Philosopher not at a table with notebooks and commentaries, but in an arm-chair. It was usually the *Metaphysics* or the *Logic*, which he explored in the historical spirit, seeking to trace the development of doctrine. This was to have been the subject of the doubtless remarkable book which he intended, but did not live, to write. His talent for writing, as for organization, first showed itself in journalism.

In 1895 Cannan was elected a delegate of the University Press; and the direction of his career was determined when in 1898 the delegates appointed him their secretary in succession to Philip Lyttelton Gell. He held the office for over twenty years, and died in harness. He devoted to the Press, or to objects connected with it, almost the whole of his energies; and he will be remembered as an outstanding figure in the long history of that institution. During his secretaryship Cannan promoted the great growth in the volume of the Press's business, in the variety of its publications, and in the number of its branches overseas. By nature conservative and cautious, he seldom seemed to initiate far-reaching changes of policy. He conceived of the Press as an institution possessing inherited characters and a natural growth; and of himself as fostering its growth rather than as giving it new directions. In effect, however, his dominant personality exercised a profound influence, both directly and through the subordinates whom he chose and trained. His method of instruction may be illustrated from the recollections of one of his assistants. This very young man paid his first visit to the Press, to be looked at; and found the secretary in conversation with a gentleman who—as appeared—had undertaken something which he had failed to perform. When he had escaped, Cannan turned to his second visitor, and regarded him, without speech. The young man presently made bold to inquire what kind of work, in the event of appointment, he should be expected to do. 'Oh, can't you see? You heard me talking to that fellow.'

Cannan's greatest reform was in the London office of the Press, where the distribution of Oxford books, and in particular the management of the business in bibles and prayer books, had been conducted with great skill by Mr. Henry Frowde. Cannan saw that the time had come for this side of the business to be directed by Oxford men. The changes which he was able to effect, and especially the appointment in 1913 of Mr. Humphrey Milford as publisher to the university (Mr. Frowde having retired at an advanced age), made the London office what it had never been, a real department of the university. He did much also to broaden the activities of the Press in the production of books, notably in the fields of modern politics and imperial history. He was not a believer in the promotion of research by endowment; but he spared no pains to help and encourage researchers of proved competence and to facilitate the publication of their work.

In politics Cannan was a conservative and a strong imperialist; but he was not a party man. He was interested in local affairs, and was for a time a member of the Oxford city council. He served on a number of university boards, where his opinion was valued on financial questions. He made few public appearances, and seldom left Oxford except to visit Switzerland or other mountainous districts; he was an ardent climber.

Cannan had a passion for anonymity His one book—*Selecta ex Organo Aristotelio Capitula* (1897)—was anonymous. He contrived to conceal his share, which was great, in making university appointments. He would not allow his name to appear in the prefaces of books in which he had a hand, and in which his characteristic style, smooth yet incisive, may sometimes be detected. His manner was formidable; his tone was dry, and even cynical; his last weapon, which he used ruthlessly, was silence; his enthusiasms were unspoken; he had a mean opinion of human intelligence in general, and not a very high one of human probity. This is, perhaps, not the description of a great man, or of a lovable one; yet Cannan was both. Those who knew him well became aware that they had to do with a man of great intellectual power and subtlety; of rare force of will; of unselfish devotion to the things he loved; and of a singularly tender heart.

Cannan married in 1891 Mary Wedderburn, daughter of A. Wedderburn Maxwell, of Glenlair, Kircudbrightshire, by whom he had three daughters. He died at Oxford 15 December 1919. His portrait was never painted; but photographs give a good impression of his piercing glance and of his salient feature, the beautifully modelled nose.

[*The Times*, 16 December 1919; articles in the *Oxford Magazine* by A. Quiller Couch and W. A. R[aleigh], January and March, 1920; *Oxford and the War* (by G. S. Gordon) in *The Times Literary Supplement*, 24 February 1921; personal knowledge.]

R. W. C.

CAPES, WILLIAM WOLFE (1834–1914), historical scholar, the third son of Joseph Capes, who had a post at the Royal Mint and was also a bookseller in Paternoster Row, London, by his wife, Anne, daughter of Joseph Wolfe, of Reading, was born in London 1 January 1834 in the parish of St. Michael le Querne, probably in Paternoster Row. He was admitted to St. Paul's School, London, 31 January 1843, under Herbert Kynaston [q.v.], then high master. He used daily to walk to school from Norwood, where his parents then resided. At sixteen he began his practice of foreign travel, which he continued throughout his life, by an expedition, mainly on foot, extending from Holland as far as Rome. In 1852 he proceeded to Oxford, having been elected to a Michel exhibition at Queen's College. His chief instructors there were George Henry Sacheverell Johnson, afterwards dean of Wells, and William Thomson, afterwards archbishop of York. Under their influence admission to the foundation of the college was then being thrown open, and in June 1854 Capes, with Antony Benn Falcon and John Percival, afterwards bishop of Hereford, was elected to a taberdarship of the college, an emolument previously reserved to natives of Cumberland and Westmorland. He had before this, in 1853, obtained first classes at moderations in classics and mathematics, and in the final honour schools in 1855 he obtained a first class in classics and a second class in mathematics. He was elected fellow of Queen's College 11 December 1856.

As an undergraduate Capes does not seem to have taken any part in the games then played in Oxford, but after graduation he rowed in the college torpid, and before he left Oxford he had bought a riding-horse. On election to his fellowship he was at once appointed tutor, and soon found himself responsible for the whole of the teaching in the college for the honour school of *literae humaniores*. He was very successful. Of a number of distinguished pupils those who became eminent were, besides Percival, Ingram Bywater, Walter Horatio Pater, and Archibald Henry Sayce. Having determined to take holy orders he was ordained in 1865, and served a while as curate at Abbot's Anne, near Andover. He returned to college work, was junior proctor in 1865–1866, and examiner in *literae humaniores* 1867–1869, and again 1873–1875 and 1878–1879. In 1869 he was presented by his college to the rectory of Bramshott, Hampshire, and in 1870 he married Mary (died 1907), daughter of John Leadbeater, of Blackburn. He held the rectory for thirty-two years. But Oxford could not spare him. The parish was an extensive agricultural one and needed the multiplication of services on Sunday. At one time there were as many as fourteen gatherings on a Sunday for teaching and worship, and the services of his wife, his curate, the schoolmasters, and other laymen were pressed into the work. But on week-days the calls of duty were comparatively few, and Capes accordingly gave three or four days in the middle of each week of term to Oxford, and held from 1870 to 1887 the university readership of ancient history. In 1876 he was elected fellow of Hertford College, and he held that fellowship with a tutorship from 1876 to 1886.

To this period of his life belong Capes's earliest publications: *The Early Roman Empire* (1874), *The Age of the Antonines* (1877, both in a series of Epochs of Ancient History), *University Life in Ancient Athens* (1877), a brilliant course of lectures based on the Greek inscriptions, and *Stoicism* (1883). The extension and variation at this time of the 'books' offered in the university honours courses induced him to prepare some editions of the texts newly introduced. An edition of Livy, books xxi, xxii (1880), was followed by one of Sallust (1884) and the part of Polybius containing the history of the Achaean League (1888). Capes was select preacher to the university 1873–1874, rural dean of Petersfield, and honorary canon of Winchester from 1894 to 1903. During his last days at Bramshott he contributed to Stephens's and Hunt's *History of the English Church* the volume covering the fourteenth and fifteenth centuries, which appeared in 1900.

Capes resigned the rectory of Bramshott in 1901 and settled for a while at Addington, Kent. While there he wrote *Rural Life in Hampshire*, an account of the neighbourhood of Bramshott, published in 1903. In that year he was collated to a residentiary canonry in Hereford Cathedral, and began a fresh course of historical work on the documents of the chapter and see. In 1908 he published the *Charters and Records of Hereford Cathedral* with a long introduction containing a valuable account of the constitution of a cathedral of the old foundation. Before this, acting on a suggestion of Prebendary J. R. Burton, rector of Bitterley, he had founded the Cantelupe Society, which succeeded in a few years in printing all the pre-Reformation registers of the bishops of Hereford. Six of these he himself edited, and he took an active interest in the work of his colleagues. He also set to work upon arranging and cataloguing the valuable cathedral library, but this he had not succeeded in finishing at his death, 31 October 1914. He and his wife are both buried at Bramshott. They had no children.

[R. B. Gardiner, *Registers of St. Paul's School*; Bishop Percival, *A Memoir of Canon Capes*, 1916; private information; personal knowledge.] J. R. M.

CAPPER, Sir THOMPSON (1863–1915), major-general, the third son of William Copeland Capper, Bengal civil service, by his wife, Sarah, daughter of W. T. Copeland, M.P., owner of the Copeland potteries, was born at Lucknow 20 October 1863. He was gazetted lieutenant in the East Lancashire regiment in 1882, and was promoted captain in 1891. He saw his first war service in Chitral in 1895, and distinguished himself in the Sudan campaigns of 1898–1899, when serving with the Egyptian army; he was present at the battles of the Atbara and Omdurman and received a brevet majority.

In the South African War he served on the staff of the Natal army at the relief of Ladysmith (January–February 1900) and in the subsequent operations in northern Natal and in the south-eastern Transvaal. In 1901–2 he was employed in Cape Colony, commanding a mobile column with conspicuous success. For his services in South Africa he received the D.S.O., was mentioned in dispatches four times, and promoted to brevet lieutenant-colonel, receiving substantive rank in November 1900.

Capper's next important employment was as professor at the Staff College, where his teaching made such a mark that he was selected to be the first commandant of the Indian Staff College at Quetta. In 1910 he received the C.B., and from 1911 to 1914 he commanded the 13th infantry brigade at Dublin. As a trainer of troops he made a great impression on those who served in his brigade, and they profited greatly by his lucid, practical, and suggestive instruction. In 1914 he was promoted to major-general and appointed Inspector of Infantry.

Shortly after the outbreak of war in August 1914 Capper was appointed to command the 7th division, the first addition to the original six, which was mainly composed of units from South Africa and the Mediterranean. It was an improvised formation, staff and units were strangers to each other, though the proportion of serving soldiers to reservists was much higher than in the Expeditionary Force. The division was dispatched to Belgium at the beginning of October, being intended to relieve Antwerp; instead of which, after covering the Belgian retreat to the Yser, it took a leading part in the defence of Ypres against the German effort to reach the Channel ports, holding a line out of all proportion to its numbers and bearing the brunt of the earlier attacks. When, after nearly three weeks' fighting, it was relieved on 7 November, its 14,000 infantry had been reduced to 4,000, and if it had more than once lost ground it had re-formed its line and had beaten back repeated attacks by greatly superior forces. Of Capper's share in the division's splendid achievement it has been well said 'no one but Capper himself could, night after night, by the sheer force of his personality have reconstituted from the shattered fragments of battalions a fighting line that could last through to-morrow' (*The Times*, 1 October 1915).

Capper, whose services at Ypres were rewarded by a K.C.M.G., retained command of the 7th division until April 1915 when he was accidentally wounded at some experiments with hand-grenades. In this period the division was in the line facing the Aubers Ridge, and took part in the battle of Neuve Chapelle (10–13 March). Capper was at home most of the summer, but recovered in time to resume command of his old division shortly before the battle of Loos (25 September). In this the 7th division captured its first objectives between Hulluch and the Hohenzollern redoubt, but lost too severely to achieve anything against the German second line position, and was itself heavily counter-attacked. Capper, who had gone forward to investigate the exact situation, was badly wounded, 26 September, and died next day. In him the army lost a commander of real achievement and promise, an original and inspiring teacher, a man of high standards and high attainments.

Capper married in 1908 Winifride Mary, eldest daughter of the Hon. Robert Joseph Gerard-Dicconson, of Wrightington Hall, near Wigan, who survived him. They had one son.

[Army Lists; '*The Times*' *History of the War in South Africa*, 1900–1909; J. E. Edmonds, (Official) *History of the Great War. Military Operations, France and Belgium*, 1914, vol. ii, 1925. C. T. A.

CARLISLE, COUNTESS OF (1845–1921), promoter of women's political rights and of temperance reform. [See HOWARD, ROSALIND FRANCES.]

CARNEGIE, ANDREW (1835–1919), manufacturer and philanthropist, the elder son of William Carnegie, a damask linen weaver of Dunfermline, by his wife, Margaret, daughter of Thomas Morrison, of the same town, was born at Dunfermline 25 November 1835. In the 'hungry forties' an unprecedented depression was experienced in the linen trade of Dunfermline, and in 1848 the Carnegie family emigrated to the United States of America, and took up residence in Allegheny city, Pennsylvania. At the age of thirteen Andrew Carnegie began work as a bobbin-boy in a cotton factory at a weekly wage of one dollar and twenty cents. Within a few months he had changed to a bobbin manufacturing establishment, where his duties included the firing of the furnace of a small engine in a cellar. Feeling like a 'bird in a cage' in the cellar, he applied for a post as a messenger boy in Pittsburg telegraph office (1850), and was appointed at a weekly wage of two and a half dollars. As he entered on his new duties Colonel James Anderson, the founder of free libraries in Western Pennsylvania, announced that he intended to open his private library of 4,000 volumes 'to working boys in Pittsburg'. As telegraph messengers did not 'actually work with their hands' it was proposed to exclude them. The youthful Carnegie wrote a letter to the *Pittsburg Dispatch* arguing that telegraph messengers were 'working boys', and so impressed was the colonel that he enlarged the classification. Every Saturday a new volume was obtained by Carnegie, and in after life, when he had become a great founder of free libraries, he declared that it was his own personal experience which led him to value a library beyond all other forms of beneficence.

In 1853 Carnegie was appointed clerk and telegraph operator to Thomas A. Scott, assistant superintendent of the Pennsylvania Railroad Company. Two years afterwards Scott asked his youthful clerk if he could find five hundred dollars to invest in the Adams Express stock. The dollars were raised by mortgaging a small cottage which the Carnegie family had acquired. The Adams Express investment was followed by a successful railway sleeping-car venture with T. T. Woodruff. Having been shown a model of a car by Woodruff, Carnegie divined that the invention was destined to become an 'important adjunct of railway travelling'. The Woodruff Company was ultimately absorbed by the famous Pullman Car Company. In 1859 Scott became vice-president of the railroad company, and appointed Carnegie superintendent of the western division of the line. On the outbreak of the Civil War, Carnegie accompanied Scott, then assistant secretary for war, to the front. During the Civil War iron reached 130 dollars a ton and, new rails being scarce, the railway systems of America were regarded as 'fast becoming dangerous'. Quick to grasp the situation, Carnegie organized a rail manufacturing company, and at the same time launched the Pittsburg Locomotive Works. Fires in connexion with railway wooden bridges led to the formation of the Keystone Iron Bridge Company. Wealth flowed in to Carnegie from all three concerns, and he and his colleagues found another profitable investment in the oil wells of Pennsylvania and Ohio.

A visit to England in 1867 convinced Carnegie that the Bessemer converter would revolutionize the iron industry, and, hurrying back, he formed a new combination and raised capital for the Edgar Thomson Steel Works, which were erected on a site of 1,200 acres near Pittsburg. By 1881 Carnegie was the foremost ironmaster in America, and the capital of the concerns controlled by Carnegie Brothers and Company was estimated at five million dollars. Of the total, Carnegie was credited with 2,737,977 dollars. By 1888 his wealth had increased sixty times over, and in 1899 when the various interests were vested in the Carnegie Steel Company, the profits were forty million dollars.

In 1900 Carnegie issued his book *The Gospel of Wealth* to emphasize a doctrine which he had proclaimed from many platforms that 'the man who dies rich dies disgraced'. He then decided to 'cease to struggle for more wealth' and to take up 'the more serious and difficult task of wise distribution'. The great Carnegie steel concern was accordingly sold to the United States Steel Corporation for the colossal sum of £89,000,000 (1901), and Carnegie retired from business the same year. Of this total, £60,000,000 represented Carnegie's share. Free from the cares of the steel company, Carnegie inaugurated his task of 'wise distribution' of surplus wealth by making a grant of four million dollars for the establishment of an accident and pension fund for the workmen who had 'contributed so greatly' to his success, and another of one million dollars for the maintenance of the libraries and other institutions which he had founded for his workers in and about Pittsburg.

Carnegie's first gift of a library had been made to his native city in 1882, and one of the conditions attached to acceptance was that the local authority should adopt the Free Libraries (Scotland) Act (1867), and provide site and maintenance. On the plea that, when a library is supported financially by a community, 'all taint of charity is dispelled', Carnegie imposed a similar condition in connexion with most of the libraries which he endowed. In glancing over a newspaper immediately after he had founded the pension fund for his old workers he read: 'The gods send thread for a web begun.' The words sank into his heart, and his first 'web' thereafter took the form of five and a quarter million dollars for sixty-eight branch libraries in New York city. Between the date of the opening of the Dunfermline library and the year 1919, Carnegie and (after 1911) the Carnegie Corporation of New York made gifts amounting approximately to 60,600,000 dollars in order to endow libraries in the United States, the British Isles, Canada, and other countries. Of this sum about twelve million dollars were devoted to the endowment of 660 libraries in the British Isles.

Carnegie also made, among others, the following benefactions:

In the United States	dollars
1896, The Carnegie Institute and Carnegie Library of Pittsburg	27,000,000
1902, The Carnegie Institute of Washington . . .	22,300,000
1904, The Carnegie Hero Fund Commission . . .	5,000,000

	dollars
1905, The Carnegie Foundation for the Advancement of Teaching . . .	29,250,000
1910, The Carnegie Endowment for International Peace .	10,000,000
1911, The Carnegie Corporation of New York . . .	125,000,000
In the British Isles	
1901, The Carnegie Trust for the Universities of Scotland .	10,000,000
1903, The Carnegie Dunfermline Trust	3,750,000
1908, The Carnegie Hero Fund Trust	1,250,000
1916, The Carnegie United Kingdom Trust . . .	10,000,000
In Europe	
1903, The Palace of Peace at the Hague	1,500,000
1909–1911, The Carnegie Hero Fund Commissions (France, Germany, Norway, Switzerland, the Netherlands, Sweden, Denmark, Belgium, Italy)	4,290,000

The 'hero' funds provide for the recognition and compensation of those who lose their lives or receive injuries in their efforts to serve or save their fellows; the objects of the Scottish Universities fund are the improvement and expansion of the four Scottish universities and the payment of the whole or part of the class fees of students of Scottish birth or extraction; the trust deed of the United Kingdom Trust directs that the income shall be applied for the well-being of the masses of the people of Great Britain and Ireland by such means as are embraced within the meaning of the word 'charitable'; the Foundation for the Advancement of Teaching embraces the Ten Million Dollar fund for pensions for the teachers of universities, colleges, and technical schools in the United States, Canada, and Newfoundland; the Institute of Washington was founded to 'encourage research and discovery, and the application of knowledge to the improvement of mankind'; while the Carnegie Corporation of New York was established to support and develop the institutions which Carnegie had founded. Carnegie had a great affection for his native city. His benefactions began with public baths; then came the free library, a technical school, new baths, the purchase of the romantic Glen of Pittencrieff, and the formation of the Carnegie Dunfermline Trust. Three-quarters of a million pounds were placed in the hands of the trust 'to bring into the lives of the toiling masses of Dunfermline more sweetness and light'.

Carnegie was installed as lord rector of St. Andrews University in 1902, and received the honorary degree of LL.D. He was also lord rector of Edinburgh University in 1906, and of Aberdeen University from 1912 to 1914. He could lay no claim to education in the scholastic sense of the term; but he showed a wonderful affinity with men of letters, and was on terms of close friendship with Gladstone, Herbert Spencer, Matthew Arnold, and especially with Viscount Morley of Blackburn. His association with these men quickened and strengthened his love for English literature, and, viewing things more from the point of view of culture than he had done in early life, he became less inclined to 'weigh up national wealth' in the language of commerce. A desire to live in romantic surroundings led him to purchase the estate of Skibo, of some 30,000 acres, in Sutherlandshire, where he built a mansion and delighted in maintaining the traditions of the Scottish Highland laird, his guests being led to meals by a piper.

Carnegie, who was a member of the Peace Society of Great Britain, became in 1907 the first president of the Peace Society of New York, and in 1913, when the palace of peace was opened at the Hague, he had visions of the establishment of an international court of justice. He thought Wilhelm II 'a man of destiny', and in 1912 had the distinction of presenting the Kaiser with 'an address of congratulation on his peaceful reign of twenty-five years'. Two years later, in the closing chapter of his *Autobiography*, Carnegie wrote: 'What a change! The world convulsed by war as never before. Men slaying each other like wild beasts.'

Carnegie died at Lenox, Massachusetts, 11 August 1919. He married in 1887 Louise, daughter of John W. Whitfield, of New York, by whom he had one daughter.

Carnegie wrote extensively, beginning with two books of travel, *An American Four-in-Hand in Britain* (1883) and *Round the World* (1884). These volumes were followed by *Triumphant Democracy* (1886), *The Gospel of Wealth* (1900), *The Empire of Business* (1902), *Life of James Watt* (1905), and *Problems of To-day* (1908).

A three-quarters length portrait of Carnegie by W. W. Ouless, R.A., is reproduced in *Royal Academy Pictures* for 1900; Edouard Lanteri executed a bust in 1907; a portrait painted by E. A. Walton, R.S.A., in 1913 belongs to the university of St. Andrews. A life-size bust in marble by Sir W. Goscombe John, R.A., was sculptured in 1914 to be placed in the palace of peace at The Hague (*Royal Academy Pictures*, 1914).

[*Autobiography of Andrew Carnegie*, 1920; John Ross, *The Carnegie American Benefactions in Operation*, 1912; Andrew Carnegie, *The Gospel of Wealth*, 1900; *A Manual of the Public Benefactions of Andrew Carnegie*, published by the Carnegie Endowment for International Peace, 1919; H. N. Casson, *The Romance of Steel*, 1907; private information.]
A. S. C.

CARPENTER, WILLIAM BOYD (1841–1918), bishop of Ripon, the second son of the Rev. Henry Carpenter, incumbent of St. Michael's, Liverpool, by his wife, Hester, daughter of Archibald Boyd, of Londonderry, was born at Liverpool 26 March 1841. His mother's brother, Archibald Boyd [q.v.], was dean of Exeter. Educated at the Royal Institution, Liverpool, he won an open scholarship at St. Catharine's College, Cambridge, and graduated B.A. (senior optime) in 1864. Ordained the same year, he served as curate at All Saints, Maidstone (1864–1866), St. Paul's, Clapham (1866–1867), and Holy Trinity, Lee (1867–1870). He rapidly gained a reputation as a preacher, his last vicar nicknaming him 'the extinguisher'. In 1870 he was appointed vicar of St. James's, Holloway, and became known as a capable parish priest. In 1879 he passed to the fashionable parish of Christ Church, Lancaster Gate. He was much liked by Queen Victoria and was appointed a royal chaplain in 1879 and canon of Windsor in 1882. Later he was clerk of the closet to Edward VII (1903–1910), and to George V (1911–1918), by whom he was created a K.C.V.O. in 1912. In these offices he came into close contact with the German court and enjoyed the friendship of the Empress Frederick and of Kaiser Wilhelm II, who made him a knight of the Royal Crown of Prussia.

In 1884 Mr. Gladstone selected Boyd Carpenter for the see of Ripon. This he administered successfully for twenty-five years. He helped to create the see of Wakefield, and prepared the way for that of Bradford; he instituted the Queen Victoria clergy fund to provide pensions for poor clergy, and founded the Ripon clergy college in 1897 to train graduates for holy orders. This foundation (renamed Ripon Hall) was moved to Oxford in 1919. He supported many forms of philanthropic endeavour, and keenly advocated the national league of physical training, the passing of the Children Act (1908), and the old age pensions scheme. A lover of the drama, he promoted the British Empire Shakespeare Society. He delivered the Hulsean lectures at Cambridge in 1878, the Bampton lectures at Oxford in 1887, the Noble lectures at Harvard in 1904 and 1913, the pastoral theology lectures on preaching at Cambridge in 1895, and the Liverpool lecture (translated into German) in 1913. In these utterances he showed himself a persuasive exponent of Victorian religious liberalism. He was a most prolific writer; commentaries, reviews, religious poetry, books of devotion, and popular expositions of the poets, particularly Dante, flowed from his pen. His *Introduction to the Study of the Scriptures* (1902) is perhaps the best example of his popular religious teaching. In 1905 under the *nom de plume* Delaval Boyd he produced a tragedy, *Brian*; and earlier, under the same name, a 'shilling shocker', *The Last Man in London*. His reputation, however, rests mainly on his oratory. He spoke, without manuscript or notes, with extreme rapidity, and in a beautifully modulated voice; this caused him to be known as 'the silver-tongued bishop of Ripon'. His most notable sermon was that before the House of Commons at the Queen's jubilee in 1887.

On resigning his bishopric in 1911 Boyd Carpenter became canon, and was later sub-dean, of Westminster. He died in London 26 October 1918. His body is buried in the cloisters at Westminster. There is a memorial window erected to him in Ripon Minster: portraits of him by H. G. Riviere (see *Royal Academy Pictures*, 1916) hang at Ripon Hall and Ripon palace.

Boyd Carpenter married twice: first, in 1864 Harriet Charlotte, only daughter of the Rev. J. W. Peers, of Chiselhampton, Oxfordshire; and secondly, in 1883 Annie Maude, daughter of W. W. Gardner, publisher. He had five sons and six daughters.

[Boyd Carpenter's published works; H. D. A. Major, *Life and Letters of William Boyd Carpenter, Bishop of Ripon*, 1925; unpublished correspondence and diaries; personal knowledge.]
H. D. A. M.

CARRINGTON, Sir FREDERICK (1844–1913), general, was born at Cheltenham 23 August 1844, the second son of Edmund Carrington, J.P., by his wife, Louisa Sarah Henney. Educated at Cheltenham College, he entered the army, 24th Foot (South Wales Borderers), in

1864. He quickly made himself expert in musketry, and became instructor to his regiment in 1870; five years later a rebellion in Griqualand West melted before a small force commanded by Lieutenant Carrington, who had been selected for the duty on the strength of this special qualification. For the Transkei War in South Africa (1877–1878) he raised and commanded the Frontier Light Horse, which he led with extraordinary success against the Kaffirs, the Transkeian territories subsequently being annexed to Cape Colony. Early in 1878 he was given his captaincy, and in the same year he commanded the Transvaal volunteer force, with temporary rank, against the native chief, Sekukuni, in the Transvaal. In recognition of his previous work and of his services in this campaign he was gazetted brevet major, and later (1880) given a step in brevet rank and the C.M.G. After a brief respite Carrington was soon in action again, commanding the native levies against the Zulus. In the Basuto War, while in command of the colonial forces, he was surrounded at Mafeteng for nearly a month (September–October 1880) by 5,000 well-mounted Basutos. Though rations were so much reduced that horse-flesh had to be eaten, he and his little force gallantly held out until relieved by Brigadier-General (Sir) Charles Mansfield Clarke. Carrington was promoted colonel in 1884, and in the following year accompanied Sir Charles Warren's expedition to Bechuanaland in command of the 2nd Mounted Infantry, better known as Carrington's Horse. Subsequently he raised and commanded the Bechuanaland Border Police (1885–1893). He received the K.C.M.G. in 1887, and, in the Matabele War of 1893 he was appointed military adviser to the high commissioner.

In 1895, on promotion to major-general, Carrington took command of the infantry at Gibraltar; but before his time in that appointment expired he was again sent to South Africa, where he succeeded in quelling the rebellion in Rhodesia (1896). For his services in this campaign he was created K.C.B. (1897). On the outbreak of the Boer War (October 1899) Carrington's unique experience of irregular warfare in South Africa made his appointment to a high command natural; and, with the temporary rank of lieutenant-general, he was selected to organize and lead an expedition which, starting from the east coast and marching through northern Rhodesia, entered the Transvaal soon after Lord Roberts had captured Pretoria (5 June 1900). In 1904 Carrington retired from the army, and pursued his favourite recreations—hunting, shooting, and fishing—at Cheltenham, where he died 22 March 1913. He married in 1897 Susan Margaret, only daughter of Henry John Elwes, F.R.S., of Colesborne, Cheltenham, by whom he had two daughters.

[*The Times*, 24 March 1913; Sir J. F. Maurice and M. H. Grant, (Official) *History of the War in South Africa*, 1906–1910.] C. V. O.

CASEMENT, ROGER DAVID (1864–1916), British consular official and Irish rebel, the younger son of Captain Roger Casement, third Light Dragoons, of Ballymena, co. Antrim, by his wife, Anne Jephson, of Dublin, was born at Kingstown, co. Dublin, 1 September 1864, and educated at the Academy, Ballymena. He belonged to an Ulster protestant family, whose ancestors had come from the Isle of Man early in the eighteenth century. He travelled widely in Africa as a young man. In 1892 he was appointed travelling commissioner to the Niger Coast Protectorate. Shortly afterwards he entered the British consular service, and in 1895 was appointed British consul at Lourenço Marques; in 1898 he was transferred to the west coast as consul successively at Loanda for Angola and at Boma for the Congo Free State. In 1903 the agitation against the administration of the Congo Free State had reached its height, and public opinion in England made it necessary for the British government to take the lead in investigating the charges made. Casement was therefore ordered to report on the conditions prevailing in connexion with the rubber trade in the interior, and visited the Upper Congo. He had seen this region in 1887, and he admitted that much advance had been made in transport and European building since that time. But his report, dated 11 December 1903, disclosed that the whole system of collecting rubber was based virtually on unpaid labour enforced by penalties of which mutilation was among the commonest. The report was all the more damning because of its moderation in tone; its testimony was never shaken; it was, in fact, confirmed by the report of the official Belgian commission of inquiry two years later, and it was the solid foundation for the movement which ended in the extinction of the Congo Free State (1908).

Casement's report had brought his name into prominence, and his personal distinction of manner and dark beauty added to the impression created wherever he appeared. He received the C.M.G. in 1905. Having been transferred to Brazil he became consul at Santos in 1906 and at Para in 1908; he was promoted to be consul-general at Rio de Janeiro in 1909. In 1910 he was directed by the Foreign Office to accompany a commission of inquiry sent out by the Peruvian Amazon Company to investigate charges of ill-treatment of the natives in the rubber-bearing regions by agents of the company. He accordingly went with the commission to the company's stations on the Putumayo river, and returned after eight weeks spent there. His report had the concurrence of the company's commission, and it charged the agents with 'crimes of the most atrocious kind, including murder, violation, and constant flogging'. A list was appended of those agents against whom the charges were worst and the evidence strongest, and their punishment was demanded. This report was submitted in December 1910, but was withheld from the public by Sir Edward Grey until it was seen that the Peruvian government was taking no steps to punish adequately the atrocities disclosed. Its publication as a Blue Book in 1912 created an immense sensation, enhanced by the authority which its writer had already acquired. But the advent of the European War prevented effective action from being taken and the whole matter was allowed to drop.

Casement was knighted for his services in 1911. In acknowledging the honour done him, he wrote to the foreign secretary a letter beginning, 'I find it very hard to choose the words with which to make acknowledgement of the honour done to me by the King'. He begged that his 'humble duty' might be presented, and that his 'deep appreciation' of the honour might be conveyed. He retired on pension shortly after, having completed nineteen years of valuable and conspicuous public work. He returned to Ireland in 1913.

The European War showed Casement in a new light. From boyhood an extreme nationalist, in spite of his Ulster protestant stock, he identified himself in 1904 with the Gaelic League. This was then a non-political organization; but while still employed by the British government he contributed articles to separatist papers signed 'Sean Bhean Bhocht'. When the Irish National Volunteers were formed in 1913, to counter the Ulster force, he formed one of the governing committee; and, when the European War broke out in 1914, he sided with the minority of volunteers who separated themselves from Mr. Redmond. His first thought was to gain German aid to win complete Irish independence. He made his way to America, and thence, by way of Sweden, to Berlin in November 1914. Here he saw important political and military personages, and wrote a letter, which was published in the Irish separatist papers, indicating Germany's intentions to recognize Ireland's independence and to send her friendly assistance. He made an attempt also to induce Irish soldiers who had been captured by the Germans to join an Irish brigade in the German service. His appeal was solely to their nationalist ideals: but even when the Germans reinforced his efforts by bribes and threats, only a handful were persuaded to join.

Before long Casement found that he neither trusted the Germans nor was trusted by them: he felt that he was spied on both by German and by British agents; and he became convinced that Germany had no intention of risking an expedition to Ireland, without which he considered rebellion hopeless. By means of submarines he conveyed to the Irish volunteer head-quarters verbal messages designed to deter action. But a rising was in preparation for Easter 1916, and a German vessel, the *Aud*, was being laden with arms and ammunition for dispatch, under the Norwegian flag, to Ireland. Casement persuaded the Germans to send him also in a submarine, his purpose being to reinforce in person his advice against the projected rebellion. They set out on 12 April; but the adventure miscarried. The British government had been warned. The *Aud* was captured by a patrol boat on 21 April off the Kerry coast, and sunk by her crew while being taken to Queenstown. Casement, with two companions, was successfully landed from the submarine at Banna, near Tralee, but was arrested by the police and taken to London (24 April). He had succeeded, however, in sending a message to Dublin, announcing the capture of the *Aud* and urging postponement of the rebellion. He was brought up at Bow Street police court on 15 May and charged with high treason. After three days' trial at the Old Bailey (26–9 June) he was convicted and sentenced to death. Strong efforts for a reprieve were made on the ground of Casement's public services in the past. The Court of Criminal Appeal dismissed his appeal (18 July), and he was hanged at Pentonville prison 3 August 1916. He had been previously received into the Church of Rome. His knighthood had been annulled on 30 June, and his name taken off the companionage. His acceptance of these honours is difficult to reconcile with the limitations to his allegiance; but, when they were bestowed, all the world thought them richly earned. And those who knew Roger Casement knew him to be honourable and chivalrous as well as able far beyond the ordinary measure of men.

[Parliamentary Papers, vol. lxii, 357 (Congo), 1904, and vol. lxviii, 819 (Putumayo), 1912–1913; P. S. O'Hegarty, *The Victory of Sinn Fein*, 1924; Evelyn, Princess Blücher, *An English Wife in Berlin*, 1920; L. G. Redmond Howard, *Sir Roger Casement*, 1916; private information; personal knowledge.] S. G.

CASSEL, Sir ERNEST JOSEPH (1852–1921), financier and philanthropist, born at Cologne 3 March 1852, was of Jewish descent, the youngest of the three children of Jacob Cassel (died 1875) by his wife, Amalia Rosenheim (died 1874). Jacob Cassel had a small banking business in Cologne which yielded a moderate competence. His elder son Max (born 1848) died in 1875. Ernest was educated in Cologne for a business career. He left school at fourteen to start work with the banking firm of Eltzbacher; but in January 1869 he went to Liverpool and entered the office of Blessig, Braun, & Co. Here he remained till April 1870, when he obtained a clerkship in the Anglo-Egyptian Bank at Paris. On the outbreak of the Franco-German War he was obliged, being a German subject, to leave Paris. He returned to England with an introduction to the financial house of Bischoffsheim and Goldschmidt (in London), which was interested in the Franco-Egyptian Bank.

In the service of this house the foundations of Cassel's immense fortune were laid with amazing rapidity. Engaged at a salary of £200, he soon gave such evidence of a remarkable aptitude for finance that he obtained early promotion. In 1874, at the age of twenty-two, he was appointed manager at £5,000 a year. The firm, in conjunction with various foreign associates, had incurred heavy commitments in America and elsewhere, out of which had arisen at this period certain claims and lawsuits. Cassel was entrusted with the negotiations for settlement, and it was arranged that he should participate in the amounts recovered. His success in this work, and notably in the disentanglement of the affairs of the New York, Pennsylvania, and Ohio Railway, resulted in substantial additions to his emoluments. Moreover, in the course of his visits to New York, he formed an intimate friendship with Jacob H. Schiff, of the banking house of Kuhn, Loeb, & Co., through whom he became profitably interested on his own account in other American enterprises.

Thus Cassel was already in flourishing circumstances in 1878, when he married Annette, daughter of Robert Thompson Maxwell, of Croft House, Croft, Darlington. On the day of his marriage he became a British subject by legal naturalization. A happy married life was cut short by the early death of Mrs. Cassel three years later. She was a convert to the Church of Rome; and, by her dying wish, Cassel himself was soon afterwards received into the Church of Rome, though the fact was not generally known till his own death. Their only daughter married in 1901 Lieutenant-Colonel Wilfrid W. Ashley; she died in 1911.

By the time of his wife's death Cassel had already accumulated a capital of £150,000; and in the next fifteen years the increasing magnitude of his operations made him one of the wealthiest and most powerful financiers in the city of London, where his high reputation for integrity and sureness of judgement, particularly in the placing of foreign issues, inspired the utmost confidence. He remained associated with the Bischoffsheim firm, though he was never made a partner, till 1884; and even then, though he began to undertake business independently, he continued to occupy part of their office in Throgmorton Street. It was not till 1898 that he took premises of his own at 21 Old Broad Street. These were his business head-quarters until the end of 1910, when he retired from active work in the City; he then purchased 51 Green Street, Grosvenor Square, from which address his affairs were subsequently administered.

While still with the Bischoffsheim firm Cassel showed great far-sightedness in connexion with what appeared to be a losing venture which the firm had made in financing the Swedish Central Railway in the early 'seventies. This railway connected the port of Oxelösund with the phosphoric iron-ore mines of the Grängesberg district. The working of these mines proved unremunerative; and Cassel realized that the success of the railway depended on its obtaining a larger revenue from the conveyance of iron ore. When

Sidney Gilchrist Thomas [q. v.] and Percy Carlyle Gilchrist made known in 1878 their new basic process for the conversion of phosphoric iron ores, which in England was generally disregarded, he took a keen interest from the first in the possibility of its application to the product of the Swedish mines. Through him the Thomas-Gilchrist process, which was eventually taken up in Germany, was introduced into Sweden with highly successful results. The mines and the railway (of which Cassel became a director in 1885) were turned into profitable concerns; and this led to a considerable enlargement of Cassel's field of enterprise in Sweden. More mines were acquired, new railways were created, and large interests in docks and shipping rounded off an extensive business from which ultimately Cassel derived a substantial part of his wealth. In 1894 he acquired a large interest in the Swedish Association, Ltd., which had a considerable holding in these concerns; and in 1896 he took part in the formation of the Grängesberg-Oxelösund Traffic Company which incorporated them.

Among the other important operations undertaken by Cassel when he had become independent of the Bischoffsheim house in 1884, one of the first was the reorganization of the Louisville and Nashville Railway in America. This he carried through successfully in conjunction with Kuhn, Loeb, & Co., of New York, and Wertheim and Gompertz of Amsterdam. He also became interested in the Mexican Central Railway, and arranged its finances throughout a considerable period; and in this connexion he subsequently formed (in 1899) the Mexican Central Railway Securities Company, Ltd., for receiving deposits of the consolidated mortgage bonds of the railway and thus securing a position of influence over the American company by a preponderating holding of the bonds. In 1893 he issued the Mexican government 6 per cent. loan; in 1895 the Chinese government 6 per cent. loan; and in 1896 the Uruguay government 5 per cent. loan. At home he took a leading part in the financing of the Electric Traction Company, Ltd., formed in 1894, which in 1895 underwrote the construction of the Central London Railway, opened in 1900. In 1897 he was instrumental in purchasing the Barrow Naval and Shipbuilding Construction Company for amalgamation with Vickers Sons and Company, and, after the amalgamation of the Maxim Gun and Nordenfelt companies, in acquiring them also for Vickers. For some years thereafter he underwrote the chief financial issues for the Vickers Company and its subsidiaries.

From early years Cassel had been interested in Egyptian affairs, and in 1898 he cemented a very important connexion with Egypt by financing the construction of the great Nile dams at Assuan and Assiut through the formation of the Irrigation Investment Corporation. He was subsequently prime mover in the formation of the National Bank of Egypt; of the Daira Sanieh Company, which purchased the Daira Sanieh estates from the Egyptian government; of the Agricultural Bank of Egypt; of the Daira Sanieh Sugar Corporation, which purchased from the Daira Sanieh Company certain sugar factories, 292 miles of railway with rolling-stock, and the benefit of contracts with the Egyptian government; of the Société Anonyme de Wadi Kom Ombo, for the development by irrigation of the great desert plain extending from the Nile to Gebel Silsileh—a daring enterprise, the later success of which, with all its benefits to the native cultivators, was another typical proof of Cassel's farsightedness; and in 1908 of the Mortgage Company of Egypt, Ltd. In 1906 the State Bank of Morocco, and in 1909 the National Bank of Turkey, were created under his auspices; in both these cases, as indeed in some others concerned with international finance, he was acting under unofficial encouragement from the government, in British national interests.

The first public recognition of Cassel's importance in the financial world was the K.C.M.G. conferred on him by Queen Victoria in 1899; under King Edward he received the further distinctions of K.C.V.O. (1902), a privy councillorship (1902), G.C.M.G. (1905), G.C.V.O (1906), and G.C.B. (1909). He was also the recipient of various foreign decorations; commander, first class, of the royal order of Vasa, Sweden (1900); grand cordon of the imperial Ottoman Order of the Osmanieh (conferred by the khedive of Egypt, in 1903); commander of the French legion of honour (1906); Crown of Prussia, first class (1908), grand cross of the Polar Star, Sweden (1909); order of the Rising Sun, first class, Japan (1911); and Red Eagle of Prussia, first class, with brilliants (1913).

Though in private life there was an element of stoicism in Cassel's character, shown in his personal abstemiousness and in an habitual reticence and reserve which made him somewhat of a mystery to the public, he kept house on the scale of his abundant means, and enjoyed offering hospitality to his acquaintances. From 1879 to 1889 his London residence was 2 Orme Square, Bayswater; from 1889 to 1908, 48 Grosvenor Square; and in 1905 he bought Brook House, Park Lane, to which he moved in 1908. He purchased the estates of Moulton Paddocks, Newmarket (1899, adding thereto in 1908, 1914, and 1920); Six Mile Bottom, Cambridge (1912); Branksome Dene, Bournemouth (1913); and Upper Hare Park, Cambridge (1917). He was a collector of old masters, old French and English furniture and *objets d'art*, including valuable examples of Renaissance bronzes, Dresden china, and Chinese jades. His pictures comprised important works by Van Dyck, Franz Hals, Romney, Raeburn, Reynolds, and Murillo. Among his fine collection of old English silver were such unique historical pieces as the 'Bacon cup' of 1573–1574 and the 'Blacksmith's cup' of 1655–1656. From early life he was a fearless rider and devoted to hunting, and his interest in horses resulted, in 1889, in his forming a stud for breeding, jointly with Lord Willoughby de Broke. This arrangement continued till 1894, when the partnership ceased and Cassel carried on the stud on his own account. Among the chief stallions owned by him were 'Cylgad' and 'Hapsburg', and among his chief mares 'Gadfly', 'Sonatura', and 'Doctrine'. In 1896 he began racing his own horses, and in later years had a fair number of successes on the turf, though he got no nearer to winning the Derby than second with 'Hapsburg' in 1914.

It was at race-meetings that he became acquainted with King Edward VII, then still Prince of Wales, and a close friendship was formed. The King, both before and after he came to the throne, held Cassel in high esteem, readily accepting his hospitality and enjoying his society at Newmarket and elsewhere, while Cassel admired and respected his royal friend, to whom in personal appearance he bore a noticeable resemblance. Some of the greatest of Cassel's public benefactions were made in honour of, or in memory of, King Edward. Contemporary gossip credited Cassel with loans or gifts of money to the King. There was no foundation for any such legends; what is true is that the King most sensibly sought, and availed himself of, Cassel's opinion about his own private money matters, and he could not have gone to a sounder or a more straightforward adviser.

Shortly after the outbreak of the European War in 1914, when anti-German feeling was acute in England, an agitation was set on foot by extremists, who were blind to Cassel's unsullied British patriotism, to have his name removed from the Privy Council; but they were deservedly frustrated. He was in fact a most valuable counsellor to the government on the financial problems arising out of the crisis; he was one of the largest individual subscribers to the successive war loans, and in September 1915 he went over to New York specially in order to use his influence there in support of the issue of the Anglo-French loan in America. Cassel died at Brook House 21 September 1921, and was buried according to the rites of the Church of Rome, at Kensal Green. His estate was proved at £7,551,608 (net personalty, £7,329,033).

As a public benefactor during his lifetime Cassel gave away altogether about £2,000,000. His most important charitable and philanthropic gifts were the following: In 1902 he gave £200,000 for founding the King Edward VII Sanatorium for Consumption, Midhurst; in 1903, £41,000 for the Egyptian Travelling Ophthalmic Hospital; in 1907, £10,000 for the Imperial College of Science and Technology; in 1909 and after, £46,000 as his half-share in founding (with Viscount Iveagh) the Radium Institute; in 1911, £210,000 for creating the King Edward VII British-German Foundation (half for relief of distressed English in Germany, and half for distressed Germans in England); £30,000 for the benefit of workmen at Kizuna and Malmberget mines in Sweden, and £50,000 (in memory of his daughter, Mrs. Ashley) to hospitals and King Edward's Hospital Fund; in 1912, £10,000 for the Deaconesses' Hospital, Alexandria; in 1913, a further £20,000 for the King Edward Sanatorium, and £50,000 for relief of sick and needy in Cologne; during the war years, £114,000 to the Red Cross, £48,000 to hospitals, £12,000 for a convalescent home for officers at Sandacres, and £222,000 in donations to the National Relief Fund, Officers' Families Fund, Salvation Army, Church Army, Young Men's Christian Association, &c.; in 1919, £472,000 (in securities of £500,000 face value) for creating an educational trust, to be applied by the trustees (Viscount Haldane, the Earl of Oxford and Asquith, the Earl of Balfour, Mr. H. A. L. Fisher, Sir George H. Murray, Mr. Sidney Webb, and Miss Fawcett) to objects generally indicated in the trust-deed (establishment of a faculty of commerce in London University; support of the Workers' Educational Association; scholarships for technical and commercial education of workmen; promotion of the study of foreign languages by professorships, lectureships, or scholarships; endowments for the higher education of women, and £212,000 for founding a hospital for functional nervous disorders at Penshurst, Kent.

Portraits of Cassel were painted by P. A. de Laszló in 1900, and by A. L. Zorn in 1907.

[Private information; personal knowledge.]

H. Ch.

CAVELL, EDITH (1865–1915), nurse, was born at Swardeston, Norfolk, 4 December 1865, the eldest daughter of the Rev. Frederick Cavell, vicar of Swardeston, by his wife, Louisa Sophia Walming. She was educated at home, at a school in Somerset, and in Brussels. In 1888, having inherited a small competency, she travelled on the Continent. When visiting Bavaria, she took much interest in a free hospital maintained by a Dr. Wolfenberg, and endowed it with a fund for the purchase of instruments. In 1895 she entered the London Hospital as a probationer. In 1897 she took charge of an emergency typhoid hospital at Maidstone. Having attained the position of staff nurse at the London Hospital, she engaged in poor law nursing, serving in the Highgate and Shoreditch infirmaries. Subsequently she took temporary charge of a Queen's district nursery in Manchester. In 1906 she went to Brussels to co-operate with Dr. Depage in establishing a modern training school for nurses on the English system, the best nurses hitherto obtainable in Belgium having been sisters belonging to Catholic religious orders. Edith Cavell was appointed in 1907 the first matron of Depage's clinic—the Berkendael medical institute—the success of which soon made it of national importance. Shortly before the European War it obtained official recognition, a new and larger building being added to it from state funds. She also organized and managed the hospital of St. Gilles. In August 1914 Dr. Depage went away to organize military hospitals, and Miss Cavell remained in charge. The German authorities gave her permission to continue her work in Brussels, the institute became a Red Cross Hospital, and she and her assistants devoted themselves to the care of the wounded, Germans as well as Allies.

When, in the latter part of 1914, the French and British forces were compelled to retire from Belgium, many soldiers from both these armies were cut off from their units. They hid themselves as best they could, for some, at least, of those who fell into German hands were summarily executed. But many escaped with the aid of the Belgian farmers and peasants. A regular system grew up under which these men were enabled to escape from the country. Miss Cavell was naturally one to whom those who needed aid applied; and she readily responded. Her conduct, careful as it was, aroused suspicion. Suspicion led to espionage. On 5 August 1915 she was arrested and placed in solitary confinement in the prison of St. Gilles. Nine weeks later (7 October) she was brought to trial together with some thirty-five other prisoners. The charges against all were of a similar kind; the tribunal before which these persons, many of them women, were arraigned was a court martial; the proceedings were conducted in German, though a French interpreter was provided.

During the weeks when Miss Cavell lay in prison Mr. Brand Whitlock, the United States minister in Brussels, was active on her behalf. He wrote to Baron von Lancken, the civil governor of Belgium, stating that he had been instructed to take charge of her defence, and he asked that a representative of his legation might see her. This letter elicited no reply. When Mr. Whitlock wrote again he was told that the prisoner had already confessed her guilt, and that a M. Braun had been engaged by her friends to conduct the defence. In fact the defence was handed over to a member of the Brussels bar, M. Sadi Kirschen, who did everything possible under the circumstances. But, as the event showed, the conviction of Miss Cavell was a foregone conclusion. In accordance with the usual procedure of such courts in Germany, the prisoner was not allowed to see her advocate before the trial, nor was he granted access to the documents in the case. The allegation was that she had enabled no less than 130 persons to escape from Belgium. Merely assisting these men to escape to Holland would have constituted no more than an *attempt* to 'conduct soldiers to the enemy'. Under German military law this is not a capital offence. But the confession which Miss Cavell is alleged to have signed on the day previous to the trial stated that she had actually assisted

Belgians of military age to go to the front, and that she had also concealed French and English soldiers, providing them with funds and with guides whereby they had been enabled to cross the Dutch frontier.

That such a confession was made by Miss Cavell is probable enough. Nine weeks of solitary confinement, the absence of any adviser who might have insisted that she should put her accusers to the proof of their charges, the conviction that what she had done was morally right, though legally wrong—all these considerations might well have induced her to tell the full story. But for her confessions, however, the capital charge would seem not to have been sustainable. The prosecution appears to have had no evidence that she had succeeded in enabling military refugees to reach England. She stated at the trial, however, that she had received letters of thanks from those whom she had helped to repatriate. In the absence of this admission she could only have been found guilty of an attempt to conduct soldiers to the enemy. Her statement showed that her attempt had been successful. So the penalty was death. The trial ended on Friday, 8 October. At eight o'clock on the evening of the following Monday (11 October) an official of the United States Legation was told unofficially that three hours previously sentence of death had been pronounced on Miss Cavell and that she would be shot at 2 a.m. on the following morning (12 October). Strenuous, but unavailing, efforts were made both by Mr. Whitlock and the Spanish minister to obtain at least a respite. All that they were granted was permission for the chaplain of Christ Church, Brussels, the Rev. H. S. T. Gahan, to visit her before the end, and he brought away her last messages.

Memorials of Miss Cavell have been set up in England and elsewhere. On 15 May 1919 her body was brought to Norwich Cathedral after a memorial service in Westminster Abbey. A statue of her, the work of Sir George Frampton, R.A., stands in St. Martin's Place, London, to record the price which she paid for doing what she conceived to be her duty.

To many English minds the execution of Miss Cavell was a judicial murder. British tribunals throughout the War avoided passing sentence of death upon women, even when found guilty of the most dangerous espionage. There is no evidence that Miss Cavell was in any sense a spy. She did nothing for pecuniary reward. Charity and the desire to aid the distressed were the mainsprings of her life. But the German military code prescribed the penalty of death for the offence of which she was found guilty. The procedure in this case was the same as that in other courts martial. Deference to her sex and some allowance for honourable motives might have been expected from humane judges. Presumably the judges were afraid to be humane and thought that the obedience of the Belgian population must be assured by severe sentences. The execution then was justified according to German standards. But, if legally justifiable, it was assuredly a blunder. Popular opinion in the allied countries considered Nurse Cavell to be a martyr.

[*The Times*, 16 and 22 October 1915; *Correspondence with the United States Ambassador respecting the Execution of Miss Cavell at Brussels*, Cd. 8013, 1915; *La Vie et la Mort de Miss Edith Cavell*, 1915; private information. Portraits, *Royal Academy Pictures*, 1916 and 1917.] B. W. G.

CECIL, Lord EDWARD HERBERT GASCOYNE- (1867–1918), soldier and civil servant, was born in London 12 July 1867, the fourth son of Robert Arthur Talbot Gascoyne-Cecil, third Marquess of Salisbury [q. v.], by his wife, Georgiana Caroline, daughter of Sir Edward Hall Alderson [q. v.]. Educated at Eton, Edward Cecil entered the army (Grenadier Guards) in 1887. At the earliest opportunity he escaped from routine duties. He served in the Dongola expedition (1896), accompanied a diplomatic mission to Abyssinia (1897), witnessed the capture of Khartoum (1898), and was besieged in Mafeking (1900). Still seeking experience, he joined the Egyptian army, and was appointed in 1903 agent-general of the Sudan government and director of intelligence at Cairo. He then passed into the Egyptian government, becoming under-secretary of state in the ministry of finance in 1905, and financial adviser in 1912. As adviser, he was not greatly concerned to increase Egyptian revenues, counting a contented people a greater blessing than an overflowing treasury. But he was not always able to reconcile his ideals with the stern responsibilities of his office.

The European War of 1914–1918 disclosed Cecil's reserve of courage and resource. Being the chief British adviser, he had to assume both direction of, and responsibility for, the conduct of the Egyptian civil administration in the difficult interval between Lord Kitchener's suspension of his own functions as high commissioner and their devolution upon Sir Henry McMahon—an interval during which Turkey, the sovereign of Egypt, took up arms against the Allies. Moreover, all the difficulties of establishing a war-time protectorate and of governing under unprecedented circumstances had to be met. He became the link between civil and military powers, and counsellor of all in perplexity. The temper of Egypt, and particularly of Cairo, was less certain in 1914–1915 than later, when large military forces were at hand; and expectation of attacks from the East by the Turks, and from the West by the Senussis, added to the internal danger. Cecil's confidence, however, never deserted him. When Sir Henry McMahon took over the high commissionership, he remained the 'power behind the throne'; but with the succession of Sir Reginald Wingate in 1917 his position became less satisfactory, and, feeling himself no longer necessary, he grew anxious to do war service at home. In 1918 his functions were delegated, and he left Egypt. Shortly after his return to England, however, he was stricken without warning by a fatal illness. He met it with his habitual resolution and composure, and died at Leysin, Switzerland, 14 December 1918.

Cecil was a notable and inspiring figure of the British occupation of Egypt—a civil servant of sympathy and insight and a polished gentleman. He was a generous almsgiver, a brilliant talker, and a witty writer, as is seen in the pages of *The Leisure of an Egyptian Official* (published after his death in 1921), his single contribution to literature.

Cecil married in 1894 Violet Georgina, younger daughter of Admiral Frederick Augustus Maxse [q.v.], by whom he had one son and one daughter.

[Official records; private information; personal knowledge.] P. G. E.

CHAMBERLAIN, JOSEPH (1836–1914), statesman, was born at Camberwell Grove, London, 8 July 1836. His father, Joseph Chamberlain, was the master of the Cordwainers' Company, with which his family had been connected for four generations, carrying on the business of wholesale boot and shoe manufacturers in the same house and under the same name for one hundred and twenty years. His mother was Caroline, daughter of Henry Harben, a provision merchant in London. In 1850 Joseph, who was their eldest son, was sent to University College School; but after a short stay, during which he showed no little promise, he was put into his father's business at the age of sixteen. Two years later an opening occurred to expand the business of Mr. Nettlefold, screw-manufacturer, the brother-in-law of Mr. Chamberlain senior, at Birmingham, and Joseph was sent there to represent his father's interests. He remained an active member of the firm for twenty years, displaying such business capacity that he was able to retire at the early age of thirty-eight with a substantial income. His relations with his employees were always of a most friendly character; and when a charge of ruthlessness was afterwards made by a political opponent regarding his dealings with the smaller manufacturers, the accuser, after careful inquiry, acknowledged the complete untruth of his allegations.

Chamberlain's apprenticeship in public speaking was served in the Birmingham and Edgbaston Debating Society. He became in 1869 a member of the city council, and in 1870 of the first school board. Politics appealed to him from the first. An intimate friend has asserted that, at the outset, it was uncertain whether foreign policy would make him a tory, or home affairs a radical; and at the election of 1859 he canvassed on behalf of the opponent of John Bright, because he was opposed to Bright's pacificism. But very soon the impulse of social reform drove him to radicalism. It was on the subject of education that his interest was first excited. He became chairman of the National Education League of Birmingham in 1868. At the time education in Birmingham was at a low ebb; and both by agitation and by practical experiment Chamberlain sought to find a remedy. He started classes at his own works, and taught history, French, and arithmetic in connexion with a Unitarian Sunday school; whilst, simultaneously, he flung himself into the campaign for a national system of education. He held the Church of England to be the enemy; and, when Mr. W. E. Forster's Bill of 1870 was found to contain provisions which seemed to encourage the maintenance of the denominational system, he attacked it with great bitterness. He had become, in March 1870, the chairman of the National Education League, and voiced with extreme vigour the case of the nonconformists.

But education was only one plank in the platform of social reform, and there were other questions, less controversial, upon which Chamberlain was able to give the lead not only to his adopted city but to England at large. He became mayor of Birmingham in 1873, and was re-elected in 1874 and 1875. If he was a radical, he maintained it was because political means were necessary to deal effectually with the evils standing in the way of social reform. Ignorance, and the existence of insanitary and disgraceful housing, were the two main evils. But, whilst free education could only be secured by act of parliament, the improvement of sanitary conditions lay with the municipalities themselves; and here there can be no question of the results achieved by Chamberlain. They included the purchase by the Birmingham corporation of the gas-works, water-works, and sewage farm, the destruction of the slums in the heart of the city, and the provision of artisans' dwellings. He worked for the extension of free libraries and art galleries, and sought in every way to make Birmingham a place in which its inhabitants should take a civic pride. Nor were his interests confined to Birmingham. At the close of 1874 he arranged a conference of municipal authorities and others interested in the sanitation of large towns, in order to create a sound public opinion on the subject. It took place in January 1875 and was a starting-point in the development of municipal social reform.

Holding the view that legislation was needed for effecting improvements, it was natural that Chamberlain should seek a yet wider field for his activities. In 1874 he stood for parliament unsuccessfully at Sheffield; but, at a by-election in 1876, he became the colleague of Bright in the representation of Birmingham. From this time till the final split over Home Rule, Chamberlain was closely associated with (Sir) Charles Dilke [q.v.]. Forming a close offensive and defensive alliance, they agreed that neither should accept office unless the other was also satisfied. In 1877 Chamberlain reorganized the liberal party in the constituencies by forming large local associations on a representative basis, and federating these in a central organization. He thus became the Carnot of the liberal victory of 1880. But Mr. Gladstone did not at first intend to admit either Dilke or Chamberlain to the Cabinet, his personal sympathies being with the more moderate type of liberal. His hand was forced, however, by Dilke, who refused to join the ministry unless either Chamberlain or he became a Cabinet minister. Queen Victoria raised strong objections to Dilke, because of the line which he had taken on grants to the royal family; and thus Chamberlain, though in his earlier years he had seemed to coquette with republican views, and though at the time his parliamentary reputation was less than Dilke's, became president of the Board of Trade, whilst Dilke was put off with the subordinate office of under-secretary of state for foreign affairs. When, at the end of 1882, room was at last found for Dilke in the Cabinet, there was at first some question of Chamberlain taking the vacant office of chancellor of the duchy of Lancaster, so that Dilke should go to the Board of Trade. The Queen was unwilling to have Dilke as chancellor of the duchy, and, indeed, afterwards showed some reluctance to accept Chamberlain. The difficulty was met by Mr. J. G. Dodson (afterwards Lord Monk-Bretton) exchanging the Local Government Board for the duchy, so that Dilke might fill his place. The episode, however, enabled Chamberlain to show the staunchness of his friendship. 'Your letter', he wrote to Dilke on 13 December, 'has spoilt my breakfast. The change would be loathsome to me for more than one reason and will give rise to all sorts of disagreeable commentaries. But if it is the only way out of the difficulty, I will do what I am sure you would have done in my place and accept the transfer.'

The intimate letters of Chamberlain to Dilke reveal the absence of sympathy between Chamberlain and most of his colleagues in the ministry of 1880–1885. In any case, in the words of Dilke, 'the holding of strongly patriotic and national opinions in foreign affairs, combined with extreme radical opinions upon internal matters, made it difficult to act with anybody for long without being attacked by some section with which it was necessary to act at other times, and made it difficult to form a solid party'. But the special circumstances regarding Ireland and foreign and colonial questions made the situation still more difficult. As to Ireland, Chamberlain distrusted and disliked a policy of coercion. He had an uneasy conscience at having accepted it in 1880; at the same time he was at a loss for an alternative. He recognized in October 1881 that Parnell had now got beyond the radicals. The Irish leader was demanding 'no rent' and 'separation'; and Chamberlain was not prepared to say that the refusal of such terms as these constituted an Irish grievance. His own inclination was to stand aside and let the coercionists and Parnell fight out their quarrel; but this was now impossible.

Altogether it was an awkward situation, and he did not see his way out of it.

The imprisonment of Parnell shortly followed (October 1881), but no improvement took place in the situation. Accordingly, the pressure of the radicals caused another change of policy. It was reported that Parnell was in a more pliant mood, and Chamberlain, 'taking his life in his hands', with the approval of Gladstone, entered into negotiations, the outcome of which was the so-called Kilmainham Treaty (2 May 1882). Parnell promised, if released, to advise payment of rent and the cessation of outrages. The absence of a public promise, however, diminished the force of this undertaking. Parnell and two other members of parliament were thereupon released, W. E. Forster in consequence resigning the post of Irish secretary. Dilke and Chamberlain had expected that the latter would be Forster's successor, and the appointment of Lord Frederick Cavendish [q.v.] took them by surprise. Again, after the murder of Lord Frederick (6 May), Chamberlain would have accepted the post, had it been offered him, with the intention of attacking the whole Dublin Castle system. But Gladstone had no desire to see Chamberlain Irish secretary, nor did he desire an Irish secretary who would be a Cabinet minister.

Chamberlain never wavered in his belief in the necessity of an Irish Local Government Bill; and a speech in which he compared the position of England and Ireland with that of Russia and Poland (February 1883) showed his discontent with the existing state of things. The pressure of foreign and domestic questions for a time diverted attention from Ireland; but in 1885 Chamberlain, in despair of a solution, suggested that Parnell or some other Irishman should become chief secretary. At the same time he proposed a more practicable plan. He advocated the creation of a system of representative county government. In addition to elected county boards, there should be a central board for all Ireland, in its essence municipal and not political, mainly executive and administrative, but with the power to make by-laws, raise funds, and pledge public credit, in such modes as parliament should provide. The central board should take over primary education, poor law, sanitary administration, and the control of public works, without dealing, however, in any way with the administration of justice, police, or prisons. It should not be elected directly by the Irish people, but chosen by the county boards. The scheme had the approval of the Irish bishops, and Parnell, according to Captain O'Shea, promised to give it his support, and not to obstruct a limited Crimes Bill. It obtained the half-hearted approval of a committee of the Cabinet; but, on being submitted to the full Cabinet, met with defeat. All the peers, except Lord Granville, voted against it; all the commoners, except Lord Hartington, were in its favour. As the Cabinet broke up (9 May) Gladstone said to a colleague, 'Ah, they will rue this day'.

Meanwhile drafts not only of a Coercion Bill but also of a Bill for Land Purchase came before the Cabinet. The latter Bill, however, was dropped for the time being, on the protests of the radical members of the Cabinet; nevertheless, Lord Spencer, the viceroy, remained convinced of its necessity; and Gladstone, under the impression that the objections of Chamberlain and Dilke would be met if, under the Bill, funds were only provided for a single year, gave notice of its introduction. But Chamberlain had not moved from the position that there should be no Land Purchase Bill, unless it was accompanied by a Bill for Local Government. He and Dilke, therefore, sent in their resignations. They afterwards agreed to suspend them; so that their resignations had not taken effect when the government was defeated in the House of Commons (8 June 1885). The situation is made clear by a letter from Chamberlain to Gladstone (21 May 1885): 'I doubt very much if it is wise or was right to cover the serious differences of principle that have lately disclosed themselves in the Cabinet. I think it is now certain that they will cause a split in the new parliament, and it seems hardly fair to the constituencies that this should only be admitted after they have discharged their function, and are unable to influence the result'.

But it was not only on Irish and domestic questions that the Cabinet was divided. On foreign and colonial questions also there was much difference of opinion. With regard to the Transvaal, Chamberlain had no doubts respecting the wisdom and justice of the policy that prevailed; but as to Egypt his position was much less easy to summarize. On the one hand he maintained that strong measures were called for after the Alexandria massacre (11 June 1882), earning thereby Lord Granville's description of him as 'almost the greatest Jingo' in the Cabinet. On the other hand he was determined that Great Britain should not become the tool of the bondholders' interests. He wrote a memorandum to this effect in October 1882. Our first duty, he insisted, was to our principles and to our supporters and not to other powers; and, if the powers insisted on financial control, we should at least identify ourselves with the legitimate aspirations of Egyptian national sentiment. When, in April 1884, the relief of General Gordon was under consideration, Chamberlain agreed with Dilke and Hartington that, whether Gordon had acted against his instructions or not, an expedition for his relief was necessary. As early as February Chamberlain had proposed to telegraph to Sir Evelyn Baring (afterwards Earl of Cromer, q.v.), giving him authority to concert measures with Sir Evelyn Wood [q.v.] for the relief of the beleaguered garrisons in the Sudan. But Gladstone and Granville broke up a meeting of the Cabinet, so as to prevent the adoption of this policy. Still, though differences in the Cabinet might delay an expedition till it became useless, they could not prevent it. Dilke and Chamberlain were consistently in favour of relieving Gordon, though Chamberlain strongly opposed the grandiose campaign of Lord Wolseley, believing that a small striking force of picked men was all that was required to avert the coming tragedy. He did not intend to be forced any further in the direction of a protectorate. He was in favour of an international guarantee of the neutrality of Egypt, and was ready to declare that country bankrupt. Two subjects, he wrote to Dilke, occupied the time of successive Cabinet councils, the finances of Egypt, and Gordon; but, whereas the former took up some two or three hours, the latter received about five minutes at the fag-end of business. Thus neither by what it did nor by what it left undone did the Egyptian policy of the Gladstone ministry of 1880–1885 win the approval of its radical members.

Chamberlain was even less in sympathy with the prevailing tendencies in other parts of the world. In 1883 a committee of the Cabinet was appointed to deal with affairs on the west coast of Africa; and this committee, according to Dilke, by its delays and hesitations, lost England the Cameroons. 'The Cameroons!' wrote Chamberlain to Dilke in September 1884, 'It is enough to make one sick. As you say, we decided to assume the protectorate eighteen months ago. If the Board of Trade or the Local Government Board managed their business after the fashion of the Foreign Office and the Colonial Office, you and I would deserve to be hung.' If he had had the direction of affairs, he would have demanded explanations from Germany regarding New Guinea; and he shared Dilke's resentment at the policy of truckling to Germany, which was adopted in the case of Samoa and of Zanzibar and East Africa.

Nevertheless, while these causes of dissatisfaction were at work, Chamberlain was proving his capacity in his own special department, where his business experience stood him in good stead. In the session of 1880 he had in charge two measures relating to merchant shipping, the one concerning grain cargoes, the other the payment of seamen's wages. In 1881 he was responsible for an Electric Lighting Bill, which entitled municipalities, with the consent of the Board of Trade, to adopt electric lighting, without the cost and trouble of a private Act of parliament. An Act of 1883 effected a valuable reform in the law of bankruptcy, by subjecting the accounts of trustees to the control of an independent authority, and by setting on foot a searching inquisition into the conduct of insolvent debtors. The Act has been improved by subsequent legislation, but at the time was recognized by lawyers and business men as marking a great advance. The Patent Act of 1883 made easier the road for the inventor, by reducing greatly the scale of provisional fees and subsequent payments. More generally interesting and more adapted to the temperament of a fighting politician was the Merchant Shipping Bill of 1884, directed against shipowners who insured unseaworthy vessels beyond the value of the ships or of their cargoes. In a speech at Newcastle in January 1884 Chamberlain asserted that in the preceding year one seaman in every sixty had met his death by violent means; three thousand five hundred men had thus come to a premature end, many of them in the prime of life and many of them leaving behind them widows and orphans. So strongly did he feel on the subject that, when parliamentary reasons dictated the withdrawal of his measure, he at once proffered his resignation; which, however, he afterwards withdrew in view of the need of a united front until the question of the vote for the agricultural labourers should be finally settled. Moreover, he was able to secure the appointment of a royal commission, which in the end bore good fruit; for subsequent Acts accomplished most of the objects at which the Bill of

1884 had aimed. As an instance of Chamberlain's courage may be noted the fact that at Hull (6 August 1885) he stood on the same political platform with Samuel Plimsoll [q. v.] whose name was anathema to all shipowners.

On the question whether the Bills for equalizing the county and town franchise and for redistribution should be introduced simultaneously, Chamberlain strongly supported the view that the measures should be kept separate, and that no more than a promise of a Redistribution Bill to follow should at the time be given. While the question remained open his relations with Lord Hartington were far from friendly, and Gladstone's mediation was necessary. It seemed to Dilke that Chamberlain was anxious to make Hartington resign on the question of the franchise. For the time being Chamberlain was full of wrath against the House of Lords; and, whilst his friend Dilke was working for a peaceful solution of the Redistribution question with Lord Salisbury, he himself was busy denouncing the iniquities of the Upper House.

The violence of Chamberlain's language at this time gave grave offence to the Queen, who made Gladstone's life a burden by her strictures on the indiscretions of this *enfant terrible* of the Cabinet. In a dramatic speech at Birmingham on 5 January 1885, Chamberlain confessed his faith in the doctrine of 'ransom' for private property. After explaining how, as a radical minister in a liberal government, he had at times to reserve and even to sacrifice his opinions, he went on to ask what was to be the nature of the domestic legislation of the future? It would be more directed to social objects than had hitherto been the case. How to promote the greater happiness of the masses of the people, how to increase their enjoyment of life, this was the problem of the future. Private ownership had taken the place of communal rights, and this system had become so interwoven with our habits that it might be very difficult, and perhaps impossible, to reverse it. But then, what ransom would property pay for the security it enjoyed? Society was banded together in order to protect itself against the instincts of those of its members who would make very short work of private ownership if they were left alone. That was all very well, but society owed to these men something more than mere toleration in return for the restraints which it placed upon their liberty of action.

But in the same speech there were utterances more in keeping with Chamberlain's future career. 'If, however,' he said, 'occasion should come to assert the authority of England, a democratic government, resting on the confidence and support of the whole nation and not on the favour of a limited class, would be very strong. It would know how to make itself respected, how to maintain the obligations and honour of the country. I think foreign nations would be very ill advised if they were to assume that, because we are anxious to avoid all cause of quarrel with our neighbours, we are wanting in the old spirit of Englishmen, and that we should be found very tolerant of insult, and long-suffering under injury.' Again: 'We are not unmindful of our obligations. If foreign nations are determined to pursue distant colonial enterprises, we have no right to prevent them. . . . But our fellow-subjects may rest assured that their liberties, their rights, and their interests are as dear to us as our own; and if ever they are seriously menaced, the whole power of the country will be exerted for their defence, and the English democracy will stand shoulder to shoulder throughout the world to maintain the honour and integrity of the Empire.' In further speeches he emphasized the necessity of enlarging the programme of the liberal party. Free education, the provision of healthy dwellings and fair rents in the large towns, and compulsory powers for local authorities to acquire land at a fair price, that is to say, the price which a willing purchaser would give to a willing seller in the open market—these were the objects at which to aim. Payment of members, the abolition of plural voting, and a revision of the existing system of taxation were also urgent reforms. He told the Eighty Club (April 1885) that to a large and ever-increasing number of persons politics was the science of social happiness, as its half-sister, political economy, was the science of social wealth; and the inferences to be drawn from the statement were sufficiently obvious.

These utterances from a Cabinet minister caused a flutter in the ministerial dovecots, and Gladstone sent a grave remonstrance regarding the 'unauthorized programme', which Chamberlain interpreted as a dead set against himself. He saw, however, that he had gone too far, and excused himself on the ground that the present was an exceptional moment, new political vistas having been opened by the recent measure of reform. Moreover, his actual proposals had not been extravagant; he only demanded a revision of taxation, which Gladstone himself had advocated, and the extension of the powers of local authorities, on lines already conceded in Ireland. It was, perhaps, not so much the proposals themselves as the manner in which they were advocated, that deeply shocked the political feelings of men of the type of Goschen. Lord Fitzmaurice has described Chamberlain's proposals as 'innocuous and almost meaningless'; and in fact many of them became law under subsequent unionist legislation.

Strong as were Chamberlain's views on social reform, he was no less firm in his determination to uphold the supremacy of the imperial parliament in regard to Ireland. When the liberal ministry of 1880 had come to its somewhat inglorious end, and the conservative government, which succeeded it, seemed to be coquetting with the idea of Home Rule, the situation became more strained; both because Parnell saw his opportunity of playing upon the needs of the rival parties, and because the apparent movement in the mind of the conservative ministry led Gladstone to believe that Home Rule was within the range of practical politics. For the moment, however, other questions than that of Ireland occupied Chamberlain's attention. With regard to the future, the radicals were not willing to be mere lay figures in a Cabinet of Goschens; and, if a liberal government attempted to do without them, they were determined to make trouble. Gladstone, however, recognized the importance of placating the redoubtable radical leader, and summoned him to Hawarden for a friendly discussion (8 October 1885). Three points were indispensable, in Chamberlain's opinion, to the programme of a liberal government: first, the granting of authority to local bodies for compulsory expropriation; secondly, a readjustment of taxation (as had been foreshadowed in Gladstone's election address); and thirdly, a recognition of the right of a Cabinet minister to support free education, notwithstanding that the other members of the ministry might not share his views. The questions of the future of the House of Lords and of church disestablishment he was willing to leave for decision to the future. According to Gladstone, he and Chamberlain were pretty well agreed on the subject of Ireland. But the latter insisted that he had always excluded Home Rule as impossible, proposing a Local Government Bill which he thought Parnell might accept. The impression left on Chamberlain was that Gladstone had as yet no definite plan. If he got a majority, his first effort would probably be to find a *modus vivendi* by entering into communications with Parnell. A little later Chamberlain was made uneasy by a note from Gladstone, confessing a presentiment that the Irish question might elbow out all others. He was further alarmed by a report from another source that Gladstone was trying to get Parnell's ideas in detail. 'It is no use,' he wrote. After the liberals had gained their Pyrrhic victory at the general election of December 1885, and Gladstone had outlined an 'admissible plan' of Home Rule, Chamberlain commented: 'My view is that Mr. G's Irish scheme is death and damnation; that we must try and stop it; that we must not openly commit ourselves against it yet; that we must let the situation shape itself before we finally decide; that the Whigs are our greatest enemies, and that we must not join them if we can help it'.

On 26 December, in a very interesting letter, Chamberlain proposed a new solution of the Irish difficulty. His own inclinations were still in favour of the extension of local liberties on municipal lines; but the fatal objection was that the nationalists would not accept such a solution. Apparently the only logical alternative was separation, with its attendant dangers. Between these lay 'the hazy idea of Home Rule', which would mean an independent Irish parliament; while all guarantees and securities, whether for the protection of minorities or for the security of the Empire, would prove altogether illusory. To this he would prefer separation, towards which, indeed, Home Rule was but a step. There still remained the possibility of an arrangement which might secure the integrity of the Empire, whilst allowing Irishmen to manage Irish affairs in their own way. He then suggested a scheme of federation, involving separate parliaments for England, Scotland, Wales, Ulster, and South Ireland. To make the scheme workable it would be necessary to set on foot a supreme court, to decide the limits of the powers of the several local legislatures. Such changes had no terrors for a radical such as he was, but was it conceivable that such a clean sweep could be made in order to meet the Irish demand for Home Rule? The obvious answer to this question decided Chamberlain's future policy. In the general confusion of affairs, of one thing he was certain. He would sooner that the tories remained in office for the next ten years than agree to what he thought would be the ruin of his country. Nevertheless, it was his friend and follower, Jesse Collings [q.v.], who moved the so-called 'three acres and a cow' amendment which gave the tory government its quietus; it resigned on 28 January 1886.

Chamberlain believed that he ought to accept, for the time being, a post in the new liberal ministry; though he recorded another protest against Home Rule in a letter to Gladstone. He would have preferred to become secretary for the Colonies. Gladstone's surprised comment: 'Oh! a Secretary of State!' bears out the assertion of Lord Randolph Churchill that Gladstone never really understood Chamberlain's capacity till he faced him as a foe. There was some question of Chamberlain going to the Admiralty; but he finally became president of the Local Government Board, though 'not very willingly'.

Starting under such auspices, it was not likely that the ministry would long remain united. Chamberlain intended to resign on the proposal of a Land Purchase Bill, but it was not till after a discussion in the Cabinet on the question of Home Rule that he finally left the government (15 March). On 21 April he justified his action before a meeting of Birmingham electors; after the Redistribution Act he had in 1885 become member for West Birmingham. 'Fifteen or sixteen years ago', he said, 'I was drawn into politics by my interest in social questions . . . and from that time to this I have done everything that an individual can do. I have made sacrifices of money and time and labour, I have made sacrifices of my opinions to maintain the organization and to preserve the unity of the liberal party.' Home Rule, he urged, now blocked the way of social reform, and the persistency of Parnell and the pliancy of Gladstone had altered the whole course of British politics. But Chamberlain knew that he must walk warily; and, after a destructive analysis of the two measures, he was careful to explain that as far as the Home Rule Bill was concerned his opposition was conditional. If the representation of Ireland were preserved on its present footing, the imperial parliament thus maintaining its control over imperial taxation in Ireland, and if there were conceded to Ulster a separate assembly, he might be able to support the measure. But these were not matters for committee; and on the answer to them depended his vote.

The speech was a great personal triumph, and although Mr. Francis Schnadhorst, the master of the 'caucus', had thrown in his lot with Gladstone and did what he could to thwart Chamberlain, the meeting passed, almost unanimously, a vote of confidence. The news of Dilke's intention to vote for the second reading was a great blow. 'The party', Chamberlain wrote, 'is going blindly to its ruin; and everywhere there seems a want of courage and decision and principle which almost causes one to despair.' For him the retention of the Irish representatives at Westminster was the touchstone. With their removal, separation must follow; with their retention, some system of federation might be possible. He would vote against the second reading, unless the ministry gave definite pledges on this point. 'The present crisis', he added, 'is, of course, life and death to me. I shall win if I can; if I cannot, I will cultivate my garden. I do not care for the leadership of a party which shall prove itself so fickle and so careless of national interests as to sacrifice the unity of the Empire to the precipitate impatience of an old man, careless of the future in which he can have no part, and to an uninstructed instinct which will not take the trouble to exercise judgement and criticism.' In a subsequent letter (6 May) Chamberlain made an illuminating admission: 'I do not really expect the government to give way, and, indeed, I do not wish it. To satisfy others I have talked about conciliation and have consented to make advances, but on the whole I would rather vote against the Bill than not, and the retention of the Irish members is with me only the flag that covers other objections.' On 26 May he wrote: 'I shall fight this matter out to the bitter end, but I am getting more and more doubtful whether, when it is out of the way, I shall continue in politics. I am wounded in the house of my friends, and I have lost my interest in the business.' Nevertheless, he threw out in parliament on 1 June the suggestion of yet another scheme, under which the position of Ireland with regard to the imperial parliament should be that of a Canadian province to the Dominion; but there was no support for this proposal.

On 7 June came the defeat of the Home Rule Bill by a majority of thirty; Chamberlain, along with Bright, voting against it. Various motives have in the past been ascribed to him. It has been supposed that he desired to oust Gladstone from the leadership. But the leadership was already, as it seemed, assured to him in the near future. The defection of the whigs under Lord Hartington must have inured to the benefit of the radical wing of the liberal party; Gladstone was a very old man, and Chamberlain was marked out as his natural successor. Chamberlain sacrificed this prize by voting with the whigs, who had been his special aversion, and with the tories, who had regarded him as Jack Cade; he risked political extinction sooner than comply with the demands of Parnell. Nevertheless, considering his past, considering the nature of his relations with most of the dissentient liberals, who, like Lord Hartington, had merely reached a goal to which for a long time they had unconsciously been moving, it was natural that Chamberlain should, for some time, retain hopes of reunion with his old associates; and the Round Table Conference at the beginning of 1887, attended by Sir William Harcourt, (Lord) Morley, and Lord Herschell from the one side, and by Chamberlain and Sir George Trevelyan from the other, was an attempt to find a *modus vivendi* between men who were in fact fundamentally at issue. In this state of things, a provocative letter by Chamberlain in *The Baptist* merely killed what could never have survived. The resignation of Lord Randolph Churchill (December 1886) had seriously affected Chamberlain's position. The tory democracy of Churchill attracted him; and the idea of organizing, along with Churchill, a new national party occurred to him, though he soon recognized its impossibility. Still, he thought that the tory government was doomed, and formed the gloomiest anticipations of the probable result of another general election, with coercion again to the fore.

Chamberlain's mission, however, to the United States to negotiate a treaty regarding the North American fisheries (November 1887–March 1888) gave him a few months' peace from party politics. The Bayard-Chamberlain Treaty of 15 February 1888 sought to make a satisfactory settlement of the questions relating to the interpretation of the Convention of 1818. That Convention gave, to a limited extent, the same territorial advantages over certain portions of the island of Newfoundland and of Canada as were given under the Treaty of 1783, and in return secured the renunciation by the United States of the liberty of their fishermen to enter on any other portion of the recognized waters of British North America, except for certain specified purposes. The Treaty was rejected by the American Senate in the following August. Nevertheless, when the Hague Tribunal arbitrated on the meaning of the Convention of 1818, the basis of their settlement was the same as that adopted in the Bayard-Chamberlain Treaty. Moreover, the *modus vivendi* which was continued after the failure of the Treaty removed all causes of irritation between the United States and Canada; and Sir Charles Tupper [q.v.], the Canadian commissioner, bore witness to the tact, ability, and firmness with which Chamberlain met and overcame all but insurmountable difficulties. The visit served to strengthen those feelings of friendship towards the United States which so profoundly influenced his later policy.

After Chamberlain's return to British politics there was a noticeable movement in the direction of support to the conservative government. He was found jeering at the 'crazy-quilt' of Lord Randolph's professions, and supporting the ministry against his attacks. The return to power of a Home Rule ministry in August 1892 further tended to unite all enemies of Home Rule; and no one worked more ably or persistently against the measure of 1893 than Chamberlain.

In other directions Chamberlain's views were crystallizing. A visit to Egypt in 1889 had deeply impressed him with the benefits accruing to that country from the British occupation, and had led him to modify his earlier opinions. In a speech urging the retention of Uganda (20 March 1893) he anticipated his future rôle as colonial secretary. He laid stress on the need for following in the footsteps of our ancestors, who had not been ashamed to 'peg out' claims for posterity, thereby creating that foreign trade without which the population of Great Britain would starve. Very characteristic of the future colonial secretary was his defence of Captain Lugard, whose pledges for the continuance of the protectorate were then in danger of being repudiated by the Gladstone Cabinet: 'Captain Lugard was on the spot—Let me say in passing that I sometimes think we do not do justice to our bravest and noblest citizens. Any man, who reads his accounts impartially, will agree in this, that he was at all events a man of extraordinary power, capacity, tact, discretion, and courage.' Equally characteristic was the statement: 'Make it the interest of the Arab slave-traders to give up the slave trade, and you will see the end of that traffic. Construct your railway and thereby increase the means of traffic and you will take away three-fourths, if not the whole, of the temptation to carry on the slave trade'.

Such being the bent of his mind, it was natural that, after the electors in July 1895 had completely vindicated the action of the House of Lords in rejecting the Home Rule Bill of 1893, Chamberlain should have chosen the office of secretary of state for the Colonies when he joined Lord Salisbury's government. He informed a supporter that he had accepted the Colonial Office with two objects: first, to see what could be done to tighten the bond between Great Britain and the self-governing Colonies; and, secondly, to attempt to develop the resources of the Crown Colonies, and to increase the trade between them and Great Britain. In a speech (22 August 1895) he described the British tropical colonies as possessions in which it would be necessary to sink British capital. In small things no less than in great, the Colonial Office felt the hand of its new master. It was cleaned up and refurnished, and the maps were brought up to date. A circular of November 1895 instituted an inquiry into the extent of foreign competition in colonial markets, and the reasons for its existence. In the same spirit a Commercial Intelligence Branch of the Board of Trade was opened some four years later, and four trade commissioners were appointed. In the same year (1899) the Treasury was authorized by act of parliament to advance to certain Crown Colonies a sum of nearly three and a half million pounds at $2\frac{3}{4}$ per cent. repayable in fifty years. Although Chamberlain was by no means the first British minister to show interest in the material development of the Crown Colonies, none before him displayed such energy and capacity in the task. Like many other colonial secretaries, on his assumption of office he found the West Indies in a lamentable plight. The royal commission of 1896 considered the causes of West Indian depression to be permanent, inasmuch as they were largely due to the system of foreign sugar bounties which was not likely to be abandoned. Nevertheless the energy of Chamberlain achieved the apparently impossible; and the Brussels Convention (3 March 1903) abolished, for the time being, the bounty form of protection. Meanwhile, in consequence of the report of the royal commission, a department of agriculture for the West Indies was set on foot, an example that has been followed in Africa and the Far East. West Indian interests were further benefited by an arrangement (April 1900) with Messrs. Elder, Dempster & Co. for a fortnightly service of steamers between England and Jamaica. At the same time Chamberlain's handling of the Jamaica constitutional question in 1899 proved that he could be as firm as he was sympathetic.

Nor were Chamberlain's sympathies confined to the West Indies. No one was quicker to realize how essential to the complex life of the modern world is the supply of tropical products; and he at once saw that the policy already adopted of placing the scientific resources of Kew at the disposal of the West Indies was capable of unlimited extension, with the object of making the Empire, as far as possible, self-sufficient.

Perhaps, on this side of his work, Chamberlain's most unchallenged title to fame was the campaign which he waged on questions of health in tropical countries. In 1897 he realized the necessity of scientific inquiry into the causes of malaria, and of special education for the medical officers of Crown Colonies. He followed eagerly on the trail which had been blazed by Sir Patrick Manson [q.v.]. A circular was issued in 1898, addressed to the General Medical Council and the leading medical schools in Great Britain, which urged the necessity of including tropical diseases in the medical curriculum. A special school of tropical medicine was set on foot in connexion with the Albert Dock branch of the Seamen's Hospital. The Treasury contributed half the cost; and the colonial governments were asked to concur in arrangements for the training of their medical officers at this school. A little later Chamberlain wrote to Lord Lister [q.v.], inviting the co-operation of the Royal Society in a thorough investigation into the origin, the transmission, and the possible prevention and cure of tropical diseases, especially of the malarial and black-water fevers prevalent on the West African coast. The Royal Society gave a ready response; so that within a year of an address by Sir P. Manson, which gave a lead to the profession, both a school of tropical medicine and a systematic inquiry into the nature of malaria had become accomplished facts. Nor was this all. Another school of tropical medicine was founded in Liverpool, which also owed its origin to the initiative of Chamberlain. Improvements were effected in the form of the medical and sanitary annual reports from the Crown Colonies;

and the enlargement of the British pharmacopoeia, so as to adapt it to Indian and colonial needs, received the powerful support of the Colonial Office. Unofficially, also, Chamberlain was able to leave his mark on this side of the work, as the establishment of the Colonial Nursing Association was mainly due to him and to Mrs. Chamberlain.

Turning to a wholly different subject, we note that under Chamberlain the British possessions in West Africa were extended by the effective occupation of the territories behind the Gold Coast and Lagos, and by the placing of the Royal Niger Company's territories under the control of the Colonial Office (1900). Chamberlain also gave his strong support to the federalizing of the protected Malay States and to the extension of their railway system.

But, valuable as was his work for the benefit of the Crown Colonies, it is in his relations with what are now known as the Dominions that Chamberlain is chiefly remembered. As early as 1888 he had told a Toronto audience that the federation of Canada might be 'the lamp to lighten our path' to the federation of the British Empire. Soon after he came to the Colonial Office the Jameson Raid (December 1895), and the events that followed in South Africa, obliged him to concentrate his attention, for the most part, on that one subject. But the symptoms of general European hostility which followed that unfortunate episode served to point the moral: 'Let us do all in our power by improving our communications, by developing our commercial relations, by co-operating in mutual defence; and none of us will ever feel isolated . . . and in the time to come, the time that must come, when these colonies of ours have grown in stature, in population, and in strength, this league of kindred nations, this federation of Great Britain, will not only provide for its own security, but will be a potent factor in maintaining the peace of the world' (21 January 1896). In too confident a mood he seemed to think that the opportunity had already arrived for consolidating the scattered parts into 'a great self-sustaining and self-protecting empire'.

But the South African difficulty, though it might suggest such ideals, prevented any immediate attempt at their realization. Chamberlain had already given a proof of his mettle in one sharp encounter with President Kruger. The president, in 1895, closed the Vaal drifts in pursuance of his policy of obtaining for the Delagoa Bay Railway Company the monopoly of conveying overseas goods into the Transvaal. Chamberlain, having first obtained an assurance that the government of Cape Colony was prepared to share equally in the expense of any military operations that might be necessary, sent an ultimatum to the president, and the drifts were promptly reopened. But the after-effects of the Jameson Raid undoubtedly made Chamberlain's position more difficult. During the anxious years that followed he was assailed with great bitterness. He was accused of complicity in the Raid; and after his solemn denial had been unanimously accepted by the House of Commons committee which dealt with the matter, it was still insinuated that there was more behind, which should have been divulged. In fact, Chamberlain's prompt and immediate action in denouncing the Raid before he knew of its failure, is sufficient proof that he could not have had previous knowledge regarding it. There may have been some confusion between a rising of the Johannesburg Uitlanders, which was expected in England, and the Raid, which was a bolt from the blue. In any case, the atmosphere of suspicion and hate, which the Raid created, made almost hopeless the attempt to secure civic rights for the Transvaal Uitlanders. Moreover, the attitude of the high commissioner, Sir Hercules Robinson (afterwards Baron Rosmead, q.v.), who concentrated all his efforts on securing lenient terms for the prisoners, made still more difficult the task of the colonial secretary. An ultimatum might lead to war; and such a war, he told the House of Commons on 8 May 1896, would be in the nature of a civil war—long, bitter, costly, leaving behind it the embers of strife, which generations might not extinguish. But success in dealing with the Jameson trouble had both hardened Kruger's heart and increased his confidence in his own wisdom; whilst the Raid had aroused a strong nationalist spirit throughout Dutch South Africa. An agreement which was practically an offensive and defensive alliance between the Orange Free State and the Transvaal (1897) was a serious menace to British interests, and the temporary eclipse of Cecil Rhodes made the English in Cape Colony as sheep without a shepherd.

The appointment, in 1897, of a high commissioner—Sir Alfred (afterwards Viscount) Milner—who combined strength with caution, gave the colonial secretary an adviser in whom he could place complete confidence. Read now, the controversy between the Transvaal and British governments on the question whether the Republic was a sovereign state, and whether foreign arbitration was admissible, may seem academic. But the practical interests of many British subjects were deeply involved ; whilst there were additional complaints—of the dynamite monopoly, of maladministration in Swaziland, and of other grievances. For a year Milner remained silent, studying the situation. When he spoke, it was to counsel the Dutch in Cape Colony to warn their kinsmen in the Transvaal against any fatal rashness. Henceforth, though Chamberlain was always ready to interfere if necessary, British policy was mainly directed by the man on the spot. It was the fashion amongst a certain school of radicals to regard Chamberlain as a firebrand, who was only kept in order by the influence of his more moderate colleagues. If his speeches showed moderation it was assumed that this was only because Lord Salisbury was holding him back. There appears, however, not to be a tittle of evidence for such a reading of the history.

In any case, the Bloemfontein Conference (May–June 1899) was an honest attempt on the part of the British authorities to reach a *modus vivendi* on the questions at issue. Its starting-point was as follows: On 4 May Milner, in a powerful and plain-spoken telegram, stated the case for intervention. 'The true remedy', he said, 'is to strike at the root of all these injuries, the political impotence of the injured. What diplomatic protests will never accomplish, a fair measure of Uitlander representation would gradually but surely bring about.' 'The case for intervention', he insisted, 'is overwhelming. . . . The spectacle of thousands of British subjects kept permanently in the position of helots, constantly chafing over undoubted grievances and calling vainly to Her Majesty's government for redress, does steadily undermine the influence and reputation of Great Britain and the respect for the British government within the British dominions.' Chamberlain's considered reply, sent on 10 May, covered the whole ground. After summarizing the details of the Uitlanders' grievances, the most serious of which affected their 'personal rights', placing them 'in a position of political, social, and educational inferiority to the Boer inhabitants of the Transvaal, and even endangering the security of their lives and property', the dispatch finally stated the conclusions at which the British government had arrived. Recognizing the exceptional circumstances of the case, they had, since February 1896, intentionally refrained from any pressure on the government of the South African Republic, except in cases where there had been a distinct breach of the Convention of 1884. Reluctant as they were to depart from this attitude of reserve and expectancy, still, 'having regard to the position of Great Britain as the paramount power in South Africa, and the duty incumbent on them to protect all British subjects residing in a foreign country, they cannot permanently ignore the exceptional and arbitrary treatment to which their fellow-countrymen and others are exposed, and the absolute indifference of the government of the Republic to the friendly representations which have been made to them on the subject'. 'With the earnest hope of arriving at a satisfactory settlement and as a proof of their desire to maintain cordial relations with the South African Republic', the British government proposed that a meeting should be arranged between President Kruger and Sir Alfred Milner at Pretoria. Meanwhile, the idea of a conference was already in the mind of leaders of the Dutch in Cape Colony and the Orange Free State; and the Bloemfontein Conference, which lasted from 31 May to 4 June, was welcomed by moderate men of all parties. The question was complicated by Kruger's desire to offset any concessions he might make with regard to the franchise by gains in other directions ; and by Milner's insistence that there were other questions, besides the franchise, about which it might be necessary to make complaints. On the main subject of the Conference Milner proposed as a settlement a five years' retrospective franchise, and a substantial increase in the number of seats in the Volksraad to be allotted to the Rand. On the third day of the Conference a counter-scheme was put forward by Kruger, which included a six months' notice of intention to apply for naturalization ; naturalization after two years' continued registration ; and the right to the franchise after continuous registration for five years after naturalization. It proved impossible to arrive at an agreement, and the Conference came to an end.

It is easy to maintain that the Bloemfontein Conference broke down on petty points ; but, in fact, throughout the negotiations Kruger never showed that spirit of conciliation without which paper concessions would have proved practically worthless. No one recognized more clearly than Chamberlain how great a calamity would be a war in South Africa, of the nature of a civil war; but the question was whether the situation had not become so serious that even war might be the less of two evils. Moreover, if the British government had really aimed at putting an end to the Republic, they would not have counselled measures that would have secured to it a new lease of life.

Even after the failure of the Bloemfontein Conference Chamberlain did not behave as if the door was finally closed to a settlement. In the words of Lord De Villiers, he 'held out an olive branch' by proposing a joint inquiry into the franchise proposals. The Dutch members of the Cape ministry were strongly in favour of the acceptance of the offer, and the European governments gave similar advice; but Kruger's mind was apparently made up, and a peaceful issue had become impossible. The conciliatory attitude of Chamberlain was all to no purpose. When he offered, as part of a general settlement, to give a complete guarantee against any attack upon the independence of the Republic, either from within any part of the British dominions, or from the territory of a foreign state, the only reply was a curt ultimatum demanding that the points at issue should be settled by arbitration, and that the troops on the borders should be withdrawn, the reinforcements removed, and the troops on the high seas forbidden to land. It is true that Chamberlain's dispatch had also contained the warning that Kruger's attitude made it necessary to consider the whole situation afresh, and that final proposals would be made after such consideration. But this warning can hardly be said to excuse the curt and peremptory tone of Kruger's ultimatum.

From this time the sword had to decide the issue, and a minister, however active and able, was forced to play a secondary part. In the darkest hour of the War, however, Chamberlain never lost heart or courage. 'Never again', he said on 5 February 1900, 'shall the Boers be able to erect in the heart of South Africa a citadel from whence may proceed disaffection and race animosities; never again shall they be able to endanger the paramountcy of Great Britain; never again shall they be able to treat an Englishman as if he belonged to an inferior race'; and in a powerful dispatch of July 1900, which tore in pieces the analogy set up by the Cape ministry between the situation at the time of the Canadian rebellion and the situation in South Africa, we may recognize Chamberlain's handiwork. There was, moreover, much in the attitude of the other colonies to give consolation. These had shown their sympathy with the wrongs of the Uitlanders and with the cause of Great Britain by deeds as well as by words. The Australian colonies sent during the War no less than 15,502 men to South Africa; New Zealand sent 6,129, and Canada 5,762. There was force in Chamberlain's boast that these young nations were beginning to recognize the duties and responsibilities, as well as the privileges, of empire.

With the coming of peace more direct opportunities for statesmanship presented themselves. Few now will question that Chamberlain's visit to South Africa at the end of 1902 was a very wise move. No secretary of state had before this time visited a British colony in connexion with political questions; but there was enough of the old radical left in Chamberlain for this not to stand in his way. It seems clear that his influence and persuasive powers helped forward a reconciliation between the rival races and parties in Cape Colony; and this reacted favourably upon the general South African situation. Nor was he less successful in his dealings with the Boers of the Transvaal. In open discussion with their leaders he did much to clear the air of dislike and suspicion. 'The terms of Vereeniging', he told them, 'are the charter of the Boer people, and you have every right to call upon us to fulfil them in the spirit and in the letter; and, if in any respect you think we have failed, or that in the future we do fail, in carrying out these terms, bring your complaints to us, and they shall be redressed.' Again: 'In the terms of peace it was promised that Dutch education should be given to the children of all parents who desired it; that promise we will keep.' 'What are the qualities', he asked, 'which we admire in you? Your patriotism, your courage, your tenacity, your willingness to make sacrifices for what you believe to be right and true. Well, those are the qualities which we desire to imitate; and which we believe we shall.' He looked forward with confidence to the day when Boer and Briton would be one free people, under a common flag. It must be noted that these sentiments represented no new doctrine on the part of Chamberlain. During the heat of the War, when racial and political animosities were at their height, he had written (2 August 1900): 'It is the desire of Her Majesty's government that the inhabitants of these territories, assuming that they peaceably acquiesce in British rule and are ready to co-operate, irrespective of race, in maintaining the peace and furthering the prosperity of the country, should, as soon as circumstances permit, have all the advantages of self-government similar to that which is enjoyed by the inhabitants of the Cape Colony and Natal.' At the same time it was obvious that there would have to be a period of Crown Colony government, between the annexation and the grant of full self-government. Chamberlain does not, however, seem to have recognized the expediency of a period of representative, without responsible, government, such as that afterwards set on foot by Alfred Lyttelton [q.v.].

Nor were Chamberlain's utterances less successful when addressed to the capitalists of the Rand. An eyewitness has testified that a speech of his at Johannesburg actually persuaded an audience, that had come with intent of refusing, to promise a loan of thirty million pounds, the proceeds of which should be paid to the British government, as a contribution to the cost of the War. It is true that this loan was never raised, bad times and a shortage of labour having disappointed the high hopes raised by the British successes. But such failure cannot be laid to the charge of the colonial secretary.

In dealing with the Rand magnates, Chamberlain was no less open than when dealing with the Boer leaders. Already the demand was beginning to be made for Asiatic labour, and his remarks on the subject are significant, in the light of its future history. 'It is clear to me, and no doubt to you,' he said at Johannesburg (17 January 1903), 'that an overwhelming popular opinion in this very colony is opposed to such a solution. You have first to convert the people. Then you will have seen that the other great colonies of the Empire, that the opinion of the mother country itself, regard a step of this kind as retrograde and dangerous. And, lastly, if these difficulties are removed, there are serious practical obstacles in the way, which will meet you at the outset, and which, I think, justify my opinion that it would be very long indeed, even if all other difficulties were removed, before you would obtain any reliable supply from the sources which have been suggested.'

Another proof of Chamberlain's moderation was his vetoing, in 1902, the suspension of the Cape Colony constitution as proposed by the English party in the House of Assembly, although the line taken by Sir Wilfrid Laurier [q.v.] at the Imperial Conference of that year may have influenced his decision. Whilst emphasizing his desire for South African federation he recognized, in a dispatch of 23 February, that nothing could be worse than federation forced upon a people before they had time thoroughly to grasp its meaning and to understand how it would affect them personally in their several states, and to come to something like a general conclusion on the subject. The harvest could not yet be reaped; but, when the Union of South Africa came into being, it owed something at least to the seed sown by Chamberlain.

He had already done good work in the cause of federation by piloting the Commonwealth of Australia Bill through the House of Commons (1900). In his attempt to maintain unimpaired the appellate jurisdiction of the Privy Council, he may have exaggerated its importance as a bond of imperial union; and the conclusion finally reached, which was that no appeal should be allowed in cases in which the question at issue was the limits *inter se* of the constitutional powers of the commonwealth and those of any state or states, or the limits *inter se* of the constitutional powers of any two or more states, without the leave of the commonwealth high court, was, in fact, a 'confession of failure'. Nevertheless, the birth of the Commonwealth of Australia seemed a distinct step forward in the direction of Chamberlain's ideals.

With his return from South Africa in March 1903, Chamberlain entered upon the last stage of his political life. During the South African War a tax of one shilling a quarter on imported corn had been imposed, which produced some two and a half million pounds a year without apparently affecting the price of bread. Chamberlain was in favour of retaining this small tax with the view of giving a rebate to imperial wheat; and he was bitterly disappointed by its abolition during his absence in South Africa. He was under the impression that, before his departure for South Africa, his policy had received the assent of the Cabinet with the exception of the chancellor of the exchequer, Mr. C. T. (afterwards Lord) Ritchie [q.v.]. The absence at the time of Cabinet ministers and other circumstances prevent certainty on the subject. Later, Chamberlain wrote to the Duke of Devonshire (21 September): 'For my part I care only for the great question of imperial unity. But for this . . . I would not have taken off my coat. . . . While I was slaving my life out, you threw it (my policy) over as of no importance; and it is to this indifference to a great policy, which you had yourselves accepted, that you owe the present situation.' On 9 September 1903 he wrote to the prime minister, Mr. Balfour, recognizing that as an 'immediate and practical policy' the question of preference to the Colonies could not be pressed with any success at the time, and saying that, as colonial secretary, he stood in a position different from any of his colleagues and would justly be blamed if he accepted its exclusion from the programme of the government. He therefore tendered his resignation so that he could, from outside, devote his attention to explaining and popularizing those principles of imperial union which his experience had convinced him were essential. It was not, however, till 16 September that the prime minister reluctantly acquiesced in this decision.

Chamberlain, while in the unionist government, was mainly preoccupied with colonial questions. He had not, however, altogether forgotten his zeal for social reform, and the Workmen's Compensation Act of 1897 was mainly due to his efforts. The weakest side of his statesmanship was, perhaps, shown in his excursions into the field of foreign policy. His attack upon Russia in 1898, with its remark that 'who sups with the devil must have a long spoon', cannot have made easier the path of Lord Salisbury's diplomacy. Nor was his grandiose scheme for an alliance between Great Britain, Germany, and the United States (1898–1901) likely, in the circumstances, to meet with success. Its object, the prevention of a great European war, was assuredly worth the price of granting a free hand to Germany in Asia Minor, and, if the negotiations had been left in the hands of Count Hatzfeldt, a conclusion might have been reached; but, with the Kaiser's jealousy and dislike of England, with the narrow persistence of Herr von Holstein, the permanent head of the German foreign office, in regarding the proposal as an opportunity to exact the hardest terms from the needs of Great Britain, and with Prince Bülow's subserviency to his royal master, the attempt was apparently from the first foredoomed to failure. It is a proof, however, of Chamberlain's flexibility of mind, since in March 1896 he had seemed to Count Hatzfeldt 'especially hostile to Germany and German interests'.

Whatever were the immediate circumstances of Chamberlain's resignation, in any case views were developing in his mind that foreshadowed a revolutionary change of policy. It must be remembered that, although it was easy enough to put side by side, as has been done, conflicting statements of his economic views at different periods, he had never, in theory or in practice, belonged to the Manchester school of free traders, to whom free trade was but one item in a general creed of *laissez-aller* and anti-socialism. From his first entrance into politics he had advocated a modified form of state socialism. He had, indeed, accepted free trade as part of the orthodox faith of a good liberal; but during those years he had failed to realize the importance of the imperial factor in the decision of the question. It was the consideration of this factor that accounted for his change of policy. On the fiscal side he had for some years been in favour of some kind of imperial *Zollverein*, and in 1896 he had protested against the proposal that, while the Colonies should be absolutely free to impose what protective duties they pleased, our whole system should be changed, in return for a small discrimination in favour of British trade. The foreign trade of Great Britain was so large and that of the Colonies comparatively so insignificant that a small preference would give a merely nominal advantage; he did not think the British working classes would consent to make so revolutionary a change for what would seem to them an infinitesimal gain. Even as late as the opening of the Imperial Conference of 1902 he declared: 'Our first object is free trade within the Empire.'

But during the sitting of this conference the conviction was borne home to him that an imperial *Zollverein* was, for the time being, an impossibility; whilst the need for closer union became more and more urgent. Unless such union could be achieved between the component parts of the Empire, he thought that separation must sooner or later be the end. The enthusiasm aroused throughout the Empire by the South African War had seemed to give him his opportunity, and at the Imperial Conference he had suggested 'a real council of the Empire to which all questions of imperial interest might be referred. Such a council would be at first merely advisory; but its object would not be completely secured until it had attained executive functions and perhaps some legislative powers'. It was the chilling reception accorded to this suggestion, and the failure of the attempt to organize closer union on the lines of imperial defence, which led him to seek elsewhere for bonds of union. A statement made in October 1903 throws light on the trend of his political development. Discussing the subject of a federal council he said: 'The Colonies want to know what it is they are to discuss before they come to your council. When you have got a commercial union, there will be something to discuss. . . . You cannot approach closer union by that means (a federal council). I tried next in connexion with imperial defence. Again I was beaten by the difficulties of the situation; but I did not on that account give it up, and I come back therefore to this idea of commercial union, which will bring us together, which will necessitate the council, which council may in time do much more than it does in the beginning, and may leave us, though it will not find us, a great united, loyal, and federated Empire.' A little later he declared: 'I hope to lay firm and deep the foundations for that imperial union which fills my heart when I look forward to the future of the world.'

Welcoming the statement made by an opponent in the press that the real issue in question was between imperialism and 'Little Englandism', Chamberlain nailed his colours to the mast as a convinced imperialist (Liverpool, 27 October 1903). He would never have raised the question, as he avowed next day, if he had not been moved by his own personal experiences, and by the responsibilities which he felt he had towards the Colonies. If he had not felt, in connexion with that experience and responsibility, that the whole future of the Empire depended upon a readiness to review the past history, he would have left the subject, so far as it concerned the immediate interests of Great Britain, to younger men. But a constructive policy was essential, and during his long stay at the Colonial Office he had had more opportunities than most men to meet and consult with distinguished colonial statesmen, and he had found that this matter of closer union was much in their thoughts. 'I found very soon that these men agreed that all progress must be gradual, and that the line of least resistance would be a commercial union on the basis of preference between ourselves and our kinsmen.' Starting from different premises, he arrived at the same conclusion as Adam Smith, that the British Empire was a potentiality, a project of empire, not an empire—'a loose bundle of sticks'—bound together by no tie but that of sentiment and sympathy. In the same speech he spoke of the sacrifices by which the Empire had been created; and a sympathetic critic may regret that more stress was not throughout laid on the necessity of sacrifice for the attainment of great objects. But it must be remembered that Chamberlain was an old campaigner in politics, and if, in the course of his appeal to the British voters, he seemed sometimes to be absorbed in considerations other than those which had launched him on his adventure, he perhaps only followed in the usual steps of the practical politician. Whilst his resignation gave him complete liberty of action, matters were not made easier for him by the hesitating attitude of some of his old colleagues, and especially of the prime minister, Mr. Balfour. Moreover, the ministry had become unpopular by reason of the Education Act of 1902, of which Chamberlain strongly disapproved, though he was too loyal to express his views openly. The effect of all this was to make him concentrate more and more upon the one object, of bringing the British people round to his views of tariff reform. He had, in any case, a difficult task before him. Arrayed against him were the political and economic beliefs of the majority of educated Englishmen; whilst vague memories of 'the starving 'forties' made any kind of protection suspect to the labouring classes.

Still, whether we agree or disagree, we must recognize the strength of Chamberlain's convictions; and it was fitting that the last words in his three years' campaign, which ended on 9 July 1906, should have been these: 'The union of the Empire must be preceded and accompanied by a better understanding, by a closer sympathy. To secure that, is the highest object of statesmanship now at the beginning of the twentieth century; and, if these were the last words that I were permitted to utter to you, I would rejoice to utter them in your presence and with your approval. I know that the fruition of our hopes is certain. I hope I may live to congratulate you upon our common triumph; but, in any case, I have faith in the people. I trust in the good sense, the intelligence, and the patriotism of the majority, the vast majority of my countrymen. I look forward to the future with hope and confidence, and

"Others I doubt not, if not we,
The issue of our toil shall see".'

But it was not given him to see the issue of his toil. Only two days later (11 July), a sudden attack cut him off, for his remaining years, from active life. He did not, indeed, lose the control of his faculties, but the aphasia which had come upon him made further public life impossible. He died at Highbury, Birmingham, 2 July 1914. A funeral in Westminster Abbey was offered, but the family preferred that he should be buried near his home.

Turning from the statesman to the man, we find a unanimity of opinion among those who knew Chamberlain intimately. If, in Lord Morley's words, he had the 'genius of friendship', he had no less the genius both of family and of official life. Chamberlain was married three times: first, in 1861 to Harriet (died 1863), daughter of Archibald Kenrick, of Berrow Court, Edgbaston; secondly, in 1868 to Florence (died 1875), daughter of Timothy Kenrick, of Birmingham, and a cousin of his first wife; thirdly, in 1888 to Mary, only daughter of William Crowninshield Endicott, a distinguished American judge and statesman, belonging to a family well known in New England history. Chamberlain had become engaged to Miss Endicott when he was working on the fisheries commission, but the marriage could not be announced or take place until after the American presidential election, for fear of prejudicing the chances of the democrats. By his first wife Chamberlain had one son (Joseph) Austen, and one daughter; by his second, one son (Arthur) Neville, and three daughters. He was a devoted husband and father, and perhaps one of the happiest moments of his life was when Mr. Gladstone gracefully alluded to the merits of his elder son's maiden speech; when he and Mr. Ritchie both resigned in 1903, it must have been some consolation that the latter was succeeded by the same son, (Sir) Austen Chamberlain, as chancellor of the exchequer. Mr. Neville Chamberlain, also, entered the Cabinet as chancellor of the exchequer in Mr. Baldwin's ministry in 1923.

Although on one occasion Chamberlain lamented the loss of a university education, the loss was made up by intercourse with the best books and with a few choice spirits at Birmingham. According to Mr. T. H. S. Escott, the writer who, more than any other, formed his mind and style, was the French publicist, Paul Louis Courier. Lord Morley, who went abroad with him frequently, bore witness to his interest in pictures, buildings, and history. In 1896 he was elected lord rector of Glasgow University, and delivered a characteristic address on patriotism, in which he protested his faith in one race and one nation: 'I believe that with all the force and enthusiasm of which democracy alone is capable they will complete and maintain that splendid edifice of our greatness.' Further, he was in a yet closer way connected with the university of Birmingham, the foundation of which in 1900 was largely due to his efforts; he became, as was meet, its first chancellor.

Chamberlain belonged to a Unitarian family, and seems always to have remained faithful to the creed of his fathers. Lord Morley has given a vivid picture of him as a companion, 'alert, not without a pleasant squeeze of lemon, to add savour to the daily dish'. Spare of body, sharp and pronounced in feature, careful of dress, Chamberlain looked ever ready. Caricaturists everywhere fixed eagerly on the monocle in his eye and the rare orchid bloom, culled from his favourite greenhouse, habitually worn in his button-hole. No physiognomy was better known to contemporaries, either at home or abroad. Gladstone, who was by no means a friendly critic, bore witness to Chamberlain's merits in serious discussions. What impressed Froude about him was that he knew his own mind. There was no dust in his eyes; and he threw no dust in the eyes of others. He was naturally open and spontaneous; and, in Lord Morley's words, 'when he encountered a current of doubt, dislike, suspicion, prejudice, his one and first impulse was to hasten to put his case, to explain, to have it out'. He was a hard hitter, and not always careful to remember that others were more thin-skinned than himself, but he was of a nature essentially generous and forgiving. After a temporary quarrel with Lord Randolph Churchill, at the time of the Aston riots (1884), he wrote to Lord Randolph who was starting for India, a characteristic letter, burying the hatchet, which received a cordial response. He seems to have been totally devoid of jealousy; and he carried loyalty to those who had once obtained his confidence to its extreme limits. With these qualities he naturally attracted friendship; and his relations with men so different as were Dilke, Churchill, Morley, and Balfour, were the best witness to that attraction. 'To him', again in Lord Morley's words, 'the friend was not merely a comrade in a campaign. He was an innermost element in his existence; whilst, if he stood by his friend, he counted on his friend to stand by him.'

The same loyalty that endeared him to his friends called forth the devoted attachment of his official subordinates. Lord Milner described him as an incomparable chief. He always, if possible, consulted those who served under him. He gave the fullest consideration to all their representations. He went thoroughly into every aspect of the case, for he was a most industrious minister; and finally, he laid down firmly and deliberately the policy which he wished to be followed, leaving a large latitude to those who had to work it out. Sir Harry Wilson, who was principal private secretary to Chamberlain from 1895 to 1897, has also described his methods of dealing with business. His 'minutes' were almost invariably concise, and always strictly to the point. While he generally accepted the advice of his under-secretaries, often making illuminating additions to their drafts, he sometimes reversed their conclusions, though not without full discussion. The vigour of his methods is attested by the fact that, at the time of the Jameson Raid, he made a personal invasion, at one o'clock a.m., of the office of the Eastern Telegraph Company, to discover why an important telegram had not been delivered. Through his whole life he justified the words of his son: 'He never rested. To his last day he seemed too young to leave things as they are.' When party animosities are forgotten, men will probably recognize the truth of the Earl of Balfour's testimony —'He was a great statesman, a great friend, a great orator, a great man.'

Chamberlain's speeches are contained in the following editions: C. W. Boyd, *Mr. Chamberlain's Speeches*, 2 vols. (1914); H. W. Lucy, *Speeches, with sketch of Life* (1885); *Speeches on Home Rule and the Irish Question, 1881–1887* (1887); *Foreign and Colonial Speeches* (1897); *Imperial Union and Tariff Reform 15 May–4 November 1903* (2nd edition, 1910). He was the author of *Patriotism* (1897) and of a preface to *The Radical Programme* (1885). He also wrote the following articles in the *Fortnightly Review: The Liberal Party and its Leaders*, and *The Next Page of the Liberals* (1874); *The Right Method with the Publicans*, and *Lapland and Swedish Licensing* (1876); *Free Schools, Municipal Public-Houses*, and *The New Political Organization* (1877); *The Caucus* (1879); *Labourers' and Artisans' Dwellings* (1883). In the *Nineteenth Century* he wrote: *Shall we Americanise our Institutions?* (1890); *The Labour Question* (1892); *A Bill for the Weakening of Great Britain* (1893); and in the *New Review, Municipal Reform* (1894).

The chief portraits of Chamberlain are those by Frank Holl (1886), by J. S. Sargent (1896), by Sir H. von Herkomer (1903, *Royal Academy Pictures*, 1904), and by C. W. Furse (1904, unfinished owing to the artist's death). A bust in Westminster Abbey was unveiled on 31 March 1916 by Lord Balfour, and another, executed by F. Derwent Wood in 1915, belongs to the Corporation of the City of London (*Royal Academy Pictures*, 1915).

[*The Times*, 4 July 1914; Stephen Gwynn and Gertrude Tuckwell, *Life of Sir Charles W. Dilke*, 2 vols., 1917; Lord Morley, *Recollections*, 2 vols., 1917, and *Life of William Ewart Gladstone*, 2 vols., 1905; Winston S. Churchill, *Lord Randolph Churchill*, 2 vols., 1906; Bernard Holland, *Life of Spencer Compton, Eighth Duke of Devonshire*, 2 vols., 1911; G. M. Trevelyan, *Life of John Bright*, 1913; Lord Edmond Fitzmaurice, *Life of Granville George Leveson Gower, Second Earl Granville*, 2 vols., 1905; Hon. A. R. D. Elliot, *Life of George Joachim Goschen, First Viscount Goschen*, 2 vols., 1911; E. A. Walker, *Lord De Villiers and his Times, South Africa 1842–1914*, 1924; A. G. Gardiner, *Life of Sir William Harcourt*, 2 vols., 1923; N. M. Murrell Marris, *Joseph Chamberlain, the Man and the Statesman*, 1900; S. H. Jeyes, *Mr. Chamberlain; his Life and Public Career*, 2 vols., 1904; Alexander Mackintosh, *Joseph Chamberlain; an honest biography*, 1906; Louis Creswicke, *Life of Joseph Chamberlain*, 4 vols., 1904; H. von Eckardstein, *Lebenserinnerungen*, translated by George Young as *Ten Years at the Court of St. James, 1895–1905*, 1921; Sir Willoughby Maycock, *With Mr. Chamberlain to the United States and Canada, 1887–1888*, 1914; Sir C. Tupper, *Recollections of Sixty Years*, 1914; Sir C. Bruce, *The Broad Stone of Empire*, 2 vols., 1910; A. W. W. Dale, *Life of R. W. Dale of Birmingham* (3rd ed.), 1899; R. Barry O'Brien, *Life of Charles Stewart Parnell*, 2 vols., 1898; W. Basil Worsfold, *Reconstruction of the New Colonies under Lord Milner*, 2 vols., 1913; R. Jebb, *The Imperial Conference*, vol. i, 1911; L. C. A. Knowles, *The Industrial and Commercial Revolutions in Great Britain during the Nineteenth Century*, 1921; '*The Times*' *History of the War in South Africa*, edited by L. C. M. S. Amery, vols. i and vi, 1900–1909; Sir Sidney Lee, *Life of King Edward VII*, vol. i, 1925; Articles on Chamberlain in the *United Empire*, vol. viii, pp. 102–11, 1917; by T. H. S. Escott in *Britannic Review*, vol. vii, pp. 321–41; and by M. Woods in *Fortnightly Review*, August 1914; *Parliamentary Papers; Hansard's Parliamentary Debates; Die Grosse Politik der Europäischen Kabinette 1871–1914*, vol. xi, 1923; E. Fischer, *Holstein's Grosses Nein. Die Deutsch-Englischen Bündnisverhandlungen von 1898–1901*, 1925.]

H. E. E.

CHEYNE, THOMAS KELLY (1841–1915), Old Testament scholar, the second son of the Rev. Charles Cheyne, a master at Christ's Hospital and curate of St. Olave Jewry, London, by his wife, Sarah Anne, daughter of Thomas Hartwell Horne [q.v.], was born in London 18 September 1841. He was educated at Merchant Taylors' School, at Worcester College, Oxford, to which he came as scholar in 1859 after a short period at Magdalen Hall, and at Göttingen. He took a pass degree at Oxford in 1862, having devoted himself to Hebrew and other subjects outside the usual course of studies; but he gained many university distinctions. After taking orders in 1864, he was appointed vice-principal of St. Edmund Hall, where he remained until elected to a fellowship at Balliol College in 1868. He was fellow of Balliol until 1882, and rector of Tendring, Essex, from 1880 to 1885. He joined the Old Testament revision company in 1884, on which he acted with a small band of critical scholars, including Andrew Bruce Davidson [q.v.], William Robertson Smith [q.v.], Samuel Rolles Driver [q.v.], and A. H. Sayce. In 1885 he was elected Oriel professor of the interpretation of Scripture at Oxford, and he held the professorship, with the canonry of Rochester attached to it, until 1908. His first wife, whom he married in 1882, was Frances, daughter of the Rev. D. R. Godfrey, fellow of Queen's College. Oxford; she died in 1907. In 1911 he married Elizabeth, daughter of John Pattison Gibson. He had no children. He died at Oxford 16 February 1915.

The son of a clergyman, and the grandson of Thomas Hartwell Horne, the author of the celebrated *Introduction to the Holy Scriptures*, Cheyne was naturally attracted to the study of the Bible. He chose the Old Testament as his special field. Whether, had he remained in England, he would have held to the rigid conservatism which the controversies that raged about Samuel Davidson, Bishop Colenso, and *Essays and Reviews*, had done little to relax, it is impossible to say. But the teaching which he received in Germany made a decisive change in his attitude to biblical problems. Above all the stimulus he received from Heinrich von Ewald at Göttingen freed him from the restraining influence of tradition. Ewald was at the time the dominant authority on the language, the literature, the history, and the religion of Israel. His personality was stimulating and inspiring to an extraordinary degree, and his pupils were men of such outstanding eminence as Hitzig, Nöldeke, Schrader, Dillmann, and Wellhausen. His influence left deep marks on Cheyne's early work, shown especially in his *Book of Isaiah Chronologically Arranged* (1870). Yet it did not enslave him, for as early as 1871 he had accepted, in spite of Ewald's scornful rejection, the 'Grafian' theory that the priestly code was the latest of the four main pentateuchal documents—a theory adumbrated by Reuss and Vatke in 1834–1835, revived by Graf in 1865, defended and applied by Kuenen in his *Religion of Israel* (1869–1870) and carried to triumph by Wellhausen in his *History of Israel* (vol. i) in 1878.

Though he had predecessors, it is to Cheyne that the distinction belongs of initiating with adequate scholarship the critical movement in his native country. When he was barely twenty-eight, *The Academy* was founded and he was placed in charge of the biblical department. His own reviews were characterized by a maturity, a width of knowledge, a familiarity with the best continental literature, and a grip of critical principles, results, and problems, remarkable in one so young. The educational work thus begun was continued in the ninth edition of the *Encyclopaedia Britannica* and in a large number of books, among which special mention should be made of *The Prophecies of Isaiah* (1880–1881), *Job and Solomon* (1887), *The Book of Psalms* (1888), *The Origin and Religious Contents of the Psalter* (1891), *The Founders of Old Testament Criticism* (1893), *Introduction to the Book of Isaiah* (1895), and *Jewish Religious Life after the Exile* (1898).

Cheyne's career, alike in criticism and religion, was of singular and, in its latest phase, of painful interest. In other respects than in his early adhesion to the Grafian theory, he was in the van of the critical movement. From first to last he probably adhered consistently to the principle, laid down in his first book, that 'preconceived theological notions ought to be rigorously excluded from exegesis'. But in 1880 he became an evangelical, though of an individual type. 'Johannine religion reasserted its supremacy over criticism and speculation.' He did not abandon his critical position; but he combined faith with criticism, and was more concerned than before to make Scripture an instrument of edification. The sense that biblical criticism untouched by the apologetic interest 'cramped the moral energies' led him to a less uncompromising statement of results and a more considerate regard for the weaker brethren. But, as time went on, accommodation seemed less necessary, and his utterances became more and more outspoken. With this there went a tendency to more extreme positions, and a growing impatience, not perhaps untouched by scorn, with those who adhered to a more moderate attitude. More and more of the Old Testament literature was relegated to the post-exilic period. More serious still was the growing recklessness of his textual criticism. This crossed at last the boundary beyond which sanity ceases. He had undertaken, in collaboration with Dr. Sutherland Black, to edit the *Encyclopaedia Biblica* (1899–1903). In the second volume (1900) the 'Jerahmeelite theory' made its appearance in a comparatively modest form. It was omnipresent in his contributions to the later volumes (1901, 1903), and in all his subsequent Old Testament work. The writing of numerous articles on proper names had convinced him that many had been incorrectly transmitted ; while Hugo Winckler's theory of a North Arabian land of Musri caused him to attribute to North Arabia an exaggerated part in Hebrew history. The whole of Cheyne's work on the Old Testament from this point has little value except for specialists. The development is one of the most tragic episodes in the history of scholarship.

Cheyne had a philological equipment of great range and high competence, a profound and intimate knowledge of the Old Testament, an amazing familiarity with the literature upon it, and a willingness to consider novel theories, however extravagant. He had a singular exegetical gift ; his commentaries are marked by originality, sympathy, and insight, and delicate literary instinct. His command of the whole field saved him from the danger of isolating its individual problems. His theological position became in his later years more and more indefinite. His last work, *The Reconciliation of Races and Religions* (1914), was not concerned with the Old Testament, but was noteworthy for its sympathy with Babism and the Bahai movement. He still spoke of himself as an anglican Christian ; but he considered most of the synoptic narrative, including the Crucifixion, to be open to the gravest doubt. It may accordingly be questioned whether at the end he could be regarded as a Christian in any tenable sense of that elastic term ; but at least his heart was set on the highest things, and in a world tortured by the strife of nations and distracted by the conflict of religions he cherished the vision of unity and peace.

[A. S. Peake in *Expository Times*, vol. vi, 1894–1895 ; G. A. Cooke in *Expositor*, May 1915 ; R. H. Charles in *Proceedings* of the British Academy, vol. vii, 1915–1916. There is much autobiographical matter in the prefaces to many of Cheyne's books.]

A. S. P.

CHILD-VILLIERS, VICTOR ALBERT GEORGE, seventh EARL OF JERSEY and tenth VISCOUNT GRANDISON (1845–1915), colonial governor. [See VILLIERS.]

CLANRICARDE, second MARQUESS OF (1832–1916). [See BURGH CANNING, HUBERT GEORGE DE.]

COHEN, ARTHUR (1829–1914), lawyer, was born in London 18 November 1829, the youngest son of Benjamin Cohen, a prosperous bill-broker. His grandfather, Levy Barent Cohen (1740–1808), came to London from Holland about 1770. Through his mother, Justina, the youngest daughter of Joseph Eliahu Montefiore and sister of Sir Moses H. Montefiore [q.v.], he was connected with the great Jewish families of Montefiore and Mocatta. At an early age he was sent to a tutor at Frankfort. When about seventeen he became a student at University College, London. His family, conscious of his ability, were anxious that he should go to Cambridge. Entrance to Trinity College was found to be impossible for a Jew, and it required the help of his uncle, Sir Moses, who invoked that of the Prince Consort as chancellor of the university, to secure his admission to Magdalene. Even then he had to pass in Paley's *View of the Evidences of Christianity*, as part of his entrance examination. He became a fellow-commoner in 1849, wore the gold-laced gown and velvet cap of that rank, and dined at the high table. He had not hitherto enjoyed much youthful companionship, and, furnished with a good allowance, he entered with zest on the life of an undergraduate. He was secretary of the Union Society in 1852, and its president in 1853. He rowed for at least one year in the Magdalene boat, and this is the only recorded instance of his indulgence in strenuous exercise. It was probably due to these diversions that his name appeared only as fifth wrangler in 1853, to the disappointment of his family, who with reason hoped to see him in a higher place, if not in the first. As a Jew he could not take his degree until after the passing in 1856 of 19 & 20 Vict., cap. 88. He was the first professing Jew to graduate at Cambridge. Later on the university made him amends; in 1879 he became counsel to the university, and in 1883 an honorary fellow of Magdalene College.

On leaving Cambridge Cohen became a member of the Inner Temple. He was a pupil of Mr. Dodgson, a special pleader. In May 1857 he won the studentship of the Inns of Court, and in November of the same year he was called to the bar. He was helped in his start by his uncle, Sir Moses Montefiore, who was chairman of the Alliance Assurance Company. But he had enough of ability and of industry to get on without backing, and he was soon busy, especially in commercial cases. He was fortunate in his time. Commercial law, the creation of Lord Mansfield in the days of small ships, was being adapted to the larger problems of steamers and of the growth of trade, and for many years Cohen appeared in nearly every important case. In 1872 he was selected by Sir Roundell Palmer, the attorney-general, to be junior counsel for Great Britain in the Alabama arbitration at Geneva. In 1873 he was given by Chief Baron Kelly the ancient post of 'tubman' in the court of Exchequer, having previously been 'postman'. In the same year he was a member of the royal commission on unseaworthy ships, the result of the agitation of Samuel Plimsoll [q.v.]. In 1874 he became a Queen's Counsel, being the junior but one in a batch of fourteen. In 1875 he was appointed judge of the Admiralty Court of the Cinque Ports, a sinecure which he only resigned in the year of his death. In 1876 he became a bencher of the Inner Temple, and he filled the office of treasurer in 1894.

In 1874 Cohen stood unsuccessfully for Lewes as a liberal. In April 1880 he headed the poll at Southwark, his fellow-member being Thorold Rogers. In 1881 Lord Selborne offered him the senior of two judgeships then vacant. At the request of Mr. Gladstone, who feared a by-election in the borough, Cohen declined. There was an understanding that Cohen should be offered a judgeship later on. But he never had another chance; and for many years new judges, answering letters of congratulation from Cohen, uniformly assured him that he ought long ago to have been on the bench himself. Cohen sat for Southwark from 1880 to 1887. He was not very successful in the House of Commons and seldom spoke, but when he did so he was listened to with respect. Even in court, at least to a younger generation who heard him in his later years, his manner of speaking was somewhat artificial, and it was probably too forensic for the House of Commons. In 1887 Cohen resigned his seat, chiefly because of the serious illness of his wife. In the year following he suffered a severe blow by her death. He had become engaged to Miss Emmeline Micholls, of Manchester, when she was a schoolgirl of fifteen, and they were married in 1860 when she was seventeen. It was a happy marriage, and they were happy in their family of three sons and five daughters.

In 1893 Cohen was appointed standing counsel to the India Office. In 1903 he was counsel for Great Britain in the Venezuela arbitration at The Hague. In the same year he was made a fellow of the British Academy, chairman of the Bar Council, and a member of the royal commission on trade unions—not a bad record for a man of seventy-four. In 1905 he was made a privy councillor by the conservative government. It was thought at the time that he would sit as one of the Judicial Committee, but there were technical difficulties which made this impossible. In 1906 he was appointed chairman of the royal commission on shipping combinations. In 1910 he wrote the article on *Insurance* in Lord Halsbury's *Laws of England.* This was his only published work of any length, and being upon a subject of which he had been long the acknowledged master it forms perhaps the most valuable section of that vast encyclopaedia. He continued his practice at the bar until about 1911, appearing at times with some junior who was born after his leader had taken silk. When he died, Lord Halsbury alone was his senior among the benchers of his Inn.

Cohen was a very great lawyer. To a fine intellect he added an untiring industry, and a passion for legal principles. In dedicating to Cohen his learned *Conflict of Laws*, A. V. Dicey said that 'his mastery of legal principles was surpassed only by the kindness with which his learning and experience have been placed at the service of his friends'. He was a slow worker, and made elaborate notes of his arguments. He was not a great advocate, in the popular sense, and in a court of first instance might be outmanœuvred by a man of much less ability. But for the argument of a question of law before an appellate tribunal he has had few equals. In all probability no advocate has so often addressed the House of Lords and the Judicial Committee.

Cohen was tall and handsome, with a

mass of dark hair, brown eyes, and a fresh complexion. He was a kindly man, with very courteous but rather stately manners. Although reserved and somewhat shy, he had many friends, and was universally esteemed by the members of the bar; to his juniors there he was ever kind and helpful. His main intellectual interest, apart from the law, was in mathematics; within a few months of his death he was reading books on the differential calculus. For his vacations his chief diversion was in foreign travel. As he would never take more work than he could properly do, and was slow and conscientious in doing it, he was never a rich man. About the acquisition of money he was as careless as he was lavish in spending it. His daughter records that he only once tried the experiment of riding in an omnibus; his brother, a bill-broker who died a millionaire, was never known to ride in anything else. Cohen was always a professing Jew, and proud of the traditions of the race. He was for many years president of the Jewish board of deputies. It was characteristic of him that he resigned when the first of his children married outside the Jewish community. His portrait was painted by J. S. Sargent in 1897. He died 3 November 1914, at his house in Great Cumberland Place, and was buried by the side of his wife in the Jewish cemetery at Willesden.

[*The Times*, 4 November 1914; *Memoir* by his daughter, 1919; *Law Quarterly Review*, January 1915; private information.]

F. D. M.

COLERIDGE-TAYLOR, SAMUEL (1875–1912), musical composer, was born in London at 15 Theobalds Road, Holborn, 15 August 1875. His father, Dr. Paul Taylor, was a native of Sierra Leone. He was brought up by his mother, Alice, *née* Hare, at Croydon, where he lived practically all his life and where he died. His mother was poor, and Coleridge-Taylor's education began at an elementary school where his musical ability was sufficiently evident for the schoolmaster to get him admitted into the choir of St. George's Presbyterian church, Croydon. Education might have gone no farther but for the interest of Colonel Herbert Walters, who discovered the boy's talent, removed him into the choir of St. Mary's church, Addiscombe, and in 1891 sent him as a student of the violin to the Royal College of Music. Here he came under the notice of (Sir) Charles Villiers Stanford, who advised him to take to composition as his principal study. In 1893 he won a scholarship at the College. He held it for four years, and during that time gained general recognition as one of the most talented of young composers. Over twenty of his works were first heard at College concerts, including a string quartet in D minor, a clarinet quintet (which so greatly impressed Joseph Joachim that he led a performance of it in Berlin in 1897), a nonet for piano, wind, and strings, and three movements of a symphony in A minor. As a composition pupil of Stanford, Coleridge-Taylor was firmly grounded in the classics, but even in these student days his highest admiration was given to the music of Dvořák, whom he loved to extol above Brahms. Spontaneity of melody, piquancy of rhythm, and glowing colour meant more to him than the subtle intellectualities of the great Germans.

Coleridge-Taylor had surrendered his scholarship when, on 11 November 1898, the concert was given, at the College, which produced his 'Hiawatha's Wedding Feast' and made him famous. Sir Hubert Parry wrote (*Musical Times*, October 1912): 'It had got abroad in some unaccountable and mysterious manner that something of unusual interest was going to happen, and when the time came for the concert the "tin tabernacle" (i.e. the temporary concert hall of the Royal College of Music) was besieged by eager crowds, a large proportion of whom were shut out, but accommodation was found for Sir Arthur Sullivan and other musicians of eminence. Expectation was not disappointed, and "Hiawatha" started on a career which, when confirmed by the production of "The Death of Minnehaha" at the North Staffordshire festival in the following year (1899) and of a final section by the Royal Choral Society in 1900, established it as one of the most universally beloved works of modern English music.'

The production of the whole work by the Royal Choral Society at the Albert Hall on 22 March 1900 set the seal on Coleridge-Taylor's unique achievement, and he was asked to compose for one festival after another. But he could never find another book with just that simplicity of narrative, that naïve human interest combined with exotic imagery, which made Longfellow his ideal partner in song. 'The Blind Girl of Castel Cuillé' (Leeds 1901), 'Meg Blane' (Sheffield 1902), and an oratorio 'The Atonement' (Hereford 1903) were all failures in comparison with 'Hiawatha'.

The only later choral work which came near to that ideal fitness between words and music was 'A Tale of Old Japan' (London 1911). Here a poem by Alfred Noyes provided the composer with a story and an 'atmosphere', the two things which he needed from words. The stage offered a similar impetus to his genius, and the incidental music which he wrote to a series of plays by Stephen Phillips [q.v.], produced at His Majesty's Theatre—*Herod* 1900, *Ulysses* 1902, *Nero* 1906, *Faust* 1908—was successful because of his power of giving vivid musical characterization to externals. The personal factor, too, was easily recognizable in his purely instrumental music from the early ballade in A minor to the 'Othello' suite, the 'Hiawatha' ballet music (distinct from the cantata), and the violin concerto, which were among his latest works. The 'catchy' rhythmic phrase and its repetition in varied tones, the capacity for indulging unrestrainedly in the simple human emotions of joy and sorrow without reflection and without cant, are the qualities which come from his negro ancestry.

In appearance and manners Coleridge-Taylor was very much of his father's race. There was a sweetness and modesty of nature which was instantly lovable. Success made him happy but he was easily cast down. He had little power of self-criticism, but sometimes he would accept the criticism of others too readily. In his student days on one occasion when his work had been sharply criticized by his teacher, the manuscript was found by a fellow-student thrown aside in the waiting-room of the College as not worth carrying home. It was only after his best work had been done that he conceived a desire to study African negro music and to become its apostle by composing works on native folk themes. His later publications show that he did this to a considerable extent, but it is noteworthy that after having planned the violin concerto which he wrote for the Norfolk (Connecticut) festival on these lines, he redrafted it in a more original style. His visits to America no doubt did something to awaken his racial sentiment, though he was received there, especially by his host, Mr. Carl Stoeckel, in the most warm and generous spirit. He was also stimulated in this direction by the example of Dvořák's group of works 'From the New World', but he lacked the stamina to become the leader of a movement. His compositions amount to 82 opus numbers, with many to which no number is assigned, and amongst them there is much that is ephemeral. But 'Hiawatha' holds its own, and twenty-five years after its production it was given in the form of a pageant opera in the arena of the Albert Hall (19 May 1924 and again in 1925), the composer's son, Hiawatha Coleridge-Taylor, taking part as conductor of the ballet.

Coleridge-Taylor married in 1899 Jessie, daughter of Major Walter Walmisley, a member of the same family as the composer and organist, Thomas Forbes Walmisley [q.v.], and the musician, Thomas Attwood Walmisley [q.v.]. There were two children of the marriage, the son Hiawatha, and a daughter. Coleridge-Taylor died 1 September 1912.

[W. C. Berwick Sayers, *Samuel Coleridge-Taylor, Musician; his Life and Letters*, 1915; *Musical Times*, March 1909 and October 1912; Manuscript catalogue of compositions, by J. H. Smithers Jackson (Croydon Public Libraries); published compositions; private information; personal knowledge.]

H. C. C.

COLLINGS, JESSE (1831–1920), politician, the youngest son of Thomas Collings, of Littleham, Exmouth, Devon, by his wife, Anne Palmer, was born at Littleham in December 1831. His father was a bricklayer, afterwards proprietor of a small building business; but in later life Jesse Collings was fond of tracing his descent from the Palmers, because they had, he believed, been yeoman farmers. He was educated at a dame's school 'for tradesmen's sons', and also spent a year at Church House School, Stoke, Plymouth, which was kept by a cousin. At the age of fifteen he became a shop assistant, later a clerk and commercial traveller in the ironmongery trade. Entering in 1850 the firm of Booth & Co., of Birmingham, as a clerk, he became a partner in the business, under the style of Collings and Wallis, fourteen years later, and retired in 1879. While living at Exeter and representing his firm he obtained much knowledge of rural conditions by his travels through the west of England. His first public work was done when he helped to establish the Devon and Exeter Boys' Industrial School in 1862. His interest in education developed when he went to live in Birmingham in 1864, and in 1868 he published a pamphlet which was the immediate cause of the formation of the National Education League for the advocacy of free and non-sectarian elementary education. He was elected a town councillor for the Edgbaston division of Birmingham in that year, and thereafter became prominently associated with the programme of municipal reform in Birmingham carried out by Mr. Joseph Chamberlain [q.v.]. He was elected mayor in 1878, after ten years' service on the council.

Outside municipal affairs Collings was becoming widely known as an advocate of free education and of land reform. In the latter connexion he, with a number of other radicals, was closely associated with Joseph Arch [q.v.] and the National Agricultural Labourers' Union. Collings was for a time a trustee of this Union. In 1880 he was returned to parliament in the liberal interest as one of the members for Ipswich, and in 1882 he secured the passing of the Allotments Extension Act. In 1886 Collings and his fellow-member for Ipswich were unseated on petition; they were, however, personally blameless. Returned to parliament for Bordesley, Birmingham, in the same year, he retained the seat until his retirement in 1918. Always the close associate and personal friend of Joseph Chamberlain, Collings became a liberal unionist on the occasion of the Home Rule split. In the Salisbury administration of 1895 he was under-secretary to the Home Department, retaining office until 1902. In 1892 he had been made a privy councillor. A loyal colleague and good party servant, his work in office was mainly administrative, and unconnected with his life interests.

From the days when he appeared on the platforms of the National Agricultural Labourers' Union until he retired from public life, Collings was an enthusiastic advocate of land reform. It was he who in 1885 began to use the phrase 'three acres and a cow' which for many years was the war-cry of the land reformers. During the debate on the Queen's speech at the opening of parliament in January 1886 he moved an amendment on the subject of small holdings, and thereby brought about the defeat of the conservative government. But the Home Rule controversy of that year scattered the group of radical land reformers which had gathered round the agricultural labourers' movement. They were henceforth in different and opposing political camps. Arch and his associates adhered to the Gladstonian party, Collings and his associates became unionists, and the effectiveness of both groups was destroyed. In 1883 Collings had formed the Allotments Extension Association; and in 1888 he became its president, but was deposed, partly as a result of differences on the question of Home Rule. He then formed the Rural Labourers' League (afterwards known as the Rural League) with which he was connected until 1919. He continued his interest in rural affairs, including education, allotments, small holdings, and the administration of charitable trusts. In education he was the advocate of a vocational system of elementary education in rural areas, and in land reform the advocate of a system of peasant proprietorship. His educational views were never embodied in legislation, though to a small extent they were adopted in teaching practice and administration. His ideas on land reform were partly embodied in the ineffective Small Holdings Act of 1882, and again in the Land Settlement Act of 1919. He published *Land Reform* (1906), *The Colonization of Rural Britain* (1914), and *The Great War: its Lessons and Warnings* (1915).

Beloved by all with whom and for whom he worked, Collings was the recipient of many presentations, including one from working-men of Birmingham and one from rural workers. He died at Edgbaston, Birmingham, 20 November 1920. He married in 1858 Emily, daughter of Edward Oxenbould, a master at King Edward VI's grammar school, Birmingham, and had one daughter.

[*Life of . . . Jesse Collings*, Part I by Jesse Collings, Part II by Sir John L. Green, 1920.]

A. W. A.

COOK, Sir EDWARD TYAS (1857–1919), journalist, the youngest son of Silas Kemball Cook, secretary of the Seamen's Hospital, Greenwich, by his wife, Emily, daughter of William Archer, born at Brighton 12 May 1857, educated at Winchester and New College, Oxford (first-classes in moderations and *literae humaniores*), was one of the most influential of London journalists in the last fifteen years of the nineteenth and first ten years of the twentieth century. During many of these years and subsequently until his death in 1919 he was actively engaged in literary work of all kinds and was the author of many books and biographies. In 1915 he was appointed joint-manager (with Sir Frank Swettenham) of the Press Bureau for the censoring of English newspapers during the European War, and he discharged that office until August 1919. He was knighted in 1912 and made a K.B.E. in 1917. He married in 1884 Emily Constance (died

1903), daughter of John Forster Baird, of Bowmont Hill, Northumberland. They had no children.

From his boyhood Cook was a keen politician and a strong liberal. He was president of the Oxford Union in 1879 and enjoyed the reputation among his contemporaries of being an extremely accomplished and resourceful debater. After leaving Oxford he was for a time secretary of the London Society for Extension of University Teaching, and gradually found his way into journalism by means of contributions to the *Pall Mall Gazette*, then under the editorship of John (afterwards Viscount) Morley. In 1883 William Thomas Stead [q.v.] became editor, and shortly afterwards invited Cook to join the staff. Here he had for a colleague another distinguished Oxford man, Alfred (afterwards Viscount) Milner, with whom he established a lifelong friendship. Stead, Milner, and Cook made one of the most remarkable trios in London journalism, the first being a vehement innovator and zealot, the other two men of the scholarly and academic type, who were sometimes left breathless by the brilliant indiscretions of their chief. To the end of his life Cook acknowledged the debt that he owed to Stead and applied not a few of Stead's ideas to the papers that he afterwards edited, but, as a writer, his own methods were the opposite of Stead's, and he relied rather on quiet and incisive argument than on emphatic assertion and remonstrance. He was in fact a most skilful debater with his pen, and few people fell into controversy with him without discovering the variety of his weapons and the deadly accuracy of his memory for facts.

When Stead resigned the editorship of the *Pall Mall Gazette* in 1890, Cook was appointed to succeed him, and instantly made his own mark as an editor. He carried on Stead's liberal imperialism, his zeal for the ' big navy ', and his admiration for Cecil Rhodes, whom the paper had been mainly instrumental in popularizing with the general public ; but he also made his own quiet but very tenacious personality felt both in public affairs and in matters literary and artistic. In the autumn of 1892 the *Pall Mall Gazette* was sold to Mr. William Waldorf (afterwards Viscount) Astor, and in the absence of guarantees for the future policy of the paper Cook and his political staff immediately resigned. Within a month he was at work again preparing to found a new paper to fill the gap in liberal journalism, and at the end of January 1893 the *Westminster Gazette*, for which the capital had been found by Sir George Newnes [q.v.], was started under his editorship and carried on the tradition of the old *Pall Mall*. At the end of 1895 Cook was offered and accepted the editorship of the *Daily News*. For four years he conducted this paper with great success, but his objection to ' little Englandism ' and the strong views that he held on imperial policy were unacceptable to some of its readers ; and when the South African War broke out, his espousal of the war policy brought him into collision with a large section of the liberal party, and caused a sharp division of opinion among the proprietors of the *Daily News*. His editorship was ended abruptly in January 1901 by the sale of the paper to new proprietors, and for the next ten years he had to content himself with expounding his views as a leader-writer in the *Daily Chronicle*, which offered him this refuge after his departure from the *Daily News*. In these years he edited, in collaboration with Mr. Alexander Wedderburn, the monumental library edition of Ruskin's *Works* in thirty-eight volumes (1903–1911), and followed it up with the standard biography of Ruskin (1911), which was entirely his own work. From his boyhood onwards he had been, if not a Ruskinian, a great admirer of Ruskin's writings, and he devoted to his works as much industry and research as the most erudite scholar could apply to a classical text. He next undertook the *Life of Florence Nightingale* (1913), and two years later wrote a study of John Delane (*Delane, of The Times*, 1915), which has been described as ' the best book ever written about a journalist '.

To those who knew him but little Cook seemed to be a reserved and rather silent man ; but he was a warm friend, and a man of unshakable loyalty both to his own convictions and to those to whom he pledged his support. He took a high view of journalism as a profession, and claimed to exercise complete independence as an editor. Though a convinced liberal, he was fearless in criticism of his party when he thought the public interest required it, and was no respecter of persons, however eminent. For many years he was an intimate friend and counsellor of liberal politicians, and though his sympathies were with the liberal imperialist group, he remained on good terms with all sections of the party and contributed not a little to the liberal revival of 1906. His long experience of journalism and intimate knowledge of

London newspapers were of the greatest service to the Press Bureau, and enabled that difficult office to be conducted with comparatively little friction. His labours during these years undoubtedly undermined his health and contributed to his comparatively early death. He died at South Stoke, Oxfordshire, 30 September 1919.

[J. Saxon Mills, *Sir Edward Cook. A biography*, 1921 ; personal knowledge.]

J. A. S.

CORNISH, FRANCIS WARRE WARRE- (1839–1916), teacher, author, and bibliophile. [See WARRE-CORNISH.]

COURTHOPE, WILLIAM JOHN (1842–1917), civil servant, poet, and literary critic, the elder son of William Courthope, was born 17 July 1842 at South Malling, near Lewes, of which parish his father was rector. His mother was a sister of John Charles Ryle, first bishop of Liverpool [q.v.]. Courthope's father died in 1849 and the three children were brought up by their uncle, the head of this ancient Sussex family, at Whiligh, near Wadhurst. William John was sent to Blackheath and then placed at Harrow, under C. J. Vaughan and (from 1859) H. Montagu Butler. In 1861 he matriculated at Corpus Christi College, Oxford, and in 1862 became an exhibitioner of New College, then a small and close society, where he was a pupil of Edward Charles Wickham, afterwards dean of Lincoln. On the introduction of John Addington Symonds the younger who had preceded him from Harrow, he formed a close friendship with John Conington, then Corpus professor of Latin, which lasted with increasing intimacy till Conington's death in 1869. He gained first classes in moderations and *literae humaniores*, and the Newdigate prize (1864). In 1868 he won the Chancellor's prize with an English essay on *The Genius of Spenser*, a composition of more than academic interest, since the author more than once returned to its principles of criticism, and even made use of some of its pages.

A modest patrimony making him ineligible for a fellowship, he was called to the bar, and in 1869 entered the Education Office as an examiner. In 1887 he became a civil service commissioner, and as senior commissioner, a post which he held from 1892 until his retirement in 1907, he did much to humanize the examinations for the higher appointments. In 1895 he was elected for five years to the professorship of poetry at Oxford and made a C.B., and in the following year he was made an honorary fellow of New College. The closing years of his life were spent in Sussex, near Whiligh. They were full of literary activities and domestic interest, until a gradual failure of strength ended in his death on 10 April 1917.

The two periods of Courthope's official life correspond nearly with his two chief literary undertakings. Of the present standard edition of Pope's works in ten volumes (1871–1889), five volumes, edited by Whitwell Elwin [q.v.], had appeared by 1872. In 1881 a sixth followed, bearing Courthope's name as joint editor, with an intimation that he would be solely responsible for the remainder. On the text, which had previously followed that of Bishop Warburton (1751) without examination of his sources, much labour was bestowed. The *Life*, which closed the series in 1889, involved questions of much delicacy, owing to Pope's strange methods in correspondence. In spite of difficulties added by the results of research then recent, the biographer dealt with his material in the generous spirit of Johnson, seeking not to condemn wholly, nor to condone, but to understand. A volume on Addison, contributed in 1884 to the series of *English Men of Letters*, had brought him into the congenial atmosphere of the eighteenth century.

In his *History of English Poetry* (1895–1910) Courthope undertook a work which had been projected by Pope, and passed on to Gray and to Thomas Warton, but never carried out. After laying sure foundations in philology, the author set himself to trace through successive poets the continuity of English poetry, and its correspondence with the great movements of English history, the great poets being those who felt the impact of conflicting forces and were able to reconcile them ; a standard which Spenser had failed to attain. The *History* was carried down to the romantic reaction of the later eighteenth century, and was completed in six volumes. In 1901 Courthope published the lectures given in his five years as professor under the title *Life in Poetry, Law in Taste*, in which he contended that poetry is a social art, and the history of English poetry a continuous one.

Of Courthope's other writings *Ludibria Lunae* (1869), an allegorical burlesque on an Italian model, is more successful, perhaps, in its passages of beauty and deep feeling than as a political satire on the ' women's rights ' question of the day. It was followed in 1870 by the *Paradise of Birds*, which echoes the mingled gaiety and pathos of Aristophanes, with something added, and has delighted successive generations of young readers. Later on he sang the praises of his native Sussex in *The Country Town* (Lewes), contributed to the *National Review* in 1886, and *The Hop Garden* (*Blackwood's Magazine*, 1905), in which, with sure Virgilian touch and perfect accuracy of detail, he set out the charms of a waning industry. Both poems were brightened by passages of glowing hopefulness for the future of the race. His remains, *The Country Town and other poems* (1920), include many smaller pieces of great charm, as *The Chancellor's Garden* (1888) and some lines suggested by war-time (1900 and 1914). He wrote frequently in the *National Review*, and contributed valuable papers to the newly founded British Academy. His last published work was a selection of translations and imitations in English verse of Martial's *Epigrams* (1914).

In 1870 Courthope had married Mary, daughter of John Scott, H.M. inspector of hospitals at Bombay, who, with four sons and two daughters, survived him.

[J. W. Mackail, *W. J. Courthope*, in *Proceedings* of the British Academy, vol. ix, 1917–1918; *The Country Town and other poems by the late William John Courthope, C.B.* (1920) with a *Memoir* by A. O. Prickard; personal knowledge.] A. O. P.

COURTNEY, LEONARD HENRY, first Baron Courtney of penwith (1832–1918), journalist and statesman, eldest son of John Sampson Courtney, banker, of Alverton House, Penzance, by his wife, Sarah, daughter of John Mortimer, was born at Penzance 6 July 1832. As a boy he worked in Bolitho's bank at Penzance. His mathematical talents attracted attention, and he won a sizarship at St. John's College, Cambridge. His university career was distinguished; for he became second wrangler (1855), Smith's prizeman, and fellow of his college. In 1857 he went to London and in 1858 was called to the bar at Lincoln's Inn. But journalism drew him from the law, and he threw himself into the study of politics and political economy. In 1865 he was appointed leader-writer to *The Times* under John Delane [q.v.], and during the next sixteen years wrote some 3,000 articles for its columns. He also contributed to the *Fortnightly Review*, forming a lifelong friendship with its editor, John (afterwards Viscount) Morley. From 1872 to 1875 Courtney occupied the chair of political economy at University College, London. Some years later he became interested in bimetallism and expressed admiration for Bryan's 'silver' speeches in the presidential campaign of 1896 in the United States.

Courtney entered parliament in 1875 as liberal member for Liskeard, and made his mark on the left wing of the party with Henry Fawcett, Joseph Chamberlain, and Sir Charles Dilke. In 1880 he became under-secretary for the Home Office in Mr. Gladstone's second administration, then under-secretary for the Colonies, and in 1882 secretary of the Treasury, a speedy promotion which promised him Cabinet office. Two years later he fell out with the government. Having become a zealous believer in proportional representation as a means of protecting minorities, he urged its inclusion in the Redistribution Bill. When the Cabinet declined to adopt this novel proposal, Courtney rather quixotically resigned. In 1886 he rejected Gladstone's Home Rule policy, holding that Ireland was unfit for self-government. At Gladstone's suggestion he became chairman of committees and deputy-speaker. In that office, which he held until 1892, his decisions were wittily, but a little unjustly, described as 'impartially unfair to both sides'. In 1892, though a liberal unionist, he was pressed by the liberal government to accept the speakership, but declined, partly owing to unionist opposition, partly because he preferred political freedom and influence to dignity and opulence.

The growing spirit of imperialism found an obstinate opponent in Courtney. He resisted consistently and conscientiously the 'forward' policy in Egypt, the Sudan, and South Africa. His interest in South African affairs dated from 1877 when he had strenuously opposed the annexation of the Transvaal. In 1896 he denounced the Jameson Raid, and afterwards the Rhodes-Chamberlain-Milner policy which ended in the Boer War. After its outbreak in October 1899, Courtney's persistent advocacy of 'forbearance and conciliation' made him one of the leaders of the anti-war party. As chairman of the South African conciliation committee he did all that was in his power to counteract the demand for annexation and unconditional surrender. This severed Courtney's official connexion with the unionist party, and made him for the first time a national figure, though it lost him his seat in the general election of 1900. For the next six years Courtney lived the life of a political sage in Chelsea. Some years before his eyesight had partially failed, but his vigour was unimpaired.

In 1901 appeared his first book, *The Working Constitution of the United Kingdom*, and in 1904 *The Diary of a Churchgoer* was published anonymously. His old zeal for proportional representation also revived, and he made many converts.

After the liberal victory of 1906 Courtney accepted a peerage and became Baron Courtney of Penwith. During the last twelve years of his life he spoke often in the House of Lords. He had agreed to the principle of Home Rule, and opposed everywhere the spirit of domination. After the death of Sir H. Campbell-Bannerman (1908) his distrust of Sir Edward Grey's foreign policy grew apace. He repeatedly urged a reduction in armaments, and demanded that the understanding with France should not be exclusive, but should be followed by a similar understanding with Germany. The European War confirmed his fears, and he criticized the British government for the failure of its diplomacy, agreeing in this with his old friend, Lord Morley. As the fearful conflict progressed, he opposed all measures which seemed likely to prolong it. At home he pleaded for freedom of speech and freedom of conscience. He explored all avenues that might lead to peace, and would have closed no door to negotiations, however unpromising. Only a few days before his death he wrote to the *Manchester Guardian*, arguing that neither side could be overwhelmed and that reconciliation should be tried. Courtney died in London 11 May 1918. He had married in 1883 Catherine (Kate), daughter of Richard Potter, at one time chairman of the Great Western Railway. They had no children.

Courtney was perhaps the greatest British statesman, since Cobden, of those who have never held Cabinet office. He was a genial host, fond of society, in argument dogmatic and sometimes pragmatical, stiff in opinions, and always ready to sacrifice his career to his convictions. To a mathematical mind and a strong logical sense, which insisted on arguing out every question, he united a very warm and emotional disposition.

There is a portrait of Courtney by Alphonse Legros in the Fitzwilliam Museum, Cambridge.

[G. P. Gooch, *Life of Lord Courtney*, 1920; personal knowledge.] F. W. H.

COWANS, Sir JOHN STEVEN (1862–1921), general, was born 11 March 1862 at Carlisle, the eldest son of John Cowans, civil engineer, of Woodbank, Carlisle, by his wife, Jeannie, elder daughter of Samuel Steven, of St. John, New Brunswick. He was educated for the navy, at Dr. Burney's academy at Gosport, but did not pass the examination. In 1878 he went to Sandhurst, and in 1881 joined the Rifle Brigade in India, where he served as aide-de-camp to Sir John Ross [q.v.], commanding the Poona division of the Bombay army. In 1891 he passed the Staff College with distinction, and after holding several staff appointments he became deputy assistant quartermaster-general in the movements branch of the War Office to supervise the transport of troops to Egypt. He was promoted major in 1898 and lieutenant-colonel in 1900. So well did Cowans perform his duties that he was retained at the War Office through the South African War in spite of his efforts to be employed on active service. He was gazetted colonel in 1903, and then served at Aldershot (1903–1906) and subsequently in India, where he held the posts of director of military education (1906–1907) and director of staff duties (1907–1908), and later commanded the Bengal Presidency brigade (1908–1910). In 1910 he returned to the War Office as director-general of the Territorial Force. Here he organized the horse census, which contributed greatly to the efficiency of the army in 1914. In 1912 he became quartermaster-general, the member of the Army Council responsible for the provision of the accommodation, food, transport, horses, clothing, and equipment, of the army, and for its movement by land and sea to the scene of operations. He was created K.C.B. in 1913.

Thus the critical moment of the outbreak of war in 1914 found Sir John Cowans in the position of supreme administrator of the most vitally important services of the army; and before many weeks had passed it was seen that a strain was to be placed upon those services to an extent not only unapproached hitherto in British military history, but hardly even dreamed of by those responsible for the military policy of the country. Fortunately, contemporary opinion recognized from the outset that in Cowans the country possessed an administrative genius, with the foresight and ability to grasp and solve the problems—of extraordinary complexity and magnitude—which faced his department. Statistics will furnish the best evidence of the success with which Cowans and his staff carried out, practically without a hitch during more than four years of war, the enormous expansion in the necessary services.

At the outbreak of war, barrack accommodation existed for only 262,000 men, so that every expedient had to be adopted in order to meet the rush of recruits and the mobilization of the Territorial force. Troops were quartered under canvas, in public institutions, but largely in billets. As men joined the army, houses were left solely in the occupation of women, and to avoid the billeting of troops in such houses, large hutted camps were built. The arrival of Dominion and Allied troops, of Belgian and Russian refugees, and of German prisoners, the creation of tank units, and the formation of the Women's Auxiliary Army Corps, continually increased the strain. In 1917, exclusive of volunteers, there were one and three quarter million troops billeted throughout Great Britain. In addition, storage had to be found for munitions and supplies, and ever-increasing hospital accommodation. In 1917 there were 1,090 hospitals with 320,000 beds, but these were only just enough, since at the time of the greatest strain, in October 1918, when the average number of wounded arriving daily was 6,000, there were at one time only 3,697 available beds.

Cowans, who was promoted lieutenant-general in 1915, recognized from the first that the War would last a long time. During 1914 he had established supply-depots all over England, and from the earliest moment he made every effort to achieve economy, as, for instance, by making changes in the items of the ration according to the state of market prices. So far as practicable, supplies which otherwise would have gone to Germany—such as Norwegian fish—were purchased for the army; and, in order to save shipping, stores were bought locally, and cultivation encouraged in the areas occupied by British troops overseas. The meat imported was all frozen; at first it came to England, but later it went direct to stores at Havre and Boulogne. In the provision of forage great difficulty was found owing to the lack of shipping, but practically all the hay required was provided from England and France. In dealing with the transportation of supplies Cowans showed equal ingenuity in order to ensure that they should reach the right place at the right time. He strongly advocated the scheme for utilizing Richborough harbour.

One important feature of the War was the use of motor transport. In August 1914 250,000 gallons of petrol were being used per month; this rose to 10,500,000 per month in 1918. In 1914 the army owned only 80 motor vehicles, but subsidized vehicles were called up in order to equip the Expeditionary Force. Large contracts for construction were placed both in England and America, and steps were taken on a large scale to train drivers and mechanics. In 1918 the personnel numbered 173,570, the four-wheeled vehicles 85,138, and the cycles 34,711; in addition the War Office provided motor transport for the Ministry of Munitions, the General Post Office, and other bodies. In order to regulate everything Cowans established a motor transport board under his own chairmanship, with three committees dealing respectively with technical questions, land and buildings, and general purposes.

In 1914 the army owned 25,000 horses, to which were added 140,000 from the reserve created by Cowans, and 115,000 were impressed. In 1918 the total numbered 735,409, most of the remounts having been imported from America. Great difficulty was found in breaking in horses owing to the want of fit men. The supply of veterinary surgeons was heavily taxed, but it just lasted out, and assistance was rendered by the Royal Society for the Prevention of Cruelty to Animals in the training of farriers. Glanders fortunately were kept under, and over two and a half million doses of mallein were supplied for the purpose. In 1914 there was accommodation in hospital for 2,000 animals; in 1918 for 64,450.

The supply of clothing and general stores also devolved on the quartermaster-general's department, and the expansion was as rapid as it was extensive. In a normal peace year, for instance, the requirements were 45,000 water-bottles, 2,500 spades, 57,000 ground-sheets, and 123 miles of rope. During the War 12,500,000 water-bottles, 10,500,000 spades, 15,750,000 ground-sheets, and 45,000 miles of rope were supplied. Every effort was made to economize material. Thus in all the back areas overseas boot-repair shops on a large scale were instituted, for which nearly all the tallow wanted was derived from mutton cloths, and the cloths themselves were used for cleaning rags. Moreover, sudden demands were often made for special needs. Thus when the British troops went to Italy, ropes, ice-axes, and mountaineering gear had to be supplied immediately. Newly devised articles were constantly needed for trench warfare; and on one occasion Cowans supplied at 48 hours' notice 30,000 tins of special grease for 'trench feet'. Tropical clothing and kit was required at short notice for minor expeditions, and the necessities of camouflage caused a sudden demand for special canvas and paint.

As the War went on, the difficulty of maintaining the personnel increased. In 1914 the Royal Army Service Corps consisted of 450 officers and 9,976 other ranks, and the Royal Army Ordnance Corps of 248 officers and 2,273 other ranks. In 1918 these had increased respectively to 11,564 and 2,253 officers and 314,313 and 38,193 other ranks. The demands of the infantry were heavy, and Cowans released from the Army Service and Ordnance Corps all officers born after 1887, and gave no commissions to men under thirty-five. The constant 'combing out' of tradesmen was met by employing women and 'C 3' men. The extension of the war areas continually threw fresh duties on the quartermaster-general. Thus in 1916 responsibility for the operations in Mesopotamia was taken over by the War Office from the Indian government; the operations in the Eastern Mediterranean were based on Egypt; and in 1918 the feeding of the troops and civilians in North Russia, in the Archangel zone, was taken over. In 1914 the ration strength of the army was 164,000 men and 27,500 animals; in 1918, 5,363,352 men and 895,770 animals.

Cowans relinquished the post of quartermaster-general in March 1919. He was promoted general in 1919 and had received the G.C.M.G. (1918) and G.C.B. (1919), besides numerous foreign orders. On leaving the army he became associated with an important oil group in the City on behalf of which he visited Mesopotamia; but the strain of the War had seriously impaired his health, and after some months of illness he died at Mentone on 16 April 1921. He had been received into the Church of Rome shortly before his death, and a public funeral was held in Westminster Cathedral.

Cowans' achievement can best be judged by the fact that he held the post of quartermaster-general throughout the War, and that in spite of the necessity for expanding the army from a six-division basis to such vast numbers, no breakdown occurred except in Mesopotamia, for which campaign he had no responsibility until in 1916 his services were required to place it on a proper administrative footing, a task he soon accomplished.

Cowans possessed an immense power of work and unusual quickness of perception. His methods were unusual and sometimes surprised orthodox staff officers and officials, but they very soon learnt to appreciate his remarkable powers of getting things done, while his genial and kindly nature endeared him to all those who served with him. Outside his work his chief interests lay in sport and society. Sometimes his recommendations for appointments were criticized, and not without reason; but there is no doubt that the chief secret of his success lay in his power of selecting the best men available to serve him in the really responsible positions. He married in 1884 Eva May, daughter of the Rev. John Edmund Coulson, vicar of Long Preston, Yorkshire, who survived him. There was no issue of the marriage.

A portrait of Cowans was painted by Sir W. Orpen (*Royal Academy Pictures*, 1917), and another is included in J. S. Sargent's picture 'Some General Officers of the Great War', painted in 1922, in the National Portrait Gallery.

[*The Times*, 18 April, 1921; War Office records; Mesopotamia Commission *Report*, 1917; *Statistics of the Military Effort of the British Empire*; Sir C. E. Callwell, *The Life of Sir Stanley Maude*, 1920; D. Chapman-Huston and O. Rutter, *General Sir John Cowans*, 1924; private information.] O.

COZENS-HARDY, HERBERT HARDY, first BARON COZENS-HARDY, of Letheringsett (1838–1920), judge, was born at Letheringsett Hall, Dereham, Norfolk, 22 November 1838, the second son of William Hardy Cozens-Hardy, a Congregationalist solicitor in good practice at Norwich, by his wife, Sarah, daughter of Thomas Theobald, of the same city. Educated at Amersham Hall School and at University College, London, Cozens-Hardy graduated at London University in 1858. He took the degree of LL.B. in 1863, and afterwards became a member of the senate of London University and a fellow of University College, London. In 1862 he was called to the bar at Lincoln's Inn, after obtaining a studentship and a certificate of honour. He read in the chambers of Thomas Lewin and James Dickinson, both eminent as equity draftsmen. Between 1871 and 1876 he was an examiner for London University in equity and real property law.

Cozens-Hardy soon acquired practice as a Chancery junior, his nonconformist connexions being of considerable service to him. After twenty busy years he took silk in 1882. Attaching himself at first to the court of Mr. Justice Fry, he took his seat before Mr. Justice North when Fry went to the Court of Appeal in 1883. He proved so successful as a leader that in 1893 he joined the small band of 'specials' of which (Sir) John Rigby and Horace (afterwards Lord) Davey were also members. In this distinguished company he held his own, and was constantly employed in heavy cases both in the Chancery division and before the appellate tribunals. Of unimpressive appearance, and without the vigour of Rigby or the subtlety of Davey, Cozens-Hardy had industry, knowledge, and lucidity of speech, and judges listened to him with respect. Kindly and courteous to all, his popularity with the practising members of the profession was shown by his election as chairman of the general council of the bar. Amongst the important cases in which he appeared as counsel were *Sheffield* v. *London Joint Stock Bank* (1888, the right of a bank to sell securities deposited by a borrower with limited authority), *Bradford Corporation* v. *Pickles* (1895, the effect of a malicious motive upon the lawful use of property), *Trego* v. *Hunt* (1896, the right of the seller of a business to canvass his old customers), and *Attorney-General* v. *Beech* (1899, the liability of a remainderman who has bought a life interest to pay estate duty).

At the general election of 1885 Cozens-Hardy was elected member of parliament for North Norfolk in the liberal interest, and continued to sit for the constituency till his elevation to the bench in 1899. In the House of Commons, although never a prominent figure, he was a not infrequent speaker. As a rule he confined himself to matters of which he had professional or local knowledge. Such subjects as married women's property, the winding up of companies, bankruptcy, and the law relating to trustees, he was able to discuss with authority. In 1886, when the liberal party split on the subject of Home Rule for Ireland, Cozens-Hardy remained faithful to Mr. Gladstone.

In 1899 the death of Lord Justice Chitty and the promotion to his place of Sir Robert Romer created a vacancy in the Chancery division. Lord Halsbury, who was not ordinarily predisposed towards political opponents, disregarded Cozens-Hardy's liberalism, and with the full approval of the profession raised him to the bench. He received the customary knighthood. As a judge Cozens-Hardy showed the industry and care that had marked his work at the bar. His findings of fact were more often criticized than his decisions on points of law. In 1901, on the resignation of Lord Justice Rigby, he became a lord justice of appeal and was sworn of the Privy Council. In March 1907 Cozens-Hardy succeeded Sir Richard Henn Collins (afterwards Lord Collins) as master of the Rolls. In this onerous office he performed his duties with ability and dignity. Appeals under the Workmen's Compensation Act were numerous, and Cozens-Hardy, although unversed in this branch of the law, dealt with them satisfactorily. His familiarity with equity law and practice made him a strong president of the court when Chancery appeals were being heard. In 1913 he was one of the three commissioners of the great seal during the absence in Canada of the lord chancellor, Lord Haldane, and the following year he was raised to the peerage. For some years he was chairman of the Council of Legal Education; he was also a chairman of quarter-sessions in Norfolk. His health had been failing for many months before his retirement in 1918. He died at Letheringsett Hall 18 June 1920, and was buried at Kensal Green.

Cozens-Hardy married in 1866 Maria (died 1886), daughter of Thomas Hepburn, of Clapham Common, by whom he had two sons and two daughters. He was succeeded as second baron by his eldest son, William Hepburn Cozens-Hardy, K.C., who died in 1924.

A portrait by R. G. Eves is in the possession of the family; there was a caricature in *Vanity Fair*, 24 January 1901.

[*The Times*, 19 June 1920; *Law Journal*, 26 June 1920; personal knowledge.]

T. M.

CRADOCK, Sir CHRISTOPHER GEORGE FRANCIS MAURICE (1862–1914), admiral, was born 2 July 1862 at Hartforth, Yorkshire, the fourth son of Christopher Cradock, of Hartforth, by his wife, Georgina, daughter of Major Gordon Duff, 92nd Highlanders. Christopher Cradock entered the navy in 1875, and three years later, as midshipman of the *Pallas*, was present at the British occupation of Cyprus. In 1884, as a sub-lieutenant, he landed with the naval brigade for garrison duties in Upper Egypt and as first lieutenant of the *Dolphin*, served with the Eastern Sudan field force, being chosen by the governor-general of the Red Sea to act as his aide-de-camp. He subsequently took part in the occupation of Affafit, receiving the khedive's bronze star with clasp for the battle of Toker, and the medjidie of the fourth class. Cradock afterwards served in the royal yacht, from which he was promoted to commander. As commander of the *Alacrity*, he commanded the naval brigade which led the Allied forces at the storming of the Taku Forts, 17 July 1900, and was noted for promotion for gallantry. Later on, as commander of the British naval brigade, he directed the British, American, Japanese, and Italian forces when they advanced to the relief of the Tientsin Settlement; and he took part in the subsequent relief of Sir Edward Seymour's column at Siku, besides assisting in the capture of the Peiyang arsenal, Tientsin.

Cradock's career in later years followed the normal course. He filled every appointment with credit to himself, and brought to his duties not only abounding energy, but the sporting instinct. He never married. His outlook on life and his attractive conception of the naval career found expression, after his promotion to captain, in a little book entitled *Whispers from the Fleet* (1907). Cradock had already written *Sporting Notes in the Far East* (1889), and *Wrinkles in Seamanship* (1894), but in his latest book he addressed himself in particular to young officers who were entering upon their careers. In view of his subsequent fate, this volume has peculiar interest. He packed it with sound common sense and did not disdain to bring to his aid anecdotes and humorous pictures. He adopted and emphasized the maxim that 'a naval officer should never let his boat go faster than his brain; a dash into a basin at 20 knots even in the strongest winds and cross tides is unnecessary. Should it come off, there is only a matey or two to see, and if it does not, there is a stone wall and a court of inquiry ahead.' He expressed a contempt for those who were 'for ever writing to the newspapers to prove that because one nation would have six and a half battleships built in three years, and another four and a quarter commenced next month, unless we immediately *do something* we shall in ten years time be seven-eighths of a battleship behind the combined navies of the world—not forgetting Timbuctoo'. The strength of the navy, he suggested, consisted in the complete loyalty and good comradeship between officers and men and 'the sacred laws of naval discipline'. To him the navy was not a collection of ships, but a community of men with high purpose, and he had confidence that, 'though it had lost its masts and sails, our personnel (after a few hard knocks) will prove as good as ever'.

Cradock was promoted rear-admiral in 1910, and created K.C.V.O. in 1912. In February 1913 he was appointed to the command of the North America and West Indies station. At the outbreak of war, he was faced with a task of great difficulty. With his flag in the armoured cruiser *Suffolk*, he had, it is true, a much larger force under his command than the two German light cruisers immediately opposed to him; but the area under his control extended from the St. Lawrence to Brazil; and, as the admiral in charge of a force designed for commerce protection, he had the duty of seeing that enemy merchant ships in Atlantic ports were shadowed and that the flow of British trade was maintained. He performed this varied work very skilfully; during the first week of the war he drove both German cruisers off the trade routes, and only missed destroying one of them—the *Karlsruhe*—by a very narrow margin. On 14 August 1914 the Admiralty was able to telegraph to Paris: 'The passage across the Atlantic is safe; British trade is running as usual.'

Cradock was now compelled to take similar measures for the southern Atlantic, whither he had driven his opponents. Before proceeding south, he hoisted his flag in the *Good Hope*, and early in September arrived at Pernambuco, where he was told by the Admiralty that the German admiral, von Spee, with the enemy's China squadron, was assumed to be moving eastwards across the Pacific with the Falkland Islands as a possible objective. This message quite altered the nature and scope of Cradock's duties, as he was now faced with the double problem of countering every possible move on the part of a powerful, concentrated squadron, and, at the same time of protecting trade against the *Dresden* which was still at large. Either task was extraordinarily difficult; if he went in search of his principal opponent it would be quite possible for Admiral von Spee to slip past, and then fall upon our trade and coaling bases in the Atlantic. In these circumstances, Cradock telegraphed to the Admiralty that the only way of dealing with the situation was to concentrate two forces, one to the east and one to the west of the Magellan Straits, and to make each sufficiently powerful to crush Admiral von Spee's squadron. This the Admiralty, with urgent demands at the moment for naval force elsewhere, did not do; it sent Cradock orders to search and protect trade, with the ships then under his command: the armoured cruisers *Good Hope* and *Monmouth*, the light cruiser *Glasgow*, and the armed merchantman *Otranto*, reinforced by the old battleship *Canopus*, mounting four 12-inch guns, which was being sent to join him. He at once pointed out that this addition was of no use, as it reduced the speed of his squadron to twelve knots, and so made the first part of his orders impossible of fulfilment. The Admiralty's instructions were in any case very ambiguous; Admiral Cradock understood them as an order to seek out the enemy and fight, and this he now proceeded to do. Taking his squadron to the west coast of South America during the latter part of October, he arrived off Coronel on 31 October, having assigned to the *Canopus* the duty of escorting the colliers of his squadron. Meanwhile, a new board of Admiralty had been appointed with Lord Fisher as first sea lord. They at once telegraphed to him that he was to keep his squadron concentrated and form a junction with the *Defence*—a powerful armoured cruiser which had been ordered out from home—and that he was not expected to fight without the *Canopus*. The new orders never reached him. At 4.20 in the afternoon of 1 November he fell in with Admiral von Spee's squadron consisting of the *Scharnhorst*, *Gneisenau*, *Leipzig*, *Dresden*, and *Nurnberg*; a force which outmatched him in gun power, armour, and speed. Cradock was quite unable to adjust the balance, as the *Canopus* was still 250 miles away; and, deeming it his duty to engage at once he formed his squadron in line of battle and endeavoured to close. Until sunset he still had the advantage of the light; but Admiral von Spee, making skilful use of the higher speed of his force, kept between Cradock's squadron and the land until after sunset. It was not until about 7 o'clock p.m. that the action began. The German ships were then almost invisible with the land behind them, and the British cruisers were sharply silhouetted against the glow in the western sky. In spite of a very heavy southerly sea, the German fire was extraordinarily good, their broadside was heavier, and by eight o'clock all was over. The *Good Hope* sank with all on board at 7.35; the *Glasgow*, after taking such part in the action as was possible with her light armament, withdrew and, joining the *Otranto*, made good her escape; and the *Monmouth* succeeded, for a time, in getting away. Her condition was, however, almost hopeless, as she was making water badly and every gun was out of action. At about 9 o'clock whilst the captain was struggling to keep his vessel afloat she fell in with the *Nurnberg*, which had been too far behind to take part in the action. Though incapable of resistance, Captain Brandt refused to surrender, and his ship went down with all hands.

When the news of the engagement arrived in England, public opinion was critical of the action of the British admiral. The disaster was imputed to recklessness, in engaging a squadron superior to his own, and to his disregard of the orders he had received. Later investigations showed that it was impossible for him to carry out the orders sent to him and, at the same time, keep his squadron concentrated on the old and slow battleship *Canopus* which had been sent to him as a reinforcement. More than that, his messages home and the Admiralty's replies proved that he had pointed this out; and that the new board of Admiralty had realized the difficulty of his position and the ambiguity of his orders.

When, later on, a memorial to Cradock was unveiled in York Minster, Mr. (afterwards the Earl of) Balfour, who was then first lord of the Admiralty, recounted the circumstances of the action and paid tribute to the memory of the admiral and his companions. 'Admiral Cradock could only judge by the circumstances which were before him, and if he judged that his squadron, that himself and those under him, were well sacrificed if they destroyed the power of this hostile fleet, then I say that there is no man, be he sailor or be he civilian, but would say that such judgement showed not only the highest courage, but the greatest courage of unselfishness, and that Cradock, by absolute neglect of personal interest and personal ambitions, had shown a wise judgement in the interests of his country.'

Cradock is represented in Sir A. S. Cope's picture 'Some Sea Officers of the Great War', painted in 1921, in the National Portrait Gallery.

[Sir J. S. Corbett, *Official History of the Great War. Naval Operations*, vol. i, 1920.]

A. H.

CRANE, WALTER (1845–1915), artist, the second son of Thomas Crane, of Chester, portrait painter, by his wife, Marie Kearsley, was born in Liverpool 15 August 1845. Two months later his parents moved to Torquay where, in due course, he attended a private school until, in 1857, they went to London. In 1859 Crane was apprenticed for three years to William James Linton [q.v.], the wood engraver, though he studied painting at the same time. In 1862 a picture by him, 'The Lady of Shalott', was accepted by the Royal Academy, but it was not until the opening of the Grosvenor Gallery in 1877 that he was able freely to exhibit his work in oils. The opportunities for the water-colourist were less restricted, and he made the most of these, becoming an associate of the Royal Society of Painters in Water Colours in 1888.

Meanwhile, in book decoration, Crane was by no means content to confine himself to reproducing the work of others. In 1863 his first illustrated book, *The New Forest*, appeared; a set of designs for *The Lady of Shalott* gained the approval of Linton; and an introduction to the engraver, Edmund Evans [q.v.], led to the publication of a number of picture books, chiefly for children, engraved and printed in colours by Evans from the drawings of Crane; a first series began in 1864 and was followed by a second in 1873. Other works of the same nature were *The Fairy Ship* (1869), *The Baby's Opera* (1877), *The Baby's Bouquet* (1879), *A Romance of the Three R's* (1885–1886), *The Baby's own Æsop* (1887), *Flora's Feast, a Masque of Flowers* (1888), three poems of his own, *The Sirens Three* (1886), *Queen Summer* and *Renascence* (1891), and an edition of Spenser's *Faerie Queene* in twelve parts (1894–1896).

In all of these Crane revealed a remarkable talent for designing beautiful accessories, and before long he began to direct this to practical ends. To record the various purposes to which he applied it would be to make a list of wellnigh every article of household decoration. It soon became apparent, however, that progress in this direction was seriously hampered by the difficulty of placing work before the public. In the endeavour to overcome this obstacle the Art Workers' Guild was established in 1884; and Crane, who had taken the principal part in its promotion, was elected first president. Subsequently he served for two periods (1888–1890 and 1895–1915) as president of the Arts and Crafts Exhibition Society, which at the New Gallery in 1888 first showed the full importance of the movement. Another development in that year was the meeting at Liverpool of the Art Congress Association; but at its second meeting held at Glasgow in 1889 William Morris and Crane so upset the harmony of the proceedings by their insistence upon their socialistic doctrines that the congress never met again. Some five or six years before Crane had been swept, by the enthusiasm of Morris, into the Socialist League which the latter had founded, financed, and provided with head-quarters in his house at Hammersmith. Crane was not highly effective as an orator; but when his subject lent itself to illustration on the blackboard he delighted his audiences with his facility, and it was chiefly with his pencil that he assisted such progress as was made. He designed a banner which was embroidered by Miss May Morris, and he contributed to the weekly periodicals *Commonweal* and *Justice* a long series of cartoons, many of which were subsequently republished in a volume entitled *Cartoons for the Cause* (1896).

In 1891 Crane exhibited at the Fine Art Society's gallery a collection of his varied artistic works, which he afterwards took to the United States, and in 1892 to Germany, Austria, and Scandinavia. His position in decorative art was recognized by his appointment in 1893 as director of design at the Manchester Municipal School of Art; in 1896 he became art director of Reading College; and in 1898 principal of the Royal College of Art, South Kensington. He published in the last-mentioned year *The Bases of Design*; this was followed by *Line and Form* in 1900, in which year he took a collection of his works to Budapest. In 1903 he arranged a display of British arts and crafts at Turin, and in acknowledgement he was awarded the order of the Royal Crown of Italy; in 1911 he received the order of SS. Maurizio and Lazzaro. In addition to many foreign medals, he received in July 1905 the gold medal of the Society of Arts of London, and in 1912 he painted a portrait of himself at the request of the authorities of the Uffizi Gallery, Florence.

Although the painting of pictures was the least significant of his activities Crane by no means neglected it. He was indefatigable in the production of landscapes, chiefly in water-colours, and he also painted a number of more ambitious works in oil. 'The Renaissance of Venus' (1877) is notable as having been purchased by G. F. Watts, by whose desire it was subsequently (1913) presented to the nation. In 1881 (Sir) Edward Burne-Jones selected Crane to complete a series, 'Cupid and Psyche', begun by himself, for the house of Mr. George

Howard (afterwards ninth Earl of Carlisle) in Palace Green, Kensington. Other important canvases by Crane are 'The Bridge of Life' (1884), 'The Mower' (1891), and 'Neptune's Horses' (1893). A tapestry panel, 'The Goose Girl', woven by Morris from one of the illustrations in Crane's *Household Stories from Grimm* (1882) is in the Victoria and Albert Museum.

Crane married in 1871 Mary Frances, daughter of Thomas Andrews, of Winchlow Hall, Hempstead, Essex, and had two sons and one daughter. He died at Horsham 14 March 1915.

G. F. Watts's portrait of Walter Crane, painted in 1891, is in the National Portrait Gallery.

[P. G. Konody, *The Art of Walter Crane*, 1902; Otto von Schliehitz, in the *Künstler Monographien* series, 1902; *Art Journal*, Easter number, 1898; J. Bruce Glasier, *William Morris and Early Days of the Socialist Movement*, 1921; private information.]

M. H. B.

CRAWFORD, twenty-sixth EARL OF (1847–1913), astronomer, collector, and bibliophile. [See LINDSAY, JAMES LUDOVIC.]

CROCKETT, SAMUEL RUTHERFORD (1860–1914), novelist, was born at the farm of Little Duchrae in the parish of Balmaghie, Kirkcudbrightshire, 24 September 1860. He was the natural son of a daughter of William Crocket, farmer, of Balmaghie, who is reputed to have been descended from refugees who fled from the Continent to Scotland to escape religious persecution. From his fifth to his seventh year Crockett went to Laurieston Free Church school, and for the next nine years attended at Castle Douglas the Free Church school, better known under the name of its head master as Cowper's school. There Crockett was remarkable for gaiety of disposition, a vivid imagination, and fondness for boyish adventure. At the age of sixteen (1876) he went to Edinburgh University with a bursary of £20 a year, and while still in his 'teens began a connexion with the daily press by means of which he helped to maintain himself. In 1878 he had six months' experience of journalism in London, and after finishing the arts course at Edinburgh University in 1879 travelled as a tutor through Germany, Switzerland, and North Italy, and attended classes at Heidelberg University. The impressions received on this tour developed those romantic inclinations which he had exhibited at school and university, with the result that in later life he had frequent recourse to continental scenes for the background of his stories, and spent much of his time abroad.

Crockett decided in 1881 to enter the ministry of the Free Church of Scotland, and studied at New College, Edinburgh (1882–1886); but he was comparatively little known to his contemporaries owing to the rigour of his life, continuing, as he did, the pursuit of journalism while engaged on theological study. At this period he felt his first definite impulse towards novel-writing; his sketches in the *Christian Leader*, which appeared in book form in 1893 under the title *The Stickit Minister*, give an indication of his potentialities. He published a volume of poems, *Dulce Cor*, in 1886. In that year he was ordained to the ministry of the Free church at Penicuik, Midlothian, where he became a popular and hardworking minister. In 1887 he married Ruth Mary, daughter of George Milner, of Moston House, Manchester; two sons and two daughters were born of the marriage. During this period he wrote, among others, his best-known novels, *The Raiders* (1894) and *The Lilac Sun-Bonnet* (1894), and the enthusiastic reception of these works confirmed him in his intention to retire from the ministry and devote himself entirely to novel-writing. He accordingly resigned in 1895, and between that year and 1914, when he died (21 April) at Avignon, published over forty books, mainly novels.

Crockett wrote with rapidity and zest, but it cannot be said that his exclusive devotion to novel-writing made for the development of his talent. His vogue, even in his lifetime, suffered a steady decline, and he will be remembered chiefly as the spirited chronicler of Galloway, which he called his 'little fatherland'. The natural beauties of this district, through which runs the Galloway Dee, inspired all that is most lasting in his work. By utilizing as a background to his best stories the variegated scenery of the district with its meadows and heaths, its rugged sea-coast and lonely lochs, and by writing about this land of feudal forays and covenanting struggles with vigour and a gay, if somewhat crude, humour, he claimed the admiration of men like Robert Louis Stevenson, who dedicated to Crockett one of his best-known poems.

[*The Times*, 22 April 1914; *Glasgow Herald*, 22 April 1914; *Scotsman*, 22 April 1914; Malcolm M. Harper, *Rambles in Galloway*, 1896.]

J. R. P.

CROMER, first EARL OF (1841–1917), statesman. [See BARING, EVELYN.]

CROOKES, SIR WILLIAM (1832–1919), man of science, was born in London 17 June 1832, the eldest son of Joseph Crookes, a tailor of north-country origin, by his second wife, Mary Scott. He received some instruction at a grammar school at Chippenham, but his scientific career began when, at the age of fifteen, he entered the Royal College of Chemistry in Hanover Square, London, under August Wilhelm von Hofmann. From 1850 to 1854 he filled the position of assistant in the college, and soon embarked upon original work, not indeed in the region of organic chemistry whither the inspiration of his distinguished teacher might have been expected to lead him, but on certain new compounds of the element selenium, the selenocyanides. These form the subject of his first published papers (1851). Leaving the Royal College, he became in 1854 superintendent of the meteorological department at the Radcliffe Observatory in Oxford, and in 1855 was appointed lecturer in chemistry at the Chester training college. In 1856 he married Ellen, daughter of William Humphrey, of Darlington, by whom he had three sons and a daughter. From this time his life was passed in London, and devoted mainly to independent work, journalistic, consulting, and academic. In 1859 he founded the *Chemical News*, which he edited for many years and conducted on much less formal lines than is usual with journals of scientific societies. After 1880 he lived at 7 Kensington Park Gardens, where in his private laboratory all his later work was carried out.

Crookes's life was one of unbroken scientific activity. He was never one of those who gain influence by popular exposition; neither was he esoteric. The breadth of his interests, ranging over pure and applied science, economic and practical problems, and psychical research, made him a well-known personality, and he received many public and academic honours. He was knighted in 1897, and in 1910 received the order of merit. At various times he was president of the Chemical Society, the Institution of Electrical Engineers, the Society of Chemical Industry, the British Association, and, from 1913 to 1915, of the Royal Society. He died in London 4 April 1919, two years after his wife, to whom he had been much devoted.

The work of Crookes extended over the regions of both chemistry and physics. Its salient characteristic was the originality of conception of his experiments, and the skill of their execution. It is probably just to say that his theoretical speculations, imaginative and stimulating as they may have been, were of less permanent importance. He was always more effective in experiment than in interpretation. His first great discovery was that of the element thallium, announced in 1861. By this work his reputation became firmly established, and he was elected a fellow of the Royal Society in 1863. The method of spectrum analysis, introduced by Bunsen and Kirchhoff, was received by Crookes with great enthusiasm, and, on applying it to the examination of the seleniferous deposit from a sulphuric acid factory, he discovered an unknown green line in the spectrum. The isolation of the new metallic element, thallium, followed, and the investigation of the properties of its compounds, which are of great chemical interest. Finally, in 1873, he determined the atomic weight of the new element in a research which is still a model of analytical precision.

Two main lines of research now occupied the attention of Crookes for many years. These were the properties of highly rarefied gases, with which he began to occupy himself immediately, and the investigation of the elements of the 'rare earths', upon which he embarked shortly after 1880. His attention had been attracted to the first problem in using a vacuum balance in the course of the thallium researches. He soon discovered the phenomenon upon which depends the action of the well-known little instrument, the Crookes radiometer, in which a system of vanes, each blackened on one side and polished on the other, is set in rotation when exposed to radiant energy. He did not, however, provide the true explanation of this apparent 'attraction and repulsion resulting from radiation'. Of more fundamental importance were his researches on the passage of the electrical discharge through rarefied gases. He found that as the attenuation of the gas was made greater the dark space round the negative electrode extended, while rays, now known as cathode rays, proceed from the electrode. He investigated the properties of the rays, showing that they travel in straight lines, cause phosphorescence in objects upon which they impinge, and by their impact produce great heat. He believed that he had discovered a fourth state of matter, which he called 'radiant matter'. But his theoretical views on the nature of 'radiant matter' proved to be mistaken. He believed the rays to consist of streams of particles of ordinary molecular magnitude. It remained for (Sir) J. J. Thomson to discover their subatomic nature, and to prove that cathode rays consist of streams of negative electrons, that is, of negatively electrified particles whose mass is only 1/1,800 that of the atom of hydrogen. Nevertheless, Crookes's experimental work in this field was the foundation of discoveries which have changed the whole conception of chemistry and physics. Moreover, it is characteristic of him that, though already advanced in years, he readily and enthusiastically accepted the new interpretation of his work.

For many years Crookes conducted laborious experiments on the elements of the rare earths, elements so similar to one another in chemical properties that special methods for their separation had to be devised. Throughout the work he employed spectroscopic methods for following the course, and testing the completeness, of the separation of one element from another. What had been one of the most obscure regions in inorganic chemistry gradually became clear. In the course of the years during which he was thus occupied, Crookes was led to views on the existence of 'meta-elements', or clusters of elements resembling one another so closely that in most ways the cluster behaves as a single individual. The 'meta-elements' of Crookes bear a superficial resemblance to the mixtures of isotopes of which some elements are now known to consist; but the theory of meta-elements cannot justly be said to anticipate the discovery of isotopes, since it was based upon facts of a fundamentally different kind from those on which more recent views on isotopic elements are founded.

Turning his attention to the newly discovered phenomena of radio-activity, Crookes, in 1900, achieved the separation from uranium of its active transformation product, uranium-X. He observed the gradual decay of the separated transformation product, and the simultaneous reproduction of a fresh supply in the original uranium. At about the same time as this important discovery, he observed that when 'α-particles', ejected from radio-active substances, impinge upon zinc sulphide, each impact is accompanied by a minute scintillation, an observation which forms the basis of one of the most useful methods in the technique of radioactivity.

Crookes published numerous papers on spectroscopy, a subject which always had a great fascination for him, and he made researches on a large variety of minor subjects. In addition to various technical books, he wrote a standard treatise on *Select Methods in Chemical Analysis* (1871), and a small book on *Diamonds* (1909), a subject to which he had devoted some study during two visits to South Africa. He frequently served the government in an advisory capacity, and his work on the production of a glass which should cut off from molten glass the rays which are injurious to the eyes of the work-people, may be cited among his many public services.

Sir William Crookes was a great experimenter. His material discoveries are of lasting and fundamental value, though his theoretical speculations have not stood the test of time so well. While it is true that all scientific theories serve primarily only for the suggestion of further research, it must be admitted that Crookes's analytical power hardly equalled his gift as an investigator of new facts. His excursions into psychical research have been strongly criticized, and they certainly led him into some very curious situations, but they show that he thought all phenomena worthy of investigation, and refused to be bound by tradition and convention. He was a man of science in the broadest sense, an influential personality, and a doyen of his profession.

There is a portrait of Crookes by E. A. Walton in the rooms of the Royal Society, and another by P. Ludovici in the National Portrait Gallery.

[*Proceedings* of the Royal Society, vol. xcvi, A, 1919–1920 (portrait); P. Zeemann, *Scientific Worthies, Sir William Crookes*, in *Nature*, 7 November 1907; E. E. Fournier D'Albe, *Life of Sir William Crookes*, 1923; Crookes's own papers and addresses in *Transactions* of the Chemical Society and *Proceedings* of the Royal Society.] C. N. H.

CROOKS, WILLIAM (1852–1921), labour politician, was born in Poplar 6 April 1852. His parents were very poor, his father having become a cripple, and at the age of eight Crooks, who had been already at work as a milkman's boy, was sent to the workhouse, and later to the Poor Law school at Sutton, Surrey, where he was separated from all his family. This period left an enduring impression on his mind. When his parents were able to resume charge of him, he became first a grocer's boy and then, at eleven years of age, labourer in a blacksmith's shop. At fourteen, his mother, at a financial sacrifice, contrived to get him apprenticed to a cooper, and this trade he followed for the rest of his working life. In 1874 he married Miss Matilda South. Already he was reading widely, and had adopted radical ideas. He became a full journeyman, but was dismissed by his employer as an agitator, and for some years was either out of work or only casually employed. Working for a time at the docks, he came to realize fully the evils of casual labour. He began lecturing and teaching in Poplar, and his open-air meetings got the name of 'Crooks's college'. His exertions in the London dock strike of 1889 brought on a serious illness. Shortly after his recovery his wife died (1892); and in 1893 he married Miss Elizabeth Lake, formerly a professional nurse. Meanwhile, he had become active in municipal politics. He helped to start the Poplar labour league. In 1892 he was elected to represent Poplar on the London County Council and on the Poplar board of guardians, of which he was chairman from 1897 to 1906. He refused an offer from the progressives to become vice-chairman of the County Council and also refused a managerial post in a coopering works, then, as ever, preferring complete independence. After 1892 he ceased to work at his trade, being supported by the 'Will Crooks's wages fund', raised by voluntary labour subscriptions. He never received from this, his only source of income, more than £4 a week. In 1901 he became mayor of Poplar—the first labour mayor in London. In 1903 he was returned by a huge majority as labour M.P. for Woolwich, becoming the fourth independent labour member in the House of Commons. He was re-elected in 1906, lost his seat at the general election in January 1910, but regained it in that of December 1910, and was returned unopposed in 1918, holding the seat till his retirement owing to ill-health in February 1921, a few months before his death, which took place at Poplar 5 June 1921. In 1906 he was involved in certain charges made against the Poplar board of guardians, but was completely vindicated. He was active on recruiting platforms during the War, and was made a privy councillor in 1916.

Will Crooks, as he was always known, excelled as a speaker, mingling humour and pathos with immense effect. He had an unfailing fund of anecdotes, and was unequalled in his power of moving large audiences to support the causes in which he believed. He was universally popular with political opponents as well as sympathisers. Mr. G. K. Chesterton once aptly described him as 'very like a poor man in Dickens', and it is characteristic of him that Dickens was his favourite author. By his first marriage he had two sons and five daughters. One of his daughters died during his early struggle for work: the other children survived him.

[George Haw, *From Workhouse to Westminster: The Life Story of Will Crooks, M.P.*, 1907; private information.] G. D. H. C.

CROSS, RICHARD ASSHETON, first Viscount Cross (1823–1914), statesman, was born at Red Scar, near Preston, Lancashire, 30 May 1823, the third son of William Cross, of Red Scar, by his wife, Ellen, eldest daughter of Edward Chaffers, of Liverpool and Everton, a collateral relative of Richard Chaffers [q.v.], the well-known potter and rival of Josiah Wedgwood, and of William Chaffers [q.v.], the virtuoso. Cross was educated at Rugby under Thomas Arnold, and at Trinity College, Cambridge, where he rowed in the First Trinity eight at the head of the river, and in 1845 was president of the Cambridge Union Society. Called to the bar by the Inner Temple in 1849, he went the Northern circuit. As his father and grandfather had held legal office in the County Palatine Court of Common Pleas at Preston, he started with the advantage of a well-known name, and quickly built up a substantial practice. He became leader of the Preston and Salford quarter-sessions bar; wrote a book on pauper settlement (1853), and collaborated in another on the jurisdiction of quarter-sessions in non-criminal matters (1858), which remained the standard manual for practitioners until that jurisdiction, save for a few fragments, was abolished on the creation of county councils. In 1857 his position was sufficiently assured to permit of his standing for parliament. He won Preston for the conservative interest and held the seat till 1862. The only pledge on which his supporters insisted was that he would not join the Carlton Club; and he signalized his independence by being the only conservative member to vote in favour of Mr. Gladstone's repeal of the paper duties, as well as by voting against the same proposal when Gladstone unconstitutionally, as he held, tacked it to a money-bill in order to circumvent opposition in the House of Lords.

In 1860 the death of his father-in-law led to Cross's becoming a partner in Parr's bank at Warrington, a step which involved giving up both his practice at the bar and his seat in parliament. But the years 1862–1868 were of great importance in his career ; for to the legal ability which he had already shown he was now to add financial experience as partner in a great bank in times of exceptional difficulty (the 'cotton famine'), and an intimate knowledge of the problems of local government. In 1865 when Parr's bank became one of the pioneers of limited liability as applied to banking, Cross became deputy chairman, and he succeeded to the chairmanship in 1870. During these years he also became chairman or deputy chairman of every local government body then existing in his neighbourhood, including two courts of quarter-sessions, a highway board, a board of guardians, and the governing bodies of many charitable institutions. The eminent services which he afterwards rendered to the state were based on the intimate knowledge thus gained of local conditions in an industrial area.

In the general election of 1868 Cross again stood for parliament, this time for the new constituency of South-West Lancashire, where he achieved a sensational success by defeating Gladstone, then at the height of popularity and power, and heading the poll. Family connexions and the influence of his old school and college friend, the fifteenth Earl of Derby, had their share in this, but Cross's personal popularity was the decisive factor. Yet, though he returned to parliament a marked man, he was entirely without that sparkle which attracts attention in debate : and it was, therefore, as Disraeli himself said, an 'almost unexampled mark of confidence' when Cross was in 1874 put at the head of the Home Office without undergoing a probation in some minor post.

From the very start, however, Cross was an unqualified success as home secretary. Disraeli had shown in his early novels, and in his Manchester speech of 1872, an appreciation of the need for social reform ; but he had no idea what direction it should take, and the only promise on the subject made in his election address of 1874 was that he would give the country a rest from 'incessant and harassing legislation' ; moreover, he not only allowed but expected his colleagues to have policies of their own. It is certain, therefore, that Cross was not merely responsible for the details, but had a large part in shaping the principles of the social reforms which are perhaps the greatest achievement of the ministry of 1874–1880.

Cross's first bill, the Licensing Act, 1874, was dictated by the necessity of redeeming pledges which had been given to the licensed victuallers in the general election : 'not much to be proud of' was his own admission in after years, but at least he cut down concession to a minimum and spoke very plainly about the increase in drunkenness which had taken place. A measure more congenial to him was the Artisans' Dwellings Act, 1875. Its preamble was apparently intended to disarm criticism by a disavowal of socialist tendencies. Nevertheless, the Act marks the definite introduction of collectivist principles into legislation, for it armed municipal authorities with compulsory powers to acquire and pull down unhealthy slums ; it authorized them to undertake the building of suitable houses and to embark on the business of owning and letting them ; it forbade the enhancement of compensation on the ground of compulsion ; and it substituted the award of a departmental arbitrator for the proprietary and local sympathies of juries. At the same time a home office order was issued requiring all local authorities to appoint medical officers of health and sanitary inspectors ; in other ways also Cross showed that the executive was determined to enforce the policy of the legislature. Joseph Chamberlain afterwards said that the reforms which have made a model city of Birmingham would have been impossible without this Act. The Factory Act, 1875, dealt with the employment of women and children in textile factories ; and the Factories and Workshops Act, 1878, consolidated and codified the mass of legislation on this subject. The latter embodies the recommendations of a royal commission appointed in 1876. The Employers and Workmen Act, 1875, and its concomitant, the Conspiracy and Protection of Property Act, on the other hand, owe little or nothing to the royal commission which preceded them. We have Disraeli's authority for saying that the policy of these Acts was initiated by Cross and would have been vetoed by the rest of the Cabinet but for his own support. However, the boldness and statesmanship of the policy were warmly applauded by the representatives alike of employers and employed, and provided a satisfactory settlement of their legal relations for many years. Other Acts introduced by Cross dealt with friendly societies and with the preservation of open spaces near large towns ; the management of prisons throughout the three kingdoms was transferred to the central government, and the cost of their maintenance from local to imperial funds, uniformity and economy of administration being thus secured without abolishing the visitatorial powers of the justices. Cross's last proposal, to acquire and transfer to a single authority all the undertakings which supplied London with water, was sharply criticized on the ground of extravagance: but the main idea was sound.

In opposition (1880–1885) the school of business men in politics to which Cross belonged was speedily thrown into the shade by Lord Randolph Churchill, whose dislike for them was open and violent. Accordingly, although Cross returned to the Home Office in the short-lived ministry of 1885, it was no surprise when in 1886 that department was given to Lord Randolph's nominee, and Cross received the lighter India Office, being at the same time raised to the peerage as Viscount Cross, of Broughton-in-Furness. His tenure of the India Office, which lasted till 1892, was uneventful, its only important piece of legislation being the India Councils Act, 1892. This was regarded at the time as a bold advance; but it was highly successful, and Cross is entitled to a considerable share of the credit. In 1895 he accepted the office of privy seal, which he retained till 1900, and he finally retired in 1902. After this his appearances in parliament were few, but he voted and spoke against the 1909 Finance Bill. He died 8 January 1914 at Eccle Riggs, Broughton-in-Furness.

Lord Cross was a fellow of the Royal Society, a bencher of the Inner Temple, and an ecclesiastical commissioner, and was keenly interested in the affairs of the Church. His honours included, besides the viscounty, the G.C.B. (1880) and G.C.S.I. (1892). Cross was among the small band of her ministers whom Queen Victoria honoured with her close personal friendship, and he was a trustee of more than one royal marriage settlement. But the picturesque story that he was the queen's confidential business agent is unfounded. Very far from being a brilliant man, Cross was yet gifted with unfailing good sense; and he had the knack of securing the affection and trust of his subordinates. His speeches were of a type which the House of Commons listens to with respect rather than enjoyment, well-documented and clear statements such as might be made at a meeting of a business company. Only twice did he rise to a note of passion in oratory, namely, when introducing the Artisans' Dwellings Act (1875) and when repudiating on behalf of the Cabinet the charge of indifference to the sufferings of Bulgaria. The last-named speech (7 May 1877) also contains a cogent defence of the whole policy of the government over the treaty of San Stefano, and created a widespread impression.

Lord Cross married in 1852 Georgiana (died 1907), third daughter of Thomas Lyon, of Appleton Hall, near Warrington, by whom he had four sons and three daughters. His two elder sons predeceased him, and he was succeeded as second viscount by his grandson, Richard Assheton Cross (born 1882).

[*The Times*, 9 January 1914; *Annual Register*, 1914; Lord Cross's own *Family History* and *Political History* (printed for private circulation, 1903); Sir Spencer Walpole, *The History of Twenty-five Years (1856–1880)*, 4 vols., 1904–1908; W. F. Monypenny and G. E. Buckle, *Life of Benjamin Disraeli*, 6 vols., 1910–1920; Herbert Paul, *History of Modern England*, 5 vols., 1904–1906; private information.] S. V. FG.

CROSTHWAITE, Sir CHARLES HAUKES TODD (1835–1915), Anglo-Indian administrator, was born at Donnybrook, co. Dublin, 5 December 1835, the second son of the Rev. John Clarke Crosthwaite, vicar-choral of Christ Church Cathedral, Dublin, and later rector of St. Mary-at-Hill, London, by his wife, Elizabeth Haukes, daughter of Charles H. Todd, M.D., of Sligo and Dublin. After education at Merchant Taylors' School and St. John's College, Oxford, he entered the Indian civil service in August 1857, and served in various revenue and judicial posts in the North-Western Provinces and the Central Provinces. From March 1883 to February 1884 he was in Burma, acting as chief commissioner during the absence on leave of Sir Charles Edward Bernard [q.v.]. After his return to the Central Provinces Crosthwaite became officiating chief commissioner there, and was confirmed in that post in January 1885. Towards the end of the following year he was made a member of the public service commission; but this employment was interrupted in March 1887 by his appointment to succeed Sir Charles Bernard as chief commissioner of Burma. He had already been made a C.S.I. in February 1887, and in June 1888 he was promoted K.C.S.I.

Crosthwaite's period of service in Burma lasted till December 1890, and during that time he did notable work in clearing the province of the rebels and dacoits who infested it, and in settling the administration. He was then recalled to join the viceroy's council as home member; but this post he had to give up in February 1891, when he went to England on furlough. He was, however, reappointed on his return in April 1892, and retained his seat until the following November, when he was selected to succeed Sir Auckland Colvin [q.v.] as lieutenant-governor of the North-Western Provinces and Oudh. In this position he again proved himself a strong and able official, at once determined and conciliatory.

Crosthwaite went home on leave at the beginning of 1895, and in the following March was appointed to a vacancy on the Council of India, where he served the customary ten years. After his retirement he devoted himself to writing. He had already (1870) published *Notes on the North-Western Provinces of India* and had collaborated in a work on *The Land Revenue Law of the North-Western Provinces* (1875). He now wrote a full account of *The Pacification of Burma* (1912), and followed this up by *Thakur Pertab Singh and other Tales* (1913). He also contributed many letters to the daily press, especially on the subject of the Morley reforms, of which he was a trenchant critic. He died 28 May 1915, at Long Acre, Shamley Green, Surrey.

Crosthwaite married twice: first, in 1863 Sarah (died 1872), daughter of William Graham, of Lisburn; secondly, in 1874 Caroline Alison (died 1893), daughter of Sir Henry Lushington, fourth baronet, of Aspenden Hall, Hertfordshire. By his first wife he had three sons and three daughters, and by his second, two sons and one daughter.

[*The Times*, 31 May 1915; *India Office List*; private information.] W. F.

CUMMINGS, BRUCE FREDERICK (1889–1919), diarist and biologist, more generally known by the pseudonym W. N. P. **Barbellion** (the initial letters concealing the bravado of Wilhelm Nero Pilate), was born at Barnstaple, Devon, 7 September 1889, the sixth and youngest child of John Cummings, a member of the staff of the *Devon and Exeter Gazette*, by his wife, Maria Elizabeth Richards. His interest in natural science awoke about his twelfth year, and shortly afterwards he began to keep a journal. In 1911, self-taught, and having already contributed in his spare time to *The Countryside*, *The Zoologist*, and other journals, he won in open competition a post at the Natural History Museum, South Kensington. His health, however, began to fail, with the result that he turned his attention more and more upon his journal and himself, and, while contributing to such scientific periodicals as the *Proceedings* of the Zoological Society, the *Journal of Botany*, and *Science Progress*, began to write articles of a more general nature. In 1915 he married Miss Eleanor Benger. But his disease, disseminated sclerosis, the nature of which had not been disclosed to him, though it had been revealed to his wife before their marriage, steadily gained ground, and in 1917 he was compelled to resign his museum appointment. He died at Gerrard's Cross, Buckinghamshire, 22 October 1919, leaving a widow and one daughter.

Cummings's fame will rest upon the record of his life, *The Journal of a Disappointed Man*, consisting of extracts from his voluminous diaries (1903–1917) edited by himself and published in March 1919. It presents the picture of a sensitive, courageous, critical personality, ambitious and greedy of life, but thwarted by limited opportunity and persistent ill-health; the style is exceptionally nervous and vivid; and the outlook, tragic and humorous in turn, is characterized by a scientific and intellectual objectivity that raises Barbellion to the rank of the great diarists; 'A self-portrait in the nude' was his own description. Two posthumous books followed. *Enjoying Life and Other Literary Remains* (published November 1919), which he himself passed for press, contains several essays too long for the *Journal*, and other papers on literary and scientific subjects; and *A Last Diary* (published 1920), a pendant to the *Journal*, is important chiefly for showing how in his last months the bias of his life, to use his own words, had 'gone across from the intellectual to the ethical'.

[The works cited; preface to *A Last Diary* (*The Life and Character of Barbellion*, by his brother, Arthur J. Cummings); private information.] C. H. C. P.

CUNNINGHAM, WILLIAM (1849–1919), economic historian, was born at Edinburgh 29 December 1849, the third son of James Cunningham, writer to the signet, of Edinburgh. His mother, who was his father's second wife, was Elizabeth Boyle, youngest daughter of Alexander Dunlop, of Keppoch, near Cardross. She was descended from William

Dunlop, the elder [q.v.], a celebrated principal of Glasgow University in the reign of William III. Cunningham was educated at the Edinburgh Institution and Academy, and at the universities of Edinburgh, Tübingen, and Cambridge. He entered Caius College, Cambridge, in 1869, but won a scholarship at Trinity College in 1872 and read philosophy, being bracketed senior with Frederick William Maitland in the moral science tripos in 1872. He also won the Hulsean prize (1873) and the Maitland and Kaye prizes (1879). He was ordained in 1873, being successively curate of Horningsea, near Cambridge, chaplain of Trinity College (1880–1891), and curate of Great St. Mary's church, Cambridge, of which he was vicar from 1887 to 1908. He was appointed archdeacon of Ely in 1907. A thoughtful and original preacher, he attracted large congregations. He was a proctor in convocation, took a considerable share in the work of the diocese, and was always ready to help the clergy in his archdeaconry, often taking their duty in order to enable them to enjoy an otherwise impossible holiday.

Through his appointment in 1878 as an examiner for the history tripos at Cambridge, Cunningham became impressed with the need for the teaching of economic history in the university. He undertook to teach the subject, but was embarrassed by the want of a suitable text-book. He accordingly set himself to supply the defect, a task of considerable magnitude since he had to begin at the roots of the subject. The result of this inquiry appeared in 1882 under the title of *The Growth of English Industry and Commerce*. This book established Cunningham's reputation as an economic historian. In 1891 he was elected Tooke professor of economics and statistics at King's College, London, an appointment which he held for six years. In the same year (1891) he was elected to a fellowship at Trinity College, Cambridge. He also served for a time in 1899 as lecturer on economic history at Harvard University; he returned to the United States as Lowell lecturer in 1914. In addition he was Birkbeck and Hulsean lecturer at Cambridge (1885), an original fellow of the British Academy, and honorary fellow of Caius College (1895).

The six subsequent editions of *The Growth of English Industry and Commerce* (1892–1910) occupied much of Cunningham's energies, since each edition was to a considerable extent a new book. In addition he developed certain aspects of the subject in separate treatises, as, for instance, *Modern Civilization in some of its Economic Aspects* (1896), *Alien Immigrants to England* (1897), and *Western Civilization in its Economic Aspect in Ancient Times* (1898), and in *Medieval and Modern Times* (1900).

Cunningham was a many-sided man. From 1872 he took an interest in social questions and wrote on them at various times. In 1884 he published *Christian Opinion on Usury*, *An Alternative to Socialism* (1885), *The Gospel of Work* (1902), *The Moral Witness of the Church on the Investment of Wealth* (1909), *Christianity and Social Questions* (1910), *Christianity and Politics* (1916), and *Increase of True Religion* (1917). He was also a great traveller, and journeyed not only throughout Europe, but in India, the Holy Land, South Africa, and the United States. This may have been the cause, or one of the causes, which made him an enthusiastic supporter of Mr. Joseph Chamberlain's scheme for imperial preference. To popularize this scheme he wrote another group of works, amongst which may be mentioned *The Case against Free Trade* (1910).

Cunningham was a pioneer in the teaching and writing of the economic history of Great Britain. Adam Smith's work had been largely historical, but under the dominance of the classical school of economists historical investigation had been pushed more and more into the background. Probably what lay deepest in Cunningham's mind was the conception that economic inquiry had to be related to economic progress, and that in order to secure this it was necessary to get at the facts. At the same time Cunningham's point of view was quite distinct from that of the historical school in Germany, in so far as he desired to see and, indeed, insisted on seeing the facts group themselves in an orderly process of development.

Cunningham married in 1876 his first cousin, Adèle Rebecca, daughter of Andrew Anderson Dunlop, of Dublin. They had one son and one daughter. He died at Cambridge 10 June 1919.

[William Cunningham, *Progress of Capitalism in England* (containing a bibliography of his works on economic subjects), 1916; H. S. Foxwell, *Archdeacon Cunningham*, and Lilian Knowles, *Dr. Cunningham*, in *Economic Journal*, vol. xxix, 1919; *Edinburgh Academy Chronicle*, July 1919; W. R. Scott, *William Cunningham, 1849–1919*, in *Proceedings* of the British Academy, vol. ix, 1920; private information.]

W. R. S.

CUST, HENRY JOHN COCKAYNE (1861–1917), politician and journalist, was born in London 10 October 1861, the elder son of Major Henry Francis Cockayne Cust, M.P., of Cockayne Hatley, Bedfordshire, grandson of the first Baron Brownlow, by his wife, Sarah Jane, daughter of Isaac Cookson, of Meldon Park, Northumberland, and widow of Major Sidney Streatfeild. He was educated at Eton and in 1883 gained a scholarship at Trinity College, Cambridge. Called to the bar in Paris, and a bar student in London, he deserted the law and went early into politics. He was returned to parliament for the Stamford division of Lincolnshire in the unionist interest in 1890, resigning the seat in 1895. Five years later he was returned for Bermondsey, which he represented until the general election of 1906. In 1892 he proposed, as an amendment to the Small Holdings Bill, that small holdings should be dealt with as personal property, and he had the satisfaction of seeing his amendment accepted.

Meanwhile, in 1892, Cust had made a sudden and accidental incursion into journalism. Asked across the dinner-table by Mr. William Waldorf (afterwards Viscount) Astor if he would edit the *Pall Mall Gazette*, he assented immediately. It was an adventure after his own heart. He knew nothing of newspapers; he had never been in Fleet Street; but he had confidence in his own powers, and in the end he proved a worthy successor of Frederick Greenwood [q.v.] and John (afterwards Viscount) Morley. He possessed all the qualities of a good editor: he was a quick judge of men, and when once he had formed his staff he had the good sense to trust it. Thus, under his editorship, the *Pall Mall Gazette* maintained a definite and consistent policy both in letters and in politics. In 1896 this episode came to an end, and Cust made no further experiments in journalism.

During the European War Cust was tireless in the work of propaganda. The founder, in August 1914, and chairman of the Central Committee for National Patriotic Organizations, he found full scope for his tact and activity in the information of neutrals and allies, while, looking ahead, he devised schemes for employment after the War both at home and overseas. For the services rendered by him as chairman of the Central Committee he was thanked by Mr. Asquith in the House of Commons, and a Cust annual lecture 'on some important current topic relating to the British Empire' was endowed at Nottingham University College in order to commemorate his work. He died in London 2 March 1917.

In spite of what he achieved Cust was remarkable rather for what he was than for what he did. It was in society that he won his greatest triumphs. He was, before all things, a talker, born and trained, and few of his contemporaries added more than he did to the stock of harmless pleasures. An assiduous traveller from his youth upwards, he knew both men and cities, and he spoke fully and amply, not only from the books which he had read and remembered, but from his own gay and vivid experience of life. After his death a volume of his *Occasional Poems* was printed at Jerusalem (1918).

Cust, who in 1893 became heir to the barony of Brownlow, married in that year Emmeline, only daughter of Sir William Welby-Gregory, fourth baronet, of Denton Manor, Grantham. They had no children.

[*The Times*, 3 and 6 March 1917; *Blackwood's Magazine*, April 1918; personal knowledge.] C. W.

DANIEL, CHARLES HENRY OLIVE (1836–1919), scholar and printer, the eldest son of the Rev. Alfred Daniel, perpetual curate of Frome, Somerset, by his wife, Eliza Anne, daughter of Clement Wilson Cruttwell, was born at Wareham, Dorset, 30 September 1836. He was educated at Grosvenor College, Bath, King's College, London, and Worcester College, Oxford, where he was elected scholar in 1854. After taking his degree in 1858, with a first class in *literae humaniores*, he returned to King's College as classical lecturer in 1859. Four years later he was elected to a fellowship at Worcester College, and there he spent the remainder of his life. In 1878 he married his cousin Emily, third daughter of Edmund Crabb Olive, by whom he had two daughters.

From a very early age Daniel was interested in printing. His first 'book', printed 'by the use of types and thumb and inking', appeared about 1845. From that time until 1903 when he was elected provost of Worcester—he was the first provost of the college elected by the fellows—the Daniel Press continued at intervals to produce books. Some of these were reprints: *Desiderii Erasmi Colloquia Duo* (1880); *Hymni Ecclesiae* (1882); *Sixe Idillia* of Theocritus (1883), probably translated by Sir Edward Dyer [q.v.] from the unique copy in the Bodleian Library; *Love's Graduate*, an attempt by (Sir) Edmund Gosse to separate Webster's work from that of William Rowley in *A Cure for a Cuckold* (1885); Blake's *Songs* (1885) and *Songs of Innocence* (1893); Herrick, *His Flowers* (1891) and *Christmas* (1891); *Odes, Sonnets, and Lyrics of John Keats* (1895); Robert Jones, *The Muses' Garden for Delights* (1901). Other books contain the work of contemporaries and of friends. Chief among these are the plays and poems of the future poet laureate, Mr. Robert Bridges, which form the contents of fifteen pieces printed between 1883 and 1903. Richard Watson Dixon, Henry Patmore, Mrs. Margaret Woods, Sir Herbert Warren, Walter Pater, Laurence Binyon and others are represented by one or more volumes. Two of the most interesting productions of the Daniel Press are *The Garland of Rachel* (1881) and *Our Memories* (1893). The latter, of which a second series was begun, but only two numbers printed, consists of personal reminiscences of Oxford by a number of senior members of the university. The former is the best known of all the Daniel Press books. At the suggestion of Mr. T. Humphry Ward, her father the printer, and seventeen 'unknown friends', celebrated in verse the first birthday of Rachel Anne Olive Daniel. Few of the seventeen names are unfamiliar. This is the first book in which large ornaments and miniation by Mrs. Daniel were used.

The smaller Daniel books are dainty, the larger, particularly such volumes as the *Keats* and the *Shorter Poems* of Bridges in five parts, are fine and handsome, but none of them reaches the typographical perfection of the best work from later famous presses. Daniel had admirable taste, but he did not set out with any serious intention of reforming or improving English printing. He was an amateur who did his own work and aimed at pleasing himself and his friends by printing as well as the means at his disposal would allow, rather than at showing how beautiful a book could be made. He was a pioneer who began printing at Oxford in 1874, seventeen years before William Morris founded the Kelmscott Press. None the less his hobby had considerable influence. This was largely due to his use of the Fell type which had lain unused at the Clarendon Press for one hundred and fifty years. Caslon's old-faced type had been revived by William Pickering [q.v.] and Charles Whittingham 'the nephew' [q.v.] for the Chiswick Press some thirty-six years earlier. Fell type was first used by Daniel in *A New Sermon of the Newest Fashion* (1876), the second book which he printed at Oxford. He also used a black letter, of which the first example is Bridges's *The Growth of Love* (1890).

Daniel first used a toy press; from 1850 to 1882 he used a small Albion press; and from 1882 onwards a large Albion hand-press. The large press was first used to print *Hymni Ecclesiae*. In 1920 it was presented by Mrs. Daniel to the Bodleian Library, and on it in 1921 was printed *The Daniel Press*, the first book printed in the Library.

Daniel died at Oddington, Gloucestershire, 6 September 1919. For fifty-three years he had been connected as fellow and provost with Worcester College, the history of which he wrote with W. R. Barker. He was chiefly responsible for the decoration of the chapel and the hall, carried out from the designs of William Burges. The former is, perhaps, the most important example in Oxford of the influence of pre-Raphaelite work. The years during which he was provost were uneventful so far as the internal history of the college is concerned. There is an unfinished portrait of Daniel by Charles Furse in Worcester College hall.

[*The Daniel Press* contains 'Memorials of Dr. Daniel' by Sir Herbert Warren, W. W. Jackson, Mrs. Margaret Woods; poems by John Masefield, W. Stebbing, Don F. de Arteaga y Pereira, F. W. Bourdillon; and a full and minute bibliography of every piece printed on the Daniel Press both at Frome and at Oxford, written by Falconer Madan.]

C. H. W.

DARWIN, Sir GEORGE HOWARD (1845–1912), mathematician and astronomer, was born at Down, Kent, 9 July 1845, the second son of Charles Darwin, the naturalist [q.v.], by his wife, Emma, daughter of Josiah Wedgwood. He was descended on both sides from men of intellectual and scientific distinction. His eminent father, his grandfather, Robert Waring Darwin, a physician, and his great-grandfathers, Erasmus Darwin [q.v.], physician, poet, and philosopher, and Josiah Wedgwood of Etruria [q.v.], the originator of the famous Wedgwood pottery, were all fellows of the Royal Society. At the age of eleven Darwin was sent to Clapham grammar school, then kept by the Rev. Charles Pritchard [q.v.], afterwards Savilian professor of astronomy at Oxford, who catered specially for scientific families by putting more mathematics and science into his curriculum than was then to be found at the great public schools. Having competed unsuccessfully for an entrance scholarship at St. John's College, Cambridge, in 1863, and again at Trinity in 1864, Darwin entered Trinity in the autumn of 1864 without a scholarship, and read mathematics with Edward John Routh [q.v.], the well-known 'coach'. Two years later Trinity elected him to a foundation scholarship, and in January 1868 he graduated as second wrangler and was awarded the second Smith's prize. The autumn of the same year saw him elected a fellow of his college.

Although Darwin had generally been expected to do well in his examinations, no one, and least of all himself, had so far recognized that he possessed quite exceptional mathematical ability, and his place in the tripos was higher than he had ventured to hope for. Having at this time no idea of finding his life's occupation in mathematics or science, he began reading for the bar; he was called in 1874, but he never practised. His health, which had frequently given trouble in his boyhood, grew much worse after he had taken his degree, and he began to suffer seriously, as his father had done before him, from digestive troubles and general weakness. Successive treatments at Malvern, Homburg, and Cannes produced no cure, although from 1873 onwards he gradually improved under the care of (Sir) Andrew Clark.

This period of ill-health resulted in Darwin's abandoning all thought of a legal career; and in October 1873 he returned to Cambridge and settled in rooms in Trinity. At this time he was writing articles on oddly miscellaneous subjects, such as 'Development in Dress', 'Restriction to Liberty of Marriage', a 'Defence of Jevons', and 'Cousin Marriages'. About 1875 a more distinctly scientific trend became noticeable, in papers on slide-rules, equipotential lines, elliptic integrals; and finally the memoir *On the Influence of Geological Changes on the Earth's Axis of Rotation*, read before the Royal Society in 1876 and published in the Society's *Philosophical Transactions* (1877), marked his definite entry into serious scientific life. He was proposed for the Royal Society in 1877 and elected a fellow in 1879. After his Trinity fellowship had expired (in 1878) he continued to live in Cambridge, holding no official position but pursuing research on cosmogony. In 1883 the Plumian professorship of astronomy and experimental philosophy fell vacant through the death of James Challis [q.v.], and Darwin was elected, although only, if we may trust a note in his diary, by the votes of five out of the nine electors. In 1884 he married, and his family life was conspicuously happy in spite of the continual handicap of his indifferent health.

The main part of Darwin's scientific life was occupied by lines of research which originated out of his memoir of 1876. Sir William Thomson (afterwards Lord Kelvin) had been asked by the Royal Society to report on the suitability of this paper for publication; and out of the ensuing correspondence and conversations resulted a friendship which terminated only with the death of the older man, as well as a lifelong devotion of the younger to problems of the past history of the earth and of the solar system. Generally speaking, Darwin's earliest papers dealt solely with the earth; those of his next epoch were concerned with the earth-moon system; later papers survey the whole solar system and even to some extent the whole universe of stars, but always with reference to the problems of past history and development. The object of most of these papers is to put general conjectures to the test of precise numerical calculations. The method is well illustrated in his 1876 paper already mentioned. Geologists, impressed by the apparent evidence of successive ice-ages, and naturalists, arguing from the present and supposed past distributions of terrestrial life, had promulgated the hypothesis of former extensive wanderings in the position of the earth's pole and violent variations in the obliquity of the ecliptic. Darwin showed, by numerical calculation, that so long as the earth has remained rigid, the north pole can never have been distant more than about 3° from its present position. The possibility of cataclysmic adjustments of the earth's shape may somewhat increase this figure, but in no event is a change to the extent assumed by geology dynamically possible.

The next series of papers, on the earth-moon system, are marked by the hypothesis that 'tidal friction' played a prominent part in the development of the system. As a result of viscosity, the tides raised in our earth by the moon will always have their points of high tide a little in advance of the positions they would occupy if the whole earth were perfectly fluid. The result is a force ever checking the speed of the earth's rotation and increasing the distance between the moon and the earth, with a consequent lengthening of the month. Tracing this effect back into the past Darwin arrived at a stage, 54 million years ago or more, at which the moon was only about 6,000 miles from the earth's surface, while the two bodies rotated together, each always turning the same face to the other. The day and month, at this time equal, were each rather less than a quarter of our present day. He concluded that the earth and moon must originally have formed a single mass, and he was led to study the process by which this mass had broken up.

A further application of the theory of tidal friction to the motion of the planets round the sun opened up the wider question of the genesis of the solar system. Darwin had at first believed that tidal friction would account for the evolution of the whole solar system, but he subsequently adopted the view that tidal friction had been of primary importance only in the one case of the earth-moon system, which he consequently supposed to form a unique example in the solar system of this special method of evolution. At this time the generally accepted theory of the origin of the planets and their satellites was that propounded by Laplace, according to which each planet and satellite had been formed by the condensation of a ring of matter shed by the primary body around which it revolved. Darwin's researches led him to contemplate the simpler possibility of an astronomical body breaking directly into two detached masses, and he tried to reconstruct the details of the process by tracing back the history of such a pair of bodies as our earth and moon still farther than had already been done. In the meantime Jules Henri Poincaré was attacking the same problem from the other end, examining the sequence of events in a mass which, owing to continued shrinkage, was rotating so fast that it could no longer hold together as a single body. Darwin adopted Poincaré's line of attack with enthusiasm, and devoted much of the last period of his life to this problem. He was still at work on it at the time of his death, which took place at Cambridge 7 December 1912.

Although the main stream of Darwin's work was always associated with the evolution of the solar system, yet no small part of his time was spent on quite other problems, many of which were brought to his notice through his membership of various scientific committees. He dealt, as a recognized authority, with a very wide range of subjects, including tidal theory, geodesy, and dynamical meteorology. Of the four large volumes in which his collected works are published [*Scientific Papers by Sir George Howard Darwin*, 1907–1911], the first is devoted entirely to *Oceanic Tides*, while the fourth and largest is entitled *Periodic Orbits and Miscellaneous Papers*. When invited to deliver a course of lectures in Boston, U.S.A., in 1897, he chose as his subject 'The Tides'. The lectures were subsequently published (1898) in a book which is a masterpiece of semi-popular scientific exposition; it passed through many editions in English, as well as two in German, and has also been translated into Italian, Spanish, and Hungarian.

To the end of his life Darwin's personality suggested a certain boyish eagerness; he seemed always on the look-out for adventures. He conveyed no suggestion of midnight-oil; his own estimate of his average hours of work was only three a day. That he achieved so much must be ascribed first to a *flair* for starting each problem in the right way, and secondly to an obstinacy which insisted on probing every problem to the bottom. He lost no time over false starts. His mathematical technique was simple; his method was always that of the direct frontal attack; his skill was of a type which he described just before his death, although with undue self-depreciation, as similar to the skill 'of a house-breaker who blows in a safe-door with dynamite instead of picking the lock'. Probably his special ability lay in getting his problem set out in perfect order before the dynamiting process began. As a lecturer and speaker he gave a quiet impression of reserve power; his pronouncements being entirely free, as was his whole character, from anything of the nature of display or self-consciousness. His unassuming modesty, no less than his personal charm and eagerness, endeared him to all who met him. He gave his time and energy freely to service on various scientific committees, being especially attracted by such as connected his university or country with the wider world. He acted with conspicuous success as president of the British Association on the occasion of its visit to South Africa in 1905 and was created K.C.B. on his return. In 1909 he presided over the International Geodetic Association, and in 1912, three months before his death, over the International Congress of Mathematicians. His scientific eminence was recognized by numerous honours and by membership of most of the leading scientific societies of the world.

Darwin married in 1884 Maud, daughter of Charles du Puy, of Philadelphia, U.S.A., by whom he had two sons and two daughters. The eldest son, Charles Galton Darwin, has followed with distinction his father's career of applied mathematics.

There is a portrait of Darwin by Mark Gertler in the National Portrait Gallery, which was painted in 1912 and presented by Lady Darwin in 1923.

[Sir Francis Darwin, *Memoir of Sir G. Darwin* in vol. v of *Scientific Papers by Sir George Howard Darwin*, 1916; obituary notices in *Proceedings* of the Royal Society, vol. lxxxix, A, 1913–1914, and in *Monthly Notices* of the Royal Astronomical Society, vol. 73; Francis Galton and Edgar Schuster, *Noteworthy Families*, 1906; *Emma Darwin: A Century of Family Letters (1792–1896)*, edited by Henrietta Litchfield; *Life and Letters of Charles Darwin*, edited by Francis Darwin, 3 vols., 1887; personal knowledge.] J. H. J.

DAVIDSON, JAMES LEIGH STRACHAN- (1843–1916), classical scholar. [See STRACHAN-DAVIDSON.]

DAVIES, JOHN LLEWELYN (1826–1916), theologian, was born at Chichester 26 February 1826, the eldest son of the Rev. John Davies, D.D., an evangelical divine, rector of Gateshead from 1840 to 1861, by his wife, Mary Hopkinson. He was educated at Repton School and at Trinity College, Cambridge. In 1848 he was bracketed fifth in the classical tripos with his friend, David James Vaughan [q.v.], also of Trinity, with whom he had been elected to a Bell university scholarship in 1845; in 1850 the friends were elected fellows of their college together, and they subsequently (1852) collaborated in translating Plato's *Republic*. Davies as an undergraduate was already interested in political and social questions, and he became president of the Union Society. After taking his degree he for a time taught private pupils, among whom was (Sir) Leslie Stephen. About this time he came under the influence of Frederick Denison Maurice [q.v.], whose teaching his clear mind was to make acceptable to many who found Maurice himself elusive. Taking orders in 1851 Davies first held a curacy, unpaid, at St. Anne's, Limehouse, and was then for four years (1852–1856) incumbent of St. Mark's, Whitechapel. He now became closely associated with Maurice's circle, especially Thomas Hughes, Charles Kingsley, and John Malcolm Forbes Ludlow, in the work of the co-operative movement and in the establishment of the Working Men's College in Great Ormond Street in 1854. In 1856 he was appointed to the crown living of Christ Church, Marylebone, which he held for thirty-three years. It was mainly a poor parish, but the rector's preaching drew hearers from other parts of London.

With his clerical work Davies combined other public activities and interests. He was a warm friend of the movement for the higher education of women, in which his sister, Sarah Emily Davies [q.v.], played a prominent part. From 1873 to 1874 and again from 1878 to 1886 he was principal of Queen's College, Harley Street, which had been founded by Maurice in 1848 for the advancement of women's education. He supported the extension to women of university degrees and of the parliamentary franchise. He was a member of the first London School Board; he favoured unsectarian religious teaching in elementary schools, and he suggested the formula known as the 'Cowper-Temple clause', which was embodied in the Education Act of 1870. In politics Davies was a strong but independent liberal: he was opposed to Gladstone's Home Rule measures, but rejoined the liberal party when free trade was threatened. He was strongly in sympathy with trade unionism, and raised his voice to vindicate the movement at a time when it was far from popular. Thus in 1872 he addressed a great meeting at Exeter Hall in support of combinations amongst agricultural labourers, and the next year at the Church Congress he vigorously combated clerical prejudice against trade unions.

It is chiefly, however, as a broad churchman that Davies will be remembered. He joined in establishing the National Church Reform Union (1870), which aimed at making the Church of England more truly national and comprehensive. His views on the relation between church and state probably stood in the way of ecclesiastical preferment, for which he seemed marked out by his practical ability, his earnestness, moderation, and fairness of mind, as well as by the position which he held in the religious and social life of London. There he was esteemed by many who held widely different opinions. His marriage brought him into close relation with the English advocates of positivism, two of whom, Henry Crompton and Edward Spencer Beesly, were his wife's brother and brother-in-law respectively.

Bishop Westcott spoke of his 'quiet wisdom', and John Stuart Mill generously acknowledged his 'intellectual and moral fairness' in controversy. He held strongly that Christian theology should seek instruction 'from the progressive development of life and knowledge' [preface to *Theology and Morality*]. While he gave his allegiance especially to Maurice, his standpoint was in general that of his friends Westcott, Lightfoot, and Hort, the contemporary leaders of liberal theology at Cambridge. His preaching was not rhetorical and made no parade of learning, the qualities which rendered it remarkable being depth of conviction, independence of thought, and an unfailing clearness of exposition. When Davies left London in 1889, on being presented to the Trinity College living of Kirkby Lonsdale, Westmorland, a valedictory address, to which was attached a remarkable list of signatures, recognized the combination in him of a 'clear and firm assertion of Christian truth with a generous appreciation of all earnest thought and feeling', and an 'habitual sympathy with rich and poor alike'.

Davies held his Westmorland living for twenty years, adapting himself successfully to the new conditions of life and work, and throwing himself vigorously into the educational business of the town and county. In 1895 he lost his wife, Mary, the eldest daughter of Sir Charles John Crompton [q.v.], whom he married in 1859, and shortly afterwards two sons of great promise. He had six sons, three of whom were fellows of Trinity College, Cambridge, and one daughter. He retired in 1908 at the age of eighty-two, and passed the remaining eight years of his life with his daughter at Hampstead. He died there 18 May 1916.

Davies, always a great walker, was in his younger days a keen lover of mountain climbing: he was one of the original members of the Alpine Club, and made the first ascents of the Dom and the Täschhorn.

Davies's published works, besides several volumes of sermons, include *St. Paul and Modern Thought* (1856), a commentary on *The Epistles of St. Paul to the Ephesians, Colossians, and Philemon* (1866), *Theology and Morality* (1873), *Social Questions* (1884), *Order and Growth* (Hulsean lectures, 1891). He wrote the article on St. Paul in Smith's *Dictionary of the Bible*, that on Thomas Hughes in this DICTIONARY and the memoir of Charles Buxton [q.v.] prefixed to the latter's *Notes of Thought* (1873). He was the author of several papers in *Peaks, Passes, and Glaciers* and in the *Alpine Journal*.

[*The Times*, 19 May 1916; *Contemporary Review*, June 1916 (article by his eldest son); *Modern Churchman*, July 1916; *Cornhill Magazine*, October 1916; *Cambridge University Magazine*, May 1879; private information.] A. F. H.

DAVIES, SARAH EMILY (1830–1921), promoter of women's education, generally known as Emily Davies, was born at Southampton 22 April 1830, the fourth child of the Rev. John Davies, D.D., who was rector of Gateshead from 1840 to 1861, by his wife, Mary Hopkinson. She was educated at home. From girlhood she felt a strong interest in the efforts made to raise the position of women by Elizabeth Garrett (afterwards Mrs. Garrett Anderson, M.D., q.v.) and Barbara Leigh Smith (afterwards Mme Bodichon, q.v.). Visits to her brother, the Rev. John Llewelyn Davies [q.v.], in London, enabled Miss Davies to do occasional work for the *Englishwoman's Journal* (founded in 1858 by Mme Bodichon and Miss Bessie Rayner Parkes, afterwards Mme Louis Belloc) and for the Society for Promoting the Employment of Women (founded in 1859).

On her father's death in 1860, Miss Davies, with her mother, moved to London and engaged actively in helping Miss Garrett to enter the medical profession. This led to the formation in 1862 of a committee, with Miss Davies as secretary (1862–1869), for obtaining the admission of women to university examinations. The committee's efforts secured in 1865 the admission of girls to the Cambridge senior and junior local examinations. In 1866 she founded the London Schoolmistresses' Association, of which she was honorary secretary till its dissolution in 1888. A memorial promoted by Miss Davies in 1864 caused girls' schools to be included in the scope of the Schools Inquiry Commission (1864–1868), before which she and Miss Frances Mary Buss, principal of the North London Collegiate School for Ladies, gave evidence of great value. The local examinations and the commission led to the modernization of girls' schools.

As nothing equivalent to university education was then available for women, Miss Davies began in 1867 to organize a college for women, with the help of Mme Bodichon, Henry Richard Tomkinson, Henry John Roby [q.v.], James (afterwards Viscount) Bryce, Sedley Taylor, Lady Stanley of Alderley [q.v.], and others.

The college, which was opened at Hitchin in 1869 and transferred to Cambridge (Girton College) in 1873, was henceforth Miss Davies' main interest, and its finance and general policy were directed by her. She insisted that the students should submit to the same tests and, as far as possible, to the same conditions as university men, and she opposed all attempts to organize separate educational schemes for women.

In suffrage work also Miss Davies was a pioneer. With Mme Bodichon and Miss Parkes she organized the first petition, which was presented by John Stuart Mill to parliament on 7 June 1866; and in 1866–1867 she acted as secretary to the first women's suffrage committee. In 1870 she was elected one of the first women members of the London School Board, but she withdrew in 1873 and devoted herself entirely to Girton College, where she resided as mistress from 1873 to 1875. In 1904 she resigned the honorary secretaryship of the college, which she had held since 1867, except for a brief interval during which she was treasurer. She then turned again to suffrage work, and became chairman of the London Society for Women's Suffrage. She died at Hampstead 13 July 1921.

Miss Davies's chief writings are *The Higher Education of Women* (1866) and *Thoughts on Some Questions relating to Women, 1860–1908* (1910). She had a remarkable power of carrying her schemes into effect; rational and clear-sighted, she combined tenacity of purpose with such caution, forethought, and moderation in action as to earn for herself the description of 'this very unrevolutionary woman', although in reality she was one of the chief figures in the movement which revolutionized the position of women.

[Miss Davies's writings; Minute Books of Girton College; Barbara Stephen, *Emily Davies and Girton College*, 1927; private information.] M. T. B. S.

DEAKIN, ALFRED (1856–1919), Australian politician, was born at Melbourne 3 August 1856. He was the only son of William Deakin, an accountant, by his wife, Sarah Bill, daughter of a Shropshire farmer. Educated from 1864 to 1871 at the Church of England grammar school, Melbourne, he decided to adopt the law as a profession, and, after study at the university of Melbourne, he was admitted in September 1877 to the Victorian bar. But he was more attracted by literature, and was persuaded by David Syme [q.v.], who then controlled the Melbourne *Age*, to take up journalism. Under Syme's influence he finally abandoned the belief in free trade which he had learned from the works of John Stuart Mill, and was induced in 1879 to stand for the constituency of West Bourke as a supporter of (Sir) Graham Berry [q.v.] in his violent conflict with the conservatives, who had the support of the legislative council, that body being elected on a high property franchise.

Successful at the polls, Deakin insisted as soon as parliament met on resigning his seat, as the validity of his election was challenged on a technicality. In the ensuing by-election he was defeated, and also at the general election of February 1880; in July 1880, however, he won the seat at the new general election necessitated by the fall of the new ministry. He immediately sought to promote a coalition between Berry and a section of the conservatives, and, when this failed, declined the attorney-generalship offered by Berry, though he supported his ministry and in 1882 won attention by a forcible denunciation of the errors of Victorian land legislation. In 1883 coalition came about between Berry and James Service [q.v.], and Deakin entered the ministry in March as minister of water supply and commissioner of public works, accepting in November the solicitor-generalship also. At the end of 1884, as president of a commission on water supply, he undertook a mission to America, the results of which were recorded in his *Irrigation in Western America* (1885). On the close of the coalition ministry, he formed, as leader of the liberal party, a new coalition with Duncan Gillies [q.v.], taking office in 1886 as chief secretary and minister of water supply; and in this capacity secured the passage of the Irrigation Act of 1886 and the adoption of an irrigation policy, which, at first seriously defective, finally proved a marked success. Next year he visited England as representative of Victoria at the colonial conference summoned to mark the jubilee of the Queen's reign. His strictures on the failure of British policy as regards New Guinea and the New Hebrides were combined with an insistence on the unity of the Empire, which attracted favourable attention; while his democratic spirit was exhibited in his refusal of the then much coveted order, the K.C.M.G. An outcome of his visit to Europe was his *Irrigation in Egypt and Italy* (1887). Disaster, however, awaited the reckless finance of the ministry, which fell in November 1890, and, though Deakin was offered office in every subsequent Victorian government up to 1900, he preferred to remain a private member. By Syme's invitation he visited India in 1891; his investigations of irrigation and his comments on British rule and Indian life, religion, and art are recorded in *Irrigated India* (1892) and *Temple and Tomb* (1893).

From 1892 Deakin worked seriously at the bar as a means of livelihood, and his main political work was devoted to furthering the federation of Australia. While still in office, he had been a member of the conference at Melbourne in 1890, and he was asked to represent Victoria at the conventions of 1891 and 1897–1898. Never a great constitutional lawyer, his direct contribution to the framing of the constitution was of small account, but he excelled in effecting the essential compromises between conflicting views, and it was largely due to his platform advocacy that the people of Victoria were induced in 1898 to approve federation by an overwhelming vote. In 1900 he was sent by the Victorian government to London to take part in the discussions with Mr. Joseph Chamberlain as to the passage of the Constitution Bill through the imperial parliament, and he played an important part in securing the compromise which reserved to the Commonwealth high court the power of deciding all constitutional issues.

Deakin's services to federation were naturally rewarded by his appointment as attorney-general in the first Commonwealth ministry (January 1901) of (Sir) Edmund Barton [q.v.], and he was the moving spirit of the ministry. On Barton's retirement in September 1903 to become a judge of the newly established high court, Deakin became prime minister. Convinced that responsible government could only be worked on the basis of two parties, and confronted by two opposition parties, the supporters of a revenue tariff, led by (Sir) George Reid [q.v.], and the labour party, he invited overtures for coalition. Neither party responded, and, as a convinced federalist, Deakin refused the labour demand to subject the public services of the States to the control of the Commonwealth court of conciliation and arbitration. Defeat ensued, and a labour ministry held a feeble tenure of office from April to August 1904, when it was ousted by a coalition between Reid and a section of Deakin's following. Deakin had declined to serve under Reid, but had consented to a compact to last until May 1906; in June 1905, however, dislike of Reid and anxiety lest a truce should prove harmful to protection induced him to break his compact. Reid naturally resented this act, and labour would not do more than give the new ministry lukewarm support, so that its period of office, terminated by the defection of labour in November 1908, was largely barren of achievement.

In 1907 Deakin revisited England for the colonial conference; his chief endeavour on that occasion was to convince the public of the necessity of consolidating the Empire by preferential tariffs, despite the decisive verdict of the British electorate in 1906 against protection; but he also sought the concurrence of the Admiralty in his scheme for an independent Australian navy. His defence bill of 1908 was taken up in part by his successor, Andrew Fisher; and from June 1909 to April 1910 he enjoyed, by coalition with (Sir) Joseph Cook, a brief term of office, marked by the participation of the Commonwealth in an imperial naval and military conference which sanctioned Deakin's naval scheme in its main idea. The public, however, resented as dishonourable this coalition of old enemies, and the general election of 1910 terminated Deakin's period of office. His mental powers, fatally overstrained by his efforts of 1907, had long been impaired, and though loyalty kept him leader of the opposition until the end of 1912, it was at the cost of any chance of recuperation. A brief tenure of the chairmanship of a royal commission on food supplies, appointed in August 1914, and a visit to San Francisco in 1915 to represent Australia at the Panama-Pacific international exhibition, ended his official work; his memory, and his power of co-ordinating his ideas, were steadily failing; a flying visit to London in 1916 brought no relief, and thereafter until his death at Melbourne 7 October 1919, his time was spent there or at his seaside cottage. He was survived by his wife, Pattie, eldest daughter of H. Junor Browne, a Melbourne merchant, to whom he was married in 1882, and by three daughters.

Deakin's contemporaries reproached him with an unpractical idealism and lack of understanding of the character of the Australian public. His ideals were in fact sane and moderate, but his anxiety to secure rapid results led him throughout his career to seek coalitions which were not very effective. He aimed at protection for manufacturers, with improved conditions for workers and regard for consumers, but only the first of these objects was achieved by his ministries.

He was able to expel the Kanakas and close the door to Asiatics, but he could effect nothing for British immigration into the Commonwealth. He failed to promote imperial unity, and his defence schemes were matured by others. But his genius for compromise served the federal cause in the inception of the Commonwealth, and no Australian of his time surpassed him in personal integrity and devotion to what he deemed duty. His oratorical power was undoubted, though the wealth of his ideas and the rapidity of his delivery often confused his hearers. His interest in literature, religion, spiritualism, philosophy, and art was insatiable, but among his copious writings on these and political topics he left nothing ripe for publication. A devoted husband and father, a charming friend, and a brilliant conversationalist, he yet felt himself, as his private papers show, in a sense isolated in life, a fact which doubtless explains in some measure his comparative failure in politics.

[Walter Murdoch, *Alfred Deakin*, 1923; Victorian and Commonwealth *Parliamentary Debates*; John Quick and R. R. Garran, *Annotated Constitution of the Australian Commonwealth*, 1901; B. R. Wise, *Making of the Australian Commonwealth*, 1913; H. G. Turner, *History of the Colony of Victoria*, 1904, and *First Decade of the Australian Commonwealth*, 1911; Sir G. H. Reid, *My Reminiscences*, 1917; personal knowledge.] A. B. K.

DE BURGH CANNING, HUBERT GEORGE second MARQUESS and fifteenth EARL OF CLANRICARDE (1832–1916). [See BURGH CANNING.]

DE MORGAN, WILLIAM FREND (1839–1917), artist, inventor, and author, was born in London at 69 Gower Street 16 November 1839, the eldest son in a family of seven children. His father was the well-known mathematician, Augustus De Morgan [q.v.]; he was named after his maternal grandfather, William Frend [q.v.]. Both his father and mother were remarkable personalities, at once brilliant and unworldly, and the boy grew up in a home circle full of happy and varied interests, though soon shadowed by untimely deaths. William was educated at University College School and at the College itself; when he entered the College he also began studying art at the school of Francis Stephen Cary [q.v.]. He remained at University College until nineteen, when he was admitted to the Academy schools (1859). Early in the 'sixties he made the acquaintance of Burne-Jones, Rossetti, William Morris, and their friends, and amid this group of artists experimenting and finding new modes of expression, De Morgan, instinctively a discoverer, found himself drifting away from the routine work of the art schools. He began tentatively by designing for stained glass and tiles, but soon felt the necessity of carrying out experiments in their manufacture. Many years later he wrote of these days: 'I certainly was a feeble and discursive dabbler in picture-making. I transferred myself to stained glass window-making and dabbled in that too till 1872.' The early experiments in stained glass and tiles were pursued at 40 Fitzroy Square for a year or two, and of this period he writes: 'The attempt to fire kilns connected with an ordinary house-chimney led to the roof being burnt off.'

After his father's death in 1871, the sadly diminished family came to live at 30 Cheyne Row; and here a kiln was built in the back garden and a pottery industry definitely established. All the work was removed before long to Orange House in the same row. It was in this Chelsea period that De Morgan rediscovered the process of making various coloured lustres, and developed the magnificent thickly-glazed blues and greens, that helped to make his pottery famous. Here, too, he and Morris made some experiments in mosaics, crowded out, however, by other interests and not pursued. When the business outgrew the Cheyne Row premises, he thought of joining with Morris to take a factory at Blockley, Worcestershire; this being found impracticable, De Morgan followed his friend to Merton Abbey, near Wimbledon (1882), erecting buildings and kilns there and, to quote his own words, 'retaining the show-room in the Chelsea house until '86, when the shop in Great Marlborough Street was taken'. He remained at Merton Abbey until 1888, but was then obliged through delicate health to bring the factory nearer his home. A partnership was entered into with Halsey Ralph Ricardo, the architect, and a new factory was built at Sands End, Fulham, the show-room in Great Marlborough Street being retained. This arrangement lasted until 1898; but, in spite of the magnificent work produced, the fortunes of the industry were now waning; and after a partnership with Frank Iles, his kiln-firer, and with Charles and Fred Passenger, painters, De Morgan retired from practical work about 1905, the firm of De Morgan, Iles, and Passenger breaking up in 1907. His late partners continued to decorate dishes and vases for a few years at a factory in the Brompton Road.

In 1887 De Morgan married Mary Evelyn, the eldest daughter of Percival Andree Pickering, Q.C., and sister of Spencer Umfreville Pickering, F.R.S. She was a pupil and niece of R. Spencer-Stanhope, and was herself an artist of talent. More than twenty years of their married life were spent in the Vale, Chelsea, where they bought a little house. The impending destruction of the Vale obliged them to leave in 1909, and the next year they settled at 127 Church Street, their last London home. About 1890 a serious pronouncement of the doctors on De Morgan's health (it was feared that he had the family predisposition to lung trouble) decided them to spend part of the year abroad, and thenceforth until the spring of 1914 they wintered in Florence. This decision, so serious for the fortunes of the pottery, spurred De Morgan to an invention whereby the tiles, which formed a large part of the industry, could be painted on paper by Italian workmen in Florence and sent to London to be transferred to the clay and fired. In the decoration of the Peninsular and Oriental Company's liners, undertaken by De Morgan, the tiles and panels were done by this process, which of course could only be employed for flat surface decoration.

When De Morgan's activities as a potter and designer were coming to an end, a new phase of his life began. A life's labour with all its brilliant achievements had brought him no monetary success; this now came to him from work lightly undertaken to keep his thoughts occupied in days of disappointment and enforced idleness. He began to write a few years before he actually retired from the business, and he speaks to a friend of 'this scribbling that keeps me quiet and prevents my being sulky'. At a time of ill-health and depression, Mrs. De Morgan brought to his notice two chapters of a story written some time before and rescued by her from being burned as rubbish. This was the beginning, leisurely and discursive, with no thought of publication, of *Joseph Vance* and of the series of novels by which De Morgan is known. It was not the first time that his wife's sympathy and encouragement had helped him in a difficult moment in his life. *Joseph Vance* was refused by the first publisher to whom it was offered, and a second novel was half finished before the first was accepted for publication in England and America. To the author's great surprise, *Joseph Vance*, published in the summer of 1906, had an immediate success, and thenceforth De Morgan, artist, potter, and inventor, became known in two worlds as a novelist. The following is a list of his subsequent novels in the order of publication: *Alice-for-Short* (1907), *Somehow Good* (1908), *It Never Can Happen Again* (1909), *An Affair of Dishonour* (1910), *A Likely Story* (1911), *When Ghost Meets Ghost* (1914).

De Morgan began two other stories which, owing to the outbreak of the European War, he never finished. One is *The Old Madhouse* (1919), which Mrs. De Morgan, with whom he always discussed his work, skilfully completed, condensing the remainder of the plot and revealing the mystery of the story. She dealt with equal skill with *The Old Man's Youth* (1921), undertaking a yet more difficult task in piecing material together to make the story coherent. This latter work is of special interest, as it is largely autobiographical, and full of revelations of De Morgan's personal character. As the War went on, De Morgan became preoccupied with the question of aircraft and submarine defence, and spent more and more time in experiments and in working out schemes. 'I have got no end of inventions afoot,' he writes, 'though I am not absolutely certain of any but one—a new airship.' He died in London 15 January 1917 from a sudden attack of trench fever. He had no children.

De Morgan wrote two treatises on his craft as a potter: a paper read before the Society of Arts in 1892 (*Journal*, vol. xl) and a *Report on the Feasibility of a Manufacture of Glazed Pottery in Egypt* (1894), the latter being the result of a visit to Egypt (by invitation) in the previous year. This *Report* considers interesting technical points, including the question of kilns suitable for the light fuel of Egypt. In the Society of Arts paper occurs the following epitomized description of his lustre-process: 'As we now practise it at Fulham, it is as follows: the pigment consists simply of white clay mixed with copper scale or oxide of silver, in proportion varying according to the strength of the colour we desire to get. It is painted on to the already fused glaze with water and enough gum-arabic to harden it for handling and make it work easily—a little lamp-black or other colouring matter makes it pleasanter to work with. I have tried many additions to this pigment . . . but without superseding the first simple mixture.'

Besides fireplace tiles and pots, &c., the De Morgan ware was used for decorative panels. One such decoration was made for the Duke of Bedford's dairies at Woburn; another, in which the tiles were used with startling success, was planned by Mr. Halsey Ricardo for Mr. Ernest Debenham's house in Addison Road. The decoration of the steamships was of a late period, the first work of the sort having been done for the Tsar's yacht *Livadia*, years before. Six liners were thus decorated, the *Arabic*, the *Palawan*, the *Sumatra*, the *China*, the *Malta*, and the *Persia*. De Morgan wrote of some of these designs: 'My pictures represent a voyage of a ship round the world and all the strange dangers she meets with. First she runs on a rock—then an earthquake shakes her off—then I propose to do her dangers from the Sirens and the Sea Serpent, only the Sea Serpent will also be attracted by the Sirens and eat them—so the ship will get off scot free. . . .' De Morgan's Italian work had no connexion, as is sometimes supposed, with the Cantagalli works in Florence, beyond the fact that certain experimental pieces were fired for him there, and that a few were painted and produced from his design.

There is a large collection of De Morgan's drawings and plans in the Victoria and Albert Museum, given by his wife before her death (1919). Among the designs are many fugitive sketches full of spontaneity and movement, and of humour too. Superb as is the achievement of the pottery, the drawings themselves should be studied to realize to the full the quality of De Morgan's work. His love for the sea shows itself in many of these designs which give curious effects of transparencies and imaginative renderings of the 'depths of the sea'. There are some fine examples of his work in the ceramic galleries of the museum.

De Morgan had a strong scientific bent, and all through his life took pleasure in problems and experiments mostly in connexion with his work. One of his inventions was a mill for grinding clay for the pottery to an extreme fineness; in fact, as Mr. Ricardo says, 'the factory was equipped with machinery (for power), and the ovens, kilns, mills, and the appliances were built and devised under his superintendence and from his designs. His power of invention was boundless: almost every article and tool in the place was the outcome of his observation and invention.'

De Morgan had great personal charm and a sweetness of nature that endeared him to all. With a level and sober judgement on men and events, he was never known to speak bitterly, talking of people with whom he had troublesome dealings with a quaint indulgence of human weakness. He was full of jokes and quips, but the streak of tragedy that seemed to cling to the De Morgan family was at times apparent in himself. William was the only one of the large family that lived to old age; these losses and the shadow of ill-health could not fail to leave their mark. He wrote to a relative some three years before his death: 'You know, I daresay, how queer a life I have had. I was seized with the unhappy fancy that I had a turn for the Fine Arts. I paid no heed to the wisest and best man I have ever known—my father of course—and went my own headstrong way. His words to me were, "If you work hard and read, Willy, especially Latin and Greek, you will live to write something worth reading. But as to painting, how can I tell, knowing nothing of it." Well! I went my own way and wasted an odd 40 or 50 years. All one can say is, things have turned out better than I deserved. I put a good deal of myself into Charles Heath in *Alice-for-Short*.'

A portrait of De Morgan, painted by his wife in 1909, was bequeathed by the artist to the National Portrait Gallery. De Morgan is shown in full face, clasping an iridescent jar made by himself.

[Mrs. A. M. W. Stirling, *William De Morgan and his Wife*, 1922; private information; personal knowledge.] M. M.

DENNEY, JAMES (1856–1917), theologian, was born at Paisley 5 February 1856, and was brought up at Greenock, whither his family removed when he was four months old. He came of Cameronian stock; his father, John Denney, who was a joiner, was a deacon in the Reformed Presbyterian Church. His mother's maiden name was Barr. James Denney was their eldest son. In 1876 the family, with the great majority of the members of the denomination, joined the Free Church of Scotland. He attended the Highlanders' Academy, Greenock, where for four years he served as a pupil teacher, with John Davidson [q.v.], the poet, for a colleague. He entered the university of Glasgow in November 1874, where he had a brilliant career in classics under (Sir) Richard C. Jebb, in philosophy under Edward Caird. He graduated in 1879. He studied theology at the Glasgow Free Church college under James S. Candlish, Alexander Balmain Bruce, and

Thomas Martin Lindsay, completing his course in 1883. His first and only pastoral charge was that of east Free church, Broughty Ferry (1886–1897). He married in 1886 Mary Carmichael, daughter of John Brown, of Glasgow. In 1897 he succeeded Candlish as professor of systematic and pastoral theology in Glasgow Free Church college; and, two years later, on the death of Bruce, he was appointed to the chair of New Testament language, literature, and theology. In 1915 he became principal of the college in succession to T. M. Lindsay, and held this position till his death on 15 June 1917. The death of his wife in 1907 had left him very lonely (all the more that he had no children), with the memory of a union of ideal happiness.

Denney did admirable work as pastor and preacher. He was not a 'popular' preacher, but he steadily grew in influence and power. The preacher's duty was, he thought, 'to make the obvious arresting'. He said, 'Though it is my business to teach, the one thing I covet is to be able to do the work of an evangelist, and that at all events is the work that needs to be done.' His volumes in the *Expositor's Bible*, viz. *The Epistles to the Thessalonians* (1892) and *The Second Epistle to the Corinthians* (1894), remain to show how high a standard his expository preaching reached. In his later years he was drawn more and more into ecclesiastical affairs, especially after the decision given by the House of Lords against the United Free Church (1904). At great cost to himself he became in 1913 the convener of the central fund on which the maintenance of the ministers largely depended. He took a leading part in the negotiations for reunion with the Established Church of Scotland, abandoning his earlier objections to establishment on the ground that they had become obsolete in the new situation. On him more than on any man the result of the negotiations was felt to depend. The toils and anxieties of his later years probably shortened his life.

Denney's chief title to remembrance will rest on his work as a theologian. Before his ordination he published an acute anonymous criticism of Henry Drummond's *Natural Law in the Spiritual World*. His *Studies in Theology* (1895) gave him fame in the field of systematic theology, while his commentary on *The Epistle to the Romans* (1900) in the *Expositor's Greek Testament* enhanced his reputation for exegesis. His chief writings were devoted to the doctrines of the person and the work of Christ. *Jesus and the Gospel* (1908), his most important work, argued that the estimate of Jesus formed by the Church was corroborated by the testimony of Jesus to Himself. His interest was especially concentrated on the doctrine of the Atonement, which he expounded in *The Death of Christ: its Place and Interpretation in the New Testament* (1902) and in his posthumous Cunningham lectures, *The Christian Doctrine of Reconciliation* (1917). The doctrine he interpreted as purely substitutionary, laying an unusual emphasis on the physical death of Christ. He cordially disliked all mysticism, and did not shrink from denying that St. Paul taught a mystical union of the believer in Christ. Nor could he discern any meaning in the interpretation of the Passion as a racial act.

His theological outlook, which had tended to be 'broad', changed after his ordination, largely under his wife's influence, into one much more definitely evangelical. He was liberal in his views of inspiration, and fully recognized the legitimacy of criticism, though his position on the New Testament problems was on the whole conservative. His faults of temperament made sympathy with his position more difficult. He had his own point of view very firmly held; and he surveyed the universe, so far as it could be seen thence, with a clear and penetrating gaze. He had a trenchant style and on great themes he wrote with distinction and power. What he could see he saw with exceptional lucidity. What he could not see, had for him no existence and no right to exist. His pungency of expression and his impatient contempt for those who differed from him seriously limited the range of his influence. Yet he was a man of lofty character, with great richness and depth of nature beneath his superficial austerity and reserve. Among his friends he was the most genial of men, full of humour, fond of hearing and telling good stories. And if his theology was expounded with a somewhat repellent harshness and narrowness, even in his latest and mellowest book, it must not be forgotten that his faith was held with an intense conviction, born of a profound and vivid religious experience, which was at once chastened and elevated by moral passion.

[No biography has been published. T. H. Walker, *Principal James Denney*, 1918, a slight and not always accurate sketch; *Letters of Principal James Denney to W. Robertson Nicoll*, 1920; *Letters of Principal James Denney to his Family and Friends*, edited by J. Moffatt (n.d.); personal knowledge.]

A. S. P.

DE VILLIERS, JOHN HENRY, first Baron De Villiers (1842–1914), South African judge, was born of Huguenot stock at the Paarl, Cape Colony, 15 June 1842. He was the second son of Carel Christiaan de Villiers, government land-surveyor, of the Paarl, by his wife, Dorothea Elizabeth Retief, also of the Paarl. In 1861 he went from the South African College, Cape Town, to Utrecht to study for the Dutch reformed ministry. He soon departed thence to Berlin to read law, but finally entered the Inner Temple, London, in June 1863, and was called to the bar in November 1865. Early in 1866 he began to practise at the Cape bar. In 1871 he married Aletta Johanna (died 1922), daughter of Jan Pieter Jordaan, a wine farmer, of Worcester, Cape Colony. Two sons and two daughters were born of the marriage. From 1867 he sat as member of the house of assembly, for Worcester, advocating railway construction, the withdrawal of state aid from the churches, and the institution of responsible government. In 1872 he became attorney-general in the ministry of Sir John Charles Molteno [q.v.], but, at the urgent request of the premier and of William Porter [q.v.], he resigned in December 1873 in order to become chief justice. In spite of his youth he speedily established his reputation, not only in South Africa but with the judicial committee of the Privy Council. Though now a judge, he never lost touch with politics. He was *ex officio* president of the legislative council; thrice, in 1888, 1893, and 1895, he was invited to stand for the Free State presidency; once, in 1892, at the suggestion of Cecil Rhodes, he contemplated standing for election as president of the Transvaal; once he was offered the premiership of Cape Colony, and twice, in the crises of 1896 and 1902, he volunteered his services, which were not accepted. De Villiers' chief political aim was federation. He tried to arrange this with President J. H. Brand of the Orange Free State in 1871; in 1877 they actually agreed upon a scheme, which would have been submitted to the high commissioner, Sir Bartle Frere, but for Sir Theophilus Shepstone's annexation of the Transvaal. In 1881 he was a member of the royal commission which drew up the Pretoria convention. He had already been knighted in 1877, and he now received the K.C.M.G. (1882).

De Villiers' influence on politics, though indirect, was considerable, through his intimacy with Cape and republican politicians and with the high commissioners, Sir Hercules Robinson (afterwards Baron Rosmead) and Sir Henry (afterwards Baron) Loch. In 1887 he was chairman of the diamond law commission; in 1893 at the invitation of Cecil Rhodes he was preparing to take office as prime minister, when Rhodes suddenly re-formed his cabinet without him. Next year, however, he went to the Ottawa colonial conference to further Rhodes's schemes of intercolonial preference and communications. Personally he was on good terms with Rhodes, but, like Loch, he feared the use to which Rhodes might put his wide and indefinite powers, and he began to turn against him early in 1894. After the Jameson Raid (January 1896), De Villiers urged President Kruger to show mercy to his prisoners; and early in 1897 he hurried to Pretoria to mediate between Kruger and the judges in their quarrel over the power claimed by some of the judges to test the validity of laws by the touchstone of the *grondwet* (constitution). For some time past De Villiers had endeavoured to form a South African court of appeal as a step towards federation, and had urged the inclusion of colonial judges in the Privy Council. In July 1897 he himself was sworn in as privy councillor, the first colonial judge to take his seat on the judicial committee.

During 1899, in spite of failing health, he worked hard for peace. He was not robust, but he had never spared himself; and now the shock of the South African War nearly killed him. He lay dangerously ill for many weeks in England and on the Riviera in 1901; but he recovered and helped to resist the proposed suspension of the Cape constitution in 1902. By 1906 his hopes of federation revived, and early in 1907 he joined in the correspondence already begun on the subject by J. X. Merriman, the Cape premier, and General Smuts. A visit to Canada as representative of the four South African colonies at the Canadian tercentenary convinced him that union was better than federation. On his return, he was unanimously elected president of the national convention; he conducted the negotiations personally with the imperial government on the future of the native protectorates; and in the convention itself, thanks to the confidence that men had in him, secured the adoption of motions which, moved by any other man, must have been rejected. He headed the drafting committee which watched the passage of the Union Bill through the imperial parliament; was created baron, with the title De Villiers of Wynberg; and returned home to become first chief justice of the Union (1910). In 1912, and again in July 1914, he was acting governor-general. He died after a very short illness at Pretoria 2 September 1914. He was succeeded as second baron by his elder son, Charles Percy (born 1871).

In person De Villiers was moderately tall, lean, and active, a man of immense dignity which was relieved by a kindly spirit and a certain dry humour. He was a good shot, a keen fisherman, a lover of animals, especially dogs, and of bees, and an ardent farmer and grower of vines. In politics he cherished the best traditions of Cape native policy, upheld the British connexion and South African liberties, and, throughout his life, saw South Africa whole. His chief claim to remembrance is as a judge, and a great one. Other South Africans have been more learned in the letter of the law, but none have understood its spirit so well. Some say that at times he dispensed 'De Villiers' law', and his judgments have been reversed on one or two points since his death; but in spite of the rapidity with which he gave his decisions, the Privy Council questioned his judgments only four times. For the space of forty-one years he did substantial justice, delivering a series of weighty judgments on a far greater variety of subjects than usually falls to the lot of any British judge. He outlived the judges of his own generation, and, when a new generation arose, he was already an institution.

He had become chief justice at a critical time. In 1873 the gold and the diamonds were drawing a flood of new men to the interior, and the various states and colonies into closer contact. Besides the supreme court at Cape Town, there were by 1882 five similar courts in South Africa under four separate legislatures, unchecked by a common court of appeal. Their law and practice were fundamentally the same, but divergences were bound to occur. These divergences were checked by the fact that the Cape supplied many of the judges to the other courts, and by the growing prestige of De Villiers. Even so the law of the colony was in a state of confusion. The criminal law had become practically English. But the Roman-Dutch civil law was being anglicized in a haphazard manner. De Villiers' great achievement was to incorporate in the main body of the Roman-Dutch code as much of the English civil law as was necessary to meet rapidly changing circumstances. And the new system, which owes more to him than to any other single man, has spread from the borders of the South Africa of 1873 northward to the Zambesi.

[Unpublished papers and correspondence; notices in the *Cape* (*South African*) *Law Journal*, passim; B. Williams, *Cecil Rhodes*, 1921; J. H. Hofmeyr, *Life of J. H. Hofmeyr*, 1913; E. A. Walker, *Lord De Villiers and His Times: South Africa, 1842–1914*, 1924; private information.] E. A. W.

DOBELL, BERTRAM (1842–1914), bookseller and man of letters, was born at Battle 9 January 1842, the eldest son of Edward Dobell, a journeyman tailor, by his wife, Elizabeth Eldridge. His father migrated to London, where he was stricken with paralysis. Bertram began earning his living as errand-boy to a grocer, and afterwards served in the business. Even then he collected old books out of penny boxes on bookstalls. He married Eleanor Wymer in 1869, and with a capital of ten pounds opened a stationer's and newsagent's shop at Queen's Crescent, Haverstock Hill. Here in 1876 he printed his first catalogue of second-hand books. His final move to Charing Cross Road was made in 1887.

In 1874 Dobell first met James Thomson [q.v.], whose *City of Dreadful Night* was appearing piecemeal in Charles Bradlaugh's *National Reformer*. Dobell arranged for its independent publication in 1880, and steadily befriended the poet till his death in 1882. He edited Thomson's *Voice from the Nile* and *Shelley* (1884), *Poetical Works*, with memoir (1895), *Biographical and Critical Studies* (1896), a selection from the poems (1899), and *Leopardi's Essays* (1905). He planned facsimile reprints of Shelley, and issued *Alastor* (1885); the Shelley Society reissued it, and printed his edition of *The Wandering Jew* (1887). He published Shelley's *Letters to Elizabeth Hitchener* (1908). Other pioneer work was his publication of Goldsmith's *A Prospect of Society* (the earliest form of *The Traveller*) in 1902, and *Sidelights on Charles Lamb* (1903), tracing Lamb's work in the *London Magazine*.

Dobell's great achievement was the recovery of the poetical works of Thomas Traherne (1903), followed by the prose *Centuries of Meditations* (1908). The manuscripts, originally sold for a few pence, were bought by Alexander Balloch Grosart [q.v.], who intended to publish them as the work of Henry Vaughan; Dobell acquired them, and followed up a clue by which he identified the author. His recovery of Traherne gives him a secure place in literary history. He also collected and edited *The Poetical Works of William Strode* (1907), and in 1908 printed from manuscript an anonymous play, *The Partiall Law* (*c.* 1615–1630). Other discoveries were printed in periodicals: notably, letters of Chapman and Ben Jonson in the *Athenæum* (March and April 1901) and *New Light upon Sir Philip Sidney's 'Arcadia'* in the *Quarterly Review* (July 1909). His carefully annotated *Catalogue of Books Printed for Private Circulation* was completely issued in 1906; and he liked to fill the inner covers of his trade catalogues with criticism, quaint humour, and literary gossip. He always spoke modestly of his own poems—*Rosemary and Pansies* (1903) and *A Century of Sonnets* (1910). *Cleon in the Palace of Truth*, by 'Lucian Lambert', was a satire on the politician (1904). Since his death, *Sonnets and Lyrics of the Present War*, *The Close of Life*, *The Approach of Death*, containing some impressive sonnets, *The Dreamer of the Castle of Indolence*, have been issued by his son (1915), the two last privately. *A Lover's Moods* was issued by the Rowfant Club (1923). He died at Haverstock Hill 14 December 1914. He had three sons and two daughters. The business passed to his sons, Percy John and Eustace Arthur Dobell.

There is a process engraving of Dobell in the National Portrait Gallery.

[S. Bradbury, *Bertram Dobell*, 1909; private information; personal knowledge.]

P. S.

DOBSON, HENRY AUSTIN (1840–1921), poet and man of letters, was born at Plymouth 18 January 1840, the eldest son of George Clarisse Dobson, civil engineer, by his wife, Augusta Harris. He was educated at Beaumaris grammar school and at a private school at Coventry, before being sent to the gymnase at Strasbourg, then a French city. At the age of sixteen he came home and entered the Board of Trade, in which he served from 1856 to 1901. His service was chiefly in the marine department, of which he was a principal clerk from 1884 till his retirement. William Cosmo Monkhouse [q.v.] and Samuel Waddington were in the same branch with him, and (Sir) Edmund Gosse was attached to the commercial department as translator, so that the Board of Trade of those days was lyrically described by an American observer as 'a nest of singing birds'. Lord Farrer, one of the official heads, put another view when he wrote of 'certain civil servants who would have been excellent administrators if they had not been indifferent poets'. It is not contended by Austin Dobson's friends that Farrer's unkind observation was not meant to include him, or that he was more than conscientious in his official duties. The *Bibliography of Austin Dobson*, published in 1900, before he retired, contains over 300 pages and makes it clear that his mind was principally applied to literature. A shy, nervous man, he was always anxious lest the evidences of his unofficial industry should jeopardize his post. After his retirement he received (1904) a civil list pension of £250.

It would be idle to deny that all the work of importance which Dobson did was in literature. For more than half a century he was constantly producing printed work, and during the first twenty years it was almost entirely in rhyme. His first publication, the verses 'A City Flower', appeared in *Temple Bar* for December 1864—immature work, as is also 'Incognita' dated 1866. But 'Une Marquise', written in 1868, and 'The Story of Rosina' in 1869, showed his gift in its perfection. The two last, with much else, appeared in *St. Paul's*, and to its editor, Anthony Trollope, was dedicated Dobson's first volume, *Vignettes in Rhyme* (1873), which reached its third edition in 1875. It contained some of his most characteristic pieces, mixed with inferior stuff. *Proverbs in Porcelain*, published in 1877, was almost all in his best vein. These two works, blended in one volume with certain additions and omissions, appeared in America in 1880 as *Vignettes in Rhyme*. In 1883 this selection, again somewhat altered, was published in London as *Old World Idylls* and achieved immense popularity. Two years later a companion book, *At the Sign of the Lyre*, had an equal success. The latter contained some of his best things—'The Ladies of St. James's', 'The Old Sedan Chair', and the enchanting verses 'My Books', written as late as 1883–1884. But though he continued to write verse intermittently for the rest of his life, and at least a quarter of his collected *Poetical Works* is dated after 1885, none of this later verse has much importance. He had ceased to be a poet, and had become a most industrious journeyman of letters.

Dobson's first prose volume, *The Civil Service Handbook of English Literature*, published in 1874, was probably written as a piece of hack work. But in 1879, when he was at his best in verse writing, appeared his *William Hogarth* in the

'Great Artists' series. By this time everybody knew that Dobson had the eighteenth century by heart, and in 1883 John (afterwards Viscount) Morley persuaded him to write the *Fielding* for the 'English Men of Letters' series. He next wrote *Thomas Bewick and his Pupils* (1884) and biographies of *Steele* (1886) and *Goldsmith* (1888). In 1890 he reprinted, under the title *Four Frenchwomen*, essays on Charlotte Corday, Madame Roland, the Princesse de Lamballe, and Madame de Genlis, which had appeared as early as 1866 in the *Domestic Magazine*. Then came a memoir of *Horace Walpole* (1890), with an appendix giving the books printed at Strawberry Hill, an extended memoir of *Hogarth* (1891), and a series of *Eighteenth Century Vignettes* (1892–1894–1896). In 1902 he published *Samuel Richardson* and in the next year *Fanny Burney*, both for the 'English Men of Letters' series. From this time onwards any publisher intending to reissue an eighteenth-century work went to Austin Dobson for an introduction. Altogether, some fifty such volumes with Dobson's editorial superintendence are catalogued. Of complete prose works, over and above his *Handbook* of English literature, there are to his credit eight biographies and ten volumes of collected essays.

Austin Dobson's immense knowledge of eighteenth-century literature and art should have made the past live again in his biographies, but his achievement varied, and perhaps the slighter the interest of his main subject the better the result. His *Fanny Burney* shows him at his best, *Fielding* at his least good. His style, though simple, serviceable, and pleasant, never for an instant suggests a poet's prose. Perhaps indeed he never was a poet, but only a most accomplished writer of verse. No one ever exceeded his mastery of artificial rhythms, and no verses are more likely than his to appeal to those who care little about poetry. But at his lightest he lacks gaiety; at his gravest he lacks weight; his sentiment is perilously near the mawkish, and he is always a little shocked by the elegance of the French eighteenth century, from which he derived so much enjoyment. In short, what Dobson lacked to be a poet was personality: there is nowhere any strong vibration of his nature. Yet nobody can read the best of his verses—and at least fifty pieces are of his best—without delight in the exquisite finish, the witty invention, and the ease of movement. And for any one with whom he can 'assume a common taste for old costume, old pictures, books', Austin Dobson will always be a favourite author.

Dobson died at Ealing 2 September 1921. He married in 1868 Frances Mary, daughter of Nathaniel Beardmore, civil engineer, of Broxbourne, Hertfordshire, and had five sons and five daughters.

There is a portrait of Dobson by Sylvia Gosse in the National Portrait Gallery.

[*The Times*, 3 and 5 September 1921; Alban Dobson, Preface to *Austin Dobson: An Anthology of Prose and Verse*, 1922; private information.] S. G.

DOHERTY, HUGH LAWRENCE (1875–1919), lawn-tennis player, the third son of William Doherty, of Oakfield, Clapham Park, was born 8 October 1875. Like his elder brother, Reginald F. Doherty (1872–1911), with whom he was intimately associated in his lawn-tennis triumphs, he began the game young in life, and at the age of fifteen won the most important junior event of that time, the Renshaw singles cup, at Scarborough. He was educated at Westminster School, where he showed himself to be a good runner, and at Trinity Hall, Cambridge. It was here that he and his brother made their name at lawn-tennis. Before they went down from Cambridge they were in the forefront of the game, and no two players have had a more triumphant career both in singles and doubles play. R. F. Doherty won the All England singles championship at Wimbledon in 1897, 1898, 1899, and 1900. Lawrence Doherty won in 1902, 1903, 1904, 1905, and 1906, and then resigned the title. The brothers, playing together, were eight times double champions between 1897 and 1905, being only once defeated (1902) by S. H. Smith and F. L. Riseley. In the Davis international cup contests, their record, and particularly that of the younger Doherty, was very fine. The latter's appearances in these matches cover the years from 1902 to 1906, and, although he was once on the losing side, he himself never lost a match, and he met all the best American players of the time. Up to the present time he is the only Englishman who has ever won the American national championship; that distinction fell to him in 1903.

After 1906, H. L. Doherty retired from competition lawn-tennis and took up golf. In a short time he became very proficient at the game, and he played in the amateur championship on several occasions. On the outbreak of the European War he joined the anti-aircraft branch of the Royal Naval Reserve, and it is possible that his hard work in the service hastened the breakdown of a constitution that had always been delicate. He died 11 August 1919, after a long illness.

The Dohertys will be remembered as two of the greatest players of lawn-tennis, and perhaps as the two greatest artists at the game that have yet appeared. If the brothers Renshaw were the pioneers, the Dohertys brought the game to the highest pitch of perfection. In size they were a contrast. Reginald Doherty was tall, very thin, and yet very graceful in all his movements. He had supreme control over the ball, a fine service, and every kind of stroke. His anticipation was wonderful, and he seemed to cover the court with no difficulty. As a master of the game he was possibly greater than his younger brother, and his style came near to perfection. Lawrence was below medium height, but well knit though lightly built. He, too, had command of every stroke. He was a better match player than his brother, and thought out the game more thoroughly. In doubles they were an ideal pair, and so good that they could play with success from unorthodox positions. They were as expert on covered courts—as at Queen's Club, Kensington, where some of their best games were played—as they were on grass. Indeed, it may be said that every gift for the game of lawn-tennis was theirs, except good health. Had they been more robust and had they continued to compete, their supremacy might have lasted over a longer period ; for at the time that he retired from the championship, H. L. Doherty was only thirty years of age. Wherever they went, and they travelled much, to play lawn-tennis, the brothers Doherty were as popular figures as they were successful exponents of the game.

[R. F. and H. L. Doherty, *On Lawn-Tennis*, 1903.] E. B. N.

DONALDSON, Sir JAMES (1831–1915), educationist, classical and patristic scholar, was born at Aberdeen 26 April 1831. Of humble parentage, he owed his education at the grammar school and university of Aberdeen to the discernment of friends who noted his early promise, and his subsequent career was due entirely to his own determination and to his genuine love of learning. After the completion of his university course he studied for some time at New College, London, with a view to entering the Congregationalist ministry ; but he soon abandoned that intention and proceeded to Berlin, where he continued his classical and theological studies, devoting his attention at the same time to the psychology of education as represented by Herbart and Beneke. The impression produced upon him by German ideals of scholarship and by the systematic organization of school and university instruction in Prussia remained strong with him to the end of his life, and is reflected in his *Lectures on the History of Education in Prussia and England* (1874).

On his return from Germany Donaldson became assistant for two years to John Stuart Blackie, professor of Greek in the university of Edinburgh, and in 1854 was appointed rector of Stirling High School. In 1856 he returned to Edinburgh as one of the classical masters in the High School, and, after serving ten years in that capacity, was appointed rector, a position which he held till 1881. It was during his twenty-five years at the High School that most of his literary work was done. His most important book, *A Critical History of Christian Literature and Doctrine from the Death of the Apostles to the Nicene Council* appeared in three volumes (1864–1866). Marked by sound scholarship and impartial insight, this comprehensive survey was immediately recognized as a most valuable contribution to our knowledge of Christian thought during the period in question. There was, indeed, at that time nothing in English to compare with it, and a second edition of the first volume, *The Apostolical Fathers*, was called for in 1874. Another piece of work in the same field was the translation of the Ante-Nicene fathers in twenty-four volumes—' The Ante-Nicene Christian Library ' (1867–1872)—which Donaldson edited along with Professor Alexander Roberts [q.v.].

During these years also Donaldson became widely known throughout Scotland as an educationist of enlightened views. He took an active part in the movement which resulted in the Education Act of 1872, establishing primary education in Scotland on a national and compulsory basis, and he contended warmly, both then and later, for an improvement in the status of the teachers as the foundation of a sound educational policy. In 1881 he became professor of humanity in the university of Aberdeen, and five years later (1886) he was appointed principal of the United College of St. Salvator and St. Leonard in the university of St. Andrews. On the passing of the Scottish

Universities Act of 1889, he became principal and vice-chancellor of the reconstituted university. He was knighted in 1907. It was his custom at St. Andrews on the opening of each session to address the students on some topic of academic or general interest, and in 1911, after a quarter of a century in office, these addresses were gathered into a volume, *Addresses delivered in the University of St. Andrews from 1886 to 1910*. In the same year, at the age of eighty, he presided with a simple dignity over the ceremonies and festivities with which the university celebrated the quincentenary of its foundation, and he continued to discharge all the duties of the principalship till within a few days of his death on 9 March 1915. Other works from his pen were *Expiatory and Substitutionary Sacrifices of the Greeks* (1875), *The Westminster Confession of Faith and the Thirty-Nine Articles of the Church of England* (1905), and *Woman: Her Position and Influence in Ancient Greece and Rome, and among the Early Christians* (1906).

Donaldson was twice married and twice left a widower. His son, the only child of his first marriage, also predeceased him. He had no children by his second wife.

[The *Scotsman*, 10 March 1915; personal knowledge.] A. S. P-P.

DOUGHTY-WYLIE, CHARLES HOTHAM MONTAGU (1868–1915), soldier and consul, was born at Theberton Hall, Leiston, Suffolk, 23 July 1868, the son of Henry Montagu Doughty, of Theberton, by his wife, Edith, only daughter of David Cameron, chief justice of Vancouver; British Columbia. He won a scholarship at Winchester College, passed high into Sandhurst, and was gazetted in 1889 to the Royal Welch Fusiliers. He saw active service in India, on the Black Mountain or Hazara expedition of 1891, being severely wounded, and in 1895 he went through the Chitral campaign as transport officer on the staff of Sir William Forbes Gatacre [q.v.]. After garrison service in Malta and Crete he was seconded to the Egyptian army in May 1898, being attracted by the prospect of a Nile campaign, and, as brigade-major, he took part in the battle and capture of Khartoum, and in the subsequent operations against the Khalifa. In the Boer War he was again severely wounded while commanding a battalion of mounted infantry in the Wittebergen district. Going next with his regiment to Tientsin, he raised and commanded a corps of mounted infantry in the China field force (1901), and subsequently he served for two years in Somaliland as special service officer.

Doughty married in 1904 Lilian Oimara, widow of Lieutenant Adams, Indian medical service, and daughter of John Wylie, of Westcliff Hall, Hampshire, whose surname he added to his own. He now sought political employment, and in September 1906 was appointed military consul for the Konia province of Asia Minor. Here again he proved his worth as a soldier. In 1909, after Cilicia had been added to his area, a revival of the Armenian pogroms, due to the general upheaval in the provinces which followed the first successes of the Committee of Union and Progress, caused an attempted massacre at Adana, where Doughty-Wylie was stationed. Donning his military uniform, he collected a half-company of Turkish regulars, and riding at their head through the town, beat back the infuriated mob from the Christian quarters. A stray bullet broke his right arm, but undeterred he again faced the mob when it returned to the attack, and taking virtual command of the town, saved its Christian communities. He is still, and long will be, gratefully remembered in Adana by Moslems and Christians alike. He received the C.M.G. and was promoted the same year (1909) to be consul-general at Adis Ababa in Abyssinia.

The Balkan War lured Doughty-Wylie back to Turkey in 1912. He became chief director of the Red Cross units on the Turkish side, and, with his wife to superintend the nursing staffs, organized two emergency hospitals in Constantinople. On the conclusion of the war he did not return at once to Adis Ababa, but served as British representative on the commission appointed to delimit the Greek and Albanian frontier, and became its chairman. For these services he received the C.B. In 1913 Doughty-Wylie returned to his consulate, but not for long. On the entry of Turkey into the European War (October 1914) he came back to England, and in February 1915 was attached, with the rank of lieutenant-colonel, to Sir Ian Hamilton's staff for the Gallipoli expedition. On the strength of his knowledge of Turkish, he begged leave to be among the first to land on the Gallipoli Peninsula, and embarked on the collier *River Clyde* which, on 25 April, was beached and landed half her troops with terrible loss. He remained on the bridge under fire during the day, and volunteered at nightfall to go ashore and explore the ground. At midnight he returned with valuable information and advice, and on the morning of the 26th went back to the shore with a fellow staff-officer, Captain Walford, and, on orders from General Hunter-Weston, took command of 'V' beach and of the attack on the village of Sedd-el-Bahr. Collecting remnants of the Munsters, Dublins, and Hampshires, he led a charge on the Old Castle, and captured it by 8 a.m. The village could only be approached through the castle, and here hand-to-hand fighting went on till noon, Doughty-Wylie, armed only with a cane, leading the rushes after Walford had been killed. Behind, on the left, lay the final objective, 'Hill 141', which commanded the beach. He went back to the shore to arrange for a preliminary bombardment of the hill by the ships. As soon as it ended he formed up his men, without waiting for reinforcements, and led them up in one rush through wire entanglements to the summit which was surrounded by a deep moat and crowned with a redoubt. The Turks fell back before his charge, and the hill, and with it the whole beach, were already won, when a bullet struck Doughty-Wylie in the head. He was buried where he fell, and to the end of the War at least the Turks respected his grave. Doughty-Wylie's achievement in thus redressing a desperate situation at 'V' beach with previously shaken and dispirited troops almost deprived of officers, and the gallantry of his leadership and death were recognized by the posthumous award of the Victoria cross.

Tall, and slightly though vigorously built, Doughty-Wylie, with his fair complexion and keen blue eyes, was a typical officer of the old army, which had always held him in high esteem. He was an ardent sportsman, good rider, and good shot, who hunted big game as well as small, but he always retained the literary interests of a Winchester scholar. Simple, tenacious, chivalrous, and humorous, he quickly won sympathy and obedience, and was a born leader of fighting men.

A window and a tablet commemorate him in Theberton church, but no painted portrait is known to exist.

[*The Times*, 4 May 1915; *The Bond of Sacrifice*, vol. ii, n.d.; information from the Historical Section, Committee of Imperial Defence; private information.] D. G. H.

DOUGLAS, Sir CHARLES WHITTINGHAM HORSLEY (1850-1914), general, was born 17 July 1850 at the Cape of Good Hope, the second son of William Douglas, of Lansdown, near Bath, by his (second) wife, Caroline, daughter of Captain Joseph Hare. He entered the army (92nd Highlanders) in 1869, and became lieutenant two years later. He first saw active service as adjutant of his regiment in the Afghan War of 1879–1880. In this campaign he took part in (Earl) Roberts's famous march from Kabul to Kandahar, and was present at the action of Kandahar on 1 September 1880. He served as captain with his regiment in the Boer War of 1880–1881, and was made brevet major in the latter year. His chief engagement in this campaign was the battle of Majuba Hill on 27 February 1881. Three years later he was given a staff appointment (deputy assistant adjutant and quartermaster-general) for the Suakin expedition, and in 1885 was promoted to the substantive rank of major. In 1893 he was appointed brigade-major to the 1st infantry brigade, and two years later became lieutenant-colonel on his appointment as deputy assistant adjutant-general at Aldershot. He was promoted assistant adjutant-general, Aldershot, with brevet rank of colonel in 1898. In this year he was appointed aide-de-camp to Queen Victoria and made full colonel. He was engaged in the South African War (1899–1901), being at first assistant adjutant-general on the head-quarters staff of the South Africa field force, subsequently commanding the 9th brigade, and finally, in 1900, commanding a column of all arms of the South Africa field force, with the rank of major-general.

In 1901 Douglas was given the command of the 1st infantry brigade at Aldershot, and in the following year of the 2nd division of the first army corps. In 1904 he became adjutant-general at the War Office. He was one of the four generals who formed, with three civilian members and a secretary, the first Army Council under the system introduced by the Esher committee in 1904. In this appointment he was very closely associated with the many reforms effected by Viscount Haldane when secretary of state for war. His long experience in administrative posts made his services at the War Office, during this period of reorganization, of peculiar value; and, in 1909, when his term of duty there expired, he was made general officer commanding-in-chief, Southern command. In his second year as adjutant-general he was made lieutenant-general, and full general in 1910. He was created K.C.B. in 1907 and promoted G.C.B. in 1911. In 1912 he was appointed inspector-general, home forces, and carried out the duties of that office with the conscientiousness that had characterized all his previous activities, with the result that the staff tours conducted under his direction were regarded as models. In 1914 he was appointed aide-de-camp to King George V, and became chief of the Imperial General Staff. In the early days of the European War (1914–1918) he was of great assistance to Earl Kitchener, the secretary of state for war; for no one had a clearer perception of administrative necessities, or a more intimate knowledge of the army generally. He was a great worker, and was still on duty in his high position when he died in London on 25 October 1914. He married in 1887 Ida de Courcy, daughter of George Tomlin Gordon, J.P., of Cuckney, Nottinghamshire. There were no children of the marriage.

[*The Times*, 26 October 1914; private information.] C. V. O.

DOWDEN, EDWARD (1843–1913), critic, the fourth son of John Wheeler Dowden, merchant and landowner, by his wife, Alicia Bennett, was born at Cork 3 May 1843. His elder brother, John Dowden [q.v.], became bishop of Edinburgh in 1886. He was educated at Queen's College, Cork, and in Trinity College, Dublin, where he graduated in 1863. Only four years later he was appointed to the newly-founded chair of English literature in Trinity College—a post which he held till his death.

The foundations of Dowden's literary reputation were laid by the publication in 1875 of *Shakspere, His Mind and Art*. It was followed by his *Shakspere Primer* (1877) and many editions of single plays. Of his other volumes of criticism the most important are *Studies in Literature* (1878), *Transcripts and Studies* (1888), *New Studies in Literature* (1895), *Essays, Modern and Elizabethan* (1910), with the short biographies of Southey, Browning, and Montaigne. His largest work is the *Life of Shelley* (1886); but his first study of Shakespeare has probably had more influence than any of his other books.

Dowden's critical method is psychological; he attempts to find the dominant law of a writer's mind and to exhibit his work as the expression of a single character and temperament. His criticism is not a record of personal impressions, nor does he dwell on the sensuous and aesthetic aspects of poetry. Ethical interests predominate with him; the first masters of his mind were the moralists and prophets, Wordsworth, Browning, George Eliot, Walt Whitman. It is significant that he found Balzac antipathetic and that it cost him an effort to enter into full sympathy with Shelley. Yet his mind was catholic in range and he interpreted successfully authors of the most dissimilar natures. His account of *Sordello* (reprinted in *Transcripts and Studies*) led to an acquaintanceship and correspondence with Browning, while with Whitman, whom he was among the first to appreciate, he formed a close and lasting friendship. Dowden had thought at one time of devoting himself to creative work, and in 1876 he published a volume of poems; but he was turned aside by the duty of bread-winning, perhaps too by a self-depreciation which showed itself in a faint, habitual irony. Tolerant and undogmatic, he seemed to verge on scepticism, but the ground of his nature was a deep seriousness, incapable of sophisticating moral issues and peremptory in matters of conduct. A cosmopolitan liberal, he disliked Irish nationalism and fought vigorously against Home Rule. He was eager to help and encourage young men, and his house became an intellectual centre. Dowden died in Dublin 4 April 1913. He was twice married. His first wife, Mary, daughter of David Clerke, whom he married in 1866, died in 1892. They had one son and two daughters. In 1895 he married Elizabeth Dickinson, daughter of John West, dean of St. Patrick's Cathedral, Dublin, a lady whose friendship had been a principal influence in his life. For her he wrote the little volume of poems, *A Woman's Reliquary* (1913). There were no children of the second marriage.

[*Letters of E. Dowden and his correspondents*, edited by E. D. and H. M. Dowden, 1914; *Fragments of Old Letters (E. D. to E. D. W.)*, 1914; personal knowledge.] E. J. G.

DRIVER, SAMUEL ROLLES (1846–1914), regius professor of Hebrew and canon of Christ Church, Oxford, was born at Southampton 2 October 1846, the only son of Rolles Driver, of that city, by his wife, Sarah Smith, of Darlington. His parents were originally Quakers. At the age of sixteen he entered Winchester as a commoner, and it was at school that he began the study of Hebrew. From Winchester he passed with a classical scholarship to New College, Oxford. An undergraduate career of exceptional distinction was followed by a fellowship (1870) and a tutorship in classics (1875) at his college. His training had been unusually wide, and the scientific bent of his mind had declared itself early. During this period he wrote *A Treatise on the Use of the Tenses in Hebrew* (1874, revised 1881 and 1892). It was the first attempt in English to expound the principles of Hebrew syntax on lines at once philosophical and scientific. The work of Heinrich von Ewald served as a starting-point, but Driver developed it in a way altogether his own. All modern study of Hebrew has been founded on the *Tenses*: it remains perhaps the most interesting and original book that Driver wrote. His reputation as a hebraist, thus early established, gained him a seat in the Old Testament revision company (1875–1884).

Meanwhile, on 16 September 1882, Dr. Pusey died; and on 23 October Mr. Gladstone offered Driver, on behalf of the Crown, the vacant regius professorship and canonry of Christ Church. At the time Driver was only in deacon's orders (December 1881); he was ordained priest in December 1882, and the letters patent were dated 5 January 1883. From June of that year until his death he resided in Christ Church. Dr. Pusey was a scholar of the old school, and had problems of his own to face; Driver, by temperament and training a very different man, was called to a different task. The way had been prepared for him. In England, some time before, John William Colenso [q. v.] and Samuel Davidson [q. v.] had questioned traditional views of the Old Testament; later on, through the translation and popularizing of the works of Ewald, Kuenen, and Wellhausen, the new learning had made its way into theological schools. The teaching of Andrew Bruce Davidson [q.v.] and W. Robertson Smith [q.v.] in Scotland, and the writings of Thomas Kelly Cheyne [q.v.], had influenced a widening circle; at the same time the religious world was agitated by a general unsettlement of opinion. Driver more than any one else came to be trusted as a guide through the period of transition: 'he taught the faithful criticism, and the critics faith.'

During the thirty-one years of his professorship Driver devoted himself, with deliberate concentration, to teaching and writing and encouraging the work of younger men. The output of this period was remarkable. In the philological department his *Notes on Samuel* (1890, enlarged 1913), and his contributions to the Oxford *Hebrew Lexicon* (1891–1905), set a standard which raised the whole level of Hebrew scholarship. He wrote commentaries in one form or another on nearly half of the Old Testament, distinguished rather by sound judgement and exactness than by original or creative thought; he took Dillmann for a model; he was at his best when dealing with objective facts; imaginative insight and passion for ideas were not his gifts. Of all his books the *Introduction to the Literature of the Old Testament* (1891, ninth edition, 1913) had the widest influence. Characteristically Driver did not accept the Graf-Wellhausen theory of the Pentateuch until he had worked over the field for himself; but between 1882 and 1889 he became convinced; and in the *Introduction* he set out the critical process in detail, and surveyed the entire literature from the modern point of view. To ardent spirits Driver's caution and moderation seemed disappointing; in general, however, the book was welcomed as authoritative, and it was singularly well-timed.

At close quarters with his pupils Driver followed the inductive method; he would insist upon a thorough discipline with grammar and lexicon before any attempt was made to enter the higher regions. Retiring and self-effacing by nature, he did not shrink from controversy if the need arose; while many a preface acknowledges the time and trouble he would spend on the work of others. Through all the changes of opinion which he helped to bring about, his loyalty to the Christian faith remained unshaken.

He married in 1891 Mabel, elder daughter of Edmund Burr, of Burgh, Norfolk, and had three sons and two daughters. He died 26 February 1914, aged sixty-seven.

[*Ideals of the Prophets*, edited by G. A. Cooke, 1915, Appendix B, giving a full bibliography; *Expository Times*, ix and xxv; W. Sanday, *The Life-Work of S. R. Driver*, 1914; *Oxford Magazine*, March 1914; *Contemporary Review*, April 1914; *Expositor*, May 1914; *Proceedings* of the British Academy, 1915; *Harvard Theological Review*, 1916; personal knowledge.]

G. A. C.

DRUMMOND, JAMES (1835–1918), Unitarian divine, was born in Dublin 14 May 1835. He was the third and youngest son of the Rev. William Hamilton Drummond, D.D. [q.v.], minister of Strand Street chapel, Dublin, who was known as a scholar and poet. His mother (his father's second wife) was Catherine, daughter of Robert Blackley, of Dublin. He entered Trinity College, Dublin, in 1851 and graduated in 1855, gaining the first classical gold medal. He had dedicated himself to the ministry under the influence of the biography of the American theologian, William Ellery Channing (1780–1842), and in 1856 entered on his theological training at Manchester New College, London, under John James Tayler [q.v.], the principal, and James Martineau [q.v.], then professor of philosophy there. His first and only pastorate was at Cross Street chapel, Manchester, where he became the colleague of the Rev. William Gaskell [q.v.] in 1860. In 1861 he married Frances, the youngest daughter of John Classon, of Dublin. Their family consisted of two sons and six daughters. In 1869 he left Manchester to succeed his old teacher, J. J. Tayler, as lecturer at Manchester New College in biblical and historical theology. He succeeded Martineau as principal in 1885; and when the college was removed to Oxford (1889), he went with it. He retired from the principalship in 1906, but continued to live in Oxford till his death, which took place 13 June 1918.

As theologian and scholar Drummond exhibited great independence. He was a loyal and trusted member of the Unitarian denomination, but it was not the dogmatic negations with which Unitarianism is popularly identified that appealed to him. It was rather its resolute affirmation of the principle of theological freedom and its repudiation of doctrinal tests for its ministers or members. 'A pledge,' he said, 'which binds teacher or learner to any foregone conclusion, even if that conclusion should be true, may yet bias the intellect and strain the conscience, and so impair the faculty by which truth is apprehended.' He had little use for *a priori* methods in his critical or historical inquiries. For example, he set aside with decision Hume's argument that miracles are antecedently incredible, and treated the whole problem as a question of fact. By close examination of the narratives he reached the conclusion that the evidence for the nature miracles in the gospels and for the Resurrection is insufficient. On the other hand he broke away from Tayler and Martineau and the general body of advanced New Testament critics in his acceptance of the Johannine authorship of the fourth gospel. But here again his independence came out, not simply in the way in which he rested his case on the external far more than on the internal evidence, but especially in his contention that though apostolic in origin the gospel is largely unhistorical in its record of the ministry of Jesus. He had a dislike of over-curious theological speculation. He was profoundly conscious of the limitations of human faculties and felt that speculation on high theological mysteries might easily become irreverent. Naturally he did not accept the Christology of the Christian Church; but he regarded Jesus as Lord and Saviour, the religious and moral leader of the race and the supreme revelation from God to man.

As a preacher Drummond displayed great eloquence and passion. Vividly conscious of the divine presence, profoundly assured of the great truths on which his whole ministry rested, he searched the conscience of his hearers, braced their moral energies, kindled their spiritual imagination, and communicated some sense of those unseen realities of which he was himself so intensely aware.

His longer contributions to theological literature were all of them important, and in some instances opened out new paths for British scholarship. They exhibit full acquaintance with the best authorities of the day but they rest even more on close and prolonged study of the original documents. *The Jewish Messiah* (1877), *Philo-Judaeus* (1888), *Via, Veritas, Vita* (the Hibbert lectures for 1894), *The Character and Authorship of the Fourth Gospel* (1904), and *Studies in Christian Doctrine* (1908), are his most notable works.

The *anima naturaliter Christiana* was eminently exemplified in Drummond. His natural virtues had been transfigured by a deep religious experience and his impetuous temper had been disciplined by rigorous self-control. His ardent humanitarian zeal and his sympathy with the oppressed made it natural for him to work for peace, for temperance, for the enfranchisement of women; this made him a liberal and a Home Ruler in politics. His character was one of great elevation and nobility; his high integrity and his loyalty to his principles were balanced and completed by a singular graciousness of disposition.

[Memorial Introduction by Edith Drummond and George Dawes Hicks to Dr. Drummond's posthumous work, *Pauline Meditations*, 1919; personal knowledge.] A. S. P.

DUFF, Sir BEAUCHAMP (1855–1918), general, was born 17 February 1855, the second son of Garden William Duff, of Hatton Castle, Turriff, Aberdeenshire, by his wife, Douglas Isabella Maria, daughter of Beauchamp C. Urquhart, of Meldrum. He was educated at Trinity College, Glenalmond, and entered the Royal Artillery from Woolwich in 1874.

He served regimentally in the Afghan War of 1879–1880, and in 1881 entered the Bengal Staff Corps and was appointed to the 9th Bengal Infantry (afterwards the 9th Gurkha regiment) with which he did some years' duty as lieutenant and captain. Having gone through the staff college course, passing out with distinction in 1889, he was appointed a deputy assistant adjutant-general in September 1891, and from that time his recognized abilities brought him almost uninterrupted employment in staff and administrative appointments, not, however, without the disadvantage arising from lack of regimental experience. He was a brigade-major in the small Isazai expedition of 1892, and with the escort sent to Waziristan on a delimitation commission in 1894; on that occasion a treacherous attack at Wana led to a punitive expedition in which he again served as brigade-major. He was twice mentioned in dispatches, and after promotion to major in 1894 was advanced to brevet lieutenant-colonel in 1895 in recognition of his services. Appointed in the same year military secretary to the commander-in-chief, Sir George Stuart White [q.v.], he held this post for more than three years, being made a C.I.E. in 1897, and promoted to substantive colonel in 1898. In January 1899 he became assistant military secretary for Indian affairs at the War Office, a post which had been created some years earlier to assist the War Office in the conduct of Indian business and to provide personal liaison with the India Office.

In September 1899, on the outbreak of war in South Africa, Duff went to Natal as military secretary to Sir George White, and served through the defence of Ladysmith. After the relief he served as assistant adjutant-general on Lord Roberts's staff during operations in the Orange Free State, the Transvaal, and Cape Colony, until October 1900. These services brought him mention in dispatches, the C.B., and five clasps to the Queen's medal (1901).

On his return to India Duff was deputy adjutant-general at head-quarters for eighteen months (1901–1902). He next held command of the Allahabad district as brigadier-general for some nine months, during part of which, however, he was acting as adjutant-general with the commander-in-chief, Lord Kitchener [q.v.]; he then succeeded to the substantive appointment of adjutant-general with the rank of major-general (June 1903). For more than six years he was Lord Kitchener's right-hand man in working out his proposals for reorganization of the army in India and its preparation for war. He wrote with facility, and his experience, industry, and trustworthiness made him invaluable to his chief. In 1905 Lord Kitchener's scheme abolishing the dual control by a military member of council and a commander-in-chief and substituting control by one person in both these capacities, was adopted by the government against Lord Curzon's opposition; and Duff was appointed to the newly created post of chief of the staff (March 1906). In 1907 he was sent to England to give detailed explanations required by the secretary of state, Mr. (afterwards Viscount) Morley, regarding further proposals of Lord Kitchener for the reorganization of army commands. When Sir O'Moore Creagh succeeded Lord Kitchener as commander-in-chief (1909), Duff, who had been made K.C.V.O. in 1906 and K.C.B. in 1907, became secretary of the military department at the India Office. His success in this post was recognized by the grant of the K.C.S.I. in 1910, and he was promoted G.C.B. in 1911.

Creagh's period of command (1909–1914) was one of quiescence and of rigid financial restriction by government both of the expansions not completed in Lord Kitchener's time and of Creagh's proposals for remedying deficiencies in equipment. In April 1913 a committee, of which Lord Nicholson [q.v.] was president and in which finance was represented by Sir William Meyer, reviewed the entire military organization of India, and deprecated any reforms which could not be introduced without additional expenditure; and its recommendations to this effect were impressed on the government of India by a dispatch from the secretary of state. Thus, when Duff took over command from Creagh in March 1914, the army in India being equipped primarily for frontier warfare and the maintenance of internal security, was poorly prepared for the demands shortly afterwards made upon it. Within less than five months from his arrival in India Duff's dual responsibilities as commander-in-chief and member of council under the changes of 1905 were intensified by the outbreak of war. He was at the same time deprived of the services of Sir William Birdwood, his secretary in the army department, who left India to command Australian troops in Egypt, and later in Gallipoli, and Flanders.

In response to urgent demands from the home government, large expeditions, fully organized and equipped, were quickly dispatched from India: to France and

Egypt two mixed divisions and two divisions of cavalry, with four extra brigades of field artillery; to East Africa twelve battalions of infantry with auxiliary services. These were soon followed, for service in France and Egypt, by fifty-two British and Indian battalions and twenty batteries of artillery, to be replaced in India by territorial troops from England; while reinforcements for Aden and British Colonies absorbed nearly 6,000 additional troops from India. Before these demands had been fully met Turkey had entered the War (29 October 1914), and the home government ordered an expedition to be sent to Mesopotamia. By the end of November 1914 a fully equipped Indian division of all arms had been landed, and Basra, the base of future operations, had been captured. To equip so many expeditions India was depleted of her supplies and reserves, and for the replacement of them, especially of medical stores, she was almost entirely dependent on England. But the requirements of the War Office and Admiralty at home left little for India, and with the gradual extension of operations in Mesopotamia it became more and more difficult to keep up the necessary supplies, and the Indian reserves of medical personnel were exhausted.

The home government had enjoined 'a safe game' in Mesopotamia. The operations were at first strategically defensive, and the advance halted after successful operations resulting in the occupation of Nazariyeh, Kut el Amara, and Aziziyeh. The possibility of a further advance was, however, discussed in the summer and autumn of 1915. The value of a resounding blow against the Turks to set off against events in the Dardanelles was recognized in England and in India, but all agreed that to capture Bagdad and afterwards to be beaten back would be worse than never to have attacked it. Moreover, to hold it, an additional division, if not two, would be necessary. Duff advised against such an advance as unwise with existing forces, and in a draft telegram to the secretary of state, submitted to the viceroy, Lord Hardinge of Penshurst, he expressed doubt 'whether in the present state of the river combined with our present insufficient number of light-draught steamers, we could adequately supply our troops there' [*Report, Mesopotamia Commission*, pp. 22–3]. This doubt, however, was not communicated by the viceroy to the secretary of state, and the urgent need of greatly increased river transport for any further advance, for the conveyance of supplies and reinforcements, and for the evacuation of sick and wounded, seems never to have been realized by the government in England. In August 1915 a large supply of tugs and barges was ordered from England by the government of India on requisitions from Sir John Nixon [q.v.], commanding in Mesopotamia. These had to be built, and could not arrive in India for many months; but on 23 October the secretary of state telegraphed to the viceroy that Nixon might march on Bagdad if he was satisfied that the force which he had available was sufficient; and it was promised that a reinforcement of two divisions from France should be sent out as soon as possible. The telegram was sent on to Nixon, without comment, by Duff, who, whatever his doubts might be, seems to have considered that, when the government had decided on the advance, it was not for him to interfere with the man on the spot. Sir Charles Townshend, advancing under orders from Nixon, but against his own judgement and with anxious misgivings, met a largely reinforced Turkish army in a prepared position at Ctesiphon, and after severe engagements retreated fighting to Kut el Amara, where, after a gallant defence of nearly five months, he surrendered (29 April 1916). In the conveyance of the very numerous wounded and sick of Townshend's force, and of the still greater numbers from the forces which successively attempted the relief of Kut el Amara in the face of great difficulties, the hopeless insufficiency of the river transport proved disastrous; it was also impossible to convey up the river large numbers of troops, guns, and supplies, which were waiting at Basra—instalments of the promised reinforcements.

The failure of the attempt on Bagdad, after the brilliant success of the earlier operations, and the reports of the sufferings of the sick and wounded, caused great excitement in England, and a royal commission was appointed in August 1916 to inquire into the origin, inception, and conduct of the operations in Mesopotamia, and the responsibility of the government departments concerned. Duff, who had received the G.C.S.I. in January 1916, was recalled from India in order to give evidence, and in consequence vacated his appointment as commander-in-chief. In December he underwent four days of examination and cross-examination. The commission's report (17 May 1917) assigned to him a large share of blame, ranking him next after Sir John Nixon and Lord Hardinge, the viceroy, in the gradation of responsibility of officials in India for the shortcomings of the expedition. The main grounds of censure were: the shortage of medical personnel and supplies; the delay in investigating the unofficial reports of medical break-down, which were subsequently confirmed; the deficiency, after the offensive movement towards Bagdad, of transport by water for the greatly increased forces, and of provision for the sick and wounded. The commission also blamed Duff for not quitting his post and visiting Mesopotamia or Bombay in order to ascertain what was happening, though he appears to have felt himself bound to stay with the viceroy, having no deputy to leave in charge of the army department. The commission's censures were, however, qualified in part by the statement that 'the combination of duties of commander-in-chief and military member of council cannot adequately be performed by any one man in time of war' [*Report*, p. 116]. Duff had, in fact, been set a task wellnigh impossible in the circumstances, and it is due to him to recognize—though he was too generous to avail himself of this defence—that in many matters he is shown to have suffered for the failures of subordinates. The Mesopotamian expedition differed from any war-scheme contemplated by previous Indian administrations, and in conjunction with so many other undertakings it involved difficulties which would have strained the most efficient organization.

Duff did not live to complete the defence which he proposed to write. From the spring of 1915 the mental strain of the war had gradually worn down his health, and he suffered much from sleeplessness. When he returned to England the effects were evident to those who had known him before 1914, He died in London 20 January 1918.

Duff married in India in 1877 Grace Maria, daughter of Oswald Wood, Indian civil service, of Glenalmond, Perthshire, and had two sons and one daughter; his daughter died in 1897, and the elder son, Captain Beauchamp Oswald Duff, fell in action near Ypres 7 November 1914.

[*East India Army Administration. Correspondence presented to Parliament* 1905–1906, Cd. 2572, 2615, 2718, 2842; Official Army Lists and India Office List; Naval and Military Dispatches, *London Gazette*, January–December, 1916; *Mesopotamia Commission Report*, 17 May 1917, Cd. 8610; Sir C. Townshend, *My Campaign in Mesopotamia*, 1920; personal knowledge.] J. H. S.

DUNLOP, JOHN BOYD (1840–1921), inventor and pioneer of the pneumatic rubber tyre, was born 5 February 1840 at Dreghorn, Ayrshire, of a farming family. As a boy he attended the local parish school and, being considered too delicate for farm work, was allowed to continue his studies at Irvine's Academy, Edinburgh. Reared in a farming atmosphere, it was natural that he should be interested in horses, and later he studied veterinary surgery so successfully that at the age of nineteen he secured his diploma. For eight years he worked at his profession in Edinburgh, and in 1867 migrated to Belfast, where he established a practice in Glouchester Street. His personal and professional qualities brought success, and within twenty years the practice was one of the largest in Ireland.

The invention which made Dunlop's name famous was devised in October 1887. His son John, then nine years of age, who had a tricycle fitted with solid rubber tyres, complained of being jarred as he rode over the rough setts with which the streets were paved. Dunlop's mind was attracted by the problem. He obtained a disk of wood and, being skilled at working in rubber, constructed an air-tube and laid it round the periphery of the disk, fastening it down by a covering of linen tacked to the wood. He tested this disk against one of the tricycle wheels by throwing the two along the cobbles of a long courtyard, and the enormously greater resilience and liveliness of the air-tyred disk was at once obvious. Developing the idea further, Dunlop made two rims of wood, fastened air-tubes and covers to them, and fixed them over the existing tyres of the rear wheels of his son's machine. A trial of this device in February 1888 proving eminently successful, a new tricycle frame was ordered, for which wheels with pneumatic tyres were built and fitted; and a demonstration took place before several Belfast business men, with the result that, on 23 July 1888, the first application for a provisional protection was lodged at the Patent Office. This was finally accepted on 7 December.

After exhaustive tests on a bicycle, Dunlop began to procure from Edinburgh tyres made to his specification and, in conjunction with Messrs. Edlin & Co., of Belfast, who built the tricycle, he put on the market machines complete with pneumatic tyres. A racing bicycle was also built to the order of W. Hume, captain of a local cycling club, who rode the new machine at a local sports meeting on 18 May 1889 and easily beat a number of superior riders mounted on solid-tyred cycles. Among the defeated riders were the sons of William Harvey Du Cros, who, being impressed with the possibilities of the new tyre, made the acquaintance of the inventor and eventually, late in 1889, refloated with him the business of Booth Brothers, cycle and agricultural implement agents, of Dublin, as the Pneumatic Tyre and Booth's Cycle Agency. Dunlop, who had been on the point of retiring from his practice, made over his patent to Du Cros for a moderate sum and took 1,500 shares in the company, the capital of which (£25,000) was not at first fully subscribed. In 1892 Dunlop removed to Dublin.

Dunlop continued to play an important part in the business for several years, but was overshadowed by Du Cros, whose ability helped to guide the company through many struggles. It was found that the pneumatic principle had already been patented in 1846 by a certain Mr. Thompson, a fact which invalidated the Dunlop patent. The company had, however, secured valuable patents for rims, valves, and fixing methods ; and, after a brief fight with the short-lived cushion tyre and much litigation, it prospered, and in time pneumatic tyres achieved worldwide popularity. The pneumatic tyre revolutionized cycling and made possible the motor road vehicle. Dunlop himself did not profit greatly from the success of his invention, and he took no further part in its development after the original company had been sold in 1896 for £3,000,000 to the financier, Ernest Terah Hooley, who refloated it for £5,000,000. Eventually it became the Dunlop Rubber Company, Ltd., with a huge capital and many subsidiary companies. Dunlop lived quietly at Balls Bridge, Dublin, his only business interest being in a drapery establishment there. He died there 23 October 1921. He married in 1876 and had a son and a daughter (Mrs. McClintock) ; the latter in 1923 published some of her father's reminiscences as *The History of the Pneumatic Tyre*.

[Jean McClintock, *History of the Pneumatic Tyre*, 1923 ; private information ; personal knowledge.] B. W. B.

EADY, CHARLES SWINFEN, first BARON SWINFEN (1851–1919), judge, was born at Chertsey 31 July 1851, the second son of George John Eady, surgeon, of Chertsey, by his wife, Laura Maria, daughter of Richard Smith, physician, of Chertsey. He was educated privately and at London University, where he took the degree of bachelor of laws in 1874. The year before this he had been articled to a Mr. Jenkins, solicitor, of Chertsey. He was admitted a solicitor in 1874 but soon determined to enter the higher branch of his profession. He was accordingly admitted as student of the Inner Temple in 1876 and was called to the bar in 1879. He read as a pupil in the chambers of (Lord) Cozens-Hardy, into whose shoes he was destined to step on more than one occasion. Eady had great capacity ; his experience as a solicitor had given him confidence, and he speedily built up a good practice on the Chancery side. In 1893 Cozens-Hardy 'went special', thus creating a vacancy for a Q.C. in the court of Mr. Justice North. Eady at once applied for and obtained a silk gown, and quickly succeeded to Cozens-Hardy's place. For the next six years he had the leading practice before Mr. Justice North. His arguments, although a little prolix, were lucid and learned, and he was always master of the facts of his case. In 1899, on Cozens-Hardy's elevation to the bench, Eady himself 'went special', and in 1901 was selected by Lord Halsbury to fill the Chancery judgeship left vacant by Cozens-Hardy's promotion to the Court of Appeal. In the same year he was knighted. Although he fell short of greatness Eady proved an admirable judge, being expeditious, learned, and courteous.

In 1913, on the resignation of Sir George Farwell, Eady was promoted to the Court of Appeal and created a privy councillor. In the Court of Appeal he rendered effective service in common law as well as Chancery cases. After the death of Lord Justice Kennedy in 1915, Eady frequently presided in the second Court of Appeal, and in May 1918, on Cozens-Hardy's resignation, was selected to succeed him as master of the Rolls. In 1919 he was raised to the peerage as Baron Swinfen, of Chertsey. But his health soon began to fail, and after the Easter sittings of 1919 he was unable to resume his duties. In the autumn he resigned, and a few weeks later, on 15 November 1919, he died at his London house.

Eady married in 1894 Blanche Maude, younger daughter of Sydney Williams Lee, of Dereham, Putney Hill. He had one son and two daughters.

[*The Times*, 17 November 1919 ; *Law Journal*, 22 November 1919 ; private information. Portrait, *Royal Academy Pictures*, 1902.] D. D.

EAST, Sir ALFRED (1849–1913), painter and etcher, was born at Kettering 15 December 1849, the youngest son of Benjamin East, who was in the Kettering boot trade, by his wife Elizabeth Wright. He was educated at Kettering grammar school, and at the age of twenty-five (1875) entered the government school of art in Glasgow. He subsequently studied in Paris at the École des Beaux-Arts and the Académie Julian under Tony Robert-Fleury and Adolphe William Bouguereau. On his return from France East lived for a time in Glasgow and then settled in London; he made, however, frequent journeys abroad, including a noteworthy visit to Japan in 1889. He exhibited for the first time at the Royal Academy in 1883, showing 'A Dewy Morning', painted at Barbizon the previous year. He was ever afterwards a regular exhibitor at Burlington House, and his work was also to be seen in other London exhibitions, notably those of the Royal Society of British Artists, of which he was elected president in 1906, and of the Society of Painter-Etchers. East was also a frequent contributor to art exhibitions abroad, and gained many distinctions, among them the gold medal at the Paris exhibition of 1900. He was elected A.R.A. in 1899 and R.A. in 1913, a few months before his death; he was also an honorary member of several foreign art academies and societies. He was knighted in 1910, and was awarded by the Italian government the decoration of cavaliere of the crown of Italy for his services in connexion with the Venice international exhibition in 1903. His self-portrait was ordered for the celebrated collection of artists *autoritratti* of the Uffizi Gallery at Florence; (this collection is at present housed in the Pitti Palace).

In his art East is, first and foremost, an interpreter of landscape. His sensitiveness to the moods of nature is very keen, and although he mostly expresses himself in a quiet, idyllic vein, a more dramatic expression is not outside his range. As a painter East did not undergo a long evolution which can be followed step by step; but, at the same time, his art never became a slave to convention. His qualities of design, drawing, colouring, and atmosphere all attain a uniform level of excellence; and, altogether, his pictures are entitled to rank among the most distinguished products of English academic art of his period.

East is not, up to the present, represented at the National Gallery of British Art at Millbank (Tate Gallery), but pictures by him may be seen in a number of English provincial galleries; Manchester owns 'The Silent Somme' and 'Autumn', Liverpool 'Gibraltar from Algeciras', and Birmingham 'Hayle from Lelant'. His 'Passing Storm' is at the Luxembourg, Paris; 'The Nene Valley' at the Gallery of Modern Art, Venice; 'Returning from Church' at the Carnegie Art Gallery, Pittsburg, U.S.A., and 'The Morning Moon' at the Art Institute, Chicago. Shortly before his death East presented a collection of his works to his native town, Kettering, where they are housed in a special building.

The etchings of East form a distinguished section of his work. About the year 1902 he began to devote himself with particular interest to this branch of art, adopting a very vigorous style and working on zinc or copper plates of considerable size. East was also active as a writer; *The Art of Landscape Painting in Oil Colour* (1906) is especially noteworthy for its excellent practical advice.

East married in 1874 Annie, daughter of Henry Heath, of High Wycombe, Buckinghamshire; they had one son and four daughters. He died in London 28 September 1913.

[*The Studio*, vols. vii, 133–42, 1896, liv, 259–68, 1912, and xxxiv, 124–37, 1905; *Die Graphischen Künste*, vol. xxxvi, 12–20, 1913; U. Thieme and F. Becker, *Allgemeines Lexikon der bildenden Künstler*, vol. x, 1914.] T. B.

EDWARDS, MATILDA BARBARA BETHAM- (1836–1919), novelist and writer on French life, the fourth daughter of Edward Edwards, farmer, by his wife, Barbara, daughter of the Rev. William Betham [q.v.], was born at Westerfield, Suffolk, 4 March 1836. She inherited literary traditions through her uncle, Sir William Betham [q.v.] and her aunt Mary Matilda Betham [q.v.], and was herself often confused, to her annoyance, with her cousin Amelia Blandford Edwards [q.v.], the Egyptologist. In the main she educated herself, browsing at random among her father's books, but she went for a time to an Ipswich day-school, and later, after six unhappy months at a Peckham boarding-school, visited Germany and France to improve her languages. After her father's death in 1864, she carried on his farm till her only unmarried sister died in 1865, when she went to live in London. There she made many friends, among them Madame Bodichon [q.v.] who introduced her to

George Eliot and George Henry Lewes [q.v.]. She also travelled widely, especially in France, where she lived in French families, made many friends, most of them in republican and anti-clerical circles in the provinces, and in interpreting the land and its people to her own countrymen did services which were recognized in 1891 by her appointment as officier de l'instruction publique de France. From 1884 onwards she lived a retired life at Hastings, where she died on 4 January 1919.

Miss Betham-Edwards was always proud to remember that Charles Dickens accepted her first verses, *The Golden Bee*, and published them, not as she herself said, in *Household Words*, but in *All the Year Round* (vol. iii, p. 108, 1860). Her literary reputation, however, rests upon her prose writings. She had not imaginative power of the highest order ; but she had a natural gift for story-telling, combined with close observation and a retentive memory. She made repeated use, always with freshness, of a comparatively narrow range of material—recollections of Suffolk, strong anti-clerical and other prejudices, lasting enthusiasm for certain persons and certain books, and above all an intense attachment to France. She felt it her duty to hold aloof from political or other interests which might distract her from her writing, imposed upon herself a rigid rule of life, and was thus able to achieve an enormous output. When in 1917 she kept the 'diamond jubilee' of her literary life, there were only eight out of the preceding sixty years which had not seen her produce at least one new book or new edition. Her first novel, *The White House by the Sea*, appeared in 1857, herald of a long series in which *Dr. Jacob* (1864), *Kitty* (1869), and *Lord of the Harvest* (1899) are perhaps the best known. *French Men, Women, and Books* (1910) and *Twentieth-Century France* (1917) may be named among her numerous books on French subjects. She edited the *Travels in France* (1889) and the *Autobiography and Correspondence* (1898) of Arthur Young [q.v.], endeared to her by his Suffolk birth. Her own personality and the influences which most affected her are frankly revealed in her *Reminiscences* (1898) and *Mid-Victorian Memories* (1919), though the biographical details are sometimes difficult to follow.

[*The Times*, 7 January 1919 ; Miss Betham-Edwards's *Reminiscences* ; personal sketch by Sarah Grand, prefixed to *Mid-Victorian Memories* ; private information.]

H. J.

EDWARDS, Sir OWEN MORGAN (1858–1920), man of letters, the eldest of the four sons of Owen Edwards, of Coedypry, Llanuwchllyn, Merionethshire, by his wife, Elizabeth Jones, was born at Coedypry on Christmas Day 1858. The scene of his childhood, beautiful in itself, and romantic in its associations, left upon the mind of Owen Edwards a profound impression. His intense love of nature and his sense of humour he derived from his father; from his mother came the felicity and aptness of diction which, with personal qualities of his own, form the groundwork of his literary style.

The foundations of Edwards's real education were laid in his home and in the activities of his nonconformist chapel. He began his more formal education at the Church of England village school, where for a time he was also a pupil-teacher. Later, he went to the grammar school at Bala, and from there to the theological college in the same town. During his last year at the college he acted as lecturer and, under the persistent pressure of influential friends, he joined the ministry of the Welsh Calvinistic Methodists. In the course of his journeys as an itinerant preacher he acquired a very intimate knowledge of Welsh life and thought and social conditions. From Bala he went in 1880 to the University College of Wales, Aberystwyth, whence he took his London B.A. degree. Subsequently, he spent one session (1883–1884) at the university of Glasgow. In 1885 he was elected a Brackenbury scholar in modern history at Balliol College, Oxford. He won the Stanhope essay prize in 1886, and in 1887 obtained the Lothian prize and a first class in modern history. After spending a year in France, Germany, and Italy, he came back to Oxford to teach. He was soon appointed lecturer in modern history at Corpus Christi and Trinity Colleges, and later at Balliol and Pembroke. In 1889 he was elected a tutorial fellow of Lincoln College, a position which he held till 1907. He remained an honorary fellow of the college until his death.

In 1899 on the death of Tom Ellis, M.P., Edwards was chosen, unopposed, to represent his native county of Merioneth in parliament, but he had no taste for politics and he resigned his seat in 1900. His views on Welsh nationalism began to take form in his undergraduate days at Oxford. He was one of the founders and the dominating influence of the Dafydd ap Gwilym Society. Later, he found an outlet for his views in journalism. He was joint-editor of the short-lived periodical *Cymru Fydd* (1890), but resigned when it became too political in character. In August 1891 he launched his own monthly *Cymru*, and in 1892 *Cymru'r Plant*, a monthly magazine for children, both of which he continued to edit to the day of his death. In 1895 he founded *Y Llenor*, a quarterly, and he also edited *Wales*, a magazine in English. In 1889 there appeared *O'r Bala i Geneva*, a book of travel, so written as to strike an entirely new note in Welsh prose ; it was followed in rapid succession by others full of that charm of style which captured the imagination of Welsh readers. The principal work that he published in English was *Wales* (1901) in the 'Story of the Nations' series. Besides his own personal contribution to Welsh literature, Edwards published cheap reprints of the Welsh classics (*Cyfres y Fil*, and others), ranging from Dafydd ap Gwilym to Ceiriog. He did more than any other man to revive Welsh as a literary language. He was knighted in 1916 'for his services to Welsh literature'.

Edwards's two main interests in life were education and Welsh culture. He reported on 'the state of education in Wales' to the committee of the Privy Council on education, before the first charter of the university of Wales was granted in 1893. He was a member of the royal commission which reported in 1918 before the granting of the second charter. In 1907 he became chief inspector of education for Wales under the Board of Education. As chief inspector he was an untiring administrator; but he was also the prophet of a new ideal of education. His conception of Welsh nationalism as based on culture and entirely exempt from political and sectarian partisanship, was peculiarly his own, and he made it effective.

In 1891 Edwards married Ellen, daughter of Evan Davies, of Prys Mawr, Llanuwchllyn. They had two sons and one daughter. His wife died in April 1919. That blow, together with the heavy burden of his work, hastened his death, which took place at Llanuwchllyn on 15 May 1920.

[*The Times*, 18 May 1920 ; *Oxford Magazine*, 11 June 1920 ; personal knowledge.]

G. P. W.

EGERTON, Sir CHARLES COMYN (1848–1921), field-marshal, the third son of Major-General Caledon Richard Egerton, by his wife, Margaret, third daughter of Alexander Cumming, of the island of St. Vincent, was born 10 November 1848. Educated at Rossall School, he proceeded thence to Sandhurst, entering the army in 1867. His first commission was to the 31st Foot and was dated 9 June of that year ; but a few days later he was transferred to the 76th Foot, now the 2nd battalion of the Duke of Wellington's regiment. After four years in the British service Egerton decided to adopt the Indian army as a career, and was accordingly posted to what was then known as the Staff Corps, i. e. the general list of British officers selected from applicants from the British forces for service with the Indian army. This was in 1871, and the army to which Egerton was posted was that of Bengal. In June 1879 he was promoted to the rank of captain.

The Afghan War of 1879–1880 gave Egerton his first chance of active service. He took part in the famous march from Kabul to Kandahar, being mentioned in dispatches for his services during the campaign. Then followed a long period of hard and incessant work in frontier operations, which brought him to the front. He served as assistant adjutant-general during the Hazara expedition of 1888, and three years later, for further service in the same country, was awarded the D.S.O. and received very high praise from Sir William S. A. Lockhart. Staff duty with Miranzai expeditions (1891) followed, in which Egerton was severely wounded; he received a brevet lieutenant-colonelcy for his brilliant work. In 1894–1895 he was himself in command of the Bannu column in the Waziristan campaign, receiving the C.B. on the conclusion of hostilities. Egerton's work as a military administrator and a fighter had now been fully proved, and it was no surprise when he was appointed to command the Indian contingent which took part in the expedition to Dongola in 1896, for his services in which he was appointed aide-de-camp to Queen Victoria.

After his return to India Egerton was employed on the staff in the punitive expedition of 1897–1898 into the Tochi Valley, and in 1901–1902 commanded another expedition into Waziristan, for which he received the thanks of the government of India. There was another little war against Waziri tribesmen which he also directed, and he then took over command of the Punjab frontier force, a post which he held for four years. An important campaign was now entrusted to him. In Somaliland the mullah, Mohammed bin Abdullah, known as the 'Mad Mullah', was still a menace. Egerton, who had received the K.C.B. in 1903, was given the task of dealing with this fanatic. His expedition (1903–1904) was successful, and on returning to India he was promoted full general and took over command of the Secunderabad division.

In 1907 Egerton was appointed a member of the council of India, a post which he held until his retirement in 1917. His long and varied military experience in India, especially on the frontier, and in expeditions beyond its borders, gave him a position of great authority on the many political and military questions which engaged four successive secretaries of state during that period. He was much interested in, and assisted much in carrying out, the various military reforms of Lord Kitchener. In recognition of his services he was raised to the grade of field-marshal. After his retirement he lived at Christchurch, Hampshire, where he died 20 February 1921. Like many whose services have been rendered on the outposts of the Empire, Sir Charles Egerton was little known to the mass of his fellow-countrymen; but his work will endure.

He married in 1877 Anna Wellwood (died 1890), daughter of James Lawson Hill, of Edinburgh; by her he had three sons.

[Official records; *The Times*, 22 February 1921.] F. E. W.

ELGIN, ninth Earl of (1849–1917), statesman and viceroy of India. [See Bruce, Victor Alexander.]

ELLIOT, GILBERT JOHN MURRAY KYNYNMOND, fourth Earl of Minto (1845–1914), governor-general of Canada and viceroy of India, was born in London 9 July 1845. He was the eldest son of William Hugh Elliot, third earl, by his wife Emma, daughter of Sir Thomas Hislop, first baronet [q.v.]. He had ancestral connexions with India, both on his father's and on his mother's side of the family. His great-grandfather, Sir Gilbert Elliot, afterwards first Earl of Minto [q.v.], was an able and vigorous governor-general of India. His mother's father had commanded the Deccan army in the Marquess of Hastings's Pindari and Maratha war. Elliot, bearing the courtesy title of Viscount Melgund, was educated at Eton and Trinity College, Cambridge. He was in his youth a noted gentleman jockey, riding several times in the Grand National and winning the Grand Steeplechase de Paris in 1874. He held a commission in the Scots Guards 1867–1870. During the next twelve years he led a curiously adventurous life, playing a part in many wars in many lands. In 1871 he witnessed the street fighting of the Paris commune. In 1873, as war correspondent to the *Morning Post*, he was with the Carlist army in the north of Spain. In 1877, at the outbreak of war between Russia and Turkey, he at once started for Constantinople, became assistant attaché under Colonel Lennox to the Turkish army and saw the Russian bombardment of Nikopolis and the passage of the Danube that followed. In 1879 Melgund, volunteering for service in the second Afghan War, was attached to the staff of Sir Frederick (afterwards Earl) Roberts in the Kurram valley, and it was only the pressure of private affairs, necessitating a return home, that kept him from attending Sir Louis Cavagnari [q.v.] on his ill-fated mission to Kabul. In 1881 Roberts took Melgund with him as private secretary, when he was sent out to South Africa to take up the work of Sir George Colley [q.v.] after the defeat of Majuba. But on their arrival, finding peace concluded, they returned to England. In the Egyptian campaign of 1882 Melgund was attached to the mounted infantry, was wounded at Mahuta, and subsequently commanded the regiment in the march into Cairo. Then he turned from the East to the West, and from 1883 to 1885 acted as military secretary to the governor-general of Canada, Lord Lansdowne. When the North-Western rebellion broke out in 1885 under Louis Riel [q.v.] he went to the front as chief of the staff with General Middleton, and was present at the battle of Fish Creek. In 1886 he failed to gain election as liberal-unionist candidate for the Hexham division of Northumberland. Then followed a quiet period of twelve years spent mostly on his Roxburghshire estate in local and county work—especially in promoting the efficiency of the volunteer service. He succeeded to the earldom in 1891 on the death of his father.

The most important part of Minto's career was yet to come, and after this interlude of comparative ease he held in succession, without any appreciable break between the two periods of office, the governor-generalship of Canada and the viceroyalty of India. As governor-general of Canada (1898–1904)—a position requiring many of the qualities that grace a constitutional monarch—Minto was happily placed. His geniality, directness, and natural shrewdness, his reputation as a soldier and a sportsman, his unaffected manners, all made him very popular, and, in consequence, thoroughly efficient as a moderating and unifying influence. Accompanied by his wife, he visited all parts of the Dominion. It was his lot in his public life to find himself the colleague—not always an enviable position—of men of great powers and striking individuality. His time in Canada coincided largely with Mr. Joseph Chamberlain's tenure of the Colonial Office and entirely with Sir Wilfrid Laurier's long liberal premiership. His relations with both these statesmen were of the happiest character. During his period of office the Dominion enjoyed an era of great commercial and material prosperity. The revenue and population of the country increased by nearly fifty per cent. The most important events were the sudden shifting of population to the extreme north-west, on the opening of the Klondyke gold-mines; the adoption by Canada of the economic policy of preference to the goods of the mother country in the hope, which proved unfulfilled, that Great Britain would grant a reciprocal preference to Canadian products; the raising and sending forth of Canadian forces to take part in the Boer War—a policy for which the governor-general was directly responsible; and the settlement of the Alaska boundary question with America. The last was the only problem during Minto's time—apart from an indiscreet speech by Lord Dundonald, the commander-in-chief, on an army question—that strained the relations between the Dominion and Great Britain. It was finally settled in October 1903 by six jurists, three British and three American. The award was unfavourable to Canadian claims, and was only agreed upon by the concurrence of Lord Alverstone, one of the British representatives, with the American members of the commission against the two other British members, who were Canadians. The natural, though unwarranted, inference that Alverstone's decision had been 'diplomatic rather than judicial', caused some soreness, but the award was loyally accepted.

Minto left Canada in November 1904. He arrived in India as viceroy 17 November 1905, having thus had less than twelve months' rest between his two arduous offices. The task before him was no easy one. He succeeded a brilliant viceroy, Lord Curzon, whose reign, ending in storm and stress, left troubled waters for his successor to navigate. Appointed by a unionist government, Minto's tenure of office was almost exactly conterminous with the secretaryship of state of Mr. John (afterwards Viscount) Morley, the lineal descendant of the philosophical radicals, and a member of the most powerful and advanced liberal cabinet that has ever held office in England. Few could have expected smooth co-operation between colleagues of such widely different antecedents, and many must have surmised that any co-operation at all would be impossible. 'To speak quite frankly', wrote the secretary of state, 'all depends on you and me keeping in step.' This the two men succeeded in doing, and though they differed on certain matters, such as the agreement with Russia, the deportation of seditious agitators, and the embarrassing interest displayed by 'impatient idealists' in the House of Commons (which Minto was inclined to resent), they worked in harmony to the end.

In the Kitchener-Curzon controversy the solution of the late government, which had practically accepted Lord Kitchener's view, was ratified. The general result was that the purely military control over army matters was strengthened and centralized, and a system was introduced, which was afterwards condemned in unsparing terms by the commission that investigated the break-down of the transport and medical services in Mesopotamia during the European War of 1914–1918. The partition of Bengal was maintained. In 1907 a threefold convention with Russia was concluded affecting Persia, Afghanistan, and Tibet. Here Minto was mainly carrying out a policy imposed upon him by the liberal government at home, and the secretary of state made it quite clear that the policy of an entente with Russia was not an open question, however much the Indian government might be consulted as to the details. Minto's personal part in carrying the famous reforms of 1909, which made his viceroyalty so notable, was much greater. In these he claimed that the initiative came from himself—a claim which Lord Morley in his *Recollections* hardly disputes. The reforms, said the viceroy, 'had their genesis in a note of my own addressed to my colleagues in August 1906. . . . It was based entirely on the views I had myself formed of the position of affairs in India. It was due to no suggestions from home—whether it was good or bad, I am entirely responsible for it.' It was Lord Minto who took the initiative in the appointment of an Indian to the viceroy's executive council, and he was in favour of sweeping away the official majority even in the supreme legislative council—but this was too advanced a step for Lord Morley. The inauguration of the age of reform unhappily coincided with the outbreak of a campaign of outrage and murder, the pretext for which was found in the refusal to reverse the partition. In November 1909 an attempt was made on the lives of Lord and Lady Minto by bombs at Ahmedabad. It was found necessary to strengthen the laws against the holding of seditious meetings and the unchecked licence of the press (1910). The position of the government was rendered exceedingly difficult; in Lord Minto's own words, they were obliged 'with one hand to dispense measures calculated to meet novel political conditions, and with the other hand sternly to eradicate political crimes'. They were conscious, too, that, though their course was determined on before the outrages began, any reform proposals which they might now put forward would be condemned by the one side as an inadequate concession to lawful political ambition, and denounced by the other as a pusillanimous truckling to revolutionary violence. Yet they determined not to draw back. 'In the midst of such complications', said the viceroy, 'I could not enter light-heartedly on a policy of reform, but I refused to lose faith in it.' Morley and Minto were undoubtedly right in maintaining their course, but a reasonable criticism, passed at the time, was that more firmness should have been shown in the early days in putting down disorders.

A feature of Minto's viceroyalty was the increasing influence of the secretary of state upon the policy of the Indian government. This was due to the strong determination of a triumphant parliamentary majority to extend liberalizing principles throughout the Empire, the dominant personality of Lord Morley, and the viceroy's disinclination to quarrel with his colleague. Constitutional purists noted with misgiving the tendency of both the viceroy and the secretary of state to neglect their councils and permanent officials, and to raise—and all but settle—important questions through the medium of an intimate private correspondence.

Not the least valuable part of Lord Minto's work was seen in his relations with the Indian princes. No Indian viceroy, not even Lord Mayo, was so universally liked and respected by them. During the winter of 1906–1907 the Amir of Afghanistan was induced to visit India, and the foundations of a stable friendship with the British power were laid. It cannot be doubted that the loyalty and enthusiasm displayed by the ruling chiefs during the European War of 1914–1918 had been largely fostered by the geniality and camaraderie of Lord Minto.

Minto left India in November 1910. Among many other honours he received the Garter, and the freedom of the cities of London and Edinburgh. At the coronation of King George V he was one of four peers selected to hold the canopy over the King. He only lived for four years to enjoy the pleasures of retirement in his Scottish home and amidst his family circle. His health failed suddenly and unexpectedly in the autumn of 1913, and he died at Hawick 1 March 1914.

Lord Minto was one of those men who would probably never have risen to the high offices he held except in a country where some deference was still paid to the claims of birth and position; and his whole career shows how much his country would have lost, had such considerations of choice been disregarded. He proved himself a conscientious, capable, and loyal servant of the state. He was, wrote Lord Morley, 'able, straightforward, steadfast, unselfish, and the most considerate of comrades in tasks of arduous public duty'. Without being a born administrator, he was able to direct successfully the work of administration: without being an orator, he fulfilled adequately all that was required of him in the council chamber and the assembly: without any deep grasp of statesmanship, he was able by sterling qualities of heart and head to control situations which might well have taxed the powers of abler men. Above all there was the appeal that his attractive character always made to the allegiance of his colleagues.

Lord Minto married in 1883 Mary Caroline, daughter of General the Hon. Charles Grey [q.v.], brother of the third Earl Grey, and he was aided all his life by his wife's devotion, cleverness, and charm. He had two sons and three daughters. Of his sons, the elder, Victor Gilbert, born 1891, succeeded to the earldom, the younger was killed in Flanders in 1917.

An excellent portrait-sketch of Minto by P. A. de Laszlo was painted in 1912. An equestrian statue by Sir W. Goscombe John has been erected in Calcutta (*Royal Academy Pictures*, 1913).

[*Annual Register*: Lord Morley, *Recollections*, 1917; Sir Valentine Chirol, *Indian Unrest*, 1910; Sir Verney Lovett, *A History of the Indian Nationalist Movement*, 1920; Lord Minto, *Speeches*, published by the Government of India, 1911; John Buchan, *Lord Minto: A Memoir*, 1924; private information.] P. E. R.

ELLIS, ROBINSON (1834–1913), classical scholar, born at Barming, near Maidstone, 5 September 1834, was the third son of James Ellis, landowner and hop-grower. His mother, the third wife, was a Miss Robinson, who is described (disparagingly) by Keats in his first letter about Fanny Brawne [H. B. Forman's *Keats*, ed. 1901, iv. 198.] Educated first at Elizabeth College, Guernsey, and afterwards, from August 1850, at Rugby School, where he owed much to George Granville Bradley [q.v.], he won a scholarship at Balliol College, Oxford, in 1852 and matriculated in 1853. He obtained a first class in classical moderations in 1854, the Ireland scholarship and Latin verse prize in 1855, a first class in *literae humaniores* in 1856, and the Boden (Sanscrit) scholarship in 1858, in which year he was elected fellow of Trinity College, where he resided, save for partial absence in 1870–1876, for the rest of his life. He was influenced by Benjamin Jowett and John Conington, and was for a time interested in ritualism and mesmerism. In later life he was attracted, but only superficially, by the Church of Rome, since, apart from pure scholarship and literature, he cared only for classical music. After twelve years of college teaching, mostly in composition and Latin authors, varied by reading parties, he was elected in 1870 professor of Latin at University College, London; but he was not successful with the larger and less advanced classes there, and in 1876 returned to Oxford for good.

By this time Ellis's position as a latinist was well established. He had examined in classical moderations at Oxford in 1861, 1862, and 1872, was elected reader in Latin in 1883, and professor (on the death of Henry Nettleship) in 1893, thereby becoming a fellow of Corpus Christi College. Having been vice-president of Trinity from 1879 to 1893 he was made an honorary fellow in 1894 and allowed to retain his rooms in college. He suffered all his life from bad eyesight, and at the last, when nearly blind and otherwise infirm, he consented unwillingly to the appointment of a deputy; but he died a few months later, after an operation in the Acland Home at Oxford, 9 October 1913, and was buried in St. Sepulchre's cemetery, leaving to distant relations a much larger sum than any one, even the testator, had expected. He had received the honorary LL.D. of Dublin in 1882, and was made a fellow of the British Academy in 1902. He was a corresponding associate of the Accademia Virgiliana of Mantua.

Ellis was well read in standard English poetry, essays, and translations, and took great interest, as an occasional contributor, in the *New English Dictionary*. In Greek he published emendations to Herodas and other fragmentary works, but his *forte* was in Latin. He was a very fine composer; some of his best pieces, mostly in hendecasyllables, are in *Nova Anthologia Oxoniensis*, which he edited with A. D. Godley in 1899. His work on Catullus commenced in 1859; he published a plain text, with conjectures based on original study of manuscripts, in 1866, and a larger edition in 1867 (second edition, 1878; revised text, 1904). This was followed by an unexpurgated translation in the metres of the original poems in 1871, very ingenious but barely intelligible, either in sense or in metre, without the Latin. His great *Commentary on Catullus* appeared in 1876 (second edition, 1889). His erudition is shown rather by his wide knowledge of the early commentators than by skill in dealing with the codices, and he was subjected to severe criticism, e.g. by E. Baehrens and H. A. J. Munro; but his mastery of the subject was unmistakable. In later life he devoted more attention to palaeography, but in this field, owing probably to his defective eyesight, he never became really proficient.

His next work was an elaborate edition of the *Ibis* of Ovid in 1881; then, considering that it would be 'too marked to edit another amatory poet', he devoted himself to minor authors. His principal recensions were of Avianus (1887), Orientius (1888), the *Opuscula Virgiliana* (1895, 1907), Velleius Paterculus (1898), and the *Aetna* (1901). He dealt exhaustively, though less formally, with other authors in his *Noctes Manilianae* (1886–1891), and in the glosses on Apollinaris Sidonius, &c. (1885); and published a dozen of the public lectures which from time to time were read for him (from the proof sheets) in the hall of Corpus Christi College. A full list of these, beginning with his inaugural lecture on Phaedrus (1894), will be found in the catalogue of the Bodleian Library, which also records most of the articles, such as those on Maximianus (1884), which he contributed at frequent intervals to the Cambridge and the American *Journals of Philology*, to *Hermathena*, *Philologus*, &c. The same library has a quantity of manuscript volumes of collations and compositions by him. His professorial lectures to undergraduates were usually on Catullus, Propertius Lucan, or Statius, on Latin verse com position, and (later) on Latin palaeography with specimen pages selected by himself from Bodleian manuscripts. He was assiduous in maintaining friendly, though cautious, relations with foreign scholars—'not Baehrens', however; and he showed much intrepidity in visiting distant libraries in search of codices. His work both as commentator and as textual critic is characterized by vast erudition and minute investigation, but is perhaps deficient in decision and logical exactness. He was, however, under no illusions about the art of emendation; in Catullus he believed that he had 'divined the truth' in one, or perhaps two, passages only (preface to *Commentary*, second edition, p. xiv).

Both by constitution and by habit Ellis was a recluse; his simplicity, his dependence on physical help, his unconventional but frequent hospitality, and not least his impressive devotion to scholarship, attracted the interest not only of his colleagues but also of many of the undergraduates, especially the rising scholars of about 1880 to 1900. At the same time the *naïveté*, not always unintentional, of his remarks about his acquaintances and his or their tastes, opinions, appearance, and his casual familiarity with the improprieties of his favourite authors, made him somewhat embarrassing in social life, and led to the circulation of numerous stories about him. Some of these, referring to his own eccentricities or mistakes, he could be easily induced to relate and discuss; new material could be obtained by artful questions; and eventually there was a considerable body of *anecdota*, some of which have found their way into reminiscences of Oxford life in connexion with Balliol, Trinity, or Corpus. His dress and manner were peculiar, and he was frequently caricatured; but there is a fine portrait of him in the hall of Trinity College, painted by G. P. Jacomb-Hood in 1889, and a posthumous bust in bronze by A. Broadbent in the Bodleian gallery.

[*Encyclopaedia Britannica*, 11th edition, 1910, ix. 294; *The Times*, 14 October 1913; personal knowledge; an admirable appreciation of Ellis's work and character was contributed to vol. vi, 1913–1914, of the *Proceedings* of the British Academy by his successor in the Corpus professorship, Mr. A. C. Clark.]

H. E. D. B.

ELWES, GERVASE HENRY [CARY-] (1866–1921), singer, born 15 November 1866 at Billing, Northamptonshire, was the elder son of Valentine Dudley Henry Cary-Elwes, of Billing Hall and Brigg Manor, Lincolnshire, by his second wife, Alice, daughter of the Hon. and Rev. Henry Ward, and niece of the third Viscount Bangor, of Castle Ward, North Ireland. He was educated at the Oratory School, Edgbaston, under Cardinal Newman, and at Woburn School under Lord Petre; and subsequently, from 1885 to 1888, at Christ Church, Oxford. Deciding to enter the diplomatic service, he went in 1889 to Munich for a year: there he studied German and French and also the violin. Returning to London he engaged in further study for his career, and in 1891, on the advice of Sir Nicholas O'Conor, took a post as honorary attaché to the British embassy at Vienna, where he spent a year; he also widened his musical knowledge by composition lessons, and became personally acquainted with Brahms. He then moved to Brussels, where he spent three years, incidentally studying singing with Demest. This was his last diplomatic appointment. Owing to his father's failing health, he resigned his profession in 1895 and returned to England, settling down on his father's Lincolnshire property and working at forestry. Five years afterwards he was advised by Sir Alfred Scott-Gatty to adopt singing as a career; and he studied in London with Henry Russell and for two winters with Bouhy in Paris, completing his technique under his chief master, Victor Beigel. He sang in public for the first time in Paris in December 1902, and in London in the spring of 1903. He owed to Miss May Wakefield (the organizer of the Westmorland festivals) and to Professor Johann Kruse some of his earliest important engagements. Subsequently he sang several times in Belgium and Holland, and also, in 1907, toured Germany with Miss Fanny Davies. He went three times to America, and on his third visit was killed (12 January 1921) by an accident at Boston (Backbay) station, either overbalancing himself or being struck by a moving train.

Elwes married in 1889 Lady Winefride Mary Elizabeth Feilding, fourth daughter of the eighth Earl of Denbigh, and had six sons and two daughters. In 1909 he succeeded, on his father's death, to the family property: at the same time he discontinued the use of the name Cary which he had previously borne.

Some few months after his death, a 'Gervase Elwes memorial fund' was instituted by his friends and admirers, the income being utilized for the assistance of young musicians of talent and for the furtherance of various musical causes in which he had taken personal interest. On 14 December 1922 a portrait-bust of Elwes, the work of Malvina Hoffman and the gift of herself and other American admirers, was unveiled at Queen's Hall, the scene of most of Elwes's important London concerts.

For many years Elwes held a position of special prominence in the English musical world. A man of a personality both lofty and winning, he was in touch with an unusually large circle: a singer of great accomplishment and high artistic conscience, he always refused to compromise with unworthy music. His tenor voice was not in itself exceptional in power or sensuous charm, but it was more than adequate for all purposes of artistry; and his singing was marked by rare intellectual insight and, so to speak, spiritual dignity and feeling. He was especially at home with Bach and Brahms and in the title-rôle of Elgar's *The Dream of Gerontius* (a work with which he had the most intimate sympathy): but he was by no means a narrow specialist and was always active in the encouragement of young composers.

[Private information; personal knowledge.]

E. W.

EVANS, Sir SAMUEL THOMAS (1859–1918), politician and judge, was born at Skewen, near Neath, Glamorganshire, in May 1859, the only son of John Evans, grocer, of that place. After attending school in Swansea, and taking the LL.B. degree of London University, he was admitted as a solicitor in 1883, and began to practise in Neath. In 1890 he was elected member of parliament for mid-Glamorganshire, and he sat for that constituency without a break until his promotion to the bench twenty years later. Indeed, throughout his career the support of his Welsh friends never failed him either in politics or in his profession, and Evans himself always remained the most loyal of Welshmen. In 1891 he was called to the bar and soon became one of the busiest juniors of the South Wales circuit. This meant that he was attempting to combine a large practice at the local bar with parliamentary work in London; and in 1901, although he had then been less than ten years at the bar, he applied for appointment as Queen's counsel in the hope of reducing the strain upon his energies. The application was successful, but the change brought him little relief, as his practice long continued to be dependent on his Welsh connexions. In fact, while he was practising at the bar Evans never succeeded in establishing any large connexion among London solicitors, with the result that, until he obtained office, his parliamentary work always suffered from the necessity of his frequent absences from Westminster. In spite of this serious handicap he had soon made his mark as one of the more promising members of the radical wing of the liberal party. Both in politics and in private life he was by temperament impetuous and combative, and not always conciliatory to those with whom he disagreed. He was a ready and humorous debater, with a rapid delivery, and a keen fighter for his party, whether in power or in opposition. He took a particularly active part as a critic of Mr. Balfour's Education Bill of 1902, as a supporter of the Licensing Bill of 1908, and as an opponent of the movement for women's suffrage. It seemed likely that he was destined for political rather than forensic success. He was a nonconformist, and a bitter and often unfair critic of the Church of England. He was recorder of Swansea from 1906 to 1908; became a bencher of the Middle Temple in 1908; and in the same year was appointed solicitor-general in the ministry of Sir Henry Campbell-Bannerman, and retained that office in the ministry of Mr. Asquith.

In 1910 Evans definitely, but most reluctantly, abandoned his political ambitions by accepting the appointment of president of the probate, divorce, and admiralty division of the High Court in succession to Sir John Bigham. He had few apparent qualifications for his new post. The work of the division, especially on its admiralty side, is highly specialized, and Evans's work had lain largely in workmen's compensation and trade union cases. His appointment was, therefore, not popular at the bar, and he himself at first did little to remove the prejudice; for he allowed his indifference to the traditions of the court to be too apparent, and he showed a certain brusqueness and some faults of judicial manner which gave unnecessary offence. But he threw himself into the work of the court with the utmost keenness, even spending his vacations at sea for the purpose of studying the technique of admiralty work. His decision in 1911 of the dispute arising out of the collision in Cowes Roads between the liner *Olympic* and H.M.S. *Hawke* already showed that capacity of mastering technical details and of patiently reconstructing the story of an event out of a tangled mass of conflicting evidence which makes some of his later judgments so remarkable. He had already proved himself a competent, if not a particularly distinguished, judge, when the outbreak of the European War in 1914 brought him a great and unexpected opportunity.

Evans's reputation as a judge of the first rank will always rest on the series of judgments in prize which he delivered during the War. For the first time in England since the Crimean War a prize court began to sit, under his presidency, on 4 September 1914. The law which it found itself called on to administer consisted, with the exception of a few decisions of the period of the Crimean War, almost entirely of the principles which Lord Stowell [q.v.] had laid down to meet the relatively simple conditions of international commerce and maritime warfare during the Napoleonic wars. It was not possible, nor would it have been just to the naval belligerents, to apply those principles without at the same time adapting them to the vastly more complicated conditions of modern warfare. Yet it was certain that the process of adaptation must adversely affect the interests of neutral traders; and it was highly probable that diplomatic controversies would ensue. Hence it was important that the judge presiding over the prize court should be bold enough to develop the law to meet the new conditions, while preserving an even balance between the interests of his own country and those of neutrals, and at the same time should be able to express the reasons for his decisions in a form which, if it did not convince a disappointed litigant, would at least demonstrate to the world the determination of the English courts to render impartial justice.

Evans's task was, therefore, difficult and delicate, and even his friends had hardly foreseen that he possessed just that combination of qualities—courage, industry, acuteness, tact—which was needed for success in it. A more timid and conventional judge might have been content to shelter himself under the great prestige of Stowell; but Evans wisely relied on the principle that in international law 'there is room for the extension of old doctrines or the development of new principles, where there is, or is even likely to be, a general acceptance of such by civilized nations. Precedents handed down from earlier days should be treated as guides to lead and not as shackles to bind. But the guides must not be lightly deserted' (case of the *Odessa*). He brought to the work no special acquaintance with the laws of naval warfare; yet in a remarkably short time he was delivering judgments which were not only models of lucid and cogent reasoning, but notable for the admirable way in which they marshalled the results of exhaustive research into the relevant authorities. No cases illustrate this combination of qualities better than (i) the case of the *Kim*, in which Evans applied, for the first time in an English court, and basing himself mainly on the precedents of the American Civil War, the doctrine of 'continuous voyage' to the carriage of contraband goods; he held that although the immediate and ostensible destination of such goods may be neutral, they will none the less be liable to condemnation if they have an *ultimate* destination to the enemy; and (ii) that of the *Leonora*, in which he held that the so-called 'reprisals' Order in Council of 16 February 1917 was not inconsistent with established principles of international law. These two cases raised fundamental questions affecting the legality of almost the whole of the naval policy of the allies, and illustrate the magnitude of the political issues which were at stake in the cases that came before Evans for decision. Yet his judgment in the *Kim* case has already met with general acceptance; and, if his decision in the *Leonora* case is still sometimes controverted, it will not be easy to refute the arguments by which he demonstrated the inevitable legality of reprisals in naval warfare within such limits as his judgment laid down.

Other notable decisions of Evans were those given in the cases of the *Möwe*, in which he greatly relaxed the traditional rule denying to an enemy subject the right to appear and argue his claim before the court; of the *Roumanian*, in which he had occasion to consider the extent of the jurisdiction of a court of prize; of the *Hamborn*, in which he held that the national character of a ship for prize purposes is not necessarily that of the flag which she is entitled to fly, nor that of the country in which the owning company is incorporated, but rather that of the country from which the effective control over the ship's movements is exercised; and of the *Zamora*, in which he considered the obligation of an English prize court to follow an Order in Council. The last is one of the few cases in which his judgment was reversed on appeal; but it is probable that his opinion, which was that the court cannot declare an order of the king in council to be repugnant to international law and therefore not binding on itself, is, historically at least, better founded than the contrary opinion adopted by the Privy Council.

The quality of a judge's work is shown quite as much by his skill in dealing with the intricacies of facts, as by the logical development of principles of law and their application to new conditions. Some few of Evans's recorded judgments, notably that in the *Kim* case, show how he could reduce to orderly sequence a confused mass of facts; but it was even more in the ordinary unreported business of the court that he was continually called upon to unravel the most complicated commercial transactions, and often, too, to expose the highly ingenious subterfuges which were employed in order to deceive the court. He has been charged with being somewhat too ready to condemn, and he was certainly acute to detect and stern in dealing with a fraud attempted on the court; on the other hand if such a criticism is tested by inquiring whether his severity led him on any single occasion to condemn an innocent ship or cargo, it will easily be seen to be unfounded. Those who found in Evans a stalwart obstacle to the carrying on of an illicit but lucrative trade naturally resented his vigilance; but the honest trader had no grievance against him.

Evans was created G.C.B. in 1916, and he was offered, but for private reasons declined, a peerage. He was twice married: first, in 1887 to Rachel (died 1889), daughter of William Thomas, of Skewen, Glamorganshire, by whom he had a son; secondly, in 1905 to Blanche, daughter of Charles Rule, of Cincinnati, U.S.A., by whom he had a daughter. Evans died 13 September 1918.

There is a portrait of Evans in the hall of the Middle Temple, and a bust, by Sir G. Frampton, R.A., in the Royal Courts of Justice.

[*The Times*, 14 September and 19 October 1918; Earl of Birkenhead, *Points of View*, vol. ii, c. 13, 1922; private information. Evans's judgments in prize are reported in the ordinary series of Law Reports, and are also collected in *British and Colonial Prize Cases* and in *Lloyds's Prize Cases*.] J. L. B.

FAIRBAIRN, ANDREW MARTIN (1838–1912), Congregational divine, was born at Inverkeithing, Fife, 4 November 1838. He came of sturdy Covenanting stock and his religious training was of the strictest. He was the second son of John Fairbairn, a miller, and a leader in the United Secession Church, by his wife, Helen, daughter of Andrew Martin, of Blainslie, near Lauder. He had very little regular schooling, and began to earn his own living before he was ten. But he was a voracious reader, with a most retentive memory, and in his spare time prepared himself for Edinburgh University, where he afterwards studied, though he took no degree. Meanwhile he had become an adherent of the Evangelical Union founded by Dr. James Morison [q.v.]. Under his influence Fairbairn decided to become a minister, entered in 1857 the theological college of the Union in Edinburgh, and ultimately (1860) settled down to the charge of the Evangelical Union church in Bathgate. While there he visited Germany, where he studied at Berlin under Dorner, Tholuck, and Hengstenberg, and from that time onwards the advocacy of a freer and broader theology than that prevalent in the Scotland of his day became the passion of Fairbairn's life. He wrote, preached, and lectured with untiring persistence. Controversy was meat and drink to him, and he found a ready hearing among the younger men, both laymen and clergy. From Bathgate he removed in 1872 to St. Paul's Congregational church, Aberdeen, where he won a great reputation as a preacher and as a lecturer on philosophical and theological subjects. His first book, *Studies in the Philosophy of Religion and History* (1876), at once called attention to him as a new and original religious teacher. In 1877 Fairbairn was invited to become principal of the Airedale theological college, Bradford, and by accepting the invitation he cast in his lot for the future with English Congregationalism. Here again he soon showed his quality as a religious leader, and while at Airedale became chairman of the Congregational Union of England and Wales (1883). At that time also he set himself to a task which absorbed him for many years, namely, the reform and development of theological education among the Free Churches. When, therefore, it was proposed in 1886 to establish a Congregational theological college in Oxford, Fairbairn was marked out as the best man to lead the enterprise. He was made principal of the new foundation, Mansfield College, and the success which attended it from the first was largely due to his sagacity, industry, and tact. His wide learning and liberal spirit, the rugged eloquence of his style, and his deep insight into human nature made him a most attractive and stimulating teacher; and his students responded with the utmost loyalty and devotion. The substance of his teaching was published in 1893 in the volume entitled *Christ in Modern Theology*, which its author described as 'an endeavour, through a Christian doctrine of God, at a sketch of the first lines of a Christian theology'. The book speedily passed through twelve editions. It was followed by *The Philosophy of the Christian Religion* (1902), and the two together gave a fairly complete presentation of a theological position which proved both stimulating and constructive at a time of stress and uncertainty. The theology is of a mediating type and, since it expresses the reaction of Fairbairn's own mind to the intellectual conditions of his day, is perhaps more helpful *ad hoc* than of permanent value. The books, will, however, always be worth reading for their great learning, mature wisdom, and vivid and penetrating analyses of men and movements. Among Fairbairn's other writings are two volumes of sermons—one, *The City of God* (1882), a real contribution to apologetics, the other *Catholicism, Roman and Anglican* (1899), the substance of which had been the occasion of a sharp controversy with Cardinal Newman—and also a volume of *Studies in Religion and Theology* (1910). He also wrote for the second volume of the *Cambridge Modern History* (1903) chapters on *Calvin* and on *Tendencies of European Thought in the Age of the Reformation.*

All this literary work was done in the intervals of an exceedingly busy life. Before coming to Oxford, Fairbairn had won a definite position as a trusted leader of the Free Churches, and he was in request all over the country as a preacher and lecturer. He paid several visits to America and lectured in many university centres. In 1898 he went as Haskell lecturer to India. He served on a royal commission on education (1894–1895) and took a leading part in framing the regulations for the theological curriculum in the Welsh universities. Educational questions always deeply interested him; and, where they were concerned, he did not shrink from political controversy.

Fairbairn married in 1868 Jane, youngest daughter of John Shields, of Byres, Bathgate, by whom he had two sons and two daughters. He died in London 9 February 1912.

Fairbairn was loved and honoured by a wide circle of friends. He was devoted to his family and never so happy as when in his hospitable home. He was a keen conversationalist, a little dogmatic and assertive in manner, but always with a sense of humour, and a sensitive appreciation of human needs and failings. His wide knowledge of men, books, and affairs made him a most entertaining companion. Above all he was deeply religious. His monument is the college which he founded and the multitude of lives 'made better by his presence'.

[W. B. Selbie, *Life of Andrew Martin Fairbairn*, 1914.] W. B. S.

FARWELL, Sir GEORGE (1845–1915), judge, was born at Codsall, Staffordshire, 22 December 1845, the second son of Frederick Cooper Farwell, of Tettenhall, Staffordshire, agent of the Duke of Cleveland, by his wife, Louisa Whitbread, daughter of Admiral Sir Frederick Michell, K.C.B. Farwell was educated at Rugby School under Dr. Temple and at Balliol College, Oxford, where he took a first class in classical moderations and a second class in *literae humaniores* (1868). He was called to the bar by Lincoln's Inn in November 1871 and, having decided to practise on the equity side, he read as a pupil in the chambers of Sir John Wickens, the vice-chancellor [q.v.]. He then assisted Horace Davey (afterwards Lord Davey, q.v.) as 'devil'. In 1874 Farwell published *A Concise Treatise on the Law of Powers*, which was quickly recognized among practitioners as the standard work on this subject and added considerably to his practice. A third edition, revised by the author's son, was published in 1916.

Farwell's rise was steady, and in 1891 he became a Q.C., attaching himself to the court of Mr. (afterwards Lord) Justice Chitty. On Chitty's promotion to the Court of Appeal Farwell migrated to the court of Mr. (afterwards Lord) Justice Romer. He was an able and pleasing advocate, though not combative, and speedily acquired a substantial practice as a 'silk'. In October 1899 Farwell was appointed an additional judge of the Chancery division and was knighted. As a judge he displayed marked independence of mind as well as learning and ability. In September 1900, when Farwell was sitting as vacation judge, it fell to him to decide, in the well-known case of *Taff Vale Railway Co.* v. *Amalgamated Society of Railway Servants*, whether an action would lie against a trade union in its registered name in respect of a wrongful act committed by its agents. Farwell answered this question in the affirmative. His judgment was reversed by the Court of Appeal but restored and much praised by the House of Lords. Its practical effect, however, was largely destroyed by the passing of the Trades Disputes Act in 1906.

In 1905 Farwell was appointed chairman of a royal commission to inquire into the purchase of supplies for the army in South Africa and the disposal of surplus army stores after the conclusion of the Boer War. Farwell conducted this laborious inquiry with great ability and fairness. The commission reported in 1906 and, while acquitting of corruption the principal officers concerned, exposed grave faults of administration resulting in 'a preventable loss to the home taxpayer of between three-quarters of a million and one and a quarter millions sterling'.

In 1906, on the resignation of Lord Justice Stirling, Farwell was appointed a lord justice of the Court of Appeal and was sworn of the Privy Council. In 1913 he resigned for reasons of health, but he recovered sufficiently in retirement to sit occasionally on the Judicial Committee of the Privy Council. In 1915, however, his health failed again, and he died 30 September 1915 at his country house at Timberscombe, Somerset.

Farwell was elected a bencher of Lincoln's Inn in 1895. In 1908 he received the degree of LL.D., *honoris causa*, from the university of Edinburgh and in 1912 he was elected an honorary fellow of Balliol College.

Farwell married in 1873 Mary Erskine, daughter of Vice-Chancellor Sir John Wickens, and had two sons and four daughters.

[*The Times*, 2 October 1915; *Law Journal*, 9 October 1915; *Annual Register*, 1905–1906; *Report* of War Stores Commission, 1906; private information.] D. D.

FIGGIS, JOHN NEVILLE (1866–1919), historian and divine, was born at Brighton 2 October 1866, the elder son of the Rev. John Benjamin Figgis, who was minister there of Lady Huntingdon's Connexion, and a leader among evangelicals. To the deep religious influence of his home Neville Figgis owed much throughout life. He went from Brighton College as a mathematical scholar to St. Catharine's College, Cambridge, and graduated as a senior optime (1888). But his real aptitude was for historical studies; and he won a first class in the history tripos (1889), and several university prizes. Meanwhile two great figures in Cambridge life were bringing new influences upon Figgis. Frederic William Maitland [q.v.] laid the lines of his future work in political philosophy, Mandell Creighton [q.v.] those of his religious development. With Creighton he had many affinities—a critical and almost sceptical intellect, brilliant powers of conversation and epigram, and a bubbling sense of humour: to him he owed his maturing in the Christian faith through a broadening out of the tradition of his upbringing. In consequence he sought not only membership but orders in the Church of England; and deserted Cambridge (1894) for Wells theological college. A curacy at Kettering (1894–1895) proved a valuable apprenticeship, and in 1896 he returned with greater powers to six further years of academic life in Cambridge, as lecturer of his college, chaplain of Pembroke, and curate of the University church. These were followed by five years of quiet study as rector of Marnhull, Dorset, a benefice in the gift of his college (1902–1907).

His early Prince Consort prize essay on *The Divine Right of Kings* (published in 1896) had already revealed Figgis as a historian of political thought. This was followed by his book *From Gerson to Grotius* (1907), by his chapter on *Political Thought in the Sixteenth Century* in the *Cambridge Modern History* (1907), and at a later stage by his *Churches in the Modern State* (1913). Meanwhile another side of Figgis had been ripening. He realized his call to a stricter life, and resigning his rectory he entered the Community of the Resurrection at Mirfield (1907). His first reappearance after profession was to give the Hulsean lectures in 1908–1909. To many friends they were the revelation of unsuspected gifts, and to a wider circle they marked the rising of a new force in Christian apologetic and religious inspiration. As a man who had fought for his faith and made his renunciations, Figgis spoke with conviction to a widening circle both in public message and in private counsel. He started for a visit to America, for the third time, for a series of lectures and sermons; he had barely recovered from an operation, and when his ship, the *Andania*, was torpedoed on 26 January 1918, the double shock was such that he never recovered but went slowly downhill till his death on 13 April 1919. His Oxford lectures on *The Political Aspects of St. Augustine's De Civitate* were published posthumously (1921), but much of his incomplete study of Bossuet perished in the shipwreck and he was never able to rewrite it.

[Personal knowledge.] W. H. F.

FISHER, JOHN ARBUTHNOT, first BARON FISHER, of Kilverstone (1841–1920), admiral of the fleet, born 25 January 1841 in Ceylon, was the elder son of Captain William Fisher, of the 78th Highlanders and 95th Foot, by his wife, Sophia, daughter of Alfred Lambe, of New Bond Street, London. Fisher entered the royal navy on 13 July 1854, on a nomination from Admiral Sir William Parker. He was appointed as naval cadet to the *Calcutta* and served in the Baltic fleet during the Crimean War. Two years later he joined the *Highflyer* as midshipman and served in China during the war of 1859–1860, being present at the capture of Canton and the attack on the Peiho forts. He was transferred to the *Furious*, promoted acting lieutenant early in 1860, and confirmed in November of that year, after winning the Beaufort testimonial, while still on the China station. Having qualified in the gunnery school *Excellent* he joined the *Warrior*, the first 'ironclad', in 1863, and a year later was appointed to the staff of the *Excellent*, where he remained till November 1869; he was promoted commander in August of that year. Then came another three-year commission in the flagship on the China station, and in 1872 he was again appointed to the *Excellent*, this time for experimental work on the torpedo, a new weapon then being tested. He remained on instructional and experimental work at Portsmouth for the next four years, and devoted himself to the development of the torpedo. He was chiefly responsible for establishing a separate torpedo school which was developed out of the gunnery school and finally placed in the *Vernon*. In 1874 he was promoted captain at the age of thirty-three, and at the end of 1876 he came for the first time to the Admiralty to serve on a torpedo committee and to go out to Fiume to study experiments with the Whitehead torpedo. He was then at sea for six years—in command of the *Pallas*, under Sir Geoffrey Hornby, in the Mediterranean; as flag captain to Sir Cooper Key in the *Bellerophon* and *Hercules* in the North America and particular service squadron; then again commanding the *Pallas* in the Mediterranean; and from September 1879 to January 1881 in the *Northampton* as flag captain to Sir Leopold McClintock on the North America and West Indies station; finally being brought home specially to fit out and command the *Inflexible*, the greatest battleship of the day. In her he was present at the attack on the Alexandria forts (July 1882), under Sir Beauchamp Seymour (afterwards Lord Alcester), and did signal service in fitting out an armoured train and commanding it in action against Arabi Pasha. For this he was awarded the C.B. He returned from Egypt with fever and was ill for nine months.

Fisher now began a period of fourteen years' service ashore, only broken by a few weeks in command of the *Minotaur* in the evolutionary squadron of the summer of 1885. He was for three years captain of the gunnery school at Portsmouth, for four years director of ordnance and torpedoes at the Admiralty, being promoted rear-admiral in 1890; for one year superintendent of Portsmouth dockyard; and for three years third sea lord and controller of the navy. In the ordnance department he secured, after a long fight with the War Office, in which Lord Salisbury as prime minister was called in to arbitrate, the transfer of the control of naval guns from the army to the Admiralty. At Portsmouth dockyard he superintended the building of the new battleship *Royal Sovereign*. As controller he was responsible for the execution of the great programme of shipbuilding authorized by the Naval Defence Act (1889), and carried the adoption of the water-tube boiler in the face of great opposition. He had long been a marked man, noticed for his outstanding ability and originality by all first lords from Mr. Ward Hunt to Earl Spencer. He was promoted K.C.B. in 1894.

Mr. (afterwards Viscount) Goschen, on coming to Whitehall as first lord for the second time in 1895, found Fisher a member of the board, and appointed him commander-in-chief, North America and West Indies station, in 1897, after he had been promoted vice-admiral in May 1896. On that station Fisher showed his diplomatic quality by his friendly relations with the American Admiral Sampson during the Cuban War. As British naval delegate he attended the first Hague Conference in 1899, and was one of the outstanding figures in that gathering of diplomatists, international lawyers, seamen, and soldiers of the principal nations of the world. His grasp of realities and of the essential principles of modern warfare did much to keep the conference on reasonably sound lines. He was then transferred to the Mediterranean with his flagship *Renown* to take command of the greatest fleet England then possessed. His tenure of that command was remarkable for his determination to ensure in every department and detail complete naval efficiency and the instant readiness of the fleet for war. He encouraged his officers of all ranks to study for themselves the problems of modern warfare. He visited every part of his station with his mind alert to seize every opportunity of making his fleet ready for any emergency that might arise. He introduced longer ranges for firing, and insisted on the need for constant training and practice in gunnery and in testing and developing every new device, from the control of firing to the newly invented wireless telegraphy, for making his ships and squadrons more effective in action. It was typical of him that, whereas other commanders-in-chief had given cups for boat-pulling and sailing, he offered one for tactical essays. He was immensely popular on the lower deck and was an inspiration to the younger officers, who admired his dislike of routine and contempt for any customs and precedents which were not warranted by sound reason. He inspired officers to enthusiasm by personal lectures on all manner of subjects connected with the future development of their profession, couched in a language as fresh and as invigorating as it was unconventional. The preparation of these lectures was the starting-point in his own mind of a great scheme of administrative reform to fit the navy for defending the Empire, under the new conditions of modern science and the changing aspect of foreign relations. The Earl of Selborne, who had become first lord of the Admiralty at the end of 1900, paid a visit to Malta and the Mediterranean fleet in the summer of 1901. Fisher laid before him an outline of his projected reforms; and after returning home Lord Selborne invited Fisher to rejoin the Admiralty board in the following summer as second sea lord with charge of the personnel of the fleet. This post had usually been filled by the appointment of a rear-admiral, and the fact that Fisher reached the rank of full admiral in November 1901 served in itself to indicate that an unusual task was expected of him.

Fisher, who was promoted G.C.B. at King Edward's coronation (August 1902), lost no time on his arrival in Whitehall in formulating the first, and in some ways the most striking, of his proposed changes. This was the new scheme of entry in training of officers, under which executive officers, engineers, and marines were all to be entered at the early age of twelve and trained together under one common system for four years in colleges on shore before going to sea, specializing later in the particular branch of the service they were to adopt. The scheme was promulgated in a memorandum published on Christmas Day 1902. Both the naval and the civil members of the board were unanimous in its favour, and Lord Selborne, who took a personal hand in framing it, secured the sanction of the Cabinet for its issue. The novelty of training all officers in engineering for four years on shore aroused considerable hostility among many naval officers, especially of the older school, and there was abundant criticism in detail. Fisher devoted the next nine months, with a buoyant enthusiasm and indomitable energy, to carrying the reforms into immediate effect. The sudden drop of three years in the age of entry made it necessary to carry on the old scheme of entry for three years so as to prevent a gap in the flow of new officers to the fleet. A college at Dartmouth was already under construction to replace the old *Britannia* training ship; but a second college was wanted at once to accommodate the larger number of officers of the new entry system for the longer course of four years. As the navy was undertaking the entire education of the boys from the early age of twelve, a staff of masters on the public-school system, as well as of officers responsible for instilling naval training and traditions, was necessary. To prevent the evils of competitive examination for lads of such tender years, a new system of selection, after interview, was adopted; and a new college, constructed and completely equipped in nine months, was opened in September 1903 in the grounds of the Osborne House property belonging to the King. This device of selection after interview, tempered by a qualifying examination, has by its proved merit lived down much initial criticism, has been permanently adopted, and has since been imitated, with suitable modifications, in other branches of the public service. The scheme of common entry has been subjected to certain changes; the inclusion of officers intended for the Royal Marines has been abandoned, and the age of entry has been slightly raised to correspond with the normal age at which boys leave preparatory schools for public schools: but in all the main essentials it has so far stood the test of time, and seems likely to be a permanent feature of the royal navy. Alterations in the organization and training of all branches of the lower ranks in the service occupied Fisher's attention during this *annus mirabilis*. At the end of it, in September 1903, he went to Portsmouth as commander-in-chief, where he was able to superintend the birth and early growth of the college at Osborne. Before the end of the year, while still at Portsmouth, he was appointed by Mr. Arnold Forster, the secretary of state for war, to be a member of a committee, with Viscount Esher and Sir George Clarke (afterwards Baron Sydenham), which was instructed to recommend reforms in the organization of the War Office. Sir George Clarke was thousands of miles away when the committee was appointed, and Fisher, with characteristic energy, had written out the first draft of the report before the three members could meet. The chief points of Fisher's draft were adopted by the committee, and, as a result, the organization of the Army Council on the lines of the Admiralty Board, in place of the former dual control of secretary of state and commander-in-chief, was approved by the government. Fisher knew that Lord Selborne and the prime minister (Mr. Balfour) intended him to return to the Admiralty on the retirement of Lord Walter Kerr in the following October (1904), and he devoted part of his untiring energy during his remaining months at Portsmouth to working out in draft the second part of his great scheme of reforms: the redistribution of the fleet on the new alignment required by the substitution of Germany for France as England's leading naval rival, and a reconstruction of the *matériel* of the navy itself to meet the most modern fighting conditions.

Fisher took a pride in the selection of Trafalgar day, 21 October, for his entry upon the office of first sea lord, though in fact he joined the board a day earlier. Throughout his life Nelson was his hero and model. Reference to the great sailor's sayings and actions was never long absent from his conversation and writings. By the end of 1904 Lord Selborne published his memorandum on the redistribution of the fleet. Fisher had realized that the country was growing restless under increased expenditure on armaments, and that severe economies in all non-essentials would be required if the construction of new fighting weapons, the necessity for which he foresaw, was not to be hindered. During the long peace since the Crimean War the types of ships of the royal navy had completely changed; but the naval stations and dockyards throughout the world had been little altered, and many of the ships, particularly on foreign stations, would have been of little fighting value against a well-equipped and determined foe. The principles of the redistribution of the fleet were the concentration of the main fighting strength of the navy in the North Sea, the ruthless abolition of small ships of little fighting value, and the closing down of various small foreign dockyards. Halifax, Jamaica, Esquimalt, and Trincomalee were closed down; Ascension and Bermuda were reduced; and 150 of the older ships were, as Mr. Balfour said, with one stroke of the pen struck off the list of the navy. The personnel set free from these ships enabled Fisher to carry out another cherished scheme which enormously increased the efficiency of the war fleet without increasing the number of men voted by parliament. Hitherto ships not in commission had been paid off and lay in the dockyards and harbours with small care and maintenance parties. Fisher devised and carried out a nucleus crew system under which the more important ships in reserve that would be required to join the fleet on the outbreak of war had the active service part of their crews permanently on board, the balance being provided from the naval reserves when these were called up. By these measures the strength, both actual and potential, of the navy in home waters *vis à vis* the growing menace from Germany was vastly enhanced.

Fisher had long been meditating the creation of an 'all big gun' fast battleship and the use of the turbine engine, and early in 1905, at his request, Lord Selborne appointed a new designs committee to advise the board on new types of ships of war. The result was the production of the design of the famous *Dreadnought* type of battleship and battle cruiser, which, by combining great speed, produced by powerful turbine engines, with immensely increased gun power, made a revolution in warship construction throughout the world. Fisher at the same time encouraged the building of destroyers of greatly increased speed and power as well as the development of the submarine, with its torpedo weapon, particularly for coast defence purposes. At the same time a committee was appointed to examine the organization of the dockyards and the reserve of stores of all kinds kept in them, in order that all non-essentials. many of which had accumulated on principles unrevised for many years, might be got rid of.

In April 1905, when Lord Selborne left the Admiralty to become governor-general of South Africa, Fisher found in Earl Cawdor a new chief no less enthusiastic in support of his reforms. These changes had proceeded with great rapidity for such a conservative service as the royal navy, and a storm of criticism arose both in parliament and in the press. Nothing daunted, Fisher determined that, before the conservative government, which was visibly tottering to its fall, went out of office, a general statement of the Admiralty's naval policy in the many fields of its operation should be published. Lord Cawdor readily agreed, and after a wise revision by that able statesman's hand, a statement of Admiralty policy, commonly called the Cawdor memorandum, was issued to parliament, with Cabinet approval, in November 1905, just before the fall of Mr. Balfour's government. The reforms and economies introduced at Fisher's instigation made it possible to reduce the navy estimates by £3,500,000 in 1904–1905 and by £1,500,000 in 1905–1906, while the fleet under his creative hand was becoming a more powerful weapon than it had been for generations. The *Dreadnought* was laid down in October 1905, launched in February 1906, and completed in December 1906, a triumph of rapid work and organization.

In the new and not very friendly atmosphere of the liberal government of 1906, Fisher thought it prudent to consent to a diminution of the programme of four capital ships a year which had been laid down in the Cawdor memorandum, and to postponing the construction of the proposed new great dockyard at Rosyth. At this time he had to meet the unabated hostility of the critics of his reforms and the insistent demands of a considerable 'little England' party in the House of Commons. He found in Lord Tweedmouth, his new chief, as loyal, if not so enthusiastic, a supporter of the principles he advocated as Lord Selborne and Lord Cawdor. The development on sound lines of the numerous schemes and reforms he had inaugurated required his unremitting attention. He never gained the sympathy of the new prime minister (Sir Henry Campbell-Bannerman) in the same degree as he possessed that of Mr. Balfour and later of Mr. Asquith; but he was encouraged by the constant sympathy and close personal friendship of King Edward, to whom he was first and principal naval A.D.C. from 1904 to 1910. He felt that he was fighting not only for his official career but for the life of the new navy that he was building up. It was an anxious time, and feeling himself with his back to the wall, he began to show towards his opponents, particularly those who belonged to his own profession, a vindictiveness which tended to foster personal rancour and division among the personnel of the great sea service, hitherto singularly free from these evils. In 1907 Lord Charles Beresford [q. v.] was appointed commander-in-chief of the Channel fleet. That great and popular commander had been on cordial terms with Fisher, when his second in command in the Mediterranean, and had at first been an enthusiastic supporter of the common entry scheme of 1902; but from the date of his taking command of the Channel fleet he found himself continually at variance with the Admiralty on points both of detail and principle. Fisher was in no mood to welcome criticisms from the principal admiral afloat, and an unfortunate estrangement began which continued until Fisher's retirement. In April 1908 Lord Tweedmouth was succeeded at the Admiralty by Mr. Reginald McKenna, who soon made up his mind that Fisher's naval policy was in essentials right, and determined to give him the fullest support. Early in the following year, they both reluctantly became convinced that Germany, so far from responding to the slowing down of the shipbuilding programme decided on by Sir H. Campbell-Bannerman's government, was secretly accelerating her own to an extent which would soon place the naval supremacy of this country in jeopardy. The result, after a bitter contest in the Cabinet, was the famous programme of eight battleships of 1909–1910 and the hastening of the deferred construction of the Rosyth dockyard. Lord Charles Beresford's continued differences with the Admiralty resulted in the termination of his command of the Channel fleet in January 1909. He subsequently addressed a communication to the prime minister criticizing the Admiralty policy in various directions. These criticisms were examined at great length by a committee of the Cabinet, whose conclusions, though expressing anxiety at the differences of opinion revealed, were generally favourable to Mr. McKenna's and Lord Fisher's policy. At the end of the year Fisher, on whom King Edward had conferred the order of merit in 1904 and the G.C.V.O. in 1908, was raised to the peerage with the title of Baron Fisher, of Kilverstone, a Norfolk estate which had been bequeathed to his son Cecil by his old friend, Mr. Joseph Vavasseur.

In January 1910 Fisher resigned office and was succeeded as first sea lord by his old friend, Sir Arthur Knyvet Wilson [q.v.], who had followed him as controller in 1897, and was in general sympathy with his naval policy. In 1912 Fisher became chairman of the royal commission on oil fuel, the importance of which, both in saving of personnel and in rapidity of re-fuelling, he had been urging for the past ten years. The commission's report resulted in the adoption of oil-fuel for all new ships. For the next four years Fisher maintained an unabated interest in naval affairs and was in constant communication with Mr. McKenna and with Mr. Winston Churchill who became first lord in October 1911.

In October 1914, after the outbreak of the War, Mr. Churchill invited Fisher to return to the Admiralty as first sea lord, on the resignation of Prince Louis of Battenberg [q.v.]. Fisher obeyed the call with alacrity, and a period of intense activity ensued in Whitehall. At first all went well. Fisher had for years past been urging that Sir John Jellicoe was the officer to command the fleet when the threatened war with Germany broke out. The officer of his own choosing held the command, and in Mr. Churchill he found an enthusiastic chief with an activity of mind and fertility of imagination not inferior to his own. Fisher's first work was to redress the loss of Sir Christopher Cradock [q.v.] and his squadron at Coronel by sending Sir Doveton Sturdee with two battle cruisers from the grand fleet to intercept Admiral von Spee, whose squadron was met and destroyed at the Falkland Islands. The complete success of this operation was made possible by Fisher's instant grasp of the situation and his insistence on the hastened preparations which brought Sturdee's squadron on the scene of action just in time with only a few hours to spare. The battle cruiser—his own conception—was more than justified. He then devoted his energies to the building on a great scale of all types of vessels in which the navy was deficient, especially submarines and monitors, and to his long-projected scheme for securing the command of the Baltic and landing a military force on the German flank in Pomerania. A large number of specially constructed barges were ordered for immediate building, but before they were completed the attention of the government was diverted to the Dardanelles, and Fisher saw his cherished design gradually excluded in favour of an operation in which he never believed. In deference, however, to the wishes of his chief and of the Cabinet he assented to the naval attempt to force the passage of the Dardanelles and to the allocation of a considerable portion of the fleet for this purpose, although he had no faith in a purely naval attack upon fortifications which was not combined with military operations. As the operations of the spring of 1915 at the Dardanelles proceeded, Fisher grew more and more discontented, until at last, becoming convinced that the Cabinet's policy of persisting in the attack upon the Dardanelles despite the naval losses suffered and the further risks incurred, jeopardized the success of the major naval strategy of the war, he resigned office as first sea lord. The fall of the government followed almost immediately, and Mr. Balfour became first lord in the new coalition ministry. Fisher, however, was not invited to return to the Admiralty. He became chairman of the Admiralty inventions board, but his career as a naval administrator was finished. His wife, Frances, only daughter of the Rev. Thomas Delves Broughton, his devoted companion for fifty-two years, died in July 1918. After the armistice at the end of that year he diverted himself by publishing two volumes of reminiscences: compilations of a most informal character consisting chiefly of copies of letters and documents and notes dictated to a shorthand writer. His continued interest in public affairs was shown in a series of letters to *The Times* urging the necessity of cutting down expenditure on the services once the War was won. He died 10 July 1920, and was accorded a public naval funeral in London at Westminster Abbey; he was buried at Kilverstone.

Fisher was one of the most remarkable personalities of his time, and one of the greatest administrators in the history of the royal navy. Belonging to a traditionally conservative service, he offended many susceptibilities by his absence of reverence for tradition and custom; but he had a singular clarity of vision and grasp of essentials, combined with a burning patriotism and belief in the destinies of the English race. He was quick to recognize ability in every grade of the service or department of life, and he won the enthusiastic support and co-operation of most of those whose help he invited by treating them as his personal friends. In later years, when his policy aroused serious opposition, he tended to treat those who did not respond to his advances, or found themselves in direct antagonism, with a hostility that left bitter feelings behind. He accepted help from every conceivable quarter whence he thought the end in view could be promoted. He possessed a daemonic energy combined with a gaiety and charm which few of his associates could resist. His conversation was sparkling, and his voluminous correspondence was full of pithy sayings and arresting phrases couched in vigorous English, and pointed by frequent quotations, particularly from the Bible, of which he was a devoted reader. Behind all lay his constantly quoted motto: 'The fighting efficiency of the fleet and its instant readiness for war.' Fate never allowed him to command a fleet in action, but it was his creative genius that reformed the ships and personnel of the royal navy and forged the weapon which finally brought Germany to her knees in the War, the date of which he had predicted with the instinct of genius.

Fisher was succeeded in the peerage by his only son, Cecil Vavasseur, who was born in 1868, and married in 1910 Jane, daughter of Randal Morgan, of Philadelphia. His three daughters, Beatrix, Dorothy, and Pamela, all married naval officers, viz., Rear-Admiral R. R. Neeld, Captain Eric Fullerton, and Captain Henry Blackett.

Fisher's portrait was painted by Sir A. S. Cope in 1903 (*Royal Academy Pictures*, 1903).

[Lord Fisher's *Memories*, 1919, and *Records*, 1919; private information; personal knowledge.] V. W. B.

FITZALAN-HOWARD, HENRY, fifteenth DUKE OF NORFOLK (1847–1917). [See HOWARD.]

FITZCLARENCE, CHARLES (1865–1914), brigadier-general, the eldest son of the Hon. George Fitzclarence, third son of the first Earl of Munster [q.v.], by his wife, Lady Maria Henrietta Scott, eldest daughter of the third Earl of Clonmell, was born 8 May 1865, and was educated at Eton and Wellington. He was gazetted lieutenant in the Royal Fusiliers in 1885, and promoted captain in 1898. In 1899 he was sent out to South Africa as a special service officer, and distinguished himself greatly in the defence of Mafeking by his remarkable fearlessness and leadership. He was severely wounded in leading an attack at Game Tree Hill in December 1899. His repeated acts of gallantry won him the Victoria Cross and the brevet rank of major, and on the reopening of the Staff College he was among the officers specially selected as students. He had been transferred in 1900 to the newly raised regiment of Irish Guards, of which he held battalion command from 1909 to 1913. On vacating command of the battalion he received command of the regiment, an appointment which carried with it command of the 5th London infantry brigade of the territorial force.

On the outbreak of war in August 1914 Fitzclarence mobilized his territorial brigade, but was sent out to France in September to succeed Brigadier-General F. I. Maxse as brigadier-general commanding the 1st (Guards) brigade in the 1st division, joining in time to command the brigade in the battles of Ypres, October–November 1914. His most conspicuous service was on 31 October, when one of the most powerful of the German attacks broke the line in front of Gheluvelt and captured that village. Fitzclarence's brigade was holding the line south of Polygon Wood, north of the point penetrated, and although the South Wales Borderers, the battalion on his immediate right, held on to Gheluvelt Château, checking the Germans by a spirited counter-attack, there was grave danger lest the Germans should push on farther to the right and roll up the thin line of the South Wales Borderers and 1st brigade. Fitzclarence reinforced the Borderers with the few men of his immediate reserve, hurried back to divisional head-quarters to inform his divisional commander, General S. H. Lomax, of the situation, and was by him directed to throw in the 2nd Worcestershires, of the 2nd division, who were in reserve southwest of Polygon Wood, having previously been placed at the disposal of the 1st division in view of such a contingency as had occurred. The counter-attack of the Worcestershires achieved a remarkable success, restoring the line and driving the Germans back from Gheluvelt just as a retirement of the whole of the 1st corps seemed inevitable. If this counter-attack had its origin in a pre-arranged plan for the use of the 2nd division's reserves, its success was in large measure due to Fitzclarence's promptitude, judgement, and decision. [See *Military Operations, France and Belgium, 1914*, vol. ii, 322–30.]

On the night of 11 November, after the attack of the Prussian Guard had broken the line south and east of Nonne Boschen Wood, though driven back by a counter-attack which cleared the wood, Fitzclarence, who had done much to check the Prussian advance by skilful handling of his scanty reserves, was bringing up two fresh battalions to recover the lost front trenches of the 1st brigade when he was killed at the head of the Irish Guards. He was a fighting soldier of great courage and dash, and his initiative and promptitude were largely responsible for the restoration of the situation at a highly critical moment on 31 October. The official historian of the war has spoken [*op. cit.*, ii, 444] of his 'wondrous spirit that had inspired the 1st brigade and made its influence felt far beyond his own battalions'. Fitzclarence married in 1898 Violet, youngest daughter of Lord Alfred Spencer Churchill, second son of the sixth Duke of Marlborough, and left one son and one daughter.

[*The Times*, 17 November 1914; War Diaries; J. E. Edmonds, (Official) *History of the Great War. Military Operations, France and Belgium, 1914*, vol. ii, 1925.] C. T. A.

FITZPATRICK, Sir DENNIS (1837–1920), Indian civil servant, was born 26 August 1837 in Dublin, the second son of Thomas Fitzpatrick, M.D., of Dublin, by his wife, Mary Clare, daughter of Dennis Kearney, of Pernambuco, Brazil. Educated at Trinity College, Dublin, he passed the open examination for the Indian civil service in 1858 and was posted in the following year to the Punjab as assistant magistrate at Delhi. His natural bent for the law and his grasp of complicated detail soon attracted notice, and in 1866 he was chosen to prepare the official defence against the claim to the estate of the notorious Begum Samru of Sardhana preferred by her adopted son's descendants. This employment gave him the unique advantage of four years (1869–1872) on legal duty in London, which he utilized to the full. The final success of the government's case in the Privy Council, though substantial, was by no means complete (*Forester* v. *Secretary of State for India*, 1872–1873); but Fitzpatrick returned to India with an established legal reputation, which was still further enhanced by his tenure of the offices of deputy secretary (1874–1876) and secretary (1877–1885) of the legislative department of the government of India, and judge of the chief court of the Punjab (1876–1877). His judgments have always been cited with respect; and though his work in the legislative department is necessarily anonymous, the years which he spent there were years of the greatest activity in the history of Indian codification. The Specific Relief Act (1877), the Trusts Act and the Transfer of Property Act (1882), and the Civil Procedure Code (1882) were among the important measures which passed through his hands.

Fitzpatrick's all-round ability, however, was too great to be obscured even by his technical merits as a lawyer, and from 1885 onwards he held responsible administrative posts in rapid succession: secretary in the home department (January 1885); chief commissioner of the Central Provinces at the close of the same year; and member of the royal commission on the public services (1887). From this last appointment he was called away immediately to act as resident in Mysore and chief commissioner of Coorg; he was transferred at the close of the same year to the chief commissionership of Assam. In 1889 he was promoted resident at Hyderabad; amid the intrigues of that typically oriental court his tact and good sense were conspicuously effective when, for instance, he saved the Nizam's almost bankrupt government from the folly of spending forty lakhs of rupees on the purchase of a diamond. The main lines of administrative reform which have since restored Hyderabad to a healthy financial position were foreshadowed and recommended by him.

Fitzpatrick received the C.S.I. in 1887, was knighted K.C.S.I. in 1890, and in 1892 returned to the Punjab as lieutenant-governor. In spite of exceptional financial stringency, he secured large grants from the government of India for productive irrigation works; but in general he devoted his attention to improving the standard of routine efficiency rather than to new departures. Punjab tradition, inherited from the great rulers of mutiny days, rightly emphasized the importance of personality in the work of government, but was somewhat behind the rest of India in this matter of system and routine. Fitzpatrick's salutary influence was lessened, however, by his habit of recording his orders, as well as the reasons for them, at the utmost length. The same defect appears in his minutes: those for instance on the 'simultaneous examinations' question (1894) and on Lord Curzon's proposals for a frontier province (1902), brilliant and effective though they are, would certainly gain by being reduced to half their length. The Irishman's delight in dialectics had grown upon him with years. Yet he inspired complete confidence and enjoyed universal loyalty and affection; and the efficiency of his government was proved by its successful handling of famine conditions without recourse to a proclamation of famine. He retired in 1897 and was immediately appointed to the Council of India, of which in 1901 he became vice-president. He was also a member of the inter-departmental committee on the naturalization laws (1899). In 1911 he was promoted G.C.S.I.

Fitzpatrick married in 1862 Mary, daughter of Colonel Henry George Buller, commanding the 94th Foot, who survived him. Ill-health compelled her to leave India while the greater part of her husband's career was still before him; but their daughters ably discharged the hospitalities of his various residencies and government houses. He died in London 20 February 1920, leaving two sons and two daughters. A civil servant's greatness is necessarily merged in that of the service to which he belongs; but Fitzpatrick left on all who knew him the impression of a charming character, an inexhaustible energy, and a mind of exceptional acumen and breadth.

[*The Times*, 21 February 1920; *Civil and Military Gazette* (Lahore), April 1897; private information.] S. V. FG.

FLECKER, HERMAN JAMES ELROY (1884–1915), poet and dramatist, was born at Lewisham 5 November 1884, the elder son of the Rev. William Herman Flecker, D.D., sometime head master of Dean Close School, Cheltenham, by his wife, Sarah Ducat. He was educated first at Dean Close School; in January 1901 he went to Uppingham School, and in October of the next year, with a classical scholarship, to Trinity College, Oxford. Here he wrote great quantities of verse, most of it of no particular merit, talked much and well, and made some lasting friendships. He took his B.A. degree in 1906. In 1907 he went to London and spent a short time teaching in Hampstead. His first book of verse, *The Bridge of Fire*, appeared in that year. In 1908 he resolved to enter the consular service. After passing the examination he went, as was customary in the service, to Cambridge for two years' special training. Here he became a member of Caius College, and studied Oriental languages. In June 1910 he was sent to Constantinople, and almost at once his health broke down and he returned to England to recruit. In March 1911 he had apparently completely recovered and went back to Constantinople, to be transferred in April to Syria. Here, at Beirut, he remained, with two short intervals of leave, until 1913. He was not a very efficient vice-consul, and was never altogether happy in the East, being increasingly anxious to obtain employment in England where he would not be cut off from the literary world. In May 1913 the state of his health, which had been failing for some time, made necessary his immediate removal to Switzerland, and in Switzerland he died, of consumption, at Davos on 3 January 1915. During his two years at Beirut he had felt deeply the influence of the life, and of the literature, of the East, an influence obvious in a number of his best, and best-known, poems, and above all in his play *Hassan*. When on leave in Athens in May 1911 he had married a Greek lady, Mlle Helle Skiadaressi, whose influence upon his literary judgements, as well as upon his life, was very considerable. He was buried at Cheltenham.

Mr. J. C. Squire's edition of Flecker's *Collected Poems* (1916) contains all his published verse, save 'seven lyrics which there is reason to believe he did not desire to perpetuate', as well as a few poems hitherto unpublished or uncollected. Flecker's published collections of poetry were: *The Bridge of Fire* (1907), *Thirty-six Poems* (1910), reissued with additional matter as *Forty-two Poems* (1911), *The Golden Journey to Samarkand* (1913), and *The Old Ships* (1915).

Flecker's fullest achievement was reached in *The Golden Journey to Samarkand*, and this volume contained, besides the beautiful title-poem, enough to ensure its author's lasting fame. Flecker had deliberately turned his back upon the tendencies fashionable with his contemporaries, which were towards the formless, the intimate, the psychological, or the self-consciously 'shocking'. His one object was 'to create beauty'. The preface to *The Golden Journey to Samarkand* attempts to explain his own theory of his art. He believed that a poet needed a definite theory to guide him in self-criticism, and he claimed to be a disciple of the French Parnassian school, which was, he wrote, 'a classical reaction against . . . sentimentality and extravagance'. The characteristics of the Parnassians he seems to have understood to be a determination first and foremost 'to create beauty, a beauty somewhat statuesque, dramatic, and objective, rather than intimate'. It was sheer beauty and not 'the message' of poetry which mattered. Flecker certainly wrote up to this theory, and though he left no 'message', and though his work contains few intimate revelations of his own personality, it enshrines much beauty, glowing and sensuous rather than statuesque, yet certainly objective and sometimes dramatic. He is much less representative of his age than Rupert Brooke [q.v.], with whom, as an untimely loss to literature, he is inevitably associated; but his achievement was already great and his promise, for his work still bore the stamp of youth, was incalculable.

Flecker's *Collected Prose* (1920) contains, except *The King of Alsander*, a novel (1914), all the prose that he published in book form during his lifetime as well as a number of pieces reprinted from periodicals. Of the longer prose works here reprinted, *The Last Generation*, an entertaining but somewhat precious fantasy upon the end of mankind, is perhaps the most typical; but Flecker's prose was of comparatively little importance. A great number of his private letters, which are of much interest, will be found in *The Life of James Elroy Flecker* (1925) by Geraldine Hodgson.

His two plays, of which he hoped much, were both published posthumously, *Hassan* in 1922 and *Don Juan* in 1925. Of these *Hassan* has already attained a celebrity, which is partly due to most effective staging. It is the work of a student of *The Arabian Nights* and Sir Richard Burton's *Kasîdah*, but it is even more obviously the work of a poet of vivid originality, who is experimenting with dramatic forms, sometimes unsuccessfully, here and there with a startling sureness of touch. Flecker's drama stands almost as far aloof as his verse from the stream of contemporary tendency. Had he lived he would have done much to revive the poetic and imaginative drama in England.

[Introduction to the *Collected Poems*; Geraldine Hodgson, *The Life of James Elroy Flecker*; Douglas Goldring, *James Elroy Flecker*, 1922; private information. See also *Letters of J. E. Flecker to Frank Savery*, 1926.]

G. E.

FLEMING, Sir SANDFORD (1827–1915), Canadian engineer, the second son of Andrew Greig Fleming, of Kirkcaldy, Fifeshire, by his wife, Elizabeth, the eldest daughter of Sandford Arnott, was born at Kirkcaldy 7 January 1827. After studying surveying in his native town he went to Canada in 1845. From 1852 onwards he took a prominent part in the railway development of Upper Canada; and from 1855 to 1863 was chief engineer of the Northern Railway. In 1864 he was appointed chief railway engineer by the government of Nova Scotia, and charged with the construction of a line of railway from Truro to Pictou. The government policy of constructing the line by a series of small contracts did not work well, as the tenders received were so far above Fleming's estimate that he refused to entertain them. He was therefore requested by the government, in 1866, as the only method of getting them out of the imbroglio, to resign his position, and carry out as contractor the work on which he had hitherto been employed as civil servant. This offer Fleming eventually accepted, and he completed the line by 31 May 1867, with profit to himself, at a great saving to the government, and to the entire satisfaction of the government inspectors.

Fleming early advocated a Canadian trans-continental railway; and when in 1867 the construction of a railway from the River St. Lawrence to Halifax was made part of the federation pact, he was appointed by the newly formed Dominion government as its chief engineer. He at once began the construction of the Inter-Colonial Railway, and carried it to completion in 1876. His difficulties were not only those of construction through a country which was in great part unsettled; he carried on a continual struggle with the governments of the day, because they wished to award extravagant contracts to political favourites, while saving money on construction which Fleming considered essential. The great 'battle of the bridges', in which he insisted on iron bridges in places where the government desired wood, was finally won by Fleming. The struggle is told by him, with his invariable reticence and moderation, in *The Inter-Colonial, a historical sketch, 1832–1876* (1876). Meanwhile, in 1871, the construction of a Canadian Pacific Railway was made a part of the bargain by which British Columbia was induced to enter the new Dominion, and Fleming was appointed engineer-in-chief. In 1872 he headed the 'Ocean to Ocean' expedition, by which a practicable route was found through the Yellow Head Pass [see George Monro Grant]; but in 1880 the government changed its policy, abandoned the plan of government construction, and formed an agreement with the Canadian Pacific Railway Company. It was the hardest blow of Fleming's life. Over 600 miles of railway had been completed, the whole line had been surveyed, and most of the engineering difficulties overcome. All this work, together with vast subsidies of land and money, was handed over by the government to the new company, whose general manager, (Sir) William Cornelius Van Horne [q.v.], was a little inclined to undervalue the work of his predecessor. But, beyond resigning his position as engineer-in-chief of the government railways, Fleming made little protest.

From that time forward Fleming's quiet, unceasing energy was occupied in promoting a series of good causes. He became a director of the Canadian Pacific Railway, and in 1883 he crossed the continent in its service and assisted in the survey of the present main line through the Kicking Horse Pass. His party had the honour of being the first white men to cross the Rockies from side to side by this route. The story is told by him in *Old to New Westminster* (1884). After protracted negotiations from 1879 onward, he succeeded in persuading the Canadian, Australian, and Imperial governments to co-operate in laying the Pacific cable, which was completed between Vancouver and Australia in 1902 [see George Johnson, *Annals and Aims of the Pacific Cable*, 1903]. From 1876 he had taken a prominent part in forcing on the adoption of standard time, which has so greatly simplified travel in British North America and throughout the world. In 1880 he was appointed chancellor of Queen's University, Kingston, a position to which he was continuously re-elected until his death. Though not a party man he was a devoted imperialist, was prominent in the Imperial Federation League, and in 1891 came forward as an opponent of reciprocity with the United States. He died at Halifax, Nova Scotia, 22 July 1915.

Fleming was tall and handsome, gentle in speech, but absolutely immovable once his mind was made up. Several portraits of him are given in the authorized biography by L. J. Burpee, *Sandford Fleming, Empire-Builder* (1915), which also contains a bibliography of his numerous reports and other writings. Of these the chief, in addition to those already quoted, are his reports to the Canadian government on the Inter-Colonial Railway and Canadian Pacific Railway, many pamphlets on time reckoning and on the Pacific cable, and a series of small volumes of prayers and short services which grew out of those which he always provided for his engineering parties. In 1855 he married Ann Jean (died 1888), eldest daughter of James Hall, M.P., sheriff of Peterborough County, Ontario. He was survived by four sons and two daughters. During the summer he lived in Halifax, in the winter in Ottawa, though till late in life he travelled constantly. In 1877 he received the C.M.G., and the K.C.M.G. in 1897.

[L. J. Burpee, *op. cit.*; Canadian newspapers of July 1915; C. F. Hamilton in *Montreal Daily Witness*, 20 February 1911; personal knowledge.] W. L. G.

FORD, PATRICK (1837–1913), Irish-American journalist and politician, described by Michael Davitt as 'for a generation the most powerful support on the American continent of the struggle in Ireland', was born in Galway city 12 April 1837, the son of Edward Ford, by his wife, Anne, née Ford. In 1841, when he was four, Ford's parents emigrated to the United States. They settled in Boston, and he was educated at the public schools and the Latin School, and afterwards served his apprenticeship in the printing-office of William Lloyd Garrison, of Boston. He began to write for newspapers in 1855, and was editor and publisher of the *Boston Sunday Times*, which proved unsuccessful, from 1859 to 1860, and of the *Charleston (S.C.) Gazette* from 1864 to 1866. He served during the Civil War in the 9th Massachusetts regiment of the Northern army. He married in 1863 Miss Odele McDonald.

The real work of Ford's life began with the founding of the *Irish World* (1870), a weekly paper published in New York as a means of communication between Irishmen in the United States. It soon became the chief organ of the Irish, and promoted the organization throughout the United States of two thousand five hundred branches of the Irish Land League founded in 1879. Ford's articles on the Irish land question led to the frequent prohibition of his paper in Ireland by the British government, notably during the chief secretaryship (1880–1882) of Mr. W. E. Forster. In the forty-five years during which he conducted it, the *Irish World* collected and sent to Ireland a steady stream of subscriptions—amounting it is said to half a million dollars—in support of successive Irish movements. In the early 'eighties, while Forster was carrying out in Ireland a policy of repression, Ford was accused of advocating dynamite and assassination as political weapons, and association with him was one of the charges brought before *The Times* special commission (1888–1889) against the Irish constitutional leaders, Parnell, Dillon, and Davitt, all of whom on their visits to America had been welcomed by Ford. It was contended by Davitt in defence that Ford was never a member of any secret society.

In later years Ford unreservedly supported the constitutional movement, his object being 'the establishment of an Irish parliament dealing exclusively with Irish affairs, leaving all other matters to the imperial parliament'. He supported John Redmond [q.v.] in accepting the Home Rule Bill of 1912, and on his death Redmond described him as 'one of the purest patriots and best men he had ever known'. Ford's death, which took place at Brooklyn 23 September 1913, provoked from numerous Irish municipal bodies and political organizations resolutions of admiration and gratitude. In private life he was a man of quiet and unassuming manners, and was a strict Roman Catholic in religion. He was the author of two books, *The Criminal History of the British Empire* (1881) and *The Irish Question and American Statesmen* (1885).

[*New York Daily Tribune*, 24 September 1913; *New York Herald*, 24, 25 September 1913; *Literary Digest*, New York, 18 October 1913; *Irish World*, 4, 11, 18 October 1913.] W. H. B.

FORMAN, HENRY BUXTON (1842–1917), man of letters, was born in Camberwell 11 July 1842, the third son of George Ellery Forman, a surgeon (retired from the royal navy), by his wife, Maria Courthope. The family removed to Teignmouth when Henry was ten months old, and there he was educated. He discarded his first Christian name, and habitually employed the name Harry in its stead. At the age of eighteen he entered the Post Office, St. Martin's-le-Grand, and became a principal clerk in 1885, afterwards second secretary, and, in 1893, controller of the packet services. In 1897 he received the C.B., and in 1907 he retired at the age of sixty-five after forty-seven years' service. He attended as a representative of the United Kingdom four postal union congresses—at Paris in 1880, at Lisbon in 1885, at Vienna in 1891, and at Washington in 1897. In 1883 he acted as surveyor of the British post offices in the Mediterranean, and he attended the international parcel post conference in Paris the same year. He was one of the earliest workers on behalf of the Post Office library and literary association, and was its secretary for several years.

Forman's literary career began in 1869 with a series of articles in *Tinsley's Magazine*, which were reprinted in 1871 as *Our Living Poets*. These brought him into touch with D. G. Rossetti, who was just then preparing the *Poems* of 1870 for the press. From 1872 to 1874 he was writing in the *London Quarterly Review*. In 1876 appeared his edition of the *Poetical Works* of Shelley, followed by the *Prose Works* in 1880, eight volumes in all. In 1878 he edited the *Letters of John Keats to Fanny Brawne*, and in 1883 the *Poetical Works and other Writings of John Keats* in four volumes. It is his work on Shelley and Keats which constitutes Forman's chief claim to remembrance. He was scrupulously exact as a textual editor, but is open to criticism on the score of his inclusion of trivial matter. Among his other contributions to the study of Shelley were part i of the uncompleted 'Shelley Library': *An Essay in Bibliography* (1886), the *Letters of Edward John Trelawny* (1910), and *Medwin's Life of Shelley*, enlarged and fully commented (1913). He followed up his edition of Keats with *Three Essays by John Keats* (1889), *Poetry and Prose by John Keats: a Book of Fresh Verses and New Readings* (1890), and a one-volume edition of the *Poetical Works of John Keats* (1906). He took an active interest in the purchase and establishment of the Keats and Shelley house in Rome, and presented to it a large number of his books.

Because of their associations with Shelley and Keats, Forman became interested in the poets Thomas Wade [q.v.], Richard Henry Horne [q.v.], and Charles Jeremiah Wells [q.v.]. When Wells's *Joseph and his Brethren* was reissued in 1876, with an introduction by A. C. Swinburne, Forman saw it through the press; he also acquired the manuscript, and printed an additional passage in W. R. Nicoll and T. J. Wise's *Literary Anecdotes of the Nineteenth Century* (1895–1896), to which also he contributed articles on Wade and Horne, besides verses of his own. He left unpublished a narrative volume in verse of some ten thousand lines, inspired by his love of Devon. For A. H. Miles's *Poets and Poetry of the Nineteenth Century* Forman made and prefaced the selections from Wade, Wells, Horne, and William Morris. Another lifelong interest with him was the work of Mrs. Browning; he edited *Aurora Leigh* for the 'Temple Classics', and published *Elizabeth Barrett Browning and her scarcer Books* (1896) and *Hitherto Unpublished Poems and Stories by Elizabeth Barrett Browning* (1914). For the 'Temple Classics' he also edited *Sordello* and two other volumes of Browning's poems. He salved William Morris's poem, *The Pilgrims of Hope*, from the pages of the *Commonweal* newspaper, and printed it in book form (1886). This he followed up in 1897 with *The Books of William Morris*, which contains an admirable essay *The Life Poetic as lived by Morris.*

In 1869 Forman married Laura, the daughter of William Christian Selle, by whom he had two sons and a daughter. He died at St. John's Wood 15 June 1917 after a long illness. In 1919 his library was sold by his widow and executors and went to America. His elder brother, ALFRED WILLIAM FORMAN (1840–1925), man of letters, the second son of George Ellery Forman, was born in London 13 September 1840. He was educated at the Royal Naval School, New Cross, but left it for a mercantile career. He became interested in Richard Wagner, and translated the libretto of *Der Ring des Nibelungen* (privately printed 1873–1875, and favourably received by Wagner; published 1877 on the occasion of Wagner's conducting concerts of his own music in London). Further translations from Wagner were *Tristan und Isolde* (1891), *Parsifal* (1899), and *Tannhäuser* (1919). This last was still unpublished at Forman's death, as also were translations of the *Agamemnon* of Aeschylus, *Le Roi s'amuse* and other of Victor Hugo's dramas, and Grillparzer's *Hero and Leander*. Alfred and his brother Henry Buxton Forman published anonymously in the *Civil Service Review* (1874, privately reprinted in 1878 under their own names) a series of articles on 'The Metre of Dante's Divine Comedy discussed and exemplified': discussed by Henry and exemplified by Alfred in dissyllabic-rhymed *terza rima* translations of *Inferno* i and iii, *Purgatorio* i, and *Paradiso* i. Beside his translations Forman produced a privately printed volume of *Sonnets* (1886). In 1876 he married Alma, daughter of Leigh Murray, well known as an actress in poetic drama. He died 17 December 1925, leaving a widow and one daughter.

[*The Times*, 19 June 1917, 23 December 1925; private information; personal knowledge.]
T. J. W.
F. P.

FORREST, JOHN, first BARON FORREST, of Bunbury (1847–1918), Australian explorer and politician, the third son of William Forrest, of Leschenault, near Bunbury, by his wife, Margaret Guthrie, daughter of David Hill, of Dundee, was born 22 August 1847 in Western Australia. He was educated at Bishop's School, Perth, and entered the survey department of the colony in 1865. He soon displayed marked capacity for the work of exploring, and in 1874 established his reputation by his successful expedition from Champion Bay to the overland telegraph line between Adelaide and Port Darwin, a distance of 2,000 miles through the heart of the continent, accomplished with horses only, without the aid of camels. Recognition of this feat took the form of a freehold grant of 5,000 acres and appointment as deputy surveyor-general in 1876. In 1883 Forrest was promoted to be surveyor-general and commissioner of crown lands with a seat in both the executive and legislative councils of the colony; and, when responsible government was attained by the colony in 1890, he was summoned to form the first ministry, in which he took office as treasurer. He remained in power until he resigned (1901) to join the first Commonwealth administration. As premier of Western Australia Forrest was responsible for programmes of public works and railway extension which added greatly to the prosperity of the colony, including the harbour at Fremantle and the supply to the Coolgardie goldfields of six million gallons of water daily by a pipe line of 350 miles from near the coast. He instituted also the system of free land grants of 160 acres on settlement conditions, and founded the agricultural land bank to make advances to agriculturists for improvements. But he worked steadily also for Australian federation, subject to securing the concessions which he deemed necessary for Western Australian interests. He represented Western Australia at the colonial conferences in London in 1887 and 1897, playing a prominent part in each, and obtaining on the latter occasion the decision of the imperial government to entrust the administration of matters affecting the aborigines entirely to the colonial government.

In the first Commonwealth ministry, that of (Sir) Edmund Barton [q.v.], Forrest, after a few days' tenure of the postmaster-generalship, succeeded to the ministry of defence vacant through Sir J. R. Dickson's death (January 1901); subsequently, in August 1903, as the outcome of Mr. C. C. Kingston's resignation, he assumed the portfolio of home affairs, a post which he retained under the first ministry of Mr. A. Deakin [q.v.] until its fall in April 1904. In the second Deakin administration he held office as treasurer from July 1905 to July 1907, when differences with his colleagues on their attitude towards the labour party resulted in his resignation. He accepted, however, his old portfolio in the third Deakin administration (1909–1910), in the administration of (Sir) Joseph Cook (1913–1914), and in the 'national' Australian governments from February 1917 to

March 1918, when the development of a fatal disease from which he had for a considerable time suffered rendered further public work impossible. He received in 1918 a peerage—the first bestowed on an Australian politician—as the culminating reward for services which had won him the K.C.M.G. in 1901 and the G.C.M.G. in 1911, and it was his most earnest wish to proceed to England to take his seat in the House of Lords and to obtain further skilled aid for his health, but he died at sea 4 September 1918.

Forrest's greatest work was accomplished for Western Australia, and he never failed, when in federal politics, to press for the carrying out of his great project, the establishment of railway connexion between that state and the rest of the continent. For an Australian statesman his political views were conservative; they prevented him from attaining the premiership of the Commonwealth, which was the goal of his ambitions. A strong and outspoken opponent of the labour party, he nevertheless won the respect of his opponents, whose denunciations of his peerage as undemocratic were modified by personal regard. Resolute in the support of local autonomy, he attached the greatest value to the imperial connexion and was unwearied during the European War in defending British institutions and aims. In private life he was a warm and trusted friend. He married in 1876 Margaret Elvire, eldest daughter of Edward Hamersley, J.P., of Pyrton, near Guildford, Western Australia. They had no children.

[Forrest's *Explorations in Australia*, 1876; A. W. Jose, *History of Australasia*, 1921; H. G. Turner, *First Decade of the Australian Commonwealth*, 1911; Commonwealth *Parliamentary Debates*; personal knowledge.]
A. B. K.

FORTESCUE, GEORGE KNOTTESFORD (1847–1912), librarian, the fourth son of Edward Bowes Knottesford Fortescue, provost of St. Ninian's Cathedral, Perth, by his wife, Frances Anne, daughter of William Spooner, archdeacon of Coventry and rector of Elmdon, Warwickshire, was born at Alveston Manor, Warwickshire, 30 October 1847. After a short stay at St. Mary's College, Harlow, an anglo-catholic school where his high spirits brought him into trouble, he went to sea in the merchant service and then in the royal navy. In 1870 he entered the department of printed books in the British Museum, on the nomination of Archbishop Tait, his mother's brother-in-law. Though not a student he had great abilities and a sailor's quickness and versatility. He thus soon made his mark and became an expert on the French Revolution, from cataloguing the Museum collection of its pamphlets. In December 1884 he succeeded Richard Garnett [q. v.] as superintendent of the reading-room, and promptly began, mainly in his private time, to compile a subject-index of the modern books acquired since the titles of accessions were first printed (instead of transcribed) in 1880. He grasped at once the doctrine, which he continually preached, that headings must be chosen to fit books, not books classified under headings previously selected to cover the whole of human knowledge. His *Subject-Index* to the acquisitions of 1880–1885, published by the trustees in 1886, met the wants of readers, and its continuation in successive volumes to 1910 was his main achievement. It left him little energy for literary work, but he wrote the lives of eight of his ancestors for this DICTIONARY, besides a few articles and papers. In May 1899 he became keeper of printed books, and held this office (despite much ill-health) till his death on 26 October 1912, four days before he was due to retire. In 1908 he had edited a catalogue of the books and newspapers relating to the Civil War and the Commonwealth, collected by George Thomason [q. v.] and given to the Museum by George III, and became almost as much interested in these as in the French Revolution pamphlets. He was president of the Library Association (1901) and of the Bibliographical Society (1909–1910). In 1906 he received an honorary LL.D. from the university of Aberdeen. He married: first, in 1875 Ida, daughter of the Rev. William Blatch, incumbent of St. John's (episcopal) church, Perth; and secondly, in 1899 Beatrice, widow of H. Webster Jones, M.D. He had no children.

[Henry Jenner, *George Knottesford Fortescue: A Memory*, reprinted from *The Library*, 1913; personal knowledge.]
A. W. P.

FOWLER, WILLIAM WARDE (1847–1921), historian and ornithologist, born at Langford Budville, Somerset, 16 May 1847, was the second son of John Coke Fowler, stipendiary magistrate at Merthyr Tydfil and afterwards at Swansea, by his first wife, Augusta Bacon, granddaughter of John Bacon, R.A. [q.v.]. After two years at the school of the Rev. F. Kilvert at Bath, and tuition from his father, he went in 1860 to Marlborough

College, where the teaching of Francis Edward Thompson developed his powers. He entered New College, Oxford, in 1866, and after a term won a scholarship at Lincoln College, where he gained much from contact with Mark Pattison, the rector, and Henry Nettleship. After taking a second class in classical moderations in 1868 and a first class in 'greats' in 1870, he became fellow of Lincoln College in 1872, and tutor in 1873, undertaking the teaching of Roman history for his own college and Oriel. He was sub-rector from 1881 to 1906, and during that time had a leading influence in the college. Remaining tutor till 1910, he then retired to Kingham, where, since 1873, he had enjoyed a country home and entertained his pupils; there he lived with his sister Alice, and after her death in 1917, with his two younger sisters, until his death, 14 June 1921. His love and pursuit of music were lifelong: Mozart was his favourite composer. His other recreations were walking, fishing, and, in early days, climbing, always with an eye alert for the lie of the land and for everything around him. Country life, the manners of men and of animals, were his constant study. By long and patient observation, overcoming defects of sight and hearing, he became an authority on birds and their migrations, and made a special contribution to the life-history of the marsh-warbler. He loved birds and led others to love and observe them. In his books on birds and in *Kingham, Old and New* (1913) he is a Gilbert White, with equal charm and more scientific knowledge. Deafness made him retiring, but his solitude was always shared by a dog or enlivened by music and the reading of Shakespeare, Scott, Dickens, or Jane Austen.

A familiar figure in Oxford, Warde Fowler shrank from public affairs, but enjoyed being a curator of the Parks and of the Botanic Garden. His ideal of a university is expressed in *An Oxford Correspondence* (1903), which suggests that the Oxford tutorial system needs enrichment by some element of German 'research' methods, and it was enforced by his practice as a tutor, which was to question his pupils and set them thinking and searching, and not to hand them ready-made opinions. Thus he formed true scholars and made lasting friendships. His central occupation was Rome, especially Rome of the Republic. By tuition, by lectures, and by books he inspired his audience and advanced knowledge. Alive to the constitutional issues, he found his chief interest in the personal and national life of Rome. Combining political sense with historic imagination, and working on a thorough knowledge of the classical texts and their interpretation, he formed conclusions which carried conviction. 'He knew what a Roman thought', it was said. His most original work is to be found in his writings on Roman religion: the *Roman Festivals of the Period of the Republic* (1899), the Gifford lectures on the *Religious Experience of the Roman People* (1911), and a supplementary work, *Roman Ideas of Deity* (1914). Tracing the process by which the animism of an agricultural people developed into a formal religion remote from conduct, he found in the Augustan revival 'an appeal to the conscience of the people'. He threw new light on the development of particular cults, weighing evidence impartially, with no preconceived theory and with a true religious sense. His handling of special questions here and in his *Roman Essays and Interpretations* (1920) showed the insight into Roman character and grasp of Roman history as a whole which illuminate his *Social Life at Rome in the Age of Cicero* (1909). His constant communications with scholars in many fields and his wide range of interests gave a vital flavour to writing which had distinction and charm. Nothing was more characteristic than his many-sidedness; rich in varied knowledge—history, anthropology, music, birds—he brought it all to bear on the subject in hand. His three studies of the *Aeneid* (1915–1919), in which his ripe knowledge is blended with a fine sense of poetry, achieved a masterpiece of interpretation which gave new life and interest to Virgil's conception of Aeneas. These and the *Essays in Brief for Wartime* (1916) were the fruit of a gracious old age, and they reveal the man: a character in which humanity and a love of truth and justice were the dominant qualities; gentle, but roused to anger by injustice or meanness; lovable, and saved from pedantry by humour and a just sense of values. A good portrait by Alexander Macdonald hangs in Lincoln College hall.

[*Reminiscences*, printed for private circulation, 1921; W. Warde Fowler, *Kingham, Old and New*, 1913; articles by 'E' in *Oxford Magazine*, 20 October 1921, by Bernard W. Henderson in *Fortnightly Review*, January 1922, and by J. Huxley in *British Birds*, xv, 6; personal knowledge.] P. E. M.

FRASER, ALEXANDER CAMPBELL (1819–1914), philosopher, was the eldest son of the Rev. Hugh Fraser, parish minister of Ardchattan, Argyllshire, by his wife, Maria Helen, younger daughter of Alexander Campbell, the neighbouring laird of Barcaldine. Born at the manse of Ardchattan 3 September 1819, in the last year of the reign of George III, he was able at the end of his life to say that he had lived under six British sovereigns. At the age of fourteen he entered the university of Glasgow, but after a single session there was transferred for reasons of health to Edinburgh. There he heard Sir William Hamilton's inaugural lecture as professor of logic and metaphysics in 1836, and later on became a member of his advanced class and attended Dr. Thomas Chalmers's lectures on divinity in preparation for the ministry of the Church of Scotland. Scotland was at that time plunged in the ecclesiastical controversies which, in 1843, rent the church in two. When the disruption took place Fraser, following the example of his teacher and of his own father, threw in his lot with the seceders, and was ordained in 1844 as junior minister of the Free church of Cramond, a small country charge close to Edinburgh. Two years later the establishment of a chair of logic and metaphysics in the theological college of the Free Church in Edinburgh opened up to him the academic career in which he was to find his true vocation. He held this position for ten years till Hamilton's death (1856) threw open the university professorship, to which Fraser was elected after a keen contest with James Frederick Ferrier He made a reputation from the first as a stimulating teacher, and during these years he also became known to wider circles as editor, from 1850 to 1857, of the *North British Review*. His own earliest contributions to philosophical literature appeared in that *Review*, and were collected and published in 1856 as *Essays in Philosophy* in connexion with his candidature for the university chair.

Fraser's thought matured slowly, and his literary output during the next ten years amounted only to a slim volume expanding an introductory lecture—*Rational Philosophy in History and System* (1858)—and four or five articles in the reviews. Two of these, however, dealing with Berkeley, led to an invitation from the Clarendon Press to edit the works of that philosopher. Fraser was fortunate enough to unearth a real philosophical treasure in the shape of the commonplace book kept by Berkeley during the early years at Trinity College, Dublin, when his new theory of the material world was first shaping itself in his mind. Enriched with this and other unpublished matter, the edition of the *Works* in three volumes, accompanied by a volume of *Life and Letters*, appeared in 1871 and at once made Fraser's name a household word wherever English philosophy is studied. A volume of *Selections from Berkeley*, largely used in the universities, was published in 1874, and in 1881 Fraser contributed to Blackwood's series of philosophical classics a charming sketch of Berkeley's life and thought in which he utilized fresh material and outlined more firmly his own philosophical position. His work on Berkeley led him back to a closer study of Locke as the fountainhead of English philosophy, and the results were given to the world in the *Encyclopaedia Britannica* article on Locke (1882), in a volume on Locke (1890), companion to his *Berkeley*, in Blackwood's series, and finally in an elaborate edition of the *Essay concerning Human Understanding* with prolegomena and notes (1894).

In 1891 Fraser resigned his chair after a thirty-five years' tenure. He had taken an active part in the business and administration of the university as dean of the faculty of arts since 1859, and as representative of the senatus in the university court from 1877; but his chief work was in the class-room, where he left behind him the reputation of a great teacher. He possessed a notable power of awakening the philosophic interest in his students. Doubts and questions were presented to them rather than solutions. The mystery of the world was emphasized, but faith in an intellectual and moral harmony was kept alive. Intellectual eagerness and reverent feeling were thus happily combined, and an unusual number of his pupils became themselves philosophical teachers and writers.

Although Fraser was seventy-two when he retired, the main harvest of his own thought was still to be garnered. His appointment (1894–1896) as Gifford lecturer on natural theology in his old university enabled him to give independent expression for the first time to the slowly matured convictions of a lifetime. He was fond of describing his position as a *via media* between the agnosticism which would limit man's knowledge to the ascertained uniformities of physical science and the too daring gnosticism (as he called it by way of contrast) of Hegelian idealism, which seemed to him to claim a species of omniscience that would banish all mystery from the universe.

Himself not without an infusion of the sceptical temperament, he insisted strongly on the element of faith which must lie at the basis of all our conclusions. Our reliance on the constancy of physical law itself rests ultimately, he insisted, on a faith in the moral trustworthiness of the universe. This species of moral trust is the only alternative to universal scepticism. Fraser's own standpoint is, therefore, that of a theism based upon moral faith. His Gifford lectures on *The Philosophy of Theism* (1895–1896) were an impressive handling of the philosophical problem from this point of view. They were followed in 1898 by a little volume on Thomas Reid [q.v.], the father of Scottish philosophy. In 1904 he published, under the title *Biographia Philosophica*, an interesting retrospect of his long life, in which personal reminiscence is happily combined with a meditative restatement of his philosophical results. Still later, in an article in the *Hibbert Journal* for January 1907 entitled characteristically *Our Final Venture*, and in a little volume on *Berkeley and Spiritual Realism* (1908), he returned to present in short compass his fundamental positions. Fraser was in his ninety-second year when he laid down his pen. He died in Edinburgh 2 December 1914, his mental faculties unimpaired to the end and his bodily senses as keen as those of a young man.

Fraser married in 1850 Jemima Gordon, daughter of Dr. William Dyce, of Fonthill and Cuttlehill, Aberdeenshire, and sister of William Dyce, R.A. [q.v.]. They had three sons and two daughters. Fraser was buried beside his wife in Lasswade churchyard, not far from Gorton House, near Hawthornden, their home after his retirement until her death in 1907. Among the many academic honours which he received were honorary degrees from the universities of Glasgow (1871), Oxford (1883), Edinburgh (1891), and Dublin (1902); in 1903 he was elected fellow of the British Academy.

[Memorial notice by A. S. Pringle-Pattison in *Proceedings* of the British Academy, vol. vi; article in *Mind*, new series, vol. xxiv; personal knowledge.] A. S. P-P.

FRASER, Sir ANDREW HENDERSON LEITH (1848–1919), Indian civil servant, was born at Bombay 14 November 1848, the grandson of an unsuccessful claimant to the Lovat peerage, and the eldest son of the Rev. Alexander Garden Fraser, D.D., Presbyterian missionary, by his wife, Joanna Maria, daughter of the Rev. John Shaw, a minister in Skye who came of a family of Dalnaglar, Glenshee, Perthshire. After a brilliant career at Edinburgh Academy and University, Fraser passed the open examination for the Indian civil service in 1869, and was posted two years later to the Central Provinces, where he served for the next twenty-seven years, holding almost every local executive post of distinction. He was also a member of the hemp-drugs commission (1893–1894). In 1898 he was about to retire after a prominent but not exceptional career, when his ready pen and his gifts as a public speaker attracted the notice of the viceroy, Lord Curzon, who appointed him first to officiate as secretary in the home department and shortly afterwards as chief commissioner of the Central Provinces. Three years later he was selected to be president of the commission on the Indian police; and in November 1903 Lord Curzon promoted him to the lieutenant-governorship of Bengal, having kept that great office without a permanent incumbent for more than a year in order that Fraser might fill it without being prematurely taken away from the commission. He received the K.C.S.I. on appointment.

More than three-quarters of Fraser's Indian service was spent in the Central Provinces before their union with Berar (1903) and the industrial development of subsequent years had transformed that administration. Under the conditions then prevailing, though he sometimes laid himself open to the criticism of giving his confidence too freely, he undoubtedly acquired a very close first-hand knowledge of Indian village life and of the problems of district administration, a knowledge which was turned to account in the invaluable reforms which his commission was able to propose in the police systems of India. No branch of government touches more intimately the lives of the people; and the improvement in the efficiency and honesty of the police is Fraser's most substantial claim to remembrance.

No part of India, however, was more different from the Central Provinces than Bengal, where in 1903 the lieutenant-governor ruled, single-handed and with an inadequate and inelastic revenue, a population of over eighty millions. Fraser's personal charm was at a discount in a province so large that none but a minority even of his own officers could be in direct contact with him; and his anxiety to satisfy every claim that came before him gave more frequent offence than blunt refusals might have done. He lacked, also, the knack of dazzling the public eye. But the task before him was one to sap the health and expose the weak points even of the very strongest. Moreover, the partition of 1905, intended to lighten, increased the burden by the violent agitation to which it gave rise. Fraser did not originate the method of partition that was adopted; indeed, he criticized it to good effect before its adoption. But he probably hesitated to oppose a scheme which his patron, Lord Curzon, was believed to be promoting. He fully appreciated the strength of the vested interests affected, but he did not believe in the local nationalism which, as it turned out, those vested interests were able to exploit. The question was to him merely one of administrative convenience; personal modesty prevented him from realizing that the lieutenant-governor could be a symbol of national unity; his own mind was not liable to be moved by illogical sentiment, which accordingly did not enter into his estimate of the problem.

The partition became law: and in meeting the storm which arose Fraser was handicapped by a liberal dislike for all repressive measures: but he gave a fine example of personal courage in the face of repeated attempts on his own life, an example well followed not only by the British but also by the Indian public servants of the province. In 1907 Fraser was chosen moderator of the Presbyterian Church assembly in India, an honour particularly acceptable to him in view of his father's sixty years of active missionary work in India. He retired in November 1908 and settled in the highlands of Scotland. He published a book of reminiscences, *Among Indian Rajahs and Ryots* (1911), was a frequent contributor to the reviews, and, especially during the European War, discharged numerous honorary administrative offices. In 1919 he gave in the press a qualified and hesitating approval to the Montagu-Chelmsford scheme. He died in Edinburgh 26 February 1919.

Fraser was twice married: first, in 1872 to Agnes (died 1877), daughter of Robert Archibald, of Devonvale, Tillicoultry; secondly, in 1883 to Henrietta Catherine Lucy, daughter of Colonel Harry Ibbotson Lugard, Indian army and Central Provinces commission. There were one son and one daughter of the first marriage, and three sons of the second, all of whom, with his second wife, survived him.

[*The Times*, 27 February 1919; *The Statesman* (Calcutta), November 1908; *Report* of the Indian Police Commission, 1903; Blue Book on the Partition of Bengal, 1905; Sir A. H. L. Fraser, *Among Indian Rajahs and Ryots*; private information.] S. V. FG.

FRASER, CLAUD LOVAT (1890–1921), artist and designer, the elder son of Claud Fraser, solicitor, of the Red House, Buntingford, Hertfordshire, by his wife, Florence Margaret Walsh, was born in London 15 May 1890. He was educated at Charterhouse, and in 1908 entered into articles of clerkship in his father's office. The year 1911, however, found him freed from the law and at work at the Westminster School of Art. By 1912 he had already begun an independent career, and he found almost at once a style for the expression of his art from which he never really departed. His work at this period included drawings of theatrical characters and scenes, and decorations for chap-books and broadsides, which were published under the title *Flying Fame* (1913). Judged by their imaginative quality, these latter designs are perhaps the most important which he achieved. On the outbreak of the European War in 1914 Fraser joined the army, and in 1916 was invalided home from Flanders. In 1919 he held the first representative exhibition of his work, and established his reputation. In the next year his designs for the settings and costumes of *As You Like It* and *The Beggar's Opera*, produced at the Lyric Theatre, Hammersmith, brought him unusual fame, and from this time onwards he produced innumerable designs for the theatre. He made a close study also of the various approaches to process-reproduction in colour, and this resulted in a prolific output by him of booklets, rhyme sheets, end papers, trade cards, and similar matter. He had realized early the importance of visualizing design and type together as an inseparable whole; and the methods which he came to employ in his printed and published work exercised a considerable influence. Among the later books which he decorated, *Poems from the Works of Charles Cotton* (1922) and *The Luck of the Bean-Rows* by Charles Nodier (1921) are notable examples. He made designs for other theatrical productions, such as *La Serva Padrona*, Lord Dunsany's *If*, two ballets for Madame Tamar Karsavina, and Gustav Holst's *Savitri*.

Fraser's inspiration was gathered from the past rather than from contemporary life, and especially from the eighteenth and early nineteenth centuries. His work stands for a gay, brightly coloured romanticism. His personality was attractive; he enjoyed many friendships, and he was devoted to his family. He married in 1917 Grace Inez, daughter of Theron Clark Crawford, journalist and author, a citizen of the United States, and had one daughter. He died at Sandgate 18 June 1921, and was buried at Buntingford.

[Haldane Macfall, *The Book of Lovat Claud Fraser*, 1923; John Drinkwater and Albert Rutherston, *Claud Lovat Fraser*, 1923; private information; personal knowledge.]

A. D. R.

FRASER, Sir THOMAS RICHARD (1841–1920), pharmacologist, born at Calcutta 5 February 1841, was the second son of John Fraser, of the Indian civil service, by his wife, Mary Fraser (a cousin). Educated at public schools in Scotland, he afterwards studied medicine at Edinburgh University, and in 1862 obtained the degree of M.D., with gold medal, for a thesis 'On the Characters, Actions, and Therapeutic Uses of the Ordeal Bean of Calabar (*Physostigma venenosum*)'. This early thesis, describing a brilliant and mature investigation, immediately placed him in the front rank of pharmacologists. He continued his researches as assistant (1864–1870) to Sir Robert Christison [q.v.] and in 1869 was appointed assistant physician to the Royal Infirmary, a post which he held till 1874. In 1877 he succeeded Christison as professor of materia medica in the university of Edinburgh, combining with it, as was then customary, a professorship of clinical medicine. For the long period of forty years, until his retirement in 1917, he filled this double rôle, teaching and researching both in the university laboratories of pharmacology and in the wards of the infirmary. He became also a valued consulting physician.

In these spheres Fraser, who was elected F.R.S. in 1877, attained a pre-eminent position. His pharmacological researches were of the first importance. His investigations of the actions of *physostigma* and of *strophanthus* were largely instrumental in introducing these two important remedies into medical practice. His publications, in conjunction with Professor Alexander Crum Brown, on the relation between the chemical constitution and physiological action of drugs laid much more than the foundations of this fundamental domain of pharmacological inquiry, while his researches on antagonism of poisons formed a model, new in design and convincing in accuracy, for future researches. Of his many other pharmacological and medical publications, those on arrow poisons, snake poisons, and immunity, were most important. Though he contributed less to the advancement of clinical medicine, his influence as a physician was considerable. In particular, the habits of accurate observation and of precision of language, which his trained mind imposed, had a lasting effect on generations of students. His writings, as well as his spoken word, were characterized not only by originality of outlook, but by a rare lucidity and dignity.

Fraser was chairman of the Indian plague commission (1898–1901), and president of the Royal College of Physicians of Edinburgh (1900–1902) and of the Association of Physicians of Great Britain and Ireland (1908–1909). He was knighted in 1902 and was appointed honorary physician-in-ordinary to the King in Scotland in 1907. In 1874 he married Susanna Margaret, daughter of the Rev. R. Duncan, by whom he had eight sons (one of whom is professor of medicine in the university of London) and three daughters. In the latter half of his life he was much troubled by a bronchial affection which he endured and disregarded with great fortitude. He survived his retirement, with his habitual keenness of mind and of expression unblunted, for three years, and died in Edinburgh 4 January 1920.

[*Gallerie hervorragender Therapeutiker und Pharmacognosten* (early portrait and bibliography); *British Medical Journal*, 17 January 1920; *Edinburgh Medical Journal*, xxiv, 122 (portrait), 1920; *Proceedings* of the Royal Society, vol. xcii, B, 1921 (portrait); private information; personal knowledge.] J. A. G.

FREEMAN-MITFORD, ALGERNON BERTRAM, first Baron Redesdale, of the second creation (1837–1916), diplomatist and author. [See Mitford.]

FREYER, Sir PETER JOHNSTON (1851–1921), surgeon, the eldest son of Samuel Freyer, farmer, of Sellerna, a village eight miles from Clifden, Connemara, by his wife, Celia Burke, also of Sellerna, was born there 21 July 1851. He received his early education at Erasmus Smith's College, Galway, and at Queen's College, Galway, then one of the constituent colleges of the Queen's University of Ireland. In 1872 he graduated in arts, with first-class honours and the gold medal, and then went to Dublin to study medicine at Steevens's Hospital, where he was a resident pupil of Robert McDonnell [q.v.]. He spent a short time in Paris and in 1874 he took the degrees of M.D. and M.S. of the Queen's University, again winning the gold medal. In 1886 he was awarded the degree of M.A., *honoris causa*, by the Royal University of Ireland which had succeeded the Queen's University.

Freyer gained first place in the examination for the Indian medical service in 1875, becoming surgeon-major in 1887, lieutenant-colonel in 1895, and retiring from the service in 1896. Being in the Bengal army he served chiefly in the North-Western (afterwards the United) Provinces of India, and was for a time surgeon to the Prince of Wales's Hospital at Benares. Here he gained much experience in operating for cataract and in crushing stones in the bladder by the method of litholapaxy which was introduced in 1878 by Henry Jacob Bigelow, of Boston, Massachusetts.

Returning to England in 1897 Freyer was appointed surgeon to St. Peter's Hospital for Stone, Henrietta Street, London, and originated the operation of total and complete removal of the prostate gland through a suprapubic incision of the bladder. He published his first four cases in 1901 (*British Medical Journal*, ii, 125, 1901) and the results of his first thousand cases in 1912 (ibid., p. 869, 1912). He was awarded the Arnott memorial medal in 1904 for his work in this branch of surgery, and in 1920 was elected the first president of the newly constituted section of urology at the Royal Society of Medicine. Freyer rejoined the Indian medical service on the outbreak of the European War in 1914, but was employed in England as consulting surgeon to Queen Alexandra's military hospital at Millbank, London, and to the Eastern command. He received the C.B. in January 1917 and was promoted K.C.B. in the following June. He was placed on the retired list with the rank of colonel, I.M.S., in 1919. He died in London 9 September 1921, and was buried in the protestant cemetery at Clifden, county Galway. He had married in 1876 Isabella (died 1914), daughter of Robert McVittie, of Dublin, and by her had two children, a son and a daughter (married to Lieutenant-Colonel John Duncan Grant, V.C.). A three-quarter length portrait of Freyer hangs in the board room of St. Peter's Hospital, Henrietta Street, London.

Freyer was the author of the following works: *The Modern Treatment of Stone in the Bladder by Litholapaxy* (1886, second edition 1896), *Stricture of the Urethra and Prostatic Enlargement* (1901, third edition 1906), *Surgical Diseases of the Urinary Organs* (1908).

[*The Times*, 10 September 1921; *The Lancet*, 1921, vol. ii, p. 677; *The British Medical Journal*, 1921, vol. ii, p. 464; private information; personal knowledge.] D'A. P.

FRIESE-GREENE, WILLIAM (1855–1921), pioneer of kinematography. [See Greene, William Friese-.]

FRY, Sir EDWARD (1827–1918), judge, was born in Union Street, Bristol, 4 November 1827. He was the second son of Joseph Fry (1795–1879), the sixth in descent from Zephaniah Fry, a member of a Wessex family long established at Corston, near Malmesbury, who followed George Fox and was imprisoned as a recalcitrant quaker in 1684. Edward Fry's paternal great-grandfather, Joseph Fry [q.v.], abandoned medicine for business; the latter's son, Edmund Fry [q.v.], who also abandoned medicine for trade, was the most learned type-founder of his day. Joseph Fry, the father of Edward, was an omnivorous reader with strong free-trade, liberal, religious, and philanthropic interests; his wife, Mary Ann, daughter of Edward Swaine, of Henley-on-Thames, traveller for a firm of druggists, was an able, self-confident, buoyant woman, with very strong quaker convictions, very decisive judgements in practical matters, and a love of poetry. Edward's father and his quaker friends instilled into the boy an intense love of observation, and a lifelong interest in scenery, animals, and more especially plants—'which, I hope, prevented my growing into a mere lawyer'. His earliest recollections were of the Bristol riots of 1831. His home education included Latin, French, and German. The study of Greek was postponed, against his wish, till he had to prepare for Bristol College in 1841. There he and his elder brother, Joseph Storrs Fry [q.v.], were ridiculed at first for their quaker dress and language. Edward at once made his mark and gained a medal for English verse. The college, however, was closed and Dr. James Booth [q.v.], the head master, opened a private school. Edward records that at the age of fourteen he greedily devoured

Berkeley's *New Theory of Vision*, with a permanent effect on his outlook on matter. With Walter Bagehot, who was at the same school, he formed a fruitful and stimulating friendship.

At the end of 1842 schooldays were over, and from 1843 till he went to London in October 1848 Fry was in business and acquired a practical knowledge of accountancy and shipbroking. He did not take to a mercantile life, but he found time to read widely in the classics, literature, and history, and actually wrote at the age of nineteen *A Treatise of the Elective Monarchies of Europe* (1846). In the spring of the same year he sent to the Zoological Society of London a paper on *The Osteology of the Hylobates agilis*, based on a remarkable specimen which had lived in the Clifton Zoological Gardens. This paper and another on *The relations of the Edentata to the Reptiles, especially of the Armadilloes to the Tortoises*, were published by the society. He worked very hard at zoology, and in 1849 in the London matriculation examination secured the prize for that subject, beating (Sir) William Henry Flower who was to become the head of the Natural History Museum at South Kensington. But he was also interested in the study of the osteology of the skull, having seen fossil bones at Weston-super-Mare as early as 1838, and he worked with William Budd [q.v.], who encouraged his surgical enthusiasms. Fry also found time for thought on the subjects of free trade and education, and as the result of a continental tour in 1848 contributed an article on *Germany in 1848* to the *London University Magazine*.

After this visit Fry decided to go to the bar, and with this in view he entered University College, London, where Thomas Hodgkin and Walter Bagehot were fellow-students. After making a brilliant mark at the college, he took his B.A. degree in 1851. He entered the chambers first of Bevan Braithwaite, the conveyancer, then of Edward Bullen, the eminent special pleader in the Temple, and lastly of (Sir) Charles Hall, the equity draughtsman, and was called to the bar at Lincoln's Inn in 1854. The beginning was not auspicious. He was called at a moment when family financial affairs had been giving temporary anxiety, and for a long period briefs failed to flow in. But he was working all the while, and soon after the publication (1858) of his well-known book, *A Treatise on the Specific Performance of Contracts*, the tide began to turn. Fry, in the time of probation, also produced a volume, *Essays on the Accordance of Christianity with the Nature of Man* (1857), which secured the approval of Baron von Bunsen, who expressed surprise that there was any one in England who would write such a book.

The early years in London from 1848 to 1859 were haunted by fear of failure. Fry's tastes were austere and his judgement too well balanced for him to entertain what seemed like false hopes. But sadness and fear of failure ended when he married in the Friends' meeting-house at Lewes in 1859 Mariabella, daughter of the quaker barrister, John Hodgkin [q.v.]. It was about this time that Fry discarded the external peculiarities of quakerism as not being really connected with religious life. In 1859 he issued a pamphlet on this subject.

From 1859 until he was raised to the bench in 1877 Fry acquired a steadily growing practice, not only in Chancery and company work but at the parliamentary bar. He took silk in 1869 and joined the court of Vice-Chancellor James, competing with (Sir) Richard Paul Amphlett and (Sir) Edward Ebenezer Kay, who, like himself, were later to sit in the Court of Appeal. He quickly made his mark by a convincing argument in a company case in which he was opposed by Lord Westbury, Sir Roundell Palmer, and others. He succeeded and was warmly congratulated by his opponents. When James became a lord justice, Fry practised for a time before Vice-Chancellor Bacon, but eventually migrated to the Rolls court, presided over by Lord Romilly and, after 1873, by Sir George Jessel. But pressure of work in the House of Lords made it necessary for him soon to 'go special'. This did not long have the desired effect, and his work was greatly on the increase when, in April 1877, he was offered by Lord Cairns the additional judgeship in the Chancery division authorized that year by statute. He accepted the offer with considerable misgiving, and characteristically set to work to put in writing his conceptions of his new duties. His precepts are worthy of study by all judges. Fry was the first judge appointed after the Judicature Act had merged the high court of Chancery in the High Court, the first Chancery judge to bear the title of Mr. Justice and to go circuit. His knighthood followed in the usual form. He at first dreaded the circuit work, but came to like it, and impressed the bar with his judicial versatility.

Probably Fry's principal legal achievement took place before he passed in 1883, on the death of Sir George Jessel, to the court of appeal. The Judicature Acts of 1873 and 1875, in addition to the reorganization of the courts, had provided a body of rules to regulate practice in the separate divisions of the new High Court. After some years these rules needed revision as the result of experience, and it was also necessary to provide a comparatively inexpensive machinery enabling trustees, executors, and beneficiaries to secure necessary judicial aid without the ruinous costs of an administration suit, often enough undertaken for the sake of the costs. Fry was on the rule committee of the judges, and with respect to this particular evil he regarded his work as one of the best actions of his life. In fact 'he invented the procedure by originating summons which effected a beneficial revolution'. Lord Cozens-Hardy [q.v.] also says that the gradual development of the new system of practice which replaced the old practice of the high court of Chancery might almost be called the invention of Fry.

From 1883 to Whitsuntide 1892 Fry sat in the Court of Appeal with, among others, Lord Esher, Lords Justices Baggallay, Cotton, Lindley, and Bowen. Lord Esher tried Fry's patience and temper sometimes, but on the whole these two very different men got on well enough, while the relations between Fry and Lindley and Bowen were the happiest possible. Sir Alfred Hopkinson [*Memoir of Sir Edward Fry*, p. 81] says that Lindley, Bowen, and Fry together 'contributed invaluable work in the development of English case law at a time when there was a special need for men who possessed such qualities as his [Fry's] for dealing with the new conditions then arising'. The same writer says of Fry, 'no better example of this power to master fully the most complicated facts, to state the relevant matter clearly, to draw from a long series of precedents the true principles to guide a decision and to apply them fearlessly, can be given than the judgment delivered by him and adopted as the judgment of the whole Court of Appeal in the Banstead Common case' (*Robertson* v. *Hartopp*, 1889).

Sir Edward Fry decided to retire in 1892 on the completion of his fifteen years on the bench. Actually there was a quarter of a century of active life before him and he was at the height of his judicial powers. He was somewhat weary of the noise and turmoil of the courts and longed to live permanently in the country with more leisure for reading and travel. The Frys left London for their country home at Failand, near Clifton. There the ex-judge sat in the local court of petty sessions, and from 1899 to 1913 took the chair of quarter sessions and an aldermanship of the Somerset county council. He was eighty-six when he retired from this work. From time to time he also sat on the Judicial Committee of the Privy Council.

Various estimates exist of the judicial capacity of Sir Edward Fry. Probably the final estimate will be that he was a great judge, though his abilities were never tested by a seat in the House of Lords. Infinitely painstaking and versatile to an unusual degree, with a very large range of knowledge, he combined a passion for seeking out first principles and for doing justice, with a fixed determination not to move out of the ambit of the case as limited by the facts before him. His strictly logical mind in these circumstances tended not only to limit the application of a judgment, but to rely on a somewhat technical view of the facts and of the law. He was working in a difficult period of transition from the old practice to the new, and his type of mind was of peculiar value in the period 1877 to 1892. In the House of Lords he might have given freer scope to his passion for first principles than was possible in the new Supreme Court. When he was free of highly technical civil procedure he was, whether in cases at quarter sessions or in his writings on legal themes, capable of the longest outlook. Probably, when the history of English law for the period falls into perspective, it will be found that Fry did more than any other lawyer, with perhaps the exception of Lord Cairns, to secure perfect continuity in the adaptation, under purified conditions of civil procedure, of the rules of law to modern social conditions.

Fry's later life was one of singular and beneficent activity. He took more than four years of leisure and travel, and then, when on the verge of seventy years, he plunged once more into the turmoil of work. He accepted in 1897 the offer to preside over the royal commission on the Irish Land Acts, an office which he filled with such capacity, knowledge, and tact that his services were at once widely called upon. In 1898 he acted as conciliator, under the Conciliation Act of 1896, in the colliery strike of South Wales and Monmouth, and, although the conciliation failed, his report led to the termination of the strike; the men had full confidence in him. In 1901 he acted as arbitrator in the Grimsby fishery dispute; in 1902 he sat as president on the court of arbitration connected with the water companies of London. His remuneration for this heavy work was £5,000, of which he returned over £3,000 as he declined to receive more than would have made up his salary if he had been sitting as a lord justice. In 1906 and 1907 he acted as arbitrator between the London and North Western Railway Company and its men, and issued an award (February 1909) that worked smoothly and well for a time. He declined any fee for 'the most tiresome piece of business which I ever transacted'.

In the meantime Fry was brought into touch with international affairs in 1902–1903 by acting as arbitrator at the Hague between the United States and Mexico in the pious funds of California dispute, the first case to be brought before the Hague tribunal created by the first Hague Conference of 1899. In November 1900 he had been given a place on the list of judges for this court. The five arbitrators, after some difficulties, settled and issued their award. Fry's next task was to act as the British legal assessor on the commission appointed to deal with the North Sea (Dogger Bank) incident in October 1904, when the Russian fleet attacked in a moment of panic the British herring fleet—an incident that threatened war. Fry's work on the commission—the findings of which upheld the British case—was highly commended. He played an active part at the second Hague Conference of 1907, when he was the doyen of the conference as ambassador extraordinary and first plenipotentiary delegate of Great Britain. Fry, although an octogenarian, made his personality felt; he took a leading part in the debates, and was entrusted by the British government with the duty of raising the question of the limitation of armaments and of making the offer that Great Britain would exchange information with any other nation on the subject of naval construction. In the next year he again acted at the Hague as one of the arbitrators in the quarrel between France and Germany over the Casablanca incident. In May 1909 the award was made, and the two nations acted on it and exchanged apologies according to the sentence of the court.

The remaining nine years of Fry's life were occupied with the various pursuits, literary, scientific, and educational, in which he delighted. His interest in the university of London lasted for nearly half a century. He joined the council of University College during the busiest of his years at the bar, and strove hard and successfully to secure a teaching university for London. He did much on the senate of the university to bring into the university all the institutions of high educational character in the metropolis. The scheme which eventually was adopted was not very different from that for which he had always striven. His efforts were not limited to London. In 1906 he presided over a commission to inquire into the condition of Trinity College, Dublin, and of the Royal University of Ireland with a view to the solution of the problem of university education in Ireland. He dissented from the main report, and the view taken by himself, Sir Arthur W. Rücker, and (Sir) J. G. Butcher that the ancient foundation of Trinity College should be preserved was accepted by Mr. Birrell when he became chief secretary in 1907.

Fry, who on two occasions declined the offer of a peerage, was created G.C.B. in 1907; he was also elected fellow of the Royal Society (1883) and honorary fellow of Balliol College, Oxford (1894). He died 18 October 1918 at Failand. He had nine children, two sons and seven daughters, of whom one died at the age of four. Lady Fry survived him.

[The *Law Reports, passim*; J. B. Scott, *The Proceedings of the Hague Conferences*, 1920; Agnes Fry (daughter), *A Memoir of the Right Honourable Sir Edward Fry . . . compiled largely from an Autobiography* (containing a bibliography of his numerous publications from 1846 to 1913), 1921.]

J. E. G. de M.

FRY, JOSEPH STORRS (1826–1913), cocoa manufacturer and quaker philanthropist, was born in Union Street, Bristol, 6 August 1826, the eldest son of Joseph Fry, of Bristol, by his wife, Mary Ann, daughter of Edward Swaine, of Henley-on-Thames. A younger brother was the distinguished jurist, Sir Edward Fry [q.v.]. He was educated chiefly at home, but was at Bristol College for a short time. After learning business methods in an accountant's office, he entered the family business of cocoa and chocolate manufacture, established in Bristol in the middle of the eighteenth century by his great-grandfather, Joseph Fry [q.v.]. In 1855 he became a partner in the firm.

Fry's interest in local affairs of a religious and social character was deep and constant. For many years he conducted a brief service with the employees of the cocoa works, and in his will he left £42,000 to be distributed among them.

In 1871 he joined the Young Men's Christian Association in Bristol, and he became president in 1877. In 1887 he was elected a member of the committee of the Bristol General Hospital, becoming later chairman, treasurer, and president. Up to the last few years of his life he visited the hospital every Christmas Eve and spoke to each patient at his bedside. In 1909 he became an honorary freeman of the city, and in 1912 the university of Bristol conferred on him the honorary degree of LL.D.

Fry was born a member of the Society of Friends and throughout his life gave ungrudging attention to its interests. He rose to the highest position in this religious body, being 'clerk' (or president) of the 'London Yearly Meeting' for fifteen years (1870–1875, 1881–1889), the longest period for which that office has been held by any individual since 1704. He was a preacher among the Friends and a pioneer in many organizations connected with their Sunday schools and home and foreign missions.

Fry's private life was singularly uneventful. The room which he occupied on the business premises to the end of his life was, he believed, the room in which he had been born. He lived with his mother for sixty years and never married. The things which usually interest men in his position—travel, politics, art, science, intercourse with nature—had no attraction for him. The distribution of his charities occupied no inconsiderable portion of his time and thought. He died 7 July 1913. The funeral was a remarkable demonstration of the esteem in which he was held by his fellow-citizens.

[The *Annual Monitor*, 1914; *Proceedings of London Yearly Meeting*, 1914; numerous magazine articles; manuscripts in Friends' Reference Library, Devonshire House, London; personal knowledge.] N. P.

FRYATT, CHARLES ALGERNON (1872–1916), merchant seaman, was born at Southampton 2 December 1872, the second son of Charles Fryatt, merchant seaman, by his wife, Mary Brown Percy. He first attended the Freemantle school in his native town, but was transferred to the corporation school at Harwich when his father removed to that port on entering the service of the Great Eastern Railway Company, in which he eventually rose to be a chief officer. Young Charles Fryatt adopted his father's calling, served his apprenticeship, and worked his way upward in large sailing-vessels till in 1892 he entered the service of the Great Eastern Railway as an able seaman on the paddle-steamer *Colchester*, which was then the company's latest passenger vessel and was engaged on the route between Harwich and Antwerp. This vessel he eventually commanded (1913), it being the practice of the company to select its officers from those in the lower ranks of its own service. The system stood the test of war conditions; in spite of the removal of guiding lights and buoys, under the constant menace of enemy warships, submarines, and mines, the company maintained a service between British and Low Country ports throughout the European War, Captain Fryatt himself making no fewer than 143 trips before he was captured by the enemy.

Fryatt's first encounter with an enemy vessel was on 2 March 1915, when, being in command of the chartered steamer *Wrexham*, he was chased for forty miles by a German submarine but eventually made Rotterdam in safety. His own skill and determination and the exertions of the engine- and boiler-room staffs were suitably recognized alike by the directors of the company and by the lords of the Admiralty. Captain Fryatt was now transferred to the Great Eastern Railway Company's s.s. *Brussels*, and on 28 March following was again attacked by a submarine, the U. 33. The enemy was sighted off the Maas light-vessel when four miles distant, and made direct for the mail steamer. Fryatt at once realized that the attacker was far speedier than his own ship. If, therefore, he attempted to get away he would soon be torpedoed; if he stopped in obedience to the enemy's signal he would make his ship an easier mark. He accordingly made up his mind to ram his enemy. He steered straight for the submarine, discharging rockets as he went, in order to call for any aid there might be in the neighbourhood and to make it appear that his ship had been supplied with guns. As the vessels approached, the U-boat submerged, and Captain Fryatt and others aboard the *Brussels* thought that the submarine was struck as they passed over her. In this they were mistaken; but the *Brussels* got safely away. For this exploit Captain Fryatt received from the Admiralty a gold watch 'in recognition of the example set by him when attacked by a German submarine'. In the following month the lords of the Admiralty, in a letter to the Great Eastern Railway Company, stated that the attention of the secretary for foreign affairs had been called to the 'highly courageous and meritorious conduct of the masters of the Company's steamers'. The commander of the *Wrexham* and of the *Brussels* was indicated amongst others, and the letter went on to express the Admiralty's thanks to the officers concerned for conduct 'which reflected credit on British seamanship'.

These well-earned recognitions, which naturally became generally known, seem to have led to Captain Fryatt's undoing. The Germans made long and careful preparations to capture him, intending to make an example which they fondly hoped would strike terror into his comrades under the red ensign. At length on the night of 22 June 1916, when the *Brussels* was homeward bound from the Hook of Holland, she was surrounded and captured by a considerable force of German destroyers, whose action showed that their commanders had obtained full information as to the ship's intended movements, probably from spies in Holland. The prize was taken into Zeebrugge and the master and crew sent on to Ruhleben internment camp, near Berlin. Captain Fryatt, however, was soon taken back to Belgium, where he was put on his trial before a court martial at Bruges on 27 July 1916 and condemned to death. Two days later he was shot, in spite of the protests of the United States minister, who had before the trial vainly attempted to secure adequate legal assistance for the prisoner. The charge laid against Captain Fryatt was that, not being a member of a combatant force, he had attempted to ram the submarine, U. 33. The official report of the trial characterized the prisoner as a *franc-tireur* of the sea, and laid stress on the approval of his conduct by the Admiralty and in the House of Commons as an aggravation of his alleged offence.

The deepest indignation was felt by all maritime peoples. The *franc-tireur* argument was seen to be wholly unfounded. It may be observed that a *franc-tireur* is a civilian who, without being attacked, picks off enemy soldiers unaware. Captain Fryatt was a civilian, but in no other respect comparable with a *franc-tireur*. In the House of Commons two days after the execution, Mr. Asquith, then prime minister, characterized the action of the German court martial as 'murder', and declared that 'His Majesty's government had heard with the utmost indignation of this atrocious crime against the law of nations and the usages of war'. More deliberate judgement in the calmer atmosphere of peace has in no way tended to alter opinion as to the gross illegality of the condemnation of Captain Fryatt.

Charles Fryatt married in 1896 Ethel Townend, who, with one son and six daughters, survived him. On his marriage he settled at Dovercourt, near Harwich. After the conclusion of peace his body was brought from Belgium to England on 7 July 1919 by a British war vessel, and buried at Dovercourt. A memorial service was held in St. Paul's Cathedral on 8 July.

[*The Times*, 9 July 1919; private information.]
B. W. G.

FURNESS, CHRISTOPHER, first BARON FURNESS, of Grantley (1852–1912), shipowner and industrialist, was born at West Hartlepool 23 April 1852. He was the seventh son of John Furness, provision merchant, of West Hartlepool, by his wife, Averill, daughter of John Wilson, of Naisbet Hall, co. Durham. Christopher Furness was privately educated and at an early age joined the firm of Thomas Furness & Co., wholesale provision merchants, of which an elder brother, Thomas, was a partner. During the Franco-German War Christopher proved his business ability when acting as agent for this firm in Norway and Sweden. It was at his suggestion that the firm began to use its own steamers in foreign trade. In 1877 the shipping business was separated from the provision business, the elder brother retaining the latter while Christopher set up as a shipowner under the style of Christopher Furness & Co. He next acquired the interest of the principal partner in the shipbuilding firm of Edward Withy & Co., of West Hartlepool. This, in 1891, was amalgamated with his shipping company, as Furness, Withy & Co., Limited. The amalgamation was the first step in a process by which many shipping and shipbuilding organizations, and many coal, steel, and iron undertakings, were linked and co-ordinated under Furness's guidance.

In 1891, on the death of Mr. Thomas Richardson, the unionist member for the Hartlepools, Furness successfully contested that constituency as a liberal and Home Ruler, defeating another local candidate, Sir William Gray; he held the seat successfully against Mr. Richardson's son and namesake (afterwards Sir Thomas Richardson) at the general election of 1892, but in 1895 he was defeated in the debacle of the liberal party. In 1898 he was an unsuccessful candidate for York city. In 1900 he was again elected for the Hartlepools, which he represented until the general election of 1910. Though he was re-elected on this occasion, he was unseated on petition owing to an irregularity on the part of his agent. His nephew, Mr. (afterwards Sir) Stephen Wilson Furness (died 1914), carried the seat at the consequent by-election and held it for the next four years. Furness was knighted in 1895 and in 1910 was created Baron Furness, of Grantley. In 1912 he was attacked by a serious illness to which he succumbed, dying on 10 November at Grantley Hall, near Ripon, after some months of suffering endured with characteristic fortitude.

In 1876 Furness married Jane Annette, only daughter of Henry Suggit, of Brierton, co. Durham, by whom he had one son, Marmaduke (born 1883), who succeeded him in his peerage and in his business interests and was created Viscount Furness in 1918.

Furness was a man of remarkable character, and possessed extraordinary powers of organization, which were always displayed at their best in times of stress and difficulty. He was extremely energetic and never spared himself. He was not popular in his own neighbourhood, or among business competitors; and his business methods were severely criticized. But to friends and associates he was singularly loyal. The outstanding feature of his career is the ability with which he applied the policy of integration and combination to the characteristic industries of the North-East coast.

[Private information.] H. W. C. D.

GAIRDNER, JAMES (1828–1912), historian, was born at Edinburgh 22 March 1828, the second son of John Gairdner, M.D. [q.v.]. Through his mother, Susan Tennant, he was, like Archbishop Maclagan [q.v.], a great-grandson of Dr. William Dalrymple, minister of Ayr, the 'Dalrymple mild' to whom Burns devotes a stanza in *The Kirk's Alarm.* Educated privately, in 1846 he obtained a clerkship in the then newly established Public Record Office, and there laboured at the arrangement and description of records until his retirement from the public service in March 1893—an uneventful life. In 1856 he was associated with John Sherren Brewer [q.v.], whom the master of the Rolls had commissioned to prepare a *Calendar of Letters and Papers of the Reign of Henry VIII.* Brewer died in 1879, when nine bulky parts, comprising the first four volumes, of that monumental work had been issued, and Gairdner continued editor of the *Calendar* to its completion in twenty-one volumes, being assisted in the last eight by Mr. R. H. Brodie. The *Calendar* gives the purport of about a hundred thousand documents in many languages. Gairdner devoted the whole of his leisure time to historical work, beginning with *Memorials of King Henry VII* (1858) and *Letters and Papers of Richard III and Henry VII* (1861–1863), edited for the Rolls Series of Chronicles and Memorials. He afterwards edited *The Historical Collections of a Citizen of London in the Fifteenth Century* (1876), *Three Fifteenth-Century Chronicles* (1880), and *The Spousells of the Princess Mary* (1893) for the Camden Society. In 1872–1875 he published in three volumes a greatly enlarged collection of *The Paston Letters*, with a long introduction which is probably his best work. He published three later editions of the *Letters*; that of 1904 is the definitive edition. A *Life of Richard III* followed in 1878. In 1884 he collected and published Brewer's prefaces to the first four volumes of the *Letters and Papers* under the title of *The Reign of Henry VIII from his Accession to the Death of Wolsey*, and in 1889 wrote *Henry the Seventh* for the popular series known as 'Twelve English Statesmen'. After retiring from the public service he wrote the volume on the period 1509–1559 (1902) in Stephens and Hunt's *History of the English Church*, and in 1908 began to publish his longest work, *Lollardy and the Reformation in England*, in four volumes, the last of which was issued after his death under the editorship of Dr. W. Hunt. He was also the author of innumerable articles for historical publications. He died at Pinner, Middlesex, 4 November 1912.

Gairdner's power as an historian lies in describing the course of events, for the elucidation of which he marshals, with patient logic and in clear and vigorous style, his contemporary authorities, and explains their obscurities of diction or handwriting. In treating of characters and motives he is less convincing, and to some readers seems to let a natural bias in favour of constituted authority influence his judgement of documentary evidence. Yet he is never intentionally unfair, and quotes all his evidences with simple confidence that other minds will interpret them as he himself does.

Gairdner married in 1867 Annie, daughter of Joseph Sayer, of Carisbrooke, by whom he had one daughter. There is a bronze bust of him by Frank Baxter in the National Portrait Gallery.

[Preface by W. Hunt to J. Gairdner's *Lollardy and the Reformation in England*, vol. iv; personal knowledge.] R. H. B.

GARRETT ANDERSON, ELIZABETH (1836–1917), physician. [See ANDERSON, ELIZABETH.]

GASELEE, SIR ALFRED (1844–1918), general, the eldest son of the Rev. John Gaselee, rector of Little Yeldham, Essex, by his wife, Sarah Anne Mant, was born at Little Yeldham 3 June 1844. He entered Felsted School in 1853 and Sandhurst in 1861. In 1863 he received a commission in the 93rd regiment, and almost immediately had experience of active service, taking part in the campaign on the North-West frontier of India in that year. Three years later he was transferred to the Bengal Staff Corps and joined a Punjab infantry regiment. In 1867 he went with the Indian force to Abyssinia, where he acted as assistant to the director-general of transport and was present at the capture of Magdala (13 April 1868). He took part in the affair against the Bezotis in 1869, receiving the thanks of the government of India, and served with the Jowaki expedition of 1877–1878. In the Afghan War of 1879–1880 Gaselee was a deputy assistant quartermaster-general, and accompanied Sir Frederick (afterwards Earl) Roberts [q.v.] on the march from Kabul to the relief of Kandahar, obtaining a brevet majority. For his services with the Zhob Valley expedition (1884) and the Hazara expedition (1891) he received the C.B. (1891). From 1891 until the end of the century he was almost continuously employed in fighting on the frontiers of India. In 1893 he was promoted to the command of a battalion of the 5th Gurkha Rifles, and was appointed aide-de-camp to Queen Victoria. He served with the Isazai expedition (1892), the Waziristan field force (1894–1895), and commanded a brigade in the Tirah campaign (1897–1898). For his services in Tirah Gaselee was created K.C.B. (1898). He acted in 1898 as quartermaster-general at Simla and had command of a second-class district in India (1898–1901).

In the summer of 1900, when the Boxer movement in China had brought about a critical situation, Gaselee was chosen to command the British expeditionary force sent to assist in the relief of the beleaguered foreign legations in Peking. The relieving force, under the German commander, Count von Waldersee, consisted, in addition to British, of Japanese, Russian, Italian, French, American, and German troops. There were counsels of delay, and it was due to the firm attitude of the commander of the British contingent that immediate action was taken. The British column was the first to enter Peking, reaching the legations on the afternoon of 13 August 1900. The international rivalries between the component parts of the relieving forces might have given rise to the most serious complications. Gaselee showed tact and firmness in his handling of a very delicate situation. As a reward for his services he was promoted major-general and created G.C.I.E. (1901). He became full general in 1906; was in command of the Northern army in India in 1907–1908; and was created G.C.B. in 1909. He retired from the Indian army in 1911, but remained colonel of the 54th Sikhs until his death, which took place at Guildford 29 March 1918.

Few soldiers have had greater experience of Indian warfare than Gaselee. Although not endowed with the highest intellectual gifts, he was possessed of sound judgement and proved himself equal to each of the many tasks which fell to him in the course of a military career extending over nearly half a century. Absolutely straightforward, he inspired confidence in all who served with or under him. The private soldiers were particularly devoted to him, appreciating the solicitude which he invariably showed for their welfare.

Gaselee married twice: first, in 1882 Alice Jane (from whom he obtained a divorce in 1893), daughter of the Rt. Hon. William Edward Baxter [q.v.], of Kincaldrum, Forfar; secondly, in 1895 Alice Margaret, daughter of Gartside Gartside-Tipping, of Rossferry, co. Fermanagh. There was no issue by either marriage.

[*The Times*, 1 April 1918; private information.] R. J. B.

GASKELL, WALTER HOLBROOK (1847–1914), physiologist, the third child and younger twin son of John Dakin Gaskell, barrister of the Middle Temple, by his wife, Anne (a cousin), daughter of Roger Gaskell, was born 1 November 1847 at Naples, where his parents were residing for the winter. He was brought up at Highgate and there attended Sir Roger Cholmley's School until he was seventeen. In 1865 he entered Trinity College, Cambridge, where he became a scholar and was twenty-sixth wrangler in the mathematical tripos (1869). With the intention of taking a medical degree he attended the lectures of (Sir) Michael Foster on biology, and in 1872 went to University College Hospital. But he dropped medicine for a time, and in

October 1874 went to work with Karl F. W. Ludwig, professor of physiology at Leipzig, returning to Cambridge the following summer. In 1875 he married Catherine Sharpe, daughter of Reginald Amphlett Parker, solicitor, and settled in Grantchester in order to work in the Cambridge physiological laboratory. He proceeded to the degree of M.D. in 1878, and five years later (1883) was appointed university lecturer in physiology, the only teaching post he ever held. In 1889 Trinity Hall elected him to a fellowship. After living for a few years in Cambridge, he built 'The Uplands', Great Shelford, where he remained until his death (from cerebral haemorrhage) on 7 September 1914. He was survived by one son and two daughters.

It was Ludwig's custom not only to suggest to his pupils the subject of research, but to carry out most of the experiments and to write the papers which appeared under their names. Gaskell, who was set a problem in vascular innervation, pondered deeply over the subject and, on his return to Cambridge, devised an ingenious method of watching the blood-flow in the mylohyoid muscle of the frog during stimulation of its nerve. He then turned his attention to the heart, and demonstrated by many beautiful experiments the inherent rhythm of cardiac muscle and the influence on it of nervous impulses and drugs. He proved that the normal beat started in the sinus and was propagated by way of the muscular tissue of the auricle to the ventricle. This work led to his being elected a fellow of the Royal Society in 1882.

In the course of these researches Gaskell discovered that the vagus nerve of the frog contained two sets of fibres, which not only produced an opposite effect on the action of the heart, but differed in structure and in their origin from the central nervous system. He therefore extended his inquiry to viscera other than the heart. The movements of these organs were generally thought to be governed by a 'vegetative nervous system', which lay outside and was largely independent of the brain and spinal cord. Gaskell revealed on broad lines the true plan of their relationship to the central nervous system, and showed that, like the heart, they were all supplied by peculiar motor and inhibitory nerves arising from specially restricted areas of the same nerve-axis as that which governed the ordinary muscles of the body.

Gaskell did not pursue the details of this visceral innervation with the same minute experimental attention which he had given to the heart, but passed on to inquiries of a still wider scope, the consideration of function from its developmental aspect. It had been taught that one set of nerves quickened and another stopped the heart; Gaskell's aim was to discover not only the mechanical means by which this was brought about, but how these functions arose. This method of considering physiological problems had a profound effect on scientific medicine. Gaskell revolutionized current ideas of the action of the heart, and, consequently, of cardiac disease. He laid bare both the structure and functions of the involuntary nervous system. Never content simply to record a new fact, he always asked the meaning of the phenomena which he described.

From these studies Gaskell was led to consider the mode by which vertebrate animals derived from an invertebrate ancestry; for he argued that many apparently anomalous structures in the nervous system must be relics of some more primitive state. In 1889 he put forward the first indications of his theory that the vertebrates are descended from an arthropod stock, of which the king crab is the nearest living example. He accounted for the obvious differences in the relation of the principal organs by supposing that the gut of the arthropod, surrounded by its chain of ganglia, had been transformed into the central canal of the spinal cord. This theory raised a vehement storm of protest from certain zoologists, which grew in volume as new points were brought forward by Gaskell in paper after paper. Finally, when he published *The Origin of the Vertebrates* in 1908, the work passed almost unnoticed. This book is written in a fascinating manner, clear, simple, and concise. Whatever may be the ultimate fate of Gaskell's hypothesis it contains innumerable original observations marshalled with unusual skill. Shortly before his death he completed the manuscript of a small book, embodying the results of all his researches, which was published in 1916 under the title of *The Involuntary Nervous System.*

Gaskell's robust frame, sanguine complexion, and abundant dark hair and beard, which never went entirely white, gave him the appearance of a man whose occupation was in the open air; and indeed digging and the care of his garden formed his principal recreation. The clarity and half-veiled enthusiasm of his exposition, together with his somewhat slow and emphatic utterance, made him an enthralling teacher for senior students. He always treated them as if they were worthy to participate in the researches which occupied him at the moment. He was ever ready to turn aside to give counsel or encouragement, and no one was more frequently consulted by the younger physiologists. Those who came under his influence can never forget his transcendent sincerity, his gift of sympathetic attention, and the unfailing wisdom of his advice.

[Private information; personal knowledge.] H. H.

GIBSON, EDWARD, first Baron Ashbourne, of Ashbourne, co. Meath (1837–1913), lord chancellor of Ireland, was born in Dublin 4 September 1837, the second son of William Gibson, of Rockforest, co. Tipperary, solicitor, by his wife, Louisa, daughter of Joseph Grant, barrister, of Dublin. He was educated at Trinity College, Dublin, and graduated as first senior moderator in history and English literature (1858). Called to the Irish bar (King's Inns, Dublin, 1860), he took silk in 1872. He contested Waterford unsuccessfully as a conservative in 1874, but was returned the next year for Dublin University. The conservatives were then weak in debating power on Irish questions, and Gibson, speaking with informed facility, gained distinction. His appearance was striking, with his fine forehead crowned by hair prematurely silver-white; his utterance was clamant but toned by genial humour; he was shrewd and looked wise; while his declamatory, lucid style peculiarly equipped him for popular audiences. Appointed attorney-general for Ireland in 1877, a position which he held till 1880, Gibson became the effective controller at Dublin Castle, and the exponent in the Commons of the official Irish policy. During Mr. Gladstone's second administration (1880–1885), when the Irish land war raged and the Parnellites commanded an insurrectionary country, Gibson's dexterous criticism not merely of the handling by the government of the Irish chaos, but of their general conduct of affairs, enhanced his reputation. On Lord Salisbury becoming premier in 1885, Gibson was raised to the peerage and promoted lord chancellor of Ireland with a seat in the Cabinet. He held the same office in the conservative governments of 1886–1892 and 1895–1905, thus occupying an unprecedented position during an unprecedented period of eighteen years.

Ashbourne was not deemed an erudite lawyer but, supported by the learning of (Sir) Samuel Walker [q.v.], ex-lord chancellor, the genius of Lord Justice Fitzgibbon [q.v.], and the acumen of Lord Justice Holmes, he proved an admirable president of an exceptionally powerful court of appeal; while he discharged the administrative duties of the chancellorship with unwearying assiduity and solicitude. He was dignified, hospitable, and popular. When he vacated the chancellorship, Ashbourne constantly sat in the appellate tribunals of the Lords and Privy Council. He piloted the Irish Land Purchase Act of 1885, known as the Ashbourne Act, but otherwise left little impress upon legislation. His familiar text was 'Give peace in our time, O Lord', and thus he earned for himself among intimates the sobriquet of 'Tutissimus'. He was the author of *Pitt, some Chapters of his Life and Times* (1898). He died in London 22 May 1913.

Lord Ashbourne married in 1868 Frances Maria Adelaide, second daughter of Henry Cope Colles, barrister, by whom he had four sons and four daughters. He was succeeded by his eldest son, William, second Baron Ashbourne (born 1868).

[*The Times*, 23 May 1913; Burke's *Peerage*; personal and professional knowledge. Portrait, *Royal Academy Pictures*, 1899.] A. W. S.

GIFFARD, HARDINGE STANLEY, first Earl of Halsbury (1823–1921), lord chancellor, the third son of Stanley Lees Giffard [q.v.], by his first wife, Susanna Meares, daughter of Francis Moran, J.P., of Downhill, co. Sligo, was born at his father's house at Pentonville, Middlesex, 3 September 1823. His mother died when he was five years old, and in 1830 his father married a second cousin, Mary Anne Giffard, who acquired the complete affection of her step-children. Hardinge was never sent to school, but received from his father so complete an education at home that he continued throughout his life to read the Latin and Greek classics for pleasure, and retained also some knowledge of Hebrew. His father had taught him to speak in all three languages, and he had at one time and another read practically the whole of the classical authors in the first two. His memory, to the very end of his life, was quite exceptional. In 1842 Giffard went into residence at Merton College, Oxford, where he rowed in the college eight and made a great many speeches at the Union. In the matter of passing examinations, his unusual and in substance extremely effective education was not calculated to promote success, and in 1845 he took a fourth class in *literae humaniores*—a long-remembered disappointment.

On coming down from Oxford Giffard assisted his father for some years in the production of the *Standard* newspaper, of which Lees Giffard was editor for the first twenty-five years of its existence. Father and son were excellent friends, and were both, throughout their lives, the most uncompromising of tories upon every issue of party politics. As soon as he felt that he could afford it, Giffard was called to the bar at the Inner Temple (1850), of which he became a bencher in due course (1865). He shared the chambers in Chancery Lane of his eldest brother, John, and joined the Western circuit; but a year later (1851), by the advice of one of his father's friends, he migrated to the South Wales circuit, where he at once acquired a steady practice. About the same time he joined (Sir) Harry Bodkin Poland in chambers at 7 King's Bench Walk. They afterwards moved to 5 Paper Buildings, where Poland remained as long as he continued to practise. From this time Giffard obtained a steady and increasing practice at the Old Bailey and at the Middlesex sessions at Clerkenwell. He was also one of the founders of the Hardwicke Debating Society.

In 1859 (Sir) William Henry Bodkin was appointed assistant judge of the Middlesex sessions, and Giffard succeeded him as junior prosecuting counsel at the Central Criminal Court. In this capacity he appeared for the Crown in all important prosecutions at police courts, and in many of the consequent trials, until 1865, when he took silk, being one of the last barristers to receive that honour from Lord Westbury. Two years later he distinguished himself greatly as leading counsel for Governor Edward John Eyre [q.v.], when the latter was prosecuted for murder before the magistrates at Market Drayton and again at Bow Street in 1868 for alleged offences against the Colonial Governors Act. From the time of his taking silk, Giffard's practice at *nisi prius* increased largely. He was second counsel with Serjeant William Ballantine for the Tichborne claimant, Arthur Orton [q.v.], in the ejectment case before Chief Justice Sir William Bovill, which lasted 102 days (1871–1872). He obtained a very large general practice and a well-deserved reputation as pre-eminent in any case which required hard fighting and inextinguishable courage. His extraordinary memory enabled him to remember everything in a brief that he had once read, and he had a singular ability of discerning at once what were the essential points of a case, and of concentrating resolutely upon them.

At the general elections of 1868 and 1874 Giffard stood as a conservative candidate for Cardiff, and was defeated. In November 1875, when Sir John Holker succeeded Sir John Burgess Karslake as attorney-general, Mr. Disraeli appointed Giffard solicitor-general, and he was knighted in the usual course. He stood unsuccessfully for Horsham in the following year, but in February 1877 he was elected member for Launceston and retained the seat at the general election of 1880. His work as solicitor-general was sound but not especially conspicuous, Holker also being a common law barrister and an attorney-general of peculiar efficiency and eminence. As solicitor-general Giffard led for the Crown in the *Franconia* case (*R.* v. *Keyn*, 1876), wherein the master of a German ship was convicted of the manslaughter by negligence of persons drowned in a collision between his vessel and an emigrant ship, the *Strathclyde*. The conviction was quashed by the Court for Crown Cases Reserved, which held by a majority that the English court had no jurisdiction over a crime committed by a foreigner on board a foreign ship on the high seas. This decision was overruled by the Territorial Waters Jurisdiction Act of 1878, which not merely enacted that the jurisdiction covered the sea to a distance of one marine league from the coast, but declared, in a preamble suggested by Giffard, that the law had always been to that effect.

After the defeat of the conservatives in 1880, Giffard became more prominent in the House of Commons as a pugnacious and useful member of the opposition. When Charles Bradlaugh [q.v.] began his controversy with the House of Commons, Giffard moved (22 June 1880) the first amendment to the effect that Bradlaugh should neither affirm nor take the oath, and carried it against the government; he took an active part both in parliament and in the law courts in the prolonged struggle which followed. He also had the better of an animated controversy with Mr. Chamberlain concerning the alleged responsibility of the political parties for rioting at a political meeting at Aston, near Birmingham. Throughout the duration of this parliament his practice at the bar continued to increase.

Perhaps his greatest forensic triumph was in the famous case of *Belt* v. *Lawes* (1882). The plaintiff was a sculptor, and the substantial issue in the case was whether he prepared with his own hand and mind the works which issued from his studio, or employed 'ghosts', that is, paid small sums to obscure persons who were better artists than himself, to make the busts and statues by the supply of which he earned a large income. The case against Giffard's client, Belt, was almost overwhelming, and the defendants were represented by Sir Charles Russell—then at the height of his powers—and Sir Richard Webster (each of them subsequently lord chief justice) instructed by Sir George Henry Lewis, whose reputation as an exposer of impostors was unrivalled. But Giffard carried with him the judge, the jury, and a large proportion of the public, and obtained for the plaintiff a verdict for £5,000.

In 1885 Giffard was appointed lord chancellor in Lord Salisbury's first administration. His appointment came as something of a surprise both to the public and to the legal profession. His early work as an 'Old Bailey man' had never been forgotten, and his general reputation as an advocate had never been that of a Russell or a Cockburn on the one hand, or of a Palmer or a Cairns on the other. The promotion, however, had been fully earned. Holker having died in 1882, the only possible competitor was William Brett, Viscount Esher [q.v.], master of the Rolls. Brett had been, seventeen years previously, solicitor-general for less than twelve months, after which he had accepted a puisne judgeship. Giffard, besides fighting several elections, had done excellent service to his party in parliament, both in office and in opposition, for eight years. His claim to the woolsack was admitted on reflection ; his ability to occupy it with distinction was widely doubted by superficial observers. Such doubts were laid to rest before the government went out of office in January 1886. From the first Giffard took command, as much as a president should, of any court over which he presided. He was strong enough to be *primus inter pares* whoever his peers might be, and they included at different times Lords Selborne, Watson, Blackburn, Bramwell, Herschell, Davey, Bowen, Macnaghten, and Robertson. On his appointment he took the title of Baron Halsbury, of Halsbury, in the parish of Parkham, Devon, one of the former seats of the Giffard family.

When the defeat of the first Home Rule Bill and the consequent general election restored the conservatives to power in July 1886, Halsbury again became lord chancellor, and he was appointed for the third time to that office by Lord Salisbury in 1895. His third period of office, in the ministries of Lord Salisbury and Mr. Arthur Balfour, lasted until 1905. He thus held the great seal for seventeen years—longer than any one else except Hardwicke and Eldon. When he resigned shortly after his eighty-second birthday he still possessed, but for a slight degree of deafness, all the necessary powers of body and mind in full vigour. In 1898 he was created Earl of Halsbury and Viscount Tiverton.

Halsbury's dissenting judgment in *Allen* v. *Flood* (1898) taken together with his prevailing judgment in *Quinn* v. *Leathem* (1901) is a good illustration of his robust and cogent methods of thought, and incidentally exhibits his increasing control of the tribunal of which he was the chief. The wealth of his learning and his facile mastery of exceedingly complicated facts are well displayed in his judgment in the Free Church of Scotland case (1904). The cases of *R.* v. *Jackson* (1891), which denies to a husband the right to use force for the purpose of securing or retaining his wife's cohabitation, *Powell* v. *the Kempton Park Race Course Co.* (1899), as to the legality of betting on race courses, and *Cowley* v. *Cowley* (1901), as to the use of titles after remarriage, are other examples of Halsbury's confident and effective treatment of questions that came before him.

Although always a tenacious and resolute conservative, Halsbury did not for a moment suppose that English law was incapable of improvement, and he was substantially the author of two such important reforms as the Land Transfer Act (1897), and the Criminal Evidence Act (1898) by which persons accused of indictable offences, and their spouses, were made competent witnesses. Halsbury, during his occupancy of the woolsack, appointed in each division of the High Court more judges than it had ever contained at the same time, viz. eight in Chancery, seventeen in the queen's (or king's) bench, and three in the probate division. After his resignation he continued to do active service judicially and politically. He was increasingly troubled by deafness, but his other physical faculties remained almost unimpaired until the closing years of his long life. He presided, from start to finish, over the production of the complete digest of *The Laws of England* (1905–1916), which is known by his name and took its place at once as the most necessary work in any collection of books purporting to be a library of English law.

In the parliament of 1905–1910, the Marquess of Lansdowne being the conservative leader in the House of Lords, Halsbury acquiesced with reluctance in the mildness of the opposition offered in the Upper House to such measures as the Trades Disputes Act (1906), which relieved trade unions and their members of official responsibility for breaches of contract or tortious acts committed by them, and the Finance Act of 1909. After the second general election of 1910, when the Parliament Bill which most seriously curtailed the legislative powers of the House of Lords came before that House, the opposition, having regard to the great majority by which it had been carried in the House of Commons, allowed it to be read a second time, and then carried against the government amendments in committee so largely limiting its scope that there was known to be no possibility of their acceptance by Mr. Asquith's government. After the House of Commons had refused to accept these amendments, and when it became known that ministers were prepared to advise the creation of as many peers favourable to their proposals as might be necessary, and that the King had indicated that he would follow such advice, Lord Lansdowne advised his party in the Lords not to insist upon the amendments which they had carried. Halsbury's capacity for surrender was now exhausted. At the age of eighty-eight he formed and led a new party among the peers, popularly known as the 'die-hards'; and the debate which ensued, upon the question whether the Lords' amendments had been merely a formal protest or a minimum of genuine resistance to the proposed constitutional change, was not less exciting than momentous, for no one really knew how the decision would go. Halsbury fought his hardest, insisting that the House ought to stand by what it thought right, whatever the consequences might be. The division was taken on 10 August 1911, and the die-hards were defeated by the narrow margin of seventeen.

In 1913 Halsbury presided effectively over a committee of the House of Lords which inquired into the conduct of a peer—a member of the government—concerned in speculation in the shares of the American Marconi Company; and after the outbreak of war in 1914 he rendered further judicial service. His last judgment was delivered in 1916. He lived to see peace concluded, and to celebrate in 1920 the seventieth anniversary of his call to the bar, when he received and responded to an affectionate address from the bench and bar. In his ninety-eighth year his strength perceptibly failed, though his mind remained perfectly clear. He died in London, after two days' illness from influenza, 11 December 1921.

Halsbury married twice: first, in 1852 Caroline (died 1873), daughter of William Conn Humphreys, of Wood Green, Middlesex, by whom he had no children; secondly, in 1874 Wilhelmina, daughter of Henry Woodfall, of Stanmore, Middlesex, a kinsman of Henry Sampson Woodfall [q.v.], the publisher. By his second wife he had one son, Hardinge Goulburn, second Earl of Halsbury, and one daughter.

Halsbury's features were good, and expressive of power and resolution; his short and stoutly built figure lent itself to caricature. A fine portrait of him by Sir George Reid is in the possession of the family; another, by the Hon. John Collier, belongs to the benchers of the Inner Temple, and a copy of it is in the hall of Merton College (*Royal Academy Pictures*, 1898).

[*The Times*, 12 December 1921; J. B. Atlay, *The Victorian Chancellors*, 1906–1908; private information; personal knowledge.]

H. S-n.

GILL, Sir DAVID (1843–1914), astronomer, the eldest son of David Gill, a watchmaker with a well-established business in Aberdeen, by his wife, Margaret Mitchell, was born at 48 Skene Terrace, Aberdeen, 12 June 1843. His interest in physical science, first aroused by the teaching of Dr. Lindsay at the Dollar Academy, was later extended and intensified at Marischal College and the University, Aberdeen, under the inspiring influence of Clerk Maxwell [q.v.]. At his father's desire he entered the business and for a time had complete charge of it. He mastered all the details, and to the end of his life kept a clock made with his own hands. His spare time, however, he devoted to physics and chemistry in a small laboratory which he set up at home.

Gill's active interest in astronomy dates from 1863. It occurred to him that a time service similar to that established by Charles Piazzi Smyth [q.v.] in Edinburgh might be usefully installed in Aberdeen. An introduction to Piazzi Smyth followed, when he was shown the arrangements for the time-gun and ball as well as the instruments of the Edinburgh observatory. With the help of Professor David Thomson [q.v.] he re-established a disused 'observatory' of King's College, Aberdeen. A small portable transit instrument was unearthed and mounted; a mean solar clock was added, with arrangements for control to within a fraction of a second of Greenwich time; to this contact springs were fitted, establishing electric control of the turret clock of King's College and other clocks of the town. Gill next procured a small Dallmeyer refracting telescope with which he made observations of double stars. He also purchased from the Rev. Henry Cooper-Key a 12-inch speculum, the equatorial mounting for which was of his own design, and the driving-clock made by his own hands on the general plan of Airy's chronograph at Greenwich. He said, in later life, that he never found a clock which worked better. With this instrument he observed double stars and *nebulae* and took some photographs of the moon.

In 1870 Gill married Isobel, daughter of John Black, a farmer of Linhead, Aberdeenshire, and shortly afterwards the opportunity came to him of devoting his time exclusively to scientific pursuits. This arose out of the friendship which he had formed with Lord Lindsay (afterwards twenty-sixth Earl of Crawford, q.v.), an amateur astronomer who was attracted by Gill's enthusiasm and skill. Gill was offered in 1872 the charge of the private observatory erected by Lord Lindsay at Dunecht. He accepted at once, although it involved a considerable sacrifice of income. The years 1873–1874 were busily occupied in the equipment of this fine observatory. The instruments comprised a 15-inch refractor by Grubb, an 8-inch reversible transit circle by Troughton and Simms, Gill's 12-inch speculum from Aberdeen, and a 4-inch heliometer by Repsold. Visits to many European observatories were made and Gill met the leading astronomers of the day. Preparations were next made for Lindsay and Gill to take part in the observations of the transit of Venus in 1874. It was thought desirable that the longitude of their station at Mauritius should be determined with all possible accuracy. As the electric telegraph only went as far as Aden, it was necessary to transport chronometers, of which no less than fifty were hired by Gill from the best makers. These had to be carried with great care, regularly wound, and compared. Gill took his chronometers to Greenwich, checked them, and then drove off with them cheerfully to his steamer in the docks, leaving Airy and the staff at Greenwich amazed at his temerity. By incessant watchfulness, however, the journey to Mauritius and back was made without mishap. The main interest in the expedition to Mauritius centres round the observations of the minor planet Juno, made with the heliometer for the determination of the solar parallax and thus of the sun's distance from the earth. From observations on twelve evenings and eleven mornings a very good result was obtained by Gill, who was profoundly convinced of the possibilities of the heliometer for astronomical measurements of the highest precision. As is well known, the observations of the transit of Venus, carefully planned and executed at great expense of time and money by expeditions all over the world, gave a disappointing result. But the Mauritius expedition proved to be the inauguration of a successful method of determining the sun's distance, a measurement of fundamental importance in astronomy.

While at Mauritius Gill was invited by General Stone, chief of the military staff of the khedive, to return via Egypt and measure a base-line for a projected survey of the country. With the assistance of the American astronomer, Professor James Watson, a base-line was laid down near the Sphinx. This was Gill's first practical experience of geodetic work.

Gill left Dunecht in 1876. He obtained from Lord Lindsay the loan of the heliometer, and with funds obtained from the Royal Society and the Royal Astronomical Society made an expedition to the island of Ascension in order to measure the distance of Mars when it came exceptionally near the earth in the year 1877, and from the result to derive the sun's distance. In this difficult and adventurous expedition he was accompanied by his wife, who published in 1878 an interesting account of their experiences —*Six Months in Ascension: an Unscientific Account of a Scientific Expedition.* The observatory was first set up at Garrison, but, owing to interference from clouds, Gill heroically moved it in the course of five days to a new site, 'Mars Bay', just in time to secure favourable observations. The expedition was crowned with success, the sun's distance being determined with much greater accuracy than had previously been attained.

In 1879 Gill was appointed H.M. astronomer at the Cape of Good Hope.

The Cape observatory had been founded in 1822 by the lords commissioners of the Admiralty for observational work for the special benefit of navigators. This 'fundamental' astronomy was the main, and almost the sole, work of the observatory when Gill was appointed. It was continued vigorously under his direction. Many thousands of stars visible at the Cape were catalogued, and the observations of one of his predecessors, Sir Thomas Maclear [q.v.], were reduced and published. Gill found a congenial task in detecting and eliminating the causes of error, especially those of systematic character, and in improving methods of observation generally. He early came to the conclusion that a new instrument was required, but it was many years before he was enabled to carry out his wishes. In 1897 the necessary expenditure was sanctioned, and his experience and engineering skill were brought to bear on the design of a transit circle which contained many new features and proved a great success.

With the assistance of W. L. Elkin, a young American astronomer, Gill next undertook the arduous task of measuring with the 4-inch heliometer (which he had now bought from Lord Lindsay) the distances of some of the brighter southern stars, including Canopus and Sirius. Measurements of great refinement continued night after night, both after sunset and before sunrise, and results of surprising accuracy were obtained with this small instrument. But a larger one was required, and in 1887 the Admiralty sanctioned the purchase of a heliometer with a 7-inch object glass from Messrs. Repsold. With this telescope Gill, assisted by W. de Sitter, a Dutch astronomer, measured the distances of no less than twenty-two stars with an accuracy which marked an era in the determination of stellar distances. This precision was due in part to Gill's great personal skill as an observer, and in part to the admirable design of the new instrument. Gill took the first opportunity of using the new heliometer for a redetermination of the sun's distance. He found that the small planet Iris would approach near the earth in 1888, and the small planets Victoria and Sappho in 1889. Very elaborate observations were planned, in which he had the co-operation of Arthur Auwers at the Cape, Elkin and Asaph Hall, junior, at Yale, B. Peter at Leipzig, W. Schur at Göttingen, and E. Hartwig at Bamberg. Subsidiary observations were also made at twenty observatories, and very elaborate calculations made at the office of the *Berliner Jahrbuch*. The result of this fine piece of work was the determination of the sun's distance correct to one part in a thousand. The details of the observations and calculations are published in two volumes of the Cape observatory *Annals*. The determination of the mass of Jupiter was a third important research carried out with the 7-inch heliometer. Here again Gill had the assistance of the young astronomers W. de Sitter and Bryan Cookson, whose enthusiasm he had kindled.

The application of photography to astronomy made great strides at the close of the nineteenth century, and Gill was one of the pioneers. His success in photographing Finlay's comet in 1882, with a Dallmeyer lens of 11 inches focus attached to an equatorial, convinced him of the practicability of constructing star maps by photography. He obtained a larger lens of 6 inches aperture and 54 inches focus, and in February 1885 commenced a photographic survey of the southern heavens. In December of the same year he received from Professor J. C. Kapteyn, of Groningen, an offer to undertake the measurement of the plates and the derivation from them of the positions and magnitudes of the stars. Methods were discussed between them, measurements begun in 1886, and completed in 1898. The results, published in the *Annals* of the Cape observatory, show the positions and magnitudes of no less than 400,000 stars. This great survey has proved of great value to astronomers, and formed the basis of important investigations on the distribution of the stars. Gill's successful photography of Finlay's comet also contributed to the adoption of photographic charting at the Paris observatory, where, thanks to the constructive skill of the brothers Henry, the administrative ability of Admiral Mouchez, the director, and the persistence and energy of Gill, an international scheme for cataloguing and charting the heavens by photography on a large scale was launched in 1887. Naturally the Cape observatory took a share in the work, and in addition the whole scheme was largely guided by Gill's views.

Gill's power of getting a comprehensive scheme carried through is well illustrated in the geodetic survey of South Africa. But for him the different states would probably have been content with small, local surveys. He outlined a system of principal triangulation for Cape Colony, Natal, the Orange Free State, and the

Transvaal, which was carried through for the Cape and Natal between 1883 and 1886, and for the Transvaal and Free State after the close of the South African War. He further saw that these operations might be made the starting-point of the still greater project, a chain of triangulation stretching the whole length of Africa approximately on the 30th meridian. This scheme he forwarded at every opportunity, and saw the chain carried to within seventy miles of Lake Tanganyika.

Gill, who had been created K.C.B. in 1900, left the Cape in 1907 after twenty-eight years of service. When he went there the observatory was comparatively small, and possessed but one instrument of much value. He left it well equipped with modern instruments, including the Victoria (24-inch) photographic refractor, the gift of Mr. Frank McClean, of Tunbridge Wells. The staff was increased to correspond with the larger equipment, so that the observatory is now qualified to carry out work of the highest order in many different directions. After his retirement Gill settled in London, and took an active share in its scientific activities. He was president of the British Association at the Leicester meeting in 1907. He was president of the Royal Astronomical Society 1910–1912, and succeeded Lord Cromer as president of the Research Defence Society. Much of his time was given to a history of the Cape observatory. Nothing gave him greater pleasure than to invite his astronomical friends to his house, especially if an occasion was provided by the visit of a distinguished foreign astronomer, to 'have a talk with astronomers about astronomy'. His health was excellent till in December 1913 he was seized with pneumonia and passed away in London on 24 January 1914.

In his *History and Description of the Royal Observatory, Cape of Good Hope* (1913) Gill mentions the delight with which he read Struve's *History of the Pulkowa Observatory*—'the author had the true genius and spirit of the practical astronomer, a love of refined and precise methods of observation and the inventive and engineering capacity'. These words are as true of Gill as of Struve. The tedium of making similar observations night after night was counterbalanced by the pleasure of making them as accurately as possible. His enthusiasm communicated itself to his colleagues and assistants, and his kindness of heart made them devoted to him. His force of character enabled him to triumph over difficulties and carry out great projects. It was said of him at the Admiralty that if he wanted anything no one had any peace till he got it. He had a happy married life, tempered only by anxieties about his wife's health. They had no children, but brought up three orphan sons of his brother. He took a lively interest in all that was going on around him, particularly in political and social matters in South Africa, and was well acquainted with many of the men who helped to shape its history.

Gill's portrait was painted by George Henry in 1912 (*Royal Academy Pictures*, 1912).

[G. Forbes, *David Gill, Man and Astronomer*, 1916; Sir David Gill's *History* of the Cape Observatory contains records of his astronomical work at the Cape; *Proceedings* of the Royal Society, vol. xci, A, 1915 (portrait); *Monthly Notices* of the Royal Astronomical Society, vol. lxxv; *Astrophysical Journal*, vol. xl.]

F. W. D.

GINSBURG, CHRISTIAN DAVID (1831–1914), Old Testament scholar, was born at Warsaw, of Jewish parentage, 25 December 1831. His parents had migrated to Warsaw not long before, having come, it is believed, from Spain. There is a tradition in the family that an ancestor was a minister of the Catholic sovereigns, Ferdinand and Isabella. His mother was of English descent. Young Ginsburg was educated in the Rabbinic school at Warsaw, and there laid the foundations of the profound knowledge of Hebrew literature which afterwards made his name well known. At the age of about sixteen he became a Christian, and, being thereby cut off from his family, came to England, where thenceforth he made his home. For some years after his arrival in this country, Ginsburg engaged in lecturing and preaching, although he was never ordained. He found time, also, to follow up his interest in biblical literature; and in 1855 he began his monumental labours upon the critical text of the Massorah—a work which was his chief occupation during the rest of his long life. In 1858 he became a naturalized British subject, and in the same year he married Margaret, daughter of William Crosfield, of Aigburth, Liverpool, a member of an old quaker family. He was then enabled to settle down in Liverpool and devote himself to literary work. His wife died in 1867, and in the following year he married Emilie, daughter of F. Leopold Hausburg, of Woolton, near Liverpool. By his two marriages he had one son and four daughters.

Ginsburg's biblical researches were by this time becoming known. He had received an honorary LL.D. degree from Glasgow University in 1863. In 1870 it was natural that he should be invited to be one of the original members of the Old Testament revision company. He thereupon moved to a new home at Binfield, Berkshire, in order to be in closer touch with Westminster and with the British Museum. In 1872, at the invitation of the British Association, he made an expedition to Trans-Jordania, in company with Canon Henry Baker Tristram [q.v.]. Their object was to follow up, by further researches, the discovery (1868) of the Moabite stone; but their efforts were unsuccessful.

In 1880 appeared the first of the four folio volumes of Ginsburg's edition of *The Massorah.* This will long remain the standard work on the subject. Although its preparation occupied the greater part of his life, he regarded it not as an end in itself, but as the only sound foundation for the text of the Hebrew Old Testament. His revision of the text, *The Old Testament in Hebrew,* was published in 1894 (second edition, 1911). In this edition the minutiae of the vowel-points and accents were more strictly corrected in accordance with Jewish tradition than they had ever been before, but the progress made in the elucidation of the text was very small. Criticism has undergone great changes since Ginsburg began his work. It is now recognized that the Massoretic recension is not the original form of the text, that it embodies corruptions, and that the evidence of the early versions and of comparative philology must be taken into account. Moreover, the scrupulous quality of Ginsburg's scholarship suffered to some extent from the defects of the rabbinical method in which he had been trained. As a pure Hebraist, however, he was unsurpassed in his knowledge of the language at all its periods. This was shown in his Hebrew translation of the New Testament (with the Rev. Isaac E. Salkinson), and in his editions of Elias Levita and Jacob ben Hayyim. In 1883 he reported upon the alleged fragments of Deuteronomy offered for sale to the British Museum by M. W. Shapira, and pronounced them to be forgeries [*The Times,* 27 August 1883].

Ginsburg delighted in the society of scholars, and his hospitality was unbounded. Among his more intimate friends were William Aldis Wright [q.v], whose great collection of bibles was always at his disposal, and Thomas Chenery [q.v.], editor of *The Times,* who was a well-known Hebrew and Arabic scholar. Ginsburg's interests and activities were, however, by no means exclusively academic. He was a keen liberal, a personal friend of Mr. Gladstone, and for many years closely associated with the National Liberal Club. He also sat regularly as a justice of the peace for Surrey and Middlesex. He made a great collection of pre-Reformation bibles, the bulk of which he bequeathed to the British and Foreign Bible Society. From his youth he had made a study of engravings, of which he possessed a large and valuable collection.

Ginsburg died at his house at Palmers Green, Middlesex, 7 March 1914. His portrait, painted in 1914 by A. Carruthers Gould, hangs in the National Liberal Club.

[*The Times,* 9 and 11 March 1914; private information; personal knowledge.]

A. E. C.
B. W. G.

GORDON, ARTHUR CHARLES HAMILTON-, first BARON STANMORE (1829–1912), colonial governor, was born at Argyll House, London, 26 November 1829. He was the youngest son of George Hamilton-Gordon, fourth Earl of Aberdeen [q.v.], by his second wife, Harriet, daughter of the Hon. John Douglas, widow of James, Viscount Hamilton, and mother of the first Duke of Abercorn. He matriculated at Trinity College, Cambridge, in 1847, and graduated M.A. in 1851. In the following year he became private secretary to his father, who was prime minister from 1852 to 1855, and with whom he always remained on terms of special intimacy and affection. From 1854 to 1857 he sat in the House of Commons as liberal member for Beverley. In 1858 he accompanied Mr. Gladstone, in the capacity of private secretary, on his visit to the Ionian Islands as lord high commissioner extraordinary.

Gordon's work as a colonial administrator, which was to extend over a period of nearly thirty years, began in 1861 with his appointment as lieutenant-governor of New Brunswick. Some account of his impressions of that country is to be found in *Wilderness Journeys in New Brunswick,* which he contributed to the volume edited by (Sir) Francis Galton, entitled *Vacation Tourists and Notes of Travel in 1862–1863,* published in 1864. In 1866 he became governor of Trinidad, where he remained until 1870; here he acted as host to Charles Kingsley during the latter's visit to the West Indies, described in *At Last.* From 1871 to 1874 he was governor of Mauritius.

In 1875 Gordon entered upon what was probably the most important period of his career, his governorship of Fiji. The islands were ceded to the British Crown in 1874, and Gordon was appointed the first governor. He had always opposed the doctrine that a superior race may rightfully exploit an inferior one, and had maintained the equal claims of all classes to consideration; and in Fiji he was able to put his theories into practice. His views were unpopular with many of the white settlers, who resented the measures taken for the protection of native institutions, and he was attacked with much bitterness in some quarters. He proved, however, a strong governor, and was largely successful in his efforts to maintain native laws and customs and to uphold the authority of the chiefs. His period of governorship in Fiji, which he himself regarded as the most interesting of his colonial experiences, is described in detail in the four volumes entitled *Fiji: Records of Private and of Public Life, 1875–1880*, printed for private circulation in 1897. From 1877 to 1883 he also held the office of high commissioner and consul-general for the Western Pacific.

Leaving Fiji in 1880 Gordon became governor of New Zealand, and in 1883 was appointed to Ceylon, where he remained as governor until his retirement in 1890. In both countries he showed firmness in difficult circumstances, whether in his dealings with the Colonial Office or with local ministries.

On his retirement Gordon devoted himself to literary and public work of various kinds. He published in 1893 a short life of his father, *The Earl of Aberdeen* based on material collected for a fuller biography which was never published, and in 1906 *Sidney Herbert, Lord Herbert of Lea: A Memoir.* He also spent much time in collecting and editing the mass of state papers and correspondence left behind by Lord Aberdeen. Besides being chairman of the Bank of Mauritius and of the Pacific Phosphate Company and president of the Ceylon Association, he was an active member of various House of Lords' committees; he was also a member of the House of Laymen for the province of Canterbury, his views being those of a pronounced high churchman.

Gordon was created C.M.G. in 1859, K.C.M.G. in 1871, and G.C.M.G. in 1878. In 1893 he was raised to the peerage with the title of Baron Stanmore, of Great Stanmore, Middlesex. He was an honorary D.C.L. of Oxford. He married in 1865 Rachel Emily (died 1889), eldest daughter of Sir John George Shaw-Lefevre [q.v.], by whom he had one son and one daughter. He died in London 30 January 1912, and was buried at Ascot, where he had lived for many years. He was succeeded as second baron by his son, George Arthur Maurice Hamilton-Gordon (born 1871).

Stanmore's work as a colonial administrator was of permanent value. In his dealings with native races, especially in Fiji, he laid down principles which have had a lasting influence; thus the methods used with such success in New Guinea by Sir William MacGregor [q.v.] were probably suggested in part by MacGregor's experience under Stanmore in Mauritius and in Fiji. Stanmore was actuated by a high sense of duty and was a man of courage, firmness, and integrity; the friend of Charles Kingsley, Samuel Wilberforce, and Roundell Palmer, first Earl of Selborne, he possessed deeply religious convictions as well as great personal charm.

[*The Times*, 31 January 1912; Lady Frances Balfour, *Life of George, fourth Earl of Aberdeen*, 1922; Earl of Selborne, *Memorials*, 4 vols., 1896–1898; Lord Stanmore's writings above mentioned.] F. P. S.

GORDON, Sir THOMAS EDWARD (1832–1914), general, was born 12 January 1832, the fourth son of Captain William Gordon, of the 2nd Queen's regiment, by his wife, Dona Mariana Carlotta Loi Gonçalves de Mello. The descendants of his grandfather, Adam Gordon, included no fewer than thirteen soldiers; and a military education at the Scottish Naval and Military Academy indicated the career intended for him. There was, nevertheless, some financial difficulty in obtaining a commission for him, but eventually the purchase price (£450) was arranged, and Gordon entered the 4th Foot as ensign in 1849. Two years later he saw active service in India in the North-West Frontier campaign against the Mohmands, and, having been promoted lieutenant, he played a conspicuous part during the Indian Mutiny (1857–1859). He commanded the 7th Punjab Infantry in the attack upon and capture of the Oudh forts (14 and 17 July 1858). In 1859 he gained his captaincy, and ten years later was gazetted major. In that year (1869) he was present at the Ambala durbar, and in 1873 he accompanied Sir Thomas Douglas Forsyth [q.v.] as second in command of the mission to the ameer of Kashgar. Gordon has described this mission in his book *The*

Roof of the World (1876), which contains sixty-two illustrations drawn by himself. He held the appointment of assistant adjutant-general to the Lahore division from 1872 to 1874, and again, with the rank of lieutenant-colonel, from 1878 to 1879. In the latter year he became deputy adjutant-general, Bengal, and, on promotion to colonel, commanded the 4th infantry brigade of the Kabul field force in the Afghan War (1879–1880). He received the C.B. in 1881 for his attack on the camp at the village of Ali Khel in this campaign. In 1883 he was given the command of a brigade in Bengal and held the appointment for four years, being promoted major-general in 1886.

Having early mastered the Persian language, Gordon was appointed in 1889 Oriental and military secretary to the legation at Teheran, and was military attaché there from 1891 to 1893. His travels through the Persian empire in his official capacity brought him into close contact with Kurds and Beduin, among whom he succeeded in making friends, and, on occasion, he even came to terms with the professional brigands whom he met. His dealings with the Shah, especially on the subject of the defects in the military system then in force in Persia, were marked by the courageous honesty of purpose that characterized the activities of his whole life. In 1890 he was promoted lieutenant-general, and in 1894 full general. He was created K.C.I.E. in 1893 and received the K.C.B. in 1900. In 1895 he published *Persia Revisited*, which records his impressions of the situation as he found it on his return to that country in the previous year. His autobiography, *A Varied Life*, was published in 1906, and eight years later, after a hard life well spent, he died in London 23 March 1914. Gordon was twice married: first, in 1862 to Mary Helen (died 1879), daughter of Alexander Sawers, of Culnah, Bengal; secondly, in 1894 to Charlotte, daughter of Joseph Davison, of Greecroft, Durham. There was no issue by either marriage.

[*The Times*, 24 March 1914.] C. V. O.

GORELL, first Baron (1848–1913), judge. [See Barnes, John Gorell.]

GORST, Sir JOHN ELDON (1835–1916), lawyer and politician, was born at Preston 24 May 1835. He was the second son of Edward Chaddock Gorst, who took the name of Lowndes on succeeding to some family property in 1853. His mother was Elizabeth, daughter of John Douthwaite Nesham, of Houghton-le-Spring, Durham. Gorst was educated at Preston grammar school and matriculated at St. John's College, Cambridge, in 1853. He was third wrangler in 1857 and in the same year was elected a fellow of his college (1857–1860). He became an honorary fellow in 1890. He chose the bar as his profession, but after a few months of legal study took a mastership at Rossall School in order to be near his father, who was seriously ill. Mr. Lowndes died in 1859, and Gorst, instead of returning to London, determined to try his fortune in the Colonies. During a three months' voyage in a sailing ship to New Zealand, he became engaged to Miss Mary Elizabeth Moore, daughter of the Rev. Lorenzo Moore, of Christchurch, New Zealand. They were married in Australia in 1860, and arrived in the North Island of New Zealand in the summer of that year.

Almost immediately Gorst became involved in New Zealand politics. The British government was then engaged in a land dispute with the Maoris of the Waikato district, and since these were of the party which followed the Maori king, a nationalist rebellion was imminent. Gorst made friends among the native chiefs, and also won the confidence of the British and Colonial authorities. Some letters which he wrote to the *New Zealander*, deprecating the use of force to crush a weaker race, made a considerable impression in the colony, and he was shortly afterwards used as an intermediary between the government and the recalcitrant chiefs. In 1861 he was appointed inspector of native and missionary schools in Waikato, a position which he was expected to combine with that of semi-official intelligence officer. In the following year the governor, Sir George Grey [q.v.], who was experimenting with reformed institutions in the hope of averting a serious conflict, made Gorst his civil commissioner for the Waikato district. He held the position for a year, towards the end of which he edited a newspaper, the *Pitroihoi Mokemoke*, which was intended to counteract Maori propaganda. The new methods of government failed, the journal excited the active hostility of the Maoris, and in March 1863, shortly before the outbreak of rebellion on a large scale, the rebels raided the printing office and carried off the press and type. Gorst was ordered to withdraw, and he and his family narrowly escaped with their lives.

His appetite for adventure satisfied,

Gorst returned to England, and was called to the bar at the Inner Temple in 1865. He stood unsuccessfully as conservative candidate for Hastings in the same year. In 1866 he was returned for the borough of Cambridge, and during the next two years attracted the notice of Mr. Disraeli as an active and independent member. After losing his seat in 1868 he was asked to undertake the reorganization of the conservative party machinery on a popular basis. He devoted the next five years to this work, without salary, and the conservative victory of 1874 was largely attributable to his efforts. He expected office in the conservative administration of that year, but was disappointed, and his relations with the party leaders, with the exception of Disraeli, were henceforth somewhat strained. He re-entered parliament in 1875 as member for Chatham, and took silk in the same year. During the next few years he consolidated his reputation as a lawyer of note.

In the parliament of 1880 Gorst found a congenial associate in Lord Randolph Churchill who, like himself, was of democratic sympathies and naturally restive under official leadership. Originally united by the endeavour to use the Bradlaugh incident to embarrass Mr. Gladstone's government, Churchill and Gorst, with their allies, Sir Henry Drummond Wolff [q.v.] and Mr. Arthur (afterwards Earl of) Balfour, soon became, as the 'fourth party', the most effective section of the opposition. Gorst was a resourceful and persistent critic of the government, and his efforts and those of the 'party', met with a certain measure of encouragement from Lord Beaconsfield. His alliance with Lord Randolph Churchill, though chequered by differences over the Coercion Bill of 1881 and over the leadership of the conservative party, lasted for four years. As vice-chairman of the National Union of Conservative Associations he was a useful lieutenant in Churchill's fight for the party machine. When, however, control of the Union was secured in 1884, Lord Randolph made terms with Lord Salisbury without consulting Gorst, and the breach thus caused was widened by a public difference of opinion over the Franchise Bill of the same year.

On taking office in 1885, Lord Randolph Churchill obtained for Gorst the post of solicitor-general, which carried with it a knighthood. The same post was offered to him on the reconstruction of the government in the next year, but only till such time as a suitable judgeship should fall vacant. He declined the office on these terms, and was appointed under-secretary of state for India (1886). In 1890 he acted as British plenipotentiary at a labour conference in Berlin. From 1891 to 1892 he was financial secretary to the Treasury, and in 1895 he became the last vice-president of the Committee of the Privy Council on Education. Though disappointed that he had not reached higher office, Gorst was genuinely interested in education, and his zeal for social reform increased with age. He retired in 1902 with a pension of £1,200 a year, retaining his seat in the House. Mr. Chamberlain's fiscal campaign led to his final breach with the conservative party. He declared himself a free trader, and at the 1906 election was rejected by Cambridge University, which he had represented since 1892. Shortly after the election he resigned his trusteeship of the Primrose League, of which he had been one of the original founders.

The rest of Gorst's public life was devoted to speaking and writing on education, and on health, particularly the health of children. His book, *The Children of the Nation* (1906), was dedicated to the labour members of the House of Commons. In 1909 he relinquished his pension and was adopted as liberal candidate for Preston. His defeat in 1910 marked the end of his public career. That it was less successful than might have been expected from his energy and ability was probably due to the fact that he could not attach himself wholeheartedly to any political party. Gorst died in London 4 April 1916, and was buried at Castle Combe, Wiltshire. His first wife, by whom he had two sons and six daughters, died in 1914; he married in 1915 Ethel, daughter of Edward Johnson. His eldest son, Sir John Eldon Gorst, K.C.B. [q.v.], was British agent and consul-general in Egypt from 1907 to his death in 1911.

[*The Times*, 5 April 1916; Sir John E. Gorst, *New Zealand Revisited*, 1908; Harold E. Gorst (son), *The Fourth Party*, 1906; private information.]

M. C.

GOUGH, Sir CHARLES JOHN STANLEY (1832–1912), general, the second son of George Gough, Bengal civil service, of Rathronan, Clonmel, co. Tipperary, by his wife, Charlotte Margaret, daughter of Charles Becher, of Tonbridge, Kent, was born at Chittagong, India, 28 January 1832. Family tradition destined the boy to a soldier's career in India, where his great-uncle, Field-Marshal Viscount Gough [q.v.], was commander-in-chief. In March 1848 a commission was obtained for him in the 8th Bengal Cavalry, and he served throughout the second Sikh War (1848–1849). He distinguished himself during the Indian Mutiny, first in the Guide Corps and afterwards in Hodson's Irregular Horse, and took part in the siege of Delhi, in Sir James Outram's operations near Alumbagh, and in the capture of Lucknow. He received the Victoria cross for four separate acts of gallantry in the course of the Mutiny; in one of these he saved the life of his younger brother, (Sir) Hugh Henry Gough [q.v.], and in another (18 August 1857) he led a troop of Guide cavalry in a successful charge and a hand-to-hand combat. Gough saw further service in the Bhootan expedition of 1864–1865, and commanded a brigade in the Afghan campaign of 1878–1879, receiving the special praise of the commander-in-chief for an independent action on 2 April 1879, in which he defeated the Kuggianis, an Afghan tribe, at Futtehabad. At the end of the same year, when Sir Frederick (afterwards Earl) Roberts [q.v.] was besieged by the Afghans in his cantonment at Sherpur, near Kabul, he ordered Gough to advance from Gundamuk to his assistance, and the march of seventy miles through hostile country was one of the most adventurous of the war, for the transport was miserable and the weather severe. It was accomplished in less than four days, and Gough's approach (23 December) led the Afghans to attack, and thus gave Roberts his opportunity. For his services Gough was created K.C.B. (1881). He subsequently commanded the Hyderabad Contingent (1881), and his last employment was the charge of a division of the Bengal army (1886–1890). He was promoted general in 1891, and retired in 1895, receiving the G.C.B. He spent his last years in Ireland. In 1897 he published, in collaboration with A. D. Innes, a volume entitled *The Sikhs, and the Sikh War*, in which he defended the military policy of his great-uncle. He died at Innislonagh, Clonmel, 6 September 1912. Gough married in 1869 Harriette Anastasia, daughter of John W. Power, formerly M.P. for county Waterford; by her he had two sons, Lieutenant-General Sir Hubert de la Poer Gough, and Brigadier-General John Edmond Gough [q.v.].

[Army Lists; *The Times*, 7 September 1912; Lord Roberts, *Forty-one Years in India*, 1897; R. S. Rait, *Life of Field-Marshal Sir Frederick Haines*, 1911.] R. S. R.

GOUGH, JOHN EDMOND (1871–1915), brigadier-general, the younger son of General Sir Charles John Stanley Gough [q.v.], was born 25 October 1871 at Murree, India, and was educated at Eton. He received a commission in the Rifle Brigade in March 1892, and was promoted lieutenant in the following year. He served in British Central Africa (1896–1897), in the Nile expedition (1898), and throughout the South African War, taking part in the defence of Ladysmith and in subsequent operations in Natal and in the Transvaal. In 1902–1903 Gough was a staff officer in the Somaliland expedition, and, while commanding a force at Daratoleh, he, with some companions, rescued a wounded officer, returning in a shower of bullets and fighting his way back through the ranks of the enemy. For this exploit he was awarded in 1903 the Victoria cross, which, having been won by his father and his uncle, had almost become a family distinction. He was promoted brevet lieutenant-colonel in the same year, and in 1905 he graduated at the Staff College. In 1907 he became brevet colonel and aide-de-camp to the King and was appointed to the command in Somaliland, where he served in 1908–1909 as inspector-general of the King's African Rifles. From 1909–1913 he was a general staff officer at the Staff College, and, at the outbreak of the European War, occupied the position of a brigadier-general on the general staff. In the first six months of the war he served on the staff of Sir Douglas Haig, and by his scientific knowledge of his profession, his sound judgement, the vigour of his personality, and what has been described as his '*flair* and instinct for military operations', he made a deep impression on all ranks of the army and raised high expectations of his future. While inspecting trenches on 20 February 1915 he was hit by a ricochet bullet and died at Estaires two days later. Sir John French in his dispatch of 5 April expressed his 'deep sense of the loss incurred by the army in general and by the forces in France in particular', by Gough's death, and added, 'I always regarded General Gough as one of our most promising military leaders of the future'. The honour of K.C.B. was conferred upon him posthumously on 20 April. Gough married in 1907 Dorothea, daughter of General Sir Charles Keyes, and left one daughter.

[Army Lists; *The Times*, 24 February 1915.]

R. S. R.

GOULD, NATHANIEL (1857–1919), known as NAT GOULD, novelist, was born at Manchester 21 December 1857, the only child of Nathaniel Gould, tea-merchant, of that city, by his wife, Mary Wright. After leaving the private school at Southport where he was educated, Gould alternated between the tea trade and farming with an uncle in Derbyshire; and then, about 1878, became a journalist on the staff of the *Newark Advertiser*. In 1884 he went to Australia, where during eleven years he worked successively in Brisbane, Sydney, Bathurst, and Sydney again, on the staffs of different newspapers. His journalism was chiefly concerned with horse-racing, but he also wrote short stories and, later, a serial. The publication of the latter in book form was arranged for by Messrs. Routledge, who bought at the same time the book rights in two other serials. Gould ascribed the immense success of this first book, *The Double Event* (1891), to the coincidence of its publication with the Melbourne Cup meeting—the great racing event of the year in Australia. Thenceforward he and his publishers could count upon purchasers by the hundred thousand for his rapid output of new books.

Gould married at Brisbane in 1886 Elizabeth Madeleine, daughter of Francis Ruska, and by her he had three sons and two daughters. In 1895 he brought his family to England, settling in Middlesex, at Feltham and afterwards at Bedfont.

First with Messrs. Routledge and then, in 1903, with Mr. John Long, Gould entered into, and kept, engagements to supply four novels and one shorter story each year. At his death he had written about one hundred and thirty books, of which twenty-two were still waiting to be put into print at the rate of five each year. This has since been done. The number of copies of his books sold up to the present has been calculated at twenty-four millions.

Gould was on easy terms with his publishers, with life, and with his work. He never haggled for terms nor exaggerated his importance. He disclaimed any pretensions to 'literature' or 'style', setting himself to write stories that should hold the attention from beginning to end. He was proud of the verdict of a clergyman that they 'could be safely put into the hands of any youth or girl'. His stories were always concerned with horse-racing, and he seems never to have been troubled by any suspicion of the harmfulness of betting. Besides fiction he wrote two books on Australian life, *On and Off the Turf in Australia* (1895) and *Town and Bush* (1896), as well as *The Magic of Sport: mainly Autobiographical* (1909). He died 25 July 1919 at Bedfont, and was buried at Ashbourne, Derbyshire.

[Nat Gould, *The Magic of Sport*; private information.] F. P.

GOWERS, SIR WILLIAM RICHARD (1845–1915), physician, born in London 20 March 1845, was the only son of William Gowers, of Hackney, by his wife, Ann Venables. He began his education at Christ Church School, Oxford, and was apprenticed at the age of sixteen to Dr. Simpson at Coggeshall in Essex. Thence he went to complete his medical training at University College, London, where he was a pupil of Sir William Jenner [q.v.]. After qualification as M.R.C.S. in 1867, he became house-physician, and subsequently private secretary to Jenner—'the daily intercourse with that mind was a privilege inestimable'. At the age of twenty-five he was fortunate in being appointed medical registrar, and, three years later (1873), assistant-physician to the hospital for the paralysed and epileptic, Queen Square, London, where as a senior colleague he had Hughlings Jackson [q.v.], thinker and physician, under whose inspiration the research of the period was rapidly advancing. In these early years at Queen Square Gowers accumulated the great mass of material which he used ultimately in his books. In 1872 he had also been appointed assistant-physician at University College Hospital; in 1883 he became physician and, later, professor of clinical medicine there. In 1887 he was elected fellow of the Royal Society. In 1888, when pressure of work led to his retirement from University College, he was appointed consulting physician.

Gowers was interested from the outset in diseases of the nervous system, and his earliest contributions to medical literature dealt with the closely related blood-vascular system. He invented a form of haemoglobinometer, an instrument for measuring the percentage of haemoglobin in the blood, and he also improved the haemocytometer, or instrument for counting the blood corpuscles. His first important book was *Medical Ophthalmology* (1879), in which he discussed the subject more fully than previous writers and emphasized the use in medical diagnosis of the ophthalmoscope, which 'gives information not often otherwise obtainable regarding the existence and nature of disease elsewhere than in the eye'. The accuracy and clearness of the illustrations, from the author's own pen, made them for long the standard illustrations in the subject, and the book became an influential work and was translated into Italian and German. In 1880 Gowers published the revision of a previous lecture, *Diagnosis of Diseases of the Spinal Cord*, in which was described for the first time the tract of nerve-fibres in the spinal cord, subsequently known as 'Gowers's tract', a name which he always deprecated. The book was an illuminating contribution to the literature of a then obscure subject, and showed the author as an investigator who could relate clinical data with pathological facts, and develop a scheme of precise regional diagnosis. His greatest book, *A Manual of Diseases of the Nervous System* (1886), became a work of international repute. Gowers was prolific as a lecturer, and as a writer careful of fact and lucid in style. There were few neurological problems on which his published opinion was not forthcoming. The condition of epilepsy deeply interested him, and to it he gave long and close attention. His *Epilepsy* (1881) was still the standard authority at the time of his death.

Gowers made daily use of his skill in stenography and urged pupils and house-physicians to do the same, for the purpose of taking notes of cases and lectures. He founded the society of medical phonographers and was its first president. He was able to etch and draw general subjects as easily as medical, and his etchings made during holidays in East Anglia were often exhibited, once at the Royal Academy. In the 'eighties the National Hospital in Queen Square was Gowers's teaching centre, and partly through him came to have an international reputation. He was a careful observer and, thanks to his combination of knowledge from the laboratory and the hospital wards, a bold and incisive teacher. But, at most times strained and tired by overwork, he might appear to some dogmatic and impatient of criticism in his discussion of a case. The writing of the *Manual* had cost him much effort and had a lasting effect on his mental vigour. If not a neurologist with the originality and inspiration of Hughlings Jackson, Gowers was nevertheless a great clinician and by his writings made it possible for the medical world of his time to understand scientific neurology. He was knighted in 1897. Gowers married in 1875 Mary (died 1913), daughter of Frederick Baines, of Leeds, and had two sons and two daughters. He died in London 4 May 1915.

[*British Medical Journal*, 1915, vol. i, p. 1055; *Lancet*, 1915, vol. i, p. 828; private information.] E. G. T. L.

GRACE, WILLIAM GILBERT (1848–1915), cricketer, was born 18 July 1848, the fourth of five sons of Henry Mills Grace, a doctor living at Downend, near Bristol, by his wife, Martha, daughter of George Pocock, proprietor of a boarding school at St. Michael's Mill, Bristol. He was educated privately, at Bristol Medical School, and at St. Bartholomew's and Westminster Hospitals; and, after qualifying M.R.C.S. (England) and L.R.C.P. (Edinburgh), began to practise as a surgeon in Bristol (1879).

There was enthusiasm for cricket in Grace's home; both his father and his uncle (Alfred Pocock) were keen exponents, and Grace and his brothers received much careful tuition in every branch of the game. They joined in local matches at an early age, and the third son, Edward Mills Grace [q.v.], brought the family name into first-class cricket about 1862. With reference to his success, his mother, an enthusiast and a competent judge, said that she had a younger son who would be a better batsman because his back-play was sounder. This forecast was soon fulfilled, and in 1865 Gilbert Grace, as he was usually called, was chosen, while still under seventeen, to play for the Gentlemen *v.* the Players both at Kennington Oval and at Lord's. In the first match (3 July) he went in eighth and made 23, and, not out, 12. Though played, it is said, more for his bowling than his batting, he was sent in first at Lord's in the following week, and his second innings of 34 helped the Gentlemen, who had not beaten the Players since 1853, to a victory by eight wickets.

Grace was famous chiefly as a batsman, but he was first-rate both as a bowler and a fieldsman. Originally a medium pace bowler, he afterwards adopted a slower delivery, and took many wickets. Some of his greatest batting feats were followed up by bowling which, if not equally good, was equally successful. His bowling was often freely hit, but he never lost his length, and persevered with an optimism which, when he himself was captain, was thought at times to be scarcely warranted. His fielding, when he was a tall and athletic youth, was admirable in any position, but especially to his own bowling. In later life his massive figure is recalled at point, where little escaped his large and capable hands. As a captain, though he lacked the special gifts of a man like Vyell Edward Walker [q.v.], he was a keen leader and inspired his side with much of his own spirit.

It was in 1866, when he made 224, not out, for England against Surrey, and 173, not out, for Gentlemen of the South against Players of the South, that Grace opened the long series of extraordinary scores, which gave him an unchallenged position in cricket history. Between 1868 and 1876, judged by the evidence of statistics, he stood out by himself as a run-getter. Indeed, he completely altered the standard of scoring. Before his day a score of 50 on the rough wickets of the time was noteworthy, and a century the rarest event. In 1871, one of his best seasons, Grace, in addition to other substantial scores, made over 200 twice, and over 100 eight times. To cite one or two of many remarkable performances: on 29 June 1868, playing for the Gentlemen at Lord's, Grace went in first wicket down, and made, not out, 134, out of a total of 201; the next highest score in the match was 29; the ground was difficult, and he had to meet some of the best professional bowlers, but this youth of nineteen was master of the attack throughout, and hardly a ball passed his bat. In 1871, for South *v.* North at the Oval, and for the Gentlemen *v.* the Players at Brighton, he had each time the unusual experience of losing his wicket in the first over of the match, once bowled by, and once leg before to the Nottinghamshire professional, J. C. Shaw: in the second innings at the Oval he made 268 and at Brighton 217. To Shaw is ascribed an epigrammatic description (divested of some adverbial adornment) of Grace's batting: 'I puts the ball where I likes, and Grace, he puts it where he likes.'

Batting so far in advance of anything yet seen created a sensation in cricket circles. In the North there was intense eagerness to see Grace play. He paid his first visit to Sheffield in July 1869, when he made 122 for the South against the North. In July 1872 he came again, with the Gloucestershire eleven, and an enormous crowd packed the ground. Yorkshire, always one of the strongest counties, had some of the best bowlers of the day, but the first Gloucestershire wicket did not fall till 238, when Grace was out for 150. His success was continuous until 1874, and, though he was not so fortunate in the wet summer of 1875, in the following season he reached what was perhaps the zenith of his form. He made, not out, 400 in a match against odds at Grimsby, and in August he scored in three consecutive first-class matches, 344, 177, and, not out, 318.

During this, the first period of his career, Grace played in all sorts of cricket, and as a match-winner he was certainly worth half a side. His name is seldom to be found in a losing team. The Gentlemen could now almost always defeat the Players, and the Marylebone Club, of which Grace became a member in 1869, was, when he played, a formidable combination. In 1870, with two of his brothers, Edward Mills Grace and George Frederick Grace, he started the Gloucestershire county eleven, which, relying entirely upon amateur talent, was for some seasons one of the strongest county sides. Grace and his brother, E. M., were long associated with Gloucestershire cricket, but the youngest brother, G. F. Grace, an accomplished and popular player, died in 1880.

After 1877, though he remained the best batsman in England, Grace's supremacy was not so clearly marked. With improved wickets batting improved generally, and other experts came into prominence, such as Arthur Shrewsbury [q.v.], William Lloyd Murdoch [q.v.], Allan Gibson Steel [q.v.], and Walter William Read [q.v.]. The position of English cricket was now disputed by powerful elevens from Australia. Grace made, in 1880, 152 in the first match played in this country between England and Australia, and he was a member of the side which lost to Australia in 1882 at the Oval by 7 runs. He visited Australia twice, once in the winter of 1873, when Australian cricket was still in the stage of development, and eighteen years afterwards with the team taken out by the third Earl of Sheffield [q.v.] in the winter of 1891. Though he was over forty the trip was for him a personal success. He also went to the United States and Canada with a team of amateurs in 1872.

In 1895, thirty years after his entry into first-class cricket, Grace made a striking return to the form of his best days. At the beginning of the season he scored 288 for Gloucestershire against Somerset, his hundredth century in first-class cricket, and a few days later 257 and, not out, 73 against Kent. On the latter occasion he opened the first innings and was out last, and so was in the field during all three days of the match, a feat of endurance remarkable for a man who was nearly forty-seven years old. In this summer he reached his thousand runs as early as 30 May. Much public enthusiasm was shown. The Prince of Wales wrote to compliment him, and a shilling subscription fund, opened by the *Daily Telegraph*, resulted in the presentation to him of more than £5,000. Other testimonials were raised, banquets were given to him, and a suggestion was made in the press that his name should appear in the honours list.

Grace had another good season in 1896 when he played an innings of over 300, and one of over 200, for his county. In 1898 the Gentlemen *v.* Players match was fixed for 18 July in honour of his birthday. Though lame and injured he made 43 and 31, and the appearance of the 'Old Man', as cricketers now termed him, was the signal for even a louder tumult of cheers than usual. In 1899 he played for England for the last time, and made his last appearance for the Gentlemen at Lord's, though he afterwards played for them at the Oval. Though scoring less freely, and moving much less quickly between the wickets, he was still good enough for most elevens, and there was some regret that at this time he should have severed his long connexion with Gloucestershire, in order to take up the position of manager of cricket at the Crystal Palace. He played there for some years more, as well as in other matches. In 1908 a single appearance at the Oval brought his first-class cricket to a close. During his career of forty-three years he had made 126 centuries, had scored 54,896 runs, and had taken 2,876 wickets.

Grace's style of batting was solid and efficient. The bat looked curiously light in his hands, an impression created probably by the ease with which he wielded it. His defence was always first-rate: he watched the ball closely, and though at his best he was more comfortable with fast than with slow bowling, he was quick on his feet for so heavy a man. Like other famous executants he was more occupied with practice than theory, and, according to a contemporary anecdote, his contribution to a technical discussion on forward and back play was confined to an explanation that his own plan was to put the bat against the ball. While he was master of all the usual scoring strokes, his placing on the leg side was specially noted for its accuracy and power. He made runs more quickly on some days than others, and seldom sacrificed his wicket by recklessness. Above all, his energy and enthusiasm were surprising: indeed, in the days before boundaries, when all hits were run out, his huge scores were only possible to a combination of zeal and fitness, which enabled him to bat for hours without any feeling of weariness, physical or mental.

Grace, who kept up his medical practice in Bristol for twenty years (1879–1899), was much liked and esteemed. His personal ascendancy as a player, and the sternness with which he upheld the rigour of the game, made him at times a little assertive on the field. But no amount of fame or adulation was able to spoil him; and, long without a rival in his own sphere, he was quite without jealousy. A man of simple character, he was bluff and downright in manner, but his genuine kindness of heart won for him countless friends. He held a unique place in the national life. He was known to the public as 'W. G.' and was described as the 'Champion', a title which, while it had no official meaning, nobody disputed or wished to dispute. Prominent in an age when the cult of outdoor games was growing rapidly, contemporary opinion would have singled him out without hesitation as one of the best-known men in England. His burly figure and thick black beard were familiar far beyond the cricket field; his fame was celebrated constantly in prose and verse; he was the hero of anecdote and legend. It is true that when he died he was only a name to many, but a name that stood for all that was best and healthiest in open-air amusements, and his death, which took place at Eltham 23 October 1915, revived memories in strange contrast to the tragedy of the time.

Grace married in 1873 Agnes Nicholls Day, by whom he had three sons and one daughter. One of his sons, W. G. Grace, junior, who died as a young man, was in the Cambridge eleven in 1895 and 1896.

A portrait of Grace at the wicket was painted by Stuart Wortley for the Marylebone Cricket Club in 1890, and the club erected an entrance gateway in his memory in 1923. Another portrait was presented by the club to the National Portrait Gallery in 1926.

[Wisden's *Cricketers' Almanack*; Lord Hawke and others, *The Memorial Biography of Dr. W. G. Grace*, 1919; W. G. Grace, '*W. G.*'—*Cricketing Reminiscences and Personal Recollections*, 1899; W. G. Grace, *W. G.'s Little Book*, 1909.]

A. C.

GREENE, WILLIAM FRIESE- (1855–1921), pioneer of kinematography, one of the seven children of James Greene, wrought-iron worker, of Bristol, was born in that city at 69 College Street, 7 September 1855, and educated at Queen Elizabeth's Hospital, Clifton. He early made the acquaintance of William Henry Fox Talbot [q.v.] from whom he gained a good working knowledge of photography. He took up the craft for a living and for some years led a roving life as a travelling photographer. In 1882 he became acquainted with John Arthur Roebuck Rudge, of Bath, who had made a study of the photography of motion and had invented the 'bio-phantascope', an instrument which recorded movement by means of the rapid projection of lantern slides of motion-photographs. Friese-Greene helped Rudge to continue his experiments until 1884, when the latter was incapacitated by illness from further active work. Their efforts were directed to reproducing, by means of camera and projecting lantern, the synthesis of motion, and are thus distinct from the experiments of Eadweard Muybridge [q.v.], whose chief aim was the analysis of animal movement, for scientific purposes, by means of high-speed photography. Shortly after this, Friese-Greene went to London, opened a photographic business in Piccadilly, and lived at 39 King's Road, Chelsea, where he fitted up a laboratory and began a further series of experiments in motion-photography. His business flourished, and he established branches of it not only in London but in Bath, Bristol, and Plymouth.

Friese-Greene's experiments in the projection of motion-photographs began to attract attention about 1885. In that year, and again in 1887, he exhibited before the (Royal) Photographic Society machines for projecting such photographs taken upon revolving glass plates. In January 1888 he used, for the first time, a band of sensitized paper made transparent by being dipped in castor-oil; but attempts to produce satisfactory positives, for projection, from such negatives, were not successful. In the same year he was awarded at Vienna the Daguerre medal for the latest advance in photography. Having found sensitized paper impracticable, Friese-Greene turned his attention to celluloid (which had been invented in 1865), and, after many experiments directed to making this substance suitable as a flexible, transparent base for a photographic emulsion, he succeeded in the spring of 1889 in producing a sensitized celluloid ribbon-film satisfactory for his purpose. In June 1889 he lodged a provisional application for a patent, the complete specification of which was accepted in May 1890; with his name he coupled that of Mortimer Evans, an engineer who had helped him to devise the mechanism for operating the film in the camera and projector. The first film successfully taken and projected with the new apparatus was of a scene at Hyde Park Corner in October 1889; it was first publicly exhibited at Chester town hall in July 1890, and a portion of it is now in the South Kensington Museum.

Other experimenters, both English and foreign, were already in the field, and Friese-Greene's patent was quickly followed by other specifications on similar lines. There has, indeed, been much dispute as to the respective shares in the evolution of the modern kinematograph of inventors such as E. F. Marey, G. Demeny, and L. Lumière in France, C. F. Jenkins and T. A. Edison in America, and M. Skladanowsky in Germany, all of whom were at work on the problem from this time; but by a judgment of the United States circuit court in November 1910, in the action of the Motion Picture Patents Co. *v.* Steiner, Friese-Greene's patent was recognized as the master kinematographic patent of the world.

Friese-Greene had neglected his business for his laboratory (which he had moved from Chelsea to 20 Brooke Street, Holborn), and so far from being able to exploit his invention commercially, he found himself in 1891 involved in bankruptcy proceedings, the outcome of which was a short term in Brixton Prison—for contempt of court—and the loss of all his early apparatus in a sale of his effects. He was able to resume his experiments in 1892, and thereafter he laboured incessantly upon the improvement of kinematographic mechanism and, subsequently, upon the projection of motion-pictures in natural colours. He took out many more patents, and became a well-known figure in the film industry, but he remained in financial difficulties until the end of his days. He died suddenly at a trade conference in the Connaught Rooms, Great Queen Street, 5 May 1921. He was buried in Highgate cemetery, and over his grave a headstone recording his invention was erected by public subscription. Friese-Greene was twice married: first, in 1874 to Victoria Marina Friese, who died without issue; secondly, in 1897 to Edith Jane Harrison, by whom he had five sons.

[The *Optical and Magic Lantern Journal*, November 1889, and *Scientific American Supplement* (New York), 19 April 1890, for contemporary accounts of Friese-Greene's invention; *Photographic Journal*, October 1924 and July 1926; private information; personal knowledge.] W. E. L. D.

GREENWELL, WILLIAM (1820–1918), archaeologist, the eldest son of William Thomas Greenwell, of Greenwell Ford, Lanchester, Durham, by his wife, Dorothy, daughter of Francis Smales, was born at Greenwell Ford 23 March 1820. He was the elder brother of Dora Greenwell [q.v.], the poetess. He was educated at Durham grammar school and at University College, Durham, where he took his B.A. degree in 1839. Originally intended for the bar, he entered at the Middle Temple, but owing to ill-health returned to Durham in 1841 and took the theological course at University College. He graduated M.A. in 1843 and was ordained in the following year. After travelling in Germany and Italy in 1846, he was appointed to the perpetual curacy of Ovingham with Mickley, Northumberland, in 1847. Resigning in 1850 he served for a short time as curate to Archdeacon Robert Isaac Wilberforce [q.v.] at Burton Agnes, Yorkshire, and then acted as assistant to William George Henderson [q.v.], at that time principal of Hatfield Hall, Durham, afterwards dean of Carlisle. In 1852 Greenwell was appointed principal of Neville Hall, a hostel for medical students in Newcastle. This post he resigned in 1854 when he began his long connexion with Durham Cathedral as a minor canon. In 1862 he was appointed librarian to the dean and chapter and was placed in charge of the large and valuable collection of charters and rolls belonging to the cathedral. He was thus enabled to continue the work of arranging them, which had been begun by Joseph Stevenson [q.v.] during the years 1841 to 1846. In 1865 he was appointed to the living of St. Mary-the-Less in Durham, which he held until his death. He resigned his minor canonry and librarianship in 1907. He died at Durham, unmarried, 27 January 1918.

Greenwell began the study of documents by editing the *Boldon Buke* for the Surtees Society in 1852. His most important work in this line was the *Feodarium Prioratus Dunelmensis*, published for the same society in 1872: in this work he proved that the foundation charters of the Benedictine convent at Durham were forgeries. In 1856 he began his work as a collector, first of Greek coins (which were sold to America in 1901), then in 1858 of prehistoric bronze implements, which were sold in 1908 and are now in the British Museum. At the same period he began to explore barrows, the results appearing in 1877 in *British Barrows*, a work produced in collaboration with his friend, George Rolleston [q.v.]. As a result he was elected a fellow of the Royal Society in 1878.

Greenwell's great reputation as an authority on historical objects and documents, and on architecture, caused him to be much consulted; and to all genuine inquirers the benefit of his varied stores of knowledge and keen critical faculty were readily available. 'The canon', as he was popularly known, had a remarkable *flair* for documents and all the other objects of which he was to the end a keen collector. An admirable raconteur, with a keen sense of humour, he was very downright in his opinions and never hesitated to express them, when he thought right, with vigour and pungency. He continued active up to the end of his long and full life; for in addition to other work he took a considerable share in local affairs. No notice of so keen a fisherman would be complete without a reference to the salmon and trout flies named after him. His portrait, painted in 1898 by Arthur Stockdale Cope, R.A., hangs in the cathedral library at Durham.

[J. C. Hodgson, *Memoir* (with bibliography) in *Archaeologia Aeliana*, third series, vol. xv, 1918; personal knowledge.] K. C. B.

GRENFELL, JULIAN HENRY FRANCIS (1888–1915), soldier and poet, was born in London 30 March 1888, the eldest son of William Henry Grenfell, afterwards first Baron Desborough, by his wife, Ethel Anne Priscilla, daughter of the Hon. Julian Henry Charles Fane [q.v.]. He was educated at Summerfields School, Oxford, and at Eton College, where he reached the sixth form, and became one of the editors of the *Eton College Chronicle* and of a clever but ephemeral periodical called *The Outsider*. His contributions to these magazines, and, while he was still at Eton, to the London *World* and *Vanity Fair*, give an indication of his literary talent. In October 1906 Grenfell went up to Balliol College, Oxford, where he spent four happy years, surrounded by a brilliant company of friends. Only a temporary breakdown in health prevented him from taking a degree in the honour school of *literae humaniores*. A man of splendid physique and vitality, he excelled in every kind of sport, and in many branches of athletics, rowing in the college eight, which won the Wyfold cup at Henley in 1909, and boxing for the university.

Grenfell had always set his heart on a military career. In 1910 he obtained a commission, and joined the 1st (the Royal) Dragoons at Muttra; a year later, the regiment was transferred from India to South Africa. Shortly after the outbreak of the European War, Grenfell, with his regiment, returned to England, and early in October 1914 accompanied it to France. Within a few weeks his gallantry and soldierly abilities had won him a great reputation: 'he set an example of light-hearted courage which is famous all through the army in France,' wrote a distinguished officer in a contemporary letter, 'and has stood out even among the most lion-hearted'. He was awarded the distinguished service order for a daring feat of individual reconnaissance in November 1914, and in January 1915 he was mentioned in dispatches. On 13 May 1915, near Ypres, he was wounded in the head, and on 26 May he died in hospital at Boulogne. He was buried in the military cemetery on the hills above Boulogne.

On the day his death was announced (27 May), a poem by Grenfell, *Into Battle*, appeared in *The Times*. It was at once recognized as one of the finest of the many fine poems inspired by the War. Sir Walter Raleigh wrote of it, 'I don't think that any poem ever embodied soul so completely.... Those who glorified War had always, before this, been a little too romantic; and those who had a feeling for the reality of War had always been a little too prosaic. It can't be done again.' The poet laureate, Mr. Robert Bridges, included it in his anthology, *The Spirit of Man* (1916). The few other poems which Grenfell left, such as, *To a Black Greyhound*, *Hymn to the Fighting Boar*, and *The Hills*, are in a lighter vein, but all show the same power of expressing poetically his intense love of nature, his vivid delight in life, and light, and energy.

Apart from his poetry and his great military promise, Grenfell's short life is memorable for the deep impression which he made on his contemporaries of all ages. Old and young saw in him the personification of triumphant Youth. This impression is finely conveyed in a sonnet to his memory by Mr. Maurice Baring, while in a family history compiled by his mother, and privately circulated under the title *Pages from a Family Journal*, there survive not only a series of tributes to him from many pens, but also a delightful collection of his own letters.

Of his two brothers, the elder, Gerald William (born 1890), a scholar of Balliol from 1909 to 1913, who won a Craven scholarship in 1911 and obtained his 'blue' for tennis, was killed in action in July 1915, and the younger, too, died from the results of a motor accident in 1926.

[E. B. Osborn, *The Muse in Arms*, 1917; R. Bridges, *The Spirit of Man*; Maurice Baring, *Poems*, 1926; *The Balliol College War Memorial Book*, 1924.] A. F. L.

GREY, ALBERT HENRY GEORGE, fourth Earl Grey (1851–1917), statesman, was born 28 November 1851, the younger but only surviving son of General the Hon. Charles Grey [q.v.], second son of Charles, second Earl Grey [q.v.], the prime minister. His mother was Caroline Eliza, eldest daughter of Sir Thomas Harvie Farquhar, second baronet, of Cadogan House, Middlesex. He was educated at Harrow and Trinity College, Cambridge, passing out first in the old law and history tripos in 1873. From 1880 to 1885 he was member of parliament for South Northumberland, a constituency for which he had stood unsuccessfully in 1878. From 1885 to 1886 he sat for the Tyneside division of that county. Although nominally attached to the liberal party he took up from the first a somewhat independent position, being especially interested in subjects such as proportional representation and the reform of the national church. He was one of the dissentient liberals who voted against the Home Rule Bill of 1886, but he was defeated when he stood as a liberal unionist at the ensuing general election. No one was more catholic in his interests. Agriculturist, traveller, and sportsman, he was also a social reformer and a champion of unpopular causes; so that there seemed some risk lest his energies, diverted into such varied channels, might run to waste. Fortunately, however, they became mainly concentrated upon one object, the promotion of imperial unity.

In 1884 Henry George, third Earl Grey [q.v.], had transferred the entire management of his estates to Albert, who made the family seat at Howick, Northumberland, his head-quarters, although he did not succeed his uncle until 1894. During this period he made friends with William Thomas Stead [q.v.] who was then editing the *Pall Mall Gazette*. Stead introduced him to Cecil Rhodes, who in later years impressed him the most of any man that he had known.

At the time of the granting of the charter to the British South Africa Company (29 October 1889) Grey was invited to join the board of directors as one in whom the British government and the public could place confidence. Mr. Joseph Chamberlain sought to dissuade him from accepting; but, confessing his belief in Rhodes as a single-minded patriot, Grey joined the board. This 'paladin of his generation' was undoubtedly a tower of strength to Rhodes; and, throughout the difficult days that were to follow, Grey remained staunch in his loyalty to his friend and hero. It is manifest that the transparent goodness and charm of Grey brought out what was best in the enigmatic nature of the great empire-builder. After the Jameson Raid (29 December 1895) Grey accepted the thankless task of succeeding (Sir) Leander Starr Jameson [q.v.] as administrator of Rhodesia (1896–1897), although it is doubtful if it was a position for which he was specially fitted. At the outbreak of the Matabele rebellion in 1896 Grey was away on leave; and the presence of Rhodes during the subsequent proceedings inevitably made the administrator of less importance.

Grey was soon, however, to find a field more suited to his temperament and talents. From 1904 to 1911 he was governor-general of Canada. Sir Wilfrid Laurier [q.v.] has testified that from the moment that Grey landed in Canada he gave 'his whole heart, his whole soul, and his whole life' to Canada. The fervour of his imperial patriotism called forth a response even in unexpected quarters. His governor-generalship has been described as a most happy combination of the office and the man. To a country then on the wave of great financial prosperity and much occupied with material considerations, Grey bore constant witness of the importance of the things of the spirit, never swerving from the beliefs which he had learnt from the study of the life of Mazzini. Occasionally his imperialism exposed him to the shafts of the party politician, as when he applauded the plan of a Canadian navy; but generally he remained conscious of his constitutional limitations, walking 'on the tight rope of platitudinous generalities'. As an example of the independent and chivalrous character of his imperialism may be cited his defence of Laurier in connexion with reciprocity negotiations with the United States (24 October 1911 and 15 January 1913). His extraordinary tact was shown by the manner in which he prevailed upon the French Canadians to approve (in 1908) the commemoration of the victory of the Plains of Abraham. His period of office was twice extended; the first time because of his exceptional popularity; the second to suit the convenience of his successor, the Duke of Connaught. But his interest in imperial affairs did not end with the termination of his governor-generalship. In 1912 he paid his last visit to South Africa in order to unveil the memorial to Rhodes on Table Mountain, and the speech which he made on that occasion, giving expression to the faith that was in him, deeply impressed his hearers. By his suggestion and advocacy of the Dominion House scheme, which aimed at a common imperial centre in London for the Dominions, he sought to promote imperial unity; and, when this attempt proved hopeless, he threw himself, as president of the Royal Colonial Institute, into the work of extending the membership of that body, the non-political and practical character of whose activities especially appealed to him.

Although imperial patriotism was the main dogma in his political creed, Grey by no means neglected other interests. He was a keen promoter of the public house trust and 'garden-city' movements; and he gave eager support to the efforts of Sir Horace Plunkett to devise an eirenicon for the Irish question. So great was the attraction of his personal charm that Irishmen, such as 'A. E.' (George William Russell), bore witness that he had thrown new light for them upon the possibilities of the English character.

Grey was lord-lieutenant of Northumberland from 1899 to 1904. In the latter year he was created G.C.M.G., and in 1908 G.C.V.O. He died at Howick 29 August 1917.

Lord Grey married in 1877 Alice, third daughter of Robert Stayner Holford, M.P., of Westonbirt, Gloucestershire, by whom he had one son and two daughters. He was succeeded as fifth earl by his son, Charles Robert (born 1879). A charcoal-drawing by J. S. Sargent is in the possession of the family.

[*The Times*, 30 August 1917; Harold Begbie, *Albert, fourth Earl Grey; a last word*, 1917; Basil Williams, *Cecil Rhodes*, 1921; H. Henson, *A History of Rhodesia*, 1900; Castell Hopkins, *The Canadian Annual Review*, 1904 onwards; Canadian House of Commons Debates; *United Empire*, vol. viii, new series, no. 9.] H. E. E.

GRIERSON, Sir JAMES MONCRIEFF (1859–1914), lieutenant-general, born at Glasgow 27 January 1859, was the eldest son of George Moncrieff Grierson, a merchant of Glasgow, by his wife,

Allison Lyon, daughter of George Lyon Walker, of Garemount, Dumbartonshire. He was educated at Glasgow Academy, in Germany, and at the Royal Military Academy, Woolwich, whence he passed out fourth, and joined the Royal Artillery at Aldershot in 1878. Almost as soon as he joined he began to write military articles for the press. In 1879 he accompanied the Austrian armies in the occupation of Bosnia and Herzegovina, and in 1880 went to the Russian manœuvres at Warsaw as correspondent for the *Daily News*. In 1881 Grierson joined his battery in India, but soon after his arrival became attaché in the quartermaster-general's department at Simla. He was employed on intelligence work, and his pen was busy; for, besides contributions to the *Pioneer*, he produced a volume of notes on the Turkish army, an Arabic vocabulary, and a gazetteer of Egypt. When an Indian division was sent to Egypt in 1882 to take part in the operations against Arabi Pasha, he accompanied it as deputy assistant quartermaster-general, being present at the battles of Kassassin and Tel-el-Kebir. He was mentioned in dispatches, and received the medal, the khedive's star, and the fifth class of the order of the Medjidie. Grierson returned to India and in 1883 passed first into the Staff College. His time at Camberley was broken by the Sudan campaign of 1885, in which he served as deputy assistant adjutant and quartermaster-general, being present at the battles of Hashin and Tamai, and was again mentioned. At the Staff College he finished translating Grodekoff's *Campaign in Turcomania* and passed out with honours in French and Russian. On leaving he served for a time in the Russian section of the intelligence division under General (Sir) Henry Brackenbury [q.v.]. He was promoted captain in 1886, and in the following year joined a battery in India, but soon after was appointed deputy assistant quartermaster-general, first at Lucknow and then at Peshawar. In the Hazara expedition of 1888 he served as deputy assistant quartermaster-general, second brigade, was again mentioned and received the medal.

In 1889, at Brackenbury's request, Grierson returned to the intelligence division and became head of the Russian section. Antagonism between England and Russia in Asia was then growing, and Anglo-German relations became closer. There was a distinct *rapprochement* between the German General Staff and the British War Office; and Grierson, whose knowledge of Germany and of the Franco-German War was very considerable, was constantly in Berlin and the frequent guest of the Emperor and of German officers. During these years he published books on the Russian, German, and Japanese armies, *The Armed Strength of Russia* (1886), *The Armed Strength of Japan* (1886), and *The Armed Strength of the German Empire* (1888), and also a hand-book entitled *Staff Duties in the Field* (1891). After a short period in 1895 as brigade-major at Aldershot he was promoted brevet lieutenant-colonel, and in 1896 was appointed military attaché at Berlin. Grierson had hitherto been a warm admirer of the Germans, but during this period his views changed. Though cordially welcomed in Berlin and well received by the Emperor, he began to see that ultimately a breach with England must come.

Early in 1900, when Lord Roberts took over the chief command of the British forces in the South African War, Grierson was sent to the front in charge of the military attachés; but on his arrival at Paardeberg in February, Lord Roberts appointed him quartermaster-general, and as such he took part in the operations in the Orange Free State at Poplar Grove, Driefontein, and the Zand river, and in the occupation of Pretoria (5 June), and in the battle of Diamond Hill (12 June), being again mentioned and receiving the Queen's medal and four clasps. In August 1900 he was hurriedly dispatched to China as British representative on the staff of Field-Marshal Count von Waldersee, commander-in-chief of the allied forces against the Boxers, and entered Peking with him. He was of great service in smoothing the relations between the British and the Germans, but his opinion of German methods of making war was influenced unfavourably by his experience in China, where he found that jealousy of Great Britain and fear of Russia were the Germans' leading motives.

Returning home in 1901 Grierson received a brevet colonelcy and the C.B. for his services, and spent two years with the second Army Corps, first as assistant quartermaster-general and then as chief staff officer. On the reorganization of the War Office in 1904 he became director of military operations and was promoted major-general. During the next two years perhaps the most important work of his life was performed in contributing to the foundation of British friendship with France. Spending some time in

France he entered into cordial relations with many French officers and especially with Colonel Huguet, who in 1905 became military attaché in London. Between them these two men laid the foundations of co-operation between the British and French armies, and when Grierson went to command the first division at Aldershot in 1906, a post which he held till 1910, his work was carried on by his successors, Sir Spencer Ewart and (Sir) Henry Wilson. For the next eight years, with an interval on half-pay during which he took part in the coronation mission to Siam (1911) and in the official tour of Prince Henry of Prussia (1911), he was employed first at Aldershot and then (1912) as general officer commanding-in-chief, Eastern Command. In both capacities his energies were directed towards the training of troops for field warfare and especially towards securing rapidity of mobilization. The clash with Germany, which had long been foreseen by Grierson and by many other soldiers, sailors, and diplomatists, grew clearly more imminent. Had war with Germany come about as the result of the Agadir crisis (July 1911), it had been proposed that Grierson should be chief of the general staff of a British expeditionary force: but in 1914, when war was declared, he was appointed to command the second Army Corps. He only lived to land in France. He reached Havre on 16 August, and the day after his arrival he died suddenly in the train, near Amiens, of aneurism of the heart He was buried at Glasgow.

Grierson's great knowledge of languages, his strength, energy, capacity for work, and extraordinary memory, enabled him to acquire a vast store of knowledge of his profession. One of the outstanding features of his character was his admiration of the British private soldier. He was beloved by his troops, for though strict as regards training, he spared them unnecessary duties by thinking out his problems in advance and making provision for all reasonable comfort and relaxation. His early service was chiefly on the staff, and he was in advance of his times in knowledge of staff work; but this was not his predilection. 'I would rather command a battalion in war than be C.G.S.', he wrote in 1914. He was of a cheerful disposition, a good musician, an amateur actor, fond of travel and society; but he really lived for his profession, and no officer was more wholeheartedly devoted to the army. He was created K.C.B. on the occasion of the coronation of King George V in 1911, when he was in attendance on the German crown prince, and he was an aide-de-camp general to the King, knight of grace of St. John of Jerusalem, a commander of the legion of honour, and holder of many other foreign decorations. He was unmarried.

[*The Times*, 18 August 1914; War Office records; *Annual Register*; '*The Times*' *History of the War in South Africa*, 1900–1909; D. S. Macdiarmid, *Life of Sir James Moncrieff Grierson*, 1923; private information.] O.

GROSSMITH, GEORGE (1847–1912), entertainer and singer in light opera, was born in London 9 December 1847, the elder son of George Grossmith, a lecturer and police-court reporter to *The Times* and other journals, by his wife, Emmeline Weedon. His uncle, William Robert Grossmith, of Reading, had been a well-known child-actor. At seventeen, while still a pupil at the North London Collegiate School, Grossmith began to act as deputy for his father at the Bow Street police court, and from 1866 to 1869 this was his only profession. He gave it up for a time in 1877, on being engaged at the Opera Comique, but resumed it for a short period on his father's death in 1880. In boyhood he had entertained his friends by singing comic songs to his own accompaniment on the piano. Modelling his work on that of John Orlando Parry [q.v.], he began in 1864 to give performances at 'penny readings' of songs and sketches of contemporary life, most of which he composed and wrote. In 1870 he was engaged by John Henry Pepper [q.v.] to perform in his entertainment at the Polytechnic in Regent Street. Other engagements of this kind followed; and until 1877 he was much occupied in touring with his father, with Mrs. Howard Paul [q.v.], with Florence Marryat [q.v.], or alone. For performance with Miss Marryat he wrote and composed in 1876 the satirical sketch *Cups and Saucers*.

In the autumn of 1877 he was engaged by Richard D'Oyly Carte [q.v.] to take the part of John Wellington Wells in Gilbert and Sullivan's comic opera, *The Sorcerer*, produced at the Opera Comique 17 November 1877; and for the next twelve years he was regularly employed in this series of operas. He 'created' the parts of Sir Joseph Porter in *H.M.S. Pinafore* (Opera Comique, 28 May 1878), Major-General Stanley in *The Pirates of Penzance* (Opera Comique, 3 April 1880), Reginald Bunthorne in *Patience* (Opera Comique, 23 April 1881, transferred to the newly built Savoy Theatre, 10 October 1881), the Lord Chancellor in *Iolanthe* (Savoy, 25 November 1882), King Gama in *Princess Ida* (Savoy, 5 January 1884), Ko-ko in *The Mikado* (Savoy, 14 March 1885), Robin Oakapple in *Ruddigore* (Savoy, 22 January 1887), and Jack Point in *The Yeomen of the Guard* (Savoy, 3 October 1888). The agility and droll dignity of his small frame, his dry humour, his pleasant voice, and the skill in rapid enunciation which caused his 'patter-songs' to be made a regular feature of these operas, suited Grossmith perfectly to this form of dramatic and musical art.

Meanwhile he had not wholly given up his 'humorous and musical recitals', which were more remunerative than the opera; and in 1889 he left the Savoy to devote himself to them. But for three appearances on the stage in comedy, this work fully occupied him, in private houses and public buildings far and wide over the United Kingdom, Canada, and the United States, until his retirement in 1909. He would fill by himself an hour and a half with words and music of his own making; and his shrewd, superficial satire and such songs as 'The Muddle-Puddle Porter', 'The Happy Fatherland', and 'See Me Dance the Polka', with their accompanying chat, made him, perhaps, more popular even than his friend, Richard Corney Grain [q.v.]. He composed the music to Gilbert's opera, *Haste to the Wedding*, and the incidental music to several plays; he also wrote two books of reminiscences, *A Society Clown* (1888) and *Piano and I* (1910), and, with his brother Walter Weedon Grossmith [q.v.], a well-known humorous book, *The Diary of a Nobody* (1894), which first appeared serially in *Punch*. In 1873 he married Emmeline Rosa (died 1905), only daughter of E. Noyce, M.D., and left two sons (George and Lawrence, both of whom became actors) and two daughters. He died at Folkestone 1 March 1912.

Walter Weedon Grossmith (1854–1919), comedian, younger brother of the preceding, was born in London 9 June 1854. Having studied at the Royal Academy schools and the Slade School he became a painter, and exhibited at the Royal Academy and Grosvenor Gallery. In 1885 he went on the stage, and soon made a hit as Lord Arthur Pomeroy in Cecil Clay's *A Pantomime Rehearsal*. In 1888 (Sir) Henry Irving [q.v.] engaged him to play Jacques Strop in *Robert Macaire* at the Lyceum. In 1907 he appeared with (Sir) H. Beerbohm Tree [q.v.] in *The Van Dyk*. His successful career was mainly occupied, under his own management or that of others, in acting 'dudes' and small, underbred, unhappy men, in which parts he excelled. Among the plays that he wrote, *The Night of the Party*, which he produced at the Avenue Theatre in 1901, was the most successful. His artistic taste showed itself best in his *flair* for old furniture. He married in 1895 May Lever Palfrey, actress, a descendant of Charles Lever [q.v.], who, with one daughter, survived him. He died in London 14 June 1919.

[G. Grossmith, *A Society Clown*, 1888; W. Grossmith, *From Studio to Stage*, 1913; P. FitzGerald, *The Savoy Opera*, 1894; Memoir of George and Weedon Grossmith, by B. W. Findon, in *The Diary of a Nobody*, 5th edition, 1920; *The Times*, 2 March 1912, 16 June 1919; private information.]

H. H. C.

GROSVENOR, RICHARD DE AQUILA, first Baron Stalbridge (1837–1912), railway administrator and politician, the fourth son of Richard Grosvenor, second Marquess of Westminster [q.v.], by his wife, Lady Elizabeth Mary Leveson Gower, second daughter of George Granville Leveson Gower, first Duke of Sutherland [q.v.], was born at Motcombe House, Motcombe, Dorset, 28 January 1837. He was educated at Westminster School and at Trinity College, Cambridge, where he matriculated in 1855, and took his M.A. degree three years later. He became member of parliament for Flintshire as a liberal as early as 1861, and retained his seat until 1886. He was sworn of the Privy Council in 1872, and was vice-chamberlain of the royal household from 1872 to 1874. In 1886 he was raised to the peerage by the title of Baron Stalbridge, of Stalbridge, in the county of Dorset, in recognition of services rendered as patronage secretary to the Treasury and chief government whip throughout Mr. Gladstone's administration from 1880 to 1885. His experience as a liberal whip during the days of nationalist obstruction made it impossible for him to agree to Mr. Gladstone's Irish policy; and after the Home Rule crisis of 1886 he became a staunch and influential member of the liberal-unionist organization.

Lord Stalbridge's life work, however, was done in connexion with the London and North Western Railway Company, of which he was a director for more than forty years and for half that period the chairman. He became a director in 1870; he was elected chairman in succession to Sir Richard Moon in 1891, and held the office until 1911. Throughout that period he took an active interest in the progress and development of railways. He made himself conversant with the design and construction of the successive types of locomotive which were brought into use ; and it was said that no railway director had ridden more miles upon the footplate than Lord Richard Grosvenor during the early years of his directorship. He was also actively concerned with many schemes for helping the employees of his company, by such means as the improvement of their savings bank, their superannuation fund, and the fund for their widows and orphans. From 1897 he presided over the meetings of their ambulance centre, established in connexion with the St. John Ambulance Association. Lord Stalbridge's interest in railway matters was not, however, limited to the affairs of the North Western. The Universal Exhibition held at Paris in 1867 had given a great impulse to plans for bringing nations into closer contact by improving their communications : the Mont Cenis tunnel was nearly completed ; that under Mont St. Gothard was about to be undertaken ; and the project of an Anglo-French tunnel under the straits of Dover was revived. Lord Richard Grosvenor became the head of an Anglo-French company formed to promote the last project, and he continued throughout his life to advocate linking up the English and continental railway systems by a submarine tunnel.

As a sportsman Lord Stalbridge was extremely fond of hunting, an enthusiastic deer-stalker, and a member of the Royal Yacht Squadron. He died, after a prolonged illness, 18 May 1912 at his house in Sussex Square, London, and was buried at Motcombe.

Lord Stalbridge married twice : first, in 1874 the Hon. Beatrice Charlotte Elizabeth Vesey (died 1876), daughter of Thomas, third Viscount De Vesci, by whom he had one daughter ; secondly, in 1879 Eleanor Frances Beatrice Hamilton (died 1911), daughter of Robert Hamilton Stubber, of Moyne, Queen's county, by whom he had three sons and two daughters. He was succeeded in the title by his eldest son, Hugh (born 1880).

[*The Times*, 20 May 1912 ; *Daily Telegraph*, 20 May 1912 ; *Book of Matriculations and Degrees, University of Cambridge 1851–1900*.] A. C. B.

GUINNESS, Sir ARTHUR EDWARD, second baronet, and first Baron Ardilaun (1840–1915), philanthropist, the eldest son of Sir Benjamin Lee Guinness, first baronet, M.P. [q.v.], by his wife, Elizabeth, daughter of Edward Guinness, of Dublin, was born at St. Anne's, Clontarf, co. Dublin, 1 November 1840. He was educated at Eton and at Trinity College, Dublin, where he graduated in 1862. Upon the death of his father in 1868 he succeeded to the title as second baronet and became the head of the famous brewery at St. James's Gate, Dublin, founded by his grandfather, from which he retired in 1877. He was at once returned unopposed in the conservative interest as member of parliament for Dublin city in his father's place. At the next election in 1869 he lost the seat. He re-entered parliament for the same constituency at the general election in 1874 and held the seat until 1880, when he was raised to the peerage under the title of Baron Ardilaun, of Ashford, co. Galway. In 1871 he married Lady Olivia Charlotte White, daughter of the third Earl of Bantry.

Guinness's generous devotion to the interests of the city of Dublin was conspicuous from the beginning of his public life. In 1872, with his younger brother, Edward Cecil, afterwards Earl of Iveagh, he originated, and took financial responsibility for, the Dublin Exhibition of Arts and Science. He completed the restoration, begun by his father, of the fabric of Archbishop Marsh's Library, Dublin. In 1877 he rebuilt the Coombe Lying-in Hospital ; while the building by the government of the Science and Art Museum in Dublin was due to his advocacy in the House of Commons. He took a practical interest in the improvement of working-class dwellings and was president of the artisans' dwellings company, the first company inaugurated in Dublin for this purpose. It was entirely due to his munificence that the beautiful public park of some twenty-two acres in the centre of the city, known as St. Stephen's Green, was acquired, laid out, and handed over under a special act of parliament to the Board of Works for the use of the citizens of Dublin. As a mark of the general appreciation in which he was held, a bronze statue of Lord Ardilaun was erected in St. Stephen's Green by public subscription in 1891. In 1899 he purchased the Muckross estate, co. Kerry, which adjoins the lakes of Killarney, in order to save it and the lakes from falling into the hands of a commercial syndicate.

Lord Ardilaun was a generous supporter of the Church of Ireland. At the time of its disestablishment he contributed largely to its capital funds, and up to his death he bore half the expense of the choir of St. Patrick's Cathedral.

From 1897 to 1913 Lord Ardilaun was president of the Royal Dublin Society, which for close on two centuries has taken the leading part in the development of the resources of Ireland ; the publication of the Society's history was due to his initiative and liberality. When he retired from the presidency, owing to failing health, he received a presentation and address, and the Society commissioned Sir William Orpen, R.A., to paint his portrait, which hangs in the board-room.

In 1900 Lord Ardilaun became the proprietor of the *Dublin Daily Express* and the *Dublin Evening Mail* which were carried on in the unionist interest. He was so staunch a conservative that in 1898 he declined to accept the lieutenancy of the county of Dublin, because it was offered to him by a conservative lord-lieutenant of Ireland (Earl Cadogan) at a moment when the loyalists of Ireland felt bitterly that their cause had been betrayed by Lord Salisbury's government.

Lord Ardilaun's principal seat was at St. Anne's, Clontarf, where he and Lady Ardilaun entertained generously and received in 1900 a visit from Queen Victoria. A large part of each year he spent on his Galway estate at Ashford, where he gave employment on a large scale, making roads and planting trees. He was an expert in forestry, and by his judicious choice of trees transformed and beautified the countryside for miles round. He also maintained for many years a steamer on Lough Corrib between Cong and Galway for the benefit of his tenants and the neighbourhood.

Lord Ardilaun died, without issue, 20 January 1915 at St. Anne's, Clontarf, and was buried in the mortuary chapel attached to the church of All Saints which he had built on his county Dublin estate. He was succeeded, as third baronet, by his nephew, Sir Algernon Arthur Guinness (born 1883).

[*The Times*, 12 June 1874, 28 November 1899, 21 January 1915 ; *Irish Times*, 20 June 1892, 11 May 1898 ; *Dublin Evening Mail*, 13 November 1913 ; personal knowledge.]

B. J. P.

GÜNTHER, ALBERT CHARLES LEWIS GOTTHILF (1830–1914), zoologist, was born at Esslingen in Würtemberg 3 October 1830, the elder son of Friedrich Gotthilf Günther (died 1835), bursar of estates under the council of Esslingen, by his wife, Eleonora Louise, daughter of Ludwig Friedrich Nagel, pastor of Vaihingen. He came of an old-established Swabian family, and through his mother was descended from Eberhard im Bart, the founder of Tübingen University. Educated at the gymnasium of Stuttgart and on the Stift at the university of Tübingen, he was trained for the ministry and took holy orders and the degrees of M.A. and Ph.D. in 1852. But his natural bent inclining rather towards zoology, he obtained permission to attend the courses of Professor Rapp and to proceed to a medical degree. He also studied at the university of Berlin under Johannes Müller, and at that of Bonn, where he formed a friendship with Charles Milner, the father of Lord Milner. Three years later he graduated in medicine at Tübingen, publishing at the same time his *Handbuch der medizinischen Zoologie* (1858), somewhat in advance of its times. Already in 1853 he had worked out a painstaking faunistic account of the fishes of the Neckar. In 1857, having made the acquaintance of (Sir) Richard Owen [q. v.] and Dr. John Edward Gray [q. v.], respectively superintendent of the natural history collections and keeper of the zoological department of the British Museum, he was invited to prepare a catalogue of the amphibia and reptiles in the Museum. In July 1862 he was appointed on the staff of the Museum and remained in its service for thirty-three years, being keeper of the zoological department in succession to Gray from 1875 to 1895. He became naturalized as a British subject when he entered the service of the Museum.

Günther was a devoted and learned systematic zoologist, author of over four hundred memoirs which range over a wide field ; and at the same time he had an enthusiastic interest in living creatures, in the care of which he was unusually successful. He possessed a remarkable knowledge of mammals, of birds, and especially of the lower orders of vertebrates, in regard both to their anatomical features and their habits and life-history. Thus he was able to supply Darwin with so much information respecting the nuptial peculiarities and the reproduction of the lower vertebrates, that the great naturalist wrote : 'My essay [i. e. *Descent of Man*, vol. ii, c. 12], as far as fishes, batrachians, and reptiles are concerned, will be in fact yours, only written by me' [*Letters*, vol. iii, 123]. In the same way Günther's work on the *Geographical Distribution of Reptiles* (1858), taken in conjunction with that of the ornithologist, Dr. P. Lutley Sclater, on a similar subject, paved the way for the work of Alfred Russel Wallace [q.v.] on the geographical distribution of animals (1876). In addition to valuable monographs, including studies of such important types as sphenodon and ceratodus, Günther was the author of an admirable *Introduction to the Study of Fishes* (1880), a treatise that has been of great value to students. Other notable pieces of work were his great *Catalogue of Fishes in the British Museum* (eight volumes, 1859–1870), his *Reptiles of British India* (1864), *Fische der Südsee* (three volumes, 1873–1909), *Gigantic Land Tortoises* (1877), and his *Deep-sea Fishes of the 'Challenger' Expedition* (1887), in which he distinguished the chief bathymetrical zones of the ocean by the character of their fish fauna.

Günther was the founder, in 1864, and first editor of the *Record of Zoological Literature*, an invaluable bibliography of new contributions to the science. He had an important share in the development of the natural history collections of the British Museum, the specimens in which were increased in number from one million in 1868 to two and a quarter millions in 1895. He was responsible for the safe removal of all the collections to their new home at South Kensington in 1883, and for the erection of a special spirit museum for the custody of an extensive series of spirit preparations for the use of students. To him also is due the credit of establishing the zoological library which forms an important adjunct to the national collections. It was his object to stimulate travellers and collectors to visit zoologically unknown regions, and so to help on the exploration of the world, especially of remote islands and inland waters. He was vice-president of the Royal Society for 1875–1876 and president of the biological section of the British Association in 1880; he was also president of the Linnean Society (1898–1901), and received the gold medal of the Royal Society (1878) and of the Linnean Society (1904). He died at Kew 1 February 1914.

Günther was a fine type of the accurate systematic zoologist—learned, indefatigable, and disinterested, with a high standard of workmanship; he was also an accomplished field-naturalist, though the circumstances of his professional life did not bring this side of his equipment into prominence.

Günther married twice: first, in 1868 Roberta (died 1869), daughter of John McIntosh, of St. Andrews; secondly, in 1879 Theodora Dowrish, daughter of Henry Holman Drake, of Fowey, Cornwall. He had two sons, one by each marriage. His elder son, Robert Theodore, was elected a fellow of Magdalen College, Oxford, in 1896.

A bronze medallion portrait by Frank Bowcher is in the Natural History Museum.

[*Günther Family Records*, 1910; *History of Collections in the Natural History Departments of the British Museum*, vol. ii, Appendix, 1912; *Proceedings* of the Royal Society, vol. lxxxviii, B, 1914–1915; private information.] J. A. T.

GWATKIN, HENRY MELVILL (1844–1916), historian, theologian, and conchologist, was born at Barrow-on-Soar, Leicestershire, 30 July 1844, the second son of the Rev. Richard Gwatkin, senior wrangler in 1814 and afterwards fellow of St. John's College, Cambridge. Henry Gwatkin went up to St. John's with a scholarship in 1863, after seven years at Shrewsbury School. In 1867 he graduated as thirty-fifth wrangler, ninth classic, and third in the moral sciences tripos—an extraordinary feat, which he followed up in 1868 by being placed alone in the first class in the theological examinations. In the same year he was elected to a fellowship at St. John's, and when he vacated this on his marriage in 1874, the college appointed him lecturer in theology. His failure in 1884 as a candidate for the new Dixie professorship of ecclesiastical history, to which Mandell Creighton [q. v.] was appointed, was to some extent compensated seven years later by his election as Creighton's successor. He now took orders, and held the chair, with the attached fellowship at Emmanuel College, for the rest of his life. In 1903 he was Gifford lecturer in the university of Edinburgh. He died at Cambridge 14 November 1916, of a seizure, probably the effect of a street accident in the previous August.

Gwatkin was a man of wide and deep learning. As an historian he possessed a wonderful knowledge of original sources and a singularly keen eye for the vital facts and tendencies of intricate and perplexing periods. His most notable writings were *Studies of Arianism* (1882), *The Knowledge of God* (1906), based on his Gifford lectures, and *Early Church History* (1909). His *Church and State in England to the Death of Queen Anne*, printed after his death from an unrevised draft, should not be taken into account in estimating his abilities and scholarship. In his last years he gave much of his time to the *Cambridge Medieval History*, as an editor and a contributor.

His literary work was always sound and lucid, but, owing to his horror of the trivial and irrelevant, his treatment of complicated subjects was at times somewhat meagre and bald. As a conchologist, while he wrote little, he won high fame among specialists by his collection of *radulae*, to which he devoted the leisure of many years. It is, however, on his very remarkable ability as a teacher that his reputation mainly rests. Though hampered by defects of sight and utterance, and by mannerisms disconcerting to his audience, he was a clear, witty, stimulating, and (when he chose) eloquent lecturer. He was most widely known as a teacher of history, but in the opinion of himself and some of his pupils, he was at his best in the Greek Testament readings which he conducted in succession to F. J. A. Hort [q. v.]. A liberal in politics and theology, he was an outspoken critic of catholicism, whether Roman or Anglican. In private life he was somewhat shy and reserved, but had the deep affection of those of his colleagues and pupils who were brought into close touch with him.

Gwatkin married in 1874 Lucy, daughter of the Rev. Thomas Brock, vicar of St. John's, Guernsey, by whom he had a son and a daughter.

[*The Gwatkins of Herefordshire*, by E.M.G.; notices in *The Cambridge Review*, 22 and 29 November 1916; private information.]

W. T. W.

GWYNN, JOHN (1827–1917), scholar and divine, the eldest son of the Rev. Stephen Gwynn, rector of Agherton, Portstewart, Derry, by his wife, Mary Stevenson, was born at Larne 28 August 1827. He was educated at the Royal School, Inniskillen, and Trinity College, Dublin, of which he became a fellow in 1852. A refined classical scholar, he was warden of St. Columba's College, near Dublin, from 1856 to 1864. For the next eighteen years he worked as a country parson at Ramelton, co. Donegal, having been presented to the benefice of Tullyaughnish by Trinity College, and he became successively dean of Raphoe (1873) and dean of Derry (1882). In 1883 he returned to Trinity College, Dublin, as Archbishop King's lecturer in divinity, and in 1888 succeeded Dr. George Salmon [q.v.] as regius professor, a post which he held until his death, which occurred at Dublin 3 April 1917. He was serving the Church in the north of Ireland during the difficult period of the disestablishment, and he came into notice in the early days of the general synod as a conservative and moderate high churchman. But academic life provided the true sphere of his activities, and his association with the divinity school of Trinity College for thirty-four years was much to its advantage. He married in 1862 Lucy Josephine, the elder daughter of William Smith O'Brien [q.v.], the Irish nationalist, and had six sons and two daughters. His portrait by S. Purser is in the common room of Trinity College.

Gwynn set himself to the study of Syriac, as he used to tell, to relieve the tedium of long railway journeys from Donegal to Dublin; and he steadily became a master of the language. Within a few years he had contributed nearly forty articles to the *Dictionary of Christian Biography*, chiefly concerned with the early Greek and Syriac translators of the Bible; and in 1888 he wrote an erudite essay on the Peshitta version for the *Church Quarterly Review*. An important paper on *Hippolytus and his Heads against Caius*, in which these two persons were distinguished from each other, appeared in *Hermathena* (1888); and his discovery that the Syriac *Pericope de adultera* belongs to the Harkleian version, in the *Transactions* of the Royal Irish Academy (1888). These preliminary studies were crowned by the publication in 1897 of a new Syriac text of the Apocalypse, accompanied by an introductory dissertation and very full and careful notes. Gwynn's researches included also *Remnants of the Later Syriac Versions of the Bible* (1909). In short, he published all that now remains of the sixth-century Philoxenian version, and increased our knowledge of its successor, the Harkleian.

Gwynn's *magnum opus* was his superb edition of the Book of Armagh, an Irish manuscript of the ninth century, containing the whole New Testament in Latin, the Life of St. Martin of Tours, and some Patrician pieces, in Latin and Irish, of high importance for the history of early Christianity in Ireland. On this he had been at work for more than twenty years, and when it appeared in 1913 it was at once recognized as a masterly achievement. His infinite patience, his meticulous accuracy, and his sound judgement were notably illustrated by this fine book. And its welcome by scholars all over Europe was grateful not only to the editor, but to his many pupils and friends to whom he had endeared himself by his gracious courtesy and his kind heart.

[*The Times*, 4 April 1917; *Abstract of Minutes* of the Royal Irish Academy, 16 March 1918; personal knowledge.]

J. H. B.

HACKER, ARTHUR (1858–1919), painter, born in London 25 September 1858, was the second son of Edward Hacker, line engraver. He became a student at the Royal Academy schools in 1876 and continued his studies in Paris in the atelier of Léon Bonnat (1880–1881). When he was only nineteen one of his studies was hung at Burlington House; but his first Academy contribution to attract general attention was 'Her Daughter's Legacy', a scene from peasant life, which he exhibited in 1881. His 'Relics of the Brave', exhibited in 1883, was immediately purchased by an American for the town of Savannah, Georgia. About this time Hacker, together with his friend, the painter Solomon J. Solomon, went for a five months' trip to Spain and Morocco, and in after years Hacker repeatedly visited the north of Africa. In 1887 he exhibited 'Pelagia and Philammon', his first more ambitious essay in the rendering of the nude (now in the Walker Art Gallery, Liverpool); to 1890 and 1891 respectively belong 'Vae Victis: Sack of Morocco by the Almohades', and 'Christ and the Magdalen'; while 1892 saw the exhibition of 'The Annunciation', which was purchased by the trustees of the Chantrey fund and is now in the National Galley of British Art at Millbank (Tate Gallery). In 1893 Hacker exhibited 'Circe', which achieved great popular success, and 'The Sleep of the Gods'. The following year he was elected A.R.A., and sixteen years later (1910) R.A.

The work of Hacker may be divided into three groups. One is formed by his more important subject-pictures, of which several have been mentioned, the best known being his 'Annunciation', an arresting composition, somewhat melodramatic in conception, and showing the artist obviously under the influence of the more conventional type of contemporary French painting. Another notable group comprises his London street scenes, in which he favoured soft and misty effects of atmosphere; of these his diploma piece, 'Wet Night, Piccadilly Circus' (1911), is an example. Finally, Hacker was very frequently employed as a portrait painter, especially towards the end of his career. Among his sitters may be mentioned Sir John Brunner (twice), Sir Frank Short, and the sculptors Edward Onslow Ford and Sir William Goscombe John. Marked at all times by considerable facility of execution, brilliant in colouring, and popular in its sentimental appeal, the work of Hacker can, however, scarcely be regarded as being of a very profound interest.

Hacker married in 1907 Lilian, third daughter of Edward Price-Edwards. They had no children. He suffered from heart trouble, and was found dead on the doorstep of his house in Cromwell Road, South Kensington, on 12 November 1919. He bequeathed £500 to the benefactors' fund of the Royal Academy.

[The *Daily Telegraph*, 14 November 1919; *Studio*, vol. lvi, 175–182, 1912; Algernon Graves, *The Royal Academy of Arts, Dictionary of Contributors, 1769–1904*, vol. iii, 1905–1906.] T. B.

HALSBURY, first EARL OF (1823–1921), lord chancellor. [See GIFFARD, HARDINGE STANLEY.]

HAMILTON, JAMES, second DUKE OF ABERCORN (1838–1913), the eldest son of James Hamilton, first Duke [q.v.], by his wife, Lady Louisa Jane Russell, second daughter of John, sixth Duke of Bedford, was born at Brighton 24 August 1838, and educated at Harrow and at Christ Church, Oxford. In 1860 as Marquess of Hamilton he became member, in the conservative interest, for county Donegal, where the family estates mainly lay, though the seat was at Baronscourt in county Tyrone. The tradition of the family was strongly tory despite their connexion with the house of Russell. Five of the brothers sat in parliament, but, unlike the others, the Marquess of Hamilton took no active part in debates and held no ministerial position. He accompanied the Prince of Wales to Russia in 1866; was lord of the bedchamber to the Prince of Wales, from 1866 to 1886 and in 1886 became groom of the stole. In the general election of 1880, at the beginning of the Land League campaign, he lost his seat for county Donegal. In 1885 his father's death raised him to the dukedom.

The new duke, though no speaker, became the official figurehead of the Irish landlord class throughout the later phases of the land war. In 1888 he was president of the Irish landlords' convention and in 1892 the outgoing unionist ministry gave him the Garter. In 1893 he presided over a great meeting held at the Albert Hall to rally opposition to the second Home Rule Bill. The affairs of his own district interested him greatly, and when the Irish Local Government Act was passed (1898) he was elected to the Tyrone county council and became its chairman by general consent. Land purchase, though a unionist measure, had not his approval, but when the Wyndham Act was passed (1903) he was one of the first to sell to his tenants. The land war being thus abated, he continued the resistance to Irish self-government and became first president of the Ulster Unionist Association. Failing health kept him out of the active struggle ; but he made a last public appearance in 1912 at the Londonderry meeting in Sir Edward Carson's campaign, and he was acclaimed as author of Ulster's formula ' We will not have Home Rule '. But he could not leave his bed that September to sign the Ulster covenant publicly, and on 3 January 1913 he died at 61 Green Street, Mayfair. His eldest son, James, Marquess of Hamilton, member for Derry city since 1900, succeeded him ; and at the by-election thus caused the representation of Derry ceased to be unionist. The last Hamilton stronghold had fallen.

Essentially a great Irish territorial magnate who throughout his life fought a losing battle to preserve territorial power, the Duke was chiefly concerned with his home life at Baronscourt. Apart from Ireland his main interest lay in the British South Africa Company, of which he became president when Cecil Rhodes resigned after the Jameson raid.

The duke married in 1869 Lady Mary Anne Curzon, daughter of Richard William Penn, first Earl Howe, and had by her seven sons and two daughters.

[Lord Ernest Hamilton, *Old Days and New*, 1923 ; Lord Frederic Hamilton, *The Days before Yesterday*, 1920.] S. G.

HAMILTON, Sir RICHARD VESEY (1829–1912), admiral, was born at Sandwich, Kent, 28 May 1829, the younger son of the Rev. John Vesey Hamilton, vicar of St. Mary's church, Sandwich, by his wife, Frances Agnes Malone. He was educated at the Royal Naval School, Camberwell, and entered the royal navy in 1843, proceeding in the *Virago* to the Mediterranean. In 1850 he volunteered for service in one of the expeditions fitted out by the Admiralty in that year to search for the Arctic explorer, Sir John Franklin [q.v.]. He proceeded to the Arctic as mate in the *Assistance*, Captain (Sir) Erasmus Ommanney [q.v.] ; and on his return was promoted lieutenant (1851). He at once volunteered for the next search expedition and was appointed to the *Resolute*, Captain (Sir) Henry Kellett [q.v.]. In charge of a sledge he was absent from the base for fifty-four days, traversed 663 miles, and discovered the northern end of Melville Island. When he once more reached England (1854), the Crimean War had broken out, and he served with the Baltic fleet from January 1855 to February 1856 in the steam sloop *Desperate*. He was then appointed to command the gunboat *Haughty*, and reached the Far East in time to participate in the second Chinese War. He played a brilliant part in the battle of Fatshan Creek on 1 June 1857, and Sir Michael Seymour affixed his name to a blank commander's commission which the Admiralty had sent out in recognition of that affair. Many years afterwards (1875) Hamilton received the C.B. as additional award for the same service.

In June 1858 Hamilton commissioned the *Hydra* for service off the west coast of Africa, but was ordered to the other side of the Atlantic, where he served in one ship or another almost continuously until 1868. On paying off the *Hydra* in 1862 he was promoted post-captain, and married in the same year. From 1868 onwards Hamilton saw service in home waters, and in 1875 was appointed captain superintendent of Pembroke dockyard, where he remained till promoted to his flag (1877). In 1878 he became director of naval ordnance ; and from 1880 to 1883 he commanded off the coast of Ireland. After promotion to vice-admiral in 1884, he returned the next year to the China station as commander-in-chief. On the occasion of Queen Victoria's jubilee (1887) he was promoted admiral and was created K.C.B. On his return from China in 1888 he was appointed one of a committee of three whose report not only prepared the way for Lord George Hamilton's Naval Defence Act of 1889, but may be taken as the starting-point of modern naval policy. At the close of the year he joined the Board of Admiralty as second sea lord, and on the retirement of Baron Hood of Avalon a few months later, succeeded that officer as first sea lord (1889–1891). The most important transaction during Hamilton's term of office was the cession of Heligoland to Germany. Against this he entered an emphatic protest, but found that the Cabinet, before consulting him, had committed itself too far to draw back. In 1891 Hamilton became admiral president of the Royal Naval College, Greenwich, where he served until 1894 ; in 1895 he received the G.C.B. and was put on the retired list.

During his retirement Hamilton devoted himself to literary pursuits. In 1896 he completed his book on *Naval*

Administration, and between 1898 and 1903 edited for the Navy Records Society the *Letters and Papers of Admiral Sir Thomas Byam Martin* in three volumes. He died at his house at Chalfont St. Peter, near Uxbridge, 17 September 1912, and was buried at Eltham. By his wife, Julia Frances Delmé (died 1897), daughter of Vice-Admiral James Arthur Murray, and great-granddaughter of John, third Duke of Atholl, he had two sons and two daughters.

[Sir Clements Markham, *Life of Admiral Sir Leopold McClintock*, 1909 ; Lord George Hamilton, *Parliamentary Reminiscences and Reflections, 1868–1885*, 1916 ; *Geographical Journal*, vol. xl, November 1912 ; private information.] G. A. R. C.

HARCOURT, AUGUSTUS GEORGE VERNON (1834–1919), chemist, was the elder son of Admiral Frederick E. Vernon Harcourt by his wife, Marcia, sister of the first Lord Tollemache, and grandson of Edward (Vernon) Harcourt, archbishop of York [q.v.]. He was born in London 24 December 1834, and died at his house, St. Clair, near Ryde, Isle of Wight, 23 August 1919. He was educated on the old classical lines at Cheam and at Harrow, and in 1854 entered Balliol College, Oxford.

When (Sir) Benjamin Collins Brodie [q.v.], a pupil of Bunsen, came to Oxford as professor of chemistry in 1855, the Balliol laboratory was placed at his disposal, and Harcourt became first his pupil and then his assistant. In 1858 Brodie migrated to the chemical department of the new museum of the university, and took Harcourt—still an undergraduate—with him as lecture assistant. Under Brodie, at the new museum, Harcourt began his researches with the exact determination of the oxygen absorbed by the metals potassium and sodium. In 1859 he was elected Lee's reader in chemistry and a senior student of Christ Church ; in 1864 he became a tutor of Christ Church, and held that position until 1902. Meanwhile he had begun researches on the rate of chemical change, which, in conjunction with those of M. P. E. Berthelot in France and those of C. M. Guldberg in Norway, were to establish on a quantitative basis Berthollet's law of mass action. In the interpretation of his results Harcourt was associated with William Esson, the Oxford mathematician. Most chemical changes take place with a rapidity too great to be followed in detail. Harcourt investigated several cases of slow change before he found one sufficiently simple to admit of mathematical discussion, and in which the amount of change during definite intervals of time could be accurately measured. Having found such a case Harcourt and Esson proved experimentally that the velocity of the change varied directly with the quantities of each of the reacting substances. In studying the effect of temperature on the rate of this reaction, they arrived at a zero of chemical action, viz. 272·6° C., which is in wonderful agreement with the absolute zero calculated from physical data.

In applied chemistry Harcourt was chiefly drawn to questions concerning the purification and testing of coal-gas, as he was appointed in 1872 one of the three metropolitan gas referees. One of his early researches on coal-gas was his attempt to purify the gas from sulphur compounds. His 'sulphur test' came into wide use, but its application on a large scale for the purification of coal-gas has only recently been carried out with success. Perhaps his most signal improvement in the testing of gas was the introduction of the Pentane lamp as the official standard of light in place of the variable spermaceti candle. Another very useful investigation which occupied much of his time between 1899 and 1911 related to the administration of chloroform as an anæsthetic. After much patient labour he devised an 'inhaler', which his medical colleagues recommended to the British Medical Association as 'possessing the advantages of simplicity, exactness, and portability'.

Harcourt was elected a fellow of the Royal Society in 1863, and served on its council from 1878 to 1880. In conjunction with Esson, he published four memoirs in the *Philosophical Transactions*, the third of which was the Bakerian lecture for 1895. Admitted to the Chemical Society in 1859, he served as one of its secretaries for eight years, 1865–1873, and was elected president in 1895. As became the nephew of one of the founders of the British Association—the Rev. William Vernon Harcourt [q.v.]—he early took an interest in its meetings and made many contributions to the chemical section, of which he was president in 1875. A few years later he was elected one of the general secretaries of the Association, an office which he held for fourteen years with conspicuous tact.

Harcourt married in 1872 the Hon. Rachel Mary, daughter of Henry Austin Bruce, afterwards first Baron Aberdare [q.v.]. He had two sons and eight daughters. To his happy family life at

Cowley Grange, the home he built for himself on the banks of the Cherwell, many of his old Oxford pupils have borne testimony.

[Personal knowledge; *The Times*, 25 August 1919.] H. B. D.

HARDIE, JAMES KEIR (1856–1915), socialist and labour leader, was born in a one-roomed cottage at Legbrannock, near Holytown, Lanarkshire, 15 August 1856. His father was a ship's carpenter and trade unionist, and his mother, Mary Keir, had been a domestic servant. His youth was passed in extreme poverty. At seven he became a messenger boy, then he worked for a time in a ship-yard, and afterwards as a baker's errand boy. His parents having moved back from Glasgow into the coal district, he went to work at ten years of age as trapper in a Lanarkshire mine, remaining for twelve years in the pits, and rising to be a skilled hewer. During these years he attended evening school, and became an active worker in the temperance movement, in which he met his wife, Lillie, daughter of Duncan Wilson, collier, whom he married in 1879. In the later 'seventies he began to agitate among the miners, then very badly paid and practically unorganized. His activity cost both him and his two younger brothers their jobs; and Hardie was black-listed by the coal-owners.

In 1878 Hardie opened a stationer's shop at Low Waters, and began journalistic work as local correspondent for the *Glasgow Weekly Mail*. He had now set to work in good earnest to get the miners organized, and for many years he acted as an unpaid official of various new miners' associations. Thus in 1879 the Hamilton miners made him their correspondence secretary, and he used this position to get into touch with the miners in other parts of the country, with a view to forming a national union. Later in that year he was appointed miners' county agent for Lanarkshire, and a conference of miners from the various Scottish coal-fields gave him the title of national secretary, though no national organization yet existed. In 1880, still practically without organization, the Lanarkshire miners struck against a wage reduction, and, though they were defeated, the struggle prepared the way for a county union. After leading the men in this dispute, Hardie accepted an invitation from the Ayrshire miners to become their county secretary, and took up his quarters at Cumnock, where his home remained for the rest of his life. In 1881 the Ayrshire miners struck and were defeated; but Hardie continued the work of organization until, in 1886, the Ayrshire miners' union was at length formed on a stable basis, with himself as secretary. In the same year he was made secretary of the Scottish miners' federation, formed by the various county unions which he had helped to create. Hardie was paid either nothing at all or only small honoraria for his services with these bodies. He supported himself mainly by journalism, joining the staff of two local newspapers in 1882. During these years he was still a liberal; but in 1887 he was already mooting the idea of a distinct labour party, and proposing to stand for North Ayrshire as an independent labour candidate. In 1888 his rupture with the liberals was complete, and he stood as a labour candidate against both liberal and conservative at the Mid-Lanark by-election, sometimes described as the first independent labour contest. He polled only 617 votes out of 7,381. During the contest unsuccessful attempts were made by the liberals to buy him off. He was offered a safe liberal seat at the next general election and an income of £300 a year. This, as well as subsequent offers of money from several sources, he refused. The year of this election is also notable for the formation, under Hardie's chairmanship, of the Scottish labour party, the first independent labour political party in Great Britain, subsequently merged in the Independent Labour Party.

Before the Mid-Lanark election, at the beginning of 1887, Hardie started a paper of his own, *The Miner*, which was continued for two years. In 1889, the year of the great dock strike in London, generally regarded as the beginning of a new epoch in British labour history, this was succeeded by the *Labour Leader*, published monthly till 1894, and thereafter weekly. This paper, which became the principal mouthpiece of the new political socialist movement and the 'new unionism', greatly increased Hardie's influence; and in 1892 he was elected as independent labour member of parliament for South West Ham, the death of the liberal candidate shortly before the election giving him a straight fight with a unionist. At the same election John Burns was returned for Battersea. Hardie's election undoubtedly helped forward the movement for an independent working-class party, and early in 1893 the various local and sectional bodies united to form the Independent

Labour Party, with Hardie as chairman. With this body and its work his name will always be principally connected. In parliament he rapidly made his name as 'the member for the unemployed', adopting from the first a militant attitude on this question. In 1895 he lost his seat owing to the withdrawal of support by the liberals. He then visited America and, on his return, fought an unsuccessful by-election at Bradford in 1896. He incurred much odium by taking up a strong attitude against the South African War; but in 1900, after being defeated at Preston, he was elected for Merthyr Burghs with D. A. Thomas (afterwards Viscount Rhondda, q.v.). This seat he held continuously until his death. He took an active part in forming the labour representation committee in 1900. When this became the Labour Party, and a strong labour group was for the first time returned to parliament in 1906, Hardie became its first leader in the House of Commons; but he resigned the leadership, owing to illness, in the following year. In 1913 he again became chairman of the Independent Labour Party, a position which he had held from 1893 to 1900, and presided at its 'coming-of-age' conference in 1914. He was chairman of the British section of the International Socialist bureau at the outbreak of war in 1914, having taken from 1888 onwards an active part in international labour conferences and in stimulating international labour organization. The powerlessness of the working-class organizations to prevent war, to which he was strongly opposed, came to him as a severe shock, and from August 1914 his health broke down. After seeming for a while to regain his strength, he suffered a further breakdown. Pneumonia followed, and he died 2 September 1915. He left two sons and a daughter, a second daughter having died in childhood.

Hardie was, in his day, perhaps the best-hated and the best-loved man in Great Britain. To his opponents he was uncompromising and hard-hitting in his language, and he was commonly regarded as much more of an extremist than he really was. His speeches in parliament and still more, during his visit to India in 1907–1908, when his utterances were seriously misrepresented, roused furious anger. In the socialist movement, on the other hand, he was regarded with feelings almost of veneration, and his personal popularity was immense. He was an excellent speaker, relying on homely phrases and simple appeals, with some tendency to sentimentalism. Never an original thinker or theorist, he had a firm grip of practical affairs, which enabled him to carry out effectively his task of drawing the British trade union and labour movement into independent political action on semi-socialist lines. He wrote well, and his journalism had always that personal touch which is essential to popular political writing. At his best, he was not unlike William Cobbett in the manner of his appeal. Like Cobbett, too, he was an excellent companion, with an extraordinary faculty for making and keeping loyal friends. By his example and the force of his personal appeal, he certainly did far more than any other man to create the political labour movement in Great Britain, and to give to it the distinctive character of an alliance of socialist and trade union forces. His London home, in Nevill's Court, off Fleet Street, was the resort of all manner of British and foreign leaders of advanced thought and action. But, though Hardie's life was spent largely in London, he always retained both his home at Cumnock, where his wife and family remained, and his essential character as a Scottish miner. He was acutely class-conscious and clan-proud, obtruding in parliament and in private life his working-class origin and attitude. His cloth cap and tweed suit, which so scandalized parliament and the newspapers when he took his seat in 1892, were worn, partly at least, in order to help him in sustaining this character. In this he was perfectly sincere, and his egoism, like Cobbett's, arose rather from his sense of symbolizing his class than from any personal vanity. Time is already enabling even his opponents to take a more objective view of Hardie. His opportunist and even sentimental socialism exactly suited the mood of the more advanced groups of workers who, escaping from Victorian liberalism, sought a new gospel as the political expression of their economic condition.

[Apart from pamphlets, of which there are many, the only life of Hardie is William Stewart's *J. Keir Hardie: A Biography*, 1921, which contains a full account of the events of his life (with portraits). David Lowe's *From Pit to Parliament*, 1923, deals more fully with his early career. For his influence, see also volume ii of Max Beer's *History of British Socialism*, 1919–1920, and the somewhat malicious references in H. M. Hyndman's *Further Reminiscences*, 1912. Hardie's own works, in addition to a good many pamphlets and much journalism, include *From Serfdom to Socialism*, 1907, a simple piece of socialist propaganda, and *India: Impressions and Suggestions*, 1909.]

G. D. H. C.

HARDIE, WILLIAM ROSS (1862–1916), classical scholar, the elder son of William Purves Hardie, tailor, of Edinburgh, by his wife, Agnes Ross, was born at Edinburgh 6 January 1862. He entered Edinburgh University at fourteen and learned high ideals of scholarship from William Young Sellar [q.v.]. Graduating M.A. he went in 1880 to Oxford as scholar of Balliol. He was the most brilliant undergraduate classic of his generation and won an unusual number of university distinctions. Elected to a fellowship at Balliol in 1884, he spent a year abroad, mostly in Greece and Italy, and returned to his college as tutor, remaining there until his appointment as professor of humanity at Edinburgh in 1895. At Balliol he established a new tradition in the teaching of classical scholarship. He had the whole field of classical literature at his command, and in lectures and private classes discussed general literary questions in a strikingly simple manner with a wealth of illustration: some specimens of his method were published later in his *Lectures on Classical Subjects* (1903). He was a most brilliant composer with an unrivalled memory and a remarkable sense of idiom: several of his most felicitous versions are included in *Anthologia Oxoniensis* (1899). The stimulus of his teaching was perhaps accentuated by his peculiarly shy manner.

The tradition of the chair of humanity at Edinburgh concentrated Hardie's work on Latin, though at Balliol he was regarded as an even greater Greek scholar. On large classes of pass students his fine scholarship and conscientious methods were to some extent lost; but to the honour students who could appreciate these qualities he gave himself with a rare devotion; with the help of his assistants he developed a system of individual teaching on Oxford lines. He published two characteristic volumes, *Latin Prose Composition* (1908), the introduction to which expounds the art—for such it was to Hardie—in its more advanced form, and *Silvulae Academicae* (1911), a collection of experiments in Latin and Greek verse, including the *Panegyricus* composed for the five-hundredth anniversary of the university of St. Andrews. *Res Metrica* (1920), published after his death, is a penetrating analysis of some problems of Latin verse-rhythms, written with his usual sanity and caution.

That Hardie's literary production was not large was due to his complete absorption in his teaching: indeed, his devotion to the work of his professorship was the chief cause of his early death on 3 May 1916. His lasting memorial, apart from his few books, is the large number of his pupils who attained distinction in academic life, in the civil service, and in other professions. Naturally taciturn, he would often sit silent even among intimate friends—but amused and sympathetic. He had a fine eye for colour and was a naturally gifted painter in water-colours; he was also an ardent and skilled fisherman and an enthusiastic golfer.

Hardie married in 1901 Isabella Watt, third daughter of the Rev. William Stevenson, of the Madras Christian College, and had three sons and one daughter.

[*Balliol College Register*; notice in *Edinburgh University Magazine*, 1916; personal knowledge.] C. B.

HARDY, HERBERT HARDY COZENS-, first BARON COZENS-HARDY, of Letheringsett (1838–1920), judge. [See COZENS-HARDY.]

HARE, SIR JOHN (FAIRS) (1844–1921), actor, whose original name was JOHN FAIRS, son of Thomas Fairs, of London, was born 16 May 1844 at Giggleswick, Yorkshire. His early years were spent in London, where as a boy he would frequently play truant in order to see the celebrated actors of the day. On the death of his parents he was sent by his guardian to Giggleswick grammar school to be prepared for the civil service. There came, however, an opportunity of appearing in some amateur theatricals, and his natural gifts were immediately recognized. With the consent of his guardian he went to London, studied for the stage under Henry Leigh Murray [q.v.], and made his first professional appearance at the Prince of Wales's Theatre, Liverpool, on 28 September 1864. Here he played the part of an old man (the first of a famous series) in *The Lyons Mail*, and made the acquaintance of the Bancrofts. Next year he appeared for the first time in London under the management of Henry James Byron [q.v.] and Mrs. Bancroft at the Prince of Wales's Theatre as Short in *Naval Engagements*. Two months later, on 11 November 1865, he established his reputation in the part of Lord Ptarmigan in *Society* by T. W. Robertson [q.v.].

Hare was now twenty-one, but had already identified himself with the most fruitful and intelligent dramatic movement of the time. Robertson's comedies, produced during the next decade at the

Prince of Wales's Theatre, were the first clear indications that a revival of native comedy was imminent, and Hare, who began his theatrical career as one of the earliest and best-equipped recruits of the revival, was shortly one of its leading figures. He remained a member of the Prince of Wales's company for nine years, appearing in a succession of Robertson's comedies and in other plays produced at that theatre. Among his parts were Prince Perovsky (*Ours*, 1866), Sam Gerridge (*Caste*, 1867), the Hon. Bruce Fanquehere (*Play*, 1868), Beau Farintosh (*School*, 1869), Dunscombe Dunscombe (*M.P.*, 1870), Sir John Vesey (*Money*, 1872), Sir Patrick Lundie (*Man and Wife*, 1873). He concluded in 1874 with a memorable performance as Sir Peter Teazle.

Hare's success in this series of productions was unbroken, and his reputation, when he left the Prince of Wales's Theatre in 1874, was sufficient to justify him in trying his fortune as a manager. He opened his first season as actor-manager of the Court Theatre in 'silent' partnership with William Hunter Kendal [q.v.] on 13 March of the following year. His tenancy lasted until April 1879. During these four years he produced some dozen plays, including a posthumous piece, *The House of Dainley*, by Lord Lytton, and *Olivia*, by W. G. Wills. The most successful productions were *New Men and Old Acres* (December 1876) in which he played Marmaduke Vavasour, *The Queen's Shilling* (April 1879) in which he appeared as Colonel Daunt, and *A Quiet Rubber* (January 1876) in which he took the part of Lord Kildare. The last-named play he frequently revived in later years.

On leaving the Court Theatre Hare joined W. H. Kendal at the St. James's Theatre. His association with Kendal lasted from October 1879 until 1888, beginning with a revival of *The Queen's Shilling*. During this period the partners produced twenty-one plays, including such conspicuous successes as *Still Waters Run Deep*, *The Ironmaster*, and two plays by (Sir) Arthur Pinero, *The Moneyspinner* (January 1881), in which Hare took the part of Baron Croodle, and *The Squire* (December 1881), in which he took the part of the Rev. Paul Dormer. Here again Hare was well in advance of his contemporaries, for *The Moneyspinner* was the first of Pinero's longer plays to be produced in London. The partnership ended in July 1888, and in the following year Hare took possession of the Garrick Theatre, built for him by (Sir) W. S. Gilbert. There he opened on 24 April 1889 with Pinero's *The Profligate*, in which he played the part of Lord Dangars. His tenancy of the Garrick lasted until 1895. He produced there over a dozen plays, including Pinero's *The Notorious Mrs. Ebbsmith*, in which he took the part of the Duke of St. Olpherts, *A Pair of Spectacles*, by Sydney Grundy, in which he played Benjamin Goldfinch, the greatest of his popular successes, and *Diplomacy*, in which he made another hit as Henry Beauclerc. In December 1895 he went for the first time to America, and appeared at Abbey's Theatre in *The Notorious Mrs. Ebbsmith*, *A Pair of Spectacles*, and *A Quiet Rubber*.

At this point Hare's career became rather less clearly associated with a definite theatrical movement. He appeared in the title-rôle of Pinero's *The Gay Lord Quex* in April 1899, and took the part of the Earl of Carlton in *Little Mary* by J. M. Barrie in 1906. These were the only new plays of importance in which he acted. For the remainder of his career he usually revived old successes, touring in America and in the provinces, and appearing in various London theatres for an occasional season. From 1902 he was engaged by Charles Frohman, under whose management he played until he entered upon the period of farewell and command performances. This period began in 1907 with a farewell tour of the provinces; he also appeared in that year by royal command in *A Quiet Rubber* and *A Pair of Spectacles* at Sandringham and Windsor Castle respectively, and was knighted on the former occasion; in 1908 he gave farewell performances of *The Gay Lord Quex* and *A Pair of Spectacles* at the Garrick Theatre. His last appearances were in July 1917, when he revived *A Pair of Spectacles* and made a large sum of money for King George's Fund for sailors, and in September 1917 when he again appeared in the same play at Wyndham's Theatre. He died in London 28 December 1921 at the age of seventy-seven.

The art of Hare was in the modern English tradition, which he helped to a considerable extent to mould and to develop. It avoided the formality of the older English stage, and broke completely with the French school that still relies to a great extent, even in modern comedies, upon devices which are rhetorical rather than histrionic. Hare was a pioneer in the art of suggesting character by tricks of deportment and facial expression that complete or illuminate the phrases of the author. He showed how this method might be applied without degenerating into grimace or becoming either elaborate or restless. His bearing and conduct on the stage were entirely natural, but were nevertheless informed at every moment with invention, and disciplined by a graceful economy to secure the effect at which he was aiming. His comedy was founded on sympathetic observation, and a zest for the intricacies of human character. He had a simple sense of fun streaked with a sentiment which was never forced and never lost touch with reality. Behind his art was a personality of rare modesty and charm, that instinctively avoided exaggeration and had a genuine dislike of publicity.

In 1874 Hare married Adala Elizabeth, daughter of John Hare Holmes, by whom he had one son and two daughters.

[T. Edgar Pemberton, *John Hare, Comedian. A Biography*, 1895; *Who 's Who in the Theatre*, 1912; *The Times*, 29 December 1921; personal knowledge. Portrait, *Royal Academy Pictures*, 1893.] J. L. P.

HARTLEY, Sir CHARLES AUGUSTUS (1825–1915), civil engineer, born at Hedworth, Durham, 3 February 1825, was the son of W. A. Hartley, of Darlington, by his wife, Lillias, daughter of Andrew Todd, of Borrowstounness, Linlithgowshire. He acquired his early practical experience in railway and mining work in Scotland and in harbour work at Plymouth. During 1855 and 1856 he served in the Crimean War in the Anglo-Turkish contingent with the rank of captain, and constructed some defence works at Kertch.

Hartley's connexion with the Near East did not terminate with the war. At the conclusion of peace in 1856 the attention of the Powers was turned to the improvement of the navigation of the lower Danube, which was impaired by the enormous quantity of mud and sand encumbering the estuary and deposited along the sea coast. By article xvi of the Treaty of Paris the European Commission of the Danube was established in order 'to designate and cause to be executed the works necessary' to clear the mouths of the Danube below Isaktcha. The Commission was empowered by the Treaty of Berlin in 1878 to exercise its powers in complete independence of the territorial authorities, and its jurisdiction was extended to Galatz. By the Treaty of London in 1883 its jurisdiction was further extended to Braila. To this commission Hartley was appointed chief engineer in 1856. Some doubt existed at first as to which of the three principal estuaries of the Danube—the Kilia, the Sulina, and the St. George—was best adapted for improvement. After some hesitation Hartley advised that in the first place provisional works should be undertaken to improve the harbour at the Sulina mouth by utilizing the natural scour of the river. These works consisted of two piers forming a seaward prolongation of the fluvial channel. They were begun in April 1858 and completed in July 1861, and were so successful that in 1866 it was determined to replace the provisional piers by permanent solid structures. The task was completed in 1871 and the piers considerably lengthened. When the works were begun the depth of the channel at the bar was only from seven to twelve feet, but by 1861 it had increased to sixteen feet or more, and Sulina, formerly known as 'the grave of sailors', had become one of the best harbours on the Black Sea. In 1876 the depth was increased to over twenty feet, and from 1879 to 1893 it remained constant without recourse to dredging. In 1894 and 1895, owing to the increasing size of vessels using the channel, the depth was increased to twenty-four feet.

Equal success was achieved in dealing with the course of the Danube above the Sulina mouth. In 1880 was commenced the construction of a new entrance from the Toulcha channel in accordance with plans designed by Hartley in 1857. This work was completed by 1882, and by 1886 the St. George's branch also was made navigable. In consequence the Danube as far as Braila is now usable by steamers of four thousand tons net register, as compared with vessels of four hundred tons before the improvements were begun.

Hartley was knighted for his services in 1862 on the petition of merchants interested in Danube navigation and of sea-captains frequenting the river. In Roumania he was affectionately styled 'the father of the Danube'. He continued to reside in that country until 1872, when he was succeeded as resident engineer by Charles Kühl, but he retained his appointment as chief engineer until 1907. To him and to Kühl the development of the navigation of the lower Danube is principally due.

Both before and after 1872 Hartley was engaged in much important work elsewhere, chiefly of an advisory character. He was consulted by the Indian government with regard to the improvement of the river Hugli below Calcutta, and of Madras harbour. He reported for the Foreign Office in 1867 on the navigation of the Scheldt, and in the same year his plans for the improvement of the port of Odessa won a prize offered by the Tsar Alexander II. His advice was also sought by the British and other governments on the improvement of the Don and the Dnieper, on the enlargement of the port of Trieste, and on the harbours of Constanza, Varna, and Burgas on the Black Sea. In 1875 Hartley was a member of the board appointed by the president of the United States to report on the best means of opening to navigation the south pass of the Mississippi. In 1884 he was nominated by the British government a member of the International Technical Commission of the Suez Canal, on which he served for twenty-two years.

Hartley's published works were confined to papers contributed to the Institution of Civil Engineers. Two important papers on his work in the Danube delta appeared in the minutes of *Proceedings* (xxi, 277–308, 1862; xxxvi, 201–53, 1873). In 1874 he contributed *Notes on Public Works in the United States and in Canada* (*ibid.*, xl, 163–230) and in 1900 *A Short History of the Engineering Works of the Suez Canal* (*ibid.*, cxli, 157–212). An exceedingly interesting survey of *Inland Navigations in Europe* by Hartley was published by the Institution in 1885 in a volume of lectures on *The Theory and Practice of Hydro-Mechanics* delivered by members of the Institution.

Hartley was created K.C.M.G. in 1884, and he received, among other decorations, the grand cross of the crown of Roumania, the second order of the star of Roumania, and the fourth order of the Medjidie. He became an associate of the Institution of Civil Engineers in 1856 and a member in 1862. He died, unmarried, in London 20 February 1915, and was buried in Highgate cemetery.

[*The Times*, 22 February 1915; *Proceedings* of the Institution of Civil Engineers, volumes cited above, and vol. cc (part ii), 1–3, 1914–1915; *Encyclopaedia Britannica*, 11th edition, s.v. *Danube*.] E. I. C.

HAVERFIELD, FRANCIS JOHN (1860–1919), Roman historian and archæologist, the only son of the Rev. William Robert Haverfield, by his wife, Emily, sister of John Fielder Mackarness, bishop of Oxford [q.v.], was born at Shipston-on-Stour 8 November 1860. There was a foreign strain in his blood; he was a great-grandson of the miniature-painter, Jeremiah Meyer [q.v.], an immigrant from Würtemberg. His mother died when he was still in early childhood, and soon afterwards his father fell into a hopeless and prolonged decline. Growing up without experience of a normal home-life, the boy was seriously handicapped. He developed a certain abruptness of manner, which he never entirely shook off and which permanently hampered the free play of his sympathetic nature. Superimposed upon a character of marked strength and individuality, it too often prevented him, in after life, from being recognized for what he really was—one of the simplest and kindest of men, one of the most unselfish and steadfast of friends.

From a preparatory school at Clifton he entered Winchester as senior scholar in 1873. Six years later he went up to New College, Oxford, once more as scholar. He obtained a first-class in moderations with no great difficulty. A second class in 'greats' was the penalty of paying less attention to Greek philosophy than to Latin lexicography. In 1884, a year after taking his degree, he went as sixth-form master to Lancing College, where his somewhat unconventional methods proved highly successful. In his strenuous leisure he pursued various lines of original research, but finally concentrated on Roman epigraphy and Roman Britain, mainly under the influence of Mommsen, for whose work he had a profound admiration and whose personal acquaintance he had made during one of his frequent visits to the Continent. In 1892 he was invited to return to Oxford, and for the next fifteen years he resided at Christ Church as a senior student. Here his unresting energy and his more than generous hospitality soon made him a prominent figure. His pen was never idle; practically every important classical book that appeared was reviewed by him in the *Guardian* or elsewhere, and he edited Henry Nettleship's *Essays* and re-edited Conington's *Eclogues* and *Georgics* (1895). Amid his multifarious interests, Roman Britain became more and more his chief concern. In vacation he moved up and down the country, visiting Roman sites, stimulating or directing excavations, guiding and advising local antiquaries. In 1907 Henry Pelham Francis [q.v.] died, and Haverfield was chosen to succeed him as Camden professor of ancient history, the appointment carrying with it an official fellowship at Brasenose College. A month before his election he had married Miss Winifred Breakwell. They had no children. Henceforward he lived in a house which he built for himself on Headington Hill. This was his happiest and most fruitful period. Freed from college routine, he was able to devote himself whole-heartedly to advanced work. At home his influence extended year by year. Abroad he commanded a respect such as only a small minority of British scholars have ever enjoyed. His relations with colleagues in different foreign countries were of the friendliest character. With some of them he was in constant communication, giving and receiving much helpful criticism. The outbreak of war in 1914 thus came on him as a stunning blow, and its progress was to bring him the loss of intimate friends. At the end of 1915 the continuous strain and anxiety induced an attack of cerebral haemorrhage. Despite a partial recovery he never regained full vigour. On 1 September 1919 the end came quite suddenly.

When Haverfield first approached it, the subject of Roman Britain was, to use his own phrase, 'the playground of the amateur'. Before his death he could claim that 'our scientific knowledge of the island, however liable to future correction and addition, stands by itself among the studies of the Roman Empire'. He might truthfully have added that this was his own achievement. And it was accomplished almost single-handed; such good work as was done by others, was done largely through his inspiration and example. Although he did not live to produce the systematic treatise which he contemplated, the bibliography of his writings, containing as it does some five hundred entries, is a singularly impressive monument. Master of a nervous and exceptionally lucid style, he penetrated into every nook and corner of his subject, bringing to bear upon its problems, not only a vast knowledge of miscellaneous details, but a breadth of outlook, a sureness of touch, and a sanity of judgement that never failed to illuminate. Conspicuous in the long list are his two sets of *Additamenta* (1892, 1913) to the Berlin *Corpus Inscriptionum Latinarum*, his *Romanization of Roman Britain* (1905, 4th ed. 1923), and the numerous chapters which he contributed to the *Victoria County History*. His Ford lectures, *The Roman Occupation of Britain*, published posthumously in 1924, provide the most convenient conspectus of his results.

[Family papers; private information; personal knowledge. For fuller details see biographical notices in *Proceedings* of the British Academy, vol. ix and *English Historical Review*, 1920. There is a bibliography in *Journal of Roman Studies*, vol. viii. The first of these notices and the bibliography are reprinted, with additions, in the Ford lecture volume.] G. M.

HAZLITT, WILLIAM CAREW (1834–1913), bibliographer and man of letters, was born in London 22 August 1834. He was the eldest son of William Hazlitt, registrar of the court of bankruptcy, by his wife, Catherine Reynell, and a grandson of William Hazlitt [q.v.], the essayist. He was educated at Merchant Taylors' School from 1842 to 1850, and after experimenting in journalism, in civil engineering, and, during the Crimean War, as a supernumerary clerk at the War Office, he published in 1858 *The History of the Origin and Rise of the Republic of Venice*, which in revised and extended forms reappeared in 1860 as a *History of the Venetian Republic*, and in 1900 and 1915 as *The Venetian Republic, its Rise, its Growth, its Fall.*

After eating dinners at the Inner Temple Hazlitt was called to the bar in 1861, but he was now becoming interested in the old books which he recorded in a *Handbook to the Popular, Poetical and Dramatic Literature of Great Britain from the Invention of Printing to the Restoration* (1867). To listing and editing these he devoted much of the rest of his life, examining thousands of old books as they passed through the sale rooms. Three series of *Bibliographical Collections and Notes*, with two supplements to the third, were published by him during the years 1876 to 1889, followed by a *General Index*, compiled by G. J. Gray (1893), and a fourth series in 1903. Written on odd bits of paper in a difficult hand, his notes, when they appeared in print, were sometimes inexact, but the *Collections and Notes* is still a much-used book of reference. In his old age Hazlitt gave much time to bringing all his notes together, with many new ones, as a *Consolidated Bibliography*, and made the cost of printing this a first charge on a reversionary bequest to the British Museum, the balance of which was to form a fund for purchasing early English books. The preparation of his *Handbook* enabled Hazlitt to give much valuable help to Henry Huth [q.v.] in the formation of the latter's well-known library, and he frequently offered bargains from the sale rooms to the British Museum and elsewhere. His methods of work and experiences are revealed in his *Confessions of a Collector* (1897) and in his two volumes, *The Hazlitts* (1911) and *The Later Hazlitts* (1912).

Hazlitt's chief editorial undertakings were new editions of Robert Dodsley's *Select Collection of Old Plays* in fifteen volumes (1874–1876) and of Thomas Warton's *History of English Poetry* (1871); *Shakespeare's Library* in six volumes (1875), *Old English Jest Books* in three volumes (1863–1864), and the *Poems and Plays of Thomas Randolph* (1875). He also wrote *Shakespeare, the Man and his Work* (1902), *Coinage of the European Continent* (1893–1897), two volumes of poems (1877, 1897), and *Man considered in relation to God and a Church* (1905, 5th edition 1912). The record of Hazlitt's publications extends to over sixty items and is good evidence of a busy life. He died at Richmond, Surrey, 8 September 1913.

Hazlitt married in 1863 Henrietta, daughter of John Foulkes, of Ashfield House, Denbighshire, and had one son and one daughter.

[W. C. Hazlitt, *Four Generations of a Literary Family*, 1897; *The Hazlitts*; *The Later Hazlitts*; *Confessions of a Collector*; private information.] A. W. R.

HEAD, BARCLAY VINCENT (1844–1914), Greek numismatist, the second son of John Head, of Ipswich, of a quaker family descended from the quaker apologist, Robert Barclay [q.v.], by his wife, Elizabeth Bailey, was born at Ipswich 2 January 1844. Educated at the local grammar school under Hubert Holden [q.v.], he left it at the age of seventeen, and entered the department of coins at the British Museum 12 February 1864. In 1869 he married Mary Harley (died 1911), daughter of John Frazer Corkran, of Dublin, author and journalist, by whom he had one daughter. In 1893 he succeeded Reginald Stuart Poole [q.v.] as keeper of his department, a post which he held until 30 June 1906. His first contributions to numismatic literature were on Anglo-Saxon coins, but by 1868 he had settled down to his life's task. The department of coins began about 1870 to work on the great series of Greek catalogues; with Poole and Percy Gardner he produced the first volume, *Italy*, in 1873; he was to write two more volumes in collaboration, and eight alone. To these official publications must be added his useful illustrated *Guide to the Coins of the Ancients* (1881), which it has been found unnecessary to modify through six editions. Meanwhile his unofficial activity included the part editorship of the *Numismatic Chronicle* (1869–1910) and a number of remarkable monographs. As early as 1874 his *History of the Coinage of Syracuse* laid the foundations of the modern historical method in Greek numismatics. All further advance on the historical side of that subject has been upon the main lines which he there laid down. But the work by which he will be generally remembered is the *Historia Numorum* (1887), a system of Greek numismatics, which at once became the leading work of reference; a second edition appeared in 1911. Recognition of Head's work, not too ample in this country—though he received degrees from Durham in 1887 and Oxford in 1905—was ungrudging abroad, where Heidelberg University and both French and Prussian Academies, and numerous specialist societies, honoured him. The finest tribute, however, to a gentle and amiable scholar was the dedication to him, on his retirement, of *Corolla Numismatica*, written by thirty scholars of six nations. He died in London 12 June 1914. The Barclay Head prize for numismatics at Oxford commemorates him. Head's work should rank as classic in the annals of numismatics; severely as he limited his scope, he was no narrow specialist, and his judgement, though deliberate, was yet instinctively so sound that even his few mistakes are illuminating.

[The *Athenæum*, 20 June 1914; *Numismatic Chronicle*, 1914, pp. 249–55; private information; personal knowledge.]

G. F. H.

HEATHCOTE, JOHN MOYER (1834–1912), tennis player, the eldest son of John Moyer Heathcote, of Conington Castle, near Peterborough, by his wife, the Hon. Emily Frances, third daughter of Nicholas William Ridley Colborne, first Baron Colborne, was born in London 12 July 1834. He was educated at Eton and at Trinity College, Cambridge, whither he proceeded in 1852. Heathcote was a man of many interests in sports and games, an amateur artist of some repute, and a graceful writer on sporting subjects. In middle life shooting, skating, and lawn-tennis were among his diversions, but he will always be best remembered as the finest amateur tennis player of his generation and as one of the greatest who has yet appeared.

Heathcote began the game at Cambridge, and he played regularly at the court in James Street, Haymarket, from 1856 to 1866, when that famous court was finally closed. His chief professional teacher and opponent in those days was Edmund Tompkins, for some years champion of tennis. Gradually Heathcote reduced the odds between them till he could play his former master level. About the year 1869 he was the equal of any player in the world, but after that George Lambert [q.v.] began to surpass him. Meanwhile there was no amateur player who had any chance against Heathcote, and for a number of years he could give his nearest rivals fifteen. Heathcote succeeded to the position of amateur champion about the year 1859, when C. G. Taylor retired from single match play. There was at that time no formal competition for the championship, but from 1867 the Marylebone Cricket Club annually offered prizes to its members for play in the court at Lord's, and the gold prize carried with it the blue riband of amateur tennis. Heathcote won this every year till 1882, when the Hon. Alfred Lyttelton [q.v.] defeated him. The next summer he regained the title, but after this Lyttelton passed him in the race, though Heathcote won the gold prize once more in 1886, when Lyttelton was unable to play. Heathcote kept up the game for many years and played in a number of courts after he had retired from competition play, and until the end of his life he was present at most of the great matches. He died at Conington 5 October 1912.

Heathcote was a fine all-round player, but his strongest point was return. Without having such a crushing attack as some of his predecessors and successors, he could cut the ball fairly heavily and could lay short chases with some certainty. He had a sound volley and he gave both the side-wall and the drop-service effectively.

Heathcote contributed largely to *Tennis* (1890) in the Badminton Library, and also wrote on *Speed Skating* (1891) in the same series. Lawn-tennis players owe him a debt of gratitude, for in one way he did as much as anyone to develop that game. It was he who first suggested and tried the experiment of covering the ball with flannel.

[*The Times*, 12 May 1915 ; Julian Marshall, *The Annals of Tennis*, 1878 ; *Tennis, Rackets, and Lawn Tennis* (Badminton Library), 1890 ; E. B. Noel and J. O. M. Clark, *A History of Tennis*, 1924.] E. B. N.

HEATON, Sir JOHN HENNIKER, first baronet (1848–1914), postal reformer, was born at Rochester 18 May 1848, the only son of Lieutenant-Colonel John Heaton, of Heaton, Lancashire, by his wife, Helen, daughter and co-heir of John Henniker, of Rochester. Educated at Kent House School and King's College, London, Henniker Heaton went to Australia at the age of sixteen (1864), and spent some years in the Bush. He subsequently moved to Paramatta, New South Wales, and joined the staff of the *Mercury* newspaper. He acted as town clerk of Paramatta from December 1869 till February 1870. Heaton then edited a paper in Goulburn with the prophetic title of *The Penny Post*, moving thence to Sydney, where he joined the staff of The *Australian and County Journal*, owned by Samuel Bennett, a writer on Australian history, described by Heaton as 'the best friend I ever had'. In 1873 he married Bennett's only daughter, Rose. During the next ten years Henniker Heaton identified himself with the public life of Sydney, and wrote a standard work of reference, *The Australian Dictionary of Dates and Men of the Time* (1879). In 1882 he stood for parliament as a candidate for New South Wales, but was defeated by a small majority. He represented New South Wales as commissioner at the Amsterdam exhibition of 1883, and Tasmania at the Berlin International Telegraphic Conference in 1885, when he succeeded in materially reducing the cost of cable messages to Australia ; he was again commissioner for New South Wales at the Indian and Colonial exhibition held in London in 1886. Throughout his life he so consistently forwarded Australian interests that he became known as 'the member for Australia'.

In 1884 Henniker Heaton settled with his family in London, and at the general election of 1885 he was returned to parliament in the conservative interest as member for Canterbury, a seat which he held for twenty-six years. After the general election of 1892 a baronetcy was offered to him on condition of his giving up his seat to a former conservative minister who had just been defeated. Regarding the condition as degrading to his own career and disloyal to his constituents, Henniker Heaton refused, and on account of this circumstance rejected three times the offer of a K.C.M.G. as a reward for his patriotic services. During his parliamentary career he worked continuously and persistently at postal reform : owing to his exertions the cost of cabling to different parts of the world was much reduced, imperial penny postage (except with Australia) came into force on 25 December 1898, whilst Anglo-American penny postage was won in 1908, and Anglo-Australian penny postage during the years 1905 to 1911. At the dissolution of 1910

Henniker Heaton retired from parliament owing to ill-health. In 1911, while he was on a visit to Australia, a baronetcy was conferred upon him, and on his return a public welcome, held under the auspices of the British Empire League and presided over by Earl Curzon, was accorded him at the Guildhall. In September 1914 he was taken ill while returning from Carlsbad, and he died at Geneva on 8 September. He had four sons and two daughters, and was succeeded by his eldest son, John (born 1877).

Henniker Heaton had an attractive and vital personality, with the gift of imparting to others something of his own tireless enthusiasm about the things for which he cared. The campaign for postal reform opened in 1886, when he moved a resolution in the House of Commons with a view to establishing a system of universal penny postage. He was opposed on financial grounds, and defeated. From this moment Henniker Heaton preached his gospel both in and out of season, for he was of the type that does not recognize refusal. By 1890 he had succeeded in reducing international postage from sixpence to twopence half-penny. When at last he succeeded (at Christmas 1898) in making imperial penny postage an accomplished fact, Australia still stood out, and it was not until 1905 that he was able to post a penny letter to Australia. Unhappily he did not live to see the adoption of his cherished ideal of penny postage to France. The secret of his success as a reformer may be gauged by a saying of Mr. Asquith, 'If I give way to Henniker Heaton on a single point, he is on my door-step next morning with fifty more'. He had a genius for friendship and was a keen clubman, being one of the early founders of the Bath Club.

[Mrs. Adrian Porter (daughter), *The Life and Letters of Sir John Henniker Heaton, Bart.*, 1916; private information.] A. C-R.

HEINEMANN, WILLIAM (1863–1920), publisher, was born at Surbiton 18 May 1863, the eldest son of Louis Heinemann (a native of Hanover who became naturalized in 1856, shortly after settling in England) by his wife, Jane Lavino, a native of Manchester. William Heinemann received a cosmopolitan education, partly at a gymnase in Dresden and partly with a tutor in England. As a young man he intended to become a musician, and went to Germany to study music. Always a fastidious critic of himself as well as of others, he realized, although he became an accomplished musician, that he lacked the creative power necessary even for interpretative work of the highest order. His genius was for appreciation: he was as fine a judge of a painting or of a book as of music.

It was in the publication of books that Heinemann's *flair* for discovering and guiding the talent of others found full expression. He loved books, and cared not only for their content, but for the craft of book-making, in which he became an acknowledged master. He received his training as publisher in the firm of Messrs. Trübner, of Ludgate Hill, afterwards Kegan Paul, Trench, and Trübner, and set up in business for himself in London in 1890. Mr. Sydney Pawling joined him in 1893. The first book published by the firm was *The Bondman* (1890) by (Sir) Hall Caine, which had a great popular success. Among his earliest publications was J. M. Whistler's *Gentle Art of Making Enemies* (1890). Heinemann, who was a great friend of the painter, later published Mr. and Mrs. Joseph Pennell's *Life* of Whistler. During the years 1895–1897 he published *The New Review* under the editorship of William Ernest Henley [q.v.].

Although the scope of Heinemann's firm was wide, it was, perhaps, the brilliance of its fiction list that made it especially remarkable: R. L. Stevenson and Rudyard Kipling were two of the earliest names; Sarah Grand, Flora Annie Steel, Israel Zangwill, Max Beerbohm, John Masefield, John Galsworthy, Joseph Conrad, William Somerset Maugham, and H. G. Wells were also amongst the Heinemann authors. It was once said of Heinemann that he 'had a nose for merit like that of a dog for truffles'. He published many plays, including most of those by Sir Arthur Pinero, Somerset Maugham, Israel Zangwill, Henry Davies, and Charles Haddon Chambers. Heinemann himself wrote plays, which were published by the firm of John Lane—*The First Step* (1895), *Summer Moths* (1898), and *War* (1901). But, as always in his creative work, he remained the dilettante. He had brilliant ideas but he turned them off lightly and bent his serious energies towards producing beautifully the creations of other minds. Hand in hand with his appreciative and critical faculties went a strong and sound sense of business, and a gift for organization. He played a great part in founding, in 1896, the Publishers' Association of Great Britain and Ireland, and was himself president from 1909 to 1911. He was also president of the National Booksellers' Provident Association from 1913 until his death, and was very active on its council.

Heinemann numbered amongst his friends many brilliant men of his day, not only in England, but on the Continent. He spoke and read fluently French, German, Italian, and had a working knowledge of Spanish; and it is largely owing to him that the masterpieces of foreign literature are now available in sound English translations. His firm produced, under (Sir) Edmund Gosse's editorship, the International Library of translations from leading works of European fiction; and Heinemann commissioned Mrs. Constance Garnett's translations of Dostoevsky, Turgenev, and Tolstoy, and launched in England the works of Ibsen—translated by William Archer—of Björnson, and of Romain Rolland. His place amongst the publishers of Europe was unique: he was the junction where all the lines met. He was *persona grata* with his *confrères* of other lands and, at the same time, he was a spectacular figure in the English publishing world. His meeting with Dr. James Loeb, a graduate of Harvard University and formerly a partner in the New York banking firm, Kuhn, Loeb & Co., was responsible for his most impressive literary enterprise. Dr. Loeb, imbued with a great love for the classics, combined with Heinemann to produce the unique Loeb classical library of translations from well-known and little-known classical authors. When completed the library will contain all that is most valuable in classical antiquity. It already includes many authors hitherto but little studied.

Undoubtedly Heinemann's most notable quality as a publisher was his extraordinary power of recognizing not only what was good but also what the world would consider good a few years after the date of publication. As a man his chief gift was for friendship. He gathered round himself a brilliant circle. Whatever party he gave he was the centre of it, and he brought out all that was best and most interesting in his guests. His great weakness was a certain intellectual arrogance: he had a larger 'blind spot' in his mental outlook than most men of his attainments, because he was human enough to be violently prejudiced by his own personal likes and dislikes. But it may be said of Heinemann, as his best epitaph, that the ideal was always more to him than the bank balance: he was a man to whom the dream was more than the business.

Heinemann married in 1899 (but divorced in 1904) Donna Magda Stuart Sindici, a talented young Italian authoress, whose first novel, *Via Lucis*, he had published. He died suddenly in London 5 October 1920.

[Private information.] F. T. J.

HENDERSON, Sir DAVID (1862–1921), lieutenant-general, the youngest son of David Henderson, shipbuilder, of Glasgow, by his wife, Jane Pitcairn, was born at Glasgow 11 August 1862. He was educated at the university of Glasgow, and passed into the army by way of Sandhurst in 1883. He served with his regiment, the Argyll and Sutherland Highlanders, in South Africa, Ceylon, and China, returning to Edinburgh in 1892. High-minded and single of purpose, he applied himself to the study of his profession. He served in 1898 in the Sudan campaign and was promoted brevet major, and in 1899–1902 in South Africa. He was wounded at Ladysmith, promoted brevet lieutenant-colonel in November 1900, and spent two valuable years (October 1900–September 1902) as director of military intelligence under Lord Kitchener. A short period with the civil government of the Transvaal followed. When Henderson returned to England he set down the lessons which he had learned in Africa, and these were published as an official text-book, *Field Intelligence: its Principles and Practice* (1904). At home he filled various staff appointments, always with distinction, but found time to write *The Art of Reconnaissance* (1907) which went into many editions.

When the American inventor, Wilbur Wright, startled Europe with his flights in France (1908) Henderson turned his mind to the air as a new element in warfare; but it was only in 1911, at the age of forty-nine, that he learned to fly at Brooklands. The committee of imperial defence was at this time deeply concerned with the question of a national air service. Henderson served on a sub-committee appointed to consider the problem, and its report bears the mark of his wide and practical experience. It recommended the formation of a flying corps, which came into being as the Royal Flying Corps in May 1912.

In July 1912 Henderson went to the War Office as director of military training, an appointment which he held for fourteen months. During that time the expansion of the Royal Flying Corps was his special interest. In September 1913 he was given the new post of director-general of military aeronautics. He brought a keen, sympathetic, well-disciplined mind to the moulding of the new service, which, in training and spirit, was second to none at the outbreak of the European War. On 13 August 1914 he took the force to France, and six days later its aeroplanes were flying over the enemy. The air reconnaissance reports did much to help the British army to escape the enveloping movements of the German advance.

In November 1914, when the main burden of the War lay on the infantry, Henderson, who had been promoted major-general in October, took command of the first division, but a month later he was back as general officer commanding the Royal Flying Corps, and he held this command until October 1917. He remained in France until October 1915, when he handed over to Brigadier-General H. M. Trenchard and went to the War Office. There were difficulties at home which taxed all his enthusiasm and energy, and he did not escape criticism. But a sufficient answer lies in the fact that England emerged from the War with the largest and best equipped air force in the world.

Henderson was promoted lieutenant-general in 1917, and in the autumn of that year he worked hard on the plans for the amalgamation of the Royal Flying Corps and the Royal Naval Air Service into the Royal Air Force. In January 1918 he became vice-president of the newly-formed Air Council; shortly afterwards both he and the chief of the air staff, Major-General Trenchard, found themselves strongly opposed to the policy of Lord Rothermere, the first air minister. The chief of the staff resigned in April; Henderson followed suit, and the air service knew him no more. After a spell as area-commandant in France (August to October 1918) and as military counsellor at the embassy, Paris (October 1918 to June 1919), he went to Geneva to organize and direct the League of Red Cross societies. In this work his tact and the charm of his personality were of conspicuous service. He died at Geneva 17 August 1921.

Henderson was created K.C.B. in 1914 and K.C.V.O. in 1919. He married in 1895 Henrietta Caroline, second daughter of Henry Robert Dundas, and granddaughter of the first Baron Napier of Magdala. He left one daughter, his only son having been killed in a flying accident in 1918.

[W. A. Raleigh, *The War in the Air* vol. i, 1922; official records; private information.] H. A. J.

HERBERT, AUBERON THOMAS, eighth Baron Lucas and eleventh Baron Dingwall (1876–1916), politician and airman, was born 25 May 1876. He was the second son of the Hon. Auberon Edward William Molyneux Herbert [q.v.], by his wife, Lady Florence Amabell, sister of Francis Thomas de Grey Cowper, seventh and last Earl Cowper [q.v.]. His elder brother died as a child in 1882, and his mother died in 1886, leaving him heir general to his uncle, Earl Cowper. On Earl Cowper's death without issue in 1905, the baronies of Lucas and Dingwall devolved upon his nephew, who also became a co-heir to the barony of Butler.

Herbert was educated at Bedford grammar school and at Balliol College, Oxford, which he entered in 1895. In 1898 and 1899 he rowed at No. 7 in the university boat-race against Cambridge. In the South African War he acted as correspondent to *The Times*, and was wounded in the foot. The wound was mismanaged, and it was eventually found necessary to amputate his leg below the knee. After he became Lord Lucas he was private secretary for a year to the secretary of state for war, Mr. (afterwards Viscount) Haldane. As one of the few liberal peers he was marked out for preferment, and in 1908 he took office in Mr. Asquith's goverment as under-secretary of state for war; he held this position until 1911, when he was transferred to the Colonial Office as under-secretary. A few months later he was again moved, being appointed parliamentary secretary to the Board of Agriculture. In 1914 he became president of the Board of Agriculture, though without a seat in the Cabinet. He remained president until the coalition government was formed in 1915, when he retired.

During his short political career Lucas showed useful qualities, but to a man of his vigorous and daring temperament the call to more active service in the European War was irresistible. In spite of his physical disability and the fact that he had passed the standard age, Lucas joined the Royal Flying Corps, and proved himself a skilful pilot. He saw much service in Egypt, and then returned to England (1916) as an instructor. On one occasion a pupil whom he was training fell with him and was killed, but Lucas escaped. He was offered the command of a squadron but preferred to gain experience in France. He was only at the front for a short time, for on 4 November 1916 he made a flight over the German lines and did not return. He was reported missing, and on 4 December his death was officially announced by the War Office. He had made Wrest Park, his house in Bedfordshire, a hospital for the wounded, and he offered it as a home for disabled soldiers.

Lucas gained the regard and affection of many friends. He was fond of the open air, of fishing, and of observing bird life. His endurance in active pursuits was remarkable, and he walked the roughest ground like a sound man. Quiet and thoughtful, he paid much attention to the problems of the day, and had his life been prolonged he might have made a valuable statesman. After the War broke out the excitement of flying absorbed him, and it seemed to some of those who knew him best that he fell as he would have wished. He left behind him the memory of an attractive and gallant character.

Lucas was nominated a member of the Privy Council in 1912. He never married, and his only sister, the Hon. Nan Ino Herbert (born 1880), succeeded to his titles at his death.

[*The Times*, 4 December 1916; *Balliol College War Memorial Book*, 1924.] A. C.

HERKOMER, Sir HUBERT VON (1849–1914), painter, was born 26 May 1849 at Waal, in southern Bavaria, the only son of Lorenz Herkomer, by his wife Josephine Niggl. His father, a joiner, belonged to a family of craftsmen, and all through life took a keen interest in his son, who felt that he owed a great deal to his influence; his mother was a talented musician and teacher of music. In 1851 Lorenz Herkomer emigrated with his wife and child to the United States; he returned to Europe, however, after six years, and settled at Southampton in 1857. After receiving a preliminary training in his father's workshop, Hubert Herkomer at the age of fourteen entered the Southampton school of art, proceeding, after a visit to Bavaria with his father in 1865 and a brief period of study at the Munich academy, to the South Kensington art schools in 1866. After some early struggles Herkomer had a drawing of a gipsy encampment on Wimbledon common accepted by the *Graphic* in 1869, and henceforth he could derive an income from working for that paper. In the same year a water-colour drawing by him, 'Leisure Hours', was accepted for the Royal Academy exhibition, and in 1870 he achieved a success with his water-colour, 'Hoeing', at an exhibition at the Dudley Gallery.

Herkomer began now gradually to make headway, his picture of a Bavarian village scene, 'After the Toil of the Day', being purchased for £500 at the Academy exhibition of 1873. Having rented a cottage for his parents at Bushey, Hertfordshire, he used to join them there when not at work in Chelsea. In 1874 he married Anna, daughter of Albert Weise, of Berlin. The next year he sent to the Academy his picture 'The Last Muster—Sunday at the Royal Hospital, Chelsea', which at once attracted very great attention. Bought by Mr. C. E. Fry, of Watford, for £1,200, this picture, which earned for Herkomer the grande medaille d'honneur at the Paris exhibition of 1878, is now in the Lady Lever art gallery at Port Sunlight, Cheshire, having been purchased for 2,800 guineas at the Quilter sale in 1923. Shortly after this great success Herkomer's parents settled in the new home which their son had acquired for them in the little Bavarian town of Landsberg am Lech, about six miles from Waal, their old home; on his wife's death in 1879 Lorenz Herkomer rejoined his son, who had meanwhile been achieving further success and in that year was elected A.R.A.

Herkomer by now had acquired a considerable position in English art life, which he developed and consolidated during the ensuing years. As a portrait painter he had a very extensive *clientèle*, many prominent Englishmen of the time, as well as distinguished Germans and Americans, figuring among his sitters. Of his single portraits the following are specially noteworthy: 'Richard Wagner' (water-colour, 1877), 'John Ruskin' (water-colour, 1879, National Portrait Gallery), 'Archibald Forbes, War Correspondent' (Royal Academy, 1882), 'Miss Katharine Grant' ('The Lady in White', 1884, Royal Academy, 1885), 'Mrs. Sealbee, of Boston' ('The Lady in Black', 1886, Leeds municipal gallery), 'Lord Kelvin' (1891, Royal Academy, 1892), and 'The Marquess of Salisbury' (1893). Herkomer made a speciality of large portrait groups, somewhat suggestive of those characteristic of seventeenth-century Holland; such are 'The Chapel of the Charterhouse' (Royal Academy, 1889), purchased for £2,200 by the trustees of the Chantrey fund and now in the National Gallery of British Art at Millbank (Tate Gallery); two pictures of the municipal authorities of Landsberg

(1894 and 1905), presented by Herkomer to the town hall of Landsberg; 'A Board of Directors' (Royal Academy, 1892); 'The Council of the Royal Academy' (Royal Academy, 1908), presented by Herkomer to the National Gallery of British Art; and 'The Firm of Friedrich Krupp' (1914).

Among the more remarkable of Herkomer's subject-pictures not already noted are: 'Missing' (Royal Academy, 1881); 'Pressing to the West', a scene from the emigrant registration office in New York (Royal Academy, 1884); 'Found' (Royal Academy, 1885), purchased by the trustees of the Chantrey fund for £800 and now in the National Gallery of British Art; 'Hard Times' (Royal Academy, 1885), now in the Manchester art gallery; 'On Strike' (Royal Academy, 1891), diploma piece on Herkomer's promotion to the rank of R.A. in 1890; 'Back to Life' (Royal Academy, 1896); and 'The Guards' Cheer' (Royal Academy, 1898).

It is as a painter that Herkomer will chiefly be remembered, but he had an irresistible desire to make experiments in other directions. Altogether, there is in him a note of rather naïve egotism which makes him temperamentally somewhat akin to another famous painter of peasant stock—a much greater artist than Herkomer—Gustave Courbet. His artistic activity was by no means confined to painting; he did much work as an engraver, inventing and perfecting technical processes, and in enamel. He composed music and wrote some operas which were performed at his private theatre at Bushey, not only designing the scenery but also inventing a new method of stage lighting from the side, and appearing himself as an actor. He took a keen interest in cinematograph production and in motoring. In 1883 he founded at Bushey the Herkomer school of art; this he directed gratuitously until 1904, when he retired. He was constantly lecturing throughout the country, and he filled the post of Slade professor of fine art at Oxford from 1885 to 1894. At Bushey he built himself a house, 'Lululaund', and in its construction and elaborate adornment took an active part together with his father and his uncles Hans, a carver, and Anton, a weaver. In memory of his mother he built a tower, 'Mutterthurm', at Landsberg.

The published works of Herkomer include *Etching and Engraving, Lectures delivered at Oxford* (1892), *My School and My Gospel* (1908), *A Certain Phase of Lithography* (1910), and *The Herkomers* (1910–1911). He received a great number of distinctions, both English and foreign: he was created C.V.O. in 1901 and knighted in 1907; he held many honorary degrees, was an honorary fellow of All Souls College, Oxford, an associate of the Institute of France and of the Belgian Academy, and an officer of the legion of honour.

After his first wife's death in 1883 Herkomer married in 1884 Miss Lulu Griffiths (died 1885), of Stanley House, Ruthin. He married thirdly, in 1888, Margaret, sister of his second wife; as such a marriage was not then legal in England the ceremony took place at Landsberg, where Herkomer had returned to German citizenship. Some time afterwards he was again naturalized in England. He assumed the prefix 'von' on being invested with the Maximilian order *pour le mérite* in 1899. He had a son and a daughter by his first wife and also by his third wife. Herkomer died at Budleigh Salterton, Devon, 31 March 1914.

Apart from his technical equipment, which was considerable, Herkomer possessed a quick scenic gift of expression, and this explains why his work became so widely popular. But although he is interesting and illuminating as an exponent of the later Victorian era, there is little in his art which, absolutely speaking, can be regarded as being of permanent value.

[Sir H. von Herkomer, *The Herkomers*, 2 vols., 1910–1911; A. L. Baldry, *Hubert von Herkomer, R.A., a Study and a Biography* (containing a list of his works down to the year 1901), 1902; Ludwig Pietsch, *Herkomer*, 1901; J. Saxon Mills, *Life and Letters of Sir Hubert von Herkomer*, 1923; U. Thieme and F. Becker, *Allgemeines Lexikon der bildenden Künstler*, vol. xvi, 1923; A. Graves, *The Royal Academy of Arts, Dictionary of Contributors, 1769–1904*, vol. iv, 1905–1906.]

T. B.

HICKS, EDWARD LEE (1843–1919), bishop of Lincoln, was born at Oxford 18 December 1843, the elder son of Edward Hicks, who was in business in Oxford, by his wife, Catherine Pugh, also of Oxford. He was educated at Magdalen College School, and at Brasenose College, Oxford, which he entered as a scholar in January 1862. He gained a first class in classical moderations in 1863, and in *literae humaniores* in 1866. In the latter year he passed on to Corpus Christi College, the first lay fellow of that college to be elected by examination. He won the Craven scholarship in 1867, and the Chancellor's Latin essay prize in the next year. Hicks was notably successful as a tutor for classical moderations at Corpus from 1866 to 1873. Quiet and reserved in youth, he grew in confidence, charm, and versatility with years. He was one of the first of English scholars to see the importance of epigraphy to ancient history. An accident, which compelled him to use crutches for some years and made exercise difficult, was turned to the best account: he worked hard at the study of Greek inscriptions, and found his recreation in vocal and instrumental music. 'Perhaps with the exception of Bywater', wrote Sir Samuel Dill, at that time one of his colleagues at Corpus, 'no young Oxford man of that time had anything like his erudition in Greek.'

Hicks was ordained deacon in 1870 and priest in 1871, and in 1873 he took the Corpus living of Fenny Compton in Warwickshire. In a quiet agricultural village he could still pursue epigraphy: he edited *The Collection of Ancient Greek Inscriptions in the British Museum* (1874–1890), and produced his *Manual of Greek Historical Inscriptions* (1882) which became a standard text-book. But he now came into close contact with the life-problems of humble folk, and his interest in these grew rapidly. He was a devoted country clergyman, somewhat of the Charles Kingsley type. In 1876 he married Agnes Mary, daughter of the Rev. Edwin Trevelyan Smith, sometime vicar of Cannock, Staffordshire. They had four sons and two daughters.

Agricultural depression and the fall in the value of tithe made it necessary for Hicks to leave Fenny Compton for the sake of his growing family, and in 1886 he was elected principal of Hulme Hall, Manchester, a Church of England hostel in connexion with Owens College. Here he continued his archaeological studies and gave lectures at Owens College. But he also found time for much religious and social work; and to this he gave himself wholly from 1892, when he accepted a canonry of Manchester cathedral, together with the living of St. Philip's, Salford. In religion Hicks combined evangelical fervour with the love of a beautiful, well-ordered service and with a sympathetic attitude to modern criticism. For eighteen years he wielded a great influence as a pastor in the slums of Salford, a preacher at Manchester Cathedral, and a temperance orator throughout the north of England. He threw himself into the political agitation carried on by Sir Wilfrid Lawson [q.v.] and the United Kingdom Alliance.

This militant teetotalism and his sympathies with pacificism and female suffrage delayed Hicks's ecclesiastical promotion; but in 1910 Mr. Asquith offered him the bishopric of Lincoln. It was not easy for one who was suspect as a radical reformer to succeed the beloved Edward King [q.v.], and Hicks was already sixty-six. His humour, courtesy, tolerance, and lightly-worn learning gradually conquered hostile prejudices, and the devotion with which he visited all parts of his diocese encouraged and stimulated his clergy. His ideals are set forth in his visitation charge, *Building in Troublous Times* (1912). He sorrowfully approved of the participation of his country in the European War; but it shattered many of his hopes and bereaved him of his eldest son. His health failed early in 1919, and he resigned his see, but died at Worthing, 14 August, before his resignation had taken effect.

[J. H. Fowler, *Life and Letters of Edward Lee Hicks*, 1922; personal knowledge.]

J. H. F.

HICKS BEACH, Sir MICHAEL EDWARD, ninth baronet, and first Earl St. Aldwyn (1837–1916), statesman, born in Portugal Street, Grosvenor Square, London, 23 October 1837, was the elder son of Sir Michael Hicks Hicks Beach, eighth baronet, by his wife, Harriett Vittoria, second daughter of John Stratton, of Farthinghoe Lodge, Northamptonshire. Sir Michael Hicks [q.v.], secretary to William Cecil, first Baron Burghley, was an ancestor, and Baptist Hicks, first Viscount Campden [q.v.], a member of the family. Sir Michael Hicks's son, Sir William, was created a baronet by James I in 1619. The additional surname of Beach was assumed in 1790 by Lord St. Aldwyn's great-grandfather, Michael Hicks, younger son of the sixth baronet, in consequence of his marriage to Henrietta Maria, only surviving daughter and heiress of William Beach, of Netheravon, Wiltshire.

Michael Edward Hicks Beach was educated at Eton and Christ Church, Oxford, whence he matriculated in 1855. In 1858 he obtained a first class in the honour school of jurisprudence and modern history, graduating B.A. in the same year and proceeding M.A. in 1861. He was created an honorary D.C.L. in 1878. He succeeded as ninth baronet on his father's death in 1854, and in 1864 was returned to parliament in the conservative interest at a by-election as member for East Gloucestershire, a seat which his father had held in 1854 for a few months before his death, and which he himself retained until 1885. From 1885 until 1906, when he was raised to the peerage, he sat for West Bristol.

Hicks Beach's political ability early marked him out for office. In the last year (1868) of the Earl of Derby's ministry, he was appointed in February parliamentary secretary of the Poor Law Board, and in August under-secretary for the Home Department. After the resignation of the ministry in December he spent five years in opposition, but in 1874, when Mr. Disraeli became prime minister for the second time, he was appointed chief secretary for Ireland. In this office he showed a sympathy with reform which was not very much to the taste of the Irish tories, but he had the approval of Disraeli, who described him in 1874 as 'a very able and rising man' [Monypenny and Buckle, *Life of Disraeli*, v, 271] and in 1876 brought him into the Cabinet.

When the fourth Earl of Carnarvon resigned the office of colonial secretary in January 1878, in consequence of his disapproval of Disraeli's attitude towards the Eastern question, Hicks Beach, who had supported Disraeli's war policy throughout, succeeded him on 4 February. During his two years of office his chief pre-occupation was with South Africa. As Carnarvon's resignation was not directly connected with colonial questions, Hicks Beach naturally followed the general lines of his policy in South Africa and gave support to his chosen agent, Sir Bartle Frere [q.v.]. But Frere, who had been sent as governor to the Cape in 1877 with wide discretionary powers to carry out Carnarvon's policy of confederation as embodied in the South Africa Act of 1877, soon found his attention occupied by the movements of the Zulus, who were menacing Natal and the Transvaal border. In 1878 Frere became convinced that a settlement of the Zulu question was a necessary preliminary to the achievement of South African federation. When he visited Natal in September he became certain that a Zulu attack was imminent and that reinforcements should therefore be sent to Natal as speedily as possible. With this view Hicks Beach, after becoming colonial secretary, had on several occasions expressed himself in agreement. But in the meantime the prime minister was giving more attention to South African affairs than during Carnarvon's tenure of office, and by May 1878 he began to be dissatisfied with Carnarvon's policy and to be apprehensive of trouble [*ibid.*, vi, 419]. By the autumn his alarm had increased [*ibid.*, 420] and early in October, in view of the serious situation in the Balkans and Afghanistan, the government determined to limit, if possible, their commitments in South Africa. In consequence, in a dispatch dated 17 October, Hicks Beach informed Frere that the government were not prepared to send out troops, and that they had a confident hope that, by the exercise of prudence, peace with the Zulu chief, Cetywayo, could be preserved. The actual reasons for this reversal of policy—the situation in Afghanistan and the Near East—were not given in this dispatch, which Frere received on 10 November. In any case Frere considered that it was impossible at that time to avert a rupture by any concessions, and that to make the attempt would weaken British authority and almost inevitably lead to a Boer revolt in the Transvaal [Frere to Hicks Beach, 5 January 1879, Worsfold, *Life of Frere*, 139]. On 11 December 1878, therefore, he sent an ultimatum to Cetywayo, which made that chief decide to begin hostilities as soon as he was ready.

Two days later (13 December) Frere received a private letter from Hicks Beach in which the reasons influencing the Cabinet to refuse reinforcements were expressly stated. Although this letter reached Frere after he had sent the ultimatum, a summary of its contents, telegraphed from Cape Town by Lady Frere, had reached him on 30 November, and it is probable, though not certain, that the telegram included this statement. It is, therefore, unlikely that the omission from the official dispatch of the reasons determining the Cabinet had any effect on Frere's action. But it was unfortunate that the reasons were eventually given in a private letter, because it enabled the government to omit the statement of their motives and Frere's reply in justification of himself, when the official papers relating to the matter were published [Frere to Sir Robert Herbert, 23 December 1878, Martineau, *Life of Frere*, ii, 265; Frere to Hicks Beach, 5 January 1879, Worsfold, *ibid.*].

In the meantime, on 3 November, Hicks Beach explained to Disraeli that he could not control Frere without a telegraph line, that he did not know whether he could if he had one, and that 'it is as likely as not that he is at war with the Zulus at the present moment and if his forces should prove inadequate . . . we shall be blamed for not supporting him ' [Monypenny and Buckle, vi. 421]. This statement convinced the Cabinet that reinforcements must be sent, but they directed that they should be for defence only [cf. Hicks Beach to Frere, 28 November 1878, Worsfold, 137]. Frere, probably with justice, considered that the only method of defending an exposed frontier two hundred miles long against greatly superior numbers was to take the initiative, and on 11 January 1879 the British commander, Lord Chelmsford, crossed the Tugela.

On 28 December 1878 Hicks Beach wrote to Frere taking exception to certain demands contained in the ultimatum on the ground that they had been made without reference home, and that Frere had hitherto made no mention of the necessity for ' a final settlement with Cetywayo '. The latter assertion does not seem to be borne out by the earlier correspondence between Hicks Beach and Frere, which treats the Zulu danger as urgent [Worsfold, 68–72, 79, 91, 102–4, 115–16, 158–9], and it is clear that the actual position, with the Zulu forces partially mobilized near the frontier, was not one which could be indefinitely prolonged. Before the catastrophe at Isandhlwana (22 January 1879) Hicks Beach expected that Frere's policy would be successful and all would turn out for the best [Monypenny and Buckle, vi, 423], but the news of the Zulu victory greatly affected Disraeli and led the Cabinet to censure Frere. This censure was conveyed by Hicks Beach in a dispatch dated 19 March 1879 [*ibid.*, 426]. At that time Frere was requested to continue in office, but in May his functions were restricted to Cape Colony and he was replaced as high commissioner for Natal, the Transvaal, and Zululand by Sir Garnet (afterwards Viscount) Wolseley in spite of Queen Victoria's strong disapproval [*ibid.*, 429–33]. The part played by Hicks Beach in these arrangements was mainly official. There is little doubt that throughout he sympathized with Frere and was personally inclined to support him, but that after October 1878 the policy in South Africa was modified and largely controlled by Disraeli, who was apprehensive that the development of the South African situation might interfere with his other plans. The position was a difficult one for a young minister, who had only recently entered the Cabinet and owed much to Disraeli's high opinion of him.

During the second Gladstone ministry (1880–1885) Hicks Beach was in opposition, and devoted his attention chiefly to the subjects of local taxation and the land. On 12 May 1884 he attacked the government for their treatment of General Gordon, in a speech which made a great impression on the House of Commons and led Lord Randolph Churchill on the following day to indicate him as the future leader of the party in the House [Churchill, *Life of Lord Randolph Churchill*, 283–4, 310–12]. Outside parliament he exerted his influence to keep the conservative party united. After the Sheffield conference in July 1884, when a reconciliation was effected between the supporters of Lord Randolph Churchill and the Marquess of Salisbury, Hicks Beach, as a friend of both sections, was elected chairman of the council of the National Union. In October and November his conferences with the Marquess of Hartington [see Cavendish, Spencer Compton, eighth Duke of Devonshire] led to an agreement with regard to the general line of the Redistribution Bill, which facilitated the passage of the Franchise Bill through the House of Lords [Holland, *Life of the Eighth Duke of Devonshire*, ii, 54–8]. In 1885 he turned to finance, and on 8 June he moved and carried an amendment to the budget, which led to Gladstone's resignation.

When Lord Salisbury formed an administration in June 1885, Hicks Beach at first accepted the Colonial Office. But on learning that Lord Randolph Churchill refused to take office if Sir Stafford Northcote (afterwards first Earl of Iddesleigh) led the House of Commons, he withdrew his assent and thus assisted Churchill to force Northcote into the House of Lords [Churchill, 326–7, 336–9]. He became chancellor of the exchequer on 24 June and leader of the House of Commons. During his short tenure of office he displeased a section of his party by his refusal, in the Maamtrasna debate on 17 July, to make himself responsible for the coercive measures of Lord Spencer, the late lord-lieutenant of Ireland, without affording opportunity for judicial investigation in particular cases. His position was subsequently restated more strongly and more generally by Churchill, and several tory members were moved to protest [*ibid.*, 353–7 ; Hansard, *Parliamentary Debates*, vol. 289, 1085].

The general election in November 1885 was followed by the resignation of Lord Salisbury's ministry on 28 January 1886, but in the five months' session which followed, Hicks Beach, as leader of the opposition, conducted the anti-Home Rule campaign to a victorious issue, manifesting, according to Lord Morley, remarkable skill and judgement [*Life of Gladstone*, iii. 338]. He himself, however, modestly considered that he was overshadowed by his colleague, Lord Randolph Churchill, and for this reason, when the new Salisbury ministry was formed in August, he insisted on making way for Churchill as chancellor of the exchequer and leader of the House of Commons [Churchill, 527–8]. On Churchill's suggestion he was offered and accepted the position of Irish secretary, which he had held twelve years before, and which was at this time the most difficult position in the government. This appointment was not approved by the Ulstermen and the more extreme Unionists, who considered him to be too much in sympathy with the Irish point of view. What was more serious, Hicks Beach found that his views about Ireland and Irish landlords differed from those of Lord Salisbury, and he became apprehensive of being forced to administer Ireland too much on a landlords' rights basis [Lord Randolph Churchill to Lord Salisbury, 22 August 1886, Churchill, 603]. Churchill's unexpected resignation in December 1886 deprived him of support in the Cabinet, from the meetings of which his Irish duties frequently compelled him to be absent [*ibid.*, 605]. On 4 March 1887 he was compelled to resign office on account of an 'acute affection of the eyes' which several times threatened him with loss of sight. He was succeeded by Mr. Arthur (afterwards Earl of) Balfour. For some time he remained in the Cabinet without portfolio; then he withdrew, but re-entered on 21 February 1888 as president of the Board of Trade, an office which he continued to hold until the fall of Lord Salisbury's government in August 1892.

In 1895 Hicks Beach became for the second time chancellor of the exchequer, and retained office until 1902. His budgets were carefully worked out and clearly presented. The first years concluded a period of great prosperity, but beyond a reduction of the rates on agricultural land in 1896, a modification of the incidence of income tax on middle-class incomes in 1898, and an abatement of the duty on tobacco in the same year, little was done to relieve taxation. In 1899 the South African War began to affect national finance. By 1902 the income tax had risen from eightpence to one and threepence, and in that year Hicks Beach reimposed the shilling corn duty which Lowe had discontinued in 1869. It was abandoned in the following year by his successor, Mr. (afterwards Baron) Ritchie [q.v.]. Hicks Beach resigned office on Lord Salisbury's retirement in July 1902. He was entirely out of sympathy with Mr. Joseph Chamberlain's movement in favour of 'tariff reform', and during the debates on Ritchie's budget he described himself as a 'thorough-going free-trader'. During the next few years he conducted a strenuous campaign against protection and in favour of administrative economy, and by his efforts contributed to deter Mr. Balfour from committing the party to Mr. Chamberlain's programme. At the same time the decided character of his opinions prevented him from returning to office. In 1906 he was raised to the peerage with the title of Viscount St. Aldwyn, of Coln St. Aldwyn, Gloucestershire, and in 1915 he was created an earl. He died in London 30 April 1916, and was buried at Coln St. Aldwyn.

St. Aldwyn was twice married: first, in 1864 to Caroline Susan (died 1865), daughter of John Henry Elwes, of Colesbourne Park, Gloucestershire; and secondly, in 1874 to Lady Lucy Catherine, third daughter of Hugh Fortescue, third Earl Fortescue [q.v.]. By his second wife he had one son and three daughters. His son, Michael Hugh Hicks Beach, Viscount Quenington (1877–1916) predeceased him by a week, and he was succeeded as second earl by his grandson, Michael John Hicks Beach (born 1912).

St. Aldwyn was a reserved man with a vein of shyness, and he made few close political friends. The most notable of these were his early patron, Disraeli, and at a later time, Lord Randolph Churchill. In 1890 he strongly urged Lord Salisbury to readmit Churchill to office, and in 1895 Churchill's bust in the House of Commons was unveiled 'by his oldest and truest political comrade, Sir Michael Hicks Beach' [Churchill, 771, 820]. Although Churchill was entirely loyal to him it may be doubted whether the alliance was favourable to Hicks Beach's political fortunes, particularly in 1886. He has been described as 'a thorough conservative of the old school', but he had no toleration for established abuses, and was more sympathetic than the bulk of his party in his attitude towards Ireland. His inability to suffer fools gladly in public matters and his merciless logic in debate gained him a reputation for austerity of demeanour and asperity of temper which was on the whole undeserved. Goschen said of him 'Beach is the only man I know who habitually thinks angrily' [Sir Almeric Fitzroy, *Memoirs*, 623]. The nickname of 'Black Michael', applied to him by members in private conversation, found its way into *Punch*, and, according to Justin M'Carthy, the Irish members discovered a reference to him in Macaulay's line 'The kites know well the long stern swell'. In private life St. Aldwyn was a land-owner, holding about four thousand acres, which he managed without an agent and kept in excellent order, while maintaining the happiest relations with his tenants. Both in public and private business he showed remarkable assiduity combined with high intellectual qualities, and it was on this that his position in the House of Commons was based.

A three-quarter length portrait of St. Aldwyn, standing at the table of the House of Lords, was painted by Sir A. S. Cope, R.A., in 1906 (*Royal Academy Pictures*, 1906).

[*The Times*, 1 and 5 May 1916; Mrs. William Hicks Beach, *A Cotswold Family*, 1909; W. F. Monypenny and G. E. Buckle, *Life of Benjamin Disraeli*, vols. v, vi, 1920; J. Martineau, *Life of Sir Bartle Frere*, 1895; W. B. Worsfold, *Life of Sir Bartle Frere*, 1923; W. S. Churchill, *Lord Randolph Churchill*, 2nd. ed. 1907; Lord Morley, *Life of Gladstone*, vol. iii, 1903; Lord E. Fitzmaurice, *Life of the Second Earl Granville*, vol. ii, 1905; B. H. Holland, *Life of the Eighth Duke of Devonshire*, 1911; Hansard, *Parliamentary Debates*; Henry Lucy, *Diaries of Parliament*, 1885–1905, and *Memories of Eight Parliaments*, 1908; Lord George Hamilton, *Parliamentary Reminiscences*, 1917; *Quarterly Review*, July 1885, January and July 1887; Hon. A. R. G. Elliot, *Life of the First Viscount Goschen*, 1911; Justin M'Carthy, *British Political Portraits, Number Six*, 1903; Sir Almeric Fitzroy, *Memoirs*, 1925; Sir A. H. Hardinge, *Life of the Fourth Earl of Carnarvon*, 1925.] E. I. C.

HILL, OCTAVIA (1838–1912), philanthropist, was born at Wisbech 3 December 1838, the eighth daughter of James Hill, corn-merchant and banker, who was noted locally for his good work in municipal and educational reform. Her mother was Caroline Southwood Smith, daughter of Dr. Thomas Southwood Smith [q.v.], well known as an authority on fever epidemics and sanitation. Octavia came under the influence of this grandfather early in life, and from him heard much about the condition of the homes of the poor. The younger sisters of the family were educated by their mother, a woman of much character and charm, with a view to earning their living as soon as possible. Octavia, who was an energetic determined, and affectionate child with much artistic talent, began work in London about 1852 at the Ladies' Guild, a co-operative association promoted by the Christian Socialists, of which her mother became manager. She was soon put in charge of a branch engaged in teaching ragged school-children to make toys, and thus gained her first experience of the lives of the very poor. At this time she naturally came under the influence of the Christian Socialists, and more especially of Frederick Denison Maurice [q.v.]. Another decisive influence in determining her future life and work was that of John Ruskin, whom she first met in 1853, and by whom she was greatly helped in her artistic training. For some years she employed much of her spare time in copying pictures for his *Modern Painters*, for the Society of Antiquaries, and for the National Portrait Gallery.

In 1856 Octavia Hill became secretary to the classes for women at the Working Men's College in Great Ormond Street, and a few years later she and her sisters started a school at 14 Nottingham Place. It was while living here and visiting her poorer neighbours that Miss Hill first became deeply impressed with the urgency of the housing problem, and succeeded (1864) in interesting Ruskin in her schemes for improving the dwellings of the poor. In after years she maintained that it was his generosity in providing the money for the purchase of the first houses which saved her undertaking from remaining 'a mere vision'; and though their friendship was at one time interrupted, she never wavered in her allegiance and gratitude to him. In 1865 she wrote to a friend: 'One great event of the term has been the actual purchase for fifty-six years of three houses in a court close to us, which Ruskin has really achieved for us. We buy them full of tenants; but there is in each house at present a landlord, who comes between us and the weekly lodgers, and of whom we cannot get rid till Midsummer. All we can do, therefore, is to throw our classes open to the tenants, and to do much small personal work among them, so that we may get to know them. But all repairing, and preventing of overcrowding, and authority to exclude thoroughly disreputable lodgers, must wait till Midsummer. At that time we are to begin the alteration of our stables into one large room, which will enable us to get the tenants together for all sorts of purposes, much more easily than at present.'

It was Ruskin also who advised Miss Hill that if she could place the work upon a business footing, paying 5 per cent. upon capital invested in it, it would be taken up and extended by other people. This advice proved to be fully justified, and her successful management led to a steadily increasing number of houses being placed under her charge. Not only did owners of house property turn to her for help, but many who came to know and believe in her work placed large sums of money in her hands for the purchase or building of houses for the very poor. So freely was this assistance forthcoming that in 1899 she was able to write: 'There has never been a time when the extension of our work has been delayed for want of money. We have always had ample at our disposal.' Perhaps the most important accession to her responsibilities was her appointment in 1884 by the Ecclesiastical Commissioners to manage a great part of their property in Southwark. Subsequently the Commissioners placed much other property in her hands as leases fell in, and frequently sought her advice in such matters as rebuilding.

Meanwhile the increase of work and responsibility left little time for teaching or for art, and in 1874 a group of friends raised a fund which freed Miss Hill for the future from the necessity of earning money, and left her at liberty to devote herself to housing reform. But, even with this assistance, the burden upon her was so great that more than once her health gave way and she was compelled to take a complete holiday. Especially was this so in 1877, when she was taken for a prolonged tour on the Continent by her friend, Miss Yorke, who from this time was closely associated with her life and work. Her long absence from England made necessary the devolution of responsibility upon the many workers whom she had trained in her methods, more especially upon her sisters. But it was characteristic of her method and temper throughout that she always endeavoured to develop responsibility and initiative in those who assisted her. There is no doubt that the rapid extension of the work was largely due to this spirit of true co-operation. Persons desiring to be trained under Miss Hill were attracted from far and near; with the result that her system of house management was introduced into other towns not only in Great Britain and Ireland, but also in America and on the continent of Europe, as for instance, in the 'Octavia Hill-Verein' in Berlin.

Octavia Hill's influence, though centred in housing reform, was far from being limited to it. Few efforts which were wisely directed towards the raising of the very poor failed to attract her interest. She was an active supporter of the work of the Charity Organization Society from its first beginnings, and frequently spoke and wrote on behalf of its principles. But perhaps her warmest sympathies were reserved for all efforts towards preserving and securing open spaces for the use of the people. She was closely associated with the Kyrle Society (founded by her sister Miranda in 1877), was a member of the Commons Preservation Society, and, in conjunction with Canon H. D. Rawnsley and Sir Robert Hunter [q.v.], founded the National Trust for places of historic interest or natural beauty (1895). It was largely due to her efforts that Parliament Hill and many other large and small open spaces were secured for public use and enjoyment.

Again, Octavia Hill's help and advice were often sought in connexion with the promotion of social reform by legislation. But her faith lay much more in the value of voluntary work, and it was with reluctance that she took part in political measures. It was an exception to this when, in 1873, she co-operated with the Charity Organization Society in active propaganda which resulted in Mr. (afterwards Viscount) Cross's Artisans' Dwellings Act (1875). But she refused to join the royal commission on housing (1889), and though she was induced to become a member of the royal commission on the poor laws (1905), she had little expectation of useful results. Nevertheless she threw herself loyally into the arduous work, and was remarkable for the steadiness and wisdom with which she maintained her principles. She also gave valuable evidence before the royal commission on the aged poor (1893).

No account of Octavia Hill would be complete without reference to the constant co-operation and assistance of her sisters. Of these, Miranda, who lived with her, died in 1910, and Octavia did not long survive her. She died in her house, 190 Marylebone Road, 13 August 1912, having made very complete arrangements for her work to be carried on. She was buried, according to her own instructions, at Crockham Hill, Kent, a memorial service being held in Southwark Cathedral.

In order to estimate the value of Octavia Hill's achievement it is necessary to recall something of the conditions which she sought to improve, and of the methods which she employed. Writing in 1899 she said : 'In Marylebone, where I began work, nearly every family rented but one room : now there are hundreds of two- and three-roomed tenements. . . . The knowledge of sanitary matters had penetrated hardly at all, gross ignorance prevailed. . . . The Building Acts took cognisance of very few of the requirements for health and hardly any sanitary measures were enforced, or even were enforceable. . . . From these and many other causes a London court in 1864 was a far more degraded and desolate place than it can be now, even in the remotest and forlornest region, and in taking charge of it one had to do a variety of things oneself where now one finds the intelligent and willing co-operation of many other agencies.' Among the duties of good management she enumerates : 'Repairs promptly and efficiently attended to, references completely taken up, cleaning sedulously supervised, overcrowding put an end to, the blessing of ready-money payments enforced, accounts strictly kept, and, above all, tenants so sorted as to be helpful to one another.' She held that an efficient manager required a thorough knowledge of finance and accounts, of the complicated system of rates and taxes in London, and of legal matters relating to leases and yearly tenancies. A further requisite, and quite as important, she considered to be the power of dealing with people at once wisely and kindly ; throughout all the work, however strictly carried out, should run the golden thread of sympathy and helpfulness—jobs must be found for those who are out of work, help given in illness and misfortune, days in the country organized for all the tenants in turn. In these ways, and by the pressure of constant and consistent influence, the people are brought to treat their homes with respect, and to prefer living orderly lives. If some of these things now appear to be commonplaces, it must be remembered that this is largely, if not mainly, due to the teaching and influence of Octavia Hill.

A portrait by J. S. Sargent, painted in 1899 and presented to Miss Hill by her friends, is now in the National Portrait Gallery. Hydon Heath and Hydon's Ball, a tract of wooded land about three miles from Godalming, 92 acres in extent, was purchased after her death and dedicated to her memory.

[Letters and other writings by Octavia Hill ; Charles E. Maurice, *Life of Octavia Hill as told in her Letters*, 1913 ; private information ; personal knowledge.] H. B–T.

HODGKIN, THOMAS (1831–1913), historian, was the second son of John Hodgkin, conveyancer, by his wife, Elizabeth, daughter of Luke Howard. He was born on 29 July 1831 at Bruce Grove, Tottenham. His parents were quakers by descent and profession, and he received his early education at Grove House, Tottenham, a quaker school. Proceeding to University College, London, he took his B.A., with honours in classics, in 1851. He was originally intended for the bar, and was admitted at Lincoln's Inn in 1850, but within a short time he abandoned legal studies owing to weak health, and turned to banking, which he studied at Pontefract and Whitehaven. In 1859 he became a partner in the new banking firm of Hodgkin, Barnett, Pease, and Spence, at Newcastle. His connexion with this concern continued until it was absorbed (in 1902) by Lloyds Bank. In 1861 he married Lucy Anna, daughter of Alfred Fox, of Falmouth, by whom he had three sons and three daughters ; they lived until 1894 at Benwell-dene in Newcastle, but in that year removed to Bamburgh Castle ; finally, in 1899, they settled at Barmoor Castle in the same county. Hodgkin was at all times a devoted and active member of the quaker community and a public-spirited citizen of Newcastle. But from an early age he contrived to find time for archaeological and historical studies. He was a leading member of the Society of Antiquaries of Newcastle-upon-Tyne, and contributed many papers to that society's journal, *Archaeologia Aeliana.* Some fruits of this local work are to be seen in his *History of England from the Earliest Times to the Norman Conquest* (1906), probably the first history of the origins of Great Britain to be written from a Northumbrian point of view. But even in this work his antiquarian learning is subordinated to humaner interests. He resisted, for instance, the temptation to make his chapter on the Roman period a monograph on excavations and inscriptions. His English History is, however, overshadowed by the larger work, *Italy and Her Invaders*, the first two volumes of which appeared in 1879, the last in 1899. To the whole work we may apply the author's description of the first and second volumes ; it was the fruit of 'happy labour' pursued without haste or rest in hours snatched from more practical activities. Hodgkin traversed a field which Gibbon had already surveyed, but described it in a new perspective. Sensitive to the urbanity of Roman culture, admiring the solidity of the Roman administrative system, he nevertheless accorded to the wreckers of the culture and the system a more genial treatment than Gibbon would have approved. Hodgkin's imagination was fired by the epic element in his theme and in the Teutonic character. He does not altogether neglect the slow and obscure developments of legal principles and political institutions. But the story is for him the main thing. He enlivens and illuminates the story with vignettes from contemporary life, and with finely drawn sketches of men of action and men of letters. As an historian he is almost inevitably to be compared with Grote. Both were bankers by trade and scholars by inclination. Both desired to write books of scholarship for the delight and the information of the general public. Hodgkin was, however, less interested in political theories than Grote, and more interested in plain humanity and the vicissitudes of human society. A full bibliography of Hodgkin's minor writings is given in the ninth volume of the third series of *Archaeologia Aeliana*; but his reputation rests on his two principal works. He died at Falmouth on 2 March 1913.

[Louise Creighton, *Life and Letters of Thomas Hodgkin*, 1917 ; *Archaeologia Aeliana*, u.s.] H. W. C. D.

HODGSON, SHADWORTH HOLLWAY (1832–1912), philosopher, was born at Boston, Lincolnshire, 25 December 1832, the eldest son of Shadworth Hodgson, of Boston, by his wife, Anne, daughter of John Palmer Hollway, also of Boston. He was educated at Rugby and at Corpus Christi College, Oxford. He graduated in 1854, after taking a first class in classical moderations, and a second class in *literae humaniores*. In 1855 he married Ann, daughter of the Rev. Edward Browne Everard, rector of Burnham Thorpe, Norfolk. The death of his wife and only child in 1858 led to his applying himself with rare devotion to philosophy. He acquired a most unusual knowledge of philosophical literature, and collected a fine library. His chief works are *Time and Space : a Metaphysical Essay* (1865), *The Theory of Practice* (1870), *The Philosophy of Reflection* (1878), and *The Metaphysic of Experience* (1898), the last of which contains a full exposition of his philosophy. He was the first president (1880–1894) and the leading spirit of the Aristotelian Society ; its *Proceedings* contain fourteen presidential addresses and many other papers by him. He was elected an honorary fellow of his college in 1882, and fellow of the British Academy in 1901. He died in London 13 June 1912.

Hodgson thought of himself as continuing the work of Hume and also that of Kant, but as improving on both by discarding their respective assumptions. Both those thinkers start by assuming the distinction of subject and object, a distinction not immediately experienced but presupposing much naïve reflection. Empiricism assumes experience to be produced by the action of bodies ; transcendentalism assumes it to be modified by a synthetic activity of the subject ; but philosophy, Hodgson held, should not assume the activity either of subjects or of objects. What is found directly in experience is not the distinction of subject and object but that of consciousness and content : i.e. of ' thatness ', the fact that consciousness occurs, and ' whatness ', the particular nature of the consciousness. As consciousness moves towards the future, it distinguishes its past ' whatnesses ' from its present ' whatness ', and objectifies them. While we must not start with the distinction of mind and matter, the analysis of consciousness reveals features which show this distinction to be necessary. Hodgson's system is thus ultimately dualistic. It is a bold and able attempt to work out a complete metaphysic by a thorough-going analysis of experience. His precise point of view was, however, one which other philosophers found it difficult to share, and he founded no school ; the main value of his work probably resides in his detailed psychological analysis.

[*The Times*, 18 June 1912 ; memoirs by H. Wildon Carr in *Proceedings* of the Aristotelian Society, new series, vol. xii, and in *Mind*, new series, vol. xxi ; memoir by G. Dawes Hicks in *Proceedings* of the British Academy, vol. vi.] W. D. R.

HOLLAND, HENRY SCOTT (1847–1918), theologian and preacher, born at Ledbury, Herefordshire, 27 January 1847, was the eldest son of George Henry Holland by his wife, the Hon. Charlotte Dorothea Gifford, eldest daughter of Robert, first Baron Gifford [q.v.], of St. Leonard, Devon. His father was the second son of Swinton Colthurst Holland, of Dumbleton, Gloucestershire. After four years at a private school at Allesley, near Coventry, he went to Eton in January 1860, where he had the good fortune to be the pupil of William Johnson (William

Johnson Cory, q.v.). He left Eton rather early, in 1864, and, after a period under private tutors, entered Balliol College, Oxford, in January 1866. Here he made two of the most important friendships in his life—with Richard Lewis Nettleship [q.v.] and Thomas Hill Green [q.v.]—and displayed in the final school of *literae humaniores* signs of great intellectual power. In December 1870 Holland was elected by open examination to a senior studentship at Christ Church. Here he resided until 1884 when he was appointed canon of St. Paul's on Mr. Gladstone's recommendation.

The circumstances of Oxford life in that period appear to have been widely different from anything that has been common there in recent years. The letters between Holland and his friends Nettleship and Green, and the serious doubts whether their friendship could survive his ordination (1872) would not be written now. And it is probably due in no small measure to Holland's tendency to mediate between opposing points of view that this change has come about. The influence of his Balliol time had gone very deep, and was never lost: from the earliest days of his residence at Christ Church he began to be effective in the way of reconciliation. Canon Liddon, in a letter on Holland's appointment to St. Paul's, tells him that 'issues are much simpler' in London; 'we live here [i.e. in London] on terms of easy intercourse with so many to whom Catholic doctrine and indeed the whole creed of Christianity go for nothing' [*Memoir*, p. 112]. Holland could never have been a lonely scholar, researching by himself: he had an instinct for companionship, and he rapidly became the centre of a group of men who read and thought and discussed together, and at length (1899) addressed the world in *Lux Mundi*. His life at Oxford was full of varied interests and he supported many causes. He took a vigorous part in college life, and held the university office of proctor in 1882–1883, but he never allowed himself to be swept into the stream of university business.

When he passed on to London, he had already identified himself with such projects as the Oxford House in Bethnal Green and the Christ Church Mission in Poplar, and he was already studying the bearing of Christian principles upon economic questions. Nothing ever interfered with his devoted loyalty to St. Paul's and his work there, but his position was identified more and more clearly with social and economic problems. He took a large part in the founding of the Christian Social Union, and he edited for years (1895–1912) the *Commonwealth*, a paper devoted to the study of the various elements in social life in the light of Christianity. Some of his most characteristic writing is to be found in the pages of this journal. The Maurice Hostel at Hoxton—named after F. Denison Maurice [q.v.]—was founded (1898) and devotedly served by him as an embodiment of the principles and aims of the C.S.U.

Soon after he went to London, Holland began to be troubled with an illness affecting his head and eyes. He varied in health from time to time, but he was never again able to read or write for long at a time: he had to depend for both upon the help of others. It is difficult to imagine a more distressing or disabling malady. It is due to this misfortune that no comprehensive book ever came from his pen. It cut him off from much social intercourse, from concerts and other gatherings, and compelled him to live with the sole purpose of fulfilling, often under great strain and discomfort, the many and various engagements which formed his work.

In 1911 he returned to Oxford as regius professor of divinity. He had been out of residence for twenty-six years, and many generations had passed through Oxford in that time. To many he was a stranger. But he entered vigorously on his work: he raised the standard required for the divinity degrees, and he introduced in 1913, but without success, a statute to base the degrees upon theological study and get rid of the restrictions which limited them to priests of the Church of England. He was beginning again to draw round him many followers, when the university life was broken up by the European War. The anxiety and distress of the War, the long lists of the fallen, especially those of the junior members of the university, to whom he was always a devoted friend, pressed heavily upon him, and in 1917 his health began to give way. He never lost his varied interests or clearness of mind. He died in Oxford 17 March 1918. His body lies in the churchyard at Cuddesdon.

No account of Holland would be complete without a reference to his lifelong love of music. In early days he had the friendship of Otto Goldschmidt and his wife, Jenny Lind [q.v.]; in 1891 he joined with William Smith Rockstro [q.v.] in the production of a memoir of his friend, *Jenny Lind, the Artist*.

Holland's published writings consist mainly of collected sermons and articles. Since his death Canon Wilfrid J. Richmond has edited a volume, *The Fourth Gospel* (1923), containing fragments illustrating his philosophical position and certain essays introductory to a commentary upon the fourth gospel which he undertook in his later years. The sermons and addresses are all written in a strongly individual and somewhat exuberant style. But the thought is neither obscure nor loose: the exuberance almost always results from the rapidity with which different aspects of his subject come before his mind: it is an exuberance of thought, and not merely of words. All his utterances, whether upon the mysteries of the Faith, the experiences of Christian life, or social rights and wrongs, are marked by a passionate sincerity and enthusiasm.

Owing to the constant disturbance of illness, Holland was not deeply read in all the controversial literature surrounding the subjects which he studied: his letters show how fully conscious he was of this. But in all his dealing with books or opinions he had an unusual power of penetrating to the mind of the man behind them. This was the most striking feature of his lectures at Christ Church on Plato's *Republic*, and is conspicuous in the notes above mentioned for the introduction to St. John's gospel. It is, perhaps, connected with this characteristic, that he was specially interested in studying, when possible, the portraits of authors. It was his power of penetrating minds other than his own that accounted for his attitude in theology and in politics. In both he must have departed widely from the lines on which he had been brought up. His early Oxford friendships, and his interest not merely in social and other questions but in the people who were raising them, made it inevitable that he should combine in his own mind and action lines of thought that to others often seemed incompatible. He was a strong and convinced liberal in politics and in theology—as his scheme for divinity degrees plainly showed in 1913—and at the same time a high churchman with a great delight in expressive ritual, a pride in the long history of the Church, and an extraordinarily penetrating perception of doctrinal truth and spiritual reality. But his interest in men did not blind him to bad work or bad arguments: at times—like Bishop Westcott—he was almost cynically clear-sighted and relentless. His written work unfortunately gives but a broken picture of his power and influence both in thought and action.

[Stephen Paget, *Henry Scott Holland, Memoir and Letters*, 1921 (portrait); personal knowledge. See also E. Lyttelton, *The Mind and Character of Henry Scott Holland*, 1926.]

T. B. S.

HOLLAND, Sir HENRY THURSTAN, first Viscount Knutsford (1825–1914), belonged by descent to the family of Holland, derived, through the Hollands of Clifton and Mobberley, from the Hollands of Upholland. His ancestors owned various estates for many centuries in Lancashire and Cheshire. He was the elder son of Sir Henry Holland, first baronet [q.v.], a leading London physician, by his first wife, Margaret Emma, daughter of James Caldwell, of Linley Wood, Staffordshire, and was born at his father's house, 72 Brook Street, London, 3 August 1825. He was educated at Harrow, at Durham University, and at Trinity College, Cambridge, where he took his degree in 1847. At Durham he won the Durham prize for Latin verse, and he steered the Cambridge boat in the university four-oared race of 1846. He was called to the bar by the Inner Temple in 1849, and practised on the Northern circuit. In 1850 he acted as secretary to the royal commission on common law, and assisted in drafting the Common Law Procedure Acts of 1852 and 1854. He was offered by Lord Campbell the county-court judgeship of Northumberland, but declined. In 1867 he was appointed by the fourth Earl of Carnarvon to be legal adviser at the Colonial Office, and gave up private practice. In 1870 he became assistant under-secretary for the Colonies. He held this office until August 1874, and then, having in 1873 succeeded to the baronetcy, resigned it in order to stand for parliament as conservative candidate for Midhurst. He was elected without a contest, and held the seat until 1885, when, under the Redistribution Act, Midhurst ceased to exist as a constituency. Sir Henry then stood for the newly created constituency of Hampstead, where he defeated the Marquess of Lorne. In the same year he became financial secretary to the Treasury in Lord Salisbury's administration, and soon afterwards vice-president of the Committee of Council on Education. He held the same office again in Lord Salisbury's second administration (1886–1888), and at the beginning of the latter year became secretary of state for the Colonies, and so head of the department in which he had served as a permanent official. He held that office until the fall of the conservative government in 1892. In 1887 took place, upon his initiative and under his presidency, the first of those colonial conferences out of which has since developed the quadrennial imperial conference. It was held in connexion with the gathering to celebrate Queen Victoria's first jubilee. Otherwise no events took place in this period which much disturbed the calm of the Colonial Office.

In 1888 Holland was raised to the peerage under the title of Baron Knutsford, of Knutsford, Cheshire, and in 1895 he was created a viscount. He was made a privy councillor in 1885; he was also a G.C.M.G. (1888), an ecclesiastical commissioner, a knight of justice of the order of St. John of Jerusalem, a bencher of the Inner Temple, and he served on several important royal commissions. He was noted for his good looks, social charm, and the energy which he put into any work that he had to do. He was not an orator, and confined his speeches in parliament to subjects with which he had, or had had, some official connexion. He had a country residence for nearly forty years at Witley in Surrey, and, when not in office, took due part in local affairs. He died at his London house in Eaton Square 29 January 1914, in his eighty-ninth year.

Lord Knutsford married twice: first, in 1852 Elizabeth Margaret (died 1855), daughter of Nathaniel Hibbert, of Munden House, Hertfordshire, and granddaughter of the famous Canon Sydney Smith; by her he had twin sons, one of whom, Sydney Holland, succeeded him as second Viscount, and a daughter; secondly, in 1858 Margaret Jean, daughter of Sir Charles Edward Trevelyan [q.v.], and niece of Lord Macaulay, by whom he had three sons and one daughter.

A portrait of Lord Knutsford by Sir Arthur Cope, R.A., painted in 1887, is now in the possession of Lord Hambleden. There is also a Grillion Club drawing.

[Burke's *Peerage*; Bernard Holland, *The Lancashire Hollands*, 1917; W. Ferguson Irvine, *The Family of Holland of Mobberley and Knutsford*, privately printed, 1912. Portrait, *Royal Academy Pictures*, 1907.] B. H. H.

HOLMES, THOMAS (1846–1918), police-court missionary and philanthropist, was born at the small village of Pelsall, near Walsall, Staffordshire, 25 January 1846, the son of William Holmes, iron-moulder, by his wife, Cecilia, daughter of Thomas Withington. At the age of twelve Thomas became an iron-moulder himself, working fourteen hours a day and earning three shillings a week. He was dependent for education upon bible readings with his father and on general instruction from an old-fashioned teacher at the church school of Rugeley. He continued to work as an iron-moulder until he was thirty-three. On his scanty earnings he married in 1872 Margaret, daughter of Ralph Brammer, carpenter, of Rugeley, and brought up a family of five sons. In the meantime he had cultivated his mind and earned a reputation for intelligent philanthropy by devoting himself after his hard day's work to the education of his fellow-workers in evening classes and at the Sunday school.

In 1877 Holmes met with a serious accident which eventually made it impossible for him to continue his work as an iron-moulder. His friends, who appreciated the trend of his character, advised him in 1885 to apply for the post, then vacant, of police-court missionary at Lambeth police-court. To his great surprise he was appointed, and there found his true vocation. In 1889 he was transferred to the North London police court. In the course of his twenty years' service as police-court missionary he dealt with thieves, drunkards, prostitutes, and outcasts of every description, devoting himself with characteristic zeal to every side of his work. He described his experiences in his book, *Pictures and Problems from London Police Courts* (1900), which had a large sale and was widely translated.

Holmes became known both in England and abroad as a criminologist of imagination and judgement, and gained both profit and reputation from his writings. He was thought at the police court to have some resemblance to Dickens, to whose memory he was sincerely devoted. He loved his work and, although not as optimistic as some missionaries of a more robust type of Christianity, he was always ready to receive unpromising cases as guests in his house, and was often surprised by the miraculous effect of practical sympathy upon the roughest characters.

In 1905 Holmes retired from the police courts in order to become secretary to the Howard Association for the reform of prisons and criminal law. In this capacity he worked for ten years, and earned the gratitude of one home secretary after another for his advice and assistance in the matter of prison reform. His efforts, owing to the public support which they received, have effected great improvements in the prison system during the last twenty years. Instead of trying to break the spirit of offenders by harsh punishments, it is now sought to raise them above the level of their old associations and to give them a sense of pleasure and pride in honest work. In 1910 Holmes was sent to the United States as the British representative at the Penological Congress.

The rest of Holmes's life was devoted to philanthropy of his own choosing. In 1904, before he left the police courts, he founded the Home Workers' Aid Association, which rapidly developed into an important undertaking. To use his own description: 'It is not a trade union, but a union of home workers (women), employers, and the public.' Its objects were generally to improve the conditions under which home workers live, and to give them an opportunity of enjoying one good holiday every year, towards which they make a reasonable contribution, and for this purpose 'to establish and maintain homes of rest for home workers needing rest and recreation'. It is difficult for ordinary people to realize the condition of home workers before the establishment (1909) of trades boards. In a pamphlet written in 1920 on behalf of Holmes's association, Mr. William Pett Ridge wrote: 'The nation was startled to find that a woman and her daughter, of Islington, costume machinists, buying their own thread and using their own sewing machine, earned 1*s.* 10*d.* each in a day of 14 hours; that a maker of artificial flowers in Bethnal Green, working 16 hours out of the 24, managed to gain 1½*d.* per hour; that other women, engaged in making boxes, or tooth-brushes, or babies' bonnets, working similarly from break of dawn until the light failed, were able to obtain similar emoluments.' It was this state of things which Holmes, with characteristic shrewdness and sympathy, set himself to redress. In 1910 he was able to establish 'Singholm', a fine house with flower and fruit gardens at Walton-on-the-Naze, where forty women during their fortnight's holiday may enjoy fine air, good food, clean rooms, and the rare privilege of having nothing to do.

Besides his police-court experiences and various magazine articles Holmes wrote *Known to the Police* (1908), *London's Underworld* (1912), and *Psychology and Crime* (1912). He died in London 26 March 1918.

[Obituary notice (by the present writer) in *The Times*, 27 March 1918.] C. M. C.

HOLROYD, Sir CHARLES (1861–1917), painter-etcher and director of the National Gallery, London, the eldest son of William Holroyd, merchant, of Leeds, by his wife, Lucy, daughter of Henry Woodthorpe, of Aveley, Essex, was born at Leeds 9 April 1861. He was educated at Leeds grammar school and also, since he was intended for the career of a mining engineer, at the Yorkshire College of Science (afterwards Leeds University) until in 1880 he went to the Slade School of Fine Art at University College, London, where Alphonse Legros [q.v.] was then professor. William Strang [q.v.], slightly his senior, was his most distinguished contemporary at the school, and these were the two students on whom the style and teaching of Legros made the strongest impression. After winning many prizes and acting from 1885 to 1889 as an assistant teacher at the Slade School, Holroyd gained a travelling scholarship, and during two years spent in Italy (1889–1891) acquired an intimate knowledge of the art, architecture, scenery, and language of the country, for which he retained throughout his life the warmest affection. He made many etchings during his student days, but they were of little merit compared with his later work. He was elected a fellow of the Society of Painter-Etchers in 1885, and thereafter (except in 1890) was a regular exhibitor at the Society's gallery, contributing all his best work on copper or zinc to its annual exhibitions. He took the keenest interest in the affairs both of this society and of the Art Workers' Guild, of which he became a member in 1898 and master in 1905. In 1891 he married a former student of the Slade School, Fannie Fetherstonhaugh, daughter of the Hon. John Alexander Macpherson, of Melbourne, at one time premier of Victoria. Holroyd and his wife spent about three years (1894–1897) in Italy; from 1897 to 1903 they lived at Epsom.

Between 1885 and 1895 Holroyd exhibited seven pictures at the Royal Academy, and contributed to other exhibitions, such as that of the International Society of Painters and Gravers. He occasionally painted portraits, and an altar-piece by him, 'The Adoration of the Shepherds', of which he made an etching in 1900, is in Aveley church. But he was not a good colourist, in spite of his warm appreciation of the Venetian school, nor a thorough master of the technique of oil-painting. Some of his water-colour sketches are in the Tate Gallery. His etched work, amounting to 286 numbers [Illustrated Catalogue by Campbell Dodgson in the *Print Collector's*

Quarterly, October and December 1923], is by far his most considerable claim to recognition as an artist. He was uncertain, though often excellent, as a draughtsman, and his imagination was not always equal to the tasks that he essayed ; but he had a fine, and in his day rare, ambition to attempt anew the great traditional themes, sacred and mythological, of renaissance art. Among his figure subjects, the 'Icarus' series, 'The Flight into Egypt', 'The Prodigal Son', 'Prayer', some monastic subjects in the manner of Legros, and the later 'Nymphs by the Sea' (1905), deserve special mention. After the year 1900 he tended to confine himself more and more to landscape. He etched many good plates of scenes on the Medway, in the New Forest, and, above all, in the English lake district, where many holidays were spent, for both he and his wife were good pedestrians and climbers. Many good etchings were done also on their frequent visits to Italy, of subjects from Rome (the small and large 'Borghese Trees' are among his best plates), Venice, Siena, and later, Belluno and Assisi. Of his portrait etchings, 'Alphonse Legros' and some idealized heads of his wife (especially 'Night', a dry-point) are the best. His excellent drawing of trees is exemplified by 'A Yew on Glaramara' (1903), 'Under the Greenwood Tree' (1904), several of the Medway etchings, and 'The Bent Beech' (1916), one of the latest of all his plates. A fairly representative, but very incomplete, collection of his etchings is in the British Museum. The complete collection formed by the artist himself now belongs to his son, who also owns the plates, of which few have been destroyed. Another branch of art which he practised about 1900, again under the influence of Legros, was that of the medallist. He also contributed lithographs to two portfolios issued by the Art Workers' Guild in 1905 and 1907.

In his later years Holroyd's artistic work was much hampered by official duties, and etching tended to become merely a holiday recreation. In 1897 he was appointed the first keeper of the newly founded National Gallery of British Art at Millbank (Tate Gallery), a position which he held till 1906, when he succeeded Sir Edward John Poynter [q.v.] as director of the National Gallery. He was knighted in 1903. At the Tate Gallery he did much to bring into prominence some of the good, but neglected, British artists, especially Alfred Stevens [q.v.]. At the National Gallery he improved the catalogue, and the arrangement and decoration of the rooms, for the greater safety of which he initiated works of reconstruction. He had few opportunities, as director, of making great acquisitions for the Gallery, and some of his attempts to improve the representation of the French school are open to criticism ; but it was in his time that the National Art-Collections Fund became powerful, and secured for the Gallery three important pictures by Velazquez, Holbein, and Mabuse, with his full approval and active help. By his tact and perseverance Holroyd overcame great difficulties in securing for the Gallery the bequest of pictures of Sir Austen Henry Layard [q.v.]. He had much to do with disinterring from the store-rooms of the National Gallery the forgotten, unfinished paintings by Turner, the beauties of which were revealed for the first time in the new Turner gallery at Millbank, to which most of Turner's pictures were transferred from Trafalgar Square during Holroyd's directorship.

Holroyd held the directorship of the National Gallery for two periods of five years, but resigned in June 1916 on account of failing health. Difficulties with the trustees, the aggressive and dangerous tactics of the suffragettes in 1913–1914, and then the outbreak of the European War, preyed upon his mind and undermined his health. From 1915 onwards he suffered from heart disease and was rarely able to leave Sturdie House, Weybridge, the house which he had built for himself in 1901–1903, and where he died 17 November 1917. He was survived by his wife (died 1924) and by their only son Michael, afterwards fellow of Brasenose College, Oxford.

Holroyd was a stalwart man of fine presence, courteous manners, and a generous heart, ever ready to befriend other artists, and to do all in his power for visitors and students at the National Gallery. He was not in all respects a learned critic or historian of art, his strong point being a thorough knowledge of the Italian school. He was the author of *Michael Angelo Buonarrotti* (1903 ; second edition, 1911), embodying a new translation of Condivi's life of that artist, and he contributed a life of Legros to the *Encyclopaedia Britannica*, but wrote little else except occasional articles and introductions to official catalogues and guides. A portrait of Holroyd was etched by Legros in 1894.

[*The Times*, 19 November 1917 ; *Daily Telegraph*, 20 November 1917 ; *Burlington*

Magazine, December 1917 and January 1918; *Print Collector's Quarterly*, October and December 1923; private information.]

C. D.

HOOD, Sir HORACE LAMBERT ALEXANDER (1870–1916), rear-admiral (posthumous K.C.B.), the third son of the fourth Viscount Hood, by his wife, Edith, daughter of Arthur W. Ward, of Tunbridge Wells, was born at 40 South Street, London, 2 October 1870. He was a lineal descendant of Samuel, first Viscount Hood [q.v.], whose younger brother was Alexander Hood, first Viscount Bridport [q.v.]—names famous in British naval history. He joined the *Britannia* as a naval cadet at the age of twelve, and left her, after the customary two years' training, with the highest classes obtainable in all subjects. He served in the *Temeraire*, of the Mediterranean squadron, from September 1885 to June 1886, then in the *Minotaur* till January 1887, when he joined the *Calliope*, and in her was present at Samoa in the hurricane of 16 March 1889. After promotion to lieutenant (1890), in the examinations for which rank he obtained remarkable successes, he had a year's service in the *Trafalgar* (June 1891–September 1892), and then spent three years ashore studying gunnery and acting as a staff officer; he next served successively in the *Royal Sovereign*, *Wildfire*, *Sanspareil*, and *Cambrian*. In June 1897 he was lent to the Egyptian government for the Nile campaign, where he had his first experience of active service in command of a river gunboat. He was present at the battles of the Atbara and Omdurman, and at the end of the campaign was promoted to commander (1898). On the outbreak of the Boer War he was employed for three months on transport duties. After serving as commander (1900–1903) of the *Ramillies*, flagship of Lord Charles Beresford, second in command in the Mediterranean, he was promoted captain, and in July 1903 was appointed to the *Hyacinth*, flagship of Rear-Admiral G. L. Atkinson-Willes in the East Indies. He led the force sent against the Dervishes at Illig, Somaliland, in April 1904, when 627 officers and men of the *Hyacinth*, *Fox*, and *Mohawk*, with a detachment of 127 men of the Hampshire regiment, dislodged the Dervishes after landing in a heavy surf in the dark. He took a prominent part in the hand-to-hand fighting and received the D.S.O. for his services. Hood next commanded the *Berwick* (1906–1907) and, after serving one year as naval attaché at Washington, the *Commonwealth* (1908–1909). After commanding the naval college at Osborne from October 1910 to January 1913, he was promoted to rear-admiral (May 1913) and hoisted his flag on board the *Centurion* for three months. In June 1914 he became naval secretary to the first lord of the Admiralty, Mr. Winston Churchill.

The threatening and rapid movement of the German army towards the Channel ports in October 1914 created a need for naval co-operation with the British and Belgian armies. A flotilla, based upon Dover, composed of vessels of the smaller and oldest types, was formed for this work, and Hood was placed in command. Here his energy, good judgement, and courage found a free scope, and in the critical days between the 21st and 30th of October 1914 this small force contributed in a high degree to stemming the German advance. In May 1915 Hood was placed in command of the third battle-cruiser squadron of the grand fleet, with his flag on board the *Invincible*.

On 30 May 1916 Hood's squadron sailed with the main body of the fleet from Scapa Flow, and on the 31st, during the approach period of the action of Jutland, was stationed twenty-five miles ahead of the battle fleet. When news arrived at 3.40 p.m. that Admiral Beatty's cruiser squadron was engaged, Hood was detached to the east-south-eastward at full speed to support. Two hours later he came into action in support of the *Chester*, light cruiser, which, hard pressed by Rear-Admiral Boedicker's second scouting group (light cruisers), was retiring under heavy fire to the westward. Hood, hearing the gun-fire to the north-west, turned toward it. His unexpected appearance was disconcerting to Boedicker, who, abandoning chase of the *Chester*, gave his commander-in-chief, Admiral Scheer, information by wireless that the British main body was to the north-eastward. At the same time, Vice-Admiral Hipper, with the German battle cruisers, believing himself headed by the whole British fleet, turned southwest to rejoin his own battleships, firing torpedoes, which were avoided, at Hood's squadron. Hood followed to the westward, and so soon as he sighted Beatty's squadron, steered to place himself in its van, making an admirable turn into his station. Within a few minutes he was closely engaged with Hipper's battle-cruisers, now coming up again from the southward.

Standing by his flag-captain, Arthur Cay, on the bridge of the *Invincible*, pressing her into action at her highest speed, and pouring in his fire, Hood was assuredly in his element. After about ten minutes of hot fire, in which the flagship had been hit several times, Hood hailed the foretop with : 'Your firing is very good. Keep at it as quickly as you can ; every shot is telling.' Five minutes later (6.34 p.m.) a shell from the *Derfflinger* burst in the *Invincible*'s 'Q' turret. The flash went down to the magazine, which immediately exploded, and the ship, breaking in half, sank in a cloud of smoke, leaving her bow and stern standing out of the water to mark where she lay. Hood, and all his ship's company save six, perished.

In Hood the navy lost an officer of exceptional merit. To great natural capacity he added, from his earliest days, remarkable powers of application. He had an intense sense of duty and moral courage of the highest order. He took responsibility readily, and never hesitated to follow a course of action that might be unpopular or prejudicial to his personal interests. To this courage he joined a love of active pursuits and an acute and hearty sense of humour. He married in 1910 Ellen, daughter of A. E. Touzalin and widow of George Nickerson, of Dedham, Massachusetts, and had two sons.

A portrait of Hood is included in Sir A. S. Cope's picture 'Some Sea Officers of the Great War', painted in 1921, in the National Portrait Gallery.

[Admiralty records; personal knowledge. See also Sir J. S. Corbett: (Official) *History of the Great War. Naval Operations*. vol. iii 1923.]

H. W. R.

HOPE, Sir WILLIAM HENRY ST. JOHN (1854–1919), antiquary, the eldest son of the Rev. William Hope, rector of St. Peter's, Derby, by his first wife, Hester, daughter of the Rev. John Browne Williams, vicar of Llantrisant, Glamorgan, was born at Derby 23 June 1854. His taste for ecclesiology, inherited from his father, was developed in his school days at St. John's College, Hurstpierpoint, where his lifelong friend, Joseph Thomas Fowler, was then chaplain. He entered Peterhouse, Cambridge, in 1877, when he had already achieved some success in his excavations at Dale Abbey, near Derby. As an undergraduate, his knowledge of English antiquities was recognized and respected by older men, and he formed close friendships with Henry Bradshaw [q.v.] and John Willis Clark [q.v.]. His work at Dale was followed by excavations at Repton Priory, and subsequently at Lewes Priory and Alnwick Abbey. After taking his degree, he was for a short time an assistant master at the King's School, Rochester. His increasing reputation led to his election as a fellow of the Society of Antiquaries in 1883, and two years later he was appointed assistant secretary of the society.

During the twenty-five years (1885–1910) in which Hope held this congenial position his authority in antiquarian circles was unique. His keen observation and retentive memory found exercise in many directions. While his chief interest always lay in ecclesiastical architecture, and the best work of his life was done in his researches into monastic history and buildings, he kept up an exceptional acquaintance with Roman antiquities and mediaeval fortification. Heraldry, mediaeval plate, and alabaster carvings were among the studies which he pursued throughout his life ; and upon these and several branches of ecclesiology his authority was generally recognized. His life was entirely devoted to his vocation, and his holidays from his duties at Burlington House were spent in practical work upon the remains of abbeys and castles and at meetings of archaeological societies, where his clear method of exposition was of great educational value. Among his numerous activities during this period, punctually recorded in papers contributed to *Archaeologia* and other learned publications, his part in the excavation of the Roman town of Silchester deserves special mention.

After 1910, when he retired from his official post, Hope continued to work and write with unabated energy. He now completed a monograph upon Windsor Castle, undertaken some years previously by royal command, and, after its publication in 1913, was rewarded (1914) by the grant of a knighthood. He died at Great Shelford, near Cambridge, where he spent the last few years of his life, on 18 August 1919, and was buried in the churchyard at Normanton, close to Derby. He was twice married : first, in 1885 to Myrrha Fullerton (died 1903), daughter of Major-General Edward Norman Perkins ; secondly, in 1910 to Mary, daughter of John Robert Jefferies, of Ipswich. There was one son by the first marriage.

Hope's writings include more than two hundred papers, many of them of considerable proportions, contributed to *Archaeologia*, *The Archaeological Journal*, and other similar publications. Of his works, reprinted from such collections or published separately, the following are of special importance: *Fountains Abbey* (1900); *The Architectural History of the Cathedral Church of St. Andrew at Rochester* (1900); *The Stall-Plates of the Knights of the Order of the Garter* (1901); *The Abbey of St. Mary-in-Furness* (1902); *Windsor Castle, an architectural history*, 2 vols., with portfolio of plans (1913); *A Grammar of English Heraldry* (1913); *Heraldry for Craftsmen and Designers* (1913); *Cowdray and Easebourne Priory* (1919); *The History of the London Charterhouse* (1925). He was also a principal collaborator in *The Chronicles of . . . All Saints, Derby* (with J. C. Cox, 1881); *The Corporation Plate . . . of the Cities of England and Wales* (completed from the work of Llewellynn Frederick William Jewitt, q.v., 1895); *Inventories of Christ Church, Canterbury* (with J. Wickham Legg, q.v., 1902); *Kirkstall Abbey* (with J. Bilson, 1907); *Pageant of the Birth, Life and Death of Richard Beauchamp, Earl of Warwick* (with Viscount Dillon, 1914); *English Liturgical Colours* (with E. G. C. F. Atchley, 1918).

[*Proceedings* of the Society of Antiquaries, second series, vol. xxxii, 1919–1920; *Archaeological Journal*, vol. lxxvi, 1919; personal knowledge.] A. H. T.

HOPKINSON, BERTRAM (1874–1918), engineer and physicist, was born at Birmingham 11 January 1874. He was the eldest son of Dr. John Hopkinson, F.R.S. [q.v.], by his wife, Evelyn Oldenbourg, and inherited his father's combination of mathematical power with insight into physics, and with the ability to apply scientific ideas to practical problems. The family soon moved to London, and Bertram was educated at St. Paul's School, living at home in close association with his father, from whom he imbibed scientific habits of thought as well as much engineering knowledge. At the age of seventeen he went to Cambridge, entering Trinity College with a major scholarship. He missed the first part of the mathematical tripos through illness; in the final part he was placed in the first division of the first class. Soon after taking his degree (1895) he was called to the bar, but the tragic death of John Hopkinson in 1898 led Bertram to turn to engineering, in order to continue, so far as he could, his father's unfinished professional work. By 1903 he had acquired a considerable reputation as an engineer, and when, in that year, the chair of mechanism and applied mechanics at Cambridge became vacant, Hopkinson was selected to fill it. He held the professorship until his death fifteen years later. In 1903 he married Mariana, eldest daughter of Alexander Siemens, a former president of the Institution of Civil Engineers, and by her he had seven daughters.

As professor of mechanism, Hopkinson became responsible for the school of engineering at Cambridge, which, thanks to the establishment ten years earlier of a mechanical science tripos, was already vigorous. Under his management its progress was maintained, its numbers were doubled, and its position advanced both in the university and in the profession outside. Hopkinson was an effective teacher, with a passion for research which students found inspiring. A collected volume of his scientific papers, published by the Cambridge University Press in 1921, contains twenty-nine items and gives evidence of unflagging industry, originality of outlook, and ingenuity in devising methods of experiment. His chief investigations relate to the endurance of metals under varying stresses, the magnetic properties of iron and its alloys, the action of internal-combustion engines and the process of explosion in gases, and the pressure produced in the detonation of high explosives. His work is characterized by clear appreciation of practical issues, and by direct attack on the essential features of the problem in hand. He was elected F.R.S. in 1910 and became a professorial fellow of King's College, Cambridge, early in 1914.

On the outbreak of war in 1914, Hopkinson accepted a commission in the Royal Engineers. Use was soon found for his powers of experiment and design. In particular he was able to apply his previous study of explosions to the improvement of methods of attack and defence. His 'pressure bar' became a standard appliance for testing at Woolwich. His investigations determined the best form of bomb; other experiments, which he carried out for the Admiralty, led to the adoption of his invention for protecting ships of war by means of a projection or 'blister', so constructed as to absorb the energy of an exploding torpedo or mine without damage to the inner shell. For a time he was secretary of a committee set up by the Royal Society to advise the government on the scientific problems of the War, and he also took part in an organization for dealing with enemy cipher. Later he was appointed to the department of military aeronautics, where he was soon entrusted with the supply to aircraft of all items of their offensive armament. His experimental head-quarters were at Orfordness, and afterwards at Martlesham Heath where the testing of aeroplanes was put under his control. In order to carry out these duties to his satisfaction he found it was necessary to learn to fly, and very frequently took solitary flights to other air stations and to France. In one of these flights, in bad weather, he was killed by a fall near London 26 August 1918. Some months earlier he had been promoted colonel, and had received the C.M.G.

Apart from his scientific eminence, Hopkinson was a born leader of men, with a personality that was at once commanding and attractive, winning regard by his unselfishness, his fine temper, and his own constant enjoyment of work and of life.

[*The Scientific Papers of Bertram Hopkinson*, 1921; *Proceedings* of the Royal Society, vol. xcv, A, 1918–9 (portrait); *Alpine Journal*, vol. xxxii, no. 219; personal knowledge.]

J. A. E.

HORSLEY, JOHN WILLIAM (1845–1921), philanthropist, was born 14 June 1845 at Dunkirk, near Canterbury, the eldest son of the Rev. John William Horsley, the first incumbent of Dunkirk, by his wife, Susannah, daughter of William Sankey, physician, of Dover. He was educated at King's School, Canterbury, and at Pembroke College, Oxford. After holding a curacy at Witney (1870–1875), he became curate of St. Michael's, Shoreditch, in 1875, and from that time his life was devoted to the amelioration of the condition of the poor, and especially to the reclamation of prisoners. From 1876 to 1886 he was chaplain at Clerkenwell Prison; many of his suggestions for the improvement of the lot of prisoners, made while he was at this institution, though at first rejected as being impracticable, have since been adopted by prison authorities. On the abolition of the Clerkenwell jail, in 1886, Horsley became the first clerical secretary of the Waifs and Strays Society, to which he devoted much time and care. His next appointment (1889) was as vicar of Holy Trinity, Woolwich, where he was a member of the Woolwich local board and board of guardians. In 1894 he became rector of St. Peter's, Walworth, where he filled the positions of chairman of the public health committee of the borough of Southwark, chairman of its largest workhouse, and, in 1910, mayor of Southwark. In 1903 he was appointed an honorary canon of Rochester, and when the new diocese of Southwark was created in 1905 he became an honorary canon of the cathedral. Naturally all these activities, over and above the heavy work connected with a large and very poor parish, proved a severe strain on his health, and in 1911 he retired to the vicarage of Detling, near Maidstone. Here he remained till June 1921, when the state of his health compelled him to resign.

Horsley was the author of a number of works on social questions, the best known being *Practical Hints on Parochial Missions* (1877), *Jottings from Jail* (1887), *How Criminals are Made and Prevented* (1912), and *I Remember* (1911), a book of recollections, and of many papers and pamphlets. In 1905 he was installed master of the Quatuor Coronati lodge of freemasons, of which he had been a member since 1891. He was also chaplain for many years to the Saye and Sele lodge, and in 1906 was appointed grand chaplain of the freemasons of England.

Horsley was an enthusiastic Alpinist and also a great authority on botany and certain genera of Mollusca. Every year it was his custom to take a party to Meiringen, where he would act as guide on long walks and climbs, enlivening the expedition by his extensive knowledge of the topography, fauna, and flora of the Alps. Just before his death he made what he knew would be his final visit to Meiringen with a party of a hundred friends, and returned home to await the end, passing away at Kingsdown, near Deal, 25 November 1921. Almost his last work was to pass for press the proofs of a book on place-names in Kent.

Devoted to all matters connected with the moral reform and social betterment of the poorer classes, Horsley became a total abstainer for the sake of example, and was an active member of the council of the Church of England Temperance Society; he was also vice-president of the Anti-Gambling League. This lover of children, who wrote that the best way to diminish crime was to work for the welfare of children, defending their rights and recognizing their importance, had the great crypt of his church in Walworth cleared of coffins and transformed into a playground for the poor children of the neighbourhood. From first to last he dedicated his life to the service of the poor and distressed with unflinching faith and courage.

Horsley married in 1877 Mary Sophia, eldest daughter of Captain Codd, governor of H.M. Prison, Clerkenwell, and had two sons and five daughters.

[Private information.]

H. B. C.

HORSLEY, Sir VICTOR ALEXANDER HADEN (1857–1916), physiologist and surgeon, was born in Kensington 14 April 1857. His father was John Callcott Horsley, R.A. [q.v.]; his mother was a sister of Sir Francis Seymour Haden [q.v.]. He was the second son in a family of seven children. His childhood was spent in his father's country house at Cranbrook, Kent, and he became a day-boy at Cranbrook grammar school. In 1874 he matriculated at the university of London; and in his student years at University College Hospital he was already beginning studies of his own in physiology and bacteriology. In November 1880 he qualified for practice. He was house-surgeon to John Marshall [q.v.], and surgical-registrar at University College Hospital. It was at this time that he made a long series of observations on the action of anaesthetics on his own brain. From 1884 to 1890 he was professor-superintendent to the Brown Institution (University of London), in those days a place of great importance, not only as a veterinary hospital, but as the chief centre in London of advanced research in pathology and physiology. It was crippled by lack of funds, but it did admirable work. At the Brown Institution Horsley followed three main lines of study: (1) the action of the thyroid gland, (2) the protective treatment against rabies, (3) the localization of function in the brain.

(1) In 1873 Sir William Withey Gull [q.v.] had published the first description of myxoedema, and thereafter, William Miller Ord [q.v.] and others studied the disease. By 1883 myxoedema and cretinism were coming to be regarded as a result of the absence or inefficiency of thyroid tissue. In 1883 the Clinical Society appointed a committee to investigate the whole subject. Horsley was a member, and to him was entrusted the experimental work. It is important to note that his first experiments (removal of the thyroid) were made on monkeys. He proved beyond all dispute the action of the thyroid, and made certain what had only been guessed. The committee's report, published in 1898, gives a very good summary of myxoedema, but there is not a word of hope about curing the disease. Finally, in 1890, Horsley advised treatment by transplantation of a sheep's thyroid under the patient's skin, as Schiff had suggested. Later, came the work of George Murray and others on the administration of thyroid extract. Horsley's work does not stand absolutely alone; but it was he who founded in this country the modern study of the thyroid gland, and gave us the rational treatment of myxoedema and sporadic cretinism.

(2) The date of Pasteur's first use of the preventive treatment against rabies is July 1885. In 1886 the Local Government Board appointed a commission to study and report on the treatment. Horsley was secretary of this commission. He and (Sir) John Burdon Sanderson [q.v.], (Sir) Thomas Lauder Brunton [q.v.], and Sir Henry Enfield Roscoe [q.v.] went to Paris, where Horsley learned the whole method and collected many notes. It is literally true that Horsley, at the Brown Institution, was the only thorough student of rabies, and the only representative and interpreter of Pasteur's method in this country. He studied the outbreak of rabies among the deer in Richmond Park in 1886–1887, when no less than 264 deer died. In 1888 he examined and exposed the claims of a quack cure for rabies, the 'Bouisson bath treatment'. He was chairman of the society for the prevention of hydrophobia, and together with other members of the commission rendered great services to the government over the enforcement of the order for the muzzling of dogs (1897).

(3) In 1884 Horsley began his chief work in physiology, his investigations of the localization of function in the brain and spinal cord. He was associated in this work with (Sir) E. A. Sharpey Schafer, Charles Edward Beevor [q.v.], (Sir) Felix Semon [q.v.], and his brother in law, Francis Gotch. He came to the work at the time of the high tide of interest in the physiology and pathology of the brain; and his contributions to the literature of the subject are numerous and very important.

In 1885 Horsley became assistant surgeon at University College Hospital. In 1886, at the very height of his experimental studies, he was elected a fellow of the Royal Society and professor of pathology at University College. That year, also, he was appointed surgeon to the National Hospital for the Paralysed and Epileptic, Queen Square, a post which brought him the leadership in a great field of surgery. Fifty years ago the rules for surgical interference with the brain were those which Ambroise Paré had followed in the sixteenth century. Trephining is not cerebral surgery: it is skull surgery. The recorded cases of real modern cerebral surgery, on the principles of localization of function, were not more than a dozen or so, when

Horsley was appointed to the Queen Square hospital. He was only twenty-nine years old: but he was exceptionally well qualified for the work. His experimental work on monkeys, with nothing to guide him except the localization of function, had familiarized him with cerebral surgery. Before the end of 1886 he had done ten operations at Queen Square, nine of them successful. On 9 June 1887 he removed a tumour from the spinal cord: it was the first operation of its kind, and an event which takes a great place in the history of surgery. He had become familiar with the method and principles of the operation, by his experimental work on the cord. It may truly be said that the work of these two years set Horsley in the very front of his profession, and his reputation extended over the civilized world. During 1893 he made a long series of experiments on the effect of bullet wounds in the brain, which provided the evidence that the immediate cause of death in such cases is failure, not of the heart, but of the respiration. In 1906, when the British Medical Association met in Toronto, Horsley gave the address in surgery. He reviewed in it the whole field of cerebral surgery; and this address is one of the most significant among his writings.

The list of Horsley's published writings is of amazing length; so also is the list of his honours in this and other countries. He was knighted in 1902. The wonder is that he produced so much original work and writing, even in the years when he was at the zenith of his practice and was in demand everywhere. Moreover, he made time, even early in his career, to give himself zealously to the politics of his profession. He was president of the Medical Defence Union, served on the General Medical Council, and was one of the leaders of the British Medical Association. In these affairs of administration he was always on the side of reform inside the profession; and was incessantly befriending his less fortunate brethren.

The general election of 1910 brought Horsley into the rush of party politics, though he never entered parliament. He had no liking for compromises, and offended people by his vehemence and by his ardent and persistent support of the claims of women to citizenship. But there is every probability that if he had lived longer, he would have done excellent work in parliament for the national welfare. He took a leading part in the agitation against alcohol in this country, and, with Dr. Mary Sturge, published in 1907 a well-known book, *Alcohol and the Human Body*.

In the European War Horsley at first was surgeon to the British hospital at Wimereux, but in May 1915 he was sent to Egypt, and in July was appointed consultant to the Mediterranean expeditionary force. In March 1916 he went to India and Mesopotamia. Both in Egypt and in Mesopotamia he had grave reason to find fault with some of the arrangements for the wounded, and he fought hard to improve them. On 16 July 1916 at Amarah, hard at work up to the last moment, he died of heat-stroke.

No man in the profession has ever achieved a record equal to Horsley's twofold work in physiology and surgery. Envy had a good deal to do with the current criticisms of him; and there was much resentment against his occasional moods of intolerance. But his life was full of devotion to science and duty. He was generous to his patients and true to his friends; and he passionately desired to be of service to the nation, especially to its women and children.

Horsley married in 1887 Eldred, third daughter of Sir Frederick Joseph Bramwell [q.v.]. They had two sons and one daughter. Before 1892 he lived at 80 Park Street, Grosvenor Square, thereafter at 25 Cavendish Square.

[Horsley's published writings; Stephen Paget, *Sir Victor Horsley, A Study of his Life and Work*, 1919 (portraits); personal knowledge.]

S. P.

HOUGHTON, WILLIAM STANLEY (1881–1913), dramatist, the only son of John Hartley Houghton, a Manchester merchant, was born at Ashton-upon-Mersey, Cheshire, 22 February 1881. A random education ended in 1897 with a year at the Manchester grammar school; and Houghton went at once into his father's warehouse, knowing that for many years the dramatic ambition which he cherished would not provide him with a livelihood. From 1897 to 1912 the selling of 'grey cloth' occupied him eight hours a day; what remained was devoted to literature and drama with a determination and confidence which Mr. Max Beerbohm's caricature distorts into Olympian conceit. From 1900 play-making and acting were Houghton's absorbing hobby: in 1905–1906 he was unpaid dramatic critic for the *Manchester City News*; between August 1905 and April 1913 he contributed seventeen 'back-page' articles and more than a hundred theatrical notices and literary reviews to the *Manchester Guardian.*

His public career as a dramatist began with the performance of *The Dear Departed* on 2 November 1908 at the Gaiety, the Manchester repertory theatre, then in its second winter. By the autumn of 1912 the success of *Hindle Wakes* assured Houghton that without undue risk he could desert cotton for drama. He left Manchester for London; but finding it impossible to work there, in 1913 he settled in Paris, where he wrote the extant six chapters of his novel, *Life*. In the summer a mysterious illness, which had threatened for some time, overtook him at Venice. He was brought back an invalid to Manchester, where he died 11 December 1913. He never married. In February 1915 a memorial tablet was unveiled in the Manchester reference library.

Mr. H. Brighouse's edition of Houghton's *Works* (1914) gives everything which is accessible in print. It omits all the early experiments (i.e. before 1908) except *The Old Testament and the New* (1905, presented at the Gaiety Theatre, Manchester, in August 1914); the rest are still in MS., and none of these have been professionally acted. Of the plays written in and after 1908, Mr. Brighouse omits only three: *Ginger* (written 1910, performed 1913), and a sketch and a play, *Pearls* and *Trust the People*, which were written, with *Phipps*, on Arthur Bourchier's commission in 1912. These three have never been printed: *Ginger* and *Pearls* have a purely theatrical virtue, and *Trust the People* is an admitted failure. The public stage has seen all the plays written from 1908 onwards, except *Marriages in the Making* (1909) and *Partners* (1911), a three-act elaboration of the one-act *Fancy-Free*. *Hindle Wakes* was first produced at the Aldwych Theatre, London, in June 1912 by Miss A. E. F. Horniman's company at the invitation of the Stage Society; the earlier of the acted plays had their premières at the Manchester Gaiety Theatre, *The Dear Departed* in 1908, *Independent Means* in 1909, *The Younger Generation* and *The Master of the House* in 1910, and *Fancy-Free* in 1911.

The first, but not the finest, of Houghton's dramatic gifts is cleverness, and naturally it is most obvious in his technique. At the outset he divined the method most suited to his range of interests, and from *The Dear Departed* little but adaptation to larger issues was necessary. Learning, through the less compatible matter of *Independent Means* and *Marriages in the Making*, the dramatic limitations and the theatrical virtues of his art, he attained almost complete technical success in *The Younger Generation* and absolute mastery in the first act of *Hindle Wakes*. In the intervening plays his cleverness is patent in more equivocal qualities. He appropriates Shaw, he adapts St. John Hankin, he echoes Wilde, and unfortunately with an adroitness that belongs less to his genius than to his besetting sin, mere showmanship. Yet he is much more than a competent artisan. At its best, his technique is dramatic, and not merely theatrical: mere technique is plainly inadequate to account for the structural harmony of person, setting, incident, and idiom which gives to the first act of *Hindle Wakes* the relentless inevitability of supreme drama. It is 'action' in the most rigid dramatic sense, isolated from all moral and intellectual values, complete in itself, and moving only by its own momentum.

Naturally, Houghton is influenced strongly by Ibsen: but his Ibsenism differs from other English varieties. Apart from *Independent Means*, he wrote no propagandist plays; his lack of vital interest in social and political problems freed his dramatic action from their constraint. Like Ibsen, he was led to concern himself with a narrow society, the nexus of which he saw in a simple convention; for Houghton, the simpler the better. He showed it, again like Ibsen, purely in its human aspect before it had been resolved into a sociological problem. If the end of a play provides no solution that a sociologist would accept, it is partly because Houghton lacks Ibsen's penetrating imagination, but also because he preferred an issue too elemental for solution. The antipathy of age and youth is the only problem which Houghton deliberately faces as such; the more fashionable dramatic problem of sex is taken without prejudice into the *mise-en-scène*, rather than developed in the theme, of *Hindle Wakes*.

The attempt of the Gaiety Theatre to rear a local drama inspired Houghton to his best use of the Ibsen tradition. It limited him to material dramatically similar to Ibsen's, and it involved such preoccupation with manners as to exclude problematic abstractions. It diverted, of course, the Ibsen tradition toward comedy, but circumstances corrected the bias. The Manchester school of dramatists might caricature Lancashire for a London audience; but in Manchester it had to show the inside of a Lancashire house to its occupants, and the Lancashire nature to itself. *The Dear Departed* is local only in its manners, customs, and speech. *The Younger Generation* claims to depict a local creed, but as contempt for the creed creates all the fun of the piece, its professors have only a limited humanity. *Hindle Wakes* is in the main so truly local that it is universal; its interest is in human nature as it lives in Lancashire. It has glaring faults, and the whole is certainly less than the part. But its two old men are great figures; as Houghton created them, his sympathy got the better of his prejudices and cleverness, and imposed on his imagination the severe economy which his developed technique is most potent to express. As a result, *Hindle Wakes* is a great play; in promise, indeed, the greatest of our time.

[H. Brighouse's memoir in the *Works* cited; the *Manchester Guardian*, 1905–1913 *passim*; private information.]

H. B. C-n.

HOWARD, HENRY FITZALAN-, fifteenth Duke of Norfolk (1847–1917), the eldest son of Henry Granville FitzAlan-Howard, fourteenth Duke [q.v.], by his wife, Augusta, younger daughter of the first Baron Lyons [q.v.], was born in London 27 December 1847. In 1860, at the age of thirteen, he succeeded his father. In that year he was sent to the Oratory School, Edgbaston, in which John Henry Newman was endeavouring to imbue the sons of English Roman Catholics with the English public school tradition. At that time Oxford and Cambridge were not open to Roman Catholics; and at the age of seventeen the duke was sent abroad to travel. He stayed for a long time at Constantinople with his uncle, the second Lord Lyons [q.v.], to whose formative influence he owed much.

While still a young man the duke began his long career of work on behalf of his co-religionists. At the age of twenty-one he was described by William George Ward [q.v.] as a model chairman. His judgement was active and independent to a degree which must have tried the patience of great prelates and others in authority. Their arguments, except on matters of doctrine, were always subjected to his searching criticism, in spite of his profound and affectionate regard for the individuals with whom the arguments originated. He once felt it his duty to make a public protest in *The Times* newspaper against the methods of the 'plan of campaign'. This protest brought him into collision with members of the Irish hierarchy. He was a convinced unionist, though he was most unwilling to quarrel with the Irish Catholics, whose children owed much to his efforts on behalf of Catholic education, and to the financial sacrifices which he made for the benefit of Catholic schools and churches.

The duke's services to the state were but a small part of his public activities. He was, however, postmaster-general in Lord Salisbury's government from 1895 to 1900. He resigned that office in order to volunteer for active service, as an officer of the Imperial Yeomanry, in the South African War. He sat on many royal commissions, and was indefatigable in the House of Lords, particularly when educational matters were under discussion; but he never again held ministerial office. He was the first mayor of Westminster (1899); he was mayor of Sheffield in 1895, and first lord mayor of that city in 1896. The parks and recreation grounds which he gave to Sheffield covered 160 acres and were valued at £150,000. He was one of the founders of the university of Sheffield, and its first chancellor (1904).

Throughout his life the Duke of Norfolk was in close relations with the Vatican, and he had dealings with four successive popes. In 1887 he was sent by Queen Victoria as a special envoy to Pope Leo XIII, with presents and congratulations. He several times entertained papal nuncios who came on missions to this country. He liked such duties, though he was sufficiently British to find the duty of entertaining eminent foreigners rather irksome. He was, however, intensely interested in public ceremonials, both civil and ecclesiastical, and his hereditary office of Earl Marshal was for him no sinecure. He could not endure the least slovenliness or vagueness in the arrangements for which he was responsible. On the occasion of the coronation of King Edward VII (1902) he revived many historical usages which had fallen into neglect. In this matter, as also at the coronation of King George V in 1911, he collaborated happily with the Anglican bishops.

His careful attention to detail is illustrated by the architectural works for which he assumed responsibility. He was a great builder, passionately devoted to the Gothic style. His first church was that of Our Lady and St. Philip Neri at Arundel, of which Joseph Aloysius Hansom [q.v.] was the architect. As the duke's taste developed he cultivated an earlier and severer style; he preferred the great church of St. John the Baptist at

Norwich to any of his other buildings. He became more and more independent of his architects, and during years of mourning and bereavement he found a constant solace in working out his own conceptions. In all his buildings there is much stained glass of high quality, but especially in the exquisite little chapel which he built at Arundel Castle.

The duke died in London 11 February 1917. He was twice married: first, in 1877 to Lady Flora Abney-Hastings (died 1887), elder daughter of Charles Frederick, first Baron Donington; secondly, in 1904 to Mary, elder daughter of Marmaduke, eleventh Baron Herries, who succeeded to her father's barony in 1908. By his first wife the duke had one child, a son, who died in 1902; by his second wife a son (born 1908), who succeeded him, and three daughters.

The duke combined great independence of character with great loyalty to causes and individuals. Eagerly and actively interested in affairs, he showed both caution and courage as a public man. His disposition was frank and open, but he inherited the diplomatic talent of his mother's family. His high and serious interests never subdued his natural gaiety and humour or weakened his strong taste for domestic life. As a private individual he reminded his friends of Sir Thomas More; and the parallel is not without interest since the duke was the first Catholic layman, since the death of More, who had played a great and honourable part in English public life. He earned the respect and esteem which are due to strong patriotism, to sober judgement, to unassuming dignity, and to strong moral and religious convictions.

[*The Times*, 12 February 1917; private information. Portrait, *Royal Academy Pictures*, 1922.]

HOWARD, ROSALIND FRANCES, COUNTESS OF CARLISLE (1845–1921), promoter of women's political rights and of temperance reform, was born 20 February 1845. She was the youngest daughter of Edward John, second Baron Stanley of Alderley [q.v.], the whig statesman, who between 1855 and 1866 held office as president of the Board of Trade and postmaster-general. Her mother, Henrietta Maria [q.v.], eldest daughter of Henry Augustus Dillon-Lee, thirteenth Viscount Dillon [q.v.], was one of the founders of Girton College, Cambridge. Her marriage in her twentieth year (1864) with George James Howard [q.v.], who in 1889 became the ninth Earl of Carlisle, brought her at first into an artistic circle; for her husband was a landscape painter of distinction in the pre-Raphaelite tradition, and Burne-Jones and William Morris were among their friends. Politics made larger demands on them when, in 1879, George Howard was called to take the place of his dead father in the parliamentary representation of East Cumberland. In the early 'eighties his house at Palace Green, Kensington, became a political centre where the Howards foregathered with Sir George Trevelyan, John Morley, Sir Wilfrid Lawson, and Joseph Chamberlain in his radical days. But the liberal party schism over Home Rule divided the family also. George Howard followed his cousin the Duke of Devonshire into liberal unionism. His wife, never forgetting the Irish blood in her veins, was fervently for Home Rule. She would not be silent about convictions held with the intensity of a religion, and in early womanhood she had moved in thought from the whig traditions of her family to the radical left. She left London, and henceforth her life lay in her country homes at Naworth and Castle Howard. She became an active member of local governing bodies, and she found scope in the discharge of local responsibilities, in varied plans for improving the housing, education, and social conditions of her neighbourhood, and in political work through the two women's organizations of which she became president. To the last task she brought a ready flow of emotional eloquence, a musically trained voice, and a keen instinct for debate polished by the conversational battles in which she delighted. These gifts made her unquestionably the foremost woman speaker of her day.

Had she played no part in politics Lady Carlisle would have been marked out as a business woman with a real talent for administration. Her husband cared more for his art than for the management of landed property, and left the family estates mainly in her control. For the latter half of her life she was her own land agent and architect, picking her farmers with a keen eye for character, and planning the rebuilding of farmsteads and cottages, with the minute love of detail on which she prided herself. The estate finances were controlled with method and economy. Hereditary debts, including some of Charles James Fox's gambling debts, were cleared away. Froude the historian, who told her that she was born to be an empress, said that her character and actions were in diametric opposition to her political theories, of which he disapproved.

Divided in politics, the Howard family remained united in its support of total abstinence. Licensed houses were suppressed on the Howard estates. The family crusade for teetotalism left its mark for good on the hard-drinking habits of the north. As president, from 1903, of the National British Women's Temperance Association, Lady Carlisle became an ardent leader of the political temperance party; but the aims of that party were frustrated.

Fortune was kinder to Lady Carlisle's other object, the winning of the vote for women; in this cause was made her main contribution to the nation's life. The daughter of a liberal chief whip, as she often remembered, she gave unswerving support to the principles of the party as she saw them. It was difficult fighting ground; before the European War all the parties were divided on women's suffrage. She had organized many women's liberal associations in the country, primarily for aid in the Home Rule struggle. But the union of these bodies, the Women's Liberal Federation (of which she was president from 1891 to 1901 and from 1906 to 1914), was not to be the meek handmaid of the party. Lady Carlisle had the balanced task, which became delicate at by-elections, of supporting her party while pressing her claim for the vote. She saw the blunder of aiming at the enfranchisement of a limited class of propertied women; and it was her circle that demanded the broader and more democratic franchise ultimately adopted. She would have nothing to do with the phase of suffragette violence which, in spite of the self-delusion of the fanatics, was throwing back the movement before the War. The suffrage came in the end as the outcome or recognition of the war-services of womanhood; but Lady Carlisle's initiative and leadership within her own party counted along with the working of other causes and the efforts of other women in the result.

The European War in its strange reactions solved for her what seemed an insoluble problem; but, for her as for other social reformers, it shattered political ideals. She had believed in the possibilities of international arbitration; but when the War came she had no doubts as to the part England had to play. The last years of her life were overclouded. Her husband died in 1911. Five of her six sons predeceased her, the last of the five falling in the War. Broken health handicapped her in the latter part of her life, but she was capable to the end of surprising physical and mental exertions. She died in London of encephalitis lethargica 12 August 1921.

[Personal knowledge.] C. H. R.

HUGHES, ARTHUR (1832–1915), painter, the third and youngest son of Edward Hughes, of Oswestry, was born in London 27 January 1832, and educated at Archbishop Tenison's grammar school, Castle Street, Long Acre. He revealed in early boyhood so irresistible an inclination towards art that in 1846, at the age of fourteen, he was allowed to join the school of design at Somerset House, where, under Alfred Stevens, he worked with such industry that in the following year he secured an art studentship in the Royal Academy schools. There, two years later (1849), he won the silver medal for antique drawing, and attained, at the age of seventeen, a place on the walls of the annual exhibition for a painting of Musidora.

Hughes was, therefore, at a critical stage when the founding of the pre-Raphaelite brotherhood (1848), and especially the publication (1850) of the first number of its short-lived periodical, *The Germ*, determined once for all the lines along which his artistic individuality was to be developed. That art must be founded directly upon nature down to its smallest details; that nothing was insignificant; that the least leaf or flower was as deserving of loving care as the most outstanding feature in the picture, was, put very briefly, the creed which he then adopted, and followed faithfully through a long and productive career.

This adhesion to the principles of the pre-Raphaelites, though he never assumed the title of a brother, brought Hughes into intimate connexion with those young enthusiasts. He at once won the approval of Ruskin; Millais painted him in 1853 as 'The Proscribed Royalist'; William Morris bought his picture of 'April Love', now in the Tate Gallery, in 1856; and in 1857, on Rossetti's invitation, he took part in the decoration of the Oxford Union, contributing a panel depicting 'The Death of Arthur'. It was, perhaps, this preoccupation which prevented his following up at the Academy of 1857 the success in 1856 of his exquisite triptych of 'St. Agnes' Eve'; but in 1858 he exhibited 'The Nativity', which with its pendant, 'The Annunciation', and 'The Long Engagement', is now in the municipal art gallery at Birmingham. Thenceforward for fifty years, with some exceptions, he was regularly represented by one or more works, the last of which, 'The Rescue', appeared in 1908, while many of his pictures passed direct from the studio to the owners. Few of these are now accessible to the public, but among them is 'Home from Sea' (1863) in the Ashmolean Museum, Oxford, which disputes with 'The Knight of the Sun', painted about 1859, the claim to be his most perfect achievement.

Hughes's earlier works naturally received their share of the extraordinary storm of abuse which burst upon the innovators, but he cannot be said to have obtained his just proportion of the approbation which followed when the reaction came after no long time. It would be untrue to speak of him as a neglected genius, for he earned for himself no small amount of appreciation and patronage, but he never succeeded in capturing that general renown to which his accomplished workmanship and imaginative charm certainly entitled him. The tender vein of poetry which inspired all his paintings was too easily missed among more clamant appeals; the delicate schemes of colouring which he mostly favoured were too apt to be eclipsed by some glaring neighbour; and even the relatively small area to which his painstaking representation of detail was best adapted may have played its part in diverting attention to more spacious rivals.

His numerous contributions to the art of book-illustration undoubtedly gained for him a more extensive body of admirers, though it is possible that few of these were aware of the name of the man who signed his work with a little Gothic monogram. Beginning in 1855 with William Allingham's *The Music Master*, he illustrated editions of *Tom Brown's Schooldays* (1869), Tennyson's *Enoch Arden* (1866), Christina Rossetti's *Speaking Likenesses* (1874) and *Sing Song* (1872), T. G. Hake's *Parables and Tales* (1872), and George MacDonald's *At the Back of the North Wind* (1871) and *Phantastes* (1905); he also produced numbers of separate drawings for stories and poems in *Good Words* and other periodicals.

Hughes's life apart from his work was uneventful. He married in 1855 Tryphena Foord, by whom he had two sons and three daughters. For about ten years he held a position as examiner at the art schools, South Kensington, but this was his only official recognition. Residing on the outskirts of London, he remained of his own choice almost entirely apart from general society, being seldom seen even in those assemblies where his fellow-artists met together; and his death at Kew Green, 22 December 1915, in his eighty-fourth year, must have come as a surprise to many who remembered his unaggressive share in the strenuous rebellion of the pre-Raphaelite brotherhood.

[Private information.] M. H. B.

HUGHES, Sir SAM (1853–1921), Canadian soldier and politician, was born in Darlington township, Durham county, Ontario, 8 January 1853, the third son of John Hughes, a native of Tyrone, Ireland, by his wife, Caroline Laughlin. He was educated at the local schools, the Toronto normal and model schools, and at the university of Toronto, where he took honour standing in modern languages in 1880. From 1875 to 1885 he taught English literature and history in the Toronto Collegiate Institute; but he turned more and more to political life, and in 1885 removed to Lindsay, Ontario, where he became owner and editor of the *Lindsay Warder*, the chief conservative newspaper of the district, continuing to hold this position till 1897. In 1891 he stood unsuccessfully as conservative candidate for the federal house in Victoria county, Ontario; but in 1892 he was successful at a by-election, and continuously represented the constituency till his death.

From very early days Hughes took a deep interest in military matters, especially in shooting. In 1870 he was a volunteer in the defence forces raised against a Fenian raid from the United States; in 1873 he was gazetted a lieutenant in the 45th militia regiment, and steadily rose till in 1897 he became its lieutenant-colonel. Meanwhile he had offered to raise battalions for the Egyptian and Sudanese campaigns. In 1899, on the outbreak of the Boer War, he went to South Africa with the Canadian contingent as an 'attached' officer, but quarrelled with his commanding officer and joined the British forces, in which he held several positions, ending as a dashing leader of irregulars. In 1911 he attended the coronation of King George V; in October of the same year he became minister of militia and defence in the Cabinet of (Sir) Robert Borden, and did much to promote the building of drill halls and the training of cadet corps in the schools. He was promoted major-general in 1912. At the opening of the European War he showed fine energy, and it was largely owing to his efforts that the first Canadian contingent was organized with such promptitude at Valcartier camp, and sent overseas. He was responsible for the arming of the Canadian forces with the Ross rifle, which, after his retirement, was replaced by the Lee-Enfield. His turbulence, however, brought him into frequent controversy with his colleagues, and in November 1916 the Canadian premier demanded his resignation. Hughes continued to give an independent support to the conservative administration, and afterwards to the union government, but hard work had sapped his strength, and he died of pernicious anæmia at Lindsay, Ontario, 24 August 1921.

Hughes was created K.C.B. in August 1915, while in England; in 1916 he was promoted lieutenant-general. He married twice: first, in 1872 Caroline (died 1874), daughter of Major Isaac Preston, of Vancouver, British Columbia; secondly, in 1875 Mary, second daughter of Harvey William Burk, M.P., of Bowmanville, Ontario. He was survived by her and by two daughters and one son, Major-General Garnet Hughes.

Hughes was well made and handsome; in his youth he had been a famous runner and lacrosse player. He was of splendid energy, and had much personal charm, but was too undisciplined and impetuous to be an easy colleague, either in political or military life.

[*The Times*, 25 August 1921; Toronto *Mail* and *Globe*, 24 August 1921; H. J. Morgan, *Canadian Men and Women of the Time* (second edition), 1912; *Canadian Hansard*.]

W. L. G.

HUME, ALLAN OCTAVIAN (1829–1912), Indian civil servant and ornithologist, son of the radical politician, Joseph Hume [q.v.], was born 6 June 1829 and educated at Haileybury College and London University. At the age of twenty he joined the Bengal civil service, and was appointed in 1849 to the North-West Provinces. As district officer of Etawah during the Mutiny he showed the highest courage and resolution in circumstances of great peril, and, when forced to retire from his district, distinguished himself as a soldier in the field. For these services he was awarded the C.B. (1860). He was engaged in district work in the North-West Provinces for eighteen years, until, through the commissionership of customs in those provinces, he found his way to the notice of the viceroy, the Earl of Mayo, and in 1870 was appointed secretary in the revenue and agricultural department of the central government. In 1879, however, after some years of service at Simla and Calcutta, he was sent back to his own province under a cloud. His biographer, Sir William Wedderburn, who shared Hume's political views, declares that his friend's offence was over-boldness in expressing opinions unpalatable to the ruling powers. The official version of the rupture has not been published. Hume became a member of his provincial board of revenue, and retired from the civil service in 1882.

Toward the end of his official career Hume became convinced that India needed a parliamentary system, and that only thus could the economic condition of the masses be bettered and the discontent among the educated classes allayed. On 1 March 1883 he addressed a circular letter to the graduates of the Calcutta University, whom he termed 'the salt of the land'. He asked them to 'scorn personal ease and make a resolute struggle to secure greater freedom for themselves and their country, a more impartial administration, a larger share in the management of their own affairs'. The Marquess of Ripon [q.v.] was then viceroy and, in sympathy with the aspirations of educated India, was inaugurating the beginnings of popular control in the shape of municipal and district boards which were to contain a considerable elective element. But before his departure the political atmosphere had been embittered by the Ilbert Bill controversy. In December 1884 Lord Ripon was succeeded by the Earl of Dufferin, with whom, according to Wedderburn, Hume took counsel as to the desirability of organizing a representative body of educated men who would explain popular needs. The viceroy approved of the project, considering that good government would be promoted by the existence of a responsible organization which could claim to voice public opinion. The incident finds no place in the official *Life* of Lord Dufferin by Sir Alfred Lyall, although there is some support for Wedderburn's account of the viceroy's views [see Sir A. C. Lyall's *Life of the Marquess of Dufferin and Ava*, 1905, ii, 152]. Dufferin, however, never contemplated any relaxation of the British hold on the supreme administration of India.

When an association of prominent Hindus of the professional classes, under Hume's guidance, convoked the first session of the 'Indian National Congress' at Bombay in December 1885, the government adopted an attitude of passive goodwill. Both then and at subsequent sessions various speeches were delivered which breathed a loyal and reasonable spirit. But as the association made way it became a rallying centre not only for men who merely desired the gradual establishment of a parliamentary system, but also for those whose real quarrel was with British rule in any form. Partly through Hume's exertions the movement gained friends in England. In 1888 its leaders embarked on vigorous propaganda of an aggressive nature. Hume admitted that friends had warned him of the danger he incurred of fostering race hatred and arousing passions which would pass beyond his control. But he considered that the whole campaign was inevitable in view of the lack of official response to reiterated demands; and he continued to work for the congress until he left India in 1894. Thereafter, living in England at Upper Norwood, he interested himself in English politics, maintaining correspondence with his friends in India. He lived to see the Morley-Minto reforms, which were in fact the first substantial step taken by England toward the establishment of a parliamentary system in India.

Hume married in 1853 Mary Anne Grindall (who died in 1890), and had one daughter. He was a keen sportsman and a noted ornithologist. Together with Colonel C. H. T. Marshall, of the Indian army, he wrote a standard book, *The Game Birds of India, Burmah, and Ceylon* (Calcutta, 1879–1881). In 1885 he presented a collection of bird-skins and birds' eggs to the British Museum of Natural History, South Kensington. He also founded and endowed the South London Botanical Institute. For some time in India he was connected with the Theosophical Society, but subsequently separated himself from that body. He died at Norwood 31 July 1912 at the age of eighty-three.

[Sir William Wedderburn, *Allan Octavian Hume*, 1913; Sir Harrington Verney Lovett, *A History of the Indian Nationalist Movement*, 1920.] H. V. L.

HUNTER, Sir ROBERT (1844–1913), solicitor, and authority on commons and public rights, was born in London 27 October 1844, the only son of Robert Lachlan Hunter, by his wife, Anne Lachlan. He was educated at a private school and at London University. After taking the M.A. degree in 1865 he studied law and was admitted solicitor in 1867. Public opinion at that time was stirred by the enclosure of many metropolitan commons, and (Sir) Henry Peek, of Wimbledon, offered prizes for essays on the subject. Hunter, amongst many rising lawyers, competed; his essay gained a prize and was selected for publication. This led to Hunter becoming in 1869 a partner in the firm of Fawcett, Horne, and Hunter, solicitors to the Commons Preservation Society which had been founded in 1865. He was entrusted with the conduct of the suits that led to the protection of Hampstead Heath, Berkhamsted, Plumstead, and Wimbledon commons, and other threatened open spaces, and established the principles of public interest upon which the law relating to commons is now based. The most notable case effected the recovery of 3,000 acres of Epping Forest on the suit of the corporation of the city of London, when Hunter acted with the city solicitor in the conduct of the protracted legal proceedings (1871–1874).

In 1882 Henry Fawcett, then postmaster-general, appointed Hunter solicitor to the General Post Office. He held the position until shortly before his death, and was concerned in the drafting and passage of over fifty acts of parliament dealing with the department. These measures included the Conveyance of Mails Act (1893), which ensured that all differences between the railway companies and the state as to remuneration for the carriage of mails should be referred for settlement to the Railway and Canal Commission. It has been officially stated that by his initiative and able handling of this measure Hunter saved the country over £10,000,000. His most striking achievement, however, was his successful negotiation, in conjunction with Sir Henry Babington Smith, of the terms for the purchase of the National Telephone Company's system under the powers conferred on the Post Office by the Telegraph Arbitration Act, 1909. The compensation claimed by the company was £20,924,700, but the amount awarded to them was reduced to £12,515,264, after the contract, drafted by Hunter, had stood the test of bitterly fought arbitration proceedings lasting for seventy-two days. The value to the Post Office of Hunter's acumen and persuasive personality was well recognized, and Fawcett once declared that nothing in his official career had given him greater pleasure than the securing of a man of Hunter's character and ability for the country's service.

Hunter's interest in the movement for protecting commons was maintained, and until his death he remained closely identified with the Commons Preservation Society. In 1895, with Miss Octavia Hill [q.v.] and Canon Rawnsley, he founded the National Trust; and he took a leading part in many schemes for acquiring open spaces. Hunter lived at Haslemere, and was instrumental in preserving in that neighbourhood over 1,500 acres of commons, including Hindhead and the Devil's Punch Bowl. He died at Haslemere 6 November 1913, within a few months of his retirement from the Post Office. As a national memorial of his work a beautiful tract of woodland adjoining the Waggoner's Wells, near Haslemere, was purchased by public subscription.

Hunter was knighted in 1894; he was made C.B. in 1909 and promoted K.C.B. in 1911. He married twice: first, in 1869 Emily (died 1872), daughter of J. G. Browning; and secondly, in 1877 Ellen, daughter of S. Cann. He left three daughters by his second marriage.

[Sir Robert Hunter, *The Preservation of Open Spaces, Footpaths and Other Rights of Way*, 1896, and *Gardens in Towns* (published posthumously), 1915; *The Movements for the Inclosure and Preservation of Open Lands* (Royal Statistical Society), 1915. L. W. C.

HUTCHINSON, Sir JONATHAN (1828–1913), surgeon, the second son of Jonathan Hutchinson, a middleman in the flax trade, by his wife, Elizabeth Massey, was born at Selby, Yorkshire, 23 July 1828. He belongs to a group of distinguished medical contemporaries of quaker origin, which includes Thomas Hodgkin, T. B. Peacock, Lord Lister, Wilson Fox, and D. H. Tuke. His ancestors had farmed for generations the same small estate near Boston in Lincolnshire, and amongst them were some of the early followers of George Fox. His youth was passed without demur in a strict quaker circle, but by middle life he had freed himself from the outward forms of quakerism, though its serious influence upon him was obvious throughout his career. A scientific training, the close study of nature, and the influence of Darwin left him at last far from orthodox, but—to quote the words which he directed to be engraved upon his tombstone—'a man of hope and forward-looking mind'.

After being apprenticed to Dr. Caleb Williams, of York, in 1845, he spent four years at the small York school of medicine (1846–1850), and completed his training by attending lectures at St. Bartholomew's Hospital, London. Disliking at first the thought of private practice, he began his life in London by writing for medical journals, coaching, and making the elaborate clinical records for which he afterwards became famous. In 1856 he married Jane Pynsent West, and about this time began private practice at 14 Finsbury Square. He held minor hospital appointments until in 1859 he obtained a post as assistant surgeon at the London Hospital. Here, as well as at the Metropolitan Free Hospital and the special hospitals on the surgical staff of which he served (the Royal London Ophthalmic Hospital, the Blackfriars Hospital for Skin Diseases, and the Royal Lock Hospital), the greater part of his life's work was carried out. In 1862 he obtained the fellowship of the Royal College of Surgeons, and in that year he was appointed lecturer on surgery at the London Hospital; in 1863, when he became full surgeon, he took on the additional subject of medical ophthalmology. In 1874, by which time he had made a great reputation, he moved to more fashionable quarters, 15 Cavendish Square, next door to his famous medical colleague, Sir Andrew Clark [q.v.]. He left the active staff of the London Hospital in 1883 with the title of emeritus professor of surgery, and the Hutchinson triennial prize essay was then instituted to commemorate his services. He served on the council of the Royal College of Surgeons from 1879 to 1895, and was president in 1889. He was Hunterian professor from 1879 to 1883 and in 1891 delivered the Hunterian oration. In 1882 he was elected a fellow of the Royal Society. He was also president in turn of most of the London medical societies, and he received many honours from abroad and in his own country. He served on the royal commissions on small-pox and fever cases in London hospitals (1881) and on vaccination (1890–1896), and was knighted in 1908. He died at Haslemere, Surrey, 26 June 1913. He had six sons, four of whom survived him, and four daughters.

Hutchinson was a specialist of great repute in at least three subjects. He was a leading authority on ophthalmology, dermatology, to some extent on neurology, but above all on syphilis; so that he has been described as the greatest general practitioner in Europe. He was extraordinarily diligent, a laborious and accurate observer, and an inveterate note-taker. His vast collection of pathological drawings was probably unequalled. He had a retentive memory, a logical mind, a love of discussion, and an enthusiasm for diffusing knowledge. His teaching was made impressive by ingenious arguments, apt illustrations, vivid metaphors, and quaint expressions, and was driven home by the simplicity and solemnity with which it was delivered. He thus naturally attracted a large following of students, young and old, who considered him almost infallible, and in doubtful cases were always anxious to hear 'what Jonathan would say'.

Amongst other outcomes of these labours were the publication of *Illustrations of Clinical Surgery* (two volumes, folio, 1878–1884), *A smaller Atlas of Illustrations of Clinical Surgery* (1895), a series of *Archives of Surgery* (1889–1900) following, at a distance, the German model, and the formation of a large museum. This collection of specimens and drawings was first housed at 1 Park Crescent, London, and was moved in 1889 to the 'Polyclinic', a post-graduate medical college in Chenies Street, in which Sir William Broadbent [q.v.] and Dr. Fletcher Little were also greatly interested. Here courses of lectures and demonstrations were given by Hutchinson and others, and gratis consultations on impecunious patients were held in public. These became very popular and were largely attended by general practitioners and others.

Hutchinson was a voluminous writer. His works on syphilis are standard authorities. He promulgated the now generally accepted view that syphilis is a specific fever like small-pox or measles. He will be specially remembered for his observations on the eyes and teeth of sufferers from congenital syphilis; 'Hutchinson's teeth' and 'Hutchinson's eyes' are terms that have passed into medical language. He also wrote on the pedigree of disease, on leprosy, and on countless other subjects in the medical journals. He was the moving spirit of the New Sydenham Society, which was chiefly occupied in producing at a moderate cost translations of continental monographs on medical subjects.

He had many interests outside his profession. He was an omnivorous reader, and by inheritance and inclination a country man. In his early days he had a small house at Reigate, and when he became prosperous he bought a property at Haslemere to which he added from time to time till it reached 300 acres. Over this he would walk with his gun, and part of it he farmed. Here, with such companions as his lifelong friend and colleague, the learned Hughlings Jackson [q.v.], he studied natural history and geology with the same energy which he devoted to surgery in London. He also established in Haslemere about 1890 at his own expense an 'educational museum' of specimens scientifically arranged for methodical instruction and study; this, he hoped, would be a model for similar museums elsewhere. It is extensively used at the present time. Here and at a hall near his own house he gave Saturday and Sunday lectures and demonstrations to his neighbours and guests, on scientific, literary, and religious subjects. He gave a museum arranged on the same lines to his native town, Selby.

Hutchinson's fame does not rest on his achievements in general surgery. He can hardly be placed amongst the pioneers; and he was too early in the field to become identified with the advances in pathology and bacteriology which laid the foundations and raised the structure of modern surgery. He has been described as an indifferent though a successful operator. His special gift was that of observation, and the accumulation and collation of clinical facts. It was impossible to doubt their accuracy, but his deductions from them were not always equally convincing. Thus, having come to the conclusion as early as 1855 that the chief cause of leprosy was the eating of decomposed fish, he did not change his opinion even after the discovery of the *lepra* bacillus. He held that leprosy was only slightly contagious, and strongly condemned segregation. To corroborate his theory he journeyed to Norway in 1869, South Africa in 1901, and India and Ceylon as late as 1903. In his book *Leprosy and Fish-eating* (1906) he adds much to our knowledge and exposes many fallacies, but his views did not meet with wide acceptance, though he upheld them stoutly to the last. The book is likely to be of interest to those who hold the simple creed that, given the discovery of a specific micro-organism, there is no need to seek further for the *causa causans* of a disease.

[*Sir Jonathan Hutchinson*, by G. N. (Sir George Newman) in the *Friends' Quarterly Examiner*, 1913; obituary notices in the *Annual Monitor* (Gloucester), 1913, p. 113; *Lancet*, 28 June 1913; *British Medical Journal*, 28 June 1913; *Ophthalmic Review*, vol. xxxii, 1913, p. 225 (by E. Nettleship); private information; personal knowledge.]

R. J. G.

HYNDMAN, HENRY MAYERS (1842–1921), socialist leader, the eldest son of John Beckles Hyndman, barrister, by his wife, Caroline Seyliard Mayers, was born in London 7 March 1842. His grandfather made a large fortune in the West Indies, and though his father was a liberal benefactor to the East End churches, Henry Hyndman inherited considerable wealth, most of which he devoted to the socialist cause. Educated privately and at Trinity College, Cambridge, where he just failed to get his 'blue' at cricket, he spent the following years mainly in travelling and sport, playing cricket for the Sussex county eleven between 1863 and 1868. Going to Italy in 1866, he became war correspondent for the *Pall Mall Gazette*, accompanying Garibaldi's force in its advance to the Trentino. From 1869 to 1871 he was in Australasia and America, and he frequently revisited the United States on business in later years. Returning to England in 1871, he joined the staff of the *Pall Mall Gazette*, with which he remained, under Frederick Greenwood, till 1880, doing other journalistic work as well, especially on Indian and Russo-Turkish questions. From this time until the end of his life he made a special study of Indian questions, and was a prominent advocate of Indian self-government and financial and social reform. In 1876 he married Matilda Ware, of Newick, Sussex, who died in 1913.

In 1880 Hyndman became acquainted with the works of Karl Marx, reading *Das Kapital* on board ship during a business journey to America. These studies made him a socialist, and in the following year he took the lead in forming, mainly on the basis of London radical clubs, the Democratic Federation, which in 1884 became the Social Democratic Federation—the first important socialist body in England. In 1881 he also published his first socialist book, *England for All*, putting his social ideas in popular form. In the Federation he was associated with William Morris, and wrote with him *A Summary of the Principles of Socialism* (1884). This was just before the split which led Morris and his friends to form the anti-political Socialist League. In the same year (1884) the Federation started a weekly paper, *Justice*, of which Hyndman became editor. During these years he was very active in leading the agitation among the unemployed, and in 1886 he was put on trial and acquitted, with John Burns, H. H. Champion, and Jack Williams, for his part in the so-called West End riots, arising out of a meeting in Trafalgar Square. His whole remaining life was spent in socialist writing and agitation. He was a vigorous opponent of the South African War and of British imperialist policy. Among the best known of British socialists, he became the chief English exponent of political Marxism, writing several books in its support, e. g. *The Historical Basis of Socialism* (1883), *Commercial Crises of the Nineteenth Century* (1892), and *Economics of Socialism* (1896). He was the recognized leader of the Social Democratic Federation, which at that time remained aloof from the Labour Party, but had a diminishing influence after the rise of the Independent Labour Party in the 'nineties. In 1911 it was merged in the British Socialist Party. This body, since merged in the Communist Party, took up an anti-war attitude in 1914, and Hyndman and his friends, who supported the War, left it in order to form the National Socialist Party (1916), which has since resumed the old name of the Social Democratic Federation, and is now attached to the Labour Party. Hyndman stood for parliament at Burnley at several elections from 1895 onwards, but was never elected, though in 1906 he came near to success. During the War he was active as a labour representative on the consumers' council at the Ministry of Food, and in other social services. In 1914 he married again. His second wife was Rosalind Travers, a poetess, the only daughter of Major Travers, of Arundel. Hyndman died at Hampstead 22 November 1921. He had no children.

The full story of Hyndman's life, up to 1912, can be found in his two fascinating and provocative books, *The Record of an Adventurous Life* (1911) and *Further Reminiscences* (1912). After his death, his second wife, who died in 1923, wrote *The Last Years of H. M. Hyndman* (1923), carrying out the plan which her husband had entertained of a third volume of reminiscences. This book is marred by an undiscriminating hero-worship which largely destroys its historical value. In his own writings Hyndman was not always accurate and seldom impartial; but he wrote very well, and the books are invaluable as a record of his important share in the growth of British socialism. He remained always something of an aristocrat among the socialists, in temper as well as in manner, impatient of differences, but always ready to make any sacrifice for the cause. His quarrels with his fellow-socialists were many, and he described them all with lively humour in his books.

There is a bronze bust of Hyndman by

E. H. Lacey in the National Portrait Gallery.

[Besides the books mentioned above, see Max Beer, *History of British Socialism*, 1919–1920; Sidney Webb, *Socialism in England*, 1890; *Reports*, &c., of the Social Democratic Federation; J. W. Mackail, *Life of William Morris*, 1899; private information.]

G. D. H. C.

INGLIS, ELSIE MAUD (1864–1917), physician and surgeon, the second daughter of John Inglis, of the East India Company's service, by his wife, Harriet Thompson, was born at Naini Tal, India, 16 August 1864. Her father was a descendant of the Inglis of Kingsmill, Inverness-shire. Her mother was the granddaughter of John Fendall, governor of Java. Elsie Inglis spent her childhood in India until her father retired in 1878, when the family came back to Scotland and settled in Edinburgh. She was educated there at the Charlotte Square Institution, and after a year at Paris returned to Edinburgh shortly before her mother's death in 1885. Between Elsie Inglis and her father there existed a strong bond of friendship. He was a wholehearted advocate of her choice of a medical career, and a wise counsellor in all her undertakings. At the time of her entry upon her medical studies the battle for the admission of women to the medical profession had been fought and won by Sophia Louisa Jex-Blake [q.v.], although there still remained a considerable amount of opposition. Her studies were begun in Edinburgh and continued at Glasgow, with some months in Dublin for a special course of midwifery. In 1892 she received her medical diploma, and returning to Edinburgh she inaugurated there a second school of medicine for women, a successful venture which became, after the closing of the first medical school founded in Edinburgh in 1886 by Sophia Jex-Blake, the only school of medicine for women, until the doors of Edinburgh University were thrown open to them (1894).

In 1892 Elsie Inglis was appointed house-surgeon to the New Hospital for Women in London (afterwards the Elizabeth Garrett Anderson Hospital), and later received the appointment of joint-surgeon to the Edinburgh Bruntsfield Hospital and Dispensary for women and children. Realizing the serious disabilities imposed on women by their exclusion from resident posts in the chief maternity hospital and Royal Hospital in Edinburgh, she conceived the bold scheme of establishing there a maternity hospital to be staffed by women. This scheme resulted in the foundation of a hospice for women, opened in 1901, which is still the only maternity training centre in Scotland managed by women. Dr. Elsie Inglis began private practice in 1895, first in partnership with Dr. Jessie McGregor, later by herself. In her profession she won the love and esteem of her patients in all classes of life. To the poor patients of the hospital she was more than a doctor, for they found in her a friend full of sympathy with their difficulties, and always ready to help in lightening the burden of their poverty.

In 1900 Elsie Inglis joined the constitutional movement for the political enfranchisement of women, under the leadership of Mrs. Millicent Garrett Fawcett, devoting all her spare time to speaking and lecturing on women's suffrage. She was the founder of the Scottish Women's Suffrage Federation (1906), and it was at a committee meeting of the Federation in August 1914 that the idea was first conceived of forming a Scottish Women's Hospitals committee, to raise hospital units staffed by women for service in the European War. Elsie Inglis was the leading spirit of this venture, travelling all over the kingdom to make public appeals for funds to equip the units. Her enthusiasm roused a quick response from the public, resulting in a steady flow of funds and of offers from women for active service.

The first fully equipped unit left for France in November 1914, a second unit going out to Serbia in January 1915. Elsie Inglis carried on the work of organizing further units until April 1915, when she left for Serbia in order to take the place of Dr. Eleanor Soltau, who had contracted diphtheria. An epidemic of typhus, which had broken out at the end of January 1915, had nearly abated when she arrived, and she immediately proceeded to organize three hospitals in the north of Serbia in readiness for the autumn offensive of the Serbs.

The invasion of Serbia by German, Austrian, and Bulgarian armies in the autumn of 1915 drove the Serbs back, and the hospitals established at Valjevo, Lazarovatz, and Mladanovatz had to be hastily evacuated and moved to Kragujevatz, where Elsie Inglis had started a surgical hospital. The relentless tide of invasion drove the hospitals farther south to Krushevatz. Here she worked at the Czar Lazar hospital, having decided that she could give more effectual help to the Serbs by remaining at her post. This decision was welcomed by the Serbian medical authorities, who had experienced the benefit not only of her surgical aid but also of the moral support given by the Scottish Women's Hospitals units during their retreat. For three months after the entry of the Germans and Austrians into Krushevatz on 7 November 1915, she continued to work at the hospitals, until the great majority of the patients were removed to Hungary. On 11 February she and her unit were sent under a strong Austrian guard first to Belgrade and then to Vienna, where, owing to the intervention of the American embassy, they were released and allowed to return to England.

Elsie Inglis's offer to the War Office of a unit for service in Mesopotamia, where the need for medical aid seemed urgent, was refused; but, after her return from a visit of inspection to the Scottish Women's Hospitals units in Corsica, she received an appeal from the Serbian minister for aid for the Serbian division in Russia. This request met with an immediate response. The London committee of the Scottish Women's Hospitals supplied two units with motor transport attached. On 16 August 1916 Elsie Inglis left for Russia, going to the front at Megidia to join the Serbian division fighting in the Dobrudja. Here the units worked until the retreat of the Russians in October brought her to Braila, where perhaps the hardest task, and what to most would have seemed a hopeless one, was presented to her. Braila was one vast dumping ground for the wounded, who streamed in every day. Only seven doctors were in the town, and no nurses, when she arrived. The units were now attached to the Russian division, until the Serbs, whose losses were very heavy owing to the lack of Russian support, had been reformed. From Braila the units went first to Galatz and then on to Reni.

The revolution in Russia had broken out in the meantime, and the difficulties of the units were increased, but despite the general confusion and the suspicion with which spy-hunters regarded a foreign hospital, they managed to work smoothly until the hospital was evacuated in August 1917 and Elsie Inglis rejoined the Serbs at Hadji-Abdul. Their position, however, became serious, for there was not much hope of the Russians making a stand; and efforts were made to get the Serbs out of Russia. Moreover, Dr. Inglis's health showed grave signs of failure, and her condition was aggravated by the intense cold and the lack of food, fuel, and clothing. The Scottish Women's Hospitals committee sent a cable advising her withdrawal, but leaving the decision in her hands. Her reply was: 'If there were a disaster none of us would ever be able to forgive ourselves if we had left. We must stand by. If you want us home, get them [the Serbs] out.' Enfeebled as she was, she met the situation courageously. Her plans for the future work of the hospital, should the Serbs be called upon again to fight, were all laid down to the smallest detail, but fortunately, before these plans had been put in operation, the order came for the Serbs to leave for England.

Dr. Inglis's cable home on 14 November announced their departure: 'Everything satisfactory, and all well except myself'—the first intimation which the committee had received of her being ill. She bore the journey home with great fortitude and endurance of physical pain, and on arriving at Newcastle (25 November) refused to allow herself to be carried, but walked down the ship's gangway. Almost to the last her thoughts were of future plans, and in her message to the London committee was a request to them to continue their support of the Serbs, whom she had served so faithfully. One of those present among her family and friends spoke to her of the great work which she had accomplished. She replied: 'Not I, but my unit.' The end came at Newcastle on 26 November. The intrepid spirit met death as calmly as she had faced life. She was buried in the Dean Cemetery, Edinburgh, on 29 November.

[Lady Frances Balfour, *Dr. Elsie Inglis*, 1918; Mrs. Shaw McLaren, *A History of the Scottish Women's Hospitals*, 1919, and *Elsie Inglis*, 1920.]

E. P.

JACKSON, HENRY (1839–1921), regius professor of Greek at Cambridge, was born at Sheffield 12 March 1839, being the eldest son of Henry Jackson, an eminent surgeon of that town, by his wife, Frances, third daughter of James Swettenham, of Wood End, near Winksworth. He was educated at the Sheffield Collegiate School and Cheltenham College, from which he went up to Trinity College, Cambridge, in 1858, taking his B.A. degree in 1862. He became a fellow of Trinity in 1864, assistant tutor in 1866, praelector in ancient philosophy in 1875, and vice-master in 1914. In 1906 he succeeded Sir R. C. Jebb as regius professor of Greek in the university, and in 1908 received, as crown of many other distinctions, the order of merit. As professor he continued to lecture on ancient philosophy in his deeply interesting and fascinating manner, as one talking familiarly out of fullness of knowledge. His principal contribution to learning was his doctrine of Plato's 'later theory of Ideas', published in a series of articles in the *Journal of Philology*, of which he was one of the editors from 1879 to his death. These articles were invaluable not only in themselves but in giving an impulse to later speculation: he insisted that Plato criticized and modified his own views, not remaining content with the crude form in which they were first put forth; he showed that various statements of Aristotle's chimed in with what he found in Plato's later dialogues; and he held that the Ideas finally became 'natural kinds' like John Stuart Mill's. He also published an edition of Aristotle's *Ethics*, book V (1879), translations, papers, articles in encyclopaedias dealing with ancient philosophy, and a book *About Edwin Drood* (1911).

But all who knew Jackson felt his personality to be more wonderful than any printed book, and every one fell under the spell of it. The secret of this was an extraordinary power of sympathy, inherited from his father, and such an interest in others that he remembered details about them forgotten by themselves. His interest in school and college life was intense, and great was his pleasure at becoming a governor of Winchester College. He took a leading part in university reform; his last appearance in public was when he was carried to the senate house to vote for women's degrees. An ardent politician, he was a Home Ruler before Gladstone. He was deeply interested in anthropology. In literature, after his beloved Greek philosophers, he was devoted to French and English fiction, Thackeray most of all; many years before his death he had read *Esmond* forty times. His rooms were crowded with all sorts of people, especially on Sunday evenings, and every distinguished visitor to Trinity would be taken under his wing. But he had some strong dislikes, hating all pretension and affectation. No man was ever more free from envy, jealousy, or self-conceit.

His constitution was strong indeed. In teaching he never spared himself, and he was constantly occupied with college and university business during the day. He would often sit up late talking with any visitor till three or four o'clock, then work at a lecture, go to bed sometimes as late as six, and lecture at ten. And he took infinite pains over his work, spending much care over testimonials and letters of importance, and keeping up a large and delightful correspondence. Yet for many years all this had no visible effect upon him, and though he had to become more careful when about seventy, the breakdown only came just after eighty. For two years he was a helpless invalid, yet even then was carried into the hall to lecture several days a week with indomitable spirit. He died at Bournemouth 25 September 1921.

He married in 1875 Margaret, daughter of the Rev. Francis Vansittart Thornton, vicar of South-Hill with Callington, Cornwall, and had two sons and three daughters. His married life was clouded by the illness of his wife, many years bedridden and unable to live at Cambridge.

[Private information; personal knowledge. See also R. St. John Parry, *Henry Jackson*, 1926 (portrait).] A. P.

JACKSON, WILLIAM LAWIES, first BARON ALLERTON (1840–1917), politician, was born at Otley in the West Riding of Yorkshire 16 February 1840, the eldest son of William Jackson, a leather merchant and tanner of Leeds. His education at a private school at Adel and later at the Moravian school at Fulneck was cut short at an early age. His father had once already compounded with his creditors, and his business was again almost bankrupt when, on his death, young Jackson succeeded to it at the age of seventeen. An iron will, exceptional health, and unremitting hard work before long enabled him to pay off all his father's creditors in full; and while still a young man he found himself at the head of an unencumbered and very valuable business which, under his continued care, grew to be one of the largest tanning and leather currying concerns in the kingdom. Jackson was an originator of the Leeds leather fair, and one of the earliest tanners to grapple seriously, and at great cost, with the problem of river pollution.

In 1869 Jackson entered the Leeds borough council, where he speedily made a name not only in debate and in the organization of the conservative party, at that time a feeble minority, but also in finance. It was on his initiative that the heavy debts of the borough were funded, the old mortgage system abolished, and the civic budget reduced to order. His services to Leeds continued throughout his life and were recognized by his election to the lord mayor's chair in 1895, and to the honorary freedom of the city in 1908.

After an unsuccessful attempt in 1876, Jackson was elected to parliament in the conservative interest for North Leeds in 1880, and continued to represent Leeds, or one of its divisions, till his elevation to the peerage as Baron Allerton, of Chapel Allerton, Yorkshire, in 1902. After only five years in the House of Commons he was selected (1885) by Lord Randolph Churchill for the financial secretaryship to the Treasury, a post which he held till 1891. He was thus assistant to (Viscount) Goschen [q.v.] in March 1888 when that great financier carried his scheme for the conversion of the national debt, and also in November 1890 at the time of the Baring crisis. In the latter month Jackson was sworn of the Privy Council; and in February 1891 was elected a fellow of the Royal Society. In November 1891 Jackson succeeded Mr. Balfour in the thankless office of chief secretary for Ireland, which he held till the fall of the ministry a few months later. His chief secretaryship was uneventful: its two legislative projects, a Local Government Bill and an Education Bill, proved abortive; the former was wholly the work of his predecessor.

Jackson was a more than ordinarily silent member of the House of Commons; but he sat on important committees, which dealt with Indian railways, financial relations between the Indian and home governments, trade, bankruptcy law, War Office contracts; on all these he did valuable work, and he was also chairman of the royal commission on the coal resources of the United Kingdom (1901–1905). His tact and thoroughness were most conspicuously displayed as chairman of the inquiry (1896–1897) into South African affairs necessitated by the Jameson Raid. After the disastrous failure of the Liberator building society in 1892, his influence in the city of Leeds enabled him to make a thorough personal investigation into the affairs of building societies; and his proposals for more effective audit and financial control were embodied in the Building Societies Act of 1894. On the fiscal controversy he was at first a strong free trader, but in 1910 had so far modified his first position as to accept Mr. Balfour's programme. His last important office was that of chairman (1895–1908) of the Great Northern Railway Company, which he successfully defended against the threatened competition of the Great Central Railway, at that time first extended to London; he eventually became chairman of a common purposes committee of the two companies.

Lord Allerton was a devout churchman and a keen and prominent freemason, and very generous both with time and money, particularly in the cause of education. He was one of the earliest promoters of the Yorkshire College, now the university of Leeds; he was also active in the maintenance and defence of church schools and in the extension of church work in Leeds. As financial secretary to the Treasury he conciliated men of all parties, and throughout his life his geniality and charm were usually successful in disarming opposition.

Lord Allerton died in London 4 April 1917. He married in 1860 Grace (died 1901), only daughter of George Tempest, of Otley. He was survived by two sons, of whom the elder, George Herbert (born 1867), succeeded him as second Baron Allerton, and by five daughters. His younger son, Francis Stanley, who was well known in early life as a county and international cricketer, was appointed financial secretary to the War Office in 1922–1923, and again in 1925.

[*The Times*, 5 April 1917; *Yorkshire Post*, 5 April 1917; J. S. Fletcher, *The Making of Modern Yorkshire*, 1918; *Annual Register*, 1891, 1892.] S. V. FG.

JACOB, EDGAR (1844–1920), bishop of Newcastle and of St. Albans, was born at Crawley rectory, near Winchester, 16 November 1844, the fifth son of the Rev. Philip Jacob, archdeacon of Winchester, by his wife, Anna Sophia, daughter of the Rev. the Hon. Gerard Thomas Noel, canon of Winchester. He was grandson of John Jacob, the Guernsey topographer [q.v.], great-grandson of Edward Jacob, the antiquary [q.v.], great-nephew of General John Jacob [q.v.], and nephew of Sir George Le Grand Jacob [q.v.]. He was educated at Winchester, and at New College, Oxford, of which he was a scholar. He obtained a first class in classical moderations (1865) and a third class in *literae humaniores* (1867). Jacob was ordained in 1868 by Samuel Wilberforce, bishop of Oxford, and held curacies at Taynton, near Burford (1868), and Witney (1869–1871), and finally at St. James's, Bermondsey (1871–1872), which he left to become domestic chaplain to Robert Milman [q.v.], bishop of Calcutta and metropolitan of India. He went reluctantly, but stated forty-seven years later that he had learned more from his four years in India than in any other way. Much of the work of administering the immense diocese of Calcutta (in those days about two-thirds of India) seems to have fallen gradually into Jacob's hands, and the experience, which left an indelible mark on his personality, was the foundation of his deep interest in all missionary work overseas, and of his wide sympathy with all work for the spread of Christianity through whatever persons and agencies it was carried on.

In 1876 Jacob returned to England and became the first warden of the Wilberforce mission in South London, and examining chaplain to Edward Harold Browne, bishop of Winchester. The latter post he retained under successive bishops till 1896, but in 1878 he left London to become vicar of Portsea. There he found a population of 20,000, a dilapidated and half-empty church, and one curate; on his departure eighteen years later the population had nearly doubled, there was a magnificent and well-filled parish church, several mission churches, and twelve curates. The new church of St. Mary he erected at a cost of about £50,000, of which sum he received nearly £30,000 from his great friend, the Rt. Hon. William Henry Smith [q.v.]. It is not too much to say that his parochial work at Portsea influenced the whole Church of England, and eloquent testimony has been borne to it by two of his successors at Portsea, Archbishop Lang of York and Bishop Garbett of Southwark.

Jacob was made an honorary canon of Winchester in 1884, an honorary chaplain to Queen Victoria in 1887, a chaplain in ordinary in 1890, rural dean of Landport and chaplain to H.M. Prison, Portsmouth, and select preacher at Oxford and proctor in Convocation in 1895. At the end of 1895 he accepted the bishopric of Newcastle and was consecrated 25 January 1896 by the archbishop of York. Here his great powers had full scope; although he only held the see for seven years, his organizing and administrative ability left a permanent mark on the diocese. In wider matters of policy his influence was felt, particularly in the passing of the Burials Act (1901), which he felt to be an act of justice to nonconformists. In 1903 he was translated to the see of St. Albans, leaving a compact diocese for an unwieldy charge of two large counties and 630 benefices, with its centre, in the words of Bishop Claughton, 'outside its circumference'. His presence not far from London was greatly desired for the central work of the Church, and the problem of the spiritual care of London-over-the-Border attracted him personally, while it elicited his most vigorous and unremitting efforts. The incessant strain of administering his great diocese and of raising money for its prospective division, which he saw to be essential, injured his health, and in 1911 he fell seriously ill. After his recovery he saw his efforts crowned in 1913 when, after many obstacles in the House of Commons, the bill was passed for the division of the see into the new units of Chelmsford (Essex with London-over-the-Border) and St. Albans (Hertfordshire and Bedfordshire). He had desired to be first bishop of Chelmsford, but ill-health necessitated his remaining at St. Albans, where he devoted himself to the incorporation of the county of Bedford in the reconstructed diocese. His health gradually failed, and after delivering an interesting and touching farewell charge in June 1919, he resigned the see in December of that year, and retired to Winchester. He died at St. Cross 25 March 1920, and was buried at St. Albans. He was never married, and his sister, Edith Jacob, the foundress of the Society of Watchers and Workers, was, as he said, 'the inspiring partner of his life'.

Bishop Jacob used his great financial ability for the good of the central and local organizations of the Church, but himself cared little for money, and characteristically refused to accept any pension when he resigned his see. Of a simple nature, kindly, unpretentious, and sympathetic, his entire interest lay in the world-wide work of the Church. A great administrator with a well-earned reputation for business capacity and legal acumen, an eloquent preacher, a man of broad and statesmanlike vision, for many years he was a trusted leader in the Church of England. His views on the pastoral work of the Church found expression in *The Divine Society* (Cambridge lectures on pastoral theology, 1890), *Five Addresses to the Clergy of the Diocese of St. Albans* (1916), and many lectures and addresses.

[*The Wykehamist*, 21 May 1920; A. H. Jacob and J. H. Glascott, *An Historical and Genealogical Narrative of the Families of Jacob*, 1875; G. W. Kitchin, *Edward Harold Browne*, 1895; C. F. Garbett, *The Work of a Great Parish*, 1915; Sir Herbert Maxwell, *Life and Times of the Rt. Hon. W. H. Smith*, 1893; Church Missionary Society *Reports*; Newcastle and St. Albans *Diocesan Gazettes*; E. Jacob, *Farewell Charge to the Diocese of St. Albans*, 1919; private information; personal knowledge.]

K. F. G.

JAMES, HENRY (1843–1916), novelist, was born at 2 Washington Place, New York, 15 April 1843. He came of a stock both Irish and Scotch, established in America from the eighteenth century. His father, Henry James, senior, was an original and remarkable writer on questions of theology. His mother's name was Mary Walsh. Henry James the younger was the second son, the elder being the distinguished philosopher William James. They received a very desultory education, at first in New York, afterwards (during two lengthy visits of the family to Europe) in London, Paris, and Geneva. Henry James entered the law school at Harvard in 1862, and lived with his parents at Cambridge, near Boston, until he finally settled in Europe in 1875. From 1865 onwards he was a regular contributor of reviews, sketches, and short stories, to several American periodicals; his life as a writer began from that year, and owed much to his acquaintance, soon a close friendship, with the novelist W. D. Howells. James's first piece of fiction long enough to be called a novel, *Watch and Ward*, appeared serially in 1871; his first volume of short stories was published in 1875, and *Roderick Hudson*, the novel which definitely marked the end of his literary apprenticeship, in 1876.

It was during the years spent in Europe as a boy that James had absorbed once for all what he afterwards called the 'European virus', the *nostalgia* for the old world which made it impossible for him to live permanently elsewhere. In 1869, and again in 1872, he came to Europe as a tourist, lingering chiefly in Rome, Florence, and Paris. These visits intensified his desire to find a fixed home on this side of the Atlantic; and when he came again, in 1875, it was with the decided intention of remaining for good. He proposed at first to settle in Paris; but after a year there he began to see that London (which he then knew very slightly) was the place where he could best feel at home, and he removed thither in 1876. He lived constantly in London, in lodgings off Piccadilly or in a flat in Kensington, for more than twenty years. In 1898 he moved to Lamb House, Rye, Sussex, where he mainly lived for the rest of his life, and where all his later novels were written. He was never married.

Henry James was thus thirty-three years old when he established himself in the country he was to make his own, and the fact is important for an understanding both of his character and his work. His youth, so far as it was European, had been almost entirely continental; his culture was French; he was a highly civilized, very critical and observant young citizen of the world. He came to England almost as a stranger, in spite of the fact that English life seemed to him in many ways barbarously insular; and he came because he was convinced that here only could an American really strike root in European soil. He accordingly proceeded with intense application to study and assimilate his chosen world—a narrow world, it may be said, for it was practically bounded by the social round of well-to-do London, but quite large enough, as he felt, to task his powers of absorption and to give him what he sought, a solid home in his expatriation. This was one side of the matter. The other concerned the exercise of his keen and unresting imagination, which found in London, and even in a small section of London, the inexhaustible material that it needed.

It is commonly said that James's work as a novelist falls into three distinct 'periods' or 'manners'; and the classification is convenient, though it may tend to obscure the unbroken steadiness with which his art was developed from book to book. In the first of these periods he was chiefly occupied with the 'international' subject, the impact of American life upon the older, richer, denser civilization of Europe; and it was not until he had been living for a good many years in England that he felt ready to drop the many possibilities of this fruitful theme and to treat a purely English subject. By that time he had written all those of his novels which were ever likely to be popular with the public at large; and though their simplicity may seem rather thin and their art ingenuous compared with his later work, books like *Roderick Hudson* (1875), *The American* (1877), *Daisy Miller* (1879), and more especially *The Portrait of a Lady* (1881), have a charm of freshness and neatness, which their author himself recognized when many years later he re-read and to some extent revised them. He had come to Europe at the right moment for the effect of the contrast which he found so pictorial, the clash of new and old, while the American in Europe (particularly the American girl) was still inexperienced and unfamiliar enough to create a 'situation', seen against the background of London or Paris or Rome. In half a dozen novels and a long series of shorter pieces James recurred to this situation, so rich in variety and so expressive of national character.

The Tragic Muse (1890) may be said to inaugurate James's second period, partly because the peculiar development of his art begins to show plainly in this book, partly because he here for the first time treated on a large scale a subject from English life, social, political, and artistic. In *The Spoils of Poynton* (1897), *What Maisie Knew* (1897), *The Awkward Age* (1899), and in several volumes of short stories, he continued to explore the field of English character, though it remained true that the England of his knowledge was confined to a comparatively small circle of London life. His sensitive appreciation of the minute distinctions, the fine shades, the all but inaudible tones, in the intercourse of very civilized people, together with his now complete mastery of his craft, began to give his work the strange and deeply individual aspect which it wore increasingly to the end. His style, matching the extreme subtlety of his perceptions and discriminations, developed an intricacy which might sometimes appear perversely obscure, though at its best it is really the simple expression of the effects he sought—suggestive, evocative effects, that gradually shape out a solid impression. (It is worth mentioning that all his later books were dictated by him to his secretary, a practice that fostered and perhaps exaggerated the natural amplitude of his style.) His fiction thus passed imperceptibly into its final phase, culminating in his three last novels, *The Wings of the Dove* (1902), *The Ambassadors* (written before *The Wings*, but not published till 1903), and *The Golden Bowl* (1904). In these books he returned once more to the 'international' theme, the contrast of American and European character, bringing the maturity of his experience and his imagination to bear on the subject which had occupied so much of his early work. After *The Golden Bowl* he wrote no more fiction, save a few short stories, till 1914, when he began to work upon two long novels, *The Ivory Tower*, and *The Sense of the Past*, both of which he left unfinished at his death. These two fragments were published posthumously in 1917, together with the extremely interesting notes which he had composed for his own guidance—a kind of leisurely rumination over the subject in hand which more than anything else reveals the working of his imagination.

For the revised and collected edition of his novels and tales, the issue of which began in 1907, James wrote a series of prefaces, partly reminiscent, mainly critical, which are of the highest importance as a summary of his view of the art of fiction. This view he had elaborated by degrees through many years of uninterrupted work; and he was certainly the first novelist in any language to explore with such thoroughness the nature and the possibilities of the craft. Even the passionate absorption in technical matters of such a writer as Flaubert seems slight and partial compared with the energy, the concentration, and the lucidity of James's thought upon the question of the portrayal of life in a novel. The form and design of a story had preoccupied him from the first; and if much of his early work was curiously thin, as though he were shy of plunging into the depths of human nature, it was largely because he would not attempt anything that he felt to be beyond his means, while he was engaged in consciously perfecting these. The most obvious influences under which he began to write were those of Hawthorne and Turgenev; but he was soon pursuing his own way in the search for a manner of presentation that should satisfy his more and more exacting criticism. It is not possible to describe in a few words the complexity of the art which reached its highest point, to the author's mind, in *The Ambassadors*; but what is perhaps most characteristic in it is the rhythmical alternation of 'drama' and 'picture' (they are James's words) in the treatment of the subject. By 'picture' he meant the rendering of life as reflected in the mind of some chosen onlooker (as the hero, Strether, in *The Ambassadors*), watching and meditating upon the scene before him; by 'drama' the placing of a scene directly before the reader, without the intervention of any reflecting, interpreting consciousness. All his later books (with one exception) are built up by the use of these contrasted methods, the old-fashioned device of 'telling' the story ('on the author's poor word of honour', as he put it) being entirely discarded. The single exception is *The Awkward Age*, in which the dramatic method alone is used, and there is no 'going behind' any of the characters, to share their thought. It may be said very roughly that he employs 'picture' for the preparation of an effect, 'drama' for its climax; the purpose throughout being to make the story *show itself* (instead of being merely narrated), to the enhancement of its force and weight. It was only when this process had been carried so far as to leave no relevant aspect of the subject in hand unillustrated and unaccounted for that he could regard the story as truly and effectually 'done'—a favourite word of his, expressing his highest praise. But, for a full understanding of the originality of his methods of criticism and creation it is necessary to study carefully the prefaces written for the collected edition.

Even the most enthusiastic admirers of James's later work have sometimes felt that the importance of his subjects was hardly equal to the immense elaboration of his treatment of them—a judgement more crudely expressed by saying that 'nothing happens' in his books, for all their densely packed extent. It is true that his central theme, baldly stated, is often a small affair, and that he seldom allows a glimpse of the fiercer passions that are the common stock-in-trade of the novelist. But this criticism implies some misunderstanding of his view of a subject—the importance of which he held to depend primarily on the value, the intelligence, and the sensibility, of the people involved. An event is nothing in itself; the question is what a fine mind will make of it; and more and more, in James's books, the characters tended to become men and women of rare and acute perception, capable of making the utmost of all their experience. A very simple theme, entrusted to a few such people, would give him more than enough for dramatic development; and if their deeper feelings remain all but hidden under the delicate surface-play of their reflections and reactions, it was because the last results and furthest implications of a thing were to him always more significant, more charged with history, than the thing itself in its nakedness could possibly be. Hence his dislike of the raw, the crude, the staring, his love of the toned and seasoned and civilized, both in literature and in life. In the immense procession of characters that he created, while it is the American girl (Daisy Miller, Isabel Archer of *The Portrait*, and many more) who predominates in his earlier books, the type nearest his mind in his later fiction is perhaps the 'poor sensitive gentleman' of stories like *The Altar of the Dead*, *The Great Good Place*, *Broken Wings*, with Strether of *The Ambassadors* at the head of them—elderly men, slightly worn and battered and blighted in the struggle of life, but profoundly versed, to use another characteristic phrase of James's, in the 'wear and tear of discrimination'.

Besides some twenty novels and nearly a hundred short stories, James published several volumes of sketches of travel and of literary criticism. He also wrote a number of plays; indeed for several years, from about 1890 to 1894, he devoted himself almost entirely to a determined attempt to win fame and fortune as a dramatist. The venture, which on the whole was certainly against the set of his genius, was not successful; very few of his plays have been acted, and none has had any lasting success on the stage. In *The American Scene* (1906) he recorded the profusion of impressions that he received from a visit to America after an absence of twenty years. Towards the end of his life he wrote two volumes (and part of a third) of reminiscences of his childhood and youth, an evocation of early days in America and Europe which shows how intense had been the activity of his imagination from his earliest years. A collection of his singularly rich and copious letters was published in 1920.

During the earlier years of his life in London, James probably seemed to those who knew him but slightly a somewhat critical onlooker, highly correct in style and manner, with a cautious reserve not easily to be penetrated. He was engaged in exploring the social world that readily opened to him; he was seen at innumerable dinner-parties and country-house visits, observantly making his way; but it was long before he felt able to lay aside the guarded prudence of a stranger and to take his ease in his acquired home. Meanwhile, among a host of acquaintances his intimate friends were few—among them may be named Burne-Jones, George du Maurier, J. R. Lowell, R. L. Stevenson; and perhaps it was only to his own family, and particularly to his brother William, to whom he was very deeply attached, that he freely confided his mind. Gradually a remarkable change took place in him; after twenty years of England he seemed at last to feel at home, and no one who met him in later days could think of him as other than the most genial, expansive, and sympathetic of friends. To a wide and ever increasing circle he became a figure uniquely impressive for the weight, the authority, the luxuriant elaboration of his mind, and lovable to the same degree for his ripe humour, his loyalty, his inexhaustible kindness—as also for something more, for a strain of odd and unexpected simplicity, that survived in him after a lifetime of ironic observation and experience. Yet those who knew him best remained conscious of something secluded and inaccessible in his genius, sufficient to itself and shared with no one.

James's published letters give a very complete picture of his habit of life, which from the time of his settlement in England varied little from year to year. The chief break was made in 1898, when Rye became his head-quarters instead of Kensington; but he was never very long absent from London, and he retained a room at the Reform Club for his frequent visits. Both there and in his charming old house at Rye he was lavish in entertainment of his many friends; as a host his standard of hospitality was very high —so high, indeed, as to make him at times impatient of the consequences it entailed. He could take nothing lightly, and the burden of sociability roused him to much eloquent lamentation. Yet he soon missed it in solitude, and he was easily tempted by any congenial call; he was not less generous as a guest than as a host, and in a circle which was not exactly that of society or of the arts or of the professions, but mingled of all three, he enjoyed himself and gave enjoyment. Nothing, however, not even his occasional excursions abroad, to Paris and Italy, was ever allowed to interrupt the industrious regularity of his work. Though his health was sometimes a difficulty and always a matter of a good deal of anxiety to himself, his constitution was remarkably strong, and he never seemed to feel the need of a holiday. In his seventy-second year, at the outbreak of the European War, his zeal in his work was as keen as ever, and his imagination teemed with material to be turned into art before it should be too late.

His portrait by J. S. Sargent, R.A., now in the National Portrait Gallery, was presented to him by a large group of friends in 1913, in commemoration of his seventieth birthday; and in 1914 a bust of him was executed by Mr. Derwent Wood. The portly presence, the massively modelled head, the watchful eye, the mobile expression, recall him as he was in his later years (till about 1900 he wore a close beard, and Mr. William Rothenstein made and possesses a drawing showing him with a moustache and beard), and may suggest the nature and manner of his talk. This, in a sympathetic company, where he could take his time to develop a topic or a description in his own way, was memorably opulent and picturesque. To listen to him was like watching an artist at work; the ample phrases slowly uncoiled, with much pausing and hesitating for the choice word, and out of them was gradually constructed the impression of the scene or the idea in his mind; when it was finished the listener was in possession of a characteristic product of Henry James's art. It was hardly to be called conversation, perhaps; it was too magnificent, too deliberate, for the give-and-take of a mixed gathering; but his companionable humour, his quick sensibility, his ornate and affectionate courtesy, set it further still from any appearance of formality or display. Though in any company he was certain to be the dominant, preponderant figure, his interest and his participation in the life around him were unfailing, and he seemed to have the gift of creating a special, unique relation with every one who came his way.

The shock of the War fell very heavily upon him; but he withstood it in a passionate ardour of patriotism that brought him at last, after nearly forty years of life in England, to take a step which he had never contemplated before. In July 1915 he became naturalized as a British subject. At the following new year he was awarded the order of merit; but by that time he was already lying ill and near his death. Three years before he had acquired a flat in Cheyne Walk, Chelsea, and it was there that he died on 28 February 1916. His body was cremated, and a commemorative tablet placed in Chelsea Old Church, close to his last home by the London riverside.

[Correspondence, published and unpublished; the autobiographical volumes, *A Small Boy and Others*, 1913, *Notes of a Son and Brother*, 1914, *The Middle Years*, 1917 (the dates and order of events in these books are not always to be relied on); personal knowledge. A bibliography of Henry James's works (to 1905), compiled by Le Roy Phillips, was published in America in 1906.] P. L.

JAMESON, Sir LEANDER STARR, baronet (1853–1917), South African statesman, the youngest of the eleven children of Robert Jameson, writer to the signet, by his wife, Christina, daughter of Major-General John Pringle, of Symington, Midlothian, was born in Edinburgh 9 February 1853. Not long afterwards his father, having given up the practice of the law, took to journalism, and in 1860 moved with his family to London, where he died in 1868. Leander was educated at the Godolphin School, Hammersmith, and afterwards at University College, Gower Street, where he studied medicine. After qualifying himself to practise (M.R.C.S. 1875, M.D. 1877) he seemed destined for a brilliant career in the medical profession in England; but the strain of overwork threatened his health. Moreover, he had the blood of the wandering Scot in his veins, and in 1878, at the age of twenty-five, having entered into partnership with a Dr. Prince, of Kimberley, he set sail for South Africa.

At this date Kimberley was a great diamond-mining camp, where a large number of independent diggers worked their individual claims, and sold the stones which they found, each man for himself. Jameson found there a restless, busy, light-hearted, cosmopolitan, gambling community, where money was made, spent, or lost with equal rapidity. He made his way rapidly, helped alike by great professional skill and daring and by a ready wit, an infectious gaiety, and an irresistible personal charm. It was not long before he was known in Kimberley as 'The Doctor'—'Dr. Jim' was a later invention of the English press. But he was destined to throw up his practice, to abandon an assured professional career, and to start afresh on a very different road, as the result of the close friendship which he formed with Cecil John Rhodes [q.v.]. Rhodes, of the same age as Jameson, was already in the early 'eighties the outstanding figure on the diamond fields, and had entered the parliament of the Cape Colony in 1881. After the death (1886) of Neville Pickering, who until then had been Rhodes's most intimate confidant, Jameson took and kept till Rhodes's death the first place in his affection.

It was to Jameson that Rhodes now began to develop his ideas and to unfold his dreams for the expansion of British civilization northwards through South Central Africa to the great lakes and onwards until it should extend from the Cape to Cairo. The first step necessary was to obtain a foothold in Matabeleland and Mashonaland, now known as Southern Rhodesia, but then the territory of Lobengula, chief of the Matabele. By the end of 1888 Rhodes had amalgamated in the hands of one great company, De Beers Consolidated Mines Limited, all the diverse interests in the Kimberley diamond fields; and could command ample funds for the prosecution of his objects. He had also obtained through his emissaries a concession from Lobengula of the mineral rights in that chief's territory, which was to form the original basis of the British South Africa Company, Rhodes's instrument for the expansion of the British Empire north of the Transvaal. But there were signs that Lobengula was repenting of his grant, and it was necessary to send up to him a trusted friend of Rhodes's to restore him to good humour, to keep him to his bond, and to defeat the designs of rival would-be *concessionaires* at his elbow. Asked by Rhodes to undertake this perilous mission, Jameson without a moment's hesitation left his patients in Kimberley to the care of a partner and, accompanied by Dr. Rutherfoord Harris, afterwards secretary to the British South Africa Company, started through the wilderness to Bulawayo, arriving there 2 April 1889.

This was the first of three such visits paid by Jameson to Lobengula between April 1889 and May 1890. The effect on the chief's mind of Jameson's winning personality was excellent; Jameson's medical skill relieved the pain of the gout from which Lobengula suffered; and, as a special mark of favour, the chief made him an 'induna' of one of his Matabele regiments. But, when Jameson was not actually by his side, Lobengula was prone to listen to those who warned him that in admitting the white men to dig for gold he would be giving away his country. He actually put to death the induna whom he held responsible for having advised him to grant the mineral concession; and it was not until Jameson's last interview with him (2 May 1890) that he definitely 'gave him the road'—that is, undertook to admit into his dominions those whom Rhodes should send up to work the concession. The concession meanwhile had been acquired by the British South Africa Company, incorporated by royal charter dated 29 October 1889, and the Company's preparations for sending into Mashonaland an expedition of 200 pioneers and 500 mounted police were well advanced. This expedition, which Jameson, coming south from Bulawayo, joined in the Bechuanaland Protectorate, crossed Lobengula's border at the beginning of July 1890, guided by the well-known big-game hunter Frederick Courteney Selous [q.v.], and accompanied by Archibald Ross Colquhoun, who was designated as the first administrator of Mashonaland. Jameson was not in command of the expedition, but went with it as the personal representative of Rhodes, and inspired it with his own spirit of cheerful audacity. There was constant danger that Lobengula's authority might not suffice to restrain the Matabele from falling on the column upon its way; but the danger was averted. The column avoided entering Matabeleland proper. Marching in a north-easterly direction to the plateau of Mashonaland, it safely reached its objective and planted the

Company's flag (11 September) at Fort Salisbury, where the capital of Southern Rhodesia now stands. The first great step in the occupation of Rhodes's 'North' had been taken. Rhodes himself had now become prime minister of the Cape Colony.

The next six months of Jameson's life were mainly occupied by two journeys of incredible arduousness. The first was undertaken to find the nearest means of access to the sea for the young community which could not for long be dependent on a land route from the Cape of nearly 2,000 miles, much of it passing through an uninhabited waste. In ill-health and with ribs broken by a fall from his horse, Jameson with his friend, Frank Johnson, made his way from Salisbury to the mouth of the Pungwe river in Portuguese East Africa, and thus marked out the route afterwards followed by the railway to Salisbury from Beira. On his second journey he obtained certain concessions for the Company from native chiefs to the eastward of Lobengula's sphere of authority. But here the Portuguese claimed sovereign rights. Jameson was arrested by the Portuguese authorities and taken as a prisoner to Delagoa Bay, whence, however, he was speedily released. The territorial dispute was settled by a treaty between Great Britain and Portugal (June 1891) which defined the spheres of the two nations in Central Africa.

From 1891 to 1893 Jameson, who had now been appointed administrator of Mashonaland in succession to Colquhoun, was engaged in establishing the nucleus of a civilized administration for the embryo colony of Rhodesia, and in cutting down the heavy expense of supplying a white settlement established in the remote wilds to such an amount as the overstrained finances of the Company could bear.

In 1893 came a new trial. The Matabele were not disposed to abandon their traditional practice of periodically raiding, slaying, and plundering their defenceless Mashona subjects. The practice was not one which a white authority, responsible for setting up an orderly administration of Mashonaland, could be expected to tolerate. Frontier incidents at Fort Victoria, and a claim by the Matabele to be allowed to slaughter some of the Mashona whom they accused of cattle-thefts, precipitated a conflict which in reality had been inevitable from the first. Jameson, hastily equipping a handful of volunteers and police, hurled them at the hitherto invincible 'impis' of Lobengula. The force numbered in all under 700 white men. It was commanded by Major Patrick William Forbes, and accompanied by Jameson himself as administrator but with no military authority. It was completely successful. Lobengula's best regiments were defeated in two pitched battles. Bulawayo was occupied (4 November 1893), and Lobengula himself died soon afterwards, a fugitive in the veld. The tragic fate of the Shangani patrol, under Major Allan Wilson, did not affect the completeness of the military success which had been achieved. The rule of the Matabele was at an end, and the Company's government under Jameson as administrator was, by the Matabeleland Order in Council of 1894, extended over the whole of what is now Southern Rhodesia.

Jameson, who had been Rhodes's chief instrument in the carrying out of his policy, was now at the zenith of his fame. On a visit to London at the end of 1894 he received the C.B. and could not wholly avoid, much as he disliked it, the notoriety of a popular hero. But the great catastrophe of his career was at hand.

The discontents of the 'Uitlander', mainly British, population of the Transvaal with the government of the South African Republic were coming to a head. By the autumn of 1895 the 'reform committee' in Johannesburg were making plans for the forcible overthrow of that government. Rhodes was supporting them, as he afterward said, 'with his purse and influence', hoping that the outcome of the movement might be the substitution for President Kruger's government of one more enlightened, which might render possible the federation, or at least the co-operation, of the South African states and colonies for common ends. Kruger had refused all proposals for reform; and an armed rising was prepared for the end of the year. To Jameson, who had returned to South Africa from England early in 1895, was allotted the task of raising a mounted force in Rhodesia and of holding it in readiness on the border of the Transvaal, to be used if events in Johannesburg should make it necessary. Accordingly, about 500 Mashonaland mounted police were by the end of October collected at Mafeking and at Pitsani Potlugo, in a portion of the Bechuanaland Protectorate which had been handed over by the imperial government to the administrative control of the British South Africa

Company. For many weeks Jameson was moving backwards and forwards between Bulawayo, Johannesburg, Capetown, Kimberley, Mafeking, and Pitsani Potlugo, interviewing the various persons concerned in the prospective rising and arranging for common action. He seems to have become convinced that the Johannesburg rising could only succeed with his active intervention, and he took it as settled that the rising was to take place on a certain date at the end of December. As that date drew near, however, he began to feel, rightly or wrongly, that the reformers' counsels were divided and that, unless he himself took the initiative, their preparations would never be completed and the whole plan would end in fiasco. On 29 December, in spite of messages from Johannesburg and from Rhodes's subordinates at Capetown calling upon him to stay his hand, he entered on his famous 'Raid' by marching his force, under the military command of Sir John C. Willoughby, across the Transvaal border. It was doomed to disaster. Boer commandos gathered round it on its way. The force which Jameson expected to be dispatched by the reformers from Johannesburg to join hands with him was never sent, and Jameson's little band, after gallant fighting and heavy losses, was forced to surrender to the Boer commandant, P. A. Cronje, at Doornkop, fourteen miles from Johannesburg (2 January 1896).

The rash decision to invade the Transvaal, in defiance of all requests for delay, was Jameson's own, nor did he ever in after life seek to minimize his sole responsibility for it. Undoubtedly he underrated the military value of the Boer commandos, but he had often before dared and achieved the impossible. He felt that Rhodes, in his position as prime minister at Capetown, was in duty bound to tell him not to start, as no outbreak had occurred at Johannesburg, but that if he did not start against orders and succeed, a scheme on which Rhodes had set his heart would fail; whereas if he started and failed the consequences would fall upon himself alone. Afterwards he bitterly reproached himself for not having foreseen that Rhodes must be involved in those consequences.

Taken captive to Pretoria, Jameson and his officers were handed over to the British authorities and sent to England to be tried for an offence against the Foreign Enlistment Act. They were convicted, and Jameson with Willoughby was sentenced in July 1896 by the lord chief justice, Lord Russell of Killowen, to fifteen months' imprisonment, the other officers receiving shorter sentences. Broken in health by all the hardships which for years he had so cheerfully borne, Jameson nearly died in Holloway prison and was released after a few months (December 1896) in a condition of great physical weakness. His robustness never returned, but a long rest restored his activity and he was able in March and April 1897 to give his evidence before the parliamentary select committee which inquired into the origin and circumstances of the Raid. From that evidence it will be enough to quote one sentence: 'I know perfectly well that as I have not succeeded the natural thing has happened; but I also know that if I had succeeded I should have been forgiven.'

The story of the remainder of Jameson's life is that of a marvellous recovery from a catastrophic fall. For two years he was travelling in Africa and in Europe and making some kind of return to health. Then upon the outbreak of the South African War (October 1899) he threw himself into Ladysmith. Here he nearly died of enteric fever, and was left after the relief of that town with a physique permanently broken, but with an unbroken and unbreakable spirit and with a fixed resolve to make amends for the past. In pursuance of this resolve he joined the board of De Beers Consolidated Mines and entered the Cape parliament as member for Kimberley in June 1900. He was content to sit silent under the taunts and abuse of opponents, who seemed to hold him answerable for all the troubles of South Africa, until October, when that parliament was prorogued, not to meet again till August 1902, after the close of the South African War. In March 1902 Rhodes died, and Jameson, who had nursed his friend devotedly, was left alone. But it was not long before he had succeeded him in the leadership of the progressive party at the Cape; and, his parliamentary silence once broken, he rapidly established his position in the House.

At the general election which followed the defeat of the ministry of Sir John Gordon Sprigg [q.v.] in 1903, Jameson's party obtained a majority of one in the legislative council and a majority of five in the assembly. It was a narrow majority indeed; and but for the fact that many of the Dutch voters in the Cape Colony had been disfranchised for rebellion during the South African War it is probable that there would have been no progressive majority at all. But it sufficed for the time, and, in less than eight years from the date of his conviction, Jameson, the ex-raider, became prime minister of Cape Colony (February 1904). He held office for four years at the head of a loyal party kept together mainly by his own magnetic personality. He bent his whole energies to the task of racial reconciliation; and when finally his small majority had dwindled away and the general election of March 1908 had restored his opponents to power, he had won their respect and, in many cases, their affection, and was incontestably the foremost figure in South African politics. He could feel that, in his own phrase, he had 'got square'—at the cost of what physical suffering and what sacrifice of every personal inclination was known to few.

As prime minister, Jameson attended the Imperial Conference held in London in 1907, and worked hard, along with Alfred Deakin [q.v.], prime minister of Australia, in the then hopeless cause of imperial preference. During this visit to England he was made a privy councillor and received the freedom of the cities of London and Edinburgh. It also fell to his lot to invite the Earl of Selborne, as high commissioner for South Africa, to review the mutual relations of the South African colonies, whose internal quarrels, over such matters as customs and railway rates, appeared impossible of settlement so long as the several colonies remained politically separate. Lord Selborne's memorandum, prepared in response to Jameson's invitation, was the immediate cause of the assembling in October 1908 of the South African National Convention, of which the outcome was the scheme of South African union, which was embodied in the South Africa Act of the British parliament in 1909. By the time the Convention met Jameson had fallen from power in Cape Colony; but he retained his seat in the legislative assembly and was leader of the opposition. As such he was a member of the Convention. He was also the acknowledged leader of the British section of the whole South African population, and played, along with General Botha [q.v.] at the head of the Dutch section, the chief part in the Convention's proceedings. The two men, inspired by a common ideal of racial amity (and sharing, it may be added, a common taste for the game of bridge), became fast friends, and to their co-operation the success of the Union movement was mainly due.

When Union had been achieved, Jameson favoured the formation of what he called a 'best man' government, that is, a government formed of the leading men of both races, irrespective of party. Botha's personal feeling was probably in sympathy with Jameson's, but other forces were too strong for him; and when called upon to form the first government of the Union of South Africa he felt compelled to form it on the old party lines. Jameson therefore entered the first parliament of the Union in 1910 (member for the Harbour division of Capetown) as leader of the opposition, an opposition anything but factious and conducted by him with unabated personal friendliness towards General Botha. He stayed at his post till April 1912, when his constant ill-health and pain obliged him finally to retire from politics, to leave South Africa, and return to England. A baronetcy was conferred on him in 1911.

In England Jameson, who was never married, lived with his brother Middleton, who survived him. He occupied himself mainly with the affairs of the British South Africa Company, of which he had been a director since 1902. He became president on the death in 1913 of the second Duke of Abercorn. In this capacity he paid two more visits to Rhodesia, in 1913–1914 and in 1915; and his work for Rhodes's Company, into which he infused new energy and spirit, ended only with his life. In the European War, though he was almost a dying man, he added to his other labours those of chairman of the committee formed by the War Office to look after the welfare of British prisoners of war. But his strength was now spent; and after a short but terribly painful illness, he died in London on 26 November 1917. When the War was over, his remains were removed from the place of their temporary interment, and finally laid to rest by the side of Rhodes's grave in the Matoppo Hills, near Bulawayo, at the place which Rhodes had named 'The view of the World'.

A portrait of Jameson was painted by Sir Hubert von Herkomer in 1895.

[G. Seymour Fort, *Dr. Jameson*, 1908; Ian Colvin, *Life of Jameson*, 1922; personal knowledge.] D. O. M.

JAYNE, FRANCIS JOHN (1845–1921), bishop of Chester, the eldest son of John Jayne, J.P., colliery-owner, of Pant-y-bailea House, near Abergavenny, by his second wife, Elisabeth Haines, was born at Llanelly, Breconshire, 1 January 1845. He was educated at Rugby under Dr. Temple, where he carried off the gold medal, and, it is said, had no superior as a football player. From Rugby he went to Oxford as a scholar of Wadham College (1863), and had a distinguished career at the university. He gained first classes in classical moderations, in *literae humaniores*, and in law and modern history, the senior Hall-Houghton Greek Testament prize, and a fellowship at Jesus College (1868). He was appointed tutor of Keble College in 1871, Whitehall preacher in 1875, and select preacher at Oxford in 1884. Among Jayne's private pupils at Oxford were Randall Davidson (afterwards archbishop of Canterbury), E. A. Knox (afterwards bishop of Manchester), and Francis Chavasse (afterwards bishop of Liverpool). At Oxford, as at Rugby, he interested himself keenly in athletic sports and was in the front rank as an oarsman. Having been ordained deacon and priest in 1870, he became curate of St. Clement's, Oxford.

In 1879 Jayne was appointed principal of St. David's College, Lampeter. Under him the college was affiliated to Oxford and Cambridge, its curriculum was extended, the number of its students more than doubled, the college school established, and the Canterbury buildings erected. The revival of the Church in Wales during the subsequent forty-five years is largely due to the new life which Jayne infused into the college, where the majority of the clergy in Wales have been trained. At Lampeter he had the assistance as tutor and Welsh professor of John Owen, afterwards bishop of St. David's, who said of Jayne, ' Personally I owe all to him, and I have always looked upon him as an ideal principal.' Jayne left Lampeter in 1886 to become vicar of Leeds in succession to Dr. John Gott. He held that important living only two years and a half, but in that time he put the financial and other business of the parish into excellent order, and extended the work of the Church in various ways, especially among men. One who worked with him has recorded his recollection of his ' wonderful personal courtesy ', which, however, was associated with ' an impatience of any idleness or pettiness '.

A man of such gifts and so vigorous was marked out for high preferment, and at the comparatively early age of forty-four Jayne was nominated by Lord Salisbury to the see of Chester (1889). Under its two previous bishops, William Jacobson [q.v.], and William Stubbs [q.v.], both eminent scholars, the diocese of Chester had been ably organized and administered, and Jayne set himself to build zealously on the foundations which they had laid. Not only were his talents for administration exceptional, but he was a shrewd judge of men, with a rare insight into character, quick to see both sides of a question and to hit upon a happy adjustment. His energies and sympathies were far from being confined to the ordinary ecclesiastical routine. Nothing that concerned the general well-being of the people was without interest for him. His tact and decisiveness together with his clear, strong, musical voice and fine presence made him an admirable chairman on all public occasions, and he had the happy knack of saying something fresh and forcible on almost every subject. Though capable of impassioned oratory, as he showed on some occasions, his manner in public speech, whether in the pulpit or on the platform, was ordinarily quiet and restrained ; to nothing was he more averse than to unguarded loquacity. His manner of life was of the simplest, and his dislike of self-parade perhaps prevented him from occupying a larger place in the public eye. Yet his hand was felt for good in every quarter, with the result that in an address to him signed by over 1,500 clergy and laity in 1917, he was alluded to as ' the spiritual head of what is, perhaps, the most peaceful and orderly diocese in England '.

Jayne's scholarly instincts and balance of mind attached him closely to the principles and tenets of the Church of England as set forth in the Prayer Book and Articles and in the writings of her leading divines, and his teaching on those lines was in exact conformity with that of his two immediate predecessors. It was thought by some that he changed his ecclesiastical leanings during the later years of his episcopate. It would be truer to say that he ' changed his front without changing his position '. His personal convictions remained unaltered, but he came to look with grave apprehension on developments of doctrine and ritual which were becoming more and more marked towards the close of his episcopate. In Convocation he was a conspicuous figure and his counsel there was much valued. Amongst other questions, he specially interested himself in the modification of the Church's use of the *Quicunque Vult*, and he was opposed to any change in the substance or structure of the Communion office.

Jayne's unremitting attention to his duties in the end quite overtaxed even his robust powers, and in May 1919 he resigned his see. He lived for two years longer in retirement at Oswestry in a condition of extreme weakness and helplessness, borne with cheerful courage and patience. He died 23 August 1921, and was buried at Bowdon in Cheshire.

Jayne married in 1872 Emily, eldest daughter of Watts John Garland, of Lisbon and Dorset. He had six sons and three daughters. It was his express wish that there should be no memorial of him, and he left nothing for posthumous publication. In 1910 he published an edition, with introduction and notes, of Richard Baxter's *Self-Review*; his other publications were *Anglican Pronouncements upon Auricular Confession and Fasting Communion* (1912) and some charges printed locally. Extracts from these have since been reprinted as an appendix to *Anglican Essays*, by various authors (1923).

[*The Times*, *Manchester Guardian*, and *Yorkshire Post*, 25 August 1921; *Chester Diocesan Gazette*, May 1919 and October 1921.] W. L. P. C.

JERSEY, seventh Earl of (1845–1915), colonial governor. [See Villiers, Victor Albert George Child-.]

JESSOPP, AUGUSTUS (1823–1914), schoolmaster and historical writer, was born at Cheshunt 20 December 1823, the third son and youngest of the ten children of John Sympson Jessopp, J.P., of Cheshunt, by his wife, Elizabeth, daughter of Bridger Goodrich, of Bermuda. The family moved to Belgium about 1832, and Augustus Jessopp received a roving education at schools abroad and later at Clapham under the Rev. A. J. Plow. He was a studious boy and, much to his relief, was sent in 1844 to St. John's College, Cambridge, after three irksome years in a merchant's office in Liverpool. In 1848 he took a pass degree, and was ordained to a curacy at Papworth St. Agnes, Cambridgeshire. In the same year he married Mary Ann, daughter of Charles Cotesworth, R.N., of Liverpool. They had no children. In 1855 he returned to Cambridge, but shortly afterwards moved to Helston, Cornwall, as master of the local grammar school, which had fallen on evil days and had hardly any pupils left. Jessopp soon restored its fortunes, leaving in 1859 to become head master of King Edward VI's School, Norwich, where a bigger task awaited him.

Norwich School was at a low ebb: it had few day-boys and but one boarder; discipline was bad, the buildings dilapidated. Under Jessopp's twenty years' rule it was transformed into a modern public school, with buildings enlarged, teaching and equipment improved, and with a good record at the universities. Jessopp was an imposing, if unconventional, head master; not a great scholar, but a teacher of originality and enthusiasm. He set the boys new standards in work, in discipline, in games; was admired by them for his vigour, fine presence, and noble voice; beloved for his kindliness and magnificent moments of indiscretion and frivolity. He interested himself for a time in larger educational questions, took some part in public discussion, and wrote one or two school-books; but his tastes were mainly antiquarian.

As early as 1855 Jessopp had published an edition of Donne's *Essays in Divinity*, and since 1866 he had been at work upon the records of the Walpole family, of several members of which he has given an account in this Dictionary. His *One Generation of a Norfolk House*—perhaps the best of his works—appeared in 1878, and the next year the Camden Society issued his edition of a seventeenth-century text, *The Oeconomy of the Fleete* (prison). In 1879 Jessopp retired from Norwich School to the rectory of Scarning, Norfolk, in order to find leisure for studies which had become his chief interest. There for many years he lived the life of a well-to-do country parson of wide accomplishments, active in his poor parish, well known in East Anglia as a learned antiquary, and outside it as an attractive writer on mediaeval England, and a vigorous critic of the conditions of village and clerical life of the day. The last question was much to the fore in the 'eighties, and Jessopp's racy, provocative articles were readily taken by (Sir) James Knowles for the newly founded *Nineteenth Century* magazine; many were later reissued by Jessopp in his volumes, *Arcady, for Better for Worse* (1887), and *Trials of a Country Parson* (1890). Of his historical articles—many of them also written for the *Nineteenth Century*—the best collections are *The Coming of the Friars* (1889), a well-known book, *Studies by a Recluse* (1893), and *Before the Great Pillage* (1901); they give popular, sympathetic accounts of parish life in the middle ages. Of more lasting value are

Jessopp's edition of the *Visitations of the Diocese of Norwich*, 1492–1532 (Camden Society, 1888)—the first English monastic visitations to be printed—his text of the *Life of St. William of Norwich* (with Dr. M. R. James, 1896), and his reports on MSS. of the bishop and chapter of Ely, at Shadwell Court, and at Holkham House, for the Historical Manuscripts Commission (1891, 1903, 1907). He also wrote biographies of Donne (1897) and Lord Burghley (1904), of Queen Elizabeth and others for this Dictionary, besides many minor works.

Jessopp's work and record brought him popular repute, eminent friends—especially George Meredith—and, in time, academic recognition. For high preferment his name was passed over. He incorporated at Oxford (from Worcester College) and took the degree of D.D. in 1870; he was select preacher there in 1890. In 1895 his Oxford and Cambridge colleges elected him honorary fellow on the same day. In that year also he was made honorary canon in Norwich Cathedral, and in 1902 a chaplain in ordinary to the King. After the death of his wife (1905) his circumstances were much reduced, and he was granted a civil list pension. Later, his mind became affected and, having sold his library, he resigned his living in 1911, retiring to Norwich, where he died 12 February 1914.

Jessopp disclaimed the title of historian, called himself 'a smatterer and a fumbler', but he had some of the gifts and equipment of the best historians. Had his powers been directed to more solid historical work it would at least have redeemed his 'exile' at Scarning from the futility which he was wont to deplore; 'I was burning my boats in taking a country living', he used to say. Yet his achievement was not without merit. He called attention to much unworked material for English parochial and monastic history, and encouraged the sympathetic study of those subjects; while by many who never read his books he was remembered as one of the most stimulating head masters of his time.

[*The Times*, 13 February 1914; *Norvicensian* (Norwich School magazine), 1914; *Letters of George Meredith*, edited by his son, 2 vols., 1912; *Cornhill Magazine*, November 1921; private information. Photographic portraits of Jessopp are prefixed to his *Arcady* and *Random Roaming* (1894).] J. R. H. W.

JEX-BLAKE, SOPHIA LOUISA (1840–1912), physician, born at Hastings 21 January 1840, was the youngest daughter of Thomas Jex-Blake, of Bunwell, Norfolk, and Brighton, proctor of Doctors' Commons, by his wife, Maria Emily, youngest daughter of Thomas Cubitt, J.P., of Honing Hall, Norfolk. She was sister of Thomas William Jex-Blake [q.v.], head master of Rugby and dean of Wells. In 1858 she entered Queen's College for Women, London, as a student, and became mathematical tutor there (1859–1861). After various educational experiments she went in 1865 to the United States and worked in Boston under Dr. Lucy Sewall, with whom she formed a lifelong friendship and from whom she gained a deep conviction of the 'incalculable blessings' conferred on her own sex by a woman physician. In 1868 she began a regular course of medical study in New York under Dr. Elizabeth Blackwell [q.v.]. Recalled to England in 1868 by the death of her father, she began to seek for medical education at home. All avenues to the profession seemed to be closed, both by the Medical Act of 1858, which excluded from the register foreign qualifications, and by the unwillingness of medical authorities at home to teach or to examine women. After being refused by the university of London, she turned to Edinburgh, where, though her first application was refused, a second was successful. Regulations were made for the admission of women and for their instruction 'for the profession of medicine' in separate classes.

From this point Sophia Jex-Blake became virtually the leader of the movement to open the medical profession to all, without distinction of sex. Five women matriculated at Edinburgh in 1869 and for three sessions carried on their medical studies, though under increasing difficulties. These difficulties came to a head in 1872, and an appeal to the university court only brought the suggestion that the women students should give up their claim to graduation (the only legal passport to practice), and should receive informal 'certificates of proficiency'. Finally, the matriculated women students, seven in all, brought an action against the university in the court of Session, claiming that the university was legally bound to enable them to complete their studies. Judgment in their favour was reversed on appeal (1873), chiefly on the ground that in admitting women to matriculation the university had acted *ultra vires*.

The failure seemed complete, yet it is clear that the struggle had been of great value in forming public opinion. Quite undaunted, Sophia Jex-Blake attacked at their base the twin difficulties of instruction and of legal qualification. Having secured Dr. Arthur Trehern Norton as dean, and a staff of recognized lecturers, she founded the London School of Medicine for Women, which opened in October 1874 on its present site in Hunter Street (formerly Henrietta Street). Clinical work was not secured till 1877, when the London (afterwards the Royal) Free Hospital opened its doors to women students. The legal question was ventilated in parliament from 1873 onwards, Sophia Jex-Blake, as the moving spirit behind the scenes, constantly supplying facts, arguments, and even, at the request of Mr. Cowper-Temple (afterwards Baron Mount-Temple), a draft Bill. Meanwhile her last attempt to qualify under existing conditions, through the licence in midwifery of the College of Surgeons, registrable for general practice, was foiled by the resignation of the examiners *en masse* (1876). This probably hastened parliamentary action, and in August 1876 the Russell Gurney Enabling Act became law. All medical examining bodies were now empowered to examine women, and through the Irish College of Physicians, the first to use the power, Sophia Jex-Blake, already an M.D. of Berne, at length gained a legal title to practise in Great Britain (1877).

In 1878 Sophia Jex-Blake settled in Edinburgh. There, in addition to private and dispensary practice, she founded a women's hospital in 1885, and in the next year a school of medicine for women which continued for more than ten years. In 1894, when the university of Edinburgh admitted women to graduation in medicine, the last of the barriers against which she had launched herself in 1869 was down. Able, energetic, determined, a born combatant and leader, she had been an unselfish and generous protagonist in the cause. In 1899 she gave up active work and retired to Rotherfield in Sussex, where she died on 7 January 1912. Her portrait by Samuel Lawrence (1865) hangs in the rooms of the Royal Society of Medicine.

[Sophia Jex-Blake, *Medical Women*, 1872, 2nd edition, 1886; Margaret Todd, *Life of Sophia Jex-Blake*, 1918; personal knowledge.] K. J-B.

JEX-BLAKE, THOMAS WILLIAM (1832–1915), schoolmaster and dean of Wells, was born at 2 Cumberland Terrace, Regent's Park, London, 26 January 1832, the eldest surviving son of Thomas Jex-Blake, of Bunwell, Norfolk, and Brighton, proctor of Doctors' Commons, and J.P. for Sussex, and grandson of William Jex-Blake, J.P., of Swanton Abbotts, Norfolk. His mother was Maria Emily, youngest daughter of Thomas Cubitt, J.P., of Honing Hall, Norfolk. He was educated at Rugby, where he was a pupil of Archibald Tait, afterwards archbishop of Canterbury, and of Edward Meyrick Goulburn, afterwards dean of Norwich. He matriculated as a scholar of University College, Oxford, in 1851, and obtained a first class in classical moderations (1853) and a first class in *literae humaniores* (1855). During his undergraduate days at University College, Frederick Charles Plumptre was master of the college, Goldwin Smith and John Conington, fellows. In 1855 Jex-Blake was elected a fellow of Queen's College, and in the following year he was ordained deacon at Oxford, and in 1857 priest at Winchester.

The calling of a public-school master was Jex-Blake's chosen career, and he followed it for thirty-two years. His apprenticeship was served at Marlborough College, where, for one 'half', he was sixth-form master under George Edward Lynch Cotton [q.v.], an inspiring head. He married in 1857 Henrietta, second surviving daughter of John Cordery, India merchant, of London. After foreign travel with his wife, Jex-Blake became assistant master (1858–1868, taking the 'Twenty') at Rugby under Frederick Temple, his second experience of an inspiring chief. In 1868 he was elected principal of Cheltenham College, a tribute to his reputation, which his services to Cheltenham enhanced.

In 1874 Jex-Blake became head master of Rugby. He took the reins at a dangerous time. His predecessor, Henry Hayman [q.v.], had been unfortunate and unpopular, and internal divisions had dimmed the lustre of the school. By tact and wisdom, and with the help of old friends, Jex-Blake restored it to prosperity, his courteous manners and knowledge of the world being helpful to Rugby in its relations with parents and with the county. He was the first public-school head master in England to appreciate the value of art in a liberal education. Owing to his initiative Rugby had an art museum before any other school in England. That his taste for fine pictures owed much to John Ruskin is gracefully acknowledged in the introduction to his book, *A Long Vacation in Continental Picture Galleries* (1858). At Rugby Jex-

Blake built the Temple reading-room and art museum, a new Big School with class-rooms under it, completed the new quadrangle, started the modern side, gave a swimming-bath in the Close, equipped school workshops under the gymnasium, and enriched the art museum with generous gifts, which he made ' in the hope that leisure hours would be given by many boys to a delightful form of culture often too little thought of at home and school, and with the conviction that some few boys would draw great enjoyment, lifelong interest, and a new faculty from it '.

Jex-Blake's sermons preached at Cheltenham and Rugby (published under the title *Life in Faith*, 1876) illustrate the influence of Arnold, Jowett, and Temple on the school pulpit. He was in the school tradition which was derived from Thomas Arnold, cooled by the influence of John Stuart Mill and of Oxford liberalism of the 'fifties, energized a second time by Frederick Temple, and coloured by the culture of Ruskin. To his contemporary, Edward Thring [q.v.], of Uppingham, he stands as a portrait by Millais stands to a portrait by Manet. As a cultivated gentleman he recalled some of the attractive types sketched by Anthony Trollope.

In 1887, fatigued by his scholastic labours, Jex-Blake withdrew from Rugby, though not from his efforts on behalf of its further endowment, to the rectory of Alvechurch, Worcestershire. Four years later (1891) he became dean of Wells. Late in 1910 he resigned the deanery and passed the last years of his life in London, where he died 2 July 1915. He had striking beauty and grace of person, great dignity in address, and a kind disposition. He had two sons and nine daughters ; two of the latter held high academic office, Henrietta being principal of Lady Margaret Hall, Oxford (1909–1921), and Katharine mistress of Girton College, Cambridge (1916–1922). His youngest sister, Sophia Louisa Jex-Blake [q.v.], was a brave pioneer in the medical education of women. The best portrait of Jex-Blake, that by Sir J. E. Millais, is in the possession of his son, Dr. A. J. Jex-Blake. There is also a portrait by Hermann Herkomer at Rugby School.

[*The Times*, 3 July 1915 ; W. H. D. Rouse, *A History of Rugby School*, 1898 ; H. C. Bradby, *Rugby*, 1900 ; private information ; personal knowledge.] M. E. S.

JOHNS, CLAUDE HERMANN WALTER (1857–1920), Assyriologist, was born at Banwell, Somerset, 4 February 1857. He was the eldest son of the Rev. Walter Pascoe Johns, Wesleyan minister, of a yeoman family settled for generations at Wendron, Cornwall, by his wife, Eleanor, daughter of Charles Gilbert, of Mutford Hall, Suffolk. Educated at Queen Elizabeth's grammar school, Faversham, Johns won an exhibition at Queens' College, Cambridge (1875), after previously declining two scholarships. At Queens' he was presently elected to a minor scholarship, a foundation scholarship, and to a Goldsmiths' exhibition ; and in 1880, while a master at the Leys School, Cambridge, he graduated as twenty-seventh wrangler, an accident having prevented him from taking the tripos examination earlier. His health, never very good, then compelled him to go abroad to Tasmania, where he became second master at Horton College (1880–1883) ; but he returned to England for family reasons in 1883 and, after a short period as a master at Paston grammar school, North Walsham (1883–1886), was ordained in 1887, becoming tutor at Peterborough training college (1887–1891). He served curacies at Helpston, Northamptonshire (1887–1888), and in Peterborough (1888–1892), in conjunction with his work at the training college. He returned to Queens' College as assistant chaplain in 1892, and was presented by his college to the living of St. Botolph's, Cambridge, in the same year. He held this living till 1909.

It was now that the interest which Johns had taken in Assyriology since 1875 began to bear fruit. The expedition to Nineveh undertaken in 1873 by George Smith [q.v.], of the British Museum, resulted in the further discovery of Deluge-tablet fragments, and the discussion on these roused Johns's interest. Subsequently, urged by the Orientalist, Sandford Arthur Strong [q.v.], he took up the study of cuneiform to such good purpose that he was made lecturer in Assyriology at Queens' College in 1895, and in 1904 lecturer in Assyrian at King's College, London. In 1903 he was elected to the Edwardes fellowship at Queens', and in 1909 proceeded to the degree of Litt.D., Jesus College making him a research fellow. A few months later he was elected to the mastership of St. Catharine's College, with its accompanying canonry at Norwich, which, while it conferred well-deserved recognition on Johns's capacity, unfortunately for Assyriology, absorbed the greater part of his time. Yet he did not lose touch with his Assyrian studies, for in 1910 he visited

America and delivered in Philadelphia the Bohlen lectures on *The Religious Significance of Semitic Proper Names*, and in 1912 he gave the Schweich lectures at the British Academy on the *Relations between the Laws of Babylonia and the Laws of the Hebrew Peoples*.

Unhappily the stress of his labours proved too much for him. His devotion to his work not only in Assyriology but also in raising the status of St. Catharine's caused a break-down in his health, and he resigned his mastership and canonry in 1919. He died at Winchester 20 August 1920, and is buried at Twyford, Hampshire. He had married in 1910 Agnes Sophia, daughter of the Rev. John Griffith, principal of Brighton College and later vicar of Sandridge, Hertfordshire. He had no children.

In 1904 Johns published *Babylonian and Assyrian Laws, Contracts, and Letters*, a collection of documents illustrated by full, ingenious, often brilliant discussions of the problems raised. His *magnum opus* was a corpus of eleven hundred contract tablets, in four volumes (one issued posthumously in 1923 by his wife), *Assyrian Deeds and Documents* (1898–1923). *An Assyrian Domesday Book* (1901) dealt with cuneiform records of plantations and their proprietors round the city of Harran. One of the results of Johns's familiarity with the contract literature was his vast collection of Assyrian proper names, which was embodied in *Assyrian Personal Names*, K. L. Tallqvist's work on the subject. He wrote two historical volumes, *Ancient Assyria* (1912) and *Ancient Babylonia* (1913), both containing much original work. In addition to numerous papers in scientific journals, Johns also wrote *The Oldest Code of Laws in the World* (1903), *Ur-Engur* (1908), *A List of the Year Names of the First Dynasty of Babylon* (1911), and *A Survey of Recent Assyriology* (1914–1915). The only drawback to his careful work was that he had never travelled in the Near East.

Johns's election to the mastership of St. Catharine's brought about a surprising change in the college. By his energy and attractive personality he raised it from a comparatively unimportant position in a way that astonished those who had known the college in the 'nineties. The number of its undergraduates greatly increased, and Johns entirely reorganized its management.

[Private information; personal knowledge.]

R. C. T.

KEKEWICH, ROBERT GEORGE (1854–1914), major-general, was born 17 July 1854 at Brampford Speke, near Exeter, the second son of Trehawke Kekewich, of Peamore, Exeter, and nephew of the judge, Sir Arthur Kekewich [q.v.]. His mother was Charlotte, daughter of Captain George Peard, R.N. He was educated at Marlborough College and entered the army (102nd regiment) in 1874. He was transferred to the Buffs (East Kent regiment) in the same year, however, and soon saw active service, going to the Malay Peninsula with the Perak expedition of 1875–1876. In 1883 he received his captaincy, and afterwards served with the Sudan expedition of 1884–1885 as deputy assistant adjutant and quartermaster-general. For his services in this campaign he was awarded the brevet rank of major. Three years later he served as deputy assistant adjutant-general in the Sudan (Suakin), and in 1890 was made major in the Royal Inniskilling Fusiliers. In the following year he was appointed military secretary to the commander-in-chief, Madras, a post which he held until 1897. He was promoted lieutenant-colonel in command of the first battalion Loyal North Lancashire regiment in 1898, and in the Boer War of 1899–1902 served as lieutenant-colonel, commanding all the troops in Griqualand West and Bechuanaland.

With the War in South Africa Kekewich's name will live in history, for it fell to him to defend the town of Kimberley, which was besieged by the Boers from 15 October 1899 to 15 February 1900. The masterly dispositions of the small and almost entirely improvised force under his command marked him as a soldier of extraordinary acumen. The extremely difficult nature of the area besieged demanded far more than average military skill for its defence, and his conduct of it elicited admiration and commendation in the highest terms from the commander-in-chief, Lord Roberts, and from Lord Kitchener. Colonel Kekewich's task, a heavy responsibility under any conditions, was made far more exacting by the presence in the town of Cecil Rhodes and his co-directors of the De Beers Company, whose outlook seemed to be affected by personal considerations, with little regard for the actual military situation. The ready tact of the commander, however, and his steady devotion to duty, reduced the dangerous possibilities of the situation to a minimum; and, though his subsequent career was prejudiced by the influence of Rhodes, yet his reputation as a brilliant soldier suffered nothing. He was created C.B. in 1900. After the relief of Kimberley by Major-General (afterwards Earl) French, Colonel Kekewich returned to the command of his battalion which formed part of the column under Lord Methuen. It was not until December 1901 that Kekewich was given command of a column of the South Africa field force. He took a prominent part in the actions of Moedville (30 September 1901) and Rooival (11 April 1902), and as a reward for his services throughout the campaign was made major-general (1902). He died 5 November 1914 at Whimple, near Exeter. He never married.

[The *Standard and Diggers' News*, 10 November 1899; *The Times*, 6 November 1914; Lieut.-Colonel W. A. J. O'Meara, *Kekewich in Kimberley*, 1926; private information.] C. V. O.

KELLY, FREDERICK SEPTIMUS (1881–1916), musician and oarsman, was born at Sydney, New South Wales, 29 May 1881, the seventh child and fourth son of Thomas Hussey Kelly, of Glenyarrah, Sydney, by his wife, Mary Dick. He was educated at Eton (1893–1899) and at Balliol College, Oxford (1900–1903), where he was Lewis Nettleship musical scholar. There can have been few in whom *γυμναστική* and *μουσική* were more happily combined, and his excellence in either field would have made him a remarkable man. Kelly was one of the most promising English musicians of his day, a fine oar, and one of the greatest scullers of all time. He stroked the Eton eight in 1899, rowed for Oxford in 1903, won the Grand Challenge cup at Henley in 1903, 1904, 1905, the Stewards' cup in 1906, and rowed in the veteran English crew which won the Olympic eights in 1908. His sculling was beautiful to see: unspoilt by professional coaching, he sculled as he rowed, and his natural sense of poise and rhythm made his boat a live thing under him, perfectly controlled. His swing was not very long, but the length of his stroke in the water was considerable, the blades being instantly and evenly covered and driven through with a steady, equal pressure and a simultaneous finish, so that no ounce of his strength was wasted. Few scullers have ever equalled the precision of his blade work and the perfect counterpoise of the two sides of his body. His style was so easy that when going his fastest at the hardest moment of a race it looked as if he were paddling. He first won the Diamond sculls at Henley in 1902 (in 8 minutes 59 seconds) when he entered as a novice, the final heat being probably the finest, though it was not the fastest, race of his life. Both by his style and his determination he recalled the classic win of T. C. Edwards-Moss in 1878. He won again in 1903 (in 8 minutes 41 seconds), was beaten in 1904 when he was not properly trained, and won in 1905, lowering the record by 13 seconds to 8 minutes 10 seconds, a time which has never since been beaten. In 1903 he won the Wingfield sculls with great ease.

As a child Kelly had a remarkable talent for the pianoforte, but his real musical education did not begin until he left Balliol in 1903, when he settled down in earnest to a prolonged course of study (1903–1908) in Frankfort-on-Main under Professors Knorr and Engesser; and until 1914 his life was devoted to realizing his dual ambition—'to be a great player and a great composer'. As in sculling, so in music, his genius lay in the direction of infinite painstaking, and he set himself a most exacting standard of musical discipline. In 1912 he gave a series of concerts in London, in which he played some of the great test pieces. No one could question the soundness of his craft or the brilliance with which he engaged. A strong masculine touch, clear articulation, abundant power of attack, an even-handed facility, and thoroughly safe command—these were some of the results, wholly admirable, of his intensive cultivation of 'technique'. But there was a certain immaturity; traces of the workshop were still evident in his performance. Even so, the concerts were a fine achievement and gave great promise for the future.

Although musical ideas came to him only fitfully, Kelly left a wide range of compositions, two volumes of songs, several pieces for the pianoforte, a serenade for the flute and string orchestra (1911), a violin sonata (1915), and two organ preludes which were masterpieces of small genre. All his work had individuality; he owed little to others except perhaps to Chopin, and here and there to Schubert. The predominant note was lyrical, and he had a great sense of orchestration and colour.

At the outbreak of the European War in 1914 Kelly joined the Royal Naval division, and was in the Hood battalion with Rupert Brooke [q.v.] and Charles Lister. He served throughout the Gallipoli campaign, and won the distinguished service cross for his conspicuous gallantry. In

1916 the division went to France, and on 13 November Kelly was killed at Beaucourt-sur-Ancre when rushing a German machine gun that was holding up the attack. He was unmarried.

No record of Kelly would be complete without a mention of almost his last work, a lovely elegy for string orchestra written in memory of his friend, Rupert Brooke, who was buried in Scyros in April 1915. Kelly wrote in his diary: 'As we slowly made our way behind the coffin to the olive grove, the phrase

constantly occurred to my mind. The work is a true portrayal of my feelings on that night—the passionless simplicity of the surroundings with occasionally a note of personal anguish.'

Kelly died just as he seemed to be entering on a period of great fertility; in composition as in playing he was freeing himself, finding himself—throwing off, in his playing, restrictions acquired through a long routine and habit of practice, and gaining for his composition not only greater vigour and freshness in his ideas, but a new judgement and discrimination in the use of all resources.

He wrote an article on sculling in *The Complete Oarsman* (1908), and published the following musical compositions (the dates being those of composition): Op. 1, Two Songs (1902 and 1904); Op. 2, Waltz Pageant for Pianoforte Duet (1905), for Pianoforte Solo (1911); Op. 3, Allegro de Concert for Pianoforte (1907); Op. 4, A Cycle of Lyrics for Pianoforte Solo (1908); Op. 5, Theme, Variations, and Fugue for two Pianos (1913); Op. 6, Six Songs (1910); Op. 7, Serenade for Flute and String Orchestra (1911); Two Organ Preludes (1915); Elegy for String Orchestra in memoriam Rupert Brooke (1915). He also left several volumes of unpublished compositions.

[*Balliol College War Memorial Book*, 1924; personal knowledge.] H. B. H.

KELLY-KENNY, Sir THOMAS (1840–1914), general, son of Mathew Kelly, of Tuanmanagh, Kilrush, county Clare, was born at Tuanmanagh 27 February 1840. In 1874 he took the additional surname of Kenny. In 1858 he received a commission in the 2nd Foot, and in 1860 took part in the China War, was present at the capture of the Taku forts, and was mentioned in dispatches. In 1866 he took part as a captain in the Abyssinian expedition and was again mentioned in dispatches. After twenty-four years of regimental service, he was promoted in 1882 to the command of the 2nd battalion of the Queen's regiment, as the 2nd Foot had become, and he first attracted notice in consequence of the very high state of efficiency to which he brought this battalion. On giving up this command he was employed in a succession of staff appointments, in which he made a name for himself as an administrator.

In 1896 Kelly-Kenny was promoted major-general and given command of an infantry brigade at Aldershot, and in the following year he was made inspector-general of auxiliary forces at the War Office. He was holding this position when the Boer War broke out (1899), and, after the first five divisions had left for South Africa under the command of Sir Redvers Buller, he was chosen to organize and command the 6th division at Aldershot. After the 'black week' (December 1899) of Magersfontein, Stormberg, and Colenso, and after the appointment of Lord Roberts [q.v.] to the supreme command, Kelly-Kenny took this division out to South Africa and led it during the operations for the relief of Kimberley. After a night march (14–15 February 1900) the 6th division arrived at Klip Drift on the Modder river and relieved Major-General (afterwards Earl) French's cavalry division, which was thus enabled to gallop through the Boer lines towards Kimberley. On discovering General Piet Cronje's movement eastwards from Magersfontein, Kelly-Kenny followed him up, engaged his rear-guard at Klip Kraal Drift (16 February), and by hampering the Boer retreat enabled Lord Roberts two days later to bring up the 9th division to join the 6th, while French's cavalry returned from Kimberley and prevented Cronje from escaping by the right bank of the Modder. Cronje had entrenched himself in a laager at Vendutie Drift, just east of Paardeberg. During the first attack on the laager (18 February) Kelly-Kenny was the senior general on the spot, but Lord Roberts had sent forward his chief of staff, Lord Kitchener [q.v.], to co-ordinate the movements of the various divisions, a measure which placed Kelly-Kenny in a difficult position, particularly as he did not agree with Kitchener's radical methods. After Cronje's surrender (27 February) Kelly-Kenny led his division in the action of Poplar Grove (7 March), but the Boers, finding their flank turned by the British cavalry, did not await the attack of the infantry. Three days later (10 March) they made a determined stand at Driefontein and there the brunt of the fighting fell on the 6th division, which Kelly-Kenny handled with such skill that the Boers never again accepted a pitched battle. After the occupation of Bloemfontein and Lord Roberts's advance to Pretoria, Kelly-Kenny was left in command in the Free State, where his chief business was to protect the long railway communications against General Christian De Wet's numerous raids. In the autumn of 1900 he came home with Lord Roberts.

Kelly-Kenny had been promoted lieutenant-general in 1899, and in 1902 he received the K.C.B. for his services in the war. He was adjutant-general of the forces from 1901 to 1904. In 1904 he received the G.C.B., and he was promoted general in 1905. In the latter year he accompanied Prince Arthur of Connaught on the mission sent to confer the order of the Garter on the Mikado. He retired in 1907 and died 26 December 1914 at Brighton. He was unmarried.

[Sir J. F. Maurice, *History of the War in South Africa, 1899–1902*, vols.i, ii, 1906–1908 ; personal knowledge.] F. M.

KENDAL, WILLIAM HUNTER (1843–1917), actor-manager, whose real name was WILLIAM HUNTER GRIMSTON, the eldest son of Edward Hunter Grimston, by his wife, Louisa Ryder, was born in London 16 December 1843. He made his first appearance on the stage at the old Soho (afterwards the Royalty) Theatre 6 April 1861, as Louis XIV in *A Life's Revenge*, assuming the name of Kendal for his debut. He remained at this theatre nearly a year. In 1862 he went to the Moor Street Theatre, Birmingham, and subsequently became a member of the stock company at the Theatre Royal, Glasgow, where he remained four years, playing a great number of parts and acquiring much experience. He then returned to London and was engaged by John Baldwin Buckstone [q.v.] for the Haymarket Theatre, making his first appearance there 31 October 1866 as Angus Mandeville in *A Dangerous Friend.* He remained a member of this company for eight years, playing numerous leading parts. Among those of which he was the original exponent were Bob Levitt (*Mary Warner*, June 1869), Prince Philamir (*The Palace of Truth*, November 1870), Pygmalion (*Pygmalion and Galatea*, December 1871), Ethais (*The Wicked World*, January 1873), and Frederick Smailey (*Charity*, January 1874). In addition he played numerous parts in revivals of old comedy and standard plays, such as Master Wildrake (*The Love Chase*), Charles Surface, Orlando, Romeo, Captain Absolute, Young Marlow, and Dazzle (*London Assurance*). During 1874–1875, in conjunction with his wife Margaret (Madge) Robertson, sister of the dramatist Thomas William Robertson [q.v.], whom he had married in August 1869, he fulfilled engagements at the Opera Comique and Gaiety Theatre ; and then in 1875 he entered into 'silent' partnership with (Sir) John Hare [q.v.] at the Court Theatre. Here he played Harry Armytage (*Lady Flora*, March 1875), Christian Douglas (*A Nine Days' Wonder*, June 1875), Prince Florian (*Broken Hearts*, December 1875), and Colonel Blake (in a revival of *A Scrap of Paper*, March 1876). Together with his wife he was then engaged by the Bancrofts for the Prince of Wales's Theatre, first appearing there in *Peril* (September 1876), in which he made a great success as Dr. Thornton. For two years he continued there successfully, as George Clarke (*The Vicarage*), Charles Courtly (*London Assurance*), and Julian Beauclerc (*Diplomacy*), the last-mentioned part being one of his greatest successes. In 1879 he rejoined John Hare at the Court Theatre, and played in *A Scrap of Paper*, *The Ladies' Battle*, and *The Queen's Shilling*. In October 1879, at the St. James's Theatre, he entered into an open partnership with Hare which lasted until July 1888. Many notable productions were made during this period, in most of which Kendal played leading parts. An early production (December 1879) was Lord Tennyson's one-act play, *The Falcon*, in which Kendal played Count Alberighi. Subsequently he played John Mildmay (in a revival of *Still Waters Run Deep*), William (*William and Susan*, a new version of *Black-Eye'd Susan*), Lord Kingussie (*The Moneyspinner*), Lieutenant Thorndyke (*The Squire*), Captain Crichton (*Impulse*), Philippe Derblay (*The Ironmaster*, in which he was very successful), Orlando, Geoffrey Roydant (*Mayfair*), Lord Clancarty (*Lady Clancarty*), and Sir Walter Amyot (*The Wife's Secret*).

After July 1888 Kendal and his wife spent much time in touring the English provinces and the United States, though many London engagements under their own management intervened. At the Court Theatre (March 1889) he played Ira Lee in *The Weaker Sex*, which was followed by a fine performance of the part of Sir John Molyneux in *A White Lie.* In October 1889, on their first visit to America, they opened at the Fifth Avenue Theatre, New York, in *A Scrap of Paper*. Further tours followed and several new productions were made. A season at the Avenue Theatre, London, was begun in January 1893, but was not very successful. While on tour in 1893–1896 Kendal added to his repertory Aubrey Tanqueray (*The Second Mrs. Tanqueray*), Sir John Frosdyke (*The Fall of the Leaf*), Mr. Armitage (*The Greatest of These*). The last of these plays was performed with success at the Garrick Theatre in June 1896. In the course of a subsequent tour *The Elder Miss Blossom* was produced, and this proved so successful that it was staged for a season at the St. James's in September 1898. Kendal played through two more London seasons at the St. James's, in 1901 and 1905, and he made several appearances at the King's Theatre, Hammersmith, and the Coronet Theatre, Notting Hill; but he produced no new play of striking importance, and in 1908 he retired from the stage.

Kendal was a 'safe' actor, but from 1869 he was more or less overshadowed by his more brilliant wife, with whom he acted constantly. He will be best remembered as an excellent comedian, although occasionally his serious work was sound. Probably his best parts were those in *Peril*, *The Queen's Shilling*, *Diplomacy*, *A White Lie*, and *The Elder Miss Blossom*. In his younger days he was a handsome and attractive man, and he was an admirable manager, with fine business ability. He died in London 6 November 1917, leaving a fortune exceeding £66,000.

Kendal had five children by his marriage—two sons and three daughters.

[*The Times*, 8 November 1917; *Who's Who in the Theatre*; private correspondence; personal knowledge.] J. P.

KENNEDY, Sir WILLIAM RANN (1846–1915), judge, the eldest son of the Rev. William James Kennedy, was born at 9 Campden Hill Villas, Kensington, 11 March 1846. His father, the fourth son of the Rev. Rann Kennedy [q.v.], was successively secretary to the National Society, H.M. inspector of schools, and vicar of Barnwood, Gloucestershire. His mother was Sarah Caroline Kennedy, who was her husband's cousin. Kennedy came of a family of distinguished classical scholars, three of his uncles, Benjamin Hall Kennedy [q.v.], Charles Rann Kennedy [q.v.], and George John Kennedy, having been senior classics and winners of the Porson prize, while his father was also Porson prizeman as well as Powis medallist. Kennedy himself was educated at Eton and King's College, Cambridge, and carried on the family tradition by gaining the Craven and Bell scholarships and the Powis and Browne medals, and by becoming senior classic in 1868. He was also president of the Cambridge Union Society. After taking his degree he taught the sixth form at Harrow for a year under Dr. Henry Montagu Butler [q.v.]. From 1868 to 1874 he was fellow of Pembroke College, Cambridge. From 1870 to 1871 he acted as private secretary to Mr. (afterwards Viscount) Goschen at the Poor Law Board. He was called to the bar by Lincoln's Inn in 1871 and read in the chambers of R. J. Williams. After call he joined the Northern circuit and settled as a 'local' barrister at Liverpool in 1873. He soon acquired a substantial practice, particularly in commercial and shipping cases. He moved to London in 1882 and in 1885 he took silk. In 1891 he published a work on the *Law of Civil Salvage*, which became the recognized authority on the subject. A keen liberal in politics, he made several unsuccessful attempts to enter the House of Commons, contesting Birkenhead in 1885 and 1886 and St. Helens in 1892. In 1892, at the unusually early age of forty-six, he was nominated by Lord Herschell to a judgeship in the Queen's bench division in succession to Mr. Justice Denman, and was knighted. As a judge of first instance he tried two cases which attracted popular interest, namely *Allen* v. *Flood* (1895), *Flood* v. *Jackson* (1898), a case on the liability of trade union officials, and *Ashby's Cobham Brewery Co.* (1906), a compensation case under the Licensing Act of 1904. From 1897 onwards Kennedy frequently sat in the 'commercial court' which had been set up in 1895.

On the appointment of Lord Cozens-Hardy [q.v.] to the mastership of the Rolls in 1907, Kennedy was appointed a lord justice of the Court of Appeal, and was sworn of the Privy Council. In the Court of Appeal he enhanced his judicial reputation, and on more than one occasion his dissenting judgments were upheld by the House of Lords. He died on 17 January 1915 at his London home, at the age of sixty-eight.

Kennedy's judgments were the fruit of great experience and learning, of an intellect which, though acute, was never the victim of its own subtlety, and of a complete mastery of lucid expression.

His self-effacing nature kept him free from any trace of intellectual vanity or legal pedantry. His care and patience in weighing the merits of the weakest case were as unvarying as his courtesy and kindness to practitioners, especially to the less experienced among them, and he was regarded with affection as well as admiration by a wide circle of colleagues and friends. He was deeply interested in the study of international law, and long played a leading part in the work of the International Law Association, of which he was president from 1908 to 1910. He became a member of the Institut de Droit International in 1913. He kept up his classical scholarship to the end of his life, and published a translation of the *Plutus* of Aristophanes in 1912. He was elected an honorary fellow of Pembroke College, Cambridge, in 1893, and a fellow of the British Academy in 1909.

Kennedy married in 1874 Cecilia Sarah, daughter of George Richmond, R.A. [q.v.]. He had four sons and one daughter.

[*The Times*, 18 January 1915; *Law Quarterly Review*, April 1915; *Journal of the Society of Comparative Legislation*, July 1915; *Proceedings* of the British Academy, 1915–1916; the Law Reports; Reports of Commercial Cases; private information.]

D. D.

KEPPEL, Sir GEORGE OLOF ROOS- (1866–1921), soldier and Anglo-Indian administrator. [See Roos-Keppel.]

KIDD, BENJAMIN (1858–1916), sociologist, born 9 September 1858, was the eldest son of Benjamin Kidd, sometime of the Royal Irish Constabulary. He had few early advantages of education or social position. In 1877, at the age of nineteen, he obtained a post in the civil service, and entered the Inland Revenue department at Somerset House. Here he worked in obscurity for seventeen years till the publication of his *Social Evolution* in 1894 made him famous; but during all that time he had been striving incessantly to extend his knowledge and improve his material position. The success of *Social Evolution* was so great that Kidd was able to resign his official post and devote himself entirely to writing. Between 1894 and 1902, when his *Principles of Western Civilization* appeared, he travelled extensively in the United States and Canada (1898), and in South Africa (1902), and also became acquainted with many important people in London in the circles of politics, science, and literature. While in America he wrote for *The Times* the series of articles afterwards published in 1898 under the title *The Control of the Tropics*. The last twelve years of his life he spent in ever increasing seclusion. In 1903 he left the neighbourhood of London and lived, first at Tonbridge, and later at Ditchling, Sussex. In 1908 he delivered the annual Herbert Spencer lecture before the university of Oxford, entitled *Individualism and After*; in 1911 he wrote the article *Sociology* for the eleventh edition of the *Encyclopædia Britannica*. In 1910 he began to work upon his last book, *The Science of Power*, which his son, Franklin Kidd, published in 1918, two years after his father's death. It was finished in its earlier form in 1914; but the outbreak of the European War necessitated a complete revision, which was not finished till the very close of the author's life. After a short period of ill-health Kidd died of heart disease at South Croydon 2 October 1916.

The remarkable success of *Social Evolution*, which was translated all over the world, needs some explanation at the present day. Its main idea is that religion is the central feature of human history. Moral progress consists in compelling individual selfishness to subordinate itself to the common good. Reason gives no help in this struggle; all our help comes from religion. It is religion which has been the chief agency in promoting philanthropy and the political enfranchisement of the masses. Reason is always selfish and short-sighted. Superior intelligence is not really a quality conducing either to virtue in the individual or to survival in the race. The book also contains a violent attack on socialism, and achieved a large measure of success by commending itself to some powerful but reactionary sections of public opinion. Kidd certainly was not wanting in the gifts of the popular philosopher: a sense of the great issues involved in social and political history, a power of emphasizing and reiterating his points, and a boundless self-confidence and conviction of the importance of his message. Some of his views are interesting and a few of them are true, especially his insistence on the importance of the emotional element in man, which was less of a commonplace thirty years ago than it is to-day. But he had no power of forming his ideas into a coherent system. His literary style was bad, and became worse as he went on writing; it is full of pretentious rhetoric, more suitable to sensational journalism than to the exposition of philosophic ideas. No wonder that academic circles always refused to take his books seriously.

The *Principles of Western Civilization*, which was announced as the 'first volume of a system of evolutionary philosophy', is very long, verbose, and obscure, and was much less successful than *Social Evolution*. It does not add much to the content of the earlier book. There is the same glorification of religion and attack upon reason. Kidd surveys an immense field of history to support his arguments, but is nowhere convincing. *The Science of Power* has more novelty and repeated his earlier success. Power, he says, consists in 'the enthusiasm of the ideal'. The great agent in creating and diffusing this enthusiasm is woman. Woman is naturally anti-pagan, i.e. unselfish, and devoted to the interests of the race, which is in accordance with the spirit of Christianity. Thus does Kidd appeal simultaneously to devout churchmen and to the supporters of feminism.

Kidd was an enthusiastic naturalist, and his son, Franklin, published in 1921 a volume of his father's papers on natural history, entitled *A Philosopher with Nature*.

Kidd married in 1887 Maud Emma Isabel, daughter of John Perry, of Weston-super-Mare, and had three sons.

[*The Times*, 3 October 1916; *Who's Who*, 1916; private information.] H. S—T.

KINGSBURGH, Lord (1836–1919), lord justice-clerk of Scotland. [See Macdonald, Sir John Hay Athole.]

KINNEAR, ALEXANDER SMITH, first Baron Kinnear, of Spurness, Orkney (1833–1917), judge, was born in Edinburgh 3 November 1833, the son of John Gardiner Kinnear, merchant, of Glasgow, by his wife, Mary, daughter of Alexander Smith, banker. He was educated at the universities of Glasgow and Edinburgh, passing advocate at the Scots bar in 1856. Business did not flow in apace for many years, but he was making himself all the time. His bent was toward what, in England, would have been a Chancery practice. He had a knowledge of law, especially of the feudal system, which few could equal, none could excel. His opportunity came with the mass of litigation consequent on the failure of the City of Glasgow Bank in 1878. The liquidators sent him a general retainer, and he was called upon to lead counsel in much larger practice. He came triumphantly out of the ordeal, helped doubtless by the fact that the lord president, John Inglis, Lord Glencorse, had a high opinion of him, and listened with respect to all that he said. In 1881 he was elected dean of the Faculty of Advocates and became a Q.C. In 1882 he went on the bench. After being a lord ordinary for eight years he entered the first division (1890), when Inglis, for whom Kinnear had a veneration, was still in the chair. Kinnear remained in the division until he resigned in 1913. Throughout thirty-one years he proved himself to be, without doubt, a great judge. His courtesy was unwavering, his patience inexhaustible. His powerful and receptive intellect responded to every current in the course of an argument. He took great pains that the form of the opinions which he delivered should leave no doubt as to their meaning. He was a model of what an appellate judge should be.

Outside the court Kinnear rendered signal service to the state. He acted as chairman of the Scottish Universities commission from 1889 until 1897, when he received a peerage in recognition of his services. At the 251st meeting of the commission, which had framed 169 ordinances, Lord Kelvin paid a tribute to his unremitting attention. In 1904–1905 Kinnear was a member of the royal commission appointed after the judgment of the House of Lords in the Free Church case. He bore a heavy burden in acting on the executive commission thereafter set up to settle the rival claims of the churches. He occasionally sat to hear appeals in the House of Lords, and continued to do so after his resignation. Two masterly essays from his pen remain, written before he was thirty, on Catullus (*North British Review*, xxxvi, 204) and on Shelley (*Quarterly Review*, cx, 289). To read these is to realize that in Kinnear Scotland gained a lawyer and lost a man of letters. He loved Sir Walter Scott, all the more because he shared Scott's 'infinite love and sympathy with humanity'. He was given to hospitality, and ever ready to impart the treasures of his well-stored mind to those who penetrated his reserve. He took no part in politics. He died unmarried, in Edinburgh, 20 December 1917.

[Personal knowledge.] C. K. M.

KITCHENER, HORATIO HERBERT, first Earl Kitchener, of Khartoum and of Broome (1850–1916), field-marshal, the second son of Lieutenant-

Colonel Henry Horatio Kitchener, of Cossington, Leicestershire, and Crotter House, Ballylongford, co. Kerry, by his first wife, Anne Frances, daughter of the Rev. John Chevallier, M.D. [q.v.], vicar of Aspall, Suffolk, was born at Crotter House 24 June 1850. Colonel Kitchener before settling in Ireland had served in the 13th Dragoons and 9th Foot. Owing to the illness of Mrs. Kitchener the family moved, when Herbert was thirteen years old, to Switzerland, where he was educated in a French school and acquired a knowledge of the French language which he never afterwards lost. In 1868 he passed into the Royal Military Academy, Woolwich, and passed out in December 1870, having qualified for a commission in the Royal Engineers. It was at this time, while he was waiting for the gazette, that the French, fired by Gambetta's eloquence, were attempting to create new armies to resist the Germans and to relieve Paris, their regular forces having been almost completely destroyed. Kitchener's parents were living at the time at Dinan, and his affection for France inspired him to offer his services to the army of the Loire. His time with it was short, for he fell ill, but it was remembered by the French Republic, which in 1913 conferred on him the medal commemorative of the campaign. On his return to England he was reprimanded by the commander-in-chief, the Duke of Cambridge, for a breach of discipline, but none the less he received his commission in the Royal Engineers (1871). After a few years of routine service at home, he was lent in 1874 to the Palestine Exploration Fund, and so began a connexion with the East which was to last almost for the remainder of his life. His work in Palestine enabled him to acquire a sound knowledge of the Arabs and of their language, and at the same time his exploration of the Holy Land developed the religious bent in a mind naturally devout. Kitchener's sympathies were then, and remained throughout his life, with the high church party of the Church of England; and though never either a zealot or a bigot he was always a convinced and professing Christian. In 1878, when Great Britain acquired Cyprus under the Treaty of Berlin, Kitchener was sent to survey the island. The work was broken off for lack of funds, to be resumed in 1880; he spent the interval as vice-consul at Kastamuni in Asia Minor.

In 1882, when the Egyptian army under Arabi Pasha rebelled, Kitchener was naturally eager to join the expedition under Sir Garnet (afterwards Viscount) Wolseley [q.v.]. The high commissioner of Cyprus said that he could not be spared; but, obtaining short leave of absence, he went to Alexandria and was able to take a small and entirely unofficial part in the campaign. He and another officer disguised themselves as Levantines and reconnoitred the route up the Nile valley from Alexandria towards Cairo, this being the first of a long series of such adventures which he was later to undertake. On his return to Cyprus after the enterprise he had some difficulty in placating the high commissioner. At the end of 1882 the survey of Cyprus was nearly completed, and Kitchener then accepted from Sir Henry Evelyn Wood [q.v.], who had been appointed first British sirdar of the Egyptian army, the offer of the post of second in command of the Egyptian cavalry. In 1883 he devoted two months' leave to a survey of the Sinai Peninsula, which he linked up with his survey of Palestine. In the following year the insurrection of the Sudanese under the Mahdi assumed serious proportions, and Kitchener was sent up the Nile to the frontier of Egypt proper, to endeavour to establish communication with Berber, which was besieged by the Mahdists. Berber surrendered 20 May 1884, and the men on the spot at once realized the gravity of the situation. Kitchener said that it would take 20,000 British troops to crush the Mahdi, but the home government shuddered at the thought of so serious an enterprise. Kitchener's task on the frontier then became that of endeavouring to establish communications with Khartoum, in which General Gordon was shut up, and to confirm the allegiance of wavering Mudirs. This work involved many adventurous rides into the desert, often in disguise. It was not until August that the British government took the step of sending an expedition up the Nile, too late as it proved, to relieve Gordon. Throughout this expedition Kitchener served in Wolseley's intelligence department, and in that capacity guided across the Bayuda desert the ill-fated column under Sir Herbert Stewart [q.v.]. It fell to him to receive the first refugees from Khartoum and to send up the first authoritative report of Gordon's death (26 January 1885). In July 1885 Kitchener resigned his commission in the Egyptian army and returned to England. He was now a brevet lieutenant-colonel with an established reputation as an authority on the habits and customs of the Arabs, Sudanese, and Egyptians, and as a keen, hard-working, and able soldier. After a short spell of leave at home he was nominated, at the request of the Foreign Office, as the British member of a joint English, French, and German commission appointed at the close of 1885 to delimit the territory of the sultan of Zanzibar, a work made necessary by the general scramble of the European powers for territory in Africa, which was then in full course.

On his way home from East Africa in the summer of 1886, Kitchener received the news of his appointment as governor-general of the Eastern Sudan, with head-quarters at Suakin; this post he held till 1888. Here he was in constant conflict with Osman Digna, the local leader of the Dervishes, and on 17 January 1888 he was severely wounded in the jaw in a raid on that chief's head-quarters. For his work at Suakin he was made brevet colonel and aide-de-camp to Queen Victoria. After his recovery he was appointed in September adjutant-general of the Egyptian army, of which Sir Francis (afterwards Baron) Grenfell was then sirdar. In the summer of 1889 the Dervishes threatened an advance down the Nile into Egypt, and a considerable part of the Egyptian army was concentrated to meet them, Kitchener being given the command of the cavalry. On 2 August Grenfell heavily defeated the Dervishes at Toski, a success in which Kitchener's handling of the cavalry had no small part, and all fear of an invasion of Egypt was removed. For his services in this campaign Kitchener received the C.B. Then, at the request of Sir Evelyn Baring (afterwards Earl of Cromer, q.v.), Kitchener undertook the reorganization of the Egyptian police, and acquired Baring's confidence to such an extent that, when Grenfell resigned the sirdarship (April 1892), Baring pressed for and obtained Kitchener's appointment as his successor. Kitchener had always maintained that the only possible solution of the problem of the Nile valley was to advance into the Sudan and to defeat the Dervishes; and for the next four years he devoted himself to the preparation of the Egyptian army for that task. He attracted to the service of that army a body of young, able, and energetic British officers, before whom he set, both by example and precept, a high standard of keenness and enterprise. With their help he infused a new spirit into the Egyptian Army, the fighting power of which had been materially increased by the formation of battalions of Sudanese. Kitchener's reforms were not always pleasing to the pashas, who intrigued against him with the khedive, but he was now sufficiently acquainted with the methods of Eastern courts to be able to forestall these manœuvres, and he found in Lord Cromer an unwavering ally. He was created K.C.M.G. in 1894. The preparations for the conquest of the Sudan revived the old controversy as to the rival merits of the desert and the Nile routes, but Kitchener obtained the approval of the home government for his plan of a methodical advance up the river.

In 1896 the River War was inaugurated by an advance on Dongola, the first stage of which was completed by the defeat of a Dervish force at Firket on 7 June. By the end of September Dongola was occupied and the Dervishes had been driven from the province of that name into the Bayuda desert. Kitchener was now promoted major-general and for his services in this campaign was created K.C.B. The winter of 1896–1897 and the following spring were spent in persuading the home government to agree to a further advance, and in making preparations for that end. The plan on which Kitchener had decided was first to move up the Nile and secure Abu Hamed, where the river bends westward to make a great loop round the Korosko desert, and then to build a railway across that desert from Wadi Halfa. The first of these undertakings was entrusted to Major-General Sir Archibald Hunter, who seized Abu Hamed with small loss on 7 August, and thereby created such a panic amongst the Dervishes that, to the general surprise and delight, he was able on 5 September without opposition to occupy Berber, which had been seized by friendly tribesmen on 31 August. These successes brought the reoccupation of Khartoum and the complete reconquest of the Sudan within reach; and the British Cabinet, and Lord Salisbury in particular—converted to reliance on Kitchener's judgement—promised him for the following year the support of British troops and the leadership in the last stage of the enterprise. By the end of January 1898 the greater part of the Egyptian army, with a British brigade under Major-General Sir William Forbes Gatacre [q.v.], was concentrated south of Berber, near the mouth of the Atbara river. The successor of the Mahdi, the Khalifa Abdullah, now thoroughly alarmed at Omdurman, sent a force of 20,000 men under Mahmud, his leading emir, to recapture Berber; but Mahmud, finding that Kitchener had so far anticipated him on the Atbara as to make a march on Berber impossible without fighting, established his army in a strong zariba on the river. The zariba was stormed by the combined Anglo-Egyptian force on 8 April, Mahmud himself was captured with 4,000 other prisoners, and his army dispersed.

The British government had for some time been aware that a small French expedition under Major Marchand had started from the Congo for the White Nile; and this fact, together with the completeness of the success won on the Atbara, decided the Cabinet to authorize an advance on Omdurman at the next high Nile, and to increase the British force under Kitchener to the strength of a division. By the end of August 8,200 British and 17,000 Egyptian troops were concentrated under Kitchener's command at the head of the Sixth Cataract, about 120 miles north of Omdurman. The greater part of this distance was covered without opposition, and by 1 September the whole force was assembled on the Nile some seven miles north of Omdurman, to find a Dervish army of 50,000 men, under the Khalifa himself, encamped in the plain between it and the Dervish capital. The battle of Omdurman, which took place on 2 September, was fought in two phases. In the first the Dervishes in a determined advance upon the Anglo-Egyptian troops, who were in position on the river bank, were mowed down by artillery, rifle, and machine-gun fire. Kitchener then ordered an advance on Omdurman, and during this movement the Khalifa's reserve attacked the first Egyptian brigade under Colonel (Sir) Hector Archibald Macdonald [q.v.], and the situation, which was for a time critical, was saved by the steadiness of the brigade and the prompt arrival of support from the British division. Organized resistance then ceased and the Dervish army was dispersed with enormous loss. The Khalifa fled to Kordofan; and on 4 September the British and Egyptian flags were hoisted over the ruins of Gordon's palace in Khartoum, which for twelve years had been Kitchener's goal. The next step was to convince Major Marchand, who with seven French officers and eighty native troops had arrived at Fashoda, that he could not hoist the French flag in the khedive's dominions. For this purpose Kitchener went with an escort up the White Nile. The interview was conducted with perfect courtesy and the Egyptian flag was hoisted over Fashoda with the customary salute. After a fierce but brief outburst of popular wrath in France, the French government gave way, and the last serious incident with France which preceded the *entente cordiale* was amicably settled.

Kitchener then came home to be received with great enthusiasm. He had wiped out the unpleasant memory of the sacrifice of Gordon, and had removed an outstanding menace to Egypt, at the cost of 60 British and 160 Egyptian lives. He was hailed by Lord Salisbury as not only a distinguished general but a first-class administrator. He was raised to the peerage as Baron Kitchener, of Khartoum, received the thanks of parliament, and was fêted in England, Scotland, and Wales. The first use which he made of his popularity was to raise a fund for the establishment and endowment of a college at Khartoum, which should at once perpetuate Gordon's memory and fulfil one of Gordon's plans for the benefit of the Sudan. He returned as governor-general of the Sudan, with sufficient money for that purpose and with the task of creating a civil administration for the country. Throughout the River War Kitchener's part had been rather that of a brilliant improviser of ways and means than of a commander in the field or of a profound student of war. He had left most of the fighting to Hunter, though he was present himself at the principal actions, and his triumph was one of firmness of purpose and of driving power in the face of great natural difficulties. In the light of the subsequent collapse of Mahdism it is easy to underrate his achievement; but up to the time of the final advance on Omdurman the Dervishes were a name of terror, and it required courage, character, and judgement of a high degree to persuade a government, rendered doubtful and cautious by previous failures, to authorize the successive steps which led to the overthrow of the Khalifa.

The greater part of the year 1899 was devoted to completing the pacification of the Sudan, and to hunting down the Khalifa, who was at large in Kordofan with a dwindling band of followers. This last task was brought to an end by Sir Reginald Wingate, who was destined to be Kitchener's successor as sirdar, on 22 November when the Khalifa was killed in a final stand. Within a month of this event Kitchener was called to other and more important duties.

The critical weeks which followed the outbreak of the South African War in October 1899, culminating in the second week of December in the successive reverses of Stormberg, Magersfontein, and Colenso, made both the government and the public realize that a struggle with the Boers was a serious matter. The decisions, therefore, to send large reinforcements to South Africa and to appoint Lord Roberts [q.v.] to the chief command with Kitchener as his chief of the staff were received with general approval. Kitchener was at Khartoum on 18 December when he received his orders, and, starting at once, was able to join Lord Roberts at Gibraltar on 27 December. During Roberts's command Kitchener rarely performed the functions of chief of the staff. He was employed far more as a second in command and the representative of the commander-in-chief in his absence, so that his duties were executive rather than advisory, and he had very free scope for the employment of his limitless energy and readiness to accept responsibility. His first business was to reorganize the transport, and to make that increase in the number of mounted troops which was needed to give the force the mobility required for the execution of Roberts's plans. When, early in February, the movement for the relief of Kimberley had begun and General Piet Cronje had retreated from Magersfontein, Kitchener was with the leading troops urging on the pursuit, and not at Lord Roberts's side. So when Cronje was forced to stand at Paardeberg, it was Kitchener, with full powers from the commander-in-chief in his pocket, who ordered the attack and directed the operations. The first attack (18 February) on Cronje's laager failed, and failed largely because of Kitchener's faulty tactical dispositions. He had with him only a small personal staff and could not effectively direct the movements of a considerable body of troops scattered over a wide area. Methods applicable to troops in the close formation used in the Sudan against ill-armed natives were not suited to the wide extensions necessary against a determined enemy armed with modern rifles. The attacks were therefore disconnected and were repulsed in succession. Kitchener wished to renew them the next day, but Roberts arrived and decided to blockade the laager instead. There can be no doubt that Kitchener's original decision to attack was right, and it is highly probable that a new and better-arranged attack on the laager on the day following the battle would not only have been successful but would have been less costly than the direct and consequential losses of the blockade, while the time gained might have been of great value. The incident is indeed typical of Kitchener's character and career. His judgement on larger issues was almost always uncannily correct, and he never lacked the courage to put his judgement to the test. His failures were generally due to a lack of knowledge of technical detail, and to a dislike, amounting almost to contempt, of deliberate methods, which he was disposed to regard as red tape. He was accused, but with injustice, of callousness and disregard for the lives of his men. His natural shyness and reserve, accentuated by years of solitary work in the East, made him almost incapable of expressing deep feeling; but he was essentially tender-hearted, and certainly not lacking in consideration for the soldier.

Five days before the surrender of Cronje at Paardeberg (27 February), Kitchener was sent by Roberts to open up railway communications across the Orange river towards Bloemfontein, and was next employed in suppressing a rebellion of the Cape Boers about Priska, and in clearing the southern portion of the Orange Free State. Everywhere he went he endeavoured to infuse the spirit of energy which he had inculcated in Egypt, but found sadly lacking in South Africa, where he said the War was taken 'too much like a game of polo with intervals for afternoon tea'. During Roberts's advance through Pretoria to Koomati Poort, Kitchener varied intervals of office work at head-quarters with expeditions to clear the lines of communication from the Boer raiders, who were becoming increasingly numerous and were usually led by that bold and enterprising leader of guerrillas, Christian De Wet. In one of these Kitchener was all but captured in a night surprise, and had to ride for his life. In November 1900 Roberts's forces had reached the frontiers of Portuguese East Africa; President Kruger had fled, and organized resistance seemed to be at an end. Lord Roberts therefore came home, and Kitchener was left as commander-in-chief to wind up the campaign.

It soon appeared that De Wet had taught the Boers the possibilities of guerrilla warfare, and that the War was far from over. Kitchener met these tactics of the Boers by employing an elaboration of the methods which he had already used in the Orange Free State. Lines of block-houses were established criss-cross through the country, and a series of drives by mounted troops, starting from these barriers, was organized against the guerrillas. This was a slow and wearisome business. Again and again the elusive Boers avoided the mounted columns and broke through the barriers; but gradually, and after many failures, the resistance of the Boers was worn down. One feature in this scheme of subjugation provoked much criticism. The Boers were without any organized systems of supply, and every farm was for them a depot. Flocks and herds were therefore removed, grain was carted away or destroyed, and farms were gutted. This made it necessary to provide for the Boer women and children, who were assembled in concentration camps where sickness soon became prevalent and the rate of mortality was for a time very high. This sickness could not, in fact, be ascribed to any neglect on the part of the British authorities, but the result was that sympathisers with the Boers were provided with apparent grounds for agitation. Moreover, the plan almost certainly had the adverse effect of prolonging the enemy's resistance by relieving the Boers in the field of the responsibility of caring for their dependents. In June 1901 there appeared to be some prospect that the Free State and Transvaal would surrender, but the waverers were rallied by an appeal from Kruger to hold out, and by a series of risings in the Cape Colony, ably led by General Johannes Smuts. But, as in Egypt, Kitchener, having formed his plan, adhered to it, and continued to multiply lines of block-houses, and to organize drives. The end did not come till 31 May 1902, and was then reached largely because of Kitchener's moderating influence upon the terms which Lord Milner, the high commissioner, desired to impose. On his return to England in July Kitchener received a viscounty, with special remainder, and became one of the original members of the order of merit.

After a few months' rest Kitchener left England in October to take up the post of commander-in-chief in India, breaking his voyage in order to go to Khartoum and open the Gordon Memorial College. The distribution of troops in India had not been varied materially since the reorganization which followed the Mutiny, and the system of military administration was in many ways too much centralized. Kitchener had little difficulty in gaining official acceptance of his plans for removing many of the details of army administration from headquarters to the commands, and for arranging a grouping of the garrisons more in accordance with the existing problems of the defence of India, and better calculated to promote the health and efficiency of the troops. But in his attempts to improve the higher administration of the army in India he encountered serious obstacles. He found in Lord Curzon a masterful viceroy convinced of the necessity of making the civil power predominant, and suspicious of any measures that had the appearance of increasing the authority of the soldier. The existing system provided for a military member of the viceroy's council, independent of the commander-in-chief. He had what amounted to the power of vetoing any proposal of the commander-in-chief which involved expenditure. Kitchener, while recognizing the importance of maintaining the supreme authority of the viceroy, urged the abolition of the system of dual control in a long controversy, in which his arguments prevailed with Mr. (afterwards Viscount) Morley, then secretary-of-state for India. As commander-in-chief he initiated more reforms than any of his predecessors, not excepting even Lord Roberts, who had the advantage of a life-long knowledge of the Indian army. Kitchener not only succeeded in improving the central administration and the machinery for mobilization, but he also modernized the system of training, and gave a great stimulus to military education by establishing a Staff College in India. It is certain that without the reforms which he instituted India could not have given the Empire the assistance which she furnished during the European War.

On leaving India in September 1909, Kitchener was promoted field-marshal, and after a visit to the battlefields of the Russo-Japanese War, went to Australia and New Zealand to advise the dominion governments as to their organization for defence. He reached England in 1910 in order to receive the field-marshal's baton from the hands of King Edward VII. He then enjoyed some fifteen months of comparative leisure, broken only by his duties as a member of the Committee of Imperial Defence; and he profited by this to visit Turkey and the Sudan and to make a tour through British East Africa. In September 1911 he was appointed British agent and consul-general in Egypt. The prestige of that position had not unnaturally fallen somewhat with the departure of Lord Cromer, but Kitchener almost immediately succeeded in restoring it to its former height. The best tribute to his administration is that, during a period of great unrest in the Near East, when Turkey was engaged in two wars, it was uneventful. He succeeded in keeping Egypt quiet, and was able to devote himself almost entirely to social reforms, and to developing the commerce and resources of the country. The British government showed its gratitude by advising the King to confer on him an earldom, which he received in July 1914. He then returned to England for his annual holiday. When, a month later, war with Germany became imminent, he was on the point of returning to his post, but on 3 August he was recalled from Dover by Mr. Asquith in order to take over the seals of the secretary-of-state for war.

There was no other man then alive who, as head of the War Office, could have commanded so much of the confidence of the public, and that was in itself sufficient reason for Kitchener's appointment; nor was there anyone who had such first-hand knowledge of the military resources of the Empire as a whole. Within recent years he had examined on the spot the military problems of Egypt, India, Australia, New Zealand, Singapore, and East Africa, and from that knowledge the Empire was to reap great benefit. The gaps in his equipment were that he had little experience of the organization of the army at home, and none at all of the methods and machinery of the War Office, or of the system of Cabinet government; but there was more than compensation for these drawbacks in the fact that he entered the War Office fully conscious of the magnitude of the problem before the nation, and of the lamentable deficiencies in the preparations which had been made to meet that problem. Both soldiers and statesmen, in making plans for the event of war with Germany, conceived a struggle in which England should give full naval, but limited military, support to France; and the general conviction was that the complexity of modern international relations, more especially in the realm of finance, made a long war impossible. Of the statesmen and soldiers of Europe Kitchener alone envisaged from the first a war which would last three years, and he alone believed in the possibility of raising and putting in the field large new armies during the War. On entering the War Office he immediately made plans for the expansion of the British army of six regular and fourteen territorial divisions to seventy divisions; and it is not too much to say that this provision not only saved the British Empire from destruction, but Europe from German domination. It is probably true that the expansion of the British army could have been carried through more smoothly and expeditiously by expanding the territorial army than by creating new armies; but Kitchener was not familiar with the effect of Lord Haldane's work upon the territorial army, and his experience in South Africa led him to distrust the influence of county magnates in the formation of new units, while it is also probable that he was to some extent led away by his taste for improvisation. The fact remains that he brought his plans to completion, and in the third year of the War he had seventy divisions either in, or ready for, the field, an achievement which no one in 1914 had believed to be possible. When the public learned in May 1915 that the British forces in France were severely hampered by the lack of high explosive shell, Kitchener was made the target of a bitter attack in a section of the press. The Ministry of Munitions and the systematic mobilization of industry for the manufacture of munitions which resulted therefrom were very necessary additions to the machinery for the conduct of the War; but no arrangements could have made up in the early part of 1915 for the lack of provision for the manufacture of high explosive shells and guns before the War, and until April 1916 the armies in the field were entirely supplied with shell under contracts made by Kitchener in the War Office. Munitions could not be improvised, nor very speedily manufactured, but in all other respects no armies in the field were ever better provided with what was needed both for efficiency and for comfort; this was made possible by Kitchener's immediate anticipation both of the length and of the extent of the War.

The newspaper attacks did not affect the confidence of the public in Kitchener, and the King's action in conferring on him the order of the Garter in June 1915 was widely approved. But at this time the relations of the war minister with some of his colleagues in the Cabinet were becoming strained, and as the difficulties of the war increased these relations did not tend to become more happy. Kitchener had from the first, and retained to the last, the confidence of Mr. Asquith; but, from the formation of the first coalition in May 1915, Mr. Asquith's influence declined, and other members of the government became anxious to know more about the conduct of the War, and to have a more active share in it. Kitchener's fine presence, his European reputation, his command of the French language, and his proved sympathy with France, made him an admirable negotiator. He was instrumental in smoothing over many of the early difficulties of the alliance, notably at the end of August 1914, when the enforced retreat of the British army after the battle of Le Cateau caused grave anxiety both to the French government and to the French commander-in-chief. But these qualities had not much influence with his colleagues in the Cabinet, where his natural reticence, his lack of experience of work in committee, and his inability to throw his ideas into the common stock, raised suspicions, usually groundless, but hard to meet. Nor was his administration of the War Office happy. He did not understand the methods of a government department, and most of the soldiers who were familiar with them had gone to France with the Expeditionary Force. This led to his taking too much work upon himself, and he became at one and the same time the adviser of the Cabinet on strategy and the organizer of an immense expansion of the British army. His methods often lacked system, and not infrequently produced friction; while, for lack of competent advice and of time for due consideration, his conduct of the strategy of the War was more than once open to criticism, though he was often right when others were wrong. Just as he foresaw the length of the War, so he foresaw also that the Germans would march through Belgium north of the Meuse in great strength, and soon after he entered the War Office he pointed out that the British army at Mons would be in an exposed and dangerous position. He deferred, however, to the opinion of the French and British soldiers who had prepared the plans of campaign. But, when the plans for attacking the Dardanelles were under discussion, he allowed himself to be influenced by those who believed that the navy could force the Straits unaided, and he was dragged into the military operations in circumstances which greatly prejudiced their success. Throughout this unfortunate campaign he was torn in divergent directions, on the one hand by his desire with limited means to sustain the British armies in France, and on the other by the need of prosecuting with vigour the attack upon the Straits. Thus there were at times hesitation and doubt when there should have been vigour and decision. When the failure of the Dardanelles campaign was evident, the government, some members of which were not reluctant to be relieved of his presence, sent him to the Near East to report on the possibility and advisability of evacuation. Reluctantly he came to the conclusion that the only course was to abandon the enterprise, and he returned to England at the end of November 1915 to advise the Cabinet to that effect. On his arrival he tendered to the prime minister his resignation, which was at once refused. He was now fully conscious of the defects in the administrative machinery at the War Office; and at the end of the year he brought Major-General Sir William Robertson from France to be chief of the Imperial General Staff, gave him greater powers than former chiefs of the staff had possessed, and authorized him to reorganize the general staff at head-quarters. Thenceforward there was little creaking of the wheels of military administration, though it was many months before the effect of the change could be seen, and Kitchener himself did not live to see it. On the morning of 5 June 1916 he sailed from Scapa Flow in H.M.S. *Hampshire* to visit Russia. The Russian government had long been anxious for his presence and advice; the British government hoped through his influence to revive the waning enthusiasm of the Russian armies, and to establish some method of co-operation between the Allied armies of Eastern and Western Europe. The circumstances of the loss of the *Hampshire* are not absolutely clear, but it appears that the cruiser, when off the Orkneys in bad weather, struck a mine and went down with the loss of all on board save a few of the crew [*The Loss of H.M.S. 'Hampshire'. Official Narrative*, 1926.]

The news of Kitchener's death was received with universal mourning and was treated as a public calamity of the first magnitude; a memorial service was held in St. Paul's Cathedral, where a chapel, in the north-west tower, is dedicated to his memory. Though his countrymen felt deeply the extent of their loss, the great work with which Kitchener's name will always be associated was in a measure completed. At his call and under his inspiration, more than 3,000,000 men had voluntarily joined the colours and had been organized into armies, an achievement without parallel in history. On the very day on which he left for Russia the last of the divisions to which his name was given by the public also sailed from

England. He had planned that the British armies in France should be at their greatest strength in the third year of the War, and he hoped that victory would be achieved in that year. He adhered to that plan with the same resolution which had brought him to Khartoum, and had ended the South African War. The British armies in France did reach their highest strength in 1917, and it is at least within the bounds of probability that had he lived he would have prevented some of those divided councils and divergences of purpose which contributed to the prolongation of the War into 1918.

Kitchener never married, and, in accordance with the special remainder, his brother, Colonel Henry Elliott Chevallier Kitchener, succeeded as second Earl.

A portrait of Kitchener was painted by Sir H. von Herkomer in 1891 against a background of Egyptian architecture executed by F. Goodall; this picture was presented to the National Portrait Gallery by Mr. Pandeli Ralli in 1916. There is also in the same gallery a portrait in pastel executed by C. Horsfall in 1899, and presented in 1916 by Sir Lees Knowles. There are other portraits by Sir A. S. Cope (1900) and the Hon. John Collier. A bronze bust by Sir William Goscombe John, is placed in the Gordon Memorial College at Khartoum; another, in marble, by Sir Hamo Thornycroft, was sculptured in 1917. The full-length effigy in marble executed in 1923 for the monument in St. Paul's Cathedral is by W. Read Dick. A statue by John Tweed was erected on the Horse Guards Parade in 1926. (See *Royal Academy Pictures* 1891, 1900, 1917, and 1923).

[W. S. Churchill, *The River War*, 1899; Sir J. F. Maurice and M. H. Grant, (Official) *History of the War in South Africa, 1899–1902*, 1906–1910; Sir George Arthur, *Life of Lord Kitchener*, 1920.]

F. M.

KITCHIN, GEORGE WILLIAM (1827–1912), dean of Winchester and of Durham, was born at Naughton, Suffolk, 7 December 1827, the fifth child of the Rev. Isaac Kitchin, rector of St. Stephen's, Ipswich, by his wife, Mary, daughter of the Rev. J. Bardgett, rector of Melmerby, Cumberland. He went to Ipswich grammar school and King's College School, London, and in 1846 was elected to a studentship at Christ Church, Oxford. In 1850 he graduated, with first classes in classics and mathematics; two years later he took orders and became a tutor of his college. In 1861, after some years as head master of a preparatory school at Twyford, Hampshire, he was appointed censor of Christ Church, a post which he held until 1863, when he married. During the next twenty years he lectured for several colleges, mainly on history. He also did good work for the University Press; he was secretary from 1866 to 1868 to the board of delegates, and for many years to the school-books committee; in the latter capacity he organized the first Clarendon Press editions of English classics, which did much to promote the serious study, if not the sympathetic appreciation, of English literature in schools. It was, however, as the first censor of non-collegiate students that Kitchin rendered his greatest services to Oxford. He held the position from 1868 to 1883; the organization which he established has been little altered, and it is largely due to his energy and tact that the experiment of admitting such students to the university has proved successful.

In 1883 Kitchin was appointed to the deanery of Winchester, and eleven years later to that of Durham. In both places he threw himself with characteristic ardour into the duties of his office, but he seems to have found Durham the more congenial, partly because of the close association of the cathedral and the university. Kitchin was ex-officio warden of University College, Durham, and after 1908 he was chancellor of the university. He died 13 October 1912.

Kitchin was a man of handsome presence and much charm of manner. His habitual zeal in the performance of the daily task was doubtless in part responsible for his failure to produce a great work of learning. His most ambitious literary undertaking—a *History of France*, in three volumes (1873–1877) — is interesting and still useful, but too slight in texture to be placed in the highest class of historical writings. While at Oxford he also wrote a *Life of Pope Pius II* (1881). At Winchester and Durham he busied himself largely with local history and archaeology. Among his later writings were a history of Winchester (1890) and a *Life of E. Harold Browne, Bishop of Winchester* (1895); he also edited several volumes of records for the Hampshire Record Society and the Surtees Society. Kitchin was a strong liberal in politics, and incurred much public disfavour by his outspoken support of the Boers during the South African War.

Kitchin married in 1863 Alice Maud, daughter of Bridges Taylor, British consul for Denmark, by whom he had three sons and two daughters.

[Notices in the *Guardian*, 18 October 1812, and other newspapers; Foster's *Alumni Oxonienses*; private information.] W. T. W.

KNOX-LITTLE, WILLIAM JOHN (1839–1918), divine and preacher, the sixth son of John Little, J.P., of Stewartstown, co. Tyrone, by his wife, Emily Kyle, was born at Stewartstown 1 December 1839. He was educated, as were several of his nine brothers, at the royal grammar school, Lancaster, whence he proceeded to Trinity College, Cambridge. He graduated B.A. with a third class in the classical tripos of 1862, and proceeded M.A. in 1865. He was ordained deacon in 1863, priest in 1864, and was an assistant master at his old school and curate of Christ Church, Lancaster, 1863–1864. He was next an assistant master at Sherborne School from 1864 to 1870. In 1870 he became curate-in-charge of Turweston, Buckinghamshire, a parish of 330 inhabitants. Here he worked devotedly as a parish priest, and discovered, it is said, by chance his powers as a preacher. Taking duty for a neighbour one winter afternoon, he was obliged to preach extempore. The effect was remarkable and his gifts soon became known.

In January 1874 Knox-Little (he transferred his third Christian name, Knox, to his surname at this time) took part in a general mission in London as missioner at St. Thomas's, Regent Street, and became curate there to the Rev. W. J. Richardson. His mission preaching made him famous, and in 1875 the dean of Manchester, Dr. Cowie, persuaded him to accept the benefice of St. Alban's, Cheetwood, Manchester, a parish of 15,000 people. Here he worked zealously, and his church rapidly became an important religious centre. In January 1877 he took Manchester itself by storm as preacher at the cathedral in a general mission; the effects were comparable with those produced by the Wesleys and Whitefield, and the services at the cathedral had to be duplicated.

Knox-Little was an uncompromising high churchman, and insisted frankly on the benefit of sacramental confession—teaching at that time most unpopular; but he never flinched before the fiercest puritan opposition, and he became a religious force both in England and in the United States. He conducted remarkable missions at Leeds parish church in 1883, and at St. Paul's Cathedral in 1884; at St. Paul's he was for some years the preacher at the Passion-tide services and drew vast congregations. His appeal was especially to men: naturally an orator, his experience as a public-school master had trained him to be a clear expositor, and in addition his strong vein of sympathy and his earnestness and sincerity were a great part of his charm to men in every rank of life.

In 1881 Knox-Little was appointed by the Crown to the residentiary canonry in Worcester Cathedral vacated by Dr. George Granville Bradley. He resigned St. Alban's, Cheetwood, in 1885 and accepted the vicarage of Hoar Cross, Staffordshire, where G. F. Bodley had built what was reputed to be the most beautiful modern parish church in England. He resigned it in 1907 and henceforth lived in Worcester, where he was sub-dean from 1902 and proctor in Convocation for the chapter from 1888 to 1911. For part of the South African War (1899–1902) Knox-Little served as a chaplain, first with the Brigade of Guards, later with the Household Cavalry. Officers and men alike were devoted to him, he was mentioned in dispatches, and received the Queen's medal and clasp. He was fearless of danger and used to carry the Sacrament to soldiers under fire. On their return he marched with the Guards through London. For many years the cathedral at Worcester was crowded when he preached; latterly his health, always delicate, broke; his voice began to fail, and he preached written sermons. But his pastoral zeal was unabated, and up to the end he exercised a deep individual influence on young men and lads in Worcester.

Between 1877 and 1891 Knox-Little published nine volumes of sermons and two short stories, *The Broken Vow* (1887) and *The Child of Stafferton* (1888); in 1893 he addressed to his old friend, Dr. W. J. Butler, dean of Lincoln, a controversial work, *Sacerdotalism, if rightly understood, the Teaching of the Church of England: a Letter in Four Parts.* In 1905 he published an interesting book on *The Conflict of Ideals in the Church of England.*

Few preachers have won a reputation so quickly as Knox-Little, or have enjoyed such wide popularity, but his success never weakened his character; he was utterly free from self-seeking, and he never flinched from taking the unpopular side. He was a man of unfailing humour, an omnivorous reader, a pianist, and a good linguist (he could preach as readily, it is said, in French as in English), and he was a spiritual guide of great integrity and wisdom. He had a thoughtful Irish face with the mouth of an orator. In appearance he was of middle height with broad shoulders and a pronounced stoop. His slight Irish accent added to the attraction of his low but most agreeable voice.

Knox-Little died at Worcester 3 February 1918, and is buried at Turweston. He married in 1866 Annette, eldest daughter of Henry Gregson, of Moorlands, Lancashire. They had ten children, six sons and four daughters, seven of whom survived their father.

[No memoir of Knox-Little has been published. The *Fountain*, 7 July 1881; *Yorkshire Post*, 6 February 1883; *Court and Society*, 30 September 1886; private information.]

S. L. O.

KNUTSFORD, first VISCOUNT (1825–1914). [See HOLLAND, Sir HENRY THURSTAN.]

LABOUCHERE, HENRY DU PRÉ (1831–1912), journalist and politician, was born in London 9 November 1831. He came of a French protestant stock established in Holland since the revocation of the Edict of Nantes. His grandfather, Pierre César Labouchere, was head of the great financial house of Hope, at Amsterdam, and left a very large fortune. The first of the family to settle in England, Pierre Labouchere purchased the estates of Hylands, Essex, and Over Stowey, Somerset, and married Dorothy Elizabeth, third daughter of Sir Francis Baring [q.v.]. The elder of their two sons was the whig politician, Henry Labouchere [q.v.], who held office in several governments, and was created Baron Taunton in 1859. His brother John, of Broome Hall, Dorking, was a partner in the firm of Hope, and later a partner in the bank of Williams, Deacon, Thornton, and Labouchere. He married Mary Louisa, second daughter of James Du Pré, of Wilton Park, Buckinghamshire. Henry Du Pré Labouchere was the eldest child of their family of three sons and six daughters.

All his life Labouchere was a rebel against constituted authority. He was educated at Eton, and afterwards went to Trinity College, Cambridge, where in two years he ran up debts amounting to £6,000. At the age of twenty-one he was sent to South America, where his family had important commercial interests. He found his way to Mexico and there wandered about for a year or two, fell in love with a circus lady, and joined the troupe. For six months he lived in a camp of Chippeway Indians.

Meanwhile, without his knowledge, his family had secured for Labouchere a place in the diplomatic service, and he learned, while in Mexico in 1854, that he had been appointed an attaché at Washington. He remained in the service for ten years and, after leaving Washington, was stationed in succession at Munich, Stockholm, Frankfort, St. Petersburg, Dresden, and Constantinople. According to his own accounts, he was insubordinate and indolent; and his passion for gambling shaped and coloured this period of his life wherever he went. But a man of his independence of mind would not have remained in the service for ten years unless he were really interested in it. The end came oddly. In 1864, at Baden-Baden, he was informed by the foreign secretary, Lord John Russell, of his appointment to a second secretaryship at Buenos Aires. He replied accepting the post, if he could fulfil the duties of it at Baden-Baden. This was not the first joke that he had tried on Lord John, and he was dismissed the service. It was his impish way of resigning. He had inherited a great fortune from his uncle, Lord Taunton, and his mind was turning to a political career.

In 1865 Labouchere was elected member of parliament for Windsor, in the liberal interest, but was unseated on petition. Two years later he was returned for Middlesex. He lost this seat in 1868, failed at Nottingham in 1874, and had to wait till 1880 before he was again in the House of Commons. Meanwhile, he won fame as a journalist. He wrote much for the *Daily News*, of which he had become part-proprietor; his letters from Paris during the siege of 1870 were republished as *The Diary of a Besieged Resident* (1871). For *The World*, founded (1874) and edited by his friend Edmund Yates [q.v.], he wrote on finance. Then, in 1876, he established a weekly journal, *Truth*, which for many years was by far the most successful of personal organs in the press. Labouchere was a first-class journalist. His reputation as a wit was well established; he had an easy style unsurpassed in clearness, and he wrote with candour about his own adventurous life and the follies and failings of his contemporaries. Above all, *Truth* won admiration and gratitude by its fearless exposure of fraudulent enterprises of all sorts. This brought upon him a long series of libel actions. Most of them he won, and they were such good advertisements of his paper that he could afford to be indifferent to his irrecoverable costs amounting to scores of thousands of pounds.

In 1880, with Charles Bradlaugh [q.v.] as his colleague, Labouchere began his twenty-five years' parliamentary representation of Northampton. For a dozen years an influential section of the nonconformist electors of Northampton had successfully opposed the candidature of Bradlaugh because he preached atheism. Labouchere, too, was a lifelong agnostic, but a silent one, and these same people gave him enthusiastic support: in his scoffing way Labouchere used to call himself the 'Christian member for Northampton'. He soon became one of the most powerful radicals in the Commons. His only hatred in politics was reserved for the whigs, who still retained an influence in the liberal party disproportionate to their numbers and to their support in the country. He attacked their methods and their purposes alike in home and foreign policy, and although publicly he always treated Gladstone with respect, privately he mocked at his fervour and 'mystifications'. He did not object, he once said, to Gladstone's always having the ace of trumps up his sleeve, but only to his pretence that God had put it there. Throughout the parliament of 1880–1885 Labouchere worked for an 'all-radical' government with Joseph Chamberlain [q.v.] at its head. Even before Gladstone 'flew' his first Home Rule 'kite', towards the end of 1885, Labouchere exploited his intimacy with the Irish nationalists in his campaign against the moderate liberals. A resourceful intriguer, he employed all his arts in the early months of 1886 to bring Chamberlain, Gladstone, and the Irish nationalists into agreement, using each in turn to further his plan of 'dishing the whigs'. When Chamberlain decided to vote against the first Home Rule Bill, it was the greatest disappointment of Labouchere's life, for it ruined his main enterprise. Thereafter his political zeal, though unabated, was diverted. The reorganization of the liberal party and doctrine, for which he had worked, and which might have altered the course of history, had become impossible. The cause of Home Rule owed much to him, and he assisted in exposing the forgeries of Richard Pigott [q.v.], by which it was sought to represent Parnell as inciting to assassination. Pigott's confession, after his cross-examination by Sir Charles Russell, was written at Labouchere's house.

If political services were the chief qualifications, there were strong reasons why Labouchere should have been given a place in the liberal government of 1892–1895. His exclusion, it was understood, was due to the objection of Queen Victoria, who held that the proprietor and editor of *Truth* ought not to be given office under the Crown. Shortly afterwards he suffered another rebuff. He intimated a desire to be ambassador at Washington, but Lord Rosebery, who was then foreign secretary, would not recommend the appointment. Even if it had been a suitable opportunity, it was scarcely reasonable to expect Lord Rosebery to appoint his most unsparing critic as the mouthpiece of his policy in the United States.

Labouchere gained distinction and notoriety by being unlike any English politician of his time. His scepticism and realism were of the French rather than of the English cast, and he was the only English politician of the nineteenth century who made himself popular by cynical wit. For the forms of the British constitution he had little respect. He was hostile to the royal prerogative, to hereditary legislators, and to the formalisms and circumlocutions of diplomacy; he instinctively distrusted the appeal of idealism. An industrious student of politics, he was an especially dangerous critic in foreign affairs. His parliamentary reputation was founded on the skill with which he attacked the Egyptian policy of Gladstone's second administration. Yet—in this respect true to the tradition of the radical school to which he belonged—Labouchere was never a 'little Englander'; and in his advocacy of an independent Egypt he recognized the need for British control of the Suez Canal. The settlement for which he pleaded in the 'eighties was, indeed, much like that embodied in the treaty of forty years later. He was among the most extreme opponents of the Chamberlain-Milner policy in South Africa. He took a prominent part in the commission of inquiry into the Jameson Raid, and while he admitted that there was no proof of Colonial Office complicity, he complained that access to some important documents was denied. In the South African War he was one of the leaders of the peace party, and this was perhaps the only period of his career in which he was personally unpopular. His constituents mobbed him at Northampton, and the worries of the time injured his health. But politics had now become almost his only interest, and he went on until December 1905, when the Balfour ministry fell and Sir Henry Campbell-Bannerman formed his liberal government. He then withdrew from parliament and lived his remaining years near Florence. Although he said that he did not wish for office, he was disappointed that the liberal leader, whom he had staunchly supported, did not ask him to join the new government. His only political reward on retirement was a privy councillorship.

In spite of his brilliant gifts and of his industry for a quarter of a century, Labouchere has left no permanent mark on English politics; but his gay personality, his wit, and his unconventional ways are established in many legends. Of no other politician in his generation are so many stories told. In appearance as in mind he was more French than English. His slight, well-formed frame, shapely head and bearded face were familiar to the British public for a third of a century. Nothing seemed to ruffle his composure. The voice was gentle and the manner bland, and he delivered his witticisms in a drawl that caught the fancy of his audiences whether on the platform or in the House of Commons. In his personal relations he was kindly and sometimes generous.

Labouchere married in 1868 Henrietta Hodson [q.v.], an actress at the Queen's Theatre, Long Acre, opened in 1867 by a syndicate of which he was a member. They had one daughter, who married, first, the Marquis Carlodi Rudini, and secondly, Prince Gyalma Odescalchi. Labouchere died at the Villa Cristina, near Florence, 15 January 1912.

A portrait of Labouchere, painted by A. Baccani, was exhibited at the Royal Academy in 1882.

[Algar Labouchere Thorold, *Life of Henry Labouchere*, 1913.] H. S.

LAMBERT, GEORGE (1842–1915), tennis player, was born 31 May 1842, the third son of Joseph Lambert, who was employed at Hatfield House as professional tennis player by the second Marquess of Salisbury. George Lambert's first engagement was under Thomas Sabin at the Merton Street tennis court at Oxford where he learned the game. His progress was very rapid, and in a few years he was in the forefront of tennis. In 1866 he went to the tennis court at Hampton Court Palace, and three years later was appointed head professional at the Marylebone Cricket Club's court at Lord's, where he remained for twenty years.

It was during the earlier part of his time at Lord's that Lambert reached the zenith of his career. In 1869 he was just defeated by John Moyer Heathcote [q.v.] in a set match, but soon afterwards Lambert began to surpass that player. Finer play than he showed in the Lord's court in 1872, 1873, and 1874 has seldom been seen; and although he had a set-back in the next few years owing to illness, by 1878 he was in his best form again. In 1870 he had challenged Edmund Tompkins, the holder, for the championship of tennis; as Tompkins did not feel equal to contesting it, Lambert gained the title without a match, and for the next fifteen years there was no one to dispute his superiority. Then, in 1885, when he was nearly forty-three years of age, he was challenged and defeated in a great match at Hampton Court Palace court by Tom Pettitt, of the Boston, U.S.A., Athletic Association. Lambert was beaten in 1886 by Charles Saunders, who thereby became champion of England, and his match-playing career ended soon afterwards. In 1889 he left Lord's and for two years was manager of the East Road court at Cambridge. He died at his house in North London 1 December 1915. He married in 1869 Jane Mellows, by whom he had three sons and one daughter. The eldest son, Alfred, became tennis professional to the fourth Marquess of Salisbury at Hatfield; Henry, the youngest, held the same post to the third Baron Leconfield at Petworth.

Lambert, more than any other player, marks the transition from the old to the new tennis. He was the first leading professional trained to the use of racquets strung as they are now and not in the fashion of old days when each cross string was looped round a main one. Lambert added a pace and severity to the game which it had never known before. He had a superb fore-hand stroke which for heaviness of cut has never been excelled, and among other features of his play was the command of a particularly hard boasted force for the dedans.

[Julian Marshall, *The Annals of Tennis*, 1878; *Tennis, Rackets*, and *Lawn-Tennis* (Badminton Library), 1890; E. B. Noel and J. O. M. Clark, *A History of Tennis*, 1924.] E. B. N.

LANE, Sir HUGH PERCY (1875–1915), art collector and critic, the third son of the Rev. James William Lane, rector of Ballybrack, co. Cork, and afterwards of Redruth, Cornwall, by his wife, Frances Adelaide, daughter of Dudley Persse, of Roxburgh, co. Galway, was born at Ballybrack 9 November 1875. Much of his boyhood was spent in travelling on the Continent with his mother. Having learnt the technique of picture-dealing with Messrs. Colnaghi, whose firm (then in Pall Mall) he entered in 1893, and at the Marlborough Gallery, he set up for himself in 1898, aged twenty-three, and almost without capital, at 2 Pall Mall Place. His *flair* for recognizing the work of any given painter, allied with the surest instinct for beauty, quickly brought him a fortune and enabled him to indulge a princely generosity.

Lane had no special interest in Ireland till, in 1900, at the house of his mother's sister, Lady Gregory, in county Galway, he met William Butler Yeats and other leaders in the Irish literary revival. Attributing the absence of a corresponding movement in Irish painting to the lack of good modern examples, Lane proposed to found a gallery of modern art in Dublin, and began by commissioning John Butler Yeats to paint a series of portraits of distinguished Irishmen (continued later by (Sir) William Orpen). In 1903 he secured for exhibition in Dublin about one hundred of the best pictures in the Staats Forbes collection, and a large number were purchased as the nucleus of a gallery. Lane himself gave many more and induced artists to give; and when the corporation of Dublin provided a temporary municipal gallery in Harcourt Street (1906), he made the collection more representative by lending a group of pictures, mostly French, which he offered to give if a permanent gallery were provided. But after a vexatious controversy over a site, Sir Edwin Lutyens's plan for a building on a bridge over the Liffey being rejected by the corporation, Lane took back the loan and lent the pictures to the English National Gallery, to which he bequeathed them in 1913.

Lane acted as adviser when a collection of modern art was being formed for the municipal gallery of Johannesburg (1909), and he brought together a collection of seventeenth-century Dutch pictures for the Cape Town National Gallery (1912). In March 1914, in spite of his differences with the Dublin corporation, he was appointed director of the Irish National Gallery. He greatly improved it, and bestowed on it J. S. Sargent's portrait of President Woodrow Wilson. In February 1915, before going to America on business, he wrote a codicil to his will, restoring the French pictures to the Harcourt Street collection, on condition that a gallery should be provided within five years after his death. Returning a few weeks later on the *Lusitania,* he was drowned when that ship was torpedoed on 7 May. His intention had been expressed to several persons, but the codicil was unwitnessed: the National Gallery became possessed of the pictures and legally had no right to part with them. In Ireland it was held that the pictures should be restored to Dublin, if necessary by special legislation. In July 1924 a committee was set up to consider the matter. Its report, published in June 1926, affirmed, first, that Lane, when he signed the codicil, thought that he was making a legal disposition, but secondly, that it would not be proper to modify his will by act of parliament. It was subsequently stated by the prime minister, Mr. Baldwin, that the government had decided not to introduce a measure on the subject. Thus, at the present time neither London nor Dublin possesses what Lane planned and for a time brought together—a collection of modern pictures which for completeness and excellence had no superior within its own scope, and was unique as the expression of one unifying taste, a taste which artists recognized as approaching creative genius. Lane was knighted in 1909. He was unmarried.

[Lady Gregory, *Hugh Lane's Life and Achievement, with some account of the Dublin Galleries*, 1921, *Sir Hugh Lane's French Pictures* (pamphlet), 1917, and *The Case for the Return of Sir Hugh Lane's Pictures to Dublin*, 1926; personal knowledge.] S. G.

LANG, ANDREW (1844–1912), scholar, folk-lorist, poet, and man of letters, was born at Selkirk 31 March 1844, the eldest son of John Lang, sheriff-clerk of Selkirkshire, whose father Andrew Lang, also sheriff-clerk, had been a friend of Sir Walter Scott. His mother, Jane Plenderleath Sellar, was the daughter of Patrick Sellar [q.v.], factor to the first Duke of Sutherland, and a sister of William Young Sellar [q.v.], professor of Latin in Edinburgh University. During his childhood he spent a year at Clifton, to which he refers in the autobiographical chapter of his *Adventures among Books* (1905). He was educated at Selkirk grammar school and the Edinburgh Academy (where he 'loathed Greek', but was converted by Homer), and in 1861 matriculated at the university of St. Andrews. His three years' residence there laid the foundations of a lifelong attachment to St. Andrews, which in his later years became his second home. In 1864 he removed for a session to the university of Glasgow in order to qualify as a candidate for the Snell exhibition, and with this he proceeded in

1865 to Balliol College, Oxford. In 1868, having taken a first class both in moderations and in *literae humaniores*, he was elected to an open fellowship at Merton College.

A career of academic distinction now lay before him. But although he occasionally resided (a carved door-top and oak mantelpiece still testify to his interest in his college rooms), he was by temperament unsuited to collegiate routine, and his literary talents pointed clearly elsewhere. In 1873 the doctors passed sentence on his lungs, and he went abroad for a time; but the trouble was averted. In 1875 he married Miss Leonora Blanche Alleyne, the youngest daughter of Mr. C. T. Alleyne, of Clifton and Barbados. He vacated his Merton fellowship, and settled down in London to a life of journalism and letters.

For journalism, which he practised with unremitting diligence for nearly forty years, Lang was unusually well qualified, combining with a lively scholarship and wit a remarkable range of miscellaneous and immediately applicable knowledge, a facility in writing which astonished even Fleet Street, and a complete indifference to time or place or interruptions. 'He would turn into the pavilion during the intervals of a cricket match', says a friend, 'and begin, finish, or write some middle page of an article, on the corner of a table or the top of a locker, quite as comfortably as he would in his own study.' His essays and articles found their public at once, and kept it grateful to the end. His sparkling verses proclaimed a new and happy talent. His characteristic studies, also, were already taking shape. By 1875 he was making his name as a folk-lorist, he was hard at work on Homer, and had been selected by Spencer Baynes to write for the ninth edition of the *Encyclopædia Britannica* (1875-1889). The articles in that work on *Apparitions, Ballads, The Casket Letters, Crystal-gazing, Fairy, Family, Edmund Gurney, Hauntings, La Cloche, Molière, Mythology, Name, Poltergeist, Prometheus, Psychical Research, Scotland, Second Sight, Tale*, and *Totemism* are all from his pen.

Lang's first book was of verse, his *Ballads and Lyrics of Old France* (1872). It was followed in 1880 by *xxii Ballades in Blue China*, which became *xxxii* the next year. These two books helped to inaugurate a revival, which Théodore de Banville had already established in France and with which Swinburne had toyed, of the old French modes of ballade, triolet, and rondeau. It was a notable contribution to English prosodical resources. His *Helen of Troy* (1882) was more ambitious. It is a narrative poem in six books, in stanzas —a beautiful exercise, but in rather still life, for 'who can write at length of Helen?' This was Lang's one deliberate bid for the laurel, and it brought him more compliments than praise. He accepted the sentence perhaps too hastily; spoke of 'the unpermitted bay'; and though he continued to write and publish poetry, as one to whom verse-making was a function of being, never again attempted a poem that might not be written at a sitting. *Rhymes à la Mode* (1884), *Grass of Parnassus* (1888), *Ban and Arrière Ban* (1894), and the rest, are rallies of fugitive verse, as his *Letters to Dead Authors* (1886), his *Books and Bookmen* (1886), and their numerous successors are rallies of fugitive prose. They are all journalism, but they are the willing journalism of a man of genius. In the lighter play of the essay as in some of the daintier forms of verse, in the short causerie falling just between literature and gossip, Lang had no rival. The prose pieees which he valued most were collected in his lifetime; a collected edition of his poetical works was published posthumously in 1923; the latter contains many waifs from the files of periodicals, and leaves many uncollected. Lang's prose was always relished, but he wrote so much of it that his verse has been underrated. He was in the habit of belittling his poetical achievement, and was too readily believed. On his favourite places and heroes, on St. Andrews and the Ettrick country, on Gordon, Burnaby, and the world of ancient Greece, he has written poems not easily forgotten. His *Ballade of his Choice of a Sepulchre* and some of his sonnets are among the best of their kind; his poems in Scots stand high in a now impoverished tradition; and he boasted with justice that no man of his day could better fake a ballad. He might have been a much more considerable poet had he made the necessary sacrifice, and been a poet only; but this he could not do.

Lang valued himself most as an anthropologist. He was forty when his first book on folk-lore appeared, *Custom and Myth* (1884), but it embodied papers written and printed much earlier. He had been brought up as a boy among ballads and folk-tales, and the reading of Dasent's *Popular Tales from the Norse* and similar collections had made him a comparative mythologist while still a youth. He observed, like others, that many of these tales existed, in analogous forms, among widely distant races; he also observed that while they differed little in their incidents they differed entirely in their names. He concluded that the key to these analogies could not be language, and that the philological explanations, then fashionable, must be wrong. He announced this discovery in the *Fortnightly Review*, May 1873, in an article, *Mythology and Fairy-tales*, which has been described as 'the first full refutation of Max Müller's mythological system, and the first full statement of the anthropological method applied to the comparative study of myths' [*Quarterly Review*, April 1913, p. 311]. *Custom and Myth* was followed in 1887 by *Myth, Ritual, and Religion*. This deals chiefly with totemism, the importance of which in early human society Lang tended in his later works to minimize. He came to believe that the seeds might be found in primitive races of another source of rules, of 'a faith in a Creator and Judge of men'. This view was first systematically stated in *The Making of Religion* (1898), and so firmly held that the second edition of *Myth, Ritual, and Religion* (1899) was drastically handled in order to square with it. Lang's monotheistic heresy, as it was called, involved him in much controversy and some temporary disrepute; the biblical quotations and Hebraic parallels by which it was supported gained him, at the same time, the unwelcome applause of orthodox believers in the legends of Genesis. The misunderstanding was increased by his unprofessional attitude towards miracles. He had always been interested in abnormal psychology: he was one of the founders of the Psychical Research Society, and its president in 1911. He now appealed to its evidence to account for those miraculous phenomena from which religion in all ages has derived support, and which he refused to regard as necessarily fraudulent. 'A little more of that', said a French confrère, 'and M. Lang may be ranked among the Church Fathers!' It is acknowledged that Lang did a service, even at the expense of admitting 'degradation', by recalling attention to some higher elements in savage beliefs which the doctrine of evolutionary progress had led inquirers to neglect. It seems probable, nevertheless, that Lang's earlier work in anthropology was also his best, and that his greatest performance was his first, when he proved that folk-lore is not the debris of a higher or literary mythology, but the foundation on which that mythology rests. 'He who demonstrated that', wrote M. Salomon Reinach, 'and made it a key to the darkest recesses of classical mythology, has conferred a benefit on the world of learning, and was a genius.'

Lang was a Greek scholar, devoted to Homer. S. H. Butcher and Lang's prose translation of the *Odyssey* (1879), preceded by Lang's best sonnet, was one of the famous and even formative books of its time. The translation of the *Iliad*, which followed (1883), by Lang, Walter Leaf, and Ernest Myers, was less good, but still notable. He published, also, translations of Theocritus (1880) and of the *Homeric Hymns* (1899), the first perhaps his best translation, the second remarkable for the excellent essays which accompanied it. He was one of the principal champions of the personality of Homer and of the unity of his poems (even writing a sonnet on *Homeric Unity*), and to the Homeric question he contributed three books: *Homer and the Epic* (1893), *Homer and his Age* (1906), and, best of the three, *The World of Homer* (1910). He did excellent service, in a light-armed, raiding way, by exposing the more childish methods of the orthodox separatists, and the rather comical inadequacy of some of their tests. There were more self-contradictions, he pointed out, in *Pendennis* than in the *Iliad*. His wit and high spirits, his knowledge of anthropology, and his wide range of literary illustration made him an invaluable ally; and if the unitarian minority to which he belonged is now in the ascendant, he must share the credit.

Lang was a considerable historian. He had dabbled, as a young man, in the mysteries of Scottish history, yet his first historical work, a history of St. Andrews (1893), was a confessed piece of book-making, and he was nearly fifty when it appeared. It gave much offence, for Lang was frank about the Reformation, and careless errors in the book were triumphantly exposed. The experience was salutary, and an accident of friendship tempted him to profit by it. R.L. Stevenson had asked 'dear Andrew' for something about the Jacobites, and Lang, in the course of searching, was caught up by a historical mystery—Who was the Jacobite spy referred to by Scott in the introduction to *Redgauntlet*? He sent what he had found to Samoa, and on Stevenson's death in 1894 the papers were returned to him. His curiosity revived, and the result was *Pickle the Spy* (1897). The spy, he decided, was Alastair Ruadh Macdonell [q.v.], 'Young Glengarry', and now from another quarter his Scottish critics assailed him. *The Companions of Pickle* (1898), which put the matter beyond doubt, was his reply. He was by this time well entered in the hardy game of Scottish historiography. In 1900 appeared his *Prince Charles Edward*, his best historical composition. He had been a Jacobite from boyhood, yet he had no illusions about the prince, preferring indeed the quieter Old Pretender, whom he did much to rehabilitate. He was now labouring at a more doubtful and ambitious project. '"A History of Scotland", said the publisher of Dr. Robertson's work in the last century, "is no very attractive title".' So Lang quotes. His own *History of Scotland from the Roman Occupation to the Suppression of the last Jacobite Rising* (1900–1907) occupied him ten years, and its intended two volumes became four. It had an odd reception. His waiting critics were disappointed by its accuracy, and his admirers by its attention to detail and the business of history. History to Lang meant finding things out, and when he began an inquiry he could not be stopped. This occasioned disproportions, of which he was aware: 'I wonder anybody can read my four volumes', he wrote, 'but the chapter on Montrose in vol. iii is pretty decent.' It is one of many fine passages, but the principal merit of the work is that, in one of the most partisan fields of human history, he, a partisan, is never content with legend, and is never unfair. His studies for the *History* overflowed into detective monographs, such as *The Mystery of Mary Stuart* (1901) and *James VI and the Gowrie Conspiracy* (1902), or into biography, as in *John Knox and the Reformation* (1905) and the *Life of Sir George Mackenzie* (1909). This last had been interrupted by an enterprise in all respects characteristic of its author. In the spring of 1908 Anatole France issued his *Vie de Jeanne d'Arc*. Within six months Lang had answered M. France's cynicism, from the evidence, in his *Maid of France* (1908), vindicating the Maid from insult.

There are few forms of writing which Lang had not attempted. The last book he saw through the press was a *History of English Literature* (1912). For years he supplied the nurseries and schoolrooms of England with Fairy Books only less attractive than his budgets of True Stories:

Books Yellow, Red, and Green, and Blue
All true, or just as good as true.

He tried the novel, but without much effect, although his first, *The Mark of Cain* (1886), and his last, *The Disentanglers* (1902), are books of note, and such as no one else could have written. As a biographer he was more successful: his *Life, Letters and Diaries of Sir Stafford Northcote, first Earl of Iddesleigh* (1890) is a valuable contribution to Victorian parliamentary history, and his *Life and Letters of J. G. Lockhart* (1896) is one of the best biographies of the century. Lockhart—'the Scorpion of the loyal heart'—was a subject to his mind, and he took pleasure in righting a proud and fastidious character which in many respects resembled his own. He was also provoked by the Bacon-Shakespeare controversy to write a defence of Shakespearian authorship, which was published after his death, *Shakespeare, Bacon, and the Great Unknown* (1912).

The word commonly applied to Lang was versatile, and there was nothing he less liked to hear. He wrote too much, but the loyalty and tenacity of his mind are as striking as its variety. His characteristic tastes were formed early. His Jacobitism and ballad lore, his interest in folk-tales and his idolization of Homer, that devotion to the memory of Sir Walter Scott which may almost be regarded as the key to his life, all date, like his instructed passion for cricket, golf, and the 'ringing reel', from his boyhood or early youth. If he kept them all going, the reason is that he never grew old. He was not an affable person, and it was his pleasure to conceal his astonishing powers of work under the air of a dilettante. But no man ever helped more lame dogs over stiles. He had what is rarer than an instinct for friendship, something higher and drier, an instinct for fraternity. He was, before all things, a brother of the craft. Indeed, in his generation, he was the ambassador of all the sporting crafts at the court of letters, and the protector of all loyalties fallen upon misfortune. Though he had many admirers among his countrymen, Scotland never heartily relished Lang: he could not be serious, it was said, and he cut too near the bone. Yet he was the greatest bookman of his age, and after Stevenson, the last great man of letters of the old Scottish tradition. On two subjects only he refrained from expressing himself: on personal religion and on party politics. No man had more questions to ask of the next world, but he kept them to himself. His chance of politics was gone with Culloden.

Of the many honours that came his way Lang valued most, perhaps, his St. Andrews (1885) and Oxford (1904) doctorates, his appointment as the first Gifford lecturer at St. Andrews (1888), and the freedom of his native town of Selkirk, conferred upon him in 1889. Merton College elected him an honorary fellow in 1890. He was more than once urged, by Sir Francis Doyle and Matthew Arnold among others, to stand for the professorship of poetry at Oxford, but always refused. He died of angina pectoris after a few hours' illness at Banchory, Aberdeenshire, on 20 July 1912, and is buried in the cathedral precincts at St. Andrews. He had no children. His portrait was painted in 1887 by Sir W. B. Richmond, and is reproduced in volume i of his *Collected Poems* (1923). A memorial by Percy Portsmouth in Selkirk free library contains a profile portrait in relief. He was averse from any biography of himself or from publication of his letters, and there will be no authorized Life.

Specimens of a Bibliography of Lang's works (1889), a *Catalogue of a 'Lang' Library* (1898), and a collection of verses addressed to Lang by his contemporaries, called *A New Friendship's Garland* (1899), were privately printed at Dundee by C. M. Falconer. There is also in the Dundee reference library a manuscript collection, in one volume, of all the poems written by Lang and uncollected by him, between the years 1863 and 1904, transcribed by C. M. Falconer and revised by Lang.

[*The Times Literary Supplement*, 6 September 1912 [G. S. G.]; notice by G. Saintsbury in *Oxford Magazine*, 17 October 1912; commemorative address by W. P. Ker, 28 November 1912, in *Proceedings* of the Academic Committee of the Royal Society of Literature, 1913; R. S. Rait, G. Murray, S. Reinach, and J. H. Millar in commemorative article, *Quarterly Review*, April 1913; G. Saintsbury in *Quarterly Review*, October 1923; private information.] G. S. G.

LASCELLES, Sir FRANK CAVENDISH (1841–1920), diplomatist, was born in London 23 March 1841, the fifth son of the Hon. William Saunders Sebright Lascelles, third son of Henry Lascelles, second Earl of Harewood [q.v.]. His mother was Lady Caroline Georgiana, eldest daughter of George Howard, sixth Earl of Carlisle [q.v.]. He was educated at Harrow, and entered the diplomatic service in 1861. After serving for two years as an attaché in Madrid, he was transferred to Paris in 1864 and promoted to third secretary in 1865. Lascelles saw the Second Empire at its apogee at the time of the great Paris international exhibition of 1867. He then went on to Berlin, where he remained till the end of the Franco-Prussian War. He returned to Paris in February 1871 after the siege, and remained at the embassy under (Sir) Edward Baldwin Malet [q.v.] during the Commune, while the ambassador, Lord Lyons, accompanied the French government to Versailles. Proceeding in the same year, with the rank of second secretary, to Copenhagen, he was transferred in succession to Rome (1873), Washington (1876), and Athens (1878), and he was three times sent to take charge of the agency and consulate-general in Cairo during the last two stormy years of the Khedive Ismail's reign, which ended in Ismail's enforced abdication in 1879.

In recognition of his services in Egypt Lascelles was promoted at the end of 1879 to be agent and consul-general in Bulgaria, which country the Treaty of Berlin (1878) had virtually detached from the Ottoman Empire and constituted into an autonomous principality with Prince Alexander of Battenberg as its first ruler. He was still at Sofia when, in September 1885, a bloodless revolution at Philippopolis led to the union of Eastern Rumelia with the principality and to the first war between Bulgaria and Serbia. In the following year, owing to the hostility of the Tsar Alexander III, who resented the independent attitude of Bulgaria, Prince Alexander was kidnapped by a pro-Russian faction of the Bulgarian army, and in spite of the popular enthusiasm which greeted his return, was driven to abdicate and leave Bulgaria. Lascelles had won Lord Salisbury's approval by giving Prince Alexander his full support throughout this difficult period; he had also earned the special goodwill of Queen Victoria, who warmly favoured the prince's suit for the hand of her granddaughter, Princess Charlotte of Prussia, though Bismarck was vehemently opposed to it.

Lascelles was promoted to be British minister to Roumania at the beginning of 1887, and to Persia in 1891. In 1894 he was appointed British ambassador to Russia, and at the end of 1895 he was specially selected to succeed Sir Edward Malet who had been ambassador in Berlin for twelve years. Lascelles held this embassy for the same length of time as his predecessor, during a period when German ambitions and the menace of Germany's naval expansion led to a growing estrangement between her and Great Britain. The first public revelation of this was the famous telegram dispatched by William II to President Kruger in January 1896, only a few days after the new ambassador's arrival in Berlin. Lascelles's personal relations with William II, who was at great pains to capture his confidence, were, however, singularly cordial and even intimate. In spite of the Emperor's not infrequent outbursts of angry temper when talking of British ministers and British policy, Lascelles was generally inclined to acquit him of any hostile designs against England, and he preferred to throw the blame on the sovereign's advisers, and especially on Prince Bülow, whom he greatly distrusted. He retired in 1908, and even after his retirement continued to use his influence for the restoration of Anglo-German amity right up to the outbreak of the European War of 1914. Lascelles was created K.C.M.G. (1886), G.C.M.G. (1892), G.C.B. (1897), G.C.V.O. (1904), and a privy councillor in 1892. He married in 1867 Mary Emma (died 1897), eldest daughter of Sir Joseph Francis Olliffe [q.v.], physician to the British embassy at Paris, and had two sons and one daughter, Florence, who married Sir Cecil Spring-Rice [q.v.]. He died in London 2 January 1920.

[Official records ; private letters.]

V. C.

LAUGHTON, Sir JOHN KNOX (1830–1915), naval historian, was the second son and youngest child of James Laughton, of Liverpool (1777–1859), who, like his ancestors, was in times of peace a master mariner and in times of war captain of a privateer. James Laughton married Ann Potts, who came of yeoman stock in Cumberland ; and before the birth of his younger son forsook the sea and took to Calvinism. The future historian was born in Liverpool 23 April 1830. He was educated at the Royal Institution School in that city and later proceeded to Caius College, Cambridge, where in 1852 he sat for the mathematical tripos and graduated as a wrangler. Almost as soon as he had taken his degree the outbreak of war with Russia suggested a career; and entering the royal navy as a naval instructor, he joined his first ship, the *Royal George*, 27 December 1853, and proceeded to the Baltic. His service here extended over 1854 and 1855 ; and in 1856, as the Crimean War came to an end, he was transferred to the *Calcutta*, flagship of the commander-in-chief in the Far East. During the second Chinese War he was present at the capture of the Canton defences (1856), the battle of Fatshan Creek (1857), and the capture of the Taku forts (1858). In these engagements he distinguished himself by his gallantry ; while at the same time in pursuit of his ordinary duties he was laying the foundations of his success as a teacher. 'Sir John taught so well,' wrote Admiral Sir Edward Seymour in later years, 'that of his pupils (in the *Calcutta*) at least seventeen got on the active list of captains and eight to that of flag officers—which from one ship I believe to be a record.' For his services in the Baltic Laughton received the Crimean medal, and for the Chinese War the medal with clasps—a remarkable achievement for one whose status was that of a civilian. In 1859 he was appointed to the *Algiers*, and, while in the Mediterranean, specialized in the geography of the Holy Land, collecting as large a library on the subject as his cabin would hold. But his war experiences were over ; and after serving in one or two other ships he came ashore for good, and in 1866 was transferred to the Royal Naval College, Portsmouth.

Here Laughton's pupils were half-pay captains and commanders; and, the educational fashions of the sailing-epoch being still in vogue, the chief subject he had to teach was meteorology, though to this was added, *inter alia*, marine surveying. There were no suitable text-books, and Laughton in his thorough fashion set himself to produce what was wanted. In 1870 he published his *Physical Geography in its relation to the Prevailing Winds and Currents*, and two years later his *Treatise on Nautical Surveying*. These works attracted attention outside the service, and led to his long and valued connexion with the Royal Meteorological Society, of which he was elected a fellow in 1873 and president in 1882.

In 1873 the Admiralty decided to convert Greenwich Hospital, the primary object of which had by then ceased to exist, into a university for the navy; and Laughton was promoted from Portsmouth to take charge of the department of meteorology and marine surveying. In 1876 he obtained permission to lecture on naval history. The subject had been utterly neglected in the service, and seemed outside the scope of the Greenwich curriculum, which hitherto had been purely technical. But from this time onward Laughton transferred his allegiance almost wholly to his new study, which he attacked in all its applications with his accustomed vigour. In 1885 he reached the retiring age, and the navy lost one of its best servants ; but he did not at once cease to lecture on naval history at Greenwich ; and he became a regular contributor to the *Edinburgh Review* and to this DICTIONARY (for which he wrote more than nine hundred lives). Within six months of retiring from the navy he was installed as professor of history at King's College, London, an appointment which enabled him to continue his pioneer work in search of naval documents, and to present the special knowledge thus obtained against the broader background of general history. Of the mass of documents examined by him, he edited *Memoirs relating to Lord Torrington* for the Camden Society in 1889; and, four years later, with the help of old shipmates who by now had risen to high positions of trust in the state, he succeeded in founding the Navy Records Society, for the publication of documents illustrating British maritime history. The first two volumes, *Papers relating to the Defeat of the Spanish Armada* (1894), he edited himself; and as first secretary of the society from 1893 to 1912, he not only directed all its proceedings, but with singular and ungrudging devotion put his own vast fund of knowledge entirely at the disposal of other labourers in the same field.

Late in life honours came thickly; he was elected an honorary fellow of Caius College in 1895; he received the honorary degrees of several universities; and in 1910 he was awarded the Chesney gold medal by the Royal United Service Institution. In 1907 he received knighthood; and in 1910, on his eightieth birthday, a number of admirers, including King George V, then Prince of Wales, and all the most celebrated admirals on the flag list, presented a testimonial and an address to the 'pioneer in the revival of naval history'.

Laughton continued to lecture at King's College until the Christmas of 1914. He then complained of ill-health, and withdrew to his house at Wimbledon where his last days were spent. He died on 14 September 1915 in his eighty-sixth year. In accordance with his own request, his ashes were conveyed to sea by H.M.S. *Conqueror* and buried in forty fathoms at the mouth of the Thames 'in the track of the incoming and outgoing ships'.

Laughton married, first, in 1866 Isabella, daughter of John Carr, of Dunfermline; and secondly, in 1886 Maria Josefa, daughter of Eugenio di Alberti, of Cadiz. He had by his first marriage one son and three daughters; and by his second, three sons and two daughters. He was a man of striking personal appearance with a tall, athletic figure and handsome features.

In addition to works already enumerated, Laughton wrote two volumes about Nelson, the *Life* (1895) and *Nelson and his Companions in Arms* (1896); edited the papers of Lord Barham (1907–1911); made a selection of Nelson letters from the unmanageable mass printed by Sir Harris Nicolas (1886); and collected some of his own fugitive tracts in a volume called *Studies in Naval History* (1887). But it is not from these books that the full value of Laughton's labour can be estimated. It is noteworthy that the publication of Captain A. T. Mahan's *Influence of Sea Power upon History* (1890) approximates in date to the foundation on this side of the Atlantic of the Navy Records Society. Mahan, admittedly one of Laughton's disciples, startled the world with his complete edifice of historical philosophy in the very hour in which Laughton dug down to the foundations on which alone such an edifice could be safely erected.

[Letters and Papers in possession of the family; Greenwich archives; personal knowledge.] G. A. R. C.

LAURIER, SIR WILFRID (1841–1919), Canadian statesman, the only son of Carolus Laurier, by his wife, Marcelle Martineau, was born at St. Lin, a village near Montreal, 20 November 1841. He was of French and Roman Catholic ancestry, resident in Canada during seven or eight generations. After spending seven years at L'Assomption College he took a course in law at McGill University, and began practice in Montreal; but ill-health, linked with narrow means, led to his removal to the small town of Arthabaska. In 1868 he married Zoë, daughter of G. N. R. Lafontaine, of Montreal, who survived him. The marriage was childless.

Laurier's mind was essentially liberal, and even as a schoolboy he had expressed opinions startling to severe clericalism. In 1871 he was elected to the legislature of Quebec, and in 1874 to the parliament of Canada for Drummond-Arthabaska. In 1877 he entered the liberal cabinet of Alexander Mackenzie [q.v.] as minister of inland revenue. When the conservatives opposed the new minister's re-election he was beaten; but he soon found a seat for Quebec East, which he continued to hold during more than forty years. Laurier always avowed himself a moderate protectionist, but in 1878 the liberals went to the country on the policy of a tariff for revenue, as opposed to the conservative 'national policy' of protection. From 1878 to 1896 they remained in opposition.

In 1880 Edward Blake [q.v.] became

leader of the liberal party. Two years later the liberals were defeated in a federal election, and when, in 1887, this again happened, Blake retired from the leadership. His recommendation of Laurier, a French Canadian, as his successor, was looked upon as of doubtful wisdom, coming so soon after the strong feeling aroused among French Canadians by the execution (1885) of the agitator, Louis Riel [q.v.]; but, once leader, Laurier quickly made his position secure. In the federal election of 1891 the liberal policy was unrestricted reciprocity in trade with the United States, and it was successfully opposed by Sir John A. Macdonald [q.v.], the conservative leader, as involving union with the United States. But after Macdonald's death in 1891, the disintegration of the conservative party was rapid. In that year the liberal government in Manitoba had abolished Roman Catholic separate schools. By a special provision of the constitution, the federal government had the right to redress grievances of a minority in respect to education. The Quebec bishops in particular were insistent for a remedial bill restoring separate schools, and this Sir Charles Tupper [q.v.], the conservative prime minister, promised. Education was, however, under provincial control, and federal interference would, Laurier said, create more difficulties than it would solve. The remedy was in conciliation not defiance. The cry 'hands off Manitoba' was effective. The electors in Quebec stood by one of their own race, even against the bishops, and Laurier carried the country.

Laurier was prime minister from 1896 to 1911. He had to meet the double difficulty of redeeming his promise of freer trade, and of saving industries which had grown up under a protective tariff. He found the solution in a compromise. In 1897, while he gave to Great Britain a preferential tariff, amounting to one-third of the duty, he made few reductions in the general tariff. The preference increased imports from Great Britain, and Laurier was received with great enthusiasm and was knighted when he attended the diamond jubilee of Queen Victoria in that year. Canada's great need was population. The North-West was still almost unpeopled, but in 1900 a vigorous immigration policy, framed by the capable minister of the interior, Sir Clifford Sifton, brought in many settlers, especially from the United States. This in time caused a demand for more railways. In earlier days the liberal party had opposed the rapid building of the Canadian Pacific Railway across the continent, in advance, as they claimed, of economic needs; but, in an era of boundless optimism, Laurier gave extensive aid to the Grand Trunk Pacific Railway, a trans-continental line, and also to a second line, the Canadian Northern. When the European War broke out in 1914 these lines were already in difficulties and, in the end, they were taken over by the state with enormous financial loss.

On the outbreak of the Boer War in 1899, Laurier, in obedience to dominant public opinion, sent contingents to South Africa. But Quebec viewed sullenly this sharing in imperial wars with which Canada had no direct concern. In the election of 1900 Henri Bourassa, the nationalist leader, a former liberal, attacked Laurier so violently as to awaken his fears for his hold upon Quebec. At the Imperial Conference in 1902 he resisted firmly Mr. Joseph Chamberlain's proposals to unite the whole Empire in a common system of defence. Quebec, the source of his political strength, would oppose any form of imperialism. In 1905, when Saskatchewan and Alberta were made self-governing provinces, Laurier tried to conciliate clerical opinion by permitting to the Roman Catholic minority state-supported separate schools. When this threatened the break-up of his Cabinet, he modified his proposals. This gave Bourassa further ground of attack, but Laurier carried the general election in 1908.

After his victory in the federal election of 1908 Laurier's position seemed secure. But in 1910, when the menace of the German fleet led Canada to take the first steps in creating a Canadian navy as auxiliary to the British, Bourassa again assailed Laurier for supporting British jingoism. In a hotly contested election in Drummond-Arthabaska, liberal since 1887, Laurier's candidate was beaten. At the same time he was attacked in Ontario as yielding to clerical pressure in the French province—a religious cry which he himself believed to have led finally to his political undoing. The avowed issue, however, was that of free trade with the United States in natural products. Canada had built up her transport, her industries, and her finance in the face of a high American tariff. When, early in 1911, a trade agreement with the United States was reached, the first impression was one of approval. But Canada's railways, running east and west to the sea, were likely to be injured. Her industrial leaders feared that free trade would soon be extended from natural products to manufactures, and that these would be ruined in competition with the more highly developed American industries. Above all, the British sentiment of Canada was alarmed lest the proposal should involve union with the United States. In great confidence Laurier dissolved parliament, but he was defeated, and his long term of office ended in September 1911.

After the defeat of Laurier the naval question was still urgent. In 1913 the new prime minister, Sir Robert Borden, abandoned the plan of a Canadian navy, and, on the ground of an emergency, proposed to add three 'Dreadnought' battleships to the British fleet. Laurier held that his own policy of a Canadian navy, which the conservatives had accepted, was the true one for Canada. He put this forward as against a gift of ships. The government measure was carried in the Canadian House of Commons, after the adoption for the first time in Canada of the closure, but was defeated by the liberal majority in the Senate. When war came in 1914, Canada, unlike Australia, had no share in naval defence. While Laurier supported the government's war policy, Bourassa vigorously attacked British imperialism as only less dangerous to the world than that of Germany. In 1917, when both Britain and the United States adopted conscription, and the many military failures of the year pointed to a prolonged war, a strong movement set in for coalition government. Sir Robert Borden announced that conscription would be applied to Canada, and, at the same time, he invited Laurier to join a coalition. While this was favoured by the great mass of English-speaking liberals, bitter opposition to conscription came from Quebec. Laurier was unwilling to risk losing support in his own province. He refused to join the new government, and in the election of 1917 Quebec alone stood with him. The liberal party was shattered in English-speaking Canada. By this time Laurier's health was failing, and he died at Ottawa on 17 February 1919, before peace was finally concluded.

Laurier was tall and graceful. His dignity and his courtesy were alike impressive. This charm of manner concealed a will which was like iron when once his mind was made up. He used, with some truth, to accuse himself of indolence. He disliked detail, with the result that he sometimes allowed abuses to go far before checking them. His tastes were simple, and during most of his life he was very poor. Though he could be opportunist, his personal character always commanded high respect. By long ancestry Canadian, he had no personal ties with either England or France. While, in all great crises, his opinions ran with those of the French element in Canada, he always opposed with outspoken vigour any appeal to racial or religious passions.

[J. S. Willison, *Sir Wilfrid Laurier and the Liberal Party*, Toronto, 1903; O. D. Skelton, *Life and Letters of Sir Wilfrid Laurier*, New York, 1922; J. W. Dafoe, *Laurier, a Study in Canadian Politics*, Toronto, 1922; L. O. David, *Laurier: Sa vie, Ses Œuvres*, 1919; Sir Wilfrid Laurier, *Discours à l'Étranger et au Canada*, Montreal, 1909; personal knowledge.]

G. M. W.

LAWSON, EDWARD LEVY-, first Baron Burnham (1833–1916), newspaper proprietor. [See Levy-Lawson.]

LEACH, ARTHUR FRANCIS (1851–1915), historical writer, the third son of Thomas Leach, barrister, of Seaford Lodge, Ryde, Isle of Wight, by his wife, Sarah Green, was born in London 16 March 1851. He was educated at Winchester College, and gained a scholarship at New College, Oxford, in 1869. In 1872 he won the Stanhope historical essay prize, and in 1873 obtained a first class in *literae humaniores*. From 1874 to 1881 he was a fellow of All Souls College, and in 1876 he was called to the bar by the Middle Temple. In 1884 he was appointed an assistant charity commissioner (Endowed Schools department). From 1901 to 1903 he was administrative examiner at the Board of Education, from April to December 1903 senior examiner, and from 1904 to 1906 assistant secretary. He was appointed second charity commissioner in 1906, a post which he held till his death in 1915.

Leach was associated with the Endowed Schools department at a particularly interesting period of its development, namely that following the Public Schools Act of 1868 (which was based on the recommendations of the royal commission of 1861–1864 on the public schools) and the Endowed Schools Act of 1869 (which embodied the recommendations of the Schools Inquiry commission of 1864–1868). The latter commission had dealt with 782 grammar schools and 2,175 endowed elementary schools, and the provision of new schemes for these schools was transferred to an augmented Charity Commission, of which body Leach was a member. Appendix V of the *Report* of the Schools Inquiry commission contained a list of endowed schools, arranged in chronological order of foundation. Leach worked over this material *de novo*, and in 1896 published his *English Schools at the Reformation* (*1546–1548*), in which he showed that the attribution of fifty-one 'new' foundations to Edward VI's reign is a misreading of history. The study of the Chantry Acts of 1546–1548 (edited in the same book) showed that the government of Edward VI was the spoiler rather than the founder of schools, and that in his reign 200 grammar schools were abolished or crippled, and that other schools were apparently swept away without record. Leach investigated the provision of pre-Reformation schools connected with cathedral churches, monasteries, collegiate churches, hospitals, guilds, chantries, and independent institutions, and gave the results in his *Schools of Medieval England* (1915), the first connected history of English schools down to the accession of Edward VI. He there maintained the view (which he had first put forward in *The Times*, 12 September 1896) that the King's School, Canterbury, is the oldest English school. Originally he had preferred the claim of St. Peter's School at York to this distinction (*Fortnightly Review*, November 1892). His book established the sense of the continuity in development of English grammar schools from the time of the conversion of England to Christianity.

In the *Victoria History of the Counties of England* (1900–1914) Leach supplied, almost single-handed, the history of schools in nineteen counties. His summaries of county school-history at the head of each of his contributions are of interest for social as well as for educational history. His opinions are sometimes hasty and unsafe, but his comprehensive collection of facts puts the student in a position to judge for himself.

In addition to county school-histories, Leach wrote histories of Winchester College (1899) and Bradfield College (1900), *Early Yorkshire Schools* (for the Yorkshire Archaeological Society, 1899 and 1903), a *History of Warwick School* (1906), and *Early Education in Worcester* (1913). He produced a representative collection of materials for the study of the history of education in England, *Educational Charters and Documents, 598 to 1909 A.D.* (1911), his aim being to do for the educational history of England what Bishop Stubbs's *Select Charters* did for its constitutional history. His work placed the subject of the history of schools and education in England on a high level of research and called attention to the continuity of their development.

Leach married in 1881 Emily Archer, daughter of Silas Kemball Cook, secretary of the Seamen's Hospital, Greenwich, and sister of Sir Edward Tyas Cook [q.v.]. They had four sons and two daughters. He died at the Bolingbroke Hospital, after an operation, 28 September 1915.

[Leach's works; private information. His *Schools of Medieval England* gives a bibliography of his writings on the history of schools.] F. W.

LEDWIDGE, FRANCIS (1891–1917), poet, born 19 June 1891 at Slane, co. Meath, was the eighth child of Patrick Ledwidge, an evicted tenant-farmer, afterwards a farm labourer, by his wife, Annie Lynch. Leaving the Slane national school at twelve, Ledwidge worked in the fields and also in domestic service. At fourteen he was apprenticed to a Dublin grocer; but this, like a later episode in a draper's shop, lasted only a few weeks. He went back to his native fields, which henceforth provided the many occupations which he followed for a livelihood. He was a ganger on the roads; then a copper-miner, until dismissed for fomenting a strike; then an overseer of roads for the Slane area. These occupations were tolerable, because they kept him close to the hedgerows, the birds, and the people that he loved. His first verses had already been printed in the *Drogheda Independent*, and he contemplated training himself for journalism. In June 1912 he sent a bookful of verse to Lord Dunsany, who gave him advice, material help, and introduction to the literary world. Though reviews began to take his poems, Ledwidge stuck to his rural occupation, interesting himself more deeply in the welfare of his village. He was secretary of the county Meath farm labourers' union, served on the Navan district council, and was insurance commissioner for the county. In October 1914, although a strong nationalist, he joined the 5th battalion Royal Inniskillings, to fight 'neither for a principle, nor a people, nor a law, but for the fields along the Boyne, for the birds and the blue sky over them'. He served as lance-corporal at the Suvla Bay landing in Gallipoli (August 1915), was with the first detachment sent from Gallipoli to Salonika (October 1915), and fought through the Vardar retreat (December 1915). After a spell in hospital in Egypt, he was sent to France, and was killed in

Belgium 31 July 1917. He was well-built, tall, with an eager, gentle face, arresting eyes, and dark soft hair. In manner he was reserved and shy, but without either conceit or self-consciousness. He was unmarried.

Ledwidge has been called the Burns and the Clare of the Irish, but he was not distinctively Irish in genius. Though his inspiration was drawn from the fields along the Boyne, its themes are common to rural poets through northern Europe—may-blossoms, roses of the lane, roadside birds upon the tops of dusty hedges, and especially the blackbird's song. His joy is purely sensuous; and his sorrow is at root the pagan grief that all things pass. The oaten straw was his natural instrument. When he puts it aside for the national harp and the conventions of the Celtic revival, he is hampered by a mythology too shadowy and portentous, except where it echoes the cradle songs of the country-side. He has more instinctive sympathy for the naturalistic myths of Pan and Proserpine. He is like Keats in other ways: in fitful dissatisfaction with the sensuousness of his genius, and in his gift for the magical phrase. But he had not even Keats's opportunities for improving his technique, especially in range of verse-craft.

Ledwidge's published works are *Songs of the Field* (1915), *Songs of Peace* (1916), *Last Songs* (1918), and *Complete Poems* (1919); a play, *The Crock of Gold*, is unpublished.

[Lord Dunsany's prefaces to Ledwidge's poems; H. R. Stannard in the *Weekly Dispatch*, 19 August 1917; Katharine Tynan, *The Years of the Shadow*, 1919; private information.] H. B. C-n.

LEE-WARNER, Sir WILLIAM (1846–1914), Indian civil servant and author, was the fifth and youngest son of the Rev. Henry James Lee-Warner, honorary canon of Norwich, of Thorpland Hall, Norfolk, by his wife, Anne, daughter of the Rev. Henry Nicholas Astley, rector of East Barsham, Norfolk. He was born at Little Walsingham vicarage 18 April 1846, and went in 1859 to Rugby, where he won the regard of Dr. Temple. Elected in 1865 a scholar of St. John's College, Cambridge, he took honours in the moral science tripos in 1869. In later years Cambridge gave him the honorary degree of LL.D. Both at school and at Cambridge he made his mark in sports; he represented the university against Oxford at racquets as late as 1889, and throughout a strenuous official career he retained his athletic and open-air tastes. On passing the Indian civil service examination of 1867, he was posted to the Bombay Presidency in 1869. Two years later the governor, Sir Philip Wodehouse [q.v.], also a Norfolk man, made him his private secretary. Thereafter Lee-Warner served in an exceptional variety of posts, whereby he saw the problem of Indian administration from every side. At one time he was in charge of education in Berar, then collector, first of Poona, and next of Satara; subsequently he was political agent at Kolapur (1886–1887). He had had a period of service with the government of India as under-secretary in the foreign department in 1884, and in August 1887 he became secretary to the Bombay government in the political and judicial departments, being later promoted to the chief secretaryship. He represented the Bombay government in the viceroy's legislature in 1893–1894 and again early in 1895. In the latter year he was appointed resident in Mysore and ex-officio chief commissioner of Coorg, but he retired a few months later. The most important of the various inquiries on which he served was the epoch-making education commission of 1882–1883. His political appointments provided him with material for his *Protected Princes of India* (1894) which, as revised and enlarged in *The Native States of India* (1916), remains the standard authority.

In 1895 Lord George Hamilton brought Lee-Warner home to be secretary of the political and secret department at the India Office. In this capacity and later as a member of the secretary of state's council, to which he was appointed in November 1902 for ten years, he had important influence upon Indian affairs. He was created K.C.S.I. in 1898. Cautious in temperament and alive to the dangers of instability of policy in dealing with Eastern peoples, Lee-Warner, who had come of strongly liberal stock, was no reactionary; but he was regarded as such by many Indian politicians, who disliked his book, *The Citizen of India* (1897), which was written in order to correct prevalent misconceptions of the British rule. His own straightforwardness of purpose and acute perceptions made him quick to diagnose motives and policies which appeared to him tortuous or malign, and he probably over-estimated the secret political influence of the Brahmin hierarchy. He looked with suspicion upon the political demands of the educated classes, because he did not believe that they would inure to the benefit of the country as a whole.

An obituary notice of him in *The Times* (19 January 1914) justifiably states that no more genuine friend of the Indian people, and particularly of the agricultural classes, served India in our time. He was trusted and admired by successive secretaries of state; and though his intimate knowledge of Indian intricacies and his fearless independence of judgement were a foil to Lord Morley's radical ideals for India, that statesman recognized the value of his criticism when he put forward the recommendation whereby in 1911 Lee-Warner was promoted G.C.S.I.

Lee-Warner wrote the authoritative *Life of the Marquis of Dalhousie* (1904) and, from intimate personal knowledge, *Memoirs of Field-Marshal Sir Henry Wylie Norman* (1908). He contributed to this DICTIONARY, to the *Cambridge Modern History*, to the *Encyclopædia Britannica*, and to other works of reference, besides writing frequently for the quarterly and monthly reviews. Of marked simplicity of character, and a devout evangelical churchman, his activities in religious and philanthropic enterprise were many-sided. He used up his strength both of mind and body remorselessly. After his retirement from the India Office in 1912, he had many schemes for literary and other work for his beloved India. Refusing to rest, he broke down in health, and died 18 January 1914. He is buried in the churchyard of the home of his childhood, Little Walsingham.

Lee-Warner married in 1876 Ellen Paulina, eldest daughter of Major-General J. W. Holland, and was survived by three sons. Another son was accidentally drowned at Nanaimo, Vancouver Island, in 1906.

[Lee-Warner's books and articles; *The Times*, 19 January 1914; Lord Sydenham in the *Spectator*, 31 January 1914; personal knowledge.] F. H. B.

LEGG, JOHN WICKHAM (1843–1921), physician and liturgiologist, was born at Alverstoke, Hampshire, 28 December 1843, the third son of George Legg, of Alverstoke, by his wife, Ellen Austin. Samuel Wilberforce [q.v.] was vicar of Alverstoke from 1840 until his appointment as bishop of Oxford in 1845, and the church revival which he began in this parish probably influenced the boy. Educated locally, Wickham Legg, on leaving school, entered University College, London, in order to study medicine, and became a pupil of Sir William Jenner [q.v.]. He won the gold medal of his year, and having qualified M.R.C.S. in 1866 became, on Jenner's recommendation, resident medical attendant to Prince Leopold, afterwards Duke of Albany. He resigned this post in 1867 and went to study at Berlin under Professor Virchow; in 1868 he returned to England in order to become curator of the pathological museum at University College. In the same year he took his M.D. degree at London, and became M.R.C.P.; he was elected F.R.C.P. in 1876. In 1870 he was appointed casualty physician at St. Bartholomew's Hospital, and in 1878 was elected assistant physician; he also held various appointments in the medical school of the hospital. In addition, he had a growing consulting practice and made considerable contributions to the literature of medicine, of which his treatise on *Haemophilia* (1872) is probably the best known. 'All Wickham Legg's medical writings show the same qualities. The language is well chosen; the main thesis carefully worked out; the literature of the subject has been thoroughly mastered, and in every paper he has something definite to say' [*Memoir*, p. 3]. The range of his researches was not less remarkable than his presentation of them.

Nevertheless, in 1887, after two attacks of rheumatic fever, Wickham Legg resolved to abandon medicine; he resigned his appointments, gave away his medical books, and retired from practice. Medicine was not his only interest: as early as 1875 he had been elected a fellow of the Society of Antiquaries, while as a churchman he was greatly influenced by Dr. Henry Parry Liddon. The study of liturgies was a strong interest in his life, and he now had the leisure to bring to it the accurate scientific training which, joined to his brilliance and eagerness for research, had made his reputation as a physician. In this new field of learning he rapidly obtained a European reputation, his first great contribution to liturgical science being his edition (1888) of the Quignon Breviary of 1535. He was one of the prime movers in the foundation, in 1890, of the Henry Bradshaw Society for printing rare liturgical texts. For that society he edited the *Westminster Missal* (3 vols., 1891–1897), the *Second Recension of the Quignon Breviary* (2 vols., 1908, 1912), and seven other volumes, and he was chairman of the council from 1897 till his death. His researches in the libraries of Western Europe bore fruit in essays printed in the publications of various learned societies; some are gathered up into his *Ecclesio-*

logical Essays (1905) and *Essays Liturgical and Historical* (1917). He also edited the *Sarum Missal*, from three early manuscripts, for the Clarendon Press in 1916. His *English Church Life from the Restoration to the Tractarian Movement* (1914) is a remarkable collection of evidence to show that in the period from 1660 to 1833 traditional church doctrines and practices prevailed more commonly than is often supposed. In 1913 the university of Oxford conferred on him the honorary degree of D.Litt. in recognition of his liturgical scholarship.

In ecclesiastical as in medical matters Wickham Legg's mind was strongly sceptical of new movements. This made him extremely conservative, and although he was open to conviction, it needed almost a scientific demonstration to convince him. He relied on the general validity of the appeal to history in the church, and as time went on his mistrust of the speculations of liberal theology and his dislike of Anglo-Catholic developments increased. He would tell with keen humour how in 1886 he had been described as 'one of a conspiracy to restore the ceremonial of fifty years ago', and probably he vastly preferred that traditional ceremonial, reverently performed, to innovations introduced, without historical inquiry, from current practice in France or Belgium. He held that the present generation lacked both the knowledge and the taste successfully to revise the Prayer Book; consequently he opposed Prayer Book revision in some learned and pungent pamphlets (*The Proposed Revision of the Prayer Book*, 1909; *Shall We Revise the Prayer Book?*, 1911). He described the aim of some of the leaders of the movement as being 'under pretence of revision, to undermine the doctrinal position of the Church of England in favour of the liberals, men who profess a new religion, of such a character that it may be doubted if it have any claim at all to be considered historical Christianity'. He was elected a member of the house of laymen of the province of Canterbury in 1910, his position being that of a strong high churchman of the Tractarian type.

Wickham Legg married in 1872 Eliza Jane, daughter of Richard Houghton, of Sandheys, Great Crosby, near Liverpool. There was one son of the marriage, who was elected a fellow of New College, Oxford, in 1908. On his wife's death in that year Legg removed from his house in Green Street, Park Lane, to Oxford, where he resided till his death on 28 October 1921. He is buried at Saltwood, Kent.

In person Legg was of middle height, portly, with a handsome face and fine head. In 1917 his sight became impaired, and at the end of his life he was almost blind. He possessed a rare charm of manner, was a first-rate raconteur, and a delightful host to a large circle of friends. They included many foreign savants, among them the future Pope Pius XI who, as prefect of the Ambrosian Library, was Legg's guest at Oxford at the commemoration of Roger Bacon in 1914.

[Memoir (by Sir A. E. Garrod), with portrait, in St. Bartholomew's Hospital *Reports*, vol. lv, 1922; private information; personal knowledge.] S. L. O.

LEVY-LAWSON, EDWARD, first **Baron Burnham** (1833–1916), newspaper proprietor, was born in London 28 December 1833, the eldest of the eight children of Joseph Moses Levy [q.v.], manager of a printing establishment in Shoe Lane, Fleet Street, by his wife, Esther, daughter of Godfrey Alexander Cohen. Edward Levy assumed the additional surname of Lawson by royal licence in 1875, in consideration of a deed of gift by his father's brother, Lionel Lawson. He was educated at University College School, Gower Street, London, and, on leaving, joined as dramatic critic the staff of the *Sunday Times*, at that time owned by his father. 'It was in the back office on the ground floor at the corner of Bridge Street,' he once told an audience many years later, 'I sometimes, in the intervals of providing copy, had visions of a future, which, with the help of many kind friends, has been happily realized.' In 1855 Joseph Levy acquired the *Daily Telegraph and Courier*, after three months' precarious existence, from its original founder, Colonel Sleigh, in liquidation of a printing debt. The new owner put fresh capital and energy into the business, dropped the second half of the cumbrous title, gathered round him a vigorous staff (including his son, who shortly afterwards became editor), and turned a losing into a paying property.

The moment was exceptionally favourable for new developments in journalism. The possibilities of the electric telegraph, then still a novelty and a wonder, were just beginning to be understood, although it was not till later that the London press made extensive use of the opportunities which it provided for the rapid transmission of news. The abolition of the last of the paper duties in 1861 cleared the way for the development of the penny press, of which the *Daily Telegraph* was the pioneer in London. Edward Levy undertook his first public work in connexion with these paper duties, for he served with Mr. Cobden and Mr. Bright on a committee the report of which finally determined their abolition. He had personal knowledge of almost every department of a newspaper. He could set type; he had 'handled copy'; he could turn a neat paragraph, and dictate a telling leader. His main interest soon focussed on politics, and he was much in the lobby of the House of Commons, where he shared with John Thadeus Delane [q.v.], of *The Times*, the special privilege, rarely granted, of standing at the bar of the House of Lords with members of the House of Commons.

The dominant idea of those who conducted the *Daily Telegraph* was to break away from the ponderous stiffness of the older journalism, to brighten the paper by a more lively presentation of the news, and to appeal to the sentiment of the reader as well as to chronicle facts. The Dickens influence was strong, and the humanized newspaper succeeded so well that by 1871 the circulation of the *Daily Telegraph* had risen to the then unprecedented figure of 200,000 copies a day. (Sir) Edwin Arnold, George Augustus Henry Sala, Edward Litt Laman Blanchard, Thornton Leigh Hunt, Frederick Greenwood, William Beatty Kingston, (Sir) Campbell Clarke, Joseph Bennett, James Macdonnell, Francis Charles Lawley, and Clement William Scott were amongst the best known of those who helped Lawson to achieve and maintain 'the largest circulation', but none did more than (Sir) John Merry Le Sage, managing editor for thirty years.

Long before his father's death in 1888 the principal direction of the paper had been in Lawson's hands; he had indeed been managing proprietor and sole controller since 1885. A good judge of men, he knew also how to get the best work out of them. His instructions never left a doubt of his meaning. A few sentences scribbled in pencil in a large, round hand on the back of a used envelope would often serve to convey his wishes. His decisions were rapid and final; his industry tireless. Although few men loved social pleasures more, or had a greater aptitude for them, he rarely failed for a long stretch of years to read and pass the proofs of all the principal articles which were to appear in the next morning's issue.

Throughout the 'sixties and 'seventies the *Daily Telegraph* consistently supported Mr. Gladstone. The name of 'the People's William', which at one time enjoyed a wide vogue, was coined by Lawson himself. On occasion he sought personally to influence the liberal leader in the direction of social reform. The day before Mr. Gladstone was to make an eagerly awaited speech in Greenwich in 1874 Lawson called and sent in the suggestion through the chief liberal whip that Gladstone should commit the party to a campaign for the better housing of the working classes. Gladstone admitted the importance of the subject, but doubted the suitability of state action. When, in 1878, Gladstone's Eastern policy became strongly anti-Turkish, the *Daily Telegraph* transferred its support to Lord Beaconsfield largely owing to the influence of Edwin Arnold. The Home Rule controversy widened the paper's breach with the liberals. Lawson always claimed that the paper was strictly independent and not bound or pledged to any leader or party, but from 1886 onwards it supported, without swerving, the unionist and imperialist causes and a 'strong navy' policy.

In politics Lawson was a realist of accommodating temper, prepared to fight hard for his political principles while reasonable hope of maintaining them remained, but not prepared to tie himself or his paper to a dead cause. He was always for settling differences rather than for fighting them out to the bitter end. He was the friend of reasonable men in either camp. A warm advocate of social reform, he had strong sympathies with those who were suffering or in distress. Tolerant himself, he opposed intolerance in others.

Lawson took a special interest in the organization of appeals to the public on behalf of great national and charitable efforts. The first of the *Daily Telegraph's* many shilling funds was raised to relieve the Lancashire cotton famine distress in the winter of 1862–1863. The last great appeal which Lawson personally initiated was the *Daily Telegraph* soldiers' and sailors' widows and orphans fund during the Boer War, which raised and distributed the sum of £255,275. The 1887 jubilee was celebrated by a fund for the entertainment of 30,000 London school children in Hyde Park. Lawson received the Queen on that occasion, and the function was one of the most successful and pleasing of the jubilee ceremonies. Another effort produced £44,570 for the Prince of Wales's hospital fund for London in commemoration of the Queen's diamond jubilee in 1897.

Among the more notable enterprises

sponsored by the *Daily Telegraph* were the expedition of the archaeologist George Smith [q.v.] to Assyria in 1873, when certain cuneiform records of the Deluge story were discovered; the joint enterprise with the *New York Herald* in 1874, when (Sir) Henry Morton Stanley [q.v.] was commissioned to complete David Livingstone's work in 'Darkest Africa' and explore the sources of the Congo; and the assistance given in 1884 to the expedition of Sir Harry Hamilton Johnston to (Mount) Kilima Njaro in East Africa.

Lawson was created a baronet in 1892, and was raised to the peerage as Baron Burnham in 1903, when he retired from active control of the *Daily Telegraph* and handed over the reins to his elder son. He received the K.C.V.O. in 1904. By that time he was universally recognized as the doyen of English journalism. In 1913, on the occasion of his eightieth birthday, Lord Northcliffe presented him at his estate of Hall Barn, near Beaconsfield, with an address of congratulation from every branch of English journalism, the most striking passage of the address being that which in effect complimented Lord Burnham on having staved off so vigorously the challenge of his younger and most formidable rival. 'You have never stood still', ran the address, 'in former ways, however successful, but by signal strokes of promptitude and courage have shown how journalism may re-adapt itself to the changing circumstances both of its own technical conditions, and of the world which it reflects.' In journalistic circles the significance of the reference was well understood. Lord Northcliffe on another occasion spoke of Lord Burnham as 'the best journalist of us all'.

Lord Burnham was one of the most widely known men of his time. He wielded power through his newspaper, but he was liked for himself. He was an original member of the Beefsteak Club, and a trustee of the Garrick Club. He loved good fellowship and genial gossip, and radiated liveliness. He also had great kindness of heart. He was a good talker and a good speaker—the utterance large, the style rotund. When he spoke for the newspaper press fund, or among journalists at press conferences—he was president of the Royal Institute of Journalists in 1892–1893, and of the Empire Press Union from 1909 till his death—he was always at his best. But he rarely appeared on public platforms and he never broke silence in the House of Lords.

A Londoner born and bred, Lord Burnham loved London life, and carried on the family tradition of being a good host and giving pleasant social parties. In 1881 he purchased Hall Barn, in the hundred of Burnham, the old home of Edmund Waller, the poet, and there the Prince of Wales (afterwards King Edward VII) visited him every year from 1892 until his death. There, too, during the last twelve years of his life Lord Burnham gave himself up to the enjoyment of country pursuits and fulfilled the duties of deputy lieutenant and justice of the peace for Buckinghamshire, of which he had been high sheriff in 1886. He died in London 9 January 1916.

Lord Burnham married in 1862 Harriette Georgiana (died 1897), only daughter of Benjamin Nottingham Webster [q.v.], the actor-manager. They had two sons and one daughter. The elder son, Harry Lawson Webster Levy-Lawson (born 1862), succeeded his father in the barony and was created a viscount in 1919.

There is a whole-length portrait of Lord Burnham, seated, in robes, with the star of the Victorian order, by Sir Hubert von Herkomer (*Royal Academy Pictures*, 1910).

[*Daily Telegraph*, 10 January 1916; private information; personal knowledge.]

J. B. F.

LEWIS, WILLIAM THOMAS, first Baron Merthyr, of Senghenydd (1837–1914), engineer and coal-owner, the eldest son of Thomas William Lewis, engineer, of Abercanaid House, Merthyr Tydfil, by his wife, Mary Anne, daughter of John Watkin, was born at Merthyr Tydfil 5 August 1837. He received his early training under his father, and in 1855 became assistant engineer to William Southern Clark, mining agent for the Marquess of Bute's estate in South Wales—in Cardiff and its neighbourhood. He succeeded Clark in 1864 at an important period in the history of the coal industry and, as consulting engineer, was connected with various colliery and railway schemes in South Wales. In 1881 Lewis was given entire control of the Marquess of Bute's Welsh estates, and, by reducing the costs of working at the Cardiff docks (constructed by the Bute family), he made possible the expansion necessary for the rapidly increasing trade in steam coal. By 1887 he had constructed the Roath dock and by 1907 the Queen Alexandra dock. He also introduced new appliances, including the Lewis-Hunter crane, of which he was part inventor. When the Bute Dock Company was formed in 1887, he became managing director, and some years later helped to secure direct access to the South Wales coal-field by opening up the Cardiff Railway. Undoubtedly, the growth of Cardiff and the prosperity of the coal-field are bound up with Lewis's career.

Lewis's work for the Bute estates, however, represents but one phase of his activities. His marriage in 1864 to Anne (died 1902), daughter of William Rees, colliery-owner, of Lletyshenkin, Aberdare, brought him into close contact with the steam-coal trade, of which his wife's family were pioneers. His main colliery interests ultimately lay in the lower Rhondda valley and in the Senghenydd district. He possessed a remarkable knowledge of the South Wales coal-field and of coal-working in general, and was appointed to serve on the royal commissions on the action of coal dust in mines, on mining royalties, on coal supplies, and on accidents in mines (1878–1886). For his valuable services on the last-named commission he was knighted in 1885. From coal Lewis was drawn into iron-working, and he helped to revive the industry by applying the new Bessemer process for the production of steel. In 1908 he was elected president of the Iron and Steel Institute.

Probably some of Lewis's greatest work was done in the cause of industrial peace. Little effort had been made to organize the coal industry until after the strike of 1871, when he succeeded in persuading coal-owners and iron-masters of South Wales to form the Monmouthshire and South Wales Coal-Owners' Association. During the great strike of 1873 he counselled arbitration and urged the adoption of a sliding scale as the basis of the new wage agreement. The acceptance of this principle in 1875 brought peace and stability to the industry for many years; and, as chairman for eighteen years of the sliding-scale committee, Lewis was largely responsible for the efficient working of the scheme. The principle led to a distinct improvement in the relations between capital and labour, and later came to be adopted in other coal-fields.

Lewis had won for himself a high reputation as an industrial expert and as a conciliator. In 1881 he was president of the Mining Association of Great Britain, and he served on the royal commissions on labour (1891–1894), on trades' disputes (1903–1906), and on shipping combinations (1906–1907). He was successful in effecting a settlement of the Taff Vale Railway strike in 1900, and his proposal for the institution of permanent boards of arbitration became the basis of settlement of the general railway strike of 1907.

Lewis, who had been created a baronet in 1896 and had received the K.C.V.O. in 1907, was raised to the peerage in 1911 as Baron Merthyr, of Senghenydd, Glamorganshire. In 1912 he received the G.C.V.O. He took a keen interest in education and in the social welfare of the coal-field, and was a generous supporter of hospitals and other institutions. He had played a prominent part in the founding, in 1881, of the Monmouthshire and South Wales permanent provident fund for the relief of colliery workers in case of sickness or accident—a scheme which anticipated by many years some of the advantages of old age pensions, compensation for accident, and insurance against sickness or unemployment.

Lord Merthyr died at Newbury 27 August 1914. He had two sons and six daughters, and he was succeeded as second baron by his elder son, Herbert Clark Lewis (born 1866).

[*Shipping World*, July 1907, September 1908; *The Syren and Shipping*, January 1900, November 1905, July 1907; *Maritime Review*, March 1905, July 1907, October 1909; *The Sphere*, July 1905; *The Queen*, March 1905, November 1906, July 1907; *South Wales Daily News*, November 1906, June 1911, August 1914; *Western Mail*, June–July 1907, November 1912, August 1914; *Merthyr Times*, November 1885, June 1887; *Merthyr Express*, February 1907, June 1911; *Aberdare Weekly Post*, March 1905, July 1907, August 1914; private information.] W. R.

LIBERTY, Sir ARTHUR LASENBY (1843–1917), fabric manufacturer, the eldest son of Arthur Liberty, lace manufacturer, of Nottingham and of Chesham, Buckinghamshire, by his wife, Rebecca Lasenby, was born at Chesham 13 August 1843. He was educated at University School, Nottingham. In 1862, at the age of nineteen, he was appointed manager of Farmer and Rogers's Oriental warehouse in Regent Street, London, the first depôt in England for the exclusive sale of goods from the Far East. Liberty held this position until 1874, when the warehouse was closed, and during these twelve years came into close contact with artists interested in Oriental and other crafts, who used to meet there. Among them were Leighton, Burne-Jones, Rossetti, Whistler, and William Morris. In 1875 Liberty went into business on his own account, with three employees, at 218

Regent Street, which he called East India House. Here the same coterie of friends continued to meet. From this modest beginning sprang the important business of Liberty & Co., well known throughout Europe and America.

Liberty was a shrewd business organizer, careful in the selection and treatment of his staff, many of whom remained a lifetime in his service. One of his principal designers was the architect, Edward William Godwin [q.v.]. He was a zealous promoter of better conditions for employees and an enthusiastic supporter of the early-closing movement. But his success was mainly due to his own thorough methods, his artistic perception, and his knack of anticipating the trend of public taste. As early as 1875 he realized that the industries of the East were influencing a much wider circle than a few connoisseurs; he therefore tried to satisfy the growing demand for Oriental textiles and colours by manufacturing fine fabrics of softer texture and subtler tint than had hitherto been generally obtainable in the West. Before long he had succeeded in producing British machine-made stuffs which equalled the hand-made products of Asia. At a later date (1888–1889) he visited Japan in order to study Japanese arts and crafts and the details of their manufacture.

Liberty's influence on the British silk and woollen industry of the 'seventies was considerable. Not only did he induce manufacturers to abandon adulteration, but, in conjunction with his friend, Sir Thomas Wardle [q.v.], he succeeded in introducing fine dyes hitherto supposed to be the exclusive product of the East. His aims were closely parallel with those of William Morris, and it has been supposed that Liberty was largely guided by Morris's example. The suggestion is erroneous, for Liberty was in close touch with a large circle, and his artistic ideas were influenced by the East rather than by the mediaeval Western art to which Morris was devoted. But both men educated the artistic taste of the public, and stimulated manufacturers to higher standards of design and workmanship.

In 1913 Liberty was knighted in recognition of his services to applied and decorative arts. He was J.P. and D.L. for the county of Buckingham, and high sheriff in 1899, juror of several international exhibitions, member of the council of the London Chamber of Commerce, and an officer of numerous commercial and artistic associations. He died at Lee Manor, Buckinghamshire, 11 May 1917. He married in 1875 Emma Louise, daughter of Henry Blackmore, of Exmouth, Devon; there were no children of the marriage.

[*The Times*, 12 May 1917; private information; personal knowledge.] G. D. R.

LINDLEY, NATHANIEL, Baron Lindley (1828–1921), lord of appeal, born at Chiswick 29 November 1828, was the younger son of John Lindley, F.R.S. [q.v.], professor of botany at University College, London, by his wife, Sarah, daughter of Anthony George Freestone, of South Elmham, Suffolk, and a descendant in the female line of the great chief justice, Sir Edward Coke. The only brother of Lord Lindley died in childhood, but his two sisters survived, like himself, to a great age. He was educated at University College School in Gower Street, and for about two years at University College. His career at school and college was uneventful. When about eighteen years of age he was sent by his father to France, without a degree, to learn French with a view to entering the Foreign Office. But the tastes which he had formed in the scientific society of his father's house soon dispelled all thoughts of a diplomatic career. On the advice of an uncle who was a solicitor, he entered at the Middle Temple in 1847. From November 1848 he read in various chambers, and finally (after a few months spent in studying Roman law at Bonn) in those of the future lord justice of appeal, Charles Jasper Selwyn [q.v.]. His pupillage lasted four and a half years. So deliberate a preparation for practice is unheard of now. He records the study of fifty-seven different books of learning, from which he made careful notes on sheets collected in large covers labelled with their subjects.

In May 1854 Lindley, who had been called to the bar in 1850, painted up his name at 16 Old Square, Lincoln's Inn. Early in 1855 he published a translation with notes of the first part of Thibaut's *System des Pandektenrechts*, under the title of *An Introduction to the Study of Jurisprudence*. This work made Lindley favourably known as a student of legal principles and not merely of English law reports. During this year he began to concentrate his attention upon the law of partnership and commenced a book upon that subject which took him nearly five years to write. His first clients were the solicitors to the Horticultural Society. His first 'fighting' case came in 1856, when his leader, the future Vice-Chancellor Bacon, left him alone in the Court of Appeal before Lords Justices Knight-Bruce and Turner. He had been engaged for some years to Sarah, daughter of Edward John Teale, solicitor, of Leeds, and they decided to marry on his income of £300 a year. The marriage, which led to many decades of happiness, took place in 1858. During the next year or two practice continued to be slack and the young couple lived in lodgings, but in February 1860 Lindley's work was published under the title, *A Treatise on the Law of Partnership, including its application to Companies*. The publishers paid £150 clear for an edition of a thousand copies and the author retained the copyright. The book was at once noticed publicly by the judges. In this year his first pupil came to him. Others followed, including (Sir) Frederick Pollock, the well-known jurist, and (Sir) Francis Maclean, afterwards chief justice of Bengal. It is characteristic that Lindley never took more than two pupils at a time, and went through their drafts with them sitting by his side.

In 1866, when the failure of the old-established house of Overend, Gurney & Co. produced a financial crisis in the City, Lindley was the junior for the partners of the firm throughout the subsequent litigation. The year marked the change from a safe to a great practice, and Lindley, with his unfailing good judgement, consolidated his Chancery work by refusing to take briefs in the countless great arbitrations which followed the 1866 debacle. In the same year he received from the lord chief justice, Sir Alexander Cockburn, the office of revising barrister for Middlesex. He only held the appointment for one turn, but, when he became a judge of the common pleas, this experience had prepared him for the appeals in election cases which went to that court. In 1871 the well-known case of *Knox* v. *Gye* enhanced his reputation greatly. He appeared for Gye, the manager of the Covent Garden opera. Vice-Chancellor Page Wood had decided against his client, but the decision was reversed by the Court of Appeal and not restored by the House of Lords. This brought further work from theatrical people, including the defendants in an action concerning *Frou-frou*, in which the owners of the copyright in the novel endeavoured to prevent the performance of the English play which had been based upon it. The defence was that the play was an adaptation and not a translation, and was moreover altered to suit English tastes. In arguing this case Lindley read many pages of French, contrasting them with the English version. The court was crowded and many French and Belgian theatrical performers were present. When it was explained to the foreigners at the close that the defendants had succeeded, the tall Belgian actress who played 'Frou-frou' threw her arms around Lindley, exclaiming 'Mon sauveur! mon sauveur!' In 1872 Lindley was making £4,500 a year and was 'terribly overworked'. He took silk on the advice of Sir George Jessel, then solicitor-general, and attached himself to the court of Vice-Chancellor Wickens. At this time one of Wickens's leaders, James Dickinson, Q.C., was seriously ill, and this helped the new silk, who in his first year as a Q.C. made a larger income than in his last year in stuff. In each subsequent year of his practice the position continued to improve. In the autumn of 1874 died the uncle who had been so valued a friend to Lindley throughout his life. He left to his nephew a small house and about sixty acres of land in East Carleton, near Norwich, and also a considerable sum of money. This house became the country home of Lindley and his family. He enlarged it substantially and lived there, at first in vacations and then altogether, until his death.

In May 1875 Lord Chancellor Cairns, to the astonishment of Lindley and of the profession, offered him a judgeship in the common pleas. The Judicature Acts (1872–1875) which were to fuse common law and equity, with the provision that where they differed equity 'should prevail', were to come into operation in the following November. The extension of this 'prevalence' to appointments caused some perturbation; for neither Lord Cairns nor Lord Selborne had ever given a chancery judgeship to a common law man. While Lindley was naturally hesitating, Mr. Justice Denman, then a stranger, offered to go the coming summer circuit for him, thus giving him time to prepare for criminal work. This encouraged Lindley to accept the post and, as Denman later advised, go the circuit himself and get the novelty over. In less than a week he was sworn in and knighted, was made a serjeant-at-law, and took his seat in the Exchequer Chamber. He was the last person to put the serjeant's black patch upon his wig, and finally the last survivor of that ancient order. He had been twenty-one years at the bar and was forty-six years of age.

Lindley's judicial career lasted for thirty years. Appointed judge of the common pleas in 1875, he was a lord justice of appeal from 1881 to 1897, master of the Rolls from 1897 to 1900, and a lord of appeal in ordinary from 1900 to 1905. On his first journey he was characteristically careful to take a marshal with knowledge of sessions, an experienced common law clerk, and a butler who knew circuit. Since his appointment he had been working every day from 6 a.m., and in all spare moments, at the criminal law. On his second circuit the former chief justice of the common pleas, Sir William Erle, came into court at York and subsequently wrote Lindley's praises in a letter to one of the barristers. No doubt his pupillage with special pleaders assisted Lindley, but this rapid success in criminal work could only have come to one who was a judge by nature. From the first it was obvious that, whether in civil or criminal work, Lindley would hold his own with any common law judge in England. After six years as a puisne judge Lindley commenced his twenty years' work in the Court of Appeal. For half this time he presided usually in one court or the other. His spare time seemed to be given to drafting rules, orders, and consolidating statutes, which were sometimes used by the chancellors who had asked for them, and sometimes pigeonholed without explanation. In 1897 he succeeded Lord Esher as master of the Rolls, and became an F.R.S. and an honorary LL.D. of Cambridge. In return for his settlement of a dispute between the Royal Society and the Royal Geographical Society Captain Robert Falcon Scott [q.v.] named after him Mount Lindley, 'very far south in the map'.

In 1900 Lindley succeeded Lord Morris as lord of appeal and was created a life peer. Had he wished he could have received a heritable title. In 1905 he fell on the steps by the Duke of York's column and suffered from concussion of the brain. Soon afterwards, on his seventy-seventh birthday, he resigned and thereafter lived a life of unostentatious usefulness at his country home in Norfolk. He died at his home, near Norwich, 9 December 1921, two days before Lord Chancellor Halsbury. They had been called in the same year (1850) and had lived to the ages of ninety-three and ninety-eight respectively. Of his nine children, four sons and two daughters survived him.

Lord Lindley's reputation stands very high among lawyers, though he was little known to the world. The record of such a man is found in his work. To sit in court, term in and term out, for thirty years, and decide numberless cases with satisfaction to litigants and improvement to their counsel, implies great gifts of intellect and disposition He brought to his task a quick and logical intellect, an unwillingness to talk, and a disposition which could not be soured. He had none of the picturesqueness of Lord Justice James or the brilliance of Lord Bowen or the refulgent rhetoric of Lord Macnaghten. In manner he was unostentatious and unpretentious. A remarkable characteristic was his versatility. He appeared to have no speciality. Whether dealing with a one-man company, or the right of houses to support, or stock-exchange gambling, or the eccentricities of the river Ouse, or peaceful pickets, he was at home with his subject. Nothing seemed simpler. He merely stated the facts correctly and applied to them the proper principles of law; and impartiality was his foible.

A bust portrait of Lord Lindley in a wig was painted by W. W. Ouless, R.A., in 1897 (*Royal Academy Pictures*, 1897).

[*The Times*, 12 December 1921; unpublished Autobiography of Lord Lindley; personal knowledge.] A. J. A.

LINDSAY, JAMES LUDOVIC, twenty-sixth EARL OF CRAWFORD and ninth EARL OF BALCARRES (1847–1913), astronomer, collector, and bibliophile, the only son of Alexander William Crawford Lindsay [q.v.], twenty-fifth Earl of Crawford and eighth Earl of Balcarres, by his wife, Margaret, eldest daughter of Lieutenant-General James Lindsay, of Balcarres, was born at St. Germain-en-Laye 28 July 1847. He was educated at Eton, and after a short residence at Trinity College, Cambridge, entered the Grenadier Guards, but resigned his commission after being elected (1874) M.P. for Wigan, a seat which he held until he succeeded to his father's earldom in 1880. Attracted to astronomy, he organized a station at Cadiz in 1870 for observing the eclipse of the sun, on which occasion he rendered valuable assistance to an expedition sent by the British government. In 1872 he erected an observatory, equipped with the newest telescopes, at Dunecht, near Aberdeen, and made acquaintance with Mr. (afterwards Sir David) Gill [q.v.] who became a distinguished assistant in its management. In 1874 Lord Lindsay, with Mr. Gill and Dr. Ralph Copeland [q.v.], proceeded to Mauritius to observe the transit of Venus. Equipped with instruments at great expense by the twenty-fifth Earl of Crawford, they were enabled, though the observation was marred by clouds, to report valuable data for the determination of longitudes and the method of establishing the solar parallax. The results are contained in the *Dunecht Observatory Publications*—a series long regarded as an important source of astronomical information. In 1888 Lord Crawford presented to the nation all his telescopes, instruments, and astronomical library, for the purpose of establishing an improved observatory at Edinburgh. Dr. Ralph Copeland, who had directed the observatory at Dunecht since 1876, was appointed in 1889 astronomer royal for Scotland, and the new Royal Observatory on Blackford Hill was opened by Lord Crawford in 1896.

During the rest of his life Lord Crawford made large collections of proclamations, broadsides, documents of the French Revolution, and postage stamps; he also collected a philatelic library which he bequeathed to the British Museum. He was an enthusiastic bibliophile, and added greatly to the splendid library inherited from his father. The manuscripts are now in the possession of the John Rylands Library, Manchester, with the exception of a series of English and Oriental manuscripts illustrating the progress of handwriting, which he presented to the free library of Wigan. He issued a number of catalogues and handlists, and also collations and notes of the rarer books in a valuable series of volumes entitled *Bibliotheca Lindesiana* (1883–1913). Though not a profound mathematician, he had considerable mechanical skill and took special interest in the development of electrical engineering, acting as chief British commissioner at the electrical exhibition in Paris in 1881. He rendered other service by scientific exploration in his yacht *Valhalla*.

Lord Crawford was elected president of the Royal Astronomical Society in 1878 and 1879, fellow of the Royal Society (1878), honorary associate of the Royal Prussian Academy of Sciences (1883), and a trustee of the British Museum (1885). He also presided over the Royal Photographic Society, the Philatelic Society, and the Camden Society. He was invested knight of the Thistle in 1896 and held the volunteer decoration. In January 1913, at a meeting of the trustees of the British Museum, Lord Crawford was taken seriously ill. He died the following day, 31 January, at 2 Cavendish Square, and was buried at the old chapel of Balcarres House, Fife. He married in 1869 Emily Florence, second daughter of Colonel the Hon. Edward Bootle Wilbraham, and by her had issue, a daughter and six sons. He was succeeded as twenty-seventh Earl by his eldest son, David Alexander Edward Lindsay (born 1871).

[Obituary notices in *Monthly Notices* of the Royal Astronomical Society, vol. lxxiv; *Faraday House Journal*, February 1913; *Nature*, 13 February 1913 (by Sir David Gill); *London Philatelist*, February and March 1913; *Proceedings* of the Institution of Mechanical Engineers, February 1913; G. Forbes, *David Gill, Man and Astronomer*, 1916; M. J. Nicoll, *Three Voyages of a Naturalist*, 1908; *New Scots Peerage*.] W. A. L.

LINDSAY, THOMAS MARTIN (1843–1914), historian, the eldest son of Alexander Lindsay, by his wife, Susan Irvine Martin, was born 18 October 1843 at Lesmahagow, Lanarkshire, where his father was minister of the Relief church. He was educated at the universities of Glasgow and Edinburgh. At the latter, which he entered in 1861, his unusually brilliant achievement in the philosophical classes was crowned by the Ferguson scholarship and the Shaw fellowship, both open to graduates of any of the Scottish universities. He became assistant to Professor Alexander Campbell Fraser [q.v.], but abandoned the career of a university teacher in order to study for the ministry of the Free Church of Scotland. After completing his course at New College, Edinburgh (1869), he acted as assistant to the minister of St. George's Free church, Edinburgh.

In 1872, the general assembly of the Free Church elected Lindsay to the chair of church history in its theological college at Glasgow, to the duties of which were added, in 1902, those of principal of the college. This appointment diverted his studies from philosophy to history, and his translation of Ueberweg's *Logic* (1871), to which he appended some original dissertations, remained his only philosophical publication. He was at once recognized as an able and inspiring historical teacher, but his zeal for social work, and especially for foreign missions, at first restricted his literary output, though he found time for wide and varied reading. He reorganized the administration of the important missions supported by his Church, acquiring an acknowledged mastery of their complicated financial arrangements, and he was convener of the foreign missions committee from 1886 to 1900. He visited the mission fields in Syria and spent a year in India. Apart from brief but well-constructed text-books on the Gospels of St. Mark and St. Luke, the Acts of the Apostles, and the Reformation, the literary product of his earlier professional years is to be found in his articles (including *Christianity*) in the ninth edition of the *Encyclopædia Britannica* (1875–1888). The contributions of his friend, William Robertson Smith [q.v.], to the *Encyclopædia* led to the most famous heresy prosecution of recent years, and in the courts of the Free Church Lindsay defended Smith with no less courage than ability (1877–1881).

Lindsay's first historical work which attracted widespread attention was his book on *Luther and the German Reformation*, published in 1900. It was followed by his remarkable chapter on Luther in the second volume of the *Cambridge Modern History* (1903), and, in 1906–1907, by his largest and most important book, *A History of the Reformation in Europe*. He intended this work to be the description of 'a great religious movement amid its social environment', and he broke fresh ground in his investigations into popular and family religious life in Germany in the decades immediately preceding the Reformation, and in his exposition of 'the continuity in the religious life of the period'. This insistence upon the significance of the records of social and domestic life was Lindsay's characteristic approach to any period of history, and it found expression in his collection of caricatures and illustrations of costume. His book on the Reformation added to its learning and candour a full-blooded humanity which makes it fascinating reading, and it is much the most important Scottish contribution to European history since the works of Robertson.

While Lindsay will be best remembered as an historian of the Reformation, the literary activity of his later life, when he prepared for the press the products of many years of reading and thinking, is illustrated by his Cunningham lectures on *The Church and the Ministry in the Early Centuries* (1903), by chapters in the first volume (1911) of the *Cambridge Medieval History* (*The Triumph of Christianity*), and in the third volume (1909) of the *Cambridge History of English Literature* (*Englishmen and the Classical Renascence*), and by his estimate of the personality and the achievement of George Buchanan in *Glasgow Quatercentenary Studies* (1906). These are marked by sureness of touch, width of interest and sympathy, and clearness of exposition. He wrote vigorously and often picturesquely, and he had a remarkable power of visualizing both men and things.

Throughout his life, Lindsay was deeply interested in social problems. He organized the efforts of his students in insufficiently equipped Glasgow parishes, he took part in the crofter agitation in the West Highlands and islands, associated with the early political career of Joseph Chamberlain, and he was the friend of such labour leaders as Ben Tillett, Tom Mann, and Cunninghame Graham. He married in 1872 Anna, elder daughter of A. Colquhoun-Stirling-Murray Dunlop, of Edinbarnet and Corsock, formerly M.P. for Greenock, by whom he had three sons and two daughters; and he shared his wife's enthusiasm for the education of women. His advice was sought by many religious and social workers, who relied upon his sympathy and his robust and penetrating common sense. He died 6 December 1914. A portrait by Fiddes Watt is in the Glasgow United Free Church college.

[*Glasgow Herald*, 8 December 1914; Janet Ross, *The Fourth Generation*, 1912; personal information.] R. S. R.

LISTER, JOSEPH, first Baron Lister, of Lyme Regis, (1827–1912), founder of antiseptic surgery, the second son and fourth child of Joseph Jackson Lister, F.R.S., wine-merchant and microscopist [q.v.], was born at Upton House, Upton, Essex, 5 April 1827. His ancestors were members of the Society of Friends since the early part of the eighteenth century. He was educated at Grove House School, Tottenham, and at University College, London, which he entered in 1844. At school he was forward for his age and early showed his taste for natural history by collecting and preparing specimens of various kinds. In later life he frequently spoke of the great influence on him of his father (of whom he has written an account in this Dictionary), and how much he was indebted to him for directing his mind to scientific pursuits and especially to the study of natural history. Whilst still at school, he determined to be a surgeon. None of his near relations were in the medical profession, and it would seem that this desire was entirely spontaneous. He took the B.A. degree of the university of London in 1847, but, owing to an attack of smallpox, he did not begin his medical studies until the autumn of 1848, and was thus rather older than most of his fellow-students. While a student in the faculty of arts, he was present at the first operation under ether in this country—performed by Robert Liston [q.v.] in the theatre of University College Hospital in December 1846.

University College was a small medical school at this time, since it had only been founded in 1828; nevertheless its staff included several men of distinction, and Lister was especially influenced at an early stage of his career by two of these, Wharton Jones and William Sharpey [q.v.]. The former was professor of ophthalmic medicine and surgery, and the latter the celebrated professor of physiology who did so much to lay the foundations on which the modern school of British physiology was raised. Thomas Graham [q.v.], professor of chemistry at University College, was also one of Lister's teachers. Wharton Jones had conducted researches of far-reaching range in physiology, and it must have been largely owing to his influence that Lister's earliest researches were physiological and dealt with the structure and function of tissues. Sharpey had, if anything, an even greater influence, since he not only directed Lister's early physiological inquiries, but advised him, towards the end of his career at University College, to widen his experience by attending the practice of the celebrated Edinburgh surgeon, James Syme [q.v.]; this advice had the most profound influence in moulding Lister's life and career.

During his student career Lister served as house-physician to Dr. Walter Hayle Walshe [q.v.] and as house-surgeon to (Sir) John Eric Erichsen [q.v.], a well-known and capable surgeon but not specially distinguished for any original contributions to the advance of surgery. In 1852 he took his M.B. degree, and at once commenced original work with success. His first work was on the structure of the iris, and he confirmed and extended the demonstration of R. A. von Kölliker that this structure was muscular. This paper and another on the involuntary muscular fibres of the skin were published in 1853 in the *Quarterly Journal of Microscopical Science*. In this year he also carried on experimental work on the flow of chyle, and during the years 1853–1858 he published a series of papers dealing with physiological problems. One of the most important, on *The Cutaneous Pigmentary System of the Frog*, dealt with physiological questions of wide range and advanced considerations that have been only quite recently confirmed. Another paper of great importance, *The Early Stages of Inflammation*, published by the Royal Society in 1857, was the result of one of the most valuable researches that Lister carried out, and the main conclusions which he then formulated have not been controverted with the lapse of time.

On the completion of his career at University College, and armed with an introduction from Sharpey to Syme, Lister went to Edinburgh in September 1853. Syme was at this time fifty-four years of age, a surgeon of acknowledged eminence with much originality, and at the same time a bold and skilful operator and an inspiring teacher. He was a man of decided views, who rather enjoyed controversy but did not brook opposition. Lister, who at first attended Syme's practice as a visitor, soon became a dresser in order to familiarize himself with Syme's methods, and subsequently acted as his house-surgeon for one year. He then decided to settle in Edinburgh, and in 1856 became assistant surgeon to the Royal Infirmary and took an active part in teaching in the extra-mural school, while continuing his researches on inflammation. In 1860 he was appointed to the chair of surgery in Glasgow University, and a year later became surgeon to the Glasgow Infirmary. From this time onward his studies were mainly concerned with suppuration and the treatment of injuries and wounds, and it was during the next few years that he made the observations and discoveries which revolutionized the treatment of disease and injuries.

The wards allotted to him at Glasgow greatly enlarged Lister's clinical experience, but they 'were particularly insanitary, and all forms of septic diseases of wounds were constantly present in them'. He was greatly distressed by the mortality which followed upon injuries and operations, and gave much thought to the subject. He felt that the solution of the problem would only be arrived at by the study of inflammation and suppuration; hence these questions played a large part in his instruction and in his research work. In 1867 he clearly summarized his views in the following words: 'In the course of an extended investigation into the nature of inflammation and the healthy and morbid conditions of the blood in relation to it, I arrived several years ago at the conclusion that the essential cause of suppuration in wounds is decomposition brought about by the influence of the atmosphere upon blood or serum retained within them, and in the case of contused wounds upon portions of tissue destroyed by the violence of the injury.' At the same time Lister became aware that the causative agent was not the air itself, nor indeed any of its gases, since in some injuries where the skin is not broken, as for example, simple fracture of the ribs with injury to the lung, air might be present in the tissues and in contact with effused blood, without any inflammation or suppuration taking place. Lister was unable to afford any full explanation of the facts until his attention was directed in 1865 by his colleague, Dr. Thomas Anderson, professor of chemistry in the university, to the researches of Louis Pasteur, who had proved that putrefaction, like fermentation, was dependent upon the presence in the air of living germs, or vibrios as they were called at first. Lister saw at once the explanation that he had been seeking. Again to quote his own words: 'When it had been shown by the researches of Pasteur that the septic property of the atmosphere depended, not on the oxygen or any gaseous constituent, but on minute organisms suspended in it, which owed their energy to their vitality, it occurred to me that decomposition in the injured part might be avoided without excluding the air, by applying as a dressing some material capable of destroying the life of the floating particles.' Three methods are available for depriving the air of its germs: filtration, heat, and chemical agents; Lister selected the third as the one most obviously practicable. Prior to becoming acquainted with Pasteur's work, he had practised various methods to secure cleanliness in the routine treatment of wounds, but with no great success. So soon as he determined, in the light of Pasteur's work, to attempt to destroy germs in contact with the wound, by means of a chemical agent, he selected carbolic acid for this purpose. This choice was due to his knowledge of the striking results that had been obtained at Carlisle in the treatment of sewage by this substance when used as a disinfectant. Lister's first attempts were made in the treatment of serious injuries, such as compound fractures. This class of case was at that date a peculiarly serious one, with a very high mortality due to septic infection. Lister, from an early stage of his work, realized that the causes or agents of putrefaction might be present in the injured part before the surgeon intervened, as in the case of a compound fracture, or that they might be introduced at the time of operation, as when an incision is made through unbroken skin. The successful treatment of the former class of case is necessarily much more difficult, and it is striking that he should have selected cases of compound fracture for his first attempts in the new treatment. He first used carbolic acid in the treatment of a compound fracture in March 1865; and in the following spring treated a very severe case of compound fracture in the leg with such complete success that the case practically followed the usual course seen in instances of simple fracture, i. e. there was no general illness and no suppuration. This case formed the basis of his paper in the *Lancet*, 1867, describing the new method of treatment of compound fracture.

Lister, in his earliest cases, used liquefied German creosote, an impure carbolic acid; this he introduced into the wound and then covered the part with a layer of lint soaked in carbolic acid. After the success obtained in the treatment of compound fractures, he used a similar method in the treatment of abscess. From this time onward he constantly extended the scope of his method and the field of his operations; but he devoted himself more especially to improving the method itself, so as to avoid the irritation produced by the crude carbolic acid. Thus he introduced carbolic oil and carbolized putty, and later he employed carbolized shellac and watery solutions of carbolic acid. From the first he insisted on the necessity of disinfecting instruments and everything else that came in contact with the wound, and he also carried out a thorough disinfection of the patient's skin in the vicinity of the wound. Further, he devoted much time and thought to devising suitable dressings, such as the well-known gauze impregnated with resin and paraffin and then dipped in a watery solution of carbolic acid. He also introduced the carbolic spray apparatus for disinfecting the air in the field of the operation, being at that time impressed with the belief that the air was a most important factor in the causation of sepsis, owing to the presence of germs in its dust. Later, the spray was dispensed with, as it was recognized that the air did not play such an important part as infection derived from the skin, instruments, dressings, &c. Nevertheless the introduction of the spray showed the extreme care which he took in devising all possible means to prevent contamination of the wound.

Lister also greatly improved the technique of operations by inventing new methods of treatment, which likewise had a profound influence in preventing septic infection. Thus he introduced the use of absorbable ligatures and of drainage tubes in the treatment of wounds. Surgeons hitherto had been in the habit of arresting haemorrhage by tying the divided vessels with either hemp or silk; these ligatures had to be cut long and left hanging out of the wound to be separated at a later date, usually about the tenth day after the operation. The separation was necessarily accompanied by ulceration and suppuration, and what is termed secondary haemorrhage was a frequent and much dreaded complication. Lister studied experimentally in animals the changes undergone by ligatures in aseptic wounds, and as a result of these studies, introduced catgut as a suitable substance for ligatures, as it was ultimately absorbed. The raw catgut was, however, unsuitable, and he devoted many years to experiments on catgut, in order to prepare it in such a manner that it should retain its firmness and at the same time be aseptic. His work on ligatures is a striking example of the successful use in surgery of knowledge obtained by preliminary experiments on animals. He also introduced many other improvements in technique, such as the simple expedient of elevating a limb prior to an operation on it, and so rendering it bloodless before the application of a tourniquet, and saving the patient an unnecessary loss of blood.

As a result of his main discoveries, all made in the course of a very few years, the practice of surgery underwent a complete revolution. In Lister's wards septic diseases did not occur, post-operative pyaemia, hospital gangrene, and tetanus disappeared, and erysipelas was rare, unless introduced. Occasionally wounds did not heal without suppuration, but even this was exceptional, and whenever it occurred, all the factors in the case were carefully investigated to ascertain the cause of the failure. Very soon his methods were applied to all kinds of surgical operations. The vanishing of septic diseases enlarged enormously the field of surgery, since operations formerly dreaded, owing to this risk, could now be carried out in safety. Lister himself introduced many new operations for the treatment of diseases and disabilities, that would have been quite impracticable without the assurance that the operation wound would heal with no septic complications. The modern development of surgery in relation to disease and injury of deep-seated organs in the chest, abdomen, &c., was only possible as the result of his discoveries, and it is probable that no man's work has had a greater influence on the progress of surgery; the saving of human life and suffering that he effected is incalculable.

Lister's work as a practical surgeon is sometimes apt to be overlooked owing to the magnitude of his work as a scientific investigator. He devised many new operations in various departments of surgery that would have made the reputation of a lesser man. Throughout his life he was improving his methods and especially the materials employed to render dressings antiseptic. During the last twenty years further modifications have been introduced, and the surgeon now uses heat more and chemical agents less, for the sterilization of instruments and dressings. Modern surgical technique is often termed aseptic rather than antiseptic; this, however, is not a modification of principle but only of method. The principles are the same as those inculcated by Lister, who might, had he liked, have used the term aseptic instead of antiseptic to describe his original method. Lister's methods did not meet with ready acceptance by the surgeons of this country. His own pupils adopted his system with enthusiasm, but the older surgeons were very slow in accepting it. Abroad it met with earlier and greater recognition, especially in France and Germany.

During his tenure of the chair of surgery at Glasgow, Lister was an unsuccessful candidate for the chair of surgery at Edinburgh in 1864, and for a similar chair at his old school, University College, London, in 1866. But in 1869 he became professor of clinical surgery at Edinburgh and remained there until he was invited to King's College, London, in 1877. On accepting this invitation he made the condition that he should bring with him his house-surgeon, (Sir) W. Watson Cheyne, a senior assistant (John Stewart), and two dressers (W. M. Dobie and James Altham), in order that his new methods might be carried out efficiently. Lister filled the chair of clinical surgery at King's College for fifteen years, and during the whole of this time was actively engaged in teaching and in pursuing his researches, besides practising as a surgeon and doing much public work. Thus he played an important part in securing modifications in certain proposed enactments restricting experiments on living animals. He was firmly convinced of the necessity of such experiments for the progress of medicine and surgery, and much of his own work was of this nature. He took an active part in founding (1891) the British Institute of Preventive Medicine on the lines of the Pasteur Institute in Paris, and became its first chairman. In 1897 its name was changed to the Jenner Institute and again in 1903 to the

Lister Institute of Preventive Medicine. He was elected a fellow of the Royal Society in 1860 and was its president from 1895 to 1900. He was president of the British Association in 1896. In 1880 he was elected on the council of the Royal College of Surgeons and served for the usual period of eight years; he was unwilling to serve for a further period and thus was never president. In 1883 a baronetcy was conferred on him, and in 1897 he was raised to the peerage as Baron Lister, of Lyme Regis. In 1902 he was one of the twelve original members of the newly constituted order of merit. On the occasion of his eightieth birthday in 1907 he received the freedom of the city of London.

Lister married in 1856 Agnes, the eldest daughter of James Syme, the Edinburgh surgeon. She died in 1903. Throughout their married life she took a great part in assisting him in much of his work, the note-books of his experiments being largely written by her. They had no children. In 1908 Lister left 12 Park Crescent, Portland Place, where he had lived ever since he came to London in 1877, and went to Walmer, where he died 10 February 1912. Burial in Westminster Abbey was offered, but he had left instructions to be buried by the side of his wife. The funeral service was held in Westminster Abbey 16 February 1912, and the burial took place at the West Hampstead cemetery.

There are many portraits of Lister. A presentation portrait painted by John Henry Lorimer in 1896 is in the library hall of the university of Edinburgh. Another portrait, by W. W. Ouless, painted in 1897, is at the Royal College of Surgeons, and a replica is in the library of the Royal College of Surgeons of Edinburgh. He was painted again by Charles E. Ritchie in 1908. A marble bust, executed by Sir Thomas Brock in 1913, is at the Royal College of Surgeons, and a plaster cast of this is in the National Portrait Gallery. In the same gallery is a wax medallion executed by Mrs. Bernard Jenkin in 1898. There are other medallions at University College, London, and at University College Hospital, and one by Brock is in Westminster Abbey. A memorial bust by Brock has been erected in Portland Place, near the house occupied by Lister, 12 Park Crescent. (See *Royal Academy Pictures*, 1897, 1913.)

[R. J. Godlee, *Lord Lister*, 1917; *Proceedings* of the Royal Society, vol. lxxxvi, B, 1912–1913; Lord Lister's *Collected Writings*, 1909.]

J. R. B.

LITTLE, WILLIAM JOHN KNOX- (1839–1918), divine and preacher. [See Knox-Little.]

LLANDAFF, Viscount (1826–1913), lawyer and politician. [See Matthews, Henry.]

LOCKYER, Sir JOSEPH NORMAN (1836–1920), astronomer, was born at Rugby 17 May 1836, the only son of Joseph Hooley Lockyer, physician, of Rugby, by his wife, Anne, daughter of Edward Norman, of Cosford, Warwickshire. He was educated at private schools and on the Continent, and at the age of twenty-one obtained a clerkship in the War Office. His marked ability gained for him in 1865 the office of editor of the Army *Regulations*. But he had already acquired, probably from his father, who founded a scientific and literary society in Rugby, a taste for science, especially astronomy. He bought a refracting telescope of 6¼ inches aperture, made by Thomas Cooke [q. v.], and began to study planetary surfaces. His first scientific paper, communicated to the Royal Astronomical Society in 1863, gives a very accurate study of Mars as observed at the opposition of 1862.

In 1866 Lockyer attached a spectroscope to his 6¼ inch equatorial, observed the spectrum of a sun-spot, saw that it contained no bright lines and that certain dark lines were thickened, and thus obtained a decisive answer to the question, then under vigorous discussion, as to the cause of the relative darkness of a sun-spot. This was a pioneer observation in many ways. The actual projection of the sun's image on the slit of the spectroscope, so that the small area of a sun-spot could be isolated for observation, was new; for spectroscopy was in its infancy, and attention had previously been paid chiefly to stars and nebulae. This success was soon followed by another still more brilliant, obtained by applying the same procedure of isolation to the solar prominences. On this occasion (20 October 1868) honours were shared with the French astronomer, Dr. P. J. C. Janssen, whose observations, suggested to him in India by the total solar eclipse of 18 August 1868, were by a remarkable coincidence communicated to the Paris Academy of Sciences on the same day as those of Lockyer. The French government, however, recognized the great merit of both discoverers by striking a special medal in their honour in 1872.

Other discoveries by Lockyer soon followed, and two names coined by him at this time have passed into circulation as memorials of his pioneer work. One is 'chromosphere' for the envelope closely surrounding the sun, of which the prominences form a part: Lockyer announced its existence on 5 November 1868, and gave it this name; subsequent work has emphasized the importance of the chromosphere in the study of solar problems. The other name is 'helium' for a chemical element recognized by a special line (D_3) detected by Lockyer in the sun's spectrum; the element was not at that time (1868) known to exist on earth, but it has since been discovered and found to play a fundamental part in physics and chemistry.

Thus by 1870 Lockyer had proved himself a capable government official and a scientist of great talent; so that he was appointed secretary to the royal commission on scientific instruction and the advancement of science (1870–1875), which recommended, *inter alia*, the establishment by the government of an observatory of solar physics. As a first step Lockyer was transferred from the War Office to the Science and Art Department at South Kensington (1875), and though at that time nothing was done on a great scale, facilities were provided for his work which he utilized with unfailing skill in many directions. He started, with a loan collection, what has become the science museum; he organized courses of astronomical teaching; and not only did he work hard and devotedly at the spectroscopic side of astronomy, but he inspired his assistants with his spirit. On the foundation of the Royal College of Science at South Kensington in 1890 Lockyer was appointed director of the new Solar Physics Observatory and professor of astronomical physics. He held this post until 1913.

Lockyer's influence on the course of scientific investigation extended beyond his immediate circle or time. It has been pointed out that to him is due 'not only the idea, but also extended and elaborate studies, of the enhanced and super-enhanced lines of elements. . . . He tried to impress the idea that the enhanced lines are due to some proto-form or fractional part of chemical atoms' [*Philosophical Magazine*, December 1922]. He also anticipated modern views of the course of stellar evolution. But in both cases his speculations were hampered by the limited knowledge of the time. His *Meteoritic Hypothesis* (1890)—propounding the wide generalization that the origin of all celestial bodies is to be assigned to meteor swarms—also suffered from imperfect information, so that when one or other of its supports gave way in the general advance of knowledge, the theory was no longer acceptable as a whole. But probably much of value will be found in its constituent parts.

Lockyer's activities were so wide that only brief mention can be made of some of them. His work on solar physics led him to make enterprising observations of total solar eclipses. In *Recent and Coming Eclipses* (1897) he gives interesting accounts of some of the official expeditions which he conducted, on which occasions he was very successful in utilizing the help offered by officers and men of the royal navy. He was convinced of the connexion, in some form, between solar activity and terrestrial weather, and in collaboration with his son, Dr. W. J. S. Lockyer, made extensive investigations into this matter. A visit to Egypt led him to suggest the possibility of dating Egyptian temples by their orientation considered in relation to the heavens of the past. In 1869, in co-operation with Mr. Alexander Macmillan, he established the journal *Nature*, which he edited until a few months before his death; it became an important organ of scientific advance. As president of the British Association meeting at Southport in 1903, he gave a stirring address on the need for the extension and better endowment of university teaching in science; and, following up these ideas, he founded the British Science Guild in 1905, with himself as chairman of committees. Finally, he was a successful popular lecturer and writer. The more important of Lockyer's numerous works not already mentioned are: *Solar Physics* (1873), *The Chemistry of the Sun* (1887), *The Sun's Place in Nature* (1897), *Inorganic Evolution* (1900).

Lockyer's work received the recognition which it deserved. In 1874 he was awarded the Rumford medal of the Royal Society, of which he had been elected a fellow in 1869, and in 1875 he received the Janssen medal of the Paris Academy of Sciences, of which he was elected a corresponding member in the same year. He was Rede lecturer at Cambridge in 1871, and Bakerian lecturer in 1874. In 1894 he received the C.B., and he was created K.C.B. in 1897.

Lockyer died 16 August 1920 at Salcombe Regis, Devon. With the help of some generous friends he had erected an observatory there in 1913, when the solar observatory was transferred, to his great disappointment, from South Kensington to Cambridge. A portrait medallion of him in the Salcombe Regis observatory was unveiled by the astronomer royal on 22 July 1922.

Lockyer married twice: first, in 1858 Winifred (died 1879), younger daughter of William James, of Trebenshon, near Abergavenny, by whom he had seven sons and two daughters; secondly, in 1903 Thomazine Mary, younger daughter of Samuel Woolcott Browne, of Bridgwater and Clifton, and widow of Bernard Edward Brodhurst, F.R.C.S. Of the sons only four survived him.

[*Proceedings* of the Royal Society, vol. civ, A, 1923 (portrait); personal knowledge.]

H. H. T.

LONDONDERRY, sixth MARQUESS OF (1852–1915), politician. [See VANE-TEMPEST-STEWART, CHARLES STEWART.]

LUBBOCK, SIR JOHN, fourth baronet, and first BARON AVEBURY (1834–1913), banker, man of science, and author, was the eldest son of Sir John William Lubbock [q.v.], third baronet, of Lammas, Norfolk, by his wife, Harriet, daughter of Lieutenant-Colonel George Hotham, of York. His father was a banker of distinguished mathematical ability and was for many years treasurer of the Royal Society. John Lubbock was born at 29 Eaton Place, London, 30 April 1834; six years later, on his father's succession to the baronetcy, the family moved to High Elms, Down, Kent. This was his country home for the rest of his life, except for an interval of four years at Chiselhurst (1861–1865) subsequent to his marriage, and for periods spent on the Kent coast at Kingsgate Castle, which he acquired and rebuilt in 1901. He showed at an early age a marked aptitude for natural history, for which his country life gave full scope. It received the greatest stimulus, and Lubbock himself a lasting impress on his whole character and career, through the influence of his father's friend, Charles Darwin, who came to reside at Down in 1841, and at once took a keen interest in the boy's early efforts. After three years at a private school at Abingdon, Lubbock at the age of eleven (1845) went to Eton, where, in the intervals of freedom from steady application to studies for which he had little zest and no conspicuous talent, he pursued solitarily his hobby of natural history. The failing health of his father's partners soon caused Lubbock's withdrawal from Eton, and in 1849, before he was fifteen, he was installed at the bank, where he soon showed exceptional capacity, and before long was able to assume responsibility for an important share in the management. He improved his general and scientific knowledge by carefully ordered private study, and spent much time with Darwin.

From this early time the course of Lubbock's life flowed in three strong and steady currents without any conspicuous interruption. He worked hard at his business and acquired a leading position among bankers; he devoted his leisure largely to the pursuit of natural science and won a recognized place among the most eminent of its followers; and thirdly, he made for himself a position of peculiar importance and usefulness in public life, notably in parliament, where he effected important legislation. Lubbock was a prolific author, and as an expositor of science and an intellectual and moral mentor to the general public he had a vogue that is almost without parallel in modern times. At the same time, his home at High Elms was a social centre for a multitude of friends, including leading men of science and statesmen, and his life included a large measure of foreign travel.

Lubbock married in 1856 Ellen Frances (died 1879), daughter of the Rev. Peter Hordern, of Chorlton-cum-Hardy, Lancashire, and by her he had three sons and three daughters. He succeeded to the baronetcy in 1865. Five years after the death of his first wife he married in 1884 Alice, daughter of General Augustus Henry Lane Fox Pitt-Rivers [q.v.], the distinguished archaeologist. His second family consisted of three sons and two daughters. On being raised to the peerage in 1900, he assumed the title of Baron Avebury, of Avebury, Wiltshire.

Lubbock's long, strenuous, and successful public life made him one of the best known and most highly esteemed men of his day. His power of work, his systematic habits, and his ability to keep his mind engaged on a great variety of topics and to pass and repass from one to another without confusion were quite unusual. As the head of Robarts, Lubbock & Co. he was continuously active in the banking world, where at an early age he inaugurated both the important reform known as the system of country clearing and the publication of clearing-house returns. He was honorary secretary of the London Bankers in 1863; from 1898 to 1913 he was chairman of the committee of London clearing bankers and president of the Central Association of Bankers; and from 1879 to 1883 he was first president of the Institute of Bankers. His successful reforming zeal and wide outlook on finance led to his being invited in 1863 to stand as parliamentary candidate for the city of London. He refused the invitation, but after unsuccessful attempts for West Kent in 1865 and 1868, he was elected as liberal M.P. for Maidstone in 1870 and again in 1874. After defeat there in 1880 he was immediately returned unopposed for London University and retained the seat till he was raised to the peerage. He was made a privy councillor in 1890. Throughout his parliamentary career Lubbock addressed himself with unremitting zeal to securing the passage of acts on which he had set his mind. The best known of these was the Bank Holidays Act of 1871, which established the public holiday in August. Appreciation of this boon was reflected in a temporary currency of the term 'St. Lubbock's day' for the first Monday in August. Through his advocacy, and after many attempts, the Act for the Preservation of Ancient Monuments was passed in 1882 and the Early Closing Act in 1904. Besides these, numerous acts of parliament relating to banking and finance and to social amelioration owed much to Lubbock's efforts; and, though never a minister, he occupied important offices such as the chairmanship of the committee on public accounts (1888–1889).

Outside finance and parliament, Lubbock's interests and authority in public life are shown by his having been president of the London Chamber of Commerce (1888–1893) and an original member and subsequently chairman of the London County Council (1890–1892); in the world of education he was a member of the senate and then vice-chancellor of London University (1872–1880), chairman of the Society for the Extension of University Teaching (1894–1902), principal of the Working Men's College in Great Ormond Street (1883–1898), a trustee of the British Museum, and rector of St. Andrews University (1908).

In science, Lubbock's main interest lay in the study of the habits, life history, and ancestry of living things throughout the kingdom of plants and animals up to man himself. His studies covered a wide range of topics and bore fruit in many contributions to the proceedings of learned societies. Notwithstanding its range, Lubbock's scientific work was by no means superficial, and it is noteworthy that eleven years after his death several distinguished scientists combined to testify to its value [*The Life-Work of Lord Avebury (Sir John Lubbock)*, 1924]. He was a pioneer in the experimental study of animal behaviour, and his researches on ants are probably the most valuable of his contributions to science. Of importance also are his studies of the life histories of insects and of the problem of their metamorphosis. He also published a standard *Monograph of the Collembola and Thysanura* (1873). In botany his contributions included much that was new and of permanent value. In geology he was actively associated with Darwin, Sir Charles Lyell, Sir Roderick Murchison, Adam Sedgwick, and their successors; and his interest in the new science of anthropology led him to travel to many centres in Europe where there was news or promise of fresh evidence of man's antiquity.

Lubbock was president of many scientific societies, and a member of the council of the Royal Society; he presided over the British Association at the jubilee meeting at York in 1881. The titles of his scientific books, such as *Prehistoric Times* (1865), *On the Origin and Metamorphoses of Insects* (1874), *The Origin of Civilization . . .* (1870), *Ants, Bees, and Wasps* (1882), *On the Senses, Instincts, and Intelligence of Animals* (1888), *A Contribution to our Knowledge of Seedlings* (1892), *The Scenery of Switzerland* (1896), *On Buds and Stipules* (1899), and *Marriage, Totemism, and Religion* (1911), indicate the wide ambit of his studies.

In addition to his gifts as an investigator, Lubbock possessed a missionary zeal for the intellectual enlightenment and moral elevation of the public, and he had a remarkable power of enlisting the interest of the unlearned world. His list of the *Hundred Best Books* (1891) was a stimulus to the multitude, whilst later works with titles so common-place as *The Pleasures of Life* (1887), *The Beauties of Nature* (1892), *The Use of Life* (1894), *Peace and Happiness* (1909), ran through many editions.

In his politics, Lubbock was throughout life a pronounced liberal, but in 1885 he associated himself with the unionist wing of the party. In religion, at an early period of his life, he moved away from orthodoxy and dogma, but his nature was in the highest degree reverent. He did not dissociate himself from the observances of religion, and both in speech and in print he refrained from anything controversial or aggressive. A high optimism gave his ethical books an instant hold on multitudes of readers. Lubbock's bodily vigour was well maintained throughout his strenuous life of public service. Towards the end he suffered much from illness, which terminated in his death at Kingsgate Castle on 28 May 1913. His body was removed to High Elms and buried in Farnborough churchyard. He was succeeded in the baronetcy by his eldest son, John Birkbeck Lubbock, second Baron Avebury (born 1858).

There is a drawing of Lubbock, executed by George Richmond in 1867, and a portrait, painted by Sir Hubert von Herkomer in 1911 (*Royal Academy Pictures*, 1912). A bust by Miss Kathleen Shaw was exhibited in 1900.

[Horace G. Hutchinson, *Life of Sir John Lubbock, Lord Avebury*, 2 vols., 1914; *The Life-Work of Lord Avebury* (*Sir John Lubbock*), *1834–1913*, edited by his daughter, the Hon. Mrs. Adrian Grant Duff, 1924; *Proceedings* of the Royal Society, vol. lxxxvii, B, 1913–1914.]
A. S.

LUCAS, eighth BARON (1876–1916). [See HERBERT, AUBERON THOMAS.]

LUCAS, KEITH (1879–1916), physiologist, was born at Greenwich 8 March 1879. He was the second son of Francis Robert Lucas, managing director of a telegraph engineering company in London, and inventor of improvements in submarine cables and cable-laying. His mother was Katharine, daughter of John Riddle, head master of Greenwich Hospital schools, and granddaughter of Edward Riddle [q.v.], both of whom were fellows of the Royal Astronomical Society and noteworthy in nautical astronomy. Educated at Rugby, where he was head of the school house, he proceeded, with a scholarship in classics, to Trinity College, Cambridge, in 1898. He gained a first class in the first part of the natural science tripos in 1901; but the death of a school friend in the South African War made him give up the second part of the tripos for the rest and change of a visit to New Zealand. There he undertook his earliest piece of research, the measuring of the depth of some hitherto unsounded lakes (*Geography*, July 1904). Returning to Cambridge he was elected a fellow of Trinity College in 1904, and later (1908) lecturer in science.

Between the years 1904 and 1914 Lucas undertook a series of researches, several of them in conjunction with pupils, the results of which gave a fresh impetus to the study of muscle and nerve. The contraction response of ordinary muscle fibre was shown to be of the 'all-or-none' type, the grading of a muscle's contraction being by additive *quanta*; the influence of duration on the effectiveness of an electric stimulus was measured, and further analysis of the excitability of nerve-muscle tissue was so obtained; the temperature coefficient of nerve-conduction was determined with precision; the nerve-impulse in its travel was shown to leave in its wake a phase of lessened excitability; excitability and conduction in nerve were reduced to one process; 'magnitudes' of nerve-impulse were discriminated by finding that range of interval between two successive impulses which is able to diminish though not to extinguish the second of them; thus subnormal impulses were recognized and the time-relations of the recovery of the nerve-fibre from its refractory phase ensuent on the impulse. In the course of this work, besides putting fundamental questions and answering them, Lucas devised for so doing instruments of remarkable ingenuity, elegance, and precision. By 1914 he was recognized as a leader in this field of science. He was appointed Croonian lecturer of the Royal Society in 1912, and was elected F.R.S. in 1913.

In 1914, on the outbreak of war, the services of Lucas, who was about to enlist as a private in an infantry battalion, were secured on 4 September for the Royal Aircraft Factory at Farnborough, 'by a lucky stroke', as the superintendent, Lieutenant-Colonel Mervyn O'Gorman, later wrote. There, his autographic registration of aeroplane roll, pitch, and yaw soon led to his being entrusted with further problems. For the Air Service he evolved the air-damped pendulum, improved the 'sights' for bomb-dropping, traced to its causes the compass disturbance which vitiated aeroplane-steering and at that time constituted an unexpected difficulty in aviation, and devised, partly in collaboration with (Sir) Horace Darwin, a type of compass which largely avoided error from this cause. Meeting with indomitable, quiet energy the ceaseless urgency for new developments of aeroplane design, and with self-effacing devotion examining and testing them against the practical conditions of flight, Lucas met his death when flying near Aldershot on 5 October 1916. He married in 1909 Alys, daughter of the Rev. Cyril Egerton Hubbard, by whom he had three sons.

[Obituary notice (by H. Darwin and W. M. Bayliss) in *Proceedings* of the Royal Society, vol. xc, B, 1917–1919 (portrait); personal knowledge.]
C. S. S.

LYALL, Sir CHARLES JAMES (1845–1920), Indian civil servant, and Orientalist, was born in London 9 March 1845. He was the eldest son of Charles Lyall, banker, of Stoke Green, near Slough, by his wife, Harriet, daughter of John Matheson, of Attadale, Ross-shire. He was educated in London at King's College School and King's College, and at Balliol College, Oxford; and in the open competition for the Indian civil service held in 1865 he obtained the first place. Arriving in India in 1867, he held minor posts in the North-West Provinces and in the government of India secretariat until 1880, when he was given the C.I.E. and transferred to Assam as acting secretary to the chief commissioner. He was confirmed in this post in October 1883, and held it (with several short periods of service as acting judge and commissioner of the Assam valley districts) until August 1889, when he was summoned to Calcutta to officiate as secretary to the supreme government in the home department. In November 1890 he was confirmed in that employment, and he retained it until he took furlough in 1894, after officiating for a few months as chief commissioner of Assam. He returned to India in December 1895, and was appointed chief commissioner of the Central Provinces, holding this post until his retirement from the service in July 1898. He had been gazetted K.C.S.I. twelve months before.

Upon his return to England Lyall joined the India Office as secretary of the judicial and public department. In that capacity he served for twelve years, retiring in 1910. Political agitation in India, and the attempt to appease it by the introduction of the Morley-Minto reforms, made his period of service a difficult one; and behind the scenes Lyall's experience and cool judgement were of great value. Among minor activities may be mentioned the part which he played in the foundation of the London School of Oriental Studies, and his deputation to three Oriental Congresses (1899, 1905, 1908). In the administration of the Royal Asiatic Society he took a leading share until his death.

From his Oxford days Lyall had studied Eastern languages, especially Hebrew and Arabic; and while in India he published a *Sketch of the Hindostani Language* (1880), *Translations of Ancient Arabic Poetry* (1885), and a *Guide to the Transliteration of Hindu and Muhammadan Names* (1885). Later (1907–1908) he wrote introductions to two of the Assam ethnographical monographs, and edited a third. His chief devotion, however, was to the early literature of the Arabs, and on this subject he published a series of works, viz. *A Commentary . . . on Ten Ancient Arabic Poems* (1891–1894), *The Dīwāns of 'Abīd ibn al-Abras* (1913), *The Mufaddalīyāt: An Anthology of Ancient Arabian Odes*, 2 vols. (1921), and *The Poems of 'Amr son of Qamī'ah* (1919). The translations which he appended to the texts were particularly successful in combining an accurate rendering with a poetical diction which imitated more or less the metres of the originals. The merit of his work was widely recognized, and honorary degrees were conferred upon him by the universities of Oxford, Edinburgh, and Strassburg. He was elected a fellow of the British Academy and of King's College, London. His death took place in London 1 September 1920.

Lyall married in 1870 Florence, elder daughter of Captain Henry Fraser, of Calcutta, and had by her two sons and five daughters.

[Official records; obituary notices in *The Times*, 3 September 1920, and in the *Journal* of the Royal Asiatic Society, October 1920; private information.] W. F.

LYNE, Sir WILLIAM JOHN (1844–1913), Australian politician, the eldest son of John Lyne, of Gala, Cranbrook, Tasmania, by his wife, Lilias Cross Carmichael, daughter of James Hume, of Edinburgh, was born 6 April 1844. His political life was begun by his entering the legislative assembly of New South Wales in 1880. A strong believer in protection, he attained office as minister of public works in the ephemeral government of (Sir) George R. Dibbs at the close of 1885; a somewhat longer tenure of the same post followed under Sir Patrick Jennings (February 1886 to January 1887); and in the fifty-day government of Dibbs in January 1889 he was given the portfolio of public lands. It was not until Dibbs once again became premier in October 1891 that Lyne had an effective spell of office in charge of public works, a post which he retained until the ministry fell in August 1894. Five years of opposition followed, during which local politics were complicated by the emergence of the issue of federation, and by the hesitation of (Sir) George Houstoun Reid [q.v.] as premier to commit himself definitely to the movement, in view of the certainty that federation would spell disaster to free trade. Lyne's activity in opposition secured him the leadership on the retirement of (Sir) Edmund Barton [q.v.] from that position on 23 August 1899.

Owing to the carelessness of Reid in matters of finance, the ministry was brought down on a minor issue, and Lyne became premier and colonial treasurer of New South Wales on 14 September 1899, His tenure of this office was not prolonged, as he aimed at achieving a place in Commonwealth politics. As premier of the senior colony he was given by Lord Hopetoun, the governor-general, the opportunity of forming the first Commonwealth ministry; but it was impossible for him to secure sufficient support to do this, and he accepted office under Barton, as minister of home affairs, on 1 January 1901. On the resignation of Mr. C. C. Kingston he became, in August 1903, minister of trade and customs. He retained this portfolio in the ministry of Mr. A. Deakin [q.v.], formed on Sir E. Barton's resignation, which lasted until April 1904. In general sympathy with Labour, he observed a benevolent attitude towards the brief ministry of Mr. J. C. Watson which ensued on Deakin's defeat, and opposed the Reid-McLean coalition which ousted that ministry from office. When the second Deakin administration was formed by a fresh political shuffle in July 1905, he was given his former office. Two years later, when Sir John (afterwards Baron) Forrest [q.v.] parted company with Deakin, Lyne naturally obtained the vacant post of treasurer, which he retained until the fall of the ministry in November 1908. He was bitterly opposed to the coalition of Deakin's supporters with the party of Reid, which took place in 1909, and no place was found for him in the last Deakin administration. In 1911 he visited England, but his health was manifestly impaired, and he died at Sydney, New South Wales, on 3 August 1913.

Overshadowed in New South Wales politics by Reid and Barton, and in federal politics by Deakin, Lyne, who was created K.C.M.G. in 1900, was a man of pertinacious character, and capable of much hard, detailed work, as was shown in his elaboration of the customs tariff in 1907–1908. His views were somewhat narrowly Australian; he regarded an importer, even of British goods, as something of a traitor to Commonwealth industries; and he was a protagonist of the movement to compel British shipping to conform to Australian standards of manning and pay. But his visit to England for the Colonial Navigation Conference and the Colonial Conference of 1907 widened his outlook, and increased his appreciation of the imperial connexion.

Lyne married in 1870 Martha Coates (died 1903), eldest daughter of Edward Carr Shaw, formerly of Terenure, co. Dublin, and afterwards of Glamorgan, Tasmania. They had one son and three daughters.

[B. R. Wise, *Making of the Australian Commonwealth*, 1913; H. G. Turner, *First Decade of the Australian Commonwealth*, 1911; W. Murdoch, *Alfred Deakin*, 1923; New South Wales and Commonwealth *Parliamentary Debates*; *Dictionary of Australasian Biography*, 1892; personal knowledge.]

A. B. K.

LYTTELTON, ALFRED (1857–1913), lawyer and statesman, born at Hagley, Worcestershire, 7 February 1857, was the eighth son of George William, fourth Baron Lyttelton [q.v.], by his first wife, Mary, second daughter of Sir Stephen R. Glynne and sister of Mrs. W. E. Gladstone. Going to Eton in 1868, he inherited and surpassed the athletic fame of his brothers, and there first exhibited the extraordinary gift of personal charm which distinguished him all through his life. His unbounded popularity and the fact that he was the finest player of his time, of cricket, football, rackets, and fives, made him like a king in the school. Proceeding to Trinity College, Cambridge, he was in the Cambridge eleven from 1876 to 1879, being captain of the 1879 eleven which was never defeated. After leaving Cambridge, where he obtained a second class in the historical tripos, he continued to play first-class cricket for some years (his play was called by W. G. Grace 'the champagne of cricket'), and he long held the amateur championship in tennis. He was called to the bar in 1881. From 1882 to 1885 he was legal private secretary to Sir Henry James (afterwards Lord James of Hereford). He practised with increasing success, till he entered the Cabinet in 1903. His mind was that of the judge rather than that of the advocate, and he had latterly more business as an arbitrator than as counsel. Lord Darling has said of him that 'his influence amongst his fellows was out of all proportion to his practice'.

The years between 1881 and 1895 were a period of strenuous professional work, relieved, however, by cricket, by hunting, and above all by membership of that attractive coterie in which his own relations and connexions, the Lytteltons, Talbots, Gladstones, and Cavendishes, were united with other brilliant representatives of the political and intellectual society of that generation. Here he met his first wife, Laura, daughter of Sir Charles Tennant [q.v.], the most beloved of the group of charming ladies round whom the coterie revolved. They were married in May 1885, but she died the next year, leaving an infant son who died in 1888. In 1892 Lyttelton married another member of the same circle, Edith, daughter of Archibald Balfour. He had by her two sons, one of whom died in infancy, and a daughter.

By this time Lyttelton had been successful enough at the bar to be able to begin thinking of the political career which was so natural a prospect for a man of his connexions. The popular nephew of Mr. Gladstone seemed an obvious recruit for the liberal party. But he had the gravest doubts about Home Rule, and it was not till after Gladstone had retired that he became, in 1895, a member for Leamington as a liberal unionist. He continued his work at the bar, but his interests now became increasingly political. In 1900 Mr. Chamberlain appointed him chairman of a commission which was to visit South Africa and report on the desirability of continuing the various concessions granted by the former government of the Transvaal. There, Lord Milner was so much impressed by his work that he wrote home suggesting him for the post of high commissioner. In 1903 came the great event of Lyttelton's political life. Mr. Chamberlain resigned the Colonial Office in September, and Lyttelton was appointed in his place. He was at once faced with the difficult problem of deciding whether he could consent to the introduction of Chinese coolies into the Rand, as demanded by Milner and by the almost unanimous colonist opinion of the district concerned. He was well aware how liable to misrepresentation this policy was. But having become convinced that it was economically and socially necessary and morally unobjectionable, he adopted it and faced the violent opposition which it aroused. The scheme was denounced as one of slavery, though it was far more careful of the interests of the coolie than the scheme which had been sanctioned for Guiana by a liberal government in 1894. The Chinese labour ordinance was sanctioned in March 1904, and at once caused a revival of industry, and enabled the reconstruction of the country to be pushed forward. Its necessity was so obvious that the liberal government of 1906 allowed it to be continued, and even re-enacted it in 1908.

This was Lyttelton's most controversial work at the Colonial Office. In his last two years of office he was engaged in drawing up a scheme for representative institutions in the Transvaal, to be followed later by responsible government. The unionist ministry fell, however, before his proposals had been put into effect. But the step of most permanent importance which he took as colonial secretary was probably the preparation of a circular dispatch, which he sent in April 1905 to the self-governing Dominions, pointing the way to the development of what afterwards became the Imperial Conference. It is described by Sir Charles Lucas as 'a dispatch which no one who traces or reads the growth of imperial unity can ever leave out of sight'.

Mr. Balfour's ministry resigned in December 1905, and Lyttelton lost his seat at the ensuing general election. He did not return to the bar, but became a director of the London and Westminster Bank and other companies. In June 1906 he re-entered parliament as member for St. George's, Hanover Square. After that he took an active part in the counsels of the opposition, and especially in the resistance, in parliament and in the country, to the disestablishment of the Welsh Church. That seemed to him to involve the issue between right and wrong, which was the only one that ever greatly moved him. The same spirit of moral and social responsibility led him to give active support to housing and town-planning reform and to the Trade Boards Bill which established a minimum wage in sweated industries.

All this, with his many directorships, his arbitrations, and other business, almost exhausted his strength, which a visit to East Africa in the spring of 1913 did not restore as much as had been hoped. He had, however, resumed the full flow of his activities, when, after playing in a cricket match and making eighty-nine, he was taken suddenly ill, and, after a few days of suffering, died 5 July 1913.

The day of his funeral was one of the days of the Oxford and Cambridge match at Lord's; and a unique tribute was paid to his memory in the suspension of play for a few moments while the great crowd of spectators stood uncovered.

Neither the lawyer nor the statesman had ever reached the first rank so indisputably as the cricketer. But the truth is that, in every field, athletic or social, legal or political, Lyttelton's greatest achievement had lain in being himself. Wherever he went he brought a personal charm which all sorts of men found irresistible. Nor was that all. There was also a character and an atmosphere which, though never obtruded, and often almost imperceptible, seldom failed to inspire and elevate any circle in which he moved. He was universally loved, and no one loved him without being the better for it.

[Edith Lyttelton, *Alfred Lyttelton; an Account of his Life*, 1917; personal knowledge.]
J. C. B.

MACARTHUR, MARY REID (1880–1921), women's labour organizer. [See **Anderson, Mary Reid.**]

M'CARTHY, JUSTIN (1830–1912), Irish politician, historian, and novelist, born near Cork 22 November 1830, was the second child and elder son of Michael Francis M'Carthy, clerk to the Cork city magistrates, by his wife, Ellen FitzGerald. Brought up, as he says, in 'genteel poverty' with a view to the bar, at seventeen he found his family dependent on him. The *Cork Examiner* offered work: the Irish famine provided subjects for his pen. In 1848 he reported the trial at Clonmel for high treason of William Smith O'Brien [q.v.] and Thomas Francis Meagher [q.v.]. M'Carthy, full of the literary and political enthusiasms of Young Ireland, was himself involved in the rebel organization, but after this abortive outbreak he became 'more and more convinced that the righting of Ireland's wrongs was to be accomplished by appeal to the conscience and reason of England's best citizens'. London became his goal. In 1854 he joined the *Northern Daily Times* in Liverpool, and there, though still supporting his family, married (1855). His wife, who died in 1879, was Charlotte, daughter of W. G. Allman. They had one son, Justin Huntly M'Carthy, the novelist, and one daughter.

In 1859 M'Carthy went to London, joined the staff of the *Morning Star*, and, having learnt to read French, German, Italian, and Spanish, became foreign editor of that journal, and later editor (1864). Friendship with John Bright, then on its board of directors, followed. Contributions to the *Westminster Review* led to another friendship, with John Stuart Mill. M'Carthy commenced as a novelist successfully, and in 1868 was able to resign his editorship and visit the United States, where his brother was established. Lucrative prospects opened before him and he would have settled in America but that the opening of the constitutional movement of Isaac Butt [q.v.] led him to believe that he could serve Ireland as writer and speaker in England. In 1871 he returned to London and became a leader writer on the *Daily News*, continuing to produce novels and short stories. In 1877 was published the *History of Our Own Times*, which definitely established his success.

In 1879 C. S. Parnell asked M'Carthy to stand for county Longford, and his candidature was successful. When Parnell was elected chairman of the nationalist party M'Carthy became vice-chairman. The new party used methods not to the liking of one who loved and respected parliament; but M'Carthy never shrank from his task. In 1886 his personal prestige enabled him to win the important seat of Derry city. After the Parnell divorce case in 1890, M'Carthy, the channel through whom Gladstone's warnings were transmitted, endeavoured to persuade Parnell to a temporary retirement. Debate in committee room No. 15 at the House of Commons having shown agreement to be impossible, M'Carthy led the majority of the members out. He became chairman of the anti-Parnellite party, which carried 72 out of 81 nationalist seats at the general election of 1892. Yet he retained Parnell's friendship; in all that savage controversy he never made an enemy. He had combined writing with the closest parliamentary attendance, and the responsibility of leadership increased the strain. Also, in 1894, having joined the executive committee of an Irish industrial exhibition which lost heavily, he became liable for a large sum. He resigned the leadership of his party to John Dillon in 1896, but continued in parliament, representing North Longford, which had elected him in 1892 when he lost Derry. In 1897 his constitution broke up; almost total blindness followed. In 1900 M'Carthy ceased to be a member of parliament and the rest of his life was spent at Westgate-on-Sea. He continued to write books by dictation up to 1911; but his mind's alertness was gone. Nothing remained but his perfect charity and gaiety. In 1903 Mr. Balfour, as prime minister, recommended him for a civil list pension of £300 a year for his services to literature.

As a literary man, M'Carthy was a popularizer rather than an original writer; but he had an ease and simplicity which recall Goldsmith's; and with them went the attraction of his own personality. Had he been nothing but a writer, he would certainly have died rich, for his novels have real charm. *Dear Lady Disdain* (1875) and *Miss Misanthrope* (1878) are the best remembered; but *Mononia* (1901) has interest for its sketch of Munster life and politics in his youth. But he threw aside certainties and chances alike to give his country a perfectly unselfish service. He died at Folkestone 24 April 1912.

[Justin M'Carthy, *Reminiscences*, 1899, *Story of an Irishman*, 1904, *Irish Recollections*, 1911; T. P. O'Connor, *The Parnell Movement*, 1886; private information; personal knowledge.] S. G.

McCUDDEN, JAMES THOMAS BYFORD (1895–1918), airman, was born at Gillingham, Kent, 28 March 1895, the second son of Sergeant-Major William Henry McCudden, Royal Engineers, of Carlow, Ireland, by his wife, Amelia Emma Byford, of Chatham. He was educated at the Royal Engineers' School, Brompton Barracks, Gillingham, joined the Royal Engineers as a bugler in 1910, and became a sapper three years later, but shortly afterwards (April 1913) was transferred to the Royal Flying Corps. After a few weeks at the flying depôt at Farnborough, he was posted as mechanic to No. 3 squadron. He occasionally flew as a passenger. On 1 April 1914 he was appointed first-class air mechanic, and took charge of an aeroplane in which he would often sit, operate the controls, and imagine himself in flight.

On the outbreak of the European War McCudden went to France with No. 3 squadron in August 1914, was promoted corporal in November, and flight-sergeant in April 1915, a post which brought him responsibility for all the engines of his flight. He was now flying occasionally as a gunner, and, by December, as an observer. He had already been recommended for a course of flying, but he could not be spared from his engines until January 1916, when he was sent home to learn to fly. He qualified at Gosport on 16 April 1916, returned to France on 4 July as a sergeant pilot of No. 66 squadron, and flew a Farman Experimental machine, chiefly on offensive patrols and photographic work. He was transferred in August to No. 56 squadron, and brought down his first enemy machine on 6 September. He received his commission on 1 January 1917, returned to England on 23 February in order to instruct in air fighting, was promoted captain on 1 May, and took part in the defence of London against the enemy daylight raids in June and July. He went to France for a 'refresher' fighting course with No. 66 squadron on 11 July, was back in England on 3 August, but was almost at once appointed to No. 56 squadron as a flight-commander, returning to France on the 15th of that month.

From this time until 5 March 1918 McCudden built up his position as the leading British fighting pilot, and enhanced the prestige of his squadron and of his service. His record included fifty-four enemy aeroplanes, of which forty-two were definitely destroyed, nineteen of them in the British lines. On two occasions he destroyed four two-seater machines in one day, the second time completing his work in ninety minutes. On 13 January 1918 he shot down three aeroplanes in twenty minutes. His success was made on the Scout Experimental 5 machine, and his feeling for engines enabled him to get the best out of his machines. He was a dashing patrol leader, always eager to attack, but never hesitating to break off a fight if his judgement so prompted. McCudden's outstanding success, however, was in single-handed attacks against enemy two-seater machines, which would cross the lines at great heights on rapid reconnaissance work. He studied their habits, the psychology of their pilots, and their weak spots. He stalked them with great patience, and seldom failed to bring his enemy down when once he got to grips. He wept when he left his squadron for England on 5 March 1918 and, whilst he was instructing at home, was thinking always of what he was missing in France.

On 9 July 1918 McCudden was promoted major, and he set out the same day for France in high spirits, in order to take command of the famous No. 60 squadron. He was leaving the aerodrome at Auxi-le-Château on his way to the front when his engine was heard to stop. He turned to land again, but his machine side-slipped into the ground and he was killed.

McCudden was gay, modest, intensely loyal, and of a great courage tempered by almost faultless judgement. He admired his enemy and loved his friends. He had two brothers who were pilots in the Flying Corps: both were killed. McCudden was awarded the croix de guerre (1916), the military medal (1916), the military cross and bar (1917), the distinguished service order and bar (1917 and 1918), and the Victoria cross (1918).

[J. T. B. McCudden, *Five Years in the Royal Flying Corps*, 1918; official records; personal knowledge.] H. A. J.

MACCUNN, HAMISH (JAMES) (1868–1916), musical composer, was born at Greenock 22 March 1868, the second son of James MacCunn, shipowner, of Thornhill, Greenock, by his wife, Barbara Neill. He enjoyed to the full in childhood the advantages of favourable environment, for his father was a student and a lover of the arts, with the means to indulge his son's tastes and the enthusiasm and foresight to guide them aright. Under a wisely ordered training young MacCunn developed musical gifts of great promise from an early age, and in 1883, when the Royal College of Music was founded in London for the encouragement of native talent, was successful in winning one of its first scholarships for composition. He studied there under (Sir) Charles Hubert H. Parry [q.v.] until 1887.

With his cantata 'The Moss Rose', produced at the Royal College in 1885, and an overture 'Cior Mhor', at the Crystal Palace in the same year, came the first signs of MacCunn's remarkable individuality; and two years later this boy of nineteen began to startle and captivate the musical world with an amazing series of full-grown orchestral and choral works, of which the most conspicuous were 'The Land of the Mountain and the Flood' (1887), 'The Ship o' the Fiend' (1888), 'The Dowie Dens o' Yarrow' (1888), 'Lord Ullin's Daughter' (1888), 'The Lay of the Last Minstrel' (1888), and 'Bonny Kilmeny' (1888). He also wrote a great number of songs, frankly melodious, but rich in his distinctive qualities; many of these were produced at concerts of his works given at the home of John Pettie, R.A. [q.v.], whose only daughter, Alison Quiller, MacCunn married in 1889.

MacCunn's sense of drama soon turned his attention to opera. In 1894 'Jeanie Deans' (the libretto by Joseph Bennett) was produced in Edinburgh, and in 1896 in London; another opera, 'Diarmid' (1897), was a setting of a libretto by the ninth Duke of Argyll, then Marquess of Lorne, founded on heroic Celtic legends. Both these works met with more success than usually falls to the lot of a British opera, but lacked the staying power, chiefly in the librettos, essential to survival. The production of his operas established MacCunn's reputation as an able conductor, and first, or early, performances in English of the later Wagner operas were given under his direction by the Royal Carl Rosa company. In light opera, too, he attained a foremost position as conductor; and as a result, possibly, of this experience, he wrote a light opera, 'The Golden Girl' (the libretto by Basil Hood), produced at Birmingham in 1905.

It is perhaps to his attachment to the theatre and to his gifts as a conductor that we may attribute the comparative smallness of MacCunn's output in the later years of his life. Certain it is that as conductor of operas, both in London and in the provinces, he found his leisure for composition curtailed more and more year by year; while, towards the end, it was made almost fruitless by ill-health. He died in London 2 August 1916, leaving a widow and one son.

As a composer, MacCunn represents a type not uncommon in its early maturity, yet it is surprising that a man who did so much did not do more. Great gifts he possessed in abundance—inspiration, sensitiveness, clearness of style, an inexhaustible flow of melody, and that magical charm of utterance that goes with a vivid and imaginative personality. He was thus enabled to reveal the heart of Scotland as none had done before him, in a musical setting of great character and originality, virile and picturesque, glowing with warmth and splendour of colouring; he did all this with such tenderness and emotional beauty that he has been named, not without reason, the most Scottish of Scottish composers.

[Royal College of Music *Registers*; Crystal Palace programmes; *Monthly Musical Record*, September 1916; *Musical Times*, September 1916; Grove's *Dictionary of Music*; *Dictionary of Modern Music and Musicians*.]

C. A.

MACDONALD, Sir CLAUDE MAXWELL (1852–1915), soldier and diplomatist, the son of Major-General James (Hamish) Dawson Macdonald, by his wife, Mary Ellen Dougan, was born 12 June 1852. Educated at Uppingham and Sandhurst, he entered the 74th Highlanders in 1872 at the age of twenty. Macdonald first came to the front in the Egyptian campaign of 1882, in which year he was promoted major; he subsequently became military attaché in Cairo to Sir Evelyn Baring (afterwards Earl of Cromer, q.v.), a post which he held till 1887. He served through the Suakin expedition of 1884–1885 as a volunteer with the 42nd Highlanders. From 1887 to 1888 he was acting-agent and consul-general at Zanzibar, and in 1889 was sent by the Foreign Office on a special mission to the Niger Territories. Shortly afterwards Macdonald was sent on another mission, to Berlin, with reference to the delimitation of the boundary between the Oil Rivers Protectorate and Cameroon, and in 1891 he was appointed first commissioner and consul-general in the Protectorate. Here he established an efficient system of consular jurisdiction and customs organization, and brought the whole territory under ordered government. During the period of his consul-generalship he took part in the Brass River expedition (1895).

In 1896 Macdonald retired from the army and was promoted to the post of British minister at Peking, where his term of office covered four critical years in the history of China. The Chino-Japanese War of 1894 had revealed to the world the military weakness of China, and German and Russian imperialism lost no time in exploiting the situation. The concession to Russia in 1896 of the Chinese Eastern Railway was followed in 1898 by the seizure of Kiaochow by Germany and the Russian occupation of Port Arthur and Dalny. In order to maintain the balance of power, Macdonald secured for England the leases of Wei Hai Wei and of the Hong-Kong Extension, and waged the 'battle of concessions' so successfully that he obtained, among other things, the opening of the West river to trade, the right to navigate the inland waters, the non-alienation of the Yangtze region, several important railway concessions, and a formal undertaking that the inspector-general of customs should continue to be an Englishman. These services brought him the congratulations of Lord Salisbury and the K.C.B. in 1898.

It was fortunate that Macdonald was at Peking when the Boxer rising of 1900 occurred. He was chosen by his colleagues to assume the command of the beleaguered legations, and he organized the defence with such skill that they were able through many weeks (20 June–14 August) to withstand all Chinese assaults. Promoted G.C.M.G. in 1900, he received in 1901 the military K.C.B. for the defence of the legations, and thus had the rare distinction of being doubly a recipient of this order.

In October 1900 Macdonald was transferred to Tokio, where he became in 1905 the first British ambassador. He took part in the negotiation of the Anglo-Japanese alliance of 1902, and his presence at Tokio was invaluable to Great Britain during the Russo-Japanese War. The Anglo-Japanese agreement of August 1905 (renewed in July 1911) was concluded under his auspices, and in recognition of his services he was made G.C.V.O. and sworn a privy councillor in 1906. He retired in 1912, and died in London 10 September 1915.

Macdonald married in 1892 Ethel, daughter of Major W. Cairns Armstrong, of the 15th regiment, and widow of P. Craigie Robertson, of the Indian civil service. They had two daughters.

[*The Times*, 11 September 1915; Lieut.-Colonel A. F. Mockler-Ferryman, *Up the Niger. A Narrative of Major Claude Macdonald's Mission to the Niger and Benue Rivers*, 1892; China Blue Books, 1898–1899; *Who 's Who in the Far East*; personal knowledge.]

J. N. J.

MACDONALD, Sir JOHN HAY ATHOLE, Lord Kingsburgh (1836–1919), lord justice-clerk of Scotland, was born at 29 Great King Street, Edinburgh, 28 December 1836, the second son of Matthew Norman Macdonald (who subsequently adopted the additional surname of Hume), writer to the signet, by his second wife, Grace, daughter of Sir John Hay, fifth baronet, of Smithfield and Haystoun, Peeblesshire. He was educated at the Edinburgh Academy and the universities of Basle and Edinburgh, and was called to the Scottish bar in 1859. In the course of a professional career distinguished by practical ability rather than by profound legal learning, he became successively sheriff of Ross, Cromarty, and Sutherland (1874–1876), solicitor-general for Scotland (1876–1880), Queen's counsel (1880), sheriff of Perthshire (1880–1885), dean of the faculty of advocates (1882–1885), and lord advocate (1885–1886 and 1886–1888). In 1888 he was promoted to the bench as lord justice-clerk in succession to the first Baron Moncreiff [q.v.], and assumed the judicial title of Lord Kingsburgh, derived from the lands of that name in Skye with which his Highland ancestors (one of whom was the Jacobite heroine, Flora Macdonald) had been associated. In this capacity he presided for twenty-seven years over the second division of the Court of Session. He retired in 1915.

As a counsel, Macdonald found his most congenial sphere in jury trials, and on the bench he was at his best on questions of fact. His judgments are characterized by directness and robust common sense. From the outset he specialized in criminal law. In his early years at the bar he produced his *Practical Treatise on the Criminal Law of Scotland* (first edition 1867), and his tenure of the office of lord advocate was appropriately marked by the passing of the Criminal Procedure (Scotland) Act, 1887, which effected a great simplification of proceedings in criminal cases. As lord justice-clerk he conducted with conspicuous ability a long series of criminal trials, including the notorious Monson case (1893).

Few men were better known in Scotland in his day than Macdonald. The remarkable reputation which he enjoyed was chiefly founded on his wide range of interests outside his profession. A stalwart conservative in politics, he fought a number of elections unsuccessfully, but ultimately sat in the House of Commons as member for the universities of Edinburgh and St. Andrews from 1885 to 1888. Throughout his life he was an ardent volunteer. At the early age of twenty-five he was appointed lieutenant-colonel of the second battalion of the Queen's Edinburgh Rifle Volunteer Brigade. In 1888 he assumed command as brigadier-general of the then newly formed Forth Volunteer Infantry Brigade, and held that command until his retirement under the age limit in 1901. He was a founder of the Scottish Rifle Association, thrice captain of the Scottish Twenty, a frequent attender at the Wimbledon and Bisley meetings, and captain of the British team which took part in the international rifle match at the Philadelphia centenary exhibition (1876). He was honorary colonel of the Army Motor Reserve and successively brigadier-general, adjutant-general, and ensign-general of the Royal Company of Archers, the King's Bodyguard for Scotland. Probably no lawyer has ever attained so great an eminence as an authority on military matters. His remarkable knowledge of technical military subjects is shown in his numerous books and pamphlets on training and tactics, which enjoyed a high reputation among professional soldiers and led to many improvements in drill. His connexion with the Volunteer movement has an association with the introduction of postcards into the United Kingdom. Macdonald had realized that it would greatly facilitate communication with his men if he could send out notices and orders on halfpenny stamped cards such as had been introduced in Austria (1 October 1869), and he wrote to Mr. Gladstone (14 October 1869) advocating this innovation in the postal system. The suggestion, which was supported from other quarters and by a petition which he set on foot, received effect in the following year.

Macdonald was attracted by scientific pursuits and took a special interest in practical applications of science. Several inventions stand to his credit and brought him various international awards. He was a fellow of the Royal Society and of the Royal Society of Edinburgh, and president of the Royal Scottish Society of Arts. In the development of motor transport he was an enthusiastic pioneer, and he was president of the Scottish Automobile Association. All forms of athletics appealed to him ; he was president of the Scottish Amateur Athletic Association, captain of the Royal and Ancient Golf Club of St. Andrews, and arbiter in international football disputes. He was a jealous guardian of the beauties of the city of Edinburgh against the inroads of vandalism. An address which he delivered before the Edinburgh Architectural Association in 1907 contained a trenchant and characteristic denunciation of the city's enemies in this respect. He was also instrumental, when lord advocate, in securing Dover House for the Scottish Office.

Macdonald's personality was outstanding, his humanity all-embracing, his mind vigorous, and his sympathies warm. He was in his element at public gatherings of a social character, and the genial pages of his Volunteer experiences and of his random autobiography in *Fifty Years of It* (1909) and *Life Jottings of an Old Edinburgh Citizen* (1915) faithfully reflect his temperament and outlook. *Our Trip to Blunderland*, first published in 1877 under the pseudonym of ' Jean Jambon ', displays his sense of fun and his sympathy with children. He died in Edinburgh 9 May 1919.

Macdonald was made a privy councillor in 1885, created K.C.B. in 1900, and G.C.B. in 1916. He married in 1864 Adelaide Jeannette, daughter of Major John Doran, of Ely House, co. Wexford. She predeceased him in 1870, and he was survived by his two sons, of whom the elder is an advocate of the Scottish bar. Throughout his life he was a devoted member of the 'Catholic Apostolic' Church.

[Macdonald's own writings above mentioned ; private information ; personal knowledge.] H. P. M.

MACDONELL, Sir JOHN (1845–1921), jurist, born 11 August 1845 at Brechin, Forfarshire, was the second son of James Macdonell, of the Glengarry Macdonells, by his wife, Rachel Allardyce, of Dyce, Aberdeenshire. Their eldest son, James Macdonell [q.v.], became a well-known journalist. In 1852 his father, an official in the Inland Revenue, removed to Rhynie, Aberdeenshire, and here John Macdonell received his early education under the Rev. George Stewart, an excellent classical scholar, to whose training he always felt deeply indebted. This was followed by a year at the Aberdeen grammar school, in the old building where

Byron had been a pupil. Macdonell entered Aberdeen University in 1861, graduating with honours in classics in 1865. Although most of his boyhood was spent in a remote village, there was no lack of intellectual stimulus at home, and perhaps he owed something of his later wide outlook on life to the fact that his father was a fervent though tolerant Roman Catholic, while his mother and many of his father's friends were Protestants.

After a brief time as a classical tutor at Leamington, Macdonell obtained an appointment on the staff of the *Scotsman*, then edited by Alexander Russel [q.v.]. A series of articles contributed to that journal formed the basis of his first book, *A Survey of Political Economy* (1871). Meanwhile, he had entered at the Middle Temple in 1870. He was called to the bar in 1873. During the early years of his professional career he wrote *The Land Question, with particular reference to England and Scotland* (1873) and *The Law of Master and Servant* (1883); he also began a connexion with *The Times* which continued unbroken till the year of his death. He was at the time in good practice as counsel to the Board of Trade and to the London Chamber of Commerce. In 1889 he was made a master of the Supreme Court, and in 1912 he became senior master and King's Remembrancer, retaining both these offices until the year before his death. In 1901 he was appointed Quain professor of comparative law at University College, London, and he held the chair until 1920. He was the first dean of the faculty of law in the university of London. He was made C.B. in 1898, knighted in 1903, and promoted K.C.B. in 1914.

Macdonell edited the *Reports of State Trials*, new series, vols. 1–3 (1888–1891), and compiled for the Home Office the *Civil Judicial Statistics for England and Wales*, from 1894 to 1919. During the same period he frequently edited the *Criminal Judicial Statistics*. He was a member of Lord Gorell's committee (1909) which inquired into the relations between the High Court and the county courts; and he prepared statistical returns for the royal commission on divorce and matrimonial causes (1909–1912), and gave evidence before that commission. He also gave evidence before the joint select committee of the Houses of Parliament on the King's Bench division of the High Court (1909); and he gave evidence and prepared statistical materials for the royal commission on delay in the King's Bench division (1912–1913). He served on the royal commission on shipping combinations (1906–1907) and signed the minority report, and was one of the two sub-commissioners sent to take evidence in South Africa. In November 1919 Macdonell undertook the chairmanship of the commission to inquire into the responsibility of the German Empire for crimes committed by its armed forces on land and sea and in the air during the European War. The report of this commission, which involved immense labour, has not been published. Among the learned bodies with which Macdonell was associated the Society of Comparative Legislation, founded in 1894, whose *Journal* he edited from 1897 until his death, deserves special mention. In 1912 he edited, with Mr. Edward Manson, *The Great Jurists of the World* (Continental Legal History series), a collection of studies reproduced from the *Journal*. In 1900 he became an associate, and in 1912 a member, of the Institut de Droit International. He was one of the founders of the Grotius Society, and its president in 1919–1920 and 1920–1921. His lecture delivered in 1917 on 'True Freedom of the Seas' attracted much attention, particularly in the United States. Through his Quain lectures he influenced legal thinkers of many nationalities, among whom were jurists from China and Japan. In 1913 he was elected a fellow of the British Academy.

Macdonell possessed a broad and sane outlook on life, combined with a versatility of mind and a serene humanism rare among any but the greatest jurists.

He married in 1873 Agnes, third daughter of Daniel Harrison, of Beckenham, Kent, and niece of Mary Howitt [q.v.]. Lady Macdonell (who died in 1925) was herself a gifted writer and a constant helper of her husband in all his work. They had two daughters, who survived them. Macdonell died in London 17 March 1921.

[*The Times*, 19 March 1921; personal knowledge.] R. W. L.

McDONNELL, Sir SCHOMBERG KERR (1861–1915), civil servant, the fifth son of Mark, fifth Earl of Antrim, of the second creation, by his wife, Jane Emma Hannah, daughter of Major Turner Macan, of Carriff, co. Armagh, was born at Glenarm Castle, co. Antrim, 22 March 1861. He was educated at Eton and at University College, Oxford, and afterwards gained experience as private secretary to the fourth Earl of Carnarvon [q.v.] and to the sixth Duke of Buccleuch. These appointments, and his own natural gifts, fitted him admirably for intimate contact with the high officials of state, and in 1888 he became principal private secretary to the prime minister, the Marquess of Salisbury. In 1892, when Lord Salisbury left office and headed the conservative opposition, he retained the services of McDonnell as his political private secretary, and McDonnell took a prominent part in party organization and especially in the work of the Central Conservative Association. Three years later the conservatives returned to power, and McDonnell again took up the duties of principal private secretary to Lord Salisbury, and for four years filled that arduous office with distinction. The outbreak of the Boer War called him from this post to active service; and, as a captain in the City of London Imperial Volunteers, he took part in that campaign until 1900, when he returned to England. After a short rest, necessitated by a slight breakdown in health, he resumed his secretarial duties with Lord Salisbury; and two years later (1902), on the latter's retirement, McDonnell was appointed secretary to the Office of Works in succession to Viscount Esher, and created K.C.B.

In his new post McDonnell found great scope for his discriminating artistic taste, and he effected many striking improvements in the royal parks. The erection of the Queen Victoria Memorial (1911), the coronation of King George V (1911), and the investiture of the Prince of Wales at Carnarvon Castle in the same year, cast a great burden of additional work upon his shoulders; and the strain of these duties, which seemed at one time to threaten his life, caused him to retire in 1912. For ten crowded years he had carried out the exacting duties of his difficult post with conspicuous success, and during that time, as indeed throughout his life, he showed a genius for friendship which endeared him to all with whom he came into close contact. In the European War McDonnell, graded as staff captain, acted for some months as chief intelligence officer of the home district at the Horse Guards. He desired, however, a more active participation in the struggle than this appointment afforded, so he quietly threw up the post and joined the 5th Cameron Highlanders. Within three weeks he was mortally wounded on the Western front in Flanders, and died 23 November 1915 at Abeele, where his remains were interred. He married, in 1913, Ethel Henry, daughter of Major Alexander H. Davis, of La Floridiana, Naples. There were no children of the marriage.

[*The Times*, 27 November 1915; private information.] C. V. O.

MacGREGOR, Sir WILLIAM (1846–1919), colonial governor, was born 20 October 1846 at Hillockhead in the parish of Towie, Aberdeenshire. He was the eldest son of John MacGregor, a crofter, by his wife, Agnes, daughter of William Smith, a farmer, of Pitprone in the neighbouring parish of Leochel-Cushnie. He received his early education at the village school of Tillyduke, where his ability soon attracted attention. During his boyhood he was engaged in agricultural labour, but partly by his own efforts at self-education and partly by the help of friends he was able to go in 1865 to Aberdeen grammar school. Proceeding to Aberdeen University in 1867 he studied medicine there and at Glasgow, graduating M.B. of Aberdeen in 1872 and M.D. in 1874.

After practising medicine for a short time in Scotland, MacGregor was appointed in 1873 assistant medical officer in the Seychelles, in 1874 resident surgeon in the civil hospital at Port Louis, Mauritius, and in 1875 chief medical officer for the colony of Fiji. During the next thirteen years he gained much administrative experience and gave evidence of great capabilities. His resourcefulness was shown in his struggle against the epidemic of measles which decimated the population of Fiji in 1878, and his physical strength in his remarkable rescue of three people at once in a shipwreck near Suva in 1884, for which he received the Albert medal (1884) and the Clarke gold medal of Australia (1885). He gradually came to occupy important administrative posts and at times acted as temporary administrator of the colony.

In 1888 MacGregor was appointed the first administrator (receiving the title of lieutenant-governor in 1895) of British New Guinea (now the territory of Papua), the country with which his name will chiefly be associated. The territory was then in its infancy, having been proclaimed a British protectorate in 1884. There was much pioneer work to be done, and MacGregor, with but small resources, showed great energy and activity in laying the foundations of a sound administration. He organized an efficient native police out of poor material, insisted on a strict enforcement of the laws, tackled the difficult problems of land tenure and native labour, and generally promoted a policy of peaceful penetration, which resulted in the gradual conciliation of the unruly tribes of the country and in the development of its great natural resources. For his important work in exploring the territory he received in 1896 the founder's medal of the Royal Geographical Society. He published in 1897 *British New Guinea: Country and People*, based on a paper read to that society.

MacGregor left New Guinea in 1898 and was appointed governor of Lagos in the following year. Here, too, he performed important pioneer work in a young colony, making the tribal chiefs share in the work of government and opening up the country by means of roads and railways. He carried on an active campaign against malaria, helping (Sir) Ronald Ross in the application of his important discoveries. After five years in Lagos, during which his health suffered from the climate, he was appointed in 1904 governor of Newfoundland. Here he used his medical knowledge in efforts for the prevention of tuberculosis; and by wise handling contributed largely to the settlement of the difficult question of American fishing rights which was then at an acute stage. He also organized and himself conducted a scientific expedition to Labrador, with the object of surveying its coast and investigating its resources. The results were of great importance alike from the geographical, meteorological, and anthropological points of view. From 1909 to 1914 MacGregor was governor of Queensland, where he was already well known owing to his success in New Guinea. He interested himself in educational affairs, in promoting the agricultural development of the country, and in the progress of medical knowledge. During his term of office, and largely owing to his personal efforts, the university of Queensland was founded (1910) and he became its first chancellor.

MacGregor retired in 1914 after nearly forty years' work in colonial administration, and went to live on his estate of Chapel-on-Leader, Berwickshire. On the outbreak of the European War he offered himself for service and did useful work in serving on committees and in lecturing. In 1918 his health began to fail, and he died 3 July 1919, after an operation in a nursing home at Aberdeen. He was buried in the churchyard of Towie, his native village. He was twice married: first, in 1868 to Mary (died 1877), daughter of Peter Thomson, by whom he had a son and a daughter; secondly, in 1883 to Mary Jane, daughter of Captain Robert Cocks, of the merchant service, by whom he had two daughters. He was created K.C.M.G. in 1889, G.C.M.G. in 1907, and became a privy councillor in 1914. He was an honorary LL.D. of the universities of Aberdeen, Edinburgh, and Queensland, and an honorary D.Sc. of Cambridge. He presented to the anthropological museum of Aberdeen University a valuable collection of ethnological specimens from Fiji, New Guinea, Lagos, and Labrador.

A man of outstanding personality, MacGregor deserves a high place in the roll of Great Britain's colonial administrators. With no early advantages of position or fortune his success in life was due to his own efforts and to the courage and determination with which he faced and overcame obstacles in his youth. He was much helped in his administrative work by his wide range of knowledge; not only was he an excellent linguist, botanist, and ethnologist, but he used his medical experience with great effect in the solution of problems of health. In his work as a scientific explorer he was aided by his remarkable physical strength. His success in dealing with native races was due to the tact, patience, and firmness with which he treated them, and to his determination to prevent their exploitation by Europeans. They rewarded him with their trust and his name became a power throughout the South Pacific. Reticent by nature, and with a certain ruggedness in his character, MacGregor was essentially a strong man and an inspiring leader; yet he was entirely without boastfulness or egotism, and his qualities of strength and restraint united to make him, in the words of Lord Bryce, 'a model of what a colonial governor should be'.

[Memoir by Professor R. W. Reid in *Aberdeen University Review*, vol. vii, part 1, November 1919; notice in *Aberdeen Grammar School Magazine*, vol. xxlii, No. 1, October 1919; Charles Brunsdon Fletcher, *The New Pacific*, 1917; private information. Portrait, *Royal Academy Pictures*, 1916.] F. P. S.

MACKAY, DONALD JAMES, eleventh Baron Reay (1839–1921), governor of Bombay, and first president of the British Academy, was born at The Hague 22 December 1839. He was the elder son of Eneas, Baron Mackay, of Ophemert, Holland, tenth Baron Reay, and head of the clan Mackay, whose ancestor, Sir Donald Mackay, first Baron Reay [q.v.], raised a regiment among his clansmen and served at its head with the Danish and Swedish armies during the Thirty Years' War. His mother was Maria, daughter of Baron Fagel, privy councillor of the Netherlands. Mackay was educated at the university of Leyden, where he matriculated in 1856 and graduated in laws in 1861. On entering the Dutch Foreign Office he was attached to the Dutch legation in London, but was transferred the same year (1861) to the Dutch Colonial Office. In 1871 he entered the Chamber of Representatives as a member of the Left.

In 1875 Mackay left Holland and settled in England, succeeding to the Scottish title in 1876 and becoming naturalized in 1877. He married in the latter year Fanny Georgiana Jane, daughter of Richard Hasler, of Aldingbourne, Sussex, and widow of Alexander Mitchell, M.P., of Stow, Midlothian. In 1881 he was created Baron Reay in the peerage of the United Kingdom, and in 1885 Mr. Gladstone appointed him governor of Bombay, a post which he held till 1890. As governor he kept in his own hands the charge of the political, military, ecclesiastical, and public works departments, and, during his last year of office, that of public instruction, encouraging the development of teaching in manifold branches. He also paid much attention to the development of the railway system. He was made G.C.I.E. in 1887 and G.C.S.I. in 1890. In 1894 Lord Reay was appointed under-secretary of state for India, but held the office for only fifteen months, the liberal ministry of Lord Rosebery having terminated in the summer of 1895. During this period the expedition to Chitral [see ROBERTSON, Sir George Scott] was organized and successfully concluded.

In 1897 Lord Reay was elected chairman of the London School Board, and retained that office till the abolition of the Board in 1904. His association with University College, London, dates from 1881, when he was elected a member of the council. On his return from India he was re-elected (1891) to the council, of which he became vice-president in 1892 and president in 1897. After the incorporation of the college in the reorganized university of London (1907), he was appointed chairman of the University College committee, and he held the office until his death. He also presided, in February 1908, over the departmental committee which led to the foundation of the school of Oriental studies, since incorporated in London University.

Lord Reay took great interest in questions of international law and politics, and was elected associate (1882) and member (1892) of the Institut de Droit International. From the latter date he took an active part in nearly all the meetings of the Institut, working on its committees and making communications on such subjects as extradition and expulsion of foreigners. He attended the Geneva meeting of 1892 and nearly all those that followed, serving as vice-president at Venice (1896) and at Brussels (1902), and as president at Edinburgh (1904). In spite, however, of his interest in questions of international law he never published any work on the subject.

In 1907 Lord Reay was appointed third British delegate to the second Peace Conference at The Hague, where he served as member of the second commission on the laws and customs of war on land. He read a closely reasoned explanation of the definition of fleet auxiliaries, delivered important speeches proposing the abolition of contraband, and presented the new British draft on the subject of delays of grace.

Lord Reay was made a privy councillor in 1906 and created K.T. in 1911. He was elected rector of St. Andrews University (1884), vice-president of the Royal Asiatic Society (1892), and first president of the newly founded British Academy in 1901, retaining the last-named office until 1907.

In January 1917 an accident, which resulted in a broken thigh-bone, confined him thenceforth to an invalid's chair, but did not prevent his attendance at the meetings of University College and of the Royal Asiatic Society. He died at Carolside, Earlston, Berwickshire, 31 July 1921. His wife predeceased him in 1917, leaving no children.

Lord Reay was a devout Presbyterian, of simple tastes and habits. He took an active part in the foundation and opening (1883) of St. Columba's Presbyterian church, Pont Street, London. A statue of him commemorating his services as governor of Bombay was erected in Bombay in 1895.

[*The Times*, 1 August 1921; Viscount Bryce in *Proceedings* of the British Academy, vol. x, 1921–1922; *Journal* of the Royal Asiatic Society, October 1921; personal knowledge.]

E. M. S.

MACLEAN, SIR HARRY AUBREY DE VERE (1848–1920), the eldest son of Andrew Maclean, M.D., of Drimnin, Argyllshire, inspector-general in the Army Medical Service, by his wife, Clara, daughter of Henry Holland Harrison, was born at Chatham 15 June 1848. He first served as a clerk in the Privy Council office, but joined the 69th regiment in 1869. At the time of the Fenian border raid into Canada in April 1870 his regiment formed part of the Huntingdon field force under Colonel Bagot which attacked and defeated the Fenians at Trout River, not far from Montreal. From Canada he went with his regiment to Bermuda in 1870, and in 1873 to Gibraltar.

In 1876 Maclean retired from the army. The following year Mulai Hassan, sultan of Morocco, sent 100 men to be trained at Gibraltar in order to act as instructors to the army of 10,000 men which he proposed to raise. He asked for an English officer to accompany them back to Morocco, and Maclean accepted the appointment. He first served as drill instructor at Tangier, but was shortly after promoted to be kaid of 400 asakir (infantry) and instructor of the forces attached to the court. His pay was at the rate of 200 francs a month with the promise of an increase when he had learned sufficient Arabic to drill his men without the aid of an interpreter. About three months after his appointment he had fulfilled this condition. Eventually he learnt to speak Arabic fluently, but he never acquired a good accent, and Mulai Hassan often used to laugh at his queer pronunciation. His pay was now raised to £30 a month, with a horse, and a house wherever the sultan might reside. To instruct the Moorish army was, however, heartbreaking work; the sultan would not allow his soldiers to learn too much, nor to have proper instruction in musketry, for fear they might become dangerous as rebels.

Mulai Hassan and his successor, 'Abd-el-'Aziz, were both much attached to Maclean and confided in him, and he accompanied the court wherever it went. But his position at first was not easy. The Moorish ministers were jealous, and in 1881 obtained his dismissal. Next year, however, he was restored and accompanied Mulai Hassan on an expedition to the Sus province. A long time had elapsed since any sultan had ventured on such an expedition, but it was quite successful, and they traversed the Sus almost as far as Cape Juby. Maclean accompanied the sultan on many other journeys, visiting Tafilet—then a city barred to Europeans—as well as all the other chief towns of Morocco. He was partly responsible for the successful concealment of the news of the death of Mulai Hassan in 1894, until the grand vizier could take the necessary steps for assuring the succession of the sultan's favourite son, 'Abd-el-'Aziz. He was very popular with his men, to whom he was always considerate, though he could be firm enough on occasion. Being of powerful physique he was able to deal summarily with insubordinate individuals. His chief function was advisory, but in 1892 he was entrusted with the command of a force engaged in suppressing an insurrection of the Anjera tribe. To the British legation at Tangier Maclean was extremely helpful, acting as its unofficial agent at the sultan's court; but he was not the Machiavelli of intrigue that some of the foreign legations represented him to be. His position at court depended on his loyalty to the sultan, but his relations with the British legation did much to smooth the conduct of business. His services were rewarded by a C.M.G. in 1898, and in 1901, when he came with a Moorish mission to the coronation of King Edward VII, he received the K.C.M.G.

In 1904 Maclean narrowly escaped being kidnapped near Tangier by the followers of the rebel sherif, Mulai Ahmed er-Raisuli; his escape was due to the resource of Mr. Carleton, the British consular agent at Alcazar, who happened to be with him at the time. In July 1907, while negotiating with Raisuli on behalf of the Makhzen, he was actually kidnapped and held to ransom. For seven months he was a prisoner, and although he endured the hardships and tedium of his detention with great courage and coolness, there is no doubt that they seriously undermined his health. Raisuli at first was very exorbitant in his terms, going so far as to demand the governorship of Tangier, but gradually he was persuaded to moderate them by the efforts of Sir Herbert White, the British chargé d'affaires, and Maclean was eventually released. In 1908 'Abd-el-'Aziz was deposed; his successor, Mulai Hafid, although eager to retain Maclean's services, would not offer acceptable terms, and in 1909 Maclean resigned. After his retirement he lived partly at Richmond and partly at Tangier. He died at Tangier 4 February 1920.

Maclean was twice married: first, in 1882 to Catharine, daughter of Thomas Coe, of Gibraltar, by whom he had one son and three daughters; secondly, in 1913 to Ella, daughter of Sir Harry Prendergast, V.C. [q.v.], who, with one daughter, survived him.

Maclean in his native uniform was always an imposing figure. He was famous for the open-handed hospitality which he extended to all British visitors at the Moorish court. He devoted much of his spare time to the bagpipes, the piano, the guitar, and the accordion. He was an amateur inventor, but none of his inventions was commercially successful.

[*The Times*, 6 February 1920; *Country Life*, June 1920; Hart's *Army List*, 1871; private information.]

MACNAGHTEN, SIR EDWARD, BARON MACNAGHTEN, of Runkerry, and fourth baronet (1830–1913), judge, the second son of Sir Edmund Francis Workman Macnaghten, second baronet, of Dundarave, co. Antrim, by his wife, Mary Anne, only child of Edward Gwatkin, was born at his father's house in Bloomsbury 3 February 1830. Sir Edmund, formerly receiver of the court of chancery in Calcutta, was the elder brother of the diplomatist, Sir William Hay Macnaghten [q.v.], murdered at Kabul in December 1841. The founder of the Irish branch of the Macnaghtens had migrated from Scotland to Antrim in 1580, and Sir Edmund Macnaghten became M.P. for the county, as his uncle, Edmund Alexander Macnaghten, had been before him. Edward Macnaghten's early years were spent at Roe Park, Limavaddy, and he went to Dr. Cowan's school, The Grange, Sunderland, where many boys from the north of England and Ireland were then educated. Thence he was sent to Trinity College, Dublin, in 1847, and proceeded as a scholar to Trinity College, Cambridge, in 1850. He won the Davis university scholarship in 1851, and in 1852 was bracketed senior classic. He was also a senior optime (1852) and won the second Chancellor's medal in the same year. As, in addition, he won the Colquhoun sculls at Cambridge in 1851, the Diamond sculls at Henley in 1852, and twice rowed in the university eight (1851 and 1852), his Cambridge career was remarkable. He became a fellow of Trinity in 1853 and an honorary fellow in 1902. In 1857 Macnaghten was called to the bar at Lincoln's Inn, and for twenty-three years was an equity junior. For a time, in and after 1858, he was secretary to the Chancery funds commission, but otherwise he was absorbed in his practice and, having taken to the law rather because he could find nothing else to do than for any other reason, had now no ambition beyond the profession for which he proved to be so well fitted.

At the general election of April 1880 Macnaghten was returned for county Antrim in the conservative interest, and in the same month he accepted the offer of a silk gown from Earl Cairns just before the latter's resignation. He attached himself first to the Rolls court and then to the court of Mr. Justice (Sir Joseph William) Chitty [q.v.]; he became a bencher of his inn in 1883 and reached the treasurership in 1907. His high position at the Chancery bar is shown by the fact that in 1883 the Earl of Selborne offered him a judgeship, which he refused, since his seat would have been lost to his party. He expected after this, and on good grounds, to be appointed one of the law officers in Lord Salisbury's first administration, it having been the practice to fill one of these offices from the Chancery bar; but both appointments were given to common law men on this occasion. How good an impression Macnaghten made in the House of Commons is shown by the offer, brought to him personally by Lord Halsbury, of the home secretaryship, when Lord Salisbury's second administration was formed in 1886. This offer he refused, not then being disposed to abandon his career at the bar, and Lord Halsbury's offer of a Chancery judgeship in the following November was refused also. At last, in January 1887, he was appointed a lord of appeal in ordinary, on the retirement of Lord Blackburn. This was a promotion without precedent, for not only was it direct from the bar but it was made in the case of a man who had worn silk for no more than seven years.

Macnaghten had been elected for North Antrim after the redistribution of 1885, and had spoken in the House of Commons only on Irish topics. His speeches on the Land Law (Ireland) Bill on 12 May 1881 and on the Home Rule Bill on 31 May 1886 were long and excellent, abounding in happy quotations and equally happy sarcasms, particularly at the expense of his brother-lawyers, Sir Charles Russell (afterwards Baron Russell of Killowen) and (Sir) John Rigby; one of his jests in the former speech ruffled Mr. Gladstone himself. From the time when he first entered the House of Lords he took an active part in debate, generally, but by no means always, speaking on Irish questions and on legal bills. In 1887 he spoke eleven times and thereafter until 1900 he was completely silent only in the years 1895 and 1897. Repeatedly he took charge of bills, and on 6 August 1896 carried against the government an amendment on the Land Law Bill (Ireland) of Mr. Gerald Balfour. He was no respecter of persons, did not see why he should bridle his tongue, and in the course of much vigorous discussion bluntly told Lord Herschell that he did not understand the bill which he was talking about. In 1903 he was prominent in the committee stage of the Irish Land Bill and carried several amendments, but from that year onwards he never spoke in debate, though he never ceased to be interested in public affairs, and especially in Ulster. In spite of his high judicial office, and though he was a justice of the peace for county Antrim, where he had a country residence, he signed the Ulster covenant (28 September 1912).

From 1887 till his death Macnaghten's life is largely written in twenty-six volumes of the appeal cases and in many volumes of the Indian law reports. He undertook other work, however, in addition to his judicial duties: he was arbitrator in the questions arising out of the affairs of the Portsea Island building society in 1893; chairman of the arbitral tribunal in the boundary dispute between Chile and the Argentine Republic in 1899; and, from 1895 till his death, chairman of the Council of Legal Education, where he was the real founder of the new system of professional training, which was so greatly developed after he first took that office.

As a judge, Macnaghten's name will long endure. He possessed in a happy combination the gifts of listening with patience and deciding without doubt, after bringing to bear his great range of unobtruded learning and a clear practical appreciation of business and of character. Others in his time were as erudite and his equals in acumen, but it was remarkable that both bench and bar fell into the way of citing a sentence or two of an opinion of Macnaghten and of accepting it without discussion as an authoritative statement of the law. This was largely due to his gift of summarizing broadly the law on the question in hand as the starting-point for discussion and judgment, and of using simple yet exact terms. In narrative he presented the relevant facts with a rapidity and sweep that seemed quite spontaneous, but he never failed to give a picture of the case which needed no further touches. To all this his nature added the charm of humanity and humour. With law he found, as Dr. Johnson's friend, Edwards of Pembroke, found with philosophy, that cheerfulness was always breaking in. *Van Grutten* v. *Foxwell* (1897) is the example most often quoted of his power of combining learning, style, and humour, so as to produce out of a dry and technical discussion a delightful literary essay, but it is far from being the only one. In fact he could not help being humorous. This style had begun before he had been four months in the House of Lords with his comments in *Drummond* v. *Van Ingen* (1887) and was still lambent in 1912, when he pointed out the legal bearings of the fact that 'there was no "pickled tea" at Mi Shwe Mai's wedding' (L. R. 39, I. A. p. 6). When he was deeply moved, however, he could use the language of curt sarcasm and of righteous wrath (*Gluckstein* v. *Barnes*, 1900, quoted in *The Oxford Book of English Prose*), and his dissentient opinion in the Free Kirk case (*Free Church of Scotland* v. *Overtoun*, 1904) rises to a height of lofty and stately eloquence rare in legal judgments.

In 1903 Macnaghten was created G.C.M.G. and in 1911 G.C.B. In the latter year he succeeded his brother Francis, as fourth baronet. To the end of his life his retentive memory and his powerful judgement were unimpaired, and in spite of years he never lost his personal activity. He died in London 17 February 1913.

Macnaghten married in 1858 Frances Arabella (died 1903), only child of Sir Samuel Martin [q.v.], a baron of the Exchequer, by whom he had five sons and six daughters. Of these Edward Charles, who succeeded his father as fifth baronet and was a leader at the Chancery bar, died in 1914; his two sons, the sixth and seventh baronets, fell in the battles on the Somme in July and September 1916 respectively; Lord Macnaghten's second son then succeeded as eighth baronet. There is a portrait of Lord Macnaghten by Hugh Glazebrook at Lincoln's Inn and a replica of it is in the Privy Council chamber. There is also a miniature of him by Miss E. Grace Mitchell, executed in 1904.

[Memoir by Lord Justice Kennedy in the *Law Magazine*, fifth series, vol. xxxviii, p. 455; private information; personal knowledge.]

S.

MACPHERSON, Sir JOHN MOLESWORTH (1853–1914), Anglo-Indian legislative draftsman, was born in Calcutta 8 August 1853. He was the elder son of John Macpherson, M.D. [q.v.], of the East India Company's medical service, and nephew of Samuel Charters Macpherson [q.v.], of the Madras army, and of William Macpherson [q.v.] of the Calcutta bar. His mother was Charlotte Melusina, fifth daughter of the Rev. John Molesworth Staples, rector of Lissan and Upper Moville, co. Tyrone. Educated at Westminster School, Macpherson was called to the bar by the Inner Temple in 1876 and enrolled as an advocate of the Calcutta high court in the same year. His career at the bar, however, was brief; for in the following year he was appointed deputy secretary to the government of India in the legislative department. After officiating on several occasions as secretary, in 1896 he was promoted permanently to that post, which he held till his retirement in 1911. He received the C.S.I. in 1897 and was knighted in 1911. After his retirement he was employed by the secretary of state for India upon a measure to amend and consolidate the conflicting and piecemeal legislation of parliament with regard to India; and on this he was engaged at the time of his death, which occurred suddenly at Streatham, 5 January 1914. The measure was finally cast into shape by Sir Courtenay Ilbert, and became the Government of India Act (1915).

Macpherson's career was of a type more common at Whitehall than in India, the whole of his active life being spent in a single office. A legal draftsman's position is necessarily one of continuous self-effacement; and it is therefore difficult to estimate his exact share in the Indian legislation of his time. Its most notable monuments, such as the Transfer of Property Act (1882) and the Civil Procedure Codes (1882 and 1908), were considered in detail by specially appointed committees composed of the highest legal talent available; and such work as Macpherson may have done on them can hardly have been more than routine. Indeed, he lacked the experience of litigation necessary for more than routine work. On the other hand, as he was never the responsible head of the legislative department, he cannot fairly be charged with its conspicuous failures, which were due to a policy of excessive simplification.

Macpherson's reputation was that of a thorough and painstaking official with an intimate knowledge of all the details of his office. To this knowledge and experience the rules of procedure for the enlarged Morley-Minto councils (1910) owe much of their success. He was also a valued critic and adviser on the technique of provincial legislation, when it came before the government of India in the ordinary course for approval before enactment. It is, however, with the legislative activities of the foreign department that his name will be longest associated; for the official *Lists of British Enactments in Force in Native States in India* (6 vols., 1888–1895) was originally compiled under his guidance, and, though subsequently re-edited, is still familiarly known as 'Macpherson'.

In private life Macpherson was a man of deep piety and a staunch adherent of the Presbyterian Church. He was happy in his home life and in a gift for making and retaining a very wide circle of friends. He married in 1880 Edith Christina (died 1913), daughter of General Charles Waterloo Hutchinson, C.B., Royal Engineers, inspector-general of military works in India. They had three sons and one daughter.

[*The Times*, 6 January 1914; private information.] S. V. FG.

MAHAFFY, SIR JOHN PENTLAND (1839–1919), provost of Trinity College, Dublin, author of numerous works on Greek literature and history, was born at Chapponnaire, near Vevey, Switzerland, 26 February 1839, the seventh and youngest child of the Rev. Nathaniel B. Mahaffy, a small landowner in county Donegal, by his wife, Elizabeth Pentland, who also came of a landowning family in county Monaghan. He was thus of Irish descent on both sides. His father acted as British chaplain at Lucerne from 1840 to 1843, in which year he exchanged the chaplaincy at Lucerne for a similar post at Bad Kissingen in Bavaria, and it was there that the boy was brought up till the age of nine. His parents then returned to Ireland and settled down on their property in Donegal. Young Mahaffy was educated at home until he entered Trinity College, Dublin, in 1855. His career at the university was brilliant; he won a scholarship in classics, and graduated in 1859 as first senior moderator in classics and logics. He was elected to a fellowship in 1864, having taken holy orders earlier in the same year. In the life of the undergraduates he played a leading part; he was captain of the cricket eleven and shot in the Irish team at Wimbledon, besides taking an active interest in the music of the college. In 1865 he married Frances, daughter of William MacDougall, of Howth, co. Dublin. The issue of this marriage was a family of four children, two sons and two daughters. From his election to a fellowship down to his death he continued to serve the college in one capacity or another as tutor, professor, vice-provost, and provost, for a period of fifty-five years.

Mahaffy's interests were originally philosophical, and the first work which he published was a *Translation of Kuno Fischer's Commentary on Kant* (1866), but his election in 1869 as the first professor of ancient history in the university gave a new direction to his studies. For the next forty years Greek history and Greek literature were to form the main subject of his labours. In 1871 he published his *Prolegomena to Ancient History*, which although rendered obsolete in great measure by the progress of discovery has been declared by a competent authority to be the best book that he ever wrote [A. H. Sayce, *Reminiscences*, 1923, p. 126]. During the next few years he visited Greece twice, and the influence of his travels may be traced in his *Greek Social Life from Homer to Menander* (1874), as well as in *Rambles and Studies in Greece* (1876). His *History of Classical Greek Literature* (1880) was followed, after an interval of seven years, by *The Story of Alexander's Empire* (1887); then came in rapid succession *Greek Life and Thought from Alexander to the Roman Conquest* (1887), *The Greek World under Roman Sway* (1890), and *Problems in Greek History* (1892). The year 1890 marks the beginning of a new epoch in his literary activities. It was in this year that a quantity of mummy cartonnage was discovered by W. M. Flinders Petrie in the Fayûm, and handed over to Mahaffy for decipherment and publication. For the next ten years his interests were centred on the Egypt of the Ptolemies, and to this period belong the first two volumes of the *Flinders Petrie Papyri* (1891–1893), followed by a third volume produced in collaboration with J. G. Smyly, and *The Empire of the Ptolemies* (1895). For the rest of his life his interests were chiefly directed to the history of his university and of Ireland in general. *An Epoch in Irish History, 1591–1660* (1904), *The Particular Book of Trinity College* (1904), and a monograph on the *Plate in Trinity College* (1918), were among the fruits of his researches in the field of Irish history. He was elected president of the Georgian Society, of which he was the founder, and from 1911 to 1916 he held the office of president of the Royal Irish Academy.

Mahaffy succeeded to a senior fellowship in 1899, and it was the general belief outside Trinity College itself that in view of his eminence in the world of letters and of his long service to his own college, he was certain of the succession to the provostship. When, however, the office became vacant by the death of Dr. George Salmon in 1904, he was passed over by the Crown in favour of Dr. Anthony Traill [q.v.]. Mahaffy had every right to anticipate that he would be appointed provost, although his was not the only name that might with propriety have been submitted to the King, and it is not too much to say that Traill's appointment came as a shock to the sentiment of the whole academic world. Mahaffy had to wait another ten years for the fulfilment of his hopes, and when, on Traill's death, he succeeded to the headship of his college (November 1914), he had reached the age of seventy-five. Two years later came the Irish rebellion of Easter week 1916, during which he directed the defence of Trinity College with coolness and resource. When the Irish Convention was summoned in 1917, it was at his invitation that it held its meetings in the Regent House of Trinity College. He was created G.B.E. in 1918. He died 30 April 1919, from the effects of a paralytic stroke.

It is by his contributions to the study of the literature, the life, and the history of the ancient Greeks that Mahaffy as a writer must be judged. Few authors, indeed, have been more versatile, and his range extended to subjects as remote from Hellenism as the *Decay of Modern Preaching* (1882), the *Art of Conversation* (1889), the architecture and furniture of the great houses of Ireland, and the introduction and diffusion of the domestic ass. On all these things he wrote well, and in his treatment of some of them he made valuable contributions to Irish history. His earliest effort, the *Commentary on Kant*, provoked a reply from Mill, then at the height of his influence; and his *Sketch of the Life and Teaching of Descartes* (1880) is an excellent piece of work so far as it goes. But it is not on these multifarious writings that his reputation rests. Indeed, it is probable that the estimate of him as a student of things Greek has suffered from the variety of his interests; he was supposed to be superficial, because people thought that knowledge so extended must be shallow. 'The Provost's talents, though brilliant, were versatile rather than profound', is the verdict in one of his obituary notices. Nothing could be more unjust. Honours such as he received from universities and learned societies (he was a corresponding member of the academies of Berlin, Munich, and Vienna, and of the Lincei at Rome, an honorary D.C.L. of Oxford, and an honorary fellow of Queen's College—these were but a few of the distinctions conferred on him) are not commonly the rewards of the mere popularizer. Although, as he himself says in one of his prefaces, his object was to set down results rather than processes of investigation, an essay such as that on the Olympian Register in his *Problems in Greek History* affords a presumption that, had he chosen, he could have exhibited the processes of investigation equally well with the results. He had no claims to exact scholarship, but he had in him much of the stuff of which historians are made; industry and imagination, a memory that was superb, and a curiosity that was insatiable. His greatest gift was his power of seeing things in the concrete; of so visualizing the past as to make it as real to us as the life we live and see around us. Hence it is that the books which bear the most distinctive impress of his individuality are the three volumes which treat of the social life and civilization of the Greeks from the age of Homer to the age of Hadrian. The first of these, *Greek Social Life from Homer to Menander*, marks an epoch in the treatment of the subject. The books which had hitherto been written were little more than works of reference. Since Mahaffy published his original and brilliant sketch no writer on these subjects, in this country at least, has ventured to make dullness his professed aim. His *History* of Greek literature is a solid and useful book, and many of his literary judgements are acute and fresh, but in originality both of conception and treatment it cannot be put on the same level as the three volumes referred to. As an historian, he had limitations and defects. He was interested in persons, rather than in the play of forces or the operation of laws; his strength certainly did not lie in the grasp of historical principles. It was perhaps inevitable that one to whom the past became as real as the present should sometimes allow the present to intrude into the past. Some of his parallels, it must be admitted, are fanciful or far-fetched. In justice to his memory, it should never be forgotten that he was above all things a pioneer. His judgements, both literary and political, anticipated in many instances the verdict of the next generation. To exalt Euripides above Sophocles is one of the commonplaces of latter day criticism; it was not a commonplace when Mahaffy wrote his *Social Life*. It needs, at the present moment, neither courage nor insight to pronounce that the democratic principle is fraught with peril to the higher interests of civilization; it needed both the one and the other when Mahaffy first pointed this moral. He, too, was one of the very few scholars in this or any other country who appreciated at the outset the revolutionary character of the discoveries of Heinrich Schliemann, and he was one of the first to grasp the importance of papyrology.

When it is remembered that Mahaffy came to the study of papyri with no previous palæographical training, we may well be surprised at the measure of success which he achieved. He was at his best in the guessing of the sense of obscure passages, the suggestion of supplements, and the lucid summarizing of results; for the task of accurate decipherment he lacked the patience and the attention to detail which are indispensable. To form a just estimate of his powers in this field we must look to the third volume of the *Petrie Papyri*, where he had the assistance of Smyly, or to the Introduction which he contributed to Dr. B. P. Grenfell's edition of the *Revenue* papyrus (1896). His *Empire of the Ptolemies*, an indirect result of his papyrological interests, still remains far the best account in English of that period.

Mahaffy's reputation was not merely that of a man of letters or university professor. For nearly half a century he was one of the best-known figures in the social life of his generation. He was an inveterate diner-out, and a constant attendant at congresses and other gatherings of the learned. His versatility extended far beyond the range of his literary interests. He was a firstrate shot and angler, and a learned and accomplished musician. He was an excellent man of business, and although his provostship was brief and in troublous times, he succeeded in carrying out some useful reforms in the government of Trinity College. Thanks in part to a boyhood spent on the Continent, he could speak German like a native and French fluently. But it was as a wit and raconteur, as one of the most brilliant talkers of his time, with a fund of apposite anecdote, that he was so widely known and so generally welcome in society. 'Ireland is a place where the inevitable never happens and the unexpected always occurs', is a fair specimen of his epigrammatic power. Like Dr. Johnson, he had the gift of stripping a subject of unessentials and arriving at once at the heart of things. His caustic wit made him unpopular, especially in his own university, and it is probable that this unpopularity stood in the way of his promotion. His wit was never really ill-natured, but he loved creating a sensation, even though he excited resentment, and he had a curious incapacity for anticipating the effect of what he said. Those who were present at the Historical Congress at Berlin in 1908 are not likely to forget the scene that was occasioned by his remark that the reason why English scholars, in dealing with questions of authorship, attached far more importance than the Germans to the argument from style, was that English scholars had been drilled in writing Latin and Greek prose, while the Germans had never written a piece of either in their lives. But if he was unpopular in certain circles, he had many attached friends, for he was generous and warm-hearted, and his judgements of men were never tainted by jealousy or bitterness.

Mahaffy played hardly any part in politics until the meeting of the Convention in 1917. He was both by temperament and conviction an aristocrat, and the Ireland for which he cared and to which he belonged was the nation of Burke and Goldsmith, of Grattan and Charles Lever. He never tired of decrying the cultural pretensions of Celtic Ireland, and he was contemptuous of the provincial note of Irish nationalism. In the Convention he recommended a federal scheme on the Swiss model with provincial autonomy for Ulster.

Portraits: by Sir W. Orpen in the Modern Art Gallery, Dublin; by Walter Osborne, 1900 (*Royal Academy Pictures*, 1900); and by James Wilcox in the Provost's House, Trinity College; a bas-relief by Carre in the chapel, and a bronze bust by Miss Shaw in the rooms of the Philosophical Society, Trinity College.

[Obituary notices in the newspapers, especially *The Times*, the *Irish Times*, and the *Spectator*; *Hermathena*, No. XLII, 1920 (with complete bibliography); A. H. Sayce, *Reminiscences*, 1923; A. S. Hunt in *Aegyptus*, i, 2, 1920 (of firstrate importance for Mahaffy's papyrological work); private information; personal knowledge.] E. M. W.

MAIR, WILLIAM (1830–1920), Scottish divine, the eldest son and fifth child in a family of twelve, was born at Savoch, Aberdeenshire, 1 April 1830. His father, the Rev. James Mair, was the parochial schoolmaster, a licentiate of the Church of Scotland; his mother, Christian Johnston, a cousin, was a member of a farming family long established there. From Aberdeen grammar school he passed to King's College and to Marischal College, Aberdeen, graduating with honours in 1849, and specially distinguished in mathematics.

'I had never thought', Mair writes in his autobiography, 'of any other life-work than the ministry.' But indifferent health kept him back for seven years; he was thirty-one at the time of his ordination to the mission church of Lochgelly, Fifeshire (October 1861). In 1864 he was translated to Ardoch, and in 1869 to Earlston, Berwickshire. He retired to Edinburgh in 1903, spending his remaining years in church work generally—constant committees, daily interviews, and correspondence on church law—but particularly in the cause of church union. He died in his sleep 26 January 1920, having lived over seventy years in fragile health by an extreme carefulness in diet, clothing, temperature, and exercise. He married in 1866 Isabella, daughter of David Edward, of Balruddery, Dundee.

Mair's remarkable vitality in the midst of bodily weakness, his wisdom in counsel, and his forthrightness in speech, his legal knowledge, his evangelical zeal, and, above all, his spiritual-mindedness, made him for many years a prominent figure in the Church of Scotland and in its General Assembly, of which he was moderator in 1897. His *Digest of Laws and Decisions, Ecclesiastical and Civil, relating to the Constitution, Practice, and Affairs of the Church of Scotland*, published in 1887, became at once, and remains, the standard authority on Scottish ecclesiastical law.

It is, however, as a pioneer in the cause of church reunion that Mair will be best remembered. A series of articles in *Blackwood's Magazine* and of pamphlets from 1904 onwards, prepared the way for 'unrestricted conference' between committees of his Church and the United Free Church. In 1907 Dr. Archibald Scott [q.v.] made the first public proposal for such conference; but Mair's had been the clear vision and the moving spirit from the beginning. His labours in connexion with the enlargement of the Assembly Hall in Edinburgh (1893–1894) are commemorated on a tablet in the vestibule, and were further acknowledged by the presentation of his portrait, painted by Sir George Reid, in 1896.

Of Mair's other writings the more important are: *Speaking* (1900), *The Truth about the Scottish Churches* (1891), *Jurisdiction in Matters Ecclesiastical* (1896), and *My Life* (1911).

[*The Times*, 28 January 1920; *Scotsman*, 19 November 1896 and 27 January 1920; Dr. W. Mair, *My Life*, 1911; personal knowledge.] A. W. F.

MARKHAM, Sir ALBERT HASTINGS (1841–1918), admiral and Arctic explorer, was born at Bagnères-de-Bigorre, Hautes Pyrénées, 11 November 1841, the fourth son of Captain John Markham, R.N., by his wife, Marianne, daughter of John Brock Wood. After being educated at home and at Eastman's Royal Naval Academy, Southsea, he entered the navy in 1856 and served eight years on the China station, being promoted lieutenant in 1862. He took part in the advance on

Peking in 1860 and in the suppression of the Taiping rising in 1862–1864. After serving in the Mediterranean, Markham spent several years on the Australian station, where he was actively engaged in suppressing the abuses of the South Sea labour traffic. In 1872 he became commander, and in 1873, while on leave, he sailed in the whaler *Arctic* to Davis Strait and Baffin's Bay in order to study ice conditions. He has given an account of this voyage in *A Whaling Cruise to Baffin's Bay* (1874). In the Arctic expedition of 1875–1876 under (Sir) George Strong Nares [q.v.] Markham was in command of H.M.S. *Alert*. His sledging party, in a spirited endeavour to reach the Pole from winter quarters in latitude 82° 27′ N. on the western shore of Robeson channel, gained the latitude of 83° 20′ 26″ N. in longitude 64° W. in May 1876. This latitude was reached without the help of dogs, and the feat remained a record until broken by Fridtjof Nansen in 1895. For his services on this expedition Markham was promoted captain, and received a gold watch from the Royal Geographical Society.

From 1879 to 1882 Markham served with the navy in the Pacific; from 1883 to 1886 he was captain of H.M.S. *Vernon*, the naval torpedo school at Portsmouth, and from 1886 to 1889 commodore of the training squadron. Promoted rear-admiral in 1891, the following year he was appointed second-in-command of the Mediterranean squadron under Sir George Tryon [q.v.]. During manœuvres off the coast of Syria on 22 June 1893 Markham's ship *Camperdown* rammed the flagship *Victoria*, which sank with great loss of life. The court martial exonerated Markham from blame, since he had carried out the orders of the commander-in-chief. From 1901 to 1904 he was commander-in-chief at the Nore; in 1906 he retired from the navy.

During earlier periods of his life Markham showed a desire to return to the work of Arctic discovery, by accompanying Sir Henry Gore-Booth on a cruise to Novaya Zemlya in 1879, described by him in *A Polar Reconnaissance* (1879), while in 1886 he made a careful survey of ice conditions in Hudson Strait and Bay, for which he received the thanks of the Canadian government. During the European War of 1914–1918 he devoted himself to the interests of the mine-sweeping service. Markham was created a K.C.B. in 1903 and for some years was an aide-de-camp to Queen Victoria. Among his numerous publications the most important are *The Great Frozen Sea* (1877), *The Life of John Davis, the Navigator* (1882), *The Life of Sir John Franklin* (1890), and *The Life of Sir Clements Markham* (his cousin, 1917). He married in 1894 Theodora, daughter of Francis T. Gervers, of Amat, Ross-shire, by whom he had one daughter. He died in London 28 October 1918.

[*The Times*, 29 October 1918; *Geographical Journal*, January 1919; A. H. Markham, *The Great Frozen Sea*, 1877. See also M. E. and F. A. Markham, *Life of Sir A. H. Markham*, 1927.] R. N. R. B.

MARKHAM, Sir CLEMENTS ROBERT (1830–1916), geographer and historical writer, was born at Stillingfleet, Yorkshire, 20 July 1830, the second son of the Rev. David Frederick Markham, vicar of Stillingfleet and canon of Windsor, and grandson of William Markham [q.v.], archbishop of York. His mother was Catherine, daughter of Sir William Milner, fourth baronet, of Nun Appleton Hall, Yorkshire. After two years at Westminster School he entered the navy in 1844 and spent four years in H.M.S. *Collingwood* on the Pacific station, mainly in South American ports, where he picked up a working knowledge of Spanish. He devoted his leisure to reading books of travel and writing accounts of the countries which he visited. Many things in the service were distasteful to him, but he remained in it three years longer in order to join H.M.S. *Assistance* as a midshipman under Captain Austin on his Franklin search expedition of 1850–1851. After a visit to William Hickling Prescott, the historian, at Boston, Markham enjoyed a year of wandering (1852–1853) among the Inca ruins in Peru, which made him a lifelong friend of the Peruvian people, while South American history and politics never lost their fascination for him.

In 1853 Markham entered the civil service, and next year was transferred to the board of control of the East India Company, which in 1858 was incorporated in the new India Office. He married in 1857 Minna, daughter of the Rev. James Hamilton John Chichester, rector of Arlington and Loxhore, near Barnstaple. She was an accomplished linguist, devoted to literary pursuits, and worked with him in perfect accord for nearly sixty years. They had one daughter.

In 1860 Markham was charged with the collection of young cinchona trees and seeds in the forests of the Eastern Andes, and with the acclimatization of the plants in India. The difficulties were great, but the result was a complete success, leading in time to the supply of quinine at a very low price. From 1867 to 1877 he had charge of the geographical work of the India Office. In 1868 he accompanied Sir Robert Cornelis (afterwards Baron) Napier [q.v.] as geographer on the Abyssinian campaign; he was present at the capture of Magdala, and it was he who discovered the body of the Emperor Theodore. In 1871 he received the C.B. and in 1873 was elected F.R.S. He took an active part in promoting the revival of Arctic exploration, and sailed in 1875 as far as Greenland with the expedition of (Sir) George Strong Nares [q.v.], on which his cousin (Sir) Albert Hastings Markham [q.v.] was second-in-command.

In 1877 Markham left the India Office and retired from official life, only to redouble his geographical and historical activities, travelling widely and writing incessantly. He had joined the Royal Geographical Society in 1854, and was one of its honorary secretaries for twenty-five years (1863–1888). He became president in 1893 and during his twelve years' tenure of this position he imposed his personality on the society, concerning himself with every detail of its work and vigorously directing its policy of encouraging exploration and geographical education. His influence maintained the popularity of the society and did much to foster the rapid growth of its numbers. Markham was frequently consulted by the government, as, for example, on the difficult question of the boundary between British Guiana and Venezuela. He received the K.C.B. in 1896.

For the next few years Markham threw his whole heart into the promotion of Antarctic exploration, securing funds by urgent appeals to public and private sources. On the joint committee of the Royal Society and the Royal Geographical Society, which was responsible for the National Antarctic expedition of 1901, he opposed the proposal to appoint a man of science as leader and insisted that the expedition should consist of naval men under the sole command of a naval officer, accompanied by a small civilian scientific staff. Markham selected Commander Robert Falcon Scott [q.v.] as leader, and the expedition was highly successful. Upon the officers Markham impressed the traditions of the old Arctic service, but he admitted improvements in details. In later South Polar achievements he took but little interest until Captain Scott planned the expedition in the *Terra Nova* in 1910, when his former ardour was rekindled.

The Hakluyt Society drew from Markham equally hearty support. He served it as secretary for twenty-nine years (1858–1886), as president for twenty more (1889–1909), and he edited for it fully twenty volumes of old travels, translating most of these afresh from the Spanish. He died in London as the result of an accident 30 January 1916, in his eighty-sixth year.

For many years Sir Clements Markham's reputation was established throughout the world as the leading British geographer. Although apt to be obstinate in his opinions and vehement in his likes and dislikes, he had a genius for friendship especially with the young. Westminster schoolboys, cadets of the nautical training colleges, and, above all, young naval officers, found in him a tireless friend, abounding in sympathy and help. In addition to translations and official reports, some of great value, he published fifty volumes. Among these are eighteen biographies (which illustrate his love of paradox and his tendency to hero-worship), twenty historical or ethnographical works, several records of polar discoveries, and three historical romances. It was inevitable that much of his published work should show signs of over-hasty production. His translations sometimes take short cuts through difficulties, and although assiduous in consulting authorities, he often accepted their data uncritically, for he was in all things an enthusiast rather than a scholar.

[Sir Albert Hastings Markham, *The Life of Sir Clements Markham*, 1917; Sir John Scott Keltie, memoir in the *Geographical Journal*, vol. xlvii, 1916; private information; personal knowledge. Portrait, *Royal Academy Pictures*, 1922.] H. R. M.

MARTIN, VIOLET FLORENCE (1862–1915), novelist under the pseudonym of MARTIN ROSS, was born at Ross House, co. Galway, 11 June 1862. She was the eleventh and youngest daughter of James Martin, D.L., head of the ancient family of Martin—one of 'the tribes of Galway'—which has been seated at Ross for several centuries; hence the pen-name which she adopted. The record of her family is one of much literary and artistic activity. Her mother, Anna Selina Fox—a lady of much wit and wide culture—was a granddaughter of Lord Chief Justice Charles Kendal Bushe [q.v.], 'silver-tongued Bushe', the wittiest man of his time, who is still remembered for his 'incorruptible' opposition to the Union with England. Among her kinsfolk on her father's side were the poet, Aubrey Thomas de Vere [q.v.], and Miss Rose Barton, the water-colourist; on her mother's, William Gorman Wills [q.v.], painter and dramatist. Her brother, Robert, was well known as the author of 'Bally-Hooley' and other Irish songs.

The Ross estate, once of great extent, suffered severely during the famine of 1845, and for a time Mr. Martin took up journalism and became leader-writer to the London *Morning Herald*. The evil time tided over, he returned to Ross and lived there until his death in 1872. After her father's death Violet Martin's childhood was spent in Dublin. Her family belonged to the Protestant church, and in that city and especially at a Sunday school which she attended she gained the deep comprehension of the strata of Dublin society so faithfully delineated in the opening chapters of *The Real Charlotte*. She was educated at home, and at the Alexandra College, Dublin, and early showed remarkable proficiency in music and in English literature. Her life, unlike that of many Irish writers, was mainly lived in Ireland, at Ross and at Drishane, the home of her cousin and collaborator, Miss Edith Œnone Somerville; but the two cousins made many tours, abroad and elsewhere, which often yielded them amusing matter for their literary work. In spite of exceeding short-sight, Miss Martin was a fearless rider to hounds. She had a very serious hunting accident in 1898, from the effects of which she never thoroughly recovered, and it possibly contributed to the illness of which she died, at Cork 21 December 1915.

Quiet, and habitually rather reserved in manner, Miss Martin, in congenial society, was a brilliant talker and an amusing mimic, and the charm of her personality, together with the sweetness and sympathy that were marked features of her character, won her a host of devoted friends. From the knowledge of hunting that she shared with her collaborator (who was for twelve years master of the West Carbery foxhounds) sprang many of the books associated with this literary alliance, the best known of which is *Some Experiences of an Irish R.M.* (1899).

The books of these writers picture the life of what has sometimes been contemptuously called the 'English garrison', though no class contained persons more truly devoted to Ireland. *The Real Charlotte*, their first serious novel (1894), is admittedly one of the best pictures of this life that has ever been presented. How the society of that day is passing out of existence is well described in *Mount Music* (1919) and *An Enthusiast* (1921), which, though published after Miss Martin's death, are understood to have benefited by her inspiration. In these books, and in *The Irish R.M.* series, the future historian of Ireland will find valuable illustrations of the real life of the Irish country-side.

Miss Martin's writings, apart from those written jointly with her cousin, show the rare combination of a penetrating sense of humour with a refined and subtle literary style and a profound and sympathetic perception of character, especially of Irish character. These qualities are specially notable in her essays, the best examples of which are to be found in *Some Irish Yesterdays* (1906) and *Stray-Aways* (1920). These two volumes are mainly autobiographical and contain much of Violet Martin's individual writing. All her essays are reminiscent of times which had their own great and peculiar charm.

[The autobiographical books alluded to; private information; personal knowledge.]

B. C. A. W.

MATHEWS, Sir CHARLES WILLIE, baronet (1850–1920), lawyer, was born in New York 16 October 1850, the son of William and Elizabeth West. His mother, who was an actress at Burton's Theatre, New York, known on the stage as Lizzie Weston, married secondly A. H. Davenport, an actor, and thirdly (in 1858), as his second wife, Charles James Mathews [q.v.], the actor and dramatist. Her son assumed his second stepfather's name by deed-poll. He was educated at Eton. On leaving school he became a pupil of Montagu Stephen Williams [q.v.], the criminal lawyer, who has left on record that Mathews was the best pupil he ever had. He was called to the bar at the Middle Temple 30 April 1872, and began practice at 5 Crown Office Row, whence he moved in 1880 to 1 Essex Court. His work was chiefly in criminal cases at the Old Bailey, and on the Western circuit, though he also appeared in a good many sensational civil cases. In 1886 he was appointed one of the two junior Treasury counsel at the Old Bailey, and in 1888 one of the senior. In 1892 he stood for parliament unsuccessfully at Winchester as a liberal. In 1893 he was made recorder of Salisbury, and in 1901 a bencher of the Middle Temple. In 1907, on the occasion of the opening of the new central criminal court by the King, he was made a knight. In

1908 he was appointed director of public prosecutions, an office which he discharged until his death with ability and discretion. In 1911 he was made a K.C.B., and in 1917 a baronet. He died at a nursing home in London on 6 June 1920.

Mathews was pre-eminently what newspapers call a 'famous' lawyer, for he always appeared in criminal trials, or in notorious civil cases. He was learned in criminal law, an adroit advocate and cross-examiner, and a fluent speaker who had claims to be called really eloquent, though his style was histrionic, and he was hampered by a weak and unpleasing voice. He was a small man, with a dapper figure, and a precise manner. He was fond of riding, and of horses, and liked to attend race-meetings when he could. Socially 'Willie' Mathews, as he was familiarly known, was exceedingly popular, and his popularity extended to much wider circles than might be suggested by his membership of the Turf, the Garrick, and the Beefsteak clubs. There, and anywhere, he was an animated talker, always ready with some anecdote, in telling which he could act, as well as narrate. He was a modest man: he was once offered a brief before the Privy Council; he crept in to watch that tribunal at work, and then asked the solicitors to allow him to decline the brief as he did not consider himself equipped for the task.

Mathews married in 1888 Lucy, daughter of Lindsay Sloper, musician, who survived him. They had no children.

[*The Times*, 7 June 1920; *Law Journal*, 12 June 1920; Law Lists; private information.] F. D. M.

MATTHEWS, HENRY, VISCOUNT LLANDAFF (1826–1913), lawyer and politician, was born 13 January 1826 in Ceylon, where his father, Henry Matthews [q.v.], the author of *The Diary of an Invalid*, was a puisne judge. The judge was the son of John Matthews [q.v.], of Belmont, Herefordshire, and the brother of Byron's friend, Charles Skynner Matthews; his wife was Emma, daughter of William Blount, of Orleton, Herefordshire, a member of an old Catholic family. Matthews was brought up in his mother's faith, his father stipulating that he should not be sent to a Catholic school. He received, therefore, a varied and cosmopolitan education. Debarred by his religion from Oxford and Cambridge, he graduated at the university of Paris as *bachelier-ès-lettres* (1844), and proceeded to London University, where he took the degree of B.A. (1847) and LL.B. and won a law scholarship in 1849.

In 1850 Matthews was called to the bar at Lincoln's Inn. His unusual knowledge of the languages and systems of law of foreign countries brought him work of a special kind; and he soon acquired a large general practice both in Westminster Hall and on the Oxford circuit. His style of advocacy, which was brilliant but artificial, was admired and imitated by his circuit contemporaries; and he played a prominent part in the festivities of the bar mess. A man of considerable private means, he was not dependent upon the practice of his profession. He was fond of the pleasures of social life, and his personal charm and witty conversation introduced him to exclusive and fashionable circles. He spoke of himself as not being closely wedded to his circuit or profession.

In 1868 he took silk. The same year he stood as a conservative for the borough of Dungarvan and defeated Serjeant Barry by 157 votes to 105. His election he himself attributed to his having combined the nationalist and tory votes against the liberal candidate 'at the cost of 800 bottles of whisky' [*Dublin Review*, April 1906]. Acting with the then Home Rule party, he voted with Mr. Gladstone on the second reading of the Irish Disestablishment Bill (1869), and with the narrow majority which defeated the Irish University Bill (1873). In 1874 he lost his seat to a Home Ruler, and a subsequent attempt to win back the seat in 1880 was unsuccessful. He stood for North Birmingham in 1885, and in 1886 was elected for East Birmingham. The personal friendship of Lord Randolph Churchill led to his appointment as home secretary in 1886. He was the first Catholic since the passing of the Emancipation Act to become a Cabinet minister. An arrangement was made that the ecclesiastical patronage of the office should be transferred to the first lord of the Treasury.

In contrast with his brilliance at the bar, Matthews was unsuccessful in the House of Commons, which his foreign education never allowed him to capture. An unkindly observer likened him to a 'French dancing master'. He was regarded as 'a departmental success but a parliamentary failure'. As home secretary he had several difficult cases to deal with, in particular those of Lipski (1887), Miss Cass (1887), Mrs. Maybrick (1889), and the Davies brothers (1890). His decisions were on occasion attacked fiercely by Henry Labouchere in *Truth* and by W. T. Stead in the *Pall Mall Gazette*; in the case of Miss Cass a vote for adjournment was carried against the government and led him to tender his resignation, which, however, Lord Salisbury refused to accept. His refusal to recommend the reprieve of Lipski was followed by the condemned man's confession of guilt. Lord Chief Justice Coleridge considered Matthews the best home secretary he had known. He returned to the House of Commons in 1892, and was in opposition for the next three years. His failure to speak or vote when Mr. Gladstone introduced his Bill for the removal of surviving Catholic disabilities (popularly known as the Russell and Ripon Relief Bill) was commented upon by his co-religionists. He voted against the Bill for the disestablishment of the Welsh Church. On the return of the conservatives in 1895 he was elevated to the peerage as Viscount Llandaff. He claimed a remote connexion with the Irish family which had enjoyed this extinct title. As a peer he took little part in public life ; but he was active in securing the passing of the Accession Declaration Act, 1910, by which the old form of declaration against the doctrine of transubstantiation, regarded as offensive to the Catholics of the Empire, was abolished. He was a loyal member of his own communion, and one of the founders of Westminster Cathedral. Yet he used to admit that on literary grounds he preferred the authorized to the Douai version of the Scriptures. He was for two years the vigorous chairman of the royal commission on the London water supply, which led to the formation of the Metropolitan Water Board (1902).

Although a leading figure at the bar Matthews was never regarded as a candidate for judicial honours. Amongst notable trials in which he appeared as counsel were *Borghese* v. *Borghese* (1860–1863), which involved complicated questions as to the devolution of the property of John, Earl of Shrewsbury ; *Lyon* v. *Home* (1868), an action for the return of moneys and securities, brought against a 'spiritualist' ; the civil proceedings in the Tichborne case (1869) ; the Epping Forest case (1874), which concerned claims to common of pasture over the waste lands of the forest ; and *Crawford* v. *Crawford and Dilke* (1886). His cross-examination of Sir Charles Dilke on the intervention of the Queen's proctor in the last case was skilful and effective. During his later years he was crippled by rheumatism. He died at 6 Carlton Gardens, London, 3 April 1913 and was buried with Catholic rites in the Anglican graveyard at Clehonger, Herefordshire. He was unmarried. He was caricatured by 'Spy' in *Vanity Fair*.

[Obituary notices in *The Times*, 4 April 1913, and *Tablet*, 12 April 1913 ; memoirs in the *Dublin Review*, January 1921 ; private information. There is an unpublished biography by W. S. Lilly.]

MATURIN, BASIL WILLIAM (1847–1915), Catholic preacher and writer, son of the Rev. William Maturin, by his wife, Jane Cooke Beatty, was born at All Saints' vicarage, Grangegorman, Dublin, 15 February 1847, the third in a family of ten children. The Maturins were old-fashioned 'Tractarians': three of the sons became clergymen, two of the daughters, nuns. Educated at home, at a day-school, and at Trinity College, Dublin, where he took his degree in 1870, Basil (or Willie as he was called at home) intended to join the Royal Engineers ; but a severe illness about 1868 and the death of his brother Arthur altered his mind and he decided to take orders. He was ordained deacon in 1870 and went in that year as curate to Peterstow, Herefordshire, of which place Dr. John Jebb, an old friend of his father, was rector. In 1873 he joined the Society of St. John the Evangelist, founded in 1866 at Cowley St. John, Oxford, by the Rev. Richard Meux Benson [q.v.]. In 1876 he was sent to America in order to begin a mission in Philadelphia. He was first an assistant priest and in 1881 became rector of St. Clement's church there and gained much popularity, until, in 1888, doubts as to his position in the Anglican Church occasioned his recall. After a six months' visit (1889–1890) to the society's house at Cape Town, he spent the next seven years in preaching, conducting retreats, and holding missions. At length, in 1897, after much mental stress, he was received into the Roman Catholic Church at Beaumont, near Windsor.

Having studied theology at the Canadian College, Rome, Maturin was ordained in 1898 and returned to England, where he lived at first with Cardinal Vaughan at Archbishop's House, Westminster. After serving for a time at St. Mary's, Cadogan Street, he joined the new society of Westminster diocesan missionaries under Fr. Chase in 1905, and became parish priest of Pimlico, where his influence began to extend widely. Maturin, however, had always longed for a monastic life, and in 1910 he tried his vocation with the Benedictines at Downside, near Bath ; but he was too old for such a strain, and he returned to London, where he worked partly at St. James's, Spanish Place, but spent most of his time in preaching at different places. He visited America again in 1913. In 1914 he was offered simultaneously the parish of the Holy Redeemer in Chelsea, and the chaplaincy of the Catholics in the university of Oxford. Maturin accepted the latter task, but had hardly taken it up when the War broke out and the university was left empty of undergraduates. He went once more to the United States, preached there during the Lent of 1915, and then, in May, sailed for England on the *Lusitania*. The vessel was torpedoed and sunk on 7 May. Fr. Maturin was observed standing to give absolution to the passengers, and then lowering a child into a boat, saying, 'Find its mother'. His body had no life-belt on it when it was washed ashore, and it was generally supposed that he refused one, as there were not enough to go round.

Maturin's chief works were: *Some Principles and Practices of the Spiritual Life* (1896), *Practical Studies on the Parables of Our Lord* (1897), *Self-Knowledge and Self-Discipline* (1905), *Laws of the Spiritual Life* (1907), and *The Price of Unity* (1912); the last gives some idea of the mental course which he followed on the way to the Church of Rome. After his death a volume of *Sermons and Sermon Notes* was edited and arranged (1916) by his friend Wilfrid Philip Ward. His books reveal a deep spirituality and an active imagination. But it was the vehemence of his sermons, combined with the acute psychological insight displayed in them and in his direction of penitents, that accounted for the profound influence which he exercised and of which he remained almost unaware. Depression and exaltation alternated in his Irish soul; but he applied to himself the discipline which he so well supplied to others.

[M. Ward, *Father Maturin. A Memoir*, 1920; Works cited above.] C. C. M.

MAUDE, Sir FREDERICK STANLEY (1864–1917), lieutenant-general, the younger son of General Sir Frederick Francis Maude, V.C., G.C.B., by his wife, Catherine Mary, daughter of the Very Rev. Sir George Bisshopp, eighth baronet, dean of Lismore, was born at Gibraltar 24 June 1864. He was educated at Eton, where he boarded at the house of Francis Warre Cornish, and at the Royal Military College, Sandhurst. At Eton he won the mile and the steeplechase, was reserve for the eight and a member of 'Pop'. He joined the second Coldstream Guards in 1884, and in the Sudan campaign of 1885 accompanied them to Suakin, being present at the actions of Hashin and Tamai and the occupation of Handub, and receiving the medal with clasp and khedive's star. From 1888 to 1892 he was adjutant of his battalion. In 1895 he joined the Staff College at Camberley, and on completing the staff course became brigade-major of the Guards brigade. During the 1897 jubilee much of the military organization devolved on Maude—congenial work, as he had a liking for parade work and ceremonial. After the outbreak of the South African War, he resigned his appointment and joined his battalion on the Modder river at the close of 1899. For a month he was second in command, but was then appointed brigade-major. Lord Roberts's offensive was just beginning, and the Guards moved to Klip Drift, having been called to the front after Paardeberg (27 February 1900). They took part in the actions of Poplar Grove and Driefontein, where Maude was seriously injured by his horse falling. He was unable to receive proper attention at the time and suffered from his shoulder for the rest of his life. He accompanied the brigade to Johannesburg and Pretoria and took part in the action at Diamond Hill and in the operations north of Belfast, and in the western Transvaal. The brigade was then sent south to oppose the attack of the Boers on Cape Colony. It being generally supposed that the campaign was as good as finished, Maude accepted an offer from the Earl of Minto [q.v.], then governor-general of Canada, to be his military secretary. In February 1901 he left South Africa for England.

Maude's record in South Africa was good, but he was unlucky in not reaching the Guards brigade until after the severest fighting in which it was engaged. General Sir Reginald Pole Carew, commanding the eleventh division, applied for his services as assistant adjutant-general, but unfortunately for Maude, this was not possible. Thus he did not obtain full scope for his qualities in the campaign. He received the D.S.O., a mention, and the medal and six clasps. The next four years were spent with Lord Minto in Canada, where he visited practically the whole of the Dominion and for his services received the C.M.G. In 1905 he rejoined his regiment. Financial reasons, however, made him anxious to obtain outside employment. He was private secretary to the secretary of state for war in 1905, and after the fall of Mr. Balfour's government became deputy assistant adjutant and quartermaster-general of coast defences at Plymouth (1906–1908). From this time forward Maude continued to hold staff appointments. He served on the staff of the second London territorial division (1908–1909) and as assistant director of the territorial forces at the War Office (1909–1912). Here he had much to do with the inauguration of the territorial force, which he foresaw from the first must be used overseas in the event of war. In 1912 he went as general staff officer to the fifth division at the Curragh and in 1914 he joined the training directorate at the War Office.

On the outbreak of the European War in 1914 Maude joined the staff of the Third Army Corps under General (Sir) William Pulteney, reaching France during the retreat from Mons; after that, he took part in the battles of the Marne, the Aisne, and Armentières, and in the fighting on the Lys. In October he became brigadier-general of the fourteenth brigade then engaged in the battle of La Bassée. He took part in the counter-attack at Neuve Chapelle, but during the rest of his tenure of command the brigade was engaged in trench warfare. From La Bassée it went north to Wulverghem and thence to Neuve Eglise, Kemmel, and St. Eloi. At the last place Maude was wounded, and obliged to return to England in November. He was given the C.B. in April 1915, and rejoined the brigade in May, but only remained in France another six weeks. In July he was promoted major-general and appointed to command the thirty-first division then forming in Nottinghamshire; in August, however, he was sent to assume command of the thirteenth division at the Dardanelles.

Maude found the thirteenth division, at Anzac Cove, shattered by losses sustained in the battles for the possession of the Sari Bair heights; its total strength scarcely amounted to that of a single brigade, and none of the artillery was with the division. From Anzac it went to Suvla Bay, and after three weeks in reserve took over the front at Salajik. When the tenth division left Suvla for Salonika in October, the important Chocolate Hill position came under Maude's control. In December definite instructions arrived for the evacuation of Suvla and Anzac. After the withdrawal from Suvla the thirteenth division was sent to Helles, which was abandoned in January 1916, Maude being almost the last to leave the shore. Thus he took a prominent part in two operations which were described by the enemy as masterpieces for which there had been no precedent.

From the Dardanelles Maude's division went to Egypt, whence it was ordered to Mesopotamia and sailed in February 1916 for Basra. In March Maude proceeded to assemble his division at Sheikh Sa'ad, where he fortunately found excellent training ground to exercise his troops before their departure for the front. The division was intended to reinforce the Tigris Corps under Major-General Gorringe, with which Sir Percy Lake, the commander-in-chief, planned to attempt the relief of Major-General Townshend, besieged at Kut el Amara. On 5 April an attack launched by the thirteenth division captured the Turkish trenches at Hannah and Felahieh, but the seventh division was unsuccessful at Sanna-i-yat. Three days later Maude attempted to take Sanna-i-yat, but was equally unsuccessful. The third division captured the Turkish trenches at Beit Aiessa, but was heavily counter-attacked at night. Maude came to its aid, but failed to improve its position. A last attempt to take Sanna-i-yat was made by the seventh division, aided by Maude's artillery and machine guns, but this also failed, and after an unsuccessful attempt to reprovision Townshend by running a steamer through to Kut, it was adjudged that no more could be done. Kut surrendered on 29 April.

For the next few months little occurred on the Tigris. In July Maude, though nearly the junior major-general in Mesopotamia, was appointed to command the Tigris Corps, and in August, on the departure of Lake, assumed command of the army in Mesopotamia. For his services as a divisional commander he received the K.C.B. For the next three and a half months he devoted himself to preparations for the advance on Bagdad. His force was divided into two corps under Major-Generals (Sir) Alexander Cobbe and (Sir) William Marshall. On 13 December the first corps bombarded the Sanna-i-yat position and the third corps obtained a footing on the Hai river. This was consolidated and followed by the capture of the Hai bridgehead by the third and the clearance of the Khaidri bend by the first corps. No pause took place in the offensive, and on 15 February 1917 the Turks were cleared out of the Dahra bend. On 22 February the final attack was launched on Sanna-i-yat, the passage of the Tigris was forced at Shumran, and on 24 February the first corps occupied the whole Turkish position, and Kut was recovered. The Turks were now retreating rapidly, and

Maude's pursuing cavalry pressed them so closely that on 27 February it entered Aziziyeh, half-way between Kut and Bagdad. After a pause, to allow his supplies to come up, Maude pushed on. Ctesiphon was occupied after a stiff fight between the cavalry and the Turkish fifty-first division at Lajj. At Bawi the first corps crossed the Tigris and pressed forward to Bagdad, while the third corps forced the passage of the Diala and pursued the Turks up that river. On 11 March Bagdad was occupied. Its capture by no means concluded active operations. In spite of growing resistance on the part of the Turks, Mushaidieh was occupied on the 14th, Bakuba on the Diala on the 18th, and Feluza on the Euphrates on the 19th. The offensive was continued to the north and east of Bagdad, and proceeded throughout the summer notwithstanding attempts of the enemy to retrieve the position. Early in November Cobbe occupied Tekrit, and this was the last victory achieved during Maude's lifetime, but by that time the conquest had been consolidated and there were no longer grounds for any fear that a reverse of fortune was possible in Mesopotamia. He had been promoted lieutenant-general on 1 March.

Simultaneously with operations in the field Maude devoted himself to consolidating and administrating the conquered territory. A railway was laid down between Kut and Bagdad, agriculture encouraged, and sanitary measures undertaken. Bagdad was not a healthy city and cholera was endemic. At a party at a Jewish school on 14 November the army commander drank some milk from which it is thought he must have caught the disease, and four days later (18 November 1917) he died of virulent cholera.

Maude was a great soldier and a born fighter, but though he had the strongest faith in the offensive he had a clear understanding when a fight must be broken off, and he never undertook an offensive without the most careful and thorough preparation. Over and above great natural gifts and knowledge acquired by years of study, he had a peculiar understanding of the requirements of troops, whose devotion he commanded in a marked degree. Punctual, methodical, and hardworking, his chief fault was perhaps a desire to over-centralize and to concentrate direction in his own hands, but he was not only generous in giving credit to his subordinates, but also open and willing to hear their advice. He was a thinker, a student, a sportsman, and a man of strong religious convictions. He will be remembered chiefly for his Mesopotamian campaign, but every task of his life was pursued in the same spirit of thoroughness and care as his last great achievement.

Maude married in 1893 Cecil, daughter of Colonel the Rt. Hon. Thomas Edward Taylor, chancellor of the duchy of Lancaster, of Ardgillan Castle, co. Dublin, and had one son and two daughters.

A portrait of Maude is included in J. S. Sargent's picture ' Some General Officers of the Great War ', painted in 1922, in the National Portrait Gallery.

[*The Times*, 20 November 1917 ; Sir C. E. Callwell, *The Life of Sir Stanley Maude*, 1920 ; '*The Times' History of the War in South Africa*, 1900–1909 ; Sir Ian Hamilton, *Gallipoli Diary*, 1920 ; Edmund Candler, *The Long Road to Baghdad*, 1919 ; E. F. Egan, *The War in the Cradle of the World*, 1918 ; *Annual Register* ; Hansard, *Parliamentary Debates* ; Eton *School Register*; Army Lists; private information.] O.

MAURICE, Sir JOHN FREDERICK (1841–1912), major-general, the eldest son of Frederick Denison Maurice [q. v.], was born in London 24 May 1841. He was educated privately, mainly at home, and was thus greatly influenced by the ideals and principles of his father and of the band of men with whom his father was associated. To this influence may be largely ascribed the intense hatred of any kind of injustice or unfairness, and the readiness to sacrifice his personal interests to a cause in which he believed, which always characterized him. It was entirely his own idea that instead of going to Cambridge he should become a soldier. He passed second into Addiscombe, where the artillery cadets for the East India Company's service were trained, just before the amalgamation of the company's forces with the Crown's led to the transfer of the Addiscombe cadets to Woolwich. From Woolwich he passed out into the Royal Artillery in 1862.

His service falls into three periods. Till 1873 he was at home, passing through the Staff College and becoming instructor in tactics at Sandhurst in 1872 ; between 1873 and 1885 his time was divided mainly between the War Office, where he did notable work in the intelligence department, and active service, in Ashanti (1873–1874), South Africa (1879–1880), Egypt (1882), and the Sudan (1884–1885) ; from 1885 till his retirement in 1903 he was in succession professor of military art and history at the Staff College, in command of an artillery brigade at Aldershot, of the artillery of the Eastern district, and, after his promotion to major-general in 1895, of the Woolwich district (1895–1902). In his period of active service he was closely associated with Viscount Wolseley [q.v.] to whom he acted as private secretary in Ashanti. The origin of his lifelong friendship with Wolseley lay in the episode which first brought Maurice into notice. While he was instructor at Sandhurst a prize of £100 was offered by the second Duke of Wellington for an essay upon the mode in which the British army could under modern conditions best meet a continental army in the open field. Nearly forty officers, including Wolseley, who was then a colonel, entered for the prize, and it was a great feather in Maurice's cap that, though only a subaltern, he should have carried off the prize with an essay which was at once recognized, by no one so cordially as by Wolseley himself, to be a really remarkable work. It gave evidence not only of great literary powers and much knowledge both of the theory of war and of contemporary military literature and thought, but also of real power of drawing new and instructive deductions. Most of the reforms in the army which were ultimately adopted in the beginning of the twentieth century were, if not actually advocated in this essay, based on the broad principles there laid down.

Maurice's active service was almost entirely upon the staff, though on several occasions he was able to give proof of his great personal courage and coolness under fire—Lord Wolseley once describing him as 'the bravest man I have ever seen under fire'. In the operations against the stronghold of Sekukuni, a recalcitrant native chief in northern Transvaal, he was badly wounded when leading, with conspicuous gallantry, an attack by a contingent of native levies. He was able also to show that he possessed considerable practical ability and administrative capacity. The credit for the capture of Cetywayo was largely his, and in the Nile campaign he displayed much ingenuity and skill as an organizer; but it did not fall to his lot to hold actual command of any large unit in action. It is therefore as a military thinker and writer that his best work was done. He was closely associated with Lord Wolseley in advocating the numerous reforms of which the army of mid-Victorian days stood in so much need. As professor at the Staff College he struggled hard to improve the methods on which that institution was conducted, and had the satisfaction later on of seeing many of his ideas adopted. His writings did much to place before civilians, as well as soldiers and sailors, sound conceptions both of war and of the principles on which the military and naval organization of the Empire should be based. He was a rapid if not methodical worker, he immersed himself in the subjects with which he was dealing, and his literary activity was considerable and versatile.

Maurice's *Military History of the Campaign of 1882 in Egypt* (1888) was of much general interest as well as of professional value, his *Balance of Military Power in Europe* (1888) anticipated by some years many of the teachings of Admiral Mahan, and his *Encyclopædia Britannica* article on *War*, separately published in 1891, was a masterly analysis of the subject on non-technical lines. But it was remarkable that the man who had dealt so well with such subjects should have achieved a pronounced success in quite another literary sphere, the *Life of Frederick Denison Maurice* (1884) being acknowledged as a real contribution to the history of religious thought in England. His retirement gave him leisure to complete the work of editing the *Diary of Sir John Moore* (1904), his chief contribution to historical literature, a work marked by his characteristic enthusiasm, vigour, and power of presenting a case. In 1903 he was induced to undertake the production of the official *History of the War in South Africa, 1899–1902* (1906–1910), a task originally accepted by Colonel G. F. R. Henderson [q.v.]. It was a difficult undertaking, not made easier by the various changes in the control of the army or by the change of government in 1906. Maurice found himself much handicapped by the limitations imposed on him and would have been glad to be relieved of the undertaking, but he felt compelled to continue with it. He had produced two volumes, and was engaged on the third when, in the autumn of 1907, his health broke down completely. He died at Camberley 11 January 1912, after a long illness patiently endured.

Maurice, who had been created K.C.B. in 1900, was appointed colonel commandant of the Royal Artillery in 1906, and in 1907 received from the Royal United Service Institution the Chesney memorial medal for his services to military literature. He married in 1869 Annie, daughter of R. A. FitzGerald, taxing officer to the courts in Dublin, and had eleven children. Four of his sons fought in the War of 1914–1918, the eldest, Major-General Sir Frederick Barton Maurice, K.C.M.G., being director of military operations, Imperial General Staff, from 1915 to 1918.

[Sir F. B. Maurice, *Sir Frederick Maurice : A Record of his Work and Opinions, with Eight Essays on Discipline and National Efficiency*, 1913 ; personal knowledge.] C. T. A.

MAXIM, Sir HIRAM STEVENS (1840–1916), engineer and inventor, was born of Huguenot stock and humble parentage at Sangerville, Maine, U.S.A., 5 February 1840. He was the elder son of Isaac Weston Maxim, who in early manhood married Harriett Boston, daughter of Levi Stevens, of Maine, and started farming on a modest scale. His farm was a pioneer undertaking : the site, which was in the midst of a dense forest, had to be cleared, and a farm-house and outbuildings erected. The district was infested by bears and the nearest house was half a mile distant. In this primitive setting Hiram Maxim was born and bred. As was appropriate to such an environment, his boyhood was adventurous, and his training one of sturdy self-reliance. When he was six his father abandoned farming and took up wood-turning, at which Hiram acquired considerable proficiency. He was studiously inclined and eagerly read any books which came within his reach. In particular he was attracted to geography and astronomy, and at one time he cherished the idea of becoming a sea captain. At the age of fourteen he was put to work with a carriage-maker, named Daniel Sweat, in the village of East Corinth. Maxim tells us that he 'used to work eight hours in the forenoon and eight hours in the afternoon', with a one-hour dinner interval, and for this his wage was at the rate of four dollars a month, not paid in cash but largely taken in goods at the local store. He did not stay long, and soon obtained employment in the same trade with another master, under whom, although the hours were as long, his remuneration and treatment were much improved. Then, by turns, he found odd jobs as a bar-tender, wood-turner, and brass-fettler. He displayed also a liking for pugilism, in consequence of which he had several notable encounters. In 1864 Maxim joined his uncle, Levi Stevens, the proprietor of some engineering works at Fitchburg, Massachusetts, where he acquired a knowledge of draughtsmanship and prosecuted his technical and scientific studies with ardour. Then he entered the service of a philosophical instrument maker, named Oliver Drake, of whom he thought and spoke highly, and to whom he attributed much of his later success. At this stage his inventive genius became fairly active, and, among other contrivances, he devised a 'density regulator' for equalizing the illuminating value of coal gas. This was not his first invention, but it was more ambitious than his previous efforts.

It was not, however, till the year 1878, when he became chief engineer to the United States Electric Lighting Company—the first to be formed in the United States—that Maxim produced anything of notable importance. Then he discovered and patented with great success a method of preserving and building up carbons in an incandescent lamp by heating the filaments electrically in an attenuated atmosphere of hydro-carbon vapour. An electrical pressure regulator, which followed, was exhibited at the Paris Exhibition of 1881 and brought him the decoration of the légion d'honneur. Maxim had represented his company in Paris, but shortly afterwards he transferred his operations to London, where he opened a workshop in Hatton Garden. It was about this time that he directed his attention to gunnery and prepared a design for an automatic gun. As soon as this weapon was constructed, it attracted high official notice and was inspected by the British commander-in-chief, the Duke of Cambridge, and the Prince of Wales. Lord Wolseley was greatly struck by it, and suggested certain developments in range and power, which led Maxim to make a number of variations of his original design in order to meet different conditions. The Maxim gun was adopted in the British army in 1889 and in the royal navy in 1892. It was not the first rapid firing gun, since it was preceded by the Gatling (1862), the mitrailleuse (1867), and the Nordenfeldt (1877) ; but it surpassed these in consisting of a single barrel and possessing a completely automatic action. It fired at the rate of ten shots a second. For the development of the patents the Maxim Gun Company was formed in 1884, and in 1888 an amalgamation was effected with the Nordenfeldt Company. The works were at Erith, Kent, and were later (1896) absorbed in the firm of Vickers Sons and Maxim, of which Maxim was a director.

From gunnery Maxim turned his attention to flying, and during the period 1889–1894 produced a steam-driven flying-machine, which may be said, in a technical sense, to have flown, since, during a trial carried out at Bexley, Kent, in 1894, the runner wheels were lifted off the rail track, but otherwise the machine failed to achieve its purpose, mainly on account of its excessive weight. It was certainly a marvellous structure, compact with ingenious contrivances, and something like £20,000 was expended on its construction. It consisted of a large central plane with two curved side frames. Its engines and boilers weighed respectively 600 lb. and 1,200 lb., including casing, feed-water heater, dome, and uptake. For a horse power of 300, the total weight of the motive agency, 6 lb. per h.p., was not unreasonable, but, unfortunately, feed-water for an hour's trip added 6,000 lb. to the load.

Maxim had now permanently taken up his residence in England at West Norwood. He became naturalized and, in 1901, was knighted. After a strenuous career he died at Streatham 24 November 1916. Endowed with a powerful frame and strong constitution, he had laboured with untiring energy throughout a long life. His versatility, ingenuity, and skill were amazing. He loved to describe himself as a 'chronic inventor'. In addition to his gun he invented a smokeless powder, maximite, the predecessor of cordite; and, among innumerable patents, at one time or another produced such diverse contrivances as a mouse-trap, an inhaler for bronchitis, a merry-go-round, an automatic sprinkler, a feed-water heater, and a process for obtaining cheap phosphoric anhydride.

Maxim was married twice: first, to Louisa Jane Budden, by whom he had one son and two daughters; secondly, in 1881 to Sarah, daughter of Charles Haynes, of Boston, Massachusetts, who survived him without issue.

[Sir Hiram Maxim, *My Life*, 1915; P. Fleury Mottelay, *Life and Work of Sir Hiram Maxim*, 1920; private information.]

B. C.

MAXWELL, MARY ELIZABETH (1837–1915), better known as MISS MARY ELIZABETH BRADDON, novelist, the youngest daughter of Henry Braddon, solicitor and author of several works on sporting subjects, a member of an old Cornish family, of Skisdon Lodge, St. Kew, Cornwall, by his wife, Fanny, daughter of J. White, of county Cavan, was born in London 4 October 1837. Sir Edward Nicholas Coventry Braddon [q.v.], premier of Tasmania, was her brother, and John Thadeus Delane [q.v.], for thirty-six years editor of *The Times*, her cousin on the mother's side. Mary Braddon received a good private education and when very young showed an eagerness to write. About 1856, when she was living near Beverley in Yorkshire, a local printer offered her ten pounds for a serial story that should combine 'the humour of Dickens with the dramatic quality of G. W. M. Reynolds'. The girl of nineteen produced a lurid story, *Three Times Dead, or The Secret of the Heath*, which was prepared for publication in penny numbers illustrated with violent woodcuts. But the printer went bankrupt and, although the whole story was set up in type, it is doubtful whether publication was ever completed. Later on the story was re-written, entitled *The Trail of the Serpent*, and in 1861 re-issued.

In 1861 Mary Braddon published *Garibaldi, and Other Poems*, and a short novel, *The Lady Lisle*. A book of stories appeared in 1862, and in the same year, in response to an eleventh hour request from John Maxwell, a publisher who was preparing to launch a periodical named *Robin Goodfellow*, she wrote *Lady Audley's Secret*. *Robin Goodfellow*, after struggling through twelve numbers, died. *Lady Audley* was at the last moment transferred to *The Sixpenny Magazine*, where it attracted the attention of Lionel Brough [q.v], then acting as literary adviser to the speculative publishing firm of Tinsley Brothers. Late in 1862 it appeared as a three-volume novel and had a success both immediate and irresistible. From 1862 to the present day *Lady Audley's Secret* has not ceased to sell. In various forms nearly a million copies must have gone into circulation; it has been translated into every civilized tongue, several times piratically dramatized, and twice filmed.

It is a misfortune to any author's reputation that an early book should have a popularity so overwhelming as to obscure later and better work. *Lady Audley's Secret*, for all its daring imagination and although it is a remarkable production for a young woman of no experience, cannot be reckoned a good novel. Yet Miss Braddon is known primarily as the author of this book, and her reputation has paid the penalty. Her work has been dismissed as without proportion, thought, or character-analysis, by critics who based their judgement solely on this one preposterously successful melodrama.

Ultimate reputation apart, however, Miss Braddon was well served by *Lady Audley's Secret*. The book which made her publisher's fortune (out of the proceeds William Tinsley built himself a villa at Barnes and called it Audley Lodge) also made her own, and she became before long a wealthy woman. Her continued success was due partly to devoted industry, but mainly to her tireless inventiveness. Novel after novel appeared, and in addition to all those which she acknowledged, she published several anonymously, which to this day remain without their author's name. She wrote many plays; contributed to *Punch* and to *The World*; produced a serial in French for the Paris *Figaro*; wrote the greater part of numerous Christmas annuals (notably *The Mistletoe Bough*); and edited several magazines, of which the best known and most successful were *Temple Bar* and *Belgravia*. Prolific vitality was not a rare quality among Victorian novelists, but Miss Braddon's indefatigable zest is unrivalled. Mrs. Charles Gore, G. P. R. James, Mrs. Oliphant, Wilkie Collins, even Trollope himself, grew weary at their desks; but Miss Braddon maintained her freshness to the end, so that *The Green Curtain*, published in 1911, is rather the book of a practised writer in the prime of life than, perhaps, the eightieth novel of an old lady of seventy-four.

In 1874 Miss Braddon married John Maxwell, who became a busy publisher and the founder of numerous periodicals. She lived a great deal at Annesley Bank, near Lyndhurst, but her permanent home was always at Richmond, Surrey, in a dignified Georgian house surrounded by a lovely garden, where, on 4 February 1915, she died.

Miss Braddon was foolishly and savagely attacked during the 'seventies and 'eighties of the last century as the most dangerous of the 'sensation novelists', whose work was liable to corrupt the minds of young people by its violence and by its power to make wickedness alluring. One critic accused her of making probity purposely ridiculous and of recommending murder and bigamy to female enterprise; another declared that her books could only stand on a shelf beside the *Newgate Calendar*. Such absurdity ignores all but one aspect of her work and deals with that unfairly. The technique of crime, and not its ethic, interested her, so that wrongdoing became ingenious rather than alluring. On the other hand she was too faithful a daughter of her age ever to think of tampering with virtue's ultimate victory and reward. Rather was she liable to strain probability in her desire to prove the sad consequences of ill-doing, so that her plots, by the standards of a more candid, and maybe a more cynical, generation, lack the force that they were meant to have, so turbulent is the villainy but so easily undone the villain.

But it is an injustice to regard Miss Braddon as a mere sensationalist. She was a clever, cultivated woman with wide sympathies and interests. Not only was her response to natural beauty always quick and keen (even in her earliest books she showed great power of description alike of landscape and weather-moods), but to the end she was intensely aware of the world and eager to be part of it. This hunger for actuality gives her best work a quality beyond that of mere sensationalism, and to her joyous acceptance of life in every form must be attributed her popularity, not only among the masses but also among her fellow-writers. That her books should have delighted readers so exigent and so diverse as Bulwer, Reade, Thackeray, Sala, Labouchere, and Robert Louis Stevenson proves them to be instinct with some quality beyond that of mere dramatic ingenuity.

Her principal books are: *Lady Audley's Secret* (1862), *Aurora Floyd* (1863), *John Marchmont's Legacy* (1863), *Henry Dunbar* (1864), *The Doctor's Wife* (1864), *Birds of Prey* (1867), *Charlotte's Inheritance* (1868), *Robert Ainsleigh* (1872), *Strangers and Pilgrims* (1873), *Dead Men's Shoes* (1876), *Joshua Haggard's Daughter* (1876), *Vixen* (1879), *Asphodel* (1881), *Mount Royal* (1882), *Phantom Fortune* (1883), *Ishmael* (1884), *All Along the River* (1893), *Sons of Fire* (1895), *London Pride* (1896), *Rough Justice* (1898), *The Rose of Life* (1905), and *The Green Curtain* (1911).

Miss Braddon was the mother of two novelists, William Babington Maxwell and Gerald Maxwell; her third son, Edward Maxwell, was a barrister. She also had two daughters. Her portrait by William Powell Frith, R.A., is in Mr. W. B. Maxwell's possession.

[The *World*, 25 April 1905; *Bookman*, July 1912; *New York Evening Post*, 10 February 1915; Harriett Jay, *Robert Buchanan*, 1903; Henry James, *Notes and Reviews*, 1921; private information.] M. S.

MERRY, WILLIAM WALTER (1835–1918), classical scholar, born at Evesham 6 September 1835, was the only son of Walter Merry, of that town, by his wife, Elizabeth Mary Byrch. He entered Cheltenham College as a day boy in 1846 and was elected to an open scholarship at Balliol College, Oxford, in 1852. He obtained a first class in classical moderations (1854) and a second class in *literae humaniores* (1856). In 1858 he gained the Chancellor's Latin essay prize and in the following year he was elected a fellow of Lincoln College, where he filled the office of classical lecturer until his election to the rectorship twenty-five years later. Merry was ordained deacon in 1860, priest in the next year, and in 1862 was presented by his college to the perpetual curacy of All Saints, Oxford. As this living was also a college chaplaincy his tenure of it enabled him to retain his fellowship on his marriage later in the same year.

While holding this living Merry acquired considerable popularity as a preacher. He was select preacher before the university in 1878–1879 and 1889–1890, and Whitehall preacher in 1883–1884. He also found time to pursue his studies in the Greek classics. His friendship with James Riddell [q.v.], who had been his tutor at Balliol, at first fixed him as a student of Homer. After Riddell's early death (1866) he completed for the Clarendon Press and published in 1876 the large edition of the *Odyssey*, books i–xii, which Riddell had begun. He was also entirely responsible for the minor edition of the whole of the *Odyssey* which was issued by the Clarendon Press in two volumes in 1870 and 1878. Later he edited for the same press the plays of Aristophanes: the *Clouds* (1879), the *Acharnians* (1880), the *Frogs* (1884), the *Knights* (1887), the *Birds* (1889), the *Wasps* (1893), and the *Peace* (1900). These editions have been familiar to several generations of students. They are sufficiently erudite, full of sound learning, and spiced with congenial humour.

Merry's Latinity was at least on a par with his Greek. He had remarkable verbal knowledge of the Latin poets and of Cicero, and great facility as a writer of Latin verse. The distinctive mark of his scholarship, however, was his power of interpretation. His colleague, William Warde Fowler [q.v.], has observed that he never found any one quite so helpful in divining the meaning of a difficult passage: 'He took the bearings of it with wonderful rapidity, and then looked straight into it without the least hesitation or confusion' [*Oxford Magazine*, 15 March 1918]. In 1875 he published a volume on *Greek Dialects* and another in 1891 on *Selected Fragments of Roman Poetry*.

In 1880 Merry was appointed public orator of the university, an office which he held till 1910; and in 1884 he succeeded Mark Pattison [q.v.] as rector of Lincoln College, not long after the election of his colleague, Thomas Fowler [q.v.], as president of Corpus Christi College. His fine presence, his lively wit, and the extraordinary lucidity of his Latin, which was aided by his delivery, made him an ideal public orator. His *Orationes tum Creweianae tum Gratulatoriae* were published by the Clarendon Press in 1909. As rector of Lincoln he was distinguished by his care for the interests of that society and by the kindly feeling and genial humour which endeared him to fellows of a younger generation and to many generations of undergraduate members of the college. He had great qualities as a host, as he showed when he filled the office of vice-chancellor from 1904 to 1906 and maintained the tradition of hospitality associated with that office.

Merry died in Lincoln College 5 March 1918 and was buried beside his wife in Holywell churchyard, Oxford. He had married in 1862 Alice Elizabeth (died 1914), only daughter of Joseph Collings, jurat of the royal court of Guernsey. They had two sons and two daughters. Merry's portrait, painted by Cyrus Johnson, R.I., is in the hall of Lincoln College.

[*The Times*, 7 March 1918; *Oxford Magazine*, 15 March 1918; *Classical Review*, May–June 1918; Joseph Foster, *Alumni Oxonienses*, 1887–1891; *Men of the Time*; personal knowledge.] E. I. C.

MERTHYR, first Baron (1837–1914), engineer and coal-owner. [See Lewis, William Thomas.]

MILFORD HAVEN, first Marquess of (1854–1921), admiral of the fleet. [See Mountbatten, Louis Alexander.]

MILNE, JOHN (1850–1913), mining engineer and seismologist, the only child of John Milne, of Milnrow, Rochdale, by his wife, Emma, daughter of James Twycross, J.P., of Wokingham, was born at Liverpool 30 December 1850. After schools at Rochdale and Liverpool he went to King's College, London, where he was a contemporary of Lord Milner, who many years later (1906) was honoured by the university of Oxford at the same encænia as Milne. Having gained a scholarship, Milne attended the Royal School of Mines to study geology and mineralogy. After some practical mining experience in Cornwall and Lancashire, he studied mineralogy at Freiberg and visited the principal mining districts of Germany. At the request of Cyrus Field he spent two years (1872–1874) in investigating the mineral resources of Newfoundland and Labrador. He also visited Funk Island, once the home of the great auk, and made a large collection of skeletons of that bird. In 1874 he joined the expedition of Dr. C. J. Beke to investigate the situation of Mount Sinai, and published interesting geological notes on the environs of Cairo.

In 1875 Milne was appointed professor of geology and mining in the Imperial College, Tokio, at a time when William Edward Ayrton [q.v.], J. A. (afterwards Sir Alfred) Ewing, and John Perry were teaching physics and engineering there. To reach Japan Milne chose to travel via Siberia and Mongolia—a journey which occupied eleven months and involved much hardship. Milne proved to be an excellent teacher, and his services were retained for twenty years and were rewarded on his return to England in 1895 by a pension from the Japanese government, and the decoration of the order of the rising sun.

Milne had his first experience of an earthquake on the night of his arrival in Tokio. Subsequently he came to devote the greater part of his time to the subject, with the co-operation of the Japanese government. After the disastrous earthquake which partially destroyed Yokohama in February 1880, Milne took the lead in forming the Seismological Society of Japan. As its secretary for fifteen years he was responsible for twenty volumes of its *Transactions*. He was the first professor of seismology in the imperial university of Tokio, and established the seismic survey of Japan, involving the erection of nearly one thousand observing stations. One practical result was the revolutionizing of house and bridge building in that country.

On his return to England, Milne became secretary of the seismological committee of the British Association and retained the position until his death. His seismic survey now embraced all British territory, and he was again responsible for a series of valuable *Reports* for the Association. It was at this time that he devised a simple form of seismograph—an invention which he had forecasted as early as 1883. These instruments, which were delicate enough to record the effects of large earthquakes occurring at any place on the earth's surface, were set up at numerous stations throughout the world—chiefly on British territory. From the records communicated to him at his home in the Isle of Wight, Milne was able to deduce particulars of the disturbances which had occurred. It was soon realized that the effects of a shock travelled to any particular station by more than one route—either through the body of the earth or round its surface; and the study of the relationships of these routes has given new and valuable information on the structure of the earth's interior. Milne was thus the first to open up a new field of scientific inquiry, which has since been rapidly explored by many investigators.

Milne's travels were extensive. As a schoolboy he had shown his bent for travel by setting off, without consulting his parents, on an expedition to Iceland, where he joined in a very dangerous exploration of the Vatna Jokul. His journey through Siberia has already been mentioned; he also visited Kamchatka, calling at most of the Kuriles. He was well known in America and Canada, and he made observations in Manila, Borneo, the Australian colonies, New Zealand, and many islands of the Pacific; in 1905 he went with the British Association to South Africa.

Milne was very hospitable both in Japan and at Shide, Isle of Wight, his English home. This, and the ungrudging pains which he took to instruct intending seismologists, contributed materially to his success in organizing the network of distant observing stations. In all his seismological work he was devotedly served by his Japanese assistant, Shinobu Hirota, who died just before him. Milne died at Shide 30 July 1913.

Milne married Tone, daughter of Horikawa Noritsune, abbot of Ganjo-ji, Hakodate. She survived him without issue, returned to Japan in 1920, and died there in 1925.

[Obituary notice in *Proceedings* of the Royal Society, vol. lxxxix, A, 1913–1914, by John Perry; *Journal* of the Geological Society, 1874 *et seqq.*; *Geological Magazine*, 1874–1912; *Transactions* of the Asiatic Society of Japan; *Transactions* of the Seismological Society of Japan; *Reports* of the British Association.] H. H. T.

MINTO, fourth Earl of (1845–1914), governor-general of Canada and viceroy of India. [See Elliot, Gilbert John Murray Kynynmond.]

MITFORD, ALGERNON BERTRAM FREEMAN-, first Baron Redesdale in the second creation (1837–1916), diplomatist and author, was born in South Audley Street, London, 24 February 1837. He was the third son of Henry Revely Mitford (1804–1883), by his wife, Lady Georgiana Ashburnham, daughter of George, third Earl of Ashburnham, and great-grandson of William Mitford [q. v.], the historian. In order to retrench, Mr. Mitford withdrew to the Continent in his son's third year. The family settled first at Frankfort on Main, but from 1842 to 1846 lived principally in Paris and at Trouville. In 1846 Algernon was sent to Eton. His school career, which lasted till 1854, threw him into the company of his cousin, Algernon Swinburne, his junior in school standing by three years, and the two became fast friends. Mitford proceeded to Christ Church, Oxford, in October 1855. As an undergraduate he read voluminously, but hated Greek philosophy, and left in 1858 with 'a dismal second-class' in moderations. He was immediately appointed to the Foreign Office, worked creditably, and secured by his breeding and good looks an entry into the most exclusive London society; he was early among the associates of the Prince of Wales. He was running the risk of becoming a brilliant but rather showy 'young man about town', when in 1863 he was sent to St. Petersburg as second secretary of embassy.

Mitford's great energy was now turned into a political channel, and he made a close study of the conditions of life in Russia. Late in 1864 the lure of the East drew him to Constantinople, by way of Wallachia, and thence to Ephesus. His linguistic gifts were developing, and in 1865 he volunteered for China, where he was welcomed in Peking by Mr. (afterwards Sir Thomas) Wade. Of his adventures in China Mitford has given a full account in *The Attaché at Peking* (1900). He was transferred to Japan in 1866, not expecting that this country, then so obscure and fabulous, was to be his home for nearly four years. When the British minister, Sir Harry Smith Parkes [q.v.], decided that it was undignified for the legation to be excluded from the capital, and forced his way to Yedo (Tokio), Mitford accompanied him, thus becoming a witness of the great struggle between the daimios and the shogun (tycoon). In May 1867 Parkes and Mitford were received at Osaka by the Shogun in circumstances of extraordinary solemnity and romance. When the civil war broke out, the British legation was in great danger. Mitford was left for five months alone at Kioto, in order to preserve the prestige of England at the Japanese court, and his life was constantly threatened by the fanatics. He occupied his leisure in thoroughly mastering the Japanese language, and he conducted difficult negotiations with the Mikado to the complete satisfaction of the Foreign Office. At Kioto Mitford began to collect and to translate the 'Tales of Old Japan'. He returned unharmed to Yedo, but the anxieties and fatigues of a strenuous and isolated existence had told upon his health, and in 1870, on being invalided home, he returned to the Foreign Office, and to London society. In 1871 he published what is still the most popular of his writings, his *Tales of Old Japan*.

Mitford was now a young man of some celebrity, and he dreamed of a more interesting existence than that of secretary of legation at a humdrum European capital. Offered the embassy at St. Petersburg by Lord Granville, he refused this post and at his own desire was placed *en disponibilité* in 1871. He did not definitely resign the diplomatic service until 1873. Before that, he had started for the East again; he was soon in Damascus with his old friend (Sir) Richard Burton, at that time British consul there. Early in 1873 he chartered a tiny Genoese vessel in order to pay an improvised visit to Garibaldi in Caprera. He was received with much cordiality, and he has preserved a precious record of the great Italian's habits on his 'storm-beaten island rock'. Mitford presently returned to London, only to start immediately on a long visit to the United States' where he gratified his curiosity by waiting upon Brigham Young in Salt Lake City.

On his return to London Mitford found the whole current of his life changed through his appointment by Disraeli in May 1874 to be secretary to the Board of Works. In December of the same year he married Lady Clementine Ogilvy, second daughter of the seventh Earl of Airlie. They settled in Chelsea, having as a near neighbour James Whistler, who was perpetually in and out of their house. Mitford was present on the famous occasion when the painter cut some of his own pictures to ribands in a frenzy of rage. He was also at this time in close relations with Carlyle, Leighton, Joachim, and Millais. During his twelve years at the Office of Works he was met by great difficulties. Disraeli, when Mitford was appointed, described the Office of Works as 'an Augean stable, which must be swept clean'. Mitford carried out this labour satisfactorily, although it must be admitted that the ornamental and the antiquarian parts of the duty were most to his taste. Of the restorations which he directed at the Tower of London, he has given a fine account in *A Tragedy in Stone* (1882).

In May 1886 his cousin, John Thomas Freeman-Mitford, Earl of Redesdale [q.v.], died unmarried, and was found to have devised his very considerable fortune to Algernon Bertram. Both the earldom and the earlier barony became extinct, but the heir assumed the name and arms of Freeman, in addition to those of Mitford. He resigned his office, sold his house in Chelsea, and took possession of Batsford Park, his cousin's estate in Gloucestershire. The house was not to his liking; he pulled it down and built another of lordlier proportions, and he began to lay out the celebrated tropical garden. From 1892 to 1895 he was member of parliament for the Stratford-on-Avon division of Warwickshire. During these years literature was much neglected, but in 1896 Mitford published *The Bamboo Garden*, a charming and fantastic work which he called an '*apologia pro Bambusis meis* at Batsford'. In 1898 he visited the East again, exploring Ceylon. In 1902 he was raised to the peerage, as Baron Redesdale, of Redesdale in Northumberland; he became a constant attendant at the House of Lords, taking little part in the debates, but speaking sometimes effectively on subjects connected with the Far East. He began to suffer from a deafness, which was very painful to a man of such gay and gregarious habits. This threw him more and more upon the resources of his mind and pen, and he became an industrious writer. In 1906 he accompanied Prince Arthur of Connaught on the latter's visit to the Emperor of Japan, and published on his return *The Garter Mission to Japan* (1906), the best pages of which deal with the disconcerting changes which had taken place since he saw that country last. He further elaborated the same theme in *A Tale of Old and New Japan* (1906).

In the last decade of his life Lord Redesdale occupied himself by writing his autobiography, which appeared as *Memories* in 1915. He was also busy with translations, addresses, and pamphlets to such an extent that he seemed, after the age of sixty-five, to have turned from an amateur into a professional man of letters. In the first year of the War he had the misfortune to lose his eldest son, Clement, who fell in France after brilliantly distinguishing himself. Lord Redesdale, now almost stone-deaf, found companionship and consolation in literature; he began a book which was to be called *Veluvana*, and he threw himself ardently into the study of Dante. Having reached his eightieth year in full mental activity, he died at Batsford 17 August 1916. What he had written of *Veluvana*, and some other fragments, were edited by the present writer in 1917. He had five sons and four daughters and was succeeded as second baron by his second son, David Bertram Ogilvy (born 1878).

Lord Redesdale was an extremely lucky man, and deserved his good fortune. Few persons of our time have been accomplished in so many directions. He did many things, and most of them well; none of them, perhaps, superlatively well, since he lacked one gift, concentration. If he had devoted himself entirely to the diplomacy of his early years, to the arboriculture of his middle life, or to the literature of his old age, he might have made a more substantial impression on posterity. But, in spite of all his intelligence and his ardour, he remained an amateur—a very brilliant amateur indeed, but not a professional expert in anything. He reached his highest level as a writer, for his style was elegant, firm, and individual, though occasionally a little slip-shod. After the age of sixty-five, carefully and earnestly as a man may write without previous training, he lacks the craftsman's hand. As a human being, Lord Redesdale was a sort of Prince Charming; with his fine features, sparkling eyes, erect and elastic figure, and, in the last years, his burnished silver curls, he was a universal favourite, a gallant figure of a gentleman, solidly English in reality, but polished and sharpened by travel and foreign society. To see him stroll down Pall Mall, exquisitely dressed, his hat a little on one side, with a smile and a nod for every one, was to watch the survival of a type never frequent and now extinct. His autobiography, which will long be read and always be referred to, will preserve the memory of a man who was vivid and spirited beyond most of his fellows, and whose eighty years were brimful of vivacious experience.

[*Edinburgh Review*, April 1913; Lord Redesdale, *Memories*, 1915 (portrait); personal knowledge.] E. G–E.

MONYPENNY, WILLIAM FLAVELLE (1866–1912), journalist, and biographer of Disraeli, came of an Ulster Protestant family of Scottish extraction, which until 1898 spelt the surname 'Monypeny'. The second son of William Monypeny, a small landowner, of Ballyworkan, co. Armagh, and of Mary Anne Flavelle, his wife, he was born at Dungannon, co. Tyrone, 7 August 1866. Educated at the Royal School, Dungannon, and at Dublin University, where he graduated with high distinction in mathematics, he proceeded to Balliol College, Oxford; but temporary ill-health compelled him, after a short residence, to leave Oxford for London, and he became a regular contributor to the *Spectator*. In 1893 he joined the editorial staff of *The Times*, where his outstanding abilities were quickly recognized.

Early in 1899 Monypenny was offered unexpectedly the editorship of the Johannesburg *Star*, the foremost organ of the Uitlanders, who were suffering under the oppressive rule of President Kruger. The offer was accompanied by an assurance of unhampered editorial freedom. He accepted it, and made the journal a power in the political struggle that ensued. When this culminated in the South African War he obtained a commission in the Imperial Light Horse, fought in Natal, and, not without injury to his health, endured the siege of Ladysmith. Later, under Lord Milner's high commissionership, he became director of civil supplies and a member of the committee for regulating the return of refugees after the annexation of the Transvaal. When the *Star* was again published he resumed the editorship ; but he resigned it in 1903 from a scrupulous sense of honour, finding himself unable to countenance the importation of indentured Chinese labour. He made his way from Lake Victoria Nyanza by an exhausting tramp past Wadelai and Dufile and down the White Nile to Khartoum, and thence to England, where he rejoined *The Times* staff. In 1908 he was appointed an original director of *The Times* Publishing Company.

Monypenny's great opportunity came when he was chosen by *The Times* to write the authoritative biography of Lord Beaconsfield, from the materials bequeathed to Lord Rowton. The choice was in all respects happy. He had taken a lifelong interest in the greater issues of politics, imperial and domestic, upon which he brought to bear a judgement of conspicuous sagacity, fortified by close observation, penetrating shrewdness, and a natural gift for separating the essential from the accidental. These qualities gave weight to a lucid style, charged with thought. The first volume of his *Life of Benjamin Disraeli* appeared in October 1910, and the second, delayed by failing health, in November 1912. Ten days later, on 23 November, Monypenny died in the New Forest. The biography was continued, and completed in four more volumes, by Mr. G. E. Buckle, the editor under whom Monypenny had served *The Times*. Mr. Buckle also wrote the inscription for the memorial tablet in the parish church of Farnham Royal, Buckinghamshire, where Monypenny is buried. Monypenny was never married.

[*The Times*, 25 November 1912 ; private records ; personal knowledge.] J. B. C.

MOORE, EDWARD (1835–1916), principal of St. Edmund Hall, Oxford, and Dante scholar, was born at Cardiff, where his father practised as a physician, 28 February 1835. He was the elder son of Dr. John Moore, by his second wife, Charlotte Puckle. He was educated at Bromsgrove, and at Pembroke College, Oxford. In 1858, after obtaining four first classes (classics and mathematics) in moderations and the final schools, he was elected to an open fellowship at Queen's College. He was ordained in 1861, and three years later was appointed by Queen's College to the principalship of St. Edmund Hall, which he held for nearly fifty years. Under Moore's headship the reputation of the hall as a home of 'true religion and sound learning' was greatly increased, the numbers were more than doubled, and it was represented in almost every honours list. The university commission of 1877 prepared a new scheme for St. Edmund Hall, to take effect on the retirement or death of the existing head. Moore made it his object to defeat this scheme, which would have ended the separate existence of the hall, and to retain the hall as nearly as possible on the old lines. In 1903, on Moore being nominated to a canonry at Canterbury, the provost of Queen's carried through the hebdomadal council a statute which would have resulted in the absorption of the hall by the college. Moore successfully opposed the statute in congregation, and, retaining the headship with the sanction of the prime minister, set himself to preserve the independence of the hall. After a prolonged struggle, during which, though he had taken up his residence at Canterbury, he lived for a part of each term at the hall, his efforts were crowned with success, and in 1913 he at last felt free to resign. At Canterbury he was from the first an active member of the chapter, his special province being the library.

To the world at large Moore was best known as a Dante scholar. In 1876 he founded the Oxford Dante Society, thereby giving a powerful impulse to the study of Dante in Oxford, and consequently far beyond the limits of Oxford. In 1886 he was appointed Barlow lecturer on Dante at University College, London, an appointment which he held in all for seventeen years ; and in 1895 a Dante lectureship was specially created for him at the Taylorian Institution at Oxford. Two of his earliest works on Dante, *The Time References in the 'Divina Commedia'* (1887), and *Dante and his Early Biographers* (1890), were the outcome of the Barlow lectureship. In 1889 appeared his monumental *Contributions to the Textual Criticism of the 'Divina Commedia'*. This work, which at once placed Moore in the front rank of living Dante scholars, was the first serious attempt to deal scientifically and methodically with the complicated problems presented by the text of the *Commedia*, and it is still the chief authority on the subject. In response to a proposal from the Clarendon Press for a single-volume edition of the works of Dante, Moore brought out in 1894 the well-known *Oxford Dante*, now in its fourth edition (1924), which has been accepted as the standard of reference throughout the world. This was followed in 1896–1903 by three series of *Studies in Dante*. A fourth series was on the eve of publication at the time of Moore's death, which took place at Chagford 2 September 1916. Especially noteworthy among the essays contained in these four volumes are those on *Scripture and Classical Authors in Dante*, accompanied by elaborate tables, in the first volume; the closely reasoned article on the *Quæstio de Aqua et Terra*, which finally established the authenticity of the treatise, and the masterly vindication of the letter to Can Grande, in the second and third; and the lengthy series of studies on the textual criticism of the *Convivio*, which constitute the *pièces justificatives* of the emended text as printed in the *Oxford Dante*, in the posthumously published fourth volume.

Moore's intimate acquaintance with the whole range of Dante's writings, his attainments in the many fields covered by his subject, his acute yet cautious critical judgement, his sound scholarship, and indefatigable industry, gained him a European reputation, which was recognized by his election, among other distinctions, as a corresponding member of the Accademia della Crusca in 1906, and as a fellow of the British Academy in the same year. Moore was twice married: first, in 1868 to Katharine Edith (died 1873), daughter of John Stogdon, solicitor, of Exeter; secondly, in 1878 to Annie (died 1906), daughter of Admiral John Francis Campbell Mackenzie. He had one son and two daughters by each marriage. There is a portrait of Moore at St. Edmund Hall, Oxford.

[*The Times*, 5 September 1916; memoir by E. Armstrong in *Proceedings* of the British Academy, 1915–1916; preface (by the writer) to the fourth series of *Studies in Dante*; personal knowledge.]

P. J. T.

MOORE, TEMPLE LUSHINGTON (1856–1920), architect, the eldest son of Major-General George Frederick Moore, by his wife, Charlotte, youngest daughter of John Lushington Reilly, of Scarvagh House, co. Down, was born 7 June 1856 at Tullamore, King's county, where his father was then quartered. He received his early education at the high school, Glasgow, to which city his father had been brought by a staff appointment. In 1872 the boy, whose health was delicate, was sent as a pupil to the Rev. Richard Wilton, curate (afterwards rector) of Londesborough, Yorkshire. Three years later he was articled to the architect, George Gilbert Scott, junior, son of Sir George Gilbert Scott. In 1878 he set up as an architect himself at Hampstead, but soon moved to a London office in Old Queen's Street, Queen Anne's Gate.

Although never in formal partnership, Temple Moore and his master, George Gilbert Scott, remained for the next twelve years in close professional association. There is actually some doubt as to the share of each in the authorship of the designs of works entrusted to Scott from this time; but it is known that owing to Scott's failing health Moore had to assume increasing responsibility. The designs themselves supply no internal evidence on this point, since the sympathy between the two men was so complete that, even after Scott's withdrawal from his profession (about 1890), Moore, who became his acknowledged successor, seems to have hesitated before innovating or imposing his own idiosyncrasies upon the practice founded by Scott. Gradually, however, it became apparent that Moore's artistic destiny was not to preserve an attenuating tradition but to bring to maturity a development which otherwise would have remained incomplete.

Throughout his career Moore found constant employment, although the list of buildings designed by him is not as long as that of many a less conscientious architect. The following are the more important new churches which he designed: Peterborough, All Saints (1885–1903); Barnsley, Yorkshire, St. Peter (1892–1911); Hull, St. Augustine (1892); West Hendon, Middlesex, St. John (1896); Mansfield, St. Mark (1897); Sledmere, Yorkshire (1897–1898); Middlesbrough, St. Cuthbert (1901) and St. Columba (1905); Bradford, St. Wilfrid, Lidget Green (1904); Harrogate, St. Wilfrid (1905–1913); Eltham, St. Luke, Well Hall (1907); Leeds, St. Margaret (1907–1909); Royton, Lancashire, St. Anne

(1908); Uplands (Stroud), Gloucestershire (1908–1910); Upper Tooting, All Saints (1909); Longsight (Manchester), St. Cyprian (1914); Basingstoke, All Saints (1915–1917). Moore also designed the Anglican cathedral at Nairobi (1914), the nave of Hexham Abbey (1902–1908), and the chapels at Pusey House, Oxford, and the Bishop's Hostel, Lincoln. About sixty churches were either added to or restored by him, and in many of these there is furniture and decoration of his invention. His skill in the design of such accessories brought him also many opportunities for its display in buildings with which he was not otherwise connected.

Moore was the architect of Bilbrough Hall, near York, Southill Park, near Bracknell, Berkshire, and several other houses, including about ten parsonages. He designed alterations and additions at Warter Priory and at Allerton Hall, Yorkshire, and elsewhere, and gained great credit from his contemporaries for his restoration of the Treasurer's House and of St. William's College at York. Among his miscellaneous works are some schools and parish halls, the court house at Helmsley, a hospital at Woodhouse Spa, and the Hostel of the Resurrection at Leeds.

Moore's work, like that of G. G. Scott, his master, is important in the history of English architecture not only for its beauty but for its emancipation from the uneasy theories which had hampered its antecedents. Assuming an essential incompatibility between mediaeval architecture and modern life, Augustus Welby Pugin [q.v.], the pioneer of the Gothic revival, had striven to lead men back to mediaevalism; his successor, Sir George Gilbert Scott [q.v.], had striven to bring mediaeval architecture up to date. The school identified with the name of George Gilbert Scott, junior, held that both of these processes were unnecessary; that the Gothic style was still the most natural medium for the church architect to employ, and that its resumption meant not the adoption but the abandonment of a restrictive convention. Moore, even more than Scott, seems to have thought and built in Gothic without any effort at stylism. His designs are indistinguishable in kind from those of the Middle Ages, and as independent of exact precedent as they. The limits of his style were the limits of his predilections: his buildings, although purely Gothic, appear to have been designed with no constraint save that of his vigilant good taste. The church of St. Wilfrid, Harrogate, and that of St. Peter, Barnsley, show his style at its grandest; the chapel at Pusey House, Oxford, and that at the Bishop's Hostel, Lincoln, at its most delicate.

Moore died at Hampstead 30 June 1920. He married in 1884 Emma Storrs, elder daughter of the Rev. Richard Wilton, his former tutor, who became canon of York Minster in 1893. They had three daughters and one son, Richard Temple Moore, who assisted his father in his later work, and was drowned in the s.s. *Leinster* in 1918. Among Temple Moore's pupils was (Sir) Giles Scott, the son of his master.

[*Architectural Review*, January and February 1926 (containing a descriptive list of Moore's ecclesiastical designs, illustrated); private information.] H. S. G-R.

MOORHOUSE, JAMES (1826–1915), bishop of Melbourne and afterwards of Manchester, the only son of James Moorhouse, who was master cutler in 1840, by his wife, Jane Frances, only daughter of Captain Richard Bowman, of Whitehaven, was born at Sheffield 19 November 1826. He was educated at a private school and at St. John's College, Cambridge, and was ordained in 1853. After serving curacies at St. Neot's (1853–1855), at Sheffield (1855–1859), and at Hornsey (1859–1861), he was appointed perpetual curate of St. John's, Fitzroy Square, London, in 1862, and vicar of St. James's, Paddington, in 1868. In 1874 he was made chaplain in ordinary to the Queen and prebendary of St. Paul's. He married in 1861 Mary Lydia, daughter of the Rev. Thomas Sale, [q.v.], vicar of Sheffield. There were no children of the marriage.

In 1876 Moorhouse was consecrated bishop of Melbourne, where his episcopate was signalized by the building of a cathedral, and by his presiding over the synod in Sydney which framed the constitution of the Church in Australia. Even more memorable were his brilliant lectures, historical, philosophical, and theological, which drew audiences of some four thousand people. By these lectures, and by undaunted courage in conflict with impurity, injustice, and violence, Moorhouse contributed greatly to the recovery of Melbourne society from the demoralizing effects of the gold-fever. By unwearied journeys, during five months in each year, to distant out-stations, he stimulated the religious life of settlers, and set the type of the colonial episcopate.

From Melbourne Moorhouse was called to the see of Manchester in 1886. Besides the ordinary activities of a very extensive diocese, to which he devoted himself wholeheartedly, he undertook a personal visitation of each of his 550 parishes, entering each church, and inspecting each church school. His most notable public efforts were a sermon to the British Association in 1887, an address to the Church Congress at Manchester in 1888, a reply to Cardinal Vaughan's assertion of Roman Catholic claims in the Manchester diocese in 1894, and a speech on church schools in the House of Lords in 1902. He retired from Manchester in 1903, and died at Poundisford Park, near Taunton, 9 April 1915.

The life story of Bishop Moorhouse, as of other churchmen his contemporaries, is that of his reaction to the religious and political movements of the age. Self-taught, unfettered by the conventions of public-school education, Moorhouse enjoyed to the full the atmosphere of controversy. He was a born debater. His reading, which was extensive both in continental and English literature, scientific and metaphysical as well as theological, was steadily maintained throughout life. It was assiduously employed to confirm his clergy and congregations in the reality of the supernatural world and its intimate connexion with the natural. Had he accepted the offer of a fellowship made by his college in 1861 he might have founded at Cambridge a school of progressive orthodoxy, a valuable rival to the Hegelian Tractarianism of Oxford. He lived, however, for the work which was under his hand, keeping up his studies but giving the first place to practical activity. The unquestionable depth and sincerity of his faith contributed to deliver his biblical criticism from the suspicion of being masked infidelity. Two characteristic utterances mark his relation to his age: 'In opposing and denouncing the dictum of an arrogant science that the supernatural is impossible, there is no need to deny any of its well-established facts, or to oppose any of its logical and well-founded arguments' [*The Teaching of Christ*, 1891], and 'Let everything be sacrificed to Truth' [Hulsean Lectures, 1865].

[Bishop Moorhouse's sermons and lectures; Edith C. Rickards, *Bishop Moorhouse*, 1920; personal knowledge.] E. A. K.

MORANT, Sir ROBERT LAURIE (1863–1920), civil servant, the only son of Robert Morant, decorative artist, of Bond Street and Hampstead, by his wife, Helen, daughter of the Rev. Henry Lea Berry, head master of Mill Hill School, was born at Manaton Lodge, Hampstead, 7 April 1863. He was educated at Winchester and at New College, Oxford, where, in straitened circumstances, he lived an exceptionally studious and abstemious life, his sole athletic diversion being boxing, in which he excelled. He took a first class in the final honour school of theology in 1885. He then taught for a short time at Temple Grove preparatory school. In November 1886 he went to Siam as tutor to King Chulalongkorn's nephews, and subsequently became tutor to the Crown Prince and laid the foundations of a system of public education in Siam which is still associated with his name. He exercised great and independent influence and became the object of much jealousy, which led to his retirement from the Siamese service in 1894. On his return to England he went to live at Toynbee Hall, Whitechapel, and took part in its social and educational work.

In 1895 Morant entered the Education Department as assistant director of special inquiries and reports, contributing to the series of volumes edited by (Sir) Michael Sadler valuable reports, among which may be mentioned those on the French system of higher primary schools (1896–1897) and on the national organization of education in Switzerland (1898). In November 1899 he became private secretary to Sir John Eldon Gorst [q.v.], the elder, who was vice-president of the Committee of Council on Education; and in 1902 he was appointed assistant private secretary to the eighth Duke of Devonshire [q.v.], lord president of the Council. This gave Morant his opportunity. His achievement, as a relatively junior officer, in mobilizing and marshalling the political, municipal, and educational forces of the country for the not unhazardous enterprise of constructing an orderly and comprehensive system of public education out of incoherent and antagonistic elements, is one of the romances of the civil service. The passing of the Education Act of 1902 was largely due to his vision, courage, and ingenuity. His promotion, in November 1902, to be acting secretary of the Board of Education, and in April 1903 to the substantive post of permanent secretary, was not only appropriate but inevitable.

Although its operation was for some years embarrassed by denominational controversy and by attempts to modify the settlement effected by it in respect of voluntary schools, the Act of 1902 afforded a broad foundation for subsequent administrative and legislative development; and the organization of English education, in the spheres both of the central and local authorities, was transformed by Morant's administrative genius and indomitable energy. He showed himself a great constructive organizer, insistent on intelligible classification and clear definition of aims, but not doctrinaire in adherence to any preconceived plan or formula. He had a great sense of realities, and though revolutionary when he was convinced that pulling down was a necessary preliminary to rebuilding, he often displayed a tolerant and tentative opportunism. The impulse of his administration and the ideals which inspired it spread very widely in the country, and during his term of office the planning and provision of public education, and particularly of secondary and higher education, made large advances, and access to it was greatly facilitated. The period was by no means free from polemics, and a lively controversy over a matter of no intrinsic importance, coupled with the need for a man of outstanding ability to take charge of a new enterprise, occasioned Morant's departure from the Board of Education in 1911 and his transference to the post of chairman of the National Health Insurance Commission.

For the next eight years Morant's work had two aspects. The outstanding practical achievements were the initiation of the payment of insurance contributions, the provision of sanatorium benefit (July 1912), and the general practitioner service (January 1913). Morant had more at heart the wide potentialities, realized in the European War, of the system of national aid for medical research, founded in 1913 on principles which he elaborated, and of a closer interrelation between the whole medical profession and the public service. Above all, he was increasingly absorbed in the plan, which was in his mind at least from 1907, when the school medical service came into being, of a redefinition, long overdue, of the functions both of central and of local authorities concerned with public health. He saw its first stage accomplished in the passing of the Ministry of Health Act in June 1919, and in July he became first secretary of the new department. The means and the man had been secured for the more important task of formulating proper relationships between the separate authorities locally responsible. His knowledge and appreciation of the difficulties were unequalled ; it was a disaster to the cause of good government that time was not left him to overcome them.

Thus in seventeen out of the twenty-five years of his official life Morant conducted three large government departments. The Board of Education he entirely remodelled, adjusting it to the new division of responsibility between the central and local authorities, and making it capable of giving and receiving stimulus for a great expansion of the service of public education. The National Health Insurance Commission he organized from the beginning ; and he then passed on to the business of consolidating health functions and local government functions and constructing a new instrument of government.

The work actually done by Morant for the public services of education and health cannot be related particularly or in concrete form so as to be intelligible to those who are not intimately acquainted with the machinery of the departments in which he was engaged. The stages of design and action between the big ideas and the practical details are numerous—and for Morant no idea was too big and no detail too small. It was not without good reason that in 1917 he was asked to serve on the committee on the machinery of government. To Morant administration was a great adventure. He had a passion for making the instruments of public service more effective, and was consumed and destroyed by it. There was no intermittence in his volcanic energy. He knew no rest and enjoyed no leisure. If opportunities presented themselves he took them ; if they did not, he made them. His methods were quite unorthodox and they challenged criticism from which he never shrank. He was ambitious not of his own advancement but of establishing the dominance of the ideas which dominated him. He was impatient of opposition to them, and prone to suspect that criticism and advocacy of different methods concealed hostility to his principles. But once he was sure that his colleagues and subordinates were loyally working for the ends which he set before himself and them, no one was more generous in welcoming their criticism, in leaving them a free hand if they came up to his standard of ability and industry, and in giving them full credit for their achievement. Underlying all superficial characteristics, and reinforcing an amazing dialectical quickness, ingenuity, and grasp of detail, there was a solid core of large and simple devotion to ideals of public service, which compelled respect and commanded devoted friendship and service. The force, variety, and complexity of his character were to his contemporaries a constant source of interest, admiration, or wonder. His premature death, in London, 13 March 1920, left the civil service with the feeling that their order had lost one of the greatest figures it had ever produced—great by both character and achievement.

Morant received the C.B. in 1902 and the K.C.B. in 1907. He married in 1896 Helen Mary, daughter of Edwin Cracknell, of Wetheringsett Grange, Suffolk, by whom he had a son and a daughter.

[Private information ; personal knowledge.]

L. A. S. B.

MORRISON, WALTER (1836–1921), man of business and philanthropist, born in London 21 May 1836, was the fifth son of James Morrison, of the firm of Morrison, Dillon, & Co., by his wife, Mary, daughter of John Todd, of the same firm. Walter Morrison was heir to a share, which was largely increased during his own lifetime, of a great fortune made in business during the Napoleonic Wars. He was educated at Eton and at Balliol College, Oxford, where, like two of his brothers, he became a redoubtable oar, and he also obtained a first class in *literae humaniores* (1857). He thus gave early proofs of a mental and physical vigour which was maintained throughout a long life, together with a devotion to his old university which bore abundant fruit in his latter days and is his principal claim to a place in the national record.

Morrison went down from Oxford in 1858, made a 'grand tour', which included Egypt, Palestine, and the United States, and entered the House of Commons in 1861 as liberal member for Plymouth. He held that seat till the liberal debacle of 1874, stood unsuccessfully for the City of London in 1880, parted from Mr. Gladstone over his Irish programme, and twice subsequently (1886–1892 and 1895–1900) represented, as a liberal unionist, the Skipton division of Yorkshire, in which his home was situated. He finally retired from candidature in 1900 after a broken career in parliament extending over nearly forty years. It was a career, however, which was neither conspicuous nor, in all probability, congenial. A man of strong convictions and great independence, but neither an orator nor an ambitious politician, Morrison was never at any period an enthusiastic party man. In his early liberal days his interests were largely centred in the co-operative movement for improving working-class dwellings. In the years following his break with Mr. Gladstone all his energies and resources were thrown into the fight for the Union with Ireland and against the tyranny of the boycott and the 'plan of campaign'.

Morrison's intermittent absorption in politics did not keep him from a careful stewardship both of his private fortune and of the various business interests from which it arose. In particular he joined in 1874 the board of the Central Argentine Railway, in which his family possessed a large stake, became its chairman in 1887, and soon afterwards paid a protracted visit to South America which resulted in an elaborate report and the eventual absorption of the Buenos Ayres and Rosario line. He was also director of a number of local concerns and travelled constantly between London and Yorkshire in discharge of these duties. They were undertaken rather from a keen sense of responsibility than from any desire to increase his wealth, which grew partly by inheritance from a childless brother and sister who died before him, and partly through the simplicity of his personal tastes. He had none of the attributes of a miser and a great part of his fortune was consistently and judiciously given away during his lifetime.

Considering all his miscellaneous interests, an astonishing part of Morrison's time was spent at Malham Tarn, the wild moorland estate in Craven which had been acquired for him when he came of age, from the Listers of Gisburn. Here he could indulge his love of walking, of folklore, of a very miscellaneous range of literature, and of local leadership in many forms. He never married, and his notion of company was rather that of an audience than of a circle of friends. He was always something of an aloof and self-centred figure, greatly respected by his neighbours but never popular in the ordinary sense of the word, quite incapable of adapting himself to his society but delighted to welcome to Malham a succession of guests, among whom, at one time or another, appeared such 'eminent Victorians' as Henry Fawcett, John Ruskin, Charles Darwin, John Stuart Mill, Sir William Harcourt, and especially Charles Kingsley. It was at Malham Cove that Kingsley had the idea of *The Water Babies*, and Walter Morrison was his 'Squire'.

From Malham, too, radiated the princely benefactions for which history will best remember Morrison, though his dislike of publicity rendered their real extent almost incalculable. He played a considerable part in the development of the northern universities—a single anonymous gift of £10,000 to the new school of agriculture at Leeds was revealed almost by accident after his death. For Giggleswick School, where he was chairman of the governors for many years, he built and furnished down to the smallest detail, in celebration of Queen Victoria's diamond jubilee, that remarkable 'chapel with a dome' which was the expression both of his lifelong interest in Oriental architecture and of his personal predilections in English history. To go further afield, it is known that he was the mainstay of Lord Roberts's campaign for national service, that for some years he made an annual contribution of £10,000 to King Edward's Hospital Fund, and that innumerable relief funds owed much to his support during both the South African and the European Wars. He was one of the founders of the Palestine Exploration Fund and regarded himself in that connexion as the 'discoverer' of Kitchener. By a single gift of £15,000 he made possible the chief Hittite excavations (those of Carchemish) undertaken by the British Museum, while the Society (now dissolved) of Biblical Archaeology owed almost its whole career to his munificence.

Towards the end of his life Oxford became the special object of Morrison's benefactions. Fired perhaps by his experience at Giggleswick, he offered to rebuild the new chapel at Balliol on the lines of the old, which he greatly preferred; and, on the rejection of this somewhat startling proposal, he at once gave £30,000 to the university for the three purposes of a readership in Egyptology, a professorial pension fund, and the study of agriculture. Finally, in 1920, he endowed the Bodleian Library with a single payment of £50,000, and thus took rank among the three chief benefactors in the history of that famous foundation. The honorary degree of D.C.L., which was conferred upon him in the following year, was the only public recognition which he received, or indeed would have valued. He died at Sidmouth 18 December 1921, and was buried at Kirkby Malham.

[Geoffrey Dawson, 'Walter Morrison' in the *National Review*, February 1922.]

G. D.

MOSELEY, HENRY GWYN JEFFREYS (1887–1915), experimental physicist, the only son of Henry Nottidge Moseley [q.v.], Linacre professor of anatomy in the university of Oxford, was born at Weymouth 23 November 1887, and educated at Eton and at Trinity College, Oxford, of which he was a Millard scholar, graduating with honours in natural science in 1910. On both sides he was descended from families of great scientific ability, and he early showed marked originality of mind and interest in science. As an undergraduate he pursued his studies with great determination, with a preference for his own methods; he also rowed every year in one or other of the college boats. Immediately after graduation, he was appointed lecturer in physics in the university of Manchester and began research under the direction of Professor (Sir) E. Rutherford. He soon developed into a rapid and skilful experimenter with unusual powers of continuous work, and showed to a marked degree that combination of practical ability and philosophic insight so necessary for attacking new and difficult problems. Following a number of important investigations in the subject of radio-activity, Moseley began that work on the X-ray spectra of the elements with which his name is inseparably connected. (Sir) W. H. Bragg and W. L. Bragg had already shown that the wave-length of X-rays could be determined by the crystal method, and had found evidence of bright lines superimposed on the continuous spectrum. Moseley proceeded to examine systematically the relation between the bright-line spectra given by different elements; and found that all the elements gave similar types of spectra, and that the frequency of vibration of corresponding lines was proportional to the square of a number which varied by unity in passing from one element to the next. From these observations, he was able to draw conclusions of far-reaching importance in connexion with the constitution of atoms. He deduced that the nuclear charge of an element, in fundamental units, was equal to its atomic or ordinal number, and varied from 1 in hydrogen to 92 in uranium; he further showed that only three elements were missing between aluminium and gold, and predicted their spectra. His results brought out clearly that the main properties of an element are determined not by its atomic weight but by a whole number defining its nuclear charge. This law of Moseley ranks in importance with the discoveries of the periodic law of the elements and of spectrum analysis, and is in many respects more fundamental than either.

In 1914 Moseley travelled with his mother to Australia to attend the meeting of the British Association. He returned to England in order to enlist at once in the new army, and he obtained his commission as lieutenant in the Royal Engineers. He took part in the Gallipoli campaign, and was killed in action on 10 August 1915 at the age of twenty-seven. He was unmarried. The premature death of a young man of such brilliant promise and achievement was everywhere recognized as an irreparable loss to science. His friends and scientific admirers in many countries united to erect a memorial tablet in the physical laboratory of the university of Manchester. He bequeathed his property to the Royal Society to aid scientific research, and a studentship bearing his name has been instituted.

[Personal knowledge.] E. R.

MOULE, GEORGE EVANS (1828–1912), missionary bishop in mid-China, was born 28 January 1828 at Gillingham, Dorset, the second of the eight sons of the Rev. Henry Moule [q.v.], then curate-in-charge of Gillingham, and from 1829 to 1880 vicar of Fordington, Dorchester, by his wife, Mary Mullett Evans. He was educated at home till 1846, the year of his sudden conversion, the result of a sermon on Acts xxviii, 24, by Augustus Handley, his father's curate. The effect never passed away; it changed his whole subsequent life. In 1846 he entered Corpus Christi College, Cambridge, and in 1850 graduated with mathematical and classical honours. James Scholefield, the regius professor of Greek, and Frederick Foster Gough helped to turn his thoughts to work abroad. He was ordained deacon at Salisbury in 1851 as curate to his father, and priest in 1852, and acted as tutor to his father's pupils. From 1855 to 1857 he was also chaplain of the Dorset county hospital.

In 1857 Moule offered his services to the Church Missionary Society, and in the December of that year sailed for Shanghai. On the way, at Hong Kong, he married Adelaide Sarah (died 1909), daughter of Frederick Moule, of Melksham, Wiltshire, and widow of Captain Griffiths, the wife who was his devoted companion for fifty-one years, and the mother of his seven children. He was stationed first at Ningpo; in 1864 he was led in a remarkable way to open up work in the capital of Chekiang, Hangchow, then practically destroyed by the Taiping rebels. From 1865 to the end of his life the house in Hangchow was his only home. In 1864 he became a member of the Royal Asiatic Society, China branch, and most of his writings were papers in its *Journal*. On the death of Bishop William Armstrong Russell [q.v.], of North China, he was consecrated (October 1880) first bishop in the new diocese of mid-China, a post which he held till his resignation in 1906. In 1905 he was elected an honorary fellow by his college. He continued to work under the Church Missionary Society till his death, which took place on 3 March 1912 while he was on a visit to England. He was buried in Bow cemetery at Durham.

George Moule was a man of wide interests: music, drawing, turning, medicine, swimming, botany (he introduced some hitherto unknown plants to science), and especially literature, all attracted him, and he attained extraordinary skill in the Chinese language, literary and colloquial. All this, however, was secondary to his missionary work, at which he laboured incessantly by prayer, preaching, teaching, translating, and church administration. During his time in China he saw the church members in Chekiang increase from less than a hundred to more than four thousand. It was a son of one of his early pupils who became the first Chinese bishop—Tsaeseng Sing, assistant bishop in Chekiang. Gentleness, reverence, humour, courage, and diligence were conspicuous in Moule, and endeared him to a wide and varied circle of friends.

[G. E. Moule, *A Retrospect of Sixty Years*, 1907; Bishop Handley Moule, *A Short Memoir of George Evans Moule*, 1912, and *George Evans Moule. A Sketch*, 1920; *Journal* of the China Branch of the Royal Asiatic Society (containing bibliography), 1912.]

H. W. M-E.

MOULE, HANDLEY CARR GLYN (1841–1920), bishop of Durham, was born at Fordington, Dorset, 23 December 1841, the eighth son of the Rev. Henry Moule [q.v.], by his wife, Mary Mullett Evans. From home, where his father educated his sons and other pupils, a home full of scholarly and literary as well as of religious and missionary keenness, Handley Moule passed to a brilliant career at Trinity College, Cambridge (1860), being bracketed second classic (1864) and elected fellow of his college (1865). He also read for the voluntary theological examination, but 'the distressing pains involved in the mere growth of thinking' had raised doubts in his mind, and he hesitated to be ordained. From 1865 to 1867 he was an assistant master at Marlborough College. Then, mainly through his mother's influence, all hesitation vanished: he was ordained at Ely. He first acted as his father's curate at Fordington, keeping in touch with Cambridge, where he gained for several years the prize for a sacred poem. Recalled in 1873 to Trinity, he acted as dean, being also curate at St. Sepulchre's church, until 1877, when his mother died, and he returned home as curate until his father's death (1880).

At that moment the evangelical party in the Church of England was planning the erection of Ridley Hall at Cambridge as a theological college for ordinands: Moule accepted the principalship, and held it for nineteen years. He married in 1881 Harriot Mary, daughter of the Rev. C. Boileau Elliott, F.R.S., rector of Tattingstone, Suffolk, by whom he had two daughters. This was a period of great happiness and influence: his wife was in whole-hearted sympathy with his aims; he won the devoted allegiance of colleagues and pupils; he preached regularly at Trinity church, and often before the university; inspired and guided many religious movements in the university; spoke often at Keswick conventions and Church Congresses, and published numerous books. In 1899 he was elected Norrisian professor of divinity, and, while professor, was brought into close touch with the leaders of other sections of the Church by taking part in a round table conference on the doctrine of the Holy Communion, impressing them much by his spirituality, and being impressed by them.

In 1901 Moule was appointed to the see of Durham. As a bishop, his strength lay in his personal and spiritual appeal; he was in touch with clergy and laity alike, with quick sympathy for all suffering, with charity to those who differed from him, an enthusiastic leader in all missionary effort and in preventive and rescue work. Rather un-English in temperament—of French ancestry on his father's side, of Welsh on his mother's—he was naturally timid and high-strung, but his whole life was one of persistent development in power. He became fearless in asserting the truth, unruffled in the face of difficulty and sorrow, deepened and even brightened by the sorrows of later life, when he lost a daughter and his wife. But, while growing in power and in toleration, he remained unchangingly within the limits of the faith as he had learned it in his father's house. He wrote much—treatises theological, devotional, exegetical, biographies, poems, hymns—notably, *Outlines of Christian Doctrine* (1889), *Thoughts on Christian Sanctity* (1885), *Veni Creator* (1890), *Charles Simeon* (1892), *Christus Consolator* (1915), *Philippian*, *Colossian*, and *Ephesian Studies* (1897–1900). His writings form the most spiritual and scholarly expression in his generation of the Christian faith as held by evangelical churchmen, proud of the Reformers, and holding that their teaching is 'the most loyal in proportion and emphasis to the New Testament standard'. He died at Cambridge 8 May 1920.

[Bishop Handley Moule's *Memories of a Vicarage*, 1913; J. B. Harford, *Letters and Poems of Bishop Moule*, 1921; J. B. Harford and F. C. Macdonald, *Handley C. G. Moule, Bishop of Durham. A biography* (with bibliography), 1922.] W. L.

MOULTON, JAMES HOPE (1863–1917), classical and Iranian scholar and student of Zoroastrianism, the elder son of the Rev. William Fiddian Moulton [q.v.], head master of the Leys School, Cambridge, by his wife, Hannah, daughter of the Rev. Samuel Hope, was born at Richmond, Surrey, 11 October 1863. His father was one of four brothers, all eminent, the best known being John Fletcher Moulton, Lord Moulton [q.v.]. He was educated at the Leys School, and at King's College, Cambridge, of which he was a fellow from 1888 to 1894. Several lines of Methodist ancestry blended in him, and he entered the Wesleyan ministry in 1886, being appointed assistant to his father at the Leys. In 1890 he married Eliza Keeling Osborn, granddaughter of Dr. George Osborn [q.v.]. He had two sons (the elder fell in action in 1916) and two daughters. He left Cambridge in 1902 on his appointment as New Testament tutor at the Wesleyan College, Didsbury, Manchester. In 1908 he was appointed Greenwood professor of Hellenistic Greek and Indo-European philology in the university of Manchester. After his wife's death in 1915, he went to India specially to lecture to the Parsees on Zoroastrianism, and to qualify himself to write a volume, which was posthumously published (1917) under the title *The Treasure of the Magi*. He left India in March 1917 and joined Dr. Rendel Harris at Port Said. Their ship was torpedoed in the Mediterranean. Moulton 'played a hero's part in the boat', died from exhaustion on 7 April, and was buried by his friend at sea.

Moulton's interests were wide, but his best work was done on the Greek of the New Testament and on Zoroastrianism. To the former he was drawn by the fact that his father, who had translated Winer's *Grammar of New Testament Greek*, had chosen his son to collaborate with him in the writing of a new and independent work under that title. Nothing had been done when the father died in 1898, and the whole responsibility fell on the son. He was himself spared only to see the publication (1906) of the first volume containing the *Prolegomena*; but the greater part of the second volume had been written and the work is in course of publication under the editorship of Mr. W. F. Howard. The *Prolegomena* was immediately recognized as of the first importance. In his *Bibelstudien* Deissmann had published a mass of evidence to show that the vocabulary of the New Testament did not belong to a class by itself, but was to be put in the same category as the ordinary spoken Greek of the time, as preserved in the non-literary papyri. Moulton accepted his demonstration and applied it to the grammar. Harnack spoke of him as 'the foremost expert in New Testament Greek'. He hoped to prepare for English readers an edition of Deissmann's projected lexicon; and he lived long enough to see the publication (1914–1915) of two fasciculi of the *Vocabulary of the Greek Testament*, which he prepared in collaboration with Professor George Milligan. The most serious loss occasioned by his premature death was his failure to write the volume on the syntax in his *Grammar of New Testament Greek*.

His study of comparative philology led him to Sanskrit and Iranian; and from the language of the Avesta he naturally passed to the religion. In this field he owed much to the teaching of Edward Byles Cowell [q.v.]. Apart from articles, he published four books on the religion. *Early Religious Poetry of Persia* (1911) was an admirable introduction to the subject, and with it may be coupled *The Teaching of Zarathushtra* (1917), lectures delivered to the Parsees. His most important contribution was made in his Hibbert lectures, *Early Zoroastrianism* (1913). He was inclined to push back the date of Zarathushtra several generations behind the traditional date, 660–583 B.C.; and he sought to disengage the true Zoroastrian elements in the Avesta from accretions which he attributed to the Magi. The subject is discussed again in the first part of *The Treasure of the Magi*, the latter part of which is devoted to modern Parsism. Moulton was an enthusiast for Zarathushtra, and for his teaching, which he regarded as the purest form of non-biblical religion.

Though a scholar of the highest quality and exceptional range he was deeply interested in practical questions. Foreign missions, social amelioration at home, the commendation to doubters of the simple Christian faith in which he rested, were always very near his heart. He was eminent for the strength, the loftiness, and beauty of his character, and for the intensity of his religion.

[W. Fiddian Moulton, *Memoir*, 1919; *James Hope Moulton, 1863–1917*, in the *Bulletin* of the John Rylands Library, vol. iv, No. 1 (also printed in separate form); personal knowledge.] A. S. P.

MOULTON, JOHN FLETCHER, BARON MOULTON (1844–1921), lord of appeal in ordinary, was born 18 November 1844 at Madeley, Shropshire, the third son of the Rev. James Egan Moulton, a Wesleyan minister, as his father and grandfather had been before him, and for a time head master of New Kingswood School, Bath, by his wife, Catherine, daughter of William Fiddian, brass-founder, of Birmingham. Moulton was named after a former vicar of Madeley, John William Fletcher [q.v.], the intimate friend of John Wesley. He was a younger brother of William Fiddian Moulton [q.v.], and uncle of James Hope Moulton [q.v.]. He received his early education from his father. At the age of eleven he was sent to Kingswood School and was at once placed in the head master's class. When thirteen and a half he was head of the school; at the age of sixteen he took the highest marks in England at the first of the Oxford and Cambridge local examinations. On leaving Kingswood School he acted for a short time as an assistant-master at schools at Biggleswade and Northampton. In 1861 he matriculated at London University, winning a studentship of £30. He took his B.A. degree in mathematics (1865), being alone in the first class both at the intermediate and the final examination. Meanwhile he had been elected to a scholarship at St. John's College, Cambridge. His fame as a mathematician soon spread, and when, during his first year at Cambridge, he entered for the London University scholarship no other candidate appeared. Coached by the famous Dr. Edward John Routh [q.v.], Moulton was first Smith's prizeman and senior wrangler in 1868, with the highest total of marks ever gained; (Sir) George Howard Darwin [q.v.] was second wrangler. The same year he won the gold medal for mathematics at London University, and was elected a fellow of Christ's College, Cambridge, few of the St. John's fellowships being at that time open to laymen. Moulton worked both as college tutor and private tutor, and was a regular attendant at the debates of the Union Society, of which he was president in 1868, and thereafter treasurer till he left Cambridge in 1873. The Union records show that he was an advocate of votes for women, reform of the university system of education, and Irish conciliation.

In 1873 Moulton came to London to read for the bar, and the following year he was 'called' by the Middle Temple. He read in chambers with William George Harrison [q.v.], then a busy common law junior, and soon had work of his own of a general kind. The passing of the Patents, Designs, and Trade Marks Act (1883), which considerably increased the number of patent actions, gave him a chance which he was ready to take, and in 1885 he applied for, and received, a silk gown. Shortly before, his electrical researches had won him a fellowship of the Royal Society. For the next twenty years Moulton was engaged, as a leader, in all patent cases of any importance. In this class of work he was unrivalled. His mind worked with great rapidity; scientific facts and problems which others had to master laboriously, presented no difficulties to him; and he had the gift of easy and lucid speech. Apart from patent work his practice was large and varied. He often appeared in parliamentary committee rooms when bills relating to electrical undertakings were being promoted; and he was a favourite advocate both in compensation cases and in those concerning trade-marks and trade-names. In the lengthy litigation over the right of the Kodak Company to register the word 'Solio' as a trade-mark, he induced the House of Lords to accept the view of his clients, despite the adverse judgments of the two courts below; he appeared in the multitudinous cases which centred round the Dunlop and Welsbach patents; and he was counsel in the arbitration which settled the price to be paid for the undertakings of the London water companies when the Metropolitan Water Board was created. There were not many barristers of his time who made a larger income.

In November 1885 Moulton was elected to the House of Commons, in the liberal interest, as a member for the Clapham division of Battersea, and began a parliamentary career which received many checks. At the general election of 1886 he lost his seat; he failed to get back to parliament at the general election of 1892; and it was not till 1894 that he was elected member for South Hackney in succession to Lord Russell of Killowen, who, as Sir Charles Russell, had held the seat for eight years. This seat he lost at the general election of 1895. He returned to the House of Commons as member for the Launceston division of Cornwall in August 1898, and continued to sit for that constituency till the general election of 1906. In the House of Commons he played an active part. His support was useful to Sir William Harcourt in 1894 when the new death duties were under discussion; he spoke effectively against the Chinese Labour ordinances after the South African War; in 1904 he showed, in a speech which convinced waverers, that the supporters of a 'pure beer' Bill were neglecting valuable scientific discoveries, and that beer drinkers had nothing to fear from what was represented as adulteration; and in 1905 he carried through the House a measure which became law as the Trade Marks Act. Between 1885 and 1905 Moulton's party was only in office for about three years, and he had few chances of promotion; but in 1906, on the return of the liberals to power, he was made a lord justice of appeal in succession to Sir James Charles Mathew [q.v.], knighted, and sworn of the Privy Council.

During his six years of service in the Court of Appeal Moulton was an outstanding figure. His power of assimilation was as great as ever; and he dealt with commercial cases, appeals under the Workmen's Compensation Act, and actions of libel, as if he had been accustomed to them all his life. Notable cases in which his dissenting judgment was upheld by the House of Lords are *Scott* v. *Scott* (1913, the right to order a trial *in camera*), and *A.-G.* v. *West Riding of Yorkshire County Council* (1907, the obligation of local education authorities to pay for religious instruction in non-provided schools); and in *Cuenod* v. *Leslie* (1909) he showed characteristic independence on the question whether a husband is still liable for the torts of his wife. From time to time he formed a court with two colleagues—Lord Justices James Stirling [q.v.] and Robert Romer [q.v.]—each of whom had also been a senior wrangler. In 1912 he succeeded Lord Robson [q.v.] as a lord of appeal in ordinary, and became a life peer with the title of Lord Moulton, of Bank in the county of Southampton.

Shortly after the outbreak of the European War in 1914, Lord Moulton was called from his work in the House of Lords by the invitation of the government to preside over a committee whose duties were to arrange for the manufacture of high explosives and propellents for the British forces. Moulton organized a service which, as the Explosives Supply Department, became a branch of the War

Office, and was turning out at the date of the Armistice (November 1918) 1,000 tons of high explosives a day. At first he had to cope with great difficulties. The available factories were few; and the sources of supply of raw materials were limited. Lyddite had been replaced by trinitrotoluene, every three tons of which required two tons of toluene; 600 tons of coal produced one ton of toluene. Moulton economized by mixing ammonium nitrate with trinitrotoluene, thus producing a new compound explosive known as amatol. Nitric acid, sulphuric acid, and glycerine were needed in large quantities at a time when shipping facilities were disorganized; but he managed to secure them. He had control of the gas works, coke ovens, and fat and oil supplies of the whole country. When the retaliatory use of poison gas was decided upon Moulton undertook its manufacture. His department delivered during the War a total of 612,697 tons of high explosive and 450,487 tons of propellents.

For these extraordinary services Moulton received the K.C.B. (1915) and G.B.E. (1917). At Christmas 1920 he underwent a slight nasal operation. On 8 March 1921 he sat in the House of Lords and seemed to have recovered his usual good health. In the early hours of 9 March he died in his sleep. His death, caused by a clot in an artery, had been instantaneous. Addressing the lords of appeal two days later, Lord Birkenhead, in an eloquent speech, spoke of the intellectual force and dynamic impulse of personality which had enabled a judge to play a supreme part in the European War. Lord Moulton had strong instincts of hospitality and was a delightful companion.

Moulton married twice: first, in 1875 Clara (died 1888), widow of Robert William Thomson, of Edinburgh and Stonehaven; and secondly, in 1901 Mary (died 1909), daughter of Major Henry Davis, of Naples. By his first wife he left a son (the Hon. Hugh Fletcher Moulton), and by his second wife, a daughter.

A crayon drawing of Moulton by Trevor Haddon, R.B.A., is in the possession of the family; and a cartoon portrait by 'Spy' appeared in *Vanity Fair*.

[*The Times*, 10 March 1921; *Law Journal*, 12 March 1921; Hugh Fletcher Moulton, *The Life of Lord Moulton*, 1922; personal knowledge.] T. M.

MOUNTBATTEN, LOUIS ALEXANDER, first Marquess of Milford Haven, formerly styled Prince Louis Alexander of Battenberg (1854–1921), admiral of the fleet, the eldest son of Prince Alexander of Hesse (a younger son of Louis II, Grand Duke of Hesse-Darmstadt) by his wife, Countess Julia Theresa von Haucke, was born at Gratz, Austria, 24 May 1854. The friendship between his mother and Princess Alice, daughter of Queen Victoria and consort of Prince Frederick of Hesse (afterwards Grand Duke Louis IV), led to Prince Louis settling in this country as a boy; and, having become naturalized as a British subject, he entered the royal navy as a cadet in 1868. In 1869 he was rated midshipman, and joined the *Royal Alfred*, flagship of Vice-Admiral (Sir) Edward Fanshawe on the North America and West Indies station. When the Admiralty took over the *Serapis* in 1874 for the visit of the Prince of Wales to India, Prince Louis, then sub-lieutenant, was selected to serve as one of the complement of officers. He already gave promise of distinction. His sympathies were entirely British, and Queen Victoria watched his career with almost motherly interest. His abilities as a linguist proved of no slight advantage to him in later life. At the conclusion of the Indian tour he was promoted to lieutenant, and served in the *Inconstant* during the Egyptian War, taking part in the bombardment of Alexandria (11 July 1882). He subsequently landed with the naval brigade, in command of a Gatling gun battery, for the occupation of Alexandria. After a period of service in the royal yacht, he was promoted to commander in 1885.

At this period the defence policy of this country was undergoing a gradual readjustment in accordance with the theories of what became known as 'the blue-water school', and Prince Louis was selected by the Admiralty to act as naval adviser to the inspector-general of fortifications, with a view to co-ordinating naval and military ideas. He took up this appointment in 1892, having been promoted captain in the preceding year, and held it until October 1894. In February 1894 he was chosen to act as joint secretary of the naval and military committee on defence, which afterwards was developed into the committee of imperial defence. During these years he applied himself seriously to the study of the defence problem in its naval and military aspects and was peculiarly well qualified when, in 1900, he was made assistant-director of naval intelligence. After a short period of service in the Mediterranean, he returned to the Admiralty in 1902 as director of naval intelligence, and retained that position until 1905, having been promoted to rear-admiral in 1904.

By this time Prince Louis, who in 1884 had married his cousin, Princess Victoria, daughter of Louis IV of Hesse-Darmstadt and Princess Alice, was regarded throughout the service as an officer who had established his fitness for high command at sea. On leaving the Admiralty in 1905 he hoisted his flag in the *Drake* as rear-admiral commanding the second cruiser squadron. In these circumstances he began his career as an admiral at sea, and that he was to exercise no slight influence upon the training of the British navy soon became apparent. After two years in the second cruiser squadron, his selection as second in command of the fleet in the Mediterranean met with general approval in the navy. In the meantime Lord Fisher [q.v.] had become the dominating figure at the Admiralty, and it was no matter of surprise when in 1908 Prince Louis was directed to move his flag into the Atlantic fleet as commander-in-chief. After two years in that command he was appointed vice-admiral commanding the third and fourth divisions of the newly constituted home fleets, and from thence in December 1911 he returned to the Admiralty as second sea lord. Mr. Winston Churchill had become first lord in that year, and he selected Prince Louis as first sea lord a year later on the retirement of Sir Francis Bridgeman. This selection was probably unwise on grounds of political expediency, in view of the circumstances of Prince Louis's birth, and of the threatening situation which was developing abroad.

In July 1914 a test mobilization of the naval reserves was carried out, and the ships were due to disperse, after carrying out exercises in the English Channel, at the moment when relations between this country and Germany had become strained. Owing to the illness of his wife, Mr. Churchill was absent from the Admiralty during the critical week-end (25–27 July) when it had to be decided whether the fleet should be dispersed and the reserve ships demobilized, in accordance with the plans already made, or whether preliminary steps should be taken to place the squadrons at their various war stations. This decision rested with the first sea lord. After a telephone conversation with the first lord at Cromer, Prince Louis, as he subsequently explained in a published letter, 'directed the secretary, as a first step, to send an Admiralty order by telegraph to the commander-in-chief of the home fleets at Portland to the effect that no ship was to leave that anchorage until further orders'. War had not then been declared, but the prevision of the first sea lord ensured that when it became inevitable the navy should be in a state of readiness. Political events moved rapidly. At four o'clock on the morning of 3 August the mobilization of the navy had been completed. The prompt initiative which Prince Louis had exhibited in this emergency did not shield him from attack in subsequent months on account of his 'German origin'. On 29 October, as the final act of patriotism in his long and distinguished naval career, he resigned his position as first sea lord. He lived to see the complete triumph of the naval weapon which he had helped to forge, dying on 11 September 1921 in his chambers at Half Moon Street, Piccadilly, at the age of sixty-seven.

With the coming of peace, tribute was paid to the services which he had rendered the country, by his promotion to the rank of admiral of the fleet. In July 1917, by the request of the King, Prince Louis relinquished the style and title of serene highness and prince, assumed for himself and his descendants the surname of Mountbatten, and was raised to the peerage of the United Kingdom as Marquess of Milford Haven, Earl of Medina, and Viscount Alderney. He left two sons and two daughters, and was succeeded in the marquessate by his elder son, George Louis, Earl of Medina.

Prince Louis, who was of a commanding presence and possessed great charm of manner, looked the beau-ideal of the British naval officer, and took throughout his life a keen interest in British naval history. He was particularly interested in the Navy Records Society and was the first president of the Society of Nautical Research. He was also associated with Admiral Sir Percy Scott in the invention of the cone signalling apparatus, and introduced into the service an instrument to enable the complicated calculations, which are necessary before certain tactical manœuvres can be carried out, to be resolved mechanically.

A portrait of Prince Louis is included in Sir A. S. Cope's picture 'Some Sea Officers of the Great War', painted in 1921, which is in the National Portrait Gallery.

[Private information; personal knowledge.]

A. H.

MOUNT STEPHEN, first Baron (1829–1921), financier and philanthropist. [See Stephen, George.]

MOWATT, Sir FRANCIS (1837–1919), civil servant, the only son of Francis Mowatt, M.P. for Falmouth (1847–1852) and for Cambridge (1854–1857), by his wife, Sarah Sophia, daughter of Captain Barnes, of Romford, Essex, of the East India Company's marine service, was born in New South Wales 27 April 1837. He went to Harrow in September 1851 and left at Easter 1853, going afterwards to Winchester. He entered at St. John's College, Oxford, in March 1855, but left the next year on being appointed to a clerkship in the Treasury (May 1856). The whole of Mowatt's active life was passed in this department, in which he served for forty-seven years. He was appointed assistant secretary in 1888, and was permanent secretary, in succession to Lord Welby, from 1894 to 1903. The latter post can never be a popular one; but a keen sense of humour, a genial cynicism, unfailing good temper, and a sagacious appreciation of what was feasible, enabled him to accomplish much useful work. At no time, probably, had Treasury control been asserted and carried into effect with so little friction as during Mowatt's tenure of the office; and he undoubtedly raised the reputation of his department for promptness and efficiency.

In January 1900, at the opening of the parliamentary session, a somewhat ill-considered attack on the constitutional position of the Treasury was made by Lord Salisbury, then prime minister and foreign secretary. Referring to the preparations made by the government in view of the South African War, he observed that the British constitution as then worked was not a good fighting machine, and that the Treasury in particular exercised a power of control over the other departments which was not for the public benefit. As he expressly stated that he made no complaint against the chancellor of the exchequer of the time (Sir Michael Hicks Beach, afterwards Earl St. Aldwyn), Mowatt was led to infer that Lord Salisbury must have intended to censure the permanent staff of the department; he therefore intimated his readiness to resign his post. Lord Salisbury thereupon made the following explanation in the House of Lords (1 February 1900): 'There is now conveyed to me a letter from a most excellent public servant, Sir Francis Mowatt, who seems to think that, because I did not blame the chancellor of the exchequer, I must have meant to blame him. Nothing was further from my mind. I was blaming a system which has been the result of causes which have lasted for a considerable time, and which affect no individuals whatever; and in speaking of the action of the chancellor of the exchequer I include the action of those who are acting under him in his own office. The impression of Sir Francis Mowatt is entirely unfounded, and though my personal acquaintance is not very great, from everything I have heard the public service does not contain a more admirable minister of the public welfare than himself.'

Mowatt's services were frequently required for royal commissions and committees. One of the most important of the latter was appointed early in the South African War to consider the deficiencies which had already become apparent in the supply of military equipment and stores. The committee, of which Mowatt was chairman, reported in March 1900, and laid down for the future a definite scale of reserves for guns, ammunition, clothing, and general stores. These became known as the 'Mowatt reserves', and the scales then adopted continued in force down to the outbreak of the European War. His political opinions were those of the old school of liberals. He was a strong free trader; and the vehemence with which he took part in the fiscal controversies of the year 1903 was understood at the time to be regarded by his political chiefs as rather inopportune.

Mowatt was made C.B. in 1884, K.C.B. in 1893, and G.C.B. in 1901, and he was sworn of the Privy Council in 1906. He was a member of the royal commission for the Exhibition of 1851, and for the Patriotic Fund. After his retirement from the Treasury he became an alderman of the London County Council, and a member of the senate of the university of London, and of the council of the Imperial College of Science and Technology. He was also a director of the Great Northern Railway (in which capacity he attended the International Railway Congress at Washington in 1906), and of the Indo-European Telegraph Company. He resided for some years at Patcham, near Brighton, and was a regular follower of the South Down hunt. Later on he moved to London, and died there 20 November 1919.

He married in 1863 Lucy (died 1896), daughter of Andreas Frerichs, of Thirlestane Hall, Cheltenham, and widow of Count Stenbock, of Kolk, Estonia, by whom he had a family of three sons and three daughters. He had four sisters, Mrs. Francis Douglas Grey, Mrs. James Gleig, Mrs. Vernon Lushington, and Mrs. William Latham.

[Personal knowledge. Portrait, *Royal Academy Pictures*, 1904.] G. H. M.

MUNRO, HECTOR HUGH (1870–1916), writer of fiction, was born 18 December 1870 in Akyab, Burma, where his father, Colonel Munro, of the Bengal Staff Corps, inspector-general of police in Burma, was then stationed. He came of Highland stock, a fact of which he was always proud. Owing to the death of his mother and to his father's absence abroad, he was brought up during childhood, with his elder brother and sister, by a grandmother and two aunts, in the village of Pilton, near Barnstaple, North Devon. It seems probable that the effect of their stern and unsympathetic methods upon Munro's highly individual and sensitive nature is responsible for the strong dislike, discernible in so much of his writing, of anything that smacks of the conventional and the self-righteous, and, perhaps, for the queer heartlessness which accompanies the humour of many of his best stories. Munro was educated at a private school at Exmouth and at Bedford grammar school. After some travel on the Continent he left England in 1893 for Burma, where he had obtained a post in the police; but in fifteen months he resigned owing to ill-health. After recuperating in Devonshire, Munro moved to London, having decided to earn his living by his pen. He began as a political satirist for the *Westminster Gazette*, to which he was introduced by (Sir) Francis Carruthers Gould. His political sketches were afterwards published as *The Westminster Alice* (illustrated by Gould). The *Not So Stories* (1902) were in the same satirical vein and were also anonymous. In 1900 he published *The Rise of the Russian Empire*, a history of Russia to the time of Peter the Great. In 1902 he went to the Balkans, in 1904 to Warsaw, and thence to St. Petersburg, as correspondent for the *Morning Post*. In 1906 he was in Paris, still writing for the *Morning Post*, and in 1908 he returned to London, where he wrote political and other sketches for a number of different papers.

Meanwhile, Munro had in 1904 published *Reginald*, a collection of short stories in which he first strikes the characteristically unconventional note which was to make his reputation. In this, and in *Reginald in Russia* (1910), *The Chronicles of Clovis* (1911), and *Beasts and Super-Beasts* (1914), which are all collections of short stories, and in *The Unbearable Bassington* (1912), which is a novel, the characteristic note remains the same. The influence of Oscar Wilde and of the eighteen-nineties is apparent, but in so far as it made for paradox and impatience of conventional standards it was probably only reinforcing tendencies already present in Munro, and he was too highly individual to owe much to other writers. The witty and irrepressible non-moral young man who figures so prominently, under different names, in Munro's writings, though he is frequently met with in the fiction of the 'nineties and has certain affinities with Wilde's Dorian Gray, has nowhere been more cleverly presented. Munro's stories are seldom perfect examples of construction, and their often fantastic settings are not drawn closely from life; but their elvish humour, their biting and eccentric wit give them an individuality which is unforgettable, and in the art of the unexpected phrase Munro was a past master. Some of the most individual features of his work, the love of practical joking, the taste for queer and exotic animals, the lack of sympathy with mankind in general, have been ascribed, perhaps rightly, to the fact that in a sense Munro was always a boy. These books were published under the pseudonym of 'Saki', the name of the cup-bearer in the Rubaiyât of Omar Khayyâm.

Soon after the outbreak of the European War in 1914 Munro enlisted, and in November 1915 he went to the front in France. He proved a fine soldier, refusing to take a commission. He was killed near Beaumont Hamel 14 November 1916.

Besides the books already mentioned, Munro wrote *When William Came* (1913), an imaginary picture of English life after a successful invasion by the Germans. *The Toys of Peace* (1919) and *The Square Egg* (1924) were published posthumously; but they were below the standard of his earlier work. The second of these volumes contains a three-act play with characteristically witty dialogue; it also includes a biography of Munro by his sister, Miss E. M. Munro.

[Prefatory notes to the Collected Edition of Munro's Works; biography by Miss E. M. Munro in *The Square Egg*; private information.] G. E.

MURRAY, Sir JAMES AUGUSTUS HENRY (1837–1915), lexicographer, the eldest son of Thomas Murray, clothier, of Hawick, Roxburghshire, by his wife, Mary, fifth daughter of Charles Scott, linen manufacturer, of Hawick, was born at Denholm, near Hawick, 7 February 1837. His baptismal name was James. He was educated at Cavers school, the parish school of his native village, and then at Minto school, where he learned Latin, French, and Greek. At an early age his studious bent singled him out from his fellows. 'James Murray', they said, 'will never make a farmer; he has always a book in his pocket.' At the age of seventeen he became assistant master at Hawick grammar school and at the age of twenty head master of the Subscription Academy in the same town. This period of his life was marked by great activity in the acquirement of languages, in the pursuit of various branches of natural science, and in the study of local antiquities; to his interest in these subjects many articles in the *Proceedings* of the Hawick Archaeological Society bear witness. During the tenure of the head mastership he married, in 1862, Maggie Isabella Sarah Scott, of Belfast. Owing to the state of his wife's health, which required a change of climate, he migrated south and took a situation in the London office of the Chartered Bank of India. In 1864 his wife died after the death of their child, and in 1867 he married Ada Agnes, eldest daughter of George Ruthven, of Kendal, by whom he had six sons and five daughters. Three years later, after the reopening of Mill Hill School under Richard Francis Weymouth [q.v.], he joined the staff as a master. He graduated B.A. of London University in 1873. He remained at Mill Hill School until 1885, when he removed to Oxford in order to devote himself exclusively to the editing of the *New English Dictionary on Historical Principles*, of which he had been appointed editor in 1879 and which he had hitherto carried on in conjunction with his teaching.

Murray's appointment as editor was the outcome of proposals, editorial plans, and negotiations which took their first rise from the suggestion made in 1857 by Richard Chenevix Trench [q.v.], afterwards archbishop of Dublin, that the London Philological Society should prepare a supplement to existing dictionaries of the English language. This suggestion had resulted in the adoption of a scheme for the compilation of a comprehensive historical dictionary. In 1861, at the very time that Murray, in consequence of his philological interests and of his residence in and near London, became associated with the Society and its leaders —Alexander John Ellis, Frederick James Furnivall, Richard Morris, Walter William Skeat, Henry Sweet—the enterprise was threatened with extinction through the death of the editor designate, Herbert Coleridge [q.v.]. That scholar had devoted himself to collecting and arranging the material which voluntary workers enlisted by the Society had amassed. It was largely due to Murray's activity that the project was revived. Having been approached by publishers who desired to bring out a rival to Webster's dictionary, he had prepared a specimen. This was shown to members of the Philological Society and received with approval; but no publisher could be induced to undertake the risk involved in Murray's scheme, until in 1878 contact was established with the delegates of the Clarendon Press at Oxford. In March 1879 an agreement was entered into by which Murray, with the help of a staff, undertook to produce a dictionary of the English language extending to 6,000–7,000 pages. It had been agreed in previous discussion that the work should be completed in ten years. Thereafter Murray's philological interests were focussed on this great task; and in the 'Scriptorium' built at Mill Hill—which served as a model for the corrugated-iron building erected later in his garden at Sunnyside, Banbury Road, Oxford—he, with a few assistants, began to erect the fabric of the greatest lexicographical achievement of the present age.

His absorption in the *Dictionary* imposed the most stringent limits upon Murray's time and opportunities for independent work, which virtually came to an end with his article on the English language written for the *Encyclopaedia Britannica* in 1878. The quality of this piece of work and of his earlier original contributions to philological learning is a sure indication of the possibilities that were within Murray's reach, had his genius been left free to develop untrammelled by the necessity of supplying the printers with a regular quota of *Dictionary* copy. The editions of three Scottish texts, brought out between 1871 and 1875, Sir David Lyndesay's *Works*, part v, *The Complaynte of Scotlande*, and *The Romance and Prophecies of Thomas of Erceldoune*, are excellent examples of his talent in this kind; while his *Dialect of the Southern Counties of Scotland* (1873) is remarkable not only for the accuracy of its information and for its author's grasp of the technicalities of phonetic science (then still in its infancy), but also for the rigour of its philological method, the principles of which were at that time appreciated by but few scholars in this country; it remains to this day in many respects a pattern of method for investigations in similar fields. Among Murray's many contributions to the *Athenæum* during these years was a review of Skeat's edition of the Anglo-Saxon gospels, in which he put forward his ingenious discovery of the relations between the glosses of the Lindisfarne and Rushworth MSS.

It is no wonder that Murray looked back upon his fifteen years at Mill Hill as his golden age, for on his removal to Oxford in 1885 began the intense pressure which was to be maintained to the end of his life, taxing to the full the resources of his strong frame and constitution. To his heavy editorial task was added the burden of a perpetual struggle against time, since at an early stage it was discovered that a serious miscalculation had been made of the years necessary for the completion of the work. Henceforward the hard life of the *Dictionary*—long working hours and short holidays—left him scant opportunity for the leisurely reading in which a scholar delights, and indeed barely permitted him to keep abreast of philological discovery in the many fields which he was bound to explore. In the early days of the work, moreover, financial difficulties were superadded. It appears that during the Mill Hill period Murray had disbursed considerable sums in providing books and other materials, and in 1885 he took the London Philological Society into his confidence with regard to this. The outcome was the raising of a special fund indemnifying Murray liberally for his expenditure. There were compensations, however, in the course of the succeeding years, not only in the ever-increasing recognition of his eminence as a lexicographer but also in the friendship and support of such Oxford men as Jowett, Robinson Ellis, and Ingram Bywater, as well as in the happiness of his home life, which was enhanced by the academic and other successes of the members of his large family. He had the satisfaction of receiving honorary degrees from nine universities, Cambridge and Oxford being added to the list in 1913 and 1914; he was elected member, *honoris causa*, of several learned societies, and was three times president of the London Philological Society; he was Romanes lecturer at Oxford in 1900, and an original fellow of the British Academy. He was knighted in 1908.

At the 'Dictionary dinner' held in Queen's College, Oxford, in 1897, Henry Bradley declared that it would have been 'a national calamity' if any other than Murray had been chosen to edit the *Oxford Dictionary*. It was his brain that conceived the plan of the work and settled its scope, the lines of which are laid down in the masterly preface of the first volume. The once current name 'Murray' as a title for the whole work is therefore justified in so far as he was its chief creator, although his editorial responsibility actually covers only one half of it (A–D, H–K, O, P, T). The first *Dictionary* copy was sent to the printers 19 April 1882, and the first section of 352 pages, comprising *A–Ant*, was published 1 February 1884. This, notwithstanding some immaturities inevitable in a piece of pioneer work on so grand a scale, marked an immense advance upon all previous lexicography, and this superiority was maintained to the full in the sections which followed. Murray's colleagues and successors owed much to the example of method, organization, and executive power which he set before them. The characteristic excellences of his work were indeed supplemented by equally characteristic merits of another kind in those who subsequently became his fellow-editors; but the framework designed by him was proved, as the *Dictionary* progressed, to be sufficient to stand the test of the expansion of philological knowledge and of the evolution of lexicographical experience. It is this achievement that gives Murray enduring rank among the great dictionary-makers.

Like the majority of philologists of his generation, Murray was in early years an advocate of English spelling reform, and even imposed an unfortunate example upon the *Dictionary* itself in the spelling *ax* for *axe*; but in later life his views on this subject were modified, and he withdrew from active support of the movement. He was a lifelong advocate of total abstinence and, following the tradition of his ancestors, who belonged to the Independent body in Scotland, he staunchly adhered to the principles of Congregationalism; he was deacon for fifteen years of the George Street Congregational chapel in Oxford. As a liberal in politics he took his place in the local activities of his party. He was a keen gardener and stamp-collector, and he bicycled regularly when past his seventieth year. His tall figure, accentuated by an erect and rigid bearing and an ample beard whitened at an early age, betokened endurance and aggressive perseverance, and rendered him conspicuous in any surroundings. With a formal exterior corresponded a formality of manner which rarely permitted him to mention a personal name without its appropriate prefix. Those, however, who knew him best were aware of his capacity for quiet humour and the amenities of friendly intercourse. He did not stint his appreciation of conscientious work, but could not tolerate the irregular or fitful worker, and expected from his staff a devotion equal to that which he exacted from himself.

Murray's long-cherished hope that he would live to finish the *Dictionary* was not fulfilled. His death was immediately preceded by twelve months' illness, which began with an attack of pleurisy against which he fought desperately, rallying sufficiently to carry on his work, though in circumstances of great physical distress. He died at Oxford 26 July 1915, and was buried in Wolvercote cemetery, near Oxford. There is a portrait, by an old pupil, at Mill Hill School, and another in the possession of his family.

[Memoir by Henry Bradley in *Proceedings* of the British Academy, vol. viii, 1917–1918; private information; personal knowledge.]

C. T. O.

MURRAY, Sir JAMES WOLFE (1853–1919), lieutenant-general, the eldest son of James Wolfe Murray, of Cringletie, Peeblesshire, by his first wife, Elizabeth Charlotte Whyte-Melville, was born 13 March 1853. His grandfather was a godson of, and named after, General James Wolfe. Sent first to Glenalmond, he proceeded to Harrow in 1867, where he remained for two years in the house of the Rev. T. H. Steel. Murray entered Woolwich shortly afterwards, and on passing out was gazetted lieutenant in the Royal Artillery on 12 September 1872. In 1881 he was promoted captain, and after graduating at the Staff College began a period of staff and extra-regimental service which continued with but little interruption for over thirty years. His first appointment was as deputy assistant adjutant and quartermaster-general of the North British district in January 1884. He was transferred eight months later to the intelligence branch at the War Office, where he remained for three years. A spell of regimental duty followed, during which he received his majority, and appreciation of his work at the War Office was shown by his appointment for a further spell of two years—from April 1892 to January 1894—for special employment at Whitehall. Thence he proceeded direct to Aldershot, where he held the important post of deputy assistant adjutant-general from the beginning of 1894 to 1897. The tenure of this appointment was interrupted by special service in the Ashanti expedition of 1895, when he was employed upon the lines of communication; for this service he received the Ashanti star and a brevet lieutenant-colonelcy. Murray was offered the post of assistant adjutant-general in India early in 1898, and he was serving at army head-quarters in India as assistant quartermaster-general when the South African War broke out.

By this time Murray had won for himself a high reputation for brilliant intelligence and administrative work, and he was accordingly selected at the outbreak of hostilities for service on the lines of communication in Natal. The value of the work which he then performed was acknowledged by four mentions in dispatches, promotion to colonel, and a K.C.B. He returned to India to become a brigade commander for a short time, and then in May 1903 he was raised to the high office of quartermaster-general in India. He was already a major-general at what was then the extraordinarily early age of fifty. Early in 1904 he became master-general of the ordnance and fourth military member of the Army Council, a position which he held for three years, leaving it to assume command of the ninth (Secunderabad) division in India, during which time he became lieutenant-general (1909). This post he held until 1911, and in 1913 and 1914 he was general-officer-commanding in Scotland and in South Africa respectively.

At the outbreak of the European War, when the War Office was in a state of confusion owing to the hurried departure of the higher military officers to the front, the general staff became merely the executive agent of the highly centralized regime directed by Lord Kitchener. It was in these circumstances that Lieutenant-General Murray was appointed chief of the Imperial General Staff. In this most difficult position at that most difficult hour Wolfe Murray was at a disadvantage. His long administrative training, and even his marvellous industry, tended to make him a master of detail at the expense of breadth of view, and his patience, kindliness, and tolerance of the opinions of others caused him to be unduly diffident in his dealings both with Lord Kitchener and with the politicians. He left the War Office in September 1915, and in that year proceeded on a special mission to Russia—a task much more to his liking, for he was an expert in Russian affairs. For a year from 1916 he was general-officer-commanding in chief, Eastern command, and on 9 April 1917 was appointed colonel-commandant of the Royal Artillery. On 5 May 1918 he retired, and on 17 October 1919 he died suddenly of heart failure at Cringletie. By his death the army lost an officer of untiring industry and shrewd judgement; and one who had the happy gift of being able to inspire his subordinates with intense and affectionate loyalty.

Murray was twice married: first, in 1875 to Arabella (died 1909), daughter of W. Bray, by whom he had two sons and three daughters; secondly, in 1913 to Fanny, daughter of James Scott Robson, and widow of Sir Donald H. Macfarlane.

[Official records; private information.]

F. E. W.

MURRAY, Sir JOHN (1841–1914), marine naturalist and oceanographer, born at Cobourg, Ontario, 3 March 1841, was the second son of Robert Murray, an accountant who had left Scotland in 1834 and settled in Upper Canada, by his wife, Elizabeth Macfarlane. John was for a time at the public school of London, Ontario, and later at Victoria College, Cobourg. At the age of seventeen he left Canada and came to Scotland to complete his education under the care of his maternal grandfather, John Macfarlane, of Coney Hill, Stirlingshire. Murray attended the high school at Stirling and afterwards studied in the university of Edinburgh, on the roll of which his name appears for the years 1864–1865 and 1868–1872. He did not pursue any regular course but attended classes in those subjects which appealed to him. He never took examinations and did not graduate. He found particularly congenial conditions in the natural philosophy laboratory, and there during at least three years he spent much time under the direction of Peter Guthrie Tait [q.v.] on experimental work, e. g. on thermal conductivity and on the construction of an electrical deep-sea thermometer. In 1868 Murray shipped as surgeon on the whaler *Jan Mayen*. He left Peterhead in February and during his seven months' voyage in northern seas reached a latitude of 81° N., explored part of Spitzbergen, and landed on Jan Mayen Island. He brought back a collection of marine organisms and also records of observations on currents, on the temperature of the air and of the sea, and on the distribution of sea ice. He added to his experience by marine work off the west coast of Scotland during the next two years.

1871 and 1872 were years of exceptional scientific activity in Edinburgh owing to the organization of the equipment for the *Challenger* expedition. The government had resolved to send this ship round the world for the purpose of scientific exploration of the ocean, and (Sir) Charles Wyville Thomson [q.v.], professor of natural history in the university of Edinburgh, was appointed director of the scientific staff. Murray took a considerable share in the preparation of the scientific apparatus; and when a vacancy on the staff unexpectedly arose he was appointed, almost at the last moment, one of the naturalists, and this led to the great work of his life. During the voyage—which lasted nearly three and a half years—the physical, chemical, geological, and biological conditions of the great ocean basins were investigated, special attention being given to the greater depths, about which little was then known. Murray devoted himself particularly to the observation of the surface organisms, especially the Foraminifera and Radiolaria, and to the study of the samples of the deposits brought up from the ocean floor, and he demonstrated the part played by the surface organisms in forming certain of the deep-sea deposits. He also took much interest in the instruments used in obtaining samples of the sea bottom, and devised improved apparatus for sounding and for registering the temperature at great depths. Thomson put Murray in charge of the collections—unrivalled in their range and importance—made during the expedition. Shortly after the return, the '*Challenger* Office' was opened at 32 Queen Street, Edinburgh, for dealing with the collections, and for nearly twenty years this was the place to which marine biologists from all over the world came to inspect the new organisms and to discuss the results gathered by the expedition. Murray was appointed chief assistant in the office and, owing to the failing health of Sir Wyville Thomson, became mainly responsible for organizing the working out of the collections. In 1882, after Thomson's death, Murray became director of the office and editor of the *Report on the Scientific Results of the Voyage of H.M.S. Challenger* (1880–1895). This *Report*, in fifty royal quarto volumes, was the work of experts of many lands, who at the conclusion of their labours expressed their sense of the great services rendered by Murray, and there is no doubt that it was owing to the forcefulness of his character that this remarkable series of memoirs was completed within twenty years of the return of the expedition. During the later years of this period Murray's task was made difficult by an unsympathetic Treasury, and he spent a large amount of his own money in completing the publication.

For several of these years Murray was engaged, with his friend, Professor A. F. Renard, of Ghent, on the study of the marine deposits, and in 1891 appeared their report on *Deep Sea Deposits*, still the standard work of reference, notable alike for its detail and its clear generalizations. As a consequence of this work, samples of deposits obtained by surveying ships and by various expeditions were sent to Murray, and a unique collection was thus brought together. Another result of Murray's observations during the expedition was his well-known paper *On the Structure and Origin of Coral Reefs and Islands* (*Proceedings* of the Royal Society of Edinburgh, vol. x, 1880), in which he dissented from Darwin's view that the form of atolls was due to subsidence of the land forming the foundation of the reef. Murray put forward the view that submarine elevations were built upwards by deposition on their summits of the skeletons of pelagic organisms and other sediments, and that when they reached a height favourable for the growth of any coral polyps which became established upon them, coral plantations were formed. He held that as these approached the surface of the sea they would assume the atoll form owing to the more abundant supply of food and more vigorous growth on the outer margin, and to the removal of dead coral from the interior portion by currents and by solution. Murray's work was stimulating, and, although his explanation of the formation of atoll lagoons is not generally accepted by recent authorities, his conclusions on other points, e. g. the importance of submarine planation, have proved to be sound. Murray was joint author of the *Narrative of the Cruise of H.M.S. Challenger* (1885), and he drew up the last two volumes of the *Report* (1895), which form an impressive summary of the results of the expedition.

In 1880 and 1882 Murray engaged, with Captain T. H. Tizard, in exploring the Faroe Channel in the government surveying ships *Knight Errant* and *Triton*. He established small marine laboratories at Granton and at Millport, and the latter has developed into the Scottish Marine Biological Association. Murray's steam yacht, the *Medusa*, built and equipped for marine biological work, enabled him with the help of several younger colleagues to bring together during the years 1884–1892 a large number of records, published in 1918 by his former secretary, J. Chumley, under the title *The Fauna of the Clyde Sea Area*.

As soon as the *Challenger* work was out of his hands, Murray undertook a bathymetrical survey of the fresh-water lochs of Scotland. Supported by the councils of the Royal Societies of London and of Edinburgh, he had urged the government to undertake this survey, but without avail. In 1897 with his capable young collaborator, Frederick Pullar, he began the work, and several important papers on the results had appeared, when in 1901 Pullar was drowned while attempting to save the lives of others. His father—Laurence Pullar, Murray's oldest friend—determined that the survey should be continued, and provided funds for a staff of assistants; they began work in 1902 and carried on the investigations until 1909. Some 60,000 soundings were made in 562 lochs, and the records of these and of other scientific results, forming an admirable survey, were published in six volumes by Murray and Pullar in 1910.

When the *Challenger* office was closed (May 1895), Murray bought a house near his residence to serve as a library and laboratory. Here were arranged the series of oceanic deposits, until in 1921, with the greater part of his library, they were removed to the British Museum (Natural History); here also were the headquarters of the Lake Survey. To this centre came many investigators whom Murray inspired and assisted out of the fullness of his experience.

As the result of his detection of phosphate of lime in rock specimens brought in 1887 from Christmas Island, in the Indian Ocean, Murray urged the annexation of the island, which took place the next year. In 1891 Murray and G. Clunies Ross, of the Cocos Islands, obtained a lease of Christmas Island, and in 1897 they formed a small company to develop its valuable resources. Murray also paid the expenses of two scientific expeditions to the island in 1897–1898 and in 1908, as the result of which Dr. C. W. Andrews, of the British Museum (Natural History), brought home extensive collections. *A Monograph of Christmas Island* (1900), which embodies the results of the first expedition, is important as forming a record of the indigenous fauna and flora of an isolated tropical island before these had become affected by the animals and plants introduced by man. Murray himself made two exploring visits (1900, 1908) to the island. He used to say that the Treasury had received from the island in the form of rents, royalties, and taxes a sum which exceeded the cost of the *Challenger* expedition and the publication of its results.

In 1909 Murray visited Copenhagen and urged upon the international council for the exploration of the sea the need for systematic observations in the north Atlantic. Later he made an offer to defray all other expenses of a four months' expedition on condition that the Norwegian government lent the *Michael Sars* and her scientific staff for the purpose. The offer was accepted, and in April 1910 this vessel of 226 tons left Plymouth with Murray on board and with Dr. Johan Hjort as leader of the staff. The immediate results of this expedition—including important physical and biological observations at all depths in the tracts traversed—were published in *The Depths of the Sea* by Murray and Hjort in 1912. A description of 1,426 samples of deposits from the floor of the Atlantic Ocean, gathered during thirty-five cruising expeditions between 1857 and 1911, was being prepared under Murray's supervision at the time of his death. This work was completed by J. Chumley, who added a discussion of the results, and the monograph was published (1924) in the *Transactions* of the Royal Society of Edinburgh.

Murray received honorary degrees from several universities, was elected F.R.S. in 1896, and created K.C.B. in 1898. He acted for nearly two years (1896–1898) as scientific member of the Scottish Fishery Board, and filled various offices in the scientific societies of Edinburgh. His recreations were yachting—during which he carried on soundings, dredging, and other observations—golf, and motoring. He was killed in a motor accident at Kirkliston, near Edinburgh, 16 March 1914.

Murray married in 1889 Isabel, only daughter of Thomas Henderson, shipowner, of Glasgow; there were two sons and three daughters of the marriage.

Edward Forbes [q.v.] was the pioneer of shallow-water dredging during the earlier half of the nineteenth century; the exploration of the deep sea we owe largely to Wyville Thomson and Murray. Murray has left an enduring mark on the science of oceanography which he brought practically to its present position and outlook. He was an original, suggestive, broad-minded thinker and did not hesitate to attack established views if they did not coincide with his conclusions. A strong and forceful personality, he was confident of his own opinion and somewhat brusque, occasionally domineering, in manner, but full of good humour, and most helpful and friendly to his assistants and to other investigators who sought his aid.

Portraits of Murray were painted by Sir Daniel Macnee in 1876 and by Sir George Reid in 1912.

[*Proceedings* of the Royal Society of Edinburgh, vol. xxxv, 1915 (with list of publications); *Proceedings* of the Royal Society of London, vol. lxxxix, B, 1915–1916; personal knowledge.] J. H. A.

MYERS, ERNEST JAMES (1844–1921), poet and translator, was born at Keswick 13 October 1844, the second son of the Rev. Frederic Myers [q.v.], perpetual curate of St. John's, Keswick, and younger brother of Frederic William Henry Myers [q.v.]. His mother was Susan Harriet, youngest daughter of John Marshall, of Hallsteads, on Ullswater; and, spending there his summer holidays during many years, Myers retained throughout his life an ardent love of the fell-country. From Cheltenham, where he was head of the school, he went in 1863 as an exhibitioner to Balliol College, Oxford. He enjoyed college life to the full, rowed in the college eight, played rackets and tennis, gained a first class in classical moderations (1865) and the Gaisford prize for Greek verse (1865), but narrowly missed the Hertford scholarship and a first class in *literae humaniores*. In 1868 he was elected fellow of Wadham College, where he remained for three years as a lecturer; and here also he wrote and published his first poem, *The Puritans* (1869), a short drama intentionally reminiscent of the *Persae* of Aeschylus.

From 1871 to 1891 Myers lived in London, where he was called to the bar (1874) but never practised. During these years he published his prose translations of Pindar's *Odes* (1874) and of the last eight books of the *Iliad* (with Andrew Lang and Walter Leaf, 1882); some essays in magazines, and one, on Aeschylus, in the collection entitled *Hellenica*, edited by Evelyn Abbott (1880); an introduction to his selection of prose passages by Milton ('Parchment series', 1884); a short biography of Viscount Althorp (1890), whose services in connexion with the Reform Act of 1832 he thought to be insufficiently recognized; and three volumes of verse, *Poems* (1877), *The Defence of Rome* (1880), and *The Judgement of Prometheus* (1886), the last two containing also 'other poems'.

Myers's activities, however, during his life in London were not confined to literature. From 1876 for nearly six years he acted as secretary to the London Society for the Extension of University Teaching. He was on the council of the Hellenic Society from its foundation in 1879. Later, after abandoning the idea of parliamentary life, he worked for the Charity Organization Society, serving on its central administrative committee until he left London.

In 1883 Myers had married Nora Margaret, daughter of the Rev. Samuel Lodge, rector of Scrivelsby, Lincolnshire; they had two sons and three daughters. In 1891 the family moved to a house at Chislehurst on the edge of Paul's Cray Common [see *A Common* in *Gathered Poems*]. Here Myers remained for the rest of his life, abandoning the habit of continental travel to which some of his best poems bear witness, but paying a weekly visit to London in order to see friends and to attend the council meetings of the Society for the Protection of Women and Children. Most of the verse composed in these years is included in *Gathered Poems* (1904), a collection containing also what he thought best in the volumes previously published. He died at Fontridge, Etchingham, Sussex, 25 November 1921. He was survived by his wife, one son, and two daughters; one daughter had died in infancy, and his elder son was killed while serving in France in 1918.

The most obvious characteristic of Myers's writings is his enthusiasm for Greece. His essay on Aeschylus gained much more attention than his biography of Lord Althorp. The excellence in scholarship, diction, and rhythm of his prose translations of Homer and Pindar is generally recognized. The volume of *Gathered Poems* opens with a group entitled *Hellenica*; and the next group, *Loca Carmine Digna*, celebrates first Arcadia, Ithome, and a tomb in Athens. In a sonnet addressed to Pindar he describes Hellas as the 'first fruit and best of all the western world', and declares that 'Whate'er we hold of beauty, half is hers'. The poems on Greek subjects illustrate also a second obvious trait, his enthusiasm for the heroic. The 'crown of Being,' he writes, 'fairer far than stream, or sky, or star,' is a 'heroic soul' [*Gathered Poems*, p. 124]. And this enthusiasm is not less marked in the poems which celebrate men of later times, for instance, King Alfred, Milton [see the drama so entitled and *Gathered Poems*, p. 120], Mazzini and Garibaldi [see *The Defence of Rome*], and General Gordon.

[Private information; personal knowledge.]

A. C. B.

NARES, Sir GEORGE STRONG (1831–1915), admiral and Arctic explorer, was born 24 April 1831 at Aberdeen, the son of Commander William Henry Nares, R.N., of Aberdeen, and great-grandson of the judge, Sir George Nares [q.v.]. His mother was Elizabeth Gould, daughter of John Dodd, of Redbourn, Hertfordshire. He entered the navy in 1845 from the Royal Naval College, New Cross, and after serving some years in the Pacific was appointed mate in H.M.S. *Resolute*, one of the five vessels employed by Sir Edward Belcher [q.v.] in his expedition of 1852 in search of Sir John Franklin [q.v.]. From winter quarters at Dealy Island, to the south of Melville Island, Nares took part in several sledge journeys which gave him valuable experience in Arctic travel. Returning to England in 1854 he was promoted lieutenant, served for two years in the Mediterranean, and took part in the Crimean War. After several years' work in training-ships for naval cadets, including the *Illustrious*, *Britannia*, and *Boscawen*, he was posted to the Australia station, having been promoted commander in 1862. In 1867 he commissioned the *Newport* for hydrographical work in the Mediterranean, which included a survey of the Gulf of Suez. In the *Shearwater* he did similar work, including oceanographical researches in the Gibraltar current and a survey from Suez to Koseir.

Nares's experience earned him the post of captain of H.M.S. *Challenger*, a wooden corvette of 2,306 tons, which was dispatched by the government in December 1872 on a voyage of exploration of the Southern oceans. Nearly a year was spent by the expedition in the Atlantic, which was crossed several times, and in October 1873 Cape Town was reached. After leaving Simon's Bay in December, the *Challenger* visited the little-known islands of Marion, Kerguelen, and Heard, before making a short visit to the Antarctic regions. The vessel was not built for ice navigation and no attempt was made to push far south; it was, however, the first steamship to cross the Antarctic Circle (66°40′S., 78°22′E.). The chief geographical result of the southern venture was the dredging of glaciated fragments of continental rocks and deep-sea muds; this furnished convincing evidence of the existence of a continent in the far south. In November 1874 the *Challenger* reached Hong Kong, and Nares was recalled to England in order to lead a government Arctic expedition in the vessels *Alert* and *Discovery*, the chief aim of which was to reach the Pole. Reports of the American expeditions of L. L. Hayes, 1860–1861, and C. F. Hall, 1870–1873, had led to the belief in an open polar sea and land extending far to the north, on the west of Robeson channel. Both these theories proved to be wrong, but, at the time, they indicated the Smith Sound route as the best line of advance to the Pole. The vessels sailed on 29 May 1875 and reached winter quarters on the coast of Grant Land, the *Discovery* in latitude 81° 44′ N., and the *Alert*, with Nares, in latitude 82° 27′ N. In the following spring (Sir) Albert Hastings Markham [q.v.] in the *Alert* made the northern record, latitude 83° 20′ 26″ N., longitude 64° W., after terrible difficulties over very rough pack-ice. Lieutenant Pelham Aldrich of the *Alert* discovered and rounded Cape Columbia, the most northerly point of Grant Land, and reached Cape Alfred Ernest, while to the west Lieutenant Lewis A. Beaumont of the *Discovery* followed the coast of Greenland to Sherard Osborn fjord. Deciding that the route to the Pole was impracticable, Nares returned in 1876 and his ships reached Portsmouth in October. The discoveries made by this expedition were valuable, but were won at the cost of life and with much hardship, since the day had not yet come when scurvy was understood and could be avoided.

Nares, who had been elected a fellow of the Royal Society in 1875, was created K.C.B. in 1876, and received the founder's medal of the Royal Geographical Society in 1877 and a gold medal from the Geographical Society of Paris in 1879. In 1878 he was again in command of the *Alert* during the survey of the Magellan Straits. From 1879 to 1896 he was employed in the harbour department of the Board of Trade, having retired from active service in 1886. From 1896 to 1910 he was a conservator of the river Mersey. He was promoted rear-admiral in 1887 and vice-admiral in 1892.

Nares married in 1858 Mary (died 1905), daughter of William Grant, of Portsmouth, and had issue three sons and four daughters. He died at Surbiton on 15 January 1915. His name is commemorated in Nares harbour in the Admiralty Islands, the Nares Deep in the North Atlantic, Nares Land in Northern Greenland, Cape Nares in Grant Land, and Mount Nares in South Victoria Land.

[*The Times*, 16 January 1915 ; *Geographical Journal*, March 1915 ; *H.M.S. Challenger, Reports of Capt. G. S. Nares*, Nos. 1–3, 1873–1874; G. S. Nares, *A Voyage to the Polar Sea*, 1877 ; *Report* of the Arctic Expedition of 1875–1876, 1877 ; private information.] R. N. R. B.

NETTLESHIP, EDWARD (1845–1913), ophthalmic surgeon, was born at Kettering 3 March 1845, the fourth son of Henry John Nettleship, solicitor, of Kettering, by his wife, Isabella Ann, daughter of the Rev. James Hogg, vicar of Geddington, near Kettering. Of their six sons four became distinguished in their professions ; Henry [q.v.], John Trivett [q.v.], Edward, and Richard Lewis [q.v.]. Edward received his early education at Kettering grammar school. His boyish enthusiasm for natural history and his love of outdoor pursuits led to the decision that he should become a farmer. On leaving school he devoted several years to the study of agriculture and veterinary science. In 1867 he qualified as member of the Royal College of Veterinary Surgeons, and shortly afterwards was appointed professor of veterinary surgery at the Agricultural College, Cirencester. In 1868 he obtained the membership, and in 1870 the fellowship of the Royal College of Surgeons of England.

About the year 1867 Nettleship entered as a student at Moorfields Eye Hospital and began the study of ophthalmology, the branch of medicine in which he afterwards became an acknowledged leader. In 1871 he was appointed curator of the hospital museum and library and soon afterwards he published in the Ophthalmic Hospital *Reports* the first of a long series of papers, clinical and pathological, on ophthalmic subjects. In 1873, at the request of the Local Government Board, he inspected the metropolitan poor-law schools in reference to the prevalence of ophthalmia. His report led to some much-needed reforms in the care of pauper children.

During his professional career Nettleship held a number of public appointments. The most important were those of ophthalmic surgeon to St. Thomas's Hospital and surgeon to the Royal London Ophthalmic Hospital. At these schools his reputation as a clinical investigator, surgeon, and teacher became firmly and widely established. In addition to his hospital duties he had a large private practice, yet he found time and opportunity for the preparation of many papers of lasting value, which he read before medical societies. He was one of the founders, in 1880, of the Ophthalmological Society of the United Kingdom, of which he became the first surgical secretary and, in 1895, president.

In 1902 Nettleship retired from practice and devoted the remainder of his life to research. For many years he had been interested in the study of heredity in disease, especially in relation to disorders of the eye and vision. He now accomplished a remarkable amount of excellent work, his pedigrees of disease being characterized by a high degree of orderly observation and meticulous accuracy. The importance of his researches on heredity were recognized by his election to the fellowship of the Royal Society in 1912, and in 1922 by the republication, delayed by the War, of much of his work in a memorial volume of the *Treasury of Human Inheritance* (Eugenics Laboratory Memoirs XXI, *Anomalies and Diseases of the Eye*, 1922).

In 1902 the Nettleship medal 'for the encouragement of scientific ophthalmic work' was founded by Nettleship's colleagues and former students, as a tribute to his character and to his outstanding qualities as a scientific exponent of ophthalmology. In 1909 the medal was awarded to Nettleship himself in recognition of his researches on heredity in diseases of the eye.

Nettleship died at Hindhead, Surrey, 30 October 1913. He had married in 1869 Elizabeth Endacott, daughter of Richard Whiteway, gentleman farmer, of Compton, Devon. There were no children of the marriage.

[Biographical memoir in the *Treasury of Human Inheritance*, 1922; personal knowledge.] J. B. L.

NICHOLSON, EDWARD WILLIAMS BYRON (1849–1912), scholar and librarian, the only son of Edward Nicholson, R.N., by his wife, Emily Hamilton Wall, was born 16 March 1849 at St. Helier, Jersey. He was educated at Llanrwst grammar school, at Liverpool College, and at Tonbridge School, from which he went as a classical scholar to Trinity College, Oxford, in 1867. He gained a first class in classical moderations (1869), a third class in law and history (1871), the Gaisford prize for Greek verse (1871), and the Hall-Houghton Junior Greek Testament prize (1872). After taking his degree Nicholson was for a short time a schoolmaster, but he gave up this work in 1873 when he was appointed librarian of the London Institution, a post which he held till 1882. In 1877 he was one of the founders of the first European conference of librarians, of which he acted as joint-secretary with Henry Richard Tedder; and in the same year he helped to organize the Library Association, of which also he was joint-secretary (1877–1878). He always retained a fatherly interest in the activities of the Association. When Henry Octavius Coxe [q.v.], Bodley's librarian, died in 1881, it was evident that the great Oxford library had reached a point in its development at which modern methods and requirements must be considered. A young man of energy and experience was needed, and Nicholson, then in his thirty-fourth year, possessed both. He was appointed (1882) partly through the influence of Benjamin Jowett, shortly to be vice-chancellor, and immediately set about a thorough reorganization of the library. He introduced a detailed scheme of shelf-classification and arrangement, reformed the method of cataloguing and provided an improved code of rules for cataloguers, organized a subject catalogue, increased the staff, and added in many smaller ways to the usefulness of the collections. At the same time he worked hard to improve the financial position of the library and to promote far-reaching schemes for its extension, including the provision of an underground storage room which was only completed after his death. The need of these may be judged from the fact that the contents of the library more than doubled in amount during Nicholson's term of office.

Nicholson's personal interests were of the most varied, ranging over biblical criticism, Celtic antiquities, comparative philology (under the influence of Friedrich Max Müller), folk-lore, music, palaeography, numismatics, athletics. He was a violent opponent of vivisection, and held somewhat extreme radical views. In his many activities, some of them revolutionary, it was inevitable that he should meet with strong opposition. He was not by nature conciliatory, and received little consideration from his opponents. Yet though vigorous and even obstinate in the pursuit of his aims, he was just, honourable, and magnanimous, while to the young and to any one in need of help he showed an unexpected sympathy. His many controversies, combined with incessant work, eventually told on his strength. His health began to fail in 1902, and for the next ten years he was more and more affected by heart trouble. He died in Oxford on 17 March 1912.

Nicholson's work lay, not altogether by his own choice, in administration rather than in scholarship, but the list of his literary productions shows that he did not neglect the latter. Besides numerous controversial fly-sheets, articles in periodicals and official papers, he published the following works: *Sir John Mandeville, the English Herodotus* (1873), *The Christ-Child, and Other Poems* (1877), *Transactions . . . of the Conference of Librarians*

(1878), *The Gospel according to the Hebrews* (1879), *The Rights of an Animal* (1879), *A New Commentary on the Historical Books of the New Testament*, vol. i, *The Gospel according to Matthew* (1881), *Our new New Testament* (1881), *Jim Lord, a Poem* (1882), *New Homeric Researches*, (1882), *Jehan de Mandeville* (*Encyclopaedia Britannica*, 1883), *John of Burgundy, alias 'Sir John Mandeville'* (1884), *The Bodleian Library in 1882–1887* (1888), *The Pedigree of 'Jack'* (1892), *The North-Pictish Inscriptions* (1893–1895), *The Vernacular Inscriptions of the Ancient Kingdom of Alban* (1896), *Golspie. Contributions to its Folklore* (1897), *Sequanian* (1898), *The Man with Two Souls, and Other Stories* (1898), *French and English, a play* (1899), *Keltic Researches* (1904), '*Vinisius to Nigra*' (1904), *Can we not save Architecture in Oxford?* (1910), *Early Bodleian Music*, vol. iii (1913). He also collaborated with Sir John Stainer in his works on early Bodleian music (1899, 1902).

Nicholson married in 1876 Helen Grant, second daughter of the Rev. Sir Charles Macgregor, third baronet, by whom he had three daughters.

[*The Times*, 18 March 1912 ; H. R. Tedder, *E. W. B. Nicholson ... In Memoriam* (a paper read to the Library Association, 2 September 1913).] A. E. C.

NICHOLSON, WILLIAM GUSTAVUS, Baron Nicholson, of Roundhay (1845–1918), field-marshal, the youngest son of William Nicholson Phillips, of Leeds, by his wife, Martha, daughter of Abram Rhodes, of Wold Newton Hall, Yorkshire, was born at Roundhay Park, Leeds, 2 March 1845. His father had in 1827 assumed the surname and arms of Nicholson. He was educated at Leeds grammar school and the Royal Military Academy, Woolwich, where he was first of his term and Pollock medallist. He joined the Royal Engineers in 1865, and after a period at Chatham served at Barbados from 1868 to 1871, when he volunteered for service in India and was employed in the public works department and as assistant engineer in the Punjab irrigation branch. In 1873 he joined the military works department, becoming an executive engineer in 1877. Promoted captain, he accompanied the Kandahar force in 1878 and the Kuram field force in 1879 as field engineer, being present at the actions of Shutargardan and Charasia and greatly distinguishing himself in the defence of the Sherpur cantonment. In 1880 he marched with Sir Frederick Roberts's force from Kabul and took part in the relief of Kandahar and in the action of 1 September. For his services he was thrice mentioned in dispatches and received a brevet majority.

Returning to India, Nicholson was appointed secretary of the defence committee in 1880 and in 1882 served in the Egyptian expedition, taking part in the battle of Tel-el-Kebir. In 1884 he accompanied Sir Robert Groves Sandeman [q.v.] and Sir Charles Metcalfe MacGregor [q.v.] in an important reconnaissance in Baluchistan. From 1885 to 1890 he served as assistant adjutant-general, Royal Engineers, India, and was employed on the problem of the defence of the frontier and of the Indian ports. In 1886 he served in the Burmese expedition as assistant adjutant-general, being mentioned and receiving a brevet lieutenant-colonelcy. From 1890 to 1893 he was military secretary to Lord Roberts, then commander-in-chief in India, and afterwards served for two years in the military works department, during which time much was done to improve the defence of the North-West Frontier. In 1895 he became deputy adjutant-general, Punjab, and in 1897 served as chief of the staff with the Tirah expeditionary force. For his services he received the K.C.B. (1898) and on the conclusion of the campaign he became adjutant-general in India.

A year later came the crisis of the South African War, and Lord Roberts telegraphed to Nicholson to join him as military secretary : but he only served in that capacity for a month, being appointed in February 1900 director of transport. This service was being reorganized by Lord Kitchener ; Nicholson dealt solely with transport, the supply service being separate. He took part in the operations in the Orange Free State, including those of Paardeberg, Poplar Grove, Driefontein, and the Vet and Zand rivers. After the capture of Bloemfontein, Nicholson again reorganized the transport. In the latter part of the year he took part in the Transvaal operations, including the capture of Johannesburg and Pretoria, and returned to England in November with Lord Roberts. For his services he received two mentions, the Queen's medal and five clasps, and promotion to major-general for distinguished services in the field. In 1901, Lord Roberts being commander-in-chief, Nicholson became director of military operations at the War Office. Under him were united the mobilization section of the adjutant-general's department, with the intelligence division. He remained at the War

Office for three years, becoming lieutenant-general in November 1901.

During his tenure of office the War Office Reconstitution Committee under Viscount Esher issued its report (1904), and as a result of the determination to carry into effect the various reforms recommended, the government decided to change the heads of departments at the War Office. Nicholson was offered the post of military member of council in India, which he declined, and the Gibraltar command, which he was considering, when he was asked to go to Manchuria as chief British military attaché with the Japanese army. He reached Tokio in March 1904, but there was some delay in reaching the front. However, in July he joined the second Japanese army under General Oku at Hai Cheng, being present at the operations leading up to the battle of Lio Yang and the capture of that place in September. He had been in bad health for some time, and was pressed in consequence to return to Tokio; but he rejoined the second army in December, and remained with it till he returned to England in January 1905. It was intended that he should take up the Gibraltar command, but he never did so.

In the following December Nicholson succeeded Sir Herbert (afterwards Baron) Plumer as quartermaster-general, the appointment synchronizing with the accession of the liberals to office and the appointment of Mr. Haldane as secretary of state for war. In 1906 he was promoted general. In 1908 he succeeded Sir Neville Lyttelton as chief of the Imperial General Staff and was created G.C.B. During the years 1905 to 1912 the reorganization of the army was completed and the territorial force created. Ably assisted by Sir Douglas Haig, who was first director of training and later of staff duties, Nicholson played an important part in this work. At first he advocated compulsory service, but later came to the conclusion that it was impossible of realization. He aided considerably in the development of the Imperial General Staff, and by his wide knowledge of affairs, his gift of able and lucid draftsmanship, and his clear understanding, rendered valuable assistance in the realization of the scheme of army reform.

Promoted field-marshal in 1911, Nicholson was created a peer on retiring from the Army Council in 1912, and went to India in the same year as chairman of a commission to inquire into Indian army expenditure. He returned to England in 1913; but, owing to the outbreak of war in 1914, the recommendations of the commission were not carried out. He continued to be a member of the Committee of Imperial Defence, and served on the royal commissions of inquiry into the Dardanelles and Mesopotamia campaigns (1916). He was also chairman of the London territorial force association. He died in London 13 September 1918.

Nicholson's career was as peculiar as it was brilliant, for though he never commanded a unit in peace or war he became a field-marshal, and though he never passed the Staff College he became chief of the General Staff. Reserved in manner, he possessed great kindness of heart, and was ever at pains to encourage brains in his junior officers. He spoke brilliantly but he never courted publicity. He married in 1871 Victorie Ursula, daughter of Monsieur Dominique d'Allier. His wife survived him. He left no issue.

[*The Times*, 17 September 1918; Army Lists; Royal Engineers' *Journal*; Lord Roberts, *Forty-one Years in India*, 1897; C. E. Callwell, *Tirah*, 1897; '*The Times*' *History of the War in South Africa*; War Office records; R. C. Temple, *The Annexation of Burmah*, 1886; *Reports* of Mesopotamia and Dardanelles Commissions; private information.] O.

NIXON, Sir JOHN ECCLES (1857–1921), general, was born at Brentford 16 August 1857. He was a younger son of Captain John Piggott Nixon, of the 25th Bombay native infantry, by his wife, Ellen, daughter of G. Cooper, of Brentford. His father afterwards held various appointments in the Indian political service, and retired as a major-general in 1879. John Eccles Nixon was educated at Wellington College, and was commissioned from Sandhurst as a sub-lieutenant in the 75th Foot in September 1875. He entered the Bengal staff corps in 1878, and was appointed to the 18th Bengal cavalry, in which, in the course of twenty-five years, he passed through successive grades up to that of second in command. During ten years of regimental duty he served in the Afghan War of 1879–1880, and took part in a very successful punitive expedition by a brigade of the Kurram force into the Zaimukht country, and was mentioned in dispatches. He was also present in the Mahsud Waziri expedition of 1881. In April 1888, as a captain, he was appointed for five years to the garrison instruction staff. Owing to almost continuous employment on the staff in peace and in war, he saw little regimental service during the next fifteen years, and in May 1903, having been appointed to a district command with the rank of brigadier-general, he quitted his regiment finally without having attained to the command of it.

Meantime Nixon had served on the staff in the Chitral relief force (1895), and in the Tochi field force (1897–1898). In both cases mentions in dispatches followed, and for the former service he was promoted to brevet lieutenant-colonel in January 1896, having attained the rank of major in the previous September. Having served on the staff as assistant quartermaster-general with the rank of colonel for more than two and a half years from March 1899, he was sent to South Africa towards the end of 1901 and served there till the end of the war, commanding a cavalry column in the Transvaal and the Orange River Colony. He received four clasps with the medal, was mentioned in dispatches, and was awarded the C.B. (1902).

On returning to India Nixon resumed his appointment as assistant quartermaster-general for intelligence (November 1902), became second-class district commander (May 1903), inspector-general of cavalry (August 1906), a divisional commander (May 1908), and in October 1912 received the important appointment of general-officer-commanding the Southern army of India, from which he was transferred to the command of the Northern army in February 1915. He had meantime been promoted to major-general (March 1904), lieutenant-general (February 1909), and general (May 1914), and had been created K.C.B. in 1911. In India he had long borne the reputation of an energetic and capable staff officer and commander; but it was the part that he played in the Mesopotamian expedition during the European War which brought his name prominently before the public.

The basis of the Indian preparations for war as organized under Earl Kitchener [q.v.] was that India would make the utmost effort on the frontier and would be reinforced by men and supplies from England. The reverse of this happened on the outbreak of war in 1914. Within a few weeks large and fully equipped forces had been sent from India to France, Egypt, and East Africa, besides reinforcements to Aden and other British outposts. A great demand had thus already been made upon the Indian military establishments when, on the entry of Turkey into the War (29 October 1914), it was decided that, as a precautionary and defensive measure, Basra and its neighbourhood should be occupied by a force from India—the 6th (Poona) division, commanded by Lieutenant-General Sir Arthur Barrett. A naval force of some small vessels co-operated. Basra was occupied on 22 November, and Kurna, 47 miles up the Tigris, at its junction with the Euphrates, on 9 December. The Turks, preparing for offensive action, were in some force at Bahran on the Tigris, at Nazariyeh on the Euphrates, and at Ahwaz on the Karun river. Meantime Barrett's division was being reinforced from India by instalments of a new division, the 12th, and Sir John Nixon was appointed to the command of the whole force, taking it up on 9 April 1915. At this juncture Sir Arthur Barrett resigned the command of his division through ill-health, and was succeeded by Major-General (Sir) Charles Vere Ferrers Townshend from India; whilst Major-General (Sir) George Frederick Gorringe took command of the 12th division, incomplete and without artillery except such as he could borrow from Townshend's division. A few days after Nixon's arrival and before that of Townshend, the Turks, advancing from Nazariyeh, attacked an entrenched camp at Shaiba, west of Basra, and were dispersed after severe engagements.

The control of all operations in Mesopotamia had been reserved to the British government acting through the secretary of state for India, the government of India, and the commander-in-chief in India, General Sir Beauchamp Duff [q.v.]. On 24 April 1915 the secretary of state, telegraphing to the viceroy, stated that no advance beyond the present theatre of operations would be sanctioned at the moment, but that measures for the protection of the oil-pipe line from Persian Arabistan on the east, and an advance to Amara on the Tigris, would be approved if supported by the government of India. The telegram concluded, 'In Mesopotamia a safe game must be played.'

Nixon, before leaving India, had received his instructions from the commander-in-chief, and these were not known to the secretary of state till 2 May. He was to retain control of the Basra vilayet, of all outlets to the sea, and of such portions of neighbouring territories as might affect his operations, and as far as possible to endeavour to secure the oilfields and pipe line on the east, and after acquainting himself on the spot with the existing situation, to submit, first, a plan for the effective occupation of the Basra vilayet, and secondly, a plan for a subsequent advance on Bagdad. He was also to report on his military requirements generally, and in particular on the adequacy and suitability of the water transport expected from India, Burma, and Egypt, details of which were given to him. An advance on Bagdad was, however, at this time and for some months longer, excluded from the plans of the government of India and of the Cabinet.

Nixon lost no time in acting with vigour on his instructions to secure the control of the Basra vilayet, and his successive advances for that purpose were made with the previous approval of government. The Turks had established a strong position at Bahran, astride the Tigris, in front of Kurna, and were showing activity on the Karun river. Here a force under Major-General Gorringe repulsed them, and then, by a flank movement, threatened the force at Bahran, which Townshend was to attack. The difficulty of the latter operation was greatly increased by the Tigris being in flood and much of the surrounding marshes under water, from which there stood out a line of redoubts on low hills. The only possible attack was a frontal one, supported by artillery fire from guns at Kurna and from the naval flotilla, and it had to be made by infantry punting forward in small country boats (bellums), each of which carried only about ten men. After some weeks of preparation and training, at much of which Nixon was present, Townshend advanced on 31 May. The difficult operation, afterwards known as 'Townshend's regatta', was completely successful, and the pursuit ended with the occupation of Amara, some 90 miles up the river from Kurna, on 3 June, and the capture of its governor and many prisoners. Nixon's next movement was against the threatening force of Turks at Nazariyeh on the Euphrates, 68 miles west of Kurna, and this position Gorringe captured, with prisoners and guns, on 25 July.

Shortly after the occupation of Amara Townshend was prostrated by a sudden illness, which necessitated two months' leave to India. During this interval Nixon proposed to the government, as a means of consolidating the control of the Basra vilayet, a further advance to Kut el Amara, an important town on the Tigris, about 150 miles beyond Amara, and a little beyond the boundary of the vilayet. A few miles below Kut the Turks were entrenching with about 10,000 men in strong positions athwart the river. The government of India considered this advance a matter of strategic necessity, and suggested that a reinforcement of a brigade from Aden should be supplied. The Cabinet could not give the reinforcement, but eventually sanctioned the advance. It was skilfully carried out by Townshend. His division captured all the hostile positions by severe fighting, and entered Kut on 29 September. Pursuing the routed Turks, he arrived on 3 October at Azizieh, a village 60 miles up river, which now became the northernmost British outpost.

The conquest of the Basra vilayet was now complete. No further advance could be made without the approval of the Cabinet; but Nixon had submitted his plan, or appreciation of the situation, on 30 August, and on 3 October, a few days after the capture of Kut, he had telegraphed direct to the secretary of state, 'I consider I am strong enough to open the road to Bagdad, and with this intention I propose to concentrate at Azizieh.' Two days later he telegraphed that he saw nothing which would justify letting slip such an opportunity. Townshend at the front, however, had found it impossible to press on at once beyond Azizieh, even if permitted to do so, and he soon realized the danger of attempting the capture of Bagdad without large reinforcements. His division was weary and greatly reduced by casualties and sickness, mainly due to the torrid heat in which his recent battles had been fought. He proposed to consolidate his position at Kut, and considered it absolutely necessary, if Bagdad were to be occupied without great risk, that the further advance should be carried out by two divisions, or at least by one division closely supported by another. As Nixon took a more optimistic view, the question of an early attempt on Bagdad was for some time discussed between himself, the government of India, and the secretary of state. On 5 October, pending further consideration, he was ordered to stop the advance.

A new element, however, had come into the discussion. The Allied attack upon the Dardanelles had been brought to a standstill, and British prestige, especially amongst Eastern peoples, was held to demand some conspicuous off-set to the successes of the Turks. This consideration turned the views of the Cabinet and its military advisers in favour of an advance on Bagdad, provided always that, if captured, it could be held. The practicability of this depended: first, on large reinforcements of Nixon's fighting and auxiliary forces; and secondly, on an increase of his river transport proportionate to his increased forces and to the lengthened distance from the front to the base, some 500 miles of a narrow, winding river, varying at different seasons from very shallow water to extensive floods, and flanked by hostile or treacherous tribes. The former of these requirements was to be met by sending out two Indian divisions from France; the latter received unaccountably little attention. The doubts of the commander-in-chief in India, submitted to the viceroy for transmission to the secretary of state—'whether in the present state of the river combined with our present insufficient number of light-draught steamers, we could adequately supply our troops'—were omitted from the viceroy's telegram to London [*Report, Mesopotamia Commission*, pp. 22–3.]

Only to a very limited extent had it been found possible to meet from India and Burma Nixon's earlier demands for water transport, and that commander was aware that the large supply of tugs, barges, &c., which had been ordered from England in August could not arrive for many months. Moreover, the medical equipment of the expedition was already insufficient; the reserves in India of personnel and stores were greatly depleted, and medical stores were almost unobtainable from England. These conditions rendered a deadlock probable, unless the new advance should be exceptionally lucky and successful, and casualties few. Vague reports of Turkish reinforcements moving from Anatolia towards Bagdad had been received, but it was thought that they would not arrive for some months.

Such were the circumstances when, on 23 October 1915, the secretary of state telegraphed to India that Nixon might advance on Bagdad if satisfied as to the sufficiency of his forces, and that two divisions would be sent from France as soon as possible. Nixon, not sharing Townshend's views as to the insufficiency of his force, did not report them to India or to England, and ordered the advance. Townshend, deferring to the judgement of his superior, occupied some weeks in preparations for attacking the Turks in their entrenched position astride the Tigris near the ancient arch of Ctesiphon. He attacked on the morning of 22 November what he supposed to be a force somewhat greater in numbers than his own. But large reinforcements had arrived or were just arriving. The Turks were driven from their first entrenchments, but their increasing numbers gradually prevailed. The battle was lost by nightfall, and after standing on the defensive for some days and repelling heavy counter-attacks, Townshend, with the concurrence of Nixon, who had been present during the fighting, decided to retreat before the overwhelming Turkish force, which now consisted of several divisions. Keeping the enemy at bay, striking back effectively, and taking with him not only his wounded but 1,350 prisoners, he reached Kut without the loss of a gun. Here, with the approval of Nixon and of the Indian government, he decided to stand fast. He was closely besieged from 6 December till 29 April, when, though all assaults had been repelled, the imminent starvation of his force compelled unconditional surrender.

After the battle of Ctesiphon reinforcements of infantry and artillery were sent to Mesopotamia from India; but the two divisions from France and another ordered from Egypt had not begun to arrive, when, on 19 January 1916, Nixon, through ill-health, relinquished his command, after the first efforts of all available troops to relieve Kut had failed. The sufferings of the sick and wounded from Townshend's retreating division and from the troops under Nixon who first attempted his relief were primarily due to the inadequacy of the river transport, the disastrous results of which culminated in still worse conditions during later operations from January to April.

Nixon was summoned to England, with many other witnesses, to appear before the Mesopotamia commission of inquiry appointed in August 1916, the report of which (but not the evidence taken) was published in the following summer. The commissioners placed Nixon first in a graded list of officials, military and civil, declared to be chiefly responsible for the shortcomings of the expedition. 'The weightiest share of responsibility', they said, 'lies with Sir John Nixon, whose confident optimism was the main cause of the decision to advance' [*Report*, p. 111]. One of the commissioners, who recorded a separate report because he thought the commission's findings generally too lenient, dissociated himself from the censure of Nixon [*Report*, p. 121]. The government proposed to set up a special court to inquire further into the accusations against the incriminated officials, civil and military; but withdrew this proposal in deference to objections raised on various grounds in parliament, and decided that in respect of civilians no further inquiry should be held, but that the Army Council should call for written explanations from the soldiers, and, on receipt of them, consider what further action was to be taken. The result of this procedure in Nixon's case was an announcement in the House of Commons on 28 October 1918 that the Army Council had received and considered his explanation and had informed him that they regarded it as satisfactory. The G.C.M.G. was conferred on Nixon in 1919, and in 1922 the dignity of *grand officier* of the legion of honour was posthumously awarded him.

The nine months of command in Mesopotamia were Nixon's last active service. He lived, in gradually failing health, till 15 December 1921, when he died at St. Raphael, France. He had married in 1884 Amy Louisa, daughter of James Wilson, of Gratwicke, Billingshurst, and Felpham Manor, Sussex, and had one son.

[Official Army Lists; Naval and Military Dispatches, *London Gazette*, January–December 1916; *Mesopotamia Commission Report*, 17 May 1917, Cd. 8610; Parliamentary Debates, June–August 1917, and October 1918; Sir C. Townshend, *My Campaign in Mesopotamia*, 1920; personal knowledge.]

J. H. S.

NOBLE, Sir ANDREW, first baronet (1831–1915), physicist and artillerist, the third son of George Noble, sometime lieutenant in the royal navy, of Greenock, Renfrewshire, by his wife, Geils Moore, only daughter of Andrew Donald, of Ottercaps, Virginia, U.S.A., was born at Greenock 13 September 1831. His father came of a Dumbartonshire family which had at one time owned property in the county. His mother belonged to an Ayrshire family. He was educated at the Academy at Edinburgh, and entered Woolwich as a cadet in the spring of 1847. In June 1849 he received a commission in the Royal Artillery, and served with that regiment for eleven years. Most of his military career, which was uneventful, was passed abroad. Always interested in mathematics and chemistry, Noble showed the scientific bent of his mind in various lines before he took up the special branch of inquiry in which he gained distinction. He returned to England at the beginning of 1858, and found the attention of the naval and military authorities occupied with the question of superseding the old smooth-bore guns by a new system of rifled artillery. It is a remarkable fact that no advance in gunnery had been made between the Napoleonic and the Crimean Wars, and the armed forces of the country still relied upon weapons of the type which had served Wellington and Nelson nearly half a century earlier. It was not until after the battle of Inkermann that (Sir) William George (afterwards Lord) Armstrong [q.v.] submitted to the War Office for trial a rifled breech-loading field gun, and began a controversy which agitated public opinion for several years. The subject exactly suited Noble's aptitude for patient experiment and accurate observation, and he lost no time in taking part in it. He was appointed secretary to various committees formed to investigate the new system of artillery, which was adopted officially by the services towards the end of 1858, a step which had the effect of accentuating rather than mitigating the acrimonies of discussion.

Noble began to be recognized more and more as a specialist, and it was not long before his ability attracted the notice of Armstrong, then in want of technical assistance for the Ordnance Company at Elswick, near Newcastle-upon-Tyne, where the government orders for re-armament were being carried out. He offered Noble a partnership in the business, and in December 1860 the latter was gazetted out of the army as a captain, and threw in his lot with Armstrong. The Elswick Ordnance Company, as a result of arrangements complicated by Armstrong's official position of director of rifled ordnance, was kept at first distinct from the Hydraulic Engineering Works at Elswick. In 1863, however, when the government contracts were completed, the two concerns were amalgamated, and, as Sir W. G. Armstrong, Whitworth, and Company, Limited, the business had grown, even before the war developments of 1914, into one of the largest industrial enterprises in the country [see Whitworth, Sir Joseph]. When he joined the Ordnance Works Noble shared the management with George Wightwick Rendel [q.v.]; but he assumed active control of the entire concern when he became vice-chairman of the public company formed in 1882. On the death of Lord Armstrong in December 1900, he succeeded to the chairmanship.

Noble's new position was of undoubted advantage to the pursuit of his scientific inquiries. He had now opportunity and resources available for the study of gunnery and explosives, and he made full use of them. His observations and experiments followed the lines of those of T. J. Rodman, Sir Benjamin Thompson (Count von Rumford, q.v.), and earlier investigators, in ascertaining the conditions which follow an explosion; but he carried the examination of fired gunpowder further than any of his predecessors. Confining the charge in a closed vessel of steel, he determined the pressures created and analysed the gases and residues. From these experiments it was found possible to record the pressures in the chamber of a gun, and the velocity of the projectile in its passage through the bore. These processes, which are now in common use at all gun trials and tests, were unknown before Noble's time, and the exact science of ballistics may be said to be due to his work. The practical issue of his experiments and conclusions was a complete alteration in the composition of gunpowder and in the design of guns. The old black powder was exchanged for an explosive of regular size and shape, which burned more slowly and gave more regular pressures. Improvements in the manufacture of steel assisted progress, allowing larger chambers which were calculated to stand heavier charges; while longer guns were designed, with breech-loading instead of muzzle-loading. The English services were slow to accept these novelties, but agreed eventually to the changes suggested, and about 1881 the modern gun, as we know it, was introduced into the navy.

Recognized as the leading authority upon his own subject, Noble often acted upon committees dealing with questions of guns and gunpowder. Apart from this he took little share in public life, confining his attention to his own business and his own studies. From time to time he published the results of his researches in papers contributed to the learned societies and institutions of which he was a member. In many of his experiments he collaborated with Sir Frederick Augustus Abel [q.v.], and two of his most important papers on ballistics were published, the first in 1875 and the second in 1879, in their joint names. In 1906 he collected his papers and lectures and reprinted them in a volume entitled *Artillery and Explosives*.

Noble combined to an unusual degree scientific ability with administrative powers. He controlled for many years a large business undertaking, was in daily attendance at his office or in the workshops, and was active in the superintendence of every detail. He proved himself a successful leader of men and commanded the loyal support of those who served under him. After his day's work he continued his technical studies in his library or laboratory, often far into the night. With it all he was full of human interests and enjoyed recreation thoroughly in many forms. His hospitality was unbounded. He was happy in his domestic circumstances, and his houses were the centre of large gatherings of relations and friends.

Noble was made a C.B. in 1881, and created a K.C.B. in 1893, and a baronet in 1902. He was also the recipient of many foreign decorations and scientific honours, including the royal medal of the Royal Society (1880) and the Albert medal of the Royal Society of Arts (1909). At the end of 1911 he ceased to take an active share in the management of Elswick, though he remained chairman of the Company to the end of his life. He died 22 October 1915 at Ardkinglas, a house in Argyllshire which he had built for himself some years earlier.

Noble married in 1854 Margery Durham, daughter of Archibald Campbell, a Quebec notary, by whom he had four sons and two daughters. His eldest son, George (born 1859), succeeded to the baronetcy.

[*The Times*, 23 October 1915; private information; personal knowledge.]

A. C.

NORFOLK, fifteenth DUKE OF (1847–1917). [See HOWARD, HENRY FITZALAN-.]

NUTTALL, ENOS (1842–1916), bishop of Jamaica, primate and first archbishop of the West Indies, was born at Clitheroe 26 January 1842, the eldest son of James Nuttall, farmer and builder, of Coates, St. Mary-le-Gill, Yorkshire, by his first wife, Alice, daughter of William and Martha Armistead, of Aynhams, in the same parish. His education was such as his mother and the parish school could give him, but he developed powers of self-tuition, and being placed by his father in charge of a farm, gave his leisure to learning. James Nuttall was a Wesleyan, and Enos, while constant in his attendance at church, became at seventeen a 'local preacher' of some power. Anxious for mission-work abroad, he applied to the Rev. George Osborn [q.v.], secretary of the Wesleyan missionary society, was accepted, and, after a period of training under the Rev. Andrew Kessen, was posted by the society to Jamaica, for which he sailed on 2 December 1862 in his twenty-first year, to work as a layman.

While, however, his brother Ezra (1850–1915) won distinction in South Africa as a Methodist minister, Enos offered himself in Jamaica for the ministry of the Church of England. He was ordained deacon on 18 February 1866 in the cathedral at Spanish Town, and priest on 8 April in the parish church, Kingston, where fifty years later (23 February 1916) his last sermon was addressed to a departing war-contingent. He was appointed 'island curate' of St. George's, Kingston, with a stipend derived from the government, and technically he retained the post till his death. In December 1869 notice was given that state-endowment (saving some life interests) would cease at the end of that year, and Nuttall, young as he was, took a leading part in the reorganization of the disestablished Church of England in Jamaica, helping to draft its canons and to settle its financial system, and engaging in public controversy with the governor, Sir John Peter Grant [q.v.]. He was made secretary of synod in 1870 and of the diocesan board of finance in 1874. Archbishop Tait recognized his work by giving him in 1879 the Lambeth degree of B.D.

In 1880, on the resignation of Bishop George William Tozer, the synod chose Nuttall as bishop of Jamaica, and he was consecrated by Tait in St. Paul's Cathedral on 28 October. From 1881 to 1891 he was also responsible for the supervision of the diocese of British Honduras, while his efforts among the West Indians working on the Panama canal caused that district to be transferred temporarily in 1885 to the diocese of Jamaica. In 1883 the first meeting of the provincial synod of the West Indies was held in Jamaica, five bishops attending, and Nuttall was mainly responsible for drafting its canons and constitutions. He was elected primate of the West Indies in 1893 in succession to William Piercy Austin, bishop of Guiana, and in 1897, in consequence of a resolution of the West Indian bishops passed (30 July) during the Lambeth Conference, he assumed the title of archbishop of the West Indies.

On 14 January 1907 Jamaica was visited by a destructive earthquake. At the moment the archbishop was attending a meeting of the West India Agricultural Conference; his coolness averted a panic, and his immediate organization and guidance of all the measures for relief and reconstruction were beyond praise. Throughout his fifty-four years in Jamaica he was intimately concerned in the daily welfare of the islanders—education, nursing, housing, agriculture—and was in constant consultation with the Colonial Office at home.

Nuttall married in 1867 Elizabeth Duggan, daughter of the Rev. Philip Chapman, a Wesleyan minister, by whom he had two sons and three daughters. In his later years, in spite of frequent visits to England, his health failed, though his hold on the diocese did not relax nor did his pastoral zeal abate. He died at Bishop's Lodge, Kingston, on 31 May 1916, and was buried in the churchyard of St. Andrew, Halfway Tree. There is a portrait in oils at Bishop's Lodge. His publications, besides many charges and sermons, include *The Churchman's Manual* (1894) and *The Jamaica Day School Catechism* (1905).

[*The Times*, 3 June 1916; Frank Cundall, *Life of Enos Nuttall*, 1922; J. B. Ellis, *The Diocese of Jamaica*, 1913; *Jamaica Diocesan Gazette*, July 1924; H. Lowther Clarke, *Constitutional Church Government*, 1924; personal knowledge.]
E. H. P.

OATES, LAWRENCE EDWARD GRACE (1880–1912), Antarctic explorer, the elder son of William Edward Oates, of Gestingthorpe Hall, Essex, by his wife, Caroline Anne Buckton, was born at Putney 17 March 1880, during his parents' temporary residence in London. As a boy Oates was delicate, and for three successive winters he was taken by his father to South Africa. After two years at Eton he was educated privately until 1898, when he was gazetted to the 3rd West Yorkshire (militia) regiment. Two years later he joined the army from the militia and was posted to the 6th (Inniskilling) Dragoons, and in 1901 he went on active service in the South African War. He served with distinction, winning a name for his daring, and was mentioned in dispatches for gallantry in the field. Severely wounded in March 1901, he was invalided home for a short time, but returned to the front before the end of the year. Promoted lieutenant in 1902, he served with his regiment in Ireland, next in Egypt, where he became captain and adjutant in 1906, and later in India.

During his military career Oates devoted his spare time to hunting and steeplechasing. He was also a practised yachtsman with a passion for the sea. With these qualifications and a love of adventure which he had inherited from his father, who was a noted big game shot, Oates in 1910 applied for a post on the Antarctic expedition which Captain Robert Falcon Scott, R.N. [q.v.], was organizing. Scott accepted him and put him specially in charge of the nineteen ponies which were to be used for sledge haulage.

The expedition sailed in the *Terra Nova* in June 1910, and leaving New Zealand in November reached the Ross Sea and established a base at Cape Evans on Ross Island in January 1911. Oates took a prominent part in the depôt-laying in January and February, in preparation for the southern journey of the following summer. In November 1911 a sledging party, which included Oates, set out under Scott's leadership for the South Pole. Several of the ponies had been lost by accident during the autumn and winter, but the survivors, thanks largely to Oates's careful attention, were in good condition. These and the dog teams helped in haulage to the foot of the Beardmore glacier, where the surviving ponies were slaughtered and the dog teams sent back. From that point onwards the sledges were man-hauled. The last supporting party under Lieutenant E. R. G. R. Evans, R.N., was sent back from latitude 86° 32′ S. The men who continued south with Scott were Oates, Dr. Edward Adrian Wilson [q.v.], Lieutenant H. R. Bowers, R.I.M., and Petty Officer Edgar Evans. Soft snow, sastrugi, and low temperatures made travelling arduous and sorely tried the strength of the party, but Oates stood the strain as well as any of them. The Pole was reached on 18 January 1912, thirty-four days after Roald Amundsen had planted the Norwegian flag there.

The return journey was begun the same day. Temperatures were very low and the surface was bad for travelling. Oates showed signs of feeling the cold severely, but the party made good progress to the head of the Beardmore glacier. Petty Officer Evans was the first to break down, and marching was very slow for several days before his death (17 February). The four men reached a depôt the next day, and with more liberal food rations their hopes rose. But on the barrier travelling conditions were bad and the temperatures fell as low as −47° F. Survival depended on the ability of the weakened men to reach each depôt before their scanty food and fuel supplies were exhausted. Oates suffered much from frost-bitten feet, but his indomitable spirit never weakened and he marched as long as he was able. At length he could go no farther and asked to be left behind. This request was of course refused. For another day he struggled on. 'He slept through the night', wrote Scott, 'hoping not to wake: but he woke in the morning (17 March). It was blowing a blizzard. He said, "I am just going outside and may be some time".' He was never seen again. The self-sacrifice of Oates enabled the survivors to push on, and there was a possibility that, in spite of their extreme exhaustion, they might cover the 30 miles to the food supplies at One Ton depôt. But a heavy blizzard held them up in latitude 79° 40′ S., 11 miles from the depot. Unable to proceed, the three men perished on or about 29 March. A search party, after finding the bodies of Scott, Wilson, and Bowers on 12 November 1912, sought in vain for that of Oates. Near the site of his death was erected a cairn and cross bearing the inscription, 'Hereabouts died a very gallant gentleman, Captain L. E. G. Oates, of the Inniskilling Dragoons. In March 1912, returning from the Pole, he walked willingly to his death in a blizzard, to try and save his comrades, beset by hardships.' Oates Land, a part of the Antarctic coast-line in latitude 69° S., longitude 158° E., discovered by the *Terra Nova* in February 1911, was so named in his honour. There is a bronze portrait medallion of Oates, executed by Lady Scott, at Eton College, and an oil portrait at the family seat in Essex. He was unmarried.

[*Scott's Last Expedition*, ed. L. Huxley, 1913; *Geographical Journal*, 1913; *Cavalry Journal*, 1913; private information.] R. N. R. B.

O'BRIEN, PETER, Baron O'Brien, of Kilfenora (1842–1914), lord chief justice of Ireland, the fifth son of John O'Brien, of Ballynalacken, co. Clare, M.P. for Limerick 1841–1852, by his wife, Ellen, daughter of Jeremiah Murphy, of Hyde Park, co. Cork, was born at Carnelly House, co. Clare, 29 June 1842. Educated at Clongowes and Trinity College, Dublin, he was called to the Irish bar in 1865, and schooled soundly in law through 'devilling' for a great jurist, Christopher Palles (afterwards chief baron, q.v.), and acting as registrar for his uncle, Mr. Justice James O'Brien. Joining the Munster circuit, he soon achieved distinction by cross-examinations instinct with knowledge of the Irish character. He contested Clare unsuccessfully in the whig interest in 1879, and took silk in 1880.

Ireland was then in distraction, crime served politics, English and Irish members frequented trials for agrarian and insurrectionary offences, and distorted them on the platform and in parliament. Every judge was under police protection, prosecutors were pursued by calumny and intimidation, and required courage, firmness, and judgement. These qualities O'Brien possessed pre-eminently. Retained by the Crown in all important cases, he was rapidly promoted serjeant (1884), solicitor-general (1887), attorney-general (1888). His attorney-generalship was historic. Mr. Arthur Balfour had become chief secretary in March 1887, and in July a Crimes Act was passed to counter the conspiracies then paralysing Ireland. O'Brien's administration of it restored the reign of law. His sagacity, patience, and fearlessness revived confidence. He worked indefatigably himself and chose his lieutenants well. The discreet power of Edward Carson (afterwards Lord Carson) found a complement in the astute erudition of Stephen Ronan (afterwards lord justice). Failure was unknown, though, where possible, every prosecution was tested microscopically on appeal. Peace ensued, and the way was clear for Balfour's regenerative measures when, in 1889, O'Brien became lord chief justice.

The great attorney-general proved a great chief justice, enhancing during twenty-four years the high traditions of that office. An atmosphere of dignified power distinguished his court. Penetrating to essentials, dispelling irrelevancies, he chiselled argument with common sense to sound decision. Urbane and humorous, knowing intimately the Irish human being, he won the confidence of juries by his rectitude and leniency. The bar and public regarded him with admiring affection. Massive, genial, hospitable, a fine conversationalist and many-sided sportsman, happiest in the hunting field, he was a thorough Irishman. He retired in 1913, having been created a baronet in 1891 and raised to the peerage in 1900. He died without male issue at Stillorgan, co. Dublin, 7 September 1914. He had lived down the propagandist misrepresentations which aspersed his earlier career, the expletives were dropped by his critics, and the best criterion of his popularity and personality is that Irishmen knew him best, not as the lord chief justice, nor as Lord O'Brien, but as 'Peter'.

O'Brien, who was a Roman Catholic, married in 1867 Annie, daughter of Robert Hare Clarke, J.P., of Bansha, co. Tipperary, by whom he had two daughters.

[Hon. Georgina O'Brien, *Reminiscences of the Right Honourable Lord O'Brien*, 1916; F. Elrington Ball, *The Judges in Ireland, 1221–1921*, vol. ii, 1926; professional and personal knowledge.] A. W. S.

OPPENHEIM, LASSA FRANCIS LAWRENCE (1858–1919), jurist, was born near Frankfort-on-the-Main 30 March 1858, the third son of Aaron Oppenheim, by his wife, Adelheid Nossbaum, and was educated at the Frankfort gymnasium and at the universities of Göttingen, Berlin, Heidelberg, and Leipzig. From 1885 to 1891 he taught law in the university of Freiburg-im-Breisgau, and from 1891 to 1895 at Basle, being chiefly interested in criminal law; but in 1895 he settled in London, and henceforth devoted himself to the study of international law. He became naturalized in England in 1900. He lectured at the London School of Economics from 1898 to 1908, when he succeeded John Westlake [q.v.] in the Whewell chair of international law at Cambridge. He married in 1902 Elizabeth, daughter of Lieutenant-Colonel Phineas Cowan, and they had one daughter. He died at Cambridge 7 October 1919.

Oppenheim's chief work is *International Law: A Treatise*, of which the first volume, *Peace*, appeared in 1905, and the second, *War and Neutrality*, in 1906. It deservedly placed him among the foremost international jurists of his time, and was followed by his election to the Institut de Droit International, as associate in 1908, and as member in 1911. He belongs to the *positive* school of international jurists, who derive the rules of the science from custom and from the quasi-legislation of international conventions, and who regard it as the function of the jurist to ascertain and give precision to those rules, to criticize and suggest improvements, but not to create them, nor to select as valid only those of which he approves. Oppenheim protested against the tendency to deduce the law from phrases, too often uncritically accepted as self-evident truths; and he pleaded for the development among jurists of that wider sympathy with other nations which can only come from a study of their juristic systems and from the cultivation of an international outlook. He was joint author of the chapter on the laws of war on land in the official *Manual of Military Law* (sixth edition 1914) and was frequently consulted by the Foreign Office on points of international law.

The conduct of Germany in the European War horrified Oppenheim, and convinced him that the only hope of a better international order lay in the decisive victory of the Allies. He was not discouraged by the apparent overthrow of international law, pointing out that in any case it affected only a relatively small part of the subject, the law of war, and revealed the paramount importance of a better organization of the peaceful relations of states. He strongly advocated a league of nations.

[*The Times*, 9 October 1919 ; *British Year Book of International Law*, 1920–1921 ; R. F. Roxburgh, Preface to Oppenheim's *Treatise*, containing a list of his writings on international law (third edition, 1920–1921) ; private information.] J. L. B.

OSLER, Sir WILLIAM, baronet (1849–1919), regius professor of medicine at Oxford, was born at Bond Head, Ontario, 12 July 1849. He was the sixth son and eighth child of a family of nine, of whom several have attained to distinction. His father, the Rev. Featherston L. Osler, a brother of Edward Osler [q.v.], had emigrated from Cornwall to take up mission work in a then scantily settled district of Canada. His mother's name was Ellen Free Pickton. He was educated at Trinity College School at Weston, and Trinity College, Toronto, with the intention of proceeding to holy orders. However he soon recognized his true vocation and entered upon the study of medicine at the university of Toronto. Two years later (1870) he migrated to McGill University, Montreal, where he completed his medical course and graduated in 1872. In after years he often spoke of three of his teachers who had influenced greatly his outlook and career, and to whose memory he dedicated his text-book of medicine. These were William Arthur Johnson, head master of the Weston school, who first awakened his scientific interests and implanted in him a lifelong devotion to the writings of Sir Thomas Browne ; James Bovell, a professor at Trinity College ; and Palmer Howard, professor of medicine at McGill.

After two years spent in post-graduate study in England and on the continent of Europe, under some of the most eminent teachers of the day, Osler returned to Montreal in 1874 to take up, at the early age of twenty-five, the professorship of the institutes of medicine at McGill. The ten years during which he held that chair were years of strenuous work. He lectured on physiology and pathology at McGill, and on helminthology at the Veterinary College, was actively engaged in microscopic and pathological research, and made such good use of his opportunities as physician to the Montreal general hospital, that in 1884 he was invited to become professor of medicine in the university of Pennsylvania. The qualities which distinguished Osler in later life were fully manifested in Montreal, as the testimony of his pupils and colleagues shows. Throughout his life he retained a lively affection for his *alma mater*, McGill ; to her he bequeathed his valuable library, and he desired that his ashes should rest within her walls.

The following twenty years were spent in the United States. In Philadelphia he stayed only five years, for when, in 1889, it was decided to appoint a professor of medicine in the Johns Hopkins University in Baltimore, Osler's fame both as teacher and physician was such that the choice naturally fell upon him. He was familiar with the methods of medical teaching and research both in Europe and America, and held very definite views on the way in which a clinic should be conducted. He was given a free hand in the organization of his department and choice of his assistants. Few teachers of medicine have had such an opportunity, and under his direction and guidance there emerged the first organized clinical unit in any Anglo-Saxon country. In it he combined the teaching of small groups at the bedside, and the contact of students and patients, which are the best features of the English schools, with the close co-operation of wards and laboratories under a single director with highly trained assistants, which is the essential feature of the German clinics. He aimed as much at the advancement of medical science as at the instruction of students, and each student was made to feel that he was a fellow-worker with his teachers in the attainment of fresh knowledge. The fifteen years in Baltimore constituted the great period of Osler's life. From Johns Hopkins have gone forth teachers to many of the leading medical schools of North America, and it is not too much to claim that Osler's work there has revolutionized medical education in the United States and in Canada, and has had a profound influence upon the schools in England also.

By frequent trips to Europe Osler kept in touch with the progress of medicine, and with friends and colleagues on this side of the Atlantic. His work was recognized in England by his election to the fellowship of the Royal College of Physicians in 1884, and to the fellowship of the Royal Society in 1898. In 1892 he married Grace, the eldest daughter of John Revere, a Boston manufacturer, and widow of Dr. S. W. Gross, of Philadelphia.

Their son, Edward Revere Osler, was born in Baltimore. Another child born to them died in infancy.

As time went on, Osler felt the strain of the strenuous work at Johns Hopkins coupled with that of a large and widespread consulting practice, and when, on the retirement of Sir John Burdon Sanderson in 1904, he was offered the regius professorship of medicine at Oxford, he accepted that appointment. To Osler the atmosphere of Oxford was thoroughly congenial. The traditions of his chair, which carried with it the mastership of the ancient almshouse at Ewelme, appealed to him strongly. He was elected to a studentship at Christ Church, the college of two of his literary favourites, John Locke and Robert Burton, and was an active curator of the Bodleian Library and delegate of the Clarendon Press. In Oxford he found time for the pursuit of literary and antiquarian studies, for which the claims of his clinic and the demands of his medical practice had left little leisure in America. His wide outlook and varied interests enabled him to hold his own in any gathering of learned men, and many to whom his eminence as a physician and teacher of medicine made no strong appeal, welcomed him as a discriminating lover of books, and as a man in full sympathy with the humanities. For several years he was president of the Bibliographical Society, and in 1919, as president of the Classical Association, he delivered a memorable address on 'The old Humanities and the new Science'. At the same time he maintained his medical activities as head of the Oxford medical school, and as a clinical teacher at the Radcliffe Infirmary. He was a familiar figure in London at the College of Physicians and medical societies. He was one of the founders of the Association of Physicians and of the historical section of the Royal Society of Medicine, and senior editor of the *Quarterly Journal of Medicine*. At the meeting of the International Medical Congress in London in 1913, he presided over the section of medicine.

Osler's house in Oxford was a centre of wide hospitality, and a place of pilgrimage for numerous visitors from overseas. Many honours came to him. He was created a baronet in 1911. Universities conferred upon him their degrees, and he was an honorary member of many societies. On the day before his seventieth birthday there were presented to him two volumes of essays and papers contributed by pupils and friends on both sides of the Atlantic. The European War brought new claims and fresh activities—for work in military hospitals in Oxford, and in others established in distant places under Canadian and American auspices. When, in 1917, deep sorrow came to him in the loss of his only son, who fell in Flanders, he carried on his work bravely, and with enhanced sympathy for his fellow-sufferers. But the strain told upon him, and in September 1919 he was attacked by the illness to which he succumbed, three months later, on 29 December.

Osler's literary output was very large. His earliest papers dealt with Canadian diatomaceae, the blood-platelets, which he was one of the first to describe, and the filaria which causes the verminous bronchitis of dogs. Others record his work in morbid anatomy, and a long series of clinical papers cover a large part of the field of medicine. These reflect his special interests at the times when they were written, and formed an excellent foundation for his text-book, *The Principles and Practice of Medicine*, his *magnum opus*. This book, which first appeared in 1891 and reached a ninth edition in 1920, has been translated into French, German, Spanish, and Chinese. Its clear and individual style, the judicious use made of statistics derived from hospital records, and the stress laid upon morbid anatomy as a foundation of clinical medicine, render it one of the best works of its kind in any language. Amongst other works which call for mention are monographs on *Cerebral Palsies in Children* (1889), on *Chorea and Choreiform Affections* (1894), and lectures on *Abdominal Tumours* (1895) and *Angina Pectoris* (1897). Many of his writings make a wider appeal, such as the essays and addresses gathered together in the volume entitled *Aequanimitas* (1904) and *An Alabama Student* (1908), and lay sermons such as *Man's Redemption of Man* (1910) and *A Way of Life* (1913), addressed to students of Edinburgh and Yale. These afford an insight into his thoughts and ideals, and reflect his vivid personality.

Osler's personal magnetism and stimulating influence had no small share in gaining for him his world-wide reputation and the position which he held in the estimation of his contemporaries. A great teacher, he inspired his pupils with his own enthusiasm, and could sum up an important lesson in a terse, epigrammatic phrase. A facile orator, he could make an appropriate speech on any occasion, and his lighter sayings and speeches were permeated by his characteristic humour. Few who knew him failed to come under the spell of his friendship, for he had the gift of being interested in the work and aspirations of all with whom he came in contact. Even the youngest student recognized in Osler a counsellor and a friend. The brotherhood of medicine was his ideal, and no man ever did more to realize that aim.

A portrait of Osler was painted for McGill University in 1903, and another for the university of Pennsylvania in 1905. In the former year (1903) Mr. H. B. Jacobs had a plaque cut by E. Vernon, of Paris, showing Osler in profile. This was reproduced in bronze for distribution among friends, and one of these plaques is in the court of the University Museum at Oxford. The most important portrait is that painted by J. S. Sargent and presented to Johns Hopkins University at Baltimore by Miss M. E. Garrett in 1905. Here Osler is seen in the centre of a group of four professors. Another portrait by an American artist, Mr. Seymour Thomas, was painted in 1908.

[*Bulletin* of Johns Hopkins Hospital, July 1919 ; *Journal* of the Canadian Medical Association, July 1920 ; Obituary notice in *Proceedings* of the Royal Society, vol. xcii, B, 1921 ; M. W. Blogg, *Bibliography of Sir William Osler*, 1921 ; Professor Harvey Cushing, *The Life of William Osler*, 1925 ; personal knowledge.] A. E. G.

PALLES, CHRISTOPHER (1831–1920), lord chief baron of the exchequer in Ireland, was born at Dublin 25 December 1831, the second son of Andrew Christopher Palles, of Little Mount Palles, co. Cavan, by his wife, Eleanor, daughter of Matthew Thomas Plunkett, of Rathmore, co. Kildare. Educated at Clongowes Wood College and Trinity College, Dublin, he graduated in 1852 as a senior moderator in mathematics. Called to the Irish bar (King's Inns, Dublin) in 1853, he acquired such reputation as a junior that on becoming Q.C. (1865) he was retained in almost every important case. He ultimately limited his practice to chancery, gaining the familiarity with equity which distinguished his decisions on appeal. In 1872 he became solicitor-general for Ireland, and, later in the same year, attorney-general. In that year also he contested Londonderry city unsuccessfully in the liberal interest. In February 1874, on the eve of the fall of Gladstone's first ministry, he was promoted chief baron of the Irish court of exchequer and held that high office until his resignation in 1916. The exchequer, composed of Palles and Barons Francis A. Fitzgerald, Rickard Deasy [q.v.], Richard Dowse [q.v.], and Judge William Drennan Andrews, was a powerful court. By the Supreme Court of Judicature (Ireland) Act (1897) it was merged in the Queen's bench division of the Irish high court of justice, but Palles retained his title and precedence as lord chief baron. Under him and his colleagues the court became a practical school of law thronged by the junior bar. Palles was a dignified, courteous, and kindly chief, who delighted in the intellectual duels of leaders, and was ever ready to prompt and encourage the young advocate who displayed diligence and research ; but to attempt a fallacious or ill-supported contention ensured rebuke and disaster.

Palles lived in the law, and his decisions are his best memorial. The *Irish Reports* from 1874 to 1916 reveal the man and his characteristics : his mastery of law as a science in all its ramifications ; his penetrating research ; his remarkable 'case memory' ; his grip of common law, of equity, and of statute law ; his assimilation of every branch of jurisprudence ; his methods of historical ratiocination, convincing deduction, and lucid exposition ; his reverence for precedent ; the guarded courage with which he enunciated principles and yet safely limited their application. His judgments were delivered with restrained judicial eloquence, in a voice of clear timbre, virile and compelling. He vivified and verified Coke's dictum, 'Reason is the life of the law, nay the common law itself is nothing but reason, which is to be understood of an artificial perfection of reason begotten by long study, observation and experience.'

At the Connaught winter assizes of 1886 Palles delivered a judgment of great constitutional importance, which excited much public interest. It deals with the duty of the executive to protect the sheriff in the execution of writs, and it defeated an attempt on the part of the chief secretary, Sir Michael Hicks Beach (afterwards Earl St. Aldwyn, q.v.), and the under-secretary, Sir Redvers Buller [q.v.], to exercise a kind of dispensing power by withholding from the sheriffs the aid of the constabulary.

Palles shone in the intimate hospitalities of bench and bar on circuit. He was full of affability, an excellent raconteur, delighting in, and delighting, young men. The public universally esteemed him, and even the suspicious peasantry of Ireland looked up to him with awed admiration as the embodiment of judicial impartiality. Palles was not only a lawyer; he was also a great educationist. He acted as chairman of the Board of Intermediate Education for Ireland (1896–1910), was commissioner of Irish national education (1890–1913), and chairman of the commissioners of Irish university education (1908); and, in his eightieth year, he practically drafted the constitution of the National University. He was a privy councillor of Ireland (1872) and of England (1892). He was a devout Roman Catholic, and the most charitable and tolerant of men. He died at Dundrum, co. Dublin, 14 February 1920.

Palles married in 1862 Ellen (died 1885), only daughter of Denis Doyle, of Dublin. There was one son of the marriage.

[F. Elrington Ball, *The Judges in Ireland, 1221–1921*, vol. ii, 1926; professional and personal knowledge.] A. W. S.

PALMER, GEORGE WILLIAM (1851–1913), biscuit manufacturer, the eldest son of George Palmer [q.v.], the founder of Huntley and Palmers' biscuit factory at Reading, by his wife, Elizabeth Sarah, daughter of Robert Meteyard, of Basingstoke, was born at Reading 23 May 1851. He was educated at Grove House, Tottenham, and from his early youth was associated with the firm of Huntley and Palmers', Ltd. In 1882 he was elected a member of the town council of the borough of Reading. He served as mayor in 1888–1889. He became an alderman in due course, and remained a member of the municipal body until his retirement. In 1892 Palmer was returned to parliament as member for Reading. He was a liberal in politics. In the general election of 1895 he was defeated, and he also contested unsuccessfully the Wokingham division of Berkshire in 1898; but he was re-elected for Reading at a by-election in the latter year and retained the seat until, owing to increasing deafness, he withdrew from public life in 1904. In 1902 the freedom of the borough of Reading was conferred upon him, the only previous person so honoured having been his father. In 1906 he was appointed a member of the Privy Council. Palmer married in 1879 Eleanor, eldest daughter of Henry Barrett, of Surbiton. There were no children of the marriage. During the early part of his life he lived chiefly in Reading. Later he lived at Marlston in Berkshire, rebuilding the house there, and devoting much attention to the development of his estate. He was a justice of the peace both for Reading and for Berkshire.

Palmer conferred many benefactions upon his native town. The most notable of these related to education. From the first he took an interest in the University College (now the university of Reading), which arose from small beginnings in 1892. This interest markedly increased after his retirement in 1904. In 1902 he had become a member of the college council, and from 1905 until his death he was also a vice-president of the college. In 1905, upon the occasion of the laying of the foundation stone of the new college hall by Viscount Goschen, then chancellor of the university of Oxford, Palmer presented the college with an endowment of £50,000, to be known, in memory of his father, as 'the George Palmer Endowment Fund'. This endowment was to enable the college to develop work of university standard. In 1909 he placed a fine recreation ground at the disposal of the college, and this benefaction was subsequently confirmed in his will. In 1910 he was associated with Harriet, Lady Wantage, in purchasing for the college five and a half acres of land with the object of preserving the amenities of her adjacent foundation of Wantage Hall, a hall of residence for men students at University College. In 1911 Palmer and his wife subscribed £100,000 towards an endowment fund of £200,000, raised with the object of enabling the college to become an independent university, the other donors being Lady Wantage and Palmer's brother, Alfred. These principal benefactions did not exhaust the list of his gifts to University College and to education. He founded a scholarship open to boys at Reading School and tenable at one of the halls of residence of University College, Reading. It is also understood that, in addition to gifts made from time to time to building and other funds of the college, he contributed anonymously large sums in order to free the college of accumulated debt.

George William Palmer died 8 October 1913. He bequeathed to University College, in addition to the recreation ground already mentioned, a sum of £10,000. In 1923 his brother Alfred, and other members of the Palmer family, presented to the college a fine library building, including an endowment, as a memorial to him. Apart from business, politics, and education, Palmer's main interests were in travel, agriculture, hunting, and shooting.

[Personal knowledge.]

W. M. C.

PARKER, ROBERT JOHN, Baron Parker, of Waddington (1857–1918), judge, the second son of the Rev. Richard Parker, rector of Claxby, Lincolnshire, by his wife, Elizabeth Coffin, was born at Claxby 25 February 1857. He was educated at Westminster, Eton, and King's College, Cambridge. At Eton he was Newcastle medallist; at King's a scholar in 1876 and a fellow in 1881. In 1878 he won the Browne's medal for the Greek ode and in 1880 was bracketed fifth in the first class of the classical tripos; he took his B.A. degree in the same year. He entered at Lincoln's Inn, read with Ingle Joyce, and, after being called in 1883, remained in Joyce's chambers and helped him in his work. Thus, though without professional connexions of his own, he soon got into practice, was highly esteemed for his pleadings, and had many pupils. In 1900, when Joyce was made a judge, Parker succeeded him, though only forty-three, as junior equity counsel to the Treasury. Thenceforward he had the most important junior practice of the day at the equity bar, and, content with this and its prospects, he never applied for silk.

This meagre account covers Parker's career to the age of forty-nine. A busy barrister's life is rarely eventful. Lord Finlay, who as attorney-general had selected him for the above-mentioned post of 'devil', as it is commonly called, said of him (15 July 1918) in the House of Lords: 'the unanimous opinion of all who knew the profession and particularly that side of the profession, was that Mr. Parker was the man for the post'. To the public he was then unknown.

In 1906 Parker was made a chancery judge and rapidly gained a great judicial reputation. On several occasions he sat as an additional member of the Court of Appeal. He made his mark especially in trying patent cases and in settling the practice under the Patents and Designs Act (1907), and having delivered a masterly judgment in a case relating to the Marconi wireless telegraphy patents in 1913, he was appointed chairman of a technical committee to advise the postmaster-general as to the choice to be made among the five then competing systems. On 1 May 1913 the committee reported in favour of Marconi's. Meantime the death of Lord Macnaghten [q.v.] on 17 February of that year had made a vacancy for a lord of appeal, for which a leading equity lawyer was required, and on 4 March Parker was appointed to fill it. He was duly sworn of the Privy Council and took the title of Baron Parker, of Waddington in Yorkshire, from the younger branch of the Parkers of Browsholme, to which his family belonged. His promotion was unexampled in its rapidity; it is true that Lord Blackburn [q.v.] had only been a stuff gownsman and a puisne judge, but he had sat on the bench for many years. From the first the profession recognized Parker as a great addition of strength to the House of Lords. In the few years during which he sat there he gained a most authoritative position as a judge of final appeal. The very varied systems of law with which from time to time a lord of appeal is called upon to acquaint himself, presented to Parker no other difficulty than that of ascertaining the principle applicable to the particular case. The most striking instance of his power of assimilating new law and making it his own is the case of the prize appeals heard during the European War. From the beginning of the series until shortly before his death he sat on the board constituted to hear them, and, after Lord Mersey ceased to sit, he presided. The subject, novel even to a learned admiralty practitioner, was quite beyond the scope of chancery experience; Parker, however, not only familiarized himself with the decisions but mastered the intricate practice prevailing in the time of Sir William Scott (Lord Stowell, q.v.), and was conspicuous in harmonizing the precedents of past wars with the very special exigencies and conditions of the War of 1914. Two judgments which he delivered on behalf of the board, those in the *Zamora* and the *Roumanian* cases, particularly bear the impress of his mind and style.

As instances of Parker's method of reasoning applied to cases of very various types, both when he was a judge of first instance and when he was a lord of appeal, the following reported cases may usefully be consulted. They are given in chronological order: *Johnson* v. *Clark* (a local custom of Kendal); *Fitzhardinge* v. *Purcell* (sporting rights on the foreshore of the Severn); *Jones* v. *Pritchard* (rights and obligations as to party-walls); *Monks* v. *Whiteley* (equitable doctrine of merger); *Barry* v. *Minturn* (an early House of Lords judgment which Parker's colleagues were satisfied to adopt without additions); *Attorney-General for the Commonwealth* v. *Adelaide Steamship Co.* (combinations in restraint of trade); *Kreglinger* v. *New Patagonian Co.* (clogging the equity of redemption); *Trim School* v. *Kelly* (murder as an accident arising out of and in the course of a schoolmaster's employment); *Stickney* v. *Keeble* (of what contracts time is of the essence); *Tamplin Steamship Co.* v. *Anglo-Mexican Co.* (frustration of a commercial adventure); *Continental Tyre Co.* v. *Daimler Co.* (the doctrine of enemy character as applied to British incorporated companies during war); *Admiralty Commissioners* v. *S.S. America* (the right to sue in respect of another person's loss of life); *Bowman* v. *the Secular Society* (illegality of anti-Christian associations); and *Banbury* v. *the Bank of Montreal* (authority of agents to bind principals by representations to third parties).

The most striking characteristic of Parker's judgments was their intellectual compactness. He instinctively avoided any parade of authorities. What mattered most to his mind was to state a general legal principle comprehensively and then to bring the case in hand logically within it. Having made a judgment clear, he attached little importance to its form. In the same spirit he was relatively indifferent to the particular part he himself played in a discussion, provided a conclusion could be arrived at that was correct in law and would sustain the credit of the tribunal. On one occasion it so chanced, in a case which concerned the interests of workmen, that the House was divided as four to three, the four being of one political party and the three of the other. Parker was one of the minority and felt that this result hardly looked well. He pointed it out to a colleague on the other side and said, 'If you will read my judgment, I will read yours.' The offer was not accepted.

When the European War broke out, Parker was one of the first to see the danger of allowing prices and the cost of living to increase rapidly and unreasonably; and, at the time of the 'business as usual' cry, he took steps to urge his views upon ministers privately. He met with no success. During 1915 he gave much thought to after-war problems, and brought the subject before the House of Lords in an elaborate and characteristically condensed address on 14 December 1915. During the passage of the Representation of the People Bill, 1918, he took up the cause of those women who had passed the examinations which qualified men for a university degree, and, speaking as an old Cambridge man and as deputy high steward of the university (which he had been since 1915), he pressed on the House of Lords the right of such women to vote for the representation of their university in parliament. In this he was successful. His most noteworthy contribution, however, to debate on public affairs was made in 1918, a few months before he died. His old friend, the Marquess Curzon of Kedleston, had often pressed him to take part in discussions in the House, and, on the occasion of a motion by Lord Parmoor on 19 March 1918 in favour of a League of Nations, Lord Parker brought before the House a detailed scheme, which went far beyond the nebulous ideas of the day in definiteness, in logical construction, and in practical detail. To those who recall it, the occasion was a moving one. It was doubly a dark day, for it was the eve of the final German advance. The light had almost failed, and Parker, then no longer able to see handwriting without strong illumination, went to the table to read out the twenty articles of his scheme, so that his fine head stood out against the gloom by the light of the lamp which he was using. His most important idea was that, for the peace of the world, it was necessary to revive the Greek principle that every man and every nation must learn to take a side. Neutrality among modern states was a temptation to aggressors and an embarrassment to those prepared to defend public rights. Only by collecting an overwhelming and united force against wrongdoers could war, as the instrument alike of the commission and the suppression of wrong, be superseded. The debate, as was natural at the time, ended inconclusively, but the impression produced was profound. To say that the scheme itself was premature or idealist is merely to say that Lord Parker's was the mind of a statesman rather than of a politician. Other counsels prevailed in Paris a year afterwards, but had he lived there can be no doubt that he would have greatly developed the scheme.

Parker's health was already beginning to fail. He continued at work until the summer of 1918, and then, after an illness of no long duration, died on 12 July at Aldworth, in Surrey, the first Lord Tennyson's old home, where he had lived since 1914. He had married in 1884 Constance, only child of John Trevor Barkley, civil engineer, who, with three sons and two daughters, survived him. His name is second to none among the judges of the first two decades of the twentieth century, and will live among the most eminent in the history of English law.

[Public records; private information; personal knowledge.] S.

PARRY, Sir **CHARLES HUBERT HASTINGS**, baronet (1848–1918), composer, musical historian, and director of the Royal College of Music, was born at Bournemouth 27 February 1848. He was the second son and youngest child by his first wife of Thomas Gambier Parry [q.v.], of Highnam Court, Gloucestershire. Gambier Parry was a lover of the arts, a collector of Italian pictures, and himself a painter of more than ordinary amateur ability. He was a keen supporter of the 'high-church' movement. Though the religious forms of Hubert's youth were completely outgrown later, and the growth involved some violent reaction from them, the life at Highnam laid a stable foundation for his habit of associating seriousness with art and beauty with seriousness.

Hubert Parry's predilection towards music appeared early. Childish compositions, beginning with single and double chants, appear in note-books which have been preserved from the age of nine. A list of his compositions when he was sixteen contains every form of Anglican church music, with piano and organ pieces, fugues, canons, madrigals, and songs interspersed. He was then at Eton, and the diaries which contain this list give a vivid picture of the zest with which he entered into every phase of public school life. That the keeper of 'School Field' should take a leading part as pianist and singer in the concerts of the Eton Musical Society was sufficiently unusual. He further surprised every one by passing the examination for the degree of bachelor of music at Oxford during his last 'half' at Eton. The method is typical. Education was for him the accumulation and sorting of diverse experiences. He had no exclusions. He would learn how things were done from the men who knew, whether the thing were the structure of a fugue or the rigging of a yacht. When he knew, he would use the knowledge in his own way. In music, Handel and Mendelssohn, imbibed at a succession of Gloucester festivals, were his first heroes. At Oxford, where he matriculated as a commoner of Exeter College in 1867, concerted chamber music became an absorbing interest, and he was instrumental in founding the University Musical Club. He spent his first long vacation at Stuttgart, studying orchestration and kindred matters with Henry Hugo Pierson [q.v.], learning German, attending the opera, and also taking lessons in viola-playing.

In 1873 Parry settled permanently in London, having married in the previous year Lady Elizabeth Maude Herbert, second daughter of Sidney, first Lord Herbert of Lea [q.v.]. He was at this time a member of Lloyds, and though his diaries and correspondence show that he was fully determined to make music the central interest of his life, the idea of the musical profession as a career was naturally not then entertained. In one sense it may be said that he never was a professional musician, since he was never under the necessity of earning a living by music. Yet his desire to do something of worth imposed on him a stern discipline of study. At first his ambition was towards piano-playing, and during a winter which he spent at Cannes for his wife's health, he gave several concerts with the violinist, Guerini. In London he sought out as his piano teacher Edward Dannreuther, who soon became his closest friend and counsellor. Every new composition was submitted to Dannreuther's judgement for many years after the days of pupillage were passed, and the words 'Dann approves' occur constantly in the record of his undertakings. It was through Dannreuther that Parry went to the first Bayreuth festival (1876) and came under the spell of *Der Ring des Nibelungen*. When Wagner visited London in the following year, Parry formed an acquaintance with him through Dannreuther, and revelled in every opportunity of steeping himself in Wagner's music.

The Wagnerian gospel found the most immediate response in Parry's soul. He was going through a necessary period of revolt against many of the narrow traditions of his upbringing, social, artistic, and religious. In composition he concentrated chiefly on instrumental music. He wrote for the violin and piano a fine Partita in D minor and a Duo for two pianos in E minor, long a favourite work (published by Breitkopf and Haertel). A whole series of concerted chamber works for piano and strings came out at the private concerts which Dannreuther gave regularly at his house in Orme Square, and a Nonet for wind, 'written as an experiment', as also the now well-known Fantasia and Fugue for organ (Novello, 1913) belong to these years. A concert of Parry's chamber music given at the house of Mr. A. J. (afterwards Earl of) Balfour in Carlton House Terrace in 1879 has been generally referred to as a landmark in his career. In none of these compositions does the influence of Wagner seem peculiarly strong, but they certainly showed an independence of thought which was disquieting to some of Parry's friends. His father shook his head sadly over the heterodoxy of 'poor dear Hubert'. A letter to one of the nearest of these friends shows Parry's own standpoint. He says, 'I like my compositions as little as possible. I feel that they are far from what they ought to be; but I take a good deal of pains and do not write ill-considered reflections of Wagner, and though I feel the impress of his warmth and genius strongly I am not tempted to tread in the same path in the matter of construction, because what is applicable to the province of dramatic music is entirely alien to instrumental music. I have my own views on the latter subject. . . .'

Towards the end of 1875 Sir George Grove [q.v.] had invited Parry to collaborate with him as assistant editor of the monumental *Dictionary of Music and Musicians,* and the research which Parry's own articles entailed, together with the varied duties of editorship, stimulated that wide historical outlook which bore fruit later in his literary works, particularly *The Art of Music* (1893), *The Oxford History of Music,* vol. iii (1902), and *Style in Musical Art* (1911).

The customary division of a composer's work into periods is always dangerous; in the case of so continuous and consistent an artist as Parry it is doubly so, yet it is necessary if such a summary of his activities as this is to be anything more than a catalogue. What may be called the formative period came definitely to an end with the production in 1880 at the Crystal Palace of a piano concerto written for Dannreuther's performance. The same year 'Scenes from Shelley's Prometheus Unbound' for solo voices, chorus, and orchestra was given at the Gloucester festival and was the firstfruit of the type of work with which Parry was to make an indelible impression on the taste of his generation.

The spirit of splendid rebellion in the poem was Parry's inspiration; he brought to its expression all that growth towards freedom which he had acquired in years of probation. Naturally the technical influence of Wagner, the Wagner of *The Ring,* is evident; the subject encouraged it, for here he was nearer to 'the province of dramatic music' than he had been before. There is also more warmth of colouring and scenic suggestion in the orchestral music than in any of Parry's later work. But the quality of the melody, the sensitiveness to the English language, and the subtle beauties of the writing for the choir, are unmistakable. Here was a new voice in music; it happened to be an English voice.

In spite of the mixed reception of 'Prometheus', the way was now open for wider activities in composition. Two symphonies followed quickly on one another, that in G and the one known as the 'Cambridge', not only because it was written for the Cambridge Musical Society but because it had as background a 'programme' of undergraduate life. The Cambridge Society had rescued 'Prometheus' from its fate in an admirable performance, and in the years in which the Society was guided by (Sir) Charles Stanford many of Parry's works were given there as they appeared. A setting of Shirley's ode, 'The Glories of our Blood and State', appeared in the same year as the Cambridge symphony, and showed that Parry's mind was already turning to what became ultimately the dominating issue of his life—reflective choral music.

The music to 'The Birds' of Aristophanes (Cambridge, 1884) led to his one experiment in opera, 'Guinevere', a romantic opera in three acts, which he composed with enthusiasm in 1886, though with many misgivings about the libretto. A single attempt to get it performed led to nothing; Parry laid aside the score and with it all aspirations towards opera, the conditions of which became increasingly distasteful to him in later years. Yet his music to the comedies of Aristophanes at various times, 'The Frogs' (Oxford, 1891), 'The Clouds' (1905), and 'The Acharnians' (1914) shows that he retained a sympathy with and a certain instinct for the theatre, though he regarded these things rather as an academic 'rag' than as the serious business of his art.

The period was completed with the noble setting for double choir and orchestra of Milton's ode 'At a solemn Music' ('Blest Pair of Sirens'). It has since become the most famous of all his works. Parry, together with many of his Eton and Oxford friends, had delighted in singing the choruses of the Mass in B minor, for the first English performance of which the Bach Choir had been originally formed. He wrote 'Blest Pair' for these friends at the suggestion of Grove, and its instant success amongst them, when the Bach Choir sang it in 1887, made amends for all the carping disparagement with which professional critics had pursued his earlier works.

His first oratorio 'Judith', given at Birmingham in the following year, marks a fresh stage in Parry's career. 'Judith', like 'Blest Pair', was a popular success, and from this time onward till he succeeded Sir George Grove as director of the Royal College of Music (1895) Parry was pouring out large works with almost unparalleled activity and conducting performances of them all over the country. They covered a wide range of expression. Two further symphonies, the 'English' in C and one in E minor, were produced in London in 1889; the same year came his first work for a Leeds festival, Pope's 'Ode on Saint Cecilia's Day'; 'L'Allegro ed Il Penseroso' (Norwich, 1890) again showed his understanding of the measured stateliness of Milton's verse, and from that he turned first to the majesty of the Latin psalm 'De Profundis', written for triple choir (Hereford, 1891), then to the melody of Tennyson in the choric song from 'The Lotus Eaters' (Cambridge, 1892). Yet this is preeminently the period of oratorios, three in number, 'Judith', 'Job' (Gloucester, 1892), and 'King Saul' (Birmingham, 1894).

'Judith' has been called a reactionary work, and with a certain justice. It is distinctly disconcerting, notwithstanding the intrinsic beauty of many of the numbers, to find Parry in the very zenith of his powers reverting to the stereotyped form of the Old Testament oratorio, with all its paraphernalia of massive choruses and arias. But Parry's attitude to the form was not one of complaisant acceptance. His preface makes it clear that his main interest lay in 'popular movements and passions and such results of them as occur a hundred times in history, of which the Israelitish story is one vivid type out of many'. In these works the musical experiences of his youth are sifted. He goes back in order to go forward, reviews the whole position of oratorio, and passes beyond both the conventional religious standpoint and the dramatic attractions of narrative. In the best moments of the two Birmingham works he reaches the epic expression of human feeling. 'Job' goes farther. Every convention of oratorio, even the choral *finale*, is discarded, in order that the one purpose, the growth of the soul through pain, may be traced out in the cry of lamentation, in the answer of the Lord 'out of the whirlwind', and in the peaceful peroration for orchestra alone. In the last two scenes of 'Job' we have the clue to that long chain of works which was eventually to sum up Parry's thought on the puzzle of life.

Meantime, however, there were busy years in which Parry's responsibilities as director of the Royal College of Music (he had held a professorship there since its inception in 1883), as choragus and subsequently as professor of music at Oxford, and his literary work, all made disastrous inroads on his time for composition. Most of the larger productions of the 'nineties show signs of that hasty workmanship which has seriously damaged Parry's reputation with a generation much concerned about technique, points of effect, and especially orchestration. Even the Symphonic Variations, probably his most successful composition for orchestra alone, has suffered from his carelessness in marking *nuances*, and certain festival works have sunk into oblivion after one imperfect performance largely on that account. The wonder is that the stream of composition went on comparatively unchecked, and that in the smaller works, from the songs collected in the various series of 'English Lyrics' to the 'Ode to Music' written for the opening of the new concert hall at the Royal College of Music, there is so much of the same lofty melody and the same sure handling of the voices which are the lovable qualities of Parry's art.

In the year after the South African War, the Royal Choral Society produced at the Albert Hall 'War and Peace', a symphonic ode for solo voices, chorus, and orchestra. Parry wrote the words himself (as he had often done—partially at any rate—in the case of previous works) and threw into rough and vigorous verse, suitable to his music, his thoughts on the conflicting passions of war and peace. Musically he rose to his full stature in the treatment of this theme, and it proved to be the precursor of a series of works, which in differing forms address themselves to one or other aspect of the same problem. Several cantatas, produced at a succession of Three Choirs festivals, beginning with 'Voces Clamantium' (Hereford, 1903), use the imagery and poetry of the Biblical writers to illustrate his message. Their very titles proclaim it: 'The Love that casteth out Fear', 'The Soul's Ransom', and 'Beyond these Voices there is Peace'. Each has compellingly fine musical moments, but each left him feeling that the message 'Look where thy Hope lies' was incomplete.

In 'A Vision of Life' (Cardiff, 1907) he again wrote his own poem, and wrestled with the same theme, surveying as in a dream the greatness and pitifulness of human struggle throughout salient epochs in the world's history. Even his last orchestral symphony (1912) shares in the thought, for the first three of its four linked movements bear the titles 'Work', 'Love', and 'Play', and the whole is summed up in a mood of optimism by a *finale* labelled 'Now'. Nor was this all. for in his last years he was much occupied with a book, *Instinct and Character* (unpublished, though typed copies have been deposited, and may be seen, in the British Museum, Bodleian, and Royal College of Music libraries), which endeavoured to examine the grounds of human action, reaction, and progress and to show where his hope lay for the future of mankind.

All this shows the impossibility of estimating Parry solely as the musical artist, even though it is through his music that he has done most towards 'winning the way'. The joyous freshness of the 'Ode on the Nativity', his last work for a Three Choirs festival (Hereford, 1912), shows that his purely musical inspiration still ran clear, and the boyish sense of fun was ready to break out again in such things as 'The Pied Piper' and the music to 'The Acharnians'. Nor must it be forgotten that during these years he so steeped himself in the mind of J. S. Bach, that he was able to produce the most intimately sympathetic study of 'a great personality' in music which the literature of this country possesses.

Parry's vivid interest in many things outside music, his love of the open air and the sea (he was a member of the Royal Yacht Squadron, and sailing his own yacht was easily first among his favourite recreations), his sympathy with young people, his constant desire to explore new ways of thought, even those ways in modern music which were most antipathetic to him—all contributed to keep his nature sane and sweet. He could be intolerant, hasty, and even forbidding. He never 'suffered fools gladly', but only fools failed to get at the essential simplicity and truth of the man. It was primarily his example and presence as head of the musical profession which compelled that enlarged outlook on the part of musicians themselves and that favourable change in their position amongst their fellows which in the last generation has brought new life to the art in England. He made music a man's concern.

The 'Songs of Farewell', six motets for unaccompanied voices, together with some solo songs and organ preludes, are the product of Parry's last years. The European War had shattered everything most dear to him, and he did not see the end of it. Its shadow is cast on his music, yet in these motets he holds to the convictions he had so hardly won, and in 'Never weather-beaten Sail', 'There is an old Belief', and 'Lord, let Me know mine End', there is a serenity and confidence which places them among the really great achievements of music.

He died at Rustington 7 October 1918, and was buried in the crypt of St. Paul's Cathedral.

Parry was knighted in 1898, and was made a baronet on the occasion of King Edward's coronation in 1902. His wife and two daughters survived him, but he left no male heir. The estate of Highnam Court, which he inherited from his father, passed to his half-brother. A tablet to his memory, bearing an inscription by the poet laureate (Mr. Robert Bridges), has been placed by public subscription in Gloucester Cathedral.

[Unpublished Diaries and Letters; personal knowledge. A fairly complete list of Parry's compositions to date of publication, 1907, is included in the second edition of Grove's *Dictionary of Music and Musicians*, edited by J. A. Fuller-Maitland. For further biographical details, see C. L. Graves, *Hubert Parry: His Life and Works*, 2 vols., 1926, published since this article was written.] H. C. C.

PARSONS, ALFRED WILLIAM (1847–1920), painter and illustrator, was born at Beckington, Somerset, 2 December 1847, the second son of Joshua Parsons, surgeon, of Beckington. He was educated at private schools and entered the Savings Bank department of the Post Office as a clerk in 1865, but two years later (1867) he gave up his career in the civil service and devoted himself to painting. The first appearance of his work at a Royal Academy exhibition was in 1871, when he showed two pictures, 'A Half Holiday' and 'In a Copse, November'. Subsequently Parsons was a frequent exhibitor at Burlington House as also at the Grosvenor, the New, and other galleries. In 1887 his picture of an orchard, 'When Nature Painted All Things Gay', was purchased by the trustees of the Chantrey fund; it is now in the National Gallery of British Art at Millbank (Tate Gallery). In 1892–1894 Parsons paid a visit to Japan; he published his impressions of that country, with illustrations, in his book, *Notes in Japan* (1896). He was elected A.R.A. in 1897 and R.A. in 1911. A member of the Royal Society of Painters in Water Colours since 1905, he was chosen president of the society, in succession to Sir Ernest Albert Waterlow, in 1914, and held that office until his death.

A very important section of Parsons's artistic output is formed by his work as a book-illustrator, much of which appeared in *Harper's Magazine*. He also contributed the illustrations to *The Genus Rosa* by Ellen Willmott (1910), and collaborated with Edwin Austin Abbey [q.v.] in illustrating Herrick's *Hesperides* and *Noble Numbers* (1882), *She Stoops to Conquer* (1887), *Old Songs* (1889), and *The Quiet Life* (1890); and with F. D. Millet in providing the illustrations for the latter's book, *The Danube, from the Black Forest to the Black Sea* (1893).

Parsons was an enthusiastic gardener, and much of his work as an artist reflects his keen interest in gardens and flowers. A prolific artist of tender, delicate fibre, there is a vein of genuine poetry in his art, even if it is lacking in intensity and originality. In the history of art his position as a landscape painter is vaguely in the great following of the Barbizon school. Parsons, who was unmarried, died at his house at Broadway, Worcestershire, 16 January 1920.

[*Daily Telegraph*, 22 January 1920; A. Graves, *The Royal Academy of Arts, Dictionary of Contributors*, vol. vi, 1905–1906.] T. B.

PEACOCKE, JOSEPH FERGUSON (1835–1916), archbishop of Dublin, was born at Abbeyleix, Queen's county, 5 November 1835, the youngest son of George Peacocke, M.D., of Longford, by his wife, Catherine Ferguson. He was educated at Trinity College, Dublin, where he graduated as senior moderator in history and English literature in 1857, obtaining also a first-class divinity *testimonium* and the political economy prize of his year. Ordained deacon in 1858 and priest in 1859, his first curacy was that of St. Mary's, Kilkenny, where he served from 1858 until 1861, when he accepted the secretaryship of the Hibernian Church Missionary Society, which he held for two years. A churchman of the evangelical school, he was always a firm supporter of foreign missions and of the Church Missionary Society in particular. In 1863 he went to Monkstown, co. Dublin, as curate of the parish church. Here he stayed until 1873, when he was appointed rector of St. George's, Dublin, an important city parish. But in 1878 he was recalled to Monkstown as rector, by the affection of his old parishioners, and he remained there until his elevation to the episcopate. Along with his benefice he held for a few months in 1894 the professorship of pastoral theology in Trinity College, Dublin, a post for which he was admirably qualified both by inclination and by experience.

In 1894 Peacocke, who had proceeded D.D. in 1883, was elected to the see of Meath, in succession to Dr. Charles Parsons Reichel. In 1897 he was translated to the archbishopric of Dublin, in succession to William Conyngham, fourth Baron Plunket. No archbishop of Dublin for two hundred years had previously held a cure of souls in the diocese; and Peacocke was well known to his clergy, even before he came to rule over them, as a churchman of tolerant mind, rich pastoral experience, and holy life. 'Pastor fidelis, humilis, et sanctus corde' are the words graven on his memorial tablet in Kildare Cathedral. He presided with dignity over the dioceses of Dublin, Glendalough, and Kildare, until illness struck him down in 1915, when he resigned his see. He died at Blackrock, co. Dublin, 26 May 1916. His public utterances, whether in pulpit or synod, always commanded respectful attention, but, with the exception of some charges and occasional sermons, he did not publish anything. He had served as select preacher both at Dublin and at Cambridge.

Peacocke was a man of fine presence, and an excellent portrait by P. A. de Laszlò, presented by the diocese, is preserved in the palace at Dublin. He married in 1865 Caroline Sophia, daughter of Major John Irvine, D.L., of Killadeno, co. Fermanagh, and had four sons and one daughter. His eldest son was consecrated bishop of Derry in 1916.

[Archbishop Peacocke's Charges, 1895–1907, and Letters; personal knowledge.] J. H. B.

PEARS, Sir EDWIN (1835–1919), barrister-at-law, publicist, and historical writer, was born 18 March 1835 at York, the younger son of Robert Pears, of York (descendant of a younger branch of the family of Piers, formerly of Piers Hall, Ingleton, Yorkshire), by his wife, Elizabeth Barnett. After being educated privately, he graduated at London University with distinction in Roman law and jurisprudence. On a voyage to Australasia in 1857 he married Mary, daughter of John Ritchie Hall, surgeon in the royal navy, by whom he had four sons and three daughters. In 1870 he was called to the bar at the Middle Temple, and began to practise in London. In addition to his legal practice, he undertook literary and administrative work. He was for a time private secretary to Frederic Temple, at that time bishop of Exeter; he was also general secretary of the Social Science Association from 1868 to 1872, and of the International Prison Congress in 1872, and edited the transactions of both those bodies. In 1872 he was also editor of the *Law Magazine*. This accumulation of activities began to tell upon his health, and when, in January 1873, he learnt accidentally that the practice of Sir Charles Parker Butt [q.v.] at the Constantinople bar was vacant, he went out to Constantinople to take up this work provisionally. This accident determined his career. He became a permanent resident in Turkey, rose to the highest position open to him in that country in his own profession (becoming president of the European or consular bar in Constantinople in 1881), and made a name for himself as a newspaper correspondent and as an historian of his adopted city. He became perhaps the best-known member of the British colony in Turkey since Sir Paul Rycaut.

Pears's political attitude and activity in the Levant were determined by the facts that he was not born there and did not settle there till his thirty-ninth year, when he had already made in England political and personal connexions which he always kept up. Consequently, though he rapidly rose to be one of the leaders of the British colony, he retained an independent and critical point of view in regard to local affairs and to the Eastern Question. Holding, as he did, strong liberal convictions, he did not become imbued with that complacency towards the Turks—right or wrong—to which there has often been a tendency among Western residents in the Levant, particularly in the British and French colonies since the Crimean War. He had no more illusions regarding Sultan Abdul Hamid's intelligence than others had in regard to his character, and he expressed his views of that sovereign in his *Life of Abdul Hamid* (1917). Here he showed himself as accomplished a student of contemporary history as he was of the Middle Ages, on which he wrote two standard monographs, *The Fall of Constantinople* [in 1204] (1885) and *The Destruction of the Greek Empire* [in 1453] (1903). He played a part of European importance in 1876, when, as correspondent of the *Daily News*, he had the judgement and the courage to expose the Turkish atrocities in Bulgaria. His statements were confirmed both by diplomatic and by journalistic investigators; and on the strength of this information, Mr. Gladstone launched a celebrated political campaign. During a long career, Pears invariably acted with frankness and uprightness towards the many and diverse communities in his adopted country and yet remained in good relations with each and all of them; though his extensive practice at the local bar involved delicate relations with them and especially with the ruling race. He was knighted in 1909. Pears stayed on in Constantinople after Turkey's intervention in the European War, but was forced to leave the country in December 1914. He returned in April 1919, but died at Malta (from an accident at sea) on 27 November of the same year.

[Sir E. Pears, *Forty Years in Constantinople*, 1916; private information.]

A. J. T.

PEARSON, Sir CYRIL ARTHUR, first baronet (1866–1921), newspaper proprietor, was born at Wookey, Somerset, 24 February 1866, the only son of the Rev. Arthur Cyril Pearson, rector of Springfield, Essex; his mother, Philippa Maxwell-Lyte, was a granddaughter of the hymn-writer, Henry Francis Lyte [q.v.], author of 'Abide with Me'. Pearson went to Winchester in 1880, but the straitened circumstances of his father prevented him from staying there more than two years. He continued his education under his father till 1884, when he won a clerkship offered by (Sir) George Newnes [q.v.] as a prize for a competition in *Tit-Bits*, a new species of popular journal. A year later he became Newnes's manager, but his salary never exceeded £350, and in 1890, being a married man with two children, he set up in business for himself as proprietor of *Pearson's Weekly*. Chiefly by means of ingenious guessing competitions he won a huge circulation for this venture, and started many other popular papers. In 1900 he brought out the *Daily Express* at a halfpenny, four years after Alfred Harmsworth (afterwards Viscount Northcliffe) had produced the *Daily Mail*. He advocated a protectionist policy before Mr. Chamberlain began his crusade, and he was the founder of the tariff reform league in 1903. Mr. Chamberlain described him as 'the greatest hustler I have ever known'. In 1904, having acquired several provincial newspapers, he purchased the *Standard*, which had fallen on evil days, and at the end of 1907 entered into abortive negotiations for the purchase of *The Times*. In 1908 he underwent an operation for glaucoma, and was never afterwards able to read or to write. In 1910 he sold both the *Standard* and *Evening Standard*, and in 1912 disposed of his interest in the *Daily Express*. A year later he learned from Professor Fuchs of Vienna that he would soon be blind. He told his wife that he would never be *a* blind man: 'I am going to be *the* blind man'. He forthwith joined the council of the National Institute for the Blind, and carried its income from £8,010 in 1913 to £358,174 in 1921. At the outbreak of war in 1914 he directed the Prince of Wales's fund, and in less than six months collected over a million pounds.

Early in 1915 Pearson devoted himself to soldiers and sailors discharged from the hospitals as blind, first opening a hostel in Bayswater Road, and in March transferring this work to St. Dunstan's, in Regent's Park. He succeeded in teaching the blind not only to earn their own living, but to bear their deprivation with courage and cheerfulness. He became a popular figure and was known as 'the blind leader of the blind'. In 1916 he was created a baronet, and in 1917 received the G.B.E. On 9 December 1921 he met his death in London in a tragic manner. His foot slipped on the enamel of his bath, he was stunned by striking one of the taps, and he fell face forward into the water. He was found dead an hour and a quarter after he had entered the bathroom. He was twice married: first, in 1887 to Isobel Sarah, daughter of the Rev. F. Bennett, of Maddington, near Salisbury, by whom he had three daughters who survived him; secondly, in 1897 to Ethel Maude (created D.B.E. 1920), daughter of W. J. Fraser, of Cromartie, Herne Bay. Their only child, Neville Arthur (born 1898), succeeded to the baronetcy.

Apart from its admirable philanthropic aspect, Pearson's career is perhaps more alarming than edifying. Intellectually he was unfitted to guide, much less to form, public opinion. He knew nothing of philosophy, little of history, and less of literature and art. His opinions were the caprice of his uncriticized intuitions, and he was resentful of opposition, impatient of argument. Happily for his readers, whom he sought to stampede rather than to inform, his tastes were harmless and his nature wholesome. He had a genuine feeling for country life and a real devotion to games and sports. Wealth did not corrupt him, and the loss of sight did not deject him. He will be remembered chiefly by his work for the blind, the part which he played in helping General Baden-Powell to start the boy scout movement, and his 'fresh air fund' (1892) which for many years has sent numbers of poor children into the country. He paid in his own person most of those penalties which nature exacts of the 'hustler'.

[*The Times*, 10 December 1921; Sidney Dark, *Life of Sir Arthur Pearson*, 1922; personal knowledge.] H. B–E.

PEEL, ARTHUR WELLESLEY, first VISCOUNT PEEL (1829–1912), Speaker of the House of Commons, was born in London 3 August 1829. He was the youngest of the five sons of Sir Robert Peel, second baronet, prime minister [q.v.], by his wife, Julia, daughter of Lieutenant-General Sir John Floyd, first baronet [q.v.]. He was named after his godfather, the first Duke of Wellington. He figures as a boy in *The Private Letters of Sir Robert Peel* (1920). His early years were spent at Drayton Manor, Tamworth, and he was educated at Hatfield, Eton, and Balliol College, Oxford, taking second-class honours in *literae humaniores* in 1852.

In 1865, two years after an unsuccessful candidature at Coventry, he began his career in the House of Commons as liberal member for Warwick. He represented Warwick until 1885, and, when that borough was joined to Leamington, he sat for the new constituency until his elevation to the peerage in 1895. At the end of 1868, when Mr. Gladstone formed his first ministry, Peel became parliamentary secretary to the Poor Law Board, and then, from 1871 to 1873, served as secretary to the Board of Trade. From 1873 to 1874 he was patronage secretary to the Treasury, that is, chief whip to the liberal party. When Gladstone returned to office in 1880, Peel became under secretary to the Home Department, but resigned after a few months on account of ill-health.

In 1884, on the retirement of Sir Henry Brand (afterwards Viscount Hampden, q.v.) from the speakership, Gladstone nominated Peel, who was unanimously elected 26 February. His speech of acceptance was reckoned so much a masterpiece that *The Times* recorded that 'the House suddenly woke to the knowledge that its numbers had among them another Peel, who might fairly compare in parliamentary eloquence with the great Sir Robert himself'. In 1895 Gladstone said that none of the Speakers for two centuries past had had to contend with a tithe of the difficulties which were met with, and overcome, by Peel. The eleven years of his speakership, lasting until April 1895, coincided with an intensity of party spirit unknown since the days of the first Reform Bill. These feelings had their root in the Irish question, more especially in the two Home Rule Bills of 1886 and 1893. The Irish members, whose numbers had much increased since the election of 1880, were able to practise what their critics termed 'obstruction' with proportionate power. The House in 1882, in order to parry obstruction, had adopted for the first time in its history a closure resolution, which threw upon the Speaker the burden of determining when closure should be applied. Peel used this power in February 1885, for the first time. If, as happened, more than forty members voted against closure, then there had to be at least 200 votes cast in its favour in order to carry it. On this initial occasion only 207 votes were so cast. This critical event marked a turning-point in the procedure of the House of Commons. Warned by this instance, the House in March 1887 passed a standing order leaving it to the Speaker to accept or to refuse a motion 'that the question be now put', thus adopting the policy of distributing these self-governing powers between the Speaker and the members. Nevertheless, the parliamentary machine could not, and did not, run smoothly, the passions of that time being too hot; so that the work of the Speaker was, on the one hand, to forward such reforms of procedure as were possible, and, on the other, to carry on the life of the House of Commons from day to day. 'Theoretically Peel was the servant of the House. There were occasions when a stranger might almost have regarded him as its master. His character, and his known uprightness, carried him through all his difficulties' [*The Times*, 25 October 1912].

In 1895 Peel was created a viscount, and from this time his main public work was to be chairman of the royal commission on the licensing laws, which sat from 1896 to 1899. He took the lead in preparing the minority report, which, though agreeing with the majority report in many points, inclined to the views of temperance reformers on the main issues of the reduction of public-houses and the basis for compensation. Peel then, as in later years, opposed the creation of a perpetual interest in a terminable licence, and favoured the rapid reduction of licences by the aid of a compensation fund levied on the trade itself. When the liberals came into power, the Licensing Bill which they carried through the House of Commons in 1908, only to be defeated in the House of Lords, was based on the Peel minority report.

Lord Peel had many other activities and honours. He was visitor of Balliol College (1894–1912), and for many years chairman of the trustees of the National Portrait Gallery, as well as an active trustee of the British Museum. He was president of the Temperance Legislation League, first chairman of the State Children's Aid Association, chairman of the council of Toynbee Hall, a governor of Harrow School, and vice-chairman of the Bedfordshire County Council. He received the honorary D.C.L. at Oxford in 1887. He married in 1862 Adelaide (died 1890), daughter of William Stratford Dugdale, of Merevale, Warwickshire. They had four sons and three daughters. Lord Peel died 24 October 1912 at Sandy, Bedfordshire, where he had lived for many years. There is a portrait of him by Sir W. Q. Orchardson, as Speaker, now in the Speaker's House, Westminster, and another by Sir H. von Herkomer, in the hall of Balliol College.

[Memoir (by the present writer) in *The Times*, 25 October 1912.] G. P.

PÉLISSIER, HARRY GABRIEL (1874–1913), comedian, was born at Finchley 27 April 1874, the second son of Frederic Antoine Pélissier, a French diamond merchant, by his wife, Jennie Kean. After leaving school he was for six months employed in his father's business in Berwick Street, London. Not finding the occupation congenial, and having from his earliest years a predilection for the stage, he made up his mind to try his fortune on the music-hall stage, and he made his first appearance at a London suburban hall. In 1895 he joined a troupe of entertainers under the direction of the brothers Baddeley, the well-known lawn-tennis players, and Mr. Sherrington Chinn. A year later he took over the direction of the troupe and renamed it 'The Follies'. It was first heard at Worthing under that title on 7 August 1896. After several years of provincial and seaside engagements, the troupe appeared at the Alhambra,

London, in 1900, and this was followed by several appearances at the Palace Theatre from 1901 onwards. For a time 'The Follies' was included in the entertainment given by Mr. Albert Chevalier at the Queen's Hall, and in December 1904 Pélissier and his 'Follies' were commanded to appear before King Edward VII at Sandringham, in connexion with Queen Alexandra's birthday festivities.

So successful was his entertainment that Pélissier determined to test its capacity to stand alone as an attraction, and after a preliminary experiment at the Midland Theatre, Manchester, at the end of 1906, he opened at the Royalty Theatre, London, on 19 March 1907. The venture was completely successful. In September 1907 he removed to Terry's Theatre, and in 1908 to the Apollo, where the entertainment was given for hundreds of nights. His 'Follies' became famous for their burlesques of current theatrical pieces, and their 'potted plays' and 'potted opera' were triumphant successes. Gifted alike as composer, producer, and comedian, Pélissier was, for a time, immensely popular; but after 1911 his powers declined, and ill-health seriously impeded his work. A revue at the Alhambra, a pantomime at the Empire, and a final season of 'The Follies' at the Apollo (1912) were all unsuccessful, and after a three months' illness Pélissier died in London 25 September 1913.

Pélissier was a man of immense proportions, and his bulk undoubtedly added to his attraction as a comedian. He had an exceedingly mobile countenance, which he used with excellent effect, and an agreeable voice, and he was an accomplished musician. His facility in writing songs, humorous and sentimental, burlesques, extravaganzas, and 'potted plays' was remarkable. A series of humorous sketches entitled *Potted Pélissier* was published in 1913.

He married in 1911 Fay Compton, actress, a member of his troupe, youngest daughter of Edward Compton, actor, and left an infant son.

[*The Times*, 27 September 1913; *Daily Telegraph*, 27 September 1913; private information.] J. P.

PENLEY, WILLIAM SYDNEY (1852–1912), actor-manager, was born at St. Peter's, near Broadstairs, 19 November 1852, the only son of William George Robinson Penley, schoolmaster, by his wife, Emily Ann Wootton, widow of Walter Pilcher. His grandfather was Aaron Edwin Penley [q.v.], water-colour painter to William IV. The family had old theatrical associations; his great-uncles William, Sampson, and Belville Penley were all actor-managers, and his great-aunt, Rosina Penley, was an actress. Penley attended his father's school, Grove House Academy, St. Peter's, for a short time, and when his father removed to Charles Street, Westminster, he also attended there. He then became one of the children of the Chapel Royal, St. James's, and was subsequently a chorister of Westminster Abbey. From the Abbey he went as chief bass vocalist to Bedford chapel, Bloomsbury, where the incumbent was John Chippendall Montesquieu Bellew [q.v.], the well-known preacher, father of the actor, Harold Kyrle Bellew. He also sang at the Russian Embassy chapel. After apprenticeship with a City firm of milliners and fancy-goods manufacturers, he joined the staff of Copestake, Moore, Crampton, & Co.

Through the introduction of William Terriss, Penley obtained an engagement at the old Court Theatre under the management of Marie Litton [q.v.], and first appeared on the professional stage at that theatre on 26 December 1871 in the farce *My Wife's Second Floor* by John Maddison Morton. His salary was thirteen shillings a week. In the following October he played in T. F. Plowman's *Zampa*, and subsequently appeared at the Holborn Theatre in *Doctor Faust.* In 1875 he appeared at the Royalty Theatre, under the management of Madame Selina Dolaro, in *Trial by Jury* by (Sir) W. S. Gilbert and (Sir) Arthur Sullivan. After touring in comic opera, he returned to London to appear at the Strand Theatre (October 1876) in the comic opera, *Princess Toto*, by W. S. Gilbert and Alfred Cellier. He remained at the Strand Theatre under the management of Mrs. Swanborough for three years, appearing principally in burlesque. In April 1879, at the Royalty, he appeared with success in Sullivan's *The Zoo* and in *Crutch and Toothpick* by G. R. Sims. Later in that year he toured the provinces in Gilbert and Sullivan's opera *H.M.S. Pinafore*. In March 1880 he appeared at the Gaiety in *La Voyage en Suisse* with the Hanlon-Lees, a well-known troupe of pantomimists, and accompanied them to the United States. He reappeared in London at the Globe Theatre (July 1882) in *The Vicar of Bray*, and at the Comedy Theatre (September 1882) in Robert Planquette's *Rip Van Winkle*.

Penley made the first notable advance

in his profession when he appeared as Lay Brother Pelican in Chassaigne's *Falka* at the Comedy (October 1883), an exceedingly droll performance. A greater opportunity followed when he was chosen by (Sir) Charles Hawtrey to succeed (Sir) Herbert Beerbohm Tree in the title-rôle of *The Private Secretary*, when that play was transferred to the Globe Theatre in May 1884. He played this part for two years and firmly established his reputation. He remained with Hawtrey for some years at the Globe, at the Comedy, and at the Strand, appearing in many plays of varied merit. His long engagement with Hawtrey having terminated, Penley appeared at Terry's Theatre (1890) in *New Lamps for Old* and *The Judge*; the following January at Toole's Theatre in *Our Regiment*, and later at the Savoy Theatre in *The Nautch Girl*. In 1891 he returned to the Comedy Theatre for a short time.

Charley's Aunt by Brandon Thomas —the play with which Penley's name is chiefly associated—was produced on 29 February 1892 at Bury St. Edmunds. The humorous possibilities of the piece were only discovered a short time after its production. Gradually it was developed into the famous farce as produced at the Royalty Theatre on 21 December 1892. Penley's remarkable impersonation of the part of Lord Fancourt Babberley became the talk of the town, and the play, transferred to the Globe Theatre early in 1893, settled down to the longest run on record for any farce, being played continuously over a period of four years in 1,466 consecutive performances. *Charley's Aunt* has since been translated into several languages and played all over the world. In 1898 Penley produced in the provinces *A Little Ray of Sunshine*, and he re-opened at the Royalty Theatre with this play in December 1898. He then acquired the lease of the Novelty Theatre, which he re-named the Great Queen Street Theatre, and opened on 24 May 1900 with the same play. At this theatre he also revived *The Private Secretary* and *Charley's Aunt*, but without much success, and his acting career ended with the run of the last-mentioned play in 1901. He retired to Woking, where he lived a quiet country life, until his death at St. Leonards-on-Sea 11 November 1912. Most of the large fortune which he had made from the success of *Charley's Aunt* was lost in later years.

Penley's face was his fortune. He had a great sense of humour; but it was the expression of his countenance and the dry, metallic quality of his voice which had such irresistible effect on his audience.

Penley was an active churchman, one of the proprietors of the *Church Family Newspaper*, and also a prominent freemason. He was the author of a little work, *Penley on Himself*, published in 1884. He married in 1880 Mary Ann, daughter of William Arthur Ricketts, of Cuckfield, Sussex, who survived him, together with three sons and three daughters.

[*The Times*, 12 November 1912; *Daily Telegraph*, 12 November 1912; private information; personal knowledge.] J. P.

PERCIVAL, JOHN (1834–1918), schoolmaster and bishop, the son of William Percival, a Westmorland 'statesman' (that is, a farmer who owned his land), by his wife, Jane, daughter of William Langmire, of Bolton, Westmorland, was born at Brough Sowerby, Westmorland, 27 September 1834, and educated at Appleby grammar school. He had a strenuous boyhood, 'trudging to and from school in his clogs, with a blue linen bag of books over his shoulder', and, in his spare hours, working on the farm. To the end he retained a strong northern accent which suited well his grave and rather melancholy voice. In 1855 he went as an open scholar to Queen's College, Oxford, where he gained the Junior Mathematical scholarship and double first classes (classics and mathematics) both in moderations and in 'greats'. Immediately after taking his degree he was elected a fellow of his college; but under the strain of spare living and hard work his health broke down temporarily and he was ordered abroad to Pau. There he first met his future wife, Louisa Holland, whom he married in 1862 and by whom he had six children. In 1860 he accepted a mastership at Rugby and, two years later, on Dr. Temple's recommendation, he was appointed first head master of Clifton College. His success was immediate and complete. In less than ten years Clifton had won a recognized place among the great public schools. He was a master builder and, like Dr. Arnold, whose views on education he largely shared, he set the stamp of his personality so deeply on the place that time has not effaced it. 'One great centre', wrote Canon J. M. Wilson, 'from which his influence radiated was the chapel pulpit. His words, somehow, rang true in the ears of the not naturally religious boy and enlisted him on the side of right of public spirit, of purity, of large-heartedness and courage, of virtues which appeal to a boy. Two things struck me specially about the boys. One was their modesty and good manners, and the other was their high standard of industry and intelligence.' And his ascendancy over the parents was as great as his ascendancy over the boys. In 1879 he left Clifton to become president of Trinity College, Oxford, a post which he subsequently combined with a canonry at Bristol (1882–1887), vacating at the same time a prebendal stall in Exeter Cathedral which he had held since 1871. The atmosphere of Oxford was not wholly congenial to him. He was impatient for reforms, and less in sympathy with the average undergraduate than with the schoolboy. Bishop Gore, recalling this period, says: 'We felt that a strong righteous will was expressing itself amongst us with profound astonishment at our being content to be such fools as we were.' In spite, however, of some friction, he left a permanent mark on the college and was largely responsible for its rapid growth and intellectual success. In university politics he had two causes specially at heart—the University Extension movement, of which he was a vigorous pioneer, and the higher education of women. He was a prime mover in the foundation of Somerville College and became the first president of its council.

In November 1886 Percival was offered, and accepted, the head mastership of Rugby, and took up his new duties in May 1887. He found much to do, and set about the task with characteristic energy, creating, reforming, and transforming. To quote one of the masters, 'under Percival we were always moving towards noble ends along a sure road; but he sometimes forced the pace to such an extent that we almost dropped from fatigue'. After seven years the strain began to tell on his health, and in February 1895 he accepted the bishopric of Hereford, which was offered him by Lord Rosebery.

As bishop he was a courageous but rather lonely figure. His views on ecclesiastical, social, and political questions (he was a strong liberal) were not those of his clergy, and he was too earnest a champion of whatever he believed to be truth to keep silence or tolerate compromise. Nor did he find in a rural diocese much scope for the gifts of initiative and organization which were peculiarly his own. But his fearlessness, his sincerity, his generosity and invariable courtesy, won him the personal affection of many and the respect of all. In 1896 he lost his first wife, and in 1899 married Mary Symonds, an old family friend. In 1917 his powers were fast failing and he retired to Oxford, where he died on 3 December 1918.

He was buried, as was fitting, in Clifton chapel, for Clifton was his greatest achievement, and it was as a head master that he influenced most the life of his generation. Keenly alive to new educational requirements, he was above all a great spiritual force, with a passion for righteousness and a deep conviction of the serious purpose of life. Perhaps boys breathed more comfortably than men in the strenuous atmosphere that surrounded him. 'He was universally and profoundly respected, and he was feared, not with terror, but with awe; and in a sense—the deepest sense—he was loved.' So writes his biographer, a former pupil at Rugby, and a head master could receive no higher tribute.

There is a portrait of Percival by Hugh Riviere at Trinity College, Oxford. Another, by G. F. Watts, is in the possession of the family.

[W. Temple, *Life of Bishop Percival*, 1921; personal knowledge.] G. F. B.

PETERSON, Sir **WILLIAM** (1856–1921), classical scholar and educationist, the fifth son of John Peterson, a merchant of Leith, by his wife, Grace Mountford Anderson, was born in Edinburgh 29 May 1856. He was educated at the high school and university of Edinburgh; graduating in 1875, he went with a travelling fellowship to Göttingen; in 1876 he entered Corpus Christi College, Oxford, as Ferguson scholar, graduating in 1879. From 1879 to 1882 he was assistant professor of the humanities in the university of Edinburgh, and from 1882 to 1895 first principal of the newly founded University College, Dundee. Here he made his mark as an administrator, and secured excellent terms for his institution in the long negotiations leading to union with the university of St. Andrews; he also continued his classical studies, editing Book x of Quintilian's *Institutio Oratoria* (1891), the *Dialogus de Oratoribus* of Tacitus (1893), and Cicero *Pro Cluentio* (1895).

In May 1895 Peterson was appointed principal of McGill University, Montreal, in succession to Sir William Dawson [q.v.]. Here his talent as administrator had ample scope. He found a group of largely autonomous schools and he transformed it into a university. He won the confidence of the wealthy men of Montreal—especially of Lord Strathcona [q.v.] and of Sir William Macdonald (1831–1917), the head of the Canadian tobacco industry—and obtained from them buildings and endowments, especially for agriculture, applied science, and medicine. Faculties of law, medicine, commerce, education, and social service were added to the university; but Peterson's constant endeavours to strengthen the faculty of arts found less sympathy in a great commercial city.

As principal of McGill, Peterson continued his own classical studies and publications. In 1901 he discovered in the library of Holkham Hall a ninth-century manuscript (formerly belonging to Cluny) of Cicero's Speeches; and in 1907 he produced an edition of the *Verrines*, based upon this text. He also took an active part in educational work in Quebec, and throughout Canada and the United States, and was a very distinct personality among the university presidents of the continent. He was for some years chairman of the protestant committee of the council of public instruction in Quebec, and a most influential trustee, and for a time chairman, of the Carnegie foundation for the advancement of teaching.

During the European War Peterson spoke and worked unceasingly, and on 12 January 1919, while presiding at a meeting on behalf of the dependents of dead or disabled Scottish soldiers and sailors, he was stricken with paralysis. In May he resigned, and returned to England, dying at Hampstead on 4 January 1921.

Peterson married in 1885 Lisa, eldest daughter of William Ross, shipowner, of Glenearn, Perthshire, and had two sons. He received honorary degrees from many universities, and in 1915 was created K.C.M.G. In politics he was an imperialist, and in his later years spoke and wrote much in favour of the continued and closer connexion between Canada and Great Britain. Though deeply devoted to McGill and to Canada, Peterson always remained half Scot, half cosmopolitan. He could show a salutary hauteur on occasion, and he did not suffer fools gladly, but he had also great personal charm and distinction.

[Cyrus MacMillan, *McGill and its story*, 1921; personal knowledge.] W. L. G.

PHILLIPS, STEPHEN (1864–1915), poet and dramatist, the eldest child of the Rev. Stephen Phillips, precentor of Peterborough Cathedral, was born at Summertown, near Oxford, 28 July 1864. From his mother, Agatha Sophia (Dockray), who was related to the Wordsworths, he inherited a feeling for poetry, and also a contemplative melancholy which is the keynote of his life and of his poems. From Trinity College School, Stratford-on-Avon, he passed, after six months at the King's School, Peterborough, into Oundle School (1878). In 1883 he was recommended for a minor scholarship in classics at Queens' College, Cambridge. But, formal difficulties precluding residence at Cambridge, he read for the civil service with a London coach, W. B. Scoones, one of whose staff, John Churton Collins [q.v.], helped him to discover that poetry had claims on him. In 1884 *Orestes and Other Poems* was privately printed. About 1885 he joined the theatrical company of his cousin, (Sir) Frank R. Benson. His only histrionic assets were a six-foot athletic figure, a gift for mimicry, and a genius for speaking verse. But he began to think of writing plays to restore poetic drama to the stage. Nothing came of a play which he submitted to Benson, and there is more of lyric mood than dramatic circumstance in his next two poems, *To a Lost Love* and *A Dream* (in *Primavera*, 1890). *Eremus* (1894), in theme and texture, anticipates *Christ in Hades* rather than the dramas.

Leaving the stage in 1892, Phillips lectured on history at an army tutor's, until the success of his *Poems* (1898) encouraged him to take to letters as a profession. Amongst the contents of this volume are *The Apparition* and *Christ in Hades* (both reprinted from a booklet of 1897), *Marpessa*, and *The Wife*, four poems, each in its own distinct and non-dramatic form, but all alike illustrating Phillips's gift for charging lyric or narrative matter with dramatic sense. The success of the volume, which was 'crowned' by *The Academy* journal, revived Phillips's ambition to write poetic drama; and for the next ten years this was his chief occupation. In the meantime his fame as a non-dramatic poet stood high, until his next collected volume, *New Poems* (1908), justified the few sceptics. Its *Endymion* has less, and its *Quest of Edith* none, of the dramatic sense which gave vitality to *Marpessa*; its lyrics are largely topical; and its best poems are those taken over from *Orestes* and *Primavera*.

Meanwhile, Phillips gained a stupendous reputation as a dramatic poet. Delays in the staging of his *Paolo and Francesca*, commissioned by (Sir) George Alexander [q.v.] in 1898, allowed it to be applauded first as a printed book (1900). Eagerness to see it played was increased by the success both in the theatre (1900) and in print (1901) of his *Herod*, which (Sir) H. B. Tree [q.v.] produced with sumptuous accessories. When *Paolo and Francesca* was at last performed (1902), the author was greeted as the successor of Sophocles and Shakespeare, and his royalties rose to £150 a week. But affluence was not good for one of his generous and pleasure-loving nature. Always indolent and careless of his proof-sheets, he now left his producer to fix the fashion of his plays; and Tree's fashion is known. In *Paolo and Francesca* theatricality is thriftily employed to relieve an austere theme. In *Herod* it is more patent, but still legitimate, limelight. In *Ulysses* (1902) the Olympian prologue and the descent to Hades are merely kaleidoscopic extras. *Nero* (1906) is intermittently ablaze with melodramatic flares and wreathed in the smoke of rhetoric; while *Faust* (in which Phillips collaborated with J. Comyns Carr, 1908) is a pyrotechnic pantomime. In *Pietro of Siena* (1910) there are only fitful echoes of his first and best play. Phillips's day was over. His dramatic genius was intense, but of very limited range. He could invest a human relationship, under circumstances essentially simple though often overlaid by the pomp of empire, with an air of devastating fate. His chosen theme is maternal or fraternal love torn asunder by the intervention of some such primary force as sexual passion. Outside this field he lacks artistic pliability and moral strength; and so for variety he is tempted to specious devices. *The Sin of David* (1904, revised 1912) seems at first a return to the severity of his earlier manner; but the sterner air is accidental, due only to the Commonwealth setting (itself a device to overcome the Lord Chamberlain's ban on Biblical subjects), and there is greater effort in the play to force melodramatic situations than to depict austerity in passion. *Aylmer's Secret* (1905), a one-act prose play, and *The Bride of Lammermoor* (1908, also called *The Last Heir*) are bids for profit rather than for fame.

From 1908 Phillips passed out of sight for a while. He was penniless, and had separated from his wife. Odd guineas for poems in the press frequently saved him from starvation. *The New Inferno* (1911), his longest poem, presents in clumsy narrative a loose series of overdrawn pictures to illustrate trite moral texts. In 1912 a brighter period opened, as chance then allowed his friends to take his regeneration in hand. *Lyrics and Dramas* (1913) has flashes of the old spontaneity. But his susceptibilities are blunted, his themes more commonplace, and whereas, before, the seamy side of life was depicted with solemn pathos, now its lurid aspects are exploited. He affects at times a gay nonchalance, but usually relapses into apathetic pessimism. From January 1913 to his death, Phillips was editor of the *Poetry Review*, and in it once more urged the claims of poetic drama. In 1913 the Drama Society projected performances of three of his shorter pieces, *Iole* (written 1907), *The King* (1912), and *The Adversary* (1913)—plays recalling his finer powers, but perhaps only because their brevity confined him to simplicity of situation and of theme. The last of his plays to reach the stage, *Armageddon* (1915), has no merit beyond that of patriotic intention. His last volume of non-dramatic verse, *Panama and Other Poems* (1915), is his worst in that kind, and reveals nothing but an indifferent talent for narrative. Shortly before his death Phillips completed a verse play on the Norman Conquest, *Harold*, and wrote the scenario of one on John the Baptist. He died at Deal 9 December 1915, and was buried at Hastings. He was survived by his wife, May (Lidyard), whom he married in 1892, and by one son.

Phillips felt his life to be a losing struggle against a destiny which was himself: this is the theme of his earliest poem, written when fifteen (*Destiny* in *Orestes and Other Poems*), and recurs as a striking dramatic motive in *The Adversary*. Yet by nature he was open, hearty, and sociable, except when afflicted by recurrent fits of depression; he had a keen sense of humour, was an excellent raconteur, and a fine cricketer. As a poet, he was continually urged by varied influences to efforts alien from the bent of his genius. In the upshot, a gift for the simple and the elemental was subjected to all manner of sophistications. His shorter lyrics, in which the form itself imposes terseness and directness, are amongst his best works. Phillips's finest dramas are those in which an ancient story and an older world are used in order to exhibit such elemental impulses as still determine the common human lot. But then, almost invariably, he or his producer once more obscures what is essential by reconstructing the outer accidents for spectacular effect. The truth is that Phillips had no critical power, and especially no sense of self-criticism. He read little, and so his genius was either starved or allowed to grow unpruned. He is best in *Paolo and Francesca*, in parts of *Herod*, or in poems where lyric and drama come together as the climax of such a simple narrative as *Marpessa*. His most original work is *Christ in Hades*, but it is somewhat overweighted by its intellectual ambition. Promise of equal originality is found in *The Wife*; but in that vein the promise is frustrated. Desiring to be objective, he becomes merely squalid, and ends in conventional realism.

List of Phillips's non-dramatic works: 1. *Orestes and Other Poems*. London, printed for private circulation, 1884 (contains eight poems, of which one, *Thoughts at Sunrise*, appears again in *New Poems*; a second, *Vale Camoena*, in a revised version becomes the first poem in *Primavera*, and occurs again as *The Dreaming Muse* in *New Poems*; a third, *Orestes*, also reappears in a revised version both in *Primavera* and in *New Poems*). 2. *Primavera: Poems by Four Authors*. Oxford, Blackwell, 1890 (the collaborators were Phillips, Laurence Binyon, Manmohan Ghose, and A. S. Cripps; contains *Vale Camoena* and *Orestes*, noted above, and two more poems by Phillips, *To a Lost Love*, and two stanzas, *A Dream* (*My dead love . . .*), afterwards printed as the first section of *The Apparition* in volumes 4 and 5 of this list). 3. *Eremus: A Poem*. London, partly privately, partly Kegan Paul, Trench, Trübner, 1894. 4. *Christ in Hades*. London, Elkin Mathews, 1897 (no. 3 of the 'Shilling Garland' series, edited by Phillips's cousin, Laurence Binyon; contains the titular poem, six sections of *The Apparition* as in 5 below, and the three poems there following entitled Lyrics). 5. *Poems*. London, John Lane, 1898 (really 1897) (pp. 1–69 give poems now first printed). 6. *New Poems*. John Lane, 1908 (really 1907) (see under 1 and 2 above; amongst the new matter is *Iole, a Tragedy in one act*). 7. *The New Inferno*. John Lane, 1911. 8. *Lyrics and Dramas*. John Lane, 1913. 9. *Panama and Other Poems*. John Lane, 1915.

List of dramatic works: 1. *Paolo and Francesca*. John Lane, 1900 (really 1899); produced 6 March 1902, St. James's Theatre, by G. Alexander. 2. *Herod*. John Lane, 1901 (really 1900); produced 31 October 1900, Her Majesty's Theatre, by H. B. Tree. 3. *Ulysses*. John Lane, 1902; produced 1 February 1902, His Majesty's Theatre, by H. B. Tree. 4. *The Sin of David*. London, Macmillan, 1904; produced 30 September 1905, Stadttheater, Düsseldorf; March 1913, at Johannesburg, by H. B. Irving; July 1914, Savoy Theatre, by H. B. Irving. 5. *Aylmer's Secret*. Unpublished, manuscript burnt by Phillips; produced 4 July 1905, Adelphi Theatre. 6. *Nero*. Macmillan, 1906; produced 25 January, His Majesty's Theatre, by Tree (part of the original, omitted from Tree's version and from this volume, appears as a one-act play, *Nero's Mother*, in *Lyrics and Dramas*). 7. *Iole* (in *New Poems*); produced June 1913, Cosmopolis, Holborn, by Efga Myers and Phillips. 8. *The Bride of Lammermoor*. Unpublished; produced 23 March 1908, King's Theatre, Glasgow, by Martin Harvey; and as *The Last Heir* 5 October 1908, Adelphi Theatre, by Harvey. 9. *Faust* (in collaboration with J. Comyns Carr). Macmillan, 1908; produced 5 September 1908, His Majesty's Theatre, by Tree. 10. *Pietro of Siena*. Macmillan, 1910; produced 10 October 1911, Studio Theatre, by the Drama Society. 11. *The King*. Stephen Swift and Co., 1912 (also by John Lane in *Lyrics and Dramas*); this and *The Adversary* were to have been produced by the Drama Society, but Tree acquired the rights to *The King*, and died before producing it. 12. *The Adversary* (in *Lyrics and Dramas*). 13. *Armageddon*. John Lane, 1915; produced 1 June 1915, New Theatre, by Martin Harvey. 14. *Harold* (in *Poetry Review*, January and March 1916); not produced.

[W. Archer, *Poets of the Younger Generation*, 1901, and *Real Conversations*, 1904; Sir Sidney Colvin, in T. Humphry Ward's *English Poets*, vol. v, 1918, and in *The Bookman*, March 1916; A. Waugh, *Tradition and Change*, ed. 1919; Coulson Kernahan, *In Good Company*, 1917, and *Celebrities*, 1923; private information.] H. B. C–n.

PLATER, CHARLES DOMINIC (1875–1921), Catholic divine and social worker, was born at Brook Green, London, 2 September 1875, the third son and youngest child of Edward Angelo Plater, by his wife, Margaret Harting. His paternal grandfather, Charles Edward Plater, was co-founder of Marlborough College; his father, who resigned a War Office clerkship in 1878 in order to devote himself to music, had been received into the Roman Catholic Church in 1851 by John Henry Newman. The Harting family, which had always remained

Catholic, was distinguished in historical research and natural science. Hereditary qualities—Christian zeal, sense of scholarship, unconventional geniality, love of music, and especially the brilliancy, controlled emotionalism, and intuition of his maternal grandmother, a Scotswoman—were startlingly visible in Charles Plater. At Stonyhurst, where he was educated from 1887 to 1894, he was precociously clever and an audacious leader; he might have become a journalist, actor, or diplomat. But, sincerely pious, he entered the Jesuit novitiate in 1894 and after four years' classical and philosophical study at Roehampton and Stonyhurst (1896–1900) he went to the Jesuit house of studies, Pope's Hall (afterwards Campion Hall) at Oxford. A second class in classical moderations (1902), and in *literae humaniores* (1904), rewarded him accurately; but scientific archaeology chastened his imagination, and vacations in Holland, Belgium, and France enriched his sympathies and revealed his vocation—namely to foster and apply Catholic social principles in England and to create a system of spiritual 'retreats' for the laity, especially for working-men.

While finishing his philosophy and teaching classics at St. Mary's Hall, Stonyhurst (1904–1907), Plater displayed much journalistic ardour and became connected with every kind of Catholic social work. During his four years in Wales, at St. Beuno's, St. Asaph, 1907–1911, retreat-houses were opened and the Catholic Social Guild founded. He was ordained in 1910. Between 1912 and 1916 he was teaching psychology at Stonyhurst and classics at Wimbledon College. In the latter year he was appointed rector of the Jesuit hall at Oxford. In 1918 he obtained a university statute making his hall (which was given the name of Campion) into a 'permanent private hall' of the university. He also took an energetic share in the social work of the city; visited his own Catholic Social Guild study-circles, especially on Tyneside and in the north, and did creative work in many military centres, labouring not least for colonial and American soldiers. At the same time Plater was conducting a very large number of retreats, and writing constantly on social subjects, his *Primer of Peace and War* (1915) being his best thought-out book. His personal influence, especially among the working-classes, seemed unlimited, and his remarkable output of work was matched by the affection which he inspired. His health broke down in 1920; after a useless sojourn afloat off the west coast of Ireland, he went to Malta in November of that year and died there suddenly 21 January 1921.

[C. C. Martindale, *Life of Charles Dominic Plater, S.J.*, 1922; diaries; private information; personal knowledge.] C. C. M.

PORTER, SIR **ANDREW MARSHALL**, first baronet (1837–1919), judge, was born in Belfast 27 June 1837, the eldest son of the Rev. John Scott Porter, Unitarian minister [q.v.], by his wife, Margaret, daughter of Andrew Marshall, M.D., a surgeon in the royal navy, who had served with Nelson. Educated at the Belfast Academic Institution, Andrew Porter graduated with distinction at Queen's College, Belfast, in 1856. He was called to the Irish bar (King's Inns, Dublin) in 1860, and joined the North-East circuit. His sound legal knowledge and exceptional aptitude for commercial cases gained early recognition, and secured him a fine practice as a junior. He became Q.C. in 1872, and a bencher in 1878, and soon established his position as a leader, proving himself a great advocate among the many great advocates, his contemporaries, at the bar of Ireland. Natural gifts enhanced his legal attainments: his fine presence, good voice, and lucid, attractive style made him a most effective orator.

Porter's political affinities were with the liberal party, which possessed a great and growing influence in Ulster until its disruption as the result of Gladstone's adoption of the policy of Home Rule. He represented county Londonderry in parliament from 1881 to 1883, and was appointed solicitor-general for Ireland in 1881, and attorney-general and privy councillor in 1883. When he entered parliament the ferocious and elusive audacity of the Land League agitation was paralysing Ireland, while at Westminster Charles Stewart Parnell [q.v.] was directing the nationalists in a policy of turbulence and obstruction. Porter's sagacity and firmness in administration and his imperturbability in debate greatly impressed his colleagues, and Gladstone more than once urged him to adopt a political career, offering him in 1882 the Irish chief secretaryship with the prospect of further advancement.

Porter's ambitions, however, were essentially forensic, and he declined to deviate from the path of his profession. As attorney-general he prosecuted, under circumstances of no little personal peril, the Phoenix Park murderers, as well as the ringleaders of the 'Invincibles' and other secret societies which were then terrorizing the community; his conduct of these remarkable trials further advanced his reputation at the bar. In December 1883, when Sir Edward Sullivan, the master of the Rolls in Ireland, became lord chancellor, Porter was raised to the bench as his successor. Although his practice had been mainly on the common law side, he proved himself a great chancery judge, and many of his judgments embody illuminating expositions of doctrines of equity. Few of his decisions were ever successfully challenged on appeal. He took great care, also, to expedite the administrative progress in chambers of the causes in his court. He was in temperament sensitive and retiring, and a reserved demeanour coupled with a commendable impatience of irrelevancy sometimes led to his judicial attitude being misinterpreted as austere. But the bar regarded him with affectionate admiration, and his retirement in 1906, after he had held the mastership of the Rolls during the unprecedented period of twenty-three years, was regretted as a public loss.

Porter was created a baronet in 1902. He married in 1869 Agnes Adinston, daughter of Colonel Alexander Horsbrugh, of Horsbrugh, Peeblesshire, and had four sons and two daughters. His second son, Andrew Marshall, a promising scholar of Trinity College, Dublin, was killed on active service in the Boer War. Porter died in Dublin 9 January 1919, and was succeeded in the baronetcy by his eldest son, John Scott Porter (born 1871), who assumed the additional name of Horsbrugh.

[Private information; personal and professional knowledge.] A. W. S.

POWER, Sir WILLIAM HENRY (1842–1916), expert in public health, the eldest son of William Henry Power, M.D., of Market Bosworth, by his wife, Charlotte Smart, of Bloors Place, Kent, was born in London 15 December 1842. He came of a medical family, being the fifth representative of the profession in direct succession from father to son. Several of his paternal relatives were distinguished mathematicians, one of whom, John Power (1818–1880), became master of Pembroke College, Cambridge. Power was educated at University College School and St. Bartholomew's Hospital. After obtaining his medical qualifications in 1864, he held for some years the post of resident medical officer to the Victoria Park Hospital for diseases of the chest. In 1871 he commenced his long official career in public health on his appointment to the medical staff of the Local Government Board. During his sixteen years' service as medical inspector, Power carried out an immense amount of original work in connexion with infectious diseases, more particularly smallpox, diphtheria, and scarlet fever. His exposition of the danger to public health from the aggregation of smallpox cases formed the basis of administrative action which resulted in the removal of smallpox hospitals outside the metropolitan area, and in the general adoption of corresponding rules for the separation of these hospitals throughout the country. In 1878 he suggested the possibility of the dissemination of diphtheria by the consumption of milk. Subsequently he demonstrated the operation of the same cause in scarlet fever, discovering, moreover, that cows suffering from a vesicular disease of the teats and udder constituted the actual source of infection. As the outcome of investigations initiated by him into outbreaks of lead-poisoning traced to drinking-water, it was found that the acidity to which the plumbo-solvent action of soft moorland waters is due, is bacterial in origin; and further, that lead-poisoning can be prevented by neutralization of the water.

Power was a pioneer in study of the causes and prevention of infantile mortality; and of the injurious effects of defective environment, such as overcrowding and other conditions incidental to insanitary housing accommodation. He also planned and directed much of the work of the medical department of the Local Government Board, including the auxiliary scientific investigations. Owing, however, to his retiring disposition he was little known outside official circles, and much, if not most, of the work which he inspired or directed was published under the names of his colleagues or of his staff.

In 1900 Power succeeded to the post of principal medical officer to the Board, and four years later the food department was established on his initiative. While medical officer he served as Crown nominee on the general council of medical education, and also on the royal commissions on sewage disposal and on tuberculosis. He was elected F.R.S. in 1895, created C.B. in 1902, and K.C.B. on retirement from office in 1908. He died at East Molesey 28 July 1916. He married in 1876 Charlotte Jane, daughter of Benjamin Charles Godwin. She died in 1882, leaving two daughters (Mrs. Mervyn Gordon and Miss Constance Power).

[*Proceedings* of the Royal Society, vol. xc, B, 1917–1919; personal knowledge.]

S. A. M. C.

POYNTER, SIR EDWARD JOHN, first baronet, (1836–1919), painter and president of the Royal Academy, was born in Paris 20 March 1836, the only son of Ambrose Poynter [q.v.]. His schooldays were interrupted by delicate health. An inherited bent for art was strengthened by the influence of his grandmother, the daughter of Thomas Banks, R.A. [q.v.]; and the acquaintance of Lord Leighton, which he made in Rome in November 1853, fixed his determination to become a painter. In the following year he entered the school of James Mathews Leigh [q.v.], and worked there, at the Royal Academy, and in the studio of W. C. T. Dobson, R.A. A visit to the Paris exhibition of 1855 filled him with admiration for contemporary French painting and led to his becoming in 1857 a pupil in the *atelier* of Gleyre. Here he met Whistler, Lamont, Du Maurier, and others of the group described in Du Maurier's *Trilby*, with some members of which he shared a studio in Paris. He used later in life to complain that he had not remained with Gleyre long enough to master completely the technique of oil painting, but the insight which he obtained into French methods was afterwards of great value to him.

Returning to London in 1860 he occupied himself with decorative work, some of it, like the painted ceiling of Waltham Abbey, in conjunction with the architect William Burges [q. v.]. At the same time he earned his place amongst the 'Illustrators of the 'Sixties' by drawing for *Once a Week* and other publications, including the truncated Dalziel Bible to which he contributed several elaborate Egyptian subjects. His first exhibit in the Academy was hung in 1861. From that year until 1919 he never failed to contribute. Many of his minor works were shown at the Dudley and later at the Grosvenor and New galleries, as well as with the old Water Colour Society; but his larger pictures, with a single exception, appeared at the Academy and can be dated from the catalogues. The first to attract attention was 'Faithful unto Death' (1865), now in the Liverpool Gallery. This was followed in 1867 by 'Israel in Egypt', which at once established the artist's fame. This immense work, now in the Guildhall Gallery, London, is characteristic of Poynter's aims and limitations throughout his career. In particular a tendency is manifest to overburden his subject with accessories, selected with extreme learning and taste and painted with great patience and in a sound and workmanlike style. In 'The Catapult' (1868) this is less marked; and the admirable drawing of the nudes places it amongst his best pictures. It secured his election as A.R.A. About this time he was engaged on several important decorative designs: the mosaic of St. George in the Houses of Parliament (1869); the tile-work in the grill-room at South Kensington Museum (1868–1870); a project for painting the semi-dome of the lecture theatre in the same museum (1871), unfortunately left unexecuted, as it would have been his finest achievement; and a fresco in St. Stephen's church, South Dulwich (1872–1873), which remains one of the few successful works in true fresco by an Englishman and is one of Poynter's most striking designs, especially the predella. He next undertook for the Earl of Wharncliffe the decoration of the billiard-room at Wortley Hall, a scheme combining four large oil-pictures in an ornamental setting; in these pictures, 'Perseus and Andromeda' (1872), 'The Dragon of Wantley' (1873), 'Atalanta's Race' (1876), and 'Nausicaa and her Maidens' (1879), he reached his highest level. He was elected R.A. in 1877.

On the foundation of the Slade chair and school at University College, London (1871), Poynter was chosen as professor. He took the opportunity to adopt in the new school the principles of French art education, of the superiority of which he had personal experience; but this revolutionary policy was not universally approved. It was in the face of much opposition that he established it firmly by securing on his retirement (July 1875) the election of his friend, Alphonse Legros [q.v.], as his successor, thus giving to English art teaching a direction which it still follows. His resignation was due to his acceptance of a still more influential position at South Kensington. As director for art, he became jointly responsible for the acquisition of specimens for the museum, a task for which the uncommon catholicity of his taste and his wide knowledge of art history peculiarly qualified him; as principal of the National Art Training School, he had to superintend the system of government art education elaborated by his predecessor, Richard Redgrave [q. v.], as well as to give personal instruction. He made considerable changes, again founded on French precedents, and his appointment of Jules Dalou as head of the modelling school was not less epoch-marking than the election of Legros at the Slade School. In connexion with his office at South Kensington he edited a series of free-hand drawing-copies and another of manuals of art history, each far superior to any previously available in this country. Finding that his duties interfered with his painting—Lord Wharncliffe's four canvases had taken seven years to finish, and the only other important picture of this period was 'A Visit to Aesculapius' (1880), now in the Tate Gallery—he resigned the directorship in August 1881.

He next undertook another piece of decoration, the preparation of gigantic cartoons developing part of Alfred Stevens's sketch-design for the interior of the dome of St. Paul's Cathedral. When tested in position they were found to be invisible, and the permanent realization of the scheme was abandoned. At this time he began the picture of 'The Queen of Sheba's Visit to King Solomon', a vast canvas containing more than fifty figures and heads. It was completed in 1890 and bought by Messrs. McLean, who sold it to the National Gallery at Sydney. The price, £3,000, although the highest he ever received, was small compared with those earned by many of his contemporaries, and cannot have remunerated him for the time and research lavished on one of the most elaborate pictures of its class ever painted. During its progress Poynter maintained the reputation he had earned by a number of portraits and by those subject-pictures of Graeco-Roman *genre* which henceforth formed the staple of his output.

Public attention having been attracted to the destructive influences at work on the monuments of ancient Egypt, a society was formed for their preservation in 1889, Poynter becoming the honorary secretary. An active controversialist, he usually took part in any correspondence in the press relating to artistic matters.

In March 1894 the directorship of the National Gallery fell vacant by the retirement of Sir Frederick Burton [q.v.]. Since 1855 the gallery had been managed with conspicuous success by autocratic directors who were also practising painters. On this occasion strong efforts were made to procure the appointment of a professional critic. Doubtless in response to this agitation, the prime minister, before offering the post to Poynter, enacted a new constitution curtailing the power of the office; in practice, as Poynter found to his cost, the influence of one trustee was sufficient to reduce the director almost to a cipher and produce constant friction. In spite of this, Poynter was able to render good service to the gallery. The number of pictures, above five hundred, added during his directorship, was swollen by the Tate gift and by the absorption of the collection formed by the Chantrey trustees. The most conspicuous purchases made in his time were the De Saumarez Rembrandts and Titian's 'Ariosto'. He also acquired the Northbrook Mantegna and Antonello and the Ashburnham Pisanello, and was instrumental in securing for the gallery its first pictures by Dürer, Goya, and Alfred Stevens, as well as in filling many less serious gaps in it; he also edited the first complete illustrated catalogue (1899). He was responsible for the arrangement and opening of the Tate Gallery (1897). He retired at the end of 1904.

On the death of Millais, Poynter was elected (December 1896) president of the Royal Academy. A man of distinguished bearing, a good linguist, an artist with practical knowledge of every process of painting, possessing intimate experience of art education and long familiarity with the business of the Academy, he was well suited for this position. During his tenure the Academy was called upon to face a rancorous attack in connexion with the Chantrey bequest. A committee of the House of Lords held an inquiry (1904) and recommended some modifications in the administration. Poynter was a principal witness, and by his dignity and integrity gave strong support to an unpopular cause. In April 1917 his colleagues in the Academy made him a present to commemorate his twenty years' tenure of the chair, Reynolds and West alone among his predecessors having presided for so long a period. About this time his health and eyesight began to fail. In the autumn of 1918 he resigned the presidentship. He died at 70 Addison Road, Kensington, on 26 July 1919, and was buried in St. Paul's Cathedral.

He married in 1866 Agnes, daughter of the Rev. G. B. Macdonald, a lady of great beauty and musical talent, one of whose sisters was the wife of Sir Edward Burne-Jones. She died in 1906, leaving two sons. Poynter was knighted in 1896, created a baronet in 1902, and G.C.V.O. in 1918. He possessed a fine collection of drawings by the old masters, which was sold at Sotheby's in 1918.

There are numerous portraits of Poynter:

a drawing by Legros, the original of a well-known etching, and a bust by Dalou are in the possession of the family; an autograph portrait is in the Uffizi Gallery, and pictures by (Sir) Arthur Cope and Seymour Lucas, both painted in 1911, belong to the Royal Academy; an excellent likeness by Sir Philip Burne-Jones is in the National Portrait Gallery, and another is introduced into the vast group of the 'Hanging Committee' by Sir H. von Herkomer in the Tate Gallery; there is also a bas-relief showing his head (life-size) by W. R. Colton, R.A. (*Royal Academy Pictures*, 1911 and 1920).

Poynter was probably, with the exception of Alfred Stevens, the most versatile and accomplished academic draughtsman the English school has ever produced. He loved drawing for its own sake, and put the best of himself into the numberless studies from life which he made for even the most inconspicuous details of his paintings. As happened with the old masters in similar circumstances, the spirit frequently lost force in the process of transference to the finished picture, especially as Poynter was a deliberate worker and, as he himself was fully aware, although a sound never a brilliant manipulator of oil paint. His water-colours show perfect mastery of the medium according to the principles of the school to which he belonged. His work in fresco has been mentioned. He executed a few very original medals and designed reverses for the coinage of 1894. Representative series of his drawings are in the British and Victoria and Albert museums. In addition to the works in public galleries already noted, others are at Birmingham, Manchester, and Bristol.

[*The Times*, 28 July 1919; *Morning Post*, 20 March 1913; Poynter's MS. autobiography (to 1855), diaries, and correspondence; *The Easter Art Annual*, 1897; Lugt's *Marques de Collections*; personal knowledge.]

C. F. B.

POYNTING, JOHN HENRY (1852–1914), physicist, the youngest son of the Rev. T. Elford Poynting, Unitarian minister at Monton, near Manchester, by his wife, Elizabeth Long, of Bath, was born at Monton 9 September 1852. He received his earlier education at the school kept by his father, and then went in 1867 to the Owens College, Manchester (now the university of Manchester). He took the B.Sc. degree at London University in 1872. In the same year he gained an entrance scholarship at Trinity College, Cambridge, and came into residence at Cambridge in October. He took his degree in 1876, being placed third in the list of the mathematical tripos. Immediately afterwards he went back to the Owens College and demonstrated in the physical laboratory under Balfour Stewart [q.v.]. On his election to a fellowship at Trinity College in 1878 Poynting returned to Cambridge, and began in the Cavendish laboratory, under James Clerk Maxwell [q.v.], experiments on the mean density of the earth which occupied much of his time for the next ten years. He remained at Cambridge until 1880, when he was elected to the chair of physics in Mason College, Birmingham (now the university of Birmingham), which had just been founded. This post he held until his death. In 1887 he received the Sc.D. of Cambridge and in 1888 he was made a fellow of the Royal Society; in 1893 the Adams prize was awarded to him, and the Hopkins prize in 1903. He was president of Section A of the British Association in 1899, and president of the Physical Society in 1905. In the latter year he received a royal medal from the Royal Society 'for his researches in physical science, especially in connexion with the constant of gravitation and the theories of electro-dynamics and radiation'. He was a vice-president of the Royal Society in 1910–1911.

Poynting's most important contributions to physics are two papers communicated to the Royal Society: *On the Transfer of Energy in the Electromagnetic Field* (*Philosophical Transactions*, A, 1884), and *On the Connexion between Electric Currents and the Electric and Magnetic Induction in the Surrounding Field* (ibid., 1885). These papers revolutionized ideas about the motion of energy in the electric field. To take an example: before the publication of these papers, when a charged Leyden jar was discharged by connecting the inside and outside by a wire, the energy was supposed to travel along the wire much in the same way as hydraulic power is carried through a pipe. In Poynting's view the energy spreads out from the glass between the coatings of the jar and then converges sideways into the wire, where it is converted into heat. He showed that there was a general law for the transfer of energy, according to which it moves at any point perpendicularly to the planes containing the direction of the electric and magnetic forces, and the amount crossing unit area per second is equal to the product of these forces multiplied by the sine of the angle between them and divided by 4π. The line which represents in direction and magnitude the flow of energy at any point is now known as the 'Poynting vector' and is of fundamental importance in electromagnetic questions.

Poynting made important advances in our knowledge of the pressure of light. He established the existence of the tangential force produced when light is reflected from a surface at which there is some absorption, and the existence of a torque when light passes through a prism, and succeeded in demonstrating the recoil from light of a surface giving out radiation. These experiments, in which he was associated with William Henry Barlow [q. v.], are a good example of Poynting's skill in devising methods and apparatus. He had exceptional mechanical instincts and an excellent knowledge of the capabilities of instruments. The result was that the apparatus which he designed was always simple and effective.

Throughout his life Poynting was engaged on researches connected with gravitation. His first piece of experimental work was a determination of the density of the earth, using, instead of a torsion balance, a balance of the ordinary type. He also investigated the question whether the gravitational attraction between two crystals depends on the orientation of their axes, and whether this attraction is affected by temperature. He further made important contributions to the theory of the change of state in matter. He took great interest in the philosophical basis of physics, chose this as the subject of his presidential address to Section A of the British Association in 1899, and expressed views which, though now common, were then different from those accepted by the majority of the physicists of this country.

Poynting's *Collected Scientific Papers* were published by the Cambridge University Press in 1920. In addition to these he wrote *On the Mean Density of the Earth* (Adams prize essay, 1893), *The Pressure of Light* (1910), *The Earth* (1913), and, in conjunction with (Sir) J. J. Thomson, a series of textbooks on physics. Poynting was very successful as a teacher, and his sound judgement and conspicuous fairness and courtesy were of great service to the university of Birmingham. He became dean of the science faculty when Mason College was made the university of Birmingham, and held the office for twelve years. He died at Birmingham 30 March 1914.

Poynting married in 1880 Maria Adney, daughter of the Rev. J. Cropper, Unitarian minister, of Stand, near Manchester. They had one son and two daughters.

[Personal knowledge.] J. J. T.

PREECE, Sir WILLIAM HENRY (1834–1913), electrical engineer, was born at Bryn Helen, Carnarvon, 15 February 1834. He was the eldest son of Richard Mathias Preece, stockbroker, of Bryn Helen, by his wife, Jane, daughter of John Hughes, shipbuilder, of Carnarvon. He was educated at King's College School and King's College, London, and received his early training in electrical engineering at the Royal Institution under Michael Faraday [q. v.], who directed his inherently scientific mind towards the many unsolved problems of applied electricity and telegraphic engineering. In 1852 Preece entered the office of Edwin Clark [q. v.], as a civil engineer; but in 1853 he was appointed to the Electric and International Telegraph Company, becoming superintendent of its southern district in 1856. From 1858 to 1862 he was engineer to the Channel Islands Telegraph Company. Preece is, however, best known on account of his long connexion with the Post Office, of which he first became an official in 1870. The various telegraphic companies were at that date taken over by the government and Preece was appointed divisional engineer for the southern district of the Post Office telegraphic system. In 1877 he was made electrician in chief, and in 1892 engineer in chief. He retired from the latter position in 1899 and from that time until 1904 was consulting engineer to the British Post Office and to the Colonies.

The scientific field explored by Preece in the course of his career was extremely wide and covered telegraphy, telephony, and radio-telegraphic communication. During his career at the Post Office he was responsible for many improvements and inventions in telegraphic work. He also applied his experience to the question of railway signalling; and he regarded the improvements which he made to secure the safe working of railways as among his most useful work. He introduced the Preece block system of working single lines and the electric system of communication between different parts of a train; he also took out a patent for reproducing by miniature signals in the signal box the positions of actual signals, and a system of locking signals. Preece was one of the earliest pioneers of wireless telegraphy, and in 1892 originated a system of signalling across space by induction telegraphy with the aid of two parallel telegraph lines. This method is now of historic interest only, and the largest share which Preece had in the introduction of wireless telegraphy into this country was the encouragement which he gave to Signor Marconi by securing for him in 1896 the assistance of the British Post Office in the practical development of the work of James Clerk Maxwell [q. v.] and of H. R. Hertz. Preece was very zealous in urging the commercial introduction of telephonic communication, and he introduced into this country the first telephone receivers as patented by Alexander Graham Bell (1876). He also strongly advocated the purchase of the National Telephone Company by the government; this took effect in 1911.

Preece was made C.B. in 1894 and created K.C.B. in 1899. He was elected a fellow of the Royal Society in 1881 and president of the Institution of Civil Engineers (1898–1899). He died at Penrhos, Carnarvon, 6 November 1913. He married in 1864 Anne Agnes (died 1874), daughter of George Pocock, solicitor, of Southampton, and had four sons and three daughters. Preece's more important publications are: *Telegraphy*, in conjunction with (Sir) J. Sivewright (1876, 15th edition, 1899, new edition, 1905); *The Telephone*, in conjunction with Dr. Julius Maier (1889); and *A Manual of Telephony*, in conjunction with Mr. Arthur J. Stubbs (1893).

[*The Engineer*, 14 November 1913; *The Electrician*, 14 November 1913; private information.] A. P. M. F.

PRENDERGAST, Sir HARRY NORTH DALRYMPLE (1834–1913), general, was born in India 15 October 1834. He was the second son of Thomas Prendergast [q.v.], of the Madras civil service, by his wife, Lucy Caroline, daughter of Marten Dalrymple, of Cleland, Lanarkshire, and Fordell, Fife. His father was a linguist of distinction, and his grandfather, Sir Jeffery Prendergast, a general in the service of the East India Company. The Prendergasts are an old Irish family. Harry Prendergast was educated at Cheam School and Brighton College, and entered Addiscombe Military College in 1852. He obtained a commission in the Madras Engineers in 1854, and after passing through the prescribed course at Chatham landed at Madras in October 1856.

Prendergast took part with his regiment in the Persian War, and in the Mutiny served first with the Deccan field force under General Woodburn. It was on 21 November 1857, while reconnoitring with a small cavalry force, that he saved the life of a brother officer, Lieutenant Dew, at the risk of his own, and was severely wounded. For this and other acts of bravery he received the Victoria cross. On recovering from his wound Prendergast acted as aide-de-camp to Sir Hugh Henry Rose (afterwards Baron Strathnairn, q.v.), and was constantly in action, until, on being wounded a second time, he was invalided home in April 1858. For his services in the Mutiny he received a medal and clasp, as well as a brevet majority, to which he was gazetted on reaching the rank of captain in the spring of 1863. He was disappointed at not being accepted as a volunteer for the Chinese War of 1860, but in 1867 he accompanied, in command of the Madras Sappers, the expedition of Sir Robert (afterwards Lord) Napier [q.v.] to Abyssinia. He was present at the capture of Magdala, and was mentioned by the commander-in-chief as having rendered singularly valuable assistance. He was promoted brevet lieutenant-colonel and received a medal.

In April 1878 when Lord Beaconsfield's Cabinet contemplated the transfer of an Indian force to the Mediterranean, Prendergast, a brevet colonel in command of the Madras and Bombay Sappers, was ordered to Malta, where he had charge of the arrangements for landing the expected troops. On his return to India he became military secretary to the Madras government. He was appointed to the command of the British Burma division in 1883, and two years later led the expeditionary force against Mandalay. He arrived at Rangoon 7 November 1885, and although the resistance of the Burmese at various points was serious, the operations were carried out with promptness and success. King Thebaw surrendered on 28 November and Mandalay was occupied on the following day. Prendergast received many congratulations, was created K.C.B., and was visited at Mandalay by the viceroy, Lord Dufferin. He left Burma 23 February 1886, thus bringing to a close a military career of exceptional variety and activity. He afterwards did useful work as acting resident in different places, chiefly in Southern India, and in connexion with the Public Works department. He was promoted general in 1887 and created G.C.B. in June 1902. He died at Richmond, Surrey, 24 July 1913.

Prendergast married in 1864 Emilie

Rachel, daughter of Frederick Simpson. He had two sons and three daughters, one of whom, Ella, married Sir Harry Aubrey de Vere Maclean [q. v.].

[*The Times*, 26 July 1913.] A. C.

RAMSAY, Sir WILLIAM (1852–1916), chemical discoverer, was born 2 October 1852 at Queen's Crescent, Glasgow, the only child of William Ramsay, by his wife, Catharine Robertson. He inherited scientific ability from both parents; for, whilst his father was a civil engineer of considerable scientific attainments and his paternal grandfather a well-known manufacturer of chemicals used by dyers (and probably the discoverer of potassium bichromate and Turnbull's blue), his mother was descended from an Edinburgh family which for several generations had produced medical men of note.

From 1866 to 1869 William Ramsay studied classics, general literature, logic, and mathematics at the university of Glasgow. In 1869 he went to the chemical laboratory of Robert Tatlock, attending at the same time lectures at the university on physics, chemistry, anatomy, and geology. At the close of the Franco-Prussian War he went to Heidelberg with the intention of studying under R. W. von Bunsen, but early in 1871 he changed to Rudolf Fittig's laboratory at Tübingen, where he obtained the degree of Ph.D. for a research on toluic and nitro-toluic acids. Returning to Glasgow in 1872, he was appointed assistant in the Young laboratory of technical chemistry. In 1874 he became the assistant of Professor John Ferguson in the chemical department of the university of Glasgow. In 1880 he was appointed professor of chemistry at University College, Bristol, of which in the following year he also became principal. In 1887 he was chosen to succeed Alexander William Williamson in the chair of general chemistry at University College, London. Here he worked until his retirement in 1913. His few remaining years were spent near Hazelmere, in Buckinghamshire, where he had bought a house and built a small chemical laboratory. He was actively engaged on chemical work in connexion with the European War when death overtook him 23 July 1916 at the age of sixty-three. He had married, in 1881, Margaret, daughter of George Stevenson Buchanan, by whom he had one son and one daughter.

Ramsay's scientific work may be divided broadly into five periods, of which the first, 1874–1880, was spent in Glasgow. During this time he devoted himself chiefly to investigations in the field of organic chemistry, obtaining various pyridinic acids from a complex mixture of pyridine bases, and establishing a close relationship between the alkaloids, quinine and cinchonine, and pyridine. In the second period (Bristol, 1880–1887) he turned to the field of physical chemistry, and, in collaboration with his assistant, Dr. Sydney Young, published an important series of papers dealing with vapour-densities, critical constants, evaporation, and dissociation. His work in London (1887–1913) may be divided roughly into three periods. At first he continued the physico-chemical work which had occupied his attention at Bristol. The most remarkable research of this period was his determination (in collaboration with his pupil Dr. John Shields) of the molecular complexity of pure liquids, as deducible from the variation with temperature of their 'molecular surface-energies'.

Although Ramsay had now established his reputation as one of the most eminent physical chemists in Europe, the great work of his life was still to come—the discovery of the chemically inert elementary gases, argon, helium, neon, krypton, and xenon. Lord Rayleigh [q. v.], in the course of very accurate investigations into the densities of gases, had found a small difference between the densities of 'atmospheric' and chemically pure nitrogen. He sought the help of Ramsay, and after a few months of their joint work came the startling announcement at the British Association meeting in 1894 that there was present in the atmosphere an elementary gas new to science. Owing to its complete chemical inertness it was named argon. This discovery was soon followed by another of equal importance; for Ramsay, having had his attention directed by (Sir) Henry A. Miers to a statement by W. F. Hillebrand that the rare mineral, cleveite, gave off a considerable amount of gas on heating, repeated the experiment and found in the gas from cleveite another new inert elementary gas, identical in its spectrum with the element helium whose presence in the sun had been spectroscopically detected by Dr. P. J. C Janssen, (Sir) E. Frankland, and (Sir) Norman Lockyer. The most remarkable thing about these new elements was their total lack of any capacity for entering into chemical combination. Ramsay divined that there must exist a whole related family of such inert elements; he at once began to search for the others, and after many months of hard work in collaboration with his pupil, Dr. M. W. Travers, three new inert elementary gases, named neon, krypton, and xenon, were isolated from the atmosphere by means of the fractional distillation of liquefied air.

The last great period of Ramsay's work in London was characterized by another discovery of a different nature, but of equally fundamental importance, namely the proof that the emanation of radium produces helium during its atomic disintegration. In this work, in which he was assisted by Dr. F. Soddy, the first definitely recognizable transmutation of one chemical element into another was placed on a firm experimental basis. This was a fact of tremendous importance for chemical science. With the insight of genius, Ramsay now perceived that it might be possible to utilize the torrent of energy, carried by the particles shot out with enormous velocities during the atomic disintegration of radio-active substances, for the purpose of breaking down the atoms of the ordinary stable elements. Working with the emanation from radium, and as the result of a long series of experiments, he considered that he had in this way been able to obtain traces of lithium from copper and of carbon from thorium. Some of these experiments were afterwards repeated by Madame Curie, but with negative results. The final decision on this problem must be left to the future. The really important point was that, just as a century earlier Sir Humphry Davy had seized on the newly discovered electric 'pile' of Volts as a new weapon for the decomposition of substances, so Ramsay had grasped the immense possibilities of the atomic projectiles hurled forth by exploding atoms as a new and powerful weapon for attempting the decomposition of the ordinary stable atoms of matter. The later investigations of Sir Ernest Rutherford have amply demonstrated that Ramsay was on the right track.

The last great research carried out by Ramsay (in conjunction with his pupil, Dr. Whytlaw Gray) was a marvellous example of his skill as an experimenter. This was the determination of the density, and therefore the atomic weight, of the radium emanation, the volume of this unstable gas available for an experiment being less than one-millionth of a cubic inch. This investigation, in conjunction with others, rendered it highly probable, if not certain, that the gaseous emanation given off by radium was one of the inert elements of the argon family.

Ramsay's investigations have been of cardinal importance for the advance of chemical and physical science. The mysterious α-particles so often ejected by atoms undergoing spontaneous disintegration have turned out to be positively charged helium atoms (or helium nuclei), and the helium atom or nucleus has been shown to be one of the most important constituents of the atoms of matter. The family of inert elements occupies a fundamentally important position in the modern theory of atomic structure.

Ramsay was the greatest chemical discoverer of his time, and it is safe to predict that posterity will rank him with the greatest scientific discoverers of any age. He was gifted with rare scientific insight and imagination, and was the possessor of a most wonderful skill and dexterity in the devising, constructing, and use of apparatus for the delicate and exact investigation of gases. A man of sanguine and courageous temperament, of tireless energy, and power of instant action, he fearlessly attacked problems the experimental difficulties of which would have dismayed and deterred most men. His great example of a life devoted to research, and his cheerful optimism and encouragement spurred his students to try to follow in his footsteps, and enabled him to build up a great school of chemical research at University College.

Ramsay was endowed with extraordinary personal charm, and a most kindly, generous, and gentle disposition. No man was ever more beloved by his students, who found in him not only a great and inspiring teacher and investigator but also a true and generous friend. An excellent linguist and musician, a witty and humorous speaker both in public and in private, Ramsay's personality endeared him to an immense circle of friends and acquaintances in many countries. The quickness and receptivity of his mind were very remarkable, so that he was ever the enthusiastic friend and exponent of new advances in science. Thus he was one of the first chemists in England to teach and expound the work of W. Ostwald, J. H. van't Hoff, and S. A. Arrhenius, as in later life he was one of the first to take up work in the new field of radioactive change. His activities extended in many directions. He found time to write a number of excellent books on chemistry, was an ardent apostle of reform in converting the university of London into a great teaching university, and served as a member of the royal commission on sewage disposal, and other public bodies. A collection of his numerous public lectures given at home and abroad was published in a volume entitled *Essays and Addresses.*

Honours were showered on him from every country in the world. Elected a fellow of the Royal Society in 1888 and created K.C.B. in 1902, he received the Nobel prize in 1904. Honorary degrees were conferred on him by numerous universities both at home and abroad, and he was made a foreign member of scientific societies in practically every civilized country, and received the Prussian order 'Pour le Mérite'.

A portrait of Ramsay, painted by Mark Milbanke in 1913, hangs in the council room at University College.

[Obituary notice in *Proceedings* of the Royal Society, vol. xciii, A, 1916–1917; Sir W. A. Tilden, *Sir William Ramsay,* 1918; Introductory Memoir in Sir W. Ramsay's *Life and Letters of Joseph Black, M.D.*, 1918.]

F. G. D.

RAPER, ROBERT WILLIAM (1842–1915), classical scholar, born at Llanwenarth, Monmouthshire, 9 March 1842, was the second son of Lieutenant-Colonel Timothy Raper (died 1862), of the 19th Foot, by his wife, Christian Mary, daughter of Robert Steavenson, M.D., of Newcastle-upon-Tyne. Colonel Raper, afterwards of Hoe Court, Colwall, Herefordshire, was highly distinguished in the Ceylon expedition of 1815; and his youngest son, Major-General Allan Graeme Raper (died 1906), of the 98th Foot and North Staffordshire regiments, was assistant quartermaster-general at the War Office 1895–1900, and commanded the infantry brigade at Gibraltar 1902–1905. From Cheltenham College (1857–1859) Raper passed to Balliol College, Oxford, in 1861, but in his first term was elected to a scholarship at Trinity College, where in 1862 he obtained the university prizes for Greek and Latin verse and a first class in moderations, and in 1865 a first class in *literae humaniores* and a fellowship at Queen's College. Having from 1866 lectured in classics at Trinity, he was in 1871 elected under a special statute to a life fellowship there, and thenceforward took a leading part in the administration of the college, being tutor until 1882, then lecturer in classics, bursar from 1887, and vice-president from 1894, remaining continuously in residence until his death. He would probably have been elected president in 1878, if laymen had then been eligible; in 1887, 1897, and 1907 he declined to accept the post. In the university he soon acquired extensive though informal influence; he only once acted as examiner in the Schools, but he was a curator of the Parks from 1885 and a visitor of the Ashmolean Museum from 1895 to 1908. He lectured mainly on favourite authors, Homer, Virgil, Aristophanes, and Tacitus, but he published nothing except an ingenious but not altogether serious attempt to prove that the *Ibis* of Ovid was directed against Septimius Severus (*Journal of Philology*, 1885), a remarkable imitation of Walt Whitman in *Echoes from the Oxford Magazine* (1890), a few brilliant versions in Latin verse in the *Nova Anthologia Oxoniensis* of 1899, and a rather fantastic paper on Virgil in the *Classical Review* (1913). His skill in translation and composition is frequently acknowledged by friends, as by Andrew Lang in the preface to his translation of the *Odyssey*, and by pupils whom he had encouraged to write.

From an early date Raper's wide acquaintance with influential Oxford men enabled him to recommend Trinity undergraduates of promise and others for tutorial, scholastic, and secretarial posts; and eventually in 1894 he founded, and for a time presided over, an Appointments Committee for the university on the model of one organized at Cambridge by Professor James Stuart. As an accomplished cricketer, rider, and skater, he was familiar with athletes as well as with students; but he was best known, especially in his own college, as a genial and judicious host, a sagacious and witty counsellor, a sympathetic and, on the whole, sound disciplinarian. Though his ability was appreciated by non-residents also, he was not drawn into public life except in connexion with the preservation of open spaces. He defended with passionate and persistent vigour the rights both of the commoners and of the general public to the enjoyment of the Malvern Hills, obtained legislation for their protection, and became in 1884 one of the first conservators, giving 16 acres of land and receiving in 1887 the right to appoint a conservator in perpetuity. In later life he lost local influence and became entangled in controversy and even litigation; but he was not unsupported, and in 1905 and later he conveyed some more land and manorial rights, which he had purchased in order to prevent encroachments and to control quarrying. He also served on the council of the National Trust from 1895. As a young man he was somewhat of an invalid, but later enjoyed life fully, until he failed rather rapidly, and died suddenly in his college rooms on 15 July 1915. He was buried at Colwall. A memorial window was placed in the hall of Trinity College in 1920; and in the common room there is a sketch in oils of his head by Brian Hatton, of Hereford. His numerous objects of art and virtù, collected as an amusement without much discrimination, were sold in Oxford and London in 1915 and 1916.

[Memoir, with a vivid appreciation, by 'C' (Lord Curzon of Kedleston), in *The Times* 17 and 20 July 1915; Malvern newspapers; personal knowledge.] H. E. D. B.

RAWLING, CECIL GODFREY (1870–1917), soldier and explorer, was born at Stoke, Devonport, 16 February 1870, the second son of Samuel Bartlett Rawling, of Stoke, by his wife, Ada Bathe, daughter of S. Withers, of Purton, Wiltshire. He was educated at Clifton College and entered the army by way of the militia, being gazetted to the 13th regiment, Somerset Light Infantry, in 1891. Thenceforward most of his service was in India, where a love of sport took him into and beyond the Himalaya. In 1902 he crossed the Lanak-la Pass into Tibet as a preliminary reconnaissance for a more ambitious venture. In 1903, with Lieutenant A. J. G. Hargreaves, of his own regiment, he crossed the same pass and in nine months explored and mapped about 38,000 miles of hitherto unsurveyed country in Western Tibet and Rudok. In 1904 he was employed with the Tibet mission, and when the British commissioner, Sir Francis Younghusband, returned from Lhasa to Gyantse, he selected Rawling for the command of the very important exploration of the Upper Tsanpo (Brahmaputra) in 1904–1905. This was a very hazardous expedition, because the Tibetans were not known to be other than hostile, and the return journey over the Himalaya to Simla had to be made in the middle of winter. During that journey Mount Everest was for the first time clearly recognized from the north, and it became Rawling's ambition to lead a party in from that side. His book, *The Great Plateau* (1905), describes his journeys in Tibet. In 1909 he went as surveyor to a scientific expedition to Dutch New Guinea, and when the leader was invalided he took command with notable success. He mapped a large area of unknown country and was the first European to meet the interesting Pygmies (Tapiro), who inhabit the lower mountains of that region. His experiences are recorded in *The Land of the New Guinea Pygmies* (1913). For his explorations the Royal Geographical Society awarded him the Murchison bequest (1909) and the Patrons' gold medal (1917). He returned to his regiment in 1911.

In 1914, on the outbreak of the European War, Major Rawling, as he was then, was ordered to raise and train a service battalion of his regiment, which he subsequently commanded in France. He survived the fighting at Hooge in July–August 1915, the long winter in the Ypres salient, the battle of the Somme, the taking of Fricourt, Mametz Wood, and the capture of Gueudecourt. He was promoted brigadier-general in July 1916. All the summer of 1917 he was constantly engaged, first in the fighting on the Hindenburg line, and then in the great battle east of Ypres. He was killed on 28 October by a stray shell outside his brigade head-quarters at Hooge.

Rawling was made C.I.E. in 1909, C.M.G. in 1916, and received the D.S.O. in 1917. He was unmarried. In character he was singularly boylike; as a traveller he was indefatigable, and as a soldier he was always hopeful and without fear. A tablet to his memory was erected in the south aisle of St. Mary Magdalen's church, Taunton.

[*Geographical Journal*, December, 1917; private information; personal knowledge.] A. F. R. W.

RAYLEIGH, third BARON (1842–1919), mathematician and physicist. [See STRUTT, JOHN WILLIAM.]

REAY, eleventh BARON (1839–1921), governor of Bombay and first president of the British Academy. [See MACKAY, DONALD JAMES.]

REDESDALE, first BARON (1837–1916), diplomatist and author. [See MITFORD, ALGERNON BERTRAM FREEMAN-.]

REDMOND, JOHN EDWARD (1856–1918), Irish political leader, the eldest son of William Archer Redmond, M.P., by his wife, Mary, daughter of Major Hoey, of Hoeyfield, co. Wicklow, was born at Ballytrent, co. Wexford, 1 September 1856. The Redmonds were Catholic gentry long established in county Wexford. One of the family became member for Wexford in 1859, and on his death in 1872, was succeeded by his nephew. Redmond's father, a supporter of the Home Rule policy advocated by Isaac Butt [q. v.].

John Redmond's childhood was largely spent on the Wexford coast at Ballytrent, the home of his father's brother. Educated at Clongowes by the Jesuits, he entered Trinity College, Dublin, in 1874, but in 1876 went to live with his father in London during the sessions of parliament, and in 1880 was nominated to a clerkship in the House of Commons. He was indeed educated largely in the House of Commons itself for the career to which hereditary tradition directed him. William Redmond, though he supported Butt's authority, was on friendly terms with Charles Stewart Parnell [q.v.]; and evidently his son's sympathy was captured by the new leader, for at the general election of 1880 when Parnell was mobbed in Enniscorthy, John Redmond was felled at his side by a stone. When the elder Redmond died in November 1880, his son would have succeeded to him, but that Parnell specially desired to bring in T. M. Healy, thus, as he said when the split began, 'rebuking, restraining, and setting by the prior right of my friend, Jack Redmond.' Two months later the borough of New Ross in county Wexford became vacant. Redmond was elected unopposed. Hurrying to Westminster, he arrived at 8 o'clock in the morning of 2 February 1881 ; the House had been forty hours in session, and an hour later Speaker Brand closured further debate. Next day when all the Irish members present were suspended for refusal to obey the rules of the House, Redmond made his maiden speech—a single sentence of protest—before he was removed by the serjeant at arms.

After this turbulent beginning, Redmond's part in parliament was quiet. But his talent as a speaker was utilized on English platforms, and his power of persuasive and moderate statement caused him to be chosen in 1882 for a mission to the Irish of Australia, where much opposition to the Irish cause had to be overcome. The Phoenix Park murders had roused indignation, and many who had promised support to the mission drew back. Sir Henry Parkes, the prime minister of New South Wales, proposed that Redmond should be expelled from the colony, but the motion was defeated. The Irish working-men in the colony stood by him and saved the situation, until a telegram arrived exculpating the Irish parliamentary party. Gradually the tide turned, and ultimately Redmond collected £15,000 before going on to America, where another £15,000 was raised. The whole tour occupied two years. He had been joined by his brother W. H. K. Redmond [q. v.], who during his absence in Australia was chosen member for Wexford, Healy having won an Ulster seat. So began a comradeship in service between the brothers, which was strengthened by the fact that in Australia they married near kinswomen. John Redmond's wife was Johanna, daughter of James Dalton, of Orange, New South Wales ; their marriage took place in 1883. While Parnell's attitude to England was that of Irish Americans, Redmond's, through the affinities he formed in this early stage, was like that of the Australian Irish, a nationalism devoid of hostility to the British Empire.

The fight was hot in the years after 1886. In 1888, during Mr. Balfour's coercive rule, Redmond had experience of jail, being sentenced to five weeks' imprisonment on a charge of intimidation. But while the prestige of Parnell and his party was at its height, John Redmond did not rank in popularity, fame, or notoriety with Mr. Sexton, Mr. Dillon, Mr. William O'Brien, Mr. Healy, or Mr. T. P. O'Connor. No man was ever less ambitious. He was contented to be a member of a strong and successful movement, useful in the team but not seeking to be foremost in anything. Nor did he ever push his chances at the bar, to which he was called in 1886. He had some private means, and was happily married. He lived in Dublin at Leeson Park, where his three children, a son and two daughters, were born within this period ; and he and his wife were much in the society of other households belonging to the parliamentary group. But Redmond's social circle was always limited. In London, during the sessions, he adhered strictly to the usage which grew up during the time when Irish members were Ishmaelites in the House of Commons, and he went to no houses but those of Irish sympathizers. In Dublin, the political struggle, then virtually a class-war, estranged him from his own class and even from his kin. His childless uncle, the owner of Ballytrent, in leaving him the family estate, so arranged his will that the inheritance was financially and politically a burden.

The closest of ties, however, bound him to his brother, and the two doubly related households lived in the utmost intimacy. When, in 1889, Mrs. John Redmond died, her three children were mainly in the care of Mrs. William Redmond. But before this bereavement, the crisis had come which called John Redmond to exert for the first time all his forces. On 17 November 1890 a verdict was given against Parnell in the undefended O'Shea divorce case. Next day the standing committee of the National League held its fortnightly meeting. Redmond, who had roused his friends, attended and was moved to the chair; and on his motion a resolution was carried, promising continued support to Parnell. Two days later Redmond with his brother and other stalwarts convened a public meeting in the Leinster Hall, at which similar resolutions were passed. On 25 November parliament assembled ; by custom the Irish party met to choose a chairman for the session, and Parnell was re-elected unanimously. That afternoon Mr. Gladstone's letter was published which declared that the continuance of Parnell's leadership would render his own 'almost a nullity'. In the split in the Irish party which followed, Redmond was Parnell's chief supporter, backing a principle rather than a person. He insisted on the need for absolute independence of British parties. If, he argued, at the bidding of any English statesman the Irish party reversed their previous resolution, their independence was gone. When death ended Parnell's career on 6 October 1891, Redmond inevitably became leader of the group which had followed him after the split. In these ten months the violence of faction had been so terrible that re-union was impossible. Resigning North Wexford, which had been his seat since the Redistribution Act of 1885, Redmond stood for Cork, which Parnell had represented since 1880. He was heavily beaten. Here and everywhere the decisive influence of the Catholic clergy was thrown as strongly against this devout Catholic as against his former leader. A few weeks later, however, a vacancy occurred in Waterford, and though Michael Davitt [q. v.] was made his opponent, Redmond was returned. This was the sole seat which the Parnellites captured, and when the general election came in June 1892 their party was reduced to nine. Yet from the opening of the first session of this parliament, Redmond ranked, by common consent, among the foremost debaters in the House. His position was indeed easier than that of the main body, since his was the more acceptable rôle of laying down what a Home Rule bill should be, theirs of considering what they could get. He was essentially at this time a partisan leader. Justin M'Carthy [q. v.], chairman of the anti-Parnellites, wrote later : 'Parnell's chief lieutenant had shown in the service of his chief an energy and passion which few of us expected of him, and was utterly unsparing of the men who maintained the other side of the controversy.' Yet, though his group were by their position irresponsible, embittered by the campaign against them and especially by the part played in it by the clergy, Redmond himself avoided personal vilification and, moreover, never sank the statesman in the partisan. Thus in 1894 he served on the Childers commission on financial relations alongside of Mr. Sexton, one of his chief opponents. When the tories came into power (1895), and Sir Horace Plunkett put forward the proposal that Irish members should act together in the recess as a committee to advise on Irish affairs, Mr. M'Carthy, for the anti-Parnellites, refused, but Redmond accepted and signed the report which led to the creation of an Irish department of agriculture in 1899. In 1897 when Mr. Gerald Balfour promised a local government measure, again the larger group refused to welcome the proposal, and again Redmond promised his support. He did not share the fear that Ireland's desire for Home Rule might be killed by minor concessions.

Meanwhile Ireland was sick of faction, and proposals for re-union were constantly under discussion. Ultimately the South African War united Irishmen in a common feeling ; and at the opening of the session of 1900, Irish members assembled as one party for the first time since the split. Redmond was chosen to be chairman. It was a choice largely dictated by irreconcilable claims among the leaders of the larger group ; and it was clearly laid down that he should be chairman of the party, not leader of the movement. Probably no one contemplated that he would be irremovable. He became so by sheer merit ; above all, by total lack of jealousy. As chairman, he never sought to impose his will on the party ; but he had an extraordinary gift for so presenting a case as to carry acceptance. He always thought very far ahead and in broad outline, giving to details their just value and no more. During the first years of his chairmanship, the star of George Wyndham [q. v.] was rising, and Redmond threw his whole weight behind the policy which resulted in land purchase; yet he did not allow himself or the party to be involved in the quarrel which arose between Mr. O'Brien and Mr. Dillon over the new measure. He was rewarded with a steadily growing warmth of support from Mr. Dillon ; while Mr. Devlin, the one important figure who appeared in the parliamentary movement after Parnell's death, though coming from the anti-Parnellite wing, became more and more affectionately bound to one who for him was certainly leader rather than chairman.

In parliament, Redmond's gifts showed themselves to the greatest advantage. He understood the House of Commons as well as Parnell, but from a different standpoint; he liked and respected it, and always held the belief that from the platform which it afforded he could persuade England into accepting Home Rule. Unlike Parnell, Redmond scarcely ever missed a division in the House of Commons; but he had inherited from Parnell the belief that a leader might to some degree hold himself aloof, and the privacy which he loved was much happier after he married in 1899 his second wife, Miss Ada Beazley. Nearly all the time when parliament was not sitting was spent at Aughavanagh, an old shooting lodge of Parnell's which he had bought, remote in the Wicklow mountains.

The Irish leader's difficulties began when the liberal party attained power (1906). Mr. Asquith's section of it had pledged themselves to go no farther than the instalment of administrative Home Rule known as 'devolution', which Redmond had denounced on the eve of the election as affording 'absolutely no remedy for the state of grievances admitted'. Yet he had no choice but to give Irish support in Great Britain to liberals, except where there was a labour candidate, and the sweeping liberal victory was accepted as a triumph for Ireland.

The first important measure of the new government was an English Education Bill which roused hostility from the Roman Catholic Church. Yet on this Bill Redmond contrived by skilful management to earn the thanks of Archbishop Bourne, and still to support the Bill, in which he had gained certain amendments, in its final stage. When at the close of a year's work the Lords threw out the measure, Redmond, knowing that the liberals had shirked Home Rule because its certain rejection by the upper House meant either its abandonment or a contest to change the English constitution for the sake of Ireland, urged an immediate appeal to the electors. There was now a chance to challenge the veto of the peers on a purely English issue. But his counsel was rejected; and, for Ireland, the proposed measure of devolution became now the main interest. By the end of 1906, Redmond was convinced that the Bill would not be acceptable. Yet liberal ministers were confident that Ireland would receive their proposals gladly, and Redmond pledged himself in advance that a full convention of his supporters should decide. In the opinion of Mr. Hayden, one of his ablest and most trusted colleagues, the character of Redmond's speech on the first reading was due to a loyal observance of his pledge that the decision should be left to Ireland; and on the morning after the debate, Redmond sent for Mr. Hayden to show him the motion of rejection which he proposed to put to the convention. None the less, the House of Commons had taken his speech for a guarded acceptance, and in Ireland his moving of the rejection was considered as an enforced concession to popular feeling.

Nothing in all Redmond's career before the European War so shook his prestige or that of his party as this episode; but he recovered his ground by a powerful campaign carried throughout Ireland, speaking in every centre of importance, and thus bringing himself into touch with many thousands to whom he had been but a name. His oratory never had the power to excite; but it could convince; and wherever he spoke he left the impression not only of high eloquence but of courage and complete sincerity.

The chance given to his policy by the conflict over Mr. Lloyd George's budget of 1909 brought with it new difficulties, for many Irish interests were hard hit by the measure; and after the general election an Irish opposition under Mr. William O'Brien and Mr. Healy came back stronger than the Parnellite party had been in 1892. But the elections in England had placed the Irish leader in a position to turn the scale, and his decisive stand, when Mr. Asquith showed signs of avoiding the direct issue of the Lords' veto, greatly increased his authority both in Ireland and in parliament; while a tour in America (at the close of 1910) enabled him to refill his party chest for the election which took place in December 1910 and to assure himself of enthusiastic support throughout the Irish world. The passing of the Parliament Act in 1911 was regarded by Ireland and by himself as largely due to the power of the Irish party. In the English constituencies Redmond and the cause for which he stood were no longer unpopular. From 1908 onwards he spoke at many centres in Great Britain; and his personal dignity, the moderation of his tone, and the magnanimity which was his best characteristic, contributed more than the work of all other men to change England's policy on this question.

But the real difficulty which Redmond

had to face lay in Ulster, of which, like most Irishmen of the South, he knew little. He accepted the view that Ulster's military preparations were only a bluff; and he did not realize how strong a feeling was growing among the young generation of Irishmen that Ulster had set an example to all Ireland. When the Irish volunteer movement was started in the close of 1913, he watched it with suspicion; but in the spring of 1914 the 'Curragh mutiny', followed by the Larne gun-running, revealed to him the full seriousness of the situation. Then, and only then, he threw his support into the volunteer movement, and Ireland came into it *en masse*; but the control of the volunteer organization was already very largely in the hands of men whose purpose was different from his. Yet he was still confident of his power to direct events in Ireland. In this year he visited one of his friends, a leading priest in county Tipperary, who asked him 'Is there anything that can rob us this time?' Redmond paused, and said 'A European war might do it'.

In July 1914 he took part with Mr. Dillon in the abortive conference at Buckingham Palace. On 26 July came the attempt of Crown forces to take rifles from Irish volunteers on the road from Howth, and the subsequent affray when soldiers fired without orders on a Dublin crowd. A week later parliament was confronted with the announcement of war, and Redmond, rising in the debate, made his declaration that all troops could be withdrawn from Ireland. The Irish volunteers would guard the country—'For that purpose the armed Catholics in the south will be only too glad to join arms with the armed Protestant Ulstermen.' He had spoken without consultation; but the reception of his words in Ireland as well as in England led the party to endorse Mr. Dillon's opinion that the speech had been a 'great stroke of statesmanship'. It was, however, largely foiled by the War Office, which refused to accept Redmond's proposal that the volunteers should receive recognition and, so far as possible, arms and training. Lord Kitchener held that this would be to arm rebels. Even the project of forming a distinctively Irish division, to correspond to that already sanctioned for Ulster, met with constant rebuffs. But Redmond persisted in his endeavour to create in Ireland an atmosphere favourable to recruiting. When the Coalition was formed (May 1915), a post in the Cabinet, but not an Irish post, was offered him, and was refused: he held strongly that Sir Edward Carson also should decline office in view of the effect on Ireland. This view did not prevail, and Irish recruiting dropped from 6,000 in May to 3,000 in June. Later, mainly through Redmond's efforts, it recovered, and by November the National Volunteers had sent 27,054 men to the colours, the Ulster Volunteers 27,412. But conscription was now in sight, and Redmond plainly told Mr. Asquith that the enforcement of it in Ireland would be an impossibility. He had so far impressed old opponents that in May 1916 Mr. Bonar Law and Sir Edward Carson supported him in opposing the inclusion of Ireland in the first National Service Bill. Ireland had then furnished at least 100,000 soldiers, of whom the majority were Catholic. He himself had visited the front in November 1915 and come back with the sense that 'from the commander-in-chief himself right down through the army one meets Irishmen wherever one goes'. He was even prouder of this than of the welcome which met him everywhere.

But in Ireland disaffection was spreading. Redmond underrated the danger, but gave certain advice to the government. 'What I did suggest, they never did; what I said they ought not to do, they always did,' was his own account of these communications. The Rebellion (April 1916) however, took him absolutely by surprise, and in parliament he expressed 'detestation and horror' of the events in Dublin. He denounced it in a public manifesto as a German intrigue, 'not half so much treason to the cause of the Allies as treason to the cause of Home Rule.' He accepted as just the executions of three leaders in the rising; but for the rest he begged that the leniency shown by Botha in South Africa should be imitated. As before, his advice was rejected. 'I have had no power in the government of Ireland,' he said in parliament, 'all my suggestions have been overborne . . . and my conviction is that if we had had the power and responsibility for the government of our country during the past two years, recent occurrences in Ireland would never have taken place.' Many shared this opinion, and negotiations were begun to bring Home Rule into operation. On the faith of a written document, Redmond, with Mr. Devlin's aid, persuaded the nationalists of Ulster to agree to the temporary exclusion of six counties. The Cabinet then repudiated the agreement, which had been made by Mr. Lloyd George with Mr. Asquith's concurrence; and Irishmen who already considered that Redmond had missed his chance of driving a bargain at the opening of the War, now held that he had been ignominiously duped. Redmond knew that he had not the confidence of the country, but he remained at his post. The death of his brother in action at the Wytschaete Ridge in June 1917, followed in a few weeks by that of Patrick O'Brien, chief whip to the party, and his most devoted follower, were deadly blows to the Irish leader's spirit.

This was his state when the last phase of his work began. In May 1917 the Irish question had been re-opened, and on a suggestion from Redmond himself it was decided to try the expedient of a convention of Irishmen for the drafting of a constitution for Ireland within the Empire. Before it met on 25 July, William Redmond's seat had been captured by Mr. de Valera, and at the opening meeting Redmond was insulted in the streets of Dublin. In the Convention he refused throughout to act as leader of a party, but his personal ascendancy was admitted on all sides; and the group of southern unionists showed a disposition to make common cause with him. But their proposals did not give to Ireland the complete fiscal control on which a section of nationalists insisted; and Redmond, on a motion designed to effect agreement with them, found the Catholic prelates and Mr. Devlin against him. He withdrew his motion, and consented to act as one of a delegation to the ministers from the nationalist members of the Convention. This took him to London in February 1918; he fell ill there, and when the Convention reassembled to discuss the government's reply, he was absent. On 6 March he died suddenly and unexpectedly. A few weeks later the government passed a measure applying conscription to Ireland, and the train of events was finally set in motion which largely undid the work of his life.

In the period of Redmond's leadership three main points were carried by the Irish people in their long struggle to regain mastery of their country: control of local government, ownership of the land, and statutory establishment of an Irish parliament with an executive responsible to it. These were essential to the complete reconquest of self-government, which came within five years from his death, achieved by means which he deliberately rejected. His aim was to establish in Ireland parliamentary institutions, capable of growth to the limit of such powers as Ireland should find necessary for her free development. Separation was no object of his. He aimed at a free Ireland within the Empire, liberated by friendly means. He aimed also at a willing union of all Irishmen, and avoided all that could increase race-bitterness. The only concession to which he could not bring himself was that of excluding any part of Ulster, except for a limited period. He was not willing that in this matter the decision should rest with Protestant Ulster. But the essential generosity of his nature is revealed in the project that Irishmen on the brink of civil war should find reconciliation by rivalry in self-sacrifice against a common enemy in a good cause. This project, after many thousand Irish lives had been sacrificed, he lived to see discomfited, and he died in the full sense of disastrous defeat.

[Stephen Gwynn, *John Redmond's Last Years*, 1919; L. G. Redmond Howard, *John Redmond*, 1910; *Home Rule: Speeches of John Redmond, M.P.*, edited by R. Barry O'Brien, 1910; political literature of the time; personal knowledge.] S. G.

REDMOND, WILLIAM HOEY KEARNEY (1861–1917), Irish nationalist, the second son of William Archer Redmond, M.P., of Ballytrent, and brother of John Edward Redmond [q.v.], was born at Ballytrent in 1861. He was educated at Clongowes, and entered the Wexford militia, but, developing strong nationalist opinions, resigned his commission, and in 1881 was one of the youngest among the 'suspects' imprisoned under the coercive measures of the Irish chief secretary, William Edward Forster [q.v.] He was in Kilmainham jail with Charles Stewart Parnell [q.v.], to whom he formed a lifelong devotion. In 1883 he was sent to join his brother John, on a political mission to Australia, and in his absence was elected member of parliament for Wexford, which his father had represented before him. While in Australia he married Eleanor, daughter of James Dalton, of Orange, New South Wales, whose near kinswoman the same day married his brother. On his return from the mission, which was extended to America, 'Willie' Redmond (as he was always called) became a prominent figure among the rank and file of Parnell's party—aggressive at Westminster and very active in Ireland, where his flamboyant rhetoric and gallant bearing made him the idol of public meetings. During the land war he was for the second time imprisoned, in 1888, for a speech, and met his brother, also a prisoner, in Wexford jail.

In the split in the Irish party in 1890 William Redmond sided passionately with Parnell. He had captured an Ulster constituency, North Fermanagh, in 1885, but after Parnell's death (1891) he won East Clare in one of the stormiest contests ever known in Ireland, and held it unopposed till his death. In that year he was called to the Irish bar; but he never practised. With maturity he became one of the most popular members in the House of Commons, but he abated nothing of his fervour, and in 1902, during the recrudescence of agitation which preceded the Wyndham Land Act, he was again imprisoned. His parliamentary hobby was the promotion of tobacco-growing in Ireland; a more serious aim was accomplished when in 1909 he carried through its second reading a Bill which the government next year embodied in the Accession Declaration Act. He revisited Australia and America several times on missions, and wrote two books on Australia, *A Shooting Trip in the Australian Bush* (1898) and *Through the New Commonwealth* (1906).

But William Redmond is best remembered by his last years. When the European War broke out, he endorsed his brother's appeal to Ireland by volunteering, and was given a captaincy in the 6th (service) battalion of the Royal Irish regiment, to which the Wexford militia belonged. He threw himself into soldiering with a kind of religious enthusiasm, and when the 16th (Irish) division went to Flanders in December 1915, he was, at fifty-four, probably the oldest man commanding a company in the line. In the following winter, when the division, based on Locre, lay next to the Ulstermen, he was the centre of a notable fraternization. On leave periods he appeared now and then at Westminster, and spoke twice, each time contriving to convey, as no one else had done, the best spirit of the fighting men. But his last speech, in March 1917, was definitely political, and none of the crowded House who listened in silence will forget the appeal for a full settlement of the Irish question, spoken in the name of the Irish soldiers: 'In the name of God, we here who are about to die, perhaps, ask you to do that which largely induced us to leave our homes—and enable us when we meet Canadians or Australians and New Zealanders side by side in the common cause and the common field to say to them, "Our country, just as yours, has self-government within the Empire".'

Three months later the forecast felt in his accent rather than his words was fulfilled. On 7 June the two Irish divisions launched against Wytschaete Ridge a long-prepared attack. Redmond had in the previous year been given his majority and transferred to a post on the divisional staff, and during the battles of the Somme was kept reluctantly out of the actual fighting line. This time he insisted on rejoining his old battalion for the day. In the triumphant advance he fell, and was carried out dying by Ulster soldiers. His death drove home the lesson of his life. His grave in the garden of the hospice at Locre is a place of pilgrimage.

[Memorial volume, *Major William Redmond*, 1917; biographical notice, and reprint of his last speech, in his *Trench Pictures from France* (posthumously published in 1917); T. P. O'Connor, *The Parnell Movement*, 1886; S. Gwynn, *John Redmond's Last Years*, 1919.] S. G.

REID, Sir GEORGE HOUSTOUN (1845–1918), colonial politician, was born at Johnstone, Renfrewshire, 25 February 1845, the son of the Rev. John Reid, a minister of the Church of Scotland. When seven years old he was taken to Australia, and spent his youth in the civil service of New South Wales. Finding this too restricted a field for his ambitions, and attracted to political life by his fervent belief in free trade, he secured in 1879 admission to the colonial bar, and in 1880 was elected to the legislative assembly for East Sydney, which constituency, with a break in 1884–1885, he continued to represent until 1901. His skill in advocacy secured him ere long a large and lucrative practice, and in politics also success was not delayed. He was minister of public instruction from January 1883 to March 1884, and on the fall of Sir Henry Parkes [q.v.] in 1891, he stood out as leader of the opposition with such skill that on 3 August 1894 he attained the premiership of the colony. The general elections of 1895 and 1898 confirmed him in office, his ministry attaining the unprecedented duration of sixty-one months. Useful work was done in re-establishing the financial position, shaken by the banking crisis of 1893; system was introduced in the public accounts, and an effort was made in the Land Act of 1895 to check the aggregation of land in private ownership.

The dominant issue of the time was federation, and on this topic Reid's attitude was ambiguous. In retrospect he regarded his term of office as the period in which, as premier of the senior colony, he carried the federation movement to a successful issue, and it was he who proposed at the Hobart Conference of 1895 the resolutions for the summoning of a convention to decide the terms of the federal constitution. But the knowledge that federation would mean the overthrow of free trade, and the fear that it would impose grave financial burdens on New South Wales and injure the importance of Sydney, rapidly cooled his ardour. When the draft constitution finally emerged from the convention, his attitude towards it in a speech at Sydney (28 March 1898) was so critical that it failed to secure at the ensuing referendum the 80,000 votes necessary for its acceptance. Reid used the result in order to obtain concessions at a conference in January 1899, and only then exerted his influence to secure acceptance, on 20 June, of the amended draft.

At this juncture, when Reid might legitimately hope to become the first prime minister of the Commonwealth, sudden disaster befell him through defeat in the assembly on a minor personal issue, and he resigned office on 13 September 1899. In 1901 he entered federal politics as leader of the opposition to the movement for protection, but he found it hard to reconcile professional work in Sydney with attendance at the debates in Melbourne. For a brief period (19 August 1904 to 3 July 1905) the feuds between the followers of Mr. Alfred Deakin [q.v.] and the labour party over the Conciliation and Arbitration Bill enabled him to secure the premiership through alliance with the labour party leader, Mr. Allan McLean. But the coalition rested on no secure basis; Mr. Deakin's attacks proved irresistible, and Reid was reduced to the position of leader of a dwindling fraction of the house of representatives. From this plight he was rescued by the coalition of his supporters with those of Mr. Deakin against Mr. Andrew Fisher's labour administration in 1909 on the issue of naval assistance to the Empire. Co-operation between him and Mr. Deakin in the same government was impossible, but a solution was found by his appointment as the first high commissioner of the Commonwealth in London (1910–1915). The post was the more attractive to Reid as he had already created a favourable impression in England by his speeches in 1897, when he represented New South Wales at Queen Victoria's diamond jubilee celebrations and at the conference of colonial premiers. By temperament in sympathy with liberal opinion in England, he met with the ready support of the imperial government in his efforts to magnify his office and to insist on the importance of the Commonwealth. To official life in London he became so deeply attached that he viewed with unconcealed dread the termination of his service under the Commonwealth, and it was with the utmost satisfaction that he accepted in January 1916 the offer of a seat in the House of Commons for St. George's, Hanover Square. But it was too late for him to adapt himself effectively to the conditions of the House of Commons, or to gain ministerial office. To occupy his energies and serve the allied cause in the European War, he undertook an unofficial mission to the United States; his health suffered severely from the strain of this exertion, and his death, which took place in London on 12 September 1918, was doubtless accelerated in consequence.

Without originality of political conception or great administrative capacity, Reid was able and ready in debate, and unquestionably the best platform orator in Australia in the decade before federation. In England he won just repute as an after-dinner speaker; his fund of amusing anecdotes—often at his own expense—was endless, and his wit was delightful. Amid the acerbities of colonial politics he preserved a remarkable measure of good humour and courtesy, and his genuine kindness of heart more than compensated for a natural vanity, which exhibited itself in the eagerness with which—unlike Mr. Deakin, his chief rival—he accepted not merely a privy councillorship in 1897, but also the more formal honours of K.C.M.G. (1909), G.C.M.G. (1911), and G.C.B. (1916); his action in this regard he justified by the value which he placed on the Crown as the symbol of imperial unity, although he was strongly opposed to any scheme of imperial federation.

Reid married in 1891 Flora, daughter of John Bromby, of Thornton, Cressy, Tasmania.

[Reid, *My Reminiscences*, 1917; J. Quick and R. R. Garran, *Constitution of the Australian Commonwealth*, 1901; H. G. Turner, *First Decade of the Australian Commonwealth*, 1911; B. R. Wise, *Making of the Australian Commonwealth*, 1913; New South Wales and Commonwealth *Parliamentary Debates*; personal knowledge. Portrait, *Royal Academy Pictures*, 1916.] A. B. K.

RENDEL, Sir ALEXANDER MEADOWS (1829–1918), civil engineer, the eldest of the four sons of James

Meadows Rendel [q.v.], by his wife, Catherine Jane Harris, was born at Plymouth 3 April 1829. The family connexion with engineering is notable, for Rendel's father was a distinguished member of that profession, and his three brothers were associated for many years with Lord Armstrong's firm at Newcastle-upon-Tyne. One of them, George Wightwick Rendel [q.v.], was for a short time a civil lord of the Admiralty; another, Stuart Rendel, was raised to the peerage as Baron Rendel in 1894. Alexander Rendel was educated at King's School, Canterbury, and at Trinity College, Cambridge, of which he was a scholar. He was thirty-third wrangler in the mathematical tripos of 1851. He then became an assistant to his father, whose premature death in 1856 obliged him at the early age of twenty-seven to take over the control of the practice. He was responsible for much work in connexion with docks and harbours. As engineer to the London Dock Company he designed the large extension to the Victoria dock now known as the Royal Albert dock (1875). The Albert dock (1863–1867) and Edinburgh dock (1874–1881) for the Leith harbour and dock commissions are other important undertakings of his in this branch of engineering.

Rendel's main work, however, was done in connexion with Indian railways. He paid his first visit to India in 1857, the year of the Mutiny, when there were scarcely any railways in the country. During his early association with the East Indian Railway, as consulting engineer, he reorganized completely the tariff of passenger fares and freight rates, basing these charges on the cost per mile run. As a result the East Indian was the only railway in India to show profits on its working. His success attracted the attention of the India Office, and in 1872 he was appointed consulting engineer to the Indian State Railways. In this capacity he did admirable service, acting often in conjunction with his close friend Sir Richard Strachey [q.v.], who was for many years a member of the council of India. Rendel was responsible for designing many railway bridges in India. Two of the most important of these were the Lansdowne bridge over the Indus at Sukkur, opened in 1889, and at that time the largest cantilever bridge in existence, and the Hardinge bridge over the Ganges, completed in 1915. Nor was it only as an engineer that Rendel's assistance was valuable, for his advice was sought also upon the many administrative and commercial questions which affected the development of the railway system in India.

Rendel acted singly as a consulting engineer in London until 1888, when he took one of his sons and Mr. F. E. Robertson into partnership. Other partners were added later, and at the time of his death his firm was known as Rendel, Palmer, and Tritton. He was created K.C.I.E. in 1887. He died in London 23 January 1918.

Rendel married in 1853 Eliza (died 1916), eldest daughter of Captain William Hobson, R.N., the first governor of New Zealand, by whom he had five sons and three daughters.

[*The Times*, 25 January 1918; *Engineering*, 1 February 1918; *The Engineer*, 1 February 1918; private information.]

A. C.

REYNOLDS, JAMES EMERSON (1844–1920), chemist, was born at Booterstown, co. Dublin, 8 January 1844, the only son of Dr. James Reynolds, who kept a medical hall at Booterstown. He was named after his great-uncle, Captain Emerson, R.N. On leaving school Emerson Reynolds, as he was usually called, became assistant to his father, and developed in early youth a strong bent for chemistry. Following his father's desire, he studied medicine, and in 1865 qualified as a licentiate of the Edinburgh College of Physicians and Surgeons. In the meantime he fitted up a small laboratory in his home at Booterstown, pursued his chemical studies unaided, and tried research work from the outset. His first paper, *On the oleaginous matter formed on dissolving different kinds of iron in dilute acids*, appeared in the *Chemical News* (1861), when he was only seventeen years of age. Several other papers of chemical interest were published by Reynolds while still in his 'teens. After practising for a short time in Dublin, he abandoned medicine on his father's death, and devoted himself solely to chemistry.

In March 1867 Reynolds was appointed keeper of minerals at the National Museum in Dublin, and in the following year analyst to the Royal Dublin Society. He now had access to a properly equipped laboratory, and here he made his first important contribution to chemistry. In 1868 he discovered thiocarbamide, or thiourea, the sulphur analogue of urea, which he obtained by the isomeric transformation of ammonium thiocyanate. His discovery was not due to chance. The existence of thiourea was indicated by theory, but its isolation had already baffled the skill of such distinguished chemists as Liebig and Hofmann in Germany. This discovery, described in the *Journal* of the Chemical Society of London for 1869, attracted much attention and was quickly republished in several continental scientific periodicals. It at once established Reynolds's position as one of the most promising of the younger British chemists. In 1871 he described the preparation of an interesting compound of acetone with mercuric oxide. This was the first colloidal derivative of mercury to be made known, and its formation is the basis of Reynolds's well-known test for acetone.

Reynolds was appointed professor of chemistry at the Royal College of Surgeons, Dublin, in 1870, while he still retained his post at the Royal Dublin Society. He relinquished both positions in 1875, when he was elected to the chair of chemistry at Trinity College, Dublin, as successor to Dr. James Apjohn. He now wrote his *Experimental Chemistry for Junior Students*, published in 1882 in four small volumes, an original work in which the teaching of chemistry was developed on entirely new lines. By the aid of simple and carefully tested experiments, the student was taught to verify for himself the fundamental laws of chemistry by quantitative results—a method, now universally adopted, which Reynolds was the first to introduce. His book passed through several editions, and was translated into German.

Reynolds was an excellent teacher; the care which he bestowed upon his experimental illustrations, and his fine qualities as a lecturer, won the admiration and respect of his pupils. The duties of his chair left little time for uninterrupted research, yet he published more than a dozen scientific papers during the twenty-eight years that he remained at Trinity College. In 1903 he resigned his chair and went to live in London. At the Davy-Faraday laboratory he continued research, chiefly on silicon compounds, his last work (1913) being the synthesis of a felspar, anorthite, a calcium-aluminium silicate, which had the properties of the naturally occurring mineral.

Reynolds was elected a fellow of the Royal Society in 1880, and vice-president for 1901–1902. He was president of the Society of Chemical Industry (1891), president of the Chemical Society (1901–1903), and president of the chemical section of the British Association (1893). His mental power was active to the end, but his eyesight, never very good, gradually failed during his last years. He died suddenly 18 February 1920, at his house in Kensington.

Reynolds married in 1875 Janet Elizabeth, daughter of Prebendary John Finlayson, of Christchurch Cathedral, Dublin, by whom he had a son and a daughter.

[Private information; personal knowledge.] E. A. W–R.

REYNOLDS, OSBORNE (1842–1912), engineer and physicist, was born 23 August 1842 at Belfast. He came of a clerical family. His grandfather and great-grandfather had been rectors of Debach-with-Boulge, Suffolk. His father, the Rev. Osborne Reynolds, was fourth wrangler in 1837, and subsequently fellow of Queens' College, Cambridge, principal of a school in Belfast, head master of Dedham grammar school, Essex, and finally, in his turn, rector of Debach. His mother was Jane Hickman. For his early education Reynolds, who was a boy at Dedham school, was indebted mainly to his father. He inherited a keen interest in mechanics, and at the age of nineteen entered the workshop of a mechanical engineer in order to make himself acquainted with the practical side of the subject before proceeding to Queens' College, Cambridge. He graduated in 1867 as seventh wrangler, and was elected a fellow of Queens' in the same year. After a short period in the office of a civil engineer, he was appointed in 1868 to the newly instituted professorship of engineering in the Owens College, Manchester. This post he held until his retirement, through ill-health, in 1905.

The courses of study laid down by Reynolds as professor were somewhat exacting, but he succeeded in rousing the interest and even enthusiasm of the more capable among his students, many of whom afterwards came to occupy posts of distinction. His long tenure of the professorship is chiefly memorable, however, for the series of original investigations which he carried out, sometimes with the co-operation of his assistants and pupils, to whom he always assigned a generous share of credit. These investigations dealt almost entirely with mechanical questions, or with physical phenomena so far as they appeared to admit of a mechanical explanation, and were highly original both in conception and in execution. Reynolds's acute physical insight enabled him to explain phenomena which other minds had regarded as obscure or even paradoxical.

Examples of this are his work on lubrication, which has led to important practical inventions; on the laws of the flow of water in pipes, with the recognition of the 'critical velocity', now universally known by his name, at which the flow changes its character; and on the 'dilatancy', as he called it, of granular media. The same peculiar insight is shown in his papers on atmospheric refraction of sound, and on the 'group-velocity' of water waves, where, in both cases, he made important additions to the work of Sir George Gabriel Stokes [q.v.].

Although Reynolds made valuable contributions to engineering practice, as in the design of turbine pumps, and in the study of the laws of communication of heat from a metal surface to a fluid, his scientific reputation will probably rest mainly on his work in general physics, although this, it may be said, was suggested often by some practical question of engineering. The most extensive piece of experimental work which he carried out was a determination of the mechanical equivalent of heat from a novel point of view. The object here was the direct measurement of the amount of heat required to raise a pound of water from the freezing to the boiling point, the result being thus independent of the thermometric properties of any particular substance, such as mercury or glass. This must always rank as a classical instance of the determination of a physical constant.

The scientific papers of Reynolds were published in a collected form, *Papers on Mechanical and Physical Subjects*, in three volumes (1900–1903). Of their originality and value there is no question, but it cannot be said that they are always easy to follow. The leading idea is in most cases simple; indeed, Reynolds's bias was always to look for a simple explanation, rather than for one which depended on the concurrence of a number of independent causes. But the involved style of exposition which he adopted had a tendency to perplex all but determined students, with the result that much of his work, especially his theoretical work, was long in gaining general acceptance. By his scientific compeers his worth was early recognized. He was elected a fellow of the Royal Society in 1877, and was awarded its gold medal in 1888.

The character of Reynolds was, like his writings, strongly individual. Somewhat reserved in serious or personal matters, and occasionally combative and tenacious in matters of university politics, he was kindly and generous in all ordinary relations of life. He had a keen sense of humour, and delighted in starting paradoxes, which he would maintain, half seriously and half playfully, with great ingenuity and resource. After his retirement (1905) he lived at St. Decuman's, Somerset, where he died 21 February 1912. An admirable portrait by the Hon. John Collier hangs in the hall of Manchester University.

Reynolds married twice: first, in 1868 Charlotte (died 1869), daughter of Dr. Chadwick, of Leeds; secondly, in 1881 Annie Charlotte, daughter of the Rev. Henry Wilkinson, rector of Otley, Suffolk. By his second marriage he left three sons and a daughter.

[*Proceedings* of the Royal Society, vol. lxxxviii, A, 1912–1913; private information; personal knowledge.] H. L.

RHONDDA, first **Viscount** (1856–1918), statesman, colliery proprietor, and financier. [See **Thomas, David Alfred**.]

RHŶS, Sir JOHN (1840–1915), Celtic scholar, was born at Aber Ceirio Fach, Cardiganshire, 21 June 1840, the eldest son of Hugh Rhŷs, yeoman farmer, of Ponterwyd, Cardiganshire, by his wife, Jane Mason, who, according to family tradition, was of Scottish extraction. John Rhŷs received his elementary education at Brynhwyth (as he insisted on writing the name), Pant-y-ffynon, and at the British school at Penllwyn, near Aberystwyth. After a course of study at the Bangor Normal College he was appointed master of a school at Rhos-y-bòl in Anglesey. In 1865 he was introduced by Chancellor James Williams, of Llanfairynghornwy, Anglesey, to Dr. Charles Williams, principal of Jesus College, Oxford, who, after a brief oral examination, offered him an exhibition at that college on the spot. Rhŷs went up to Oxford in the same year, obtained a second class in classical moderations in 1867, and a first class in *literae humaniores* in 1869. Towards the end of the latter year he was elected to a fellowship at Merton College.

Visits to French and German universities in the long vacations of 1868 and 1869, and again in 1870–1871 when he matriculated at Leipzig and attended the lectures of, among others, Georg Curtius and August Leskien, turned Rhŷs's attention definitely towards linguistic research. He contributed to the first volume of the *Revue Celtique* (1870), and in the course of the following six years, during which he was inspector of schools for the counties of Flint and Denbigh, published a number of articles on Celtic grammar in the same journal. A course of lectures delivered at Aberystwyth in 1874, published later under the title *Lectures on Welsh Philology* (1877), established his reputation as a Celtic scholar of the first rank; and when the Jesus professorship of Celtic was founded at Oxford in 1877 he was elected first professor. At the same time he was made an honorary fellow of Jesus College, of which he became fellow and bursar in 1881. He filled the office of bursar till 1895, when he was elected principal of the college in succession to Dr. Hugo Harper.

Rhŷs was, first and foremost, a student, and although he served as member of the hebdomadal council from 1906 to 1911, it was clear that the administrative side of academic life had little attraction for him. On the other hand, he was for forty years an unwearied worker in the cause of educational and social advancement. Wales, in particular, owes him an inestimable debt. He served on Lord Aberdare's departmental committee on Welsh education (1881), and was secretary to Sir John Bridge's commission on the tithe agitation in Wales (1887) and to the royal commission on Sunday closing in Wales (1889). He was also a member of the royal commission on land tenure in Wales (1893), of the royal commission on university education in Ireland (1901), of Sir Thomas Raleigh's commission on the Welsh university and colleges (1907), of Chief Baron Palles's commission for a national university of Ireland (1908); and at the time of his death (1915) he was chairman of the royal commission on ancient monuments in Wales and Monmouthshire. In recognition of his public services Rhŷs was knighted in 1907, and in 1911 made a privy councillor. He received the honorary degree of LL.D. from the university of Edinburgh in 1893, and that of D.Litt. from the university of Wales in 1902.

As a scholar, Rhŷs combined with great industry and learning a singularly active, reconstructive imagination. Where a more cautious man would have decided that the data were insufficient he often preferred to suggest a series of alternative theories, sometimes without making it clear that he was presenting in each of them not something intended to be a definitive interpretation of the facts, but simply a suggestion which appeared to deserve consideration even if it should later have to be withdrawn. His researches took him into many fields. Beginning as a grammarian, he resumed and continued his linguistic and epigraphic investigations in *The Outlines of the Phonology of Manx Gaelic* (1894), in a series of papers read to the British Academy, of which he became a fellow in 1903, in *The Celtic Inscriptions of France and Italy* (1906), *Notes on the Coligny Calendar together with an Edition of the Reconstructed Calendar* with a supplement, *The Reconstruction of the Coligny Calendar* (1910), *The Celtic Inscriptions of Gaul: Additions and Corrections* (1911), *The Celtic Inscriptions of Cisalpine Gaul* (1913), and *Gleanings in the Italian Field of Celtic Epigraphy* (1914). His historical works include *Celtic Britain* (1879, 2nd ed. 1884, 3rd ed. 1904), *Studies in Early Irish History* in the *Proceedings* of the British Academy (1903), *The Welsh People* (with D. Brynmor-Jones, 1900), *Celtae and Galli* in *Proceedings* of the British Academy (1905). To the literature of the history of religion, archaeology, ethnology, and folk-lore he contributed his Hibbert lectures, *On the Origin and Growth of Religion, as Illustrated by Celtic Heathendom* (1888), his presidential address to the anthropological section of the British Association (1900), his Rhind lectures at Edinburgh on *The Early Ethnology of the British Isles* (1889), *Studies on the Arthurian Legend* (1891), *Celtic Folk-lore: Welsh and Manx* (2 vols., 1901), together with numerous articles in the publications of the Honourable Society of Cymmrodorion. Almost his only excursion into the field of literary research is represented by *The Englyn: The Origin of the Welsh Englyn and the Kindred Metres* (vol. xviii of the *Cymmrodor*, 1905). He was associated with J. Gwenogvryn Evans in the publication of the first three volumes of the series of Old Welsh Texts.

Rhŷs died at the Lodgings, Jesus College, 17 December 1915, and was buried in Holywell cemetery, Oxford. There is a portrait of him by S. J. Solomon, R.A., in the hall of Jesus College (*Royal Academy Pictures*, 1915). He married in 1872 Elspeth (died 1911), daughter of John Hughes-Davies, of Llanberis, Carnarvonshire, by whom he had two daughters.

[Memoirs in *Transactions* of the Honourable Society of Cymmrodorion, 1916; *Jesus College Magazine*, June 1919; private information. See also *Proceedings* of the British Academy, 1925.] J. F.

RICHARDS, Sir FREDERICK WILLIAM (1833–1912), admiral, was born at Ballyhally, co. Wexford, 30 November 1833, the second son of Captain Edwin Richards, R.N., of Solsborough, co. Wexford, by his wife, Mary Anne, daughter of the Rev. Walter Blake Kirwan [q.v.], dean of Killala. After education at the Naval School, New Cross, he became a naval cadet in 1848. He served for several years on the Australian station and was promoted acting mate, H.M. sloop *Fantome,* on the same station in January 1854. He was promoted lieutenant in October 1855, and on returning home in 1856 went on half-pay for a year, after which he was appointed to the *Ganges,* flagship on the China station. The commander-in-chief, Rear-Admiral R. L. Baynes, appointed him flag lieutenant in April 1859, and in February 1860 he was promoted commander in command of the paddle-sloop *Vixen* on the China station. He brought home and paid off this vessel in 1861. From March 1862 to January 1866 he commanded the *Dart,* a gunboat, on the west coast of Africa, and on his return was promoted captain in February 1866.

After four and a half years on half-pay Richards commanded the Indian troopship *Jumna* till June 1873, and was then selected to command the *Devastation,* the first steam turret battleship designed without any sail power. This command was of much importance, as the loss in 1870 of the *Captain,* a sailing turret ship of special design, had caused great anxiety as to the stability of such vessels. Richards's conduct of the exhaustive steam trials and his able reports on them completely satisfied the authorities and allayed public anxiety. In 1874 he took the *Devastation* to the Mediterranean and remained her captain till June 1877. The following January he became captain of the steam reserve, and in October 1878 he was appointed commodore and senior officer on the west coast of Africa, H.M.S. *Boadicea.* When he arrived at the Cape the disaster at Isandhlwana in the Zulu War had just occurred (22 January 1879), and he promptly proceeded up the east coast outside the limits of his station, and landed in March 1879 with a small naval brigade and commanded it at the battle of Gingihlovo (2 April) and in the relief of Echowe (3 April). For these services he was gazetted and made a C.B. (1879). He remained as commodore in South Africa until June 1882, having taken part in the battle of Laing's Nek (28 January 1881) in the Boer War, and being promoted K.C.B. for this service the same year.

After promotion to flag rank in June 1882 Richards was appointed junior naval lord at the Admiralty under the second Earl of Northbrook. In May 1885 he received the command of the East Indies station with his flag in H.M.S. *Bacchante.* In the course of this three years' command he organized and equipped the naval brigade in the Burmese War and was officially thanked by the government of India for his services. After his return to England in 1888 he was appointed, with Admirals Sir William Montagu Dowell and Sir Richard Vesey Hamilton, to report on the lessons of the naval manœuvres of that year. Their report, most of which was acknowledged to be due to the hand and brain of Richards, presented a most convincing discussion of the conditions of modern warfare and a clear statement of the vital importance of sea power to the existence of the British Empire, and set forth what became known as the two-power standard as the principle on which the British shipbuilding programme should be based. This able report, though challenged at first by official naval opinion, made a great impression, and may be regarded as one of the determining causes of Lord George Hamilton's Naval Defence Act of 1889, which in effect recreated the royal navy. Richards was also the naval representative on the royal commission on naval and military administration (1890), in the proceedings of which and in the drafting of its conclusions he bore a leading part.

Richards was promoted vice-admiral in 1888, and in 1890 went as commander-in-chief to the China station until June 1892, when he rejoined the Board of Admiralty under Lord George Hamilton as second naval lord. He was promoted admiral in September 1893, and in November of that year was selected by the fifth Earl Spencer to succeed Sir Anthony Hiley Hoskins as first naval lord, a position which he retained for nearly six years. His career as first naval lord was of great importance in the history of naval administration. Richards had a clear understanding of the needs of the navy, and he had the entire confidence of his political chiefs, Lord Spencer and Mr. (afterwards Viscount) Goschen. This period was marked by a great development of the shipbuilding programme begun under the Naval Defence Act of 1889, and, at Richards's particular instigation, by a series of big naval works carried out under the Naval Works Acts of 1895 and subsequent years. The result was that the naval ports and dockyards at home and abroad were renovated and brought up to date to meet the requirements of the modern navy. Under this scheme naval harbours were constructed at Portland, Dover, Gibraltar, and Simon's Bay, and great extensions of the dockyards at Portsmouth, Devonport, Malta, Gibraltar, Hong Kong, and Simon's Bay. In carrying his naval programme Lord Spencer had to contend with a most formidable opposition from Sir William Harcourt and from Mr. Gladstone himself, and it was only the unwavering determination of Richards and his other colleagues on the Board that enabled him to succeed—a success which had no little to do with Mr. Gladstone's final decision to retire from office.

In June 1895 Richards was promoted G.C.B. on the resignation of the Rosebery ministry. Mr. Goschen, who then again became first lord after an interval of over twenty-one years, wisely decided to follow the precedent set by Lord Spencer and to retain the naval advisers of the outgoing government. He and Richards worked together with remarkable unity of purpose during the next four years. The sending of the fleet to the Dardanelles in 1895 brought the Turkish government to a sense of its responsibility for the Armenian massacres; the commissioning of the flying squadron in 1896 indicated clearly to the German Emperor the dangerous consequence of his ill-advised telegram to President Kruger; in 1897 and 1898 it was the action of the British fleet which at length restored order in Crete; the vigorous handling of the naval situation in the Fashoda crisis in 1898 was the chief preventive of war with France over that incident; and, finally, the firm attitude of the government based on the readiness of the fleet stopped any interference by European powers in the Spanish-American War. There was thus a universal and well-founded feeling in the naval service that its interests were safe in the hands of Richards. In November 1898 Richards would have been retired for age, but Goschen obtained a special order in council promoting him to be admiral of the fleet in order that he might remain on the active list until the age of seventy. In the following August Goschen decided that it was time that Richards should give place to a younger officer as first naval lord, though Richards was much disappointed at being superseded after the special promotion to keep him on the active list. He was succeeded by Lord Walter Kerr, who was fully in accord with the policy pursued by the Board during Richards's term of office.

Richards was undoubtedly one of the leading administrators in the history of the navy. He early won the confidence of his superiors, and was selected for one important duty after another, performing them with unfailing success until he reached the position of chief naval adviser to the Crown at a time when a firm and clear restatement of the essentials of maritime policy was invaluable to the country. Richards was a man of prudent foresight, clear, if limited, vision, and firm determination that what he knew to be right should be done. His powerful intellect was somewhat slow in operation; but, though not ready in council, he could and did express his views in admirable English which left no doubt of his intention or of the strength of will that lay behind it. His official minutes were models of vigorous style and well-chosen language. As a sea officer it was not his fortune to command a battle fleet or to win the renown of such great peace commanders as Sir Geoffrey Thomas Phipps Hornby and Sir Arthur Knyvet Wilson. His great natural qualities of a clear brain and indomitable will, combined with a gift for organization, found their best opportunity in his work at Whitehall. Though he was naturally of a retiring disposition, always avoiding publicity and loathing controversy, his character was so transparently honest and just and his devotion to his service and country so marked that he was regarded throughout the naval service with a most complete confidence and trust. In private life he was a constant friend and, though a ruler among men and of a stern exterior, was full of human sympathy, and possessed a deep fund of humour and kindness of heart.

After his retirement Richards maintained his interest in naval affairs, and although he was not in sympathy with many of the changes and reforms carried out by later administrations, he seldom expressed his mind in public and took no share in controversy. In 1904, shortly after the election of Lord Goschen as chancellor of Oxford University, Richards was given the honorary degree of D.C.L. He died at Horton Court, Chipping Sodbury, Gloucestershire, 28 September 1912.

After the successful struggle over the naval programme in the Cabinet of 1893–1894, the officers of the fleet had Richards's portrait painted by (Sir) Arthur Cope, R.A., and presented it 'from the navy to the nation'. It was hung in the Painted Hall at Greenwich. In November 1912 a 'Sir Frederick Richards memorial fund' was established by a large representative meeting of admirals, friends, and admirers, the trustees of which make charitable grants to naval and marine officers and their dependants. A memorial tablet is in the crypt of St. Paul's Cathedral.

Richards married in 1866 Lucy (died 1880), daughter of Fitzherbert Brooke, of Horton Court, Gloucestershire, and widow of the Rev. Edwin Fayle. They had no children.

[Admiralty records; private information.]

V. W. B.

RICHMOND, Sir WILLIAM BLAKE (1842–1921), artist, the second son of George Richmond, R.A. [q.v.], by his wife, Julia, daughter of Charles Heathcote Tatham [q.v.], architect, was born in London 29 November 1842. While still a boy he became an enthusiastic student of the writings of Ruskin and was led by them to a keen admiration of the works of Holman Hunt, Millais, and the pre-Raphaelite school; but he never formally adopted the principles of the Brotherhood, though their influence, together with that of Leighton and Da Costa, is clearly traceable in much of his work. Richmond was educated at home till 1858, when he entered the Royal Academy Schools; there he gained in 1859 second prize (silver medal) for a drawing from the antique, and in 1861 third prize (silver medal) for a drawing from the life; in the latter year he was also represented for the first time at the annual exhibition by a portrait of his brothers Walter and John. This brought him several commissions, but he was not misled by these into the belief that he had no more to learn; and in 1865 he went to Italy, where for four years he devoted himself to sculpture, architecture, and painting in tempera and fresco. The results of his studies in sculpture were seen later in statues of 'An Athlete' and 'The Arcadian Shepherd', and a bust 'Lady Richmond'. His studies in fresco stood him in good stead when in 1873 he painted a series of frescoes illustrating 'The Life of Woman' (in the house of J. S. Hodgson, Lythe Hill, Haslemere); but his only performance in tempera seems to have been a ceiling which he painted for practice in his hotel at Assisi in 1867, and found forty-six years later as fresh as on the day when it was finished.

Continuing at the same time to work in oils, Richmond brought back with him from Italy in 1869 a picture of 'A Procession in Honour of Bacchus', and exhibited it that year at the Royal Academy. To such subjects he would have been well content to confine himself thenceforward, and he did in fact complete a considerable number, among them being 'Ariadne abandoned by Theseus' (1872), 'Prometheus Bound' (1874), 'Electra at the Tomb of Agamemnon' (1877), now in the gallery at Toronto, 'The Birth of Venus' (1881), 'An Audience at Athens during the Performance of Agamemnon' (1885), now at Birmingham, 'The Death of Ulysses' (1888), 'Venus and Anchises' (1889), now at Liverpool, 'The Bath of Venus' (1891), and many others. But the gift of pleasing portraiture inherited from his father, grandfather, and great-grandfather, was too marked to be neglected, and Richmond, had he so desired, might have fully occupied his time with that alone. He was conspicuously in favour with the peerage and the bench of bishops, but among his sitters of more important interest were W. E. Gladstone, Prince Bismarck, Charles Darwin, Theodor Mommsen, Robert Browning, and Andrew Lang.

Richmond's chief claim, however, to the attention of posterity will doubtless rest on the great scheme for the decoration of St. Paul's Cathedral, London, on which he was engaged for several years. Stirred to interest in this by the architect, George Frederick Bodley, he drew up a plan into the execution of which, when it was approved in 1891, he threw himself whole-heartedly. Convinced that mosaic was the only material suited to the London atmosphere, he found that he must first master the technique himself and then impart it to the British craftsmen. Moreover, the customary method of building up the mosaic elsewhere and then attaching it to the walls was found to be incompatible with a solution of the various problems of light which arose; he decided, therefore, to execute the work on the spot. Opinions differ as to the result, but it is beyond dispute the most complete and consistent piece of internal decoration which has been achieved in England for many years.

Preferring always to work at art rather than to talk about it, Richmond was nevertheless persuaded to accept the post of Slade professor of fine art at Oxford when Ruskin retired in 1879. He resigned the chair in 1883. Several lectures and addresses of his were published at intervals, and his *Assisi, Impressions of Half a Cen-*

tury (1919) was illustrated by reproductions of a selection from the large number of landscapes in colour and pencil with which he occupied the intervals of his weightier tasks. He received the customary honours of the successful artist, becoming associate of the Royal Academy in 1888 and academician in 1895. Oxford conferred upon him the degree of D.C.L. in 1896, and in 1897 he was created K.C.B. He married in 1867 Clara Jane (died 1915), daughter of William Richards, merchant, of Cardiff, and had six sons and one daughter. He died at Beavor Lodge, Hammersmith, 11 February 1921.

There is a portrait of Richmond by George Phoenix in the National Portrait Gallery.

[*The Times*, 14 February 1921; *Magazine of Art*, vols. xxii and xxv; A. M. W. Stirling, *The Richmond Papers*, 1926; private information.] M. H. B.

RITCHIE, SIR RICHMOND THACKERAY WILLOUGHBY (1854–1912), civil servant, was born at Calcutta 6 August 1854, the third son of William Ritchie, advocate-general of Bengal, afterwards legal member of the governor-general's council and vice-chancellor of the university of Calcutta, by his wife, Augusta, daughter of Captain Thomas Trimmer, R.N. His family had been distinguished in Indian annals for three generations. He was educated at Eton, where he was a King's scholar and Newcastle medallist, and at Trinity College, Cambridge, where also he held a scholarship, and was one of a brilliant coterie. In 1877 he entered the India Office as a junior clerk. His abilities were soon recognized. From 1883 to 1892 he acted as private secretary to a succession of parliamentary under-secretaries of state for India, including Sir John Gorst and (Lord) Curzon. From October 1892 to February 1894 he was private secretary to the permanent under-secretary, Sir Arthur Godley (afterwards Lord Kilbracken); and in May 1895 he was appointed secretary to the royal commission on Indian expenditure. The last appointment he gave up after a few weeks in order to become private secretary to the secretary of state for India, Lord George Hamilton; this post he held for seven years.

Ritchie possessed qualities which admirably fitted him for these secretarial appointments, and they provided him with a unique experience of the *arcana* of Indian administration. In November 1902 he was accordingly appointed secretary in the political and secret department of the India Office, although he lacked that service in India which had previously been considered an essential qualification.

When Mr. John (afterwards Viscount) Morley became secretary of state for India in 1905, he was at once attracted by Ritchie's literary gifts, and soon came to place great reliance on his subordinate's experience and independence of judgement. The part which Ritchie played in the momentous changes in Indian administration which followed remains confidential; but it is believed that the fact of his not having served in India absolved him from any suspicion of bias in Lord Morley's eyes and lent weight to counsels of moderation; and in particular that he was responsible for the strict adhesion to recorded precedents which was an unexpected feature of Lord Morley's policy in all questions relating to the internal affairs of native states.

Ritchie was closely concerned with the negotiations with Tibet which followed upon the armed mission of Sir Francis Younghusband to Lhasa in 1903–1904, and with those which resulted in the Anglo-Russian convention of 31 August 1907. He also took great interest in the construction of the Bagdad Railway (1904–1908). He was created K.C.B. in June 1907, and was promoted permanent under-secretary of state in October 1909, being the first member of the staff of the India Office to attain to that position. After, as before, his promotion, Ritchie was the most accessible of men; but in his new position this habit, so valuable in his previous career, made undue demands upon his time. His fastidious taste would not allow a dispatch to go out till it had received the highest polish which he could give it, a process which often entailed long hours of night work. Moreover, the demands of the secretary of state on his personal advice and assistance steadily increased during the crowded years when the Morley-Minto reforms and the revocation (December 1911) of the partition of Bengal were being carried out. Overwork brought on illness, and he died in London 12 October 1912.

Ritchie married in 1877 Anne Isabella, the eldest daughter of William Makepeace Thackeray, who was his father's first cousin. ANNE ISABELLA THACKERAY, LADY RITCHIE (1837–1919) was born in London 9 June 1837. Her future husband first proposed to her while he was still a schoolboy at Eton; and the marriage was a very happy one, the disparity in their ages being made up for by the early maturity of her husband's character and the lasting youthfulness of her own. They had one son and one daughter.

Lady Ritchie wrote a number of novels, some of which, notably *The Village on the Cliff* (1867) and *Old Kensington* (1873), deserved and obtained a considerable popularity. But her real bent was rather to memoirs and biographical sketches; and it is in social life rather than in literature that her position was unique. For seventy years, almost from the nursery until her death, she knew nearly everybody of literary, artistic, or musical note; and her eye for picturesque detail combined with her quick sympathy and unquenchable interest in character-study gave distinction to all her work. To this DICTIONARY she contributed the life of Elizabeth Barrett Browning; and through her brother-in-law, Sir Leslie Stephen, and her friend, Reginald Smith, she gave valuable information and assistance to other contributors. *The Blackstick Papers* (1908) and *From the Porch* (1913) are the best-known volumes of her essays. The latter contains the address which she delivered in January 1913 as president of the English Association, remarkable for its fine appreciation of Mrs. Oliphant, the novelist. In 1914 Lady Ritchie sat to J. S. Sargent for a black-and-white portrait, subscribed for by her friends; this is now in the possession of her daughter. She died 26 February 1919 at Freshwater, Isle of Wight.

[*The Times*, 14 October 1912 and 28 February 1919; *Cornhill Magazine*, vols. xlvi and xlvii, 1919; Gerard Ritchie, *The Ritchies in India*, 1920; Leonard Huxley, *The House of Smith Elder* (for private circulation), 1923; Lady Ritchie's Works, of which a complete bibliography is given in *Letters of Anne Thackeray Ritchie*, edited by her daughter, Hester Ritchie, 1924; Sir Malcolm Seton, *The India Office*, 1926; Lord Morley, *Recollections*, 1917; private information.] S. V. FG.

RIVIERE, BRITON (1840–1920), painter, the youngest child of William Riviere [q.v.] by his wife, Ann, daughter of Joseph Jarvis, of Atherston, Warwickshire, was born in London 14 August 1840. The family, which originally bore the name of Nerac, came to England from the Bordeaux district after the revocation of the Edict of Nantes. Briton Riviere's mother was a good musician and had some talent for drawing. His grandfather, Daniel Valentine Riviere, his uncle, Henry Parsons Riviere [q.v.], as well as his father, were painters and teachers of drawing, and altogether nine bearers of the name, including his wife, are to be found in the list of exhibitors at the Royal Academy. Another uncle, Robert Riviere [q.v.], was a well-known book-binder. Briton received his education and his first training in art at Cheltenham College, where his father was drawing-master. From thence he sent in 1851 and 1852 to the exhibitions at the British Institution, two little oil-paintings of kittens. In 1858, with 'The Broken Chain', he began the series of works annually shown at the Royal Academy, with one short interruption of four years, till the end of his long life; the last picture, 'Michael', an old shepherd with his dog, was sent in a fortnight before he died.

Between 1860 and 1863 Riviere was attracted, mainly under the influence of his future brother-in-law, Clarence Dobell, by the aims and methods of the pre-Raphaelites. He painted, in accordance with their principles, 'Elaine on the Barge', 'Hamlet and Ophelia', and other pictures, all in turn rejected by the Academy, which had previously shown itself appreciative of his work. Helped by his experience to realize his own congenial sphere, the painter returned to the path by which he was to reach artistic and popular success. Meanwhile his parents had moved in 1859 from Cheltenham to Oxford. In 1863 Briton matriculated at St. Mary Hall. The authorities did not require him to reside, and he continued to live and paint under his father's roof, while reading for a degree. He took his B.A. in 1866 and his M.A. in 1873. In 1867 he married. His wife was Mary Alice, sister of Clarence and Sydney Thompson Dobell [q.v.], and daughter of John Dobell, of Detmore, a property, near Cheltenham, which figures as 'Longfield' in *John Halifax, Gentleman*. The young couple lived first at Keston, Kent, and then at Bromley. In 1871 they moved to London, and finally settled at 82 Finchley Road.

Life in London brought Riviere the stimulating friendship of other painters. He became closely attached to, and much influenced by, the artists of the new Scottish school, Orchardson, Pettie, Peter Graham, and MacWhirter. It is not too much to say that his first conception of a colour scheme, instead of a black and white scheme, as a basis for a picture came to him from them, and that his fine use of broken, shimmering colour was developed by his association with these friends. Besides exhibiting in oil and watercolour at the Royal Academy, the Dudley Gallery, and later, the Grosvenor Gallery,

Riviere worked for *Punch*, chiefly in decorative initials, and drew illustrations for English and American magazines, notably for *Good Words*, and for some of the novels of Mrs. Craik. The list of his exhibits at the Royal Academy includes portraits and etchings, and also some sculpture. He was elected associate in 1877 and academician in 1880. After the death of Sir John Millais (1896) he narrowly missed election as president, somewhat to his relief, it was believed, as delicate health had long precluded him from social and official activities. In 1891 his university conferred upon him the honorary degree of D.C.L., and Oriel College elected him to an honorary fellowship in 1910. A man of distinguished presence, courteous manner, and wide culture, Riviere had many friends. He died in London 20 April 1920. He had five sons, one of whom, Hugh Goldwin Riviere, is the well-known portrait painter, and two daughters.

A portrait of Riviere by Sir H. von Herkomer is in the Royal Academy, and another excellent likeness, by the same painter, figures in the group of the 'Hanging Committee of the Royal Academy' in the Tate Gallery. A bronze head by Onslow Ford is in the Common Room at Oriel College.

There are six pictures by Riviere in the Tate Gallery, among which are the 'Miracle of the Gadarene Swine', 'Giants at Play', 'Beyond Man's Footsteps', and a study for 'Sympathy', the finished picture of which is, with 'An Anxious Moment', at the Royal Holloway College. 'The Last Spoonful' is in the Schwabe collection at Hamburg, 'A Roman Holiday' in the gallery at Sydney. 'The King Drinks', one of his many lion pictures, is in the Diploma Gallery, and a noble 'Prometheus', painted in 1889, was given by his family to the Ashmolean Museum, Oxford, in 1920, in accordance with his wishes. A water-colour drawing, 'Fox and Geese', is in the Victoria and Albert Museum.

In the popular mind Riviere occupied the place of successor to Sir Edwin Landseer. Without Landseer's amazingly facile draughtsmanship and *bravura* brushwork, Riviere possessed the more serious and solid mentality of his own age: this restrained him also from the over-infusion of human traits and feelings into his animals, which was Landseer's besetting fault. Riviere himself took most interest and pride in those of his pictures in which animal life, or at least its more homely and humorous aspects, played least part. Works like the beautiful 'Ganymede' (in the possession of his family), the 'Prometheus', and the 'Gadarene Swine' show how fully he was justified in this, and cause regret that the public should have fastened upon his groups of children and dogs, admirable in their way, as his most characteristic productions.

[*The Times*, 21 April 1920; Sir W. Armstrong, *Briton Riviere, R.A.*; *His Life and Work*, with list of works till 1891, illustrated, in *The Art Annual*, 1891; Wilfrid Meynell, *Some Modern Artists and their Work*, illustrated, 1883; Algernon Graves, *The Royal Academy of Arts, Dictionary of Contributors*, 1905–1906; Catalogues of the Exhibitions of the Royal Academy of Arts 1904–20.] R. E. P.

ROBERTS, FREDERICK SLEIGH, first Earl Roberts, of Kandahar, Pretoria, and Waterford (1832–1914), field-marshal, the younger son of General Sir Abraham Roberts [q.v.] by his wife, Isabella, widow of Major Hamilton Maxwell, and daughter of Abraham Bunbury, of Kilfeacle, co. Tipperary, was born at Cawnpore 30 September 1832. Roberts was one of many distinguished soldiers whom Ireland has sent to the service of the Empire, his family having long been settled in county Waterford. He was brought home from India at the age of two; when thirteen he was sent to Eton; and after one year there he passed second into Sandhurst at the age of fourteen, joining in January 1847. His father, however, wished Frederick to follow his own example and enter the East India Company's service. Accordingly, after waiting some time for a vacancy, he went to the training college at Addiscombe, from which he was gazetted on 12 December 1851 to the Bengal Artillery.

Roberts landed in India in April 1852 and in the same year joined his father, who was in command at Peshawar, to serve both as aide-de-camp and as battery officer. He obtained an introduction to the problems of the North-West Frontier and to the character and customs of the tribesmen of the Himalaya, under his father, who had much experience of active service in India and was for a time in command of a brigade of native levies in Kabul, which he left a few months before the disastrous retreat from Kabul in January 1842. In 1854 Roberts gained the distinction, coveted by every young gunner, of the Horse Artillery jacket. He was serving in the Bengal Horse Artillery when, in May 1857, news reached Peshawar of the outbreak of the Mutiny at Meerut. A mobile column was formed in the Punjab, and Roberts became staff officer to its first commander, (Sir) Neville Bowles Chamberlain [q.v.], and to the latter's successor, John Nicholson [q.v.], who won his unbounded admiration and devotion. In June he joined the staff of the force on the ridge before Delhi, and there again during the last stage of the siege did double duty as a staff officer and battery officer. In the rough and tumble fighting around Delhi he had a number of narrow escapes, and was incapacitated for a month by a blow on his spine from a bullet, which was stopped from doing more deadly mischief by the leather pouch which he was wearing. Soon after the fall of Delhi he took part in the second relief of Lucknow under Sir Colin Campbell [q.v.], by whom he was chosen to guide the force attempting the relief from the Alumbagh to the Dilkusha palace. Roberts was then attached to the cavalry division of the force under (Sir) James Hope Grant [q.v.], and it was with it, in a cavalry charge at Khudaganj in January 1858, that he won the Victoria cross for saving the life of a sowar and capturing one of the mutineers' standards. He remained with Hope Grant, and served on the staff during the British siege of Lucknow, at which his great military contemporary, Major (afterwards Viscount) Wolseley, then commanding a company of the 90th Light Infantry, was also present. In April 1858 Roberts's health broke down, and he was succeeded in his staff appointment by the man whose place he was later to take as commander-in-chief of the British army. During a year of convalescence in England (1859) he met and married Miss Nora Henrietta Bews (died 1920), daughter of Captain John Bews, who had retired from the 73rd regiment. So began a married life of mutual devotion and comradeship.

Roberts returned to India in 1859 with his wife, and in the following year was promoted captain, receiving at the same time a brevet majority for his work in the Mutiny. In 1863 he had a short experience of active service on the North-West Frontier in the Umbeyla campaign against the Sitana fanatics, and five years later he went with Sir Robert Napier (afterwards Baron Napier of Magdala, q.v.) to Abyssinia, as assistant quartermaster-general of the expeditionary force. He spent the campaign at the base, with the organization and control of which he was charged, and gained experience in the work of the quartermaster-general's department in which he was beginning to be recognized as an expert. As a reward for his services, Napier sent him to England with dispatches, and he was made a brevet lieutenant-colonel. In 1871 another of the perennial troubles of the Frontier resulted in an expedition against the Lushais. Here again the main problem was the organization of transport in a country presenting great natural difficulties; and for his work in overcoming them Roberts received the C.B. He had now made his name as a staff officer and was recognized as one of the leading figures in the quartermaster-general's department at the head-quarters of the army in India. In January 1875 he was promoted brevet colonel and became quartermaster-general with the temporary rank of major-general. In this position he came face to face with what was then one of the major problems of imperial defence. Russia's advance through Central Asia was continuous: she had seized Samarkand in 1868, occupied Khiva in 1873, and was making friendly advances to Shere Ali, the ameer of Afghanistan. The danger to India if Afghanistan became a dependency of Russia was obvious. The problem was how best to counter Russia's policy. One school maintained that the right answer was to make the Indus the northern frontier of India and to tell the Russians that any encroachment, territorial or political, in Afghanistan, would mean war with England. This policy would, it was argued, both relieve the Indian taxpayer and bring England's chief weapon, her sea power, into play. The other school argued that Afghanistan left without direct support would inevitably succumb to Russia, and that no pressure elsewhere would make India safe if Russia gained the control of the passes of the Himalaya. The policy of this school became known as the 'forward' policy and aimed at controlling the tribes and securing the passes. Roberts was from the first one of its foremost advocates. He gained the ear of Lord Lytton, who became viceroy in 1876, and of his successors; and the forward policy became, and still is, the defensive policy of India.

In March 1878 Roberts was appointed to the command of the Punjab frontier force, in which position he at once became one of the chief agents of the policy which he had advocated. A few months later the ameer refused to receive a political mission headed by Roberts's old chief and friend, Sir Neville Chamberlain, and welcomed the Russian envoy. Three columns were at once formed for the invasion of Afghanistan, one to move from Quetta to Kandahar, one to demonstrate in the Khyber Pass, and the third under Roberts to occupy the Kurram and Khost valleys and thence threaten Kabul. In November Roberts moved up the Kurram and found a large Afghan force holding the Peiwar Kotal. Roberts turned the Afghan position by a skilful night march and routed the Afghans, who abandoned their guns and baggage, the loss to the British column being less than a hundred killed and wounded. Shere Ali at once fled to Turkestan, and his successor, Yakub Khan, signed on 26 May 1879 the Treaty of Gandamuk, which conceded all that the British government had demanded. At the end of 1878 Roberts was promoted major-general, and he received the K.C.B. and the thanks of parliament for the victory at the Peiwar Kotal. Roberts, who knew the Afghans well, was not satisfied that the British position in Afghanistan was secure, and his doubts were soon justified. In July 1879 a political mission led by Sir Louis Cavagnari [q.v.] went to Kabul, and in September Cavagnari with his staff and escort was treacherously murdered. Roberts at once returned to the Kurram, and led his force, which had been strengthened, on towards Kabul. No opposition was met until at Charasia, twelve miles south of Kabul, an Afghan army was found in position. On 6 October Roberts, aided by an attack against the Afghan left, gallantly and skilfully led by Major (afterwards Sir George) White [q.v.], turned the enemy's right and again routed them with trifling loss to his own force. He then occupied Kabul without further fighting. After arranging for the administration of the capital, he transferred his force in November to the cantonments of Sherpur in its vicinity, and here he was suddenly attacked on 11 December by masses of Afghans. After enduring a short siege he repulsed decisively a great assault on his lines (23 December), and this repulse broke the Afghan resistance. In the summer of 1880 Abdur Rahman was recognized by the British government as ameer, the war appeared to be at an end, and orders were issued for the return of the troops to India. Suddenly a fresh storm broke. In July a force of Afghans, which gathered reinforcements as it advanced, invaded Western Afghanistan from Herat, and on 27 July attacked and defeated a British brigade at Maiwand, nearly half the brigade being killed or wounded, while the Afghans captured large quantities of arms and ammunition. The small garrison of Kandahar appeared to be in danger, and Roberts at once proposed that he should lead a column from Kabul to its relief. Roberts had brought his transport to a high state of perfection, and he started from Kabul on 9 August with a picked body of 10,000 men. In the first fourteen days he covered 225 miles through difficult country, but encountered no opposition. He then learned that Kandahar was in no immediate danger and he completed the remaining 88 miles to Kandahar, which he entered on 31 August, at a more leisurely pace. On 1 September he met and defeated the Afghans outside Kandahar, and the pacification of Afghanistan was completed without further difficulty. The march to Kandahar and its triumphant conclusion appealed irresistibly to a public gravely perturbed by the disaster of Maiwand and racked with anxiety as to the fate of Kandahar. Roberts became at once a popular hero. He received the G.C.B. and a baronetcy, and was made commander-in-chief of the Madras army. The march to Kandahar was made possible by Roberts's prompt and bold decision, his careful forethought, the sound organization of his transport, and by the confidence in his leadership with which he inspired his men; but, as he always maintained, it was not as a military feat to be compared with his advance on Kabul in the previous year. The actions of the Peiwar Kotal and Charasia established his reputation amongst soldiers as a tactician; as an organiser of transport in a mountainous country he was without an equal; while his neat figure, fine horsemanship, charm of manner, and constant care for the lives and welfare of his men, won from them a devotion which was not the least of the causes of his success. The name 'Bobs' became one to conjure with in India.

In the autumn of 1880 Roberts came to England for a rest, and was received with all honour. As a firm believer in the forward policy he strongly advocated the retention of Kandahar, but was unable to persuade Mr. Gladstone's government to agree. While he was in England the news came home of the disaster of Majuba Hill (27 February 1881). He was at once sent to South Africa, but on reaching Cape Town he learned that Sir Henry Evelyn Wood [q.v.] had already arranged peace with the Boers. He therefore came straight back to England, and left for India again in the autumn of 1881 to take up his command in Madras. Four years later, when Sir Donald Stewart vacated the chief command in India, Roberts was universally recognized to be his natural successor. He continued to be the commander-in-chief until the spring of 1893. During the seven years in which he was the supreme military authority in India, his chief preoccupation was Russia's advance to the frontier of Afghanistan, and he regarded the threat of the invasion of India by Russia as the chief military problem of the British Empire. He revised the schemes for the defence of the North-West Frontier, and was engaged in a constant struggle to win from the Indian Treasury money for the improvement of communications leading into the Himalaya, and for the provision of adequate transport. He also devoted himself particularly to the improvement of the shooting, both of the infantry and of the artillery, and established a system of field-training which caused the India of his day to be recognized as the most practical school of training for the British army. He was not in agreement with the military reformers at home, and in particular was opposed to the introduction of the short-service system, which, at first, undoubtedly affected the efficiency of the British troops in India. The problems of India required the army to be in a state of instant readiness for war, while a frontier expedition did not involve losses so heavy that they could not be quickly replaced by drafts from home. The need for a reserve was not therefore obvious to one who had passed his military life in India, but later experience caused Roberts to revise his judgement of the reforms which Viscount Cardwell had initiated and Wolseley brought to completion. On 1 January 1892 Roberts was created Baron Roberts, of Kandahar, and early in the following year he left India for good amidst demonstrations of affection and respect such as have rarely been won by a soldier.

In England he had two years to wait for an appointment suited to one of his rank and reputation, and he devoted these to writing his reminiscences. His *Forty-one Years in India* (1897) is at once a stirring story, simply told, and a demonstration of the generous and frank character of its author. In May 1895 he was made field-marshal, and in the same year he became commander-in-chief in Ireland. In his new command he again set himself to improve the shooting and the field-training of the soldier, while Dublin society was soon convinced that the reputation which he had gained in Simla as a charming host was well deserved.

When, in October 1899, the British government's disputes with the Boers culminated in war, few anticipated a serious campaign requiring the services of a British field-marshal, and Sir Redvers Buller's long experience of South Africa marked him as the leader of the expedition to the Cape. In December the news that Sir George White was shut up in Ladysmith was followed quickly by reports of reverses to Sir William Gatacre at Stormberg, to Lord Methuen at Magersfontein, and to Buller's main force at Colenso. The country was deeply stirred, and heard with relief on 17 December that Mr. Balfour's government had appointed Roberts to the supreme command in South Africa with Lord Kitchener [q.v.] as his chief of staff. Roberts left England in his sixty-eighth year, carrying with him the confidence and affection of his countrymen, as well as their sympathy for the loss of his only son, Lieutenant Frederick Roberts, mortally wounded a few days before in a gallant attempt to save some of Buller's guns at Colenso. Lieutenant Roberts died before the Victoria cross, for which he had been recommended, could be awarded him.

Up to the time of Lord Roberts's arrival at the Cape (10 January) two fundamental mistakes had been made in the conduct of the campaign. Reliance had been placed mainly upon the British infantry, and offers of mounted troops both from South Africa and from the Dominions were treated coldly; the consequent lack of mobility in dealing with enemy forces in which every man was mounted was a fatal handicap. Further, the provision of transport was so limited as to tie the lines of advance to the few railways. This indicated clearly to the Boers the general nature of the British plan. Roberts at once encouraged local levies of mounted men, greatly increased the number of mounted infantry, and, profiting by his long experience of transport difficulties in India, with the help of Kitchener completely remodelled the transport system. He also saw at once that the situation demanded the earliest possible invasion of the Free State from the Cape Colony, and, while reinforcements from England were on the way to him, prepared his plans with the utmost secrecy. To these plans he resolutely adhered, despite urgent calls for relief from Kimberley, the failure of Buller's third attempt to relieve Ladysmith and his despairing suggestion that he should abandon it, despite also the first flicker of revolt in Cape Colony. Disposing his troops so as to indicate a direct advance on Bloemfontein from Naaupoort, he transferred them rapidly to the Modder river on the road to Kimberley, and on 11 February began a movement round the left flank of the force with which General Piet Cronje was at once besieging Kimberley and opposing Methuen. On 15 February the cavalry division of Major-General (afterwards Earl) French at Klip Drift, on the Modder, galloped through a gap in the Boer lines and rode on into Kimberley. Cronje, finding his communications with Bloemfontein threatened, began a retreat along the Modder. Roberts's infantry hung on to the Boer rear-guard, and on 17 February French, returning in haste from Kimberley, prevented Cronje from crossing the Modder. On the 18th the Boer laager at Paardeberg Drift was attacked by the British infantry divisions under (Sir) Thomas Kelly-Kenny [q.v.] and Kitchener, but this attack was repulsed with 1,270 casualties. Roberts, who had been detained at Jacobsdal by a slight illness, arrived the next day and decided not to renew the attack but to engage in a siege of the laager. Within a week the Boer position in the bed of the river had become desperate, and on 27 February, the anniversary of Majuba, Cronje surrendered with 4,000 men. The effect of Roberts's manœuvre was immediate. The Free State commandos left Natal to defend their own country, and Ladysmith was relieved on 28 February. Deficiency of transport and supplies, due largely to a successful raid by General Christian De Wet upon a large transport column, made an immediate advance on Bloemfontein impossible, and the Free Staters gathered a force to oppose Roberts's farther advance. At Poplar Grove on 7 March they succeeded in evading serious attack, but three days later they stood at Driefontein and were severely handled. This proved to be the last attempt of the Boers to offer battle in the Free State, and Bloemfontein was occupied on 13 March without opposition. After a pause in the Free State capital in order to restore railway communications and get up supplies, Roberts began an advance on Pretoria at the beginning of May. Moving on a broad front and turning the flanks of the Boers whenever they attempted to stand, he reached Kroonstad on 12 May; here a further halt was necessary, to enable the railways to be repaired. During this halt the news arrived that Buller had cleared Natal of Boers, and that Sir Archibald Hunter and Colonel (Sir) Bryan Mahon, moving north from Kimberley, had, in conjunction with a force under Colonel (afterwards Lord) Plumer, coming south from Rhodesia, relieved Mafeking, the last of the besieged garrisons.

The advance from Kroonstad was begun on 22 May and the Vaal was crossed two days later. On 31 May Roberts entered Johannesburg and, after overcoming a feeble resistance, occupied Pretoria on 5 June. On 12 June the main Boer force under General Louis Botha [q.v.] was defeated at Diamond Hill, and it appeared that organized resistance was at an end. President Kruger had removed his government to Machadodorp on the Delagoa railway, and there held some 4,000 British prisoners of war. An advance eastwards to Komati Poort, on the frontier of Portuguese East Africa, seemed all that was needed to complete the subjugation of the Transvaal, and this task was made easier by the junction of Buller's force advancing from Natal with Roberts's main body in the Transvaal in the first week of July. It was true that De Wet and the Free State leaders had been actively engaged in guerrilla warfare in their own country, but at the end of July a large body of Free Staters was surrounded on the border of Basutoland, and their commander, Prinsloo, surrendered with 4,000 men. Before this Roberts had begun his final advance, and on 28 July captured Machadodorp after some stiff fighting. Buller, pursuing the retreating Boers, occupied Lydenberg (6 September), French seized Barberton (13 September), and Major-General (Sir) Ian Hamilton entered Komati Poort (24 September). There was then no Boer town of importance which was not in British hands. Kruger fled to Lourenço Marques and on 11 October left Africa on board a Dutch vessel. The formal annexation of the Transvaal on 25 October, following that of the Free State (28 May), created the general impression that the War was at an end. Roberts was needed at home to succeed Wolseley as commander-in-chief, and he came back to England just in time to be received by Queen Victoria, one of the last of her acts being to reward him with the Garter and an earldom.

Roberts's generalship had changed a dark and doubtful situation in South Africa, with a rapidity which was almost startling, into one which, when he left that country, seemed brilliant. He had achieved the apparently impossible in converting the slow, lumbering columns of the early days of the War into bodies of troops which could manœuvre as swiftly as could their active enemy, and above all, he had at once struck his blow in the right direction. He is open to the criticism that he did not complete his task. Influenced by his desire to save the lives of his men, and probably also by his experience of the effect of turning movements on Asiatics, he continually manœuvred the Boers out of their positions, and rarely brought them to battle. Possibly he underrated the stubbornness of the Boer character, and attached too much importance to the occupation of their towns. If so, he was not alone in holding such opinions; and though he left to Kitchener a legacy far more burdensome than he had anticipated, the issue, when he handed over the command in South Africa, was never in doubt as it had been when he took it up.

His period of service as commander-in-chief of the British army was disappointing. He reached England with an unrivalled reputation, and the public, which the events of the War had at last made aware of the defects of the British military system and training, expected great things from him. In his own special sphere of training troops for war Roberts certainly effected important reforms, and under him a new spirit of keenness and earnestness pervaded the army. A service dress was introduced, and shooting and field-training became of greater importance than pipe-clay and ceremonial, but his endeavours to reform the military system were ineffective. He found himself confronted with an intricate organization, with which, owing to his long service in India, he was little acquainted. As commander-in-chief he had no organized general staff to support him, and he did not know how to set about getting one.

The royal commission on the South African War (1903) pointed out the anomalies in the position of the commander-in-chief, and its report was followed in the autumn of 1903 by the appointment of a commission, under the chairmanship of Viscount Esher, on the organization of the War Office. This commission recommended the abolition of the office of commander-in-chief and the creation of an Army Council. Its findings were accepted by Mr. Balfour's government, and in February 1904 Lord Roberts left the War Office. He continued for a time to be a member of the Committee of Imperial Defence which Mr. Balfour had instituted, but he found himself in disagreement with the government's policy of defence, and in an article in the *Nineteenth Century* (December 1904) he advocated national service for home defence. In November 1905 he resigned, and for the next ten years devoted himself to the cause of national service, becoming in 1905 president of the National Service League. Mr. Balfour's government having been succeeded in 1905 by that of Sir Henry Campbell-Bannerman, Mr. (afterwards Viscount) Haldane, the new minister for war, brought in important measures of army reform which included the formation of the territorial force and the officers' training corps; but Lord Roberts, while agreeing that these were great steps forward, insisted on their inadequacy. The weakness of his own scheme was that what was needed was not a great army for home defence but an increase in the number of troops which could be employed abroad, while there was grave danger that the drastic change which he advocated in the constitution of the military system would injure for many years the efficiency of the voluntary regular army at a time when British relations with Germany were becoming more and more strained. Mr. Haldane had therefore no difficulty in finding, in the War Office, hostile critics of Lord Roberts's proposal; while in 1910 Sir Ian Hamilton, at that time adjutant-general, published a volume on *Compulsory Service* in which he strongly advocated the voluntary system. To this Lord Roberts replied, with the help of two anonymous contributors, in his book *Fallacies and Facts* (1911). Though the controversy continued, Mr. Haldane persevered with his plans; and it was not until the European War had raged for nearly two years that compulsory service became the law of the land. But Lord Roberts's campaign, begun at the age of seventy-two and continued into his eighty-second year, did much to awaken the country to a sense of the dangers with which it was confronted in 1914.

On the outbreak of war with Germany Mr. Asquith summoned Lord Roberts to the first war council which settled the destination of the original British expeditionary force; and when India dispatched an expedition to France the King made Roberts its colonel-in-chief. Feeling that he must go and hearten the men of the country which had been so long his military home, he left for France on 11 November 1914, caught a chill at once, and died at St. Omer on 14 November, as he would have wished, in the midst of an army on active service. His body was brought back to England, and he was buried with due pomp in St. Paul's Cathedral.

Roberts had six children, of whom three

died in infancy. His title devolved by special remainder upon his elder surviving daughter, Lady Aileen Mary Roberts; his second daughter, Lady Ada Edwina Stewart, who is the heir presumptive to the title, married in 1913 Colonel Henry Frederick Elliott Lewin, of the Royal Artillery, and has one son.

A portrait of Roberts by W. W. Ouless was painted for the Royal Artillery in 1882. A bust painting by G. F. Watts, executed in 1898, is in the National Portrait Gallery. A portrait by J. S. Sargent, painted in 1904, is in the possession of Lady Roberts, who owns another by P. A. de Laszló; a second portrait by Laszló is at Eton College. Another portrait, by C. W. Furse, belongs to Lady Hudson. A statue of Roberts by Harry Bates (1894) is in Calcutta; there is a copy in Glasgow, and another, without the pedestal, on the Horse Guards Parade, Whitehall. Busts in bronze by C. W. Roberts and Sir Hamo Thornycroft are both dated 1915, and one by W. R. Colton was exhibited in 1916. There is a bust by John Tweed in St. Paul's Cathedral (*Royal Academy Pictures*, 1882, 1894, 1915, 1916).

[Lord Roberts, *Forty-one Years in India*, 1897; *Letters written during the Indian Mutiny, by Fred. Roberts, afterwards Field-Marshal Earl Roberts*, 1924; H. Hensman, *The Afghan War of 1879–1880*, 1881; *The Anglo-Afghan War 1878–1880*, Official Account, 1881; Sir J. F. Maurice and M. H. Grant, (Official) *History of the War in South Africa 1899–1902*, 1906–1910.] F. M.

ROBERTSON, Sir GEORGE SCOTT (1852–1916), Anglo-Indian administrator, was born in London 22 October 1852, the second son of Thomas James Robertson, a pawnbroker in Southwark, by his wife, Robina Corston, daughter of Robert Scott, of Kirkwall, Orkney. He was educated at Westminster Hospital medical school, and entered the Indian medical service in 1878. In the same year he proceeded to India, where he held various appointments as medical officer and served through the Afghan War of 1879–1880 with the Kabul field force.

In 1889 the government of India decided to create a political agency in Gilgit, a district lying within the political sphere of Kashmir, in order to counteract Russian activities. The Russians were about to secure a concession from the state of Hunza, situated sixty miles north of Gilgit, and a Russian cantonment was in process of establishment there, which would have been a real menace to Kashmir and the Indian Empire. Colonel Algernon Durand was appointed British agent in Gilgit, and he chose Robertson, who thus passed into the employment of the Indian foreign department, as his surgeon. A visit with Durand to Chitral led Robertson to interest himself in the Kafirs, the aboriginal inhabitants of that country. He travelled for a year in Kafiristan (1890-1891) and gained the confidence of these primitive people in a marked degree.

On returning to his post Robertson found the political situation in and around Gilgit more satisfactory. Russian interference had been definitely stopped, and the people had accepted the rule of the British agent as representing the government of Kashmir. Moreover, the mehtar, or ruler, of Chitral had a British officer at his court as representative of the government of India, and was pledged to act by his advice in foreign affairs. Durand therefore went home on leave in 1893, and on his recommendation Robertson succeeded him in 1894 as British agent in Gilgit.

The death of the old ruler of Chitral in 1892 had been followed by an orgy of assassination, as is usual in many Oriental countries on a demise of the crown. But when Robertson assumed charge of Gilgit the claimant to Chitral who was most favoured by Simla had, after the usual struggles, been accepted as mehtar by the people. Peace was rudely broken, however, in January 1895 when the mehtar was murdered by his younger brother in Chitral itself. Had this been the murderer's irresponsible act the matter might have been peacefully settled, but more powerful influences were concerned. Umra Khan, a Pathan chief, was in control of Dir and Swat, territories which lie between Chitral and Peshawar. His aim was to extend his power over Chitral to the Oxus. The mehtar's murder afforded him a convenient excuse for interference by urging the claims of Sher Afzal (the dead mehtar's uncle) to the vacant throne. His action was approved and controlled by the Ameer of Kabul who had long coveted Chitral.

Robertson, therefore, proceeded to Chitral with an escort. At the same time Umra Khan entered that country from the south with Sher Afzal and a considerable force. Robertson handled the situation with firmness. He recognized as ruler of Chitral neither the late mehtar's murderer nor Sher Afzal, whose claims were supported by Umra Khan's invading force. The youngest legitimate male survivor of the ruling family was proclaimed mehtar, whereupon war was at once declared. After a brisk engagement Robertson's small force was driven into Chitral fort and closely besieged. This building was badly situated for defence, inconvenient for the numbers which it now contained (543 men, of whom 137 were non-combatants), and, owing to local hostility, inadequately provisioned. The water-supply was commanded by the enemy and the defenders were too weak to break the ring surrounding them. Yet for six weeks, from 4 March to 20 April, Robertson held out. Rejecting the enemy's treacherous offers of peace and repulsing their determined efforts on the crazy fort, he kept the flag flying until relieved by the simultaneous advance of a force from Gilgit under Colonel James Kelly and of an army from India under Sir Robert Cunliffe Low [q.v.].

The credit for this notable achievement must be shared by Robertson with the determined men whom he had the honour to command. He could not have succeeded in defying such formidable opposition without the unflinching loyalty and devotion of his officers and men. His military adviser, Colin Powys Campbell, of the Central India Horse, directed operations, though wounded. (Sir) Charles Townshend, afterwards famous for the defence of Kut, Henry Kellett Harley, of the 14th Sikhs, and Bertrand Gurdon, the political officer, made up for their weakness in numbers by fertility in resource and bravery in action. The Rosebery ministry decided on the evacuation of Chitral, but went out of office before evacuation had taken place, and Lord Salisbury's ministry reversed the decision of their liberal predecessors.

Robertson was created K.C.S.I. for his services in 1895, but to the surprise of the Indian public he suddenly abandoned his career, retiring from the Indian service in 1899 and returning to England. He unsuccessfully contested Stirlingshire in the liberal interest in 1900, but was elected M.P. for Central Bradford in 1906. Robertson was the author of two books; *The Kafirs of the Hindu Kush* (1896), and *Chitral: the story of a Minor Siege* (1898). He died in London 1 January 1916.

Robertson married twice: first, in 1882 Catherine Edith (died 1886), daughter of Colonel Alexander John Edwin Birch, by whom he had one daughter; secondly, in 1894 Mary Gertrude (Mrs. Bird), daughter of Samuel Laurence [q.v.], the portrait-painter.

[Private information; personal knowledge.]

C. A. S.

ROBINSON, Sir JOHN CHARLES (1824–1913), art connoisseur and collector, the son of Alfred Robinson, of Nottingham, was born 16 December 1824 at Nottingham, where he was also educated. He was brought up there by his grandfather, a bookseller, and, later, was sent for art-training to the studio of Michel Martin Drolling in Paris. There he spent much time in the Louvre, laying the foundation of his knowledge of Renaissance art. In 1847 he was appointed head master of the government school of art at Hanley, Staffordshire. In 1852 he became first superintendent of art collections of the South Kensington Museum, where he remained for seventeen years, and organized the circulation of works of art among provincial institutions. Robinson's technical knowledge and artistic appreciation of the many branches of art were unusually wide and thorough, and his taste was in an extraordinary degree in advance of his time. Until his resignation in 1869 he was frequently employed in travelling for the Museum in Italy and especially in Spain. With the small funds at his disposal he was able to acquire, at what would now be considered infinitesimal prices, a vast number of those works in marble, bronze, majolica, and terracotta which quickly gave South Kensington a unique position at the time among the museums of Europe. On retiring from the public service he continued this important work as the adviser of eminent private collectors, such as Mr. Malcolm of Poltalloch, and Sir Francis Cook [q.v.]. As an instance of his wise purchases, he acquired for Sir Francis Cook in 1872 for £335 Hubert van Eyck's 'The Three Maries', which in 1927 was the gem of the Flemish exhibition in London. Robinson's own extensive collections included at one time or another, besides paintings, drawings, and sketches, Greek gems, Renaissance jewellery, ivories, bronzes, Oriental porcelain, French furniture, Spanish and Italian embroideries, and ancient Coptic fabrics. From 1882 to 1901 he was surveyor of the Queen's pictures. He was knighted in 1887 and made C.B. in 1901.

In 1866, in conjunction with the Marquis d'Azeglio, Robinson founded the Fine Arts Club (afterwards the Burlington Fine Arts Club), and for fifteen years acted as its honorary secretary. He was a skilful etcher, excelling especially in his treatment of strong effects of light, and he joined with his lifelong friend, Sir Francis Seymour Haden [q.v.], in founding the Royal Society of Painter Etchers. Unfortunately, beyond letters and articles in *The Times*, *Nineteenth Century*, and other journals, he left no written memorials other than catalogues of various collections, chief of which was the admirable catalogue *raisonné* of the *Drawings by Michael Angelo and Raffaelle in the University Galleries* at Oxford (1870). He was a fearless and outspoken critic, who nevertheless numbered many artists and experts among his personal friends.

Robinson married in 1852 Marian Elizabeth (died 1908), daughter of Edmund Newton, of Norwich, by whom he had five sons and two daughters. He lived for many years in Harley Street, London, but latterly at Newton Manor, Swanage, where he died 10 April 1913.

[*The Times*, 11 April 1913 ; *Who 's Who* ; personal knowledge.] G. B.

ROBINSON, WILLIAM LEEFE (1895–1918), airman, was born at Tollidetta, South Coorg, India, 14 July 1895, the youngest son of Horace Robinson, an owner and planter of coffee estates, by his wife, Elizabeth Leefe. Robinson was educated at St. Bees School and, after travelling in France and Russia, entered Sandhurst, on the outbreak of the European War, in August 1914. He received his commission, in the Worcestershire regiment, in December, but on arriving in France applied for transfer to the Royal Flying Corps and was seconded, as observer, to No. 4 squadron 29 March 1915, qualifying on 15 April. He received a shrapnel wound during a flight on 8 May, and after his recovery in England learned to fly at the Central Flying School, Upavon, Wiltshire.

Robinson served with various squadrons at home until February 1916, when he was transferred to No. 39 home defence squadron. He was promoted captain on 1 September. In the early morning of Sunday, 3 September, he fought, and shot down at Cuffley, Hertfordshire, the German military Schütte-Lanz airship, S.-L. 11, one of fourteen airships which had set out to raid the London area. He had been in the air more than two hours, on his Bleriot Experimental 2 c, and had unsuccessfully attacked another airship before he met the S.-L. 11. The airship, which was of wooden construction, caught fire after Robinson had emptied into it three drums of ammunition from his Lewis gun, and it burned for two hours after striking the ground. Its descent was watched by thousands of Londoners as well as by the crews of several of the raiding airships, which at once dropped their bombs indiscriminately and made for home. The S.-L. 11 was the first enemy airship to be brought down on British soil, and by his exploit Robinson discomfited the largest airship raid attempted during the War. His success marked the beginning of the defeat of the airship as a raiding weapon. He was awarded the Victoria cross.

Robinson continued to serve at home until 17 March 1917, when he returned to France as a flight commander with No. 48 squadron. On 5 April he led his Bristol fighters in an attack upon a stronger enemy formation, but his engine was quickly shot out of action, and he was compelled to land within the German lines. The treatment, including solitary confinement, which he received during his long imprisonment, wore down his strength. He arrived in England from Germany on 14 December 1918, fell an easy victim to influenza, and died on 31 December.

[Official records ; personal knowledge.] H. A. J.

ROBSON, WILLIAM SNOWDON, Baron Robson, of Jesmond (1852–1918), lawyer and politician, was born at Newcastle-upon-Tyne 10 September 1852, the third son of Robert Robson, J.P., a merchant and philanthropist of that city, greatly esteemed by his fellow-citizens, by his first wife, Anne Snowdon. William Robson was educated privately. After passing the law examinations with a view to becoming a solicitor, he went to Caius College, Cambridge, and took a second class in the moral science tripos in 1877. His advanced radical opinions and his inability to play games (the result of an accident at school) did not lessen his popularity, and one of his college contemporaries wrote of him that though they abhorred his political principles they 'would have voted with him to a man whatever line he took'. After leaving Cambridge Robson became a member of the Inner Temple and was called to the bar in 1880. He joined the North-Eastern circuit and soon established a reputation in shipping, industrial, and commercial litigation. His personal gift of advocacy, his lucidity in presenting his case, and his skill in cross-examination enabled him to take silk in 1892. Among his pupils in King's Bench Walk were Cosmo Gordon Lang, afterwards archbishop of York, and several other distinguished men.

Robson entered politics as liberal member for Bow and Bromley in 1885, but lost his seat the next year through supporting Mr. Gladstone's Home Rule policy. Though he had made his mark in the House he failed to win Middlesbrough in 1892; but in 1895 he was returned for South Shields, the seat which he held till 1910 when his career in the House of Commons ended. Robson was responsible for placing the Children's Act on the statute book. The principle of raising the minimum age of 'half-timers' in the cotton mills had been admitted by the government in the Education Bill of 1896, but it did not become law until Robson brought in his Bill in 1899. Even then the government opposed it, and the Bill was only carried by the eloquence and tenacity with which Robson pleaded the cause of the children.

Meanwhile Robson's reputation as an advocate was increasing: he was made recorder of Newcastle in 1895 and a bencher of the Inner Temple in 1899. The part which he played in *Smith* v. *Charles Baker & Sons* (1891), the Hexham election petition (1892), *Allen* v. *Flood* (1895), the Penrhyn quarry dispute (1903), the Sackville case (1909–1910), and many others, pointed to his rapid promotion.

During the South African War Robson was one of the liberal imperialistic group which gave active support to the British cause. He took a prominent part in the campaign of 1904–1905 against the fiscal proposals of Mr. Chamberlain, and his thorough knowledge of political economy was a great asset to the cause of free trade. When Sir Henry Campbell-Bannerman took office in 1905, Robson was made solicitor-general and knighted, and on the death in 1908 of Sir John Lawson Walton [q.v.] he became attorney-general. In the strenuous times that followed, the great burden of piloting Mr. Lloyd George's budget of 1909 through the House fell on Robson. Week after week, during the committee stage of the Bill, he rarely left his seat on the front bench, and at the cost of his own health saved the budget from shipwreck.

The culminating success of Robson's legal career was his skilful presentation of the British case at the Atlantic fisheries arbitration at the Hague in 1910. Certain coastal fishing rights had caused a dispute, which had lasted nearly a century, between the United States on the one hand and Canada and Newfoundland on the other. The Canadian government appointed Sir Robert Finlay (afterwards lord chancellor) to act for it, and Robson was chosen to represent the imperial government. With him were associated Sir Arthur Frederick Peterson (afterwards judge of the High Court) and Raymond Asquith, eldest son of the prime minister. The final award met with approval from all parties, and the government of Canada attributed the credit to Robson's infinite pains in studying the early treaties and presenting the case in a fresh light in which the historical evidence led to a clear and conclusive decision. An unanimous vote of thanks from the Canadian parliament and the G.C.M.G. from the British government were his reward (1911). In the previous year he had been made a privy councillor. His arduous life at the bar and in the House had told on his health, and he accepted a life peerage as lord of appeal in ordinary on the resignation of Lord Collins in 1910; but a serious illness in 1912 forced him to resign, and he died at Battle, Sussex, 11 September 1918 at the age of sixty-six.

Robson's life was given to the public service, and though he never ranked as a great lawyer or as a man of deep learning, his absolute honesty and high moral standard earned him the respect of his colleagues and the deep affection of his constituents. One of his most distinguished contemporaries described him as 'the most valiant of comrades, the truest of friends, the most lovable of men'. In spite of his hard fighting he is said never to have made an enemy, and even when his work was overwhelming and his health failing he was always ready to give 'ungrudging help and counsel' to those who asked for it.

Durham University conferred an honorary D.C.L. on Robson in 1906, and his own college gave him an honorary fellowship and placed his arms in the window of the college hall between those of Lord Esher and Lord Thurlow.

Robson married in 1887 Catherine, daughter of Charles Burge, of Portland Place, London; she took an active share in her husband's political life. They had one son and three daughters.

[*The Times*, 12 September 1918; *The Caian* (magazine of Gonville and Caius College) vol. xxviii, 1917–1918; *Annual Register*; *Liberal Magazine*, 1905–1912; private information.] N. L. H.

ROBY, HENRY JOHN (1830–1915), educational reformer and classical scholar, was born at Tamworth 12 August 1830, the only son of Henry Wood Roby, by his wife, Elizabeth Robins. His father, a solicitor at Tamworth, died in 1833, and Roby was educated at Bridgnorth School and St. John's College, Cambridge; he was senior classic in the tripos of February 1853, became a fellow of his college in 1854 and lecturer in 1855, and lived in Cambridge till 1861. Among his friends, afterwards distinguished, were J. B. Lightfoot and Henry Philpott, G. D. Liveing, Isaac Todhunter, Joseph Mayor, J. L. Hammond, and H. M. Butler; and he himself was a leading spirit among the young Cambridge tutors who were agitating for the proper use of college revenues and for other university reforms. He was one of the founders and the first secretary of the Cambridge local examinations; and during this time he examined for the classical tripos, the moral science tripos, and the degrees in law, as well as in a great many schools.

In 1861 Roby married Matilda (died 1889), daughter of Peter Albert Ermen, of Dawlish; she was an accomplished linguist and keenly interested in women's education. Because in those days marriage put an end to a fellowship, he had accepted the second mastership at Dulwich College shortly before. There, becoming soon dissatisfied with the Latin grammar of King Edward VI, then still in use, he wrote an *Elementary Latin Grammar* (1862), which had a large sale. With this, however, he was so little content as to refuse to allow any second issue. Long-continued work led to the publication (1871–1874) of his *Grammar of the Latin Language from Plautus to Suetonius*, his greatest achievement as an author. He also continued his study of law. In 1864 he was appointed secretary to the Schools Inquiry commission, which was succeeded in 1869 by the Endowed Schools commission, an executive body. These dealt with all endowed schools in England and Wales other than the nine which had been the subject of the Public Schools commission of 1861. In 1865 he retired from Dulwich, and, although from 1866 to 1868 he also held the chair of jurisprudence at University College, London, he devoted himself almost wholly to school-reform for the next nine years—'the most interesting portion of my life' he called it afterwards.

Hand in hand with Dr. (afterwards Archbishop) Temple, Roby took a leading part in inquiries and legislation affecting over eight hundred schools for boys and girls. Most of them were in an indescribable state of inefficiency and maladministration, due partly to the inexpert control of the court of Chancery. For every one of these schools the Endowed Schools commission established, under the Committee of the Privy Council on Education, a scheme of management, which provided the necessary machinery for its own revision from time to time, but completely precluded any loose handling of the endowments. This reform was largely due to Roby's strenuous and brilliant pleading. Few public men can ever have enjoyed a greater reward than to have been the means, not merely of reforming the life and teaching of this multitude of schools, but also of enormously increasing the number of children to whom their doors were opened.

The Endowed Schools commission, of which Roby was first the secretary, and after 1872 a member, ended on 31 December 1874. He then accepted a business partnership with a relative of his wife, creating the firm of Ermen & Roby, of Manchester, sewing-cotton manufacturers; this he held for the next twenty years while his children (three sons and a daughter) grew up. The confidence with which he had come to be regarded in the commerce and society of Manchester led to his election as member of parliament for the Eccles division of Lancashire in October 1890, as a supporter of Mr. Gladstone. He lost his seat in the conservative reaction of 1895 and never re-entered parliament.

After his retirement from business in 1894 Roby settled, as became a lover of mountains and a devoted student of Wordsworth, in a beautiful corner of Easedale, below Helm Crag, near Grasmere; his garden was famous for the variety of roses which he established and improved. Here he delighted to entertain with genial hospitality a continual succession of friends, old and young; and the generous interest which he took in their concerns, and in everything that affected education or public questions, made the last twenty years of his life hardly less busy and hardly less fruitful than any that had gone before. He celebrated the completion of his eightieth year by the ascent of Scafell. He died at his home on 2 January 1915.

Roby's great *Latin Grammar* (seventh edition 1904) is distinguished from all its predecessors by the wealth of illustration drawn directly from his reading of all the authors from Plautus to Suetonius, and by its severe impartiality. Not that his statements lack precision; but they show a lawyer-like caution. Everywhere he preferred that the passages cited should speak for themselves; and that the limits of any general rule should be made plain by sharply contrasted examples. Thus in his treatment of the

Subjunctive, the seventy right-hand pages are occupied with examples of the Indicative in uses nearly approaching those of the Subjunctive which are set forth in the examples on the seventy pages opposite. Hence arises what sometimes appears to beginners a defect—his refusal to make hard and fast rules, not always warranted by the facts. But no one who seeks counsel in ' Roby ' on any difficult point will fail to find a representative collection of the evidence, worth many pages of dogma. He had a shrewd perception of degrees of probability, and an equally shrewd reluctance to accept tradition without testing it for himself. His profound knowledge of it, however, appeared everywhere; notably in his article on Priscian in the *Encyclopaedia Britannica* (ninth edition).

In one respect the *Latin Grammar* introduced among English-speaking scholars a reform so important as to amount to a revolution. Roby everywhere adopted the historical rather than the conventional point of view. He nowhere fails to make clear what older grammarians called the correct, that is, the Ciceronian usage, with abundant and striking examples; but he set it in its true perspective. He read deeply in the growing literature of comparative grammar; and chose continually that part of its teaching which made a strictly scientific use of evidence. His own carefully limited account of Latin phonology, which contributed much to the reform of Latin pronunciation, often anticipates the truth and clarity of the work of Karl Brugmann which was then just beginning; and his original investigations, especially in the preface to the second volume, still retain their full value.

Roman Law was a favourite study with Roby from his Cambridge days; but his first considerable publication was the *Introduction to Justinian's Digest* (1884), which provided students with a comprehensive account of the history, and method of compilation of the Digest, and of the jurists from whom it was drawn, such as did not exist, and does not exist, in any other language. It contained much original criticism, including a study—very valuable at the time—of ' lawyer's Latin ', though later writers have shown that the Digest, in which he had suspected some degree of interpolation, is an even more complex product than he had supposed.

Roby's study of *Roman Private Law* (1902) was an admirable presentment of what is known as the ' classical ' law, so far as it was then understood. These essays are probably the most original part of his legal work, though he had mastered what other men had written. ' Here ', writes a competent critic, ' is the real Roby; the work was better than anything that had been done before in England; he always drew from the sources and he always thought for himself.' His latest contribution to the subject of any length was the chapter (vol. ii, c. 3) on *Roman Law* in the *Cambridge Medieval History* (1913).

Roby will no doubt be best remembered for his *Latin Grammar*—a monument of open-minded research from which other grammars will long continue to be compiled. But probably his greatest service to his generation lay in the educational reforms which he carried through with keen insight, indomitable zeal, and the most genial humour; and these qualities were fruitful also in other kinds of work, such as his long service on the governing bodies of the grammar school and university of Manchester, of Girton College, Cambridge, and of University College, London, which with other good causes were deeply indebted to his far-sighted, high-minded, and always generous guidance.

[Roby's published works, cited above; an autobiography (unpublished) written for his family; private information; personal knowledge.] R. S. C.

ROGERS, BENJAMIN BICKLEY (1828–1919), barrister and translator of Aristophanes, was born at Shepton Montague, Somerset, 11 December 1828, the third son of Francis Rogers, of Yarlington Lodge, Wincanton, by his wife, Catharine Elizabeth, eldest daughter of Benjamin Bickley, of Bristol and Ettingshall, Staffordshire. He was educated at Bruton School, Somerset, and Sir Roger Cholmley's School, Highgate (now Highgate School), of both of which he subsequently became a governor. He matriculated at Wadham College, Oxford, in 1846, and was elected scholar there the same year. He obtained a first class in *literae humaniores* and a fourth class in mathematics in 1851, and in the next year was elected a fellow of his college. In 1853 Rogers joined Lincoln's Inn, and in 1856 was called to the bar. He vacated his fellowship in 1861, having in that year married Ellen Susanna, daughter of Robert Herring, of Cromer. As an undergraduate he had shown rare gifts and promise, as well as intellectual and moral bent. Already prominent in the Oxford Union, in February 1853 he took part in a memorable debate, continued over four nights, on the subject of Mr. Gladstone's political conduct, and moved an amendment condemning his coalition with the whigs. G. J. Goschen, M. E. Grant Duff, E. S. Beesly, and C. H. Pearson also spoke. Rogers, whose eloquence made a unique sensation, was followed with cheers into the street, carried to Wadham shoulder high, and elected president for the next term. As a barrister, Rogers built up a lucrative practice, and bade fair to receive high promotion, when severe deafness, at the age of about fifty, cut short his career. Among his legal pupils was Frederick William Maitland.

Rogers now fell back on his other early interest, that of the scholar and poetical translator. He had begun in 1846, as he records sixty-four years later, under the influence of his brother, Thomas Englesby Rogers, fellow of Corpus Christi College, Oxford, an edition of the *Clouds* of Aristophanes with a translation 'into corresponding metres'. This he completed while still an undergraduate, and published in 1852. The preface, dated Oxford 1851, shows wide and deep reading, both of original Greek authors and of commentators English and German; the notes, a large and varied acquaintance with English literature; and the translation, much verbal and metrical skill, and poetic feeling. The whole is a very striking performance for a young man of twenty-three. In 1855 Rogers published a pamphlet on *Napoleon III and England*, a warning against the 'faithful ally' of Tennyson's 'Riflemen, form', and in 1863 and 1865 two pamphlets, *The Difficulties suggested by Dr. Colenso* and *The Mosaic Record*, demonstrating the absurdity of the bishop's mechanical and mathematical handling of the Pentateuch. Returning to Aristophanes, he published the *Peace* (1867), the *Wasps* (1875, used for the Cambridge performances of 1897 and 1919), the *Lysistrata* (1878), the *Thesmophoriazusae* (1904), and then from 1910 to 1916 reissued all the plays in a complete edition in six volumes. To volume vi was appended a translation of Plautus's *Menaechmi*, later published separately with the Latin text. In 1909 Oxford University conferred on him the honorary degree of D.Litt. Such was his modesty that when he received the letter conveying the offer he thought that it was meant for someone else of the same name. Wadham College, where he was always greatly liked, elected him an honorary fellow in 1902.

In the final edition of the *Clouds* Rogers records how after sixty-four years he now reissued the work, having rewritten the commentary, but only slightly retouched the translation lest he should destroy its early vigour. It was a true instinct. A faithful while ardent scholar, steeped in literature dramatic and general, a man of the world, a barrister at home in the courts and in the purlieus and quillets of the law, keenly interested in politics, of an open yet thoroughly conservative temper in church and state, of personal piety, a special lover of birds, Rogers's genius was exactly suited to that of Aristophanes. He is as lively as Frere, and more literal. As Walter Headlam said, 'he permanently raised the standard of verse translation by writing verse that was verse'. His notes are a thesaurus controlled by literary discrimination, and his version, to use his own eloquent phrase, is 'fragrant', through and through, 'with the volatile wit of the poet'.

Rogers died at Eastwood, Strawberry Hill, Twickenham, 22 September 1919 in his ninety-first year. He had two sons and three daughters. He never consented to sit for his portrait, but there is a very good pencil-drawing of him in the Oxford Union. He left his classical library to Wadham College.

[*The Times*, 25 September 1919; H. A. Morrah, *The Oxford Union 1823–1923*, 1923; Foster's *Alumni Oxonienses* and *Men at the Bar*; Rogers's Prefaces to his translations; private information; personal knowledge. There is an excellent summary of the value of Rogers's work by T. L. Agar, *Classical Review*, vol. xxxiii, nos. 7 and 8, 1919.]

T. H. W.

ROMER, Sir ROBERT (1840–1918), judge, was born at Kilburn 23 December 1840, the second son of Frank Romer, musical composer, by his wife, Mary Lydia, daughter of Benjamin Cudworth. He was educated at private schools, and in 1859 matriculated at Cambridge as a scholar of Trinity Hall. In 1863 he was senior wrangler, and Smith's prizeman jointly with the second wrangler. Trinity Hall had never before produced a senior wrangler, and Romer's success is commemorated in the large picture (by Farren, a local artist), 'Degree Day, 1863,' which hangs in the combination room of the college. On leaving Cambridge his first appointment was that of private secretary to Baron Lionel Nathan de Rothschild. In 1864 he married his first cousin, Betty, daughter of Mark Lemon [q.v.], one of the founders, and first editor, of *Punch*. From 1865 to 1866 he was professor of mathematics at Queen's College, Cork. In 1867 he was elected a fellow of Trinity Hall; on 11 June of the same year he was called to the bar at Lincoln's Inn, and took chambers at 4 New Square, whence some years later he moved to 16 Old Buildings. In the law list of 1868 his connexion with the home circuit and Sussex and Brighton sessions was announced; but he soon developed a practice in the chancery courts, and the reference to sessions was not repeated in later issues. His chancery practice increased rapidly and for several years he was one of the busiest juniors. In 1881 he was made a Q.C., and practised at first for a brief time before the master of the Rolls, Sir George Jessel; but when under the Judicature Act (1881) that judge became a member of the Court of Appeal, Romer went to the court of Sir Joseph William Chitty. He was a very successful advocate, quick, learned, and lucid, with something of a genial audacity. Among chancery advocates he was especially noted for his skill in the art (at that time still a novelty in their traditions) of dealing with witnesses in the box. In 1884 he was made a bencher of Lincoln's Inn, and in the same year stood unsuccessfully for parliament at Brighton as a liberal; but he was never a keen politician.

On 17 November 1890, upon the elevation of Sir Edward E. Kay to the Court of Appeal, Romer was appointed a judge of the chancery division, and knighted. Lord Halsbury's selection of judges was not always applauded, but no one had any doubt about the propriety of this choice. Apart from his professional distinction, the new judge enjoyed a popularity of which his being almost universally known as 'Bob' Romer was significant. His career on the bench added to the distinction, and did not decrease the popularity. In 1899, on the death of Chitty, he was promoted to the Court of Appeal and made a privy councillor. Sitting in the Court of Appeal was perhaps less congenial to him than his work as a judge of first instance, and in the long vacation of 1906 he retired from the bench. In the first part of that year it was possible for the Court of Appeal to consist of three senior wranglers (Romer, Stirling, and Fletcher Moulton), as a few years before it could consist of three 'rowing blues' (Lord Esher, Chitty, and A. L. Smith).

Romer's acute and active mind was always interested in other things besides the law. In 1899 he was elected a fellow of the Royal Society, primarily in virtue of his eminence as a mathematician. In 1900 he was appointed chairman of the royal commission to inquire into the management of military hospitals in the South African War, and he received the G.C.B. in recognition of his services. After his retirement in 1906 he lived at Great Hormead, Hertfordshire, and enjoyed the pleasures of country life, of which, and of shooting in particular, he had always been fond. Lady Romer died in 1916, and Romer himself died at Bath on 19 March 1918. Five sons, of whom the second, Sir Mark Lemon Romer, has followed in his father's footsteps as a judge of the chancery division, and one daughter, survived them. A portrait of Romer, by Lowes Dickinson, hangs in the combination room at Trinity Hall.

[*The Times*, 21 March 1918; *Law Journal*, 23 March 1918; Law Lists; H. E. Malden, *History of Trinity Hall*, 1902.] F. D. M.

ROOS-KEPPEL, Sir GEORGE OLOF (1866–1921), soldier and Anglo-Indian administrator, was born in London 7 September 1866, the elder son of Gustaf Ehrenreich Roos, a Swede who had settled in England as a young man, by his wife, Elizabeth Annie, eldest daughter of George Roffey, of Twickenham. He was educated at the United Services College, Westward Ho, Devon, and afterwards at Bonn and Geneva. In 1890 he changed his name to Roos-Keppel, at the wish of his grandmother, who was the last representative of a branch of the Keppel family that had emigrated from Holland to Sweden many generations before.

After a course at Sandhurst, Roos joined the Royal Scots Fusiliers in August 1886, and served in the third Burma War (1885–1886). He was soon, however, transferred to the North-Western Frontier, where he quickly displayed his remarkable aptitude for dealing with the wild mountaineers of that region. After serving for six years as political officer in the Kurram valley he was made political agent in the Khyber in 1899, and in the following January he was gazetted C.I.E. for his successful campaign against the Para Chamkannis. From October 1903 the post of commandant of the Khyber Rifles was added to his other duties. His great influence over the border clans, particularly the Afridis, pointed him out as the natural successor of Lieutenant-Colonel Sir H. A. Deane, and accordingly, on the latter's death in July 1908, Lieutenant-Colonel Roos-Keppel became chief commissioner of the North-West Frontier Province and agent to the governor-general. At the same time he was advanced to the dignity of K.C.I.E., in recognition of the part which he had played in the recent Bazar valley campaign, which brought him also the Swedish military order of the Sword.

Roos-Keppel's service of eleven years in his new post included the period of the European War, during which his presence on the Indian frontier was of inestimable value. Skilled in all the local dialects and intimately acquainted with the customs and traditions of the border tribes, he was able to win their affection by his sympathy, while gaining their respect by the mingled patience and firmness with which he ruled them. He always had in view the permanent pacification of the province, and its material well-being; and for this reason he paid great attention to the spread of education. His popularity with the tribes enabled him to keep the frontier quiet until the spring of 1919, when war with Afghanistan became inevitable; his presence at Peshawar was then a tower of strength, and great was the regret when, in the autumn of that year, increasing ill-health forced him to relinquish his post and return to England. The government, however, was unwilling to lose the benefit of his assistance, and he was immediately appointed to the council of the secretary of state for India, where his experience and judgement gave him great weight in all political questions. His health broke down completely in August 1921, and after a trying illness he died in London on 11 December of that year. Roos-Keppel had been made a G.C.I.E. in 1917, and at the time of his death he was also a knight of grace of the order of St. John of Jerusalem. He had never married.

[*The Times*, 12 December 1921; Indian official publications; private information. Portrait, *Royal Academy Pictures*, 1916.]

W. F.

ROSCOE, Sir HENRY ENFIELD (1833–1915), chemist, was born in London 7 January 1833. His father, Henry Roscoe [q.v.], judge of the court of Passage, Liverpool, was the youngest son of William Roscoe [q.v.], banker, well known for his biographies of Lorenzo de' Medici and Pope Leo X; his mother, Maria, daughter of Thomas Fletcher, a Liverpool merchant, was granddaughter of William Enfield [q.v.], the last rector of the Warrington Academy. Roscoe began his scientific training at the high school of the Liverpool Institute under W. H. Balmain, known for his 'luminous paint'. In 1848 he entered University College, London, and worked in the Birkbeck laboratory under Alexander William Williamson [q.v.] who, on succeeding Thomas Graham [q.v.] as professor of chemistry, appointed Roscoe his assistant. Gaining his B.A. degree with honours in chemistry in 1852, Roscoe proceeded to Heidelberg to work under R. W. von Bunsen, and on graduating Ph.D. in 1854 began his long research with Bunsen on the measurement of the chemical action of light. The reaction chosen was the gradual union of hydrogen and chlorine under the influence of light, originally observed by John Dalton [q.v.]. This had been investigated in 1843 by John William Draper [q.v.], who had demonstrated the initial 'inert period' and its abolition by the sun shining on the chlorine standing over water previous to its mixture with hydrogen. Bunsen and Roscoe made many experiments without being aware of Draper's work; on learning of it they repeated his experiment on the abolition of the inert period and found that 'insolated' chlorine, when mixed with hydrogen over water, still exhibited 'photo-chemical induction'. This delay was afterwards proved to be due to a minute trace of an ammonia compound which had been destroyed in Draper's experiment. By the preparation of a standard photographic paper Roscoe secured a ready means of comparing the light of the sun at different altitudes, and of measuring the diffused light from the sky.

Soon after Roscoe's return to England he was elected (1857) to the chair of chemistry vacated by (Sir) Edward Frankland at the Owens College, Manchester. He came to Manchester when the college (opened in 1851) had reached its lowest ebb, but he grasped the great need for scientific education in an industrial centre, and the success of the chemistry school under Roscoe was a large factor in the rise of the college in efficiency and public estimation.

Roscoe's most important contribution to chemistry was the preparation of pure vanadium, and the proof which he gave from the study of its oxides and chlorides that vanadium was a member of the phosphorus-arsenic family, and not related to chromium as J. J. Berzelius had supposed. The new atomic weight assigned by Roscoe to vanadium fitted it for its rightful place in the fifth group when D. I. Mendeléeff published his *Periodic System* (1869). Roscoe's *Lessons in Elementary Chemistry* (1866) passed through many editions in England and abroad, and the inorganic portion of his *Treatise on Chemistry* (1877), written with Carl Schorlemmer, has been revised through several editions and remains a standard work. From a study of Dalton's laboratory note-books he published (with Dr. Arthur Harden) *A New View of the Origin of Dalton's Atomic Theory* (1896), showing that the law of multiple proportions was not the genesis but the sought-for confirmation of the idea of chemical atoms.

Roscoe was active in founding the Society of Chemical Industry (1880) and was its first president; he was also president of the Chemical Society (1881–1883), and of the British Association at Manchester in 1887. From 1878 he forwarded the movement to make the Owens College a university for Lancashire, but the opposition of other interests led to the establishment (1880) of the federal Victoria University, to which the Liverpool and Leeds colleges were afterwards admitted. In 1903–1904 the federated colleges received separate charters. Appointed vice-chancellor of London University in 1896, he took an active part in its reconstitution. The same year he became chairman of the 1851 Exhibition scholarship committee; in 1901 he joined the executive of the Carnegie Trust.

Roscoe served on the royal commission on technical instruction (1882–1884) which led to the Technical Instruction Act of 1889 and to the partial appropriation of the 'whiskey money' to technical education. Knighted for his services in 1884, he was elected M.P. in the liberal interest for South Manchester in 1885 and resigned the chair of chemistry at Owens College. Roscoe promoted legislation on ventilation in weaving-sheds, on sewage disposal, and on the legalization of the metric system; he asked for and served on a commission to report on Pasteur's treatment of hydrophobia, and from the first was a governor of the Lister Institute. In 1895 he began experimenting on the intermittent filtration of sewage—a process that has been largely adopted. He was made a privy councillor in 1909.

Roscoe married in 1863 Lucy (died 1910), daughter of Edmund Potter, M.P.; one son and two daughters were born of the marriage. He died at Woodcote, his summer home near Leatherhead, Surrey, 18 December 1915.

[*The Life and Experiences of Sir Henry Enfield Roscoe, written by himself*, 1906; *Journal* of the Chemical Society, 1916; personal knowledge.] H. B. D.

ROSS, MARTIN (pseudonym), novelist. [See MARTIN, VIOLET FLORENCE.]

ROSSETTI, WILLIAM MICHAEL (1829–1919), man of letters and art-critic, the second son and third child of Gabriele Rossetti, and brother of Christina Georgina Rossetti [q.v.] and Dante Gabriel Rossetti [q.v.], was born in London at 38 Charlotte Street (now Hallam Street), Portland Place, 25 September 1829, and educated with his brother at King's College School, London. In 1845 he entered the Excise Office (which became later the Inland Revenue Board), where he remained till his retirement in 1894, having attained (in 1869) the position of senior assistant secretary. From 1888 he acted as referee, for estate duty, of pictures and drawings, and he continued to hold this position till about 1905, after his retirement.

William Rossetti was the companion in boyhood of Dante Gabriel Rossetti, and his lifelong confidant, and to him were dedicated the *Poems* of 1870, 'to so many of which, so many years back, he gave the first brotherly hearing'. But after boyhood and his youthful share in the 'pre-Raphaelite' movement, William Rossetti showed a marked intellectual detachment from all his family. He was one of the seven pre-Raphaelite 'brothers' and even made some slight practice of painting. He edited *The Germ* (1850), the organ of the brotherhood, and wrote the sonnet printed on the cover of each of its four issues; in it he reviewed Clough's *Bothie* and Matthew Arnold's *Strayed Reveller*. During the following years he wrote art-criticisms for the *Spectator* and other papers, and republished them, revised, under the title *Fine Art, chiefly Contemporary* (1867). At a later date he contributed articles on art to the *Encyclopaedia Britannica*.

On the death of his brother's wife in 1862, Rossetti joined his brother, Algernon Charles Swinburne [q.v.], and George Meredith [q.v.], in a short experiment in combined housekeeping at Tudor House, Cheyne Walk, Chelsea. He published a discriminating defence in pamphlet-form of Swinburne's *Poems and Ballads* (1866) and jointly with him, wrote *Notes on the Royal Academy Exhibition* (1868); to him Swinburne dedicated his essay on William Blake (1868). With his brother he had assisted Anne Gilchrist [q.v.] to edit her husband's *Life* of Blake in 1863. William Rossetti shared the republican and antiecclesiastical opinions of Swinburne and, in 1881, had in preparation a volume of *Democratic Sonnets*, but their revolutionary sentiments alarmed Dante Gabriel, who feared for his brother's dismissal from the civil service, and they were withheld from publication till 1907.

From 1870 to 1873 Rossetti edited Edward Moxon's series of popular poets, reprinting the introductions in *Lives of Some Famous Poets* (1878). A review of this is included in Swinburne's *Miscellanies*. He introduced Walt Whitman to the British public in a volume of selections (1868). In 1870 he issued an edition of Shelley in two volumes (revised edition, 3 vols., 1878), and in 1874 an edition of Blake in the 'Aldine Poets' series. He was an active member of the Shelley Society, founded in 1886, and contributed papers afterwards privately printed. In 1887 he wrote a *Life* of Keats for the 'Great Writers' series.

The deaths of Dante Gabriel Rossetti in 1882 and Christina Rossetti in 1894 gave William Rossetti scope for that biographical and editorial work by which he will be best remembered. Editions by him of his brother's collected works appeared in 1886, 1891, 1904, and 1911, as well as various critical studies; but it was only after waiting in vain for thirteen years for the promised biography of his brother by Theodore Watts-Dunton [q.v.], that Rossetti set about the *Memoir, with Family-Letters* (2 vols., 1895). His services to Christina Rossetti are the editions of *New Poems* (1896), *Collected Poems*, with a memoir (1904), and *Family-Letters* (1908). He also published a blank-verse translation (1901) of his father's Italian 'versified autobiography'. It is not necessary to share either his sense of his brother's importance or his careful detachment from his sister's religion to find his loyalty and candour admirable, and his detachment amusing, in no derisive sense. He suppressed nothing but what the rights of the living demanded, and he was scrupulously just.

He followed the tradition of his family's devotion to Dante by a blank-verse translation (1865) of the *Inferno*, by the translation of the prose-arguments in his brother's version (1861) of the *Vita Nuova*, and by a study of *Dante and his Convito*, with translations (1910). In 1891 he delivered the Taylorian lecture at Oxford, on Leopardi. He was amongst the earliest workers on the *Oxford English Dictionary*; he edited certain texts (1866, 1869) for the Early English Text Society, and for the Chaucer Society a comparison of *Troilus and Criseyde* with Boccaccio's *Filostrato* (2 parts, 1875, 1883).

In 1874 Rossetti married Emma Lucy [see Rossetti, Lucy Madox], daughter of Ford Madox Brown [q.v.], and by her he had two sons and three daughters. He died at 3 St. Edmund's Terrace, Primrose Hill, 5 February 1919. His wife predeceased him in 1894.

A portrait in oils (1864) by A. Legros is reproduced in Rossetti's *Some Reminiscences*, vol. i (1906), and a pencil-drawing (*c.* 1846–1848), by D. G. Rossetti, in the *Family-Letters of D. G. Rossetti*, vol. ii.

[*The Times*, 6 February 1919; British Museum Catalogue; private information.]

F. P.

ROTHSCHILD, Sir NATHAN MEYER, second baronet, and first Baron Rothschild, of Tring (1840–1915), banker and philanthropist, the eldest son of Lionel Nathan de Rothschild [q.v.], baron of the Austrian Empire, by his wife Charlotte, daughter of Baron Charles de Rothschild, of Naples, was born in London 8 November 1840. Destined for membership of the famous banking house of N. M. Rothschild and Sons, which had been established in London by his grandfather, Nathan Meyer Rothschild [q.v.], Nathan Rothschild was educated privately, at Trinity College, Cambridge, where he was a contemporary of King Edward VII, and afterwards in Germany. He left Cambridge without taking a degree.

Rothschild entered the House of Commons as liberal member for Aylesbury in 1865. He retained the representation of the borough and afterwards of the county division until his elevation to the peerage as a baron in 1885. He was the first professing Jew to become a member of the House of Lords. He had succeeded his uncle, Sir Anthony de Rothschild [q.v.], as second baronet in 1876, and his father as Austrian baron in 1879. On the introduction of the Home Rule Bill in 1886 Lord Rothschild joined the liberal unionists. Ranging himself behind the Marquess of Hartington (afterwards eighth Duke of Devonshire, q.v.) on the Home Rule issue, he remained a loyal and, for the most part, silent member of the party. He gave the same statesman his support also when the questions of protection and imperial preference became a decisive issue in 1903. He served on several royal commissions, was created (1902) a privy councillor and G.C.V.O., and held the post of lord-lieutenant of Buckinghamshire from 1889 till his death.

Rothschild's support and advice, whenever sought, as well as the influence of his firm, were always at the disposal of the British government, quite independently of party, in international and also in financial affairs; and it was with the firm's assistance that Lord Beaconsfield acquired for Great Britain a controlling interest in the Suez Canal in 1875. It was four years after this, on the death of his father, that Nathan Rothschild succeeded to the headship of the firm. In 1882, when Egypt was on the verge of financial collapse, the firm came to her assistance and to that of the British government, and was largely instrumental in maintaining the financial stability of Egypt during the crisis. In the city of London Rothschild held a unique position as the personification of the best aspects of the City's finance, and the influence of his firm and himself have been compared with that of the Bank of England.

Lord Rothschild, however, stood out in the public eye as a philanthropist no less than as a financier. The generosity of himself and of his family was proverbial as well as princely. It is not known whether Lord Rothschild set out to observe strictly the Jewish law that a tithe of income be devoted to philanthropic and public purposes; but it is probable that a tithe of his firm's immense income, and possibly more, was devoted to the benefit of others. Under his headship one of the departments of the firm was devoted exclusively to the administration of the large amount set aside for charitable purposes, and it is certain that no deserving object of charity, the needs of which were known, was left unassisted. But Rothschild's charity did not consist merely in the distribution of relief to individuals or institutions. Every public subscription included a donation from his firm, and his assistance and advice were freely granted whenever a movement for the relief of any section of humanity arose in the city of London. It is not possible to give here a full list of the philanthropic offices which he held. He was president of three hospitals and treasurer of a fourth as well as of King Edward VII's hospital fund. He was also chairman of the council of the British Red Cross Society, and guided its destinies and controlled its finances during the early period of the European War. In the Anglo-Jewish community he was at one time or another officially connected with practically every institution of any consequence; and he was in later life regarded as the lay head of the community. He also showed himself a munificent benefactor of his fellow Jews in all parts of the world. The many funds for the relief of persecuted or distressed Jews abroad were always headed by a donation from the house of Rothschild. After the death in 1885 of Sir Moses Haim Montefiore [q.v.] Rothschild may almost be said to have been the generally acknowledged leader of the Jews of the world. His philanthropy even invaded the realm of business, for largely through his influence the doors of the city of London were closed to anti-Semitic powers seeking loans.

Lord Rothschild was for long out of sympathy with the Zionist movement; and although Theodor Herzl at the opening of his career endeavoured to secure Rothschild's support, he failed. Later, however, the two men came together in connexion with the royal commission on alien immigration (1902), of which Rothschild was a member, and the latter's views became somewhat modified. When the outbreak of the European War and the participation of Turkey made Zionism a matter of practical politics it is said that Rothschild's views underwent further modification, and that when he died he was no longer antipathetic to the Zionist ideals as they had in the meanwhile developed. His death took place in London 31 March 1915.

Lord Rothschild married in 1867 Emma Louisa, daughter of Baron Karl von Rothschild, of Frankfort, by whom he had two sons and one daughter. He was survived by his wife and was succeeded by his elder son, Lionel Walter, second Baron Rothschild (born 1868).

A portrait of Lord Rothschild was painted by W. W. Ouless in 1917 (*Royal Academy Pictures*, 1917).

[*The Times*, 1 April 1915; *Jewish Encyclopaedia*; *Jewish Chronicle*, 2 April 1915.]

A. M. H.

RUMBOLD, Sir **HORACE**, eighth baronet (1829–1913), diplomatist, the fifth son of Sir William Rumbold, third baronet, by his wife, Henrietta Elizabeth, second daughter of Thomas Boothby Parkyns, first Baron Rancliffe, was born in Calcutta 2 July 1829. His father had served on the staff of the second Earl of Moira (afterwards Marquess of Hastings) when governor-general of Bengal. Horace was sent home from India when he was three years old, and was privately educated in Paris, where he had many relations amongst the old French aristocracy. No examinations were required in those days for the diplomatic service, and he was nominated to it by Lord Palmerston in 1849. In the next ten years he held appointments in Washington and Turin (1849), Paris and Frankfort (1852), Stuttgart (1854), and Vienna (1856). In December 1858 he was appointed secretary of the legation in China on the staff of (Sir) Frederick William Adolphus Bruce [q.v.] and proceeded to China in March 1859. Bruce sent him back to England in January 1860 to report to the government the active resistance which was offered to the progress of the British mission to the Chinese capital. This report led to the Anglo-French expedition to Peking in that year. Promotion came slowly to Rumbold, and he held in succession a long series of minor diplomatic posts. After serving at Athens (1862, 1866–1867), Berne (1864), St. Petersburg (1868–1871), and Constantinople (1871), he became consul-general in Chile (1872–1878), minister at Berne (1878), and envoy extraordinary to Argentina (1879–1881), Sweden and Norway (1881–1884), Greece (1884–1888), and the Netherlands (1888–1896). In 1896 he was appointed ambassador at Vienna. To his friends' congratulations he replied that it was 'not promotion but reparation', and four years later he retired (1900).

Rumbold occupied his leisure in writing accounts of his wide experience as a diplomatist. He was the author of *The Great Silver River: Notes of a Residence in Buenos Ayres* (1887), *Recollections of a Diplomatist* (1902), *Further Recollections* (1903), and *Final Recollections* (1905). In 1909 he published *The Austrian Court in the Nineteenth Century*, a book which created some sensation, and was regarded as a grave indiscretion at a time when high officials had not acquired the habit of writing memoirs.

Rumbold succeeded his brother, Sir Charles Hale Rumbold, as eighth baronet, in 1877 (the baronetcy having passed in turn, since his father's death in 1833, to his three elder surviving brothers and a nephew). He was made a privy councillor in 1896 and G.C.B. in 1897. He died at Lymington, Hampshire, 3 November 1913.

Rumbold married twice: first, in 1867 Caroline Barney (died 1872), daughter of George Harrington, United States minister at Berne, of Washington, U.S.A., by whom he had three sons; secondly, in 1881 Louisa Anne, daughter of Thomas Russell Crampton, and widow of Captain St. George Francis Robert Caulfield, 1st Life Guards, by whom he had one son. He was succeeded in the baronetcy by his eldest son, Horace George Montagu (born 1869), also a distinguished diplomatist, who in 1920 was appointed British ambassador at Constantinople.

[Official records; private letters.] V. C.

RUTHERFORD, MARK (pseudonym), novelist, philosophical writer, and literary critic. [See White, William Hale.]

ST. ALDWYN, first Earl (1837–1916), statesman. [See Hicks Beach, Sir Michael Edward.]

SANDAY, WILLIAM (1843–1920), theological scholar, the eldest son of William Sanday, a well-known breeder of sheep and cattle, by his wife, Elizabeth Mann, was born 1 August 1843 at Holme Pierrepont, Nottinghamshire, where his family had been settled for more than a century. He was educated at Repton School from 1858 to 1861 and went up to Oxford as a commoner of Balliol College in 1862, but gained a scholarship at Corpus Christi College in 1863. He obtained a first class in classical moderations (1863), and in *literae humaniores* (1865), and was elected fellow of Trinity College in 1866. He remained there as a lecturer till 1869 when, having taken priest's orders, he left Oxford and held in succession the college livings of Navestock, Essex, Abingdon (1871–1872), Great Waltham (1872–1873), and Barton-on-the-Heath (1873–1876). Sanday was appointed principal of Hatfield Hall, Durham, in 1876, but was recalled to Oxford on his election in 1882 to Dean Ireland's professorship of the exegesis of Holy Scripture, a poorly paid chair which was made more acceptable by his appointment as fellow and tutor of Exeter College in the following year. From 1895 to 1919 he was Lady Margaret professor of divinity and canon of Christ Church. He was one of the original fellows of the British Academy (1903) and an honorary doctor of many universities. He married in 1877 Marian (died 1904), daughter of Warren Hastings Woodman Hastings, of Twining, Tewkesbury; they had no children. He died at Oxford 16 September 1920.

Sanday enjoyed an even academic life of thirty-seven years as professor, and spent nearly half a century in Oxford; his life's work, equally homogeneous, was dedicated to the scientific study of the New Testament and especially of the Gospels. He had no master, though his later development owed much to the influence of friends and fellow-workers, notably from 1883 to 1889 of Edwin Hatch [q.v.], and from 1895 to 1903 of

Robert Campbell Moberly [q.v.]. His first books, *The Authorship and Historical Character of the Fourth Gospel* (1872) and *The Gospels in the Second Century* (1876), already foreshadowed his mature method. He early evolved for himself a scheme of his life's work, proceeding by graduated stages through the 'lower' or textual criticism of the New Testament to the 'higher' or historical criticism, and so finally to a conception of the result as a whole. Under the first head falls his epoch-making claim for the close examination of the primitive Western authorities for the text, put forward in his *Portions of the Gospels according to St. Mark and St. Matthew from the Bobbio MS.* (1886) and in his *Novum Testamentum S. Irenaei* (posthumously published in 1923). The second of these works was produced in conjunction with one of the seminars of graduates meeting fortnightly during term, which he, as professor, had instituted. In some sense the *Critical and Exegetical Commentary on the Epistle to the Romans* (1895), written in collaboration with Dr. A. C. Headlam, admirable in many ways as it is, meant an interruption to his central purpose, prompted by the feeling that a professor of exegesis should publish something exegetical.

Sanday wanted, at least from the time that he became Margaret professor, to concentrate his energies on writing a Life of Christ, and his later books are all of the nature of preliminary studies for the *magnum opus,* which in fact was never written and, so far as actual manuscript went, never even begun. Thus, he published successively *Outlines of the Life of Christ* (1905, reprinted from Hastings's *Dictionary of the Bible*), *Sacred Sites of the Gospels* (1903), *Criticism of the Fourth Gospel* (1905), *The Life of Christ in Recent Research* (1907), *Christologies Ancient and Modern* (1910), *Personality in Christ and in Ourselves* (1911), and in conjunction with his seminar, *Oxford Studies in the Synoptic Problem* (1911); books not all of equal value, but constituting in their sum a sustained effort to look at his subject from every side. Similarly, his later courses of professorial lectures illustrated his conception of the 'praeparatio evangelica' as rooted in the history of religion in the East, and not among the Jews only, far back in the centuries before Christ. As the result of advancing years, the pressure of controversy, and the distraction of the War, the *magnum opus* was practically dropped. His theological position as a modernist, advanced at some points, conservative at others, Sanday did not reach till 1912, and then for a time the scholar was merged in the controversialist (*Bishop Gore's Challenge to Criticism,* 1914; *Spirit, Matter, and Miracle,* privately printed, 1916; *Form and Content in Christian Tradition, a friendly discussion* [with the Rev. N. P. Williams], 1916, &c.). Just at first there may have been something a little impetuous or a little pontifical in his polemic: it was difficult for him to understand how people who adopted his conclusions on critical problems did not necessarily adopt the theological conclusions which had now become to him no less certain. With the outbreak of the War his activities found another vent. His political cast of mind was rather conservative (just as in his economic views he stood up for the middle classes), and the fighting services always had a curious fascination for him. So he threw himself with ardour into the business of a pamphleteer (*The Deeper Causes of the War,* 1914; *The Meaning of the War for Germany and Great Britain: an attempted synthesis,* 1915; *In View of the End: a retrospect and a prospect,* 1916; *When should the War end?,* 1917). Possibly he turned to these questions with relief because theological controversy was no longer congenial to him. At any rate his instinct for positive statement reasserted itself in a simple but finished summary of the results, as he saw them, of the critical study of the Gospels, *The New Testament Background* (1918).

Sanday held a unique position among English theological critics as the interpreter *par excellence* to Englishmen of the immense labour that was being devoted to the New Testament abroad. His best and most characteristic work was perhaps contained in the *Life of Christ in Recent Research,* which sketched the rise of the eschatological school of interpretation of the Gospels. He was acquainted with some of the most influential scholars abroad. His ideals were in some respects of a German rather than of an English type: he was wont to lament that Englishmen produced so much less that was conceived on an encyclopaedic scale than did the Germans. For many years he read almost everything that was written on his subject in German or English; over nine hundred bound volumes of pamphlets, given to the library of Queen's College, Oxford, attest his assiduity. And he not only read; he digested. He passed through the crucible of his own sane and cautious temper the whole voluminous mass, and criticized the critics. His was not in the strict sense an original mind; he made few striking discoveries of his own; he was slow in arriving at conclusions, though very tenacious of them when once reached; patient rather than nimble or acute, comprehensive rather than brilliant. Perhaps just for that reason his critical work was trusted on all sides. A French cardinal wrote after his death that he regarded himself as 'in some sort Sanday's disciple', while if there has been during the last generation a substantial measure of agreement among English students in their attitude to the critical study of the New Testament, that is perhaps due, more than to any other single cause, to the life's work and influence of William Sanday.

A portrait of Sanday by L. Campbell Taylor, painted in 1908, hangs in the house of the Lady Margaret professor; another, painted after his death from photographs, by C. H. Shannon, was presented by Mr. S. Sanday to Christ Church and hangs in the chapter house.

[The *Church Times*, 24 September 1920; *Constructive Quarterly*, June 1921; *Oxford Magazine*, October 1920; *Expositor*, November and December 1920; *Expository Times*, January–March 1921; *Journal of Theological Studies*, January and April 1921 (with bibliography); preface to the *Novum Testamentum S. Irenaei*; W. Sanday, *Records and Reminiscences of Repton*, 1907; *Oxford Chronicle*, 15 October 1909; personal knowledge.] C. H. T.

SCHREINER, WILLIAM PHILIP (1857–1919), South African lawyer and statesman, the fifth son of Gottlob Schreiner, a Lutheran missionary sent out by the London Missionary Society, by his English wife, Rebecca Lyndall, of London, was born in the Wittebergen Reserve, Cape Colony, 30 August 1857. After a school-life which was broken by spells at the diamond fields, and a brilliant career at the South African College, Cape Town, he entered first London University, and then, in 1878, Downing College, Cambridge, and the Inner Temple. He won the senior Inns of Court studentship in 1880, and in 1881 was Chancellor's medallist and senior jurist in the law tripos at Cambridge. He was a fellow of Downing from 1884 to 1887. Called to the English bar and to the Cape bar in 1882, he became Q.C. in 1892. In 1884 he married Frances Hester, a sister of Francis William Reitz, chief justice and subsequently president of the Orange Free State. Two sons and three daughters were born of the marriage.

After serving as parliamentary draftsman and legal adviser to the high commissioner from 1887 to 1893, Schreiner entered the Cape parliament in 1893 and held office as attorney-general in the second ministry of Cecil Rhodes in that year and again from 1894 to 1896. He helped to arrange for joint action with the British government against the South African Republic (Transvaal) during the Vaal River crisis of 1895, and defended the charter of the British South Africa Company after the Jameson Raid (1896); but he introduced in the Cape parliament the report of the committee which condemned Rhodes for complicity in the Raid. He now became leader of the Afrikander Bond parliamentary party, and, in 1898, prime minister of Cape Colony. A man of peace, slow-moving in his anxiety to be just, he first tried to avert war in 1899 and then to keep his colony neutral—'a port in the storm'—till his duty as a minister of the Crown and the republican invasion rendered that course impossible. In June 1900 his Cabinet split, and he retired for a time from politics.

As leader of the bar Schreiner, by his example and influence with the younger advocates, did much to maintain the high standard of his profession at the Cape. He was a freemason, a keen sportsman, and an expert rock-fisherman. Early in 1908, believing that group politics could alone check 'radicalism', he declined to lead a combined moderate-progressive party to 'smash the Bond'. He re-entered parliament in 1908 for Queenstown as an independent, and accepted a seat in the National Convention, which he resigned before the meeting of that body in October 1908, in order to undertake the defence of Dinizulu. He favoured federation rather than union as the best safeguard of the Cape native franchise, and, mainly on this ground, fought the draft Union Bill in Cape Town and in London. In 1910 his championship of native interests earned him a seat in the senate; this he vacated in 1914 in order to go to London as high commissioner of the Union. The strain of his official duties, and still more of the manifold services rendered to others during and after the European War—for Schreiner, ever generous, suffered all men gladly—wore him out. His heart had never been strong enough for his burly frame. He died at Llandrindod Wells 28 June 1919.

His sister, Olive Emilie Albertina Schreiner (1855–1920), authoress, the fifth daughter of Gottlob Schreiner, was born at Wittebergen mission station 24 March 1855. After spending several years as a governess in South Africa, Miss Schreiner came to England in 1881. She brought with her the manuscript of her earliest and most successful published work, *The Story of an African Farm*, which, read for press and praised by George Meredith, appeared in 1883 under the pseudonym 'Ralph Iron'. In 1889 Miss Schreiner returned to South Africa, and in 1894 married Samuel Cron Cronwright, a South African politician, who took the name of Cronwright-Schreiner. Among other works, she wrote *An English South African's View of the Situation* (1899) and *Women and Labour* (1911). For the greater part of her life she was troubled by ill-health, and she died at Cape Town 11 December 1920. An uncompleted novel by her, entitled *From Man to Man*, was published, with an introduction by her husband, in 1926. She had been engaged upon it intermittently since 1876, or even earlier, and frequently refers to it in her diaries and letters. She evidently regarded it as her most important work, and wove into a story of strong emotional appeal much of her own social and moral philosophy.

[B. Williams, *Cecil Rhodes*, 1921; G. R. Hofmeyr, *Life of Jan Hendrik Hofmeyr*, 1913; private information. See also, S. C. Cronwright-Schreiner, *The Life of Olive Schreiner*, 1924, and the introduction to *From Man to Man*.] E. A. W.

SCOTT, ROBERT FALCON (1868–1912), naval officer and Antarctic explorer, was born 6 June 1868 at Devonport, the second son of John Edward Scott, of Outlands, Devonport, by his wife, Hannah, daughter of William Bennett Cuming. His ancestors were of Scots extraction, but the family had lived in Devon for three generations. He was educated at Stoke Damerel and Stubbington House, Fareham, until in 1880 he passed into H.M.S. *Britannia*. In 1882 he became a midshipman and joined the *Boadicea*; in 1888 he served as sub-lieutenant in the *Spider*, and later as lieutenant in the *Amphion* (1889). He was promoted first lieutenant in 1897. In 1899, having been appointed in the previous year torpedo-lieutenant in the *Majestic*, flagship of the Channel squadron, he was offered, on the recommendation of Sir Clements Robert Markham [q.v.] and Sir R. Egerton, the command of the National Antarctic expedition. On taking up his duties in the *Discovery* in 1900 he was promoted commander. The expedition was organized by the Royal Geographical Society and the Royal Society, and although the personnel was drawn largely from the navy, the ship sailed under the merchant flag. The objects of the expedition were the scientific exploration of South Victoria Land and the ice barrier, discovered by Sir James Clark Ross [q.v.] in 1841, and the penetration of the interior of the Antarctic continent.

The *Discovery* left England in August 1901 and reached the Ross Sea via Lyttelton, New Zealand, in January 1902. A course was made southward along the coast of South Victoria Land and then eastward along the edge of the ice barrier. Ross's 'appearance of land' was confirmed by the discovery of King Edward VII Land. The ship returned westward and entered McMurdo Sound, where an anchorage off Hut Point, Ross Island, in lat. 77° 50′ 50″ S., was selected as a suitable place for wintering. This remained the base of the expedition for about two years, since in the following summer the ice failed to break up and liberate the ship. The expedition was excellently staffed and equipped for the varied scientific work which was actively pursued throughout the two years. Of many sledge journeys the two principal were led by Scott. Accompanied by (Sir) Ernest Henry Shackleton and Dr. Edward Adrian Wilson [q.v.] he went south over the barrier along the edge of the plateau to lat. 82° 16′ 33″ S. (30 December 1902), discovering the southward continuation of the South Victoria Land mountain-range and making the southern record. Dog teams were used on the outward journey, but they were little help on the return, which was also made difficult by the serious breakdown of Shackleton and by an outbreak of scurvy which attacked the three men. A year later Scott made a long journey westward over the high plateau of Antarctica to lat. 77° 59′ S., long. 146° 33′ E. This was the first long journey towards the interior of the continent, and it amplified the work done by Lieutenant A. B. Armitage on his pioneer journey to the plateau in the previous season. Other important results of the expedition were the survey of the coast of South Victoria Land, the sounding of the Ross Sea, and investigations into the nature of the barrier and into the structure of the Antarctic continent. The researches in zoology, magnetism, and meteorology were also of great value. The *Discovery* with its two relief ships,

Morning and *Terra Nova*, returned to New Zealand in April 1904.

Scott had proved his capacity not only as a leader and sledge traveller but as a student of scientific problems and an investigator with sound judgement. On his return from the Antarctic he was promoted captain (1904) and returned to his naval duties. After serving afloat for a few years in command successively of the *Victorious*, the *Essex*, and the *Bulwark*, he became in 1909 naval assistant to the second sea lord of the Admiralty. The same year he announced his plans for a new Antarctic expedition which was to continue the work of the *Discovery* and to attempt to reach the Pole, following as far as possible the route by which Shackleton had reached lat. 88° 23′ S. in January 1909.

With the financial support of the British and Dominion governments the *Terra Nova* was able to sail in June 1910. Winter quarters were established at Cape Evans in lat. 77° 38′ 24″ S., 15 statute miles north of the *Discovery's* old anchorage. Before the *Terra Nova* returned to New Zealand she made a course eastward to King Edward Land, and discovered Roald Amundsen's *Fram*, which was landing a wintering party at the Bay of Whales on the ice barrier preparatory to making an attempt on the Pole. This news confirmed the announcement of his plans which Amundsen had made to Scott some months earlier. Scott set out on his southern sledge journey 1 November 1911. Several food and oil-fuel depôts had been laid in the previous autumn, the most southerly being One Ton depôt in lat. 79° 28′ 53″ S., 130 geographical miles from the base. Scott had hoped to put this depôt in lat. 80° S., but the condition of the ponies had compelled him to forgo the last 31 miles. After a few days march the motor sledges broke down beyond repair. This was inconvenient, but reliance was placed chiefly on ponies and dogs, which helped the transport to the foot of the Beardmore glacier. Here the last of the ponies was shot for food and the dogs were sent back with a supporting party (11 December). Depôts for the return journey were established on the outward route. Heavy haulage and fierce blizzards delayed the explorers and extremely low temperatures taxed their endurance. On 4 January 1912, in lat. 86° 32′ S., the last supporting party, consisting of Lieutenant E. R. G. R. Evans, R.N., and two seamen, left Scott to continue his journey to the Pole with Dr. E. A. Wilson, Captain Lawrence Edward Grace Oates [q.v.], Lieutenant H. R. Bowers, R.I.M., and Petty Officer Edgar Evans. In spite of the use of ski, pulling was heavy and progress slow. Temperature frequently fell to −23° F. and never rose as high as zero. On 16 January a flag was sighted, and Scott's anticipation of being forestalled by Amundsen proved true. On 18 January the Pole was reached. In the vicinity was a tent left by Amundsen with a note for Scott. The Norwegians had reached the Pole on 14 December 1911, and left three days later. Subsequent recalculation of Bowers's observations show that the possible error in the determination of the polar position was not more than 30″.

In spite of bad travelling conditions fair progress was made on the return journey till the head of the Beardmore glacier was reached (7 February). Petty Officer Evans, however, was breaking down under the strain, and he died on 17 February. His weakness had entailed dangerous delay. On the barrier temperatures of −30° to −47° F. sorely tried the four men, weak from want of warm food. A shortage of oil in the depôts by evaporation through the stoppers of the tins was a serious and unforseen calamity. Frost-bite made marching slow and painful. By the beginning of March it was a race against time to reach one depôt after another before the party's strength gave out. Progress was frequently interrupted by strong winds. On 17 March Oates, who was too badly frost-bitten to go any further, walked out into a blizzard, hoping by this sacrifice to allow the others to push on to safety. Four days later they camped in lat. 79° 40′ S. eleven miles from One Ton depôt. There seemed to be a faint hope; but a long-continued blizzard put an end to all possibility of advancing. On 29 March Scott made the last entry in his diary: 'We shall stick it out to the end, but we are getting weaker, of course, and the end cannot be far. It seems a pity, but I do not think I can write any more.'

In accordance with instructions a relief party with dog teams had set out from the base to meet Scott, but was held up by a blizzard at One Ton depôt from 3 to 10 March, when a shortage of dog food compelled a return. Eight months later a search party under Dr. E. L. Atkinson found the tent and the bodies. Scott's diaries, letters, photographs, and message to the public were recovered, as well as the valuable geological specimens from the Beardmore glacier, which, in spite of their weight, had been retained to the end. A snow cairn surmounted by a cross was built over the tent. Some months later a cross to the memory of the five men was erected at Observation Hill on Hut Point, Ross Island.

In addition to the polar journey, much valuable exploration was carried out, together with notable scientific researches. A party, under Lieutenant V. Campbell, unable to land in King Edward Land, was put ashore by the *Terra Nova* at Cape Adare and was moved in the second year to Terra Nova Bay. In face of great difficulties this party explored the coastal region of South Victoria Land and reached the expedition's main base in safety.

The news of the disaster to Scott and his companions did not reach Europe till February 1913 when the expedition finally returned to New Zealand. The achievement and the heroic end aroused world-wide admiration. A memorial service was held in St. Paul's Cathedral on 14 February, government pensions were awarded to the dependents of those who had perished, and Scott's widow received the rank and precedence of the wife of a K.C.B. A Mansion House fund was opened to commemorate the explorers, and devoted chiefly to the publication of their scientific results and to the foundation of a polar research institute at Cambridge.

Scott received the C.V.O. in 1904, the Polar medal (in that year also), and the gold medals of many British and foreign geographical societies. He also received the honorary degree of D.Sc. from the universities of Cambridge and Manchester. Statues of Scott, the work of Lady Scott, stand in Waterloo Place, London, Portsmouth dockyard, and in Christchurch, New Zealand, and there are busts, also by Lady Scott, at Devonport and Dunedin, New Zealand. There is a portrait plaque in St. Paul's Cathedral. A portrait by D. A. Wehrschmidt (Veresmith), painted in 1905, was deposited on loan in the National Portrait Gallery in 1924. Another portrait, bust size and posthumous, painted by C. Percival Small, was given to the Gallery by Sir Courtauld Thomson in 1914. A third picture, also posthumous, based upon photographs and painted by Harrington Mann, was presented to the house of the Royal Geographical Society by Scott's family.

Scott married in 1908 Kathleen, youngest daughter of Canon Lloyd Bruce, by whom he had one son.

[R. F. Scott, *The Voyage of the 'Discovery'*, 1905; L. Huxley, *Scott's Last Expedition*, 1913; E. R. G. R. Evans, *South with Scott*, 1921; *British Antarctic Expedition* (*Terra Nova*), *1910–1913: Scientific Results*, 1914; *Geographical Journal*, 1902–1913, passim; *Journal* of the Royal United Services Institution, March 1913; private information.] R. N. R. B.

SEDGWICK, ADAM (1854–1913), zoologist, was born at Norwich 28 September 1854, the eldest son of the Rev. Richard Sedgwick, vicar of Dent, Yorkshire, by his wife, Mary Jane, daughter of John Woodhouse, of Bolton-le-Moors, Lancashire. Through both his parents he came of country-bred, land-owning ancestry. His great-uncle was Adam Sedgwick [q.v.], professor of geology in the university of Cambridge, one of the founders of British geological science. Sedgwick's childhood was spent at Dent vicarage, and from Marlborough College he passed to King's College, London, with the idea of becoming a medical student; but his stay there was brief, and he entered Trinity College, Cambridge, as a pensioner, in 1874. There he came under the strong influence of (Sir) Michael Foster, at that time praelector of physiology in Trinity College, and of Francis Maitland Balfour, who was then inspiring a school of comparative embryology in the university. In 1877 Sedgwick obtained a first class in the natural science tripos, and in the following year he became Balfour's demonstrator. In 1882, when Balfour, just elected to a special chair of animal morphology, lost his life in the Alps, Sedgwick was appointed to a readership in that subject.

For many years Sedgwick was the head of a great school of zoological research, and many of his students became distinguished teachers and investigators. A visit to Cape Colony in 1883 led to a series of highly important memoirs on the structure and development of peripatus, an archaic type which many regard as a connecting link between annelid worms and arthropods. It is probably in connexion with peripatus that Sedgwick's name will be longest remembered.

In 1897 Sedgwick, who had been elected a fellow of the Royal Society in 1886, accepted a fellowship and tutorship at Trinity College, a position which he held for ten years, when he succeeded Alfred Newton as professor of zoology in the university (1907). His duties at Trinity College had already seriously interfered with his researches, and he had hardly settled down to his professorial work when, in 1909, he was called to London as professor of zoology in the new

Imperial College of Science and Technology, South Kensington. Into the reorganization of the zoological department, which in former years had been, in a sense, T. H. Huxley's special domain, Sedgwick threw himself with enthusiasm, and he had the satisfaction of seeing some of the fruits of his labours. But an old-standing pulmonary weakness grew on him, and, in spite of vigorous resistance and a winter in the Canary Islands, he died in London 27 February 1913.

Sedgwick was an independent, resolute thinker with a strong critical faculty which expressed itself in timely reactions against outworn views, notably in regard to recapitulation and the cell-theory. He was the author, and subsequently editor, of a monumental *Text-Book of Zoology* in three volumes (1898, 1905, 1909), but his greater work was as an investigator and as an inspirer of research.

Sedgwick married in 1892 Laura Helen Elizabeth, daughter of Captain Robinson, of Armagh. They had two sons and one daughter.

[*Proceedings* of the Royal Society, vol. lxxxvi, B, 1912–1913.] J. A. T.

SEEBOHM, FREDERIC (1833–1912), historian, was born at Bradford 23 November 1833. He was the second son of Benjamin Seebohm, a wool merchant and prominent minister of the Society of Friends, who had come over from Friedensthal, in the principality of Waldeck-Pyrmont, as a boy of sixteen and had settled at Bradford. His mother, Esther Wheeler, was a descendant of one of the staunchest adherents of George Fox. Both parents were profoundly imbued with the spirit of intense and active Christianity characteristic of the early quakers. There was a wide scope for charity in the 'thirties of the last century, and Frederic Seebohm kept through life the memory of the piteous struggle of the handloom weavers of the West Riding against the introduction of machinery. After going through the Bootham School, York, Seebohm read law in London and started in practice as a barrister in 1856. In 1857 he married Mary Ann, daughter of William Exton, a banker, and settled definitely in Hitchin as a partner in a bank (Sharples & Co.), which was amalgamated with the firm of Barclay & Co. in 1896. His house, 'The Hermitage', became the happy home of a family of five daughters and one son. He proved an able and hard-working man of business, but as in the case of George Grote, Sir John Lubbock (Lord Avebury), and Thomas Hodgkin, his professional duties did not prevent him from becoming a leader of research; on the contrary they seemed to sharpen his intellect and to stimulate his energy. Nor did he shirk his duties as a citizen. As a friend and supporter of William Edward Forster [q. v.] he took an active share in the campaign for organizing popular education; he was a poor law guardian, a justice of the peace, a governor of the secondary schools at Hitchin, and a member of the Hertfordshire County Council education committee. After the split of the liberal party over Mr. Gladstone's Home Rule Bill (1886) he took the side of the liberal unionists. In 1893 he acted as a member of the Welsh land commission.

Seebohm's civic activity was prompted by the atmosphere of the community of Friends—the spirit of Christian fraternity. He was well acquainted with the critical work achieved by science and philosophy, but he kept up his devotion to Christianity as the moral guide in the history of the world. Speaking of various movements towards emancipation, he wrote in his little book, *The Christian Hypothesis* (1876): 'Looking at all these broadly, they are ripples and waves in a great tide which is moving onwards towards the political development of mankind. And not only is the direction of the movement, taken as a whole, evidently towards the realization of the goal and object of Christian civilization, but Christianity itself has mainly furnished the moral force by which it has been so far accomplished.'

The subject which attracted Seebohm's attention in his early literary work was the rise of modern civilization in opposition to the organization of society under the sway of the Roman Church. He traced this process from the revival of learning in his book, *The Oxford Reformers* (1867); as he expressed it, 'Their fellow work had been to urge, in a critical period in the history of Christendom, the necessity of that thorough and comprehensive reform which the carrying of Christianity into practice in the affairs of nations and men would involve.' It seemed to him that the revolutionary crisis of the Reformation might have been avoided if the reforms advocated by Colet, Erasmus, and More had been carried out. The main lines of the conflict in the sixteenth century were sketched by Seebohm in a little volume on *The Era of the Protestant Revolution* (1874). While *The Oxford Reformers* lays stress on the new outlook in science and literature, *The Protestant Revolution* dwells on the social process underlying the intellectual revolt. The dogmatic history of the movement is treated in both cases as of secondary importance in comparison with the revival of domestic life. From this point of view the downfall of the religious orders appears as a wholesome reaction against the ' blunder ' of celibacy and its political influence.

The principal contribution of Seebohm to historical studies is embodied in his books, *The English Village Community* (1883), *The Tribal System in Wales* (1895), and *Tribal Custom in Anglo-Saxon Law* (1902). These inquiries originated from an attempt to trace the historical conditions of the problem of population in England, of which some articles in the *Fortnightly Review* (1865–1870) present an outline. Seebohm became aware that it is not the simple relation between the supply of food and the demands of individuals to be fed that provides the solution of the problem, but that this solution is conditioned by the forms of economic organization. He was struck by the peculiar character of the open-field system which had prevailed in England for more than a thousand years. Communal farming with its inconvenient intermixture of strips, compulsory rotation of crops, common pasture, common waste, were traced by him to the so-called manorial system, which, in his view, was already in existence in the Roman *villa*; the organization of rural labour had proceeded on these lines with the same uniform regularity as the building up of hexagonal cells by bees; the communism of the open-field villages was derived from the fact that the labouring population was by custom subjected to the exploitation of lords who were endowed with rights of individual property; the disruption of the open-field community was considered as one of the aspects of progressive emancipation. Seebohm's argument fitted well into a widespread movement of revolt against a romantic conception of ancient Teutonic freedom which had been preached on the Continent by German scholars and advocated in England by E. A. Freeman, J. R. Green, and others. Fustel de Coulanges in France initiated independently a crusade against the Germanistic interpretation of mediaeval history, maintaining, among other things, that there had never existed such a thing as the village community, and assigning a decisive influence in the history of Western European origins to Roman institutions. In Germany itself G. F. Knapp and A. Dopsch criticized the doctrines derived from the study of Tacitus and of the barbarian laws, and laid stress on the organizing rôle played by the great estate. In this way Seebohm's teaching came in, as it were, on the crest of a wave of critical and constructive study.

Seebohm did not entrench himself, however, behind the one-sided conception of the great estate. He addressed himself to another and equally important line of development. His eyes were open not only to the vestiges of common husbandry in the home counties of England, but also to the scattering of homesteads in Wales and other Celtic districts. He devoted considerable attention to the practice of co-aration and to the joint family in this region. In his *Tribal System in Wales* he presented an extensive study of the Welsh kindred, its ramifications, its pastoral and agricultural peculiarities. Here was clearly a case of tribal, not servile, community; and Seebohm traced it to the authority of the patriarch, as he had traced the manorial arrangement to the authority of the military lord. He exaggerated to some extent this patriarchal authority as against the collective influence of the kindred, and he did not succeed in explaining the process by which tribal arrangements were transformed into the manorial system. But the strong emphasis given by his investigations to the kindred of tribesmen supplies an effective counterblast to the shallow simplifications to which some of the followers of his *villa* doctrine have committed themselves. His *Tribal Custom in Anglo-Saxon Law* contains interesting studies leading in the same direction, but it is far from being on the same level with his preceding work. In the posthumous volume on *Customary Acres* (1914) there are valuable observations on the continuity of land measurements, but it is a collection of materials rather than a definite statement of the subject. Seebohm was still at work on it when he died at Hitchin, after a protracted illness, on 6 February 1912.

Seebohm's greatest merit as a researcher was his sense of concrete reality in describing and explaining the remote and obscure past. Working from the known to the unknown, he succeeded in making himself at home in the surroundings of old England or of Welsh tribal life, and he introduces his readers to a strange world of archaic ideas and practices. His lucid exposition made his work accessible to a large circle of readers; it achieved also signal recognition in the world of learning, and the universities of Edinburgh, Cambridge, and Oxford conferred on him honorary degrees. The books acquired in the course of his studies in economic history have been given by his family to the Maitland Library in Oxford.

[*The Times*, 7 February 1912; private information; personal knowledge.] P. V.

SELOUS, FREDERICK COURTENEY (1851–1917), hunter and explorer, was born in London 31 December 1851, the son of Frederick Lokes Selous, chairman of the Stock Exchange, by his wife, Ann Sherborn. He was sent to Bruce Castle School, Tottenham, and subsequently, in 1866, to Rugby, where he distinguished himself principally for his proficiency in games and his interest in wild bird life. His conduct and tastes as a schoolboy, his inborn spirit of adventure, and his love of natural history and sport determined his future career; and the presence of mind and resource which saved his life in a skating disaster in Regent's Park in 1867 stood him in good stead in many moments of danger in after-life.

On leaving Rugby in 1868 Selous went abroad to learn French and German before entering on a medical career. That career, however, had no attractions for him, and, deciding to take his chance, he went to South Africa in 1871, determined upon the open-air life of a sportsman. The next ten years of his life as a hunter and ivory-trader were years of strenuous effort, exciting adventures, privation, and anxiety for the future. In quest of game he traversed the interior of South Africa from east to west and penetrated as far north as Matabeleland, thus acquiring an intimate acquaintance with the natives, animals, and topography of the country.

During a short visit to England in 1881, Selous wrote his first book, *A Hunter's Wanderings in Africa*, which was instrumental in securing for him commissions from museums and dealers for trophies of big game; and since the ivory-trade was by that time practically dead in South Africa, he devoted the next few years to fulfilling those orders and acting as guide to hunting and prospecting parties. During this period his explorations resulted in some interesting discoveries, which were published in 1888 by the Royal Geographical Society. Other memoirs followed, and the Society aided him with grants, and in 1892 awarded him the Founder's gold medal. His activities during these years he subsequently described in *Travel and Adventure in South-East Africa* (1893).

In 1890 Selous embarked upon the most important undertaking of his career. In order to forestall the annexation of Mashonaland by the Portuguese he urged upon Cecil Rhodes [q.v.] the immediate occupation of that country by the British South Africa Company. Acting as intermediary between Rhodes and Lobengula, the Matabele chief, he secured from the latter a concession of the mineral rights of Matabeleland and Mashonaland; and he was appointed by Rhodes guide and chief of the pioneers who made the road to Mashonaland and secured the country for the British Crown. He left the service of the Company in 1892, but again joined it in 1893 when the Matabele War broke out. At its close he came to England, bought a house at Worplesdon, Surrey, and married. He was again in Matabeleland in 1895 and helped to subdue the second Matabele revolt. In *Sunshine and Storm in Rhodesia* (1896) he gave an account of this campaign. He subsequently devoted his time to writing, birds'-nesting and shooting at home, and to sporting trips abroad, more particularly to East Africa, whither he accompanied Theodore Roosevelt in 1909, and North America.

When the European War broke out in 1914 Selous immediately offered himself for active service; and persevering, despite repeated rejections on account of his age, was ultimately accepted for duty in (German) East Africa, and left England, with a commission in the 25th Royal Fusiliers, in the spring of 1915. He received his captaincy in the following August, and was awarded the D.S.O. in September 1916. He was killed in action at the head of his company, near Kissaki, 4 January 1917.

That Selous was endowed with indomitable courage, enduring energy, and great tenacity of purpose his achievements amply attest. But he was deliberate and painstaking rather than brilliant in his work. He was also a man of high and simple character which, coupled with engaging manners, gained the affection and respect of all who knew him. His extreme modesty was, perhaps, one of the most attractive qualities of his nature. Probably the only exploit of his career which he is known to have spoken of with pride was the part which he played in planting the British flag in Rhodesia. He repeatedly repudiated the false praise of his friends in styling him the greatest hunter of all time; and he would have been the first to protest against the mistaken estimate of his contributions to science which led to the placing of his memorial tablet and bust (see *Royal Academy Pictures,* 1919) alongside the statue of Darwin and the portrait of Alfred Russel Wallace in the British Museum at South Kensington.

Selous married in 1894 Marie Catherine Gladys, daughter of Canon Henry William Maddy, vicar of Down Hatherley, Gloucestershire, by whom he had two sons. After his death a scholarship was founded in his name at Rugby, and his collection of trophies, including heads and skins of big game, was bequeathed to the trustees of the British Museum (Natural History).

[J. G. Millais, *Life of Frederick Courteney Selous,* 1918 ; personal knowledge.]

R. I. P.

SEMON, Sir FELIX (1849–1921), laryngologist, was born at Danzig 8 December 1849, the elder son of Simon Joseph Semon, stockbroker, of Berlin, by his wife, Henrietta Aschenheim. He began his medical studies at Heidelberg, but they were interrupted by the Franco-German War (1870–1871), in which he served as a volunteer in the 2nd Uhlans of the Prussian Guard and was awarded the war medal with five clasps. After the War he returned to Berlin and took the M.D. degree in 1873 and the *staatsexamen* in the following year. He then studied in Vienna and Paris, and came to London in 1874. In 1875 he was clinical assistant at the Hospital for Diseases of the Throat, Golden Square, and in 1877 was elected to the honorary staff of the hospital. From 1882 to 1897 he was physician in charge of the throat department at St. Thomas's Hospital. The department was soon crowded by students and practitioners who were attracted by Semon's growing reputation for ability and diagnostic skill. In 1888 he was appointed laryngologist to the National Hospital for the Paralysed and Epileptic; and here he carried out, in association with Sir Victor Horsley [q.v.], experimental and clinical researches on the central motor innervation of the larynx. As a result of these investigations he demonstrated 'that in all progressive organic lesions of the centres and trunks of the motor laryngeal nerves, the abductors of the vocal cords succumb much earlier than the adductors'. This is known as Semon's law.

In 1876 Semon was admitted a member, and in 1885 elected fellow, of the Royal College of Physicians. In 1881 he was one of the secretaries of the sub-section of laryngology at the International Medical Congress in London, and managed the work of the section with remarkable efficiency. In 1893 he helped to found the Laryngological Society of London, of which he served as president for three years (1894–1896). He was twice president of the section of laryngology at meetings of the British Medical Association. In 1884 he founded the *Internationales Centralblatt für Laryngologie und Rhinologie,* and for twenty-five years was its editor. In 1912 he published *Forschungen und Erfahrungen, 1880–1910,* a collection, in two volumes, of his numerous contributions to medical literature. As a writer he was accurate and painstaking.

Semon rendered great service to the surgery of the larynx by his skill in the early diagnosis of cancer of this organ, and following on the lines laid down by Sir Henry Trentham Butlin [q.v.] he attained great success in removal of the growth by laryngo-fissure. Another valuable piece of work was his recognition of the identity of cachexia strumipriva with myxoedema. This paved the way for all subsequent work on myxoedema and led to the thyroid treatment of this disease.

Many distinctions were bestowed upon Semon. At Queen Victoria's diamond jubilee (1897) he was knighted, and in 1901 he was appointed physician extraordinary to King Edward VII. In that year (1901) he became naturalized as a British subject. In 1902 he received the C.V.O. and in 1905 he was promoted K.C.V.O. In 1888 the order of the Red Eagle was awarded him by Kaiser Wilhelm II, who in 1894 conferred on him the title of royal Prussian professor.

Semon was a man with many artistic and social gifts, who excelled in whatever he took up. He was a fine pianist and composer, and at the end of the Franco-German War his regiment entered Berlin to the strains of a march which he had composed when encamped outside Paris in the winter of 1870–1871. He was a brilliant conversationalist and raconteur, and also a keen sportsman devoted to hunting, shooting, and fishing. He was a most loyal and affectionate friend, and though his temper was easily aroused, it was quickly appeased.

In 1911, at the zenith of his professional career, Semon retired. In recognition of his services to medicine he was entertained at a banquet presided over by Sir Henry Butlin, at which a large and distinguished gathering was present. The sum of £1,040 was subscribed as a testimonial of esteem and appreciation, and at Semon's request the money was presented to the university of London to establish a Semon lectureship in laryngology. After a year's voyage round the world Semon retired to the house which he had built on the Chilterns above Great Missenden. He died there 1 March 1921.

Semon married in 1879 Augusta Dorothea, daughter of Heinrich Redeker, wholesale furniture dealer, of Cloppenburg, Oldenburg, and had three sons.

[*Lancet*, 1921, vol. i, p. 561; *British Medical Journal*, 1921, vol. i, p. 404; personal knowledge. See also *The Autobiography of Sir Felix Semon*, edited by H. C. Semon and T. A. McIntyre, 1926.] F. de H. H.

SHADWELL, CHARLES LANCELOT (1840–1919), college archivist and translator of Dante, the eldest surviving son of Lancelot Shadwell [q.v.], barrister-at-law, and grandson of Sir Lancelot Shadwell [q.v.], the last vice-chancellor of England, was born in London 16 December 1840. Educated at Westminster School and Christ Church, Oxford, where he became a junior student in 1859, he was a fellow of Oriel College from 1864 to 1898, and lecturer in jurisprudence there from 1865 to 1875. In 1898 he was elected an honorary fellow. From 1874 to 1887, as treasurer of the college, he managed with care and ability the property of the institution, for which he felt an ardent affection that amounted almost to religious fervour. Of its past history, traditions, and muniments he was an indefatigable and competent explorer. The results were shown in the *Registrum Orielense, 1500–1900*, 2 vols. (1893, 1902), in a chapter of A. Clark's *Colleges of Oxford* (1891), and in privately printed papers. It was characteristic of Shadwell that in the *Colleges of Oxford* he should dwell at length on the remote original foundation, forgotten benefactors, recondite incidents, and unknown earlier developments of the college, and dismiss in two brief sentences the work of Thomas Arnold and John Henry Newman, and ignore all that has happened since the Oxford Movement. Elected provost of Oriel in 1905, he brought to this office, held for nine years, the same intense loyalty, with a stately presence which stirred awe rather than invited closer advance. Yet, once captured, he was a firm and hearty friend, never failing to display for those whom he liked an appreciation that ignored popular prejudice and palliated individual blemish. He enjoyed dispensing a magnificent hospitality, and was also a generous benefactor of the college. Resigning the provostship in 1914 owing to ill-health, he died at Oxford 13 February 1919. He was never married.

In the affairs both of the university and of the city of Oxford Shadwell took a large share; a comprehensive grip of minute detail, a fond adherence to immemorial tradition and official form, and a high sense of fit conduct and public duty were inseparable features of his useful service in this connexion. To the study of chess problems and chronograms, his chief recreation, he joined a literary interest and aptitude that made him pursue assiduously an 'experiment in literal verse translation' of Dante's *Purgatorio* (in a metre favoured by Marvell) which was described by Walter Pater as 'full of the patience of genius'. This bent also gave him the privilege of being, in Mr. Arthur Benson's words, the 'closest friend' and 'lifelong companion' of Pater himself. They visited Italy together, and Pater's early studies on the Renaissance were dedicated to Shadwell, who, as his literary executor, fulfilled the duty, Mr. Benson says, 'with a rare loyalty and discretion'. In one of the later books thus issued, it should be added, Shadwell's own 'temperament' was finely delineated as that of an 'intellectual guilelessness or integrity that instinctively prefers what is direct and clear' and 'seeks to value everything at its eternal worth'.

There is a portrait of Shadwell by Fiddes Watt at Oriel College.

[A. C. Benson, *Walter Pater*, 1906; obituary notices; private information; personal knowledge.] L. L. P.

SHAW, JOHN BYAM LISTER (1872–1919), painter and illustrator, was born at Madras 13 November 1872, the son of John Shaw, registrar of the high court of Madras, by his wife, Sophia Alicia Byam Gunthorpe. He came to England in 1878 and to London in 1879. He was educated privately, and, after having first studied at the St. John's Wood school of art, he entered the Royal Academy Schools in 1889. In 1893 he exhibited at the Royal Academy for the first time, when his picture 'Rose Mary', an illustration to D. G. Rossetti's poem, was shown. Among his more notable subsequent exhibits are 'Whither?' (1896), 'Love's Baubles', and 'The Comforter' (1897), and 'Love, the Conqueror' (1899). For the Canadian War Records Shaw painted a large allegorical picture, 'The Flag', which was shown at the Canadian War Memorials exhibition at Burlington House in 1919. Shaw also illustrated a great number of books, among them being Browning's *Poems* (1898), *Tales from Boccaccio* (1899), *The Chiswick Shakespeare* (1900), *The Pilgrim's Progress* (1904), and Poe's *Tales of Mystery and Imagination* (1909). As an art teacher Shaw was active at the school of art on Campden Hill which he established, in partnership with Rex Vicat Cole, in 1911. He was elected an associate of the Royal Society of Painters in Water Colours in 1913.

Byam Shaw has been called 'a kind of belated pre-Raphaelite'. This description refers, however, mainly to the external trappings of his art, which, while showing the resourceful illustrator's inventiveness and considerable sleight of hand, is yet essentially of a somewhat superficial and scenic character.

Shaw married in 1899 Evelyn, daughter of J. N. Pyke-Nott, of Bydown, North Devon, by whom he had four sons and one daughter. He died in London 26 January 1919.

[A. Graves, *The Royal Academy of Arts, Dictionary of Contributors*, vol. vii, 1905–1906.] T. B.

SHAW, RICHARD NORMAN (1831–1912), architect, was born in Edinburgh 7 May 1831, the youngest son of William Shaw, by his wife, Elizabeth Brown. His mother was Scotch; the father, who died before he was two years old, came from county Meath, of Protestant Irish stock with a Huguenot strain. The boy went to school at the Hill Street Academy, Edinburgh, and afterwards for a year at Newcastle; but his education was chiefly imparted by his elder sister. At fifteen years old, when he went with the family to London, his bent for architecture was recognized. He was apprenticed to a small architect; and shortly after passed into the office of William Burn [q.v.] in Piccadilly. He was there for seven years, at a time when Burn, in the full tide of practice, was designing 'mansions' for territorial magnates in all parts of Great Britain and Ireland. Norman Shaw in this pupilage was well schooled in the art of planning country-houses, and acquired that clean, clear draughtsmanship, by which he won the silver medal of the Royal Academy in 1852, and the gold medal for design in 1853. Next year he was given the travelling studentship of the Academy, and during his year and a half of travel visited Rome, Prague, and Lübeck, as well as the French cathedrals.

At that time, thanks to the enthusiasm of George Edmund Street [q.v.] and William Burges [q.v.], the Gothic of the thirteenth century in France had become the gospel of English art. Viollet le Duc's *Dictionnaire de l'Architecture* had just been published, and for Shaw remained the classic of Gothic construction; William Butterfield [q.v.] never ceased to be his ideal of the church architect. Indeed, like Burges, Shaw proved his faith by designing furniture after French mediaeval models. The immediate fruit, however, of his travelling year was the publication in 1858 of *Architectural Sketches from the Continent*—lithograph illustrations drawn by himself from his sketches of French churches. In 1859 he entered the office of G. E. Street, succeeding Philip Webb [q.v.] as chief assistant. Yet this strict school of mediaeval ritual equipped neither Webb nor Shaw as orthodox stylists. What both gained was the conscience of the building artist—the personal sense of aesthetic creation which was to be as clear in Shaw's 'Gothic' churches as in his so-called 'free classic'.

In 1862 Shaw started practice in Argyll Street, Regent Street, with William Eden Nesfield [q.v.], who had been a fellow-student in Burn's office, and for a time his companion in France. Formal partnership did not last, but the two occupied the same office till 1876, and these fourteen years brought Shaw to the front of his profession. In 1868 he designed James Knight's bank at Farnham; and other early clients were the shipowners, Shaw, Savill & Co., his brother's company, for whom in 1871 he designed New Zealand Chambers in Leadenhall Street; the street elevation of this, with its projecting bays and Jacobean glazings, was an evident protest against humdrum city classicalities; still more was it a challenge to the mediaeval stylists. About the same time John Callcott Horsley, R.A. [q.v.], began to give Shaw work, and soon he had many commissions from members of the Royal Academy. Elected an associate in 1872, he became full academician in 1877. For a short time he had been a member of the Royal Institute of British Architects, but he never became a fellow. His attitude towards the Institute is explained in *Architecture, a Profession or an Art?* (1891), of which he was joint-editor with (Sir) T. G. Jackson.

Building for artists, Shaw was in the swim of that golden age of the Victorian painter, when, after a year or two of Academy recognition, the artist got a competency and built himself a palace-studio in the developing suburbs of Kensington or South Hampstead. In this 'artist' building Shaw was the protagonist of an architectural evolution. The red-brick walls and tiled roofs, the white sash-barred windows, the ingle-nooks and bay-recesses of studio-houses, gave a new sense of building to dwellers in square, blank-windowed rooms and monotonous, drab streets. The style was called 'Queen Anne'; but in Shaw's work it was not a revival of the eighteenth century so much as a recovery of the building art. There has followed the bathos of commercial exploitation; but the suburban inanities are not to be laid at the door of the pioneer architects, Philip Webb, John James Stevenson [q.v.], Nesfield, or Shaw. Lowther Lodge, for example, built by Shaw in 1874 (now the home of the Royal Geographical Society) is the English *maison*—the town-house, standing in its own grounds, and having style in the practical sense of its needs. Shaw's country-houses possessed the essential merit of being built to requirement and site—whether in the gable and chimney 'picturesque' of half-timber and turret, as at Leys Wood, Sussex (1868), Preen Manor, Shropshire (1871), and Cragside, Northumberland (1872); or in the broader stone-work and squarer blocking of Adcote, Shropshire (1876–1881), and Dawpool, Cheshire (1883). In these country-houses the 'hall' became the great room as distinctly as Shaw had given that office to the 'studio' for his artist clients.

In 1867 Shaw married Agnes Haswell Wood, and in 1876 with their family of three children they moved from St. John's Wood to Ellerdale Road, Hampstead. At the same time he took new offices at 29 Bloomsbury Square, a house now pulled down. His health, which gave way in 1877, much improved in 1881, after a visit to Aix-les-Bains. The next fifteen years were those of his second architectural manner, preluded indeed by a house built for himself at Hampstead (1876), and others in Queen's Gate, Kensington. The town-houses of his design on the Chelsea embankment and in Kensington, and the offices built for the Alliance Assurance Company at the corner of St. James's Street, have a composed dignity of façade along with the space and ease of interior convenience. Two good examples are the houses which he built in Hampstead for the portrait-painter, Edwin Longsden Long [q.v.]. For city architecture, however, his masterpiece of this period is New Scotland Yard; its tiers of official rooms and its official material of 'convict' granite are combined with masterly planning and monumental effect; but it is the only public building for which Shaw's genius was utilised. No commission came to him from the universities; his church-buildings, e.g. at Bournemouth, belong chiefly to the early years of his practice; and, though the Harrow Mission church in Latimer Road, Notting Hill, and All Saints', Leek, are of the later period, no cathedral building was put in his hands. The opportunity for big architecture came, however, in commissions for two great country houses, Chesters, Northumberland, and Bryanston, Dorset. The palatial expression of nobleness, as we recognize this in the Italian villa or the French château, has nowhere in this last hundred years been given such distinction as at Bryanston, built from 1890 to 1894 for Viscount Portman. Unfortunately, the lay-out of the domain was taken out of the architect's hands, and so the conception remains an incomplete one.

In the last years of the nineteenth century, Norman Shaw, owing to renewed ill-health, was relinquishing active practice. He gave up his office, and in 1909 he retired from the Royal Academy. But public authorities often consulted him about their building problems, and to his advice we owe some attempts to give our English capital city a dignity worthy of its imperial position. But, as with Wren so with Shaw, the projects for straightening out the haphazard muddle of London were mostly blocked. Before his scheme for Regent Street could be extricated from the slough of mixed opinions and vested interests he died at Hampstead, 17 November 1912.

Critics have blamed Norman Shaw for his carelessness of the constructive proprieties in which he, as a Gothic architect, had been strictly bred. In his breakaway into 'Queen Anne' he was found rearing solid house-fronts on steel skeletons, and plastering brickwork with half-timber veneers and barge-board frillings—stylistic scenery which has been vulgarized *ad nauseam* at the hands of imitators. But all Victorian architecture must needs come under the same censure—it has been a profession of pedantry paid for by fee. The architect of the 'seventies or 'eighties could not be an artist, like the painter or the sculptor, with work executed and acclaimed as his. Only by partnership with a client was a Victorian architect able to get to work at all; his genius was conditioned by the necessity of gaining and keeping a practice. It was in this that Norman Shaw stood out among his fellows. His was a magnetic personality and its influence worked on all with whom he came in contact. Alone among Victorian architects he may be credited with founding a school which is by no means limited to his pupils and immediate contemporaries. He was a great architect in virtue of a great ability, by address and mastery of mind. Yet in the eyes of those brother architects it was not the success but the sincerity of his art that made the salt of his genius; in the words of Sir R. T. Blomfield: 'Norman Shaw was an artist absolute and ingrained. His whole power was concentrated on the art that he loved and to which he dedicated his life; and from the ideal he never swerved.'

[Private information; personal knowledge.]

E. S. P.

SHERBORN, CHARLES WILLIAM (1831–1912), engraver, born 14 June 1831 at 43 Leicester Square, London, was the eldest son of Charles Sherborn, upholsterer, by his wife, Mary, daughter of Richard Bance, of Newbury. He was educated first at a local school and then at Cave House, Uxbridge, under a Mr. Wilkinson. In 1845 he left school and began attending the government school of drawing and design at Somerset House, being at the same time apprenticed to Robert Oliver, a silver-plate engraver in Rupert Street, Soho. In October 1852, having served his apprenticeship, he went abroad, staying in Paris some ten months and afterwards travelling in Italy. In September 1853 he settled in Geneva, where he remained three years, working as a goldsmith's designer and engraver. He returned to London in September 1856 and began engraving for the London jewellers, first in his father's house, and then in Jermyn Street, in a partnership which proved unsuccessful and was dissolved in 1860; but the same year he began again in Warwick Street, Regent Street.

Sherborn was a man to whom time and money meant little in comparison with perfecting himself at his craft, and he was not likely to succeed in a branch of the engraver's profession which afforded little scope for his skill. In 1872, in view of financial difficulties, he abandoned business and decided to work independently as an etcher and engraver. His early training had been limited, and it was chiefly with reproduction-work after contemporary portrait and subject painters, and later on with book-plates, that he gained a livelihood. Original work he had always done for his own pleasure, and his etchings of London architecture and riverside deserve praise for their sincerity. It is in fact a quality of sincerity which lifts his work above the level of painstaking endeavour, and entitles him to a place among British engravers. His finest achievement is a series of over 350 book-plates which he designed and engraved chiefly between 1881 and 1912. They are mostly of the armorial type, but some are pictorial and a few are portraits. His mastery of fine engraving technique was unrivalled among the working engravers of his time, and came into its own in reproducing these formal and intricate designs. He was a regular exhibitor at the Royal Academy and was elected a foundation member of the Society of Painter-Etchers in 1884.

Sherborn died at 1 Finborough Road, South Kensington, 10 February 1912. He married in 1860 Hannah Simpson (died 1922), daughter of Thomas Davies, watchmaker, and widow of Thomas Wait, draper, of Liverpool, and by her had four sons and a daughter.

Sherborn and his family presented a complete set of his book-plates, engravings, and etchings to the British Museum, and representative selections of the book-plates to the national collections in France, Germany, and the United States.

[Charles Davies Sherborn (son), *The Life and Work of Charles William Sherborn*, 1912, with three portraits, bibliography, catalogue of paintings, engravings, &c., and list of book-plates (by G. H. Viner); a typewritten catalogue, made by G. H. Viner, describing the unfinished states of the book-plates, is in the British Museum Print Room.]

H. M. H.

SKEAT, WALTER WILLIAM (1835–1912), philologist, the second son of William Skeat, architect, by his wife, Sarah Bluck, was born in London 21 November 1835. He attended King's College School, where Thomas Oswald Cockayne [q.v.], one of the best Anglo-Saxon scholars of the time, was his form-master; passed thence to Highgate School; and entered Christ's College, Cambridge, in 1854. At Cambridge, C. S. Calverley, J. R. Seeley, and Walter Besant were among his friends. He studied theology and mathematics, took the mathematical tripos (fourteenth wrangler) in 1858, and was elected a fellow of his college in 1860. In the latter year he took orders, and entered on his first curacy at East Dereham, Norfolk. In the next year he became curate of Godalming, but a serious illness affecting his throat closed his career in the Church. He returned to Cambridge and was appointed to a mathematical lectureship at Christ's College in 1864. The duties left him ample leisure, and he now began the serious study of Early English, with such results that in 1878 his election to the new Elrington and Bosworth professorship of Anglo-Saxon at Cambridge was assured. Teaching, untiring research, and writing occupied the rest of an evenly happy and full life. He died at Cambridge 6 October 1912. He had married in 1860 Bertha, eldest daughter of Francis Jones, of Lewisham ; his wife, two sons, and three daughters survived him.

Skeat's interest in Early English authors was first roused by the extracts in the history book which he used at school, and he worked back to them through the *Faerie Queen*. But it was Frederick James Furnivall [q.v.] who first set him to work as an editor. The discussion of plans for the *New English Dictionary* had revealed a dearth of trustworthy early texts, and to supply the want Furnivall and Richard Morris [q.v.] formed the Early English Text Society in 1864. Skeat was pressed into the service, and punctually edited *Lancelot of the Laik* (1865). In 1866 he began his great edition of *Piers Plowman*, which was finished twenty years later. The first part of his edition of John Barbour's *The Bruce* appeared in 1870 ; and by 1872 he had published the *Treatise on the Astrolabe*, one of many studies preliminary to his seven-volume edition of Chaucer (1894–1897). This might seem a life's work, but it is only a part of Skeat's contribution to the study of one century—the fourteenth. He produced two standard works in Anglo-Saxon, the *Anglo-Saxon Gospels* (1871–1887) and Ælfric's *Lives of Saints* (1881–1900) ; and in 1873 he founded the English Dialect Society, which prepared the way for the *English Dialect Dictionary* (edited by Joseph Wright, 1896–1905). Another important book, his *Etymological Dictionary* (1879–1882, revised and enlarged, 1910), was begun with the purpose of collecting and sifting material for the use of the *New English Dictionary*. Besides these larger works, none of which has yet been superseded, he found time to edit Chatterton (1871), to write many text-books for schools and universities, to popularize philology and modernize old authors, and to contribute freely to the learned societies and journals concerned with English studies. Furthermore, in his latter years he led the way in the systematic study of place-names, county by county. All this vast output is distinguished by accuracy in matter of fact, wide learning, and humanity ; and most of it Skeat produced without prospect of reward, out of devotion to his subject.

Skeat's own prescription for such monuments of scholarship was enthusiasm, with unremitting application, and he wasted no time. He would take part in a fireside conversation, all the while sorting glossary slips as tranquilly as a woman does her knitting. Besides, he could set practical limits to his curiosity ; in the preface to the first edition of the *Etymological Dictionary* he explains that he usually gave three hours to a difficult word : 'During that time I made the best I could of it and then let it go.' This requires self-sacrifice in a scholar, but it is the secret of Skeat's great service. The new school of philology which arose towards 1880, when the lines of Skeat's work were laid down and much of it done, produced men like Zupitza and Sievers in Germany, or Henry Sweet [q.v.], A. S. Napier, and Henry Bradley in England, who went beyond Skeat in linguistic theory and in exact methods. But Skeat's pioneer work made such advances possible. At a critical moment in English studies he saw the wisdom of Furnivall's doctrine, that the essential thing was to attract workers, and to make available for them quickly a great quantity of materials, edited as well as possible, but always with a time-limit in view rather than perfection in minutiae. And perhaps he gained as much ground for his subject by quiet sapping as Furnivall took by storm.

[Autobiography in *A Student's Pastime*, 1896 (with list of publications) ; notices in *Englische Studien*, December 1912, and elsewhere ; private information.] K. S.

SMITH, DONALD ALEXANDER, first BARON STRATHCONA and MOUNT ROYAL (1820–1914), Canadian financier, the second son of Alexander Smith, a tradesman, of Archieston, by his wife, Barbara, daughter of Donald Stuart, of Leanchoil, was born at Forres, Morayshire, 6 August 1820. In 1838 his maternal uncle, a fur-trader named John Stuart, got him a clerkship in the Hudson Bay Company. He was first employed at Lachine, in 1841 was sent to Tadoussac, and in 1847 to Labrador, where he remained for the next thirteen years. In 1853 he took as wife Isabella, the daughter of a company trader, Richard Hardisty. He rose steadily in the Company's service and on his own account began operations as a financier ; his colleagues trusted him with their salaries, he paid them interest and invested in his own name, mainly in shares of the Bank of Montreal. He became a 'chief trader', and in 1862 a 'chief factor'. A few years later his interest in the Hudson's Bay Company was much enlarged, and politics and railway building made heavy demands upon his energy.

The Hudson's Bay Company was a profit-sharing enterprise, for by the deed poll of 1821 two-fifths of its profits, divided into eighty-five shares, went to officials, a chief trader holding one of these and a chief factor two. Such officials were known as 'wintering partners'. In 1862 the capital of the company was quadrupled, and the wintering partners' interests became threatened. For some years the Canadian government had held that the company's charter did not cover all the territorial rights it claimed, and negotiations for the surrender of the trade and land monopoly were in progress.

In 1868 Smith, who had held something like a roving commission for a few years, became head of the company's Montreal department; this led the government to treat him erroneously as Canadian head of the company, and soon brought him into politics. In March 1868 a bargain was struck between the Canadian government and the company; for £300,000 and large land grants the territorial claims were bought out together with the trade monopoly. Smith, seeing that the wintering partners would suffer, began to buy the company's shares, gradually became its chief shareholder, and within three years was able with his associates to control its policy. The wintering partners, apparently unaware that he was a shareholder, asked him to represent their interests in London; in 1871 an agreement was reached there by which the traders got no share in the company's lands, and had their rights to a share of profits capitalized at a low figure. It has been claimed that Smith did everything possible for his old colleagues, but the terms of settlement make this questionable. His associations henceforth were with the shareholders, not with the local traders. He became chief commissioner of the company, in 1883 a director, and in 1889 its governor.

His entry into politics was dramatic. French half-breeds formed fully half of the scattered population in the west, just acquired by Canada. They took alarm at the arrival in 1869 of Canadian surveyors, fearing the loss of lands held only on a squatter's title. There was a tangle of intrigue, one group wanting to anglicize the west, one desiring annexation to the United States, a third working for an independent republic. The government was negligent, and unrest grew into the revolt headed by Louis Riel [q.v.]. Sir John Macdonald assumed without foundation that Smith, as the chief officer of the Hudson's Bay Company available, knew the west intimately, and sent him to negotiate. Smith reached Fort Garry (Winnipeg) in December 1869, was kept a prisoner by Riel for over two months, and could achieve little. In 1870 the rising was crushed, and Manitoba organized. Smith was elected in 1871 by Selkirk as conservative member of the federal parliament. In 1873 he took a prominent share in overthrowing Macdonald's government on the Canadian Pacific scandal; he had been counted on for support and his defection made defeat certain. The conservatives thought him a traitor and attacked him bitterly; in 1878 Macdonald interjected in the Commons 'that fellow Smith is the biggest liar I ever met'. Smith, though a conservative, invariably tended to support every ministry in power. This, and his breach with Macdonald, kept him out of the conservative party until it took up a protective tariff. In 1879 he was unseated on an election petition, and in 1880 defeated. He re-entered parliament in 1887 for a Montreal constituency. In 1896, when the conservative party was tumbling into ruin, he was suggested as its possible leader, but he was too old and had too wide business interests to desire a position so difficult.

Railways received most of Smith's attention between 1873 and 1886. His visit to the west in 1869 led him to plan lines in Manitoba. Soon after came his big opportunity. An American railway, later the Great Northern, which held valuable land grants conditional on its completion, had twice gone bankrupt; it was the property of Netherlands bondholders, who had advanced $20,000,000 but wished to cut their losses. Two Canadians, J. J. Hill and N. W. Kittson, who lived in St. Paul, saw their chance; they approached Smith, his cousin George Stephen (afterwards Baron Mount Stephen, q.v.), who in 1876 was president of the Bank of Montreal, and R. B. Angus, that bank's general manager. The group bought out the bondholders for a sum roughly equal to interest due on the bonds, and finished the line largely with money borrowed from the bank which they controlled. The railway prospered, and its owners voted themselves its common stock and a large bond issue; by 1906 they had collectively received, besides interest on their investment, about $300,000,000 in securities. From this success they, with others, turned to the Canadian Pacific. The liberal party's policy of national construction was abandoned when Macdonald came into power in 1878; in 1880 the Canadian Pacific Railway Company was organized under Stephen, and Smith, who owing to his quarrel with the conservatives did not figure openly at the beginning, soon became a director. The transcontinental line was pushed through despite great difficulties, Smith and his colleagues staking all their resources to get it completed. In November 1885 Smith drove the last spike. This made many regard him as the railway's chief builder; but, though one of the group, he was never its leader, and Stephen's was the directing brain.

In 1886 Smith was knighted, in 1897 created Baron Strathcona. In 1896 he became high commissioner for Canada; henceforward he made his home in Great Britain, and became something of an imperial figure. His great wealth allowed him to entertain more liberally than any previous occupant of the office. He gave freely to hospitals and education in Scotland, Canada, and the United States, in the last thirty years of his life distributing more than £1,300,000. He raised at his own expense a regiment of rough-riders for service in the South African War. But, though more prominent than he had been before, Strathcona had little direct influence on Canadian development during this last period of his life. He was not in sympathy or close touch with the younger liberal leaders who were in power at Ottawa after 1896, and the chief Canadian government activity in London, immigration, was not under his control. His splendid physique enabled him to remain in office long after the usual age for retirement. Till the end he attended personally to many details, and ran his office on rather autocratic lines. He showed a tendency to resent the success of other men's ideas, and largely for this reason opposed Earl Grey's plan of a central house for the offices of all the Dominions. He clung to his position when the Canadian government would not have regretted his resignation. In November 1913 Lady Strathcona died, and after a short illness his own death followed in London on 21 January 1914, at the age of ninety-three. In 1900 his patent had been modified so as to make the barony transmissible through the female line; this was done because his only child was a daughter, and in recognition of his raising of 'Strathcona's Horse'. He was succeeded in the barony by his daughter, Margaret Charlotte, who married in 1888 Robert Jared Bliss Howard, F.R.C.S. She died in 1926, and the elder son of this marriage is the present holder of the title.

Lord Strathcona has been regarded as a great statesman and financier, of the same calibre as Cecil Rhodes, and also as the man chiefly responsible for the increased corruption of Canadian public life in the 'eighties: both estimates are excessive. The immense power of finance, and particularly of the Canadian Pacific Company, was not a beneficent force in Canadian politics; but Strathcona's personal responsibility for its exercise is unproven. That he had any far-reaching political views or any deep purpose is equally doubtful. He was led from fur-trading to politics and railway building by forces which he did not create and could hardly guide. The expansion of Canada westwards, following swiftly on federation, altered the tone of Canadian politics and the scale of Canadian business. Until he was approaching fifty years of age, Strathcona's activities had hardly reached beyond Labrador and the lower waters of the St. Lawrence; and save that he acquired manufacturing interests in Montreal he showed no realization of what was coming. A mistake of the Canadian government turned his attention to the west, and with his customary shrewdness he saw its importance. Through his whole life he was a strenuous worker, an able judge of men, apt to seize opportunity. Financially generous, he was also a good hater, but never let animosity interfere with business. Had he chosen a political career it is doubtful whether he would have succeeded in it, for he lacked the three qualities—eloquence, personal charm, and strength of conviction—one at least of which is needed in a national leader. Rhodes went into finance to achieve a political end, Strathcona into politics largely for the sake of business.

A portrait of Lord Strathcona by W. W. Ouless, painted in 1890, is in the possession of the family.

[Beckles Willson, *Life of Lord Strathcona and Mount Royal*, 1915; W. T. R. Preston, *Strathcona and the Making of Canada*, 1915; O. D. Skelton, *The Railway Builders*, 1916; J. Pope, *Memoirs of Sir John Macdonald*, 1894; Canadian House of Commons Debates.]

E. M. W-G.

SMITH, REGINALD JOHN (1857–1916), barrister and publisher, was born at Brighton 30 May 1857, the second son of John Smith, of Britwell House, Oxfordshire, by his wife, Emily Jane, daughter of George Frederick Cherry, of Denford, Berkshire. A colleger of Eton and scholar of King's College, Cambridge, he took a first class in the classical tripos (1880) and a degree in law; he was then called to the bar from the Inner Temple. In addition to some casual journalism, from 1886 to 1894 he 'devilled' for Sir Charles Russell (afterwards Baron Russell of Killowen, q.v.) and, amongst other cases, acted as his junior in the defence of Mrs. Maybrick (1889). In this, as in all his legal work, he was distinguished for his painstaking care, lucid arrangement of material, and invincible courtesy.

In 1893 Smith married Isabel, youngest daughter of George Smith [see the memoir now prefixed to the first volume of this DICTIONARY], whose publishing firm of Smith, Elder, & Co., he joined in 1894. On leaving the bar he was granted the farewell distinction of silk. In 1899, the other partners having retired, he assumed sole control of the firm, and in 1901 took as his literary adviser Mr. Leonard Huxley. Smith had already in 1898 succeeded Mr. St. Loe Strachey as editor of the *Cornhill Magazine*. In 1904–1905 and again in 1916 he was president of the Publishers' Association, in 1905 strongly opposing the Times Book Club's threat to the book trade in selling off new books at second-hand prices. From the first Reginald Smith was in close sympathy with his father-in-law. Without equalling the older man's speculative dash, he shared his ideal of the publisher—in literature a trustee of the public, in business the actual partner and trustee of the author. Aiming at quality rather than quantity in his business, he rendered 'the other man' not only justice, but countless services not in the bond. The possession of independent means enabled both men to show more concern for good literature than for mere profit-making.

Smith's salient characteristic was consideration for the sensitive race of authors. Remembering Smith Williams's letter to Charlotte Brontë, he regularly sent, in his own or his lieutenant's hand, a letter of kindly criticism with each rejected manuscript. He delighted in telling young authors the private praises given by established writers. It was part of his genius that almost invariably the business client became the personal friend, and though he rarely wrote for the press, his friends recognized the soundness of his literary judgements. He continued his father-in-law's friendships with the families of Thackeray, Browning, and Mrs. Gaskell, and with Mrs. Humphry Ward; among his many newer friends special mention may be made of Dr. A. C. Benson and the Rev. W. H. Fitchett, both of whom he introduced to their English audiences, and of the Antarctic explorers, Robert Falcon Scott [q.v.] and Edward Adrian Wilson [q.v.]. No fewer than six such friends dedicated books to him, 'whom to have known', wrote Sir E. T. Cook, 'was, in itself, a liberal education in human kindliness, in thoughtful courtesy, and in love of letters'.

As editor of the *Cornhill*, Reginald Smith resolutely maintained its literary quality, undismayed by the competition of the illustrated sixpennies which had crushed other magazines, and setting literary prestige against financial loss. His warmest publishing interest attached to the centenary editions of Thackeray and Browning, the Brontë and Gaskell definitive editions, the Antarctic books of Captain Scott, the disposal of the Brontë relics (among which he secured Branwell Brontë's portraits of his sisters for the National Portrait Gallery), and the thin paper edition of the DICTIONARY OF NATIONAL BIOGRAPHY (1908). This he initiated in consultation with Mrs. George (M.) Smith, and carried it through with untiring attention to the complex details. All corrections, including those published in the volume of *errata* (1904), were incorporated in the text under the editorship of Sir Sidney Lee; the original sixty-six volumes were reduced to twenty-two, each three being fused into one and the pages renumbered. Ultimately, in 1917, Mrs. Smith's representatives gave the DICTIONARY to the university of Oxford, to be continued by the Clarendon Press.

Elsewhere the name of the 'Reginald Smith ward' commemorates his long connexion with the Poplar Hospital, as a member of the committee from 1910 onwards, and treasurer in 1915–1916. During the European War his unsparing exertions broke down his health, and death came suddenly on 26 December 1916, at his home in Green Street, Park Lane. He left no children. In appearance Reginald Smith was dark and very tall; in face and figure almost austerely spare; and a certain formality of address made him somewhat formidable to strangers upon first acquaintance. A bronze statuette by Lady Scott (Mrs. Hilton Young), in the possession of Mrs. Reginald Smith, shows him sitting in a characteristic attitude.

[Leonard Huxley, *The House of Smith, Elder*, privately printed, 1923; private information; personal knowledge.] L. H.

SMITH, VINCENT ARTHUR (1848–1920), Indian historian and antiquary, was born in Dublin 3 June 1848, the fifth of the thirteen children of the Irish antiquary, Aquilla Smith [q.v.]. His mother's maiden name was Esther Faucett, and his parents were first cousins. After a distinguished career at Trinity College, Dublin, he entered the Indian civil service in 1871, and was posted to the North-West Provinces and Oudh, as they were then styled. He retired in 1900, having held an exceptionally wide variety of appointments within the Provinces, culminating in the chief secretaryship and the commissionership of a division.

Smith inherited his father's tastes, and his work as a settlement officer early directed his attention to the antiquities in which the Ganges valley is exceptionally rich; among his earliest published works were articles on the coinage of the Gupta dynasty (1889, 1893) and on Graeco-Roman influence on the civilization of ancient India (1889). An original investigator of no mean merit, his studies gradually led him to see the need for coordinating the detailed results obtained by various independent scholars; and to this object he devoted himself, retiring from the service while it was still open to him to serve for several years. His best work, the *Early History of India*, was published in 1904; embodying the main results of the work on India done during the previous century, not only by the Royal Asiatic Society but also by a host of continental scholars, it immediately became authoritative, and in its latest (revised) edition (1924) will long remain so. Other works of importance in the same field were a *History of Fine Art in India and Ceylon* (1911), a *Life of Asoka* (1901), a *Life of Akbar* (1917), and the *Oxford History of India* (1918). Smith wrote with restraint, due in part to his overwhelming sense of the need for sobriety and caution in a field where so much necessarily remains obscure. His *Early History* thus lacks the picturesque atmosphere with which less cautious writers have invested the period; while the *Oxford History* suffers from extreme compression. But the value of his work is universally recognized by scholars, even by those most prone to the extravagances from which he was naturally averse. In addition to studies in his own subject he published a criticism of the Montagu-Chelmsford proposals for Indian reform (1919). He had been too long absent from India, and his taste for antiquarian illustrations was too great, for his criticisms to carry much weight, especially as his constructive proposals were few and small; but he made a vigorous protest against the spirit of make-believe which was too prevalent at that time in Indian politics.

Smith's life after his retirement, at Cheltenham (1900–1910) and at Oxford (1910–1920), was uneventful; though he suffered a disappointment in not being elected to the readership in Indian history at Oxford after he had acted as deputy reader. On the other hand his C.I.E. (1919), as a recognition of pure scholarship, was something outside the beaten track of official decorations. For many years his vigour and common sense were of the greatest service to the Indian Institute at Oxford and to the Royal Asiatic Society. The latter awarded him its gold medal in 1918. Save for his attack on the Montagu-Chelmsford proposals, and an occasional protest against slipshod research or muddled thinking, his published works give little indication of his private character, which was thoroughly Irish—genial, hospitable, and outspoken. He married in 1871 Mary Elizabeth, daughter of William Clifford Tute, of Sligo, who, with three sons and a daughter, survived him. He died at Oxford 6 February 1920.

[*The Times*, 7 February 1920; *Journal* of the Royal Asiatic Society, 1920 (notice by F. E. P(argiter) with full bibliography); Sister Nivedita (Margaret E. Noble), *Footfalls of Indian History*, 1915; private information.] S. V. FG.

SOLOMON, Sir RICHARD (1850–1913), South African statesman, was born in Cape Town 18 October 1850, the third son of the Rev. Edward Solomon, an Independent missionary, by his wife, Jessie Matthews, sister of James Matthews, architect and at one time lord provost of Aberdeen. He was educated at the Lovedale mission and Bedford public school, Cape Colony, and at the South African College, Cape Town. He entered Peterhouse, Cambridge, in 1871, passed out as twenty-third wrangler in 1875, and became mathematical lecturer at the Royal Naval College, Greenwich. After being called to the bar at the Inner Temple in 1879, he returned home to practise at Grahamstown, Cape Colony.

As became a nephew of Saul Solomon (editor of the *Cape Argus* and champion of the natives in the Cape parliament) he took a keen interest in native affairs and served on the Cape native law commission of 1882. In 1886 he was legal adviser to the royal commission which inquired into the administration of Mauritius. Three years later he settled at Kimberley, and secured the De Beers retainer. In 1893, after having been appointed Q.C., he entered the Cape house of assembly as independent member for Kimberley. At the elections of 1894 he was defeated by a supporter of Cecil Rhodes, but he was returned once more for Kimberley at a by-election at the end of 1896. In 1898 he became attorney-general in the ministry of William Philip Schreiner [q.v.] as member for Tembuland, and he supported his chief in the policy of punishing Cape rebels, which brought about the downfall of the Cabinet in June 1900.

Early in 1901 Solomon was appointed legal adviser to the Transvaal government. He took part in the negotiations which led to the peace of Vereeniging, and was created K.C.M.G. As attorney-general of the Transvaal from June 1902 onwards, he exercised his great powers of persuasion, his moderating influence, his industry, and his knowledge of affairs in the work of reconstruction. He revised the Transvaal native labour regulations, presided over the gold laws commission, and reorganized the statute book and the administration of justice. He represented the South African colonies at the Delhi durbar of 1903, and twice served as acting-lieutenant-governor of the Transvaal. He was elected an honorary fellow of Peterhouse in 1904, and in the next year was awarded the K.C.B.

In 1906 Solomon helped to draft the letters patent by which responsible government was established in the Transvaal, and was much talked of as the future prime minister. He resigned the attorney-generalship, and stood for Pretoria South with the support of Het Volk (the party of Louis Botha, q.v.), but was unexpectedly defeated by the progressive candidate (1907). He refused a post in Botha's ministry, and became agent-general for the Transvaal in London, where from 1910 onwards he was high commissioner for the Union of South Africa. He was created G.C.M.G. in 1911. He died unexpectedly in London, after a very short illness, 10 November 1913.

Solomon married in 1881 Mary Elizabeth, daughter of the Rev. John Walton, Wesleyan minister, of Grahamstown, and had one daughter.

[*The Times*, 11 November 1913; *Cape Times*, 11 November 1913 and 14 November 1923; private information. Portrait, *Royal Academy Pictures*, 1922.] E. A. W.

SOMERSET, Lady ISABELLA CAROLINE, Lady Henry Somerset (1851–1921), was born in London 3 August 1851. Her father was Charles Somers Cocks, Viscount Eastnor, afterwards third and last Earl Somers; her mother was Virginia, seventh daughter of James Pattle, Bengal civil service, whose wife was a daughter of the Chevalier Antoine de l'Etang, page of honour to Queen Marie Antoinette. Of Earl Somers's three children, Isabella was the eldest, Adeline—subsequently Duchess of Bedford—the second; the third, Virginia, died young. In 1872 Lady Isabella married Lord Henry Somerset, second son of the eighth Duke of Beaufort. Her husband was comptroller of Queen Victoria's household from 1874 to 1879, and M.P. for Monmouthshire, 1871–1880. In 1874 her only child, Henry Charles Somers Augustus, was born. The marriage proved an unhappy one, and in 1878 Lady Henry found herself facing life alone with her child, whose custody had been secured to her by the courts. She now devoted herself to work amongst the poor in the country town of Ledbury, near her home, Eastnor Castle, Herefordshire. It was her acquaintance with the brutalizing effects of drunkenness in this place, made poignant by the suicide, under the influence of drink, of her dearest friend, that led her to take up the cause of temperance. Henceforth it became the absorbing interest of her life. She now began to speak publicly for the cause all over England. Her beauty, her eloquence, her power to hold and move great audiences, won for her a widespread reputation.

In 1883 Earl Somers died, and Lady Henry Somerset inherited his estates. This event did not affect her temperance work. In 1890 she was elected president of the British Women's Temperance Association, and in 1891 she went to America to represent the association at the convention of the World's Women's Christian Temperance Union. It was at this convention, at Boston, Massachusetts, that she first met Miss Frances Willard. In company with her Lady Henry travelled much in the United States, everywhere receiving enthusiastic welcomes. But, later on, it became known that she could not support the prohibition movement, and her influence there came to an end. She returned to England in 1892, bent upon introducing into the English Temperance Association the wider views and the new methods which she had seen working so well in the United States. But she preached to unsympathetic ears. Eventually, in 1903, weary of controversy and with health impaired, she resigned her presidency. Meanwhile, in 1898, on the death of Miss Willard, she had been elected to replace her as president of the World's Women's Christian Temperance Union, an office which she held until 1906.

In 1895 Lady Henry founded Duxhurst, a farm colony, near Reigate, for inebriate women, adding to it afterwards a 'nest' for children rescued from bad surroundings. Duxhurst was the first institution of its kind in England. In contrast with the usual procedure of institutions for inebriates the women were treated not as criminals and outcasts under punishment, but simply as patients, and met from the first with courtesy, trust, and sympathy. Living at the Priory, Reigate, in constant contact with them, Lady Henry by her charm, artistic gifts, resourcefulness, and sense of humour, in conjunction with her higher qualities, profoundly influenced the varied characters of those who had taken refuge in the colony. Ultimately it was upon religion that she relied the most, and to religious influences she was wont to attribute the unusual success of her work. The six and twenty years of her work at Duxhurst, taken all in all, brought more satisfaction and happiness into her life than any other of her public and private ventures. All that had gone before, of labour, of suffering, and of experience led up to this and found in this its compensating fruit. She worked on with a zeal which increasing infirmity was not allowed to abate, until, with short warning, she died in London 12 March 1921.

Lady Henry's publications include: *Our Village Life* (in verse, 1884); *Sketches in Black and White* (1896); *In an Old Garden* (1900); *Under the Arch of Life* (a novel, 1906); and *Beauty for Ashes* (1913). In 1894 she founded the *Woman's Signal* (the official organ of the British Women's Temperance Association), of which she became editor, and, in addition, she contributed many articles to English and American magazines.

[Kathleen Fitzpatrick, *Lady Henry Somerset: a Memoir*, 1923; Ray Strachey, *Frances Willard, her Life and Work*, 1912; personal knowledge.]

E. F. R.

SPIERS, RICHARD PHENÉ (1838–1916), architect, was born at Oxford 19 May 1838, the eldest son of Alderman Richard James Spiers, a leading citizen of Oxford and mayor in 1854, by his wife, Elizabeth Phené, daughter of Thomas Joy, of Oxford. Walter Spiers, a younger brother, was curator of Sir John Soane's Museum, Lincoln's Inn Fields, from 1904 to 1917. Phené Spiers was educated at King's College School and in the engineering department of King's College, London. From 1858 to 1861 he was a student, in the atelier Questel, of the École des Beaux-Arts, Paris. Returning to England, he became assistant to Sir Matthew Digby Wyatt [q.v.], who was then engaged on works, particularly the grand staircase and internal courtyard, at the India Office, Whitehall. Spiers's relations with Wyatt were close and sympathetic.

In 1861 Spiers was elected an associate of the Royal Institute of British Architects; in 1863 he gained the silver and gold medals of the Royal Academy, and in 1864 the travelling studentship. In 1865 he won the Soane medallion and £50 for his designs for an 'Institute for the Study, Practice, and Performance of Music'. In the same year, in company with some artist friends, he set out on a tour of eighteen months through France, Germany, Greece, Constantinople, Palestine, Syria, and Egypt. His companions worked in water-colours, and Spiers was led to follow their example. He became, in fact, very expert, and was well known for his drawings of architecture in colour, which for many years were sold at good prices. He always felt, however, that his professional pursuits prevented him from keeping up with the artistic and technical advance of water-colour painting.

On his return from abroad in 1866 Spiers assisted William Burges [q.v.] in his mediaeval design (which was not accepted) for the new Law Courts in the Strand; in conjunction with Charles John Phipps [q.v.] he submitted a modern French design for the war memorial church of the Sacré Cœur at Montmartre; and with Professor Robert Kerr [q.v.] he competed in a design for the Criterion restaurant and theatre in Piccadilly; he also assisted in designing and building the synagogue in Seymour Street, Edgware Road.

Spiers's executed works are not numerous. They include additions to Umberslade Hall, Warwickshire; restorations of the churches of Hampton Poyle and Weston-on-the-Green, Oxfordshire; a house on Chelsea Embankment for Lord

Monkswell; various studios there and in Campden Hill Square; two board-schools in London, and alterations and additions to Beckett Hospital, Barnsley. In conjunction with M. Tronquois, of Paris, he designed Impney Court, near Droitwich.

With his appointment in 1870 as master of the Royal Academy architectural school a fresh phase of Spiers's career opened; but, although he held the post for thirty-six years (until 1906), the outcome was disappointing to his friends. His reputation as an architectural designer and as a water-colourist, his skill as a draughtsman, his close touch with continental tradition, and, above all, his gifts as a teacher, raised hopes that a fresh lead in the development of English architecture would be inspired by the new master of the Academy school. These hopes were not fulfilled. Partly because he allowed his personality and ideas to be overshadowed by those of his brilliant contemporaries, George Edmund Street and Richard Norman Shaw, but mainly because he felt that his influence with and authority over the students were subject to interference by the Academy visitors, Spiers did not give the lead expected of him. It is probable, indeed, that his best teaching was done outside the Academy school; and it was perhaps a matter of regret to his friends that he did not found a private school of his own, where his inspiration and undoubted gifts would have had free play.

In addition to his teaching Spiers pursued incessant investigation into the architecture of all periods and countries. He collected and abstracted a mass of material of all kinds bearing on the subject, and was always adding to it from the reports and studies of the many students with whom he was in constant touch. His point of view was scientific and highly cautious, and no labour was too great with him in ascertaining exact data. His papers thus embodied the results of years of research, and were very carefully compiled, but they possess little charm of style, and are apt to be found rather dry by the average student or amateur. He was in his element in the work of preparing a new edition (1893) of James Fergusson's *History of Architecture*; though it is unfortunate that his respect for the author prevented his recasting the work and eliminating much that has lost its value. His own book on *Architectural Drawing* (1887) has been commended for its explanation of technical methods, but some of the illustrations were not happily chosen. His collected papers in *Architecture, East and West* (1905) contain some of his most valuable work. The book was published in connexion with a testimonial presented to him, on his retirement, by past students of the Academy school and other friends in many parts of the world; a bronze plaque with his portrait, modelled by Edouard Lantéri, was given to him, and smaller replicas were issued to subscribers; a commemorative medal was presented at the same time by the Société Centrale des Architectes Français, of which body Spiers was an honorary and corresponding member. Spiers was president of the Architectural Association in 1867–1868, and served on the council of the Royal Institute of British Architects from 1888 to 1903, and was chairman and member of the literature committee for twenty-two years. He died in London 3 October 1916. He was unmarried.

Spiers is memorable for his modest and disinterested devotion to the study and teaching of architecture. He was a discriminating and fearless critic, who tolerated no lowering of a high artistic standard. He regarded architecture as a rational art, and believed in the prevalence, in all periods and styles, of definite principles not to be transgressed.

[*Journal* of the Royal Institute of British Architects, third series, vols. xxiii, xxiv, 21 October and 11 November 1916; *Architectural Review*, vol. xl, July–December 1916; personal knowledge.] A. T. B.

SPRIGG, Sir JOHN GORDON (1830–1913), South African statesman, was born at Ipswich 27 April 1830, the second son of the Rev. James Sprigg, Baptist minister of that town, by his wife, Maria Gardiner. After a short school career and employment in local insurance and shipbuilders' offices, he joined in 1846 the staff of Joseph Gurney [q.v.], parliamentary shorthand writer. In 1858 he travelled to the Cape for his health. He decided to remain in South Africa, and in 1861 obtained a free farm on military tenure in British Kaffraria some thirty miles from East London.

As a member of the East London divisional council Sprigg took a leading part in advocating the annexation of British Kaffraria to the Cape Colony, provided that self-government were speedily granted to the enlarged colony (1865–1866). In 1869 he was elected member for East London, a constituency which he represented without a break till 1904. He supported (Sir) John Molteno [q.v.] in the successful agitation for self-government (1872); but subsequently, when Molteno became the first premier of the Cape,

Sprigg attacked him because he opposed the scheme of the colonial secretary, Lord Carnarvon [q.v.], for South African confederation (1875), and because he refused to accept the findings of Sprigg's committee on the defence of the eastern frontier. Sprigg succeeded Molteno as prime minister upon the latter's dismissal during the Kaffir War of 1877–1878, and duly carried his defence measures, including a Bill which provided for the disarmament of the natives. He supported the confederation policy, harassed though he was by petty native wars, during one of which he courageously went unarmed with one companion to induce a hostile chief to surrender. Sprigg's ministry fell in 1881, nominally on the defeat of his measures for local railway construction in substitution for the Kimberley line desired by Cecil Rhodes [q. v.], but really because his disarmament policy contributed to the failure of the Basuto War.

In 1884 Sprigg became treasurer in the ministry of (Sir) Thomas Upington, and in 1886 prime minister for the second time. In July 1890 he was defeated once more on a railway Bill—for he was a great projector of railways in times of political crisis—and made way for Rhodes. He joined the second Rhodes ministry in May 1893, and, after the collapse caused by the failure of the Jameson Raid, formed a Cabinet of his own in 1896. The next year, on the occasion of Queen Victoria's diamond jubilee, he attended the premiers' conference in London. Relying on a resolution of the house of assembly to furnish assistance to the navy he readily offered the Admiralty a cruiser. He was enrolled as a privy councillor and received the honorary D.C.L. of Oxford and LL.D. of Edinburgh, but on his return to South Africa he had to withdraw his unauthorized promise. In 1898 he attempted to carry a redistribution Bill reducing the advantage enjoyed by the Afrikander Bond rural constituencies as against the progressive towns, but he was defeated on a motion of no confidence and appealed to the country virtually on the issue of British or Transvaal supremacy. He was defeated and had to resign. On the fall of the ministry of William Philip Schreiner [q.v.] in June 1900, Sprigg became premier for the fourth time and governed for two years without parliamentary sanction. For a time he was inclined to approve of a suspension of the Cape constitution as the best means of furthering the federation of South Africa; but on Rhodes's death (1902) he stiffened his back; and at the premiers' conference in London in 1902 he followed the lead of Sir Wilfrid Laurier [q. v.] in crushing the scheme. Sprigg appealed to the country in 1904, but was himself rejected. He dropped out of politics till 1908 when he was returned once more for East London as a federalist, and ended his political career in a vain effort to stop the passage of the draft Union Bill. On the clause setting up the parliamentary colour bar he voted with Schreiner in a minority of two (June 1909).

Sprigg was not a commanding figure and was completely lacking in humour, but his influence in parliament was great. During his thirty-six years as a member he made himself indispensable. He was always in his seat, a ready speaker, cool, patient, courteous, possessed of considerable moral courage and boundless self-confidence. As head of a department for eighteen years he was industrious and businesslike, and as premier for thirteen years he displayed great powers of party management. He was created K.C.M.G. in 1886, G.C.M.G. in 1902, and commander of the legion of honour in 1889. He died at Wynberg, Cape Colony, on 4 February 1913.

Sprigg married in 1862 Ellen (died 1900), daughter of James Fleischer, a neighbouring farmer in British Kaffraria, and had one son and three daughters.

[*The Times* and *Cape Times*, 5 February 1913; *Votes and Proceedings* of the (Cape) House of Assembly; J. H. Hofmeyr, *Life of Jan Hendrik Hofmeyr*, 1913; E. A. Walker, *Lord De Villiers and his Times*, 1924; private information.] E. A. W.

SPRING-RICE, Sir CECIL ARTHUR (1859–1918), diplomat, was born in London 27 February 1859. He was the second son of the Hon. Charles Spring-Rice, second son of the first Baron Monteagle [q.v.], by his wife, Elizabeth, daughter of William Marshall, M.P., of Halsteads and Patterdale Hall, Cumberland. Educated at Eton and Balliol College, Oxford, he achieved distinction both at school and college as a scholar, and his first efforts at poetry appeared in an Eton booklet, whilst his *Oxford Rhymes* had a more than ephemeral vogue. Later on it was in poetry of a more serious order that he often revealed his innermost thoughts, and sometimes with rare felicity of expression and depth of feeling.

Spring-Rice's father had been at one time under-secretary of state for foreign affairs, and he himself was appointed clerk in the Foreign Office on 9 September 1882. He had the advantage almost at the outset of his diplomatic career of serving directly under two secretaries of state, first as assistant private secretary to Lord Granville and then as précis-writer to Lord Rosebery. His first post abroad, as well as his last, was Washington, where, with brief intervals, he spent several years between 1886 and 1895; he was then transferred to Berlin. He remained in the German capital until 1898 and he had there the opportunity, which he always regarded as having been of the greatest educational value to him, of watching at close quarters the 'new course' upon which the policy of the German Empire was being set by William II after he had emancipated himself from Bismarck's tutelage. From Berlin Spring-Rice went in 1898 first to Constantinople and then to Teheran. He was seconded thence in 1901 as British commissioner on the Caisse de la Dette Publique in Cairo where, as he put it, he went 'back to school' under Lord Cromer, than whom he wished for no better schoolmaster. From Cairo he was promoted in 1903 to be secretary of embassy at St. Petersburg during the stormy years of the Russo-Japanese War and the first revolutionary upheavals in Russia. While serving in Russia he married, in 1904, Florence, the only daughter of his former chief, Sir Frank Lascelles [q.v.], then still ambassador in Berlin; one son and one daughter were born of the marriage. In 1906 he was created K.C.M.G. and he returned to Persia as British minister. There his sympathies were with the Persian people in their first gropings towards constitutional freedom, and in troublous times thousands used to take sanctuary within the grounds of the British legation in Teheran. None the less he faithfully carried out the policy of the Anglo-Russian agreement of 1907 which placed fresh restraints upon Persian independence. After Teheran he enjoyed from 1908 to 1913 five years of relative ease and rest at Stockholm as British minister to Sweden. It was, however, a post of observation from which he watched the heavy storm-clouds gathering on the European horizon. In April 1913 he was appointed ambassador at Washington, and shortly after his arrival there he signed the agreement renewing the Anglo-American Arbitration Convention of 1908. He was at home on leave after a somewhat serious illness when the Serajevo tragedy precipitated the European conflict, which he had long foreseen.

Spring-Rice returned to his post as soon as war had broken out in Europe, and within a few weeks affixed his signature to a document which the violent clash of arms had already turned to irony. It was a treaty for which the then secretary of state, Mr. Bryan, had long diligently laboured and had secured the adhesion of Great Britain and a number of other powers, including France, Russia, and Italy, but not of Germany, who had declined to have anything to do with it. It provided for the establishment of a permanent International Peace Commission, to which disputes were in the last resort to be referred, when diplomatic methods of adjustment had failed, the contracting parties agreeing to await the Commission's report before beginning hostilities. The sterner realities which the British ambassador had now to face were those of a state of war in Europe, which was bound to put a severe strain upon England's relations with all neutral countries, and not least with the United States. Spring-Rice's knowledge of American affairs and the many friendships he had gained in America in the early part of his career stood him in good stead at this critical juncture. He had great confidence in the sound instincts of the American democracy as a whole, but he knew that the Allies must reckon with the bitter hostility of many alien and anti-British elements. Difficult and delicate questions, moreover, were certain to arise out of the exercise, however careful, of British naval power, so long as America remained neutral and was the foremost champion of neutral rights and interests.

The State Department entered frequent protests against the seizure and detention of United States vessels and goods and the practice of British prize courts. The British order-in-council of 15 March 1915 relating to the blockade of Germany, and the proclamations of 20 August and 15 October declaring raw cotton and various cotton goods and products to be absolute contraband, gave rise to still more serious differences; while the 'black-listing' on 29 February 1916 of a number of firms, under the Trading with the Enemy Act, aroused the strongest resentment in certain sections of the American business world. In the lengthy controversies between the two governments, Spring-Rice's conciliatory influence made itself constantly felt at Washington, where his tact and forbearance, and anxiety to meet any legitimate grievance, were deservedly appreciated. Some of his fellow-countrymen were apt to criticize him for placing less faith in demonstrative forms of propaganda than in the spontaneous reaction of American public opinion against German 'methods of frightfulness'.

During the whole of the War Spring-Rice only spoke once in public as British ambassador—returning thanks at Harvard in June 1917 in a few stirring words for the honorary degree conferred upon him. His reliance on the goodwill of America found its justification when he attended on 3 April 1917 the memorable session of Congress in which President Wilson declared a state of war to exist between the United States and the German Empire. To borrow the language in which Mr. Balfour afterwards summed up the British government's appreciation of his great services, he steered his course with unfailing judgement and unwearied forbearance, at a time when a single false step might have had the most serious consequences for the cause which he represented, and he might well be proud to remember that at that great moment he was ambassador at Washington, and had done all that lay in his power to prevent any unnecessary friction and avoid any appearance of undue pressure which might have impeded or delayed the President's action. With the entry of America into the War Spring-Rice's task was consummated, and he was the first to recognize that the work of the British embassy in Washington henceforth required a man of trained business capacity rather than a diplomatist, to superintend the huge transactions involved in the effective co-ordination of the financial, industrial, and shipping resources of the two nations for the joint prosecution of the War. At the end of the year the War Cabinet decided that Lord Reading, who had already discharged important missions in that connexion in the United States, should return there as ambassador; and on 13 January 1918 Spring-Rice left Washington for Canada on leave till the appointed time for his retirement.

The strain of the three and a half years' ceaseless work and anxiety had, however, told heavily upon a constitution already undermined by illness, and, whilst waiting at Ottawa for the ship that was to take him home, he died suddenly on 14 February 1918 before the fine tribute from Mr. Balfour, to which reference has been made, had had time to reach him.

[Foreign Office lists; Parliamentary Papers; private letters.] V. C.

STALBRIDGE, first BARON (1837–1912), railway administrator and politician. [See GROSVENOR, RICHARD DE AQUILA.]

STANMORE, first BARON (1829–1912), colonial governor. [See GORDON, ARTHUR CHARLES HAMILTON-.]

STANTON, ARTHUR HENRY (1839–1913), divine, the third son and youngest of twelve children of Charles Stanton, fine cloth manufacturer, by his wife, Martha Holbrow, was born at 'Upfield', Stroud, Gloucestershire, 21 June 1839. He was educated at Rugby and Oxford, entering Trinity College in 1858. Neither at school nor at the university did he win any distinctions. He was not idle, but his ambitions and his gifts pointed another way, and books, throughout his life, were always a quite subordinate interest. Under the influence of Henry Parry Liddon [q.v.], then vice-principal of St. Edmund Hall, he went on to Cuddesdon theological college; and thence to London to take up work as curate in the newly-formed parish of St. Alban, Holborn, under Alexander Heriot Mackonochie [q.v.]. On 21 December 1862 he was ordained deacon at Whitehall by Bishop Tait, and went at once to reside in the clergy house adjoining St. Alban's church, where he lived, without break, for the fifty years of his ministry. The parish was for the most part a difficult one, uncared for, squalid, and lawless. This did not repel him; on the contrary it was the wild element in it which really attracted him, and he gave himself body and soul to work for the good of these neglected men and women. He succeeded in gaining a remarkable hold upon some of the very roughest amongst them, by the natural, unconventional way in which he identified himself with them in their homes and daily life. Before long it became widely known that a preacher of unusual type and eloquence was at work at St. Alban's, and crowds of young men flocked to hear him. He was in these early days and onwards a singularly attractive personality. The fervour of his personal devotion to Christ, his sympathy and humour, aided by a voice of great charm and a manner naturally dramatic, won for him a devoted following. Invitations to preach now came to him from all quarters. It was a time of great and fruitful activity; it was also a very happy time, for he had found himself, and a field ripe for his zeal.

But Stanton's career was abruptly checked by an experience which affected his whole later life. The first signs of coming trouble were certain letters in the newspapers which accused him of romanizing, and of disloyalty to the Church of England, and demanded that he should be silenced. This did not disturb him; but when bishops gave in to the clamour and denounced him, he was deeply hurt. For the moment, indeed, it paralysed him, because obedience to episcopal authority was to him an article of faith. One after another certain bishops, when he was announced to preach in their diocese, inhibited him, and even the chaplain-general of the forces forbade him to officiate again in any military chapel (1867). Stanton bowed to the storm; he obeyed and said very little, but it wounded him to the quick. To make matters harder, he had in time to share with his vicar, Mackonochie, the burden and worry of a series of ritual prosecutions which pursued him for nearly fifteen years. Throughout this time and to the end of his life, in spite of all, Stanton continued to work with undiminished earnestness within the limits of his own parish and diocese. As the years went on active opposition died away, leaving him in peace, until in 1906 the report of the royal commission on ecclesiastical discipline laid him open to new attacks. The effect of this was to call out at once the indignant protest of his many friends. Three thousand men, who publicly acknowledged their personal debt to his preaching and influence, signed an address assuring him of their affection and gratitude, and of their resentment at the treatment he had received. During the remaining years of his life he continued his apostolate among young men without molestation. Of official recognition of his work for half a century there was no sign, until in March 1913, the bishop of London, not knowing how seriously ill he was, offered him a prebendal stall in St. Paul's Cathedral. Stanton wrote in courteous terms declining the honour, but the offer, coming from his bishop, pleased him greatly. Within three weeks he died at Stroud (28 March). His funeral through the streets of London was a most striking public demonstration of the place which he had won in the hearts of the people. He was buried at Woking. A chapel, containing his recumbent effigy in bronze, perpetuates his memory in the church which he served.

Stanton was felt to be one of the most attractive and inspiring of the preachers of his day. To him and his quickening eloquence the Anglo-Catholic movement in the Church of England owes much. He printed nothing himself, but since his death two volumes of reports of his sermons have been published and often reprinted, and two volumes of his own sermon-notes. His life—*Arthur Stanton, a Memoir*—written by his friend, G. W. E. Russell, was published in 1917.

[Personal recollections of one who was his colleague for forty-five years. Portrait, *Royal Academy Pictures*, 1917.] E. F. R.

STEAD, WILLIAM THOMAS (1849–1912), journalist and author, the son of the Rev. William Stead, Congregational minister, of Yorkshire farmer stock, by his wife, Isabella, daughter of John Jobson, also a Yorkshire farmer, was born at the Manse, Embleton, Northumberland, 5 July 1849. In 1850 the family settled at Howden-on-Tyne. Taught only by his father until he was twelve, Stead went in 1861 to Silcoates School, near Wakefield. In 1863 he was apprenticed office-boy in a merchant's counting-house on Quayside, Newcastle-upon-Tyne. In February 1870 he began to contribute articles to the *Northern Echo*, a liberal daily paper which had just been founded at Darlington, and his contributions were held to be so remarkable that in April 1871 he was appointed editor, although he had never been inside a newspaper office. In 1873 he married Emma Lucy, daughter of Henry Wilson, of Howden-on-Tyne, by whom he had six children. During the years 1876–1879 he won high praise for the *Northern Echo* by his ardent support of Mr. Gladstone in the agitation against Turkey over the Bulgarian atrocities.

In September 1880 Stead moved to London in order to act as assistant-editor of the *Pall Mall Gazette*, which had recently become a liberal organ under the control of Mr. John (later Viscount) Morley. Morley and Stead worked together excellently until August 1883, when Stead became editor, Morley having been elected M.P. for Newcastle-upon-Tyne. Stead's reputation reached its zenith during the following seven years, when with Mr. Alfred (afterwards Viscount) Milner as his very active and sympathetic lieutenant, he inaugurated the 'new journalism', as Matthew Arnold called it. The *Pall Mall*, until then a sedate chronicle and review of the day's events, suddenly became the initiator of all kinds of new programmes and movements, political and social, besides astonishing people by its dash and unconventionality. In January 1884 General Gordon, who had been on the point of resigning from the army, was dispatched on his fateful mission to Khartoum, as the direct result of an 'interview' with him published in the *Pall Mall* and reinforced by a leading article in which Stead urged this step upon the government. Towards the end of 1884 Stead's articles in the *Pall Mall*, headed *The Truth about the Navy*, again forced the government's hand, and compelled the Earl of Northbrook [q.v.], then first lord of the Admiralty, to ask for a supplementary grant of three and a half millions in order to strengthen the naval defences. In July 1885 Stead achieved wide notoriety by an exposure of criminal vice in England under the heading *The Maiden Tribute of Modern Babylon*. As the almost immediate outcome of these revelations a Criminal Law Amendment Act, raising the age of consent to sixteen years, was passed by parliament after years of obstruction and opposition. A lack of precaution in securing the evidence requisite for his purpose entailed on Stead a sentence of three months' imprisonment. 'I cannot find words to tell you how I honour and reverence you for what you have done for the weakest and most helpless among women', wrote Mrs. Millicent Garrett Fawcett to him while he was in Holloway jail; 'I always felt that by some legal quibble you might be tripped up, as it were: but this is as nothing; your work will stand.' Mrs. Fawcett's view was shared by Cardinal Manning, Lord Shaftesbury, Dr. Temple, then bishop of London, and most of the social reformers, but Stead's action was violently condemned by the London daily press and by the British public in general, and he was reviled as a dealer in pornography.

After a great variety of other noteworthy exploits, Stead abandoned daily journalism and started his well-known *Review of Reviews* in January 1890; American and Australian editions of it were founded in 1891 and 1892 respectively. From 1893 to 1897, having become keenly interested in psychical matters, he edited also *Borderland*, a periodical devoted to this subject. In *Letters from Julia* (1897) he published a selection from communications which he said he wrote quite involuntarily with his own hand at the dictation of the departed spirit of a young American lady, Julia Ames, whom he had met not long before her death in 1891. 'If I am remembered a hundred years hence', he said once to a friend, 'it will be as Julia's amanuensis.' Throughout the 'nineties and down to the time of his death Stead's spiritualistic beliefs remained unshaken, although they subjected him to much ridicule, alienated friends, and weakened his influence and prestige. Despite this, he was perhaps the most powerful, as he was certainly the most resolute, supporter of the peace movement set on foot in 1898 by the rescript of the Tsar Nicholas II.

Although he had hitherto been one of the strongest champions in England of Cecil Rhodes, Stead was the most uncompromising of all the opponents of the war in South Africa (1899–1902), and thereby he accentuated his unpopularity. A morning journal which he founded in January 1904, the *Daily Paper*, failed completely, lasting only five weeks. He persisted in his efforts to keep up the strength of the British navy, with the watchword, 'Two keels to one'; but he devoted the best of his energies throughout the remainder of his career to the preaching of peace through arbitration. Bound for New York on the maiden voyage of the White Star liner *Titanic*, in order to take part in a peace congress, he lost his life in the tragic disaster of 15 April 1912, when the great ship struck an iceberg and sank with the loss of 1,500 lives. When last seen by survivors Stead was assisting women and children to make their escape from the vessel.

The younger generation learned with surprise from the obituary notices what a potent figure Stead once had been. Lord Esher declared roundly that 'no events happened to the country since the year 1880' which had 'not been influenced by the personality of Mr. Stead'. Mr. H. W. Massingham maintained that no pen in England had 'wielded an ascendancy comparable with Stead's' from the time of the Bulgarian atrocities down to the South African War. To Stead's goodness and unselfishness, courage and generosity there were tributes innumerable.

[Estelle W. Stead, *My Father. Personal and Spiritual Reminiscences*, 1912; Edith Harper, *Stead, the Man*, 1914; Frederic Whyte, *The Life of W. T. Stead*, 1925; *Review of Reviews*, January–June 1912.]

F. W. W.

STEEL, ALLAN GIBSON (1858–1914), cricketer, was born at Liverpool 24 September 1858, the son of Joseph Steel, of Liverpool and Kirkwood, Lockerbie, Dumfriesshire, by his wife, Margaret Gibson, who came of a Lanarkshire family. He was the sixth of seven brothers, four of whom played at one time or another in the Lancashire county cricket team. Allan Steel was sent to Marlborough, where he was in the eleven from 1874 to 1877. He was regarded as a schoolboy cricketer of exceptional promise, and when in the autumn of 1877 he went up to Trinity Hall, he was considered not only certain of a place in the Cambridge eleven, but likely to add considerably to the strength of the side. This forecast was amply fulfilled. The Cambridge team of 1873 won all its engagements, defeating Oxford with ease, and ending up with a decisive victory over the first Australian eleven to visit this country. In this series of triumphs Steel took a leading part—indeed his slow bowling was one of the features of the cricket of 1878. Breaking both ways and combining clever variation of pace with an accurate length, he was consistently effective against the best batsmen of the day. For that season he had a fine record of 164 wickets for 9 runs each. He also made runs constantly, and headed the Cambridge averages with 37.

Steel, though he remained for some years in the front rank of amateur bowlers and did many good performances, was never quite as deadly again, possibly because batsmen became more familiar with his methods. He was four years in the Cambridge eleven, and was captain in 1880. As he grew older his batting improved, and his place in the Gentlemen's eleven *v.* the Players, as well as in the early contests with Australia, was always assured. He made 42 in the first test match at Kennington Oval on 6 September 1880, and, though he did little in the single test match of 1882, he played a great innings of 148 for England at Lord's against the strong Australian team of 1884.

Steel was called to the bar (Inner Temple) in 1883, and as the claims of his profession increased he found little time for first-class cricket. His appearances were confined to important occasions, such as the Gentlemen *v.* Players matches, and special county fixtures. It was noticeable that the want of regular match practice seemed to make little difference to his skill, for his isolated efforts were often attended with great success. In 1886, for example, though he only went in four times for Lancashire, he made 232 runs for three times out, and in 1887, when he only played once for his county, he made 32 and 105 against Surrey.

Steel was a short thick-set man, full of confidence and vigour. As a batsman, he possessed no special graces of style, but the quickness of his footwork and the power of his hitting made him always attractive to watch. His career as a cricketer was comparatively short, but for a season or two his all-round ability made him second only to W. G. Grace [q.v.] as a match-winning force. He visited Australia with the side taken out by the Hon. Ivo Bligh (afterwards eighth Earl of Darnley) in the winter of 1881. He was president of the Marylebone Cricket Club in 1902, and his few contributions to the literature of the game show that he had a gift of writing pleasantly on his own subject.

As a barrister, Steel had at one time a considerable practice in Liverpool, chiefly in commercial cases. He took silk in 1901, and was appointed recorder of Oldham in 1904. He married in 1886 Georgiana Dorothy, daughter of John Philip Thomas, of Warneford Place, Highworth, Wiltshire. His wife was related to the three brothers Studd, accomplished cricketers, who were his contemporaries at Cambridge. He had two sons, both of whom lost their lives in the European War. Steel died in London 15 June 1914.

[Wisden's *Cricketers' Almanack,* 1915; private information.] A. C.

STEPHEN, GEORGE, first Baron Mount Stephen (1829–1921), financier and philanthropist, was born at Dufftown, Banffshire, 5 June 1829. He was the eldest son of William Stephen, a carpenter, of Dufftown, by his wife, Elspet, daughter of John Smith, of Knockando. After a few years at the parish school of Mortlach, and summer work as a herd boy, Stephen at fourteen was apprenticed to an Aberdeen draper, and four years later (1847) moved first to Glasgow and then to London. A chance meeting at his employer's with a cousin, William Stephen, a Montreal draper, led him to Canada in 1850. There he became buyer to his cousin's firm, partner, and, on his cousin's death in 1860, sole proprietor. He prospered, embarked on cloth manufacture, and in 1873 became a director of the Bank of Montreal, in 1876 its president. As retail trade had led to wholesale, and that to manufacture and finance, so finance led to railway building. Business took Stephen and the bank's manager, Richard Bladworth Angus, to Chicago; thence they visited St. Paul, the head-quarters of a potentially valuable but bankrupt railway, the St. Paul and Pacific. It held wide concessions conditional on speedy completion. In 1878 it was taken up by a group of six, with Stephen as president and James J. Hill as general manager; the others being Stephen's cousin, Donald Alexander

Smith, afterwards Baron Strathcona [q.v.], Norman W. Kittson, John Kennedy, and R. B. Angus. Stephen visited Holland and bought out the owners, Dutch bondholders, for a low price; the group finished the line and made their fortunes; the railway later grew, under Hill's management, into the Great Northern.

It was this same group, with a few changes, that built the Canadian Pacific Railway. Some 700 miles of the transcontinental line had been constructed by the Canadian government, but work was languishing and British Columbia dissatisfied. The ministry of Sir John Alexander Macdonald [q.v.] resolved to transfer the railway to private enterprise. Stephen was reluctant to undertake the task, but he and his group finally consented, and formed a company of which he was president from 1880 to 1888. There were enormous difficulties, natural, financial, and political; for surmounting the last two Stephen, more than any man, was responsible; (Sir) William Van Horne [q.v.] saw to construction. Stephen showed great courage and determination; with his associates he pledged all his resources; he wrung financial aid from a reluctant Cabinet. From January 1884 to April 1885 he nearly despaired, but at the last minute, bankruptcy being a matter of hours, the railway was saved by the intervention of the acting minister of railways, (Sir) Joseph H. Pope, with the government. In November 1885 D. A. Smith drove the last spike at Craigellachie. Stephen was not satisfied even with a coast to coast railway; from the first it was his aim that the company should run its own ships to England and China, and his views have proved justified by the Company's later expansion.

In 1888 Stephen retired from the railway presidency, and in 1893 made his home in England. He was created a baronet in 1886, and a peer in 1891, taking his title from a peak in the Rockies named after him by railway surveyors. He showed no political ambitions, and in England lived chiefly at Brocket Hall, Hertfordshire. He had no passion for continuing in harness, his tastes were simple, his ambition satisfied, and he cared little for publicity. He lived for nearly thirty years after his retirement, giving generously to hospitals in London, Montreal, and Aberdeen, distributing over £1,000,000 in his lifetime and leaving the residue of his estate to King Edward's hospital fund. He died at Brocket Hall 29 November 1921. He married, first, in 1853 Charlotte Annie (died 1896), daughter of Benjamin Kane; secondly, in 1897 Gian, daughter of Captain George Robert Tufnell, R.N. He had no children, but left an adopted daughter, who married Henry Stafford Northcote, Baron Northcote [q.v.].

There is a portrait of Stephen, painted by Sir George Reid in 1894, in the Canadian Pacific Company's offices, Toronto.

[*The Times*, 1 December 1921; Keith Morris, *Story of Lord Mount Stephen*, 1922; *Life and Letters of the Rt. Hon. Sir Charles Tupper*, 2 vols., 1916; *Correspondence of Sir John Macdonald*, 1921; O. D. Skelton, *The Railway Builders*, 1916.] E. M. W-G.

STEWART, CHARLES STEWART VANE-TEMPEST-, sixth MARQUESS OF LONDONDERRY (1852–1915), politician. [See VANE-TEMPEST-STEWART.]

STIRLING, SIR JAMES (1836–1916), judge, was born at Aberdeen 3 May 1836, the eldest son of the Rev. James Stirling, minister of the George Street United Presbyterian church, Aberdeen, by his wife, Sarah Irvine. He was sent to the grammar school and to the university of Aberdeen, where he showed marked ability as a mathematician. Proceeding to Trinity College, Cambridge, he was senior wrangler and first Smith's prizeman in 1860. The fact that he was not a member of the Church of England prevented his election to a fellowship. Having read in the chambers of Charles Turner Simpson, a well-known conveyancer, he was called to the bar at Lincoln's Inn in 1862.

After serving on the staff of the *New Reports*, Stirling joined that of the newly-founded *Law Reports* in 1865, and reported chancery cases in the Rolls court under two masters of the Rolls, Lord Romilly and Sir George Jessel. He did not give up this occupation till 1876. Meanwhile, unlike most reporters, he acquired a considerable practice at the bar. Learned and industrious, he was at the same time diffident and distrustful of his powers. It was said of him that his opinion was the best in Lincoln's Inn if one could only get it. In 1881 (Sir) John Rigby, the attorney-general's 'devil', became a Q.C., and Sir Henry James (afterwards Lord James of Hereford) selected Stirling as his successor. For the Treasury work which now fell to him he was well suited. In 1886 Sir John Pearson died, and Lord Herschell appointed Stirling to the vacant chancery judgeship. As a judge, he was careful and painstaking to a fault, and the slowness of his methods was a subject of criticism; but his judgments were seldom reversed. With the bar he was exceedingly popular. In 1900 Lord Alverstone became lord chief justice of England, Sir Archibald Levin Smith succeeded him as master of the Rolls, and Stirling was promoted to the court of Appeal. As a lord justice, he was inclined to defer unduly to his colleagues, whose opinion was not always as good as his own. In one well-known instance (the case of *Farquharson* v. *King*, 1902) the House of Lords preferred Stirling's dissenting judgment to those of the majority in the Court of Appeal. From time to time he found himself sitting with two other senior wranglers, Lords Justices Romer and Moulton.

Stirling retired from the bench in 1906. Thereafter he spent most of his time at his country house, Finchcocks, at Goudhurst, Kent, taking no further part in legal affairs. Knighted on his appointment to the bench, he was sworn of the Privy Council when he became a lord justice. He died 27 June 1916 at Goudhurst.

Stirling married in 1868 Aby, daughter of John Thomson Renton, of Bradstone Brook, Shalford, Surrey, who survived him. They had one son and two daughters.

An oil-portrait by Sir William Orpen is in the possession of the family, and there is a caricature by 'Spy' in *Vanity Fair*.

[*The Times*, 28 June 1916; *Law Journal*, 1 July 1916; personal knowledge.] T. M.

STODDART, ANDREW ERNEST (1863–1915), cricketer, was born at Westoe, South Shields, 11 March 1863. He was the younger of the two sons of George Best Stoddart, by his wife, Elizabeth Whinney. When he was nine years old, his father, who had owned a wine merchant's business, went south, and Stoddart was educated at a private school kept by a Mr. Oliver in St. John's Wood. His reputation was made in London club cricket, and it was as a prominent player for Hampstead that he was chosen to play for Middlesex in August 1885. He soon established himself in first-class company with an innings of 79 against the strong bowling of Nottinghamshire. In the following season, playing for Hampstead against the Stoics, he scored 485, at that time the highest individual innings on record; and in 1887, in the Marylebone Club's centenary match, he made 151, putting up, in company with Arthur Shrewsbury [q.v.], 266 for the first wicket.

For the next ten years Stoddart was in the front rank of English amateurs. Most of his finest performances were for Middlesex, a county which at this period could put into the field a powerful batting side. The captain, A. J. Webbe, Stoddart, S. W. Scott, Sir T. C. O'Brien, and F. G. J. Ford were players who attracted large crowds to Lord's cricket ground during the last decade of the nineteenth century. The best of them was Stoddart, whose great scores are too numerous to give in detail. In 1891 he made 215, not out, against Lancashire, and in 1893, his most successful season, he scored at Lord's against Nottinghamshire, 195, not out, in the first innings and 124 in the second. He was chosen to represent England against Australia in 1890 at Manchester, but rain prevented play. In 1893 he played in all three test matches against Australia, making 83 at Kennington Oval and 42 at Manchester.

Stoddart's reputation in Australia stood as high as in England. He visited the colony in the winter of 1887, and again with the eleven taken out by the third Earl of Sheffield [see HOLROYD, Henry North] in 1891, when he made 134 in the third test match. In 1894 he went out as captain of a representative English team. Australian cricket was very strong, and the five test matches constituted a struggle of giants. In the first engagement England, after following on against a total of 586, won a surprising victory by ten runs. When the fifth game took place at Melbourne on 1 March 1895, the position was two matches each, and the fortunes of the deciding contest aroused intense interest. Eventually England, put in to make 297 in the last innings, succeeded in scoring the necessary runs for the loss of four wickets. Stoddart's own share in the triumphs of the tour was considerable, his consistent batting and judicious captaincy contributing much to the result. On his return to England he was received with enthusiasm. A second trip, which he organized in 1897, proved a complete disappointment. His eleven, of whose success high hopes were entertained, was handicapped by various misfortunes, and was overwhelmed in the test matches. The captain himself was obliged to stand down on several occasions, and could show nothing approaching his proper form. He retired soon afterwards, for after the summer of 1898 he ceased to play regularly for Middlesex. Now and then he took part in a match; on his last appearance, indeed, he made his highest score in first-class cricket—

221 for Middlesex against Somerset at Lord's in June 1900.

Stoddart's style as a batsman was a model for imitation: his driving, cutting, and leg-play were admirable. Though essentially a forcing player, his defence on difficult wickets was sound. He was also a first-rate fieldsman anywhere, and a useful change bowler. He was also well-known as a three-quarter back at Rugby football. He played for the Harlequins Club as well as for Blackheath, and represented England in the international matches between 1886 and 1893. He enjoyed the uncommon distinction of captaining an English international team both at cricket and football.

Apart from his skill as an athlete Stoddart deserves to be remembered for the success with which he filled the difficult office of leader and manager of a touring side in Australia. His relations with his opponents were as pleasant as those with his colleagues, a happy result due to his genuine and unassuming character.

Stoddart as a youth was articled to a London architect, and passed into the Royal Academy School, but he did not follow the profession; he subsequently became a member of the Stock Exchange. On his retirement from first-class cricket he was for a time secretary of the Queen's Club, West Kensington. He married in 1906 Ethel Luckham, a widow, the daughter of Theodor von Sinnbech. There was no issue of the marriage. The early failure of his health, and his death at his house in St. John's Wood under sad circumstances on 3 April 1915, caused grief to his numerous friends, both in this country and in the colonies.

[Wisden's *Cricketers' Almanack*, 1916; private information.] A. C.

STRACHAN - DAVIDSON, JAMES LEIGH (1843–1916), classical scholar, the eldest son of James Strachan, merchant (who took the name of Davidson in 1861), by his second wife, Mary Anne Richardson, was born at Byfleet, Surrey, 22 October 1843. His father came of a Dundee family, and was a merchant trading and residing in Madras. His mother was the daughter of a Yorkshire land-agent who lived at Kirkby Ravensworth; she died when her eldest son was only four years old. Her husband married again in 1853 and retired to Leamington, where he resided until his death (1867). James Leigh Strachan became a day-boy at Leamington College in 1854. Thence he passed to Balliol College, Oxford, in 1862 as an exhibitioner; among those who entered the college at the same time were (Sir) William Reynell Anson [q.v.], Evelyn Abbott [q.v.], Paul Ferdinand Willert, and Francis de Paravicini, who became and remained his close friends. Strachan-Davidson (as he was now named) obtained first classes in classical moderations (1864) and *literae humaniores* (1866). In 1864 he was elected to the Jenkyns exhibition (the chief college prize for classical men), and in 1866 to a fellowship. As an undergraduate he read with three remarkable tutors, Edwin Palmer, Benjamin Jowett, and William Lambert Newman; by the last of these three he was inspired to make ancient history the avocation of his life. He was a frequent speaker at the Union Society, of which he was successively secretary (1863), librarian (1866–1867), and president (1867).

In his early years as a fellow Strachan-Davidson was much abroad, owing to the weakness of his health. He began to lecture regularly in 1874, but for many years wintered habitually in Egypt. In 1875 he accepted the office of senior dean, which he was to hold for thirty-two years. In this capacity he was Jowett's right-hand man. His own personality, which though elusive was singularly charming, made him the social centre of the senior common room and the idol of those undergraduates to whom he acted as a tutor or a *censor morum*. The subjects which he habitually taught were political economy, in which he represented orthodox individualism, and Roman history, of which he was an acknowledged master. In 1880 he contributed a study of Polybius to a volume of *Hellenica*, edited by Evelyn Abbott, and in 1888 he published *Selections from Polybius* with substantial prolegomena and appendices. In 1886 and 1890 he contributed to the *English Historical Review* two articles on 'The Growth of Plebeian Privilege at Rome' and 'The Decrees of the Roman Plebs'. In 1890–1891 he wrote articles on Roman subjects for the third edition of William Smith's *Dictionary of Greek and Roman Antiquities*. His small but learned volume on *Cicero and the Fall of the Roman Republic* (1894) was a brilliant vindication of his favourite Roman statesman and an effective rejoinder to Mommsen's eulogy of Julius Caesar. In 1901 he criticized at some length the *Römisches Strafrecht* of Mommsen in the *English Historical Review*; and out of this article developed his own searching examination of *Problems of the Roman Criminal Law* (2 vols., 1912), his most elaborate and ambitious work, which Oxford recognized by the degree of D.C.L. (1916).

Learning, however, was only Strachan-Davidson's recreation. Though essentially a scholar he gave his best energies to the service of his university—whose interests in connexion with the Indian civil service he defended strenuously and successfully on more than one occasion, but especially in the years 1903–1904 and in 1913—and of his college, which he loved with a monastic patriotism most appropriate in one of the last representatives of the race of celibate life-fellows. This patriotism was humanized, but in no sense weakened, by his strong personal friendships and by his tolerance for those who could not permanently embrace his rule of life.

In 1893, on Jowett's death, there were many who expected that Strachan-Davidson would succeed him. But the electors preferred Edward Caird, a great philosophical teacher, and Strachan-Davidson loyally placed himself at the service of the new master, who was also an old friend. Their alliance was fortunate for the college, and in 1907, when Caird resigned, Strachan-Davidson was unanimously elected in his place—but at the age of sixty-three, with his naturally weak health impaired by a recent accident and operation. His tenure of office was quiet, prosperous, and uneventful until the outbreak of the European War in 1914. He faced the crisis in college affairs with a wise and cautious statesmanship. With the help of only three fellows he kept the teaching organization in being; and he did his utmost to make the college useful for the chief purpose that it then served, the training of officer-cadets. He gave his juniors a high example of courage, patience, and unobtrusive well-doing. On 28 March 1916 he died suddenly, at the Master's Lodgings, of cerebral haemorrhage. He is buried in the cemetery of Holywell church, Oxford. A speaking portrait, painted in 1909–1910 by Sir George Reid, hangs in the hall of Balliol College.

[J. W. Mackail, *James Leigh Strachan-Davidson*, 1925; personal knowledge.]

H. W. C. D.

STRANG, WILLIAM (1859–1921), painter and etcher, was born at Dumbarton 13 February 1859, the younger of the two sons of Peter Strang, builder, of Dumbarton, by his wife, Janet Denny. He was at school at Dumbarton Academy; but before he was seventeen he went up to London (1875) and entered the Slade School of Art. London was to be his home for the rest of his life. In 1875 Alphonse Legros [q.v.] became Slade professor of fine art at University College, London; his influence on Strang's art was deep and lasting. Under Legros, Strang took to etching, while not neglecting the painter's brush. It was as an etcher of imaginative compositions, in which homeliness and realism, sometimes with a grim or fantastic element, were subdued to fine design and severe drawing, that he first made a name. The illustrations to *Death and the Ploughman's Wife* (1888) and *The Earth Fiend* (1892), two ballads written by himself, and those to *The Pilgrim's Progress* (1885) contain some of the best of his earlier etchings. Among the numerous single plates the portraits are especially good, though these were to be surpassed as the artist acquired more confident mastery and a broader style, tending to exchange the use of acid for dry point or graver. The best of the later portraits are masterpieces of their kind. Among later sets of etchings are the illustrations to *The Ancient Mariner* (1896), Kipling's *Short Stories* (1900), and *Don Quixote* (1902). A catalogue of Strang's etched work, published in 1906, with supplements (1912 and 1923), contains small reproductions of all his plates, 747 altogether. During the latter part of his life he etched less and painted more. Much of his time was given also to portrait drawings, in style founded on the Holbein drawings at Windsor. Strang did a great number of these, including many of the most distinguished people of his time. He designed and cut one of the largest woodcuts ever made, 'The Plough'. As a painter he experimented in many styles, but at his best was quite original. 'Bank Holiday' in the Tate Gallery, and the 'Portrait of a Lady' at Glasgow, are good examples of his clean, bright colour and rigorous drawing. The Tate Gallery also contains two self portraits and a landscape. The British Museum has 136 of the etchings.

Strang was elected A.R.A. in 1906, R.A. (as an engraver) in 1921, and president of the International Society of Sculptors, Painters, and Gravers in 1918. He was of middle height, strongly built. Direct in speech and combative in argument, he delighted in good company, talk, and fun. He often travelled on the Continent, and visited the United States. He made many portraits of himself, etched, drawn, and painted, including one in the Fitzwilliam Museum, Cambridge. He married in 1885 Agnes M'Symon, daughter of David Rogerson, J.P., provost of Dumbarton, and had four sons and one daughter. He died of heart disease, at Bournemouth, 12 April 1921.

[Private information; personal knowledge.]

L. B.

STRATHCONA AND MOUNT ROYAL, first Baron (1820–1914), Canadian financier. [See Smith, Donald Alexander.]

STRUTT, JOHN WILLIAM, third Baron Rayleigh (1842–1919), mathematician and physicist, was born at Langford Grove, Maldon, Essex, 12 November 1842, the eldest son of John James Strutt, second baron, by his marriage with Clara Elizabeth La Touche, eldest daughter of Captain Richard Vicars, R.E., and sister of Hedley Shafto Johnstone Vicars [q. v.]. As is said to have been the case with so many men of exceptional talent, he was a seven months' child. Throughout his infancy and youth he was of frail physique; his education was repeatedly interrupted by ill-health, and his prospects of attaining maturity appeared precarious. He entered Eton at the age of ten, but stayed only one half, a large part of which was spent in the school sanatorium. After three years at a private school at Wimbledon he went to Harrow, where his stay was almost as short as at Eton. In the autumn of 1857 he was put under the care of the Rev. George Townsend Warner, who took pupils at Torquay. Here he remained for four years, the surroundings proving more congenial and his health better than at his former schools. Having competed unsuccessfully for a scholarship at Trinity College, Cambridge, in 1860, he entered the college as a fellow-commoner in October 1861, and at once commenced reading for the mathematical tripos under Dr. E. J. Routh [q.v.], of Peterhouse. Although he was 'coached' privately during the summer he was not at first equal in mathematical attainments to the best of his contemporaries. But his exceptional abilities soon enabled him to overtake all his competitors, and it caused no surprise that the senior wranglership fell to him in January 1865. There still lingers in Cambridge a tradition as to the lucidity and literary finish of his answers in this examination. One examiner is said to have averred that they could have been printed without revision, and another that 'Strutt's answers were better than the books'. The fine sense of literary style which he displayed in the press of examinations never deserted him; every paper he wrote, even on the most abstruse subject, is a model of clearness and simplicity of diction, and conveys the impression of having been written without effort.

As a boy, Strutt had shown a distinct interest, although perhaps nothing more, in experimental science; his pocket money was spent on sulphuric acid, magnets, and an electric machine, while both in school and undergraduate days he took a great interest in the then infant science of photography. Four months before the tripos examination he had been awarded the Sheepshanks exhibition in astronomy, but astronomy at this time offered little to attract a powerful mind, and it was his earlier tastes and interests that determined his choice of occupation after he had taken his degree. He began by taking a course of chemical analysis with G. D. Liveing, the newly-appointed professor of chemistry. The choice of subject may seem strange, but the only experimental courses then available were those in chemistry, mineralogy, and certain biological sciences, a narrowness of choice which Strutt greatly resented. 'It wasted three or four years of my life', he said in later years. From now on his academic career was that normal to a man of his intellectual attainments. The first Smith's prize fell to him in 1865, he was elected a fellow of his college in the next year, and a fellow of the Royal Society in 1873.

In 1871 he married Evelyn, daughter of James Maitland Balfour, of Whittingehame, East Lothian, and sister of Mr. Arthur (afterwards Earl of) Balfour, the future prime minister. This step involved the resignation of his fellowship at Trinity and resulted in a temporary severance of his connexion with Cambridge. The year after his marriage, a severe attack of rheumatic fever led to his devoting a winter to travel in Egypt and Greece. Shortly after his return his father died (June 1873), and he succeeded as third Baron Rayleigh, taking up his residence in the family seat, Terling Place, Witham, Essex. Although, as throughout his life, his primary interest was scientific research, he now found himself compelled to devote a part of his time to the management of his estates, which were somewhat embarrassed by the prevailing agricultural depression. He acquired, or perhaps rather had forced upon him, a considerable knowledge of agriculture, which, combined with his general scientific knowledge and acumen, led to his practice in estate management being in many respects in advance of the time. He was especially interested in experimenting with artificial fertilisers, and was a pioneer in the use of nitrate of soda. After 1876 he left the entire management of the land to his younger brother, Edward Strutt.

This period saw the commencement of Rayleigh's lifelong interest in psychical research. At first he expected that investigation would rapidly lead to a definite conclusion, either positive or negative. Apparently he expected the former, in which case, his son believes, he was prepared to throw the greater part of his energies into a study of psychic phenomena. When it became clear that no such definite conclusion was being attained, he returned to orthodox scientific work. His recreations at this time were travel, tennis, and photography; a taste for music he shared with his wife. Shooting parties, which for some years he gave every winter, and ordinary social engagements, occupied but a small part of his time; it was not until later years that Terling became a gathering place for scientists from all the corners of the earth. He held strong conservative, and still stronger unionist, opinions, but the possibility of a political career did not attract him. He seconded the address in the House of Lords in 1875, and on rare occasions intervened in debate, but in general was resolute in not allowing politics to interfere with science.

Although he had taken his degree in 1865, and had immediately afterwards embarked on the experimental study of chemistry, it was not until 1869 that Rayleigh's first scientific paper appeared, bearing the title *Some Electro-magnetic Phenomena considered in connexion with the Dynamical Theory*. The paper has an interest beyond that which generally attaches to the first efforts of even the most brilliant investigators, in that it was a perfect example of the method its author was to pursue throughout his career. A dynamical theory of the electro-magnetic field had been given by James Clerk-Maxwell [q.v.] in terms of abstruse mathematical equations. Rayleigh elucidated and simplified this recondite theory—almost, one might say, made it intelligible to the average man—by showing that the intricate processes of the electro-magnetic field found practically perfect analogies in such well-understood phenomena as the bursting of a water-pipe under sudden pressure and the action of a hydraulic ram. The capacity for understanding everything just a little more deeply than anyone else, and the consequent capacity for exhibiting it in its simplest aspect, which formed so marked a characteristic of all Rayleigh's writings, was fully apparent in this, his first paper, which, as Sir Arthur Schuster remarks, 'bears the imprint of the craftsman marked as clearly as a picture by Perugino carries the signature of the artist in every square inch'. From now until his death the 446 papers which are reprinted in the six volumes of his collected works issued in a steady, unbroken flow. Except for a period of intense activity while he held the Cavendish professorship at Cambridge, these papers appeared with remarkable regularity at the rate of about nine a year. Each records some definite clear-cut advance, and records it in a perfectly direct and unambiguous manner. Limitations of space prevent reference to more than the outstanding landmarks of his scientific life.

In the period between his first paper (1869) and his election to the Cavendish professorship (1879), Rayleigh's work dealt mainly with electrical questions, problems of light and colour, and dynamical questions of resonance and vibrations both of gases and of elastic solids. His investigations in these latter subjects ultimately formed the foundation of his *Treatise on the Theory of Sound*. This, the only text-book he ever wrote, was begun during his Egyptian tour in 1873, but was not published until 1877, when it at once took rank as the leading book on the subject, a position it has retained ever since.

In 1879 Clerk-Maxwell died, after holding for only eight years the Cavendish professorship of experimental physics which had been founded for him at Cambridge. In accordance with a widely-expressed wish, the professorship was re-established specially for Lord Rayleigh, and he was duly elected in December 1879. The taking up of his professorial duties not only marks the commencement of the most active period of his scientific life, but coincides also with a change in the nature of his papers. He thought it important that the energies of the laboratory under his charge should be devoted in the main to some one big problem of research in which all who wished could take part. The subject selected was a re-determination of the electrical units in absolute measure. Measurements had been made by a committee of the British Association in 1863, but doubt had been thrown on their accuracy, and a re-determination was urgently needed. The subject had the disadvantage of giving but little scope to the originality or intellectual powers of an ambitious student, but Rayleigh succeeded in persuading a band of workers, some of whom have since risen to the highest scientific positions, to buckle down to the tedious drudgery involved in exact measurements. The result was the classical series of papers published, mainly by the Royal Society, in 1881–1883, and reprinted in volume ii of Rayleigh's collected works.

Finding his life at Cambridge rather too exacting, Rayleigh resigned his professorship at the end of 1884 and retired to Terling to pursue his researches in his private laboratory. A few months later he accepted the secretaryship of the Royal Society, vacant through the resignation of Sir George G. Stokes. The duties of this office were not so onerous as they have since become, but that he found them sufficiently so is suggested by a sentence which he wrote in the obituary notice of his predecessor. Commenting on the marked decrease of scientific output resulting from Stokes's acceptance of the secretaryship, he remarked, 'The reflexion suggests itself that scientific men should be left to scientific work and should not be tempted to assume heavy administrative duties, at any rate until such time as they have delivered their more important messages to the world'. No such falling-off occurred in Rayleigh's work, his output of work being consistently high throughout his eleven years of secretaryship. The tenure of this office gave him the opportunity to discover and rescue from oblivion the valuable memoir in which J. J. Waterston in 1846 had anticipated some of the important features of the kinetic theory of gases. During this period he began his experimental determinations of the densities of gases, of which the culminating success was the discovery of argon in 1894. In 1892 he had announced that two samples of nitrogen which he had prepared in chemically different ways had shown densities differing by as much as one part in 1,000, and had concluded that such a difference could be attributed only to a variation in the character of the gas. Gradually he was led to the view that what had so far been regarded as pure atmospheric nitrogen was a mixture of chemical nitrogen and some heavier atmospheric constituent. Sir William Ramsay [q.v.] joined the research in its later stages, the final outcome being the classical paper *Argon, a new Constituent of the Atmosphere* which was communicated to the Royal Society by Rayleigh and Ramsay jointly on 31 January 1895. About this time Rayleigh became deeply interested in physical optics. His researches in this subject will perhaps constitute his most enduring title to fame, the papers in which they are recorded, over 150 in number, are probably those in which his intellectual powers are displayed to best advantage, and he himself said, when late in life he thanked the Royal Society for the award of their Rumford medal, that they were those which had given the greatest pleasure to their author.

In his later years honours and responsibilities fell thick upon Rayleigh. He was one of the original recipients of the order of merit in 1902; he received a Nobel prize, jointly with Sir William Ramsay, in 1904, and he was made a privy councillor in 1905. In the same year he was elected president of the Royal Society, and in 1908 succeeded the Duke of Devonshire as chancellor of the university of Cambridge. Some of the most arduous, although probably also most pleasant, duties of his later life centred in his association with the National Physical Laboratory. He acted as chairman of the Treasury committee which reported in favour of its formation in 1898, and presided with unfailing regularity over the meetings of its executive committee until the onset of his last illness. In 1909 he was appointed president of the special government advisory committee on aeronautics, an appointment which led to his taking great interest in, and devoting much time to, problems of aviation.

The passing of Lord Kelvin left Rayleigh undisputed leader of British science on the physical side. It is no easy task to explain to the layman the grounds on which this supremacy was unanimously accorded him. His massive, precise, and perfectly balanced mind was utterly removed from that of the erratic genius who typifies the great scientist in the popular imagination. Of striking discoveries or inventions practically none stand to his credit with the single exception of the discovery of argon. His special aptitude was for arranging and levelling up existing knowledge rather than for taking giant strides into unexplored country. The outstanding qualities of his writings were thoroughness and clearness: he made everything seem obvious. These talents which would have been dangerous in a man of less sound judgement, or one less scrupulously careful not to lead others astray, were safe in Rayleigh's keeping. The inscription on his memorial in Westminster Abbey, 'An unerring leader in the advancement of natural knowledge', does not overstate the case. His researches covered almost the whole field of exact science; he was apparently equally at home in physics, chemistry, and mathematics. Although professing but little patience with the refinements of modern pure mathematics, he could always muster the technique necessary for the treatment of a practical problem, and his solutions, invariably direct, artistic, and workmanlike, never fail to inspire admiration for his mastery of mathematical methods. Although not directly concerned with the great strides made by molecular physics in the latter years of his life, his judgement in these matters, in strong contrast with that of some of his contemporaries, was always fair, open-minded, and acute. His record of scientific work, great though it is, would have been greater had it not been that he felt it a duty to shoulder any administrative responsibility under which he believed that he could achieve valuable work. His personal preference would have undoubtedly been for pursuing his scientific investigations in the quiet of his country seat and the detachment of his private laboratory.

Rayleigh died at Witham, Essex, on 30 June 1919, having been at work on a scientific paper only five days previously. Although his physical health had for some time been feeble his mind had retained its power to the end. By his marriage he had three sons, of whom the eldest, Robert John Strutt (born 1875), already well known as a physicist, succeeded to the barony.

A portrait of Lord Rayleigh in his robes as chancellor of the university, painted by Sir Hubert von Herkomer in 1911, hangs in the Examination Hall at Cambridge; another portrait, by Sir George Reid, is in the rooms of the Royal Society (*Royal Academy Pictures*, 1911).

[Robert John Strutt, fourth Baron Rayleigh, *John William Strutt, third Baron Rayleigh*, 1924; *Proceedings* of the Royal Society, vol. xcviii, A, 1921 (with portrait); Sir R. T. Glazebrook, *The Rayleigh Period*, in *The History of the Cavendish Laboratory*, 1910; personal knowledge.] J. H. J.

SUTTON, MARTIN JOHN (1850–1913), scientific agriculturist, born at Reading in 1850, was the eldest son of Martin Hope Sutton, senior partner in the seed firm of Sutton and Sons, which was founded by John Sutton in 1806. Martin John Sutton was educated at Blackheath Proprietary School until he reached the age of sixteen. He then entered the family business as a junior and, having become familiar with the work of every department, he was taken into partnership in 1871. In 1887 he became senior partner on his father's retirement. Before his time the firm already had a high reputation for its care in selecting and testing seeds, and for experimental work (inaugurated by his father) on the improvement of the potato and of agricultural grasses. He continued and extended these investigations in a thoroughly scientific spirit. He made searching field-trials both on the nursery grounds of the firm and on his private farms. He succeeded, by the help of the researches of the French botanist Vilmorin, in improving the methods of seed-selection, and he collaborated with Dr. J. A. Voelcker in experiments on grass-lands. Some of his results were stated in his standard book on *Permanent and Temporary Pastures* (sixth edition, 1902), to which a gold medal was awarded at the Paris Exhibition of 1900. Under his guidance the firm of Sutton became celebrated for numerous and important new strains of farm and garden plants. His own interests centred in practical agriculture. He was a successful amateur breeder of cattle, sheep, and horses. He published important papers on wheat-growing and on agricultural education. He served for twenty-three years on the council of the Royal Agricultural Society and was a leading member of the Smithfield Club and of the London Farmers' Club. He was also a fellow of the Linnean Society, and a chevalier of the legion of honour and of the ordre du mérite agricole.

In politics Sutton was a conservative, with some characteristic reservations. He refused to stand for Reading in 1898 because he disapproved of his party's attitude towards the questions of liquor control and of religious teaching in elementary schools. He took his share in the work of county and municipal administration, and served as mayor of Reading in 1904. He was a staunch churchman of the evangelical type, sat for the diocese of Oxford in the Canterbury House of Laymen, and took part in founding the Imperial Sunday Alliance (1908). He was a generous supporter of religious, philanthropic, and educational institutions, especially in Reading and its neighbourhood.

Sutton was twice married: first, in 1875 to Emily Owen (died 1911), daughter of Colonel Henry Fouquet; secondly, in 1912 to Grace, eldest daughter of Charles Thomas Studd, the African missionary. By his first wife he had two sons and a daughter, who survived him. He died of heart-failure on 14 December 1913, while staying at a London hotel, and was buried at Sonning.

[Obituary notices in *The Times, Daily Telegraph, Record, Evening Standard*, and *Nature*; private information.] H. W. C. D.

SWAN, Sir JOSEPH WILSON (1828–1914), chemist and electrical inventor, the second son of John Swan, by his wife, Isabella Cameron, was born at Sunderland 31 October 1828, and educated at Hendon Lodge and Hylton Castle, near Sunderland, under the Rev. John Wood, who interested him in science and encouraged him to study such scientific books as were then available. At the age of fourteen he was apprenticed to a firm of chemists and druggists at Sunderland, where he obtained considerable experience in operative and experimental chemistry. Before the end of his apprenticeship he joined the business of John Mawson, a chemist of Newcastle, and, encouraged by Mawson's kindly interest, he continued his experimental researches, and later became a partner in the business.

Swan was interested in photography, and, on the invention of the collodion process by Frederick Scott Archer [q.v.] in 1851, turned his attention to improvements in the manufacture of collodion; his firm soon after brought out a preparation of collodion for photographic use which has never been excelled. The experiments of W. H. Fox Talbot [q.v.] and Farguier had shown the possibility of a photographic printing process based on the hardening action of light on bichromated gelatine, but the methods were uncertain and of little practical use until Swan in 1864 patented the 'carbon process' (afterwards known as 'autotype'), which by the use of the methods of single and double transfer rendered the production of permanent prints a matter of ease and certainty. The carbon process was also used for the production of a variable resist to the etching solution in photogravure and became the basis of that widely-used form of photo-engraving. The variation of relief in a carbon print suggested to Swan the making of an electro-type matrix from which prints were mechanically produced by casting with a gelatinous pigment, and the process of 'photo-mezzotint', patented in 1865, led to the stannotype and Woodburytype methods of printing. The chrome tanning of leather was also one of the results of Swan's study of the reactions of chromic acid and gelatine. During the next fifteen years Swan experimented on the production of typographic half-tone blocks and patented the use of line screens in such work.

In 1871 Swan's attention was attracted to the improvement of the gelatino-bromide of silver emulsion invented by Dr. R. L. Maddox, and he discovered that the sensitiveness depended on the temperature at which the emulsion was formed, and also on its being subjected for some time to a somewhat high temperature. This was the real starting-point of the manufacture of rapid dry plates, and the gelatine-silver bromide plates of Mawson and Swan soon became famous. Two years later the same methods were employed in the preparation of bromide paper, the forerunner of the development papers afterwards so widely used.

Swan's name is more widely known in connexion with the development of incandescent electric lighting. Arc lights, run from primary batteries, had been in use for some time, but the subdivision of the electric light was the great difficulty, and to this Swan turned his attention. At a lecture given by W. E. Staite he had been much interested by the light given off by a fine platinum-iridium wire rendered incandescent by a battery current, and he considered that in this direction lay the solution of the problem of subdivision. T. A. Edison had already patented a lamp in which a carbon high resistance filament was heated to incandescence in a vacuous globe, but owing to the difficulty of preparing the filaments and of obtaining a good vacuum in the globe, the lamps were short-lived and of little practical use. Swan, however, succeeded in producing fine carbon filaments by squirting a solution of dissolved cellulose ('viscose') through fine apertures into a coagulating solution, and the filaments so obtained, after drying and carbonization, were mounted to the conducting 'leads' by short-circuiting under a solution of benzol and aniline, while the application of the Sprengel air-pump secured the necessary vacuum in the globe. His first lamp was shown at the Newcastle Literary and Philosophical Society in February 1879, and in that year his own house and that of (Sir) William Crookes [q.v.] were lit by these lamps. Swan's improvements in Edison's invention were a complete success, and the Edison-Swan lamp solved the problem.

In other branches of electrical science Swan made important advances. His improvements in C. A. Faure's storage batteries by the invention of the cellular-surfaced lead plate—so formed as to hold securely the lead oxide—made possible the modern electrical accumulator; and his discovery of the extraordinary influence of the presence of a small quantity of gelatine in accelerating the deposition of copper in electrolytic cells rendered the rapid production of electrolytic copper a matter of certainty.

Swan was twice married: first, in 1862 to Frances (died 1868), daughter of William White; secondly, in 1871 to Hannah, sister of his first wife. He had four sons and four daughters who attained adult age. He died at Overhill, Warlingham, Surrey, 27 May 1914.

Swan received many distinctions in recognition of his remarkable work in applied science. In 1904 he was awarded the Hughes medal of the Royal Society, of which he had been elected a fellow in 1894; and he was made an honorary fellow, and received the progress medal, of the Royal Photographic Society in 1902. He was president of the Institute of Electrical Engineers from 1898 to 1899; of the Society of Chemical Industry in 1900 and 1901; and first president of the Faraday Society from 1903 to 1904. He was made chevalier of the legion of honour in 1881, and was knighted in 1904.

There is a drawing of Swan by Miss Cohen in the National Portrait Gallery.

[*The Times*, 28 May 1914; *Photographic Journal*, June 1914; *Journal* of the Institute of Electrical Engineers, vol. lii; *Journal* of the Society of Chemical Industry, 15 July 1902; numerous papers in the *Photographic Journal* and the *British Journal of Photography* from 1864 onwards.] W. B. F.

SWEET, HENRY (1845–1912), phonetician, comparative philologist, and anglicist, the eldest son of George Sweet, barrister-at-law, of the Inner Temple, by his wife, Agnes Nicholson, was born in London 15 September 1845. His father was of Frisian and West of England origin, his mother of Scottish birth. In his early life Sweet suffered under great physical disadvantages; as a boy he was subject to fits, and also to extreme short-sightedness, which made reading inconceivably difficult, until the defect was relieved in later years. In the subjects of which he became a master Sweet was largely self-taught. He began with an interest in alphabets; but the first advance in the direction of his life's work was due to his study of Rask's grammar of Anglo-Saxon.

Sweet's formal education began in his tenth year at a private school, Bruce Castle, Tottenham. At the age of sixteen he went to King's College School, London. In 1864 he gained experience of German philological method at the university of Heidelberg. After a short time in a merchant's office, he entered Balliol College, Oxford, in 1869. He was ill fitted by nature and to some extent by the turn which his studies had taken, to adapt himself to the classical curriculum of the university. He won a Taylorian scholarship in German and gained thereby the favourable notice of Friedrich Max Müller, but his fourth class in *literae humaniores* (1873) did not commend him in the eyes of university or college authorities, and no position in Oxford was offered to him.

Sweet had, however, already contributed to the *Proceedings* of the London Philological Society, and had published in 1871 an edition of King Alfred's translation of the *Cura Pastoralis* of Gregory the Great, in which he had laid the foundations of the dialectology of Old English. He had been familiar since 1868 with the system of A. Melville Bell's *Visible Speech* (1863), and this bore fruit in his *Handbook of Phonetics: including a Popular Exposition of the Principles of Spelling Reform*, published in 1877. His *History of English Sounds from the earliest period* had appeared in 1874; this is a work of great originality, and in its enlarged form (1888) became a standard text-book.

In 1876 Sweet published the first edition of his famous *Anglo-Saxon Reader*, a selection of Old English literature that has not been surpassed in any similar compass. In the twenty years following he produced most of that pioneer work which, by its range and originality, distinguishes him as the greatest philologist that this country has produced. In *The Oldest English Texts* (1885), the result of some seven years of the closest work, he put the early history of English once for all on a sound basis. Through the medium of his *Elementarbuch des gesprochenen Englisch* (1885) and the English edition of it (1890) he taught phonetics to Europe; he must, indeed, be considered to be the chief founder of modern phonetics, and his descriptions of the sounds of the languages examined by him—for instance, Danish, Welsh, Russian, and Portuguese—will always retain their value.

Sweet applied the data of human speech with vital results to the exposition of the history of the English language and to the elucidation of wider linguistic problems. Supreme examples of his method are seen in *A New English Grammar* (1892, 1898) and *The History of Language* (1900). His last word on the subject of phonetics is contained in *The Sounds of English : an Introduction to Phonetics* (1908), where he refers to the value and possibilities of instrumental phonetics. Few scholars, native or foreign, have left their mark so plainly and permanently upon the study of the grammar and lexicography of Old English, of the relation of grammar to the laws of thought, and of the history of English in all its forms and periods.

In the accomplishment of this great and lasting work Sweet enjoyed neither an official position nor a settled endowment until 1901, when a readership in phonetics was created for him at Oxford. In 1876 he was an unsuccessful candidate for the chair of comparative philology (to which no salary was attached) at University College, London ; in 1885 he failed to obtain the newly founded Merton professorship of English language and literature at Oxford. In 1898 he accepted a lectureship in English language at University College, Liverpool, but he was obliged to resign, for private reasons, before he had taken up the duties. In 1901 the chair of comparative philology at Oxford became vacant by the death of Max Müller, and once again Sweet was an unsuccessful candidate, although supported by the testimony of several of the greatest philologists in Europe : this failure was perhaps the severest blow of all. Thus, to the astonishment of foreign scholars, he remained all his life deprived of those large opportunities which an important chair might have afforded him of working out liberal schemes for a school of linguistic study which he had adumbrated as far back as the early 'eighties.

In 1887 Sweet married Mary Aletheia, youngest daughter of Samuel Birch, the Egyptologist [q.v.], and sister of Walter de Gray Birch, for many years senior assistant in the MSS. department of the British Museum. After several changes of residence, he and his wife settled permanently in Oxford in 1895. Here he was brought into contact with a considerable group of eminent philologists. It was not long, however, before trouble arose from some obscure cause. Living somewhat remote from society, Sweet was prone to magnify chance sayings and doings out of all proportion to their significance. Misunderstandings became frequent ; feud succeeded feud, and finally Sweet became estranged from nearly all his philological contemporaries in Oxford. With a few, however, he remained in touch, among them being Max Müller ; with two others at least, Frederick York Powell and F. C. Conybeare, he remained on intimate terms. The fault was not all on his side. A more general spirit of magnanimity towards a great worker and thinker would have made his position easier. But Sweet did not understand the ways of the world, and he resented violently anything that he conceived to savour of jealousy or intrigue. More than once his irritation provoked him to outbursts which his most fervent admirers could not but deplore.

The keynote of Sweet's work and character was independence. As a philologist, he belonged to no school of thought ; as a man, he took his own way. He was widely interested in many things ; he had the gifts of humour and an open mind. He was always learning. He was close on fifty years of age when he began the study of Arabic, Chinese, and Finnish. Late in life, also, he took to music, and was at one time busy with a new system of musical notation. His teaching was an inspiration to many young scholars.

Sweet's power of literary appreciation and expression is less well known, but is clearly evident in, for instance, his lecture on *Shelley's Nature Poetry* (delivered in 1888 and privately printed in 1901), and in his sketches of persons and places in *A Primer of Spoken English* (1890). He was interested in spiritualism and Swedenborgianism, and looked forward to flying, 'real flying, not with bags and stoves.'

Sweet was of middle height and thickset, with a head remarkable at once for its length and breadth, with deep square shoulders, hair that was golden-yellow in his youth, and blue eyes, to which his excessive shortsightedness lent a glaring aspect. He died of pernicious anaemia at Oxford 30 April 1912, and was buried at Wolvercote. He had no children.

[H. C. K. Wyld in *Modern Language Quarterly*, July 1901; H. C. K. Wyld and Alois Brandl in *Archiv für das Studium der neueren Sprachen und Literaturen*, April 1913; J. A. S. in *Oxford Magazine*, 9 May 1912; *Transactions* and *Proceedings* of the Philological Society (London) 1868–1885; the several prefaces to Sweet's works, and letters in *Academy*, 23 January, &c., 1886; *Collected Papers of Henry Sweet*, arranged by H. C. K. Wyld, 1913; private information; personal knowledge.]

C. T. O.

SWETE, HENRY BARCLAY (1835–1917), regius professor of divinity at Cambridge, was the only child of the Rev. John Swete, D.D., lecturer of St. Mary Redcliffe, Bristol, afterwards vicar of Blagdon, Somerset, by his second wife,

Caroline Ann Skinner Barclay. He was born at Redlands, Bristol, 14 March 1835. Educated at Bishop's College, Bristol, King's College, London, and Gonville and Caius College, Cambridge, he graduated as seventh classic in 1858, and was elected to a fellowship at his college. After ordination he spent some years in pastoral work as curate to his father at Blagdon. Returning to Cambridge in 1865, he held the office of dean, tutor, and theological lecturer of his college. But the life of a college official was never congenial to him. Naturally diffident and shy, he showed at this period little indication of the gifts which were to mark his later career, though his first serious piece of theological work, two essays on the history of the doctrine of the Holy Spirit (1873, 1876), was published during these years. In 1877 Swete was offered the college living of Ashdon, Essex, and this appointment, while appealing to his strong pastoral instinct, also afforded him leisure for study. During this period the valuable article on the Holy Spirit, embodying the substance of the earlier essays, was written for Smith's *Dictionary of Christian Biography* (s.v. *Holy Ghost*), and the edition of the Commentaries of Theodore of Mopsuestia on the Minor Epistles of St. Paul (1880–1882) was published. Another important undertaking was an edition of the text of the Septuagint version of the Old Testament, *The Old Testament in Greek according to the Septuagint*, 3 vols. (1887, 1891, 1894), entrusted to him by the syndics of the Cambridge University Press, and intended to prepare the way for a larger edition. From 1882 to 1890 he held, with his living, the professorship of pastoral theology at King's College, London.

Swete's return to Cambridge in 1890 as regius professor of divinity was viewed with misgiving by many who recognized his learning and scholarship, but who feared that his shy and diffident manner, and the specialized character of his studies, unfitted him to succeed so great a teacher as Dr. Westcott. His twenty-five years' tenure of the professorship, however, abundantly justified his selection, and he developed quite unforeseen initiative and activity in stimulating and guiding theological study at Cambridge. In his professorial lectures he constantly bore in mind the needs of ordinands; his understanding of those needs won for him the sympathy and interest of his pupils, and his lectures became the best attended courses in the divinity faculty. To the more serious students he was always ready to offer encouragement and guidance. Probably the greatest service which he rendered as professor was the stimulus which he gave to younger men by setting them to work on some particular field of research. He also enlisted the services of scholars in joint schemes of literary work, and was the general editor of three volumes of essays dealing with theological and biblical questions of the day and with the early history of the Church and ministry. Other literary ventures which owed their inception to him were the series of *Patristic Texts* and the *Cambridge Handbooks of Liturgical Study*. It was due to his initiative that a committee of scholars from Cambridge, Oxford, and Durham brought into being the *Journal of Theological Studies* in 1899. He was also the founder of the Cambridge Theological Society. His interest in the parochial clergy and their studies was shown in another creation of his, the Central Society of Sacred Study, an organization which was founded in 1899, and has since extended its work to every English diocese and also to other English-speaking lands.

Amid these various practical schemes Swete found time for considerable literary activity of his own. His published works show a wide range of theological interests, and deal with the Greek version of the Old Testament, the exegesis of the New Testament, Christian doctrine, patristic studies, the history and interpretation of the Apostles' Creed, and Christian worship. All his work exhibits precise and careful scholarship, and a singular delicacy and grace of style. While he welcomed all the aids of the new scholarship and learning, his judgement on critical questions was cautious and sober, and on the fundamental questions of belief he remained loyal to the tradition of the Church. He resigned his professorship in 1915 and retired to Hitchin, where he died 10 May 1917. He was unmarried.

As a scholar his published works place him in the foremost rank. His practical achievement in stimulating theological study not only among professed scholars, but also among the clergy and educated Christian laity, marks his professorship as one of the most fruitful in the history of the chair. A gracious and winning personality, he was singularly modest, and inspired by a profound sense of the value of the things of the spirit.

A portrait of Swete, painted by Hugh Rivière in 1906, is at Caius College.

[*Henry Barclay Swete. A Remembrance*, 1918, containing bibliography reprinted from the *Journal of Theological Studies*; notices by Bishop F. H. Chase, *Church Quarterly Review*, October 1917, and by Dr. A. J. Mason, *Journal of Theological Studies*, July 1917; personal knowledge.] J. H. S-Y.

SWINFEN, first BARON (1851–1919), judge. [See EADY, CHARLES SWINFEN.]

SYKES, SIR MARK, sixth baronet (1879–1919), traveller, soldier, and politician, was born in London 16 March 1879, the only child of Sir Tatton Sykes, fifth baronet, of Sledmere, Yorkshire, by his wife, Jessica, elder daughter of the Rt. Hon. George Augustus Frederick Cavendish-Bentinck, M.P. At the age of three he was received, with his mother, into the Roman Catholic communion. He had no continuous schooling, being withdrawn repeatedly from private tutors to accompany his father on long journeys abroad; but for short periods he was placed under Jesuit instruction at Beaumont College, at Monaco, and at Brussels. Thus he learned to speak French fluently and acquired miscellaneous experience and interests; but after matriculation at Jesus College, Cambridge, in 1897, he showed no aptitude for the university course, and went down without a degree. Two Lent terms he spent in the Near East, and of these wanderings he published a humorous account under the title *Through Five Turkish Provinces* (1900). He joined the Yorkshire militia, and served with it in 1902 in South Africa, where, till after the peace, he was employed in guarding lines of communication. After returning home he went off to Syria, Mesopotamia, and Southern Kurdistan, about whose peoples and scenery he wrote in the most amusing of his books, *Dar ul-Islam* (1904). For a short time in 1904–1905 he served at Dublin Castle as private secretary to Mr. George Wyndham [q.v.], and gained a lasting interest in the Irish question; but in 1905 he returned to Turkey as honorary attaché to the British embassy. He had married in 1903 Edith Violet, third daughter of Sir John Eldon Gorst [q.v.], whom he met first at Cambridge, and now took her with him through the north of Asia Minor. Later, he utilised opportunities to revisit Mesopotamia and Syria, in which lands he did some mapping for the War Office. Accounts of these travels appeared in his *Five Mansions of the House of Othman* (1909), and at the end of *The Caliphs' Last Heritage* (1915), the most ambitious of his books.

In 1907 Sykes left Constantinople, and was adopted as conservative candidate for the Buckrose division of the East Riding; but he failed to secure the seat at two elections in 1910. In 1911 he was returned for Central Hull, and found no difficulty in gaining from the first the ear of the House of Commons, thanks to a turn of humour, a pleasing voice, and an unusual measure of youthful audacity. As a leading member of a small group of young conservative independents he spoke frequently on matters military, Oriental, and Irish, and became well known for pungent political caricatures and mimicry. He had been noted as an actor at Cambridge. His humour was nowhere better used than in a skit on the *Infantry Drill Book*, which he wrote in collaboration with Mr. Edmund T. Sandars and issued, in 1902, as *Tactics and Military Training by Maj.-Gen. D'Ordel.* Always a keen amateur of military theory, he showed interest also in the improvement of equipment and armament, and twice (1912 and 1914) took part in organizing military tournaments at Olympia.

In 1913 Sykes's father died and he inherited Sledmere, where he largely rebuilt the ancestral house. Before the outbreak of the European War he had raised a reserve battalion of the Yorkshire regiment, largely from wagoners and other tenants on his estates; but he was prevented from accompanying it to France in 1914 by orders from head-quarters to undertake political duties, with the rank of lieutenant-colonel. These took him to Serbia, Bulgaria, Egypt, and India, and occupied his time till the summer of 1915, when objections taken by France to proposed action by Great Britain in Syria, coinciding with a prospect of failure in the Dardanelles, rendered it expedient that preliminary agreement should be arrived at among the Allies about the future of the Near East.

Sykes's knowledge of French, his political and diplomatic training, and his general first-hand acquaintance with the field to be discussed, suggested to the Foreign Office and to Lord Kitchener his admission to the formal conversations which were instituted in London that autumn with the French Foreign Office, represented by M. Georges Picot, sometime consul-general in Syria. The British principals, overdone with other duties, soon fell out; and after the beginning of 1916 Sykes was left virtually single-handed to carry on the negotiation with M. Picot. His general instructions were to spare no effort to conciliate French susceptibilities about Syria, but to detach, so far as possible, the Palestinian question from the Syrian, and to conserve intact the special interests of Great Britain in Arabia, where steps had already been taken by the British towards bringing about a rising by the emir of Mecca. Sykes had become an enthusiast for Lord Kitchener's pro-Arab policy, and in negotiating the agreement with France he laboured to render possible the ultimate establishment of Arab independence, even in Syria. So far as he succeeded he had in the main to thank M. Picot's fixed disbelief in the possibility of such independence. Sykes was sent to communicate the draft agreement to M. Sazonof at Petrograd and to the Grand Duke Nicholas in the Caucasus; and on 16 May it was duly signed by the three governments and kept secret. It assigned definite spheres of interest to each of the signatory powers: to Russia, the north Armenian and the south Kurdish provinces, to beyond Trebizond on the west; to France, Cilicia and Cappadocia, with the south Armenian provinces down to Aintab, and the Syrian littoral; to Great Britain, southern Mesopotamia with Bagdad, and the ports of Haifa and Jaffa. The zone between the French and British territories was to be placed under Arab sovereignty, and Palestine was to be subjected to a special régime, the details of which were reserved for future settlement. Commonly spoken of since as the 'Sykes-Picot Agreement', this pact has focussed unfair criticism upon the British representative, who was acting under orders at a moment of danger to the continuance of the Entente, while neither an Arab rising nor a British conquest of Palestine and Syria seemed likely to happen. At any rate the settlement thus arrived at enabled the British to go forward without let or hindrance in the war against the Turks.

Henceforward Sykes was attached to the Foreign Office, and used as chief adviser on Near Eastern policy, with special reference to the Arab revolt. Twice (1916 and 1917) he was sent out to Egypt to consult with the military command and the Arab bureau, and he accompanied M. Picot to Jidda in May 1917, in order to persuade King Husein of the reality of the Entente, and to secure some reasonable agreement about prospective Arab claims. A habit of reading his own thoughts in the minds of others, and a politician's instinct for scoring quickly, made him an unsafe negotiator with purposeful Orientals; but usually he won their affection, and he will be remembered by Arabs not only as a champion of their nationality, but as the inventor of the quadricolor flag under which they marched to Damascus, and under which the Hejaz was subsequently ruled. In spite of his fervent Catholicism he was converted early to Zionism, which he believed to be a just cause, likely to serve England well with Russia and the United States, and not inconsistent with British pledges to the Arabs. He was employed at home throughout the autumn of 1917 to prepare public opinion for the Balfour declaration (November 1917), and no one became more popular with Zionist leaders. From the Foreign Office he was able to dictate the general tenor of the proclamation issued by General Allenby on his entry into Jerusalem (December 1917), as he had already dictated that read by General Sir Stanley Maude [q.v.] at Bagdad. With characteristic disregard of self-interest he refused from first to last all honours for these or other war services.

During the first half of 1918 Sykes exerted influence at home to impose a pro-Zionist direction on the administrative policy of General Allenby in Palestine, and to minimize difficulties raised by the French about a further British advance When Syria had fallen into British hands, and friction was imminent between the French administration in the coastal province and Feisal's administration in the interior, he asked to be sent out again on a roving commission. He was in Jerusalem when called upon to seek re-election to parliament for Hull; but despite his absence he was returned by an overwhelming majority, his wife acting for him throughout. Finally, he established himself at Aleppo, where he hoped to reconcile French aims with those of the Arabs, and also to serve the cause of the refugee Armenians—a people which he held to have been betrayed by the terms of the armistice with Turkey. By his earnestness and prestige he triumphed that winter, as few men could have done, over the disadvantages of his anomalous advisory position in territory occupied but not administered by the British; and never did he render better or more strenuous service. But the consequence was that when, in January 1919, he procured his recall, in order to lay the state of affairs in Syria before the British government, he was physically enfeebled. He halted in Paris where his wife, joined him. The Peace Conference had already assembled, and he began honestly and fearlessly to state facts unpalatable alike to French chauvinism and to British optimism and not a little derogatory of some of his own earlier enthusiasms. The mental strain of this effort further reduced his strength, leaving him but a poor chance when the influenza of that bitter spring attacked him. He died in Paris after only three days' illness, 16 February 1919, one month short of the age of forty. His body was taken to Sledmere. The concourse at his funeral betokened the personal affection that he had inspired; as did the numerous tributes paid to his memory by absent representatives of causes which he had advocated and even of some that he had discouraged.

In person, Sykes was typically Nordic—fair, tall, loosely and powerfully built—with humorous eyes and a winning smile. His laughter soon overcame his anger. Careless of appearances and manners, he paid little heed to polite conventions.

He left three sons and three daughters, and was succeeded in the baronetcy by his eldest son, Mark Tatton Richard (born 1905).

[Shane Leslie, *Mark Sykes, his Life and Letters*, 1923; *History of the Peace Conference at Paris*, vol. vi, 1924, pp. 15–17 for the terms of the Sykes-Picot agreement; private information; personal knowledge.]

D. G. H.
S. L.

TADEMA, Sir LAWRENCE ALMA- (1836–1912), painter. [See Alma-Tadema.]

TAYLOR, Sir JOHN (1833–1912), architect, was born at Warkworth, Northumberland, 15 November 1833, the son of William Taylor, of that place, by his wife, Elizabeth Bolton. After being educated privately, he entered H.M. Office of Works in 1859, and in the same year was appointed assistant surveyor of royal palaces, public buildings, and royal parks. In 1866 he became surveyor, and held this office until he retired in 1898 under the superannuation rule. His services were retained, however, as consulting architect until 1908, when he resigned. The ancient title of surveyor hardly expressed the character of the work which the holder of the office was expected to discharge in Taylor's time, and it has since been abandoned for that of architect. During the long period of his surveyorship Taylor made various additions to Marlborough House, the chief being a new storey (1886), and designed the new Bow Street police court and station (1879), the Bankruptcy Buildings in Carey Street (1892), the new wing of the Public Record Office, facing Chancery Lane (1896), and the Patent Office Library (1898), besides many smaller official buildings, including police courts and park lodges. He also added new exhibition rooms and the central staircase to the National Gallery (1887). He was charged with the general upkeep and maintenance of these buildings as well as of the Houses of Parliament, in which many alterations were made from time to time. He was also responsible for the structural arrangements for several important public functions, such as the thanksgiving services held at St. Paul's Cathedral for the recovery of the Prince of Wales (1872), and at Westminster Abbey for Queen Victoria's jubilee (1887). During the later years of his service he arranged for the rebuilding of the War Office and of the public buildings in Great George Street. Soon after his retirement, the architect, William Young, who had been appointed to design and superintend the erection of the new War Office, died, and Sir John Taylor was entrusted jointly with Mr. Young's son with the construction of these buildings. On their completion he resigned his position as consulting architect.

Taylor was regarded by the many first commissioners of works under whom he served as a sound and cautious adviser, and was much appreciated and esteemed by all those with whom he came in contact in the course of his public service. In recognition of his services he was made a C.B. in 1895 and a K.C.B. in 1897. He was elected a fellow of the Royal Institute of British Architects in 1881, and served on the council during the session 1899–1900, as a vice-president in 1905–1906, and as member of the art standing committee. He was a volunteer in the Civil Service Rifle Volunteers and, being a good shot, attended with regularity the competitions of the National Rifle Association, winning many cups, until his official duties prevented further attendance. He was also a keen golfer, and was at one time captain of the Royal Wimbledon Club; he was one of the founders of the Royal St. George's Club at Sandwich. He died 30 April 1912 at his residence at Surbiton Hill.

Taylor married in 1860 Emma Hamilton, daughter of Henry Hadland, and had three daughters.

[*The Times*, 2 May 1912.] H. T.

TENNIEL, Sir JOHN (1820–1914), artist and cartoonist, the youngest son of John Baptist Tenniel, a well-known dancing-master and instructor in arms, was born in Kensington 28 February 1820. He was educated at a private school in Kensington and received his first training as an artist at the Academy Schools. He did not remain long at the schools as he was dissatisfied with their teaching, but he afterwards joined the Clipstone Street Life Academy in Fitzroy Square, where he studied both the antique and the nude with Charles Keene [q.v.], his lifelong friend. He also attended anatomy lectures and studied the Elgin marbles and other sculpture at the British Museum. His interest in costume and armour was encouraged by Sir Frederic Madden [q.v.] of the manuscripts department of the Museum; and Tenniel now laid the foundation of a wide knowledge of both subjects which proved of great service to him in after years. In 1836, at the age of sixteen, he exhibited and sold an oil-picture at the Society of British Artists in Suffolk Street, and in the following year he began to exhibit at the Royal Academy. In 1845 he was successful in a cartoon competition for Westminster Hall and received a commission to execute a fresco (illustrating Dryden's 'St. Cecilia') in the House of Lords. For this purpose he went to Munich to study the process of fresco.

The year 1848 marks the turning-point in Tenniel's career. His illustrations to the Rev. Thomas James's version of *Æsop's Fables*, which appeared in this year, attracted considerable attention, and it was largely owing to this book that Mark Lemon [q.v.], at that time editor of *Punch*, invited Tenniel to join the staff in December 1850. The paper had been left in great straits by the sudden desertion of Richard Doyle [q.v.], the second cartoonist, and at the suggestion of Douglas Jerrold [q.v.] Tenniel was asked to take his place. As John Leech [q.v.], the first cartoonist, was still in his full vigour, Tenniel was at first mainly employed on fanciful initials, decorative borders, &c. His earliest cartoon, representing Lord John Russell as Jack the Giant-Killer advancing to attack Cardinal Wiseman, appeared in 1851. For some time he was not particularly successful as a cartoonist, but his reputation gradually increased owing to cartoons such as 'The British Lion's Vengeance on the Bengal Tiger' (1857); and in 1862 he began to contribute a weekly cartoon. When Leech died in 1864, Tenniel succeeded him as first cartoonist.

After 1864 Tenniel left London for scarcely more than a week for thirty years, with the exception of a short visit to Venice in 1878. During his fifty years' work on the staff of *Punch* he drew considerably over two thousand cartoons, rarely missing through absence or illness his regular contribution. His last cartoon appeared on 2 January 1901, immediately preceding his retirement. On the last occasion when he attended the weekly *Punch* dinner the customary course of proceedings was interrupted for him to receive a presentation from his colleagues. On 12 June in the same year a public dinner was given in his honour, at which the prime minister, Mr. (afterwards the Earl of) Balfour presided over a distinguished gathering. The warmth of Tenniel's reception was such that it overwhelmed him, and he broke down in attempting to reply to the toast of his health.

It would be impossible to enumerate here even the most striking of Tenniel's cartoons: two of the most notable were 'Dropping the Pilot' (1890), referring to the resignation of Bismarck, and 'Who said "*Atrocities*"?' (1895), showing Gladstone, as a terrier, indignant at the Armenian revelations. Several volumes of his cartoons have been published. *Cartoons from 'Punch'* (1864, second series 1870) was followed by *Cartoons from 'Punch'*, volume i, *1871–1881*, volume ii, *1882–1891* (1895), while in 1901, after his retirement, a volume was issued, entitled *Cartoons by Sir John Tenniel, selected from the pages of 'Punch'*, covering the whole period of his work.

For the remaining years of his life Tenniel lived in retirement at Kensington. In 1874 he had been elected a member of the Royal Institute of Painters in Water Colours, and in 1893 he was knighted. He died at his Kensington home 25 February 1914, within three days of his ninety-fourth birthday. Early in life Tenniel married a Miss Giani, who died two years later. They had no children.

It was said of Tenniel that 'it has been his mission, without sacrificing one iota of real power or true form, to purify parody and ennoble caricature'. He was not, indeed, a caricaturist in the usual sense of the term. Still less was he a libellist or a lampoonist. Through fifty years it was his mission to shoot at folly, to strike at fraud and corruption, to touch with delicate though firm hand the political problems of the hour. This task he accomplished with unfailing fancy and with a delightful humour which never degenerated into coarseness nor was lacking in dignity. Tenniel was never carried away by private feeling. His aim was to treat all public men with equality and fairness, and to be severe without being vindictive. Thus, he was always careful to make the politician, not the man, appear ridiculous, and the laugh raised is almost invariably good-natured. It is a remarkable fact that Tenniel never used models or nature for any of his drawings. In his portraits he was an idealist rather than a realist, since they were never taken from the life. His allegorical figures are notable for their beauty and statuesque qualities; his beasts, in which he especially delighted, for their dignity. All his designs are characterized by earnestness and directness, and his best work has great simplicity.

In addition to his drawings for *Punch* Tenniel did a certain amount of work as a book-illustrator. His illustrations to Lewis Carroll's *Alice's Adventures in Wonderland* (1865), and *Alice Through the Looking-Glass* (1872) are famous [See DODGSON, Charles Lutwidge.] He also illustrated, among other works, *Lalla Rookh* (1861), *The Ingoldsby Legends* (1864), and *Punch's Pocket-Book* (1876).

In private life Tenniel was genial and of an equable temper. Through an exceptionally long life, in which he came into contact with all sorts and conditions of men, it is safe to say that he never made an enemy, while few men have had more friends.

There is a portrait of Tenniel by Frank Holl in the National Portrait Gallery.

[*The Times*, 27 February 1914; Supplement to *Punch*, 4 March 1914; Cosmo Monkhouse, *The Life and Works of Sir John Tenniel* in *The Art Annual*, 1901; M. H. Spielmann, *History of Punch*, 1895; personal knowledge.]

H.W.L.

THOMAS, DAVID ALFRED, first VISCOUNT RHONDDA (1856–1918), statesman, colliery proprietor, and financier, was one of seventeen children born to Samuel Thomas and his second wife, Rachel Joseph. Twelve of these children died in infancy; David was the third of those who survived. He was born at Ysgyborwen, close to Aberdare, 26 March 1856. His father welcomed the news of his birth with the exclamation, 'Well, I see nothing for him but the workhouse'. This father was a remarkable man who had advanced his fortunes as a grocer in Merthyr Tydfil by dabbling in colliery speculations. Tight-fisted and despotic in the family circle, he was courageous to the point of daring in matters of business. He would sell sixpenny-worth of apples from his garden, would read the newspaper holding a candle in his hand, and would burn the garments of his young wife to punish her for extravagance: nevertheless he was ready to risk the savings of a hard and thrifty life whenever a speculation presented itself which promised fortune. At the time of his son's birth so desperate was his financial condition that had his bank known the true condition of his affairs he would have been ruined.

David Thomas was sent to a private school at Clifton, where he won two scholarships at Cambridge, one for Jesus College and another for Caius. He chose the second and went up to Cambridge in 1876, taking his B.A. degree four years later. He was slight and delicate, but notable for high spirits, a love of games, and a natural brilliance in mathematics. At Cambridge he learnt no more mathematics than he had easily acquired at school, and gave up almost all his time to rowing, boxing, and swimming. His scholarship, in consequence, was taken away from him. This love of games distinguished his character to the end of his life, giving him a certain charm of boyishness which quickly won for him the confidence and affection of men in all stations of life, from the great financial magnates of America to the most truculent of labour leaders in the South Wales coal-field. It is characteristic of him that he was still birds'-nesting as a Cabinet minister. In the year 1882 he married Sybil Margaret, daughter of George Augustus Haig, of Pen Ithon, Radnorshire, by whom he had one child, Margaret, afterwards Viscountess Rhondda. He became associated at this time with the Cambrian collieries in the Rhondda Valley. His skill in handling men and his ability in financial matters soon made him a power in South Wales, and he was returned, unopposed, as a Gladstonian liberal for Merthyr Tydfil in 1888. The elections of 1892, 1895, and 1900 found him in each case at the top of the poll, but he was ignored by the leaders of his party, even to the point of never once being asked to sit on a committee. Still at the top of the poll in 1906, and still ignored by his leaders, Thomas decided in 1910 to give himself up to business, relinquishing all the dreams he had sincerely cherished of rendering his country distinguished political service. The reason for his failure to make an impression on the House of Commons was said, falsely perhaps, to be that he was hard to get on with: a real bar to his political fortunes was the dullness of his speeches. In 1915 he was asked by

Mr. Lloyd George, then minister of munitions, to go to the United States on the business of the ministry. For his brilliant services on that occasion he was created Baron Rhondda, of Llanwern, in 1916, being promoted viscount, with special remainder to his daughter, in 1918. Mr. Lloyd George said of him: 'He organized a supply of munitions from the States and from Canada. He got the right men round him. He chose the right men, and he set things going. There were all sorts of quarrels and difficulties, but in every case he simply said, "I know only one thing: our need of guns and shells." From that hour the supply of munitions never wavered. It was Rhondda who gave to America and the Allies a breathing space and a chance. That service of his cannot be overestimated.' A few months before undertaking this mission he had been on board the *Lusitania* when it was sunk by the Germans.

Rhondda's next promotion was to be president of the Local Government Board, but it was not until 1917, when he succeeded Lord Devonport as food minister, that he became a popular figure. His success was almost entirely of a personal nature. He was accessible to the press and made many speeches up and down the country. Schemes of rationing were easily carried out under his influence. He had real genius in choosing the right man for a particular purpose, and communicated to the persons of his choice an enthusiasm akin to his own. He was a man of vision, not an organizer. He would sit up to all hours of the night covering sheets of paper with the small, scribbled figures of his calculations, but he left to others the difficult work of giving structure to his ideas. His grasp of a problem was complete, but the builder's work was too slow for his patience. However, the builder always worked the better for the inspiration of Rhondda's charm and boyish eagerness to score a success. He was accepted by the nation as a man of scrupulous honour and impartial justice. Every hardship which he called upon the people to bear was recognized as necessary and was seen to press equally on all classes. He enjoyed his popularity, spared himself no labour to carry the nation with him, and died at his home, Llanwern, under the strain of hard work, on 3 July 1918.

Lord Rhondda was a lovable man to those in whom he felt any interest. The centre of his character was an egotism without guile—the egotism of a schoolboy who loves success and is not ashamed to show it. He never lost his affection for field and hedgerow. His heart to the last was with his notable herd of white-faced Herefords at Llanwern. To the end of his days he was given to mild practical joking and to a jesting persiflage. He had no clear faith, but said his prayers every day. He surrounded himself with youthful people, calling them his 'young germs', and avoided close intimacy with the aged, believing that they were bad for his health. Clear-headed, far-sighted, ambitious, daring, and superstitious, he regarded life as a game to be played entirely for its own sake, and truly believed that money was merely the symbol of the real prize, which was success.

[*D. A. Thomas: Viscount Rhondda*, by his Daughter and others, 1921; personal knowledge. Portrait, *Royal Academy Pictures*, 1917.] H. B–E.

THOMAS, PHILIP EDWARD (1878–1917), critic and poet, born in Lambeth 3 March 1878, the eldest son of Philip Henry Thomas, staff clerk for light railways and tramways at the Board of Trade, by his wife, Mary Elizabeth, daughter of Edward Thomas Townsend, of Newport, Monmouthshire, was of pure Welsh descent on the paternal, and of Welsh and Spanish blood on the maternal side. He was educated at St. Paul's School, and matriculated at Oxford as a non-collegiate student in 1897, but in the following year was elected to a scholarship in modern history at Lincoln College. He gained a second class in that subject in 1900, and graduated B.A. in the same year. Thomas early showed a passion both for nature and for literature, his favourite authors being Richard Jefferies, Izaak Walton, and Malory. His first book, *The Woodland Life*, appeared in 1897. Two years later he married Helen, daughter of James Ashcroft Noble, the critic, who had encouraged him to write. Thomas settled at Bearsted, Kent, in 1901, moving to The Weald, Sevenoaks, in 1903, and to Petersfield in 1908, maintaining himself by reviewing, and by critical essays and studies of country life. Frequent excursions through the southern counties gave him intimate knowledge and love of rural life and scenery, and his book *Richard Jefferies, His Life and Work* (1909) is racy of the soil of Wiltshire, its character, history, and farm life. The little group of imaginative masterpieces, such as 'Home', 'July', 'The Flower Gatherer', 'Olwen', 'A Group of Statuary', in *Rest and Unrest* (1910) and *Light and Twilight* (1911), excel by clear beauty of imagery, grace of contour, and delicate, limpid English. 'Celtic magic' and a sensitive freshness and contemplative charm inspire these idylls as well as many pages of *The South Country* (1909), and *In Pursuit of Spring* (1914). The range of Thomas's cool, fastidious, critical taste, and of his subtle destructive analysis, is shown in his studies of *Swinburne* (1912) and *Walter Pater* (1913).

The incessant strain of literary journalism and of producing book after book for publishers, 'paid at one pound per thousand words', without respite or hope of popular success, had told seriously on Thomas's health by 1911, and with his deepening anxieties in the next two years his tendency to introspective melancholy steadily increased. The War solved his difficulties. In July 1915 he enlisted in the Artists' Rifles, but was transferred to the Royal Garrison Artillery. He went to France in 1917, and was killed at Arras on 9 April of that year.

Six months before joining the army, Thomas, inspired by the example of his friend Robert Frost, the American poet, bent all his energies to writing verse. In his foreword to *The Collected Poems of Edward Thomas* (1920), Walter De La Mare has said: 'This intensity of solitude, this impassioned, almost trance-like delight in things natural, simple, short-lived and happy seeming, "lovely of motion, shape and line", is expressed—even when the clouds of melancholy and of self-distrust lour darkest—on every page of this book. A light shines in it, like that of "cowslips wet with the dew of their birth". If one word could tell of his all, that word would be England. . . . When indeed Edward Thomas was killed in Flanders, a mirror of England was shattered, of so true and pure a crystal that a clearer and tenderer reflection can be found in no other than in these poems. . . .'

Sensitive and shy, Thomas guarded himself from the world by a fine, dry irony, which slightly veiled the poet both austere and ardent in his passion for beauty and the homely things of earth. His lofty, melancholy spirit burned in an eye fastidiously grave. His figure was tall and spare, his hair at thirty was bleached gold, his head noble. He left one son and two daughters. Among his personal friends were W. H. Hudson, Walter De La Mare, W. H. Davies, and Edward Garnett.

[W. De La Mare, Foreword to *The Collected Poems of Edward Thomas*, 1920; E. Garnett, *Some Letters of Edward Thomas*, in the *Athenæum*, 16 and 23 April, 1920.] E. G.

THOMPSON, SILVANUS PHILLIPS (1851–1916), physicist, was born at York 19 June 1851, the second son of Silvanus Thompson, schoolmaster, of that city, by his wife, Bridget Tatham, of Settle. He was educated at Bootham School, York, and at the Flounders' Institute, Pontefract, graduating B.A. of London University in 1869. He acted as a master at the Bootham School from 1870 to 1875, in which year he graduated B.Sc., London. He studied for one year in London at the Royal School of Mines and spent one semester at Heidelberg University. He was appointed lecturer in physics at the University College, Bristol, in 1876, and became professor in 1878, gaining the degree of D.Sc., London, in the same year. In 1885 he was appointed principal and professor of applied physics and electrical engineering of the City and Guilds Technical College, Finsbury. He held these posts until his death at Hampstead 12 June 1916. He was elected F.R.S. in 1891, and, besides holding other important posts in connexion with various scientific societies, he was president of the Institution of Electrical Engineers in 1899, of the Physical Society in 1901, and of the Optical Society in 1905.

Silvanus Thompson showed at an early age great vigour and breadth of mind, considerable literary and artistic talent, and untiring industry that never abated throughout his life. Although he was interested in scientific theory, and made important contributions to the study of optics and electricity, the coincidence of Thompson's scientific life with the inauguration of the age of electrical engineering gave an irresistible opportunity for the exercise of his special talents. In addition to his knowledge of electrical science and of magnetism, he had unusual experimental and inventive skill and the true instinct of an engineer. His mind was intensely lucid, and his power of simple and arresting exposition was certainly not excelled, if equalled, among his scientific contemporaries. He attained the position of a pioneer in the development of applied electricity. In 1881 he produced a text-book, *Elementary Lessons in Electricity and Magnetism*, which has run through many editions; while his *Dynamo-electric Machinery*, published in 1884, established itself at once as a standard work for electrical engineers. He also published *The Electro-magnet and Electro-magnetic Mechanisms* (1891). His public lectures attracted large audiences and aided greatly in promoting technical education, especially in electrical engineering. Thompson was much consulted and greatly relied upon as an expert.

As principal and professor of the City and Guilds Technical College, Thompson had a full share in bringing about the success which the college achieved by the labours of the distinguished men who filled its three chairs, and he contributed in a high degree to securing the corporate spirit and loyalty, as well as the enthusiasm and sound learning of the Finsbury students.

Thompson pursued with zest his literary, antiquarian, and artistic tastes. He wrote lives of Philipp Reis (1883), of Michael Faraday (1898), and of Lord Kelvin (1910), as well as numerous essays. He devoted much time to the study of the sixteenth-century scientist, William Gilbert [q.v.], and to the translation of his work *De Magnete*. He was a skilful painter, especially of Alpine scenery, and an accomplished linguist. He came of quaker stock and was throughout his life an earnest member of the Society of Friends, in which he was recognized as a minister in 1903. His interest in religion prompted him to write *The Quest of Truth* (1915) and *A Not Impossible Religion* (published in 1918). He married in 1881 Jane, daughter of James Henderson, of Pollokshields, by whom he had four daughters.

[J. S. and H. G. Thompson, *Silvanus Phillips Thompson. His Life and Letters*, 1920; *Proceedings* of the Royal Society, vol. xciv, A, 1917–1918 (with portrait).] A. S.

THOMSON, HUGH (1860–1920), illustrator and pen-and-ink draughtsman, was born 1 June 1860 at Coleraine, co. Londonderry, the eldest son of John Thomson, who was in a tea-merchant's business in Coleraine, by his wife, Catherine, daughter of James Andrews. He was educated at the Model School, Coleraine, and first entered a firm of linen-manufacturers; but showing an aversion from commerce and a talent for design he was placed with the publishing firm of Marcus Ward & Co., of Belfast. There he came under the influence of John Vinycomb, a member of the Royal Irish Academy, whose counsel was the only real art training that he ever received. In 1883 he removed to London. Thomson's natural ability was quickly recognized by Joseph William Comyns Carr, editor of the then newly-established *English Illustrated Magazine*. In June 1884 his work first appeared in its pages, and he soon became one of its leading illustrators. Here first appeared his *Sir Roger de Coverley* (1886), and *Coaching Days and Coaching Ways* (1888). His drawings showed not only a delightful skill in landscape work but a consummate knowledge of horses, and a keen sense of humour. His early indebtedness to the art of Randolph Caldecott [q.v.] was obvious, but by degrees he developed an original talent.

For Messrs. Macmillan, the proprietors of the *English Illustrated Magazine*, to whom he was greatly attached both as artist and friend throughout the whole of his career, Thomson illustrated, between the years 1884 and 1903, a long series of books, eighteen in number, besides twelve volumes in their well-known county series, *Highways and Byways*, alone or in collaboration (1897–1920). He illustrated also with exquisite charm and grace many of the English classics of humour, beginning with Goldsmith's *The Vicar of Wakefield* (1890), Mrs. Gaskell's *Cranford* (1891)—which was declared to be 'the book of the year'—and Mary Mitford's *Our Village* (1893). In 1894 he developed his delicate taste for sylvan scenery in *Coridon's Song*. Then, after William Somerville's *The Chase* (1896), followed a series of Jane Austen's novels—*Sense and Sensibility* (1896), and *Emma*, *Mansfield Park*, *Northanger Abbey*, and *Persuasion*, all in 1897; *Pride and Prejudice* he had already illustrated for Messrs. Allen in 1894. He continued with Fanny Burney's *Evelina* (1903), Thackeray's *Henry Esmond* (1905), George Eliot's *Scenes from Clerical Life* (1906) and *Silas Marner* (1907). He also illustrated *The Ballad of Beau Brocade* (1892) and *The Story of Rosina* (1895), both by Austin Dobson [q.v.], to whose help, encouragement, and friendship Thomson owed much of his early success. Among the other books with which he sustained his popularity were Charles Reade's *Peg Woffington* (1899), James Lane Allen's *The Kentucky Cardinal* (1900), and Mrs. Mabel Henrietta Spielmann's *My Son and I* (1908). He also supplied coloured illustrations for *As You Like It* (1909), *The Merry Wives of Windsor* (1910), *The School for Scandal* (1911), *She Stoops to Conquer* (1912), Dickens's *The Chimes* (1913), as well as for Sir James Barrie's *Quality Street* (1913) and *The Admirable Crichton* (1914), Hughes's *Tom Brown's Schooldays* (1918), and Nathaniel Hawthorne's *The Scarlet Letter* (1920). In all these he showed a fine appreciation of his author's point of view, together with much character and imagination of his own. Thomson did much work for the leading illustrated journals, mainly *The*

Graphic, being usually called upon for pictures of the dainty graces and foibles, as well as of the sports, of seventeenth- and eighteenth-century and early Victorian society.

Thomson was much hampered by indifferent health, which, allied to his natural modesty, prevented him from mixing much with the world. His life was happy, with little incident, sweetened by the devoted attachment of a small circle who appreciated his worth and nobility of character. Extreme conscientiousness——he destroyed much of his work as soon as drawn—prevented him from making a competency, but a Civil List pension eased his lot in his declining years. He died at his home on Wandsworth Common, of heart disease, 7 May 1920. He married in 1884 Jessie Naismith, daughter of Peter Miller, of Ballynafeigh, Belfast, by whom he had one son.

[*Life*, by M. H. Spielmann (in preparation); private information; personal knowledge.]

M. H. S.

TINWORTH, GEORGE (1843–1913), modeller, the fourth son of Joshua Tinworth, wheelwright, by his wife, Jane Daniel, of Woolwich, was born in Walworth 5 November 1843. He worked in his father's shop until he was twenty-four, spending his evenings first at the Lambeth School of Art (1861), and later at the Royal Academy Schools (1864). In 1867 he joined the pottery works of Messrs. Doulton, of Lambeth, and he remained with the firm until his death. He exhibited at the Royal Academy from 1866 until 1885. Three large terra-cotta panels shown there in 1874—'Gethsemane', 'The Descent from the Cross', and 'The Foot of the Cross'—are now in the Edinburgh Museum. In 1875 a number of his small reliefs were highly praised by Ruskin in his *Notes on the Royal Academy*, vi, and, as a result, Tinworth was engaged by the architect George Edmund Street to collaborate with him in the large panel of the Crucifixion for the reredos of York Minster, and in the twenty-eight panels for the Guards' Chapel in St. James's Park. These reliefs, which led to the execution of many others of a similar type, show the artist at a level of achievement which he maintained in all his subsequent works. In 1883 an exhibition of his works, many of them very large and elaborate, was held in London at the Conduit Street Gallery.

Owing to the early influence of his mother, a strict dissenter, the majority of Tinworth's reliefs were scenes from Biblical history. Although conceived as reliefs the larger works were in reality groups of figures separately modelled and fired, and placed against a background, the borders of the panels being incised with descriptive quotations from the Bible. His work is full of realism and shows much technical skill, but it is the creation of a man who took no pains to remedy his early lack of education, and Tinworth cannot in any sense be considered a great artist. He executed a number of statues, among which are those of Henry Fawcett in Vauxhall Park, Charles Bradlaugh at Northampton, and Dr. Spurgeon in the Stockwell Orphanage; other large works by him are a sacred group in Whitworth Park, Manchester, panels in the pulpit and reredos of the English church, Copenhagen, a statue in St. Augustine's, Stepney, and a relief in the church of the Mediator, New York. All these are modelled: Tinworth made no pieces of actual sculpture.

Tinworth was awarded many foreign medals and prizes, and was made an officer of the French Academy in 1878. He married in 1881 Alice, third daughter of William Digweed; they had no children. He died in the train on his way from his home at Kew to the studio at Lambeth, 10 September 1913.

[E. W. Gosse, *A Critical Essay on the Life and Works of George Tinworth*, 1883; G. Tinworth, *From Sunset to Sunset*, 1908; private information.]

R. P. B.

TRAILL, ANTHONY (1838–1914), provost of Trinity College, Dublin, was born 1 November 1838 at Ballylough, co. Antrim, the eldest son of William Traill, of Ballylough, by his wife, Louisa, daughter of Robert Ffrench, of Monivea Castle, co. Galway. His family, of Scottish origin, descended from Colonel James Traill, a soldier in the Cromwellian army, who settled in Ireland about the year 1660. Anthony Traill entered Trinity College, Dublin, in 1856, was first scholar in mathematics in 1858, and graduated B.A. in 1860, winning first place among the moderators in mathematics and in experimental science. In 1865 he was elected to a fellowship, which he held until his appointment to the provostship in 1904.

A man of restless energy, Traill took a share in every department of college life. Although trained principally in applied mathematics, he took degrees both in medicine and in law. He was keenly interested in the fortunes of the school of physic, and in later life prided himself on being the only *medicus* among the provosts of Trinity. He was equally zealous in fostering the recently founded school of engineering, and for many years was a member of its staff with the title of assistant to the professor of natural philosophy. He was also a member of the university council from its first formation in 1874, sat on innumerable committees, and was an active and somewhat turbulent participator in the college politics of his day. At the same time he was a most successful and hard-working college tutor ; the fortunes of his pupils were his personal concern, and he prided himself on their successes. His athletic distinction as captain of cricket, racquets champion, and golfer brought him into close touch with the undergraduates, who regarded him with a mixture of affection and amusement, tempered by fear.

College duties were far from exhausting Traill's energy. He was a keen politician, —a unionist of the Ulster type. Himself the owner of a small estate in Antrim and deputy-lieutenant for that county, he fought the losing battle of the landlords during the 'eighties and 'nineties, and represented them on the royal commission (1897–1898) which inquired into the working of the Land Acts. His appointment as provost of Trinity College was generally ascribed to the influence of the Ulster unionists. It was also, no doubt, in part a reward for his services to the Church of Ireland, to whose material interests he gave a lifelong devotion. He was an original member of its representative body, and for many years was entrusted with the duty of presenting the financial report to the general synod. As a commissioner of national education for Ireland (1901–1914), he watched jealously over the Church's interests, as he conceived them, in educational matters; and as a member of the educational endowments (Ireland) commission (1885–1892), he worked hard to save for the Church as large a residue as possible of her legal inheritance.

To these various activities Traill brought prodigious physical energy and a most tenacious will. Contact with him gave a dominant impression of force, physical and moral. Nothing could less resemble the conventional idea of the college don. His presence was like a perpetual gale of wind; his bearing was aggressive, his gestures unrestrained, his speech uncompromising. He was contemptuous of forms and ceremonies, careless of personal dignity, and indifferent to the amenities of life. Essentially a man of action, he cared only for getting things done. He bore down opposition, or else wore it out by sheer persistence. In his maturer years he lost nothing of his driving power, and gained from experience a shrewd judgement of affairs. Combative and self-confident as ever, he would never own himself beaten or mistaken; but he knew when to make concessions, and was always ready for a fair bargain. If he fought hard, he never lost self-command, and never bore his opponent a grudge. It was his favourite saying that he gave hard knocks, and took them.

During his provostship from 1904 till his death, Traill's rough-hewn and massive figure was familiar to all Dublin. He steered the college successfully through difficult times. He resisted Mr. (afterwards Viscount) Bryce's proposals (1906) for solving the Irish university problem by amalgamating Trinity College with the colleges of the Royal University, and when this danger was averted, he had a principal share in effecting the long-needed reform of the internal constitution of his college, which did so much to renew its vitality. His energetic rule was felt in every department of Trinity College, especially in the science schools, and no detail of administration was too petty for his personal attention.

In character and outlook, Traill was a genuine son of Ulster—in his industry, his self-confidence, his toughness of fibre, his practical view of life, his insistence on material values, his strong prejudices, and his simple and sincere piety. He married in 1867 Catherine Elizabeth (died 1909), daughter of Captain J. Stewart Moore of Ballydivity, co. Antrim, by whom he had five sons and three daughters. He died at the Provost's House, Dublin, 15 October 1914.

[Personal knowledge.] E. J. G.

TREE, Sir HERBERT BEERBOHM (1852–1917), actor-manager, the second son of Julius Ewald Beerbohm (a London grain merchant of mixed German, Dutch, and Lithuanian extraction who had become naturalized as a British subject) by his wife, Constantia Draper, was born in London 17 December 1852. He was educated in England and at Schnepfenthal College, Thuringia, and was engaged for some time in his father's business. He was, however, already a member of several amateur dramatic clubs, and known privately as a clever mimic of popular actors. As an amateur he made several public appearances under the stage name of Beerbohm Tree in 1876,

1877, and 1878, notably at the Globe Theatre (February 1878) in the part of Grimaldi in *The Life of an Actress*. His success on this occasion resulted in the offer of a professional engagement for a short tour, at the conclusion of which he was engaged by Henry Neville [q.v.] to play at the Olympic Theatre. From July to December 1878 he appeared at that theatre in several plays, and in the following year was definitely committed to a professional career, appearing in a succession of parts at several London theatres. From the first he was noticeable for his ingenuity in the playing of parts inclining towards eccentricity and giving scope for elaborate invention. He was also recognized as a cosmopolitan, and his first great success was in the part of the old Marquis de Pontsablé in *Madame Favart*, in which he toured towards the end of 1879. This brought him into prominence, and on his return to London in April 1880 he appeared at the Prince of Wales's Theatre with Geneviève Ward, as Prince Maleotti in *Forget-me-not*. Between July 1880 and April 1887, when he first entered into management on his own account, Tree appeared in over fifty plays, founding a reputation for extraordinary versatility. His repertoire included Sir Anthony Absolute, Sir Benjamin Backbite, and Joseph Surface, Malvolio, Prince Borowsky in *The Glass of Fashion* by Sydney Grundy, the Rev. Robert Spalding in *The Private Secretary*, Paolo Macari in *Called Back*, Mr. Poskett in (Sir) A. W. Pinero's *The Magistrate*, Baron Hartfeld in *Jim the Penman*, and Fagin in *Oliver Twist*. His most conspicuous successes during this period were in *The Glass of Fashion* (8 September 1883) and *The Private Secretary* (29 March 1884), the latter play owing a great deal to his invention.

On 20 April 1887 Tree became his own manager, and had the good fortune to begin with a popular success, appearing as Paul Demetrius in the Russian revolutionary play, *The Red Lamp*, by W. Outram Tristram. It was the kind of part in which he excelled, Paul Demetrius being a 'character' in the popular sense of the word. Tree might here indulge to the full an impishness which was the secret of his personal charm and of his success as a comedian. The play was so successful that in September of the same year he was able to take the Haymarket Theatre as lessee and manager, and there, with occasional absences, he remained until the opening of Her Majesty's Theatre in April 1897. During the ten years of his management he produced, and acted in, over thirty plays, appearing as Iago (7 March 1888), Falstaff (13 September 1888), Beau Austin in the play of that name by W. E. Henley and R. L. Stevenson (3 November 1890), the Duke of Guisbery in *The Dancing Girl* (15 January 1891), *Hamlet* (8 September 1891), the grandfather in Maeterlinck's *The Intruder* (27 January 1892), Lord Illingworth in Oscar Wilde's *A Woman of No Importance* (19 April 1893), Dr. Stockman in Ibsen's *An Enemy of the People* (14 June 1895), and Falstaff in *Henry IV, Part I* (8 May 1896). These productions are mentioned either as popular successes in the kind of part in which Tree personally excelled, or as bringing him definitely into relation with contemporary developments of the drama. His production of plays by Ibsen, Wilde, and Maeterlinck indicates an interest in the more important dramatic movements of the time not invariably shown by contemporary actor-managers, while the productions of Shakespeare were a preparation for the impressive exploits of his closing period. The number and variety of the plays from which these few examples are taken are a further proof of Tree's versatility and ardour in experiment. The seasons at the Haymarket were broken by journeys to America in January 1895 and November 1896, and by occasional visits to the provinces.

Her Majesty's Theatre, Tree's final theatrical home and the appropriate monument of his theatrical genius, was opened on 28 April 1897. Henceforth, with occasional diversions, all was to be done in the high Roman fashion. Shakespeare shared a noble stage with Tolstoi; and, if the author were not of the classic rank, Tree himself would appear, for the most part in illustrious disguise as the Duc de Richelieu, Mephistopheles, or Beethoven, in plays that endeavoured, if in vain, to do dramatic justice to their protagonists. The following is a selection from the list of parts in which he appeared at Her Majesty's: the Duc de Richelieu in *The Silver Key* (10 July 1897), Petruchio in *Katharine and Petruchio* (1 November 1897), Mark Antony in *Julius Caesar* (22 January 1898), D'Artagnan in *The Three Musketeers* (3 November 1898), King John (20 September 1899), Bottom (10 January 1900), Herod (31 October 1900), Malvolio (5 February 1901), Ulysses (1 February 1902), Falstaff in *The Merry Wives of Windsor* (10 June 1902), Prince Dmitri Nehludoff in *Resurrection* (17 February 1903), King Richard II (10 September 1903), Benedick in *Much Ado About Nothing* (24 January 1905), Fagin in *Oliver Twist* (10 July 1905), Colonel Newcome in a play of that name (29 May 1906), Nero (25 June 1906), Mark Antony in *Antony and Cleopatra* (27 December 1906), Shylock (4 April 1908), Mephistopheles (5 September 1908), Sir Peter Teazle (7 April 1909), Ludwig von Beethoven in *Beethoven* (26 November 1909), Cardinal Wolsey in *King Henry VIII* (1 September 1910), Macbeth (5 September 1911), and Count Frithiof in *The War God* (8 November 1911).

During the closing period of Tree's activities the natural comedian was obscured by his serious ambition to rank as a great tragedian and a producer in the grand manner. There were interludes of condescension towards fashionable romantic drama. There was one notable essay in modernism in the production of G. B. Shaw's *Pygmalion* in 1914. But the impression which he finally left on the public mind was the result of his later productions of Shakespeare and of his attempt to revive poetic drama (*Herod*, 1900 ; *Ulysses*, 1902 ; *Nero*, 1906) under the influence of Stephen Phillips [q.v]. The exuberant vitality which in Tree's earlier work had found a natural outlet in a fanciful elaboration of characters like Paul Demetrius in *The Red Lamp*, or the Rev. Robert Spalding in *The Private Secretary*, demanded in later life an ampler and more dignified expression. He fell in love with magnificence, and it was a magnificence that ran to big designs packed with extravagant detail. His stage arrangements, as in the forum scene in *Julius Caesar* or in the costly pageant of *Henry VIII*, were, like his personal performances, too elaborate and too full of invention and ingenuity to serve the purpose of tragedy, for which they lacked the necessary simplicity.

It was natural for a producer with an increasing passion for emphatic splendour to fall under the spell of Stephen Phillips, who was greeted by many serious critics of the time as the founder of a modern poetic drama. It was even more natural that he should take to its extravagant limit a method of producing Shakespeare which insisted on a sumptuous illustration of the author's lines, as close and as detailed as the arts of the scene painter and stage carpenter could compass. Tree lived to see a reaction in the art of production, which swung violently back from the method of illustrative realism to the method of suggestive decoration, and he had to encounter a good deal of hostility from younger men. But, in estimating his achievement, it must be remembered that the movement which he led to such clamant extremes began as a protest against the tawdriness and indifference of an earlier generation of producers, and that he did succeed in keeping an open house for Shakespeare in London by striking the popular imagination with splendid spectacle mounted with convincing enthusiasm and ability. The climax was his celebrated performance of Mark Antony in the forum scene, where all the complicated gestures and ingenious pantomime of his craft were displayed at leisure. In 1905 Tree began a series of Shakespeare festivals, repeated annually and culminating in 1910–1911 with an entire season during which only plays by Shakespeare were performed. His last professional adventure was a visit to Los Angeles in 1915 in fulfilment of a contract with a film company. He was in America for the greater part of 1915 and 1916. He returned to England in 1917 and died quite suddenly in London on 2 July of that year.

Tree's devotion to his profession and natural generosity of disposition prompted him to take a leading part in all that concerned its dignity and well-being. In 1904 he founded the Academy of Dramatic Art, and on the death of Sir Henry Irving he was elected president of the Theatrical Managers' Association. He was a trustee and vice-president of the Actors' Benevolent Fund and president of the Actors' Association. He was knighted by King Edward in 1909, having in 1907 received the order of the Crown from the German Emperor, and the order of the Crown of Italy from the King of Italy.

Tree was the author of several books, in which an enthusiastic personality may be seen at issue with an unpractised pen : *Some Interesting Fallacies of the Modern Stage* (1893), *An Essay on the Imaginative Faculty* (1893), *Thoughts and Afterthoughts* (1913), *Nothing Matters* (1917). He also wrote a one-act play entitled *Six-and-Eightpence*, produced in 1884. In 1882 he married Maud, daughter of William Holt, by whom he had three daughters.

There is a pencil-drawing of Tree by the Duchess of Rutland, executed in 1891, and a charcoal-drawing by J. S. Sargent.

[*The Times*, 3 July 1917; Max Beerbohm, *Herbert Beerbohm Tree*, 1920.] J. L. P.

TUCKER, ALFRED ROBERT (1849–1914), missionary bishop of Uganda, was born at Woolwich 1 April 1849, the second son of Edward Tucker, artist, of Windermere, by his wife, Julia Mary Maile. Alfred Tucker was given an art education, and in due course exhibited at the Royal Academy. He also gained a reputation as an athlete, and a famous walk of his of over sixty miles, including the ascent of Scafell, Bow Fell, Skiddaw, and Helvellyn, in twenty-four hours, is still remembered in the Lake district. He went up late to Oxford as a non-collegiate student in 1879 migrated to Christ Church in 1881, and graduated in 1882. In the same year he was ordained to the curacy of St. Andrew's, Clifton, and in 1885 became curate of St. Nicholas, Durham, where he remained for five years.

In 1890 Tucker wrote to the Church Missionary Society, offering his services as a missionary in any part of Africa. In response to his offer the archbishop of Canterbury, Dr. Benson, invited him to fill the vacant bishopric of Eastern Equatorial Africa. The first bishop, James Hannington [q.v.], had been murdered by order of the king of Uganda; and the second, Henry Perrott Parker, had died *en route* to that country. Tucker was consecrated at Lambeth on St. Mark's day (25 April) 1890, and sailed for the East African coast the same evening. In 1891 he was back in England, reporting the position, not only in Uganda but in the vast intervening territory now known as the Kenya Colony. The British East Africa Company was abandoning its attempt to represent British influence in Uganda; but Tucker's influence in obtaining special gifts from friends of the Church Missionary Society's Uganda mission enabled the company to continue for one year; and then, in 1892, the British government sent a special commissioner, Sir Gerald Herbert Portal [q.v.], to report. Eventually, in 1894, Uganda became a British protectorate.

In 1899 the huge diocese of Eastern Equatorial Africa was divided. What subsequently (1920) was known as the Kenya Colony, together with a part of the then German dominion, which from 1920 formed the Tanganyika Territory, became the diocese of Mombasa; while Tucker assumed the title by which he is best known, that of bishop of Uganda. It was his special work to organize the growing church which had been built up by the Church Missionary Society's Uganda mission, making it as far as possible self-supporting, self-governing, and self-extending. When he retired in 1911, after a vigorous episcopate of twenty-one years, there were over 100,000 Anglican Christians, with hundreds of churches and schools, and a regular synod of British and African clergy and elected lay members; the African clergy—of whom he himself had ordained forty-seven—, school teachers, and other helpers, being supported by their own people.

On his retirement Bishop Tucker was appointed to a canonry in Durham Cathedral. When the archbishops of Canterbury and York, together with the leaders of the Free churches, formed a united conference on 'faith and order' at Westminster in 1914, Tucker was one of the Anglican representatives; and it was just outside the Jerusalem Chamber, which he was entering to attend the first meeting on 15 June, that he was seized with sudden illness. He was carried into the deanery, and died within an hour. He married in 1882 Hannah Josephine, daughter of William Fisher Sim, of Southport, Lancashire, by whom he had one son. His chief literary work was his book, *Eighteen Years in Uganda and East Africa*, illustrated by his own sketches (2 vols., 1908).

[Private information; personal knowledge.] E. S.

TUPPER, Sir CHARLES, first baronet (1821–1915), Canadian statesman, was born in Amherst, Nova Scotia, 2 July 1821, the third son of the Rev. Charles Tupper, a Baptist minister, by his first wife, Miriam Lowe (*née* Lockhart). His ancestors came from England to Massachusetts in 1637, but his branch of the family removed in 1763 to Nova Scotia, and settled upon land left vacant by the expulsion of the Acadians. Tupper was educated at Horton Academy (afterwards Acadia University); and after some time spent as a medical student with a local practitioner, he studied at Edinburgh University, graduating in 1843. He then returned to Nova Scotia and began a very successful practice of medicine at Amherst. In 1855 he entered the Nova Scotia legislative assembly as conservative member for Cumberland county, defeating the liberal leader, Joseph Howe [q.v.].

On his entry into the assembly Tupper found his party a mere dispirited tory rump. He at once and fully accepted both responsible government and the state construction of railways, the chief planks in the programme of the liberal administration, and set out vigorously to shape for his own party a constructive policy of its own. In 1857 the conservatives gained power by an alliance with the Roman Catholics, and Tupper became provincial secretary. In 1860 his party was defeated, but in 1864 returned to power with Tupper as premier. In 1864–1865 he forced through, against the opposition of ill-educated farmers and of Roman Catholic supporters of separate schools, the effective system of education which is still in force, with free primary schools supported by compulsory assessment. In 1864 he organized a conference at Charlottetown to consider a maritime union of Nova Scotia, New Brunswick, and Prince Edward Island. This was soon merged in the larger project of Canadian confederation, and Tupper was the chief Nova Scotian delegate at the Quebec conference in October 1864. While here, he formed a political and personal alliance with Sir John Alexander Macdonald [q.v.], which grew ever closer till Macdonald's death. Fierce opposition to federation soon developed in Nova Scotia, led by Howe and financed by the Halifax merchants, who feared for their monopoly of the provincial trade. Howe had long been an advocate of a larger union, and his inconsistency was apparently due to his egotism. 'I will not play second fiddle to that d—d Tupper', he said. Tupper faced his opponents aggressively. The Roman Catholic archbishop offered him the votes of his flock in return for separate schools, but Tupper was obdurate. The opposition clamoured with much justice for an appeal to the electorate, but this Tupper refused, and he held together his majority in the house by Walpolean methods. In 1866–1867 he was a prominent figure at the conference in London with the imperial authorities, in which the details were worked out of the British North America Act.

When Sir John Macdonald formed the first government of federated Canada (1867), sectional and religious claims had to be placated, and Tupper unselfishly stood aside, in company with the Irish-Canadian, Thomas D'Arcy McGee [q.v.]. Meanwhile Nova Scotia had become all but unanimous in favour of the repeal of the British North America Act. Of nineteen members in the federal house Tupper was the only federationist, and of thirty-eight in the local house he had but two supporters. His private savings had been exhausted in the struggle for federation, but he refused to withdraw from public life though offered the chairmanship of the board of commissioners for constructing the Intercolonial Railway. In 1868 he went to London to counter the repeal agitation of Howe, and was so completely successful that he actually induced Howe, by the promise of financial 'better terms' for Nova Scotia, to enter the federal Cabinet. On 21 June 1870 he himself entered the Cabinet as president of the council; he was transferred on 2 July 1872 to the department of inland revenue, and on 22 February 1873 to that of customs, which post he held till the defeat of the government in the autumn of that year on the 'Pacific scandal' [see MACDONALD, Sir John Alexander].

In opposition Tupper was the chief financial critic of government measures, and did more than any other man to commit his own party to the 'national policy' of protection. On the return of the conservatives to power in October 1878 after a general election, Tupper accepted the ministry of public works in the Cabinet of Sir John Macdonald; in 1879 this post was divided into two, and Tupper became the first minister of railways and canals. In this office he reorganized and enlarged the inter-colonial railway between the maritime provinces and Quebec, and was largely concerned in changing the former policy of government construction of the Canadian Pacific Railway to that of construction by a private company with government aid. In May 1884 he suddenly and unexpectedly retired from the Cabinet in order to succeed Sir Alexander Tilloch Galt [q.v.] as Canadian high commissioner in London. This office he held till January 1896, when he resigned to enter the conservative Cabinet of Sir Mackenzie Bowell as secretary of state. As high commissioner he was vigour personified, and gave new importance to the office. Through him Canada obtained a larger influence in the making of all treaties which concerned her interests. He was an early advocate of imperial preference, and of fast inter-imperial steamship services both on the Atlantic and the Pacific; but he disliked the political activities of the Imperial Federation League, and was largely responsible for its disbanding in 1893. During his tenure of the high commissionership he returned to Canada in 1887 and 1891 to take part in the general elections, and was on each occasion Sir John Macdonald's chief assistant. For a few months of 1887–1888 he was also finance minister, and from November 1887 to February 1888 he was the Canadian representative at Washington in the negotiations for settling the fisheries imbroglio with the United States, the British representatives being Mr. Joseph Chamberlain [q.v.] and Sir Lionel Sackville-West (afterwards Baron Sackville, q.v.).

On 27 April 1896 Sir Mackenzie Bowell

resigned; and Tupper succeeded him as prime minister of Canada. Since the death of Sir John Macdonald (1891) the conservative party had disintegrated, political and personal differences being rife. On Tupper's accession to power he found the federal government committed to a bill restoring to the Roman Catholic minority in Manitoba certain privileges which had been taken away by the provincial government. He was therefore opposed both by the advocates of provincial rights, and by the extreme Protestants, while he failed to win the French Roman Catholics of Quebec, who pinned their faith on Sir Wilfrid Laurier [q.v.], the liberal leader, in spite of the exhortations of their bishops. Parliament dissolved by efflux of time before the remedial bill could be forced through, and on 23 June 1896 the conservatives were defeated in a general election. The defeat was not due to Tupper, who 'fought with amazing freshness and with indomitable courage . . . We could almost see the restoration of party unity proceed under his hand' [J. S. Willison, *Sir Wilfrid Laurier*, ii, 255].

After his defeat, but before his resignation, Tupper filled a large number of important offices with his political supporters. These appointments the governor-general, the Earl of Aberdeen, refused to ratify. Tupper had on his side constitutional precedent, but the general sympathy of the country was with the governor-general. In opposition Tupper led his party with vigour until the general election of 1900, after his defeat in which he retired into private life, though still from time to time intervening in Canadian and imperial affairs with public letters and articles. In 1909 he settled at Bexley Heath, in Kent, where he died 30 October 1915.

Tupper was perhaps the most fearless and constructive statesman whom Canada has produced. He gave free education to Nova Scotia. Without him the Canadian Dominion could not have been formed. Without him Sir John Macdonald would almost certainly not have pulled through the lean years of opposition from 1873 to 1878. Without him Canada would almost certainly have had neither a 'national policy' nor the Canadian Pacific Railway. He had great executive ability, and untiring energy and fluency. The chief defects of which he was accused were a tendency to nepotism, and a willingness to use public money and public contracts as bribes to constituencies in need of railways and other public works.

Tupper was of middle height, broad-shouldered, with an alert and vigorous frame, capable of great exertion and endurance. His face was ruddy and leonine, with heavy masses of hair, which remained black till very late in his life. Many portraits and photographs of him are easily accessible. In religion he was at first a Baptist, but later became a member of the Anglican Church. In 1879 he was created K.C.M.G.; in 1886 G.C.M.G.; in 1888 a baronet of the United Kingdom; and in 1908 a privy councillor. Though from about 1863 he gave up the active practice of medicine he always retained his interest in it, and on the foundation of the Canadian Medical Association in 1867 was elected its first president.

Tupper married in 1846 Frances Amelia, daughter of Silas H. Morse, of Amherst, Nova Scotia; she died in 1912. They had three sons and one daughter; the second son, Sir Charles Hibbert Tupper, was from 1882 to 1904 a member of the Dominion parliament, and from 1888 to 1896 a member of the Canadian Cabinet.

[Sir C. Tupper, *Recollections of Sixty Years in Canada*, 1914; E. M. Saunders, *Life and Letters of the Rt. Hon. Sir Charles Tupper*, 2 vols., 1916; J. W. Longley, *Sir Charles Tupper*, 1916; Canadian *Hansard*, 1875–1900; biographies of the chief Canadian and English contemporaries.] W. L. G.

TURNER, Sir WILLIAM (1832–1916), anatomist, teacher, and academic administrator, was born at Lancaster 7 January 1832. His father, also William Turner, an upholsterer and cabinet-maker, died in 1837, and the boy, with a younger brother who only lived to the age of fourteen, was left to the care of the widowed mother (*née* Margaret Aldren) in straitened circumstances. He was educated at a private school, which he left at the age of fifteen to be apprenticed to a local general practitioner, Dr. Christopher Johnston. In 1850, with the leave of his employer, he was freed from his apprenticeship, and allowed to complete his training in London at St. Bartholomew's Hospital. There he studied assiduously under Sir James Paget [q. v.] and other teachers, preparing himself at the same time for matriculation in London University. In 1852 he passed this examination, taking the first prize in chemistry and the second place in botany. In May 1853 he gained a scholarship at St. Bartholomew's in anatomy, physiology, and chemistry, and in the following month he obtained his diploma, after the oral examination which in those days was the only test of the successful completion of a professional course.

Turner was now qualified to practise, but he decided, with the help of his scholarship, to continue his studies for the London M.B. degree. In August 1854 he passed the intermediate examination, and in the following month he received from John Goodsir [q. v.], professor of anatomy in Edinburgh, the offer of the post of senior demonstrator in that department. The offer, which he owed to Paget's recommendation, was accepted; and in October, at the age of twenty-two, Turner crossed the Border for the first time, and entered the service of the university with which he was to be so closely associated for sixty-two years.

The thirteen years during which Turner worked under Goodsir were a testing-time in his career. His position was not at all secure nor altogether comfortable. He was very young and had no previous experience in teaching. He was merely Goodsir's private assistant, nominated and paid by the professor, without any direct commission from the university. He was English by birth and the product of an English school, thrust into a medical school which was at the height of its reputation and proudly confident of its superiority and its self-sufficiency. That Turner established his position and his reputation in spite of these disadvantages is a striking proof of his ability and strength of character. His industry was extraordinary, and was only equalled by the physical strength, derived apparently from the mother's side, which enabled him to work with the minimum of interruption from morning to night. Although his teaching work was very heavy, as Goodsir was not in good health, he found time to complete his London M.B. in 1857, to edit Paget's *Lectures on Surgical Pathology*, to produce several scientific papers, to publish his own *Atlas and Handbook on Human Anatomy and Physiology* (1857), and to take part in founding the *Journal of Anatomy and Physiology* in 1866. He also corresponded with Darwin, to whom he supplied information as to rudimentary parts in human and animal structure [see Darwin's letters in Turner's *Life*, pp. 186–90]. While he was thus establishing a position among men of science he was also steadily strengthening his position in the university. Nothing contributed more to this than his active part in the Volunteer movement of 1859. The improvement in his position was shown in 1861, when his demonstratorship became a university office with an additional salary from university funds (this enabled him to marry in 1863), and still more conclusively in 1867 when, on Goodsir's death, he was chosen by the curators as his successor in the chair of anatomy.

Turner's position was now secure, and all idea of returning to England was abandoned. At the same time the range of his activities was largely extended. The teaching of anatomy continued until 1903 to be his primary duty, and his eminence as a teacher is indisputable. He commanded the services of a series of efficient demonstrators, and he could point with legitimate pride to the fact that the chairs of anatomy throughout the Empire were largely filled by students who had received their early training at his hands. To the labour of teaching he added administrative and legislative work, for which he developed both taste and capacity. From the outset he was an active member of the senatus, and played a specially prominent part in all matters concerning the faculty of medicine, of which he was dean from 1878 to 1881. He was a leader in the opposition to the admission of women to medical classes, when the question was raised by Sophia Jex-Blake [q. v.]; and to the last he was an opponent of mixed classes in the study of medicine. He was the right-hand man of Sir Alexander Grant [q. v.] in collecting the large sums needed for the construction of the new medical buildings, and in organizing the great tercentenary celebration which in 1883 followed their completion. He found a congenial occupation in the equipment of the spacious accommodation now provided for the anatomical department, and especially in the arrangement and cataloguing of the museum, to which he himself made numerous and valuable contributions, notably of skulls from all parts of the world. On the death of Sir Alexander Grant, Turner became chairman of the extension committee; and in that capacity he obtained from his friend, William McEwan, a large benefaction to build the imposing hall for academic functions, which had been cut out of the original plans for want of sufficient funds. He was also active in securing the gift from Sir John Usher of an institute of public health and the establishment of a chair in that subject. When the Act of 1889 extended the functions and composition of the university court, Turner was elected by the senatus an original member of the new body, of which, as convener of the finance committee and later as principal, he continued to be the most prominent and influential member for the rest of his life.

Outside the university Turner played a prominent part in matters concerning the general welfare of the medical profession. He was especially active in the long controversy over the improvement of the conditions to be imposed as a qualification for professional practice. Reform was urgently needed, especially in England, but there was an acute conflict as to the direction which this reform should take. The favourite proposal of English reformers was the creation of a central examining board, with the exclusive power of conferring the licence to practise in the United Kingdom. This scheme found a powerful supporter in Robert Lowe (afterwards Viscount Sherbrooke), who sat in parliament for London University and took as his model that university's system of external examination. Against this formidable champion Turner entered the lists as the advocate of the university's privilege of conferring a licence through its degree, of the higher training given by a university as opposed to the mere cramming of knowledge for examination purposes, and of the superiority of examinations in which the teachers had a share. In 1881 he was invited by Earl Spencer to sit on a royal commission which was appointed to consider the whole matter. The majority reported in favour of the single portal to the profession; but Turner, with characteristic courage, drew up a vigorous minority report in which he defended his views. An attempt to legislate on the lines of the majority report proved a failure; and the Act of 1886, which finally settled the controversy, was a virtual victory for Turner's contentions. On the General Medical Council, created in 1858 to supervise the medical register and professional education, Turner sat from 1873 to 1883 as representative of the universities of Edinburgh and Aberdeen. When the council was re-constituted in 1886, and each university obtained separate representation, Turner again took a seat for the university of Edinburgh and retained it till his resignation in 1905. From 1898 to 1904 he was president of the council, the first Scottish representative to hold that office.

Turner had now become a man of considerable mark. He was knighted in 1886, and received many further distinctions in subsequent years. In 1897 his friends and former pupils subscribed to present to him his portrait, which was painted by Sir George Reid, president of the Royal Scottish Academy.

In 1903, on the retirement of Sir William Muir [q. v.], the curators offered Turner the principalship of the University, to which his long services had given him a substantial claim. He accepted the offer without any misgivings, but his confidence was not shared by all his colleagues. No Englishman and no occupant of a medical chair, had previously risen to the headship of a Scottish university. Turner was over seventy years of age, and he had identified himself so completely with medical interests as to inspire a fear that the other studies of the university might suffer if more weight was thrown on to the side of a faculty which was already, to some minds, too apt to assume that the university revolved around itself. But Turner, as in his younger days, speedily disarmed his critics. His English birth was already almost forgotten, as it was discovered that in all essential qualities he was as Scottish as any native of the country. His fellow-citizens recognized his virtual naturalization by conferring upon him the freedom of the city of Edinburgh in 1908. His years he carried lightly, and to the end there was no failing of his mental powers, and very little of his physical energy. Above all he showed himself to be no one-sided specialist. He had always been a man of wide general interests, and he had cultivated these by reading and by travel. But it was a remarkable achievement that he succeeded, at an age when most men are content with what they have already learned, in mastering the business and in appreciating the needs of all departments of the university. It was a recognition of the fairness and impartiality of his administration that steps were taken in 1912, on the occasion of his eightieth birthday, to obtain his portrait as a permanent possession for the university. This, as he liked to point out, was again painted by a president of the Royal Scottish Academy, Sir James Guthrie.

The thirteen years of Turner's principalship, or at any rate the first eleven of them, were a notable period of expansion in the activities of the university. This expansion was rendered possible by the foundation of the Scottish Universities Trust by Andrew Carnegie [q.v.], with the administration of which Turner was closely associated, and by a benefaction from Sir Donald Currie [q. v.] due entirely to his regard for Turner. For the material expansion of the university Turner can claim direct credit. The new medical buildings had relieved but had not remedied the congestion in the old college, and the problem was rendered the more difficult by its position in a crowded quarter of the city. But in 1905 the old city hospital, only a stone's throw from the college, was vacated; and Turner's cordial relations with the town council enabled the university to acquire the valuable site and buildings at a very moderate cost. Room was found there for the departments of physics and engineering, and a new chemical laboratory would have been built there but for the War. To meet the charge that nothing had hitherto been done for the arts faculty, a substantial building was acquired in Chambers Street, which ultimately housed the mathematical department. Its old quarters, where Turner had originally taught anatomy, were now made available for historical and other humane studies. There were many other changes in which Turner was a sympathetic helper rather than an originator. The arts curriculum was revolutionized by a new ordinance in 1908, when the traditional method of teaching by formal lectures was supplemented by tutorial instruction ; lectureships were established not only in medical and scientific subjects but also in ancient history, geography, economic history, Indian and colonial history, mercantile law, English law, banking, and military history; professorships in bacteriology, clinical medicine, and tuberculosis were created ; and finally, an agreement with the Royal Infirmary brought its surgical and medical staff into a direct connexion with the university.

In spite of his activity in academic and other administrative duties, Turner never lost interest in his own branch of science and in the kindred subject of anthropology, though the time which he could give to these studies was necessarily curtailed. He kept himself abreast of all progress in his own subjects, and from time to time he published the results of his own observations and research. Of these the most important dealt with the placentation of mammals, the comparative anatomy of sea mammals, and the craniology of man. In each of these three fields of work he did good service, clearing the ground of many fallacies and preparing the way for further advances. But while he was eminent as a man of science, as was testified by his presidency of the British Association in 1900, and by his numerous academic distinctions, it cannot be claimed that he was pre-eminent. He had none of the imagination necessary for a great pioneer. He instinctively shrank from all theories based upon inference rather than on directly provable facts ; his passion was for accurate and patient observation, for careful records and measurements, rather than for original suggestions. Caution was his watchword in scientific as in academic matters. He was a collector of bricks with which other men could build rather than a builder on his own account. What made Turner memorable was not originality but his many personal merits : a manly and fearless character ; a statesmanlike habit of mind which realized what could be done and the necessary method of doing it; a firm and resolute grip of everything which he undertook ; great clearness of view and an equal power of expressing and enforcing his opinions ; and, finally, a notable combination of geniality, which disarmed opposition and inspired affection, with a dignity which enforced respect and commanded allegiance.

Turner's last years were saddened by the European War, and all that it involved. He was intensely patriotic, and urged the enlistment of all able-bodied students and members of the staff. But the empty quadrangles and the shrunken classes, together with the enforced abandonment of his building schemes, depressed him and seemed to sap his vitality. His last illness was mercifully short. He expected to attend the university court on 13 February 1916, but this proved impossible, and he died two days later. He was buried in the Dean cemetery by the side of his wife, Agnes, the eldest daughter of Abraham Logan, of Burnhouses, Berwickshire, who had died in 1908. He left three sons, one of whom became his biographer, and two daughters. Of his two portraits, that by Sir George Reid is in the hands of his family, and that by Sir James Guthrie hangs in the senatus hall of the university.

[A. Logan Turner, M.D., *Sir William Turner: A Chapter in Medical History*, 1919; private information; personal knowledge.]

R. L-E.

TYLOR, Sir EDWARD BURNETT (1832–1917), anthropologist, the third son of Joseph Tylor, brass-founder, by his wife, Harriet Skipper, was born at Camberwell 2 October 1832, and educated at Grove House, Tottenham, a school belonging to the Society of Friends, of which his parents were members. Their second son was

Alfred Tylor, the geologist [q.v.]. Entering his father's foundry at the age of sixteen, he was obliged in 1855 to abandon business and travel for the sake of his health. In a Havana omnibus he happened to make acquaintance in 1856 with the ethnologist, Henry Christy [q.v.], whom he thereupon accompanied on an expedition to Mexico. Here, under expert guidance, he found ample opportunity for developing a taste for archaeological and anthropological studies. In 1861 appeared his first book *Anahuac, or Mexico and the Mexicans, Ancient and Modern*, in which a spirited account is given of these travels. Four years later he established his reputation as a scientific student of human origins by the publication of *Researches into the Early History of Mankind*. But his fame rests chiefly on his next work, *Primitive Culture*, which first saw the light in 1871 and has since become known throughout the world as a classic. It is in these pages, for instance, that he elaborates the theory of animism with which his name will always be associated. His only other book was a useful manual, *Anthropology*, published in 1881. But many of his scattered articles are likewise of first-rate importance, such as a paper suggesting how a statistical method may be applied to the development of institutions (*Journal of the Anthropological Institute*, 1888).

Apart from his influence as a writer, Tylor's work as organizer and teacher helped greatly to secure for anthropology a place among the acknowledged sciences. Thus, he led the movement which resulted in the creation of an anthropological section of the British Association, and in 1884 acted as its first president. Again, the university of Oxford, which awarded him its D.C.L. as early as 1875, was repaid by services extending from 1883 until the final decline of his powers. He was appointed successively keeper of the university museum (1883), reader in anthropology (1884), and professor of anthropology (1896), being the first occupant of a chair in that subject at Oxford. On his retirement in 1909 he received the title of emeritus professor. That a school of anthropology flourishes at Oxford to-day is due to Tylor's pioneer efforts, whereby a subject which students of the humanities at first regarded with suspicion became gradually invested with a dignity corresponding to the personal eminence of its originator and chief exponent. Tylor was also elected the first Gifford lecturer at Aberdeen University in 1888, president of the Anthropological Society in 1891, and honorary fellow of Balliol College, Oxford, in 1903. He was knighted in 1912. After his retirement from active work in Oxford he lived at Wellington, Somerset, where he died 2 January 1917.

The secret of Tylor's eminence lies in his infinite respect for facts. A stout Darwinian, he had all his master's patience in eliciting the universal from a multitude of particulars. With Tylor, as with Darwin, the facts seem almost of themselves to crystallize into generalizations. Yet, although building so solidly, Tylor had the literary art to make the whole construction appear graceful, because well-poised and simple in its lines. Such simplicity of design is matched by a simplicity and straightforwardness of expression which makes his writing intelligible to every educated reader. Dealing as he does with the thoughts and actions of primitive people, he eschews in his interpretations the language of the learned, deeming it more appropriate to describe such simple-mindedness, as it were, in terms of itself.

Tylor's genius, which is to say his power of divination, was shown by his ability to grasp the true scope and method of anthropology from the outset. As regards scope, he set himself to study the evolution of man from every side at once and together, comprising not only his body and its environing conditions but also his soul with all the activities issuing therefrom in the shape of language, religion, law, morality, and art. Tylor's own studies covered all this wide ground, embracing physical anthropology, ethnology, prehistorics, technology, social anthropology, and linguistics. That British anthropology retains its synthetic character to-day is largely owing to Tylor. As regards method, he realized from the first that the inward springs of human behaviour rather than its outward conditions afford the best clue to its history, and hence that a psychological method must be paramount. He was quite aware, however, that due weight must be given to outward conditions, and especially to those movements and clashings of peoples whereby culture is quasi-physically distributed through the world. Perhaps some of his psychological interpretations hardly took into sufficient account the effects of culture-contact; for, after all, his outlook was limited by the imperfections of the evidence then available. Even so, he must ever rank as a great seer—*vir sublimis ingenii qui veluti ex rupe omnia circumspiciebat.*

Tylor married in 1858 Anna, daughter of Sylvanus Fox, of Wellington, Somerset. There were no children of the marriage.

There is a portrait of Tylor by George Bonavia in the National Portrait Gallery, and another by W. E. Miller at Balliol College.

[Appreciation by Andrew Lang in *Anthropological Essays presented to E. B. Tylor*, 1907; bibliography of his writings by B. W. Freire-Marreco, *ibid.*; personal knowledge.]

R. R. M.

TYRRELL, ROBERT YELVERTON (1844–1914), classical scholar, the fifth and youngest son of the Rev. Henry Tyrrell, by his wife, Elizabeth Shea, was born 21 January 1844, at Ballingarry, co. Tipperary, of which his father was vicar. He was a first cousin of George Tyrrell, the modernist [q.v.]. Except for six weeks at a private school in Hume Street, Dublin, he received his education at home, being taught by his elder brothers. He entered Trinity College, Dublin, when sixteen, carrying off the entrance prizes in classical composition. In 1861 he obtained a classical scholarship in his first year—until that date an unheard-of feat for a first-year man who was only seventeen. He graduated with a double first class in classics and logics in 1864, and obtained a fellowship in 1868 on very brilliant answering in classics. In 1871 he was elected professor of Latin, in 1880 regius professor of Greek, in 1899 public orator, in 1900 professor of ancient history, and in 1904 senior fellow and registrar of the college. In 1901 he was chosen one of the first fifty members of the British Academy. He married in 1874 Ada, eldest daughter of Dr. George Ferdinand Shaw, senior fellow of Trinity College, Dublin, by whom he had three sons and three daughters. He died in Dublin on 19 September 1914 after a tedious illness.

Tyrrell's principal formal works were editions of the *Bacchae* (1871) and *Troades* (second edition, 1884) of Euripides, and of the *Miles Gloriosus* of Plautus (third edition, 1889), critical editions of Sophocles (1897) and Terence (1902), and especially an extensive commentary in seven volumes [mainly in collaboration with Dr. L. C. Purser] on the *Correspondence of Cicero* (1879–1900). He also published his Percy Turnbull lectures, delivered at Johns Hopkins University in 1893, under the title *Latin Poetry*, and a volume of *Essays on Greek Literature* (1909). Tyrrell was for many years editor of the Trinity College miscellany called *Kottabos*, to which he himself was the most brilliant and inspiring contributor; it had but a short life after he resigned the editorship. He was one of the founders in 1874 of *Hermathena*, to which he remained a constant contributor to the end of his life.

Tyrrell's genius lay principally in his power of translation: by instinct he knew the right style to adopt, the right tone to take, and the right word to choose, whether translating from the classics into English or the reverse. His lectures were most stimulating, and his influence on the students in literary matters all-pervading, only to be equalled by that of his friend Edward Dowden [q.v.]. He was not a very learned man in all the multifarious departments of classical study; but his criticisms on and enthusiasm for the best in classical and English literature were arresting and infectious, his opinions always being firmly grounded, sincerely felt, and courageously expressed. He was not merely a man of books. He took a keen interest in many forms of sport. He had few peers as a conversationalist; without in any way obtruding himself, by his power of elegant and terse expression he always gave life and light to any discussion. The classical school of his university owes him a debt which it must ever remember.

A portrait of Tyrrell, painted by A. Woolmark in 1907, hangs in the Fellows' smoking-room in Trinity College.

[Private information; personal knowledge.]

L. C. P.

VANE-TEMPEST-STEWART, CHARLES STEWART, sixth Marquess of Londonderry (1852–1915), politician, was born in London 16 July 1852. He was the eldest of the three sons of the fifth Marquess, George Henry Robert Charles William Vane-Tempest, by his wife, Mary Cornelia, only daughter of Sir John Edwards, first baronet, of Garth, Montgomeryshire. A year after his succession to the marquessate he added by royal licence the family name of Stewart to that of Vane-Tempest. He was educated at Eton, and spent a year at the National University of Ireland before matriculating at Christ Church, Oxford. In 1875 he married Lady Theresa, eldest daughter of Charles John Chetwynd-Talbot, nineteenth Earl of Shrewsbury.

In 1878 Vane-Tempest entered the House of Commons as member for the then undivided county of Down, and sat until, at his father's death in 1884, he took his seat in the House of Lords as Earl Vane. Two years later the political world was agitated by Mr. Gladstone's Home Rule proposals, which were rejected by the electorate in the summer of 1886. In the ensuing conservative ministry Mr.

Arthur (afterwards Earl of) Balfour was made chief secretary for Ireland, and Londonderry became viceroy. The Irish position was difficult, for nationalist feeling ran high during a period of coercion, but he filled the viceroyalty with tact and courage, so that when he left Dublin in 1889 the discontent had abated and some measure of prosperity had been restored. He was again prominent in opposition to the second Home Rule Bill of 1893, and presided over the great meeting at which the political alliance between the conservatives and liberal unionists was formally ratified. On Lord Salisbury's return to power in 1895 Londonderry held no office in the government, but he entered it in 1900 as postmaster-general. In 1902, though diffident of his capacity for the post, he became the first president of the Board of Education. He had already had some experience of educational questions, for he had been chairman of the London School Board from 1895 to 1897. As president he administered with success Mr. Balfour's Education Act of 1902–1903. From 1903 to 1905 he was also lord president of the Council.

After the liberals came into office in 1906 Londonderry, as far as politics were concerned, confined his attention almost exclusively to Irish affairs. A consistent conservative in his views, he opposed the Parliament Bill, and when Mr. Asquith's government reopened the subject of Home Rule it fell to him as president of the Ulster unionist council to lead the opposition to it. His was the second signature to the Ulster covenant (28 September 1912), and in the sessions which followed he spoke often in the House of Lords in support of Ulster. The outbreak of war in 1914 caused the suspension of party hostilities, and the Home Rule Bill, twice rejected by the Lords, was allowed to pass, on the understanding that for the present it remained inoperative. Londonderry did not live to see the measure take a different shape in 1920.

Londonderry found time for much charitable work. As lord-lieutenant of Durham and a great coal-owner, he played a considerable part in the life of the county. He was an ideal landlord, and spared no effort to improve the conditions of those about him, providing for his miners churches, schools, clubs, and institutes. His hospitality was noted, and King Edward VII was his guest on five occasions at Wynyard Park, Stockton-on-Tees. In all his social and philanthropic activities he was well seconded by his wife, who survived him only four years, dying in 1919. He was also a keen sportsman, interested in the turf and in the breeding of race-horses, although he never had the good fortune to own a winner of any of the classic events. A patron of agriculture, he farmed upon a large scale.

Londonderry was a sincere and honourable man, of the highest character. Courteous and simple in manner he was always popular, and he had a capacity for friendship. He was sworn of the Privy Council in 1886, and was created K.G. in 1888. He died of pneumonia at Wynyard Park 8 February 1915. He left a son and a daughter. The son, Charles Stewart Henry (born 1878), succeeded him as seventh Marquess, and the daughter, Helen Mary Theresa, married in 1902 Lord Stavordale, afterwards sixth Earl of Ilchester. A younger son, Charles Stewart Reginald, died in 1899.

[*The Times*, 9 February 1915; private information. Portrait, *Royal Academy Pictures*, 1919.] A. C.

VAN HORNE, Sir WILLIAM CORNELIUS (1843–1915), Canadian railway builder and financier, the eldest son of Cornelius Covenhoven Van Horne, lawyer, by his second wife, Mary Minier, daughter of Benjamin Richards, was born at Chelsea, Will county, Illinois, U.S.A., 3 February 1843. His father's ancestors had emigrated from Holland to New Amsterdam in 1635; on his mother's side he came partly of German, partly of French stock. From 1851 to 1857 he attended the common schools in Joliet, Illinois. He then became a telegraph operator on the Chicago and Alton Railway, one of the lines which was opening up the west, and by energy and ability rose steadily. From 1874 to 1879 he was general manager of the Southern Minnesota Railway, and from 1879 to 1881 general superintendent of the Chicago, Milwaukee and St. Paul line.

In 1881 Van Horne accepted the general managership of the newly-formed Canadian Pacific Railway, the construction of which was one of the terms upon which British Columbia had entered the Canadian federation. Such was his energy that, though the contract did not call for the completion of the transcontinental line until 1891, the last spike of the main line was driven on 7 November 1885. From the first he saw that settlement must go hand in hand with construction, and showed foresight and ingenuity in his methods of encouraging and assisting immigration. In 1884 he became vice-president of the company, and in August 1888 he was succeeded as general manager by Thomas George (afterwards Baron) Shaughnessy. From 1888 to 1899 he was president of the company, and from 1899 to 1910 chairman of the board of directors.

Van Horne became a naturalized Canadian in 1888, and in 1894 was created an honorary K.C.M.G. From 1883 onwards he lived in Montreal, but he travelled so constantly that he claimed to have covered more miles than any other living man. From time to time he intervened in Canadian political life, and he was influential in the defeat of reciprocity with the United States in 1891 and 1911. From 1900 till his death he was increasingly interested in the development of Cuba, was president of the Cuba Company, and was largely responsible for the railway law of that island. He died in Montreal 11 September 1915, after an operation for an internal abscess.

Van Horne was tall and strong, with great physical vitality and power of work. In his later years he became very corpulent, but his energy never slackened. After a hard day's work he would spend the night at chess or poker, and turn to the next day's work with unexhausted ardour. His interests were very wide ; he had great natural talent as a watercolourist, and made large collections of old masters, pottery, and palaeontological specimens. He was a member of the Unitarian body.

Van Horne married in 1867 Lucy Adaline, only daughter of Erastus Hurd, civil engineer, of Galesburg, Illinois, who survived him. They had one son and one daughter.

[Walter Vaughan, *Sir William Van Horne*, 1920.] W. L. G.

VERRALL, ARTHUR WOOLLGAR (1851–1912), classical scholar, was born at Brighton 5 February 1851, the eldest of a family of three brothers and two sisters. His father, Henry Verrall, was a well-known solicitor, for many years clerk to the Brighton magistrates ; his mother was Anne Webb Woollgar. In October 1864 Arthur Verrall gained a scholarship at Wellington College, where he became a favourite pupil of Edward White Benson, afterwards archbishop of Canterbury. In 1869 he was elected scholar of Trinity College, Cambridge. He had a distinguished undergraduate career : was Pitt university scholar (1872), was bracketed second classic and chancellor's medallist (1873), and became fellow of his college (1874). For the next three years he lived in London, reading for the bar at Lincoln's Inn ; he was called in 1877. He had gained the Whewell scholarship for international law in 1875. In October 1877 he returned to Cambridge, where for thirty-four years he lectured at Trinity College until, in 1911, he was chosen to be the first King Edward VII professor of English literature.

Verrall's reputation as a teacher grew year by year. He had remarkable powers of exposition ; he held large audiences spell-bound with the novelty and ingenuity of the problems which he propounded, and he would captivate them, as in his Clark lectures, with his gift of reading aloud. As his pupil, Mr. F. M. Cornford, put it, 'To him teaching was the means of expression in which he felt the passion and the joy of an artist ; a lecture by him was definitely a performance prepared down to small details with an orator's sense of effect.'

The long series of Verrall's published works begins with his edition of the *Medea* (1881). His originality, meticulous care, and audacity in pushing principles to logical conclusions, are as conspicuous here as in any of his later works. His *Studies, Literary and Historical, in the Odes of Horace* (1884) was a series of brilliant hypotheses ; to take an instance, a new turn was given to the *Ode to Lamia* (iii, 17) by treating it as a jest, the slave Lamia being playfully assumed to belong to the noble house of that name. Other Latin studies followed—of Martial, of Statius, and, above all, of Propertius. These, however, were but interludes : the Greek drama was his main theme. The first of his editions of Aeschylus was the *Seven Against Thebes* (1887) ; the *Agamemnon* (1889) he dedicated to (Sir) Richard Claverhouse Jebb ; the *Choephori* (1893) to Samuel Henry Butcher ; long afterwards appeared the *Eumenides* (1908). Verrall's treatment of the text was conservative. Others might emend : his ampler resources were lavished upon the task of interpretation. These editions established Verrall's fame and at the same time provoked fierce opposition. For subtlety and cogent argument the *Agamemnon* has no equal. It divided critics into two opposing camps, which thirty years have not reconciled. In his *Euripides the Rationalist* (1895), his *Essays on Four Plays of Euripides* (1905), and his edition of the *Bacchae* (1910), Verrall achieved more unequivocal success. Here he began with the invaluable aid of Aristophanes in the *Frogs*. His main contention is that Athens enjoyed a play by Euripides the rationalist almost in proportion to his skill in wrapping up heresy in orthodox make-believe. The hierarchy of heaven, from Athena and Apollo to Heracles and Dionysus, cut sorry figures, the keenest shafts being aimed at the Delphian god. The *Bacchae*, indeed, presents a peculiar problem ; even here Verrall made out a good case for the poet's rationalism. The net result may be summed up thus : the gods and miracles of Greek anthropomorphic religion were assumed, for artistic purposes, to be real and true ; on the other hand, the incidents and language of the plays pointed to the opposite conclusion ; the inevitable consequence was to foster disbelief ; the peculiar traditions of the tragic stage required this pretence, maintained throughout by a natural love of irony, ambiguity, and play of meaning.

Verrall's appointment to the new chair of English literature gave universal satisfaction. His Sidgwick lecture (1909) on *The Prose of Scott* and his Clark lectures (1909) on the Victorian poets had delighted crowded audiences. But the sands were running out. For fourteen years he had suffered increasingly from arthritis. He had to be carried to deliver his lectures on Dryden in the Michaelmas term of 1911. A course on Macaulay, a subject for which he was singularly well qualified, was to have come next; but, although prepared, it was never given. In his long illness his sufferings were borne with unflinching courage and without complaint ; he would still talk to intimate friends with alertness and something like the old vivacity. He died at Cambridge on Waterloo day (18 June) or, as he himself called it, ' Wellington College day ', 1912.

Verrall married in 1882 Margaret de G. Merrifield, daughter of Frederic Merrifield, barrister-at-law, by whom he had one daughter.

[*Collected Literary Essays, by A. W. Verrall*, ed. M. A. Bayfield and J. D. Duff, with *Memoir*, 1913 ; personal knowledge.] R. D. H.

VILLIERS, JOHN HENRY DE, first Baron De Villiers (1842–1914), South African judge. [See De Villiers.]

VILLIERS, VICTOR ALBERT GEORGE CHILD-, seventh Earl of Jersey and tenth Viscount Grandison (1845–1915), colonial governor, the eldest son of George Augustus Frederick Child-Villiers, sixth Earl, by his wife, Julia, elder daughter of Sir Robert Peel, second baronet [q.v.], was born 20 March 1845. He was educated at Eton and Balliol College, Oxford, and, while at school, succeeded his father in 1859. He was a lord-in-waiting to Queen Victoria from 1875 to 1877, and in 1889 was made paymaster-general. The following year he received the appointment of governor and commander-in-chief of New South Wales, and assumed office in January 1891.

The task before Lord Jersey was a difficult one, for Australia was passing through a critical period in her history. Although the burning question of Chinese immigration had been satisfactorily settled in 1888, other urgent problems had taken its place. Chief of these were the federation movement and the attitude of the working classes. Before 1889 New South Wales had stood aloof from the movement for Australasian federation, but in that year the premier of the colony, Sir Henry Parkes [q.v.], had given his adhesion to it, and New South Wales was represented at the first inter-colonial conference held at Melbourne early in 1890. A few weeks after Lord Jersey had taken up his appointment a convention to consider the question was held at Sydney ; but federation was never so popular in New South Wales as in the other colonies, and no further progress was made during Lord Jersey's term of office. The attitude of labour presented a far more serious problem. The labour movement in Australia had been gaining ground for many years, especially in New South Wales, and in 1890 the differences between employers and men came to a head over the question of reduction of wages. A great strike, of which Sydney was the centre, had at one time threatened to paralyse the trade of the colony, and had only come to an end (November 1890) two months before Lord Jersey's arrival. The result was a decisive victory for the employers, but in the following year labour representatives were able to dominate the situation in the New South Wales parliament. To complicate the situation, rash land speculations were just then contributing to the financial difficulties of Australia, and some harsh criticism in the London financial press had been deeply resented in the colony. Lord Jersey, however, showed himself capable of dealing tactfully with the situation. He set himself to win the confidence of the people of New South Wales and to show them that he recognized that they were neither dishonest nor bankrupt. In this he proved eminently successful, and although he remained governor for less than two and a half years he made himself greatly beloved, and as ex-governor became a trusted unofficial ambassador of the Commonwealth in London.

In 1893 Lord Jersey returned to England. His sound abilities and his banking experience as principal proprietor of Child's Bank were always thereafter at the service of the Empire. In 1894 he represented the United Kingdom at the Ottawa colonial conference, and in the same year he revisited Australia and received a warm welcome. In 1904–1905 he acted as agent-general for New South Wales, and on the foundation of the Australian Commonwealth (1901) was offered the position of first high commissioner. He declined on the ground that he preferred to remain an unofficial representative of the Commonwealth.

As a great landowner Lord Jersey was keenly interested in local administration and agricultural questions. He acted as chairman of the light railway commission (1896–1905), was lord-lieutenant of Oxfordshire from 1887 till his death, and a member of the Oxfordshire County Council. He died at Osterley Park, Isleworth, 31 May 1915.

Lord Jersey married in 1872 the Hon. Margaret Elizabeth, eldest daughter of William Henry Leigh, second Baron Leigh; they had two sons and four daughters. He was succeeded by his eldest son George Henry Robert Child (1873–1923).

A portrait of Lord Jersey is included in H. Jamyn Brooks's picture 'Private View at the Royal Academy, 1888', in the National Portrait Gallery.

[*The Times*, 1 June 1915.]

VOYSEY, CHARLES (1828–1912), Theistic preacher, was born in London 18 March 1828, the youngest son of Annesley Voysey, architect, by his wife, Mary, daughter of Thomas Green. His father was a direct descendant of John Wesley's sister, Susannah Ellison, and a noted architect in Jamaica. Charles Voysey passed from Stockwell grammar school to St. Edmund Hall, Oxford, where he matriculated in 1847 together with his elder brother Richard. He graduated in 1851, when he was ordained and appointed to the curacy of Hessle, Hull. Here he remained for seven years, until he became incumbent of St. Andrew's, Craigton, Jamaica. After eighteen months he returned to England and, through Dean Stanley's influence, obtained a curacy at Great Yarmouth, but six months later (1861) was appointed curate at St. Mark's, Whitechapel. Here he gave some offence by preaching a sermon in which he denied the doctrine of eternal punishment. He was recommended in 1863 by the bishop of London (Dr. Tait) to the curacy of St. Mark's, Victoria Docks, under Dr. Henry Boyd, afterwards principal of Hertford College, Oxford. After six months' service there he was invited by the patron and vicar of Healaugh, near Tadcaster, to accept the curacy of that parish, and in the following year (1864) the vicar resigned and presented Voysey to the benefice.

Voysey began his career as a religious reformer by the publication, in 1864, of a sermon 'Is every statement in the Bible about our Heavenly Father strictly true?' In consequence of the unorthodox tendency of his preaching and writings he was cited in 1869 to appear before the chancellor's court of the diocese of York, where judgment was given against him. He appealed to the Privy Council and conducted his own defence, but the judgment of that body, delivered 11 February 1871, supported the York chancellor's decision, and sentence of deprivation, with costs, was pronounced, to be rescinded if within a week Voysey expressly and unreservedly retracted the errors of which he had been convicted. This he refused to do. Before the date of judgment Voysey had begun to hold services in London at St. George's Hall, Langham Place, whither he attracted a number of sympathizers, pledged to support the 'Voysey establishment fund.' He thus started a movement which eventually took shape as an independent religious denomination under the name of the 'Theistic Church'. In 1885 he established for his followers a regular place of worship in Swallow Street, Piccadilly, where he continued to hold services for nearly thirty years.

Voysey's ultimate theological position amounted to the absolute rejection of the creeds, biblical inspiration, the sacramental system, and the divinity of Christ, and his teaching was the inculcation of a pure Theism, without any miraculous element. He was an attractive preacher, courageous and sincere in challenging doctrines which he believed to be erroneous, and he undoubtedly had a profound influence in deepening the religious sense of his followers. He was one of the founders of the Cremation Society of England, and for twenty-five years a member of the executive council of the Homes for Inebriates. In politics he was an ardent unionist. He died at Hampstead 20 July 1912. He was succeeded at Swallow Street by Dr. Walter Walsh, but within a short time two separate congregations were formed, one retaining the name of the Theistic Church, the other adopting that of the 'Free Religious Movement'. The Swallow Street building was closed in 1913 and shortly afterwards demolished.

Voysey married in 1852 Frances Maria, daughter of Robert Edlin, partner in the banking firm of Herries, Farquhar & Co. They had four sons and six daughters.

[Private information; personal knowledge.] D. W.

WALLACE, ALFRED RUSSEL (1823–1913), naturalist, was born 8 January 1823, at Usk, Monmouthshire. He was the third son and seventh of the eight children of Thomas Vere Wallace, by his wife, Mary Anne Greenell. The father, a dabbler in many subjects but master of none, had lost most of his money in a literary venture. Alfred Wallace was educated at the grammar school at Hertford, whither the family had moved in 1828, and acted as pupil-teacher there from 1836 to 1837. His tastes were those of the average intelligent boy. He was fond of reading and of making toys and mechanical devices, two traits which, in his own opinion, were of importance to his later life. When fourteen he left school, joined his brother William in London, and set himself to learn surveying with him. In connexion with the practical work of surveying he also learnt the rudiments of geology. A year later (1838) he went to live as apprentice with a watchmaker named Matthews at Leighton Buzzard, and would probably have settled down in that business had not William Wallace been enabled to take Alfred with him to Herefordshire in 1839 to help in his surveying work. Here Alfred became interested in astronomy, in agriculture, and particularly in botany and in botanical problems, such as that of a natural classification. About 1843 he began the valuable practice of systematizing his ideas on subjects which interested him by writing them down. In that year his father died; and in 1844, his brother's prospects not being good, he became a master at the collegiate school at Leicester. Here he read much and conducted experiments in hypnotism. One set of experiments in what he called 'phreno-mesmerism' is of considerable interest, although the phenomena seem more likely to shed light on suggestion and telepathy than on phrenology. Here also—a turning-point in his career—he made the acquaintance of Henry Walter Bates [q.v.], the naturalist, by whom he was introduced to the science of entomology; and he read Malthus *On Population*, a book which for him, as for Darwin, was one of the foundations for the theory of natural selection.

In 1846 William Wallace unexpectedly died. Alfred left the collegiate school in order to take up his brother's work, finding plenty of well-paid employment in connexion with the railway mania. After a short interlude at Neath, where he was joined by his brother John, and added building and architectural designing to his other work, and also gave his first public lecture, he suggested to Bates that they should join forces for a collecting trip on the Amazon. Expenses were to be defrayed by the sale of specimens. Bates agreed, and they sailed in April 1848. In March 1850 they parted company, Wallace remaining four years in all, Bates returning after a stay of no less than eleven years. In 1849 Wallace was joined by his younger brother Herbert, who, however, died of yellow fever in 1851. Wallace tells us that the three things which impressed him most in the Amazons were the majesty and variety of the equatorial forest, the beauty and strangeness of the butterflies and birds, and the contact with savage man—a contact which had made a deep impression on Darwin also. During the return voyage the ship was destroyed by fire. The ship's company, after ten days in open boats, were rescued; but all of Wallace's collections and notes which had not previously been sent home were lost—a circumstance which, he wrote in his old age, was of great service to him in the long run, as it stimulated him later to visit the Malay Archipelago. On his return he settled in London to work out his collections. He became a regular attendant at scientific meetings, and made the acquaintance of many notable men of science.

In 1854, having satisfied himself that the Malay Archipelago offered the richest field for a collector, Wallace set off thither by himself, on a voyage which lasted no less than eight years. He visited every important island in the group, often more than once, and became fascinated both by the practical and by the theoretical side of the work. When urged by his brother-in-law, in 1859, to return to England, he answered that he had set himself to work out 'the whole problem' of the Archipelago, and would not think of coming home before he had done so to his satisfaction. One of his most interesting discoveries was that the Archipelago is divided zoologically into two very distinct regions by the narrow but deep strait between Bali and Lombok (now known as 'Wallace's Line'); the western area is Oriental in the character of its fauna, the eastern, Australasian. In 1855 he published his first contribution to the species problem, an *Essay on the Law which has regulated the*

Introduction of New Species, in which he laid down the evolutionary conclusion that 'every species has come into existence coincident both in time and space with a pre-existing closely-allied species'. He gradually became a convinced evolutionist; but it was not till 1858, during an attack of fever at Ternate, in the Moluccas, that the idea of natural selection as the solution of the *method* of evolution flashed upon him, and he thought it out in the course of a few hours. The next two days he spent in writing down his views and sending them to Darwin. Darwin was fourteen years his senior, and a man of established reputation, whereas Wallace was a young collector with his reputation still to make. The result, a monument to the natural generosity of both the great biologists, was the famous joint paper at the Linnaean Society on 1 July 1858, in which the modern theory of evolution was first given to the world. Darwin had been working privately on the identical theme for years, but insisted on this joint publication; while Wallace, who might have raised a technical claim to priority as having been the first to write out his views for publication, never dreamt of such a procedure [see DARWIN, Charles Robert]. In 1860 he obtained a copy of the *Origin of Species*, and read it five or six times, 'each time with increasing admiration'. He felt that Darwin had done the work as well as it could be done, and wrote to Bates to say how thankful he was that Darwin and not himself had been called upon to set forth the theory in detail. However, he later did great service to the cause of evolution by his lucid volume, *Contributions to the Theory of Natural Selection* (1870).

Early in 1862 Wallace left Singapore for England, bringing with him the first birds of paradise to reach Europe alive. He again settled down in London to work out the huge private collections which remained in his hands, even after the rest had been sold to such good purpose that the money when invested brought him in about £300 a year. He gradually turned from purely systematic description to the broader problems of evolution and geographical distribution; and in 1869 published what is perhaps his most important book, the great work on *The Malay Archipelago*, a magnificent combination of interesting sketches of travel and vivid pictures of natural history, together with a discussion of the great generalizations of evolutionary biology.

In 1863 Wallace became engaged to be married, but, to his great pain, the lady broke off the match. In 1866 he married Mary, the eldest daughter of William Mitten, of Hurstpierpoint, Sussex, a botanist friend, and embarked upon a long and happy married life. They had two children, a son and a daughter.

During his two periods of life in London Wallace made many friends and acquaintances, scientific and otherwise, among whom were Darwin, Lyell, Huxley, Tyndall, Mivart, W. B. Carpenter, Herbert Spencer, Wheatstone, and Lecky. He also interested himself in various outstanding social questions, especially land nationalization. During the next few years he was a candidate for the posts of assistant secretary of the Royal Geographical Society, director of the Bethnal Green museum, and superintendent of Epping Forest, which had just been acquired for the public; but in every case without success. He was now in the prime of his powers, and in 1876 published another first-class work, *The Geographical Distribution of Animals*.

In 1871, seized with a desire for country life, Wallace had moved to Grays in Essex. But he was never long in one place. He moved again to Croydon in 1876, to Dorking in 1878, to Godalming in 1881, to Parkstone in 1889, and finally, in 1902, to Broadstone, near Wimborne. In the late 'seventies he had lost most of his money through speculation and very injudicious investments, but in 1881, largely through the influence of Darwin and Huxley, he was granted a Civil List pension of £200. In the same year he became president of the newly-formed Land Nationalization Society. In 1886 he spent nearly a year on a lecturing tour in the United States. On his return, stimulated by the success of a lecture on Darwin's views, he wrote the excellent semi-popular work entitled *Darwinism*, which was published in 1889.

For the next few years Wallace gave up public lecturing and devoted himself chiefly to the writing of articles on every kind of scientific and social subject. In 1898 he published *The Wonderful Century*, a resumé of human progress in the nineteenth century. Another work, entitled *Man's Place in the Universe* (1903), embodied his belief that life could have developed only once in the cosmos, a belief based upon the then generally accepted statement that the solar system was near the centre of the visible universe. In 1905 he published his autobiography, *My Life*, a very detailed two-volume work. He died at Broadstone, Dorset, 7 November 1913, aged ninety. Much of his peaceful and happy old age was devoted to gardening.

Wallace will chiefly be remembered as a great naturalist who was also an evolutionist. He was not a trained anatomist or physiologist, nor had he the prodigious range of tested knowledge which Darwin amassed. But he was an indefatigable collector, both of specimens and of facts; and he thought about what he collected with originality and vigour. Of his services to biology, not the least was the wealth of material which he sent back during his eight years in the Malay Archipelago. On the theoretical side, his most famous achievement was his independent discovery of the principle of natural selection as a key to the method of evolution. This alone would give him a permanent place in the history of thought. But further, it was he who first called attention to the importance of many colours and markings of animals for purposes of recognition at a distance—a very fruitful idea; he pointed out an important correlation between nesting-site and brilliancy of coloration in female birds; he also amplified and strengthened the theory of warning coloration and mimicry. He was an unsparing critic of Darwin's theory of sexual selection, but on illogical and insufficient grounds; his own theory of 'male vigour' as the cause of brighter male plumage has little to recommend it. He came to reject the whole of the Lamarckian element in Darwin's views, and, with August Weismann, became one of the apostles of the neo-Darwinian movement.

Wallace's most solid work was, perhaps, that on geographical distribution. Here he strengthened with various new arguments J. D. Dana's principle of the permanence of the great ocean basins; pointed out how dispersal of temperate and Arctic faunas could take place even across the tropics along mountain-chains; laid stress on the cumulative effect of snow-fall and ice-accumulation in accentuating the temperature changes which led to glacial epochs; and was emphatic in support of a single system of zoo-geographical regions for the distribution of all groups of animals. His zoo-geographical work was fundamental for all subsequent investigations in this field. He himself expressed the hope that his book on the geographical distribution of animals might bear 'a similar relation to the eleventh and twelfth chapters of the *Origin of Species* as Mr. Darwin's *Animals and Plants under Domestication* bears to the first'—a hope which has been fully justified.

As regards human evolution, Wallace was the first to point out explicitly that from an early period in man's evolutionary history, natural selection would act chiefly upon the mind, not on the body, and that therefore we should not expect further physical evolution in the human species. He also advanced some interesting observations concerning what he called 'mouth-gesture' in relation to the origin of language, extending the principle of onomatopoeia to great lengths.

On many other matters of scientific opinion Wallace took up a very unorthodox position. He was a convinced phrenologist, anti-vaccinationist, and spiritualist, and believed that natural evolution, while it would account for the development of man's body, must have been supplemented by a supernatural intervention to produce his soul. In politics also he was unorthodox. His socialism was highly theoretical, and his views on land nationalization extreme. A vegetarian 'in principle,' he found that a meat diet agreed best with him. His zeal for demonstrating scientific truth once cost him a considerable sum of money and still more vexation. In 1870 a certain Mr. J. Hampden offered £500 to any one who could prove that the earth was round. Wallace took up the challenge, and an experiment was carried out on the Bedford levels. After much dispute the stakes were awarded to Wallace; but owing to technicalities connected with the law on betting Hampden recovered the money. Not content with this, he pursued Wallace in public and private with the most violent and scurrilous invective for nearly twenty years, in spite of being twice sent to jail.

Wallace was a modest man, with a kindly nature. This showed itself in the active interest he would take in the views and plans of younger naturalists; and, together with his strong sense of justice, led him to undertake his various social crusades. It has been said that he combined the most remarkable shrewdness in dealing with natural history, with an equal credulity in dealing with his fellowmen; and, although this statement is exaggerated, there is some truth in it. There was a certain element of the crank in him; but, when he was handling the facts of nature and the ample speculations of evolutionary theory, this could not show itself; and his fondness for nature, his industry, his zeal, his love both of detailed fact and of broad generalization, and his very considerable abilities, here could find their proper scope, with the result that his name will be permanently remembered as long as the theory of evolution is discussed.

Wallace was awarded the first Darwin medal of the Royal Society in 1890; he had received the royal medal in 1868. He held the honorary degrees of LL.D. of Dublin University (1882) and D.C.L. of Oxford (1889). The order of merit was bestowed on him in 1910.

Wallace was the author of the following works, besides numerous scientific papers: *Travels on the Amazon and Rio Negro* (1853), *Palm Trees of the Amazon* (1853), *The Malay Archipelago* (1869), *Natural Selection* (1870), *On Miracles and Modern Spiritualism* (1875, new edition 1896), *The Geographical Distribution of Animals* (1876), *Tropical Nature* (1878), *Island Life* (1880), *Land Nationalization* (1882), *Bad Times* (1885), *Darwinism* (1889), *Vaccination, a Delusion* (1898), *The Wonderful Century* (1898, new edition 1903), *Studies, Scientific and Social* (1900), *Man's Place in the Universe* (1903), *My Life, an Autobiography* (1905), *Is Mars Habitable?* (1907), *The World of Life* (1910), and *Social Environment and Moral Progress* (1912).

[Wallace's *My Life*; Introduction (by G. T. Bettany) to Wallace's *Travels on the Amazon and Rio Negro*, 1889; *Proceedings* of the Royal Society, vol. xcv, B, 1923–1924 (with portrait).] J. S. H.

WALLACE, Sir DONALD MACKENZIE (1841–1919), newspaper correspondent, editor, and author, the son of Robert Wallace, of Boghead, Dumbartonshire, by his wife, Sarah, daughter of Donald Mackenzie, was born 11 November 1841. He lost both his parents before he was ten years old, and about the age of fifteen, having a sufficiency of private means, he conceived, in his own words, 'a passionate love of study, and determined to devote my life to it'. Accordingly, he spent all the years of his early manhood, until he was twenty-eight, in continuous study at various universities; about half the time at Glasgow and Edinburgh, where he was occupied mainly with metaphysics and ethics; the remainder at the École de Droit, Paris, and at the universities of Berlin and Heidelberg, where he applied himself particularly to Roman law and modern jurisprudence, taking the degree of doctor of laws at Heidelberg in 1867. During the vacations he travelled extensively over the continent of Europe, acquiring fluency in its principal languages.

While he was engaged in qualifying himself in Germany for a professorship of comparative law, Wallace accepted a private invitation to visit Russia, as he had a strong desire to study the Ossetes, a peculiar Aryan tribe in the Caucasus, with exceptionally primitive institutions. He remained in Russia nearly six years, from early in 1870 till late in 1875, studying, not the Ossetes, but the Russians themselves, whom he found much better worth attention. He familiarized himself thoroughly with the life of the people, not merely visiting the great towns and the show places, but settling for a considerable period in a remote country village; and in 1876 he came back to England with the material which he utilized in his famous work on *Russia*, published in two volumes in the beginning of 1877, just before the outbreak of the Russo-Turkish War. The book had a great and instant success, went through several editions, and was translated into many languages, the French translation being 'crowned' by the Academy. It was twice revised by its author, in 1905 and in 1912, and remains the standard authority on Russia before the revolution of 1917.

Wallace now entered active life as a foreign correspondent of *The Times*, which he represented at St. Petersburg in 1877–1878; at the Berlin Congress in June and July 1878, where he assisted M. de Blowitz, the famous Paris correspondent of *The Times*; and afterwards for six years at Constantinople (1878–1884). From that point of vantage he was able to investigate the Balkan peoples and their problems; and thence he went on behalf of *The Times*, after the battle of Tel-el-Kebir (September 1882), on a special mission to Egypt, the outcome being his book, *Egypt and the Egyptian Question* (1883). In 1884 the Earl of Dufferin, who, as British ambassador at Constantinople, had learnt to appreciate Wallace's unusual attainments, tact, and discretion, took him to India as his private secretary during his viceroyalty, and testified at its close in 1888 to the 'incomparable' nature of his assistance, which was rewarded by the K.C.I.E. in 1887. After a further period of travel in the Near and Middle East, Wallace was selected to accompany, as political officer, the Tsarewitch, afterwards the ill-fated Emperor Nicholas II of Russia, in his Indian tour during the winter of 1890–1891. Then he returned to the service of *The Times*, as director of its foreign department, a new post, in which for eight years his powers of organization, calm judgement, and encyclopaedic knowledge found congenial scope. That knowledge was utilized in 1899 in another direction, when *The Times* took over the

Encyclopaedia Britannica and prevailed on Wallace, with Mr. Hugh Chisholm as colleague, to edit the extra volumes of the tenth edition needed to bring the work up to date. In 1901 he accompanied, as assistant private secretary, the Duke and Duchess of Cornwall and York (afterwards King George V and Queen Mary) in their tour of the British Dominions—a tour which he commemorated in a book, *The Web of Empire* (1902). In 1905 he acted once more as a correspondent of *The Times*, attending the conference at Portsmouth, New Hampshire, U.S.A., which produced peace between Russia and Japan.

For the last decade and a half of his life Wallace reverted to his youthful ideal, and devoted himself to persistent study, varied by occasional travel; but he published nothing further. In spite of being essentially a student he had a genius for social intercourse, and possessed friends in all European and several non-European countries, and in many walks of life—savants, artists, journalists, travellers, diplomatists, statesmen, social magnates, great ladies, courtiers, and, to a remarkable degree, royal personages. He never married, and died at Lymington, Hampshire, 10 January 1919.

[*The Times*, 11 January 1919; private information; personal knowledge.]

G. E. B.

WALLER, LEWIS (1860–1915), actor-manager, whose real name was William Waller Lewis, was born at Bilbao, Spain, 3 November 1860. He was the eldest son of William James Lewis, civil engineer, by his wife, Carlotta, second daughter of Thomas A. Vyse, of the Howard-Vyse family. He was educated at King's College School, London, and in Germany. Intended for a commercial career, he was employed for five years in his uncle's office in the City. As an amateur he acted for several years with dramatic societies, but subsequently he made up his mind to become a professional actor, and was fortunate enough to be engaged by John Lawrence Toole [q.v.] for Toole's Theatre, where he first appeared on 26 March 1883 in a revival of *Uncle Dick's Darling*. For the next twelve months he played in Toole's repertory, and then left in order to tour the provinces. He appeared at the Lyceum Theatre with Madame Modjeska on 30 March 1885 in *Adrienne Lecouvreur*, and then went on tour until the end of 1886. He made his first substantial success in London at the Strand Theatre on 7 February 1887 in *Jack in the Box* by G. R. Sims and Clement W. Scott. Subsequently he fulfilled engagements as leading juvenile with Kate Vaughan at the Opera Comique, with Mrs. Brown-Potter at the Gaiety Theatre, with (Sir) John Hare and William Hunter Kendal at the St. James's, with Rutland Barrington at the same theatre, and with Wilson Barrett at the Princess's.

On the opening of the Garrick Theatre by John Hare on 24 April 1889, Waller played as Hugh Murray in (Sir) A. W. Pinero's play *The Profligate*, and again in November of that year as Cavaradossi in an adaptation of *La Tosca*. After fulfilling engagements at various other theatres, he appeared in January 1893 in G. S. Ogilvie's *Hypatia* at the Haymarket Theatre under the management of (Sir) Herbert Beerbohm Tree, and later in the same year in a series of Ibsen's plays at the Opera Comique. In the autumn of 1893 Waller undertook theatrical management for the first time, in conjunction with H. H. Morell (Mackenzie), son of Sir Morell Mackenzie, the physician, when he went on tour in Oscar Wilde's *A Woman of No Importance*.

At the Haymarket Theatre on 3 January 1895 Waller began his career as a London theatrical manager, producing, in conjunction with H. H. Morell, Oscar Wilde's comedy *An Ideal Husband*. In the same year he joined forces for a short time with (Sir) Charles Wyndham at the Criterion Theatre. At the Haymarket in May 1896 he gave a brilliant interpretation of the part of Hotspur in *Henry IV, Part I*. In April 1897 he was engaged by Tree for the opening of Her Majesty's Theatre; and between that date and September 1900 he appeared there in many parts, the most notable of which were Laertes in *Hamlet*, Philip Faulconbridge in *King John*, and Brutus in *Julius Caesar*. On the conclusion of his engagement with Tree, Waller resumed management on his own account. In conjunction with William Mollison he entered into the management of the Lyceum Theatre, where he revived Henry Hamilton's adaptation of *The Three Musketeers* on 3 November 1900. During a vacation from Her Majesty's Theatre in 1898 Waller had made a notable appearance in this play in the part of D'Artagnan. In December 1900 he achieved what was possibly his finest impersonation, namely that of the King in *Henry V*.

At the Shakespeare Theatre, Liverpool, 6 October 1902, Waller appeared for the first time in the title-rôle of *Monsieur Beaucaire* by E. G. Sutherland and Booth Tarkington. On 25 October he produced the play at the Comedy Theatre; it was performed 430 times in succession, and he revived it on many subsequent occasions. On 3 November 1903 Waller opened in this play at the Imperial Theatre, which he continued to manage until May 1906. He then removed to the Lyric Theatre, where he remained, with varying success, until July 1910. He made several notable productions during his period of management, especially *Miss Elizabeth's Prisoner*, *Brigadier Gerard*, *Robin Hood*, *A White Man*, and *The Fires of Fate*. He also revived *Othello* and *Romeo and Juliet*, but these ventures were unsuccessful. In September 1911 Waller visited the United States for the first time, and in October achieved success in a production in New York of *The Garden of Allah*. In May 1913 he went to Australia, where he remained for twelve months, and on his return to England reappeared on the London stage. In June 1915 he appeared at Wyndham's Theatre as John Leighton in *Gamblers All* by May Martindale, and while appearing in this play at Nottingham in the following October caught a chill and died there of double pneumonia on 1 November. He was buried in Kensal Green cemetery.

Waller was an actor of great individuality. His pleasing voice and fine presence fascinated popular audiences. No actor of his time could compare with him in such parts as D'Artagnan, Hotspur, or Henry V. But his acting appealed less to the intellect than to the eye and ear. His energy was remarkable, and during his thirty-two years' career he played nearly two hundred parts on the London stage without missing a performance. He was a great favourite with King Edward VII.

Waller married in 1883 Florence (died 1912), eldest daughter of Horatio Brandon, solicitor. First as Florence West, and subsequently under her married name, she was for many years a popular actress. Waller was survived by a son and a daughter, both of whom appeared on the stage.

A painting of Waller as 'Beaucaire', by the Hon. John Collier, was exhibited at the Royal Academy in 1903.

[*The Times*, *Daily Telegraph*, *Standard*, 4 November 1915; Clement W. Scott, *The Drama of Yesterday and To-Day*, 1899; *Who's Who in the Theatre*; private information; personal knowledge.] J. P.

WARD, MARY AUGUSTA (1851–1920), better known as MRS. HUMPHRY WARD, novelist and social worker, was the daughter of Thomas Arnold [q.v.], by his wife, Julia, daughter of William Sorell, of Hobart Town, Tasmania. Her father was the second son of Dr. Arnold of Rugby [q.v.]. She was born at Hobart Town 11 June 1851, and was the eldest of a family of eight children. At the time of her birth her father held an appointment as inspector of schools in the public education service of Tasmania, which he relinquished in 1856 on being received into the Church of Rome. He brought his family to England in the same year, and after a period of work in Roman Catholic educational establishments at Dublin and Birmingham, returned to the Church of England in 1865 and settled in Oxford. His daughter Mary, who had spent the interval at private boarding schools, came to live at home in the summer of 1867, and began, as she herself considered, her real education. She worked hard at music and early Spanish literature, and delighted in the stimulating society of the university. In 1872 she married Thomas Humphry Ward, fellow and tutor of Brasenose College, son of the Rev. Henry Ward, vicar of St. Barnabas, King Square, Holloway.

The movement for the higher education of women began in Oxford in the years succeeding Mary Ward's marriage, and in 1879 she acted as the first secretary of Somerville College. She was at that time engaged on an ambitious piece of historical work, the writing of the lives of early Spanish ecclesiastics for the *Dictionary of Christian Biography*. In 1881 her environment was changed by removal to London, but her literary activities were not interrupted. Mr. Humphry Ward had joined the staff of *The Times*, and his wife also became a contributor to that paper as well as to various reviews. In spite of writer's cramp, which now first attacked her and continued to hamper her for the rest of her life, she wrote her first novel, *Miss Bretherton*, in 1884, and translated Henri Frederic Amiel's *Journal Intime* in the same year.

Mrs. Ward had an hereditary interest in religious problems, which had been fostered by her life in Oxford. While still a young woman she arrived at the conclusion that Christianity could be revitalized by discarding its miraculous element and emphasizing its social mission, and to this she held firmly all her life. She embodied her views in her best-known novel, *Robert Elsmere* (1888), which at once excited public interest, and was the subject of elaborate comment by Mr. Gladstone in the *Nineteenth Century*. The sales of the first three editions in the United Kingdom amounted to 70,500, and pirated editions of the book had a great success in America.

Robert Elsmere brought its author into touch with many who desired, as she did, to work among the London poor, as missionaries of undogmatic religion. In 1890 she and her associates founded a settlement at University Hall, Gordon Square, for popular Bible-teaching and 'simplified' Christianity on the one hand, and for social purposes on the other. This developed a few years later into the Passmore Edwards Settlement, opened in Tavistock Square in 1897 [see EDWARDS, John Passmore.]

Though her health was always uncertain, Mrs. Ward continued for the rest of her life to accomplish an enormous amount of work. Her novels followed each other in rapid succession. *The History of David Grieve* appeared in 1892, *Marcella* in 1894, *The Story of Bessie Costrell* in 1895, *Sir George Tressady* in 1896, *Helbeck of Bannisdale* in 1898, *Eleanor* in 1900, *Lady Rose's Daughter* in 1903, *The Marriage of William Ashe* in 1905, *Fenwick's Career* in 1906, and *The Testing of Diana Mallory* in 1908. She continued to publish novels down to 1920, but except for *The Case of Richard Meynell* (1911), a return to the theme of *Robert Elsmere*, her later books did not achieve that remarkable combination of serious intellectual interest with descriptive power and skilful presentation of social types which had won her her great reputation.

Mrs. Ward's practical achievements were no less notable than her literary success. At the Passmore Edwards Settlement she instituted the 'children's play hours', which developed into the movement, so closely associated with her name, for recreational centres for London children. In 1898 she set on foot a scheme for the education, at the Settlement, of crippled children; and by many years of experiment and propaganda she succeeded in so fully awakening the public mind to the necessity for special educational facilities for physically defective children, that the provision of such facilities was made compulsory on local authorities in 1918.

Mrs. Ward's other principal activity, in the period before the European War, was the organization of opposition to the extension of the franchise to women. She was the foundress of the Women's National Anti-Suffrage League (1908), and also, since she combined anti-suffrage feeling with a personal taste for political activity, of the 'Joint Advisory Council of Members of Parliament and Women Social Workers', an organization for bringing the views of women to bear on the legislature without the aid of the vote. In 1910 she wrote a series of political pamphlets, *Letters to My Neighbours*, for the benefit of the Hertfordshire constituency in which her son was conservative candidate.

During the War Mrs. Ward undertook, at the request of Mr. Roosevelt and with the encouragement of the British government, a series of articles designed to bring home to the imagination of the American people the efforts and achievements of the Allies. She was allowed facilities for seeing the army in the field, the navy, and the munitions works, and she published the result of her tours of inspection in the press as *Letters to an American Friend*, later republished as *England's Effort* (1916), *Towards the Goal* (1917), and *Fields of Victory* (1919). In 1918 she published an autobiographical volume, *A Writer's Recollections*.

Shortly before her death Mrs. Ward was invited to act as one of the first seven women magistrates, and the university of Edinburgh offered her the degree of LL.D. She died in London 24 March 1920, and was buried at Aldbury, Hertfordshire. Her husband died in 1926. She had one son and two daughters: Arnold, who was member of parliament for West Hertfordshire from 1910 to 1918; Dorothy; and Janet, the wife of Professor George Macaulay Trevelyan.

[*The Times*, 25 March 1920; Janet Penrose Trevelyan, *The Life of Mrs. Humphry Ward*, 1923; Mrs. Humphry Ward, *A Writer's Recollections*, 1918.] M. C.

WARD, WILFRID PHILIP (1856–1916), biographer and Catholic apologist, was born 2 January 1856 at Old Hall House, Ware, Hertfordshire, the second son of William George Ward [q.v.], 'Ideal' Ward, of the Oxford Movement. His family was of old standing in the Isle of Wight and noteworthy in the cricketing world. Ward was brought up in an ultramontane atmosphere before proceeding to Ushaw College, Durham, and the Gregorian University at Rome. He lectured on philosophy at Ushaw College in 1890, was an examiner in mental and moral science for the Royal University of Ireland 1891–1892, and a member of the royal commission on Irish university education (1901). In 1906 he became editor of the *Dublin Review*, which he raised to a commanding standard of thought and influence. His vocation to the Catholic priesthood was not realized, but his younger brother, Bernard Nicholas (1857–1920), was ordained priest in 1882, and afterwards became president of St. Edmund's College, Ware, and bishop of Brentwood.

Educated outside the influences of Oxford or a public school, Wilfrid Ward developed into a thinker and a controversialist after an individual and tolerant manner. As a young man he crossed swords with Herbert Spencer and Frederic Harrison. His first work, *The Wish to Believe*, appeared in the *Nineteenth Century* (1882), and was followed by *The Clothes of Religion* (1886), a reply to popular positivism, and *Witnesses to the Unseen* (1893). But he found his most congenial field in biography, and it was here that he displayed an original talent. In 1889 he published the first volume of his father's life, *William George Ward and the Oxford Movement*, the second volume appearing in 1893, *William George Ward and the Catholic Revival*. *The Life and Times of Cardinal Wiseman*, which Cardinal Vaughan requested him to write, occupied him for five years and appeared in 1897. The first edition was sold in a week, but an interesting chapter was omitted in subsequent editions. He then wrote a memoir of Aubrey Thomas de Vere [q.v.], the poet-convert (1904). Seven years' unremitting work led to his *Life of Cardinal Newman* (1912), a work of 1,300 pages into which he wove about 1,000 of the Cardinal's letters. In it he said the last word on Newman, and identified himself with Newmanism even to the extent of opposing his father's opinions.

The *Life of Newman* was written during the Modernist controversy, when many Catholic thinkers, such as George Tyrrell [q.v.], Lagrange, the Abbé Duchesne, and Baron von Hügel, were incurring the suspicion of the Holy See. More than any single man Ward held the balance and kept comparative peace among the thinkers of English Catholicism. His apologetic was based on his axiom that since the Reformation the Catholic Church was in 'a state of siege'. He was a liberal without being found guilty of liberalism by authority. The balance which Ward held amongst his fellow Catholics corresponded with his position amongst non-Catholics. He understood and appreciated Anglicanism, enjoying the friendship of Lord Halifax, George Wyndham [q.v.], and John Neville Figgis [q.v.]. Richard Holt Hutton [q.v.] had also deeply influenced him. He helped to revive the old Metaphysical Society under the name of the Synthetic Society. He was elected to the Athenæum Club *honoris causa*. His genius for friendship and portraiture found its fulfilment in a series of books, *Problems and Persons* (1903), *Ten Personal Studies* (1908), and *Men and Matters* (1914). The *Life of Newman* led to two successful lecturing tours in America in the course of which he delivered the Lowell lectures at Boston (1914). His last days were spent in preparing for publication the letters of his friend Father Basil Maturin [q.v.]. In 1916 he retired to Hampstead, where he died on 9 April. He was buried at Freshwater in the Isle of Wight. He married in 1887 Josephine Mary, second daughter of James Robert Hope-Scott Q.C., [q.v.], of Abbotsford, and left two sons and two daughters.

[*Last Lectures* (1916) edited by Mrs. Ward; obituary notices in *The Times*, 10 April 1916, *Dublin Review*, and *Tablet*; private information.] S. L.

WARNEFORD, REGINALD ALEXANDER JOHN (1891–1915), airman, was born at Darjeeling, India, 15 October 1891, the eldest child and only son of Reginald William Henry Warneford, civil engineer, of Puddletrenthide, Dorset, by his wife, Dora Alexandra Campbell. He was educated at the English College, Simla, and at King Edward's grammar school, Stratford-on-Avon, from which he entered the merchant service. On the outbreak of the European War, Warneford joined the second ('Sportsmen's') battalion, Royal Fusiliers, in August 1914. In February 1915 he was granted a commission as probationary flight sub-lieutenant in the Royal Naval Air Service, and gained his certificate at Hendon, flying a Bristol biplane, on 25 February. He was sent to No. 1 wing at Dunkirk, where his commanding officer reported on his 'remarkable keenness and ability'. On 7 June, flying a Morane monoplane, he attacked at 6,000 feet, between Ghent and Bruges, a zeppelin airship, on which he dropped six bombs from close range. The last bomb set fire to the zeppelin, but the force of the bomb's explosion turned the aeroplane upside down, the engine stopped, and Warneford was compelled to land in enemy territory. He was able to restart his engine after fifteen minutes and to return to his aerodrome. His achievement, brilliant in itself, robbed the zeppelin of much of its terror and pointed the way to the true method of defending England against airship raids. He was awarded the Victoria cross—the first officer of the naval air service to be so honoured. He did not long survive to enjoy his fame. On 17 June he went up from the aerodrome at Buc, near Paris, to test a Henri Farman machine which he was to fly to Dunkirk. The machine broke in the air, and Warneford and an

American passenger were killed. His body was brought to England for burial in Brompton cemetery.

[Official records; personal knowledge.]

H. A. J.

WARRE, EDMOND (1837–1920), head master of Eton, born in London 12 February 1837, was the second son of Henry Warre, of Bindon, Somerset, by his wife, Mary Caroline, third daughter of Nicholson Calvert, M.P., of Hunsdon House, Hertfordshire. Born a puny infant, he went a high-spirited boy to the Rev. Edward Wickham's school, Hammersmith, whence came other great head masters, and later he passed to Eton, then under the enlightened sway of Edward Craven Hawtrey [q.v.]. With his elder brother Francis, who had been there two years as the pupil of Charles John Abraham, afterwards first bishop of Wellington, New Zealand, he boarded first at Miss Vavasour's, next at Mr. Vidal's, with Edward Coleridge for tutor. Edmond in his last year was removed to Mr. Marriott's, where he had Redvers Buller [q.v.] for fag. His energy and concentration of purpose were remarkable; though a devoted 'wet-bob', he was Newcastle scholar at seventeen, and with John (Jack) Hall (neither of them in the eight) won the Pulling in the same year. A fine drawing by George Richmond shows Warre as a lad of great beauty of feature, keen-looking, with light hair, and a delicate complexion. In 1855 he went up as a scholar to Balliol College, Oxford, where he won first classes in moderations and 'greats', and in 1859 a fellowship at All Souls. Meanwhile he had won the sculls twice, the pairs three times, and had helped Balliol to be head of the river and to win the ladies' plate at Henley. In 1856 he refused to row in the Oxford eight because of his reading, but next year was No. 6 in the boat which defeated Cambridge, and with J. A. P. (Heywood-) Lonsdale won the Goblets at Henley. In 1858 he was president of the university boat club. The Oxford university rifle volunteer corps was founded in his rooms without help from government or university. As first officer he attended a musketry course at Hythe, and gradually secured 500 members and War Office aid; also with the fifth Earl Spencer [q.v.] he helped to launch the National Rifle Association in 1859.

So far Warre's future career, whether it was to be the bar or the army, was undecided. But he had already met his future wife, Florence Dora, second daughter of Colonel C. Malet, of Fontmell Parva, Dorset, and it chanced that his Eton tutor, Marriott, fell ill and asked his temporary help. He went, and found his vocation. Dr. Goodford [q.v.] offered a mastership: the income enabled him to marry at the cost of his fellowship (1861), and to his elder sister he wrote 'I feel education is my work in life and the one in which I shall show God's work to this generation'.

For Eton that was a critical time. The Public Schools Commission (1864) impended, 'new schools' were building, chapel and hall were being gothicized, mathematics introduced, and in 1871 new statutes partly suppressed the college and altered the government of the school. On his marriage Warre boldly built himself the house called 'Penn'. Next year Edward Balston, though a fellow, became head master, and Warre received some of his Manor-house boys. Warre's Oxford reputation and the pains and ability spent on his new work naturally attracted distinguished pupils. One of the first, Sir William Anson, writes 'We all thought it creditable to work, a new idea to most of us'. Warre started with good material: of twenty-one boys whom he sent to the university in 1864 three became fellows of colleges; a Tomline and Oppidan scholar came next year. In the 'nineties all three of the Indian governors and two governors-general were from his house. No less remarkable were its athletic successes. And yet with Warre duty and learning always came before athletics: he hated 'pot-hunting' and competition, avoided Henley when it became a huge picnic, and shunned fashion and crowds. In 1867 he took up the Volunteer movement at Eton. He instructed the shooting and secured for the corps the Chalvey range. But the corps often languished, and Warre rejoined to reorganize it. It now flourishes as the Officers' Training Corps.

Not less demand was made on him by the river. He became river master, with charge of watermen and bathing, and at the special request of the captain of the boats undertook the training of the eight, involving hard physical work, as well as much delicate tact to avoid infringing the liberty or authority of the boys. This, with schoolwork conscientiously prepared, was too much even for a very strong man. He sketches a day to his sister . . . 'rise at 6.30 and, but for breakfast, be on duty till 2; half an hour's rest after lunch, and then two schools; corps drill and Duffers (pacing crew) till 8; dinner and boys till 10; nap till 11 and work till 2.30.'

In March 1867 Bishop Samuel Wilberforce ordained Warre deacon and gave him priest's orders in December. That month

Balston resigned the head-mastership, and, to the disappointment of some, the college appointed Dr. J. J. Hornby [q.v.], whom for seventeen years Warre supported and strengthened with all the loyal fidelity of his masterful will. In 1869 he moved to the larger boarding house which now bears his name. From 1882 to 1904 he gave his sons the advantages of country life at Baron's Down, near Dulverton, on the slopes of Exmoor. He became a farmer and bred sheep, a gardener and laid out beds scientifically for a son's study. He rode, shot, and fished, cleared woodlands, helped harvesters, fraternized with the peasantry, and seemed to be on intimate terms with all the wild things of wood and field. The love of gardening so grew with years that he could identify classical plant-names and meet on equal terms experts such as Sir W. Thiselton Dyer or Canon Ellacombe. In 1904 Baron's Down was left for a house at Finchampstead, nearer Eton.

In 1884, on Dr. Hornby becoming provost, Warre as head master came 'like a breeze from the sea', vigorous and refreshing. At first some petty jealousy of a few collegers in VI form vexed him, but the energy of his work and plans put fresh spirit into most. He spent incredible labour on time-tables and curricula, which, like the grammars which he set his assistants to prepare, proved inelastic for the growth of the school. He sank money in a school of mechanics too advanced for the times. But it was no longer possible for any boy to avoid working. Terminal examinations and superannuation did much; also, the moral tone of the school seemed to rise; numbers grew, and the fame of Eton spread world-wide. Much building was done in Warre's reign, but some of it was mediocre, partly through faults of the architects. Colenorton house, the drill hall, lower chapel, Queen's schools, the Warre schools, the memorial of the Boer War, are of this period; and a corner of Cloisters was converted into a residence for the head master. Queen's Eyot he secured for 'wet-bobs', and for 'dry-bobs' he planted Agar's Plough, which he daily visited even during his later illness. Warre also started the Eton mission at Hackney Wick, too far off and overbuilt, but he let G. F. Bodley [q.v.] set there one of the most beautiful of London churches. He invented the school office, the pivot of all the intricate school arrangements, perhaps his most enduring practical work, as the most triumphant, was the celebration of Queen Victoria's first jubilee, when for days there was complete and enthusiastic unity of the whole school, men and boys, under his direction. By consenting to coach the eight and the rifle corps he brought masters nearer the boys. Official dress was changed for play-time, and the boys, losing some of their free initiative and perhaps of their respect, gained by friendlier intercourse.

But Warre had lived too hard for a constitution less sturdy than his magnificent frame. In 1894 there was heart-trouble. The movement for new studies distressed him and divided the staff, injuring the tutorial system, a corner-stone of Eton. He did not find that the modern subjects were better done when classics were omitted, yet he could never long withstand outside opinion and the pressure of authorities. In 1896 the doctors sent him away for a month's rest, and next year forbade him early school. In 1903 came the terrible blow of a fatal fire in one of the boarding houses. Though he had previously been urgent about fire-drills, yet he was never quite the same man afterwards. In 1905 he resigned, and resided at 'Finch' till recalled to the provostship in 1909. But the change was too trying. Grave and impressive was his entry and reception in school yard, but after a time his bodily strength failed altogether, and his resignation in July 1918 was followed by his death at Colenorton 22 January 1920. He left five sons and two daughters.

Never was character better expressed by outward appearance than in Edmond Warre. A big frame, great-limbed but just a little clumsy, and handsome features, full of dignity and kindliness, bespoke the man. He combined a very humble simplicity and a tender heart with true religion and remarkable energy. But his commanding nature made him sometimes inconsiderate of weaker vessels, and his *μεγαλοψυχία* might seem self-centred. Had he retired when his health first failed he would have been remembered as the greatest of Eton head masters. In the long period of decline men forgot the pristine Warre. His extraordinary memory was never at a loss for a classical quotation, nor his kindly humour for a classical epigram. He was a sound scholar, not a bookworm nor yet an orator or ready preacher. To prepare sermons weighed on his spirits, but of talk he took all his share. As division-master, therefore, he was weighty rather than inspiring, active rather than vocal. His scientific boat and oar designs are now only remembered: the raft of Ulysses, Caesar's bridge, the trireme and the axe are still famous models. Compared with great head masters he seems to overtop them in humanity, genuineness, and all-round efficiency. He would have been a great soldier or a great squire. The effect of his personality in making Eton so widely famed ranks him above Edward Barnard [q.v.], John Keate [q.v.], and Edward Hawtrey: he was more complete and lovable than they, and if not the greatest of head masters a very great and typical Englishman.

There is a portrait of Warre by J. S. Sargent in the school hall at Eton.

[C. R. L. Fletcher, *Edmond Warre*, 1922; Eton school lists; Eton College *Chronicle*; intimate acquaintance since 1864.]

H. E. L.

WARRE-CORNISH, FRANCIS WARRE (1839–1916), teacher, author, and bibliophile, the second son of the Rev. Hubert Kestell Cornish, vicar of Bakewell and formerly fellow of Exeter College, Oxford, by his wife, Louisa, daughter of the Rev. Francis Warre, D.C.L., rector of Cheddon Fitzpaine, was born at Bakewell 8 May 1839. He adopted the surname Warre-Cornish in 1892. He went to Eton as a colleger, was Newcastle scholar in 1857, and passed in the same year to King's College, Cambridge. After being third classic in 1861, he returned to Eton as an assistant master in the same year. He was appointed vice-provost and librarian in 1893, resigned in April 1916, and died at Englefield Green, Windsor, on 28 August in that year. He married in 1866 Blanche, daughter of the Hon. William Ritchie, legal member of the council of the governor-general of India, and had eight children. His wife, sister of Sir Richmond Thackeray Ritchie [q.v.], wrote two successful novels and was a brilliant conversationalist.

Warre-Cornish was a singularly attractive man. Small and frail, with a gentle voice and quiet manners, he was not the typical schoolmaster. He was no martinet and was not methodical. But boys who wished to learn were inspired by his fine scholarship and his literary and historical knowledge. As a house-master, he was inclined to leave his boys to govern themselves; but their attachment to him was shown by a strong esprit de corps. When he received the charge of the manifold treasures of the college library he did most valuable work in discovering and adding to them. He had a wide knowledge of books and bindings and had made a special study of Aldines. He was a good musician. As an author he was versatile. Industrious in research, he wrote clearly and with distinction, and had a power of vivid portraiture. His chief work is a useful *History of the English Church in the Nineteenth Century* (1910). He also wrote a *History of Chivalry* (1901), a *Life of Oliver Cromwell* (1882), *Jane Austen* in the 'English Men of Letters' series (1913), and a translation of Catullus (1904), besides minor books and reviews. *Sunningwell* (1899) and *Dr. Ashford and his Neighbours* (1914) are in a different vein. They are graceful fictions, with little plot, embodying a slightly ironical view of life, expressed with a peculiar charm and sympathy. These indeed were the qualities which endeared him to his friends. He was never pontifical, and in his power of epigrammatic speech he did not spare himself. He was interested in almost everything, and there were few whom he did not fascinate. To those who knew him well he remains a model of *mitis sapientia*.

[Private information; personal knowledge.] H. B.

WARRENDER, Sir GEORGE JOHN SCOTT, seventh baronet (1860–1917), admiral, was born 31 July 1860. He was the second son of Sir George Warrender, sixth baronet, of Lochend, East Lothian, by his wife, Helen, only child of Sir Hugh Hume-Campbell, seventh baronet, of Marchmont, Berwickshire. He entered the royal navy in 1873, and saw service, while still a midshipman, in the Zulu War (1879). During the whole of his career he was entirely dependent upon his mental abilities for advancement. His family connexions gave him access to rather wider and more cultured circles than are ordinarily open to naval officers, and he made full use of his opportunities. In 1879 he qualified as an interpreter in French—a rare distinction in those days—and later obtained high honours in his lieutenant's examination. Like many of the ablest officers of the mid-Victorian navy he specialized in gunnery, as it was obvious to the more thoughtful members of the service that the rapid progress of marine engineering would be accompanied by an enormous development in the gunnery arm. After this his promotion was rapid. He was made a commander in 1893, a captain in 1899, and rose finally to flag rank in 1908. During the Boxer rising (1900) he served as flag captain in the *Barfleur* and was largely responsible for organizing the operations in which the navy was engaged.

During Admiral Warrender's service as a flag officer between 1908 and 1914, the navy was again passing through a period of rapid and drastic change. The development of the torpedo arm had shaken the principles upon which battle tactics had hitherto been based, and simultaneously British naval strategy underwent a complete revolution with the disappearance of France as a maritime rival, and the rapid growth of German naval power. Warrender commanded squadrons in all the fleet manœuvres designed to test the new situation, and was partly responsible for the new rules of naval warfare which were evolved from them.

In May 1914 he was sent to Kiel, as commander of the second battle squadron, for the celebrations of the Kaiser's birthday. Nobody realized at the moment the near approach of war; but a feeling of tension was general in naval circles, and in any case the visit had a deep political significance. Of all the naval officers of his day Warrender was perhaps the most fitted to undertake the duty of making a diplomatic naval visit to a rival power. He made a deep impression upon his hosts, and the German liaison officer attached to the British flagship has left a vivid picture of his courtesy and tact [Georg von Hase, *Zwei Weissen Völker*, 1920].

In August 1914 Admiral Warrender was in command of the second battle squadron of the grand fleet, and in December became the leading figure in one of the most remarkable operations of the War. On the 14th of that month the Admiralty became aware that the Germans intended to attack the East coast, and, assuming on purely negative evidence that the high seas fleet was not going to support the movement, detached a force of battleships and cruisers to cut off the raiders. Admiral Warrender, in command of this intercepting force, was thus left to operate in the middle of the North Sea without any possibility of being supported by the grand fleet in an emergency. As a matter of fact the high seas fleet did come out, and, but for Admiral von Ingenohl's timid leadership, the British might have suffered disaster. The German raiders, operating in advance of the high seas fleet, bombarded Scarborough, Whitby, and Hartlepool during the early morning of the 16th, and then made for home. In the meanwhile Warrender, after his destroyers had twice obtained contact with the advanced screen of the high seas fleet, got across the returning track of the raiders, and sent his faster force of battle cruisers in towards Scarborough. Unfortunately, his orders to press in to a position within sixty miles of the coast were not carried out; and the Germans escaped by a narrow margin. It would be hard to find an operation more pregnant with possibilities and dramatic changes. At six o'clock in the morning, Ingenohl had Warrender's force almost at his mercy; six hours later, all danger from the German high seas fleet had disappeared, and the utter destruction of the German raiders seemed certain; one hour after that, all the opposing forces engaged were steaming away from one another on diverging courses.

At the end of 1915 Admiral Warrender was promoted to the post of commander-in-chief at Plymouth. Throughout the year 1916 he watched the steady growth of the submarine campaign in the western approaches to the Channel, and was painfully conscious that no remedy or counter to it had yet been found. He realized quite clearly that a campaign of far greater intensity was inevitable; but he did not live to see it. On 6 December he laid down his command owing to ill-health, and died in London a month later (8 January 1917). Admiral Warrender, who succeeded to the baronetcy in 1901, married in 1894 Lady Ethel Maud Ashley, fifth daughter of the eighth Earl of Shaftesbury, and left two sons and one daughter.

[Sir Julian S. Corbett, *Official History of the War. Naval Operations*, vol. ii, 1921; private information.] A. C. B.

WATERLOW, Sir ERNEST ALBERT (1850–1919), painter, born in London 24 May 1850, was the only son of Albert Crakell Waterlow, lithographer, of London, by his wife, Maria, daughter of James Corss. Sir Sydney Hedley Waterlow [q.v.], lord-mayor of London in 1872–1873, was his uncle. After education at Eltham collegiate school and Heidelberg, Ernest Waterlow began his art studies at Ouchy, near Lausanne, and subsequently (1867) continued them at the school of art in London kept by Francis Stephen Cary [q.v.]. In 1872 he entered the Royal Academy Schools, where, in the next year, he gained the Turner gold medal for landscape-painting with his picture 'A Land Storm'. A constant exhibitor at Burlington House from 1872 onwards, Waterlow was also a frequent contributor to the exhibitions of the Royal Society of Painters in Water Colours, of which he was elected associate in 1880, member in 1894, and president in 1897, holding that office until 1914. He was also a member of the 'Society of Six', an association of landscape painters, which in 1896 held its first exhibition at the Old Dudley Gallery. He was elected A.R.A. in 1890 and R.A. in 1903; his diploma piece, painted in the latter year, was called 'The Banks of the Loing'. In 1887 his picture 'Galway Gossips' was purchased by the trustees of the Chantrey fund, and now hangs in the National Gallery of British Art at Millbank (Tate Gallery). He was knighted in 1902.

The bulk of Waterlow's production, whether in oil or water-colour, consists of landscapes, with or without figures; he displays in them the characteristics of an essentially facile art, of considerable popular appeal, but without aesthetic qualities of a more profound or lasting interest.

Waterlow was twice married: first, in 1876 to Mary Margaret Sophia (died 1899), daughter of Professor Carl Hofmann, of Heidelberg; secondly, in 1909 to Eleanor Marion, widow of Dr. George Sealy, of Weybridge. By his first wife he had two sons and two daughters. He died at Hampstead 25 October 1919.

[C. H. Collins Baker in the *Art Journal*, Christmas number, 1907. Portrait, *Royal Academy Pictures*, 1916.] T. B.

WATSON, Sir CHARLES MOORE (1844–1916), soldier and administrator, the second son of William Watson, J.P., of Dublin, by his wife, Sarah, daughter of the Rev. Moore Morgan, rector of Dunlavin, co. Wicklow, was born in Dublin 10 July 1844. He was educated at Trinity College, Dublin, and at the Royal Military Academy, Woolwich, whence he passed, as a lieutenant, into the Royal Engineers in 1866. In 1874–1875 he served in the Sudan under General Gordon, and was engaged on the survey of the White Nile. He subsequently filled an appointment at the War Office until 1878, when he was made a captain and aide-de-camp to Sir John Lintorn Arabin Simmons [q.v.]. In 1880 he commenced two years' duty in the India Office, receiving in 1882 the brevet rank of major. In the latter year Watson was selected for special duty in the Egyptian campaign. It was he who, at the head of a small force, led the advance on Cairo after the battle of Tel-el-Kebir, and received the surrender of the citadel (14 September 1882). He continued to serve in the Egyptian army until 1886, when he became governor-general of the Red Sea littoral. In 1891 he was appointed assistant inspector-general of fortifications; he was promoted lieutenant-colonel in the following year, and in 1896 became deputy inspector-general of fortifications, a position which he held, with the rank of colonel, till his retirement in 1902. He carried out the arduous duties of these posts with the care, foresight, and technical skill which had already earned him a high reputation. His long experience and outstanding success undoubtedly influenced his selection in 1904 as secretary to the royal commission for the organization of the British section of the St. Louis Exhibition and commissioner-general. Two years prior to this appointment he was chosen to be the British delegate to the International Navigation Congress at Düsseldorf, and in the same capacity visited Milan in 1905 and St. Petersburg in 1908. He was chairman of the Palestine Exploration Fund committee from 1905 until his death, which took place in London 15 March 1916. He married in 1880 Geneviève, daughter of the Rev. Russell Cook. In his later years Colonel Watson turned to account a decided literary gift, publishing in 1909 a *Life of Major-General Sir Charles William Wilson*, and in 1910 a very useful work on *British Weights and Measures*. In 1912 he published *The Story of Jerusalem*, and three years later *Fifty Years' Work in the Holy Land*. He received the C.M.G. in 1887, and the C.B. in 1902, and in 1905 was created K.C.M.G.

[*The Times*, 16 March 1916; *Journal* of the Royal Engineers, June 1916.] C. V. O.

WATTS-DUNTON, WALTER THEODORE (1832–1914), critic, novelist, and poet, was born 12 October 1832, the eldest child of John King Watts, solicitor, of St. Ives, Huntingdonshire, well known for his scientific attainments. He added to his surname that of his mother, Susannah Dunton, in 1896. At school in Cambridge he devoted himself to literature, science, and life in the open air. His meeting with George Borrow in 1872 emphasized his early delight in gipsy lore, of which another friend, Francis Hindes Groome [q.v.], was a master. Becoming a solicitor, he practised for a while in London, where his gifts as a friend, talker, and man of business, facilitated his intercourse with the 'pre-Raphaelite group' of poets. 'Watts the worldling,' as J. M. Whistler called him, was a familiar figure in London literary gatherings, such as those of John Westland Marston [q.v.]. He gave up his profession on taking to literary criticism, writing first for the *Examiner* under William Minto [q.v.] in 1874, and two years later for the *Athenæum*, where for the rest of the century he enjoyed a great anonymous reputation. He proved a steady friend to D. G. Rossetti in his declining years, and when, in 1879, A. C. Swinburne's reckless life was making his health hopeless, he took him to 'The Pines', his house in Putney. Henceforth, Swinburne, a child in many ways, was the centre of his world. He managed Swinburne's affairs, and stamped the macabre element out of his life and writing. The two lived together till Swinburne's death (1909), and the devoted and tactful control of Watts-Dunton prolonged Swinburne's life, though it involved a certain loss of his independence in material life and critical judgement. Watts-Dunton married in 1905 Clara, youngest daughter of Gustave A. Reich, of East India Avenue, E.C., but this did not change the quiet, ordered life at The Pines, where he died 6 June 1914. He had no children.

In the *Athenæum* Watts-Dunton printed from time to time scenes in verse, in which Rhona Boswell, a gipsy girl, was prominent, and the publication of these, with additions, as *The Coming of Love, and Other Poems* made a stir in 1897. On the whole the large and adventurous design of the verses did not 'command an art equal to its purpose'. He made a great success in 1898 with *Aylwin*, a novel kept back for many years, and originally called *The Renascence of Wonder*. This phrase was later announced as the very pith of his critical doctrines, a protest against materialism and pessimism. *Aylwin*, dealing partly with the same characters as *The Coming of Love*, revealed a gift for romance and scenery, some admirable gipsies, especially the girl, Sinfi Lovell, and some clever sketches after famous prototypes, such as Rossetti. It also heralded that tide of mysticism which has since become a feature of the twentieth century. Although striking in plot and detail, the book has flat passages which show that the author, a good judge of style, was not a great stylist. The same criticism applies to Watts-Dunton's *Athenæum* articles, which he himself described as 'too formless to have other than an ephemeral life'. Not lacking in good things and in generalizations of value, they are clogged with wise saws and ancient instances. They are clear-sighted, and were very widely admired; but their profundity has been exaggerated. Watts-Dunton was one of the first to applaud the verse of George Meredith, and many young authors owed much to his judicious encouragement. His best critical work is his essay on *Poetry* in the *Encyclopaedia Britannica* (9th edition, 1885). His tributes to literary friends, reprinted as *Old Familiar Faces* (1916), are notable though discursive. His agreeable reminiscences of George Borrow may be read in his editions of *Lavengro* (1893) and *The Romany Rye* (1900). Here he dwells on Borrow's refusal to 'figure in the literary arena'. He always protested against the jealousies and personalities of modern literary life. He lived for his friends, read endlessly, put off, polished, and altered his own compositions. The variety of his interests dissipated his energies. He had great kindliness, a good sense of fun, but little humour, and throughout his long life remained a boy in his eagerness for the latest discovery in letters or science.

Aylwin is Watts-Dunton's best imaginative work. His posthumous novel, *Vesprie Towers* (1916), and his collections of verses, other than *The Coming of Love*, are not likely to last. Of his sonnets, 'The Octopus of the Golden Islands' is a typical example, too close-packed with thought to read naturally. His verse in general lacks the flow and final mastery essential to great poetry. The phrasing and occasionally the rhymes have a factitious appearance. But he was a real romantic in spite of his scientific leanings, and his thoughts went beyond his achievement.

[Thomas St. E. Hake and A. Compton-Rickett, *Life and Letters of T. Watts-Dunton*, 1916; James Douglas, *Theodore Watts-Dunton, Poet, Critic, Novelist*, 1904; Clara Watts-Dunton, *The Home Life of Swinburne*, 1922; personal knowledge.] V. H. R.

WAVELL, ARTHUR JOHN BYNG (1882–1916), soldier and explorer—one of few who have made the Mecca pilgrimage successfully in an assumed character—was born in London 27 May 1882. His father, Colonel Arthur Henry Wavell, was the son of an adventurous soldier and fellow of the Royal Society, and his mother, Matilda Clara Beatrice, daughter of the Rev. John Byng, was a collateral descendant of the unfortunate admiral of that name. Before going to Sandhurst he spent three years at Winchester; the school's peculiar football game was to suggest to him ten years later a comparison between a 'loose hot' and the struggling mob of pilgrims before the black stone of the Kaaba. Commissioned in the Welsh Regiment in 1900, he saw service in the South African War before he was nineteen, and after the peace went on to Swaziland, Bechuanaland, and other ill-known northern districts to do military intelligence work. He left the army in 1906, and took a farm at Nyali, near Mombasa, where he learned Arabic, and interested himself in the religion of Islam. From this study grew a desire to explore Arabia, to which end he believed, like Sir

Richard Burton, that the accomplishment of the Meccan pilgrimage would conduce. In 1908 he proceeded to realize his idea by starting from England as a Zanzibari, with a Turkish passport, in the company of a Moslem Swahili friend, to whom he added at Marseilles an Aleppine Arab, long resident in Berlin. The trio reached Damascus and ultimately Medina without serious difficulty. What risk of detection they ran there; how they journeyed by caravan to Yambo and by ship to Jiddah; their experiences in Mecca and at Arafat, and their ultimate return to Jiddah—these things were written down by Wavell in *A Modern Pilgrim in Mecca*, published in 1912. Though he had awkward moments, and appears to have been suspected in both Medina and Mecca, he was not unmasked; and his feat, which he regarded merely as a means to greater ends, was not represented by him as in any sense a desperate undertaking. The present writer saw him both before and after his pilgrimage.

In 1910 Wavell tried to turn this success to account by pushing up to Sanaa in Yemen, in hope of finding a way thence into south central Arabia. Going without disguise as a British *hadji*, he found native Zeidite fanatics and Turkish authorities alike suspicious; and though he braved both and outwitted the latter more than once, he was rounded up in the end and sent back to Hodeida. The chief interest of his experience arises from the fact that he was in Sanaa during its siege by the Zeidite *imam*, Yahya, whom he would have joined, had he not given his word to the British vice-consul before he left the coast. Though, strictly speaking, he had a right, under the Capitulations, to travel where he would in the Ottoman dominions, the British Foreign Office accepted the not unreasonable plea of the Turkish authorities that, with Yemen in revolt from end to end, they were bound, in Wavell's interest as much as their own, to arrest his progress; and he got no satisfaction. His own account both of this journey and of his dispute with the Foreign Office appeared in the latter part of his *Modern Pilgrim in Mecca*.

Neither of Wavell's Arabian adventures did much to increase science. Both were undertaken merely as preliminaries to serious exploration, and under circumstances prohibitive of scientific work. Unfortunately, a subsequent plan of his to penetrate Arabia under the aegis of another rebel, the Idrisi of Asir, came to nothing; and he had no further opportunity to show that he was equipped with the diligent curiosity and acquired competence of a scientific explorer, as well as the ambition, address, and daring of an adventurer. In any case he had the gift of narrating adventures vividly and with humour.

Wavell returned to his farm, and was still there at the outbreak of the War, for which he had prepared as long ago as 1909 by joining the special reserve of his old regiment. Detained in East Africa, as being necessary for its defence, he raised, from water-carriers and other Arabic-speaking natives, a force widely known as 'Wavell's Own'; and as early as 25 September 1914, at the cost of severe wounds, he held the road to Mombasa against a superior force of the enemy. Promoted major and put in charge of Mwele, on the Uganda Railway, he received the military cross and proved conspicuously successful in handling natives, till, on 8 January 1916, he marched out against a German column reported in his neighbourhood, and fell into an ambush. In spite of desperate hurt in the legs from the explosion of a bomb-box, he kept on firing till shot through the chest, and the Germans, who buried him on the field, set up a cross to mark the grave of a very gallant foe. A statue stands to his honour in Mombasa as the saviour of the town. He was unmarried.

[Biographical note by Major Leonard Darwin in reissue (1918) of the first part of *A Modern Pilgrim in Mecca*; private information; personal knowledge.] D. G. H.

WEBB, PHILIP (SPEAKMAN) (1831–1915), architect, was born in Beaumont Street, Oxford, 12 January 1831, the second of the eleven children of Charles Webb, by his wife, M. E. Speakman. His grandfather was the well-known medallist, Thomas Webb, of Birmingham. His father, who died in 1848, was a medical man of standing in Oxford, with many accomplishments, including a taste for drawing and an aptitude for natural history. Philip Webb was brought up in the house in St. Giles's which formerly belonged to the dukes of Marlborough and is now used as the judges' lodgings. He was educated at Aynho grammar school. He early developed that intimate knowledge of wild life shown in all his designs. He was articled to John Billing, architect, of Reading, and after serving his time entered the office of George Edmund Street [q.v.] in Beaumont Street, Oxford. Here he met William Morris [q.v.], and their subsequent friendship brought him into the brilliant group whose story is so well known.

In the firm, known as Morris, Marshall, Faulkner, & Co., founded by Morris in London in 1861, which effected a revolution in contemporary decorative art, Webb was for long the most active member. He had left Street's office about 1856, and while building up his own professional practice, first at 7 Great Ormond Street and afterwards at 1 Raymond Buildings, Gray's Inn, he produced designs of the most varied description for Morris's firm in its Red Lion Square and Queen Square days. These include church and house decoration, designs for symbols, animals, birds, traceries for stained glass, embroideries (e.g. the altar-frontal at Llandaff Cathedral), tiles, grates, candlesticks, metal-fittings, table-glass, and jewelry. The furniture design was entirely his own, always remarkable for its distinction and practical quality. As time went on, and his practice expanded, his decorative design grew in scope and was no longer restricted to the needs of the Morris firm. Much of his early work can be seen in the churches built by George Frederick Bodley [q.v.] in Scarborough and Brighton. Some of the actual painting of the roofs is by his hand. The interior of the dining-room (1867) at the Victoria and Albert Museum is perhaps the most important of Webb's decorative schemes which have been left intact. The wall-decoration is full of variety and interest, the frieze of animals in relief with touches of bright colour, and the main walls with olive boughs in flower and fruit (also in relief) being specially noticeable. Webb's working-drawings are exquisite in colour and finish, and the pen-and-ink studies of beasts and birds show the vigour and delicacy of a great master's hand. Among his later small designs are to be noted the animals for some of the Morris tapestry. One of his last pieces of design is the mace for the university of Birmingham.

Webb's career as an architect extends from about 1856 to 1900. He built some fifty or sixty fine houses and one church (Brampton, Cumberland, 1875), refusing to undertake any work which he could not personally superintend. He was especially successful in his additions to old houses, such as Berkeley Castle and Pusey House, Berkshire, satisfying modern needs without either jarring on the harmonies of the old work or trying to reproduce its features. The addition to Forthampton Court (1891), now much altered, was a fine example of his genius. Three houses in London are notable as different types of his work: 1 Palace Green (built for the Hon. George Howard, afterwards ninth Earl of Carlisle, 1868), West House, Glebe Place, Chelsea (for G. P. Boyce, 1873), and 19 Lincoln's Inn Fields (*c.* 1870). The last-named is a 'street-house', standing unobtrusively when it was built, for all its originality, in the block of old buildings of which it formed part. Among his country houses may be mentioned Joldwynds, near Dorking (for Sir William Bowman, 1873), Rounton Grange, Yorkshire (for Sir Isaac Lowthian Bell, 1875), Clouds, Wiltshire (for the Hon. Percy Wyndham, 1881–1886), and Standen, East Grinstead (for Mr. James Beale, 1892). At Arisaig, in the Highlands, is a fine example (1863) of his use of local material. Webb's first house, Red House, Upton, Kent, built for William Morris in 1859, marks the birth of modern domestic architecture. His constant aim was to carry on and develop English architectural tradition without copying any particular style, and as a consequence he founded no school, but his influence on modern architecture is a deep and growing one.

In 1877 Webb, with William Morris, founded the Society for the Protection of Ancient Buildings, which has so powerfully influenced public opinion on the subject of 'restoration'. To this society he gave inestimable help, not the least of which was his invention of a method of strengthening the interiors of decaying walls by clearing out the loose core and filling the cavity with strong new material. This method was first used in repairing the tower of East Knoyle church, Wiltshire (1893), and has since been developed by the society's builders with the best results.

Webb avowed himself a socialist at the same time as Morris, and though he was never prominent in the public eye, his influence on the internal policy of the movement was an important factor in the building up of the party to which both men belonged.

In early life Webb was an accomplished horseman, a good shot, and interested in many field sports. But all such pursuits as dealt with the destruction of life were early given up, as his study of birds and beasts and his love for them developed. Though a town-dweller he never lost his sympathy with country life, and came back to it simply and easily in his latter days. He had a keen wit; at the same time he enjoyed greatly the humours of the country people with whom he came into relations in the course of his work. A certain dryness of manner in ordinary intercourse veiled a kindliness easily divined by those who knew him. To the group of young men around him he was an encouraging and stimulating influence; reserved by nature, he was always ready to discuss their ideas and theories and to share with them the results of his own experience.

Webb never married. He retired from practice in 1900 and lived in a cottage at Worth, Sussex, on the estate of his friend, Wilfrid Scawen Blunt. Here he died 17 April 1915, and his body was cremated at Golder's Green, his ashes being scattered by his direction.

The following are some of the notable houses built by Webb in addition to those already mentioned:—

1861—houses and shops, Worship Street, Finsbury. 1864—house in Melbury Road, Kensington, for Val Prinsep, R.A. 1868—Oakleigh Park, Barnet, for Major Gillum. 1873—house at Freshwater, Isle of Wight, for G. F. Watts, R.A. 1875—church, vicarage, and house for estate agent, at Brampton, Cumberland. 1880—house at Welwyn, Hertfordshire, for his brother, Dr. H. S. Webb. 1886—Coneyhurst, Ewhurst, Surrey, for Miss Ewart. 1887—25 Young Street, Kensington, for Sir Frederick Bowman. 1896—chapel at the Rochester Deaconess Institution, Clapham Common. 1902—cottages at Kelmscott, Oxfordshire, for Mrs. William Morris.

[Webb's papers; private information; personal knowledge. See also W. Hale White, *Letters to Three Friends*, 1924.]

M.M.

WEBSTER, RICHARD EVERARD, VISCOUNT ALVERSTONE (1842–1915), judge, the second son of Thomas Webster, Q.C. [q.v.], by his wife, Elizabeth, eldest daughter of Richard Calthrop, of Swineshead Abbey, Lincolnshire, was born 22 December 1842 in Chester Place, London. He was educated at King's College School, the Charterhouse, and Trinity College, Cambridge. He took his degree as 36th wrangler in 1865, having earlier in that year won the mile and two-mile races against Oxford. He was called to the bar at Lincoln's Inn 29 April 1868, taking chambers at 2 Pump Court, where he remained throughout his career. He soon developed a large practice as a junior, and in 1878, less than ten years from his call, he became a Q.C. When Lord Salisbury formed his government in 1885, he appointed Webster attorney-general, who then entered the House of Commons as member for Launceston. At the next election he was chosen for the Isle of Wight, and he sat for that constituency until he became a judge.

Webster was attorney-general three times, from June 1885 to February 1886, from August 1886 to August 1892, and from July 1895 to May 1900, over twelve years in all. For more than half that period (before 1895) the system allowed him to continue his great private practice, and it was in this way that in 1888 and 1889 he acted as leading counsel for *The Times* at the Parnell commission. It is unlikely that in thirty-two years at the bar any man ever had more work to do, or earned more money. In 1893 he appeared for Great Britain in the Behring Sea arbitration, and was made a G.C.M.G. In 1899 he was leading counsel in the Venezuela arbitration and was created a baronet.

On 10 May 1900 Webster was appointed master of the Rolls in succession to Sir Nathaniel (afterwards Baron) Lindley [q.v.], and made a privy councillor. A month later he was created Baron Alverstone, of Alverstone in the Isle of Wight. On 22 October 1900 he became lord chief justice of England, upon the death of Lord Russell of Killowen. In 1903 he was arbitrator, with two Canadian and three American colleagues, on the Alaska Boundary question. The decision, which was that of Lord Alverstone and the three Americans, may have been right, but it made him, and for a time Great Britain, very unpopular in Canada. In October 1913 he resigned his office on account of ill-health, and was made a viscount. In 1914 he published *Recollections of Bar and Bench*, a book which is badly written and not interesting. He died at the house which he had built at Cranleigh in Surrey 15 December 1915, and was buried in West Norwood cemetery. He had married in 1872 Mary Louisa, only daughter of William Calthrop, M.D., of Withern, Lincolnshire; she died in 1877, leaving one son and one daughter, but the son died before his father.

Perhaps the truest, and most modest, remark in Alverstone's *Recollections* is that throughout his life he had been favoured by good fortune. He was not a very clever man, nor a learned lawyer, nor a good speaker—either in the courts or in parliament. His equipment as an advocate consisted mainly in a splendid physique, a forcible personality, and immense industry. As a judge he was dignified, and sitting with a jury was satisfactory, though not distinguished; but the reports will be searched in vain for judgments of his that are valuable as expositions of the law. Socially he displayed a somewhat boisterous geniality which his detractors sometimes regarded as artificial. He was generous with his money, delighted in playing billiards and singing drawing-room songs, and was an assiduous church-goer: during forty years he sang in the choir at Kensington parish church.

[*The Times*, 16 December 1915; *Law Journal*, 18 December 1915; Memoranda in the *Law Reports*; Law Lists; *Recollections of Bar and Bench*, 1914.] F. D. M.

WELBY, REGINALD EARLE, first Baron Welby, of Allington (1832–1915), the fifth son of the Rev. John Earle Welby, rector of Harston, Leicestershire, by his wife, Felicia, daughter of the Rev. George Hole, was born at Harston 3 August 1832. His father was a younger son of Sir W. Earle Welby, first baronet, of Denton Manor, Lincolnshire. Though of tory stock young Welby proved to be a child of the Reform Bill and followed his hero Gladstone towards liberalism. From Eton and Trinity College, Cambridge, where he took his B.A. degree in 1855, he passed into the civil service, entering the Treasury in 1856, where he learned the ropes under that great civil servant, Sir Charles E. Trevelyan [q.v.], and became an enthusiastic disciple of Gladstonian and Cobdenite finance—above all a free trader and an exponent of rigid economy in all branches of the public service. As a junior at the Treasury he was instrumental in introducing treasury bills, the ingenious invention of Walter Bagehot [q.v.], into the British financial system. In 1880 he became assistant financial secretary of the Treasury, and ruled the office as permanent secretary from 1885 to 1894.

In the ordinary sense of the word Welby was not a good man of business. He loved a litter; his table was a byword. He was dilatory, inclined to potter over details, slow in coming to the point, and apt to delay a decision. But his industry was immense, and his proficiency in all the mysteries and minutiae of public finance unrivalled. His gift for estimates and for gauging the probable yield of taxes, new or old, was almost uncanny. He believed in a strong Treasury as a necessary check upon the growth of public expenditure and bureaucracy. He admired Queen Victoria for refusing to see civil servants. Her servants were the responsible ministers. It was to them, not to *their* servants, that she gave audience. On his retirement from the Treasury in 1894 he was created Baron Welby, and contributed occasionally to financial discussions in the House of Lords. Once, when he had pleaded for economy, Lord Salisbury retorted, 'Who are we that we should try to swim against the tide?' Henceforward he devoted himself to public work, mainly in connexion with the London County Council, first as alderman, then as vice-chairman, and finally in 1900 as chairman. He became almost as ardent over rates as he had been over taxes, and London is deeply indebted to him for the zeal, energy, and skill which he freely devoted to the furtherance of sound finance and economical administration.

On the death of his friend, Lord Farrer, in 1899, Welby became chairman of the Cobden Club, and assisted in some important publications directed against armaments and protection. Towards the end of his life he devoted many months to a comprehensive survey of public finance from 1815 to 1914, which was presented in the form of a presidential address to the Royal Statistical Society. His last publication was a letter to the *Economist*, 17 July 1915, exhibiting the effects of the European War on the protective tariffs of the belligerent powers. He died in London 30 October of the same year.

A few days after Lord Welby's death Lord Bryce drew attention to the remarkable group of civil servants—Ralph Lingen, Louis Mallet, Thomas Farrer, Henry Thring, Spencer Walpole, and Henry Jenkyns—to which Welby belonged. He survived them all. His life was probably shortened by the calamity of the War. From its outbreak in August 1914 until late in the following summer, when his health failed, he was an anxious and critical student of war finance. As the months wore on and the debt piled up he became oppressed by fear that all his hopes for social progress and the gradual elimination of poverty were doomed to be shattered.

Lord Welby was a clubbable man, and a bachelor of bachelors. He enjoyed London society for two generations, and few men knew it better. His dinners were perfect. To hear a conversation between him and his cook was an education in culinary science. His standard of civility was high and sometimes was enforced with severity. Though quite free from vanity, conceit, or pomposity, he was quick to resent any breach of manners or intrusiveness. His memory was well stored with odd stories about the old-world officialdom which had passed away with the reform of the civil service. Much wisdom and humour perished with him.

[Private information; personal knowledge.] F. W. H.

WEMYSS-CHARTERIS-DOUGLAS FRANCIS, tenth EARL OF WEMYSS AND MARCH (1818–1914), politician, the eldest son of Francis Wemyss-Charteris-Douglas, ninth Earl, by his wife, Lady Louisa Bingham, third daughter of Richard, second Earl of Lucan, was born in Edinburgh 4 August 1818. He was educated at Edinburgh Academy, Eton, and Christ Church, Oxford, where John Ruskin was his contemporary. He graduated B.A. in 1841. In the same year he was returned to parliament in the conservative interest as member for East Gloucestershire, which he represented until January 1846, when he resigned his seat. In 1847 he re-entered the House of Commons, having been elected member for Haddingtonshire, for which constituency he continued to sit until he was called to the House of Lords on the death of his father in 1883. On the formation of the Earl of Aberdeen's ministry at the close of 1852 he was made a lord of the Treasury. He retired with the Peelites in 1855, when Lord Palmerston became prime minister, and did not subsequently hold office. From that time he acted independently, styling himself a liberal-conservative. In 1859 he supported the Earl of Derby's Reform Bill; later he opposed the reform proposals of Lord John Russell. On the introduction of the Franchise Bill of 1866 he joined Edward Horsman [q.v.], Robert Lowe (afterwards first Viscount Sherbrooke, q.v.) and others in forming the 'cave of Adullam', and it was at his house that meetings of the 'cave' took place. Lord Elcho, as he was styled after the death of his grandfather in 1853, took an active part in the proceedings of the House. He introduced a Medical Practitioners Bill in 1854, and it was in great measure due to his exertions that the Act of 1858 creating the General Medical Council became law. On his proposal a committee was appointed to consider the law relating to master and servant, with the result that he carried through parliament an Act making a breach of contract on the part of a servant a civil, and no longer a criminal, offence (1867). He sat on the royal commission on Trades Unions in 1867. Elevation to the House of Lords did not diminish his interest in public affairs. The expression 'cross-bench mind' applied to him by Earl Granville (14 February 1884) was happily chosen, and his persistent opposition to the steady growth of state interference brought him into conflict with each administration in its turn. He was founder and, until the date of his death, chairman of the Liberty and Property Defence League, constituted in 1882 for the purpose of advocating individualism as opposed to socialism.

Lord Wemyss was extremely proficient in field sports, and was distinguished both as a painter in water-colours and as a sculptor. In 1856 he was largely instrumental in preventing the removal of the National Gallery to Kensington Gore. Throughout his career his wise counsel in matters of art and architecture was tendered to successive administrations, and by his watchfulness over the public buildings of London he rendered valuable service.

It is, however, on matters of military reform and national service that Lord Wemyss's claim to remembrance will mainly rest. His experience as a member of the Aberdeen ministry had brought home to him the deficiencies of the army. When in May 1859 the government authorized the formation of a corps of rifle volunteers, he threw himself enthusiastically into the movement and was one of those who helped to create the London Scottish regiment (originally the 15th Middlesex corps). As lieutenant-colonel of this regiment he was present at the first review in Hyde Park on 23 June 1860, when 19,000 volunteers paraded before Queen Victoria. He relinquished command of the regiment in 1879, and was made an aide-de-camp to the Queen in 1881. He was also ensign general of the Royal Society of Archers. He was a member of the royal commission of 1862 which resulted in the Volunteer Act of 1863. He presided over the meeting which inaugurated the National Rifle Association in 1859, was first chairman of the association (1859–1867), and held this office again in 1869–1870. He presented the association with the Elcho challenge shield to be competed for yearly by teams representative of England and Scotland (Ireland and Wales subsequently included), and was a regular attendant at the Wimbledon meetings of the association.

Lord Wemyss was a persistent advocate of the militia ballot. He was frankly critical of Mr. (afterwards Viscount) Cardwell's military reforms, and in 1871 printed a series of *Letters on Military Organization*. In 1907, when he had reached his ninetieth year, he vigorously protested in the House of Lords against the reforms of Mr. (afterwards Viscount) Haldane, and six years later in a letter to *The Times* (3 June 1913) he referred to the military system of the country as having been 'fatuously destroyed several years ago'.

Lord Wemyss died in London 30 June 1914. He was twice married: first, in

1843 to Lady Anne Frederica Anson (died 1896), second daughter of Thomas William, first Earl of Lichfield; and secondly, in 1900 to Grace, daughter of Major James Blackburn, 85th regiment, and niece of Colin, Baron Blackburn [q.v.]. By his first wife he had six sons and three daughters, and he was succeeded as eleventh earl by his fourth and eldest surviving son, Hugo Richard (born 1857).

A charcoal-drawing of Lord Wemyss is in the possession of the Hon. Evan Charteris, K.C.

[*The Times*, 1 July 1914; A. P. Humphry and T. F. Fremantle, *History of the National Rifle Association, 1859–1909*, 1914.]

R. J. B.

WERNHER, Sir JULIUS CHARLES, first baronet (1850–1912), financier and philanthropist, was born at Darmstadt in the grand duchy of Hesse 9 April 1850 of an old and reputable Protestant family. His grandfather, Wilhelm Wernher, had been privy councillor and president of the court of appeal in his native state; his father, Friedrich August, was an eminent railway engineer, a friend of Robert Stephenson and of Isambard Kingdom Brunel. His mother was Elise Weidenbusch. Julius was the second child and eldest son of a family of four. His father's duties took him to Mainz and, when the boy was in his ninth year, to Frankfort. There Julius was educated and, although he hankered after his father's profession, decided upon a business career. After a commercial education, and some experience in a banking house at Frankfort, an aptitude for languages secured him an appointment in Paris. On the outbreak of the Franco-Prussian War in 1870 he served as a cadet in the 4th cavalry division and in the army of occupation, without being in the least touched, as appears from his letters, by the wave of military and imperial sentiment then sweeping over Germany. His term of service over, he went to London, and then came a notable stroke of fortune. His employer in Paris had given him a warm letter of recommendation to Jules Porges, a diamond merchant of Paris and London, who, on news coming to Europe of remarkable finds in South Africa, offered young Wernher a two years' engagement as assistant to his partner, Charles Mège, then setting out to buy diamonds in the fields.

Mège and Wernher arrived at Port Elizabeth on 4 January 1871, and took over a week to get to the Vaal river, 'packed like herrings, galloping with six horses over utterly impossible roads' through country almost stripped of its inhabitants by the great diamond rush. They found the river diggings almost deserted for the 'dry diggings' at Du Toit's Pan, twenty-six miles from the river, and there the new comers set up their canvas house, opening an office a little later in the neighbouring camp of New Rush, afterwards to become Kimberley. Wernher made himself master of the infinitely difficult and delicate business of diamond buying, and by the spring of 1872 was able to write home, 'I am already indispensable to my Frenchman,' and again, 'I am proud to say that my voice has its full weight.'

It was a rough life. 'A great wide plain,' Wernher wrote, 'bounded in the far distance by hills of baroque . . . without any grass and hardly any trees; . . . now and again a little green, and the yellow sand broken by muddy water . . . That is everything that can be said of the place where we live.' Wernher, a giant in physical strength, living a wise and temperate life, outlasted most of his competitors. Mège returned to Paris in the autumn of 1873, and from that time Wernher was partner in the firm and its sole representative at the fields. Porges came to trust him absolutely. 'I am not', Wernher wrote modestly, 'one of those people who create new fortunes by genius or new combinations, and lose them again and win them again. I only walk well-known paths, but I walk steadily and only act out of conviction, without, indeed, paying too much attention to my own point of view.' Such a character was well suited to win its way through the long series of crises caused by over-production, indiscriminate selling, prolonged droughts, wars, and falls of reef, which form the chequered history of the diamond mines of Kimberley. By 1876 Wernher had persuaded Porges to visit the fields and purchase claims in the Kimberley mine, and Wernher was soon the head of one of the most important diamond producing companies in the fields. 'I have put a little order', he wrote in 1878, 'into the mining board (of which he was a director), and I am teaching them', he added significantly, 'to provide for the time when the mines are worked in common.' In the busy mining camp he was already trusted and acknowledged as a leader, as much for his integrity of character as for his intellectual power. The Kimberley mine, originally divided into surface claims thirty feet square, had gone down into great depths; claims, sometimes subdivided, had crumbled one upon another; surrounding reef had fallen in upon the whole; the mining board, with little capital or influence, was unequal to the task of control, which ever grew more complicated, and Wernher was one of the first to see that consolidation was the only solution. His company (usually called the French Company) gradually and constantly enlarged its holdings and bought up strategical points, but was unable to come to terms with the powerful Central Company, of which Barnett Isaacs, known as Barney Barnato [q.v.], was the presiding genius; and it carried on with this and other companies a wasteful war in production and underground workings.

As the work of the mine became more absorbing Wernher was forced to neglect the diamond buying business, hitherto the mainstay of the firm, and arranged with several younger men to operate on joint account, the firm supplying the capital for shipment. Thus began his partnership with Alfred Beit [q.v.]. 'I am living', he wrote in 1879, 'with Rube and Van Beek and Beit. With the last, the nicest of all, I lived for a long time in Old De Beers. He is a cheery, optimistic fellow of extraordinary goodness of heart and of very great business ability.' Now Beit had invested on his own account in the De Beers mine and was thereby brought into intimate contact with Cecil John Rhodes [q.v.]. Rhodes and his friends in De Beers were thus able to come to a firm understanding with Wernher and the French group in the Kimberley mine in the task of bringing Barnato to terms and of consolidating the whole industry. It was by the aid of Wernher that Rhodes, in a flying visit to Europe (1887), bought the French Company and so faced Barnato as an equal in his own mine. In the meantime Wernher and Beit had been quietly buying large holdings in Du Toit's Pan and elsewhere in complete understanding with Rhodes, and the result of all these combinations was that the rival holders were ultimately forced to agree to the amalgamation of the chief diamond mines of Kimberley as the De Beers Consolidated Mines (1888).

Meanwhile, in order to stop the wasteful competition and reckless selling of diamonds, Wernher set about the creation of a diamond syndicate in London. From 1880 to 1882 he directed the London office of his firm, Porges residing in Paris. He then returned to the fields, but in 1884 he was back in London and from that time controlled from Europe an immensely important business. In 1886 the London Diamond Syndicate was established, with the result that the price of diamonds became stable. In January 1890, when Porges retired, the firm of Wernher, Beit, & Co. came into being. The partnership merely confirmed the combination which had produced such important results. The junior partner was a financial genius of the first rank, and although it was a favourite joke with the senior that he was known only as the Christian name of Beit, yet Wernher supplied strength and solidity of character and wise judgement as well as a foresight which came of profound knowledge and long experience. Wernher thus stands out as one of the pioneers of Kimberley who cherished the design, and carried through the great task, of consolidation.

The discovery of the Witwatersrand gold deposits in 1887 brought the firm into the field as gold miners. Alfred Beit bought large and valuable properties on the advice of such expert prospectors as James Benjamin Taylor and (Sir) Joseph Benjamin Robinson. Wernher, however, did not visit the gold fields until many years later, but by a remarkable combination of judgement and imagination mastered from London the problems of the Rand and organized the industry on a stable and scientific basis. He showed himself, indeed, an expert in the science of mining. He put his faith in the deep levels, employed the best engineering skill to be found in the world, and developed the properties of his firm to such good purpose that in 1912, the year of his death, the gold mines under the control of his group produced 3,500,000 ounces of fine gold and paid in dividends no less than £4,250,000, that is, 51 per cent of the profits of the whole of the Witwatersrand. In 1911 he was awarded the gold medal of the Institution of Mining and Metallurgy.

Although Wernher came to live in London owing to the necessities of business, he made his choice of British nationality with deliberation. 'Undoubtedly', he wrote in December 1879, 'I shall live in London. The trend of things in Germany now and the manner in which liberal development is fettered in every conceivable way is intolerable to anybody who knows English life.' His family earnestly, even angrily, protested, and, in deference to their feelings, he did not become a naturalized British subject until 1898. But he made his home where he had not only made his fortune but his friends and his life. In 1888 he married Alice Sedgwick, daughter of James Mankievicz, of London. He bought an estate in Bedfordshire, Luton Hoo, and at his London residence, Bath House, indulged a lifelong taste in art and formed a fine collection of pictures, principally of the Renaissance period. One of the best pictures in his collection, Watteau's 'La Gage d'Amour', he left by his will to the National Gallery. He was a man of deep culture and he read widely, even during his Kimberley days.

With strength of character was joined a tenderness which runs through all his letters, and possibly had its source in his deep affection for his mother. 'I am your declared lover', he told her in one of the first letters of a never-failing correspondence. When he became rich his philanthropy took the form of great and well-considered benefactions. To King Edward's hospital fund he made enormous gifts, and by his will it benefited to the extent of some £400,000, including a twelfth part of his residuary estate; he left a further £100,000 to be distributed among charities. He was deeply concerned at the backwardness of his adopted country in practical science, and he was a member of Lord Haldane's departmental committee (1904–1907) which recommended the establishment by royal charter of the Imperial College of Science and Technology in London; this institution Wernher endowed with £250,000, and by his will with a further sum of £150,000. Like Rhodes and Beit he was deeply interested in education, and he gave £250,000 towards the scheme for a university at Groote Schuur, the home of Cecil Rhodes. He took the reform side in the Transvaal, and when the South African War broke out his firm equipped the regiment of Imperial Light Horse. He declared himself in favour of tariff reform, but never threw himself into the politics of his adopted land or accepted any office of honour in his county. His self-effacement, indeed, amounted almost to a passion; with it went a notable loyalty to old friends and to the people who worked for him; his chief pride lay in the fact that he had made his wealth honestly, and that he had earned the complete and profound trust of the industry which he had done so much to establish. He was created a baronet in 1905. On his death, which took place in London 21 May 1912, the eldest of his three sons, Derrick Julius (born 1889), succeeded to the title.

A portrait of Wernher was painted by Sir Hubert von Herkomer in 1910; the original is at Luton Hoo, and there are replicas in the possession of his son, Major H. A. Wernher, and at the Johannesburg Art Gallery.

[Letters (unpublished) of Sir Julius Wernher; family papers; private information.]

I. D. C.

WEST, Sir ALGERNON EDWARD (1832–1921), chairman of the Board of Inland Revenue, born in London 4 April 1832, was the third son of Martin John West, recorder of King's Lynn, by his wife, Lady Maria Walpole, third daughter of Horatio, second Earl of Orford, of the second creation, and great-granddaughter of the prime minister, Sir Robert Walpole. He was sent to Eton in 1843, where he made his mark as an oar, but experienced 'an almost total neglect of any kind of education beyond a very superficial smattering of Latin and Greek' [*Recollections*, i, 50]. After two years of travel and study, he matriculated in 1850 at Christ Church, Oxford, intending to take orders. The next year, having kept only two terms, he changed his plans and accepted a clerkship in the Inland Revenue department, but was transferred to the Admiralty a year later. At the end of 1854 official business took him to the seat of war in the Crimea, where he was disgusted by the 'gross mismanagement'.

Tall, handsome, and a favourite in society, West earned advancement by tact, ability, and hard work. After service as private secretary in the India Office (1860–1866) to Sir Charles Wood (afterwards Viscount Halifax) and the Earl of Ripon, his great opportunity came in 1868, when Gladstone, then prime minister, appointed him to be his private secretary. 'After nearly four years of delightful and confidential intercourse' [*Recollections*, ii, 17], Gladstone rewarded him with a commissionership of inland revenue (1872), a post in which for twenty years he served in succession eight chancellors of the exchequer from Robert Lowe (afterwards Viscount Sherbrooke) to (Viscount) Goschen. His financial capacity endeared him to Gladstone, and the two men became devoted friends. It was on West's suggestion that Gladstone abolished the malt tax in 1880. In 1883 West cruised in the *Pembroke Castle* with Gladstone and Tennyson, and was entrusted with the negotiations which ended in Tennyson's acceptance of a peerage.

West, who had been chairman of the Inland Revenue Board since 1881, was created K.C.B. in 1886. In 1892 he retired from the civil service and offered his services as private secretary to Gladstone, who was forming his last administration. His *Private Diaries* (posthumously edited) provide a lively account of Gladstone's difficulties with his colleagues. In March 1894 West retired with his chief from party politics and was made a privy councillor. He was promoted G.C.B. in 1902. Almost to the last 'Algy' West was a conspicuous figure in Brooks's Club, on the London County Council, and, as director of several companies in the City. He died at his London house in Manchester Square 21 March 1921.

West married in 1858 Mary (died 1894), daughter of Captain the Hon. George Barrington, granddaughter of Charles, second Earl Grey, and was survived by three sons and one daughter. He was the author of *Recollections* (1899), *Memoir of Sir Henry Keppel* (1905), *One City and Many Men* (1908), *Contemporary Portraits* (1920). His *Private Diaries* were edited by H. G. Hutchinson in 1922.

[*The Times*, 22 March 1921; West's *Recollections* and *Private Diaries*; private information.] F. W. H.

WEST, Sir RAYMOND (1832–1912), Indian civil servant, judge, and jurist, born at Ballyloughrane, co. Kerry, 18 September 1832, was the elder son of Frederick Henry West, journalist, by his wife, Frances, daughter of Richard Raymond, of Ballyloughrane, Ballybunnion. His father's occupation was precarious, and the boy's education was much neglected; but his mother's personality and wide culture made up for this, and he was able to secure a scholarship to Queen's College, Galway, where he graduated with the highest honours in 1855. In the same year he passed into the service of the East India Company as one of the second batch of 'competition-wallahs'. He arrived in India in September 1856, and was posted to the southern Maratha country, where he soon saw active service as civil officer with the force sent against the insurgent Sawant clan. His experiences were of lasting value; but he was always conscientiously averse from wearing in India the Mutiny medal which he received.

West joined the judicial department in 1860, and in 1863 was appointed registrar of the recently constituted high court, where he distinguished himself by the part which he took in building up the judicial service, by his annotated edition of the Bombay code, *Acts and Regulations in force in the Presidency of Bombay* (1867–1868), and by his collaboration with Dr. J. G. Bühler in their important *Digest of Hindu Law* (1867–1869) consisting of a collection of the replies of the *shastris* (Hindu law officers attached to the former Zilla courts) to questions of Hindu law addressed to them by the courts. The *Digest*, with its scholarly introduction and annotation, throws great light on the relations of custom and revelation as sources of Hindu law; and it has helped the Bombay high court to steer a wise middle course, avoiding the exaggerated deference to revelation and the unnecessary search for 'custom' which have prevailed elsewhere in India. As district judge of Canara (1866) and as judicial commissioner in Sind (1868), West had further opportunities of carrying out his ideas of judicial organization. But his tenure of the latter post was broken by two years' furlough necessitated by overwork, a 'rest' which he spent in omnivorous legal study and in obtaining a call to the Irish bar. In 1873 he was appointed a judge of the Bombay high court, where he had already officiated in 1871, and he held that position till 1886. The long series of his judgments enjoys an authority in India not exceeded by that of any other judge; and the ultra-conservatism of some of them, which has recently evoked criticism from Hindu reformers, is perhaps a judicial virtue.

West's immense and varied reading, in addition to his judicial duties, had already brought on insomnia, from which he suffered for the rest of his Indian service. In 1879 he was deputed to serve on the Indian statute law commission at Simla; the portion of its report dealing with principles of codification is from his pen, and the whole report owes much to his experience. In 1884 his services were lent to the Egyptian government as procureur-général to reform the judiciary. The root and branch reorganization which he recommended was held by Lord Cromer [q.v.] to make insufficient allowance for temporary political difficulties; but his proposals, though not immediately practicable, were partly carried out at a later date. In 1887 he became a member of the executive council of the governor of Bombay, and was created K.C.I.E. in 1888. In the extensive judicial business which came before that government West continued to add to his reputation; and it has been suggested that an edition of his judgments and minutes of this period would be of even wider legal interest than his earlier work. In the purely executive work of government he was perhaps hampered by his judicial conservatism. He retired in 1892.

West deserves to be remembered not only for his own judicial eminence, but also for his guidance of the subordinate judiciary. English law and justice in India were exotics which required personal explanation and example to render them workable or even intelligible. It was an even greater task to build up a sound tradition, an esprit-de-corps, and, above all, an efficient system of inspection and control. To the progress of Bombay West also contributed by his long connexion with the university, culminating in his vice-chancellorship (1878 and 1886–1892). He not only insisted on a high standard of examinations, but also firmly believed in an Indian nationalism which should yet be open to the best influences of Europe. In conversation with students his slight awkwardness of manner would disappear, and he was always ready to fire their imagination with frank talk on great subjects. Bombay University has only given three honorary degrees in its history, of which one was a fitting tribute to the services of Sir Raymond West. In retirement he showed as lecturer in Indian law at Cambridge (1895–1907) his love of educational work.

West was twice married: first, in 1867 to Clementina Fergusson (died 1896), only daughter of William Maunsell Chute, of Chute Hall, co. Kerry, by whom he had a son and three daughters; secondly, in 1901 to Annie Kirkpatrick, eldest daughter of Surgeon-General Henry Cook, M.D., of Prior's Mesne, Lydney, Gloucestershire, who survived him. He died 8 September 1912 at Upper Norwood.

[*The Times*, 9 September 1912; *Times of India* (Bombay), March–April 1892; *Journal* of the Royal Asiatic Society, 1913; *Report* of the Indian Statute Law Commission, 1879; Bombay High Court *Reports*, vols. viii–xii; Indian Law Reports, Bombay Series, vols. i–xii; private information.] S. V. FG.

WESTLAKE, JOHN (1828–1913), jurist, was born at Lostwithiel, Cornwall, 4 February 1828, the only son of John Westlake, a woolstapler, by his wife, Eleanora, daughter of the Rev. George Burgess, of Atherington, Devon. He was educated privately and at Trinity College, Cambridge, which he entered in 1846; was sixth wrangler and sixth classic in 1850, and a fellow of his college from 1851 to 1860. He was called to the bar in 1854, and practised, becoming a Q.C. and a bencher of Lincoln's Inn in 1874, until in 1888 he succeeded Sir Henry Sumner Maine [q.v.] in the Whewell chair of international law at Cambridge, a post which he held till his resignation in 1908. He married in 1864 Alice, second daughter of Thomas Hare [q.v.], but had no children. He died at Chelsea 14 April 1913.

As a jurist, Westlake was equally eminent in private and in public international law. His *Treatise on Private International Law*, first published in 1858 but rewritten in 1880, was the first English attempt to give systematic form to this branch of law. With a profound knowledge of continental theory Westlake combined a practising barrister's intimate understanding of English habits of legal thought; and by its influence on the courts his *Treatise* has been the main formative influence in the development of a new branch of English law which hardly existed before he wrote. On public international law his most important works were *Chapters on the Principles of International Law* (1894), and *International Law*, Part I, *Peace* (1904), and Part II, *War* (1907). While Westlake did not neglect its historical and philosophical aspects he treated international law primarily as a branch of law. He strongly advocated the judicial settlement of international disputes, and was himself a member of the Hague international court of arbitration from 1900 to 1906.

In both departments of his study one of Westlake's main purposes was to reconcile English and continental traditions by promoting on both sides a better understanding of divergent views, and greater interchange of thought between lawyers of different countries. In 1869 he was one of the founders of the *Revue de Droit International et de Législation Comparée*, the first periodical of international law; and in 1873 of the Institut de Droit International, of which he was president in 1895, and a permanent honorary president from 1910. On social and political questions Westlake was a strong liberal, with a hatred of all kinds of oppression or injustice. He was a founder in 1854, with Frederick Denison Maurice and others, of the Working Men's College in Great Ormond Street, a strong supporter of the enfranchisement of women, and an active sympathizer with the grievances of the Balkan nations and of Finland. He was elected liberal member for the Romford division of Essex in 1885, but differed from his party on the Irish question and failed to obtain re-election in 1886.

There is a portrait of Westlake by Mrs. Adrian Stokes in the National Portrait Gallery.

[*The Times*, 15 April 1913; *Memories of John Westlake*, containing a list of his writings (pp. 147–154), 1914; L. F. L. Oppenheim, Introduction to *The Collected Papers of John Westlake on Public International Law*, 1914.] J. L. B.

WESTON, DAME AGNES ELIZABETH (1840–1918), organizer of 'Sailors' Rests', the elder daughter of Charles Henry Weston, by his wife, Sarah Agnes, daughter of Robert Bayly, was born in London 26 March 1840. Her father was a barrister who retired from practice in 1845 and settled with his family just outside Bath. Agnes was his eldest surviving child. She received, at private schools in Bath, the usual education of daughters of professional men of that time; at her second school she was prepared for confirmation by the Rev. (Canon) James Fleming [q. v.], at that time curate of St. Stephen, Lansdown, Bath, whose teaching tended, like the influence of her parents, towards evangelical Christianity, and made a deep and lasting impression on her mind. For the next twelve years she divided her time between a serious study of the organ and various philanthropic activities in the neighbourhood of her home. She became an effective speaker at temperance meetings, and developed some skill as a writer of tracts. Towards the end of this period she started a coffee bar in Bath for men of the 2nd Somerset Militia, with some of whom she kept in touch by correspondence after they left the town.

This correspondence opened the way to Miss Weston's main work in life. One of her soldier friends, on his way to India, showed her parting letter to the steward on his troopship, who wished that he had such a friend 'to help him in the Christian life.' His wish was reported to Miss Weston. She wrote to him and to others whose names he gave her, and succeeded at once in establishing a genuine personal relationship with her unknown correspondents. Only three years after her first letter to a sailor (which was dated 1868), she began the issue of a printed monthly letter for distribution to ships' companies, the circulation of which rose before her death to over 60,000 copies.

At the beginning of 1873 many of Miss Weston's sailor correspondents were paid off at Devonport, and she went to the port to see them. There she stayed with the family of Miss Sophia Gertrude Wintz, who became her lifelong friend and partner. During this year she took up active work in Devonport on behalf of the Royal Naval Temperance Society, and was successful in obtaining permission to visit men-of-war and address their crews. Her popularity among the men grew steadily, and in 1874 a deputation from H.M.S. *Dryad* requested her to open a temperance house for bluejackets near the dockyard gates. After some hesitation she and Miss Wintz decided to undertake the enterprise. Meetings were organized all over the county, funds were raised, and a house in Fore Street, Devonport, was adapted as a restaurant and hostel. It was opened as the first 'Sailors' Rest' in May 1876.

The institution was an immediate success. Its organization was admirable, and it was carried on in a spirit of hearty kindliness. Deeply as Miss Weston had at heart her temperance crusade and the propagation of her religious views, she made no attempt to force them on the men who used her house. Lectures, religious services, and the pledge book were there for those who wanted them. Others who wanted only a 'cabin' for the night and a meal were equally welcome. The result was that from the first the accommodation was barely equal to the demand.

After a few years a similar establishment was started by Miss Weston and Miss Wintz at Portsmouth. For a time they carried on 'Sailors' Rests' at Portland and Sheerness also, but they found that the task of managing four such establishments was too exacting, and decided to concentrate their energies on the expansion and development of those at Devonport and Portsmouth. It was Miss Weston's policy to make the institutions self-supporting so far as the provision of food and shelter was concerned, but the cost of building was met from public subscriptions. Sufficient support was forthcoming to enable her to extend her premises till 900 men could be housed at Devonport and 700 at Portsmouth. Greatly to her satisfaction, several public houses were demolished in the process of extension.

At an early stage the two partners secured the property for its original purpose by conveying it to trustees, themselves acting as managing directors. Miss Weston was a woman of strong physique, good humour, and robust courage, and forty years of devotion to this arduous work did not abate her zeal. She was known to the seamen as 'Mother' Weston, a name she earned by her solicitude for their welfare, and the mixture of indulgence and admonition in her bearing towards them. Free 'promotion' classes and a seamen's savings bank were among her many enterprises for their benefit. She was a good friend also to their families, and on several occasions came to the help of the dependants of those who were lost by disaster at sea, administering privately funds subscribed for their support till official pensions were awarded.

The work of the 'Sailors' Rests' gradually attracted public notice. Queen Victoria endowed a cabin at Devonport in 1895, and gave permission for the word

'Royal' to be prefixed to the name of the institution. Miss Weston received the honorary LL.D. degree of Glasgow in 1901, and was created G.B.E. in 1918. She died at Devonport 23 October 1918, and was buried there with full naval honours.

A portrait of Miss Weston was presented to the corporation of Portsmouth for the town hall by the wives of sailors in 1925.

[*The Times*, 24 and 28 October 1918; Agnes Weston, *My Life among the Blue Jackets*, 1909; *Nineteenth Century*, December 1916.] M. C.

WHITE, Sir GEORGE STUART (1835–1912), field-marshal, was born at Whitehall, co. Antrim, 6 July 1835, the eldest son of James Robert White, of Whitehall, by his wife, Frances, daughter of George Stuart. Entering the army from Sandhurst in 1853 he served in the Indian Mutiny with the 27th Foot (Inniskilling Fusiliers) and subsequently transferred to the 92nd (Gordon) Highlanders. It was with this regiment, after twenty-six years of service, that he, as a major, obtained his first chance of winning distinction. In the Afghan War of 1879–1880, during the advance of Major-General (afterwards Earl) Roberts [q.v.] from Charasia to Kabul, White, in command of some 200 of the 92nd Highlanders, managed by skilful leading and great courage to outflank the Afghans in the Saug-i-nawishta gorge (6 October 1879), and so was largely instrumental in clearing the way for the remainder of the force. Roberts said of this exploit: 'From an inspection of the ground, I had no difficulty in coming to the conclusion that much of the success which attended the operations on this side was due to White's military instincts, and, at one moment, to his extreme personal gallantry.' Thenceforward White's advancement was as rapid and remarkable as it had hitherto been slow and ordinary. At the end of the Afghan War he received the V.C. for his feat at Charasia and was made a C.B. and brevet lieutenant-colonel. In 1880 he was military secretary to the viceroy of India. After a short spell of duty at home in command of the 92nd, he went again on active service to Egypt as assistant quartermaster-general (1884–1885). In the latter year war broke out in Burma, and White was given the command of a brigade for operations in that country. Mandalay was speedily taken by the force under Major-General (Sir) Harry Prendergast [q.v.], but, as was usually the case in Burmese wars, there followed a long and tedious conflict with bands of dacoits, a conflict aggravated in this instance by the action of the frontier tribes, who thought their opportunity had come for avenging themselves on their Burmese neighbours. In quelling this guerrilla warfare and in the pacification of Upper Burma White played a leading part and established his reputation both as a general and as an administrator. At the conclusion of the War in 1887 the government of India reported that 'the success of these operations, which have involved great hardship and labour on the troops, and the satisfactory progress made towards the pacification of the country, must be ascribed in a very large measure to the skill, judgement, and ability of Sir George White.' For his services he had been made K.C.B. in 1886, and he was promoted major-general in 1889.

In the latter year White was transferred from Burma to command at Quetta, where for the first time he was brought in a responsible position into contact with the problems of the North-Western Frontier of India. The controversy between those who desired to make the Indus the administrative frontier and those who desired to extend it to the borders of Afghanistan was at its height; but the 'forward' school, with the powerful support of the commander-in-chief in India, Sir Frederick Roberts, and of the viceroy, the Marquess of Lansdowne, was in the ascendant, and White, who was an enthusiastic supporter of Roberts's views, at once became an instrument of that policy. In the autumn of 1889 he was entrusted with the command of the Zhob Valley expedition. The operations, directed against a tribe which had long made their almost inaccessible mountain home a base for raids into British territory, were admirably planned and skilfully executed. White, having scaled the heights of the Maramazh, surrounded the principal village of the tribe, which surrendered at discretion. In the following years, in conjunction with Sir Robert Groves Sandeman [q.v.], he was occupied with the pacification of Baluchistan, to this day the one lasting achievement of the 'forward' policy. In this work he displayed considerable political and diplomatic gifts and was successful in the not always easy task of working harmoniously with his civilian coadjutors.

For his services in Baluchistan White was made G.C.I.E. in 1893; and when, in that year, Roberts's long term of command in India came to a close, he was chosen over the heads of a number of seniors to be his successor. His period of supreme command in India saw the greatest development of the 'forward' policy. Encouraged by his success in Baluchistan, he supported the policy of opening up communications beyond the Indus and subjugating the unruly tribesmen of the Himalaya. This policy brought about a succession of frontier campaigns. During this period the gradual approach of Russia to the northern frontier of Afghanistan and the menace of a Russian attack upon India were the principal military preoccupations, and the chief argument of the advocates of the 'forward' policy was the necessity, in view of this menace, of obtaining better control of the tribes of the North-Western Frontier, and thereby more influence in Afghanistan. White's command began with a small expedition in 1894 against the Abor tribe on the North-Eastern Frontier. This was followed in 1895 by the more considerable Chitral campaign, due to the revolt of Umra Khan, who besieged in Chitral fort the commissioner, (Sir) George Scott Robertson [q.v.], and a small garrison. The expedition of relief which was successfully carried through had more than local importance in view of Russian approaches to the Pamirs. The Chitral campaign was followed in 1897 by a succession of outbreaks along the frontier, which were the cause of expeditions into the Tochi Valley of Baluchistan, the Swat Valley, and against the Mohmands; and before these were terminated the most warlike and important tribes of the frontier, the Afridis and the Orakzais, rose and burned the British forts in the Khyber Pass. There followed the Tirah campaign, the most considerable military enterprise of which India had been the scene since the days of the Mutiny. While the responsibility for the policy of these expeditions rested with the viceroy, the Earl of Elgin, who had followed the tradition established by Lord Lansdowne, White was responsible for their planning and organization. All of them were successful in obtaining the objects immediately aimed at, but the permanent gains were small. It has been said, with reason, that a less ambitious enterprise than the Tirah campaign, more swiftly executed, would have had better results. White probably hoped that by operations on a considerable scale the problem would be solved once and for all. In that he was not successful. His term as commander-in-chief was in other respects remarkable for the training which he inaugurated (particularly of the British troops) in the intricacies of mountain warfare, and for the advancement of the musketry instruction of the Indian army. For his services as commander-in-chief he was made G.C.B., and at the end of 1897 he was appointed quartermaster-general at the War Office.

In September 1899, on the outbreak of the Boer War, White was sent in command to Natal with the task of saving that province from invasion. There he was confronted with a far more serious problem than any created by the tribes of the Indian frontier, a problem more serious indeed than had confronted any British general then alive. His predecessor in command in Natal, Sir William Penn Symons [q. v.], had taken up a forward position on the frontier at Dundee; and though White desired to concentrate his whole force in the neighbourhood of Ladysmith, which was the strategically wise course, he allowed himself to be overruled by the dashing and adventurous Symons, and the campaign in Natal began with the British forces divided. At that time no one believed that the Boers would show the tactical skill and cohesion which they in fact displayed, and the advantage which their mobility conferred upon them was much underrated. There were, therefore, arguments on behalf of the plan adopted, mistaken though it proved to be. After a successful engagement with the Boers at Talana (20 October), in which Symons lost his life, the Dundee column made good its retreat to Ladysmith. The next day the Boers were again repulsed by Major-General French at Elandslaagte, but by that time the horns of the invasion had extended far into Natal. An unfortunate night enterprise at Nicholson's Nek, which ended in a complete failure, ruined White's plan for engaging the enemy at Lombard's Kop (30 October), and the whole of his forces were shut up in Ladysmith (2 November). It would have been possible for White to retreat across the river Tugela, but it would have been a hazardous undertaking, entailing the abandonment of a large quantity of ammunition and stores, while the moral effect would have been even more considerable than was that of the investment. White maintained that by attracting the Boers to Ladysmith he preserved the rest of Natal from invasion. In this he was shown by the result to have been right. The balance of military argument is in favour of White's decision in a very difficult and critical situation. It has been said that White's defence was lacking in enterprise and that his choice of the lines of defence was not the best. Mistakes—common in war—there may have been, yet there is no question but that he kept the enemy at bay; for only once, in the rough and tumble fights of Waggon Hill and Caesar's Camp (6 January), did they make any attempt to close, while his indomitable courage inspired a defence which more than once had cause for despair. After a siege of 118 days, Ladysmith was relieved (28 February) by the advance of the Natal field force, Lord Roberts's invasion of the Free State having drawn away a number of besiegers. It is with the defence of Ladysmith that White's name will always be associated, and he deserves to be honourably remembered for his reply to the suggestion of Sir Redvers Buller [q.v.], after the latter's defeat at Colenso (15 December), that he should make terms: 'The loss of 10,000 men would be a heavy blow to England; we must not think of it.' Broken in health as a result of the siege, he came home to be appointed governor of Gibraltar, where on the occasion of a visit by King Edward he received the baton of field-marshal. In 1905 he was awarded the order of merit, and was made governor of Chelsea Hospital, where he died 24 June 1912.

White married in 1874 Amy, the only daughter of the Venerable Joseph Baly, archdeacon of Calcutta, and had one son and four daughters.

[Earl Roberts, *Forty-one Years in India*, 2 vols., 1897; Howard Hensman, *The Afghan War of 1879–1880*, 1881; A. Durand, *The Making of a Frontier*, 1889; L. James, *The Indian Frontier War*, 1898; Sir J. F. Maurice, and M. H. Grant, (Official) *History of the War in South Africa*, 3 vols., 1906–1910.] F. M.

WHITE, WILLIAM HALE (1831–1913), novelist (under the pseudonym of MARK RUTHERFORD), philosophical writer, literary critic, and civil servant, was born in High Street, Bedford, 22 December 1831. He was the eldest son of William White, bookseller and printer, of Bedford, by his wife, Mary Anne Chignell, of Colchester. His father, a strong dissenter and whig politician, was a man of some note in the public life of Bedford, and later became a famous doorkeeper of the House of Commons; he was the author of a series of lively parliamentary sketches for the *Illustrated Times*, a collection of which, edited by Justin M'Carthy [q.v.], appeared under the title *The Inner Life of the House of Commons* (1897). Hale White was educated at Bedford Modern School, and after a rather mechanical process of 'conversion', entered, at seventeen, the Countess of Huntingdon's college at Cheshunt, with a view to becoming an independent minister. He passed thence to New College, St. John's Wood, from which he was expelled, with two other students, for unorthodox views concerning the Biblical canon. Later he occasionally preached in Unitarian chapels, at Ditchling and elsewhere, and also in the London chapel of the famous Welsh preacher, Caleb Morris, for years Hale White's friend and spiritual guide. But his most definite early connexion with London was his engagement in the early 'fifties with John Chapman [q.v.], the publisher and editor of the *Westminster Review*, in whose office he met George Eliot and enjoyed her friendship. There are traces of this association in the sketch of 'Theresa' in the *Autobiography*, while Chapman is obviously 'Wollaston'. In 1854 he passed into the civil service as a clerk in the office of the registrar-general, Somerset House; but was transferred in 1858 to the Admiralty, where he rose (1879) to be assistant director of contracts, frequently acting as director. He retired on a pension at the age of sixty. For a short time he was registrar of births, marriages, and deaths for Marylebone. He died 14 March 1913 at Groombridge, Kent, and was buried in the churchyard there. He was twice married: first, in 1856 to Harriet (died 1891), daughter of Samuel Arthur, a dress-trimmings maker, and a pupil of Sir Charles Hallé; by her he had five sons, the eldest of whom was Sir William Hale White, the physician, and one daughter; secondly, in 1911 to Dorothy Vernon, daughter of Horace Smith, metropolitan police magistrate for Westminster.

Hale White's work in literature virtually began with the appearance in 1881 of *The Autobiography of Mark Rutherford*, followed in 1885 by its sequel, *Mark Rutherford's Deliverance*. For the two books he invented a posthumous editor, 'Reuben Shapcott'. He maintained the pseudonyms of 'Mark Rutherford' and 'Reuben Shapcott' through the series of novels which followed these works of spiritual biography, never formally acknowledging his authorship even when his place in contemporary literature had become assured. The novels closed in 1896 with *Clara Hopgood*. The intervening volumes, *The Revolution in Tanner's Lane* (1887), *Miriam's Schooling, and other Papers* (1890), and *Catharine Furze* (1893), yield, with the autobiographical books, the flower of his thought on life and religion, while his later imaginative work appears in *Pages from a Journal, with other Papers* (1900), *More Pages from a Journal* (1910), and the posthumous *Last Pages from a Journal* (1915), consisting of aphorisms, Biblical notes and sketches, a brilliant analysis of the book of Job, and some short stories which exhibit the poetic quality and delicate texture of his prose writing.

Hale White was a man of varied intellectual equipment, a scholar, an amateur astronomer, and an exact and painstaking literary critic. His work as a translator and exponent of Spinoza's ethical philosophy, as a student of Wordsworth's MSS. and his champion against the charge of political and religious apostasy, was of excellent quality, and his political journalism as London letter-writer for the *Scotsman* and many provincial journals was shrewd and broadly human. But his thought on life and literature received its deepest colouring through the religious and philosophic thinkers whose minds interested and fertilised his own, Spinoza and Wordsworth, with the great puritans, Milton and Bunyan. Spinoza drew him away from the 'artificial God of the churches' to a rational and also a transcendental view of religion, to which Wordsworth gave poetic expression, at the same time quickening his deep love of natural beauty. But throughout his passage from the theological to the philosophic position Hale White remained a puritan in temper and inclination.

The distinction of Hale White's writing lies in its intimate spiritual quality. Its main theme is that of provincial dissent in the early and middle nineteenth century; its setting the quiet scenery of his native Bedford and the eastern Midlands. Half dreamer, half thinker, his special appeal is to the lonely and the sensitive, and to the devout sceptic whose will is at issue with his intelligence. Under the veil of fiction, his work is essentially one of self-disclosure. In that respect the *Autobiography* and the *Deliverance* are as penetrating as Rousseau's *Confessions*, save that 'Mark Rutherford' is a reticent Englishman, and his more disturbing adventures are of the soul, not of the body. Slight as is their form, his novels impress the imagination by their sincerity and depth of feeling, touched and relieved with ironic humour, and by their still, if rather sombre, beauty of atmosphere; while as studies of nonconformist England they take high, and almost solitary, rank in Victorian literature.

Hale White wrote under his own name: translations of Spinoza's *Ethic* (1883) and *Emendation of the Intellect* (1895), *A Description of the Wordsworth and Coleridge MSS. in the possession of Mr. T. Norton Longman* (1897), *Examination of the Charge of Apostasy against Wordsworth* (1898), and *John Bunyan* (1905).

[*The Early Life of Mark Rutherford*, by himself, 1913; Sir William Robertson Nicoll, *Memories of Mark Rutherford*, 1924; William Hale White, *Letters to Three Friends*, 1924; Dorothy V. White, *The Groombridge Diary*, 1924; private information; personal knowledge.] H. W. M.

WHITE, Sir WILLIAM HENRY (1845–1913), naval architect, born at Devonport 2 February 1845, was the youngest child of Richard White, a currier, of Devonport, by his wife, Jane, daughter of W. Matthews, of Lostwithiel, Cornwall. He was educated at a private school at Devonport and apprenticed as a shipwright in the royal dockyard there. In 1864 he and seven fellow-apprentices were appointed by the Admiralty to the then newly-founded royal school of naval architecture at South Kensington to undergo a training in naval architecture, higher mathematics, physics, and chemistry; and in 1867 he passed out from this school, obtaining its highest honours. He and five others were at once appointed to the Admiralty staff by Sir Edward James Reed [q.v.], the chief constructor of the navy, White being engaged as a professional secretary to Sir Edward. Many warships with iron hulls were then building, in private yards as well as in the royal dockyards, in succession to vessels with wooden hulls. New methods of construction were therefore being devised, and numerous structural features were under discussion. It was desirable to collate and publish these. Reed did this in his book, *Shipbuilding in Iron and Steel*, published in 1869; in the preparation of this White was given a large share, as also in Reed's *Our Iron Clad Ships* (1869), and in the paper *On the Stresses of Ships* contributed by Reed to *Philosophical Transactions* (1871). In 1870 Reed retired from the position of chief constructor of the navy, when the office was put into commission with Mr. (afterwards Sir) Nathaniel Barnaby [q.v.] as president of the council of construction. This council appointed White as its secretary (1872).

Shortly after Reed's retirement, H.M.S. *Captain*, a fully-rigged, low-freeboard turret ship, designed by Captain Cowper Phipps Coles [q.v.] and built by a private firm, capsized, most of her crew being drowned. Amongst the ships then building from Reed's designs were the 'all big gun' battleships *Devastation* and *Thunderer*, of comparatively low freeboard but with no sail. The loss of the *Captain* drew especial attention to these vessels, and a committee was appointed to report on their safety. The council of construction proposed certain alterations, which were finally approved by the committee and adopted by the Admiralty, largely through White's advocacy. The first important design approved by the council of construction (Barnaby being the responsible designer) was that of the 'all big gun' *Inflexible* of 1876. She carried four muzzle-loading 16-inch 80 ton guns, mounted *en échelon*, two in each of two turrets on a central citadel. The side armour was limited to the central part of the vessel, and the ends, which had thin side plating, were fitted with high and thick cork belts and strong under-water decks. The design was attacked by Reed and was referred for report by the Admiralty to a naval and scientific committee. The committee was convinced of its merit by the defence, which was left largely to White. The *Inflexible* and four other vessels, of the same type but somewhat smaller, were built and passed into the fleet.

The breech-loading gun was now so far developed as to be adopted in the *Collingwood*, a vessel of Barnaby's design, laid down in 1880. Turrets were abandoned, and the main armament, of four 12-inch guns in pairs in two barbettes, was mounted on the middle line, one pair towards each end of the vessel. The weights of the revolving material and of the power to actuate it were much reduced, and a secondary armament of six 6-inch guns was carried between the barbettes of the main armament. The cost then considered permissible for a battleship, about £650,000, made it necessary to accept a comparatively narrow belt of armour of about half the length of the ship, leaving the sides at the ends unprotected with armour as in previous vessels. The lower portions of the ends were protected by strong under-water decks, but cork buoyancy was not provided. This design also was very adversely criticised by Reed, and by many naval officers, and others. The defence was again left largely to White; the Admiralty eventually accepted the design, and built the *Collingwood* and five similar vessels with somewhat more powerful armament—*Rodney*, *Howe*, *Anson*, *Camperdown*, and *Benbow*.

White gave much consideration to the design of cruisers, and particularly to that of the *Iris*, laid down in 1875—the first steel vessel built for the navy. He was also one of Barnaby's principal assistants in designing the cruisers *Mersey*, *Severn*, *Thames*, and *Forth*, commenced in 1883. These were by far the most powerful of the smaller cruisers then in the navy; they had a speed of 17 knots, a powerful armament, and were protected for their whole length by a strong deck, rising above the water at the middle line of the ship from well below water at the sides. For many years this remained the accepted type of Admiralty cruiser, culminating in 1894 (after White had become director of naval construction) in the *Powerful* and *Terrible*.

In 1883 White left the Admiralty to become designer and manager to Armstrong & Co. at their warship-yard then being constructed at Elswick-on-Tyne. There he did much good work, assisting in laying out the yard and organizing the staff, and designing and building several of the earlier Elswick vessels. He left Armstrong's in 1885 when, on Sir Nathaniel Barnaby's retirement, he was appointed director of naval construction. On his return to the Admiralty as the head of the construction department (1885) he made various improvements in each class of vessel, embodying advances made in machinery, gunnery, and quality of materials. He designed the *Barfleur* and *Centurion*, of 11,000 tons, for service in eastern waters. Step by step he progressed through the eight vessels of the *Royal Sovereign* class of 1889, and thirty-five additional battleships, to the *King Edward VII* class, the building of which began in 1902. This class was of 16,500 tons, with an armament of four 12-inch guns, four 9·2-inch guns, and ten 6-inch guns, and a speed of 18½ knots. The cost had risen from £650,000 in the *Collingwood* to £1,500,000 in the *King Edward VII*. Several of these vessels were employed in service during the European War. Much improvement was made in the large cruisers. In the 'protected' class (without side armour) these ranged from the *Crescent* of 7,700 tons and a speed of 19½ knots to the *Powerful* and *Terrible* of 14,200 tons and a speed of 22 knots. In all, twenty 'protected' cruisers were built for the royal navy to White's designs. Owing to improvements in the quality of armour the next design for large cruisers—that for the six vessels of the *Cressy* class—provided for 6-inch side armour, 12,000 tons displacement, and a speed of 21½ knots. A bigger design was that for the four vessels of the *Drake* class of 14,100 tons and a speed of 23½ knots. Twenty-eight large armoured cruisers were built to White's designs. Many smaller cruisers, torpedo boat destroyers, and miscellaneous vessels, were designed by White and built for the royal navy, but space is not available for their description. In 1902 White retired on account of ill-health. During his seventeen years' service as director of naval construction larger additions were made to the navy than in any preceding period of the same length.

In the early days (1870–1873) of his career White was appointed lecturer on naval design at the royal school, South Kensington, and he continued (until 1881) to act in this capacity on the transfer of the school to the Royal Naval College at Greenwich. While there he formulated a scheme of instruction in naval architecture for the executive officers of the royal navy which has been continued to the present time. In association with Sir Nathaniel Barnaby, Admiral Sir Houston Stewart [q.v.], and Sir Thomas Brassey (afterwards Earl Brassey, q.v.) he devised the organization of the royal corps of naval constructors, dating from 1883. During his year of office as master of the Worshipful Company of Shipwrights, he, with the assistance of the first Lord Norton [q.v.], founded the educational trust fund, which during the past forty years has helped hundreds of young naval architects to obtain a technical education. He was for some years on the governing body of the National Physical Laboratory, during which time he took much interest in the installation of the William Froude tank. He had considerable literary ability: his *Manual of Naval Architecture* (first edition, 1877) is a model of clear, popular exposition of a difficult subject; it is enriched by many data that reached the Admiralty during his period of service, especially results of original scientific investigations obtained by William Froude [q.v.]. He contributed twenty papers, all of great merit, to the *Transactions* of the Institution of Naval Architects. He also wrote many important articles for leading magazines, and several pamphlets on special subjects connected with naval architecture.

Many honours were awarded White, among them his appointment in 1885 as assistant controller of the navy; he received the K.C.B. in 1895. He was of genial personality, much liked by his fellows, a ready debater, lucid in his statements and convincing to his opponents. He was a welcome guest at the dinners of many City companies, at which he frequently exercised his influence to obtain donations for assistance in educational matters.

White, who left three sons and one daughter, was twice married: first, in 1875 to Alice (died 1886), daughter of F. Martin, of Pembroke, chief constructor, R.N.; and secondly, in 1890 to Annie (who survived him), daughter of F. C. Marshall, J.P., of Tynemouth. He died suddenly in London 27 February 1913, leaving behind him a brilliant record of work and an example to the corps which he did much to inaugurate. During his lifetime the 'wooden walls of old England', wooden ships carrying what are now regarded as feeble armaments, were replaced by iron and steel armoured vessels carrying guns of very great power. In this revolution Sir William White played an important part.

[Admiralty records; *Transactions* of the Institution of Naval Architects; *Proceedings* of the Royal Society, vol. lxxxix, A, 1913–1914; personal knowledge.] P. W.

WHYTE, ALEXANDER (1836–1921), divine, was born at Kirriemuir, Forfarshire, 13 January 1836, of parents who never married. Brought up by his mother, Janet Thomson, who earned her living as a weaver and harvester, the boy owed much to her influence as well as to that of two local ministers and several keenly intelligent artisans. Abandoning the shoemaking trade to which he had served his apprenticeship, Whyte taught for four years in village schools. At the age of twenty-two (1858) he matriculated in King's College, Aberdeen, and, supporting himself mainly by teaching evening classes, succeeded in graduating as M.A. with second-class honours in mental philosophy in 1862. (Sir) William Duguid Geddes and Alexander Bain were the professors who made the deepest impression on him. During this period he became acquainted with the writings of Thomas Goodwin, the elder [q.v.], and Goodwin's influence persisted to the end of his life.

Whyte decided to enter the ministry of the Free Church of Scotland, and four years (1862–1866) devoted to the study of theology at New College, Edinburgh, enabled him to become a licentiate. After serving as colleague at St. John's Free church, Glasgow (1866–1870), he became colleague to Robert Smith Candlish [q.v.] at St. George's Free church, Edinburgh, and, on Candlish's death in 1873, sole minister of the congregation. Alone for the next twenty-two years, and subsequently with the assistance of a colleague, Whyte held this charge till 1916, when he resigned. In 1898 he was elected moderator of the General Assembly, and in 1909 principal of New College, Edinburgh, a position which he held till 1918. The freedom of the city of Edinburgh was presented to him in 1910. The union of 1900, whereby the Free Church and the United Presbyterian Church of Scotland were merged into one communion, was warmly welcomed by him; and the movement, which began some years later, for the union of the Church of Scotland and the United Free Church won his enthusiastic support.

Whyte married in 1881 Jane Elizabeth, daughter of George Freeland Barbour, of Bonskeid, Perthshire, and was survived by her and by three sons and three daughters. He died at Hampstead 6 January 1921. His eldest son, Sir Alexander Frederick Whyte, was member of parliament for Perth in the liberal interest from 1910 to 1918, and afterwards the first president of the legislative assembly of India.

A traditionalist himself, Whyte championed the cause of liberty in Biblical criticism; a Calvinist in theology, he was catholic in his sympathies with exponents of the devotional life. His preaching was distinguished by a rich imagination, with a streak of humour, genial or grim, running through it; by a passion for righteousness which betrayed him at times into exaggerated confessions and attributions of evil motives; and by a mysticism which expressed itself in rapturous and moving eloquence. He was the author of *A Commentary on the Shorter Catechism* (1882) and a number of biographical studies of Biblical characters and others.

[Whyte's works; G. F. Barbour, *Life of Alexander Whyte, D.D.*, 1923; personal knowledge.] A. B. M.

WILDING, ANTHONY FREDERICK (1883–1915), lawn-tennis player, was born at Opawa, near Christ Church, New Zealand, 31 October 1883, the eldest son of Frederick Wilding, Q.C., of the firm of Wilding and Acland, solicitors, of Christ Church, by his wife, Julia, daughter of Alderman Charles Anthony, J.P., of Hereford, England. Frederick Wilding, an all-round sportsman and games player, gave his son his first lessons in cricket and lawn-tennis. Anthony Wilding was educated first at Mr. Wilson's school at Christ Church, and while there won his first lawn-tennis success of importance when he defeated Richard D. Harman in the championship of the province of Canterbury. He went up to Trinity College, Cambridge, in 1902, and during his first summer term won the freshmen's lawn-tennis tournament, although he had been chiefly playing cricket, at which he was good enough to be chosen for some of the university trial matches and to be awarded his Crusader colours. From 1904, however, Wilding's chief recreation was lawn-tennis. He was secretary of the university lawn-tennis club in 1904, president in 1905, and represented Cambridge against Oxford in both years, when he was certainly the best singles player. In the doubles he was partnered by Kenneth Powell.

Henceforth Wilding made steady progress at the game. Considerable help was given to him by great players of that day, such as H. S. Mahony and Hugh Lawrence Doherty [q.v.], but it was by constant practice and training that he made himself into one of the first dozen players which the game has yet known. From 1903 onwards he won prizes and championships in all parts of the world where the game was played, for he was very fond of travelling, and made journeys half across Europe on his motor-bicycle. He was one of the representatives of Australasia for the Davis international challenge cup from 1905 onwards. He first became All England singles champion at Wimbledon in 1910 when he defeated the holder, A. Wentworth Gore, and he retained the title until 1914, defeating in turn H. Roper Barrett, A. W. Gore, and M. E. McLoughlin in the challenge round. Wilding also won the championship doubles in 1907, partnered by Norman E. Brookes; in 1908 and 1910, partnered by M. J. G. Ritchie; and in 1914, partnered by Brookes.

On leaving Cambridge, Wilding read for the bar and was called by the Inner Temple in 1906, qualifying as barrister and solicitor of the supreme court of New Zealand in 1909. After the outbreak of the European War he was gazetted lieutenant in the Royal Marines (October 1914). Later he was employed at the Head-Quarters Intelligence Corps. In 1915 he was attached to the armoured car force, and on 9 May of that year he was killed in the fighting in Artois, near Lestrem, the dug-out in which he was stationed being shattered by a large shell.

Although Wilding had not such a natural genius for lawn-tennis as the Renshaws or the Dohertys displayed, he possessed many assets for proficiency. He had a good eye, health and physical strength in abundance, while his patience and perseverance in practice were inexhaustible. In his early days he would practice for hours against a wall. His name will live in the annals of the game, not as one of the most brilliant or graceful of lawn-tennis players, but as one of the most difficult to beat. He wrote a book describing his experiences, entitled *On the*

Court and Off, which was first published in 1912. He was unmarried.

[A. Wallis Myers, *Captain Anthony Wilding*, 1916; A. F. Wilding, *On the Court and Off*; Ayres, *Lawn-Tennis Almanac*.] E. B. N.

WILLETT, WILLIAM (1856–1915), builder, and the originator of 'daylight saving', the eldest son of William Willett, builder, by his wife, Maria Box, was born at Farnham, Surrey, 10 August 1856. He was educated at the Marylebone grammar school. After acquiring some commercial experience, he entered his father's business. Between them they created a remarkable reputation for 'Willett-built' houses in London, Chislehurst, Hove, and other places. On Earl Cadogan's estate round Sloane Square, London, they replaced small houses and alleys by well-planned streets of large houses. Other examples of their methods of development are to be seen in South Kensington, in Avenue Road, Regent's Park, and in the roads round Eton Avenue, South Hampstead, which are laid out on 'garden city' lines. The typical Willett house differs from the ordinary stucco-fronted London dwelling in the use of good bricks, tiles, and Portland stone, giving to the exterior an effect of warmth, colour, and interest. Variety of elevation was aimed at and achieved. Great care was devoted to internal planning, ample window light, domestic convenience, and good craftsmanship. Although an architect was constantly employed in the firm's office, and others were commissioned from time to time, much of the credit for the success of these houses was due to the Willetts themselves, father and son, who took great pains to make every detail satisfactory.

William Willett, the younger, will be remembered chiefly, however, as the pioneer of 'daylight saving'. The idea is said to have occurred to him early one summer morning in 1907 as he returned from his customary canter over a Kentish common, when he noticed how many blinds were still down in the large houses that he passed. As the result of his advocacy, the first Daylight Saving Bill was introduced by Mr. Robert Pearce in the House of Commons in the following March. From the first inception of his scheme up to the date of his death Willett devoted much energy, time, and money to the furtherance of this measure. Between 1907 and 1914 he wrote and published nineteen editions (in English and other languages) of a pamphlet entitled *The Waste of Daylight*, containing his arguments in favour of this reform. Nevertheless, in spite of many influential supporters, the Bill met with much opposition and ridicule, and, although introduced again in 1909 and 1911, did not become law until 1916, and then only as a war-time measure of economy. This continued in force until August 1925, when a new Summer Time Act received the royal assent. Thus Willett failed to see the realization of his hopes, for he died at Chislehurst, Kent, 4 March 1915. In 1923 his portrait, by Charles Shannon, R.A., publicly subscribed for as a memorial to his work, was unveiled in the council chamber of the Chelsea town hall.

Subsequently, more prominent recognition was given to Willett's efforts to establish 'summer time', by the purchase and handing over to the public of over eighty-seven acres of Pett's Wood, near Chislehurst, in May 1927. This beautiful wooded common is the place where the idea of daylight-saving first occurred to him.

[*The Times*, 5 March 1915, 1 October 1926, 9 April 1927, 23 May 1927; *The Builder*, 19 March 1915; private information.] M. S. B.

WILLIAMS, Sir ROLAND BOWDLER VAUGHAN (1838–1916), judge, who on his marriage assumed the name of Lomax in place of Bowdler, was born in Queen Square, Bloomsbury, 31 December 1838, being the fifth son of Sir Edward Vaughan Williams (q.v., justice of the court of common pleas from 1846 to 1865) by his wife, Jane Margaret Bagot, and the grandson of Serjeant John Williams [q.v.], author of the well-known commentary on Saunders's *Reports*. This Welsh family thus furnishes a remarkable illustration of the inheritance of legal genius. In numbers its record has been equalled and surpassed by other legal families; but in sustaining through three successive generations the highest level of erudition and the ability to apply it in practice, it can claim a pre-eminent position in the annals of English law.

Vaughan Williams was educated at Westminster School, whence he was elected to a junior studentship at Christ Church, Oxford, in 1856. He graduated with second-class honours in the school of jurisprudence and modern history in 1860. He then proceeded to read in chambers with Mr. Dodgson, the special pleader, and was called to the bar by Lincoln's Inn in 1864, joining the South Eastern circuit. In 1870 he published *The Law and Practice of Bankruptcy*, a work which reached its thirteenth edition in 1925 and is still the standard authority on the subject. He eventually obtained a large common law practice; but his reputation at the bar was one of learning rather than of advocacy, and it was not until 1889, when he was over fifty, that he became a Queen's counsel. He practised within the bar for less than a year; for in 1890, on the death of Sir Henry Manisty, Lord Halsbury, for whom, when solicitor-general, Vaughan Williams had acted as 'devil', appointed him to be a judge of the Queen's bench division. In 1891 the bankruptcy jurisdiction of the High Court was assigned to him; and during the next seven years he rendered conspicuous service in applying from the bench his wide experience to the problems of bankruptcy and liquidation, subjects in which the law was then still in a stage of development. Amongst the few *causes célèbres* that came before him was that of the New Zealand Loan and Mercantile Agency, of which Anthony John Mundella [q.v.], president of the Board of Trade, was a director. The case was one with political complications of peculiar difficulty, and Vaughan Williams conducted it with rigid independence and impartiality (1894).

In 1897, upon the resignation of Lord Justice Lopes (Baron Ludlow), Vaughan Williams was promoted to be a lord justice of appeal, with the dignity of a privy councillor, and he sat as a member of the Court of Appeal for no less than seventeen years. During this long period of service he was naturally called upon to deal with every kind of civil litigation; and, apart from the common law and bankruptcy, upon which he was clearly a recognized authority, he showed a thorough grasp of such subjects as local government and revenue law; while for several years it fell to his lot to preside over and to give the leading judgment in the equity side of the court. The work of an appellate court is not of a nature that attracts the notice of the public; and it would be too long a task to attempt to enumerate all the decisions of importance and interest to the profession in which he took part.

Vaughan Williams's judgments have met with the criticism that his mind was too subtle, too prone to be side-tracked by logical niceties and to allow the main issue to be obscured by a minor point. But he was never guilty of the much commoner judicial fault of failing to get to the bottom of a difficult case. His investigation of every problem was attentive and essentially thorough; and this fact, together with his old-world courtesy to counsel, helped to make him one of the most popular judges of his time. By ancestry and by training he was imbued with the best traditions of the bench; and, without ever lapsing into pedantry, he maintained throughout his long career the high standard of accuracy and refinement of the old common law judges at a time when there was some danger of the relaxation of their old and well-tried principles at the hands of a generation of lawyers less thorough in their methods. Even in his personal appearance, Vaughan Williams, on the bench, looked a strikingly picturesque survival from a bygone age.

Almost the only occasion upon which Vaughan Williams undertook external work was in connexion with the royal commission on the disestablishment of the Welsh Church, of which he was appointed chairman in 1906. This was a difficult rôle in view of the contentious nature of the subject under inquiry, but he handled the commission effectively and with a complete freedom from political bias; and the quick solution of the difficulties attending Welsh disestablishment and disendowment may largely be attributed to him. He retired from the bench in 1914, and died 8 December 1916 at High Ashes Farm, Abinger, near Dorking, where he had spent his leisure time in farming and other country pursuits during the whole of his professional career.

Vaughan Williams married in 1865 Laura Susanna, daughter of Edmund Lomax, of Netley, Shere, Surrey, and their mutual devotion was proverbial in legal circles of that generation. His eldest son, Roland Edmund Lomax, became King's counsel in 1913, and was appointed recorder of Carmarthen in 1919 and of Swansea in 1923; he was also British representative on the Anglo-German Mixed Arbitral Tribunal under the Treaty of Versailles (1920). Two other sons died in childhood.

A portrait of Vaughan Williams by Robert Brough is in the possession of his elder daughter, Mrs. W. T. Barkworth.

[Private information.] P. A. L.

WILSON, Sir ARTHUR KNYVET, third baronet (1842–1921), admiral of the fleet, the third son of Rear-Admiral George Knyvet Wilson, by his wife, Agnes Mary, younger daughter of the Rev. William Yonge, vicar of Swaffham, Norfolk, was born at Swaffham 4 March 1842. He entered the navy in 1855, and was twice employed on active service as a midshipman. On the first occasion he served in the *Algiers* in the Black Sea during the Crimean War, and on the second he assisted at the capture of the Peiho forts in 1858, and marched on Canton with the naval brigade. After his promotion to lieutenant, he was invited by the Japanese government to take up a post as instructor to the Yedo naval college; so that the Japanese navy may thus be said to have received its first lessons from one of the greatest naval commanders of the nineteenth century. In 1870 he was made junior member of the committee appointed to inquire into the capacity of the Whitehead torpedo. Six years later the Admiralty decided to create a special course of training in torpedo work; and Commander Wilson was placed in charge of the instructional staff in the *Vernon* at Portsmouth, where the school had been installed. It was an employment well suited to his genius: during the three years for which he held it he invented the aiming apparatus of the new weapon, and worked out a system of submarine mining and countermining adapted to naval needs.

In 1882 Wilson commanded the *Hecla* at the bombardment of Alexandria, and took an active part in the subsequent operations; the armoured train, and the mounting of a 40-pounder gun on a railway truck, both of which were improvised for the defence of the town, were due to him. Two years later, whilst still commanding the *Hecla*, he landed at Trinkitat with the force sent to relieve Tokar, and earned the Victoria cross for great gallantry at the second battle of El Teb (29 February 1884). In 1889 he was appointed to command the *Vernon*. Once again his specialized studies were productive; for it was during this period of his career that he devised the submerged torpedo tube, the double-barrelled tube for torpedo craft, and an instrument which enabled a torpedo to shear its way through protective wire nets.

Wilson was promoted rear-admiral in 1895, and vice-admiral in 1901, when he was given command of the Channel squadron, after serving for four years at the Admiralty as controller of the navy and third sea lord. At this date the first line battleships of the fleet incorporated the improvements and inventions of an entire generation; but construction had outpaced other branches of naval science. Battle tactics in particular were in an elementary state; and naval commanders of the day were still very vague about the principles which ought to govern the employment of ships in action. Admiral Wilson spent the remainder of his active career in elaborating a tactical system which was, in the main, adopted by his successors. To give one example: the formation from which a fleet can best deploy for battle is one of the most arduous problems in tactics. As rules were slowly elaborated for the scientific and calculated manœuvring of fleets, the question came into great prominence, and was much discussed. Opinion was, however, sharply divided as to the best solution. On the one side a group of fleet commanders maintained that a squadron should approach its adversary in a single line, and that it should engage by altering course to the direction in which the battle has to be fought out. The other party were convinced that a fleet formed in columns, from which it can deploy into a single line, had every chance of getting a decisive tactical advantage in the first stages of a battle, if its opponent followed the other practice. Admiral Wilson's success in the manœuvres of 1901 showed that the second opinion was right; and thenceforward it became the rule in the British service. In Germany the opposite doctrine prevailed; and when Admiral Jellicoe outmanœuvred his adversary between 6 and 7 p.m. on 31 May 1916 he was simply applying the tactical principles which Wilson had established. As a fleet commander Wilson had no equal. Between 1901 and 1907, when he commanded the Channel and Home fleets, his manner of handling masses of ships during fog, and his skill in manœuvring in narrow waters, set up a standard of seamanship which has admittedly never been surpassed. In 1907 he was made an admiral of the fleet by special order in council, and in January 1910 was appointed first sea lord of the Admiralty. He held the office for two years; and then went into retirement. The immediate reason for his withdrawal was the difference of opinion which existed between him and the first lord, Mr. Winston Churchill, on several important questions of administration and policy. Admiral Wilson was supported by the majority of the sea lords, and Mr. Churchill saw clearly that he would not be able to carry through the measures which he wished to introduce without a new board.

When Lord Fisher [q.v.] was summoned to the Admiralty in October 1914 Mr. Churchill invited Admiral Wilson to return to the Admiralty to help the first sea lord. The answer he gave was typical of his disinterestedness and elevation of mind. He would come, he said, so long as he was not given an official post or a salary. The country was thus given the services of the greatest seaman of his day as a sort of anonymous gift. He preferred that it should be so; and worked on in seclusion until June 1918. The order of merit was conferred upon him in 1912, but he was careless of formal honours, and resolutely declined a peerage on retirement. In 1919 he succeeded to the baronetcy, on the death of his brother, Sir Roland Knyvet Wilson. On 25 May 1921 he died at Swaffham after a short illness. He was unmarried.

[Admiral Sir E. E. Bradford, *Life of Admiral of the Fleet Sir Arthur Knyvet Wilson*, 1923; private information.] A. C. B.

WILSON, Sir CHARLES RIVERS (1831–1916), civil servant and financier, was born in London 19 February 1831, the eldest son of Melvil Wilson, of independent means, by his wife, Louise, daughter of Major-General Sir Benjamin Stephenson. He passed through Eton to Balliol College, Oxford, and graduated B.A. in 1853. Three years later he entered the Treasury, and was appointed private secretary to James Wilson [q.v.], the financial secretary. From 1869 to 1874 he performed the same function for Robert Lowe (afterwards Viscount Sherbrooke, q.v.), while Lowe was Gladstone's unpopular chancellor of the exchequer. Promotion came at the end of this administration, and Rivers Wilson was appointed comptroller-general of the National Debt Office (1874). This post brought him into touch with the critical position of Egyptian finance; and when, a year later, Disraeli's purchase of the khedive's shares in the Suez Canal made its prosperity of primary importance to Great Britain, Rivers Wilson was deputed by the British government to serve on the council of the Canal company, while retaining his comptroller-generalship.

The experience which he acquired in this capacity, and during a short mission to Cairo in 1876, marked him out as the natural representative of Great Britain when Egypt's default of payment in that year led Great Britain and France to agree upon a joint investigation of khedivial revenue and expenditure. This was delayed for some time by the obstructive tactics of Khedive Ismail; but on 4 April 1878 a commission was appointed, of which M. de Lesseps was president, and Rivers Wilson, in the capacity of vice-president, the effective head. A first report (rendered in August) not only prescribed drastic financial reforms, but also recommended limitations of the khedive's absolutism. On 23 August Ismail summoned Rivers Wilson to hear his acceptance of the report, and a few days later authorized Nubar Pasha to form a ministry in which Wilson should take the portfolio of finance—the first foreigner to hold a cabinet position under a khedive. Wilson went home to negotiate a loan upon the hypothecated khedivial estates, and did not take up office in Cairo until nearly the end of November. The ministry was destined to brief life. Though supported by the powers, it was barely tolerated by Ismail, who avenged his restriction to a constitutional position by declining responsibility for the extrication of his country from the financial straits to which his own extortions, and a recent low Nile, had condemned it. In view of his attitude, Wilson agreed with Nubar that the doctrine of ministerial responsibility should be logically enforced by the exclusion of the khedive from the deliberations of his council. In this policy Wilson undoubtedly was influenced by Nubar, for whom he had much respect and affection. Within three months it became clear that an irresponsible khedive of Ismail's prestige and power could nullify any measures taken by a ministry without his previous advice. Proof was offered by the military mutiny in February 1879, when Nubar and Wilson were dragged out of a carriage, hustled violently into the ministry of finance, and held there, the animus of the crowd being directed against Nubar, and only against Wilson when he stood by his colleague. The ministers were rescued by Ismail in person, and on the following morning Nubar resigned. The finance minister, however, and the minister for public works, M. de Blignières, carried on under Sherif Pasha, Wilson stout-heartedly refusing to find money for the mutineers till it could be procured by loan at a reasonable rate. But his position was rapidly becoming untenable. His views about restricting the khedive's share in government had not only exasperated Ismail, but caused difficulties with the British political representative, (Sir) Hussey Vivian; and when he proposed a plan for dealing with the April coupon by postponement, the khedive appealed confidently to his other ministers, the chamber, and the country against an act of insolvency. The end came on the eve of the publication of the final report of the commission of inquiry, which, it was known, would declare Egypt bankrupt. Both European ministers were dismissed by Ismail on 7 April. During the following twelve months, which saw the deposition of Ismail and the establishment of Tewfik as a constitutional president of his council, Wilson performed no function in Egypt. But he was recalled from his London office in April 1880 to be president of the international commission of liquidation, which was to formulate a scheme for the regular payment of the Egyptian coupon. After much division of opinion about the shares of the revenue to be allotted respectively to the bondholders and to the Egyptian administration, the commission made recommendations which the khedive accepted in July; but it never reported formally for fear of exposing its lack of accord; and the general effect of its activities was to starve the Egyptian administration and to embitter national feeling.

Wilson then left for London and was rewarded with a K.C.M.G. Except that he continued till 1896 to serve on the council of the Suez Canal (to which he did good service by negotiating, in 1884, the addition of seven representatives of British mercantile interests) he passed for good from Egypt. He had occupied a conspicuous position there, and proved himself a master of the technicalities of finance; but Lord Cromer, who worked under and with him, has qualified his warm appreciation of Wilson's ability and quickness of intelligence with words implying that he lacked political sense, and adaptability to conditions different from those with which the normal Treasury official has to deal. He had regarded Egypt from the single point of view of international finance; and, since that aspect was to become ever less important in the years to come, he left little mark on the country and cannot be called one of its makers.

After representing Great Britain at the Brussels monetary conference in 1892, he resigned his comptroller-generalship in 1894, and two years later also his seat on the Suez Canal council. His first wife, Caroline, daughter of Mr. R. Cook, whom he married in 1860, had died in 1888, and he married secondly, in 1895, the Hon. Beatrice Mostyn, sister of the seventh Baron Vaux, of Harrowden. He had no children by either marriage.

Wilson now put his expert knowledge at the service of industrial finance, becoming in 1895 president of the Grand Trunk Railway of Canada, and subsequently accepting office on the boards of the Grand Trunk Pacific Railway, the Rand Control electric works, and the Alliance assurance company. Failing health led in 1909 to his retirement from active service on these boards and from the chair of the Grand Trunk Railway. His tenure of the last had been marked by important developments of the system, notably by the construction of the great Victoria tubular bridge at Montreal, and the replacement of the Niagara suspension bridge by a single span double track. Wilson had to conduct the negotiations with the Canadian government which resulted in the formation of the Grand Trunk Pacific Company in 1903 and the construction of the western part of the transcontinental line to a Pacific terminus at Prince Rupert. He lived in his later years in Berkeley Square and had a country place at Chertsey; and it was at the former that he died 9 February 1916, being within a few days of completing his eighty-fifth year.

[Personal knowledge.] D. G. H.

WILSON, EDWARD ADRIAN (1872–1912), naturalist and Antarctic explorer, was born at Cheltenham 23 July 1872, the second son and fifth child of Edward Thomas Wilson, M.B., consulting physician to the Cheltenham General Hospital, by his wife, Mary Agnes, daughter of Bernhard Whishaw, of Hadleigh, Suffolk. After his early education at Cheltenham College he entered Gonville and Caius College, Cambridge, in 1891. He was chiefly interested in zoology, which he read for the natural science tripos, taking his B.A. degree in 1894. Later he went to St. George's Hospital, London, to study medicine. During his residence in London his wide human sympathies found outlet in strenuous work at the Caius College mission in Battersea. A breakdown in health compelled him to go abroad for some time, but after making a complete recovery he returned to his medical studies and qualified M.B., B.C. (Cambridge) in 1900.

In the same year Wilson applied for a post on the National Antarctic expedition under Commander Robert Falcon Scott, R.N. [q.v.], and was appointed junior surgeon with special work in vertebrate zoology. The *Discovery* left England in August 1901 and spent over two years in the Ross Sea, being frozen into McMurdo Sound from February 1902 to February 1904. Owing to the customary good health on modern polar expeditions Wilson's medical duties were light, and he was able to devote his time to zoological research and to the preparation of many striking paintings of Antarctic scenery. His researches into the habits and breeding of Emperor penguins were of special importance. In the summer of 1901–1902 Wilson took part with Commander R. F. Scott and (Sir) Ernest Henry Shackleton in the southward sledge journey over the ice barrier to lat. 82° 16′ 33″ S. Cape Wilson, on the edge of the plateau, marks the highest latitude reached. Symptoms of scurvy and the breakdown of Shackleton made the return journey difficult. After the return of the expedition to England, Wilson prepared the monograph on the mammals and birds observed and collected. In 1905 he served on the royal commission on grouse disease, and he was the author of various papers in the published report. He also prepared many of the illustrations for G. E. H. Barrett-Hamilton's *History of British Mammals* (1910).

In 1910 Scott invited Wilson to join his new Antarctic expedition in the *Terra Nova* as chief of the scientific staff. The value of the detailed exploration and researches in Victoria Land made by this expedition were overshadowed by the loss of the entire party of five on the return journey from the Pole (February–March 1912). From the expedition's base at Cape Evans, Wilson, with Apsley Cherry-Garrard and Lieutenant H. R. Bowers, R.I.M., made a remarkable five weeks' journey (June to August 1911) to Cape Crozier and back in mid-winter darkness, fierce blizzards, and temperatures as low as −70° F., in order to obtain chicks of the Emperor penguin. The journey was a great test of endurance and proved Wilson's perfect fitness. The journey to the Pole began 1 November 1911. After the last supporting party returned, from lat. 86° 32′ S., Scott had with him Wilson, Captain Lawrence Edward Grace Oates [q.v.], Lieutenant Bowers, and Petty Officer Edgar Evans. The Pole was reached 18 January 1912. On the return journey the party was delayed by difficult surface conditions, strong winds, and low temperatures. Evans died 17 February, and Oates heroically sacrificed himself when he saw that his weak condition impeded his comrades' progress; but eventually, overcome by bad weather and lack of food, Scott, Wilson, and Bowers perished on or about 29 March in lat. 79° 40′ S. The bodies were found in the following November by a search-party from the base, and buried beneath a cairn of snow, surmounted by a cross. Scott's diaries speak in terms of warm praise of Wilson's courage and steadfastness in the face of all difficulties: he was one of the most valued and best loved members of the expedition.

Wilson received the Polar medal (1904) and posthumously (1913) the Patron's medal of the Royal Geographical Society. Some of his paintings are in the house of the Royal Geographical Society. A statue of him, the work of Lady Scott, stands on the Promenade, Cheltenham.

Wilson married in 1901 Oriana Fanny, daughter of the Rev. Francis Abraham Souper, of Bedford, and had no children.

[R. F. Scott, *The Voyage of the Discovery*, 1905; *Scott's Last Expedition*, ed. L. Huxley, 1913; A. Cherry-Garrard, *The Worst Journey in the World*, 1922; *British Medical Journal*, 22 February 1913; *Geographical Journal*, March and April 1913; private information.]

R. N. R. B.

WILSON, JOHN COOK (1849–1915), philosopher, the only son of the Rev. James Wilson, a Methodist minister, by his wife, Hannah, daughter of John Cook, of Newcastle-under-Lyme, was born at Nottingham 6 June 1849. Educated at Derby grammar school and Balliol College, Oxford, where he obtained first classes in classics and mathematics, both in moderations and the final examinations, he was elected to a fellowship at Oriel College in 1874; he also won the Chancellor's Latin essay prize in 1873, and the Conington prize in 1882. After holding a tutorship at Oriel he was elected Wykeham professor of logic in 1889, and retained the chair until his death. He resided continuously in Oxford, except for a brief period of study in Germany, where he came strongly under the influence of Hermann Lotze, and met his future wife, Charlotte, daughter of A. D. Schneider, of Gifhorn, Hanover, whom he married in 1876. There was one son of the marriage. Mrs. Wilson's health failed for many years, and the burden thus thrown upon him materially hampered his academic activities and in the end wore him out. He died at Oxford 11 August 1915.

He was singularly human—appreciative of the simpler pleasures, generous, warm-tempered but easily appeased, and resentful of anything which he thought unjust. Unselfish, affectionate, and loyal almost to a fault, he had a great capacity for friendship with people of all ages and many different kinds.

Cook Wilson's equipment as a philosopher was such as only one or two in a generation can attain. He was at once a good mathematician and a good scholar. An intensive study in his earlier years of the great philosophers, and especially of Plato and Aristotle, gave him an unrivalled background for his own inquiries. He had a great feeling for facts. His mind was independent, cautious, and intensely critical. Thus equipped, he seemed one of the few capable of doing philosophical work of that rare kind which does not need to be done over again. Yet he published little beyond a number of papers on the text, interpretation, and doctrine of Plato and Aristotle. This failure, which to his friends seemed tragic, was due largely to his wife's ill-health. But there were other causes. The multiplicity of his interests was a continual source of distraction. A chance statement to which he objected would set him researching, and once this process had begun, no one could say when it would stop, for, to him, all critical problems were equally fascinating. He had a passion for detail, and his hatred of error in any form constrained him to deal faithfully with any statement which he considered erroneous. Again, a sense of the pitfalls to which philosophers are exposed steadily grew on him. He considered writing on philosophy, when young, mere presumption, and cleverness a snare. He dreaded, too, the petrifying effect of publication. Moreover when, as he said, he began to think things out again from the beginning, he found himself led in a direction very different from the idealist views of those whom he regarded as his main teachers, Thomas Hill Green [q.v.] and Lotze, and this made him increasingly anxious to avoid committing himself, until he felt sure not only of the truth, but of his ability to state it in a form which would compel conviction. It was not surprising, therefore, that he threw his energies mainly into teaching, as the best means of developing his own thought. He was not, indeed, a prophet with a gospel—unless the conviction that above all things a man must not let himself be put off with shams gives a right to the title. His lectures, too, though not unrelieved by humour, were apt to seem abstract and rather dry. But his real powers stood out in informal discussions. There he cast aside reserve, and his audience could watch his mind at work. His acuteness seemed a revelation, and there was infection in his conviction that the truth was a matter of high importance.

He was certainly the strongest philosophical influence in Oxford of his generation. He influenced his fellow-teachers, to whom he was an unfailing source of help and inspiration, quite as much as his pupils; and in his later years most of his colleagues had been his pupils and looked up to him as a kind of master.

The starting-point of Cook Wilson's views lay in his unwavering conviction of the truth of mathematics. In mathematics we *know*. Hence the scepticism inherent in the philosophy of those who follow the metageometricians was wholly alien to him. So also was the position represented in F. H. Bradley's *Appearance and Reality* (1893). Reflection on our experience, he held, doubtless gives rise to puzzles in plenty, but where contradictions are alleged to be involved in our fundamental notions of the world, the cause lies in some fallacy, usually simple and often merely verbal, in which we have been involved. Not unfairly the first principle of his philosophy may be described as the principle that there is no first principle—that, in Aristotle's words, there are *ἴδιαι ἀρχαί*. He never tired of insisting on the impossibility of general criteria, whether of knowledge, of beauty, or of morality. The key to particular problems lay in consideration of their particular subject-matter. Yet the knowability of single facts by themselves, and the existence of irresolvable differences, were compatible with the unity of reality; they only showed that reality had not that unity which some philosophers expected it to have. Further, as he came more and more to maintain, much that is ultimate in our experience is in itself intelligible to us, and our difficulties about such realities only arise because we treat them as if they were, or try to express them in terms of, or to explain them by, something else. In particular he became convinced that this was true of knowledge itself, and that for that reason the teaching of the idealists, which for long he had accepted, was based on a fallacy.

In giving his lectures on logic—which formed the nearest approach to a systematic expression of his philosophy—Cook Wilson found himself driven from time to time to subject portions of them to drastic modification. Gradually a general doctrine seemed to be emerging which involved a greater break with tradition than was consistent with his lectures, even in their latest form; and for his friends the dominant feeling awakened by the posthumous publication of these lectures must be regret that he was not given ten more years of health and strength in which to work out his thought to the full. Unfortunately it was only towards the close of his life that he really seemed to find himself, and then it was too late.

[Notice in *Proceedings* of the British Academy, vol. vii, 1916; personal knowledge. See also *Statement and Inference. With other Philosophical Papers by John Cook Wilson*, edited by A. S. L. Farquharson, 2 vols., 1926.]

H. A. P.

WOLFE-BARRY, SIR JOHN WOLFE (1836–1918), civil engineer, was the youngest son of Sir Charles Barry [q.v.], the architect of the Houses of Parliament. He assumed the additional surname of Wolfe in 1898. He was born in London 7 December 1836, and educated at Trinity College, Glenalmond, and King's College, London. He then became a pupil of Sir John Hawkshaw [q.v.], under whom he subsequently acted as assistant resident engineer for the railway bridges and stations at Charing Cross and Cannon Street, London. In 1867 he began a long and disguished career as a consulting civil engineer; for many years before his death his wide experience, sound judgement, and untiring energy made him the leader of his profession in Great Britain. He was created K.C.B. in 1897.

Only a brief account can be given here of the principal works for which he and his firm were responsible. He was engineer for the Earl's Court station, and for the extension of the District Railway to Ealing; also, with Sir John Hawkshaw, for the completion of the Inner Circle Railway to Aldgate and Whitechapel, a work involving great technical difficulties. In 1899 he persuaded the metropolitan companies to experiment with electric traction, and the results were so satisfactory that electric traction is now widely adopted. He was engineer of the Blackfriars arched bridge, and of the King Edward VII bridge at Kew. In association with Sir Horace Jones [q.v.] he constructed the Tower bridge, completed in 1894, with a bascule opening span. The ponderous bascules had to be erected in a vertical position so that navigation should not be arrested. To prevent delay to foot passengers when the bascules were raised, a special high-level foot-bridge was provided, but the opening and closing of the span takes so short a time that the footway is no longer used. Wolfe-Barry was almost continuously occupied from 1885 with the construction of the Barry docks and railway in South Wales, and with other similar undertakings, including the Alexandra dock, Newport, the lock entrance, dock, and graving dock at Immingham, near Grimsby, and the extensions of the Surrey commercial docks (1895–1906). With Sir Benjamin Baker [q.v.] and Mr. Hurtzig he was engineer for the Avonmouth docks, near Bristol, completed in 1908.

Wolfe-Barry acted as consulting engineer to many railways and public undertakings, and was a member of many royal commissions, including the Port of London Commission. He was one of the three members of the court of arbitration which arranged, under the terms of the Metropolitan Water Act (1902), the purchase of the eight London water companies. From 1892 to 1906 he was one of the two representatives of the British government on the International Suez Canal Commission. He was specially interested in the problems of town traffic, served on the royal commission on London traffic (1903–1905), and expressed his views on the subject in two addresses delivered to the Society of Arts (1899). He contributed a paper to the Institution of Civil Engineers in 1868 on the city terminus of the Charing Cross Railway, and, with Sir Benjamin Baker, one on the metropolitan railways in 1895. His other publications were *Railway Appliances* (1874–1892), *Lectures on Railways and Locomotives*, 1882, *The Tower Bridge*, 1894.

Not the least important of Wolfe-Barry's services was the part which he took in founding (1901–1902) the Engineering Standards Committee, now the British Engineering Standards Association. Of this body he remained the chairman till his death. He saw that, as the adoption of standards must be voluntary, it was necessary to co-operate, in formulating them, with the great technical societies, with representatives of the manufacturers and the consumers, with the spending departments of the government, and with public companies and registration societies. The great advantage of the standardizing policy is that it cheapens and simplifies the process of manufacture and renders mass production possible. To give only two examples of the economies which have been effected: it has been found possible to reduce the number of patterns of tramway-rail from seventy to nine, and one uniform specification for Portland cement has been found to combine the best qualities of the many different specifications formerly in use. The principle of standardization has been extended to almost every class of engineering production, and the example of Great Britain in this respect is now being followed by other countries.

Wolfe-Barry had many interests and activities outside his professional work. He was much interested in technical and scientific education. He was chairman of the City and Guilds of London Institute for promoting technical education, and afterwards on the governing body of the Imperial College of Science and Technology, in which the Central Engineering College of the Guilds of London has been merged. He was on the senate of the university of London, and took a prominent part in the establishment of the National Physical Laboratory. He took a deep interest in the Institution of Civil Engineers, of which he was a member for fifty-four years; he sat on its council for forty years, and held the office of president for two years; it was at his instance that an examination test was prescribed for candidates for membership.

Wolfe-Barry married in 1874 Rosalind Grace, youngest daughter of the Rev. Evan Edward Rowsell, rector of Hambledon, Surrey, by whom he had four sons and three daughters. He died at Chelsea 22 January 1918.

Wolfe-Barry's portrait was painted by Sir Hubert von Herkomer in 1900.

[*Proceedings* of the Royal Society, vol. xciv, A, 1917–1918; *Engineering*, 25 January 1918.]

W. C. U.

WOLSELEY, GARNET JOSEPH, first VISCOUNT WOLSELEY (1833–1913), field-marshal, the eldest son of Major Garnet Joseph Wolseley, 25th Borderers, by his wife, Frances Anne, daughter of William Smith, of Golden Bridge House, co. Dublin, was born at Golden Bridge House 4 June 1833. His family, a junior branch of the Staffordshire Wolseleys, had obtained land in county Carlow under William III. Major Garnet Wolseley died when his eldest son Garnet was only seven years old, leaving a widow, four sons, and three daughters in somewhat straitened circumstances. Garnet was educated at a day school in Dublin, and at a very early age determined to be a soldier. Eager to improve his education to this end, and unable to afford special tuition, he took service in a surveyor's office in Dublin, and there acquired a sound knowledge of draughtsmanship and surveying, which knowledge was to bring him at an early stage of his career to the notice of his superior officers.

Wolseley's mother was a woman of remarkable character. Intensely religious, with a simple form of Irish Protestantism, she took the Bible as her one guide, and from her Wolseley acquired a profound belief, which lasted until his death, that his life was in God's hands. To this faith he added from the first a keen ambition to make a name for himself, while his parentage made him turn naturally to the army for a career. In after-life he said that the first business of the young officer who wishes to distinguish himself in his profession is to seek to get himself killed, and he did his best to apply that principle to himself. His faith in God's providence made him a fatalist. The resultant of this faith joined to an eager temperament and an ambitious nature was a rare degree of courage.

Wolseley received his commission as second lieutenant in the 12th Foot on 12 March 1852, and at once transferred to the 80th Foot, which was engaged in the second Burma War, in order that he might see active service. He arrived in Calcutta at the end of October 1852 to hear the guns of Fort William firing a salute on the death of the Duke of Wellington. Thus, the soldier destined to create a new phase in the history of the British army began his service just when the great leader of the régime which he was to modernize passed away. A few months later Wolseley, not yet twenty, won his first distinction by leading with judgement and gallantry an assault upon Meeah Toon's stockade, in which at the moment of victory he fell severely wounded in the left thigh. For this service he was mentioned in dispatches, was promoted lieutenant on 16 May 1853, and received the Burma War medal. He was sent home to recover from his wound, and transferred to the 90th Foot in Dublin, where, as the crisis in the Near East which culminated in the Crimean War developed, he grew more and more restless until orders arrived for his battalion to embark. When he landed in the Crimea the siege of Sebastopol was in progress, and his knowledge of surveying was soon of service. In January 1855 he was appointed an assistant engineer and served in that capacity in the trenches, becoming, owing to a run of promotion, captain at the age of twenty-one. In the trenches he first met Charles George Gordon [q.v.], the common bond of religion drawing the two men together and cementing a close friendship which was to last till Gordon's death. In June 1855 he distinguished himself greatly in the attack on the Quarries, in which he was slightly wounded, the success of the operation being in a great measure due to his personal example and initiative. On 30 August, a few days before the fall of Sebastopol, he was severely wounded by a shell, losing the sight of one eye. On recovery he was appointed to the quartermaster-general's staff and remained with it till the end of the War. For his services he was recommended for a brevet majority, which he could not receive till he had completed (24 March 1858) six years' service. Returning home from the Crimea he was for a short time with the 90th at Aldershot. Then orders came for the battalion to go to China, where risings were threatening the security both of Shanghai and Hong Kong. On its way to the Far East the transport was wrecked, and, owing to the mutiny of the Bengal army, a second vessel took the three companies of the 90th, with which Wolseley travelled, from Chinese waters to Calcutta, where they were landed in 1857. In November of that year he took part in Sir Colin Campbell's first relief of Lucknow, and so distinguished himself in the leading of his company that with it he accomplished what Sir Colin had planned to be undertaken the next day by his pet regiment, the 93rd Highlanders. After the withdrawal from Lucknow, the 90th was shut up with Sir James Outram in the Alumbagh until Sir Colin was able to return on 5 February 1858 for the final capture of Lucknow. This achieved, Wolseley was appointed by Sir Colin quartermaster-general on Sir Hope Grant's staff, and served throughout the campaign of Oudh. He was mentioned five times in dispatches, and at the end of the Mutiny was promoted brevet lieutenant-colonel at the age of twenty-five.

Hardly was the Mutiny over before Wolseley was sent to China, still on Sir Hope Grant's staff, for the campaign which the war in India had postponed. Reaching China in April 1860, he took part in the capture of the Taku Forts and of the Summer Palace at Pekin. During the looting of the treasures of the palace he was observed looking sadly upon a scene which he was powerless to stop, and he paid for such few treasures as he could afford to buy, a very real piece of self-denial to a man with great natural taste for works of art, of which as soon as he had any money he became an ardent and judicious collector. Throughout his life he was strongly opposed to looting, which he regarded as immoral and injurious to discipline, and on the first occasion when he had authority, at the capture of Kumassi (1874), he insisted on King Koffee's treasure being regularly valued and systematically sold. The close of the China campaign, at the end of which he was awarded a substantive majority, marks the end of the first period of Wolseley's career. With less than eight years' service he was a brevet lieutenant-colonel, he had distinguished himself in four campaigns, each very different in character, he had established a reputation for personal courage, cool leading and judgement in action, and had proved himself to be a staff officer of ability. He was marked out as a coming man. But his experiences had done more for him than the laying of the foundation of a successful career. They had taught him to respect profoundly the fighting quality of the British soldier, but also they had taught him the grave defects of organization and training from which the British army suffered. In the Crimean winter and the Indian summer he had marked the suffering and want of efficiency due to lack of preparation and organization. He had noted the evils of a long-service system which provided no reserves to fill the losses due to battle and disease, the weakness of the purchase system, and the lack of inducements to officers to study their profession. He left China resolved to devote himself to the remedying of these evils.

After his four campaigns he was entitled to a period of long leave, which he occupied partly in the writing of his first book, *Narrative of the War with China in 1860* (1862), partly in sketching and painting, in which he had considerable skill, and partly in hunting in Ireland, and it was while enjoying this sport that he was suddenly in 1861 ordered to Canada as assistant quartermaster-general. The American Civil War was then in progress, and the *Trent* incident had decided the British government to increase the forces in Canada. During his period of staff service there he had opportunities of testing his theories of military organization and training, and also of increasing his experience of war by a visit to the United States while the Civil War was in progress.

During that visit Wolseley met Robert Lee and 'Stonewall' Jackson, of whose character, generalship, and ability he expressed unbounded admiration in a vivid article on the War which he wrote for *Blackwood's Magazine* in 1863. The Canadian service also gave him more leisure than his campaigns had allowed him for serious study, particularly of military history. In June 1865 he was promoted full colonel, and not long afterwards was made deputy quartermaster-general in Canada. Two years later, during a period of leave, he married Louisa, daughter of Mr. Alexander Erskine; and since he was a man capable of great devotion and very responsive to all that is best in woman's influence, his wife filled during the remainder of his life the place in his mind which his mother had occupied. How large that place was and how much Lady Wolseley's keen wit and shrewd observation influenced and aided her husband are shown in *The Letters of Lord and Lady Wolseley, 1870–1911*, edited by Sir George Arthur (1922).

In 1869 Wolseley increased his reputation by publishing *The Soldier's Pocket Book*, a manual of military organization and tactics, the keynote of which is preparation for war in time of peace. At that time the official manuals and regulations were almost solely concerned with peacetime drill and administration, and Wolseley's book, which ran through many editions, was the forerunner of the modern field service regulations. The next year he obtained his first chance of displaying his ability as a commander. During his period of service in Canada, the Fenians had been giving constant trouble by raids from the United States into Canada, and by their endeavours to enlist the sympathy of the French Canadians. These disturbances culminated at the end of 1869 in the rebellion of Louis Riel [q.v.], the direct cause of which was the transfer of the Hudson Bay Territory to the Canadian government. Riel proclaimed a republic of the North West and established himself at Fort Garry. It was necessary to send an expedition, known as the Red River expedition (August–September 1870) against him, and Wolseley was chosen to command it. The problem was chiefly one of organization, and consisted in transporting a little force of 1,200 men with all their stores some 600 miles from Lake Superior to Fort Garry mainly by river. For this Wolseley relied largely on the services of the Canadian voyageurs, and he was completely successful, receiving the K.C.M.G. and C.B. for his services. In May 1871 he was brought home to the War Office as assistant adjutant-general, and was from the first an ardent supporter of the reforms which Mr. (afterwards Viscount) Cardwell [q.v.], then secretary of state for war, was inaugurating. He became the military leader of the reformers and was deeply involved in the fierce struggle which resulted in the establishment of short service, the creation of an army reserve, the abolition of purchase, and the amalgamation of the regular army, auxiliary forces, and reserve under the commander-in-chief.

While this struggle was still in progress, the outrages of King Koffee of Ashanti brought about the first Ashanti War, (1873–1874) and Wolseley was sent out in command of the expedition. He took with him a band of men most of whom were to serve with him for the remainder of his career. This band, which became known as the 'Wolseley ring', was the target of much unreasoning jealousy. He had made a practice of noting down the names of soldiers of ability and character, who were keen students of their profession, wherever he met them, and these were the only passports to his favour. The men whom he selected were little known even in the army at the time when he chose them, and included those known later as Sir Evelyn Wood, Sir Henry Brackenbury, Sir Redvers Buller, Sir George Pomeroy Colley, Sir William Butler, and Sir Frederick Maurice. The last of these he picked out for the sole reason that he (Maurice) had beaten him in a competition for a prize offered by the second Duke of Wellington for an essay on the lessons of the Franco-Prussian War. Wolseley's essay, entitled *Field Manœuvres*, was published in *Essays written for the Wellington Prize* (1872). Wolseley landed at Cape Coast Castle in October 1873. The chief difficulties to be overcome were those of country and a pestilent climate. He made his plans so as to keep British troops as short a time as possible in the country. These reached him early in January 1874, and on the 21st of that month he had defeated King Koffee at Amoaful; the capital, Kumassi, was occupied four days later. For this swift success he received the thanks of parliament, was promoted major-general, created G.C.M.G. and K.C.B., and given a grant of £25,000.

These rewards may seem excessive in relation to the scope of the expedition, but Wolseley had come to be regarded by the government as a political asset. The Franco-Prussian War had opened men's eyes to the immense importance of military organization, and there were loud outcries about British unpreparedness. Strangely enough, the man who was the leader of the military reformers was used to show that all was well. Wolseley became a popular hero. 'All Sir Garnet' was the slang equivalent of the day for 'all correct', and George Grossmith [q.v.] made himself up as Wolseley to sing 'The Modern Major-General' in *The Pirates of Penzance*. After a short spell at the War Office as inspector-general of the auxiliary forces, Wolseley was sent in 1875 as administrator and general commanding to Natal, where difficulties had arisen between the colonists and the Kaffirs. He settled these difficulties with tact and judgement. On his return home he became a member of the council of India at the India Office, and in 1878 was promoted lieutenant-general. In that year Lord Beaconsfield acquired Cyprus from the Turks and sent Wolseley to take over the island and to be its first administrator. While he was there the Zulu War broke out, and after the disaster of Isandhlwana (22 January 1879) he was chosen by the government to restore the situation. Before he landed, Lord Chelmsford [q.v.] had defeated the Zulus at Ulundi (4 July), and Wolseley's military tasks consisted in the pursuit and capture of the Zulu king, Cetywayo, and the defeat of Sekukuni, a native chief who had long harried the Boers. The problem of civil administration in South Africa had few attractions for Wolseley, and he was anxious to be rid of them as soon as possible. His instructions from the government separated him from Sir Bartle Frere [q.v.], who, until his arrival, had in preparation a scheme for the federation of South Africa, with results that were not altogether happy. After establishing an administration in Zululand which was not unjustly criticized, and granting to the Transvaal the constitution of a Crown colony in accordance with the orders of the government, Wolseley returned home to the more congenial duties of quartermaster-general at the War Office.

Wolseley then entered with increased power and authority into the struggle for army reform, and for the completion of the Cardwell programme. This threw him at once into violent opposition to the second Duke of Cambridge [q.v.], then commander-in-chief. The Duke had a profound knowledge of the personnel of the army, and was very popular in the service, but he believed that drill and discipline were the chief, if not the only, means to military efficiency, and held that long service was essential to discipline. He had not the imagination to enable him to envisage the requirements of modern war, and was satisfied with troops who made a fine show on parade. Wolseley made preparation for war the first principle of his policy, and in order to further that, obtained, after a fight for each item on his programme, an extension of the intelligence department, the preparation of plans for mobilization, the completion of the territorialization of the army, the encouragement of professional study, the simplification of equipment, and a gradual development of training for field warfare. His keenness, his intense belief that he was right, his impatience of opposition, and his quick temper often caused him to make enemies unnecessarily, and placed him in an unfavourable light. The Queen and the Duke of Cambridge, though both later changed their opinions, were disposed to regard him as a pushing upstart. Lord Beaconsfield, who had a high appreciation of Wolseley's qualities, did not think that they were altogether wrong, and he wrote to the Queen in 1879: 'It is quite true that Wolseley is an egotist and a braggart. So was Nelson. . . . Men of action when eminently successful in early life are generally boastful and full of themselves. It is not limited to military and naval heroes' [Monypenny and Buckle, *Life of Disraeli*, vi, 435]. Amongst the very conservative class to which most of the officers of the army belonged, a class which he did not always trouble to conciliate, Wolseley figured as an iconoclast who cared nothing for regimental history or tradition. This was far from the truth. No man had a greater belief in the value of regimental esprit de corps, but he believed in it as a thing which made for proficiency, and not as a thing to delight nursemaids. He could get little money for his plans, and in order to provide clothing economically for the reservists on mobilization, dress had to be made uniform; he was therefore driven to abolish the cherished facings of line regiments, an innovation for which he was roundly abused. This is but one example of the kind of struggle which went on throughout Wolseley's periods of service in the War Office. He won, because all the arguments were on his side; but the struggle wore him out.

In 1882 Wolseley became adjutant-general, the official then responsible for the military training, and while in this office his campaign for reform was interrupted by his last two and most famous expeditions. In 1882 Arabi Pasha headed a rebellion of the Egyptian army, and on France's refusal to intervene, the British government took the law into its own hands and sent Wolseley to enforce it. After a futile naval bombardment of Alexandria, which Wolseley condemned, there followed a short and brilliant military campaign. Wolseley left England on 15 August, and after a feint at Alexandria, swiftly and secretly transferred his troops down the Suez Canal to Ismailia. A sharp action at Kassassin brought him before Arabi's fortified lines at Tel-el-Kebir, and these were carried on 13 September by a night attack, a more daring enterprise at that date than it sounds to-day. Arabi's force was routed, and Cairo promptly occupied. For this achievement Wolseley was promoted general, received the thanks of parliament, a grant of £30,000, and was created Baron Wolseley, of Cairo and Wolseley. Eighteen months after his return from Egypt Wolseley saw his friend Charles Gordon off to Khartoum (January 1884), and as soon as the extent of the Mahdi's rising became evident, urged upon a reluctant government the necessity for a relief expedition. He did not prevail in time, and in the Nile campaign he led what was from the first a forlorn hope. It has been said that Wolseley in his choice of the route for the advance to Khartoum was prejudiced by his experiences on the Red River, and he certainly used that experience to the fullest extent, for he had 800 special boats built and employed some 400 Canadian voyageurs in their navigation. Whether the rival school which advocated the Suakin-Berber route across the desert was right can never now be determined, but it is certain that (Lord) Kitchener [q. v.], who served under Wolseley in the Nile campaign, chose in different circumstances to follow the Nile, and that Gordon himself strongly advocated the same route. As it was, Wolseley's steamers, after the Mahdi's followers had been defeated in a number of engagements, reached Khartoum (28 January 1885) just too late, but it is at least probable that a somewhat earlier arrival would merely have hastened Gordon's death. With this expedition, for which he was created viscount, and knight of Saint Patrick, Wolseley's long series of campaigns ended, and he returned to complete his work as an army reformer.

In October 1890 he was made commander-in-chief in Ireland, an appointment which gave him opportunity for experiment in modernizing the system of military training, and at the same time left him more leisure to indulge his tastes. Though he disliked society functions, he was a delightful host and greatly enjoyed the conversation of men and women of wit, with whom he was well able to hold his own. In furnishing Kilmainham Hospital he was able to give scope to his ardour as a collector of bric-à-brac, and there too he found time both for reading and writing. He again became a fairly constant contributor to the magazines, and in 1894 wrote for the *Pall Mall Magazine* a series of articles on *The Decline and Fall of Napoleon*, which were republished in book form (1895). He also began to write a work for which he had long been collecting material—the *Life of Marlborough*. Of this he only completed two volumes (published 1894), for in 1895, on the resignation of the Duke of Cambridge, he was appointed commander-in-chief. His struggles for reform now entered upon a new phase. He had won his battle within the army, and he now became engaged in an almost continuous effort to get ministers to give him the means to make the army efficient in war. He found his powers more cramped than he had expected. One of the Duke of Cambridge's chief efforts had been to preserve the prerogative of the Crown, particularly as regards army patronage, and in this he had received the full support of Queen Victoria. Ministers, on the other hand, were anxious to make their control complete, and they had the political sagacity to see that this would be best achieved by curbing the power of the commander-in-chief and giving the secretary of state for war a number of military advisers. Thus, Wolseley found himself not supreme but *primus inter pares*, a position which added to his difficulties in preparing for the South African War, which he foresaw, and for the great European struggle which he anticipated. In those days it was difficult to get the government to spend money upon stores and preparations which made no show in time of peace. But Wolseley so far won his way that, when the South African War broke out, for the first time in our military history brigades and divisions, which had been trained as such in time of peace, were swiftly mobilized and dispatched with adequate equipment to the theatre of war. It had taken Wolseley forty years to get the lessons of the Crimean War applied. The struggle with the Boers taught the army the defects in its training, and the truth of all that Wolseley had been preaching for years. Thereafter the training and preparation which enabled Great Britain in 1914 to place in the field an incomparable expeditionary force went forward without controversy.

But the long struggle for efficiency had worn out the protagonist. Wolseley retired in 1899. In 1903 he published *The Story of a Soldier's Life*, an interesting but not very adequate account of his life down to the Ashanti expedition. Thereafter his brain began to fail rapidly, and he died at Mentone 25 March 1913, to be buried with fitting pomp in St. Paul's Cathedral. Lady Wolseley survived her husband seven years, and the title devolved by special remainder upon their only daughter.

As a commander in the field, Wolseley never endured the supreme test of war against an equal adversary, and of his generalship it is only possible to say that everything he was asked to do he did well. His real title to fame is that he recreated the British army, which had fallen into inanition and inefficiency after the Napoleonic wars. It is he who laid the foundations upon which were built up, both the expeditionary force which saved France in 1914, and the great national army which brought victory to the Allies in 1918.

A whole-length portrait of Lord Wolseley standing by his charger, painted by Albert Besnard in 1880, was presented to the National Portrait Gallery by Lady Wolseley in 1917; a bronze bust by Sir J. E. Boehm, modelled in 1883, was also given to the Gallery by Lady Wolseley in 1919. An equestrian statue for Trafalgar Square was designed by Sir W. Goscombe John in 1918.

[Viscount Wolseley, *The Story of a Soldier's Life*, 2 vols., 1903, and *Narrative of the War with China*, 1862; C. R. Low, *A Memoir of Lieutenant-General Sir Garnet Wolseley*, 2 vols., 1878; G. L. Huyshe, *The Red River Expedition*, 1871; Sir Henry Brackenbury, *Narrative of the Ashantee War*, 2 vols., 1874; J. F. Maurice, *The Military History of the Campaign of 1882 in Egypt*, 1888; H. E. Colvile, *The History of the Sudan Campaign*, 2 parts, 1890; Sir F. Maurice and Sir George Arthur, *The Life of Lord Wolseley*, 1924.] F. M.

WOOD, Sir HENRY EVELYN (1838–1919), field-marshal, the youngest son of the Rev. Sir John Page Wood, second baronet, rector of St. Peter's, Cornhill, London, and vicar of Cressing, Essex, by his wife, Caroline, youngest daughter of Admiral Sampson Michell, of Croft West, Cornwall, was born at Cressing 9 February 1838. He was sent to Marlborough College, and entered the royal navy as a midshipman in 1852. In 1854 he was in the *Queen* in the Black Sea during the Crimean War. In that war he served ashore with the naval brigade, took part in the battle of Inkermann, was in the trenches before Sebastopol, and was wounded in the assault on the Redan (18 June 1855) while acting as aide-de-camp to Captain Peel, commander of the brigade. Finding service ashore more to his taste, Wood applied to be transferred to the army and received a commission as cornet in the 13th Light Dragoons. During the Crimean War he was twice mentioned in dispatches, and on its conclusion he received the medal with two clasps, became a knight of the legion of honour and a member of the 5th class of the Medjidie, and obtained the Turkish medal—not a bad beginning for a youth of seventeen.

In 1857 Wood transferred to the 17th Lancers, and in the following year went with his regiment to India to take part in the suppression of the Mutiny. From May 1858 until October 1860 he was employed in the operations in central India, chiefly with a regiment of native cavalry which he raised and commanded. He was mentioned in dispatches for great gallantry in the action of Sindwaha (19 October 1858), and received the V.C. for routing, with ten men, a party of eighty rebels at Sindhara (29 December 1859). On becoming a captain in the 17th Lancers (April 1861) he was, after some delay, made brevet major (August 1862) for his services during the Mutiny. In 1862 he passed the entrance examination for the Staff College, but, as another officer of the 17th Lancers had passed above him and only one officer at a time could be at the college from one cavalry regiment, he transferred in October 1862 to the 73rd Foot. On passing out of the Staff College (1864) he obtained a succession of staff appointments. In 1867 he married the Hon. Mary Paulina Anne Southwell, a sister of the fourth Viscount Southwell; there were three sons and three daughters of the marriage. In 1871 Wood purchased a majority in the 90th Light Infantry, being one of the last officers to obtain promotion in this way, and in January 1873 he was promoted brevet lieutenant-colonel in consequence of his seniority as a brevet major. A few months later, when the crimes of Koffee, king of Ashanti, demanded punishment, it was decided to send an expedition under Sir Garnet (afterwards Viscount) Wolseley [q.v.] to the Gold Coast. Wolseley, in his search for officers of ability and energy, had come across Wood, and took him to Ashanti as special service officer. Wolseley desired to expose British troops for as short a time as possible to the fevers of the West coast, and the preliminary work of the campaign fell to the native levies, of whom Wood raised and commanded a regiment. At Amoaful, the chief action in the campaign, he commanded the right attack and was slightly wounded (January 1874); he was also present at the capture of the Ashanti capital, Kumassi. On the conclusion of the campaign he received the C.B. and was promoted brevet colonel. After three years on the staff at Aldershot, he went (1878) with his regiment to South Africa, where he was to make his name, already known in the army, familiar to the general public.

At that time the conflicting interests of Briton, Boer, and native had caused general unrest throughout South Africa. Wood went out with Lieutenant-General Thesiger, afterwards second Baron Chelmsford [q.v.], and their first task was the suppression of a rising of the Gaikas in the north-east of Cape Colony. In this campaign Wood commanded a column with the ability and resolution which the army had learned to expect of him. Hardly was this work completed, when the rising of the Zulus under Cetywayo took place. In the invasion of Zululand Wood was again in command of a column, which escaped the disaster of Isandhlwana (22 January 1879). This disaster to one column made the position of the others precarious, but Wood's resolution was unshaken. Having occupied with his force the Kambula Mountain he sallied out to attack the Zulus in Inhlobana (28 March), and after defeating them returned the next day to Kambula, where he beat off a determined attack. This gave Lord Chelmsford, as Thesiger had now become, time to reorganize and receive reinforcements, and a fresh invasion of Zululand ended in the complete defeat of Cetywayo's army at Ulundi (4 July). During this campaign the Prince Imperial, the only son of Napoleon III, was killed, while on a reconnaissance, in circumstances which were not creditable to the officer in charge of the party. Wood, who had a great affection for the young prince, conducted the Empress Eugénie to Zululand (1880) to see the place where her son had been killed, and so began a friendship which lasted until Wood's death. For his services in the Zulu War Wood was many times mentioned in dispatches and was created K.C.B. (1879).

After a short interval in command at Chatham, Wood was again sent to Natal early in 1881. The Boers of the Transvaal, resentful of the terms of the annexation of 1877, had revolted, and a field force under Sir George Pomeroy Colley [q.v.] was sent to Natal. Wood served as Colley's second in command, but was not present when Colley was killed and a portion of his force driven from Majuba Hill (27 February 1881). Again, as after Isandhlwana, it fell to Wood to retrieve a dangerous situation. The British troops were shaken by the death of their commander and by the losses at Majuba Hill, and Wood informed the government that he could not attack the Boers with success for some weeks. Strong feeling was expressed in England that no settlement should be concluded with the Boers until the disgrace of Majuba had been wiped out; but Mr. Gladstone's Cabinet was not disposed to subordinate peace to the restoration of military prestige, and directed Wood to open negotiations with the Boers. Wood, after pointing out to the government that he could attack the Boers successfully by the middle of March, loyally carried out his instructions, came to terms with the Boers on 21 March 1881, and was thereafter appointed one of the royal commissioners for the settlement of the Transvaal. He was attacked by the parlamentary opposition for being a party to what they termed a disgraceful surrender, but maintained stoutly that in matters of policy a soldier's duty is to carry out the orders of his government unless in his opinion the safety of his troops would be prejudiced by doing so, a question which in this instance did not arise.

On the conclusion of the work of the royal commission, Wood left for good what he termed 'the land of his fortunes', and resumed command at Chatham in February 1882. He was promoted major-general and created G.C.M.G. for his work in the Transvaal. During his command at Chatham (Sir) William Robert Robertson, who later was to succeed to Wood's baton as field-marshal, served as a lance-corporal in the 3rd Dragoons in charge of his mounted orderlies. In August 1882, on the outbreak of Arabi Pasha's rebellion in Egypt, Wood went out with Sir Garnet Wolseley in command of the 4th brigade, and had the dull but anxious task of keeping the Egyptian forces around Alexandria occupied, while Wolseley, with the main body, went down the Suez Canal to Ismailia and Tel-el-Kebir. In December 1882 he was appointed first British sirdar of the Egyptian army, which had been disbanded after the rebellion and which it was his task to recreate. This he did in a remarkably short space of time, and the foundations which he laid have endured. The greater part of the force with which (Lord) Kitchener defeated the Mahdi at Omdurman was organized in the main on the lines designed by Wood. While he was still in Egypt, General Gordon was isolated and besieged in Khartoum; and in September 1884, when Lord Wolseley came out to attempt the relief of Gordon, Wood was appointed to the command of the long and difficult line of communications.

On the conclusion of the Nile campaign, Wood came home to be appointed, first, in April 1886, to the Eastern command with head-quarters at Colchester, and later, in January 1889, to the Aldershot command. Both at Colchester and at Aldershot he was busily engaged in giving practical application to Lord Wolseley's plans for modernizing the training of the army by abolishing useless drill and ceremonies and giving much greater attention to exercises in the field. At the same time he did much to improve the conditions of the soldier's life. In 1891 he became lieutenant-general and was created G.C.B. In 1893 he went to the War Office as quarter-master-general, and was responsible for a complete reorganization of the system of transporting troops. He abolished the old transports and instead entered into contracts with the great shipping companies, not only effecting a considerable economy, but adding greatly to the comfort of the troops conveyed overseas. He also made new and more economical arrangements with the railway companies, and incidentally obtained many valued concessions for officers and men proceeding on leave. In October 1897 he became adjutant-general to the forces, and in that position was responsible for the mobilization on the outbreak of the South African War (1899–1901) and for the raising of the large number of new formations which that war required. In October 1901 he was appointed to the command of the Second Army Corps, with head-quarters at Salisbury, and was responsible for organizing that command, which had developed out of the purchase of a great part of Salisbury Plain for military training. This was Wood's last active command. He had been promoted full general in 1895, and in 1903 was created field-marshal.

Throughout his life Wood was a keen and bold rider to hounds and he hunted almost down to his death. On becoming prime warden of the Fishmongers' Company in 1893 he invited thirty-five masters of hounds to dine with the company. He was a regular contributor to the military magazines, and published, among other books, *The Crimea in 1854 and in 1894* (1895), *Cavalry in the Waterloo Campaign* (1896), *Achievements of Cavalry* (1897), and *From Midshipman to Field-Marshal* (1906). He died 2 December 1919 at Harlow, Essex.

There is a portrait by W. W. Ouless in the hall of the Fishmongers' Company (*Royal Academy Pictures*, 1906).

[*From Midshipman to Field-Marshal*, 1906; J. Morley, *Life of W. E. Gladstone*, 1903; D. Moodie, *History of the Battles and Adventures of the British, Boers, and Zulus in South Africa to 1880*, Cape Town, 1888.] F. M.

WOODGATE, WALTER BRADFORD (1840–1920), oarsman, was born at Belbroughton rectory, Worcestershire, 20 September 1840, the eldest son of the Rev. Henry Arthur Woodgate, rector of Belbroughton and canon of Worcester, by his wife, Maria Bradford. His younger brother was Major-General Sir Edward Woodgate [q.v.]. He entered Radley College in 1850, matriculated at Brasenose College, Oxford, as a scholar in 1859, graduated in 1863, and was called to the bar (Inner Temple) in 1872. For more than half a century Woodgate was the outstanding figure on the upper Thames. He rowed his first race in 1858 for Radley against Eton over the Henley course; he rowed his last race at Henley in 1868. His racing record is amazing: he was in the Oxford winning crews of 1862 and 1863, and won the university pairs three times and the sculls twice; at Henley he won the Grand Challenge cup in 1865, the Stewards' cup in 1862, the Diamond sculls in 1864, the Goblets in 1861, 1862, 1863, 1866, and 1868. He also held the Wingfield sculls in 1862, 1864, and 1867. Woodgate was not only a great oar, but his knowledge of oarsmanship was unsurpassed and it covered almost a century of rowing. He entered the rowing world soon enough to meet the giants of its early days; he had known Thomas Staniforth, Oxford stroke in the first university boat race in 1829, and he was present at Henley regatta in 1920. As a judge of pace he was unequalled, and his textbook, *Oars and Sculls, and how to use them* (1875), is a classic.

Woodgate's life, however, was full of other interests, and his full-blooded activities and mental versatility were as remarkable as his rowing. His varied interests jostle one another in the pages of his *Reminiscences of an Old Sportsman* (1909), where he writes of country life, steeplechasing, school and college life (he was the founder of Vincent's Club at Oxford), of the parentage of James I, the inner history of the search for Dr. Livingstone by the Royal Geographical Society, his own indirect share in Pasteur's researches, of politics, and police morality. The law he never took too seriously. As a journalist he assisted at the birth of *Vanity Fair* and *Land and Water*; he was associated with the *Pall Mall Gazette* in its early days, and contributed to the *Field* for half a century. He wrote a few novels under the pseudonym of 'Wat Bradwood', and in 1893 he published *A Modern Layman's Faith*.

The question why, with his undoubted ability, Woodgate did not go further, may perhaps be answered in his own words: 'I am who and what I am, and my best and truest friends (of both worlds) have been just who and what they are and beyond price. If one shift of the helm had steered my bark into some other channel wherein I should have failed to know and revere any single one of those elect, I should feel myself the poorer, even if that course had led me to a coronet.' Woodgate fashioned his life, as he chose his clothes, for his own use and satisfaction, and was careless of the world's ways. He was a man of unflinching rectitude, of decided opinions, but of great kindliness, and an excellent raconteur. As a young man he was strikingly handsome; in later years his fine, stern face and stalwart figure made him a typical John Bull, an effect accentuated by a low-crowned top hat. He died 1 November 1920, in his sister's house at Southampton, of heart weakness brought on by bronchial trouble. He never married.

[*The Times*, 2 November 1920; *The Field*, 6 and 13 November 1920; personal knowledge.] H. C. W.

WOOLDRIDGE, HARRY ELLIS (1845–1917), painter, musician, and critic, had a wide personal influence on the educated taste of his time. Born 28 March 1845, his father, who held a literary post in Smith, Elder's house, articled him to Lloyd's, but he soon changed his office-desk for an easel in the Royal Academy School. Friendship with Burne-Jones encouraged his pre-Raphaelite sympathies; his Academy pictures were always well hung, the first being bought by Sir F. Leighton; and a cabinet which he decorated for some upholsterer was placed in the South Kensington Museum. Critical sensibility gradually checked his creativeness, and he undertook commissions—from G. F. Watts, Sir T. G. Jackson, and others—to execute wall-paintings or design stained glass. Of this period are his large reredos at St. Martin's church, Brighton, and many of Messrs. Powell's windows, worked in Renaissance manner with correct drawing and predetermined colours. But he had another love, smiling perhaps more kindly upon him, and his daily recreation was to explore the old Italian music in the British Museum. From his youth an accomplished singer, he now became an expert contrapuntist, and as an unrivalled specialist was chosen to re-edit Chappell's *Popular Music of the Olden Time*, under the new title *Old English Popular Music*; the first volume (1893) is an example of his scholarship. Sir Hubert Parry used to consult him, and Sir John Stainer invited him to lecture for his chair. But he was recalled to painting by being appointed Slade professor of fine art at Oxford in 1895. There, with his honorary M.A. degree, he personated academic propriety, teaching logical principles in rounded periods of Caroline diction and rhythm.

Reviewing inaugurally the theory of art from Plato to Hegel, he proclaimed the Greek notions to be inadequate, and, accepting much of Hegel's analysis, alleged this to be philosophically one-eyed, through ignorance of actual experience; objecting also that it encouraged a literary criticism which, in ascribing development of art to moral causes and political events, neglected the predominant influence of new materials or methods; and it was these, he contended. and the personal delight of artists within their own circle, exploiting new means of expression, that provoked the developments of any art. This thesis, which he would have applied with even greater confidence and could have illustrated by more convincing detail in music, was maintained throughout his discourses. He was twice re-elected, retiring in 1904.

While at this work he was retained to contribute the initial volume to *The Oxford History of Music*; and, judging that in such a work the art should be traced to its Greek foundations, he was led off into obscure antiquarian research; and although experts say of his two volumes (vol. i, 1901 and vol. ii, 1905) that 'they are monuments of erudition and insight . . . unlikely to be superseded . . . and his explanations of controverted points though challenged at the time have won general acceptance', yet, since he had exceeded the limits of his space before he arrived at the period of his special knowledge, he left undone the one great work for which he was exclusively qualified. Under this double strain his health failed; and he became more and more invalided until his death, which took place in London 13 February 1917.

Except some late photographs, a silhouette, and a sketch by Mr. Roger Fry, there is no portrait of Wooldridge. He had a well-formed thick-set frame, massive bust, and noble head which early baldness forced on the attention; blue eyes in wide orbits, fine and muscular features, ruddy auburn beard trimmed like a Frenchman's. In dress and manners punctilious, in character brave and generous, of philosophical conviction and strict morality, he was gentle-hearted and indulgent towards others, genial in conventional chatter but intolerant of pretence, especially in the talk of artists, to whom his undisguised amusement and devastating irony were obnoxious. With but a smattering of Latin and Greek, his rare intuition, wide reading, and full memory distinguished him in any company. He had a good knowledge of French literature and was a fair Italian scholar, pronouncing both languages like a native; was a good raconteur and mimic, and a loud laugher. Although he truly loved romance, his solid figure, deliberate movements, and searching common sense seemed unromantic, and gave the impression of ease and indolence—and that was not untrue to his nature, for he would have preferred a world that was not always calling for the delicate adjustment of his serious intelligence.

Among his musical remains are *The Yattendon Hymnal*, 1895–1899, edited with the present poet laureate, his lifelong friend, with whom he lived for years in London and afterwards constantly visited at Yattendon, where he sang in the choir and set music for it. There are also church settings and compositions by him in *Musica Antiquata* (1907–1908, 1913). The rare combination of delicate aesthetic sensibility with complete scholarly and artistic sympathy identifies the best of these simple four-part polyphonic settings with the workmanship of the original masters. He was called upon to serve on the committee for the revision of *Hymns Ancient and Modern*, but retired after two or three meetings through dissatisfaction with the quality of the work.

He married in 1894 Julia Mary, daughter of Stephen Olding. To her knowledge of German he owed much in his antiquarian research. He left no children.

[Personal knowledge.] R. B.

WRIGHT, WILLIAM ALDIS (1831–1914), Shakespearian and Biblical scholar, born at Beccles 1 August 1831, was the second son of George Wright, baptist minister there, by his second wife, Elizabeth Higham, sister of Thomas Higham [q.v.], the engraver. After education at the Northgate house academy and from 1847 at the Fauconberge grammar school, Beccles, he was admitted in 1849 to Trinity College, Cambridge, and was eighteenth wrangler in 1854. He taught in a school at Wimbledon in 1855, returned to Cambridge, and, on the removal of the religious tests, graduated B.A. in 1858 and M.A. in 1861. His first publication was an essay on Herrick in the *Oxford and Cambridge Magazine* for September 1856. He found regular employment on (Sir) William Smith's *Dictionary of the Bible* (1860–1863), and made his name as a scholar by his contributions to it, by his edition of Bacon's *Essays* (1862), and by the part which he played with Henry Bradshaw [q.v.] in the exposure of the falsehoods of Constantine Simonides [*Guardian*, 3 September 1862, 26 January and 11 November 1863]. In 1863 he was appointed librarian of Trinity College, but could not be elected fellow till October 1878, when the university commission of 1877 had removed the last disabilities of dissenters. He was senior bursar from June 1870 (when he resigned the librarianship) to December 1895, and vice-master from February 1888 till his death at Cambridge, 19 May 1914. He had occupied the same rooms in Nevile's Court since 1865. Although one of the great figures in the university, he took no part latterly in its politics, and he neither taught nor lectured. Few undergraduates ventured to speak to him, and even the younger fellows of his college were kept at a distance by the austere precision of his manner. His old-fashioned courtesy made him a genial host, but his circle of chosen friends was small.

Wright's edition (Golden Treasury series) of Bacon's *Essays* foreshadowed his later work in the accuracy of its text and the concise learning of its notes, and remains a model edition of an English classic. He insisted on keeping the old spelling and punctuation, and was the first to point out emphatically that editors of Elizabethan texts must expect variations in different copies of the same issue. He had used ten copies of the text which he reprinted, and found that some of the sheets were in three stages. He thus anticipated much that is supposed to be recent in editorial methods. He showed that the older punctuation was 'rhetorical and not grammatical' in a memorandum (unpublished) *On the use of the Comma in the Annexed Book* (i.e. the copy of the Prayer Book annexed to the Act of Uniformity of 1662), which he presented in 1894 to the Oxford and Cambridge University Presses.

In 1863, after the publication of the first volume of the *Cambridge Shakespeare*, Wright succeeded John Glover as joint-editor with William George Clark [q.v.], and brought out the remaining eight volumes from 1863 to 1866. He was solely responsible for the second edition (1891–1893), which remains the great monument of his industry and accuracy. But he was not responsible for its plan. In conversation he admitted the disadvantages of a modernized text, and said that an editor who knows his business is better without a colleague. While the *Cambridge Shakespeare* was in progress, he edited with Clark the *Globe Shakespeare* (1864); and when it was complete he edited with him in the Clarendon Press series *The Merchant of Venice*, *Richard II*, *Macbeth*, and *Hamlet* between 1868 and 1872. Thereafter he carried on the series alone, and added thirteen plays between 1874 (*The Tempest*) and 1897 (1 *Henry IV*). Besides presenting a mass of new material he was the first editor to give due attention to the Elizabethan usage of words. Every later editor has recognized the value of this series. It was in his nature to be silent about poetic beauty and dramatic genius; but learning, accuracy, and common sense combined to make him our greatest Shakespearian scholar since Edmund Malone.

In 1864 Wright undertook to collaborate with John Earle [q.v.] and Henry Bradshaw on an edition of Chaucer which ultimately became the *Oxford Chaucer*, edited by Walter William Skeat [q.v.]; but he retired in 1870, partly under the pressure of new duties. In 1867 he printed privately the *Clerk's Tale* from MS. Dd. 4.24 in the University Library, Cambridge. His other publications during the busy years of his librarianship were an abridgement of the *Dictionary of the Bible*, called the *Concise Dictionary* (1865); *The Bible Word-Book*, begun by Jonathan Eastwood [q.v.], (1866, second edition 1884); the Clarendon Press edition of *Bacon's Advancement of Learning* (1869), and the Roxburghe Club edition of Guillaume de Deguileville's *Pilgrimage of the Lyf of the Manhode* (1869). In 1868 he edited with W. G. Clark and John Eyton Bickersteth Mayor [q.v.] the first number of the *Journal of Philology*, and he continued as editor till 1913.

In 1870, when Wright became bursar of his college, he also became secretary to the Old Testament revision company. Of its 794 meetings from June 1870 to May 1885, he attended 793. His work on Smith's *Dictionary of the Bible* had made him highly proficient in Hebrew, a study which he had begun as a schoolboy; but he had the rarer qualification of knowing sixteenth-century English. None of the revisers could have had greater respect than he had for the English of Coverdale, and he is understood to have been largely responsible for the conservatism of the revision. All his official papers, showing every stage of the revision, are now in the Cambridge University Library. While engaged on the revision, he edited *Generydes* for the Early English Text Society (1873–1878) and ten plays of Shakespeare in the Clarendon Press series. He also contributed to Smith's *Dictionary of Christian Antiquities* (1875–1880) and *Dictionary of Christian Biography* (1877–1887). In 1887 he completed for the Rolls Series his edition of the *Metrical Chronicle of Robert of Gloucester*, which he had been forced to lay aside in 1870.

From 1889 to 1903 Wright edited, as literary executor, the writings of his friend Edward FitzGerald, a pleasant duty which was accompanied till 1895 by his laborious task as bursar, and varied by his exacting revision of the *Cambridge Shakespeare* and by his editing of separate plays, as well as of a *Facsimile of the Milton MS. in the Library of Trinity College, Cambridge* (1899). He brought out FitzGerald's *Letters and Literary Remains* in three volumes in 1889, and published the *Letters* by themselves, with additions (Eversley series) in 1894, the aim of the collection being 'to let FitzGerald tell the story of his own life'. *Letters to Fanny Kemble* followed in 1895, *Miscellanies* (Golden Treasury series) in 1900, and *More Letters* in 1901. All were combined in the final edition of FitzGerald's *Letters and Literary Remains* (7 vols., 1902–1903). Wright took care never to come between the author and the reader, but his notes give the information that the reader requires. In all respects he provided an example of how a contemporary ought to be edited.

Till his first serious illness, two years before his death, Wright's energies were unwearied. His work after the age of seventy continued to show the same wide range; in quality it never varied. For the Pitt Press (of which he was a syndic from 1872 to 1910) he edited *Milton's Poems with critical notes* (1903), the *English Works of Roger Ascham* (1904), and the Authorized Version of the Bible as printed in the original two issues (5 vols., 1909). In 1905 he brought out the third edition of Bishop Westcott's *History of the Bible* (undertaken at Westcott's request in 1901) and a *Commentary on the Book of Job from a Hebrew MS. in the Cambridge University Library*. Then he turned to Anglo-Norman and presented the Roxburghe Club with an edition of the long-lost Trinity College MS. of *Femina* (1909). For his last work he fittingly chose an edition of the six English translations of the Psalms from

Tyndale to the Revised Version, and produced his *Hexaplar English Psalter* in 1911, at the age of eighty. In the same year he contributed to the second Lord Tennyson's *Tennyson and his Friends* an account of James Spedding [q.v.]. Since 1871 he had been engaged on an edition of Burton's *Anatomy of Melancholy,* and had succeeded in tracing all but a few of the quotations. Before his death he distributed many of his books among the Cambridge libraries, and by his will he left £5,000 to the University Library, and £5,000 to the library of his college.

The amount of Wright's work is the more remarkable seeing that he suffered from writer's cramp and had to learn to use his left hand; but he allowed nothing to interfere with his methodical habits, and faced all his tasks with an iron will. As an editor he held it his duty to present his material in such a way that it would speak for itself. He distrusted theories and intuitions, and all the short cuts that cleverness is tempted to adopt. 'Ignorance and conceit', he said, 'are the fruitful parents of conjectural emendation', and he would quote the rabbinical saying, 'Teach thy lips to say "I do not know"'. He never forgot that he was the servant rather than the master of his material, and consistently, throughout a career of over fifty years, was the most impersonal of our great editors. A superficial reader may find his work dry, and may even think of him as a mere scholiast, but every worker in the same fields continually finds that Wright has taken account of facts which others have failed to see, and every one learns to trust him. His one mistake was over the Squire Papers (*Academy,* 11 April and 2 May 1885; *English Historical Review,* April 1886); FitzGerald had believed in their authenticity, and for once Wright's judgement was misled by friendship. In conversation, as in his writings, he might seem to be incapable of any display of sentiment, but the friends who were permitted to get behind his somewhat rigid sincerity found a warm heart and great depth of feeling. He never married.

He received the honorary degrees of LL.D., Edinburgh (1879), D.C.L., Oxford (1886), and Litt.D., Dublin (1895). The portraits by Walter William Ouless at Trinity College (1887), and by William Strang in the Fitzwilliam Museum (1910), fail to convey his vigour. The best likeness is the photograph by A. G. Dew-Smith of Trinity College (1894).

[*The Times,* 20 May 1914; *Morning Post,* 20 May 1914; *Cambridge Review,* 27 May 1914; *Journal of Philology,* 1914, pp. 299–304; *Admissions to Trinity College, Cambridge,* vol. iv; S. K. Bland, *Memorials of George Wright,* 1875; G. W. Prothero, *Memoir of Henry Bradshaw,* 1889; *Letters of Alexander Macmillan,* 1908; C. L. Graves, *Life and Letters of Alexander Macmillan,* 1910; private information; personal knowledge.] D. N. S.

WYNDHAM, Sir **CHARLES** (1837–1919), actor-manager, whose original name was Charles Culverwell, was born in Liverpool 23 March 1837, the only son of Major Richard Culverwell, doctor. He was educated abroad, at King's College, London, and at the College of Surgeons and Peter Street anatomical school, Dublin. He took the degree of M.R.C.S. in 1857 and that of L.M. in 1858. His first appearance on the stage was in amateur theatricals at Sir Hugh Lyon Playfair's private theatre at St. Andrews. In 1862 he went on the stage in London. Later in that year he went to America, and took service as an army surgeon in the federal army during the Civil War. He served till the War was nearly over, though during the winters he appeared on the stage in New York, at one time in a company which included John Wilkes Booth (who shortly afterwards assassinated Abraham Lincoln). In 1865 he returned to England and, after some appearances in provincial theatres, came to London, where during the next two years he was engaged at the Royalty Theatre, at the St. James's under Miss Herbert, and at the Queen's Theatre in a company which included (Sir) Henry Irving and Ellen Terry. In May 1868 Wyndham began a brief and unsuccessful management of the Princess's Theatre. Then, in the summer of 1869, he sailed for the United States, where, after playing leading comedy parts in New York, he began in 1871 a two years' tour with his own company, the repertory including the comedies of Thomas William Robertson [q.v.]. Subsequently he acted in the United States in 1882–1883, 1888, 1904, 1909, and 1910.

In May 1874 Wyndham appeared in London in one of his most popular parts, Bob Sackett in the farce *Brighton,* an anglicized version of *Saratoga,* by Bronson Howard. In 1875 he began a series of afternoon performances at the Crystal Palace, where in three years he produced more than one hundred plays ranging from Greek tragedy to farce. In December 1875 he took the play *Brighton* to the Criterion Theatre, and in April 1876 became manager of that theatre, which he made his London stage till 1899. His earliest successes here were in farce especially in *Pink Dominoes*, by James Albery; and he maintained his fame as a light comedian of grace and gaiety and a skilful producer of plays. Always anxious to increase the range of his acting, he appeared in 1886 in the title-part of *David Garrick*, by T. W. Robertson, and this became his best-known character: in January 1888 he gave the play in German (his own translation) before royal audiences in Germany and Russia. As Charles Surface and in other parts in the old comedy he was much admired. In the last decade of the nineteenth century, the comedies of Henry Arthur Jones (*The Bauble Shop*, *The Case of Rebellious Susan*, *The Liars*) showed Wyndham's varied powers at their ripest.

In November 1899 Wyndham opened a new theatre, which he had built and which took his name, in Charing Cross Road. Here he played the title-part in *Cyrano de Bergerac*; but his excursions into romance were not appreciated by the public. At Wyndham's Theatre, too, he produced *Mrs. Gorringe's Necklace*, the first of four comedies by Hubert Henry Davies, which gave him the best parts of his later years. In 1903 he opened another theatre, the New Theatre, which he had built in St. Martin's Lane. Till his failing memory led to his retirement he continued to act well in revivals of his former successes. In 1902 he was knighted on the occasion of the coronation of King Edward VII. He died in London 12 January 1919.

Wyndham married twice: first, in 1860 Emma Silberrad (died 1916), granddaughter of Baron Silberrad, of Hesse-Darmstadt; by her he had four children of whom one son and one daughter survived him; secondly, in 1916 Mary, youngest daughter of Charles Moore, parliamentary agent, and widow of the dramatist, James Albery; she had first acted in Wyndham's company in 1881, and was its leading lady from 1885 to the end of his career; she was also his partner in the management and building of his theatres.

[*The Times*, 13 January 1919; T. E. Pemberton, *Sir Charles Wyndham*, 1904; private information. Portrait, *Royal Academy Pictures*, 1917.] H. H. C.

WYNDHAM, GEORGE (1863–1913), statesman and man of letters, was born in London 29 August 1863, the elder son of the Hon. Percy Scawen Wyndham, third son of the first Baron Leconfield; his mother, Madeleine, sixth daughter of Sir Guy Campbell, first baronet [q.v.], and a granddaughter of Lord Edward Fitzgerald [q.v.], the Irish rebel, was a woman of remarkable talents and character, and had much influence upon him. He was educated at a private school, at Eton, and at Sandhurst, and joined the Coldstream Guards in March 1883; he served through the Suakin campaign of 1885. In 1887 he married Sibell Mary, daughter of the ninth Earl of Scarbrough and widow of Earl Grosvenor. In the same year George Wyndham became private secretary to Mr. Arthur (afterwards Earl of) Balfour. In 1889 he was elected to the House of Commons, unopposed, as conservative member for Dover, and he held the seat till his death.

In 1892 the conservatives went into opposition, and for the next four or five years Wyndham devoted himself mainly to literature; he made the acquaintance of William Ernest Henley (q. v.) in 1892 and became in a sense his disciple, writing for his weekly papers, the *National Observer* and the *New Review*. He also wrote an introduction to North's *Plutarch* (1895–1896) in Henley's Tudor Classics. An edition of *Shakespeare's Poems* (1898) prefaced by an essay on the conditions of Shakespeare's literary life, and a short essay, *Ronsard and La Pléiade* (1906), with a few selections and verse translations, are the chief of Wyndham's other literary works. His writings are eloquent and interesting, and show a characteristic determination to understand the subject and see it in the concrete; they have much merit, but more promise, a promise which was not fulfilled, as in 1898 Wyndham was appointed parliamentary under-secretary in the War Office, and thereafter never had the leisure for a serious literary undertaking.

In the autumn of 1899 came the South African War. The first British defeats caused intense dissatisfaction with the government. Wyndham defended its policy in a remarkably fine speech in the House of Commons (1 February 1900), perhaps the most effective which he ever made there. His administrative work during the first part of the War was very hard, and as successful as the conditions permitted. In 1900 he was made chief secretary for Ireland. His Irish administration (November 1900 to March 1905) was his chief political achievement, and is noteworthy as the last attempt (successful while it lasted) to govern that country on the lines laid down by Mr. Arthur Balfour, that is, the maintenance of the Union—which in practice meant personal government by the chief secretary—combined with a policy of economic development (land purchase, light railways, assistance to agriculture). Wyndham's personal administration was on the whole successful, as he worked very hard, was fair-minded, and had a more sympathetic understanding of the Irish than most English statesmen. His only important contribution to the economic policy was his Land Act (1903). It followed the general lines of Mr. Arthur Balfour's Land Purchase Act of 1891, but by several new provisions made sale much more profitable to the landlords without increasing the immediate payment by the tenant-purchasers; hence an immense extension of sales, which had nearly come to an end under the former acts. The Act of 1903 made a very bold use of imperial credit (the terms were modified in 1906); it encountered much opposition in the Cabinet, and was discussed at great length in the House of Commons; its passing marks the zenith of Wyndham's political career. In 1904 he attempted, without success, to devise a scheme of university education for Irish Catholics, which would at the same time meet their views and those of a unionist government; and in March 1905 he resigned as the result of a scheme of 'devolution', that is, half-way Home Rule, brought forward by his permanent under-secretary, Sir Antony (afterwards Baron) MacDonnell, with the approval of the lord lieutenant, the Earl of Dudley. Wyndham was savagely attacked at the time for a betrayal of unionist principles, and has since been praised for having devised a solution of the Irish question. He deserved neither the praise nor the blame; he did not know what his colleagues were doing and would certainly have stopped them if he had. He might possibly have extricated himself from the embarrassment had he been physically fit, but in fact six years of overwork had broken him down. He retired from politics for a few months to recuperate, and then came in again gradually, but did not take any considerable part before the conservatives went out of office in 1906.

In the last seven years of his life (he died suddenly in Paris from a clot of blood, 8 June 1913, not having reached the age of fifty), Wyndham was associated mainly with the tariff reform wing of the unionist party, though he never renounced his personal loyalty to Mr. Balfour. But he showed some signs of a desire to leave politics altogether, especially after he succeeded his father (1911) and had the management of a small landed estate on his hands. He took this duty very seriously, for he was an English tory in the best sense; his love of England, which was intense, was bound up with a belief in the monarchy, the church, and the landed gentry, as the best institutions for England. He was an imperialist, and he was not a believer in democracy. But his ideal for the nation, or for the class which he thought called to the function of government, was so high that he grieved less at the gentry's loss of power than at any manifestation of their abandoning their traditions. In his last years he found politics very depressing, and saw nothing clearly in the future except war with Germany.

Wyndham's career in office was less than seven years, and his literary output was small; the impression which he made on those who knew him personally was greater than can be justified by his actual achievements. He had a very keen appreciation of beauty in nature, in some kinds of art, and in some departments of literature; a passion for life, and a passion for ideas; he loved hunting and open-air life, he loved talking—and his conversation was most inspiring. His public speaking was, at its best, admirable, but very uncertain. He had many friendships, and an inner devotion to his family. He entered political life with a good deal of ambition, but was retained in it mainly by a sense of duty; his delicate feeling of honour was a contributing cause of his fall from power. He had not so much a faculty of concentration as an inability to escape from any subject which he took up seriously; and this characteristic, while it made him very powerful in council and in administration, probably led to overstrain and shortened his life.

Wyndham was survived by his wife and by one son.

[Letters; J. W. Mackail and Guy Wyndham, *Life and Letters of George Wyndham*, 2 vols., 1924; C. Whibley's edition of Wyndham's *Essays in Romantic Literature*, 1919; private information; personal knowledge.] P. H. H.

YOUNG, Sir ALLEN WILLIAM (1827–1915), sailor and polar explorer, was born at Twickenham 12 December 1827, the son of Henry Young, of Twickenham. After being educated at home he joined the merchant service in 1842 and rose quickly. During the Crimean War he transferred from the *Marlborough*, an East Indiaman, to the command of the troopship *Adelaide*, but remained in the merchant service. In 1857, when (Sir) Francis Leopold McClintock [q.v.] was fitting out the yacht *Fox* in order to follow up the discoveries of Dr. John Rae [q.v.] bearing on the fate of the expedition of Sir John Franklin [q.v.], he chose Young as navigating officer. Young declined any salary and contributed to the cost of the expedition. During the two years spent in following Franklin's tracks Young took an active part in sledging, and explored about 380 miles of new coast line, including the southern and western coasts of Prince of Wales Land and both shores of Franklin Strait. He also discovered McClintock Channel, but was unable to cross its rough ice. In 1860 Young had command of the *Fox* in the North Atlantic Telegraph expedition, which surveyed a telegraph route between Europe and America via the Faroes, Iceland, and Greenland. He visited the east coast of Greenland, but, believing it to be impracticable for a cable route, did not land. Sailing for the west coast he landed with Rae, who was in charge of the land part of the expedition, ascended to the ice cap near Julianehaab, but returned on deciding that a telegraph line could not be carried across Greenland. Young next went to China to assist Admiral Sherard Osborn [q.v.] in equipping the Chinese navy, and commanded the *Quantung* during the Taiping rebellion, 1862–1864. In 1871 he was commissioner to the Maritime Congress at Naples, and in 1875 he was present at Suakin as commissioner of the National Aid Society.

With the object of assisting the government Arctic expedition which set out in May 1875 under the command of (Sir) George Strong Nares [q.v.], Young took his steam yacht *Pandora* to Baffin's Bay and picked up Nares's dispatches from the Carey Islands. He then tried to make the North-West passage, but was stopped by heavy ice in Peel Strait. The next year he again took the *Pandora* north, and in spite of great difficulties landed dispatches for Nares at Cape Isabella and Littleton Island. On his return he sighted Nares's ships homeward bound off Cape Farewell. In 1882 he commanded the whaler *Hope*, chartered with government help, in order to search for the explorer, Benjamin Leigh Smith, who had sailed for Franz Josef Land in July of the previous year. In August 1882 the *Hope* found Leigh Smith and his party at Matochkin Shar, on the west coast of Novaya Zemlya, which they had reached in boats after the destruction of their vessel off Franz Josef Land.

Young was knighted in 1877, and received the C.B. in 1881 and the C.V.O. in 1903. He also held orders from the crowns of Denmark, Sweden, Austria, and the Netherlands. He was a commander in the Royal Naval Reserve (1862) and a younger brother of Trinity House. He died in London, unmarried, 20 November 1915. He wrote comparatively little and had a strong dislike of publicity. He contributed to the *Cornhill Magazine* in 1860 an account of his experiences in the *Fox* expedition in search of Franklin, and was the author of *The Cruise of the Pandora* (1876) and *The Two Voyages of the Pandora* (1879).

[*The Times*, 23 November 1915 ; Sir F. L. McClintock, *The Voyage of the Fox*, 1859; T. Zeilau, *Fox Expeditionen in Aaret, 1860* (Copenhagen, 1861) ; *Proceedings* of the Royal Geographical Society, July and September 1882 and April 1883 ; *Geographical Journal*, January 1916 ; private information.]

R. N. R. B.

CUMULATIVE INDEX
TO THE TWENTIETH CENTURY
DICTIONARY OF NATIONAL BIOGRAPHY
1901-1921

Any Worthy who died in or before 1911 is in the *D. N. B.* **1901–1911** in *three* volumes (now *bound* in one volume).

Any Worthy who died after 1911 is in the *D. N. B.* **1912–1921** (one volume).

The position (within his period) of any Worthy depends on the initial of his *surname* (not of his title or pseudonym, if any).

Abbey, Edwin Austin . . 1852–1911
Abbott, Evelyn 1843–1901
À Beckett, Arthur William . 1844–1909
Abel, Sir Frederick Augustus, baronet 1827–1902
Abercorn, second Duke of. See Hamilton, James.
Abney, Sir William de Wiveleslie 1843–1920
Abraham, Charles John . . 1814–1903
Acton, John Adams. See Adams-Acton.
Acton, Sir John Emerich Edward Dalberg, first Baron Acton . 1834–1902
Adam, James 1860–1907
Adams, James Williams . . 1839–1903
Adams, William Davenport . 1851–1904
Adams-Acton, John . . . 1830–1910
Adamson, Robert 1852–1902
Adderley, Charles Bowyer, first Baron Norton 1814–1905
Adler, Hermann 1839–1911
Agnew, Sir James Willson . 1815–1901
Agnew, Sir William, first baronet 1825–1910
Aidé, Charles Hamilton . . 1826–1906
Aikman, George 1830–1905
Ainger, Alfred 1837–1904
Aird, Sir John, first baronet . 1833–1911
Airedale, first Baron. See Kitson, James.
Aitchison, George . . . 1825–1910
Alcock, Sir John William . . 1892–1919
Aldenham, first Baron. See Gibbs, Henry Hucks.
Alderson, Henry James . . 1834–1909
Alexander, Boyd 1873–1910
Alexander, Sir George . . 1858–1918
Alexander, William . . . 1824–1911
Alexander, Mrs, *pseudonym*. See Hector, Annie French.
Alger, John Goldworth . . 1836–1907
Alington, first Baron. See Sturt, Henry Gerard.
Alison, Sir Archibald, second baronet 1826–1907
Allan, Sir William . . . 1837–1903
Allen, George 1832–1907
Allen, John Romilly . . 1847–1907
Allen, Robert Calder . . 1812–1903
Allerton, first Baron. See Jackson, William Lawies.
Allies, Thomas William . . 1813–1903
Allman, George Johnston . 1824–1904
Alma-Tadema, Sir Lawrence . 1836–1912
Almond, Hely Hutchinson . 1832–1903
Alverstone, Viscount. See Webster, Richard Everard.
Amherst, William Amhurst Tyssen-, first Baron Amherst of Hackney 1835–1909
Anderson, Alexander . . 1845–1909
Anderson, Elizabeth Garrett . 1836–1917
Anderson, George . . . 1826–1902
Anderson (formerly Macarthur), Mary Reid 1880–1921
Anderson, Sir Thomas McCall . 1836–1908
Andrews, Thomas . . . 1847–1907
Angus, Joseph 1816–1902
Annandale, Thomas . . . 1838–1907
Anson, Sir William Reynell, third baronet 1843–1914
Arber, Edward 1836–1912
Arbuthnot, Sir Alexander John . 1822–1907
Arbuthnot, Forster Fitzgerald . 1833–1901
Arbuthnot, Sir Robert Keith, fourth baronet . . . 1864–1916
Arch, Joseph 1826–1919
Archer, James 1823–1904
Archer-Hind (formerly Hodgson), Richard Dacre 1849–1910
Ardagh, Sir John Charles . . 1840–1907
Ardilaun, first Baron. See Guinness, Sir Arthur Edward.
Arditi, Luigi 1822–1903
Ardwall, Lord. See Jameson, Andrew.
Argyll, ninth Duke of. See Campbell, John Douglas Sutherland.

Armes, Philip 1836–1908
Armour, John Douglas . . 1830–1903
Armstead, Henry Hugh . . 1828–1905
Armstrong, Sir George Carlyon Hughes, first baronet . . 1836–1907
Armstrong, Thomas . . 1832–1911
Arnold, Sir Arthur . . . 1833–1902
Arnold, Sir Edwin . . . 1832–1904
Arnold, George Benjamin . 1832–1902
Arnold, William Thomas . . 1852–1904
Arnold-Forster, Hugh Oakeley . 1855–1909
Arrol, Sir William . . . 1839–1913
Arthur, William . . . 1819–1901
Ashbourne, first Baron. See Gibson, Edward.
Ashby, Henry . . . 1846–1908
Asher, Alexander . . . 1835–1905
Ashley, Evelyn . . . 1836–1907
Ashmead Bartlett, Sir Ellis. See Bartlett.
Aston, William George . . 1841–1911
Atkinson, Robert . . . 1839–1908
Atthill, Lombe . . . 1827–1910
Aumonier, James . . . 1832–1911
Austen, Sir William Chandler Roberts-. See Roberts-Austen.
Austen Leigh, Augustus . . 1840–1905
Austin, Alfred . . . 1835–1913
Avebury, first Baron. See Lubbock, Sir John.
Ayerst, William . . . 1830–1904
Ayrton, William Edward . . 1847–1908

Bacon, John Mackenzie . . 1846–1904
Badcock, Sir Alexander Robert . 1844–1907
Baddeley, Mountford John Byrde 1843–1906
Bailey, Philip James . . 1816–1902
Bain, Alexander . . . 1818–1903
Bain, Robert Nisbet . . 1854–1909
Bainbridge, Francis Arthur . 1874–1921
Baines, Frederick Ebenezer . 1832–1911
Baird, Andrew Wilson . . 1842–1908
Baker, Sir Benjamin . . 1840–1907
Baker, Shirley Waldemar . 1835–1903
Balfour of Burleigh, sixth Baron. See Bruce, Alexander Hugh.
Balfour, George William . . 1823–1903
Balfour, John Blair, first Baron Kinross 1837–1905
Ball, Albert 1896–1917
Ball, Sir Robert Stawell . . 1840–1913
Banks, Sir John Thomas . . 1815 ?–1908
Banks, Sir William Mitchell . 1842–1904
Bannerman, Sir Henry Campbell-. See Campbell-Bannerman.
Barbellion, W. N. P., *pseudonym*. See Cummings, Bruce Frederick.
Bardsley, John Wareing . . 1835–1904
Baring, Evelyn, first Earl of Cromer 1841–1917
Baring, Thomas George, first Earl of Northbrook . . 1826–1904
Barker, Thomas . . . 1838–1907
Barlow, William Hagger . . 1833–1908
Barlow, William Henry . . 1812–1902
Barnaby, Sir Nathaniel . . 1829–1915
Barnardo, Thomas John . . 1845–1905
Barnes, John Gorell, first Baron Gorell 1848–1913
Barnes, Robert . . . 1817–1907
Barnett, Samuel Augustus . 1844–1913
Barrett, Wilson . . . 1846–1904
Barry, Alfred 1826–1910
Barry, Sir John Wolfe Wolfe-. See Wolfe-Barry.
Bartholomew, John George . 1860–1920
Bartlett, Sir Ellis Ashmead . 1849–1902
Bartley, Sir George Christopher Trout 1842–1910
Barton, Sir Edmund . . 1849–1920
Barton, John 1836–1908
Bashforth, Francis . . . 1819–1912
Bass, Michael Arthur, first Baron Burton 1837–1909
Bates, Cadwallader John . . 1853–1902
Bateson, Mary . . . 1865–1906
Battenberg, Prince Louis Alexander of. See Mountbatten.
Bauerman, Hilary . . . 1835–1909
Baxter, Lucy, 'Leader Scott' . 1837–1902
Baylis, Thomas Henry . . 1817–1908
Bayliss, Sir Wyke . . . 1835–1906
Bayly, Ada Ellen, 'Edna Lyall' 1857–1903
Beach, Sir Michael Edward Hicks, first Earl St. Aldwyn. See Hicks Beach.
Beale, Dorothea . . . 1831–1906
Beale, Lionel Smith . . 1828–1906
Beattie-Brown, William . . 1831–1909
Beckett, Sir Edmund, first Baron Grimthorpe 1816–1905
Beddoe, John 1826–1911
Bedford, William Kirkpatrick Riland 1826–1905
Beecham, Thomas . . . 1820–1907
Beeching, Henry Charles . . 1859–1919
Beevor, Charles Edward . . 1854–1908
Beit, Alfred 1853–1906
Belcher, John 1841–1913
Bell, Charles Frederic Moberly . 1847–1911
Bell, Horace 1839–1903
Bell, Sir Isaac Lowthian, first baronet 1816–1904
Bell, James 1824–1908
Bell, Valentine Graeme . . 1839–1908
Bellamy, James . . . 1819–1909
Bellew, Harold Kyrle . . 1855–1911
Bellows, John . . . 1831–1902
Bemrose, William . . . 1831–1908
Bendall, Cecil 1856–1906
Benham, William . . . 1831–1910
Bennett, Alfred William . . 1833–1902
Bennett, Edward Hallaran . 1837–1907
Benson, Richard Meux . . 1824–1915
Benson, Robert Hugh . . 1871–1914
Bent, Sir Thomas . . . 1838–1909
Bentley, John Francis . . 1839–1902
Beresford, Lord Charles William De La Poer, Baron Beresford . 1846–1919
Bergne, Sir John Henry Gibbs . 1842–1908
Berkeley, Sir George . . 1819–1905
Bernard, Sir Charles Edward . 1837–1901
Bernard, Thomas Dehany . 1815–1904

Berry, Sir Graham . . . 1822–1904
Bertie, Francis Leveson, first Viscount Bertie of Thame . 1844–1919
Besant, Sir Walter . . . 1836–1901
Betham-Edwards, Matilda Barbara. See Edwards.
Bevan, William Latham . . 1821–1908
Bewley, Sir Edmund Thomas . 1837–1908
Bickersteth, Edward Henry . 1825–1906
Biddulph, Sir Michael Anthony Shrapnel 1823–1904
Biddulph, Sir Robert . . 1835–1918
Bidwell, Shelford . . . 1848–1909
Bigg, Charles 1840–1908
Binnie, Sir Alexander Richard . 1839–1917
Birch, George Henry . . 1842–1904
Bird, Henry Edward , . . 1830–1908
Bird, Isabella Lucy. See Bishop.
Birdwood, Sir George Christopher Molesworth 1832–1917
Birdwood, Herbert Mills . . 1837–1907
Birrell, John 1836–1901
Bishop, Edmund . . . 1846–1917
Bishop (formerly Bird), Isabella Lucy 1831–1904
Blackburn, Helen . . . 1842–1903
Blackley, William Lewery . 1830–1902
Blackwell, Elizabeth . . 1821–1910
Blackwood, Frederick Temple Hamilton-Temple, first Marquess of Dufferin . . . 1826–1902
Blake, Edward . . . 1833–1912
Blandford, George Fielding . 1829–1911
Blaney, Thomas . . . 1823–1903
Blanford, William Thomas . 1832–1905
Blaydes, Frederick Henry Marvell 1818–1908
Blennerhassett, Sir Rowland, fourth baronet . . . 1839–1909
Blind, Karl 1826–1907
Bloomfield, Georgiana, Lady . 1822–1905
Blouet, Léon Paul, 'Max O'Rell' 1848–1903
Blount, Sir Edward Charles . 1809–1905
Blumenthal, Jacques [Jacob] . 1829–1908
Blythswood, first Baron. See Campbell, Archibald Campbell.
Bodda Pyne, Louisa Fanny . 1832–1904
Bodington, Sir Nathan . . 1848–1911
Bodley, George Frederick . 1827–1907
Body, George 1840–1911
Bompas, Henry Mason. See under Bompas, William Carpenter.
Bompas, William Carpenter . 1834–1906
Bond, William Bennett . . 1815–1906
Bonwick, James . . . 1817–1906
Booth, Charles . . . 1840–1916
Booth, William ['General' Booth] 1829–1912
Boothby, Guy Newell . . 1867–1905
Borthwick, Algernon, Baron Glenesk 1830–1908
Boswell, John James . . 1835–1908
Bosworth Smith, Reginald. See Smith.
Botha, Louis 1862–1919
Boucherett, Emilia Jessie . 1825–1905
Boughton, George Henry . . 1833–1905
Bourchier, James David . . 1850–1920
Bourinot, Sir John George . 1837–1902
Bourke, Robert, Baron Connemara 1827–1902
Bourne, Henry Richard Fox . 1837–1909
Bousfield, Henry Brougham . 1832–1902
Bowen, Edward Ernest . . 1836–1901
Bowes, Robert . . . 1835–1919
Bowler, Henry Alexander . 1824–1903
Boyce, Sir Rubert William . 1863–1911
Boyd, Sir Thomas Jamieson . 1818–1902
Boyd Carpenter, William. See Carpenter.
Boyle, Sir Courtenay Edmund . 1845–1901
Boyle, Sir Edward, first baronet 1848–1909
Boyle, George David . . 1828–1901
Boyle, Richard Vicars . . 1822–1908
Brabazon, Hercules Brabazon . 1821–1906
Brackenbury, Sir Henry . . 1837–1914
Braddon, Sir Edward Nicholas Coventry 1829–1904
Braddon, Mary Elizabeth. See Maxwell.
Bradford, Sir Edward Ridley Colborne, first baronet . . 1836–1911
Bradley, George Granville . 1821–1903
Brampton, Baron. See Hawkins, Henry.
Bramwell, Sir Frederick Joseph 1818–1903
Brand, Henry Robert, second Viscount Hampden . . 1841–1906
Brand, Herbert Charles Alexander 1839–1901
Brandis, Sir Dietrich . . 1824–1907
Brassey, Thomas, first Earl Brassey 1836–1918
Bray, Caroline . . . 1814–1905
Brereton, Joseph Lloyd . . 1822–1901
Brett, John 1831–1902
Brewtnall, Edward Frederick . 1846–1902
Bridge, Thomas William . . 1848–1909
Bridges, John Henry . . 1832–1906
Bridges, Sir William Throsby . 1861–1915
Briggs, John 1862–1902
Bright, James Franck . . 1832–1920
Bright, William . . . 1824–1901
Brightwen, Eliza . . . 1830–1906
Broadbent, Sir William Henry, first baronet . . . 1835–1907
Broadhurst, Henry . . . 1840–1911
Brodribb, William Jackson . 1829–1905
Brodrick, George Charles . . 1831–1903
Bromby, Charles Hamilton. See under Bromby, Charles Henry.
Bromby, Charles Henry . . 1814–1907
Brooke, Sir Charles Anthony Johnson 1829–1917
Brooke, Rupert Chawner . 1887–1915
Brooke, Stopford Augustus . 1832–1916
Brooking Rowe, Joshua. See Rowe.
Brotherhood, Peter . . . 1838–1902
Brough, Bennett Hooper . . 1860–1908
Brough, Lionel . . . 1836–1909
Brough, Robert . . . 1872–1905
Broughton, Rhoda . . . 1840–1920
Brown, George Douglas, 'George Douglas' 1869–1902

Brown, Sir George Thomas . 1827–1906
Brown, Joseph . . . 1809–1902
Brown, Peter Hume . . 1849–1918
Brown, William Haig-. See Haig-Brown.
Browne, Sir James Frankfort Manners 1823–1910
Browne, Sir Samuel James . 1824–1901
Browne, Thomas 1870–1910
Bruce, Alexander Hugh, sixth Baron Balfour of Burleigh . 1849–1921
Bruce, Sir George Barclay . 1821–1908
Bruce, Victor Alexander, ninth Earl of Elgin . . . 1849–1917
Bruce, William Speirs . . 1867–1921
Brunton, Sir Thomas Lauder, first baronet . . . 1844–1916
Brushfield, Thomas Nadauld . 1828–1910
Brydon, John McKean . . 1840–1901
Buchan, Alexander . . . 1829–1907
Buchanan, George . . . 1827–1905
Buchanan, Robert Williams . 1841–1901
Buckton, George Bowdler . 1818–1905
Bullen, Arthur Henry . . 1857–1920
Buller, Sir Redvers Henry . 1839–1908
Buller, Sir Walter Lawry . . 1838–1906
Bulwer, Sir Edward Earle Gascoyne 1829–1910
Bunsen, Ernest de . . . 1819–1903
Bunting, Sir Percy William . 1836–1911
Burbidge, Edward . . . 1839–1903
Burbidge, Frederick William . 1847–1905
Burbury, Samuel Hawksley . 1831–1911
Burdett-Coutts, Angela Georgina, Baroness Burdett-Coutts . 1814–1906
Burdon, John Shaw . . 1826–1907
Burdon-Sanderson, Sir John Scott, baronet . . . 1828–1905
Burgh Canning, Hubert George De, second Marquess of Clanricarde 1832–1916
Burn, Robert 1829–1904
Burn-Murdoch, John . . 1852–1909
Burnand, Sir Francis Cowley . 1836–1917
Burne, Sir Owen Tudor . . 1837–1909
Burnham, first Baron. See Levy-Lawson, Edward.
Burns, Dawson 1828–1909
Burroughs (afterwards Traill-Burroughs), Sir Frederick William 1831–1905
Burrows, Montagu . . . 1819–1905
Burton, first Baron. See Bass, Michael Arthur.
Bushell, Stephen Wootton . 1844–1908
Busk, Rachel Harriette . . 1831–1907
Butcher, Samuel Henry . . 1850–1910
Butler, Arthur Gray . . 1831–1909
Butler, Arthur John . . 1844–1910
Butler, Henry Montagu . . 1833–1918
Butler, Josephine Elizabeth . 1828–1906
Butler, Samuel . . . 1835–1902
Butler, Sir William Francis . 1838–1910
Butlin, Sir Henry Trentham, first baronet 1845–1912
Butterworth, George Sainton Kaye 1885–1916
Buxton, Sir Thomas Fowell, third baronet 1837–1915
Byrne, Sir Edmund Widdrington 1844–1904
Bywater, Ingram . . . 1840–1914

Cadogan, George Henry, fifth Earl Cadogan . . . 1840–1915
Caine, William Sproston . . 1842–1903
Caird, Edward . . . 1835–1908
Cairnes, William Elliot . . 1862–1902
Calderon, George . . . 1868–1915
Calkin, John Baptiste . . 1827–1905
Callaghan, Sir George Astley . 1852–1920
Callow, William . . . 1812–1908
Calthorpe, sixth Baron. See Gough-Calthorpe, Augustus Cholmondeley.
Cambridge, second Duke of. See George William Frederick Charles.
Campbell, Archibald Campbell, first Baron Blythswood . 1835–1908
Campbell, Frederick Archibald Vaughan, third Earl Cawdor . 1847–1911
Campbell, Sir James Macnabb . 1846–1903
Campbell, John Douglas Sutherland, ninth Duke of Argyll . 1845–1914
Campbell, Lewis . . . 1830–1908
Campbell, William Howard 1859–1910
Campbell-Bannerman, Sir Henry 1836–1908
Cannan, Charles . . . 1858–1919
Canning, Sir Samuel . . 1823–1908
Capel, Thomas John . . 1836–1911
Capes, William Wolfe . . 1834–1914
Capper, Sir Thompson . . 1863–1915
Cardew, Philip . . . 1851–1910
Carey, Rosa Nouchette . . 1840–1909
Carlisle, ninth Earl of. See Howard, George James.
Carlisle, Countess of. See Howard, Rosalind Frances.
Carnegie, Andrew . . . 1835–1919
Carnegie, James, ninth Earl of Southesk 1827–1905
Carpenter, George Alfred . . 1859–1910
Carpenter, Robert . . . 1830–1901
Carpenter, William Boyd . . 1841–1918
Carrington, Sir Frederick . . 1844–1913
Carte, Richard D'Oyly . . 1844–1901
Carter, Hugh 1837–1903
Carter, Thomas Thellusson . 1808–1901
Carver, Alfred James . . 1826–1909
Casement, Roger David . . 1864–1916
Cassel, Sir Ernest Joseph . . 1852–1921
Cassels, Walter Richard . . 1826–1907
Cates, Arthur 1829–1901
Cavell, Edith 1865–1915
Cavendish, Spencer Compton, Marquess of Hartington, afterwards eighth Duke of Devonshire 1833–1908
Cawdor, third Earl. See Campbell, Frederick Archibald Vaughan
Cecil, Lord Edward Herbert Gascoyne- 1867–1918

Cecil, Robert Arthur Talbot Gascoyne-, third Marquess of Salisbury 1830–1903
Chads, Sir Henry 1819–1906
Chalmers, James 1841–1901
Chamberlain, Sir Crawford Trotter 1821–1902
Chamberlain, Joseph . . . 1836–1914
Chamberlain, Sir Neville Bowles 1820–1902
Chamier, Stephen Henry Edward 1834–1910
Chance, Sir James Timmins, first baronet 1814–1902
Channer, George Nicholas . 1842–1905
Chapman, Edward John . . 1821–1904
Charles, James 1851–1906
Charley, Sir William Thomas . 1833–1904
Charteris, Archibald Hamilton . 1835–1908
Chase, Drummond Percy . . 1820–1902
Chase, Marian Emma . . 1844–1905
Chase, William St. Lucian . 1856–1908
Cheadle, Walter Butler . . 1835–1910
Cheetham Samuel . . . 1827–1908
Chelmsford, second Baron. See Thesiger, Frederic Augustus.
Cheylesmore, second Baron. See Eaton, William Meriton.
Cheyne, Thomas Kelly . . 1841–1915
Child, Thomas 1839–1906
Child-Villiers, Victor Albert George, seventh Earl of Jersey. See Villiers.
Chrystal, George 1851–1911
Clanricarde, second Marquess of. See Burgh Canning, Hubert George De.
Clanwilliam, fourth Earl of. See Meade, Richard James.
Clark, John Willis . . . 1833–1910
Clarke, Sir Andrew . . . 1824–1902
Clarke, Sir Caspar Purdon . 1846–1911
Clarke, Charles Baron . . 1832–1906
Clarke, Henry Butler . . 1863–1904
Clarke, Sir Marshal James . 1841–1909
Clasper, John Hawks . . 1836–1908
Clayden, Peter William . . 1827–1902
Clerke, Agnes Mary . . . 1842–1907
Clerke, Ellen Mary. See under Clerke, Agnes Mary.
Cleworth, Thomas Ebenèzer . 1854–1909
Clifford, Frederick . . . 1828–1904
Close, Maxwell Henry . . 1822–1903
Clowes, Sir William Laird . 1856–1905
Clunies-Ross, George . . 1842–1910
Clutton, Henry Hugh . . 1850–1909
Cobb, Gerard Francis . . 1838–1904
Cobbe, Frances Power . . 1822–1904
Cohen, Arthur . . . 1829–1914
Coillard, François . . . 1834–1904
Cokayne, George Edward . 1825–1911
Coke, Thomas William, second Earl of Leicester . . . 1822–1909
Coleman, William Stephen . 1829–1904
Coleridge, Mary Elizabeth . 1861–1907
Coleridge-Taylor, Samuel . . 1875–1912
Collen, Sir Edwin Henry Hayter 1843–1911
Collett, Sir Henry . . . 1836–1901
Collings, Jesse . . . 1831–1920
Collingwood, Cuthbert . . 1826–1908
Collins, John Churton . . 1848–1908
Collins, Richard Henn, Baron Collins 1842–1911
Collins, William Edward . . 1867–1911
Colnaghi, Martin Henry . . 1821–1908
Colomb, Sir John Charles Ready 1838–1909
Colton, Sir John . . . 1823–1902
Colvile, Sir Henry Edward . 1852–1907
Colvin, Sir Auckland . . 1838–1908
Colvin, Sir Walter Mytton. See under Colvin, Sir Auckland.
Commerell, Sir John Edmund . 1829–1901
Common, Andrew Ainslie . 1841–1903
Compton, Lord Alwyne Frederick 1825–1906
Conder, Charles 1868–1909
Conder, Claude Reignier . . 1848–1910
Connemara, Baron. See Bourke, Robert.
Conquest, George (Augustus) . 1837–1901
Cook, Sir Edward Tyas . . 1857–1919
Cook, Sir Francis, first baronet . 1817–1901
Cooper, Sir Alfred . . . 1838–1908
Cooper, Sir Daniel, first baronet 1821–1902
Cooper, Edward Herbert . . 1867–1910
Cooper, James Davis . . 1823–1904
Cooper, Thomas Sidney . . 1803–1902
Cooper, Thompson . . . 1837–1904
Copeland, Ralph . . . 1837–1905
Copinger, Walter Arthur . . 1847–1910
Coppin, George Selth . . 1819–1906
Coppinger, Richard William . 1847–1910
Corbet, Matthew Ridley . . 1850–1902
Corbett, John 1817–1901
Corbould, Edward Henry . 1815–1905
Corfield, William Henry . . 1843–1903
Cornish, Charles John . . 1858–1906
Cornish, Francis Warre Warre-See Warre-Cornish.
Cornwell, James . . . 1812–1902
Corry, Montagu William Lowry, Baron Rowton . . . 1838–1903
Cory, John 1828–1910
Couch, Sir Richard . . . 1817–1905
Couper, Sir George Ebenezer Wilson, second baronet . . 1824–1908
Courthope, William John . . 1842–1917
Courtney, Leonard Henry, first Baron Courtney of Penwith . 1832–1918
Cousin, Anne Ross . . . 1824–1906
Cowans, Sir John Steven . . 1862–1921
Cowell, Edward Byles . . 1826–1903
Cowie, William Garden . . 1831–1902
Cowper, Francis Thomas De Grey, seventh Earl Cowper . 1834–1905
Cox, George (called Sir George) William 1827–1902
Cozens-Hardy, Herbert Hardy, first Baron Cozens-Hardy . 1838–1920
Cradock, Sir Christopher George Francis Maurice . . . 1862–1914
Craig, Isa. See Knox.
Craig, William James . . 1843–1906
Craigie, Pearl Mary Teresa, 'John Oliver Hobbes' . . 1867–1906
Cranbrook, first Earl of. See Gathorne-Hardy, Gathorne.
Crane, Walter 1845–1915

Craven, Hawes 1837–1910
Craven, Henry Thornton . . 1818–1905
Crawford, twenty-sixth Earl of. See Lindsay, James Ludovic.
Crawfurd, Oswald John Frederick 1834–1909
Creagh, William . . . 1828–1901
Cremer, Sir William Randal . 1838–1908
Cripps, Wilfred Joseph . . 1841–1903
Crocker, Henry Radcliffe-. See Radcliffe-Crocker.
Crockett, Samuel Rutherford . 1860–1914
Croft, John 1833–1905
Crofts, Ernest . . . 1847–1911
Croke, Thomas William . . 1824–1902
Cromer, first Earl of. See Baring, Evelyn.
Crompton, Henry . . . 1836–1904
Crookes, Sir William . . 1832–1919
Crooks, William . . . 1852–1921
Cross, Richard Assheton, first Viscount Cross . . . 1823–1914
Crossman, Sir William . . 1830–1901
Crosthwaite, Sir Charles Haukes Todd 1835–1915
Crowe, Eyre 1824–1910
Cruttwell, Charles Thomas . 1847–1911
Cubitt, William George . . 1835–1903
Cullingworth, Charles James . 1841–1908
Cummings, Bruce Frederick, 'W. N. P. Barbellion' . . 1889–1919
Cuningham, James McNabb . 1829–1905
Cunningham, Daniel John . 1850–1909
Cunningham, William . . 1849–1919
Currie, Sir Donald . . 1825–1909
Currie (formerly Singleton), Mary Montgomerie, Baroness Currie, 'Violet Fane' . . . 1843–1905
Currie, Philip Henry Wodehouse, Baron Currie . . . 1834–1906
Curzon-Howe, Sir Assheton Gore 1850–1911
Cust, Henry John Cockayne . 1861–1917
Cust, Robert Needham . . 1821–1909
Custance, Henry . . . 1842–1908
Cutts, Edward Lewes . . 1824–1901

Dale, Sir David, first baronet . 1829–1906
Dallinger, William Henry . 1842–1909
Dalziel, Edward . . . 1817–1905
Dalziel, George . . . 1815–1902
Dalziel, Thomas Bolton Gilchrist Septimus 1823–1906
Daniel, Charles Henry Olive . 1836–1919
Daniel, Evan 1837–1904
Danvers, Frederic Charles . 1833–1906
Darbyshire, Alfred . . 1839–1908
Darwin, Sir George Howard . 1845–1912
Daubeney, Sir Henry Charles Barnston 1810–1903
Davenport-Hill, Rosamond. See Hill.
Davey, Horace, Baron Davey . 1833–1907
Davidson, Andrew Bruce . . 1831–1902
Davidson, Charles . . . 1824–1902
Davidson, James Leigh Strachan-. See Strachan-Davidson.
Davidson, John . . . 1857–1909
Davidson, John Thain . . 1833–1904
Davies, Charles Maurice . . 1828–1910
Davies, John Llewelyn . . 1826–1916
Davies, Robert . . . 1816–1905
Davies, (Sarah) Emily . . 1830–1921
Davis, Charles Edward . . 1827–1902
Davitt, Michael . . . 1846–1906
Dawson, George Mercer . . 1849–1901
Dawson, John 1827–1903
Day, Sir John Charles Frederic Sigismund 1826–1908
Day, Lewis Foreman . . 1845–1910
Day, William (Henry) . . 1823–1908
Deacon, George Frederick . 1843–1909
Deakin, Alfred . . . 1856–1919
Deane, Sir James Parker . . 1812–1902
De Burgh Canning, Hubert George, second Marquess of Clanricarde. See Burgh Canning.
De la Ramée, Marie Louise, 'Ouida' 1839–1908
De la Rue, Sir Thomas Andros, first baronet . . . 1849–1911
De Montmorency, Raymond Harvey, third Viscount Frankfort de Montmorency . . 1835–1902
De Morgan, William Frend . 1839–1917
Denney, James . . . 1856–1917
Derby, sixteenth Earl of. See Stanley, Frederick Arthur.
De Saulles, George William . 1862–1903
Des Vœux, Sir (George) William . 1834–1909
Detmold, Charles Maurice . 1883–1908
De Vere, Aubrey Thomas . 1814–1902
De Vere, Sir Stephen Edward, fourth baronet . . . 1812–1904
De Villiers, John Henry, first Baron De Villiers . . . 1842–1914
Devonshire, eighth Duke of. See Cavendish, Spencer Compton.
De Winton, Sir Francis Walter . 1835–1901
De Worms, Henry, Baron Pirbright 1840–1903
Dibbs, Sir George Richard . 1834–1904
Dicey, Edward James Stephen . 1832–1911
Dickinson, Hercules Henry . 1827–1905
Dickinson, Lowes (Cato) . . 1819–1908
Dickson, Sir Collingwood . . 1817–1904
Dickson, William Purdie . . 1823–1901
Digby, William . . . 1849–1904
Dilke, Sir Charles Wentworth, second baronet . . . 1843–1911
Dilke, Emilia Francis Strong, Lady Dilke 1840–1904
Dillon, Frank 1823–1909
Dimock, Nathaniel . . . 1825–1909
Dixie, Lady Florence Caroline . 1857–1905
Dobell, Bertram . . . 1842–1914
Dobson, (Henry) Austin . . 1840–1921
Dods, Marcus 1834–1909
Doherty, Hugh Lawrence . 1876–1919
Dolling, Robert William Radclyffe [Father Dolling] . . 1851–1902
Donaldson, Sir James . . 1831–1915
Donkin, Bryan . . . 1835–1902
Donnelly, Sir John Fretcheville Dykes 1834–1902

Donnet, Sir James John Louis . 1816–1905
Doughty-Wylie, Charles Hotham Montagu . . . 1868–1915
Douglas, Sir Adye . . . 1815–1906
Douglas, Sir Charles Whittingham Horsley . . . 1850–1914
Douglas, George, *pseudonym*. See Brown, George Douglas.
Douglas, George Cunninghame Monteath 1826–1904
Douglas-Pennant, George Sholto Gordon, second Baron Penrhyn 1836–1907
Dowden, Edward . . . 1843–1913
Dowden, John . . . 1840–1910
Dowie, John Alexander . . 1847–1907
Doyle, John Andrew . . 1844–1907
Dredge, James . . . 1840–1906
Dreschfeld, Julius . . . 1846–1907
Drew, Sir Thomas . . . 1838–1910
Driver, Samuel Rolles . . 1846–1914
Drummond, Sir George Alexander 1829–1910
Drummond, James . . . 1835–1918
Drummond, William Henry . 1854–1907
Drury-Lowe, Sir Drury Curzon . 1830–1908
Drysdale, Learmont . . . 1866–1909
Du Cane, Sir Edmund Frederick 1830–1903
Duckett, Sir George Floyd, third baronet 1811–1902
Dudgeon, Robert Ellis . . 1820–1904
Duff, Sir Beauchamp . . . 1855–1918
Duff, Sir Mountstuart Elphinstone Grant. See Grant Duff.
Dufferin, first Marquess of. See Blackwood, Frederick Temple Hamilton-Temple.
Duffy, Sir Charles Gavan . . 1816–1903
Duffy, Patrick Vincent . . 1836–1909
Dunlop, John Boyd . . 1840–1921
Dunmore, seventh Earl of. See Murray, Charles Adolphus.
Dunphie, Charles James . . 1820–1908
Dupré, August . . . 1835–1907
Dutt, Romesh Chunder . . 1848–1909
Dutton, Joseph Everett . . 1874–1905
Duveen, Sir Joseph Joel . . 1843–1908

Eady, Charles Swinfen, first Baron Swinfen . . . 1851–1919
Earle, John 1824–1903
East, Sir Alfred . . . 1849–1913
East, Sir Cecil James . . 1837–1908
Eastlake, Charles Locke . . 1836–1906
Eaton, William Meriton, second Baron Cheylesmore . . 1843–1902
Ebsworth, Joseph Woodfall . 1824–1908
Eddis, Eden Upton . . . 1812–1901
Edouin, Willie . . . 1846–1908
Edward VII, King . . . 1841–1910
Edward of Saxe-Weimar, Prince 1823–1902
Edwards, Sir Fleetwood Isham . 1842–1910
Edwards, Henry Sutherland . 1828–1906
Edwards, John Passmore . . 1823–1911
Edwards, Matilda Barbara Betham- 1836–1919
Edwards, Sir Owen Morgan . 1858–1920
Egerton, Sir Charles Comyn . 1848–1921
Elgar, Francis . . . 1845–1909
Elgin, ninth Earl of. See Bruce, Victor Alexander.
Eliot, Sir John . . . 1839–1908
Ellery, Robert Lewis John . 1827–1908
Ellicott, Charles John . . 1819–1905
Elliot, Sir George Augustus . 1813–1901
Elliot, Gilbert John Murray Kynynmond, fourth Earl of Minto 1847–1914
Elliot, Sir Henry George . . 1817–1907
Elliott, Sir Charles Alfred . 1835–1911
Ellis, Frederick Startridge . 1830–1901
Ellis, John Devonshire . . 1824–1906
Ellis, Robinson . . . 1834–1913
Elsmie, George Robert . . 1838–1909
Elwes, Gervase Henry (Cary-) . 1866–1921
Elworthy, Frederick Thomas . 1830–1907
Emery, William . . . 1825–1910
Etheridge, Robert . . . 1819–1903
Euan-Smith, Sir Charles Bean . 1842–1910
Eva, *pseudonym*. See O'Doherty (formerly Kelly), Mary Anne.
Evans, Daniel Silvan . . 1818–1903
Evans, Edmund . . . 1826–1905
Evans, George Essex . . 1863–1909
Evans, Sir John . . . 1823–1908
Evans, Sir Samuel Thomas . 1859–1918
Evans, Sebastian . . . 1830–1909
Everard, Harry Stirling Crawfurd 1848–1909
Everett, Joseph David . . 1831–1904
Everett, Sir William . . 1844–1908
Ewart, Charles Brisbane . . 1827–1903
Ewart, Sir John Alexander . 1821–1904
Eyre, Edward John . . 1815–1901

Faed, John 1819–1902
Fagan, Louis Alexander . . 1845–1903
Fairbairn, Andrew Martin . 1838–1912
Falcke, Isaac 1819–1909
Falconer, Lanoe, *pseudonym*. See Hawker, Mary Elizabeth . 1848–1908
Falkiner, Cæsar Litton . . 1863–1908
Falkiner, Sir Frederick Richard . 1831–1908
Fane, Violet, *pseudonym*. See Currie, Mary Montgomerie, Baroness Currie.
Fanshawe, Sir Edward Gennys . 1814–1906
Farjeon, Benjamin Leopold . 1838–1903
Farmer, Emily . . . 1826–1905
Farmer, John 1835–1901
Farningham, Marianne, *pseudonym*. See Hearn, Mary Anne.
Farquharson, David . . 1840–1907
Farrar, Adam Storey . . 1826–1905
Farrar, Frederic William . . 1831–1903
Farren (afterwards Soutar), Ellen [Nellie Farren] . . . 1848–1904
Farren, William . . . 1825–1908
Farwell, Sir George . . . 1845–1915
Fausset, Andrew Robert . . 1821–1910
Fayrer, Sir Joseph, first baronet 1824–1907
Fenn, George Manville . . 1831–1909
Ferguson, Mary Catherine, Lady 1823–1905
Fergusson, Sir James, sixth baronet 1832–1907
Ferrers, Norman Macleod . 1829–1903

Festing, John Wogan . . 1837–1902
Field, Walter 1837–1901
Field, William Ventris, Baron Field 1813–1907
Figgis, John Neville . . . 1866–1919
Finch-Hatton, Harold Heneage . 1856–1904
Finlayson, James 1840–1906
Finnie, John 1829–1907
Fisher, John Arbuthnot, first Baron Fisher . . . 1841–1920
Fison, Lorimer 1832–1907
Fitch, Sir Joshua Girling . . 1824–1903
FitzAlan-Howard, Henry, fifteenth Duke of Norfolk. See Howard.
Fitzclarence, Charles . . 1865–1914
FitzGerald, George Francis . 1851–1901
FitzGerald, Sir Thomas Naghten 1838–1908
FitzGibbon, Gerald 1837–1909
Fitzpatrick, Sir Dennis . . 1837–1920
Fleay, Frederick Gard . . 1831–1909
Flecker, James [Herman] Elroy 1884–1915
Fleming, George 1833–1901
Fleming, James 1830–1908
Fleming, Sir Sandford . . . 1827–1915
Fletcher, James 1852–1908
Flint, Robert 1838–1910
Floyer, Ernest Ayscoghe . . 1852–1903
Forbes, James Staats . . 1823–1904
Ford, Edward Onslow . . 1852–1901
Ford, Patrick 1837–1914
Ford, William Justice . . 1853–1904
Forestier-Walker, Sir Frederick William Edward Forestier . 1844–1910
Forman, Alfred. See under Forman, Henry Buxton.
Forman, Henry Buxton . . 1842–1917
Forrest, John, first Baron Forrest 1847–1918
Forster, Hugh Oakeley Arnold-. See Arnold-Forster.
Fortescue, George Knottesford . 1847–1912
Fortescue, Hugh, third Earl Fortescue 1818–1905
Foster, Sir Clement Le Neve . 1841–1904
Foster, Joseph 1844–1905
Foster, Sir Michael . . . 1836–1907
Foulkes, Isaac 1836–1904
Fowle, Thomas Welbank . . 1835–1903
Fowler, Henry Hartley, first Viscount Wolverhampton . 1830–1911
Fowler, Thomas 1832–1904
Fowler, William Warde . . 1847–1921
Fox, Samson 1838–1903
Fox Bourne, Henry Richard. See Bourne.
Foxwell, Arthur 1853–1909
Frankfort de Montmorency, third Viscount. See De Montmorency, Raymond Harvey.
Fraser, Alexander Campbell . 1819–1914
Fraser, Sir Andrew Henderson Leith 1848–1919
Fraser, Claud Lovat . . . 1890–1921
Fraser, Sir Thomas Richard . 1841–1920
Fream, William 1854–1906
Fréchette, Louis Honoré . . 1839–1908
Freeman, Gage Earle . . 1820–1903
Freeman-Mitford, Algernon Bertram, first Baron Redesdale. See Mitford.
Frere, Mary Eliza Isabella . 1845–1911
Freyer, Sir Peter Johnston . 1851–1921
Friese-Greene, William. See Greene.
Frith, William Powell . . 1819–1909
Fry, Danby Palmer . . . 1818–1903
Fry, Sir Edward 1827–1918
Fry, Joseph Storrs . . . 1826–1913
Fryatt, Charles Algernon . . 1872–1916
Fuller, Sir Thomas Ekins . 1831–1910
Fulleylove, John 1845–1908
Furness, Christopher, first Baron Furness 1852–1912
Furnivall, Frederick James . 1825–1910
Furse, Charles Wellington . 1868–1904
Fust, Herbert Jenner-. See Jenner-Fust.

Gadsby, Henry Robert . . 1842–1907
Gairdner, James 1828–1912
Gairdner, Sir William Tennant . 1824–1907
Gale, Frederick 1823–1904
Gallwey, Peter 1820–1906
Galton, Sir Francis . . . 1822–1911
Gamgee, Arthur 1841–1909
Garcia, Manuel (Patricio Rodriguez) 1805–1906
Gardiner, Samuel Rawson . 1829–1902
Gargan, Denis 1819–1903
Garner, Thomas 1839–1906
Garnett, Richard . . . 1835–1906
Garran (formerly Gamman), Andrew 1825–1901
Garrett, Fydell Edmund . . 1865–1907
Garrett Anderson, Elizabeth. See Anderson.
Garrod, Sir Alfred Baring . 1819–1907
Garth, Sir Richard . . . 1820–1903
Gaselee, Sir Alfred . . . 1844–1918
Gaskell, Walter Holbrook . 1847–1914
Gatacre, Sir William Forbes . 1843–1906
Gathorne-Hardy, Gathorne, first Earl of Cranbrook . . 1814–1906
Gatty, Alfred 1813–1903
Gee, Samuel Jones . . . 1839–1911
Geikie, John Cunningham . 1824–1906
Gell, Sir James 1823–1905
George William Frederick Charles, second Duke of Cambridge . 1819–1904
George, Hereford Brooke . . 1838–1910
Gerard (afterwards de Laszowska), (Jane) Emily 1846–1905
Gerard, Sir Montagu Gilbert . 1842–1905
Gibb, Elias John Wilkinson . 1857–1901
Gibbins, Henry de Beltgens . 1865–1907
Gibbs, Henry Hucks, first Baron Aldenham 1819–1907
Gibson, Edward, first Baron Ashbourne 1837–1913
Giffard, Hardinge Stanley, first Earl of Halsbury . . . 1823–1921
Giffen, Sir Robert . . . 1837–1910
Gifford, Edwin Hamilton . . 1820–1905
Gigliucci, Countess. See Novello, Clara Anastasia.

Gilbert, Sir Joseph Henry . 1817–1901
Gilbert, Sir William Schwenck . 1836–1911
Gill, Sir David . . . 1843–1914
Gillies, Duncan . . . 1834–1903
Ginsburg, Christian David . 1831–1914
Girouard, Désiré . . . 1836–1911
Gissing, George Robert . . 1857–1903
Gladstone, John Hall . . 1827–1902
Glaisher, James . . . 1809–1903
Glenesk, Baron. See Borthwick, Algernon.
Gloag, Paton James . . 1823–1906
Gloag, William Ellis, Lord Kincairney 1828–1909
Godfrey, Daniel . . . 1831–1903
Godkin, Edwin Lawrence . 1831–1902
Godwin, George Nelson . . 1846–1907
Goldschmidt, Otto . . . 1829–1907
Goldsmid, Sir Frederic John . 1818–1908
Goodall, Frederick . . . 1822–1904
Goodman (formerly Salaman), Julia 1812–1906
Gordon, Arthur Charles Hamilton, first Baron Stanmore . 1829–1912
Gordon, James Frederick Skinner 1821–1904
Gordon, Sir John James Hood . 1832–1908
Gordon, Sir Thomas Edward . 1832–1914
Gordon-Lennox, Charles Henry, sixth Duke of Richmond . 1818–1903
Gore, Albert Augustus . . 1840–1901
Gore, George 1826–1908
Gore, John Ellard . . . 1845–1910
Gorell, first Baron. See Barnes, John Gorell.
Gorst, Sir John Eldon . . 1835–1916
Gorst, Sir (John) Eldon . . 1861–1911
Goschen, George Joachim, first Viscount Goschen . . 1831–1907
Gosselin, Sir Martin le Marchant Hadsley 1847–1905
Gott, John 1830–1906
Gough, Sir Charles John Stanley 1832–1912
Gough, Sir Hugh Henry . . 1833–1909
Gough, John Edmond . . 1871–1915
Gough-Calthorpe, Augustus Cholmondeley, sixth Baron Calthorpe 1829–1910
Gould, Nathaniel . . . 1857–1919
Goulding, Frederick . . 1842–1909
Gower, (Edward) Frederick Leveson. See Leveson-Gower.
Gowers, Sir William Richard . 1845–1915
Grace, Edward Mills . . 1841–1911
Grace, William Gilbert . . 1848–1915
Graham, Henry Grey . . 1842–1906
Graham, Thomas Alexander Ferguson 1840–1906
Graham, William . . . 1839–1911
Grant, Sir Charles. See under Grant, Sir Robert.
Grant, George Monro . . 1835–1902
Grant, Sir Robert . . . 1837–1904
Grant Duff, Sir Mountstuart Elphinstone 1829–1906
Grantham, Sir William . . 1835–1911
Gray, Benjamin Kirkman . 1862–1907
Green, Samuel Gosnell . . 1822–1905
Greenaway, Catherine [Kate] . 1846–1901
Greene, William Friese- . . 1855–1921
Greenidge, Abel Hendy Jones . 1865–1906
Greenwell, William . . . 1820–1918
Greenwood, Frederick . . 1830–1909
Greenwood, Thomas . . 1851–1908
Grego, Joseph . . . 1843–1908
Gregory, Sir Augustus Charles . 1819–1905
Gregory, Edward John . . 1850–1909
Gregory, Robert . . . 1819–1911
Grenfell, George . . . 1849–1906
Grenfell, Hubert Henry . . 1845–1906
Grenfell, Julian Henry Francis 1888–1915
Grey, Albert Henry George, fourth Earl Grey . . . 1851–1917
Grey (formerly Shirreff), Maria Georgina 1816–1906
Grierson, Sir James Moncrieff . 1859–1914
Griffin, Sir Lepel Henry . . 1838–1908
Griffith, Ralph Thomas Hotchkin 1826–1906
Griffiths, Arthur George Frederick 1838–1908
Griggs, William . . . 1832–1911
Grimthorpe, first Baron. See Beckett, Sir Edmund.
Groome, Francis Hindes . . 1851–1902
Grose, Thomas Hodge . . 1845–1906
Grossmith, George . . . 1847–1912
Grossmith, Walter Weedon. See under Grossmith, George.
Grosvenor, Richard De Aquila, first Baron Stalbridge . . 1837–1912
Gubbins, John . . . 1838–1906
Guinness, Sir Arthur Edward, first Baron Ardilaun . . 1840–1915
Guinness, Henry Grattan . . 1835–1910
Gully, William Court, first Viscount Selby . . . 1835–1909
Günther, Albert Charles Lewis Gotthilf 1830–1914
Gurney, Henry Palin . . 1847–1904
Guthrie, William . . . 1835–1908
Gwatkin, Henry Melvill . . 1844–1916
Gwynn, John 1827–1917

Hacker, Arthur . . . 1858–1919
Haden, Sir Francis Seymour . 1818–1910
Haig-Brown, William . . 1823–1907
Haigh, Arthur Elam . . 1855–1905
Haines, Sir Frederick Paul . 1819–1909
Haliburton, Arthur Lawrence, first Baron Haliburton . . 1832–1907
Hall, Christopher Newman . 1816–1902
Hall, FitzEdward . . . 1825–1901
Hall, Sir John . . . 1824–1907
Hallé (formerly Norman-Neruda), Wilma Maria Francisca, Lady 1839–1911
Halliday, Sir Frederick James . 1806–1901
Halsbury, first Earl of. See Giffard, Hardinge Stanley.
Hamblin Smith, James. See Smith.
Hamilton, David James . 1849–1909
Hamilton, Sir Edward Walter . 1847–1908
Hamilton, Eugene Jacob Lee. See Lee-Hamilton.
Hamilton, James, second Duke of Abercorn 1838–1913
Hamilton, Sir Richard Vesey . 1829–1912

Hampden, second Viscount. See Brand, Henry Robert.
Hanbury, Charlotte. See under Hanbury, Elizabeth.
Hanbury, Elizabeth . . 1793–1901
Hanbury, Sir James Arthur . 1832–1908
Hanbury, Robert William . 1845–1903
Hankin, St. John Emile Clavering 1869–1909
Hanlan (properly Hanlon), Edward 1855–1908
Harben, Sir Henry . . . 1823–1911
Harcourt, Augustus George Vernon 1834–1919
Harcourt, Leveson Francis Vernon-. See Vernon-Harcourt.
Harcourt, Sir William George Granville Venables Vernon . 1827–1904
Hardie, James Keir . . 1856–1915
Hardie, William Ross . . 1862–1916
Hardwicke, sixth Earl of. See Yorke, Albert Edward Philip Henry.
Hardy, Frederic Daniel . . 1827–1911
Hardy, Gathorne Gathorne-, first Earl of Cranbrook. See Gathorne-Hardy.
Hardy, Herbert Hardy Cozens-, first Baron Cozens-Hardy. See Cozens-Hardy.
Hare, Augustus John Cuthbert . 1834–1903
Hare, Sir John . . . 1844–1921
Harland, Henry . . . 1861–1905
Harley, Robert . . . 1828–1910
Harrington, Timothy Charles . 1851–1910
Harris, Thomas Lake . . 1823–1906
Harrison, Reginald . . . 1837–1908
Hart, Sir Robert, first baronet . 1835–1911
Hartington, Marquess of. See Cavendish, Spencer Compton.
Hartley, Sir Charles Augustus . 1825–1915
Hartshorne, Albert . . . 1839–1910
Hastie, William . . . 1842–1903
Hatton, Harold Heneage Finch-. See Finch-Hatton.
Hatton, Joseph . . . 1841–1907
Havelock, Sir Arthur Elibank . 1844–1908
Haverfield, Francis John . . 1860–1919
Haweis, Hugh Reginald . . 1838–1901
Haweis, Mary. See under Haweis, Hugh Reginald.
Hawker, Mary Elizabeth, 'Lanoe Falconer'. 1848–1908
Hawkins, Henry, Baron Brampton 1817–1907
Hayes, Edwin 1819–1904
Hayman, Henry . . . 1823–1904
Hayne, Charles Hayne Seale-. See Seale-Hayne.
Hayward, Robert Baldwin . 1829–1903
Hazlitt, William Carew . . 1834–1913
Head, Barclay Vincent . . 1844–1914
Headlam, Walter George . . 1866–1908
Hearn, Mary Anne, 'Marianne Farningham' . . . 1834–1909
Heath, Christopher . . . 1835–1905
Heath, Sir Leopold George . 1817–1907
Heathcote, John Moyer . . 1834–1912
Heaton, Sir John Henniker, first baronet 1848–1914
Hector, Annie French, 'Mrs. Alexander' 1825–1902
Hector, Sir James . . . 1834–1907
Heinemann, William . . 1863–1920
Hellmuth, Isaac 1817–1901
Hemming, George Wirgman . 1821–1905
Hemphill, Charles Hare, first Baron Hemphill . . . 1822–1908
Henderson, Sir David . . 1862–1921
Henderson, George Francis Robert 1854–1903
Henderson, Joseph . . . 1832–1908
Henderson, William George . 1819–1905
Henley, William Ernest . . 1849–1903
Hennell, Sara. See under Bray, Caroline.
Hennessey, John Bobanau Nickerlieu 1829–1910
Hennessy, Henry . . . 1826–1901
Henry, Mitchell . . . 1826–1910
Henty, George Alfred . . 1832–1902
Herbert, Auberon Edward William Molyneux . . . 1838–1906
Herbert, Auberon Thomas, eighth Baron Lucas 1876–1916
Herbert, Sir Robert George Wyndham 1831–1905
Herford, Brooke . . . 1830–1903
Herford, William Henry . . 1820–1908
Herkomer, Sir Hubert von . 1849–1914
Herring, George . . . 1832–1906
Herschel, Alexander Stewart . 1836–1907
Hertslet, Sir Edward . . 1824–1902
Hibbert, Sir John Tomlinson . 1824–1908
Hicks, Edward Lee . . . 1843–1919
Hicks Beach, Sir Michael Edward, first Earl St. Aldwyn . 1837–1916
Hiles, Henry 1828–1904
Hill, Alexander Staveley . . 1825–1905
Hill, Alsager Hay . . . 1839–1906
Hill, Frank Harrison . . 1830–1910
Hill, George Birkbeck Norman . 1835–1903
Hill, Octavia 1838–1912
Hill, Rosamond Davenport- . 1825–1902
Hills, Sir John . . . 1834–1902
Hind, Henry Youle . . . 1823–1908
Hind, Richard Dacre Archer-. See Archer-Hind.
Hingeston-Randolph (formerly Hingston), Francis Charles . 1833–1910
Hingley, Sir Benjamin, first baronet 1830–1905
Hingston, Sir William Hales . 1829–1907
Hipkins, Alfred James . . 1826–1903
Hoare, Joseph Charles . . 1851–1906
Hobbes, John Oliver, *pseudonym*. See Craigie, Pearl Mary Teresa.
Hobhouse, Arthur, Baron Hobhouse 1819–1904
Hobhouse, Edmund . . 1817–1904
Hodgetts, James Frederick . 1828–1906
Hodgkin, Thomas . . . 1831–1913
Hodgson, Richard Dacre. See Archer-Hind.
Hodgson, Shadworth Hollway . 1832–1912

Hodson (afterwards Labouchere), Henrietta 1841–1910
Hoey, Frances Sarah [Mrs. Cashel Hoey] . . . 1830–1908
Hofmeyr, Jan Hendrik . . . 1845–1909
Hogg, Quintin 1845–1903
Holden, Luther 1815–1905
Holder, Sir Frederick William . 1850–1909
Hole, Samuel Reynolds . . 1819–1904
Hollams, Sir John . . . 1820–1910
Holland, Henry Scott . . 1847–1918
Holland, Sir Henry Thurstan, first Viscount Knutsford . 1825–1914
Hollingshead, John . . . 1827–1904
Hollowell, James Hirst . . 1851–1909
Holman Hunt, William. See Hunt.
Holmes, Augusta (Mary Anne) . 1847–1903
Holmes, Sir Richard Rivington . 1835–1911
Holmes, Thomas . . . 1846–1918
Holmes, Timothy . . . 1825–1907
Holroyd, Sir Charles . . 1861–1917
Holroyd, Henry North, third Earl of Sheffield . . . 1832–1909
Holyoake, George Jacob . . 1817–1906
Hood, Arthur William Acland, Baron Hood 1824–1901
Hood, Horace Lambert Alexander 1870–1916
Hook, James Clarke . . 1819–1907
Hooker, Sir Joseph Dalton . 1817–1911
Hope, John Adrian Louis, seventh Earl of Hopetoun and first Marquess of Linlithgow . 1860–1908
Hope, Laurence, *pseudonym*. See Nicolson, Adela Florence.
Hope, Sir William Henry St. John 1854–1919
Hopetoun, seventh Earl of. See Hope, John Adrian Louis.
Hopkins, Edward John . . 1818–1901
Hopkins, Jane Ellice . . 1836–1904
Hopkinson, Bertram . . 1874–1918
Hopwood, Charles Henry . . 1829–1904
Hornby, James John . . 1826–1909
Horniman, Frederick John . 1835–1906
Horsley, John Callcott . . 1817–1903
Horsley, John William . . 1845–1921
Horsley, Sir Victor Alexander Haden 1857–1916
Hoskins, Sir Anthony Hiley . 1828–1901
Houghton, William Stanley . 1881–1913
Howard, George James, ninth Earl of Carlisle . . . 1843–1911
Howard, Henry FitzAlan-, fifteenth Duke of Norfolk . 1847–1917
Howard, Rosalind Frances, Countess of Carlisle . . 1845–1921
Howell, David 1831–1903
Howell, George 1833–1910
Howes, Thomas George Bond . 1853–1905
Howitt, Alfred William . . 1830–1908
Howland, Sir William Pearce . 1811–1907
Hubbard, Louisa Maria . . 1836–1906
Huddart, James 1847–1901
Hudleston (formerly Simpson), Wilfred Hudleston . . 1828–1909
Hudson, Charles Thomas . . 1828–1903
Huggins, Sir William . . 1824–1910
Hughes, Arthur . . . 1832–1915
Hughes, Edward . . . 1832–1908
Hughes, Hugh Price . . 1847–1902
Hughes, John 1842–1902
Hughes, Sir Sam . . . 1853–1921
Hulme, Frederick Edward . 1841–1909
Hume, Allan Octavian . . 1829–1912
Hume, Martin Andrew Sharp . 1843–1910
Hunt, George William. See under Macdermott, Gilbert Hastings.
Hunt, William Holman . . 1827–1910
Hunter, Colin 1841–1904
Hunter, Sir Robert . . . 1844–1913
Hunter, Sir William Guyer . 1827–1902
Huntington, George . . 1825–1905
Hurlstone, William Yeates . 1876–1906
Hutchinson, Sir Jonathan . 1828–1913
Huth, Alfred Henry . . 1850–1910
Hutton, Alfred . . . 1839–1910
Hutton, Frederick Wollaston . 1836–1905
Hutton, George Clark . . 1825–1908
Hyndman, Henry Mayers . 1842–1921

Ibbetson, Sir Denzil Charles Jelf 1847–1908
Ibbetson, Sir Henry John Selwin-, Baron Rookwood. See Selwin-Ibbetson.
Ignatius, Father. See Lyne, Joseph Leycester.
Ince, William 1825–1910
Inderwick, Frederick Andrew . 1836–1904
Inglis, Elsie Maud . . . 1864–1917
Ingram, John Kells . . . 1823–1907
Ingram, Thomas Dunbar . . 1826–1901
Innes, James John McLeod . 1830–1907
Irby, Leonard Howard Loyd . 1836–1905
Ireland, William Wotherspoon . 1832–1909
Irvine, William . . . 1840–1911
Irving, Sir Henry . . . 1838–1905
Iwan-Müller, Ernest Bruce . 1853–1910

Jacks, William . . . 1841–1907
Jackson, Henry . . . 1839–1921
Jackson, John . . . 1833–1901
Jackson, John Hughlings . . 1835–1911
Jackson, Mason . . . 1819–1903
Jackson, Samuel Phillips . . 1830–1904
Jackson, William Lawies, first Baron Allerton . . . 1840–1917
Jacob, Edgar 1844–1920
James, Henry, Lord James of Hereford 1828–1911
James, Henry 1843–1916
James, James 1832–1902
Jameson, Andrew, Lord Ardwall 1845–1911
Jameson, Sir Leander Starr, baronet 1853–1917
Japp, Alexander Hay, 'H. A. Page' 1837–1905
Jardine, Sir Robert, first baronet 1825–1905
Jayne, Francis John . . 1845–1921
Jeaffreson, John Cordy . . 1831–1901
Jebb, Sir Richard Claverhouse . 1841–1905
Jelf, George Edward . . 1834–1908
Jenkins, Ebenezer Evans . . 1820–1905
Jenkins, John Edward . . 1838–1910
Jenner-Fust, Herbert . . 1806–1904
Jephson, Arthur Jermy Mounteney 1858–1908

Jersey, seventh Earl of. See Villiers, Victor Albert George Child-.
Jessopp, Augustus . . . 1824–1914
Jeune, Francis Henry, Baron St. Helier 1843–1905
Jex-Blake, Sophia Louisa . 1840–1912
Jex-Blake, Thomas William . 1832–1915
Johns, Claude Hermann Walter 1857–1920
Johnson, Lionel Pigot . . 1867–1902
Johnston, William . . . 1829–1902
Joly, Charles Jasper . . 1864–1906
Joly de Lotbinière, Sir Henry Gustave 1829–1908
Jones, Sir Alfred Lewis . . 1845–1909
Jones, Henry Cadman . . 1818–1902
Jones, John Viriamu . . 1856–1901
Jones, Thomas Rupert . . 1819–1911
Jones, William West . . 1838–1908

Kane, Robert Romney . . 1842–1902
Keay, John Seymour . . 1839–1909
Keetley, Charles Robert Bell . 1848–1909
Kekewich, Sir Arthur . . 1832–1907
Kekewich, Robert George . 1854–1914
Kelly, Frederick Septimus . 1881–1916
Kelly, Mary Anne, 'Eva'. See under O'Doherty, Kevin Izod.
Kelly, William 1821–1906
Kelly-Kenny, Sir Thomas . 1840–1914
Kelvin, Baron. See Thomson, William.
Kemball, Sir Arnold Burrowes . 1820–1908
Kemble, Henry 1848–1907
Kendal, William Hunter . . 1834–1917
Kennedy, Sir William Rann . 1846–1915
Kensit, John 1853–1902
Kent (William) Charles (Mark) . 1823–1902
Kenyon, George Thomas . . 1840–1908
Kenyon-Slaney, William Slaney 1847–1908
Keppel, Sir George Olof Roos-. See Roos-Keppel.
Keppel, Sir Henry . . . 1809–1904
Kerr, John 1824–1907
Kerr, Robert 1823–1904
Kidd, Benjamin . . . 1858–1916
Killen, William Dool . . . 1806–1902
Kimberley, first Earl of. See Wodehouse, John.
Kinahan, George Henry . . 1829–1908
Kincairney, Lord. See Gloag, William Ellis.
King, Edward 1829–1910
King, Sir George . . . 1840–1909
King, Haynes 1831–1904
Kingsburgh, Lord. See Macdonald, Sir John Hay Athole.
Kingscote, Sir Robert Nigel Fitzhardinge . . . 1830–1908
Kingston, Charles Cameron . 1850–1908
Kinnear, Alexander Smith, first Baron Kinnear . . . 1833–1917
Kinns, Samuel 1826–1903
Kinross, first Baron. See Balfour, John Blair.
Kitchener, Horatio Herbert, first Earl Kitchener . . . 1850–1916
Kitchin, George William . . 1827–1912
Kitson, James, first Baron Airedale 1835–1911
Kitton, Frederick George . . 1856–1904
Knight, Joseph . . . 1837–1909
Knight, Joseph . . . 1829–1907
Knowles, Sir James Thomas . 1831–1908
Knox (formerly Craig), Isa . 1831–1903
Knox-Little, William John . 1839–1918
Knutsford, first Viscount. See Holland, Sir Henry Thurstan.
Kynaston (formerly Snow), Herbert 1835–1910

Labouchere, Henrietta. See Hodson.
Labouchere, Henry Du Pré . 1831–1912
Lafont, Eugène 1837–1908
Laidlaw, Anna Robena . . 1819–1901
Laidlaw, John 1832–1906
Lambert, Brooke . . . 1834–1901
Lambert, George . . . 1842–1915
Lane, Sir Hugh Percy . . 1875–1915
Lang, Andrew 1844–1912
Lang, John Marshall . . 1834–1909
Langevin, Sir Hector Louis . 1826–1906
Langford, John Alfred . . 1823–1903
Lascelles, Sir Frank Cavendish . 1841–1920
Laszowska, (Jane) Emily de. See Gerard.
Latey, John 1842–1902
Latham, Henry 1821–1902
Laughton, Sir John Knox . 1830–1915
Laurie, James Stuart . . 1832–1904
Laurie, Simon Somerville . 1829–1909
Laurier, Sir Wilfrid . . . 1841–1919
Law, David 1831–1901
Law, Sir Edward FitzGerald . 1846–1908
Law, Thomas Graves . . 1836–1904
Lawes (afterwards Lawes-Wittewronge), Sir Charles Bennet, second baronet . . . 1843–1911
Lawes, William George . . 1839–1907
Lawley, Francis Charles . . 1825–1901
Lawson, Edward Levy-, first Baron Burnham. See Levy-Lawson.
Lawson, George 1831–1903
Lawson, George Anderson . 1832–1904
Lawson, Sir Wilfrid, second baronet 1829–1906
Leach, Arthur Francis . . 1851–1915
Leader, John Temple . . 1810–1903
Leake, George 1856–1902
Lecky, Squire Thornton Stratford 1838–1902
Lecky, William Edward Hartpole 1838–1903
Ledwidge, Francis . . . 1891–1917
Lee, Frederick George . . 1832–1902
Lee, Rawdon Briggs . . 1845–1908
Lee-Hamilton, Eugene Jacob . 1845–1907
Lee-Warner, Sir William . . 1846–1914
Lefroy, William . . . 1836–1909
Legg, John Wickham . . 1843–1921
Legros, Alphonse . . . 1837–1911
Lehmann, Rudolf . . . 1819–1905
Leicester, second Earl of. See Coke, Thomas William.

Leighton, Stanley . . . 1837–1901
Leiningen, Prince Ernest Leopold Victor Charles Auguste Joseph Emich 1830–1904
Leishman, Thomas . . . 1825–1904
Le Jeune, Henry . . . 1819–1904
Lemmens-Sherrington, Helen . 1834–1906
Lempriere, Charles . . . 1818–1901
Leng, Sir John . . . 1828–1906
Leng, Sir William Christopher . 1825–1902
Lennox, Charles Henry Gordon-, sixth Duke of Richmond. See Gordon-Lennox.
Leno, Dan 1860–1904
Leveson-Gower, (Edward) Frederick 1819–1907
Levy-Lawson, Edward, first Baron Burnham . . . 1833–1916
Lewis, Bunnell . . . 1824–1908
Lewis, David. See under Lewis, Evan.
Lewis, Evan 1818–1901
Lewis, Sir George Henry, first baronet 1833–1911
Lewis, John Travers . . 1825–1901
Lewis, Richard . . . 1821–1905
Lewis, William Thomas, first Baron Merthyr . . . 1837–1914
Liberty, Sir Arthur Lasenby . 1843–1917
Lidderdale, William . . 1832–1902
Lindley, Nathaniel, Baron Lindley 1828–1921
Lindsay, James Gavin . . 1835–1903
Lindsay, James Ludovic, twenty-sixth Earl of Crawford . . 1847–1913
Lindsay (afterwards Loyd-Lindsay), Robert James, Baron Wantage 1832–1901
Lindsay, Thomas Martin . . 1843–1914
Lingen, Ralph Robert Wheeler, Baron Lingen . . . 1819–1905
Linlithgow, first Marquess of. See Hope, John Adrian Louis.
Lister, Arthur 1830–1908
Lister, Joseph, first Baron Lister 1827–1912
Lister, Samuel Cunliffe, first Baron Masham . . . 1815–1906
Little, William John Knox-. See Knox-Little.
Littler, Sir Ralph Daniel Makinson 1835–1908
Livesey, Sir George Thomas . 1834–1908
Llandaff, Viscount. See Matthews, Henry.
Loates, Thomas . . . 1867–1910
Lockey, Charles . . . 1820–1901
Lockyer, Sir (Joseph) Norman . 1836–1920
Loftie, William John . . 1839–1911
Loftus, Lord Augustus William Frederick Spencer . . 1817–1904
Lohmann, George Alfred . . 1865–1901
Londonderry, sixth Marquess of. See Vane-Tempest-Stewart, Charles Stewart.
Longhurst, William Henry . 1819–1904
Lopes, Sir Lopes Massey, third baronet 1818–1908
Lord, Thomas . . . 1808–1903
Lotbinière, Sir Henry Gustave Joly de. See Joly de Lotbinière.
Lovelace, second Earl of. See Milbanke, Ralph Gordon Noel King.
Lovett, Richard . . . 1851–1904
Low, Alexander, Lord Low . 1845–1910
Low, Sir Robert Cunliffe . . 1838–1911
Lowe, Sir Drury Curzon Drury-. See Drury-Lowe.
Lowry, Henry Dawson . . 1869–1906
Lowther, James . . . 1840–1904
Löwy, Albert or Abraham . 1816–1908
Loyd-Lindsay. See Lindsay, Robert James, Baron Wantage.
Luard, Sir William Garnham . 1820–1910
Lubbock, Sir John, first Baron Avebury 1834–1913
Luby, Thomas Clarke . . 1821–1901
Lucas, eighth Baron. See Herbert, Auberon Thomas.
Lucas, Keith 1879–1916
Luckock, Herbert Mortimer . 1833–1909
Ludlow, John Malcolm Forbes . 1821–1911
Luke, Jemima 1813–1906
Lupton, Joseph Hirst . . 1836–1905
Lusk, Sir Andrew, baronet . 1810–1909
Lutz, (Wilhelm) Meyer . . 1829–1903
Lyall, Sir Alfred Comyn . . 1835–1911
Lyall, Sir Charles James . . 1845–1920
Lyall, Edna, *pseudonym*. See Bayly, Ada Ellen.
Lyne, Joseph Leycester [Father Ignatius] 1837–1908
Lyne, Sir William John . . 1844–1918
Lyons, Sir Algernon McLennan . 1833–1908
Lyttelton, Alfred . . . 1857–1913
Lyttelton, Arthur Temple . 1852–1903

Macan, Sir Arthur Vernon . 1843–1908
McArthur, Charles . . . 1844–1910
Macarthur, Mary Reid. See Anderson.
M'Carthy, Justin . . . 1832–1912
Macartney, Sir Samuel Halliday 1833–1906
Macaulay, James . . . 1817–1902
Macbain, Alexander . . 1855–1907
Macbeth, Robert Walker . . 1848–1910
MacCallum, Andrew . . 1821–1902
McCalmont, Harry Leslie Blundell 1861–1902
McClean, Frank . . . 1837–1904
McClintock, Sir Francis Leopold 1819–1907
McCoan, James Carlile . . 1829–1904
MacColl, Malcolm . . . 1831–1907
MacColl, Norman . . . 1843–1904
MacCormac, Sir William, first baronet 1836–1901
McCudden, James Thomas Byford 1895–1918
Maccunn, Hamish [James] . 1868–1916
MacDermot, Hugh Hyacinth O'Rorke, The MacDermot . 1834–1904
Macdermott, Gilbert Hastings . 1845–1901
MacDermott, Martin . . 1823–1905
Macdonald, Sir Claude Maxwell . 1852–1915
MacDonald, George . . . 1824–1905
Macdonald, Sir Hector Archibald 1853–1903

McDonald, John Blake . . 1829–1901
Macdonald, Sir John Denis . 1826–1908
Macdonald, Sir John Hay Athole, Lord Kingsburgh . . . 1836–1919
MacDonell, Sir Hugh Guion . 1832–1904
Macdonell, Sir John . . . 1846–1921
McDonnell, Sir Schomberg Kerr 1861–1915
Mace, James [Jem Mace] . . 1831–1910
Macfadyen, Allan . . . 1860–1907
Macfarren, Walter Cecil . . 1826–1905
MacGregor, James . . . 1832–1910
Macgregor, Sir William . . 1846–1919
Machell, James Octavius . . 1837–1902
Machray, Robert . . . 1831–1904
Macintyre, Donald . . . 1831–1903
Mackay, Æneas James George . 1839–1911
Mackay, Alexander . . . 1833–1902
Mackay, Donald James, eleventh Baron Reay . . . 1839–1921
Mackennal, Alexander . . 1835–1904
Mackenzie, Sir Alexander . 1842–1902
Mackenzie, Sir George Sutherland 1844–1910
M'Kenzie, Sir John . . . 1836–1901
Mackenzie, Sir Stephen . . 1844–1909
MacKinlay, Antoinette. See Sterling.
Mackintosh, John . . . 1833–1907
McLachlan, Robert . . . 1837–1904
Maclagan, Christian . . 1811–1901
Maclagan, William Dalrymple . 1826–1910
Maclaren, Alexander . . 1826–1910
Maclaren, Ian, *pseudonym*. See Watson, John.
McLaren, John, Lord McLaren . 1831–1910
Maclean, Sir Harry Aubrey de Vere 1848–1920
Maclean, James Mackenzie . 1835–1906
Maclear, George Frederick . 1833–1902
Maclear, John Fiot Lee Pearse . 1838–1907
Macleod, Fiona, *pseudonym*. See Sharp, William.
Macleod, Henry Dunning . . 1821–1902
Maclure, Edward Craig . . 1833–1906
Maclure, Sir John William. See under Maclure, Edward Craig.
McMahon, Charles Alexander . 1830–1904
Macmillan, Hugh . . . 1833–1903
Macnaghten, Sir Edward, Baron Macnaghten 1830–1913
McNair, John Frederick Adolphus 1828–1910
McNeill, Sir John Carstairs . 1831–1904
Macpherson, Sir John Molesworth 1853–1914
McQueen, Sir John Withers . 1836–1909
Macrorie, William Kenneth . 1831–1905
McTaggart, William . . 1835–1910
MacWhirter, John . . . 1839–1911
Madden, Frederic William . 1839–1904
Madden, Katherine Cecil. See Thurston.
Madden, Thomas More . . 1844–1902
Mahaffy, Sir John Pentland . 1839–1919
Mair, William 1830–1920
Maitland, Agnes Catherine . 1850–1906
Maitland, Frederic William . 1850–1906
Malet, Sir Edward Baldwin, fourth baronet . . . 1837–1908
Malone, Sylvester . . . 1822–1906
Manley, William George Nicholas 1831–1901
Manners, (Lord) John James Robert, seventh Duke of Rutland 1818–1906
Manning, John Edmondson . 1848–1910
Manns, Sir August . . . 1825–1907
Mansel-Pleydell, John Clavell . 1817–1902
Mansergh, James . . . 1834–1905
Mansfield, Robert Blachford . 1824–1908
Maple, Sir John Blundell, baronet 1845–1903
Mapleson, James Henry . . 1830–1901
Mapother, Edward Dillon . 1835–1908
Mappin, Sir Frederick Thorpe, first baronet . . . 1821–1910
Marjoribanks, Edward, second Baron Tweedmouth . . 1849–1909
Markham, Sir Albert Hastings . 1841–1918
Markham, Sir Clements Robert . 1830–1916
Marks, David Woolf . . 1811–1909
Marriott, Sir William Thackeray 1834–1903
Marsden, Alexander Edwin . 1832–1902
Marshall, George William . 1839–1905
Marshall, Julian . . . 1836–1903
Martin, Sir Theodore . . 1816–1909
Martin, Sir Thomas Acquin . 1850–1906
Martin, Violet Florence, 'Martin Ross' 1862–1915
Marwick, Sir James David . 1826–1908
Masham, first Baron. See Lister, Samuel Cunliffe.
Maskelyne, Mervyn Herbert Nevil Story-. See Story-Maskelyne.
Massey, Gerald . . . 1828–1907
Masson, David . . . 1822–1907
Massy, William Godfrey Dunham 1838–1906
Masters, Maxwell Tylden . . 1833–1907
Matheson, George . . . 1842–1906
Mathew, Sir James Charles . 1830–1908
Mathews, Charles Edward . 1834–1905
Mathews, Sir Charles Willie . 1850–1920
Mathews, Sir Lloyd William . 1850–1901
Matthews, Henry, Viscount Llandaff 1826–1913
Maturin, Basil William . . 1847–1915
Maude, Sir (Frederick) Stanley . 1864–1917
Maurice, Sir John Frederick . 1841–1912
Mawdsley, James . . . 1848–1902
Maxim, Sir Hiram Stevens . 1840–1916
Maxwell (formerly Braddon), Mary Elizabeth . . . 1837–1915
May, Philip William [Phil May] 1864–1903
Mayor, John Eyton Bickersteth 1825–1910
Meade, Richard James, fourth Earl of Clanwilliam . . 1832–1907
Meakin, James Edward Budgett 1866–1906
Medd, Peter Goldsmith . . 1829–1908
Medlicott, Henry Benedict . 1829–1905
Meiklejohn, John Miller Dow . 1836–1902
Meldrum, Charles . . . 1821–1901
Mellon (formerly Woolgar), Sarah Jane 1824–1909
Melville, Arthur . . . 1855–1904
Meredith, George . . . 1828–1909
Merivale, Herman Charles . 1839–1906
Merriman, Henry Seton, *pseudonym*. See Scott, Hugh Stowell.
Merry, William Walter . . 1835–1918

Merthyr, first Baron. See Lewis, William Thomas.
Meyrick, Frederick 1827–1906
Michie, Alexander 1833–1902
Micklethwaite, John Thomas . 1843–1906
Midlane, Albert 1825–1909
Milbanke, Ralph Gordon Noel King, second Earl of Lovelace 1839–1906
Milford Haven, first Marquess of. See Mountbatten, Louis Alexander.
Miller, Sir James Percy, second baronet 1864–1906
Milne, John 1850–1913
Minto, fourth Earl of. See Elliot, Gilbert John Murray Kynynmond.
Mitchell, Sir Arthur . . 1826–1909
Mitchell, John Murray . . 1815–1904
Mitford, Algernon Bertram Freeman-, first Baron Redesdale . 1837–1916
Moberly, Robert Campbell . 1845–1903
Mocatta, Frederic David . . 1828–1905
Möens, William John Charles . 1833–1904
Moir, Frank Lewis 1852–1904
Molloy, Gerald 1834–1906
Molloy, James Lynam . . 1837–1909
Molloy, Joseph FitzGerald . 1858–1908
Molyneux, Sir Robert Henry More-. See More-Molyneux.
Moncreiff, Henry James, second Baron Moncreiff 1840–1909
Moncrieff, Sir Alexander . . 1829–1906
Mond, Ludwig 1839–1909
Monkhouse, William Cosmo . 1840–1901
Monro, Charles Henry . . 1835–1908
Monro, David Binning . . 1836–1905
Monson, Sir Edmund John, first baronet 1834–1909
Montagu, Lord Robert . . 1825–1902
Montagu, Samuel, first Baron Swaythling 1832–1911
Montagu-Douglas-Scott, Lord Charles Thomas. See Scott.
Montgomerie, Robert Archibald James 1855–1908
Montmorency, Raymond Harvey de, third Viscount Frankfort de Montmorency. See De Montmorency.
Monypenny, William Flavelle . 1866–1912
Moor, Sir Ralph Denham Rayment 1860–1909
Moore, Arthur William . . 1853–1909
Moore, Edward 1835–1916
Moore, Stuart Archibald . . 1842–1907
Moore, Temple Lushington . 1856–1920
Moorhouse, James . . . 1826–1915
Moran, Patrick Francis . . 1830–1911
Morant, Sir Robert Laurie . 1863–1920
More-Molyneux, Sir Robert Henry 1838–1904
Morfill, William Richard . . 1834–1909
Morgan, Edward Delmar . . 1840–1909
Moriarty, Henry Augustus . 1815–1906
Morley, third Earl of. See Parker, Albert Edmund.
Morris, Sir Lewis . . . 1833–1907
Morris, Michael, Lord Morris and Killanin 1826–1901
Morris, Philip Richard . . 1836–1902
Morris, Tom 1821–1908
Morris, William O'Connor . 1824–1904
Morrison, Walter 1836–1921
Moseley, Henry Gwyn Jeffreys . 1887–1915
Moule, George Evans . . 1828–1912
Moule, Handley Carr Glyn . 1841–1920
Moulton, James Hope . . 1863–1917
Moulton, John Fletcher, Baron Moulton 1845–1921
Mountbatten, Louis Alexander, first Marquess of Milford Haven (formerly Prince Louis Alexander of Battenberg) . . 1854–1921
Mountford, Edward William . 1855–1908
Mount Stephen, first Baron. See Stephen, George.
Mowat, Sir Oliver . . . 1820–1903
Mowatt, Sir Francis . . 1837–1919
Muir, Sir William . . . 1819–1905
Müller, Ernest Bruce Iwan-. See Iwan-Müller.
Mullins, Edwin Roscoe . . 1848–1907
Munby, Arthur Joseph . . 1828–1910
Munro, Hector Hugh . . 1870–1916
Munro, James 1832–1908
Murdoch, William Lloyd . . 1855–1911
Murray, Alexander Stuart . 1841–1904
Murray, Charles Adolphus, seventh Earl of Dunmore . . . 1841–1907
Murray, David Christie . 1847–1907
Murray, George Robert Milne . 1858–1911
Murray, Sir James Augustus Henry 1837–1915
Murray, Sir James Wolfe . . 1853–1919
Murray, Sir John . . . 1841–1914
Musgrave, Sir James, baronet . 1826–1904
Muybridge, Eadweard . . 1830–1904
Myers, Ernest James . . 1844–1921

Nares, Sir George Strong . . 1831–1915
Neil, Robert Alexander . . 1852–1901
Neil, Samuel 1825–1901
Nelson, Eliza. See under Craven, Henry Thornton.
Nelson, Sir Hugh Muir . . 1835–1906
Neruda, Wilma Maria Francisca. See Hallé, Lady.
Nettleship, Edward . . . 1845–1913
Nettleship, John Trivett . . 1841–1902
Neubauer, Adolf . . . 1832–1907
Neville, Henry 1837–1910
Newmarch, Charles Henry . 1824–1903
Newnes, Sir George, first baronet 1851–1910
Newton, Alfred 1829–1907
Nicholson, Sir Charles, first baronet 1808–1903
Nicholson, Edward Williams Byron 1849–1912
Nicholson, George . . . 1847–1908
Nicholson, William Gustavus, first Baron Nicholson . . 1845–1918
Nicol, Erskine 1825–1904
Nicolson, Adela Florence, 'Laurence Hope' 1865–1904

Nicolson, Malcolm Hassels. See under Nicolson, Adela Florence.
Nightingale, Florence . . 1820–1910
Nixon, Sir John Eccles . . 1857–1921
Noble, Sir Andrew, first baronet 1831–1915
Nodal, John Howard . . 1831–1909
Norfolk, fifteenth Duke of. See Howard, Henry FitzAlan-.
Norman, Conolly . . . 1853–1908
Norman, Sir Francis Booth . 1830–1901
Norman, Sir Henry Wylie . 1826–1904
Norman-Neruda, Wilma Maria Francisca. See Hallé, Lady.
Northbrook, first Earl of. See Baring, Thomas George.
Northcote, Henry Stafford, Baron Northcote 1846–1911
Northcote, James Spencer . 1821–1907
Norton, first Baron. See Adderley, Charles Bowyer.
Norton, John 1823–1904
Novello (afterwards Countess Gigliucci), Clara Anastasia . 1818–1908
Nunburnholme, first Baron. See Wilson, Charles Henry.
Nunn, Joshua Arthur . . 1853–1908
Nutt, Alfred Trübner . . 1856–1910
Nuttall, Enos 1842–1916

Oakeley, Sir Herbert Stanley . 1830–1903
Oates, Lawrence Edward Grace . 1880–1912
O'Brien, Charlotte Grace . . 1845–1909
O'Brien, Cornelius 1843–1906
O'Brien, James Francis Xavier . 1828–1905
O'Brien, Peter, Baron O'Brien . 1842–1914
O'Callaghan, Sir Francis Langford 1839–1909
O'Connor, Charles Yelverton . 1843–1902
O'Connor, James . . . 1836–1910
O'Conor, Charles Owen [O'Conor Don] 1836–1906
O'Conor, Sir Nicholas Roderick . 1843–1908
O'Doherty, Kevin Izod . . 1823–1905
O'Doherty (formerly Kelly), Mary Anne. See under O'Doherty, Kevin Izod.
Ogle, John William . . . 1824–1905
O'Hanlon, John . . . 1821–1905
Oldham, Charles James. See under Oldham, Henry.
Oldham, Henry . . . 1815–1902
O'Leary, John . . . 1830–1907
Oliver, Samuel Pasfield . . 1838–1907
Olpherts, Sir William . . 1822–1902
Ommanney, Sir Erasmus . . 1814–1904
Ommanney, George Druce Wynne 1819–1902
Onslow, William Hillier, fourth Earl of Onslow 1853–1911
Oppenheim, Lassa Francis Lawrence 1858–1919
Orchardson, Sir William Quiller . 1832–1910
Ord, William Miller . . 1834–1902
O'Rell, Max, *pseudonym*. See Blouet, Léon Paul.
Ormerod, Eleanor Anne . . 1828–1901
Orr, Alexandra Sutherland . 1828–1903
Osborne, Walter Frederick . 1859–1903
O'Shea, John Augustus . . 1839–1905
O'Shea, William Henry . . 1840–1905
Osler, Abraham Follett . . 1808–1903
Osler, Sir William, baronet . 1849–1919
O'Sullivan, Cornelius . . 1841–1907
Otté, Elise 1818–1903
Ouida, *pseudonym*. See De la Ramée, Marie Louise.
Overton, John Henry . . 1835–1903
Overtoun, Baron. See White, John Campbell.
Owen, Robert . . . 1820–1902

Page, H. A., *pseudonym*. See Japp, Alexander Hay.
Paget, Francis . . . 1851–1911
Paget, Sidney Edward . . 1860–1908
Pakenham, Sir Francis John . 1832–1905
Palgrave, Sir Reginald Francis Douce 1829–1904
Palles, Christopher . . . 1831–1920
Palmer, Sir Arthur Power . . 1840–1904
Palmer, Sir Charles Mark, first baronet 1822–1907
Palmer, Sir Elwin Mitford . 1852–1906
Palmer, George William . 1851–1913
Parish, William Douglas . 1833–1904
Parker, Albert Edmund, third Earl of Morley . . . 1843–1905
Parker, Charles Stuart . . 1829–1910
Parker, Joseph . . . 1830–1902
Parker, Robert John, Baron Parker 1857–1918
Parr (formerly Taylor), Louisa . *d.* 1903
Parry, Sir Charles Hubert Hastings, baronet . . . 1848–1918
Parry, Joseph . . . 1841–1903
Parry, Joseph Haydn. See under Parry, Joseph.
Parsons, Alfred William . . 1847–1920
Parsons, Laurence, fourth Earl of Rosse 1840–1908
Paton, John Brown . . 1830–1911
Paton, John Gibson . . 1824–1907
Paton, Sir Joseph Noël . . 1821–1901
Paul, Charles Kegan . . 1828–1902
Paul, William . . . 1822–1905
Pauncefote, Julian, Baron Pauncefote 1828–1902
Pavy, Frederick William . . 1829–1911
Payne, Edward John . . 1844–1904
Payne, Joseph Frank . . 1840–1910
Peacocke, Joseph Ferguson . 1835–1916
Pearce, Stephen . . . 1819–1904
Pearce, Sir William George, second baronet . . . 1861–1907
Pears, Sir Edwin . . . 1835–1919
Pearson, Sir Charles John, Lord Pearson 1843–1910
Pearson, Sir Cyril Arthur, first baronet 1866–1921
Pease, Sir Joseph Whitwell, first baronet 1828–1903
Peek, Sir Cuthbert Edgar, second baronet 1855–1901
Peel, Arthur Wellesley, first Viscount Peel . . . 1829–1912

Peel, Sir Frederick . . . 1823–1906
Peel, James 1811–1906
Peile, Sir James Braithwaite . 1833–1906
Peile, John . . . 1837–1910
Pelham, Henry Francis . . 1846–1907
Pélissier, Harry Gabriel . . 1874–1913
Pell, Albert 1820–1907
Pember, Edward Henry . . 1833–1911
Pemberton, Thomas Edgar . 1849–1905
Penley, William Sydney . . 1852–1912
Pennant, George Sholto Gordon Douglas-, second Baron Penrhyn. See Douglas-Pennant.
Penrhyn, second Baron. See Douglas - Pennant, George Sholto Gordon.
Penrose, Francis Cranmer . 1817–1903
Percival, John . . . 1834–1918
Percy, Henry Algernon George, Earl Percy 1871–1909
Perkin, Sir William Henry . 1838–1907
Perkins, Sir Æneas . . . 1834–1901
Perowne, Edward Henry . . 1826–1906
Perowne, John James Stewart . 1823–1904
Perry, Walter Copland . . 1814–1911
Peterson, Sir William . . 1856–1921
Petit, Sir Dinshaw Manockjee, first baronet . . . 1823–1901
Petre, Sir George Glynn . . 1822–1905
Petrie, William . . . 1821–1908
Pettigrew, James Bell . . 1834–1908
Phear, Sir John Budd . . 1825–1905
Phillips, Stephen . . . 1864–1915
Phillips, William . . . 1822–1905
Piatti, Alfredo Carlo . . 1822–1901
Pickard, Benjamin . . . 1842–1904
Picton, James Allanson . . 1832–1910
Pirbright, Baron. See De Worms, Henry.
Pitman, Sir Henry Alfred . 1808–1908
Plater, Charles Dominic . . 1875–1921
Platts, John Thompson . . 1830–1904
Playfair, William Smoult . . 1835–1903
Pleydell, John Clavell Mansel. See Mansel-Pleydell.
Plunkett, Sir Francis Richard . 1835–1907
Podmore, Frank 1855–1910
Pollen, John Hungerford . . 1820–1902
Poore, George Vivian . . 1843–1904
Pope, George Uglow . . 1820–1908
Pope, Samuel 1826–1901
Pope, William Burt . . . 1822–1903
Portal, Melville 1819–1904
Porter, Sir Andrew Marshall, first baronet . . . 1837–1919
Pott, Alfred 1822–1908
Powell, Frederick York . . 1850–1904
Power, Sir William Henry . 1842–1916
Poynter, Sir Edward John . 1836–1919
Poynting, John Henry . . 1852–1914
Pratt, Hodgson . . . 1824–1907
Pratt, Joseph Bishop . . 1854–1910
Preece, Sir William Henry . 1834–1913
Prendergast, Sir Harry North Dalrymple 1834–1913
Price, Frederick George Hilton . 1842–1909
Price, Thomas . . . 1852–1909
Prinsep, Valentine Cameron [Val Prinsep] 1838–1904
Prior, Melton 1845–1910
Pritchard, Sir Charles Bradley . 1837–1903
Pritchett, Robert Taylor . . 1828–1907
Probert, Lewis . . . 1841–1908
Procter, Francis . . . 1812–1905
Proctor, Robert George Collier . 1868–1903
Propert, John Lumsden . . 1834–1902
Prout, Ebenezer . . . 1835–1909
Prynne, George Rundle . . 1818–1903
Puddicombe, Anne Adalisa, 'Allen Raine' 1836–1908
Pullen, Henry William . . 1836–1903
Pyne, Louisa Fanny Bodda. See Bodda Pyne.

Quarrier, William . . . 1829–1903
Quilter, Harry . . . 1851–1907
Quilter, Sir William Cuthbert, first baronet . . . 1841–1911

Radcliffe-Crocker, Henry . 1845–1909
Rae, William Fraser . . 1835–1905
Raggi, Mario 1821–1907
Railton, Herbert . . . 1858–1910
Raine, Allen, *pseudonym*. See Puddicombe, Anne Adalisa.
Raines, Sir Julius Augustus Robert 1827–1909
Rainy, Adam Rolland. See under Rainy, Robert.
Rainy, Robert . . . 1826–1906
Ramé, Maria Louise, 'Ouida'. See De la Ramée.
Ramsay, Alexander . . 1822–1909
Ramsay, Sir William . . 1852–1916
Randall, Richard William . 1824–1906
Randegger, Alberto . . 1832–1911
Randles, Marshall . . . 1826–1904
Randolph, Francis Charles Hingeston-. See Hingeston-Randolph.
Randolph, Sir George Granville . 1818–1907
Ransom, William Henry . . 1824–1907
Raper, Robert William . . 1842–1915
Rassam, Hormuzd . . . 1826–1910
Rathbone, William . . . 1819–1902
Rattigan, Sir William Henry . 1842–1904
Raven, John James . . 1833–1906
Raverty, Henry George . . 1825–1906
Rawling, Cecil Godfrey . . 1870–1917
Rawlinson, George . . . 1812–1902
Rawson, Sir Harry Holdsworth 1843–1910
Rayleigh, third Baron. See Strutt, John William.
Read, Clare Sewell . . . 1826–1905
Read, Walter William . . 1855–1907
Reade, Thomas Mellard . . 1832–1909
Reay, eleventh Baron. See Mackay, Donald James.
Redesdale, first Baron. See Mitford, Algernon Bertram Freeman-.
Redmond, John Edward . . 1851–1918
Redmond, William Hoey Kearney 1861–1917

Redpath, Henry Adeney . 1848–1908
Reed, Sir Edward James . 1830–1906
Reeves, Sir William Conrad . 1821–1902
Reich, Emil 1854–1910
Reid, Archibald David . . 1844–1908
Reid, Sir George Houstoun . 1845–1918
Reid, Sir John Watt . . 1823–1909
Reid, Sir Robert Gillespie . 1842–1908
Reid, Sir Thomas Wemyss . 1842–1905
Rendel, Sir Alexander Meadows 1829–1918
Rendel, George Wightwick . 1833–1902
Reynolds, James Emerson . 1844–1920
Reynolds, Osborne . . . 1842–1912
Rhodes, Cecil John . . . 1853–1902
Rhodes, Francis William . . 1851–1905
Rhondda, Viscount. See Thomas, David Alfred.
Rhys, Sir John 1840–1915
Richards, Sir Frederick William 1833–1912
Richmond, sixth Duke of. See Gordon-Lennox, Charles Henry.
Richmond, Sir William Blake . 1842–1921
Riddell, Charles James Buchanan 1817–1903
Riddell, Charlotte Eliza Lawson [Mrs. J. H. Riddell], 'F. G. Trafford.' 1832–1906
Ridding, George 1828–1904
Ridley, Sir Matthew White, first Viscount Ridley . . . 1842–1904
Rieu, Charles Pierre Henri . 1820–1902
Rigby, Sir John . . . 1834–1903
Rigg, James Harrison . . 1821–1909
Ringer, Sydney . . . 1835–1910
Ripon, first Marquess of. See Robinson, George Frederick Samuel.
Risley, Sir Herbert Hope . . 1851–1911
Ritchie, Anne Isabella, Lady. See under Ritchie, Sir Richmond Thackeray.
Ritchie, Charles Thomson, first Baron Ritchie . . . 1838–1906
Ritchie, David George . . 1853–1903
Ritchie, Sir Richmond Thackeray 1854–1912
Rivière, Briton . . . 1840–1920
Roberts, Alexander . . . 1826–1901
Roberts, Frederick Sleigh, first Earl Roberts . . . 1832–1914
Roberts, Isaac 1829–1904
Roberts, Robert Davies . . 1851–1911
Roberts-Austen, Sir William Chandler 1843–1902
Robertson, Douglas Moray Cooper Lamb Argyll . . . 1837–1909
Robertson, Sir George Scott . 1852–1916
Robertson, James Patrick Bannerman, Baron Robertson . 1845–1909
Robinson, Frederick William . 1830–1901
Robinson, George Frederick Samuel, first Marquess of Ripon 1827–1909
Robinson, Sir John . . . 1839–1903
Robinson, Sir John Charles . 1824–1913
Robinson, Sir John Richard . 1828–1903
Robinson, Philip Stewart [Phil Robinson] 1847–1902
Robinson, Vincent Joseph . 1829–1910
Robinson, William Leefe . . 1895–1918
Robson, William Snowdon, Baron Robson 1852–1918
Roby, Henry John . . . 1830–1915
Rogers, Benjamin Bickley . 1828–1919
Rogers, Edmund Dawson . 1823–1910
Rogers, James Guinness . . 1822–1911
Rolls, Charles Stewart . . 1877–1910
Romer, Sir Robert . . . 1840–1918
Rookwood, Baron. See Selwin-Ibbetson, Sir Henry John.
Rooper, Thomas Godolphin . 1847–1903
Roose, Edward Charles Robson . 1848–1905
Roos-Keppel, Sir George Olof . 1866–1921
Roscoe, Sir Henry Enfield . 1833–1915
Ross, Sir Alexander George . 1840–1910
Ross, Sir John . . . 1829–1905
Ross, Joseph Thorburn . . 1849–1903
Ross, Martin, *pseudonym.* See Martin, Violet Florence.
Ross, William Stewart, 'Saladin' 1844–1906
Rosse, fourth Earl of. See Parsons, Laurence.
Rossetti, William Michael . 1829–1919
Rothschild, Nathan Meyer, first Baron Rothschild . . . 1840–1915
Rousby, William Wybert . . 1835–1907
Routh, Edward John . . 1831–1907
Rowe, Joshua Brooking . . 1837–1908
Rowlands, David, 'Dewi Môn' 1836–1907
Rowton, Baron. See Corry, Montagu William Lowry.
Rumbold, Sir Horace, eighth baronet 1829–1913
Rundall, Francis Hornblow . 1823–1908
Rusden, George William . . 1819–1903
Russell, Henry Chamberlaine . 1836–1907
Russell, Thomas O'Neill . . 1828–1908
Russell, William Clark . . 1844–1911
Russell, Sir William Howard . 1820–1907
Russell, William James . . 1830–1909
Rutherford, Mark, *pseudonym.* See White, William Hale.
Rutherford, William Gunion 1853–1907
Rutland, seventh Duke of. See Manners, (Lord) John James Robert.
Rye, Maria Susan . . . 1829–1903
Rye, William Brenchley . . 1818–1901

Sackville-West, Lionel Sackville, second Baron Sackville . 1827–1908
St. Aldwyn, first Earl. See Hicks Beach, Sir Michael Edward.
St. Helier, Baron. See Jeune, Francis Henry.
St. John, Sir Spenser Buckingham 1825–1910
St. John, Vane Ireton Shaftesbury. See under St. John, Sir Spenser Buckingham.
Saladin, *pseudonym.* See Ross, William Stewart.
Salaman, Charles Kensington . 1814–1901
Salaman, Julia. See Goodman.
Salisbury, third Marquess of. See Cecil, Robert Arthur Talbot Gascoyne-.

Salmon, George . . . 1819–1904
Salomons, Sir Julian Emanuel . 1835–1909
Salting, George . . . 1835–1909
Salvin, Francis Henry . . 1817–1904
Sambourne, Edward Linley . 1844–1910
Samuelson, Sir Bernhard, first baronet 1820–1905
Sanday, William . . . 1843–1920
Sandberg, Samuel Louis Graham 1851–1905
Sanderson, Edgar . . . 1838–1907
Sanderson, Sir John Scott Burdon-, baronet. See Burdon-Sanderson.
Sandham, Henry . . . 1842–1910
Sandys, Frederick . . . 1829–1904
Sanford, George Edward Langham Somerset . . . 1840–1901
Sanger, George [' Lord ' George Sanger] 1825–1911
Sankey, Sir Richard Hieram . 1829–1908
Saumarez, Thomas . . . 1827–1903
Saunders, Edward . . . 1848–1910
Saunders, Sir Edwin . . 1814–1901
Saunders, Howard . . . 1835–1907
Saunderson, Edward James . 1837–1906
Savage-Armstrong, George Francis 1845–1906
Savill, Thomas Dixon . . 1855–1910
Saxe-Weimar, Prince Edward of. See Edward of Saxe-Weimar.
Schreiner, Olive. See under Schreiner, William Philip.
Schreiner, William Philip . 1857–1919
Schunck, Henry Edward . . 1820–1903
Scott, Archibald . . . 1837–1909
Scott, Lord Charles Thomas Montagu-Douglas- . . 1839–1911
Scott, Clement William . . 1841–1904
Scott, Hugh Stowell, 'Henry Seton Merriman' . . . 1862–1903
Scott, Sir John . . . 1841–1904
Scott, John 1830–1903
Scott, Leader, *pseudonym*. See Baxter, Lucy.
Scott, Robert Falcon . . 1868–1912
Seale-Hayne, Charles Hayne . 1833–1903
Seddon, Richard John . . 1845–1906
Sedgwick, Adam . . . 1854–1913
See, Sir John 1844–1907
Seebohm, Frederic . . . 1833–1912
Seeley, Harry Govier . . 1839–1909
Selby, Thomas Gunn . . 1846–1910
Selby, first Viscount. See Gully, William Court.
Selous, Frederick Courteney . 1851–1917
Selwin-Ibbetson, Sir Henry John, Baron Rookwood . . 1826–1902
Selwyn, Alfred Richard Cecil . 1824–1902
Semon, Sir Felix . . . 1849–1921
Sendall, Sir Walter Joseph . 1832–1904
Sergeant, (Emily Frances) Adeline 1851–1904
Sergeant, Lewis . . . 1841–1902
Seton, George 1822–1908
Severn, Walter . . . 1830–1904
Sewell, Elizabeth Missing . 1815–1906
Sewell, James Edwards . . 1810–1903
Shadwell, Charles Lancelot . 1840–1918
Shand (afterwards Burns), Alexander, Baron Shand . . 1828–1904
Shand, Alexander Innes . . 1832–1907
Sharp, William, writing also under the pseudonym of Fiona Macleod 1855–1905
Sharpe, Richard Bowdler . . 1847–1909
Shaw, Alfred 1842–1907
Shaw, Sir Eyre Massey . . 1830–1908
Shaw, James Johnston . . 1845–1910
Shaw, John Byam Lister . . 1872–1919
Shaw, Richard Norman . . 1831–1912
Sheffield, third Earl of. See Holroyd, Henry North.
Shelford, Sir William . . 1834–1905
Shenstone, William Ashwell . 1850–1908
Sherborn, Charles William . 1831–1912
Sherrington, Helen Lemmens-. See Lemmens-Sherrington.
Shields, Frederic James . . 1833–1911
Shippard, Sir Sidney Godolphin Alexander 1837–1902
Shirreff. See Grey, Maria Georgina.
Shore, Thomas William . . 1840–1905
Shorthouse, Joseph Henry . 1834–1903
Shrewsbury, Arthur . . 1856–1903
Shuckburgh, Evelyn Shirley . 1843–1906
Sieveking, Sir Edward Henry . 1816–1904
Simmons, Sir John Lintorn Arabin 1821–1903
Simon, Sir John . . . 1816–1904
Simonds, James Beart . . 1810–1904
Simpson, Maxwell . . . 1815–1902
Simpson, Wilfred Hudleston. See Hudleston.
Singleton, Mary Montgomerie. See Currie, Baroness.
Skeat, Walter William . . 1835–1912
Skipsey, Joseph . . . 1832–1903
Slaney, William Slaney Kenyon-. See Kenyon-Slaney.
Smeaton, Donald Mackenzie . 1846–1910
Smiles, Samuel . . . 1812–1904
Smith, Sir Archibald Levin . 1836–1901
Smith, Sir Charles Bean Euan-. See Euan-Smith.
Smith, Donald Alexander, first Baron Strathcona . . 1820–1914
Smith, Sir Francis (afterwards Sir Francis Villeneuve) . . 1819–1909
Smith, George Barnett . . 1841–1909
Smith, George Vance . . 1816 ?–1902
Smith, Goldwin . . . 1823–1910
Smith, Henry Spencer . . 1812–1901
Smith, James Hamblin . . 1829–1901
Smith, Lucy Toulmin . . 1838–1911
Smith, Reginald Bosworth . 1839–1908
Smith, Reginald John . . 1857–1916
Smith, Samuel . . . 1836–1906
Smith, Sarah, ' Hesba Stretton ' 1832–1911
Smith, Thomas 1817–1906
Smith, Sir Thomas, first baronet 1833–1909
Smith, Thomas Roger . . 1830–1903
Smith, Vincent Arthur . . 1848–1920
Smith, Walter Chalmers . . 1824–1908
Smith, William Saumarez . 1836–1909

Smyly, Sir Philip Crampton . 1838–1904
Smyth, Sir Henry Augustus . 1825–1906
Snelus, George James . 1837–1906
Snow, Herbert. See Kynaston.
Solomon, Sir Richard . . 1850–1915
Solomon, Simeon . . . 1840–1905
Somerset, Lady Isabella Caroline [Lady Henry Somerset] . 1851–1921
Sorby, Henry Clifton . . 1826–1908
Sotheby, Sir Edward Southwell 1813–1902
Soutar, Ellen. See Farren.
Southesk, ninth Earl of. See Carnegie, James.
Southey, Sir Richard . . 1808–1901
Southward, John . . . 1840–1902
Southwell, Thomas . . . 1831–1909
Spencer, Herbert . . . 1820–1903
Spencer, John Poyntz, fifth Earl Spencer 1835–1910
Spiers, Richard Phené . . 1838–1916
Sprengel, Hermann Johann Philipp 1834–1906
Sprigg, Sir John Gordon . . 1830–1913
Spring-Rice, Sir Cecil . . 1859–1918
Sprott, George Washington . 1829–1909
Stables, William (Gordon) . 1840–1910
Stacpoole, Frederick . . 1813–1907
Stafford, Sir Edward William . 1819–1901
Stainer, Sir John 1840–1901
Stalbridge, first Baron. See Grosvenor, Richard De Aquila.
Stamer, Sir Lovelace Tomlinson, third baronet 1829–1908
Stanley, Frederick Arthur, sixteenth Earl of Derby . . 1841–1908
Stanley, Henry Edward John, third Baron Stanley of Alderley 1827–1903
Stanley, Sir Henry Morton . 1841–1904
Stanley, William Ford Robinson 1829–1909
Stanmore, first Baron. See Gordon, Arthur Charles Hamilton.
Stannard, Henrietta Eliza Vaughan, 'John Strange Winter' 1856–1911
Stannus, Hugh Hutton . . 1840–1908
Stanton, Arthur Henry . . 1839–1913
Stark, Arthur James . . 1831–1902
Stead, William Thomas . . 1849–1912
Steel, Allan Gibson . . . 1858–1914
Steggall, Charles 1826–1905
Stephen, Sir Alexander Condie . 1850–1908
Stephen, Caroline Emelia. See under Stephen, Sir Leslie.
Stephen, George, first Baron Mount Stephen . . . 1829–1921
Stephen, Sir Leslie . . . 1832–1904
Stephens, Frederic George . 1828–1907
Stephens, James 1825–1901
Stephens, James Brunton . 1835–1902
Stephens, William Richard Wood 1839–1902
Stephenson, Sir Frederick Charles Arthur 1821–1911
Stephenson, George Robert . 1819–1905
Sterling (afterwards MacKinlay), Antoinette 1843–1904
Stevenson, David Watson . 1842–1904
Stevenson, John James . . 1831–1908
Stevenson, Sir Thomas . . 1838–1908
Stewart, Charles . . . 1840–1907
Stewart, Isla 1855–1910
Stewart, James . . . 1831–1905
Stewart, Sir William Houston . 1822–1901
Stirling, Sir James . . . 1836–1916
Stirling, James Hutchison . 1820–1909
Stoddart, Andrew Ernest . . 1863–1915
Stokes, Sir George Gabriel, first baronet 1819–1903
Stokes, Sir John . . . 1825–1902
Stokes, Whitley . . . 1830–1909
Stoney, Bindon Blood . . 1828–1909
Stoney, George Johnstone . 1826–1911
Story, Robert Herbert . . 1835–1907
Story-Maskelyne, Mervyn Herbert Nevil 1823–1911
Strachan, John 1862–1907
Strachan-Davidson, James Leigh 1843–1916
Strachey, Sir Arthur. See under Strachey, Sir John.
Strachey, Sir Edward, third baronet 1812–1901
Strachey, Sir John . . . 1823–1907
Strachey, Sir Richard . . 1817–1908
Strang, William 1859–1921
Strathcona, first Baron. See Smith, Donald Alexander.
Stretton, Hesba, *pseudonym*. See Smith, Sarah.
Strong, Sir Samuel Henry . 1825–1909
Strong, Sandford Arthur . . 1863–1904
Strutt, John William, third Baron Rayleigh 1842–1919
Stubbs, William 1825–1901
Sturgis, Julian Russell . . 1848–1904
Sturt, Henry Gerard, first Baron Alington 1825–1904
Sutherland, Alexander . . 1852–1902
Sutton, Henry Septimus . . 1825–1901
Sutton, Martin John . . 1850–1913
Swain, Joseph 1820–1909
Swan, John Macallan . . 1847–1910
Swan, Sir Joseph Wilson . . 1828–1914
Swayne, Joseph Griffiths . . 1819–1903
Swaythling, first Baron. See Montagu, Samuel.
Sweet, Henry 1845–1912
Swete, Henry Barclay . . 1835–1917
Swinburne, Algernon Charles . 1837–1909
Swinfen, first Baron. See Eady, Charles Swinfen.
Sykes, Sir Mark, sixth baronet . 1879–1919
Syme, David 1827–1908
Symes-Thompson, Edmund . 1837–1906
Symons, William Christian . 1845–1911
Synge, John Millington . . 1871–1909

Tait, Frederick Guthrie. See under Tait, Peter Guthrie.
Tait, Peter Guthrie . . . 1831–1901
Tallack, William . . . 1831–1908
Tangye, Sir Richard . . 1833–1906
Tarte, Joseph Israel . . 1848–1907
Taschereau, Sir Henri Elzéar . 1836–1911
Taschereau, Sir Henri Thomas . 1841–1909
Tata, Jamsetji Nasarwanji . 1839–1904
Taunton, Ethelred Luke . . 1857–1907

Taylor, Charles . . . 1840–1908
Taylor, Charles Bell . . . 1829–1909
Taylor, Helen 1831–1907
Taylor, Isaac 1829–1901
Taylor, Sir John 1833–1912
Taylor, John Edward . . . 1830–1905
Taylor, Louisa. See Parr.
Taylor, Walter Ross . . . 1838–1907
Tearle, (George) Osmond . . 1852–1901
Temple, Frederick 1821–1902
Temple, Sir Richard, first baronet 1826–1902
Tennant, Sir Charles, first baronet 1823–1906
Tennant, Sir David 1829–1905
Tenniel, Sir John 1820–1914
Thesiger, Frederic Augustus, second Baron Chelmsford . 1827–1905
Thomas, David Alfred, Viscount Rhondda 1856–1918
Thomas, (Philip) Edward . . 1878–1917
Thomas, William Moy . . . 1828–1910
Thompson, D'Arcy Wentworth 1829–1902
Thompson, Edmund Symes-. See Symes-Thompson.
Thompson, Francis 1859–1907
Thompson, Sir Henry, first baronet 1820–1904
Thompson, Lydia 1836–1908
Thompson, Silvanus Phillips . 1851–1916
Thompson, William Marcus . 1857–1907
Thomson, Hugh 1860–1920
Thomson, Jocelyn Home . . 1859–1908
Thomson, William, Baron Kelvin 1824–1907
Thomson, Sir William . . . 1843–1909
Thornton, Sir Edward . . . 1817–1906
Thring, Godfrey 1823–1903
Thring, Henry, Baron Thring . 1818–1907
Thrupp, George Athelstane . 1822–1905
Thuillier, Sir Henry Edward Landor 1813–1906
Thurston (formerly Madden), Katherine Cecil 1875–1911
Tinsley, William 1831–1902
Tinworth, George 1843–1913
Todd, Sir Charles 1826–1910
Tomson, Arthur 1859–1905
Toole, John Lawrence . . . 1830–1906
Torrance, George William . 1835–1907
Townsend, Meredith White . 1831–1911
Tracey, Sir Richard Edward . 1837–1907
Trafford, F. G., *pseudonym*. See Riddell, Charlotte Eliza Lawson.
Traill, Anthony 1838–1914
Traill-Burroughs, Sir Frederick William. See Burroughs.
Tree, Sir Herbert Beerbohm . 1852–1917
Trevor, William Spottiswoode . 1831–1907
Tristram, Henry Baker . . 1822–1906
Truman, Edwin Thomas . . 1818–1905
Tucker, Alfred Robert . . 1849–1914
Tucker, Henry William . . 1830–1902
Tupper, Sir Charles, first baronet 1821–1915
Tupper, Sir Charles Lewis . 1848–1910
Turner, Charles Edward . . 1831–1903
Turner, James Smith . . . 1832–1904
Turner, Sir William . . . 1832–1916
Turpin, Edmund Hart . . . 1835–1907
Tweedmouth, second Baron. See Marjoribanks, Edward.
Tyabji, Badruddin 1844–1906
Tyler, Thomas 1826–1902
Tylor, Sir Edward Burnett . 1832–1917
Tylor, Joseph John 1851–1901
Tyrrell, George 1861–1909
Tyrrell, Robert Yelverton . 1844–1914

Underhill, Edward Bean . . 1813–1901
Urwick, William 1826–1905

Vallance, William Fleming . 1827–1904
Vandam, Albert Dresden . . 1843–1903
Vane-Tempest-Stewart, Charles Stewart, sixth Marquess of Londonderry 1852–1915
Van Horne, Sir William Cornelius 1843–1915
Vansittart, Edward Westby . 1818–1904
Vaughan, David James . . 1825–1905
Vaughan, Herbert Alfred . . 1832–1903
Vaughan, Kate . . . . 1852?–1903
Veitch, James Herbert . . 1868–1907
Vernon-Harcourt, Leveson Francis 1839–1907
Verrall, Arthur Woollgar . . 1851–1912
Vezin, Hermann 1829–1910
Vezin (formerly Mrs. Charles Young), Jane Elizabeth . 1827–1902
Victoria Adelaide Mary Louise, Princess Royal of Great Britain and German Empress . . 1840–1901
Villiers, John Henry De, first Baron De Villiers. See De Villiers.
Villiers, Victor Albert George Child-, seventh Earl of Jersey 1845–1915
Vincent, Sir (Charles Edward) Howard 1849–1908
Vincent, James Edmund . . 1857–1909
Voysey, Charles 1828–1912

Wade, Sir Willoughby Francis . 1827–1906
Wakley, Thomas. See under Wakley, Thomas Henry.
Wakley, Thomas Henry . . 1821–1907
Walker, Sir Frederick William Edward Forestier-. See Forestier-Walker.
Walker, Frederick William . 1830–1910
Walker, Sir Mark 1827–1902
Walker, Sir Samuel, first baronet 1832–1911
Walker, Vyell Edward . . . 1837–1906
Wallace, Alfred Russel . . 1823–1913
Wallace, Sir Donald Mackenzie 1841–1919
Wallace, William Arthur James 1842–1902
Waller, Charles Henry . . . 1840–1910
Waller, Lewis 1860–1915
Waller, Samuel Edmund . . 1850–1903
Walpole, Sir Spencer . . . 1839–1907
Walsh, William Pakenham . 1820–1902
Walsham, Sir John, second baronet 1830–1905
Walsham, William Johnson . 1847–1903
Walter, Sir Edward . . . 1823–1904
Walton, Sir John Lawson . . 1852–1908
Walton, Sir Joseph . . . 1845–1910
Wanklyn, James Alfred . . 1834–1906

Wantage, Baron. See Lindsay (afterwards Loyd-Lindsay), Robert James.
Ward, Harry Leigh Douglas . 1825–1906
Ward, Harry Marshall . . 1854–1906
Ward, Henry Snowden . . 1865–1911
Ward, Mary Augusta [Mrs. Humphry Ward] . . . 1851–1920
Ward, Wilfrid Philip . . 1856–1916
Wardle, Sir Thomas . . 1831–1909
Waring, Anna Letitia . . 1823–1910
Warington, Robert . . . 1838–1907
Warne, Frederick . . . 1825–1901
Warneford, Reginald Alexander John 1891–1915
Warner, Charles . . . 1846–1909
Warre, Edmond . . . 1837–1920
Warre-Cornish, Francis Warre . 1839–1916
Warrender, Sir George John Scott, seventh baronet . . 1860–1917
Waterhouse, Alfred . . . 1830–1905
Waterlow, Sir Ernest Albert . 1850–1919
Waterlow, Sir Sydney Hedley, first baronet . . . 1822–1906
Watkin, Sir Edward William . 1819–1901
Watson, Albert . . . 1828–1904
Watson, Sir Charles Moore . 1844–1916
Watson, George Lennox . . 1851–1904
Watson, Henry William . . 1827–1903
Watson, John, 'Ian Maclaren' . 1850–1907
Watson, Sir Patrick Heron . 1832–1907
Watson, Robert Spence . . 1837–1911
Watts, George Frederic . . 1817–1904
Watts, Henry Edward . . 1826–1904
Watts, John 1861–1902
Watts-Dunton, Walter Theodore 1832–1914
Waugh, Benjamin . . . 1839–1908
Waugh, James . . . 1831–1905
Wavell, Arthur John Byng . 1882–1916
Webb, Alfred John . . . 1834–1908
Webb, Allan Becher . . 1839–1907
Webb, Francis William . . 1836–1906
Webb, Philip (Speakman) . 1831–1915
Webb, Thomas Ebenezer . . 1821–1903
Webber, Charles Edmund . 1838–1904
Webster, Richard Everard, Viscount Alverstone . . 1842–1915
Webster, Wentworth . . 1829–1907
Weir, Harrison William . . 1824–1906
Welby, Reginald Earle, first Baron Welby . . . 1832–1915
Weldon, Walter Frank Raphael . 1860–1906
Wellesley, Sir George Greville . 1814–1901
Wells, Henry Tanworth . . 1828–1903
Wemyss-Charteris-Douglas, Francis, tenth Earl of Wemyss . 1818–1914
Wernher, Sir Julius Charles, first baronet 1850–1912
West, Sir Algernon Edward . 1832–1921
West, Edward William . . 1824–1905
West, Lionel Sackville-, second Baron Sackville. See Sackville-West.
West, Sir Raymond . . 1832–1912
Westall, William (Bury) . . 1834–1903
Westcott, Brooke Foss . . 1825–1901
Westlake, John . . . 1828–1913
Westland, Sir James . . 1842–1903
Weston, Dame Agnes Elizabeth 1840–1918
Weymouth, Richard Francis . 1822–1902
Wharton, Sir William James Lloyd 1843–1905
Wheelhouse, Claudius Galen . 1826–1909
Whistler, James Abbott McNeill 1834–1903
White, Sir George Stuart . . 1835–1912
White, John Campbell, Baron Overtoun 1843–1908
White, William Hale, novelist under the *pseudonym* of Mark Rutherford 1831–1913
White, Sir William Henry . 1845–1913
Whitehead, Robert . . . 1823–1905
Whiteley, William . . . 1831–1907
Whiteway, Sir William Vallance 1828–1908
Whitman, Alfred Charles . . 1860–1910
Whitmore, Sir George Stoddart 1830–1903
Whitworth, William Allen . 1840–1905
Whymper, Edward . . . 1840–1911
Whymper, Josiah Wood . . 1813–1903
Whyte, Alexander . . . 1836–1921
Wickham, Edward Charles . 1834–1910
Wiggins, Joseph . . . 1832–1905
Wigham, John Richardson . 1829–1906
Wigram, Woolmore . . . 1831–1907
Wilberforce, Ernest Roland . 1840–1907
Wilding, Anthony Frederick . 1883–1915
Wilkins, Augustus Samuel . 1843–1905
Wilkins, William Henry . . 1860–1905
Wilkinson, George Howard . 1833–1907
Wilks, Sir Samuel, baronet . 1824–1911
Will, John Shiress . . . 1840–1910
Willes, Sir George Ommanney . 1823–1901
Willett, William . . . 1856–1915
Williams, Alfred . . . 1832–1905
Williams, Charles . . . 1838–1904
Williams, Charles Hanson Greville 1829–1910
Williams, Sir Edward Leader . 1828–1910
Williams, Sir George . . 1821–1905
Williams, Hugh . . . 1843–1911
Williams, John Carvell . . 1821–1907
Williams, Sir Roland Bowdler Vaughan 1838–1916
Williams, Rowland, 'Hwfa Môn' 1823–1905
Williams, Watkin Hezekiah, 'Watcyn Wyn' 1844–1905
Williamson, Alexander William 1824–1904
Willis, Henry 1821–1901
Willis, William . . . 1835–1911
Willock, Henry Davis . . 1830–1903
Willoughby, Digby . . . 1845–1901
Wills, William Henry, Baron Winterstoke 1830–1911
Wilson, Arthur. See under Wilson, Charles Henry, first Baron Nunburnholme.
Wilson, Sir Arthur Knyvet, third baronet 1842–1921
Wilson, Charles Henry, first Baron Nunburnholme . . 1833–1907
Wilson, Sir Charles Rivers . 1831–1916
Wilson, Charles Robert . . 1863–1904
Wilson, Sir Charles William . 1836–1905
Wilson, Edward Adrian . . 1872–1912
Wilson, George Fergusson . 1822–1902
Wilson, Henry Schütz . . 1824–1902

Wilson, Sir Jacob . . . 1836–1905
Wilson, John Cook . . . 1849–1915
Wilson, John Dove . . . 1833–1908
Wilson, William Edward . . 1851–1908
Wimshurst, James . . . 1832–1903
Windus, William Lindsay . 1822–1907
Winter, Sir James Spearman . 1845–1911
Winter, John Strange, *pseudonym*. See Stannard, Henrietta Eliza Vaughan.
Winterstoke, Baron. See Wills, William Henry.
Winton, Sir Francis Walter De. See De Winton.
Wittewronge, Sir Charles Bennet Lawes-. See Lawes-Wittewronge.
Wodehouse, John, first Earl of Kimberley 1826–1902
Wolfe-Barry, Sir John Wolfe . 1836–1918
Wolff, Sir Henry Drummond Charles 1830–1908
Wolseley, Garnet Joseph, Viscount Wolseley . . . 1833–1913
Wolverhampton, first Viscount. See Fowler, Henry Hartley.
Wood, Sir (Henry) Evelyn . 1838–1919
Woodall, William . . . 1832–1901
Woodgate, Walter Bradford . 1840–1920
Woods, Sir Albert William . 1816–1904
Woods, Edward . . . 1814–1903
Woodward, Herbert Hall . . 1847–1909
Wooldridge, Harry Ellis . . 1845–1917
Woolgar, Sarah Jane. See Mellon.
Wordsworth, John . . . 1843–1911
Worms, Henry De, Baron Pirbright. See De Worms.
Wright, Charles Henry Hamilton 1836–1909
Wright, Edward Perceval . 1834–1910
Wright, Sir Robert Samuel . 1839–1904
Wright, Whitaker . . . 1845–1904
Wright, William Aldis . . 1831–1914
Wroth, Warwick William . 1858–1911
Wrottesley, George . . . 1827–1909
Wylie, Charles Hotham Montagu Doughty-. See Doughty-Wylie.
Wyllie, Sir William Hutt Curzon 1848–1909
Wyndham, Sir Charles . . 1837–1919
Wyndham, George . . . 1863–1913
Wyon, Allan 1843–1907

Yeo, Gerald Francis . . 1845–1909
Yonge, Charlotte Mary . . 1823–1901
Yorke, Albert Edward Philip Henry, sixth Earl of Hardwicke 1867–1904
Youl, Sir James Arndell . . 1811–1904
Young, Sir Allen William . 1830–1915
Young, Mrs. Charles. See Vezin, Jane Elizabeth.
Young, George, Lord Young . 1819–1907